THE DICTIONARY OF CRIMINAL JUSTICE

Seventh Edition

Connie Ireland
George E. Rush

California State University, Long Beach

With Summaries of Supreme Court Cases Affecting Criminal Justice

Judy Hails

California State University, Long Beach

Connect
Learn
Succeed™

The McGraw-Hill Companies

Connect
Learn
Succeed™

THE DICTIONARY OF CRIMINAL JUSTICE: WITH SUMMARIES OF SUPREME COURT CASES AFFECTING CRIMINAL JUSTICE, SEVENTH EDITION

Published by McGraw-Hill, a business unit of The McGraw-Hill Companies, Inc., 1221 Avenue of the Americas, New York, NY 10020. Copyright © 2011 by The McGraw-Hill Companies, Inc. All rights reserved. Previous editions © 2003, 2000, 1995. No part of this publication may be reproduced or distributed in any form or by any means, or stored in a database or retrieval system, without the prior written consent of The McGraw-Hill Companies, Inc., including, but not limited to, in any network or other electronic storage or transmission, or broadcast for distance learning.

Some ancillaries, including electronic and print components, may not be available to customers outside the United States.

This book is printed on acid-free paper.

1 2 3 4 5 6 7 8 9 0 DOC/DOC 1 0 9 8 7 6 5 4 3 2 1 0

ISBN 978-0-07-352780-2
MHID 0-07-352780-7

Managing Editor: *Larry Loeppke*
Senior Development Editor: *Jade Benedict*
Senior Permissions Coordinator: *Lenny Behnke*
Senior Marketing Communications Specialist: *Mary Klein*
Project Manager: *Erin Melloy*
Design Coordinator: *Brenda Rolwes*
Cover Designer: *Studio Montage, St. Louis, Missouri*
Buyer: *Susan K. Culbertson*
Media Project Manager: *Sridevi Palani*

Compositor: *Laserwords Private Limited*
Cover Image: © *Photodisc/Getty Images RF*

All credits appearing on page or at the end of the book are considered to be an extension of the copyright page.

Library of Congress Cataloging-in-Publication Data

Ireland, Connie.
   The dictionary of criminal justice / Connie Ireland, George E. Rush; with summaries of Supreme Court cases affecting criminal justice [by] Judy Hails. – 7th ed.
      p. cm.
   George E. Rush's name appeared first in earlier eds.
   ISBN 978-0-07-352780-2 (alk. paper)
   1. Criminal justice, Administration of–Dictionaries. 2. Criminal justice, Administration of–United States–Dictionaries. I. Hails, Judy. II. Rush, George E. (George Eugene), 1932- Dictionary of criminal justice. III. Title.
   HV7411.R87 2011
   364.97303–dc22
                              2010033329

www.mhhe.com

CONTENTS

DEDICATIONS

G. R.: To my family—my children, Susan and Michael, and their families
C. I.: To Jim, my dearest friend and soul mate; our children, Dane,
*Drew and Sarah, who bring joy daily; and J. C., who is **always** there for me.*
J. H.: To Miriam and Kahina, my wonderful daughters

ABOUT THE AUTHORS

George E. Rush, after retiring from the United States Air Force (Security Police, MSGT), received his B.S. and M.S. degrees in criminology from California State University, Long Beach, and his Ph.D. in government from Claremont Graduate School. He is an emeritus professor at California State University at Long Beach, in the Department of Criminal Justice, and served as the editor-in-chief for the *Journal of Contemporary Criminal Justice,* which he helped establish. He is a past member of the California Peace Officers Associations' Standards and Ethics Committee; past director of the Center for Criminal Justice Research and Training; served two years as the chairman of the Public Safety Committee, City of La Mirada, CA; and was a reserve officer with the Los Alamitos Police Department. Dr. Rush is also a founding member of Death Penalty Focus, a California-based abolitionist movement, and holds memberships on the American Society of Criminology, the Academy of Criminal Justice Sciences, and the Western Society of Criminology. He is the author or coauthor of eleven books. His research and writing have been published in numerous academic and professional journals.

Connie Ireland earned her BA in psychology and social behavior in 1996, followed by a second BA in criminology, law & society in 1997 from the University of California, Irvine. She earned her MA in social ecology in 2001, and her Ph.D. in criminology, law & society in 2003 from the University of California, Irvine. Dr. Ireland began her position in the Department of Criminal Justice at California State University, Long Beach in 2003, where she is currently an associate professor and graduate director. Dr. Ireland is also the director for the Evaluation of Mandatory Conditions of Parole, a research group that evaluates drug treatment and rehabilitation services for parolees. Her primary research interests are in corrections, especially parolee reintegration, parolee service delivery, and the operations of correctional agencies. She maintains active memberships with the Western Society of Criminology, for which she was a board member between 2004–2007, the Academy of Criminal Justice Sciences, and the American Society of Criminology. Dr. Ireland received official recognition from the California Senate and the California Assembly and a Certificate of Special Congressional Recognition from the United States House of Representatives for her research on *Women in Parole,* which was exhibited at the T. H. Pendergast Parole Museum in 2005. Since her appointment at CSULB, she has published two books and more than a dozen peer-reviewed articles and delivered more than 50 conference presentations.

PREFACE

The criminal justice student, researcher, or practitioner continually encounters certain words, names, personalities, court cases, events, phrases, and terms that by their selective nature have somewhat special meaning. *The Dictionary of Criminal Justice* is intended to compile in one reference volume information that could otherwise be found only by tediously searching through a myriad of interdisciplinary literature—for the study of criminal justice and its process crosses, blends, and overlaps several disciplines. As a result, this book satisfies a long-recognized need. This ready-reference volume will enable the instructor as well as the student, practitioner, and layperson to quickly pinpoint the object of a search. The scope goes far beyond conventional coverage, as medical, political, psychological, historical, sociological, economic, statistical, and organizational aspects are included. This dictionary is a comprehensive attempt to cover terms associated with the wide spectrum of law enforcement, courts, probation, parole, and corrections, and cites information and information sources particular to each area. To reduce the overall length, cross-references have been minimized by listing most multiple-word entries under their first word. In some cases, it is necessary to look under the more important word to find the desired entry. This edition includes organization address and Web sites that will lead the reader to key statistics, research, and resources that expand the scope of this book; details and contact information for organizations of interest to law enforcement and criminal justice professionals; and resources for students, including a listing of graduate programs in criminology and criminal justice. It also includes key criminal justice events and people omitted from previous editions, such as AMBER alerts, BTK killer, Department of Homeland Security, Jack the Ripper, Jonestown, USA Patriot Act, September 11 attacks, OJ Simpson, and Aileen Wournos. *The Dictionary of Criminal Justice, Seventh Edition,* defines the terms commonly used in the broad, interdisciplinary field of criminal justice.

ACKNOWLEDGMENTS

The authors are indebted to the following individuals who contributed their time, effort, and expertise in the several editions of *The Dictionary of Criminal Justice:*

From George Rush: My colleague Judy Hails, LL. M., Department of Criminal Justice CSULB, who compiled all legal cases cited in this dictionary, and my other supporting faculty members: Drs. Paul M. Whisenand and Ronald Vogel. Professional assistance was provided by SEARCH Group; NIJ Reference Service; John Mattingly, Los Angeles Police Department; City Manager Oliver (Lee) Drummond (retired); Lt. Gen. Robert Carter, Ph.D., U.S. Military Academy, West Point; Capt. James Nunn, San Bernardino County Sheriff's Department, G. Thomas Gichoff, D.Crm., San Diego State University, who provided a wealth of information, data, and charts; and Catherine Leonard, who diligently and professionally edited the fourth and fifth editions. Special thanks goes to Bob Weaver, of Veritech Publishing Services, for his help in editing the Seventh Edition.

From Connie Ireland: I wish to thank my colleagues at CSULB for their ongoing support of my work, including the dedicated Connie Rae McCarroll, Durrell Dew, and Joseph Aubele, who keep this place running; Doug Butler and Sue Stanley for their commitment to service and excellence, which shows in all they do; Drs. Jolae Brocato, Ryan Fischer, Judy Hails, Stacy Mallicoat (CSU Fullerton), Harv Morley, Tracy Tolbert, Sam Torres, Brenda Vogel, John Wang; and the late Drs. Bruce Berg and Libby Deschenes, both of whom were extraordinary mentors. I am indebted to the following colleagues who provided terms and information included in this edition: Drs. Aili Malm, Lisa Murphy, and Robert Schug, CSULB; Sergeant Gregory Gibbs, J.D., Irvine Police Department; captain Ron Mark, Signal Hill Police Department; investigator Damon Tucker, Orange County District Attorney's Office; agents Arthur J. Ramirez and Houston, Whisenton, California Department of Corrections and Rehabilitation; Ms. Monica Todd, J.D., who reviewed legal terminology; and my son, Dane Stivers, the walking thesaurus who contributed valuable ideas, prose, and alternate interpretations to terms included in this work. I owe special thanks to the following CSULB graduate students, who will undoubtedly continue to make outstanding contributions to the field during their careers: Jennifer Jacqueline Doyle, who painstakingly reviewed information for all government agencies included in this edition, updated information on drugs of abuse and scheduling, and added homicide tables; Richard Porter, who tirelessly searched journal articles and books for new terms included in this edition and developed many of the new tables included herein; and Marcus Galeste, whose exceptional skill in APA citation is unsurpassed. I am also grateful to students who have shaped my career, including Nicholas Athey, Alyson Boehler, Paola Contreras, Weston Morrow, Sonia Munoz-Duran, Rebecca Nash, Norma Palacios, Emily Ragsdale, Christina Ramirez, Jennifer Stumpp, Samuel Vickovic and others who remind me why I entered this field. Last, I wish to thank Dr. Henry Fradella, who not only contributed important terms, cases, and people to this edition, but who is the quintessential servant-leader, a superb mentor to me, an extraordinary chair, and a dear friend.

THE
DICTIONARY OF
CRIMINAL
JUSTICE

Seventh Edition

With
Summaries of
Supreme Court
Cases
Affecting
Criminal Justice

Part I

THE
DICTIONARY
OF
CRIMINAL
JUSTICE

A

AAFS. *See* Forensic Sciences, American Academy of

Abagnale, Frank William, Jr. (1948–) an American forger and imposter who successfully passed $2.5 million in forged checks across 26 countries over a five-year period in the 1960s. During his crime spree, which occurred when he was 16–21 years of age, he impersonated an airline pilot (accruing nearly 1 million miles), a supervising physician, a prison inspector, and an attorney, all without detection. He was convicted and served time in France, Sweden, and the United States, although he also escaped from custody at least twice. After serving five years for federal crimes in the United States, he was paroled. He eventually developed a successful security consulting firm, Abagnale & Associates, for which he is CEO. His exploits are depicted in the book and film entitled *Catch Me If You Can.*

abandonment. The relinquishment of a claim or privilege.

abate. To do away with; annul; remit. To become void.

abatement. A legal process designed to rid properties of nuisances that occur in the course of gang, narcotic, and/or vice activity. In order for a property to be abated, the illegal activity must be prolonged and continuous. If the owner is uncooperative, the abatement procedures require an extensive investigation followed by civil court proceedings. *See also* nuisance

ABA transit numbers. A unique nine-digit number assigned by the American Bankers Association (ABA) to route checks to the bank of origin. The code, which is printed in the upper right-hand corner, identifies the city or state of the bank the check was drawn against, the name of the bank, and the Federal Reserve Bank district. The code key is held by the ABA.

abduction. The taking of a person, without his or her consent or consent of parents or guardian, by fraud, persuasion, or open violence. In common law, a taking for money and a marriage or defilement are essential to the completion of the offense. *See also* seduction

Abel. An Old Testament shepherd, son of Adam and Eve, known as world's first murder victim, killed by his brother Cain, a farmer.

Abel Assessment for Sexual Interest: A computer-based screening instrument developed by Abel Screening, Inc. (Gene Abel, M.D.) that aims to identify deviant sexual interest in children.

abeyance. A state of suspension; being undetermined; in expectation; awaiting determination of true owner.

ab inconvenient (Lat., lit. "from inconvenience or hardship"). A term applied in cases where, because of inconvenience or practical impossibility, the prosecution can't establish a fact which is part of its case.

ab initio (Lat., lit. "from the beginning"). The first act or the beginning of a state or condition. (A void marriage is of no effect *ab initio*.)

abjuration. The renunciation under oath of one's citizenship or some other right or privilege.

abnormal psychology. The specialized field that studies behavioral disorders such as mental illness. Abnormal psychologists search for causes, explain behavioral disorders, and provide principles to guide prevention and treatment.

abnormal sex. A generic term for all criminalized or devalued sexual behaviors except masturbation, adultery, and fornication.

abolitionists. Historically, one who opposes the practice of slavery. Term now applies to those who oppose capital punishment.

abortion. The termination of a pregnancy by the removal of the fetus or embryo from the uterus. Abortion can be spontaneous (called

3

a miscarriage) or induced (intentional). Induced abortion can be achieved by surgical or pharmaceutical means.

abortion and birth control laws. Historically, controversy over abortion centers on whether a fetus, before the 20th week of pregnancy, is a living human being, as the Roman Catholic Church asserts it is. Since 1869, Church leaders have stated the belief that life begins at the moment of conception. Feminists and other pressure groups argue for a woman's right to control her own body. A century ago, the dissemination of birth control information was prohibited by the Comstock Law of 1873. Through the efforts of pioneers like Margaret Sanger, however, such dissemination by physicians was legalized in 1937. In 1965 the Supreme Court, in *Griswold v. Connecticut,* declared laws regulating birth control unconstitutional on the grounds that they infringed on the right to marital privacy. Demand for abortion had risen in the 1960s with evidence that rubella (German measles) and drugs like thalidomide could cause fetal deformities. Decisions as to whether an abortion was legal—that is, necessary to preserve the mother's life—were being made by boards of doctors. In 1962 the American Law Institute (ALI) recommended, in its proposal for a Model Penal Code, that abortion be permitted (a) when the mother's mental or physical health was in jeopardy, (b) when there was significant risk of fetal deformity, and (c) in cases of rape or incest. In 1967 the American Medical Association reversed its opposition to abortion and supported the ALI recommendation. The same year, Colorado became the first state to liberalize its abortion laws according to the new guidelines, and several other states followed— sometimes with slight variations from the ALI model. There are no abortion laws that force a woman to undergo abortion against her will. Restrictive abortion laws have been challenged in the federal courts. It has been contended that the right to have an abortion is protected by the Ninth Amendment, since at the time this amendment was adopted in 1791, women enjoyed such a liberty under common law. This view was upheld in 1973 in a landmark Supreme Court decision, *Roe v. Wade,* which ruled that abortion could be barred only during the last 10 weeks of pregnancy. In June 1994, the federal Freedom of Access to Clinic Entrances Act was passed in an attempt to prevent harassment of women entering health clinics known to provide abortion services. In 2003, the Partial-Birth Abortion Ban Act was passed in the United States, prohibiting abortions by the medical procedure known as "intact dilation and extraction." Current abortion controversy centers around spousal notification (in cases where the woman seeking an abortion is married), and parental notification (in cases where the woman seeking an abortion is a minor child). As of September 2008, 35 states require some form of parental notification when a minor seeks abortion.

Selected Supreme Court decisions on abortion:

1973: *Roe v. Wade.* Legalized abortion during the first six months of pregnancy.

1976: *Planned Parenthood of Central Missouri v. Danforth.* Invalidated requirement that a married woman obtain consent from her husband or a minor from one parent.

1981: *H. L. v. Matheson.* Upheld law requiring doctors to notify parents of minors seeking abortions.

1983: *City of Akron v. Akron Center for Reproductive Health.* Struck down requirements for preabortion counseling, parental consent, and waiting period.

1986: *Thornburgh v. American Counsel of Obstetricians and Gynecologists.* Struck down requirements for preabortion counseling.

1989: *Webster v. Reproductive Health Services.* Upheld law restricting use of public facilities and funds for abortions.

1991: *Rust v. Sullivan.* Barred federally funded family planning clinics from providing information about abortion.

1992: *Planned Parenthood v. Casey.* The Court upheld Pennsylvania law: (a) doctors must counsel women on risks of abortion and alternatives; (b) 24-hour waiting period; (c) a minor must get one parent's consent or judge's approval; (d) doctors must keep detailed records of abortions and the reason for performing late-term abortions. This decision overturned the provision that a married woman must notify her husband of her intent to obtain an abortion.

1993: *Bray v. Alexandria Women's Health Clinic.* Limits causes of action against persons obstructing access to abortion clinics.

2000: *Stenberg v. Carhart.* Laws banning partial-birth abortion are unconstitutional if they don't make exceptions for maternal health or if they appear to extend to other abortion methods.

2004: *McCorvey v. Hill.* McCorvey (who was "Roe" in the original abortion case) sought to have Roe v. Wade overturned based on her rights as the original litigant. The court ruled that too much time has lapsed and denied certiorari.

2006: *Ayotte v. Planned Parenthood of New England.* The Court ruled that states have the right to require parental notification if a minor seeks abortion but cannot restrict access to abortions that are necessary to preserve life or health of mother.

2007: *Gonzales v. Carhart.* U.S.S.C. upheld the Partial Birth Abortion Ban Act of 2003.

abrogate. To annul by authority or by a later enactment; abolish, repeal.

ABSCAM. This term is a contraction from "Arab scam" referring to an FBI undercover investigation in the late 1970s and early 1980s. The investigation, which initially targeted stolen property that led to political corruption involving several members of the U.S. Congress and a number of state and local political figures. Agents posing as wealthy Arab businessmen offered bribes to several members of Congress in exchange for political favors. The resulting exchanges were secretly video-taped and used to secure the conviction of one senator and five members of the House of Representatives and five other government officials.

abscond. To leave one's usual residence or to conceal oneself, usually in order to avoid legal proceedings or sanctions.

Absence without leave. (AWOL), Abandonment of position or responsibilities. *See also* desertion

abstinence. Voluntary self-deprivation of a pleasurable activity, generally used in reference to sexual activity, drugs, or alcohol.

Academy of Criminal Justice Sciences (ACJS). Founded in 1963. Address: 7339 Hanover Parkway, Suite A, Greenbelt, MD 20770. Tel: (301) 446-6300 (800) 757-2257. Web: www.acjs.org.

accelerant. A substance that increases the speed of a reaction; for example, a flammable liquid used by an arsonist.

access control. The control of pedestrian and vehicular traffic through entrances and exits of a protected area or premises.

accessory. A person who helps a criminal either before or after a crime is committed, but who is not present during the crime.

accessory after the fact. Anyone who, after a felony has been committed, knowingly harbors or conceals the felon, or helps him or her avoid arrest, trial, conviction, or punishment.

accessory before the fact. One who helps another to commit a crime but is absent when the crime is committed.

accident investigation (AI). Includes search for physical evidence; taking measurements and photographs, interviews, sketching/diagrams. The goals of AI are to determine the causes of traffic collisions, which can include human behavior, mechanical failure, or environmental factors.

accomplice. One who knowingly and voluntarily aids another in committing a criminal offense.

accountability. The state of being responsible and punishable for a criminal act; this responsibility is reduced or abolished in some cases because of age, mental defect, or other reasons.

Accreditation for Corrections, Commission on. The Commission on Accreditation for Corrections is a private, nonprofit body that is comprised of corrections professionals from across the country. The main responsibility of this board is to conduct the accreditation hearings to verify that those agencies applying for accreditation comply with the applicable standards. The commission operates under the auspices of the American Correctional Association (ACA). Address: 206 North Washington Street, Suite 200, Alexandria, VA 22314; telephone (800) ACA-JOIN. Web: www.aca.org.

Accreditation for Law Enforcement Agencies, Inc., Commission on. Provides assistance to agencies in the accreditation process. Address: 10302 Eaton Place, Suite 100, Fairfax, VA 22030; telephone (800) 368-3757. Web: www.calea.org.

accuracy of firearms. The accuracy of firearms depends on many factors, including the firearm, the cartridge, and the shooter. Within the firearm, the barrel must be as nearly perfect as mechanical skill can make it. It must be of uniform size of bore its entire length, and the grooves of the rifling must be of uniform width and depth throughout, with no defects. The fit of the bullet is next in importance: it must be of correct diameter, hardness, density, lubrication, etc. The powder charge must be exactly the same for any given cartridge, and the same lot of powder must be used. The primers must have a uniform amount of priming composition.

accusation. Accusations of guilt may be made by complaints or affidavits, and sworn to by injured persons or by police officers, especially in minor offenses. Accusations of felonies are made by indictments found by grand juries or by information filed by prosecuting attorneys, generally following preliminary examinations in magistrates' courts.

accusation, modes of. A person charged with a crime may be prosecuted following (a) an indictment or a presentment upon oath by a grand jury; (b) a coroner's inquisition in cases of homicide (where authorized by law); (c) information proffered by the proper prosecuting officer without the intervention of a grand jury; and (d) a complaint or information given under oath by a private person.

accusatorial system. A system of administering criminal justice law, like those of the United States and Canada, that is based on the assumption that justice and truth can best be attained through a process that resembles a con test between opposing parties—the accused, or defendant, and the accuser, or plaintiff, who can be either an individual or a government.

accusatory stage. The part of a police investigation that is carried out once suspects have been identified.

accused. The defendant in a criminal case; a prisoner.

accused persons, rights of. The U.S. Constitution, in particular the Bill of Rights, protects individuals from unjust punishments by the state. Amendments 4, 5, 6, 8, and 14 are most commonly associated with rights of the accused.

The Fourth Amendment protects individuals from unreasonable search and seizure of their persons and property. It provides conditions for search and seizure (arrest), most notably "probable cause."

The Fifth Amendment provides various procedural protections for the accused.

Specifically, the government may not hold an individual for a serious crime unless the prosecution presents appropriate evidence to a grand jury that indicates likely guilt; prosecute an individual more than once for the same offense; force an individual to testify against himself in a criminal matter; deprive an individual of life, liberty, or property without due process of law.

The Sixth amendment protects individuals against the power of government. Specifically, these include the rights to a speedy and public trial by an impartial jury in the state where the crime was committed; the right to be informed of the nature and cause of the accusation; the right to confront witnesses in court (cross-examination); the right to subpoena witnesses in favor of the accused; and the right to counsel.

The Eighth Amendment provides protection against overly harsh punishments and excessive fines and bail.

Although these protections originally applied only to federal courts, Supreme Court decisions interpreting the due process clause of the Fourteenth Amendment have found that most of these restrictions also apply to state courts. The Supreme Court has clarified provisions of these Amendments.

acid bombs. Sometimes called a "bottle bomb" or a "MacGyver bomb," an acid bomb is a crude, home-made bomb constructed by combining a strong acid (chemical with a low pH) and a strong base (chemical with a high pH, or aluminum foil). The two substances are mixed in a plastic bottle, and their chemical reaction produces a gas that builds up until the bottle explodes. While acid bombs are sometimes used as a teenage prank, such bombs can cause serious injury. On Thanksgiving Friday, 2006, two 15-year old boys detonated acid bombs in Walmart. Homeland Security arrested and charged them criminally.

acquittal. The legal judgment that a criminal defendant has been found not guilty beyond a reasonable doubt by a judge or jury for a criminal charge against him/her.

act of God. An inevitable event, one that occurs without human aid or intervention (e.g., hurricane, flood, or tornado) and thus, for which no one can be blamed. On this ground, carriers are released from liability for loss, and a person is, in some cases, discharged from covenant or contract.

acts of state legislatures. State legislatures, unlike Congress, have inherent power to declare acts criminal and to impose penalties for acts. Their power in these respects,

however, is not absolute. Their enactments must adhere to all provisions of the U.S. Constitution, the state constitution, and valid acts of Congress.

acts of territorial legislatures. Territorial legislatures are created by Congress, and their powers are limited to those conferred upon them by that body. Their legislative power extends to all rightful subjects of legislation not inconsistent with the Constitution and laws of the United States.

ACT-UP (AIDS Coalition to Unleash Power). Founded in 1987 by Larry Kramer, ACT-UP is a direct action advocacy group designed to raise public awareness regarding inadequate government funding for AIDS research. The organization targets government agencies and corporations' lack of attention to AIDS issues.

actus reus (Lat.). The requirement that, for an act to be considered criminal, the individual must have committed an overt act that resulted in harm.

ADAM. *See* Arrestee Drug Abuse Monitoring Program

Adam Walsh Child Protection Safety Act. Named after six-year old Adam Walsh, who was abducted from a mall and murdered in 1981, and whose father, John Walsh, later helped form the National Center for Missing and Exploited Children (NCMEC) and became host to TV's *America's Most Wanted*. This is a federal law that created a national sex offender registry, strengthens federal penalties for crimes against children, and makes it harder for sexual predators to contact kids on the Internet.

Adamsite. (Diphenylaminechlorarsine chloride, DM). This war gas (also a mob- and riot-control gas) has a rapid rate of action. Only about one minute is required for temporary incapacitation. It causes the same symptoms as dishenychloroarsine (DA), but the long-term effects develop more slowly. Also called a "sternutator" or "sneeze gas," and can cause vomiting and diarrhea. It was developed at the end of World War II by Roger Adams, an American. DM is widely regarded as obsolete today and has been replaced by other riot control agents such as CS gas (o-Chlorobenzylidene Malononitrile), which is less toxic and has a more rapid onset.

addict. One who habitually uses drugs despite adverse consequences or to such an extent that cessation of such use causes severe physical or psychological trauma.

addiction. (From Lat. verb *addicere,* to bind a person to something). Socially, this term refers to compulsive use or pursuit of a substance, e.g., alcohol, or activity, e.g., gambling, despite adverse consequences. Pharmacologically, addiction has three components: tolerance, the need for progressively higher doses of a substance to produce the desired effect; dependence, the need to maintain a certain dosage or level in order to avoid withdrawal symptoms; and compulsion, or a powerful craving for the substance or activity. The World Health Organization (WHO) has replaced the term in favor of "substance use disorder." *See also* drug abuse

ad hoc committee. A committee established for the purpose of investigating or otherwise handling a specific matter. Generally an ad hoc committee is created as a temporary subcommittee of a standing committee. Both houses of Congress establish numerous such committees.

ad hominem (Lat., lit. "to the man"). An argument against an opponent personally instead of against the substance of the argument.

adipocere. Also called grave wax, adipocere is a waxy substance that accumulates on corpses in the initial stages of decomposition. Adipocere is composed of insoluble salts of fatty acids, oleic, palmific, and stearic acids.

adjective law. That part of law prescribing the method or procedure for carrying out the rights and obligations of persons. Includes the code of procedure, e.g., the manner of

executing a warrant of arrest, extradition proceedings, the presenting of an indictment, and appeal procedure. Conversely, "substantive law" defines the rights of persons that the courts are bound to administer and protect.

adjournment. Termination of a session or hearing; postponement to some other time or place.

adjudge. To rule upon judicially; to grant through a judicial process.

adjudication. The process of judicial settlement; the settlement itself.

adjudication withheld. A court decision, made at any point after filing of a criminal complaint, to continue court proceedings but stop short of pronouncing judgment. The usual purpose of such a decision is to avoid the undesirable effects of conviction, which can include both unnecessary harm to the offender and unnecessary expense or harm to the public interest. "Withholding adjudication" places the subject in a status where the court retains jurisdiction but will not reopen proceedings unless the person violates a condition of behavior.

adjudicatory hearing. In juvenile justice usage, the fact-finding process wherein the juvenile court determines whether or not there is sufficient evidence to sustain the allegations in a petition. An adjudicatory hearing occurs after a juvenile petition has been filed and after a detention hearing, if one is necessary. If the petition is not sustained, no further formal court action is taken. If it is sustained, the next step is a disposition hearing to determine the most appropriate treatment or care for the juvenile. These last two stages of judicial activity concerning juveniles are often combined in a single hearing, referred to as a "bifurcated hearing," meaning a process that encompasses both adjudication of the case and disposition of the person.

administration of criminal justice. Comprises the following subjects: criminal procedure, police organization and administration, prosecution, accusation, the defense of accused persons, the organization of courts, pleadings, arraignment and trial, evidence, judgment and sentence, appeals, probation, parole, pardon, penology and prison administration, rehabilitation and reentry, juvenile courts, special procedures for crime prevention, and laws designed to change social and industrial conditions in order to prevent crime.

administrative case closure. The termination of community supervision (probation or parole) for administrative reasons, including death, deportation, extradition or transfer to another jurisdiction, medical issues (e.g., coma or long-term hospitalization), term of incarceration for new charge, or another such discretionary administrative reason.

administrative courts. (1) Specialized courts in western Europe that are organized in a separate hierarchy from general courts, which apply administrative law, generally concerning the exercise of public power. Administrative courts typically have a reputation for fairness in protecting the interests of citizens, for rendering speedy justice, for invalidating administrative orders that lack proper statutory authority, and for granting compensation for injuries suffered at the hands of officers or employees of the government. (2) Those courts not created under Article II of the U.S. Constitution and that are usually called legislative courts.

administrative judge. A judicial officer who supervises administrative functions and performs administrative tasks for a given court, sometimes in addition to performing regular judicial functions. Typical duties of administrative judges are (a) assigning cases to other judicial officers within a court; (b) setting court policy on procedure; and (c) performing other tasks of an administrative nature, such as those concerned with personnel and budgets.

administrative law. *See* law, administrative

administrative services. The specialized bureau in a traditionally organized police department responsible for community

relations, planning and development, code enforcement, personnel recruitment and training, and disciplinary review.

administrator (m), administratix (f). One to whom letters of administration have been granted by a court and who administers an estate.

admiralty The court dealing with maritime questions; the branch of law administered by such courts.

admiralty jurisdiction. The authority to try cases arising under maritime law. It is concerned with (a) wartime captures, collisions, piracy, crimes, and torts on the high seas, navigable lakes, and rivers; and (b) with contracts for shipments of goods, insurance, and wages of seamen. It is not concerned with crimes and other incidents committed on board ships in port. Original jurisdiction in admiralty cases is exercised by federal district courts acting as admiralty courts.

admiralty law. Maritime law dealing with ships and the sea, including events and transactions, both civil and criminal, occurring at or involving the sea. Although now administered by national courts and affected by municipal law, the legal principles of admiralty law, being a composite of customs of the sea and maritime nations, antedate even Roman law and transcend national borders.

admissible. Capable of being admitted; in a trial, such evidence as the judge allows to be introduced into the proceeding.

admission. (1) A voluntary statement or acknowledgment, made by a party, that is admissible in court as evidence against that party. (2) The act by which attorneys and counselors become officers of a court and are licensed to practice law. The requirements for admission to the bar vary greatly in different states.

adolescence. The transitional stage of human development that occurs between childhood and adulthood. Adolescence generally begins around the onset of puberty, which occurs on average around age 10 for girls and age 12 for boys and ends at the age of majority, generally around age 18.

Adult Education and Family Literacy Act (1998). This act organized employment, adult education, and vocational rehabilitation programs into an integrated system of workforce investment and education activities for adults and youth.

Adult Internal Management System (AIMS). Also known as the Quay system, AIMS is a type of prison inmate classification system.

adultery. Voluntary sexual intercourse between a married person and a partner other than his or her spouse. Most societies have customs or laws relating to adultery. Some have treated it as a private wrong to be handled by the families concerned; others have made adultery a crime subject to severe penalties, even death. Today, adultery is still a crime in many parts of the United States, although the law is rarely enforced. Adultery is grounds for civil divorce in all states and is a court-martial offense in the U.S. military.

ad valorem tax. Tax on a percentage of an item's value, such as real estate or personal property taxes.

adversary proceeding. A legal proceeding involving contesting or opposing parties.

adversary system. The Anglo-American system for resolving both civil and criminal disputes. It is characterized by a contest between the initiating party, called the plaintiff in civil proceedings and the prosecutor (representing the state) in criminal proceedings, and the responding party, called the defendant in most instances (also called the respondent in family law). The case is presided over by a judge, who adjudicates and renders final judgment. The judge sometimes has the aid of a jury for finding disputed facts, acts on the basis of the evidence presented by the parties in court, and makes a decision in light of the applicable law. *See also* inquisitorial system; party-dominated process

advertising, legal. The American Bar Association (ABA) traditionally prohibited lawyers from advertising, but in June 1977 the Supreme Court ruled that lawyers may advertise their services and customary fees for those services. The Court held that a ban on advertising was a violation of the free speech guarantees of the First Amendment. The ABA then adopted a code of guidelines for advertising for ABA members.

advocate. Traditionally, an advocate is the attorney who speaks or writes in support of a client's cause. The term *advocate* is also used to describe court-appointed volunteers who provide support and resources to victims of crime during criminal proceedings.

affiance. To assure by a pledge, such as a mutual promise or agreement between a man and a woman that they will marry.

affiant. A person who creates and signs an affidavit.

affidavit. Written statement made under oath usually before a notary public or other authorized person.

affinity fraud. A type of investment fraud in which con artists target religious, ethnic, cultural and professional groups or deceitfully represent themselves as representing such groups. *See also* fraud, investment

affirm, affirmance. A pronouncement by a higher court that the case in question was rightly decided by the lower court from which the case was appealed.

affirmation. Positive declaration or assertion that the witness will tell the truth; an affirmation is not made under oath.

affirmative action. A general term for statutes and procedures designed to redress wrongs committed against minority groups in hiring and promotion practices. The Office of Federal Contract Compliance Programs (OFCCP) requires that all federal contractors do not discriminate and take affirmative action to ensure that all individuals have an equal opportunity for employment, without regard to race, color, religion, sex, national origin, disability, or status as a Vietnam era or special disabled veteran.

affray. A fight involving two or more persons in some public place, and which disturbs the peace. An affray differs from a riot in that it is not considered premeditated.

AFIS. *See* Automated Fingerprint Identification System, a database for storing and making rapid comparisons of fingerprints

aflatoxin. A naturally occurring toxin created by bacteria that grow on stored foods, especially on rice, peanuts, and cotton seeds. It is present in minute quantities in almost all commercially available peanut butter, and it is highly carcinogenic in larger doses. Iraq developed and stockpiled alfatoxin for use as a biological weapon through the late 1990s.

Afro-American Police Association. Formerly the Black American Police Association. Address: 256 E. McLemore Avenue, Memphis, TN 38106.

aftercare. (1) Traditionally, the status or program membership of a juvenile who has been committed to a treatment or confinement facility, conditionally released from the facility, and placed in a supervisory and/or treatment program. (2) treatment or confinement of an adult following a term of incarceration.

agar composition. A substance derived from seaweed, which is used as a medium for serology analysis through electrophoresis.

age. In common law, children under the age of 7 were incapable of committing a crime. In modern times, each state determines the age at which a juvenile can be adjudicated in juvenile court or tried as an adult. The National Center for Juvenile Justice (NCJJ) reports that juveniles as young as 6 years of age (North Carolina) are subject to juvenile court jurisdiction, and 35 states do not define the lowest age for jurisdiction.

agent. A person employed to act for another (the principal) in dealing with third parties.

Principals are generally bound and liable for (other than criminal) acts by their agents.

Agent Orange. Common name for the compound comprised of 2,3,7,8-Tetrachlorodibenzodioxin (TCDD), a polychlorinated dibenzodioxin (dioxin). This substance is an herbicide (kills plants) and defoliant (causes leaves to fall off), that effectively kills plants exposed to this substance. The United States used Agent Orange as a type of agricultural warfare in the Vietnam War. In 2010, the U.S. department of Veterans Affairs announced the addition of "presumptive diseases" attributed to Agent Orange exposure by Vietnam soldiers. The Veterans Administration now names "B-cell leukemias, such as hairy cell leukemia; Parkinson's disease; and ischemic heart disease as associated with Agent Orange exposure."

agent provocateur. (1) An unofficial police agent who associates with politically disaffected groups or persons suspected of crime to win their confidence or encourage them to resist authority and commit illegal acts, and who subsequently informs on them. (2) An undercover individual hired by one nation to encourage disaffected elements of another nation's citizenry to commit acts of sabotage, sedition, or treason.

age of consent. The youngest age at which a person may consent to sexual intercourse without subjecting the partner to a statutory rape charge. In most states it is 16, although the range is 14–18 nationwide.

age of maximum criminality. That age, when judging from criminal statistics, a person is most likely to get into conflict with the criminal law. In the case of serious offenses against property (robbery, burglary, and larceny is generally 16 to 20 years; a slightly older age group leads in offenses against the person. Offenses against public order are most common in the third decade of life. Generally speaking, crime rates decline somewhat after the age of 20, and very rapidly after the age of 40.

agglutinin. Antibody substance that causes a clumping of blood cells or bacteria in liquid suspension. This property is used in blood typing.

aggravated assault. Unlawful, intentional causing of serious bodily injury with or without a deadly weapon; unlawful, intentional attempting or threatening of serious bodily injury or death with a deadly or dangerous weapon.

aggravating circumstances. Circumstances relating to the commission of a crime that cause its gravity to be greater than that of the average instance of the given type of offense. Examples: the causing of serious bodily injury, the use of a deadly or dangerous weapon, or the accidental or intentional commission of one crime in the course of committing another crime or as a means to commit another crime.

aggravation. (1) Any action or circumstance that increases the magnitude of a crime or its penalties. (2) Any action or circumstance which intensifies the seriousness of a dispute and makes its solution more difficult.

aggregator. A Web application or software program that searches and retrieves news feeds from other sources and combines them. Once stored, the contents can be sorted by date, title, topic author, and key word.

aggression. The attempt by one state to impair another state's political sovereignty or territorial integrity by forcible means devoid of moral or legal justification. Aggression remains one of the most challenging areas of study because of the elusiveness of an adequate definition of the term. Some researchers have applied it to any act that inflicts pain or suffering on another individual; others feel that a proper definition must include some notion of intent to do harm. Still others use a situational definition, so that what might be described as aggression in one context might not be considered as such in others.

agnomen. A nickname or additional name.

agricultural violation. Unlawful conduct that falls under federal statutes, such as Agricultural Acts, violations of plant quarantines (such as transportation of prohibited produce), violations of laws related to national parks (such as fishing or hunting in protected area).

agroterrorism. a type of bio-terrorism in which terrorists attack the food supply by destroying livestock or crops. Generally, such attacks use animal diseases (e.g., anthrax), natural pests (e.g., the potato beetle), defoliation (e.g., Agent Orange), molds, or other plant diseases.

aid and abet. To assist in the commission of a crime through words, acts, presence, or other encouragement and support.

AIDS (acquired immune deficiency syndrome). A chronic, life-threatening condition caused by a virus known as the human immunodeficiency virus (HIV), which infects and destroys certain white blood cells, undermining the body's ability to resist infection. A person can be infected with HIV for years without developing symptoms of AIDS, and can transmit the virus in the absence of symptoms. Patients do not die from AIDS itself, but from "opportunistic infections" such as pneumonia, malignancies, and a type of skin cancer. AIDS is transmitted via exposure to contaminated blood, semen, and vaginal secretions; it occurs primarily through sexual intercourse, needle-sharing by intravenous drug users, and blood transfusions. By 2007 the Center for Disease control estimated that 1,106,400 people were living with the HIV infection.

Aid to Incarcerated Mothers. Founded in 1980. Serves women inmates' needs throughout Massachusetts, providing counseling on parenting and substance abuse, weekly visits with children, HIV/AID support, and advocacy. Address: 434 Massachusetts

Ave., Boston, MA 02118; telephone (617) 536-0058.

Air Pollution Index. *See* Pollution Standard Index

Air Quality Index. *See* Pollution Standard Index

alarm, class A. A fire protection specification that requires alarm operation even in the event of a single break or ground fault in the signal line. Class A alarm is a "redundant" or "ring circuit" and is generally a more expensive specification than class B alarm.

alarm, class B. A fire protection specification that requires the detection of an alarm, a single break, or a ground fault in a signal line. A break or ground fault causes further alarms to go undetected.

alarm station. (1) A manually activated device installed at a fixed location to transmit an alarm signal in response to an emergency, such as a concealed alarm in a bank teller's station. (2) A well-marked emergency control unit, installed in fixed locations usually accessible to the public and used to summon help in emergencies. The control unit contains either a manually activated switch or an automatic connection to emergency dispatch.

alarm system. An assembly of equipment and devices designed and arranged to signal the presence of a situation urgently requiring attention, such as an unauthorized entry.

Albastone. A commercially prepared material for casting footprints and similar indentations and used by some investigators instead of Plaster of Paris.

Alcatraz. A 12-acre rock island in the middle of the San Francisco harbor, discovered by the Spanish land expedition of Portola in 1769 and named *Isla de Alcatraces* (island of the pelicans), since it was white with pelicans and guano. The island was the site of the first lighthouse on the West Coast, and of the first army garrison. When it had been refitted as a maximum-security prison, James Johnson served as the first warden from 1934 to 1948, followed by Edwin Swope (1948–1955), Paul Madigan (1955–1961), and Olin Blackwell (1961–1963), who was the last warden. Alcatraz accepted only high-risk prisoners from other federal prisons. Upon its closing, inmates were sent to the federal prison in Marion, IL. Alcatraz was occupied by activists several times in the 1960s, most notably during the 19-month occupation of Indians of All Tribes (IAT) from November 20, 1969, to June 11, 1971. The group maintained that, under the Treaty of Fort Laramie between the United States and Sioux Indians, all abandoned or out-of-use federal land must be returned to the native people from whom it was acquired. Thus, when Alcatraz was declared surplus property in 1964, many activists felt the island qualified for reclamation. The group was forcibly removed by federal forces in 1971.Today, Alcatraz Island is part of the National Park Service and daily tours of the island are available for a fee.

Alcohol and Drug Abuse Information, National Clearinghouse for. Operated by the U.S. Department of Health and Human Services Substance Abuse and Mental Health Services Administration, the focal agency for federal information on drugs and their abuse. Provides information through publications and a computerized information service. Address: P.O. Box 2345, Rockville, MD 20847-2345. Web: http://ncadi.samhsa.gov/.

Alcohol and Tobacco Tax and Trade Bureau (TTB). Created in 2003, the mission of the ATF is "to collect alcohol, tobacco, firearms, and ammunition excise taxes; to ensure that these products are labeled, advertised, and marketed in accordance with the law; and to administer the laws and regulations in a manner that protects the consumer and the revenue, and promotes voluntary compliance." TTB serves regulatory functions; law enforcement functions related to alcohol, tobacco, and firearms are with the Bureau of Alcohol, Tobacco, Firearms and Explosives.

Address: Alcohol and Tobacco Tax and Trade Bureau, Public Information Officer, 1310 G Street, NW., Suite 300, Washington, DC 20220, Web: http://www.ttb.gov/. *See also* Bureau of Alcohol, Tobacco, Firearms and Explosives

Alcoholics Anonymous (AA). A voluntary fellowship, founded in 1935 by New York stockbroker Bill Wilson and surgeon Bob Smith from Akron, OH, concerned solely with the personal recovery and continued sobriety of the alcoholic members who turn to the organization for help. AA is self-supporting through its own membership and declines contributions from all outside sources. Although AA may cooperate with other organizations concerned with problems of alcohol abuse, and its members often take part in outside endeavors related to alcoholism research or treatment, the members preserve personal anonymity in the public information media. AA has been the major influence in gaining acceptance of the disease concept of alcoholism. The AA program consists basically of Twelve Suggested Steps designed for personal recovery from alcoholism. The General Service Board of Alcoholics Anonymous publishes the monthly *AA Grapevine* and other materials. Alcoholics Anonymous also runs Alateen and AlAnon for families of alcoholics.

alcoholism. Historically, alcoholism is the continued consumption of alcohol despite adverse consequences. In modern medical terms, it is the chronic, progressive disease of alcohol dependency, defined by continued consumption despite adverse consequences.

Alford plea. An Alford plea is a type of no contest plea; a guilty plea in which the defendant asserts his innocence. Often used in plea bargaining, this technique of refusing to admit guilt is often rooted in an unwillingness to risk trial when sufficient evidence exists to result in guilty verdict. *See also* no contest *or nolo contendre*

algolagnia. Sexual satisfaction derived from inflicting or experiencing pain or suffering; it is associated with both sadism and masochism. Current research suggests algolagnia is a physical phenomenon, in which the brain misinterprets pain signals as pleasurable.

alias dictus (Lat.). In its common use, this term is contracted to "alias" and means "otherwise called."

alibi. A type of defense in a criminal prosecution that demonstrates the accused could not have committed the crime with which he or she is charged, since evidence offered shows the accused was in another place at the time the crime was committed.

alien. Noncitizen, resident, or transient, who owes allegiance to a foreign government. Aliens are subject to the laws of their country of residence. In the United States, resident aliens can be drafted and own property, but have no voting rights.

alienate. To transfer property or a right to another.

alienation. A sense of estrangement or separation of individuals from community or society; a lack of cohesion with the surrounding environment, people, and social institutions, or estrangement of a married couple.

alimony. The allowance made by court order to an individual for support from his or her spouse in a divorce case. Courts typically award two types of alimony: alimony pendente lite," or temporary alimony ordered while the divorce is pending, and permanent alimony.

Alito, Samuel (1950–). Alito is an Associate Justice of the United States, appointed by President George W. Bush in 2006. Alito was born in Trenton, New Jersey, raised in Hamilton, NJ and received his degrees from Princeton and Yale. Between 1987–1990, Alito was a U.S. Attorney for the District of New Jersey; he was appointed by President George H. W. Bush as a judge on the United States Court of Appeals for the Third Circuit between 1991–2006. In 2006, he was confirmed to the U.S.S.C.

Allaway, Edward Charles (1939–). Allaway was a janitor employed by California State University, Fullerton, who shot and killed seven men, wounding two others, at the CSUF library in July of 1976, accusing them of "messing around with my wife." Allaway's wife informed him of her intention to divorce, and he believed it was due to an affair with one of his co-workers. Allaway was found not guilty by reason of insanity and sent to Atascadero State Hospital in California. In 2001, his treatment providers determined that his schizophrenia was in remission. Although eligible for discharge, he was determined to be a danger at his release hearing, a decision that was upheld by the California Supreme Court.

allegation. An assertion of what a party to an action expects to prove in court.

allege. (1) To assert; to set forth. (2) To plead.

Allen charge. Named for the case *Allen v. United States,*164 U.S. 492, 501–502, 17 S.Ct. 154, 41 L.Ed. 528 (1896), this is the term for instructions given by a judge to a jury that is having difficulty reaching a decision. Such instructions are prohibited in some states.

Alliance Against Fraud in Telemarketing (AAFT). Formed by state, federal, trade union, industrial, law enforcement, and consumer groups in 1989. Agency will forward complaints to the appropriate agency to investigate and prosecute fraudulent practices. Address: AAFT, National Consumers League, 1701 K Street NW, Suite 1200, Washington, DC 20006. Telephone: (202) 835-3323. Web: http://www.fraud.org/aaft/aaftinfo.htm.

allocution. (1) A defendant's response to the court following conviction and before sentencing; this is generally the defendant's statement addressing the injury or expressing remorse for a criminal act; (2) the victim's statement of injury to the court.

alpha (code). A set of authorized words standing for the letters of the alphabet, used in transmitting messages when a possibility of a misunderstanding exists. It supersedes the old ABLE code. The following are authorized code words: Alpha, Bravo, Charlie, Delta, Echo, Foxtrot, Gold, Hotel, India, Juliet, Kilo, Lima, Mike, November, Oscar, Papa, Quebec, Romeo, Sierra, Tango, Uniform, Victor, Whisky, X-ray, Yankee, and Zulu. *See also* Code, International

ALS. *See* Alternative Light Source

Alston Wilkes Society. Founded in 1962 and named for the late Rev. Eli Alston Wilkes, Jr., the Methodist minister who founded it, this private correctional services agency assists prison inmates, their families, and those being released. In recent years the AWS has extended its services to assist homeless veterans, at-risk families, and disadvantaged youth. Publishes a quarterly newsletter. Has different locations in South Carolina, with the state office at 3519 Medical Drive, Columbia, SC 29203-6517. Telephone: (803) 799-2490. Web: http://www.alstonwilkes-society.org/.

altercation. A fracas, fight, fuss, or noisy quarrel. *See also* affray; riot

Alternative Light Source (ALS). Used for bringing out latent fingerprints, blood, fibers, and other trace materials that are difficult to see under regular light conditions. An ALS is a white light source that emits lights from multiple spectrums, including near-ultraviolet and visible light depending on the filter used. ALS replaced "blue light" for forensic use. As of 2007, the field began moving away from ALS towards the use of portable laser OPS (optically pumped semiconductor) technology.

alternative writ. A writ granted on ex parte affidavits and requiring the person to do a certain thing or show cause why he or she should not be compelled to do so. *See also ex parte*

altruism. Helping behavior that occurs at some cost to the helper. Altruism is usually motivated intrinsically, not by observable rewards or threats of punishment, and is therefore characterized by an unselfish motive.

AMA. *See* American Medical Association

amateur radio. *See* American Radio Relay League

AMBER alert (America's Missing: Broadcast Emergency Response). Created in 1996, AMBER Alert "is a voluntary partnership between law-enforcement agencies, broadcasters, transportation agencies, and the wireless industry, to activate an urgent bulletin in the most serious child-abduction cases." AMBER Alert system is coordinated out of the United States Department of Justice, Office of Justice Programs. Since its inception, AMBER Alerts have helped authorities safely recover nearly 500 abducted children in the United States. The acronym AMBER is a memorial to Amber Hagerman, a nine-year old girl who was kidnapped while riding her bike and later found murdered. For further information, visit: http://www.amberalert.gov/.

ambisexual. Another term for bisexual.

amentia. Historical term used to describe developmental disabilities. *See* developmental disability or lack of development of mental capacity. In medical jurisprudence, insanity or developmental disability, or other diminished mental capacity.

amercement. The act of punishing by an exactment, assessment, or deprivation. A financial penalty. While often used synonymously with the term "fine," a fine is generally a fixed sum prescribed by statutes, while an amercement is a discretionary sum.

American Academy for Professional Law Enforcement. Founded in 1974 after the merging of the Academy of Police Sciences and the Law Enforcement Association on Professional Standards, Education and Ethical Practice. The Academy focuses on education and development programs in the areas of law enforcement professional and ethical standards. Its membership consists of practitioners, educators, planners, and research personnel. Address: P. O. Box 917, Peck Slip Station, New York, NY 10272. Web: www.aaple.org.

American Bar Association (ABA). A professional association, comprising attorneys who have been admitted to the bar in any of the 50 states and a registered lobby. ABA is the largest voluntary legal professional association in the world, with over 400,000 members. ABA provides law school accreditation, continuing legal education, information about the law, programs to assist lawyers and judges in their work, and initiatives to improve the legal system for the public. The ABA mission is serve members, the profession, and the public by defending liberty and delivering justice as the national representative of the legal profession. Through its committees, the ABA provides information, research, and technical assistance on various issues including substance abuse, crime prevention, and children's needs. The Standing Committee on Substance Abuse, for example, addresses medical marijuana dispensing, teenage drug abuse, and medical parity. Address: 740 15th Street, N.W., Washington, DC 20005-1019. Web: http://www.abanet.org/.

American Bar Foundation (ABF). Founded in 1952, the ABF is a research entity affiliated with the ABA. Address: 750 N. Lake Shore Drive, Chicago, IL 60611. Web: http://www.americanbarfoundation.org/index.html.

American Civil Liberties Union (ACLU). Founded in 1920 with the purpose of defending the individual's rights as guaranteed by the Constitution. Toward this end, the group's primary activities are direct involvement in test cases, organized opposition to legislation considered unconstitutional, and public protests. Among the many prominent cases in which the ACLU has participated is the Sacco-Vanzetti trial. The ACLU played a vital role in decisions citing the unconstitutionality of prayer in public schools, state-administered loyalty oaths for teachers, and illegal police search and seizure. In recent years the organization has been involved in the fight for civil rights. Privately sponsored, the

ACLU reports a membership of over 500,000, with offices in every state. Headquartered at 125 Broad Street, 18th Floor, New York, NY 10004. Web: http://www.aclu.org/.

American common law. Similar in most respects to English common law. The Supreme Court of the United States has decided, however, that English statutes that were enacted before the emigration of our ancestors, which were in force at that time, and which are applicable to our conditions and surroundings, do constitute a part of our common law. The common law of many states is expressly defined by each state's legislature; in most states there are no criminal offenses except those expressly declared by statute. In the absence of evidence to the contrary, the courts of any state presume that the common law prevails in other states. Federal courts have no common law jurisdiction in criminal cases.

American Correctional Association (ACA). Originally formed in 1870 as the National Prison Association, the organization changed its name to ACA at the Congress of Corrections held in Philadelphia. Address: 206 N. Washington Street, Alexandria, VA 22314; telephone: (703) 224-0000. Web: http://aca.org/.

American Criminal Justice Association-Lambda Alpha Epsilon (ACJA-LAE). Founded in 1937, this organization is dedicated to improving criminal justice through educational activities, fostering professionalism in law enforcement, promoting awareness of criminal justice issues, and promoting standards of ethical conduct in criminal justice. Address: P.O. Box 61047, Sacramento, CA 95860. Web: http://www.acjalae.org/.

American Federation of Labor (AFL). Organized and founded by Samuel Gompers in 1886 as a labor union, the AFL represented the members of skilled trades who did not want to be associated with the Knights of Labor. In 1955, the union merged with the Congress of Industrial Organizations to form the AFL-CIO. *See also* Hoffa, James

American Federation of Labor and Congress of Industrial Organizations (AFL-CIO). Under the leadership of AFL vice president John L. Lewis, several industrial unions sought charters with the AFL. When the AFL ordered these groups to disband, they left the AFL and joined the CIO in 1938. Both organizations enjoyed success in the late 1930s and early 1940s. However, union power was curtailed in 1947 with the passage of the Taft-Hartley Act. This prompted the merger of the AFL and CIO in 1955. The only major unions not affiliated with the AFL-CIO are the United Mine Workers and the National Education Association. Address: 815 16th St., N.W., Washington, DC 20006. Web: http://www.aflcio.org/. The International Union of Police Associations (IUPA), an AFL-CIO charter, has established locals throughout the United States and claims to represent over 200 law enforcement agencies (IUPA Address: 1549 Ringling Blvd, Suite 600 Sarasota, FL 34236 Web: http://www.iupa.org/).

American Federation of Police and Concerned Citizens (AFP & CC). Founded in 1960, the AFP & CC is committed both to supporting the law enforcement community and providing programs and financial assistance to the family members left behind by officers killed in the line of duty. Publishes the *Police Times Magazine* (quarterly). Address: 6350 Horizon Drive, Titusville, FL 32780. Web: http://www.afp-cc.org/.

American Humane Association. Founded in 1877, its objectives are to provide information, advice, and training to prevent animal abuse and child abuse, and to promote better services for both groups. Address: 63 Inverness Drive East, Englewood, CO 80112. Web: http://www.americanhumane.org/.

American Indian Movement (AIM). An activist group of Native Americans founded in 1968 in Minneapolis to address issues concerning the Native American community including poverty, housing, treaty issues, and police harassment. Since its inception, AIM has expanded its activities throughout the

Midwest and its interests to a broad range of concerns. It has brought successful suits against the federal government for the protection of the rights of Native Nations guaranteed in treaties, sovereignty, the United States Constitution, and laws. In February of 1973, AIM members conducted a siege at Pine Ridge Reservation, Wounded Knee, South Dakota, which lasted seventy-one days. AIM members staged the siege in response to the 1890 massacre of at least 150 Lakota Sioux men, women, and children by the U.S. Cavalry near Wounded Knee Creek. During the stand-off, actor Marlon Brando missed his acceptance speech at the Academy Awards for his role in the 1972 film *The Godfather,* sending a native American woman to accept the award in his place. The event garnered national and world support. Web: http://www.aimovement.org/.

American Institutes for Research. Founded in 1946, the institute examines various facets of education, including crime in school. Address: 1000 Thomas Jefferson Street, NW, Washington, DC 20007-3835. Web: http://www.air.org/.

American Judges Association. Founded in 1959 as the National Association of Municipal Judges, the organization changed its name to AJA in 1973. The purpose of the organization is to promote and improve the effective administration of justice; to maintain the status and independence of the judiciary; to provide a forum for the continuing education of its members and the general public; and for the exchange of new ideas among all judges. Address: 300 Newport Avenue, Williamsburg, VA 23185-4147. Web: http://aja.ncsc.dni.us/.

American Judicature Society. Founded in 1913, the organization works to maintain the independence and integrity of the courts and increase public understanding of the justice system. Publishes *Judicature* (bimonthly) and *Judicial Conduct Report* (quarterly). Address: The Opperman Center at Drake University, 2700 University Avenue, Des Moines, Iowa 50311. Web: http://www.ajs.org/.

American Law Institute. A national association of prominent lawyers and legal scholars who voluntarily draft model laws, such as the Model Penal Code. Address: 4025 Chestnut Street, Philadelphia, PA 19104, Phone: (215) 243-1600; Web: http://www.ali.org/.

American Law Institute (ALI) model. A legal standard for insanity developed by the American Law Institute in its Model Penal Code. This standard is a combination of several other tests and holds that a defendant is not responsible for criminal acts "if at the time of such conduct as a result of mental disease or defect he lacks *substantial capacity* either to appreciate the criminality of his conduct or to conform his conduct to the requirements of the law." *See also* insanity defense; M'Naghten Rule, irresistible impulse, Durham rule, Brawner rule; substantial capacity test, and temporary insanity. *See also* Insanity Defense Reform Act of 1984 (U.S.); *See also* Table 25. Types of Insanity Defense in the United States, page 232

American Medical Association (AMA). A national organization designed to promote the art and science of medicine and the betterment of public health. Address: 515 N. State Street, Chicago, IL 60610. Web: http://www.ama-assn.org/.

American Society of Questioned Document Examiners (ASQDE). Formally established in 1942, the oldest organization of questioned document examiners in the United States. Publishes *Journal of the American Society of Questioned Document Examiners* (biannually). Address: P.O. Box 18298, Long Beach, CA 90807; Web: http://www.asqde.org/.

American Probation and Parole Association (APPA). Developed in 1975, international association of members involved with probation, parole, and community-based corrections, in both adult and juvenile sectors. Provides technical assistance and information regarding probation and parole systems and related court-ordered treatment programs, including community supervision. Address:

Council of State Governments, Ironworks Pike, P.O. Box 11910, Lexington, KY 40578. Web: http://www.appa-net.org/eweb/.

American Prosecutors Research Institute (APRI). Founded by the National District Attorneys Association (NDAA) in 1984, the APRI "provides state and local prosecutors knowledge, skills and support to ensure that justice is done and the public safety rights of all persons are safeguarded. To accomplish this mission, APRI serves as a nationwide interdisciplinary resource center for research and development, technical assistance, training, and publications reflecting the highest standards and cutting-edge practices of the prosecutorial profession." Address: 44 Canal Center Plaza, Suite 110, Alexandria, VA 22314 http://www.ndaa.org/apri/about/index.html.

American Psychological Association (APA). A scientific and professional society of psychologists and educators founded in 1892. APA is a scientific and professional organization representing psychology in the United States and which APA seeks to advance psychology as a science, as a profession, and as a means of promoting human welfare. It is the largest professional psychological organization worldwide, with over 150,000 members. Headquartered at 750 First Street, NE, Washington, DC 20002-4242. http://www.apa.org/.

American Radio Relay League. Organization for amateur radio operators, or "hams." Many have assisted police efforts during emergencies in which normal communications channels have been overtaxed or disabled. Headquarters: 225 Main Street, Newington, CT 06111.

American Society for Industrial Security. Founded in 1955, ASIS changed its name to ASIS International in 2002 to reflect the organization's worldwide growth to more than 35,000 members. It is an international organization of industrial security officers. Publishes *Security Management.* Address: 1625 Prince Street, Alexandria, Virginia 22314-2818.

American Society of Crime Lab Directors (ASCLD). Organized in 1973, ASCLD is a "nonprofit professional society of crime laboratory directors and forensic science managers dedicated to providing excellence in forensic science through leadership and innovation." The organization offers guidelines on the management and operations of crime labs. Address: ASCLD, Inc., 139K Technology Drive, Garner, NC 27529. Web: http://www.ascld.org/.

American Society of Criminology, The (ASC). Founded in Berkeley, CA, in 1941, the ASC is an interdisciplinary international organization whose members pursue scholarly, scientific, and professional knowledge concerning the measurement, etiology, consequences, prevention, control, and treatment of crime and delinquency. Publishes *Criminology: An Interdisciplinary Journal* (quarterly) and the *Criminologist* (bimonthly). Address: 1314 Kinnear Road, Suite 212, Columbus, OH 43212. Web: http://www.asc41.com/.

Americans for Effective Law Enforcement, Inc. (AELE). Founded in 1966, AELE provides research assistance in civil liability for law enforcement agencies and administrators. Publishes *AELE Monthly Law Journal* (monthly), *Law Enforcement Liability Reporter* (monthly); *Fire and Police Personnel Reporter* (monthly), *Jail and Prisoner Law Bulletin* (monthly). P.O. Box 75401, Chicago, IL 60675-5401. Web: http://www.aele.org/.

Americans with Disabilities Act, The (ADA). The U.S. Supreme Court's 1896 decision in *Plessy v. Ferguson* allowed the continuation of segregation and other discriminatory employment practices based not only on race, but also on age and disability. The Court reversed that decision and declared segregation to be inherently unequal treatment in *Brown v. Board of Education* in 1954. *Brown,* along with the Civil Rights Act of 1964 and the results of advocacy group activities, brought about the passage of the Rehabilitation Act of 1973, which specifically addressed disabled Americans for the first time but applied only to the employment practices of the federal government. The Air Carrier Access Act (1968) and the Fair Housing Amendments Act (1988) broadened legislation to include private-sector businesses. The ADA was signed into law on July 26, 1990, and amended in the ADA Amendments Act of 2008. The ADA defines a covered disability as "a physical or mental impairment that substantially limits a major life activity." The 2008 amendment added examples of "major life activities" including such factors as "caring for oneself, performing manual tasks, seeing, hearing, eating, sleeping, walking, standing, lifting, bending, speaking, breathing, learning, reading, concentrating, thinking, communicating, and working." The ADA is organized around five Titles: employment (Title I), public entities and transportation (Title II), public accommodations and commercial facilities (Title III), telecommunications (Title IV), and miscellaneous technical provisions (Title V). The courts have consistently held that ADA applies to prisons and jails (*Pennsylvania Dept. of Corrections v. Yeskey,* 524 U.S. 206 (1998)) Multiple class-action lawsuits have been filed by jail and prison inmates citing ADA violations in custody (*Armstrong v. Davis,* 2000; *Beckford v. Irvin,* 1999; *Beckford v. Portuendo,* 2000; *Berthelot v. Stadler,* 2000; *Bradley v. Puckett,* 1998; *Brady v. Griffith,* 1998; *Frost v. Agnos,* 1998; *Gorman v. Bartch,* 1998; *Gleish v. Hardiman,* 1993; *Grant v. Schuman,*1998; *Hallett v. New York State Dept of Correctional Services,* 2000; *Jones v. St. Tamany Parish Jail,* 1999; *Lawson v. Dallas County,* 2000; *Mills v. Lee,* 2000; *Miller v. Tanner,* 1999; *Nelson v. Norris,* 2001; *Owen v. Chester County,* 2000; *Parkinson v. Goord,* 2000; *Rainey v. County of Delaware,* 2000; *Schmidt v. Odell,* 1999; *Shariff v. Artuz,* 2000).

America's Missing: Broadcast Emergency Response. *See* AMBER alert

amicus curiae (Lat., lit. "friend of the court"). One who is permitted or invited by a court to participate in a legal proceeding but who is not a party to it. In cases involving civil and criminal rights where a question of general applicability is being decided, courts have increasingly allowed "amicus briefs," which give legal argument or facts. The practice can be of value in providing the court with a clear analysis of both the factors it should consider in making its decision and the possible implications of that decision.

amphetamine. Alpha-methylphenethylamine, a synthetic (analog) drug that stimulates the central nervous system. The effects are similar to those of cocaine, with mental and physical hyperactivity, including increased breathing rate and rapid or irregular heartbeat, increased blood pressure, increased/distorted sensations, dilated pupils, flushing, restlessness, impaired speech, numbness, dry mouth, sweating, headache, dizziness, and blurred vision, tremors, insomnia, reduced appetite, diarrhea, and constipation,and erectile dysfunction. Overdose can lead to convulsions and death. Street names include meth, speed, ice and uppers. Amphetamines can be taken orally (affecting the central nervous system within 30 minutes for up to 14 hours), inhaled as a white powder, or by injection when in solution (with immediate effects that last only one–two hours). Amphetamines are highly addictive, with tolerance developing within two–four weeks, causing users to increase the dosage. Withdrawal symptoms include depression, irritability, extreme fatigue, intense hunger, and disturbed sleep patterns. Amphetamines were first synthesized in 1887 and marketed under the name Benzedrine in 1932 as inhalants for use as nasal decongestants. *See also* ephedrine

Amplified Fragment Length Polymorphism (AmbFLP). A low cost method of DNA analysis using a relatively simple procedure using PCR to amplify DNA samples. This method examines variable number tandem repeat (VNTR) polymorphisms, which show variations between individuals. Not widely used in the United States today. *See* also Deoxyribo nucleic acid; DNA analysis; Restriction Fragment Length Polymorphism (RFLP) test; Polymerase Chain Reaction (PCR); PCR-based Short Tandem Repeat (STR) method; Short Tandem Repeat on the Y-chromosome (Y-STR); and mitochondrial DNA (mtDNA)

amygdala. Almond-shaped structures in the medial temporal lobes of the brain, the amygdala is part of the limbic system and is responsible for emotional memory.

anabolic steroids. Also called **anabolic-androgenic steroids (AAS)**, synthetic drugs which mimic the effect of the male sex hormone testosterone, a natural substance responsible for the development of such secondary sexual characteristics as facial hair and deep voice. Testosterone also plays a major role in increased muscle size and strength, which is the primary reason for high rates of steroid misuse among professional athletes. The use of anabolic steroids for this purpose is a criminal offense in most U.S. jurisdictions. Long-term use of anabolic steroids can cause many adverse effects, including harmful changes in cholesterol levels, high blood pressure, liver damage, and changes in the structure of the left ventricle of the heart, which may be associated with hypertension, cardiac arrhythmias, congestive heart failure, heart attacks, and sudden cardiac death. It can also increase the risk of cardiovascular disease and coronary artery disease. Excessive use has also been associated with acne, premature baldness, reduced sexual function, and temporary infertility in males.

anal eroticism. Sexual behavior focusing on the anus, which may include oral/anal contact (rimming), insertion of the penis into the anus (sodomy), digital insertion into the anus, and sexual stimulation by anal odors. The additional term "analism" refers to a preoccupation with the anus as a focus of sexual stimulation.

anaphrodisiac. A drug or substance which repressed or quells sexual desire.

anarchism. The political philosophy that equality and justice may be obtained only through the abolition of the state and its organs. It opposes capitalism and free enterprise. In the United States, anarchists exercised some influence in the trade union and radical political movements in the last third of the nineteenth century. Anarchists were accused of perpetrating the Haymarket affair in Chicago in 1886, leading to the arrest of seven anarchists and the ultimate execution of four of them. An anarchist assassinated President William McKinley in 1901. Sacco and Vanzetti, two anarchists, were arrested in 1921 and executed in 1927.

anarchist. One who proposes the violent overthrow of the government; one who advocates a lack of government.

anarchist bombings. A series of bombings in the United States carried out in 1919 by followers of Luigi Galleani, a self-proclaimed anarchist. Between April and June of 1919, at least 30 bombs were mailed to prominent members of the U.S. government; although no one was killed, the attacks resulted in several injuries before authorities tracked down nearly 16 undetonated bombs traveling via U.S. post. In June of 1919, eight large bombings targeting politicians were completed by the same group; no deaths occurred. One suspect, Andrea Salsedo, committed suicide prior to arrest. Another suspect, Roberto Elia, was deported after he failed to testify. The U.S. Attorney General Palmer, who was targeted in the attacks, led a series of raids (known as Palmer raids) and arrests related to the bombings, which fueled the Red Scare. An estimated 500 people associated with Galleani were subsequently deported under the Anarchist Act; see also domestic terrorism; Galleanist anarchists

anarchy, criminal. Advocacy of the overthrow of any authorized government or the assassination of any of its executive heads.

anasyrma. The intentional exposure of a woman's naked vagina, exposed by lifting a skirt when no underwear is worn. Anasyrma is generally done for the arousal of the viewer, as opposed to exhibitionism, which is generally done for the arousal of the exhibitionist and viewer. *See also* exhibitionism, flashing

androgynous. A term referring to individuals who possess both male and female characteristics.

angel dust. *See* phencyclidine

angel of death. *See* hero-homicide complex

animal abuse. All 50 states have legislation relating to animal abuse; however, definitions vary by jurisdiction. A common definition includes causing the intentional infliction of unnecessary pain, suffering, distress, or death of an animal. However, it can also include intentionally causing deprivation of shelter, water, food, socialization or medical care. *See* child abuse

annulment. (1) The act, by competent authority, of canceling, making void, or depriving of all force, as a contract. (2) The legal procedure for declaring a marriage null and void.

anomalies, physical. The physical signs that criminologist Cesare Lombroso held would identify a criminal. It was Lombroso's contention that criminals were born, not made, and that evidence of criminality could be seen in the peculiar shape of various body parts, particularly the head and face. Although the theory has been discredited, it has been revived in recent years by physical anthropologists. *See also* Lombroso, Cesare

anomalous plea. A court plea that is partly affirmative and partly negative.

anomie. A concept first formulated by sociologist Emile Durkheim to describe a state of normlessness in which social control of individual behavior has become ineffective. The concept is fundamental to Durkheim's sociology and provides the reference point for his critical analysis of the problems of modern society. The concept was later used by Robert Merton (American sociological theorist, 1910–2003) to describe the conflict between culturally instilled goals and socially approved means of attaining those goals. *See also* Genovese, Kitty

anonymity. In sociological theory, the conditions that occur when an individual is masked or not highly visible. Under normal conditions, people's antisocial impulses are held in check by fear of embarrassment or punishment. But one factor that can free individuals from these restraints and provide them with the opportunity to engage in nontypical behavior is anonymity. Thus, many burglars work at night, bank robbers wear masks, and members of the Ku Klux Klan wear white sheets. In an experiment testing the effects of anonymity on aggression, it was found that girls whose identities were masked with hoods delivered more than twice as much shock to a "victim" as did girls whose identities were not masked. Individuals are thought to seek anonymity as a defense against hostile environments in which they fear punishment or retribution. *See also* deindividuation

anonymous groups. Patterned after Alcoholics Anonymous, the most notable self-help movement of its kind, and often involving a 12-step process of recovery along with reliance on fellow group members who have all experienced similar problems, usually addictions. Groups include (but are not limited to): Co-Dependents Anonymous, Compulsive Stutterers Anonymous, Debtors Anonymous, Divorcees Anonymous, Drugs Anonymous, Gamblers Anonymous, HIV+ or HIVIES Anonymous, Incest Anonymous, Narcotics Anonymous, Nicotine Anonymous, Obsessive-Compulsives Anonymous, Overeaters Anonymous, Parents Anonymous, Pill Addicts Anonymous, Sex Addicts or Sexaholics Anonymous, Workaholics Anonymous.

anorexia nervosa. An eating disorder, most commonly found in adolescent girls, characterized by extremely low body weight, distorted body image, and fear of gaining weight. Has the highest fatality rate (20 percent) of all psychiatric disorders. *See also* bulimia nervosa

answer. A defense in writing to charges contained in a bill or complaint filed by the plaintiff against the defendant.

Antabuse therapy. A treatment for alcoholism using the drug disulfiram (Antabuse), a relatively inert chemical compound which causes acute sensitivity to alcohol. It interferes with the metabolism of alcohol, resulting in a buildup of the toxin acetaldehyde in the blood. If an individual on Antabuse consumes alcohol, he or she experiences increased blood pressure, flushing of the skin, rapid breathing, and accelerated heart rate. If drinking continues, dizziness, nausea, and vomiting occur, eventually followed by a rapid fall in blood pressure, unconsciousness, and possibly death. Giving disulfiram is not in itself a sufficient therapeutic program. Many physicians, however, regard the drug as a useful tool to help patients overcome the urge to drink while pursuing psychological rehabilitative techniques, such as group therapy. Although primarily used in the treatment of alcoholism, antabuse has also been reported or researched for use in the treatment of cocaine dependence, giardia, scabies, and cancer.

antecedent. Prior to; preceding.

anthrax attacks. The first known bioterrorist attack on U.S. soil, the anthrax attacks occurred in the fall of 2001, shortly after the September 11 attacks. The attacks were involved letters laced with anthrax spores mailed to U.S. senators and the media between September 18 and October 9, 2001. The attacks killed five persons and infected 17 others (some reports claim 68 exposures). Bruce Edwards Ivins a microbiologist and biodefense researcher at the United States Army Medical Research Institute of Infectious Diseases (USAMRIID) who was a key suspect in the attacks, committed suicide prior to the filing of formal charges. *See also* domestic terrorism; Ivins, Bruce Edwards

anthropology. Scientific study of mankind and its development in relation to its physical, mental, and cultural history. It is a comprehensive science, touching upon such other disciplines as criminology, biology, physiology, psychology, comparative anatomy, and sociology. Specifically, anthropology may be considered the science of man's natural history in relation to his physical character, rather than the general science of man.

anticipated strain: theoretical expectation that current strain will continue in the future.

Anti-Money Laundering/Combating the Financing of Terrorism (AML/CFT). Division within the International Monetary Fund (IMF) which coordinates global regulation and tracking of money laundering and the financing of terrorism. The goals of AML/CFT are: "protecting the integrity and stability of the international financial system, cutting off the resources available to terrorists, and making it more difficult for those engaged in crime to profit from their criminal activities." Address: International Monetary Fund, 700 19th Street, N.W., Washington, DC 20431 Web: http://www.imf.org/external/.

antisocial behavior. Disruptive acts characterized by covert and overt hostility and intentional aggression; acts that impose physical or psychological harm on other people or their property.

antisocial personality disorder. According to the Diagnostic and Statistical Manual-IV (DSM-IV) of the American Psychiatric Association, antisocial personality disorder is "a pervasive pattern of disregard for, and violation of, the rights of others that begins in childhood or early adolescence and continues into adulthood." Research suggests the prevalence of this disorder is higher in correctional and substance abusing populations than in the general population.

anti-trust violation. Unlawful conduct which violates federal antitrust statutes, including such offenses as price fixing, monopolies, etc.

anthropometry. The study of the measurements of the human body for the purpose of anthropological comparison; also known as the Bertillon system. *See also* Bertillon method

anthropophagy. Cannibalism; the act or practice of human consumption of human flesh.

anti-lynch bills. Federal bills that, since the early 1920s, have attempted to provide the protection of the U.S. courts against lynching, a crime that still results in virtually no arrests, presentments, or court convictions. In 1922 the Dyer Anti-Lynch Bill was passed in the House but rejected by the Senate. Subsequent attempts at legislation, consistently been opposed on states' rights grounds, all failed. On June 13, 2005, members of the U.S. Senate unanimously passed a resolution apologizing to the victims of lynching and their descendants for the failure of the Senate to enact anti-lynching legislation. (S. Res. 39, 109th Cong. [2005] [enacted]). *See also* lynching

antipsychotic drugs. A group of psychoactive prescription medications that are used to relieve or control, but not to cure, the symptoms of psychosis and other mental and emotional conditions.

Anti-Racketeering Act. A law of Congress, passed on June 18, 1934, which made it a criminal offense to interfere with foreign or interstate commerce by violence, threats, coercion, or intimidation. In 1946, an amendment to this Act was passed in the form of the Hobbs Anti-Racketeering Act, which includes heavy criminal penalties for acts of robbery or extortion that affect interstate commerce. The Hobbs Acts has been interpreted broadly, resulting in prosecutions for intrastate robberies and public corruption.

antitrust cases. Federal cases against large business conglomerates, or trusts. Prosecutions are conducted under the provisions of the Sherman Antitrust Act of 1890, which barred any joint action by business "in restraint of trade" and made it a criminal offense to attempt to monopolize interstate commerce. The act expressed the traditional American hostility to monopoly and "privilege." In 1914 President Woodrow Wilson introduced the Clayton Antitrust Act to strengthen the Sherman Act. A notable recent case was the U.S. Department of Justice's suit against the Microsoft in 1998, which was settled when Microsoft agreed to share its application programming interfaces with other companies.

Apalachin Meeting. A meeting of high officials of the Cosa Nostra held at Apalachin, New York, in 1957. The meeting was interrupted by law enforcement officers who had obtained the identity of several persons in attendance. Nearly 60 indictments followed.

apathy. Indifference. In an increasingly urban and impersonal society, apathy has become a problem of growing concern to social scientists. In 1964 at least 37 individuals watched the stabbing murder of 28-year-old Kitty Genovese in New York City; not one of them called for help during or after the stabbing. Anonymity and deindividuation play a large role in creating such a climate of indifference. A second factor contributing to indifference is perceived loss of control. As individuals perceive themselves to be less and less in charge of their own lives, their willingness to try to change things decreases. *See also* anonymity; deindividuation; Genovese, Kitty

aphrodisiac. A chemical substance that is alleged to stimulate sexual interest and/or capability.

apocrypha. Writings or statements of doubtful authorship or authenticity.

Apodysophilia. A psychological compulsion to expose one's naked sex organs, including bare breasts for women and genitals (or buttocks) for either sex. *See also* exhibitionism, sex offender

apparent danger. Used in reference to self-defense, to justify a killing as necessary for self-preservation. The danger must be presumable, or clear and manifest.

appeal. A proceeding found in many ancient legal codes, appeal in civil law was the removal of a case from a lower to a higher court for retrial as to both law and fact. Most modern appellate proceedings (appeals) are now governed by statute. The term in modern-day usage connotes any form of appellate review of errors of law rather than of fact, and distinguishes appellate review as a matter of right (direct appeal) from appellate review at the discretion of the higher court (*certiorari*).

appeal bond. The bond posted by an individual who is appealing a case; the appellant guarantees to pay damages and costs if he or she fails to go forward with the appeal.

appeal case. A case, filed in a court having incidental or general appellate jurisdiction, to initiate review of a judgment or decision of a trial court, an administrative agency, or an intermediate appellate court.

appeal proceedings. The set of orderly steps by which a court considers the issues and makes a determination in the appeal case before it. The major steps in appeal proceedings are: (a) the appeal is initiated by the filing of a formal document in the court having appellate jurisdiction; (b) a record of the original proceedings (the court reporter's transcript) in the trial court is obtained by the appellate court; (c) briefs are filed in court by the opposing parties (appellant and respondent); (d) if there are to be oral arguments, a hearing is scheduled and the arguments heard; and (e) following completion of arguments or submission of briefs, the court deliberates, reviewing the record of the earlier proceedings and considering the allegations and arguments of the parties, and announces its decision in the case. This decision may be embodied in an opinion that also gives the reasons for the decision.

Appeals, U.S. Court of. An intermediate federal court, with jurisdiction above the U.S. District Courts. There are 13 such courts in the United States, and decisions made by each U.S. Court of Appeals apply to all cases within that district. Such decisions are subject to review by the United States Supreme Court.

appearance. An individual's formal presentation of him- or herself in court, usually to present testimony in a lawsuit.

appellant. Relating to appeals; the individual who appeals, especially from a lower to a higher court.

appellate. Relating to or having jurisdiction to review appeals.

appellate court. A court that reviews cases originally tried and decided by lower courts. The appellate court acts without a jury and is primarily interested in correcting errors in procedure or in the interpretation of law by the lower court.

appellate judge. A judge in a court of appellate jurisdiction who primarily hears appeal cases and also conducts disciplinary or impeachment proceedings.

appellate jurisdiction. The authority of a superior court to review and modify the decisions of an inferior court.

appellee. The party in a lawsuit against whom an appeal is taken; the respondent.

appose. To examine an officer of a business firm for the purpose of reviewing the firm's accounts.

apprehend. To make an arrest on a charge of a crime.

approver. In English common law, one who confesses a crime and at the same time accuses others to save him- or herself.

appurtenance. A right (such as a right-of-way) attached to something else; an accessory or adjunct.

aquaeroticism. Sexual gratification from submerging the head and/or the entire body in water so as to produce a sensation of losing consciousness during orgasm.

arbitration. Often used in labor management, a process by which disputes may be resolved, using a third party to render a decision. Arbitration may deal with controversies arising in the determination of a new contract (interest arbitration) or with disagreements over the interpretation of an existing contract's provisions (grievance arbitration). More flexible and less expensive than court proceedings, arbitration is usually preferred by both labor and management. *See also* collective bargaining; conciliation; mediation

arbitrator. The person chosen by parties in a controversy to settle their differences; a private judge. Arbitrators are usually chosen from the National Academy of Arbitrators American Arbitration Association, the Federal Mediation and Conciliation Service, or an agency of the federal, state, or city government.

archives. Records preserved as evidence; public papers and records.

area, delinquency. An area of a city marked by an unusually high delinquency rate compared to other areas of the city of similar size and population. Such areas are often located in zones of transition and are marked by industrial buildings, waterfronts, railroad yards, and deteriorated buildings.

area, metropolitan. A region including a large concentration of population together with the surrounding areas, where the daily economic and social life is predominantly influenced by the central city.

aristocracy. A high social class, especially one that is a nation's governing or ruling class.

Armed Career Criminal Act (ACCA) of 1984. Federal law that provides sentencing enhancements for offenders who commit crimes with firearms, if they have two or more prior "serious" or "violent" crimes as specified in the statute. Offenders sentenced under this provision receive a minimum sentence of fifteen years imprisonment. 18 U.S.C. § 924(e)(1).

armory. (1) A place or building where arms are stored. (2) Aboard ship, a compartment where small arms and light machine guns are stowed and serviced. (3) Formerly, a place or building where arms were manufactured.

arms, right to bear. A provision of the Second Amendment that prohibits Congress from interfering with the right of the people to arm themselves. Enacted at a time of strong popular distrust of standing mercenary armies and a fear of the creation of an overly powerful central government, the Second Amendment allowed the establishment of state militia free of congressional restraints. The amendment and the inherent power of the states to control firearms have bred considerable controversy over gun control.

Arpaio, Joseph M. "Joe." (1932–). Born in Springfield, Illinois, Arpaio's mother died in childbirth. He was raised by his father, a grocery store owner, and various family members. He served in the Army from 1950–1954. He was a police officer in Washington DC in 1954–1957 and reportedly earned the title "most assaulted WDCPD officer" in 1957. After a brief tenure in Nevada law enforcement, he had a 25-year career with the Drug Enforcement Agency (DEA), with assignments in Turkey, Mexico, and as head of the Arizona office. He was elected Maricopa County Sheriff in 1992, and was subsequently reelected in 1996, 2000, 2004, and 2008. Arpaio is most noted for his reforms to corrections in his jurisdiction, most notably the development of "Tent City," which has received numerous complaints of civil rights violations. Arpaio also instituted the only known volunteer juvenile chain gang in the world. *See also* Tent City

arraign. To bring a person before a court to answer a charge.

arraignment. (1) Strictly, the hearing before a court having jurisdiction in a criminal case, in which the identity of the defendant is established, the defendant is informed of the charge(s) and of his or her rights, and the defendant is required to enter a plea. (2) In some usages, any appearance in court prior to trial in criminal proceedings.

array. The group of persons summoned into court for jury duty; the order in which these people are ranked in the jury box.

arrest. The legal detainment of a person to answer for criminal charges or (infrequently

TABLE 1 VICTIMIZATION, ARREST, CONVICTION, AND INCARCERATION
FOR INDEX CRIMES, 2004

Crime type	Victimizations*	Arrests	Felony Convictions	Incarcerations	Prison sentences
Homicide	(16,140)+	12,360	8,400	7,730	7,480
Rape/sexual assault	209,880	21,840	12,310	10,960	8,490
Robbery	501,820	83,710	38,850	33,800	27,970
Aggravated assault	1,030,080	377,580	94,380	68,900	40,580
Burglary	3,427,690	213,030	93,870	70,400	46,000
Motor vehicle theft	1,014,770	109,100	16,910	14,540	6,930
Larceny	13,814,920	1,160,085	4,508	----	----
Drug trafficking	-----	282,590	201,760	139,210	78,690

*NCVS victimization data are based on interviews with victims and thus cannot measure homicide.

+Homicide estimate (16,140) based on preliminary FBI data as reported by BJS. Compiled from Bureau of Justice Statistics data.

at present) civil demands. Constitutional limitations prevent arrest or detention under false or assumed authority and harassment of persons without warrants properly issued. *See also habeas corpus See also* Table 1. Victimization, Arrest, Conviction, and Incarceration for Index Crimes, 2004, on page 27.

arrest by officer without warrant, when lawful. A peace officer may, without a warrant, arrest a person when: (a) the person to be arrested has committed a felony or misdemeanor in the officer's presence (in the case of such arrest for a misdemeanor, the arrest shall be made immediately or on fresh pursuit); (b) the person to be arrested has committed a felony, although not in the officer's presence; (c) a felony has in fact been committed, and the officer has reasonable grounds to believe that the person to be arrested has committed it; or (d) the officer has reasonable grounds to believe that a felony has been or is being committed and

reasonable grounds to believe that the person to be arrested has committed or is committing it.

arrest by private person, when lawful. A private person may make an arrest when (a) the person to be arrested has in the former's presence committed either a misdemeanor amounting to a breach of the peace or a felony, or (b) a felony has been in fact committed and the private citizen has reasonable grounds to believe that the person to be arrested has committed it.

arrestee dispositions. The class of law enforcement or prosecutorial actions that terminate or provisionally suspend proceedings against an arrested person before a charge has been filed in court. Such actions, permanent or provisional, are: (a) police release—arrestee released after booking because of law enforcement agency decision not to request complaint; (b) complaint rejected—prosecutor declines to prosecute case on grounds such as insufficient evidence, lack of witnesses, or interests of justice (c) prosecution withheld—prosecutor suspends proceedings conditional upon behavior of arrestee with referral to probation or other criminal justice agency, or with referral to a noncriminal justice agency, or with no referral.

Arrestee Drug Abuse Monitoring Program (ADAM). The Arrestee Drug Abuse Monitoring (ADAM) program began in 2000, under the National Institute of Justice, within the U.S. Department of Justice. The ADAM program absorbed the Drug Use Forecasting (DUF) program, established in 1987. ADAM collects data about drug using, drug and alcohol dependency and treatment, and drug participation among recently booked arrestees. The program was canceled in 2004. However, archived copies of reports from 1987–2003 are available at: National Archive of Criminal Justice Data, P.O. Box 1248 Ann Arbor, MI 48106-1248, Web: http://www.ojp.usdoj.gov/nij/topics/drugs/adam.htm.

arrest rate. The number of arrests as a percentage of the crimes known to the police; also, the number of arrests as a percentage of a certain population group, such as the rate for males or for youths under the age of 16.

arrest record. A list of a person's arrests and charges made against him/her, usually including those dismissed or dropped and those of which he/she was found innocent. The arrest record also contains information on dispositions and sentences if there was adjudication of guilt. *See also* security and privacy

arrest register. The document containing a chronological record of all arrests made by members of a given law enforcement agency, each entry containing at a minimum the identity of the arrestee, the charges at time of arrest, and the date and time of arrest. This kind of record is also called an "arrest register book" or "initial entry record." In some agencies the information is entered directly into an electronic processing system. These records and arrest reports are key sources of statistical information. A "police blotter" is used in some jurisdictions to record arrests and other information about police activity. All these types of records, being chronological accounts of government activity, are usually open to public inspection. Jail registers or jail books are records of "bookings," that is, admissions of persons into detention facilities. In some jurisdictions these may be the chief or only source of information about completed arrests.

arrest upon hue and cry. An old common law process of pursuing with horn and with voice all felons and individuals who have dangerously wounded others. The hue and cry could be raised by officers, private persons, or both. The officer and his or her assistants have the same powers, protection, and indemnity as if they were acting under a warrant.

arrest upon order of magistrate. When an offense is committed in the presence of a magistrate, he or she may, by an oral or written order, command any person to arrest the offender immediately, and may then proceed as though the offender had been brought before him or her on an arrest warrant.

arrest warrant. An official document signed by a judge or other authorized court official accusing an individual of a crime and authorizing law enforcement personnel to take that person into custody.

arson. maliciously, voluntarily, and willfully setting fire (or attempting to set fire) to structures or wildlife areas for an improper purpose, such as to collect insurance. Arson in children is one element of the MacDonald Triad, suggesting precursors for sociopathy. *See also* MacDonald Triad

Arson Investigators, International Association of. Founded in 1949. Publishes *The Fire and Arson Investigator* (quarterly). Address: 2151 Priest Bridge Drive, Suite 25, Crofton, MD 21114. Web: http://firearson.com/.

arsonist. A person who deliberately starts a fire for the purpose of destroying life, property, or evidence, or for collecting insurance.

artifice. Trickery; false or insincere behavior.

artificial. Having an existence presumed in law or on paper only, such as a corporation.

Artificial Intelligence (AI). Coined in 1956, AI is the branch of computer science that aims to study and create intelligence in computer software. Artificial intelligence technologies are used by most federal agencies to process and analyze large amounts of data. The use of AI is considered indispensable in the antiterrorism efforts of the FBI and the Department of Homeland Security.

artificial presumption. A presumption that derives its force and effect from the law rather than from belief or actual events. Thus, a legal presumption that a person is dead after continued absence is an artificial presumption created by law. The period of absence varies from state to state, but the majority hold seven years as the mark.

Aryan Brotherhood. Also called "The Brand," "Alice Baker," "the AB," or "the One-Two," a white prison gang which originated in San Quentin Prison and has spread throughout the nation. The gang has an alliance with La Eme (The Mexican Mafia), as the two are mutual enemies of the Black Guerilla Family. With an estimated 15,000 members both in and out of prison as of 2010, the FBI estimates that the Aryan Brotherhood is responsible for nearly 20 percent of all murders in the federal prison system. Members can be identified by distinctive tattoos, including "Aryan Brotherhood," "AB," SS 666, shamrocks, and Nazi and Celtic symbols.

ASCLD. *See* American Society of Crime Lab Directors

asportation. Taking and carrying away. If a defendant, having taken possession of goods, has not moved them from their original location, the *asportation* necessary to constitute larceny is lacking.

assassination. (1) Murder of a public figure. A wide range of U.S. political officials—from presidents and cabinet members to local judges and tax collectors—have been targets of assassination attempts, as have other prominent public figures such as leaders of protest movements and candidates for office. Motives for assassination have included gaining revenge for a real or imagined wrong, earning fame or a reward, and removing a political enemy or group from office. Four presidents have been struck down: Abraham Lincoln, James A. Garfield, William McKinley and John F. Kennedy. Five other presidents (Jackson, both Roosevelts, Truman, and Reagan) escaped death by assassins. In 1965 it became a federal crime to kill, kidnap, or assault a president, vice president, president-elect, or acting president. It had already been illegal to threaten the life of a president. (2) Any murder in which the distinguishing feature is resort to treachery or stealth. The word *assassin* comes from the Arabic *hashshashin*—or hash eaters. The original assassins were followers of Hasan Al-Sabah, "The Old Man of the Mountains," a political and religious leader of eleventh-century Persia. They terrorized the Middle East for two centuries. *See* Table 2. Infamous U.S. Assassinations/Assassination Attempts, page 30.

assault. Occurs when an individual, without lawful authority, places another person in fear of receiving, or actually delivers to that person, a battery (that is, touching with the possibility of physical harm or death). If performed with intent to inflict severe bodily injury, the act is called aggravated assault; if performed with intent to kill, the act is called attempted murder (*State v. Smith,* 621 A.2d 493 (N.J. 1993)).

assault weapon. Essentially a civilian, semi-automatic version of a military weapon.

text continues on page 31

TABLE 2   INFAMOUS U.S. ASSASSINATIONS/ASSASSINATION ATTEMPTS

Target	Date	Location	Victim Outcome	Offender	Offender Outcome
Abraham Lincoln	April 4, 1865	Ford's Theatre, Washington, D.C.	Dead	John Wilkes Booth	Tracked down and killed 12 days later
James A. Garfield	July 2, 1881	6th Street Station, Washington, D.C.	Died of his wounds 6 months after	Charles J. Guiteau	Executed June 30, 1882
William McKinley	September 6, 1901	Buffalo, New York	Died 8 days after being shot	Leon Frank Czolgosz	Beaten by crowd; found guilty; executed October 29, 1901
John F. Kennedy	November 22, 1963	Dallas, Texas	Dead	Lee Harvey Oswald	Killed by Jack Ruby on November 24, 1963
Andrew Jackson	January 30, 1835	Washington, D.C.	Uninjured	Richard Lawrence	Deemed insane and institutionalized
Theodore Roosevelt	October 14, 1912	Milwaukee, Wisconsin	Slightly injured	John Schrank	Sentenced to state mental hospital
Franklin Roosevelt	February 1933	Miami, Florida	Uninjured, Mayor Cermak killed	Giuseppe Zangara	Executed March 20, 1933
Harry S. Truman	November 1, 1950	Washington, D.C.	Uninjured	Griselio Torresola, Oscar Collazo	Torresola shot dead at scene; Collazo sentenced to life in prison
Ronald Reagan	March 30, 1981	Washington, D.C.	Wounded, punctured lung	John Hinckley Jr.	Not guilty by reason of insanity
Robert F. Kennedy	June 5, 1968	Los Angeles, California	Dead	Sirhan Sirhan	Sentenced to death; commuted to life in prison
Malcolm X	February 21, 1965	Manhattan, New York	Dead	Talmadge Hayer, Norman Butler, Thomas Johnson	Hayer paroled 1993; Butler paroled 1985; Johnson released in 1987

(continued)

Target	Date	Location	Victim Outcome	Offender	Offender Outcome
Martin Luther King Jr.	April 4, 1968	Memphis, Tennessee	Dead	James Earl Ray	Sentenced to 99-year prison term
Lee Harvey Oswald	November 24, 1963	Dallas, Texas	Dead	Jack Ruby	Died of cancer following his conviction
John Lennon	December 8, 1980	New York, New York	Dead	Mark David Chapman	Sentenced to 20 years to life
Huey P. Long	September 8, 1935	Baton Rouge, Louisiana	Died 2 days later	Carl A. Weiss	Shot at the scene
William J. Gaynor		Hoboken, New Jersey	Died three years later from wounds	James J. Gallager	
George C. Wallace	May 15, 1972	Wheaton, Maryland	Paralyzed	Arthur Herman Bremer	63 years in prison
Gerald Ford	September 5, 1975	Sacramento, California	Uninjured	Lynette "Squeaky" Fromme	Sentenced to life in prison; paroled in 2009
Gerald Ford	September 22, 1975	San Francisco, California	Uninjured	Sarah Jane Moore	Served 32 years; paroled in 2007
George H. W. Bush	May 10, 2005	Country of Georgia	Uninjured	Vladimir Arutyunian	Sentenced to life in prison
George Tiler	May 31, 2009	Wichita, Kansas	Dead	Scott Roeder	Life in prison

Compiled by Richard Porter, CSULB.

Features often used to characterize or differentiate assault weapons from "normal" rifles, pistols, and shotguns usually include folding stocks, bayonet mounts, detachable ammunition magazines, pistol grips (on rifles and shotguns), and the ability to attach flash suppressors or silencers to the barrel. Assault weapons have been banned by the federal Violent Crime Control and Law Enforcement Act of 1994. Most statutes outlaw the manufacture, transfer, or possession of assault weapons after that date. However, possession of weapons possessed prior to the enactment of legislation is in many cases permitted so long as the weapon is not sold or transferred. In 1999, California enacted legislation specifically exempting many pistols used in Olympic and international competition because of the general nature of the definition of an assault weapon found in California law.

assembly. The meeting of a number of persons in one place, for a common objective.

assignation house. A house of prostitution; brothel.

assigned counsel. An attorney in private practice who is appointed to represent an indigent defendant.

assigned counsel system. This method of providing legal defense for individuals accused of crimes exists in many U.S. counties, particularly in smaller counties in which there are not enough cases to justify the cost of a salaried public defender. The system is funded primarily by local units of government; the states and the federal government generally provide only a small proportion of funds to operate indigent defense services. *See also* public defender's organization

assistance, writ of. A written order, issued by the court, requiring specific action. For example, in aid of the execution of a legal judgment, to put the complainant into possession of lands adjudged to him or her. *See also* chancery procedure

assisting officer in making arrest. An officer authorized to make arrests may call upon private persons for assistance in doing so. Originally derived from the English common law term *posse comitatus,* the term refers to the power of the county to command any male person over 18 years of age either to aid and assist in taking or arresting any person against whom a legal complaint may be lodged or to prevent breach of the peace or any criminal offense.

Association of Certified Fraud Examiners. International antifraud training and education organization with over 50,000 members. Association of Certified Fraud Examiners, World Headquarters—The Gregor Building, 716 West Ave, Austin, TX 78701-2727 ; Web: http://www.acfe.com/.

Association of Law Enforcement Intelligence Units (ALEIA) According to its Web site, the mission of ALEIA is "providing leadership and promoting professionalism in the criminal intelligence community in order to protect public safety and constitutional rights." Address: 4949 Broadway Sacramento, Ca 95820; Web: http://leiu.org/.

association, differential. The distribution of a person's associations in a manner different from those of other persons; generally stated as a hypothesis of criminal behavior, namely, that a person who develops criminal behavior differs from those who do not both in the quantity and quality of associations with criminal patterns and in his or her relative isolation from anticriminal patterns, and that differential association with these criminal and anticriminal patterns is therefore the cause of criminal behavior.

assumpsit. A suit based on the breach of a simple contract.

asylum state. The state in which a fugitive from justice from another state, which is demanding his or her return, is found.

asymmetric threat. The use of primitive, crude or low-tech methods to attack an enemy with more advanced or high-tech methods of combat.

atavism. A theory of criminal behavior, developed by Lombroso and other evolutionists in the post-Darwinian era. It postulates that criminality diminishes in the evolutionary development of humanity, and that its appearance as a biological predilection in some persons is a hereditary throwback on the evolutionary scale. *See also* Lombroso, Cesare

Atcherley system. Based on the book *Modus opperandi in criminal investigation and detection* by Llewelyn William Atchreley. *See modus operandi*

Atkins, Susan (1948–2009). Manson family member convicted in 1966 of the Tale and La Bianca murders in Los Angeles, CA. Atkins was initially sentenced to death, but this was commuted to life due to a court case questioning the constitutionality of capital punishment in 1972. She was denied parole 18 times prior to her death. *See also* Manson, Charles

Atlanta serial murders. On July 28, 1979, Atlanta police found the bodies of Alfred

James Evans, age 13, and Edward Hope Smith, age 14. Over the next 22 months Atlanta citizens were terrorized by the abductions and murders of 29 African American children (27 males and two females). The FBI entered the case and in May 1981, after 29 nights of surveillance, stopped Wayne Bertram Williams near the James Jackson Parkway Bridge; two days later, a third victim's body was recovered from the Chattahoochee River 1½ miles from the bridge. A search warrant was issued for Williams' home, automobile, and person, and significant fiber evidence was collected linking him to a number of the victims. On February 26, 1982, Williams was convicted of two counts of murder in Fulton County Court, Georgia. *See also* serial murders

attachment. Taking into custody an individual being sought by the court, or seizing the assets or property of an individual who has been asked to appear in court and has failed to do so.

attainder. The annihilation of all civil rights and privileges, which, in early English law, followed a condemnation for treason or felony. The person attained forfeited all property and lost all capacity to inherit or transmit property to his descendants; nor could he appear in court or claim the protection of law. A bill of attainder, which is prohibited by the U.S. Constitution, is a legislative condemnation without the formality of a judicial trial.

attaint. To convict of a crime; also, a writ to inquire whether a jury has given a false verdict.

attempt to commit a crime. An act done with intent to commit a crime and tending to, but falling short of, its commission. (1) The act must be such as would be closely connected with the completed crime. (2) There must be an apparent possibility to commit the crime in the manner proposed. (3) There must be a specific intent to commit the particular crime at the time of the act. (4) Voluntary abandonment of purpose after

an act constituting an attempt is no defense. (5) Consent to the attempt will be a defense if it would be a defense were the crime completed, but not otherwise. All attempts to commit a crime, whether the crime be a felony or a misdemeanor, in common law or by statute, are misdemeanors in common law.

attestation. The act of verifying or affirming, orally or in writing, the genuineness or validity of some legal document, such as a will or an affidavit.

attorney. Lawyer, counsel, advocate; a person trained in the law, admitted to practice before the bar of a given jurisdiction, and authorized to advise, represent, and act for other persons in legal proceedings. He or she may represent private individuals, corporations, or the government. The *prosecuting* attorney acts on behalf of the government ("the people") in a criminal case. The *defense* attorney advises, represents, and acts for the defendant (or, in post-conviction proceedings, the offender). *Retained counsel* is a defense attorney selected and compensated by the defendant or offender or by other private person(s). *Assigned counsel* is a defense attorney assigned by the court on a case-by-case basis to represent indigent defendants and offenders, compensated from public funds or not compensated at all (*pro bono*). A *public defender* is a defense attorney regularly employed and compensated from public funds to represent indigent defendants and offenders. When a defendant acts as his or her own defense attorney, that person is said to be represented *pro se* or *in propria persona*.

attorney at law. The official name for a practicing attorney.

attorney general, state. The chief legal officer of a state, representing that state in civil and, under certain circumstances, criminal matters; furnishes legal advice to the governor and state departments.

Attorney General, United States. A member of the president's cabinet and head of the

U.S. Department of Justice; appointed by the president as the chief legal officer of the federal government, representing the national government in civil and criminal matters; also gives legal advice to other federal agencies and the president. This post was created by the 1789 Judiciary Act.

attorney in fact. A private attorney; one who is authorized by his client to perform a particular service. One who exercises power of attorney. *See also* power of attorney

Attorney, United States. The chief law officer (federal) in the Federal Judicial District; represents the U.S. government in civil and criminal matters; acts under the direction of the U.S. Attorney General, who heads the U.S. Department of Justice. The U.S. Attorney usually has assistants, who aid in performing the duties of the office.

Auburn system. A prison system or procedure first created in Auburn (NY) State Prison in 1816. It demanded silence on the part of the inmates, who were assigned to individual cells at night and forced to work in silence during the day.

audita querela, **writ of.** A remedial writ that sets aside execution of a judgment because of some injustice performed by the party obtaining the judgment but which could not be pleaded at the time of the trial; an arrest of judgment.

Augustus, John. Founder of the probation system in the United States. In 1841 he became the first probation officer, with supervision over minor offenders.

authentic document. A document bearing a signature or seal attesting that it is genuine and official.

authoritarianism. (a) A type of government or (b) a type of individual personality. In the first sense, the term refers to rigidly hierarchical, undemocratic structures. In the second sense, it refers to a personality syndrome that finds comfort in such structures. The authoritarian personality is associated with a mind that is closed to new ideas and subject to ethnic and racial prejudice and discrimination, chauvinistic nationalism, willingness to restrict civil rights and liberties, and punitiveness as a response to deviance.

authority. (1) The power or right conferred on a person by another to act on his or her behalf. (2) A public officer or body having certain powers of jurisdiction. (3) Constitutions, statutes, precedent cases, opinions of text writers, and other material cited in arguments.

autocracy. A government of a monarch or other absolute ruler who is not limited by law; a dictatorship.

autoerotic death. An accidental death, usually by asphyxiation (suffocation or strangulation), in which the victim dies while intentionally restricting oxygen to the brain for sexual arousal. The goal is to increase sexual pleasure by coming close to, but stopping just short of, death.

autoeroticism. Masturbation and other forms of sexual self-gratification.

automated data processing (ADP). Data processing performed by computer system(s). Also called electronic data processing.

Automated Fingerprint Identification System (AFIS). The national automated fingerprint identification and criminal history database maintained by the Federal Bureau of Investigation (FBI), this database is used for storing and making rapid comparisons of fingerprints. *See also* Integrated Automated Fingerprint Identification System (IAFIS)

automatic fire. Continuous fire from an automatic weapon, lasting until the pressure on the trigger is released. Automatic fire differs from semiautomatic fire and single-shot fire, both of which require a separate trigger pull for each shot fired.

automatic firearm. Any firearm that fires, automatically ejects the used cartridge case from the barrel.

automobile theft. The stealing of an automobile or motor vehicle. Under state law it is theft of a motor vehicle. Under federal law it is a violation to transport a vehicle, or cause it to be transported, from one state to another, knowing the vehicle has been stolen. *See also* motor vehicle theft, vehicle identification number

automonosexual perversion. Sexual activities performed on or with one's own body, such as self-fellatio or self-mutilation.

autonomy. The state of being self-governing or self-directing.

autopsy. Examination and dissection of a dead body to discover the cause of death.

Auto Theft Investigators, International Association of. Founded in 1952. Publishes *The APB* (quarterly). Address: P.O. Box 223, Clinton, NY 13323. Web: http://www.iaati.org/.

autrefois. (Fr., "convict or acquit"). A plea made by a defendant that he or she has previously been tried and convicted or acquitted of the same offense.

Avatars. Graphical images representing people. In criminal justice, Avatars are often used in computer generated reenactments of crime

aversion therapy. A form of psychological treatment in which the patient is exposed to a stimulus while simultaneously experiencing an unpleasant stimulus, such as discomfort or pain. Such conditioning is intended to modify undesirable or antisocial habits or addictions by creating a strong association with the unpleasant stimulus. *See also* Antabuse therapy; behavior modification

Aviation Crime Prevention Institute. Founded in 1986, a nonprofit organization dedicated to the elimination of aviation-related crime. Address: 226 N. Nova Road, Ormond Beach, FL 32174.

avowtry. Adultery.

axiom. In logic, a truth that is self-evident.

B

baby boom. A demographic term referring to the 76 million Americans born between 1946 and 1964. This is relevant to criminal justice, as these people reached their peak crime ages during the 1960s and 1970s.

Baby Face Nelson. *See* Nelson, Charles

badges and shields, law enforcement. The five-pointed pentacle is the symbol of the U.S. Marshal's Service. It is the star in the American flag, in the insignia of an army general, and on the Medal of Honor. In ancient eras, the pentacle was used by sorcerers and believed to impart magical powers. As late as the sixteenth century, soldiers wore pentacles around their necks in the belief they would be invulnerable to enemy missiles. Over time, the six-star shield emerged as the local badge of choice, simply because it is easy to manufacture.

bad-tendency test. A legal test used to analyze free speech issues, it was originally dervied from English common law. This test measures the legality of speech by its propensity to cause illegal action. The USSC cited the test in *Patterson v. Colorado* (1907), *Fox v. Washington* (1915), and Gitlow v. New York (1925). *See also* dangerous tendency test

bail. A form of pretrial release in which a defendant pledges property or posts cash with the court in order to be released from jail pending a criminal matter. The property or cash bail is typically refunded at the conclusion of trial, provided the defendant has met the terms of bail (generally refraining from criminal activity and making all court appearances. *See also* bail bondsman. *See* Table 3. Types of Pretrial Release, page 36.

bail bondsman. A person, usually licensed, whose business it is to effect releases on bail for persons charged with offenses and held in custody, by pledging to pay a sum

---

TABLE 3   TYPES OF PRETRIAL RELEASE

Both financial bonds and alternative release options are used today.

Nonfinancial Conditions:

Personal Recognizance: Defendant is released subject to no financial or other conditions.

Unsecured bond: No money is required to be posted before the defendant is released, but defendant is liable for full bail amount if s/he fails to appear.

Conditional release: Any combination of restrictions that are deemed necessary to guarantee the defendant's appearance at trial or the safety of the community. Nonfinancial conditions commonly place restrictions on the defendant's movements, association, and/or actions. They may also involve employment or treatment for medical, psychological, or substance abuse conditions.

Third-Party Custody: Although not tracked by BJS, third-party custody is practiced in some jurisdictions.

Citation release: Arrestees are released pending their first court appearance on a written order issued by law enforcement personnel.

Financial conditions: Defendants may also be released on financial conditions, which can include:

Deposit bond: The defendant is required to post a percentage of the total bail amount, usually 10%.

Surety bond: The defendant is released subject to guarantees by a third person that the full amount will be paid. Surety bonds are generally privately secured through the services of a bail bondsman, who signs a promissory note to the court for the bail amount and charges the defendant a fee for the service (usually 10% of the bail amount). If the defendant fails to appear, the bondsman must pay the court the full amount. Frequently, the bondsman requires the defendant to post collateral in addition to the fee.

Collateral bond: Collateral equal to the full bail amount must be posted by the defendant before release.

Financial conditions may occur in combination with nonfinancial conditions.

Source: Bureau of Justice Statistics.

---

of money if the defendant fails to appear in court as required. In law, a bail bondsman is also called a surety. Typically, the defendant posts 10 percent of the total bond amount to the bondsman, which is the fee charged for securing bail.

Bailey, F. Lee. (Francis Lee Bailey, 1933–). Attorney born in Waltham, MA. While in law school he organized and operated a detective agency. First gained notoriety in the retrial of Dr. Samuel Sheppard of Cleveland, convicted in 1954 of murdering his wife (widely believed to be the basis for the series and film entitled *The Fugitive*). Bailey helped to force a review of the trial by the Supreme Court, which ruled in 1966 that the pretrial publicity may have prejudiced the jury. In a retrial, completed in 1966, Bailey secured Sheppard's acquittal and thus became one of the country's leading trial lawyers. He gained further notoriety as the lead defense attorney in the 1971 court marshall case against Captain Ernest Medina for the My Lai Masasacre in Vietnam, in which he helped secure an acquittal for defendant Medina. He was also part of the "dream team" of defense attorneys in the O.J Simpson homicide trial of 1995. He was disbarred from Florida (2001) and Massachusetts (2002) and served time in prison (for contempt) due to his mishandling of stock in a 1994 marijuana case (DuBoc). Known for employing tactics that bordered on the flamboyant, Bailey was occasionally censured formally for his trial conduct, but his method of tirelessly pursuing every possible line of investigation and legal action made him one of the most sought-after legal defenders in the country.

bailiff. An officer of the court. This office evolved from the Statute of Winchester in 1285, by which King Edward I tried to establish a uniform system of law enforcement in England. Original responsibilities were to keep persons under surveillance who were traveling town streets after dark, and to check on strangers. Currently is responsible for keeping order in the court and protecting the security of jury deliberations and court property.

bailiwick. The territorial jurisdiction of a sheriff or bailiff.

bail revocation. The court decision withdrawing a defendant's previously granted release on bail.

bail system. Developed by the early common law courts to secure the defendant's appearance in court at trial. Originally required in both civil and criminal cases, bail has come to be used primarily in criminal cases. In the bail system, the defendant is released to his or her surety, who undertakes to produce the defendant at trial, usually giving a bail bond to secure that obligation. The bail system also provides for a defendant's release on "recognizance," an obligation entered into in court to do some act, usually to appear at trial. The bail system has been criticized as a violation of civil liberties and due process. With the bonds' nonrefundable cost being approximately 10 percent of the face amount, not uncommonly in excess of $50,000, the system has served to keep many defendants in jail pending trial, depriving them of their liberty before they have been found guilty of any crime. However, efforts at reform face the problem that this system has been more effective than most in ensuring the end for which it was designed: that the defendant appear at trial. Also know as the Illinois plan.

balance of sentence suspended. A type of sentencing disposition, consisting of a sentence to prison or jail that credits the defendant for time already spent in confinement awaiting adjudication and sentencing, suspends the execution of the time remaining to be served, and results in the defendant's release from confinement.

ballistics. The science that deals with the motion and impact of such projectiles as bullets, rockets, and bombs. Ballistics also involves the behavior, appearance, or modification of missiles or other vehicles acted upon by propellants, wind, gravity, temperature, or any other modifying substance, condition, or force.

banditry. Consistent and organized robbery and other forms of theft with violence; especially, such behavior when committed by persons who reside in mountainous or other sparsely populated regions.

banishment. The sending away of a criminal from his or her place of residence.

bank fraud. A scheme to (a) swindle a federally chartered or insured financial institution or (b) obtain any of the moneys, funds, credits, assets, securities, or other property owned by or under the custody or control of these institutions by means of false pretenses, representations, or promises. The term "federally chartered" or "insured financial" institution means any type of bank or financial institution organized or operating under the laws of the United States.

bank robbery, the first. Occurred Saturday, March 19, 1831, when two doors of the City Bank, on Wall Street, New York City, were opened by duplicate keys and the bank was robbed of $245,000. Edward Smith, an

Englishman (alias Jones, James Smith, and James Honeyman), was indicted by a grand jury and arraigned May 2, 1831, at the Court of General Sessions. On May 11, 1831, he was sentenced to five years at hard labor at Sing Sing. Over $185,000 was recovered.

bankruptcy. The legally declared inability to pay creditors The financial status of a person or organization when a court has determined an inability to pay creditors. A person may file a voluntary petition of bankruptcy, listing his or her assets and liabilities, or may be forced into bankruptcy on petition of his or her creditors. Generally, the individual's assets are disposed of by an officer appointed by the court, creditors are paid pro rata, and the individual is discharged from further obligation. There are six types of bankruptcy under the Bankruptcy Code, Title 11 of the U.S. Code: *Chapter 7,* sometimes called "straight bankruptcy," which allows businesses and individuals to keep some exempt property, such as real estate. *Chapter 9,* which covers municipal bankruptcy; *Chapter 11,* often called "corporate bankruptcy" provides businesses with protection from creditors while they reorganize operations and establish a payment plan; and *Chapter 12,* which covers farmers and fishermen; *Chapter 13,* sometimes called "Wage Earner Bankruptcy,' which allows individuals with regular income to develop repayment plan; *Chapter 15,* which covers foreign and international bankruptcy. The 2005 Bankruptcy Abuse Prevention and Consumer Protection Act substantially revised bankruptcy law. The most notable changes are that it requires a "means test," which makes it more difficult to qualify for Chapter 7 bankruptcy. In practice, many individuals who file for bankruptcy are now required to pay back at least a portion of their debts. Further, there must be an eight-year gap between bankruptcies for those wishing to file multiple bankruptcies.

bankruptcy fraud. (also called criminal bankruptcy). The intentional concealment of assets or destruction of documents, filing of fraudulent claims, false statements or declarations, and fee fixing in a bankruptcy declaration, for the purpose of avoiding payment of debts.

Bank Secrecy Act of 1970 (also called the Currency and Foreign Transactions Reporting Act). A law requiring U.S. financial institutions to assist the federal government in detecting money laundering. Under this Act, financial institutions must file Currency Transaction Reports (CTRs) on all cash transactions of more than $10,000. CTRs must be filed with the IRS within 15 days of the transaction. Cash Purchases of Monetary Instruments (such as cashier's checks, money orders or traveler's checks) greater than $3,000 must be recorded in a Money Instrument Log (MIL) and kept for federal review for five years. In addition, any transaction in which it appears someone is attempting to launder money must be logged in a Suspicious Activity Report (SAR) and filed, without the suspicious person's knowledge, with the Financial Crimes Enforcement Network. The reports require specific information regarding customers' identities.

bar. (1) The railing separating the judge, counsel, and jury from the general public. (2) The whole body of attorneys and counselors who have been admitted to practice in a court. *See also* bench

barbed wire. Commonly used to supplement prison fencing, barbed wire is fencing with sharp edges arranged at intervals. Barbed wire was first patented in 1867 in New York by William D. Hunt, but perfected and marketed in 1874 by J. F. Glidden of Illinois. Barbed wire is sometimes used as perimeter fencing in jails and prisons, although the use of razor wire is generally used for this purpose. Today, barbed wire is most commonly used for agricultural purposes.

barbiturates. Drugs that can produce a state of depression of the central nervous system resembling normal sleep. In smaller doses these drugs are referred to as sedatives and can cause effects including sedation, drowsiness and depression; unusual excitement;

fever; irritability; poor judgment; slurred speech; dizziness; reduced anxiety; feeling of well-being; lowered inhibitions; slowed pulse and breathing; lowered blood pressure; poor concentration/fatigue; confusion; and impaired coordination, memory, judgment. In larger doses they are known as hypnotics and can produce anesthesia; respiratory depression and arrest; coma; and even death. Barbiturates are made from barbituric acid, which was first synthesized in Germany in 1863 by Nobel Prize-winning chemist Adolph Baeyer. The first barbiturate was synthesized in 1882 but not marketed until 1902, when it was released under the name Veronal and known generically in the United States as barbital.

bargain, implicit. A sentencing practice by which the defendant pleads guilty and seeks the mercy of the court, with the implied understanding that he or she will receive a lighter sentence in this way than by pleading not guilty and demanding trial.

Barker, Arizona Donnie Clark (AKA Kate, Ma Barker). (1872–1935). Born outside Springfield, Missouri, in 1872, Ma Barker was the leader of the nefarious Barker Gang, comprised of Ma and her four sons (the Barker Boys). In the 1920s, the Gang committed several bank robberies under Ma Barker's direction. Ma Barker also operated a hideout for escaped convicts and fugitives near Tusla, Oklahoma. In the 1930s (after two of her four sons were released from prison, planned several more bank and payroll robberies and orchestrated two kidnappings. On January 16, 1935, Ma and her son Fred were killed in a shoot-out with FBI in Florida. She was never arrested a single time for any crimes, although she is believed to have been the mastermind behind the Barker Gang, using her influence to get her sons and other criminals to carry out the crimes she planned. *See also* Barker Gang

Barker, Arthur (Doc Barker) (1899–1939). Born in Aurora, Missouri in 1899 to George and "Ma" Barker, Doc Barker was arrested multiple times as an adolescent, and released to his mother's custody. He was sentenced to life imprisonment when he was just thirteen years old, although he was paroled after 20 years at the age of 33. After his parole, he resumed a very active criminal career. He was in and out of prison for multiple felonies, including bank robberies, murders, and kidnappings for ransom. His final conviction, for kidnapping, resulted in a life sentence to Alcatraz. He died in 1939 in a failed escape attempt. *See also* Alcatraz; Barker Gang

Barker, Fred (1902–1935). Son of George and "Ma" Barker born in Aurora, Missouri in 1902, Fred Barker was arrested for robbery as an adolescent and released to his mother's custody. He committed countless bank robberies, murders, and kidnappings for ransom as an adult and escaped from jail multiple times. Fred was killed on January 16, 1935, along with his mother Ma Barker, in a shootout with FBI in Florida. *See also* Barker Gang

Barker Gang. The Barker Gang was a notorious criminal gang comprised of "Ma" Barker and her four sons (Herman, Lloyd, Arthur [Doc], and Fred) and various other criminals who migrated in and out of the Barker hideout. As adolescents, each of the boys was arrested for serious crimes and released to the custody of their mother, Ma. The Barker Gang committed countless crimes in the late 1920s–1930s, including bank robbery, postal payroll robbery, kidnapping for ransom, and murder. Despite multiple arrests, convictions, and prison terms when one or two of the gang were occasionally apprehended, the gang evaded authorities for nearly a decade by changing their criminal patterns and activities. Ma, the leader of the gang, planned and orchestrated the crimes, although she was never arrested. The Barker Gang was stopped in 1935, when Ma and Freddie (the youngest Barker) were killed in an FBI shoot-out. *See also* Barker, Arizona; Barker, Arthur; Barker, Fred; Barker, Herman; Barker, Lloyd

Barker, Herman (1894–1927). Born to George and "Ma" Barker in Aurora, Missouri in 1894, Herman was the oldest of the Barker Boys. He was arrested as a juvenile and returned to the custody of his mother. At age 16, he organized the "Central Park Gang," a group of adolescents who committed multiple burglaries. Herman was a murderer and bank robber who, on September 19, 1927, killed himself with a Luger firearm to avoid capture after a failed robbery in Kansas. *See also* Barker Gang

Barker, Lloyd (1896–1949). Second son of George and "Ma" Barker, Lloyd was born in Aurora, Missouri, in 1896. Lloyd Barker was arrested as a juvenile and released to his mother's custody. Along with his brother Herman, organized the "Central Park Gang" of juvenile burglars in 1910. He was apprehended in a post office robbery in Tulsa, Oklahoma, in 1922 and sentenced to 25 years in Leavenworth. After serving his entire term, Barker was released in 1947 and found employment managing a snack shop. Perhaps due to his extended incarceration during the Barker Gang's most active criminal period, Lloyd was the only Barker who neither joined a gang nor recidivated after prison. He was killed by his wife in 1949. *See also* Barker Gang

barratry. The criminal offenses of exciting groundless quarrels or lawsuits. (1) In criminal law, the practice of bringing repeated legal action with the intent to harass. (2) In maritime law, any act of gross misconduct by the master or crew of a ship that damages the vessel or cargo.

Barrow, Clyde (1909–1934). Clyde Barrow was born in Telice, Texas, to Henry and Cumie Barrow in 1909. He was one of eight children. At the age of nine he was sent to a school for incorrigible boys. After his release, he was a farmer, then joined a gang of burglars and robbers with his brother Ivan (Buck). Barrow met Bonnie Parker in Dallas in January of 1930 and began a stream of crimes in multiple states which gained them national attention, including bank robbery, murder, and escape. Barrow and Parker were shot and killed by a posse in Louisiana. *See also* Parker, Bonnie

BARS (behaviorally anchored rating scale). A method of evaluating an individual's job performance.

basic car plan The assignment of one or two officers in a motor vehicle to permanently patrol a designated geographic area. The "basic car" officers are responsible for all activities reported in that area, and for interacting with the community in formal and informal meetings. Other patrol units serve as back-up or to handle calls as needed.

Bastille. (Fr., "small fortress"). La Bastille, the infamous fortress-prison of Paris, was destroyed by revolutionaries on July 14, 1789—a day celebrated in France ever since. A synonym for all prisons, especially those holding political prisoners.

Bates, Sanford. (1884–1972). First director of the U.S. Bureau of Prisons

bathroom phobia. Also known as toilet phobia, this is a fear of falling into a toilet or of being attacked, especially in the genitals, by creatures emerging from the toilet. This phobia is alleged to afflict males who are anal erotic. *See also parauresis*

baton. Often called a truncheon, cosh, Paddy wacker, billystick, billy club, nightstick, sap, blackjack, stick, batons are a stick used by law enforcement for less-lethal self defense. Most frequently made of hardwood, plastic or metal, batons come in lengths of 24 to 29 inches. The "side-handle" baton, 24-inches long with a short protruding handle, is a variation on the traditional baton. Some agencies have replaced the traditional baton with a spring-loaded telescoping metal baton, commonly referred to as an "ASP."

battered child syndrome. The set of physical and emotional symptoms associated with long-term physical violence against a child, generally caused by parents or caretakers.

battered person syndrome. (sometimes called battered woman syndrome) The set of physical and emotional symptoms associated with deliberate and repeated assault of a female by her spouse or domestic partner. Spousal assault did not begin in the twentieth century, nor is it limited to assault against females by their male partners. Battered person syndrome is so named because, in the opinion of some experts, the condition refers to a collection of characteristics that appear in both parties in such a relationship. Initially coined by Walker in 1979 as the Battered Woman Syndrome, the cycle has three distinct phases: tension-building phase, explosion or acute battering incident, and the honeymoon phase. One hallmark of the syndrome is that the victim often presents depressed and is unable to take independent action that would allow him or her to escape further abuse. The syndrome explains why abuse victims often do not seek help, fight their abuser, or leave. Under the 1994 U.S. Violence Against Women Act, congress mandated a report on Battered Women Syndrome in the courtroom. Based on the report, congress rejected the validity of the syndrome. However, BWS is still sometimes invoked in criminal proceedings. In 1992, testimony on battered person syndrome was made admissible in the state of California. In 2002, California Penal Code §1473.5 allows women convicted prior to 1992 to petition for a new trial in cases where evidence of battered woman syndrome was not allowed into evidence during their original trial. In 2004, SB 1385 was passed in California, which allows those convicted of violent crimes and not allowed to present evidence of intimate partner battering to submit *habeus corpus* challenges to their original conviction. *See also* domestic violence; battered woman defense

battered woman defense. A legal defense that the person accused of an assault or murder was suffering from *battered person syndrome* at the time s/he committed the crime.

battered woman syndrome. *See* battered person syndrome

battery. Any unlawful application or use of force upon an individual; intentional offensive or harmful contact with a person, likely to cause bodily harm.

Baumes' laws. The restrictive penal legislation sponsored by a committee of the New York State Senate in 1926, of which Senator Caleb H. Baumes was chairman. These laws provided an increase in penalty with each successive offense and an automatic life sentence for the fourth offense, whether known at the time of conviction or discovered after sentencing. The term "Baumes' laws" has been widely applied to similar habitual-offender laws subsequently enacted in other states. *See also* three strikes

bayonet. An edged steel weapon with a tapered point, a blood groove, and a formed handle designed for attachment to the muzzle end of a rifle, shotgun, or the like. Bayonets were first introduced in Bayonne, France, in the seventeenth century, and the earlier forms were made to be fitted into the bore of a musket or rifle.

beam test. Introduced in the 1940s, a microscopic examination of crushed marijuana as a means of accurately distinguishing it from similar-looking material. The technique has been replaced in modern times by the Duquenois-Levine presumptive marijuana test.

Bean, Roy. (1825–1903). An eccentric outlaw who became a saloon-keeper and Justice of the Peace in the old west. Born in Mason County, KY, Bean worked at various jobs, sought gold in the West, and traded in Mexico. In 1848 he shot a man in a barroom brawl; several years later, he killed a Mexican army officer in a gun duel over a woman, after which he was hanged (but survived). Bean's career in frontier justice began in 1882, when he drifted across the Pecos River into West Texas, dispensing whiskey from a tent. The records of Pecos County, TX, document that Bean was appointed justice of the peace on August 2, 1882, by the County Commissioner's Court and that he fully qualified for the position by submitting a $1,000 bond. He held court sessions in his saloon, where he dispensed rough-and-ready justice and hung a sign designating himself "the law west of the Pecos." Although he was not elected to the bench after 1896, he continued to try cases. In his final years, Bean spent much of his profits to help the poor of the area. Bean died March 15, 1903, after a bout of heavy drinking precipitated by the building of a power plant.

beastiality. *See* bestiality

Beccaria, Marchese de (Cesare Bonesana). (1738–1794). Referred to as the "father of criminology," and one of the founders of the classical school of criminology. His major work, *An Essay on Crimes and Punishments,* became the manifesto of the liberal approach that led to major changes in European criminal laws. Besides denouncing torture and excessive use of the death penalty, he further argued that penalties should equal offenses and that certainty of penalties is more effective as a deterrent than severity. He also advocated the prevention of crime and rigid rules of criminal procedure.

bedlam. A place of uproar or confusion; an asylum for the mentally ill. The word originated as a contraction of St. Mary of Bethlehem, the name of a hospital in London. Used for mental patients as early as 1402, the institution was formally designated a "lunatic asylum" by King Henry VIII in 1547. Conditions in Bedlam were so terrible that the word became a general term for confusion and uproar.

behavioral model of crime. An approach in criminology that seeks to explain crime in terms of the individual pathology of the offender, the social pathology of the society, or a combination of the two.

behavior modification. The use of empirically based techniques to promote behavior change. Behavior modification is based on the belief that all behavior is learned and that socially acceptable behavior can be learned as a replacement for deviant behavior. There are two basic types of behavior modification: (a) classical conditioning, spawned by the Russian physiologist Ivan Petrovitch Pavlov in the 1920s, which has usually been associated with negative reinforcers, such as shock treatments and deprivation of privileges for undesirable behavior; and (b) operant conditioning, which is best exemplified in the research and writings of B. F. Skinner. The distinction between the two theories appears to be that classical conditioning seeks to modify basic emotional responses, while operant conditioning is used to teach individuals how to act or how to manage their emotions.

Beltway shooters. *See* Beltway sniper attacks

Beltway sniper attacks. In October of 2002, the Interstate-95 highway between Virginia, Washington, DC, and Maryland was plagued by sniper attacks. Over the course of three weeks, 10 people were dead and three more seriously injured by the "Beltway sniper," who seemed to pick targets at random. On October 24 of that year, two suspects were arrested for the crimes: John Allen Muhammad and Lee Boyd Malvo. The pair were tried and convicted. Malvo, a minor at the time of his involvement in the crime, was sentenced to six consecutive life terms in prison. At age 41, Muhammad was sentenced to death. He was executed by lethal injection in 2009.

bench. The place where judges sit in court; the collective body of judges sitting as a court.

bench probation (bench parole). The process of allowing individuals on probation to remain at liberty in the community, with the sentencing judge as their only direct supervisor, on the basis of their pledge not to engage in any further illegal behavior.

bench trial. In this procedure, also called a court trial, no jury is present, and only a judge hears all evidence and determines the guilt or innocence of the defendant. Bench trials are held when the accused waives his or her right to a jury trial and requests or agrees to be defended only before a judge.

bench warrant. A document issued by a court, directing that a law enforcement officer bring before the court the person named therein, usually a person who has failed to obey a court order or a notice to appear.

benefit of clergy. A thirteenth-century practice that allowed members of the clergy to escape capital punishment and other severe sentences by transferring their cases to church courts, where they were routinely acquitted. Eventually, this became a practice in which first time offenders were afforded leniency.

benzidine test. Historically used as a preliminary chemical test for the presence of blood. Use of benzidine in blood testing has largely been replaced by the use of phenol-phthalein/hydrogen peroxide and luminol, as benzidine is highly carcinogenic.

bequeath. To give personal property by will.

Berkowitz, David Richard. (1953–)("Son of Sam"). From July 1976 through most of 1977, Berkowitz terrorized more than 12 million residents of greater New York City. Born in 1953 as Richard David Falco, Berkowitz was adopted by local hardware owners who changed the order of his first and middle names and gave him their surname. He was a troubled child who engaged in petty theft and arson; his adolescence was strained following his adoptive mother's death due to breast cancer, and his father's remarriage. He served in the U.S. army from 1971 until his honorable discharge in 1974. He subsequently held various blue-collar jobs and was employed by the U.S. Postal Service. Berkowitz claims to have joined a cult in 1975, which practiced drug use, watched sadistic pornography, and engaged in animal killing. On Christmas Eve 1975, he committed his first act of violence by stabbing two women. Six months later he struck again, with a .44 caliber revolver, and by July 1977, he had fired his weapon a total of 32 times, killing six of his victims and wounding another seven. A special detective squad known as the Operation Omega Task Force was formed to hunt down the ".44-caliber killer." On April 17, 1977, after killing two more victims, Berkowitz left a note in the street addressed to Joseph Borelli, a police detective assigned to supervise the investigation. In it, Berkowitz remarked that he was not a woman-hater but a monster and wrote the sentence that would make him the centerpiece of thousands of headlines on the following day: "I am the Son of Sam." The police subsequently published a psychological profile describing the suspect as neurotic, suffering from paranoid schizophrenia, and under the belief he was possessed by a demon. The Omega Task Force traced hundreds of leads each day and investigated a total of 3,167 suspects. Berkowitz was traced through a parking ticket and arrested on August 10, 1977. He readily admitted his guilt and was sentenced, on several counts of murder, attempted murder, assault, and possession of a deadly weapon, to a total of 365 years in prison. Although eligible for parole, Berkowitz has been denied parole four times. Berkowitz is in Sullivan Correctional Facility, a maximum-security prison in Falsberg, New York. Based on speculation that Berkowitz would sell his story for profit, New York became the first state to enact "Son of Sam laws," used to keep criminals from profiting from crime. *See also* serial murders

Bertillon method of identification. A system of determining whether an individual under investigation is the same individual as one whose anthropometric measurements are on record. It was invented by Alphonse Bertillon when he was head of the Paris police department in 1883, and applied to the identification of criminals. It consisted of measuring certain parts of the body, standardizing forensic photography, noting peculiar markings, and classifying the data to make easy the location of thousands of records. His method, based on the unreliable observation that physical maturity fixes the skeletal dimensions for life, has been widely superseded by the fingerprint method.

beryllium oxide (BeO). A poisonous ionic chemical substance used as an electrical insulator.

best evidence rule. One coming into court must bring the best available original evidence to prove the questions involved in the case. If a written document is involved, it is the best evidence and must be produced, unless it is shown to have been lost or destroyed.

bestiality. Sexual intercourse between humans and animals. Bestiality occurs predominantly in rural areas and most commonly involves male adolescents and farm mammals.

beyond a reasonable doubt. A legal term used in relation to proof by evidence. In cases where the state (prosecution) uses direct evidence in whole or part as proof of the offense, such evidence must convince the jury, or the judge if no jury is used, of the guilt of the accused *beyond a reasonable doubt. See also* doubt, reasonable

Bianchi, Kenneth (The Hillside Strangler) (1952–). Kenneth Bianchi was born in Rochester, New York, and adopted when he was two months old. He was raised by his adoptive parents in Rochester and was a troubled child, diagnosed with petit mal seizures and passive-aggressive disorder before adolescence. He moved to Los Angeles in 1977. Along with his roommate and cousin, Angelo Buono, Bianchi embarked on the killing rampage of 12 women in a 15-month period. The crimes brought Los Angeles into panic. Meanwhile, Bianchi applied to be a Los Angeles police officer and went on several ride-alongs, including to a few of his own murder scenes. Bianchi moved to Washington where he gained employment as a security guard before resuming his killing spree. Witnesses identified Bianchi as the man seen with two of his victims shortly before their deaths, and he was subsequently arrested. Upon arrest, Bianchi claimed to be insane. Bianchi was convicted and sentenced to life imprisonment. He was eligible for parole in 2005, but was denied. Although never convicted, he is also suspected of being the "Alphabet murderer," who raped and killed three young girls in Rochester in the early 1970s. *See also* Buono, Angelo; Hillside Strangler

bias. The theoretical or emotional preconceptions or prejudices of individuals or groups, which may lead to certain subjective interpretations that are radically different from objective reality.

bibliotherapy. An expressive therapy grounded in the notion that reading can bring healing. Bibliotheraphy is often used in conjunction with writing assignments.

bifurcated trial. A two-part trial proceeding in which the issue of guilt is tried in the first step and, if a conviction results, the appropriate sentence or applicable sentencing statute is determined in the second step. The two steps of a bifurcated trial generally take place in separate hearings. Typical issues in the second step of a bifurcated trial are (a) what sentence to impose (e.g., for capital offense convictions, whether to impose death penalty) and (b) what statute section should determine the convicted person's sentence (e.g., whether or not the convicted person meets the statutory definition of habitual criminal).

bifurcation. The dividing or forking of one line into two or more branches. Division of issues at trial into two parts. A term used in describing fingerprint patterns. *See also* fingerprints

bigamy (1) Unlawful contracting of marriage by a person who, at the time of the marriage, knows himself or herself already to be legally married. (2) A statutory and not a common law crime; involvement in two monogamous marriages at one time. In most states the second marriage is void, the partners are criminally liable, and any children of the second marriage are illegitimate. Bigamy is often interchangeable with polygamy; however, bigamy is generally used when two or more spouses are unaware of other spouses, whereas polygamy is generally used when all spouses are aware of the others. *See also* monogamy, polygamy

Big Brothers Big Sisters. (1) Historically, "big brother" is a plan for reducing juvenile delinquency by securing the cooperation of recognized community leaders to act as "big brothers" to wayward youth who appear before the juvenile court. The plan aims to organize the economic and social resources of the community to assist juveniles who need a helping hand and practical guidance in growing into adulthood. The organization now exists as an official mentoring program in the United States, providing mentors to children aged 6–18. (2) Big Brother is also the name of a popular reality television show.

Big Floyd. FBI supercomputer system developed in the 1980s that can search criminal records and draw conclusions about those responsible for an individual crime.

bill of attainder. A legislative act declaring an individual or a group of persons guilty, without trial, of a crime such as treason. The U.S. Constitution specifically forbids bills of attainder.

bill of exceptions. A written statement of objections made, or exceptions taken, by either side to the court's rulings or instructions during a trial. The statement becomes an integral part of the record when the case is appealed and is used by the appellate court in reaching its decision.

bill of exchange. A written order from one person to another, requiring the person to whom it is addressed to pay a certain sum on demand or at a fixed date. A common bank check is one example.

bill of indictment. A document, usually prepared by a prosecutor, which charges a person with the commission of a crime and is submitted to a grand jury for its consideration. If the jury finds there are sufficient grounds to support the charge, it returns the document with the endorsement "true bill." If

there are not sufficient grounds, the endorsement reads "not a true bill."

bill of pains and penalties. A legislative conviction similar to a bill of attainder, except that it imposes a penalty of less than death. It, too, is prohibited in the United States.

bill of particulars. A formal itemized listing of charges or claims in a legal action.

Bill of Rights. A brief statement of certain fundamental rights and privileges that are guaranteed to the people against infringement by the government. The English Bill of Rights, from which some provisions of American bills of rights have been derived, is a statement of Parliament passed in 1689. The Virginia Bill of Rights, 1776, incorporated some common law principles. The first 10 amendments to the Constitution of the United States, popularly called the Bill of Rights, were added to the Constitution in 1791, after state ratifying conventions had objected to the absence of such guarantees in the original document. They were originally limitations on the federal government only (*Barron v. Baltimore*). Beginning in 1925, many of the substantive provisions of the federal Bill of Rights have also become limitations on state governments by judicial interpretation. A bill of rights is nearly always the first article of a state constitution. *See* Table 4. The Bill of Rights, page 46

bill of sale. A written document transferring the rights and interest in certain personal property or chattels.

Billy the Kid. *See* Bonney, William

bind over. (1) The decision by a court of limited jurisdiction requiring that a person charged with a felony appear for trial on that charge in a court of general jurisdiction, as the result of a finding of probable cause at a preliminary hearing held in the limited jurisdiction court. (2) To require by judicial authority that a person promise to appear for trial, appear in court as a witness, or keep the peace. (3) The basic meaning of *bind over* is to send forward; the contrasting term, *remand,* means to send back.

TABLE 4   THE BILL OF RIGHTS

First Amendment
Congress shall make no law respecting an establishment of religion, or prohibiting the free exercise thereof; or abridging the freedom of speech, or of the press; or the right of the people peaceably to assemble, and to petition the Government for a redress of grievances.

Second Amendment
A well regulated Militia, being necessary to the security of a free State, the right of the people to keep and bear Arms, shall not be infringed.

Third Amendment
No soldier shall, in time of peace, be quartered in any house, without the consent of the Owner, nor in time of war, but in a manner to be prescribed by law.

Fourth Amendment
The right of the people to be secure in their persons, houses, papers, and effects, against unreasonable searches and seizures, shall not be violated, and no Warrants shall issue, but upon probable cause, supported by Oath or affirmation, and particularly describing the place to be searched, and the persons or things to be seized.

Fifth Amendment
No person shall be held to answer for a capital, or otherwise infamous crime, unless on a presentment or indictment of a Grand Jury, except in cases arising in the land or naval forces, or in the Militia, when in actual service in time of War or public danger; nor shall any person be subject for the same offence to be twice put in jeopardy of life or limb; nor shall be compelled in any criminal case to be a witness against himself, nor be deprived of life, liberty, or property, without due process of law; nor shall private property be taken for public use, without just compensation.

Sixth Amendment
In all criminal prosecutions, the accused shall enjoy the right to a speedy and public trial, by an impartial jury of the State and district wherein the crime shall have been committed, which district shall have been previously ascertained by law, and to be informed of the nature and cause of the accusation; to be confronted with the witnesses against him; to have compulsory process for obtaining witnesses in his favor, and to have the Assistance of Counsel for his defence.

Seventh Amendment
In Suits at common law, where the value in controversy shall exceed twenty dollars, the right of trial by jury shall be preserved, and no fact tried by a jury, shall be otherwise re-examined in any Court of the United States, than according to the rules of the common law.

Eighth Amendment
Excessive bail shall not be required nor excessive fines imposed, nor cruel and unusual punishments inflicted.

Ninth Amendment
The enumeration in the Constitution, of certain rights, shall not be construed to deny or disparage others retained by the people.

Tenth Amendment
The powers not delegated to the United States by the Constitution, nor prohibited by it to the States, are reserved to the States respectively, or to the people.

---

bio-assay. (also called biological assay) The estimation of the amount of potency of a drug or other physiologically active substance by its action on a suitable living organism.

biochemterrorism. The use of biological or chemical agents as weapons in an act of terrorism.

biocriminology. A branch of criminology that attempts to explain criminal behavior using biosocial factors.

biological ammunition. Munitions, such as warheads and bombs, specifically designed to release a biological agent when used.

biological determinism. The theory that certain qualities inherent in an organism cause its behavior. In this view the substantive concerns of social science are eliminated or at least enormously subordinated. A number of theories of human development are biologically deterministic. Cesare Lombroso claimed that those who become criminal are degenerate and animalistic, with identifiable atavisms—or qualities suggesting genetic or evolutionary throwback. *See also* Lombroso, Cesare

biometry (also called biometrics or biostatistics). (1) Historically, biometry is measuring or calculating of the probable duration of human life; the attempt to correlate the frequency of crime between parents and children or siblings. (2) In modern usage, biometry is the application of statistics to a wide range of topics in biology. *See also* Goring, Charles

biometrics. (1) A security measure that relies upon measurable physiological or individual behavioral characteristics for authentication, such as fingerprint or iris scans. (2) application of statistics to biological topics.

biosocial criminology. A contemporary resurgence of early criminological explanations of the sources of crime. According to these theories, criminal behavior is often rooted in biological and social factors.

bio-terrorism. Terrorism by intentional release of biological agents such as toxins, viruses, and bacteria to cause illness or death in people, animals, or plants; A biological or chemical assault on persons or property. The Center for Disease Control (CDC) lists three categories of bio-terrorism agents/diseases. Category A includes high-priority agents rarely seen in the United States, but posing a risk to national security because they can be easily disseminated or transmitted from person to person; result in high mortality rates and have the potential for major public health impact; might cause public panic and social disruption; and require special action for public health preparedness. Examples of Category A agents include: Anthrax (*Bacillus anthracis*); Botulism (*Clostridium botulinum* toxin); Plague (*Yersinia pestis*); Smallpox (*variola major*); Tularemia (*Francisella tularensis*); Viral hemorrhagic fevers (filoviruses [e.g., Ebola, Marburg] and arenaviruses [e.g., Lassa, Machupo]). Category B agents are the second highest priority and include agents which: are moderately easy to disseminate; result in moderate morbidity rates and low mortality rates; and require specific enhancements of CDC's diagnostic capacity and enhanced disease surveillance. Category B agents include: Brucellosis (*Brucella* species); Epsilon toxin (*Clostridium perfringens);* Food safety threats (e.g., *Salmonella* species, *Escherichia coli* O157:H7, *Shigella*); Glanders (*Burkholderia mallei*); Melioidosis (*Burkholderia pseudomallei*); Psittacosis (*Chlamydia psittaci*); Q fever (*Coxiella burnetii*); Ricin toxin from *Ricinus communis* (castor beans); Staphylococcal enterotoxin B; Typhus fever (*Rickettsia prowazekii*); Viral encephalitis (alphaviruses [e.g., Venezuelan equine encephalitis, eastern equine encephalitis, western equine encephalitis]); and water safety threats (e.g., *Vibrio cholerae, Cryptosporidium parvum*). Category C agents are the third highest priority agents. These include emerging pathogens that could be engineered for mass dissemination in the future because of: availability; ease of production and dissemination; and potential for high morbidity and mortality rates and major health impact. Examples of Category C Agents include emerging infectious diseases such as Nipah virus and hantavirus. In 2001, there were several cases of Anthrax reported in the United States, contracted through letters that were deliberately contaminated and mailed. *See* terrorism

Birdman of Alcatraz. *See* Stroud, Robert Franklin. *See also* Alcatraz

birth order. The chronological order or rank of siblings born into a family. Criminological research has explored the role birth order plays in the development of certain personality disorders and possibly criminality.

bisexuality. Engaging in sexual acts with or being attracted both to members of the opposite sex (heterosexuality) and to members of the same sex (homosexuality).

bits. The smallest unit of information used on a computer on in telecommunications. Bits have a single binary value either 0 or 1.

Black Dahlia (1924–1947). The term *Black Dahlia* references the murder of Elizabeth Short, found murdered and mutilated in Los Angeles on January 15, 1947. Short's body was severed at the waist, and her face was cut from the corners of her mouth to her ears. Her murder was never solved and remains the source of continued speculation.

Black Gangster Disciples. A gang formed in Chicago around 1969 with the merging of the Disciple Nation and Gangster Nation. Since around 1990, many members have dropped the word "black," and refer to themselves as Gangster Disciples. This gang is known for narcotics sales, gambling, and the use of violence to maintain order within the organization.

Black Guerrilla Family. (AKA **Black Family** or **Black Vanguard**) A prison gang formed at San Quentin in 1966 by the late George Jackson. Members were initially characterized by prison officials as having tight internal discipline and a left-wing political ideology that held that blacks were essentially political prisoners. Authorities said the group, which had ties to the Black Panther Party and Symbionese Liberation Army in the mid-1970s, once had a political strategy that included plans to kidnap Department of Corrections officials. More recently BGF members had reported alliances with the following gangs: 415s, Crips, Bloods, and Black Gangster Disciples. Both Mexican Mafia and Aryan Brotherhood consider Black Guerilla Family to be their main rival. Symbols of the gang include Crossed Sabres, Machetes, Rifles, Shotguns with the letters "BGF" or the numbers "276."

Black Hand. (1) In the United States, the use of the term *Black Hand* is derived from La Mano Nera in Italian. In this usage, it refers to a type of extortion in which the victim was given a letter demanding money to avoid assault or destruction of property/business, signed with a black hand. It is not a criminal organization per se, although it was practiced by criminal organizations. (2) The term is also reference to the first Mafia family in the United States, which later became the Genovese crime family. (3) A nickname given to particularly brutal gangsters. (4) A secret society in the Kingdom of Serbia founded around 1911. *See also* Mafia; organized crime

Black, Hugo Lafayette. (1886–1971). An associate justice of the U.S. Supreme Court (1937–1971) who pursued a judicial career marked by the absolute defense of civil rights as they are literally defined in the Bill of Rights and the Constitution. Born in Alabama, he practiced law before his election to the Senate in 1924. As a senator he supported President Franklin D. Roosevelt's plan to add six justices to the Supreme Court, which became known as the "court packing" plan, and was appointed by Roosevelt to the Supreme Court in 1937. Black held that the First Amendment freedoms of speech, press, and religious liberty were "absolutes." His position resulted in occasional intellectual confrontations with those who held that individual rights should be weighed against the need for governmental authority.

Black Law Enforcement Executives, National Organization of (NOBLE). Founded in 1976. Publishes NOBLE Actions (quarterly). Address: 4609 Pinecrest Office Park Dr., Suite F, Alexandria, VA 22312. Web site: http://www.noblenatl.org.

black-light stamps. A security measure in which visitors to a given site have their hands stamped with ink that reflects ultraviolet light, which is then visible when a black-light device is shone on it.

blacklist. Generally, any list or register of people who are denied certain benefits, privileges, services, or access. For example, the specific list of names of prominent union leaders, organizers, and members. Such a list was used before the 1930s by anti-union business firms in their attempts to avoid hiring pro-union employees. The most notorious example is the Hollywood blacklist, which stemmed from an investigation launched in 1947 by the House Un-American Activities Committee (HUAC) into Communist influence on the motion picture industry.

blackmail. The extortion of money from a person by threats of accusation or exposure. *See also* extortion

blackout dates. In criminal justice, the term blackout dates generally refer to the initial period of confinement or treatment in which no outside contact is permitted, except for protected communication such as attorney and pastoral visits. The blackout period, which generally lasts seven days–three months, is designed to facilitate classification and allows the inmate/resident time to adjust to the rules and routines of the institution.

Black Panther Party. (initially called the Black Panther Party for Self-Defense) Founded in Oakland, California in 1966, a militant black organization established to promote black power. In October 1966, two black students from Merritt College in Oakland, CA, Bobby Seale and Huey P. Newton, purchased guns and drafted their 10-point self-defense program. In 1967 they opened their first storefront headquarters in Oakland. They called for complete equality for black people, including demands for black exemption from military service, the freeing of all imprisoned blacks, and the calling of all-black juries for blacks accused of crime. Between 1968 and 1971 the Panthers (never more than 2,000 strong) established headquarters across the nation, claiming they were armed and would defend themselves if attacked. The police systematically harassed the Panthers, killing a score of them and jailing their leaders (including Seale and Newton, who were eventually exonerated). In 1972, the Panthers discontinued their armed-defense tactics and moved into black community-development programs. Seale ran for mayor of Oakland in 1973, and Newton was shot and killed in Oakland in 1989. The group's political goals, which eventually focused on socialism without racial exclusivity, were overshadowed by their confrontational, militant tactics, and by the suspicions they engendered within law enforcement. The party collapsed in the mid-1970s.

Blacks in Criminal Justice, National Association of. Founded in 1974. An association of criminal justice professionals concerned with the impact of criminal justice policies and practices on the minority community. Compiles statistics on minority involvement in the criminal justice field. Address: N.C. Central University, P.O. Box 19788, Durham, NC 27707. Web: http://www.nabcj.org/.

blog. A portmanteau of the words "web" and "log," a blog is an Internet-based article or column.

blogosphere. A term used to define a collection of interrelated blogs, or all blogs currently published on the Internet.

blogroll. A list of links on one blog referencing others.

blood alcohol. A chemical test for determining the concentration of alcohol in the blood. The test refers to the weight of the alcohol measured in grams per 100 milliliters of blood, given in percentage figures. Also called blood alcohol concentration.

blood alcohol level (BAL). The measurement of breath, blood, or urine samples to determine intoxication. It is expressed in terms of the percentage of alcohol in a person's blood: a BAL of .10 percent means one part alcohol to 1,000 parts blood. Generally, a BAL of 0.20 percent is significant intoxication, BAC above 0.35 percent is can lead to coma and death. *See* Table 5. Blood Alcohol Level (BAL), page 50

blood-borne pathogens. Disease-causing organisms, such as bacteria or viruses, which are carried by means of the circulatory system.

TABLE 5 BLOOD ALCOHOL LEVEL (BAL): EFFECTS AND IMPAIRMENTS		
Blood Alcohol Level	**Changes in Feelings and Personality**	**Physical and Mental Impairments**
0.01—0.06	Relaxation Sense of Well-being Loss of Inhibition Lowered Alertness Joyous	Thought Judgment Coordination Concentration
0.06—0.10	Blunted Feelings Disinhibition Extroversion Impaired Sexual Pleasure	Reflexes Impaired Reasoning Depth Perception Distance Acuity Peripheral Vision Glare Recovery
0.11—0.20	Overexpression Emotional Swings Angry or Sad Boisterous	Reaction Time Gross Motor Control Staggering Slurred Speech
0.21—0.29	Stupor Lose Understanding Impaired Sensations	Severe Motor Impairment Loss of Consciousness Memory Blackout
0.30—0.39	Severe Depression Unconsciousness Death Possible	Bladder Function Breathing Heart Rate
=> 0.40	Unconsciousness Death	Breathing Heart Rate

Source: Virginia Tech.

blood feud. A quarrel between families or clans. The feud between the families of Hatfield and McCoy is one of the more famous.

Bloodhound Association, National Police. Founded in 1962. Publishes *Nose News* (quarterly). Address: P.O. Box 338, Waterford, CT 06385; Web: http://www.npba.com/.

Bloods. Street gang founded in Los Angeles, California, in the 1970s widely known for its rivalry with the Crips, another street gang. The Bloods are often identified by the color red, worn by their members as an insignia, and by distinctive hand signs.

Bloodstain Pattern Analysis (BPA). A specialty field of forensic science, BPA is the scientific study of the size, shape, and distribution of bloodstains to ascertain the causes of, and events resulting in, the bloodstain patterns found. One method of categorizing such patterns is through the mechanism by which the stain was created; when categorized this way, types of bloodstains include: passive, projected, and transfer/contact. Blood stains can also be categorized by velocity, referring to the amount of force transferred to a blood source to create the stain; when categorized this way, types of bloodstains include: low-, medium-, and high-velocity impact spatter.

bludgeon. Also called cudgel, baton, truncheon, night stick, and sap. A short stick with one thick, heavy, or loaded end, used as an offensive weapon; any clublike weapon.

blunt force trauma. A type of physical injury caused by sudden impact, often due to attack. Blunt force trauma injuries can be received from weapons such as clubs, sticks, or the butt of a gun; they can be caused by fists or as a result of a fall. Blunt force trauma injuries generally do not penetrate the body as stabbings or gunshot wounds do, but they cause damage such as bruising, internal bleeding, concussions, and broken bones while leaving the skin generally intact. In February of 2010, a Sea World animal trainer was attacked and killed by a whale she trained: she died of traumatic injuries due to blunt force trauma of the whale attack.

blue-collar workers. A term used to designate employees who are not involved in supervision or administration of a business. The term originated when factory-floor workers wore blue collars and office personnel wore white collars. Blue collar does not imply a skill level.

blue laws. (1) A puritanical code regulating public and private morality in the theocratic New Haven, CT, colony during the seventeenth and eighteenth centuries. (2) All laws prohibiting commercial businesses on Sunday.

blue-ribbon jury. A petit jury selected for its special qualifications, either because the case is too complex for a regular jury or because some expert knowledge is required. Such juries existed from the earliest period of development of the common law and were common in London by the mid-fourteenth century. Because of the modern emphasis on impartial selection of jurors, blue-ribbon juries have fallen into disfavor. They were abolished in U.S. federal courts in 1968.

blue sky laws. Laws intended to prevent the sale of fraudulent securities. The term is attributed to a facetious remark made by a Kansas bank commissioner, who said that certain skillful promoters were able to "sell blocks of the blue sky" to gullible victims. The U.S. Supreme Court upheld the law on the ground that prevention of deception is within the competency of government. This law requires companies selling stock to file financial statements with state banking commissioners in all operating locations.

board of pardons. A state board, having various official names, that acts alone or with the governor in granting executive clemency to criminals or advises the governor in the exercise of that function.

board of parole. A state board that grants or revokes paroles of convicts within the jurisdiction. If authorized by a court, the board determines the date of a convicted person's eligibility for parole.

board of review. An administrative appeals board which, after hearing evidence, determines whether an assessment, action, or decision of an officer was correct.

Body Orifice Security Scanner (BOSS). BOSS is a non-intrusive device that detects metal objects hidden in body cavities. Persons being screened sit on the BOSS chair, or place their face against a BOSS screening place, and the device scans for metal, weapons, and other contraband hidden in anal, vaginal, oral, and nasal cavities. This device is used at correctional facilities to screen inmates at intake or following movement, visitors, and employees. According to the BOSS Web site, this device is highly sensitive and can identify: "razor blades, handcuff keys, paper clips, knives, shanks and tools, cellular telephones, metal foils and objects such as detonator caps." For more information, visit: http://www.bodyorificesecurity scanner.com/us/.

body types. Human physical structures or builds. Constitutional psychologist William Sheldon created a typology consisting of three categories, each of which he related to a characteristic temperament. The endomorph was flabby and easygoing, the skinny ectomorph was inclined to be introspective, and the mesomorph was restless and tended to translate impulse into action.

boiler rooms. A call center used to sell questionable goods, stocks and commodities by telephone, or to engage in other types of telemarketing fraud. In such centers, unscrupulous organizations instruct their employees in the use of using high-pressure techniques and dishonest (often illegal) practices in making telephone sales. According to the SEC, examples of such practices include: "lying about the firm's reputation and expertise, claiming it had a 'research department' that analyzed stocks when it didn't; refusing to say *anything* negative about the stocks they pushed, including the 'risk factors' discussed in the prospectus; making baseless price predictions, promising that certain stocks would double in price within a short time period; impersonating other salespeople at the firm; and discouraging customers from selling the stocks they recommended without regard to the customers' best interests. *See also* telemarketing fraud

bolo Be on the look-out for.

Bomb Technicians and Investigators, International Association of. Founded in Sacramento, CA, in March 1973. Publishes *The Detonator Magazine* (bimonthly). Address: IABIT, P.O. Box 160, Goldvein, VA 22720-0160. Web: https://www.iabti.org/.

Bombing of Los Angeles Times building. On October 1, 1910, the Los Angeles Times building was bombed by dynamite, killing 21 people and injuring more than 100. Suspects John (JJ) and James (JB) McNamara were members of the Iron Workers union, reportedly unhappy about LA Times publisher Harrison Otis' use of the paper to disseminate anti-union information. JB McNamara pled guilty of murder and was sentenced to life; JJ McNamara pled guilty to a related bombing and was sentenced to 15 years in prison. *See also* domestic terrorism

bona fide. In good faith; honestly, without fraud or unfair dealing; genuine.

bona fide occupational qualification (BFOQ). Any attribute and/or skill that an employer has proven is necessary for satisfactory performance of a particular job, as distinguished from characteristics that have sometimes been required, such as race, height, gender, property-owning status, or passing grades on tests, but that can't be shown to be related to job performance.

Bonanno, Joseph (Joe Bananas) (1905–2002). Born in Sicily, Italy, in 1905,

Bonanno entered the United States illegally in 1924. In the United States, Bonanno lived in Chicago and became one of Al Capone's hijackers and a rumrunner. He moved to New York and began loan sharking and running gambling rackets. He bought a funeral home around 1927, which served as a mafia corpse disposal operation. Despite the fact that Bonanno grew into the head of a La Cosa Nostra family in New York City, he had only one conviction during his criminal career, for violating minimum wage law. Bonnano ended his own criminal career and retired in Tuscon, Arizona, in the early 1980s. He died of heart failure in 2002. *See also* mafia

Bonaparte, Charles. (1851–1921). United States Secretary of the Navy (1905–1906). Bonaparte is best known as the U.S. Attorney General (1906–1909) credited for establishing the FBI.

bond. A pledge of money or assets offered as bail by an accused person or his or her surety (bail bondsman) to secure temporary release from custody; forfeited if the conditions of bail are not fulfilled.

bondsman. An individual, bound by a contract, who is responsible for the performance of an act on behalf of another person.

Bonin, William (The Freeway Strangler). (1947–1996). Born in 1947 to an alcoholic father and domineering mother, Bonin was first arrested at the age of 10. He lived in multiple juvenile facilities in his adolescence. As an adult, he worked as a truck driver and was arrested for several sex offenses, and was twice paroled for sex crimes. Between 1978–1980, Bonin is believed to have tortured, raped and murdered between 20–35 teenage males in the Los Angeles area, using his truck to cruise the freeways of southern California looking for his prey. Bonin was convicted and sentenced to death in 1982. He was executed in 1996, the first person to be executed by lethal injection in California.

Bonney, William (Billy the Kid) (1859–1881). Born in New York, Billy the Kid began his notorious outlaw life after the murder of John Tunstall, a rancher who hired Bonney. Bonney vowed to avenge the murder, and he did, killing the men who murdered Tunstall, among others with his notoriously fast draw. In all, Billy the Kid killed 21 men by his twenty-first birthday; he was shot and killed by police a few months before his twenth-second birthday.

boodle. Money accepted or paid for the use of political influence; bribe money. The term originated in New York City about 1883.

bookie. A person who operates a racing "book"; one who takes illegal bets on horse races.

booking. A law enforcement or correctional process that officially records an entry into detention after arrest; involves recording the identity of the arrestee, place, time, reason for arrest, and name of arresting authority.

bookmaking. The practice of receiving and recording bets made on the results of horse racing and other sporting events; often illegal.

boot camps. Generally run by private organizations and modeled after military recruit training camps, boot camps are based on shock incarceration techniques and military routine. Boot camp programs generally offer (1) intervention to parents with incorrigible teens or (2) an alternative sanction in juvenile court. In either case, the consent of the teen is not required. *See* shock incarceration

Booth, John Wilkes. After the fall of Richmond and General Lee's surrender at Appomattox, Booth decided on assassination, enlisting one accomplice to murder Vice President Andrew Johnson and another to kill Secretary of State William H. Seward. On the evening of April 14, 1865, Booth shot Abraham Lincoln in the head at Ford's Theater. He leaped to the stage, crying, "Sic semper tyrannis! The South is avenged!" and escaped through the rear of the theater. His accomplices were unsuccessful in their assassination attempts, although Seward was badly beaten. Booth was located April 26, when

he was found hiding in a barn near Bowling Green, VA, and was killed by his captors. *See also* assassination; Table 2. Infamous U.S. Assassinations/Assassination Attempts, page 30

bootlegging. Illegal manufacture, transportation, and/or sale of alcoholic beverages.

booty bump. The rectal ingestion of drugs or alcohol. This method is used in severe dependence, and is known for being a speedy delivery method. Also, rectal (or genital) ingestion generally produces greater pharmacological effects than other methods, thus substances are generally ingested in much smaller doses when taken this way. This method has a higher rate of overdose than other methods of ingestion.

Borden, Lizzie (1860–1927). Lizzie Andrew Borden was suspected of killing her father and stepmother in 1892. Lizzy and the maid (Sullivan, who was sleeping) were the only persons home when the bodies were found. Borden was prosecuted for the double homicide and acquitted. She led an isolated life thereafter, due in part to widespread public belief that she "got away with murder." She died of pneumonia in 1927. *See also* parricide

border. Geographical boundary of legal jurisdiction, such as city, county (parish in Louisiana), state, or country. *See* U.S.-Mexico border

borstals/borstal system. (1) English institutions that were organized for the treatment of youthful offenders. Borstals were abolished in the U.K. with the Criminal Justice Act of 1982, replaced by youth custody centers; (2) term used loosely to apply to juvenile institution or reformatory.

BOSS. *See* Body Orifice Security Scanner

Boston Massacre. Name applied to the killing of five men and the wounding of others when British troops fired into a crowd of men and boys in Boston in 1770. The incident occurred as a result of the quartering of two regiments of troops in Boston, sent to protect British officials in executing the Customs

Acts. John Adams acted as counsel for the British in the trial that followed. The British officer in command was acquitted of the charge of giving the order to fire. Two British soldiers were given light sentences for manslaughter.

Boston Police Strike. A strike of 72 percent of the Boston police force on September 9, 1919, following the police commissioner's refusal to recognize the policemen's union. Boston Mayor Petes called sections of the militia, which broke the strike. Governor Coolidge subsequently commanded the police commissioner to assume charge and called out the entire state guard, after order had already been established. The striking officers were not permitted to return to work and, despite legislation supporting their reinstatement, were not rehired. Coolidge's often-quoted declaration that "there is no right to strike against the public safety by anybody, anywhere, anytime" projected him into the national limelight as a supporter of law and order. This led to his nomination for president by the Republican Party in 1920.

Boston Strangler. *See* DeSalvo, Albert Henry

bounty. A reward or premium, usually offered as an inducement for some act.

bounty hunter (sometimes called bail enforcement agent, fugitive recovery agent, and bail fugitive investigator). Person who captures fugitives for a monetary reward (bounty). The practice of bounty hunting is only legal in the United States and Philippines. In March of 2010, President Obama authorized the use of high-tech bounty hunters to detect fraud in Medicare/Medicaid billing using sophisticated software. *See* thief-takers

bourgeoisie. In Marxist theory, the owners of the means of production; the ruling class in capitalist societies.

Bow Street Runners. A unit of the police force organized in the London, England, metropolitan area in 1749 by John and Henry Fielding to prevent crime. This concept was developed into "the new science of preventive police." Some called this unit the first police detective squad, as its function was to arrive at the scene of the crime quickly and investigate the case.

brachioproticism. Also known as brachioprotic eroticism, this practice involves inserting one's hand into another's rectum for sexual pleasure. *See also* fisting

Brady Bill. *See* Brady Handgun Violence Prevention Act.

Brady Handgun Violence Prevention Act of 1983. The Brady Handgun Violence Prevention Act requires purchasers to pass a federal background check prior to purchasing a firearm in the United States. Certain persons are prohibited from possessing a firearm, including: those convicted of a felony; fugitives from justice; drug addicts; those adjudicated as criminally insane or committed to a mental institution; unlawful immigrants; those dishonorably discharged from the military; persons who have renounced U.S. citizenship; those named in an active restraining order; and persons convicted of misdemeanor domestic violence. This last provision impacts some law enforcement personnel, who can no longer carry a firearm, and thus can no longer perform their job, if they perpetrate domestic violence. The Brady Bill was named for James Brady, White House Press Secretary, shot in 1981 by John Hinkley, Jr. in an assassination attempt on President Ronald Regan. *See also* Bureau of Alcohol, Tobacco, Firearms and Explosives (ATF); Federal Assault Weapons Ban of 1994; Federal Firearms Act of 1938; Firearm Owners' Protection Act of 1986; Gun Control Act of 1968; National Firearms Act of 1934; Omnibus Crime Control and Safe Streets Act of 1968; Violent Crime Control and Law Enforcement Act of 1994.

Brady Issue. Colloquial term used by law enforcement officers in reference to the U.S.S.C. case *Brady v Maryland,* which prohibits police and/or prosecutors from withholding exculpatory evidence in criminal investigation and prosecution. The term is used to reference potentially exculpatory issues identified during investigation which must be presented to the defense. The issue has far-reaching implications for law enforcement, prosecutors, and criminal defendants.

Brady, James. (1940–). James Brady was the White House Press Secretary under President Ronald Reagan when, on March 30, 1981, he was shot in the head by John Hinckley, Jr., in a botched assassination attempt against President Reagan. The injury left Brady permanently paralyzed. Brady became an advocate for stricter handgun control. The Brady Handgun Violence Prevention Act was named in his honor. *See also* Brady Bill

brain death. A legal definition of death adopted by many states. Under it, an individual is dead when there is an irreversible end to all brain activity. Brain death is a condition in which the brain is no longer capable of sustaining the rest of the body's systems without advanced life support. This definition of death became necessary once the medical profession developed the ability to maintain heart and lung functions by artificial means. Should not be confused with *persistent vegetative state*.

brain imaging. The use of various technologies to view structures and function within the brain. Examples include *computed axial tomography* (CAT), which is a series of X-rays to view brain structures; *diffuse optical tomography* (DOT), which relies on infrared light to view hemoglobin absorption in the brain; e*lectroencephalography* (EEG), which uses electrodes on the scalp to measure electrical activity in the brain; *functional magnetic resonance imaging* (fMRI), which provides a view of brain structures activated by various stimuli; *magnetic resonance imaging* (MRI), which relies upon magnetic fields to view cross-sectional images of the brain; and *positron emission tomography* (PET) imaging, which uses the injection of radioactive chemicals to image brain function.

Brandeis, Louis Dembitz. (1856–1941). Associate justice of the Supreme Court from 1916, when he was appointed by President Woodrow Wilson, until 1939. Born in Louisville, KY, Brandeis was educated in public schools, in the severe academic discipline of Dresden, Germany, and at Harvard Law School. He gained recognition for his expertise in litigation in his private law practice in Boston. Brandeis disdained the traditional lawyer's brief, which was filled with narrow procedural points. Instead, he filled his legal presentations with social and economic arguments. "The Brandeis brief" became the label given to this type of argument. While he was a lawyer, he became an ardent Zionist. Once on the Court, Brandeis became associated with Justice Oliver Wendell Holmes, Jr., and his advocacy of judicial restraint. Brandeis believed that legislative regulations in the economic sphere were necessary, but he held that the judicial branch had to remain aloof from them. A thorough scholar, Brandeis filled his opinions with cross-references and footnotes. Brandeis is also associated with Holmes in the formulation of the "clear and present danger" test of laws restricting speech and press, although, if anything, Brandeis was more emphatic in his defense of the First Amendment freedoms. Nonetheless, he is still generally associated with the tradition of judicial restraint. He consistently argued for a limited role in judicial decision making, and he was a dedicated defender of federalism.

Brawner Rule (insanity). This insanity rule derived from the 1972 U.S. District Court of Appeals case *United States v. Brawner.* Brawner effectively replaced the Durham benchmark for insanity. In Brawner, the court relied heavily upon the American Law Institute (ALI) standard, under which a defendant must lack substantial capacity to appreciate that his conduct is wrongful" or must lack "substantial capacity to conform his conduct to the law." As this was a Court of Appeals case, it affected all trials between 1972–1984 within the DC Circuit only. The Insanity

Defense Reform Act (1984) replaced the Brawner rule. *See also* insanity, M'Naghten Rule, Irresistible Impulse; The Durham/New Hampshire Test; American Law Institute Model; The Insanity Defense Reform Act of 1984 (U.S.); The substantial capacity test; Temporary insanity. *See* Table 25. Types of Insanity Defense in the United States, pages 232 &233.

breach of peace. A violation of the public tranquility and order. Acts or conduct which seriously endanger public peace and order. Such violations include blocking the sidewalk, fighting, cursing, spitting on the sidewalk, loitering, panhandling, using obscene language in public, resisting arrest, trespassing, vandalism and other types of disorderly behavior defined as illegal in various jurisdictions. Such offenses are crimes against the state.

breach of trust. Willful acts that use knowledge or power acquired through one's official position to gain unfair advantage in competitive situations or to achieve monetary or other gain. Many such acts are not regarded as crimes but are merely subject to ethical sanctions. To constitute a crime, there must be a breach of some official duty sufficient to justify the state's intervention. *See also* fiduciary; organized deception of the public

breaking. A forcible destroying, removing, or putting aside of something material that constitutes a part of a building and is relied on as security against intrusion; forcible entry of a building.

breathalyzer. Initially the trade name of a device used to test the blood-alcohol ratio via exhaled breath. The term is now used as the generic for all models used to analyze blood alcohol level by breath.

breath-testing equipment. Equipment designed to test the breath to determine blood-alcohol level. There are several brands of such products. *See also* passive alcohol sensor

bribe. A price, reward, gift, or favor bestowed or promised with a view to perverting the judgment, or corrupting the conduct of a judge, witness, or other person in a position of trust or power.

bribery. The giving or offering of anything of value with intent unlawfully to influence persons in the discharge of their duties; the receiving or asking of anything of value with unlawful intent to be influenced.

briefs. Summaries of the law relating to a case, prepared by the attorneys for both parties and given to the judge.

Brink's Armored Car Service. Established in 1859 in Chicago, IL, by Washington Perry Brink as an armored transportation service.

British North America Act. Legislation passed by the Canadian Parliament in 1867 that created the structure of the Canadian criminal justice system.

broken window syndrome. A public safety theory that neighborhoods deteriorate rapidly if initial cases of vandalism, such as broken windows or graffiti, are ignored by law enforcement and/or neighborhood residents. The premise is that police officers should take cases seriously and residents should repair damage promptly, since neglect indicates no one is concerned, thereby inviting additional incivilities.

brothel. Also called a bordello or whorehouse, an establishment dedicated to prostitution that provides clients with a location to meet and have sexual intercourse with prostitutes.

BTK Killer (bind, torture, kill). *See* Rader, Dennis Lynn

bug. (1) To plant a microphone or other sound sensor or to tap a communication line for the purpose of surreptitious listening or audio monitoring; loosely, to install a sensor in a specified location. (2) The microphone or other sensor used for the purpose of surreptitious listening.

buggery. An anti-sodomy law adopted in England in 1533 under King Henry VIII, defining buggery as "unnatural sexual acts." The term was later defined as anal penetration and bestiality. *See* sodomy

bulimia nervosa. An eating disorder in which the patient engages in binge eating or gorging and then deliberately regurgitates the food and/or takes excessive laxatives to purge it from his or her system. Fasting and the use of diuretics is also common. The word bulimia is derived from Latin for "ravenous hunger."

bullet. A projectile made for firing in a rifle or pistol; the part of a cartridge, usually made of lead, that is discharged from a firearm. Common types of bullets include: lead—common in most handguns; nontoxic—made of non-lead metals with the goal of reduced leakage of lead and other toxic metals into the environment; jacketed lead—generally used for high velocity firearms; armor piercing—generally a jacketed design with high-density metal; tracer—hollow, filled with material to illuminate the direction of aim; incendiary—generally made with an explosive component that ignites upon impact; and frangible—generally breaks into particles upon impact, minimizing through-shots. *See* Table 6. Types of Bullets, page 58; *see also* Table 7. Bullets: Caliber, Weight, Feet per Second, Stopping Percentage, and Typical Weapon, page 59

bunco game. (1) A parlour or gambling game originating in England in the 1700s, played with teams and using three dice; (2) Act or trick contrived to gain the confidence of a victim, who is then defrauded.

Bundy, Theodore (Ted) (1946–1989). Born to Eleanor Louise Cowell on November 24, 1946, Ted Bundy was raised by his maternal grandparents to avoid stigma and grew up believing his mother was his sister. Ted changed his surname to Bundy in 1951, after his biological mother (Eleanor Cowell) married John Bundy, who legally adopted five-year-old Ted. Ted Bundy was a charming, handsome, and intelligent young man who was educated at Stanford University; he was the well-liked assistant director of the Seattle Crime Commission and volunteered on a suicide hotline. He was also one of the nation's most nefarious serial killers, murdering at least 21 young women in Washington, Oregon, Utah, and Florida between 1974 and 1979. His crime spree included two known jail breaks, after which he continued killing. Bundy was finally apprehended and convicted in Florida. He was sentenced to death by electrocution, a sentence carried out on January 24, 1989. Shortly before his execution, thought by many to have been a ploy to delay his death, Bundy admitted to killing 30 women. Although some estimates are as high as 100 women, additional victims have never been confirmed.

Buono, Angelo (1934–2002). Born in Rochester, New York, Buono was convicted of failure to pay child support, auto theft, assault, and rape became close to his cousin Kenneth Bianchi around 1975. The two moved to Los Angeles in 1977. Over the next two years, the pair, who became known as the Hillside Stranglers, killed at least 10 women before their arrest in 1979. At trial, Bianchi testified against Buano in exchange for leniency. Buono was convicted of nine murder counts and was sentenced to life imprisonment. While incarcerated, he met and married a California State employee in 1986. He died of a heart attack in prison on September 21, 2001. *See also* Bianchi, Kenneth; Hillside Strangler

burden of proof. Duty of establishing the existence of fact in a trial.

bureaucratic model of legislation. The view that a society's laws are enacted as a result of power exerted by clearly identifiable bureaucratic organizations.

Bureau of Alcohol, Tobacco, Firearms and Explosives (ATF). According to their Web site, the ATF "protects our communities from violent criminals, criminal organizations, the illegal use and trafficking of firearms, the illegal use and storage of explosives, acts of arson and bombings, acts of terrorism, and the illegal diversion of alcohol and tobacco products. We partner with communities, industries, law enforcement, and public safety agencies to safeguard the public we serve through information sharing, training,

text continues on page 59

TABLE 6   TYPES OF BULLETS

Type	Generally made of	Application	Problems
Lead	Lead with tin or antimony	Generally low velocity and used for practice.	Leaves deposits of corrosive residue in gun.
Jacketed Lead	Lead core plated with steel, cupronickel, or copper alloys	Soft and hollow points are generally used for self-defense.	More expensive than regular load bullets.
Armor Piercing	Tungsten, tungsten carbide, steel, depleted uranium	Used to defeat armor, usually in war.	Can penetrate farther than necessary or wanted.
Tracer	Magnesium perchlorate and strontium salts	Useful for aiming streams of fire; also used to signal friendly forces.	Not as effective at long ranges since it burns out.
Incendiary	Phosphorous	Used in fighter planes and for armor penetration. Great because they are explosive.	Their explosive properties can make them hazardous.
Frangible	Copper/tin powder	To cause maximum damage with minimum penetration on human targets.	Will not penetrate body armor as readily.
Nontoxic	Tungsten, bismuth, steel	Used for hunting. Cuts down on lead poisoning in animals.	No widespread use as of yet.
Practice	Wood, wax, plastic	Good for short-range target work.	Limited range.
Less Lethal	Rubber, plastic, beanbags	Used by police and military to cut down on casualties when subduing crowds.	May not effectively neutralize intoxicated targets.
Blanks	Plastic, wax	Used to simulate live gunfire.	Can still be fatal at short distances.
Blended Metal	Made with powders and bound with another substance.	Can be modified to penetrate thicker, harder surfaces.	Illegal for most applications, even military purposes
Exploding	Made with lead with an explosive tip.	Intended for use on human targets.	Can be unstable if dropped.

Compiled by Richard Porter, CSULB

TABLE 7   BULLETS: CALIBER, WEIGHT, FEET PER SECOND,
STOPPING PERCENTAGE, AND TYPICAL WEAPON

Caliber	Common Bullet Weights (grains)	Estimated Speed in Feet per Second	Estimated One Hit Stopping Percentage	Type of Firearm Used
10 mm	150, 155, 175, 180	900–100	85	Semiautomatic pistol
.22 LR	20, 35, 60	575–1750	30	Rifle, semiautomatic pistol, revolver
.223 Remington	40, 52, 55, 62, 68, 69	3025–3300	95	Rifle
.25 ACP	33, 35, 45	855–1081	25	Pistol
.30 Carbine	110	2000	84	Rifle
30-30	110, 130, 150, 160, 170	1616–2684	93	Rifle

Compiled by Richard Porter, CSULB.

research, and use of technology." In 2003, regulatory functions of the ATF were transferred to the new Alcohol and Tobacco Tax and Trade Bureau under the Department of the Treasury. Address: Bureau of Alcohol, Tobacco, Firearms and Explosives, Office of Public and Governmental Affairs, 99 New York Avenue, NE, Room 5S 144, Washington, DC 20226 USA; Web: http://www.atf. gov/. *See also* Alcohol and Tobacco Tax and Trade Bureau; Brady Handgun Violence Prevention Act; Federal Assault Weapons Ban of 1994; Federal Firearms Act of 1938; Firearm Owners' Protection Act of 1986; Gun Control Act of 1968; National Firearms Act of 1934; Omnibus Crime Control and Safe Streets Act of 1968; Violent Crime Control and Law Enforcement Act of 1994

Bureau of Consumer Protection (BCP). Organization within the Federal Trade Commission (FTC) that works "to prevent fraud, deception, and unfair business practices in the marketplace." In the United States, the Federal Trade Commission (FTC) tracks consumer fraud. In 2005, consumers reported $680 million in fraud losses. Internet-related complaints accounted for 46 percent of all reported fraud complaints, with identity theft as the most common complaint filed with FTC. Other consumer fraud complaints included: Internet auctions; foreign money orders; shop-at-home and catalog sales; prizes, sweepstakes, and lotteries; business opportunities and work-at-home plans; advance loans and credit protection. Address: Federal Trade Commission, Consumer Response Center, 600 Pennsylvania Avenue, NW, Washington, DC 20580. Web: http://www.ftc.gov/bcp/.

Bureau of Industry and Security. The mission of the BIS, which is operated under the Department of Commerce, is to "Advance U.S. national security, foreign policy, and economic objectives by ensuring an effective export control and treaty compliance system and promoting continued U.S. strategic technology leadership." Address: Bureau of Industry and Security, 14th Street & Constitution Ave., NW, Washington, DC, 20230. Web: http://www.bis.doc.gov/about/index.htm.

Bureau of Justice Assistance. Established in 1984 and authorized to provide block grants to assist state and local governments in carrying out programs to improve the criminal justice system, with special emphasis on violent crime and drug abuse. Located at Bureau of Justice Assistance, 810 Seventh Street NW, Fourth Floor, Washington, DC 20531. Web: http://www.ojp.usdoj.gov/BJA/.

Bureau of Justice Statistics. The Bureau of Justice Statistics was first established on December 27, 1979, under the Justice Systems Improvement Act of 1979. The mission of BJS is "To collect, analyze, publish, and disseminate information on crime, criminal offenders, victims of crime, and the operation of justice systems at all levels of government." Address: 810 Seventh Street, NW, Washington, DC 20531, Web: http://bjs.ojp.usdoj.gov/. *See* National Institute of Justice

Bureau of Narcotics and Dangerous Drugs. Formed April 8, 1968, by a merger of the Bureau of Narcotics of the U.S. Treasury Department and the Bureau of Drug Abuse Control of the Department of Health, Education, and Welfare. Became the Drug Enforcement Administration in 1973. Web: http://www.justice.gov/dea/.

Burger, Warren Earl. (1907–1995). Fourteenth chief justice of the Supreme Court (1969–1986), appointed in 1969 by President Richard Nixon, who wanted a "law and order" jurist with "strict constructionist" views. Born in St. Paul, MN, Burger developed a successful law practice and also taught law. In 1953, he was appointed assistant attorney general by President Dwight Eisenhower and in 1956 was named to the U.S. Court of Appeals for the District of Columbia. He made a reputation as a conservative judge in a generally liberal appellate court. When appointed to the Supreme Court, Burger indicated that it was not the place for the type of liberal judicial reform practiced by the Warren Court. Several of his more notable contributions were to define obscenity legally, establish busing as a tool to end school segregation, force Nixon to release the Watergate tapes, lead the national celebrations of the Constitution's 200th anniversary in 1987 and the Bill of Rights' 200th anniversary in 1989, uphold affirmative action, and establish the right to abortion.

burglar alarm. A system used to detect unwanted entry into a residence, business or other building. In earlier versions, openings such as windows and doors are fixed with a connective electronic mechanism. Entrance through the opening breaks the connection and initiates an alarm signal. There are two main categories for alarm systems: those designed for indoor use, and those designed for outdoor use. Types of alarms include, but are not limited to: passive infrared detectors; ultrasonic detectors; microwave detectors, photo-electric detectors; vibration/motion detectors; magnetic or electromagnetic field detectors; fencing systems; and fiber-optic systems.

Burglar and Fire Alarm Association, National. Founded in 1948. A clearinghouse for all materials related to the business of security alarm systems and services. Address: 2300 Valley View Lane, Suite 230, Irving, TX 75062.

burglary. An early legal definition was trespassing and breaking and entering of the dwelling house of another in the nighttime with the intent to commit a felony. The term now means entry of any fixed structure, vehicle, or vessel used for regular residence, industry, or business, with or without force, with intent to commit a felony or larceny. Next to larceny-theft, burglary is the most frequent major crime.

burglary, safe. (also called safe cracking) The illegal entry of a safe, generally without combination or key. Several methods are used: lock manipulation—generally by feeling or hearing the sound of a rotary combination lock in order to determine the combination; guessing the combination—generally by using manufacturer installed "try-out combinations" or in cases where the owner uses a combination that is easy to guess, such as a birthdate; autodialer—commercially produced device that tries every combination of numbers until the correct combination is found; weak-point drilling—based on manufacturer-published drill-point diagrams, this method is generally used by locksmiths to gain access to a safe if the owner does not have the combination or key, or in gaining access to a compromised or tampered safe; brute force methods such as explosives or "jam shots," which are aimed at the safe's doors. This method often trips "relockers" in most safes, which semi-permanently locks the safe, making it impenetrable by key or combination; radiological methods—technology such as X-ray can be used to view the angles in the lock's internal mechanism to ascertain the combination. This technique does not work on newer safes, which use nonmetal interiors to thwart this method; tunneling—generally used to gain access to vault safes, as are generally used in banks. Most vault safes employ underground passages to detect such attempts.

burglary tools. Tools suitable for gaining illegal entry to a safe. Possession of such tools is illegal in many states, but the intent to use them to commit a crime must also be shown. The courts have held that it is immaterial that the tools might also be used for lawful purposes.

burn. A skin injury caused by intense heat, often secondary to accidental exposure to fire, chemical agents, or electrical conduction. *See* Table 8. Burn Classification Causes, Symptoms, and Treatment, this page.

burnese. A slang term for cocaine.

burnout. The depletion of an individual's mental and physical resources, often due to excessive stress, characterized by long-term exhaustion and diminished interest. Symptoms of burnout can include feelings of exhaustion, boredom, and impatience, as well as psychophysiological problems such as headaches, ulcers, and heart disease. Although it can occur in anyone, burnout appears to be more prevalent among caring professionals, such as counselors, social workers, doctors, police officers, and teachers. Treatment includes relaxation techniques, social support networks, variation of activities, and control of responsibilities. *See also* stress

TABLE 8 BURN CLASSIFICATION, CAUSES, SYMPTOMS, AND TREATMENT

Traditional types	Depth	Typical causes	Symptoms	Treatment
First degree	Superficial—epidermis	Sunburn, steam	Pain, no blisters	First aid, pain management
Second degree	Superficial—papillary dermis	Scalding, holding hot metal	Blisters, fluid, pain	First aid, sterile dressing, pain management
Third degree	Deep—reticular dermis	Fire	White appearance, red stain appearance, diminished sensation	First aid, sterile dressing, intravenous fluids
Fourth degree	Full thickness—involves epidermis, dermis, subcutaneous fat/connective tissue to bone	Fire	Charred, leathery, absence of flesh to bone in severe cases	Skin graft

Burns, William John. (1861–1932). Founder of Burns International Detective Agency and chief of the Bureau of Investigation (BOI), a predecessor agency to the Federal Bureau of Investigation (FBI). Burns was born in Baltimore, MD. He served in the Secret Service and in the Department of the Interior. In 1909 with William P. Sheridan he formed the Burns and Sheridan Detective Agency, headquartered in Chicago. On March 11, 1910, Sheridan sold his interest to Burns, and the Burns National Detective Agency was born.

C

CA. (1) Abbreviation for the federal Circuit Court of Appeals. The letters are followed by the designation for the circuit; that is, CA5 = Fifth Circuit and CADC = the District of Columbia Circuit Court. (2) Also the abbreviation for the state of California.

cache. A hidden quantity of materials or items, often used in reference to weapons, as an arms cache.

cadaver. A corpse; dead body.

cadre. Trained and dedicated activists in an organization, forming its core and capable of training others.

Cain. An Old Testament farmer, son of Adam and Eve, known as world's first murderer for killing his brother Abel, a shepherd.

calendar. In criminal justice, a listing of pending cases and the date and place of the next step in their processing; a listing of all cases in any particular court for a given day.

caliber. A term that derives from the Latin *qua libra,* "what pound," first applied to the weight of a bullet and then to its diameter. The bore diameter is measured in hundredths of an inch. A .22 caliber gun has a barrel measuring 22/100 of an inch in diameter. This term is similar to gauge, used in shotguns, but caliber is measured differently. *See also* gauge

Calley, William L., Jr. On March 16, 1968, U.S. Army Lieutenant Calley and his platoon were transported via helicopter into My Lai, Vietnam, with orders to "clean the village out." They expected to find forces of the 48th Battalion of the Viet Cong but instead found several hundred civilians. The soldiers herded their captives to the center of the village, where Calley ordered them shot. By the end of the day, an estimated 567 civilians had been executed. Many soldiers refused to take part in the "My Lai Massacre," claiming the order was unlawful. On September 5, 1969, the day before Calley was scheduled to be discharged, he was accused of killing 104 Vietnamese civilians. He claimed innocence on the grounds that he was acting under orders given by his superior, Captain Ernest Media (Medina was acquitted in a separate trial). Calley was tried by a general court martial, convicted, and sentenced to life imprisonment. Calley was the only one within the chain of command who was convicted. After three and one-half years under house arrest and confined to quarters, he was released and his life sentence commuted. Calley lived in Columbus, OH, with his wife from 1975–2006; following his divorce, he moved to Atlanta, GA, in 2007. In August 2009, he apologized for his role in the My Lai massacre in a speech to the Kiwanis Club of Columbus; however, he still maintained that he was following orders.

calumny. A false and malicious accusation of some offense or crime, generally made to injure the reputation of another; slander; defamation.

Camarena, Enrique (Kiki). A DEA agent assigned to the Guadalajara, Jalisco DEA office in Mexico from 1981 until his death in 1985. Camarena was a well-known undercover agent, although he was able to keep his face out of the media. He assisted in various raids on Mexican drug cartels, including one against drug lord Rafael Caro Quintero. Camarena was kidnapped in Guadalajara in February 1985, tortured, and murdered. The United States was unsuccessful in extraditing those suspected of the murder. In December 1989 Caro Quintero and Ernesto Fonseca Carrillo, another drug kingpin, were convicted of Camarena's murder in Mexico City. In April 1990, Dr. Humberto Alvarez Macham, a physician suspected of prolonging Camarena's life to sustain additional torture prior to the murder, was abducted from Guadalajara and delivered to DEA agents in Texas. He was transferred to Los Angeles, where a district court judge granted Avarez' petition for summary acquittal. Alvarez was returned to Mexico, and won a $25,000 settlement against the United States, in 1993, which was overturned by the U.S.S.C. in 2003. Four others were found guilty in U.S. District court of Camarena's kidnapping. As a legacy of his service, Camarena posthumously received the DEA Administrator's Award of Honor. A foundation was started in his memory. Most notably, national Red Ribbon week, which promotes drug abstinence to schoolchildren, was begun in his honor.

Camorra. An underworld, secret, criminal organization that began in the Campania region of Italy (capital city of Naples) around 1830, and thrived until about 1922. While the Camorra was identified with the underworld of Neapolitan life, it also had contacts with civil, political, and religious authorities. It represented a nineteenth century version of an entrenched "racket" protected by civil and political authorities.

CAMP. The Campaign Against Marijuana Planting. Established in California in 1983, this program operates under the Bureau of Narcotics Enforcement, with a goal of eradicating illegal marijuana cultivation and trafficking in the state. In 2006, the program seized over 1,675,681 plants with an estimated street value of $6.7 million. Since its inception CAMP agents have eradicated more than 6.9 million marijuana plants with an estimated wholesale value of $27.6 billion. Web: http://ag.ca.gov/bne/camp.php.

Campus Law Enforcement Administrators, International Association of. Founded in 1958 to advance public safety for educational institutions by providing educational resources, advocacy, and professional development. Publishes *Campus Law Enforcement Journal* (bi-monthly). Web: http://www.iaclea.org/.

Campus Unrest, President's Commission on. A nine-member panel commissioned on June 13, 1970, to explore the causes of campus violence and recommend ways of peacefully resolving student grievances. The impetus for the commission, chaired by William Scranton, former Republican governor of Pennsylvania, was the shooting of students by National Guardsmen and police, respectively, at Kent State University in Ohio and Jackson State University in Mississippi in May 1970. On September 26, 1970, the commission issued separate reports on the two incidents, pointing to an "unparalleled crisis" on the nation's campuses. The studies saw the prolonged agonies of the Vietnam War and domestic economic instability as causes of student violence, which the commission vigorously condemned.

Canadian Criminal Justice Association. Founded in 1919, the association "exists to promote rational, informed, and responsible debate in order to develop a more humane, equitable, and effective justice system" through "balanced information and education on justice issues through publications; conferences, seminars, and congresses; and training opportunities." Sponsors the Canadian Congress on Criminal Justice and publishes the *Justice Report* (quarterly newsletter) and *Canadian Journal of Criminology* (quarterly). Address: 320 Parkdale Avenue, Suite 101, Ottawa, Ontario, Canada, K1Y 4X9. Web: http://www.ccja-acjp.ca/en/.

Candaulism. A man's intentional exposure of his female partner to others for the purpose of his sexual gratification. Candaulism can include actual exposure of her sex organs, exposure of depictions through photographs or images, or the fantasy of such.

canine (K-9). Police, detection, or security dogs. Detector dogs and handlers are used by multiple law enforcement agencies throughout the United States. Federally, the U.S. Customs and Border uses detection dogs to screen arriving aircraft, cargo, baggage, mail, ships, vehicles, and passengers. *See also* Bloodhound Association, National Police;

Canine Association, United States Police; Detector Dogs, U.S. Customs and Border Patrol; Dog Association, North American Police Work

Canine Association, United States Police. Organization founded in 1971 with the merging of the Police K-9 Association and the United States K-9 Association. Address: P.O. Box 80, Springboro, OH 45066. http://www.uspcak9.com/.

cannabis. The term *cannabis* refers to a type of flowering plant and includes three distinct species: *cannabis sativa, cannabis indica, and cannabis ruderalis*. In common usage, cannabis generally refers to cannabis sativa, the species which is the source of marijuana and hashish. The psychoactive quality of cannabis sativa comes from Δ^9-tetrahydrocannabinol, or "THC," the effects of which are generally relaxation and euphoria. *See also* hashish; marijuana

cannabism. Poisoning from cannabis, generally due to habitual or excessive consumption.

canon. A standard or principle accepted as fundamentally true and in conformity with good usage and practice; ecclesiastical law.

canon law. Church law, developed by the ecclesiastical courts of the twelfth and thirteenth centuries, with sources in Roman law. When the Roman Empire collapsed (A.D. 476), the popes found themselves acting as temporal rulers, and the influence of canon law grew rapidly. In 1140, Gratian, a Benedictine monk, made the first great codification of church law, assisted by professors of the University of Bologna. Church law has left its mark on the common law. In such areas as crimes against morality involving adultery, incest, and sodomy, and in regulations concerning marriage and probate, the influence of the Church can be seen. Perjury and defamation were also once within the jurisdiction of the ecclesiastical courts. The element of guilt and criminal intent, together with the correctional theory of penitence, can be viewed as part of the overall impact of the Church on ethics and morality in the legal process.

canons of police ethics. Standards, principles, and policies governing the conduct of law enforcement officers. Adopted by the International Association of Chiefs of Police in 1957, the canons include the following articles: Article 1: primary responsibility of job; Article 2: limitations of authority; Article 3: duty to be familiar with the law and with the responsibility of self and other public officials; Article 4: utilization of proper means to gain proper ends; Article 5: cooperation with public officials in the discharge of their authorized duties; Article 6: private conduct; Article 7: conduct toward the public; Article 8: conduct in arresting and dealing with law violators; Article 9: gifts and favors; Article 10: presentation of evidence; and Article 11: attitudes toward profession.

cap. (1) Historically, a colloquial term meaning murder. (2) Crownwork: dental appliance consisting of an artificial crown for a tooth.

capacitance alarm system. An alarm system in which a protected object is electrically connected to a capacitance sensor. The approach of an intruder causes sufficient change in capacitance to upset the balance of the system and trigger an alarm signal. Also called proximity alarm system.

capacity. (1) the legal ability of a person to commit a criminal act; the mental and physical ability to act with purpose and to be aware of the certain, probable, or possible results of one's conduct. (2) the maximum bed space of an institution. When exceeded, inmates often claim conditions of confinement violate Eighth Amendment protections against cruel and unusual punishment. However, the USSC generally considers the totality of conditions, not just capacity alone, in evaluating such claims.

capias (Lat., lit. "that you take"). A generic name for writs (usually addressed to the sheriff), ordering the arrest of the individuals named in them. Capias warrants can also be generated in civil court, in which case they compel someone to comply with a court order, such as a civil judgment for payment of fines or debt; they can also be used to arrest someone who has failed to comply with a civil judgment, including failure to pay traffic tickets.

capital offense. (1) A criminal offense punishable by death. (2) In some penal codes, an offense that may be punishable by death or by imprisonment for life.

capital punishment. *See* punishment, capital

Capone, Alphonse (Al, Scarface) (1899–1947). Born in New York City in 1899, Capone was one of the most notorious gangsters in U.S. history. Capone ran the Chicago mafia, a criminal enterprise that included racketeering, bootlegging, extortion, and murder. In all, Capone is believed to have ordered more than 500 murders in Chicago alone, and more than 1,000 people were killed in turf wars over bootlegging. Capone was convicted of income tax evasion in 1931 and sentenced to prison. Capone served eight years in Leavenworth and Alcatraz prisons before his parole in 1939. After his parole, Capone suffered brain paresis from untreated neurosyphilis, a stroke, and pneumonia. He died of a heart attack in 1947. *See also* Capone Gang

Capone Gang. The criminal organization of more than 300 thugs run by Al "Scarface" Capone in Chicago in the 1920s. The gang specialized in bootlegging, gambling, and prostitution. *See also* Capone, Al

capper. A person employed by an attorney to solicit clients or business. In some jurisdictions, it unlawful for a paralegal to engage in such activities.

carbineer, carabiniere. A term derived from the French *carabinier* (also called *Carabinero* in Spanish, *Carabiniere* in Italian). Historically, a cavalry soldier armed with a carbine (as short musket). In modern Italy the *Carabinieri* is now a branch of the armed forces. Also spelled *carabineer.*

carbofuchsin. A chemical dye which, when mixed with a slow-drying glue, is applied on doorknobs, drawer handles, coins, or other objects. It stains the hand and is difficult to wash away, rendering it useful in crime prevention and detection. The use of carbofuchsin for this purpose has waned in recent years.

carbon monoxide poisoning. The result of inhaling the odorless, poisonous element contained in illuminating gases and in exhaust gases of motor vehicles or incompletely oxidized coal in a dampened furnace. Early symptoms can include: headache, nausea, vomiting (especially in children), dizziness, and fatigue. With prolonged exposure, more severe symptoms may include: confusion, drowsiness, rapid breathing or pulse, vision problems, chest pain, convulsions, seizures, loss of consciousness and death.

cardiopulmonary resuscitation (CPR). An emergency revival procedure involving chest compression to assist the heart and forcing air into the lungs by breathing into the unconscious victim's mouth, both techniques aimed at maintaining the flow of blood to the brain.

Cardozo, Benjamin Nathan. (1870–1938). Lawyer and jurist of distinction whose liberal but balanced judgments profoundly influenced the Supreme Court in its consideration of New Deal legislation. Born in New York City, Cardozo was educated at Columbia University and admitted to the bar in 1891. He was elected to the New York Supreme Court in 1913 and was a U.S. Supreme Court Justice from 1932 until his death in 1938. Cardozo held that the intent of historical law, not its form, should guide justice. He believed the value of the Constitution lay in its intrinsic generality and that the function of the judiciary was to apply established principles to current trends.

career criminal. A person having a past record of multiple arrests or convictions for serious crimes or an unusually large number of arrests or convictions for crimes of varying degrees of seriousness. This term has a formal effect of initiating additional penalties, often in the form of habitual offender or three-strikes laws. The Bureau of Justice Statistics defines a career offender as someone who is 18 years or older, with two or more prior violent felony or felony drug convictions, and who has a current conviction of a violent felony or felony drug crime. While the definition varies by jurisdiction, the term generally describes offenders who: have an extensive record of arrests and convictions; commit crimes over a long period of time; commit crimes at a very high rate; commit relatively serious crimes; use crimes as their principal source of income; specialize (or are especially expert) in a certain type of crime; or have some combination of these characteristics. Such criminals are often described as chronic, habitual, repeat, serious, high-rate, or professional offenders. *See also* habitual offender

career criminal, armed. A person who receives, possesses, or transports, in commerce or affecting commerce, any firearm and who has three previous convictions for a serious or violent crime. *See also* Armed Career Criminal Act of 1984

career criminal laws. *See* habitual offender laws

career offender. *See* career criminal

Cargo Criminal Apprehension Teams (Cargo CATS). Operated by various county, state, and federal law enforcement officials, these groups conduct investigations to identify, apprehend, and prosecute cargo thieves.

carjacking. The completed or attempted robbery of a motor vehicle by a stranger to the victim perpetrated by force, threats, or coercion. In 1992, the United States passed legislation making carjacking a federal crime. Provisions of this law mandate a 15-year sentence for convicted carjackers and impose an automatic life sentence if a victim is killed during the commission of the crime. According to the Bureau of Justice, a weapon was used in 74 percent of carjacking victimizations between 1993–2002.

carnal abuse. (1) Historically, a male's contact with a female's sexual organs with his genitals. (2) In modern usage, and more typically, the term refers to an adult's lascivious contact with the genitals of a child. In either usage, the term does not necessarily involve penetration.

carnal knowledge. A general term for sexual activity, usually applied to males who engage in intercourse in a way that violates a law. This term is defined by the criminal code of a given jurisdiction and often involves specific sex acts, including contact between a penis and vagina, sodomy, and/or oral sex.

carotid choke hold. Also called lateral vascular neck restraint; sleeper hold. A controversial hold historically used by law enforcement officers to subdue violent subjects. Pressure is applied with the arm, a baton, or a flashlight to the carotid artery, located below the jaw at the side of the neck, which causes unconsciousness. The carotid is the principal artery of the neck, supplying blood to the head. Because this hold is potentially lethal, its use is discouraged or banned in most U.S. jurisdictions.

Carrier's Case. A legal precedent of 1483 that changed the definition of larceny in England in a way that favored the interests of traders and merchants. The ruling held that a person transporting merchandise or goods on behalf of someone else, but who keeps the goods for himself, is guilty of larceny.

Carroll Doctrine. An automobile exception to the Fourth Amendment search warrant requirement. In *Carroll v. United States* (1925), petitioner George Carroll was convicted of transporting liquor for sale in violation of the federal prohibition law and the Eighteenth Amendment. The liquor, used as evidence, was taken from his car by agents acting without a search warrant. The Supreme Court sustained Carroll's conviction against his contention that the seizure violated his Fourth Amendment rights. Known as the Carroll Doctrine, the Court's decision maintained that an automobile or other vehicle may, upon probable cause, be searched without a warrant. In 1931, the Court upheld the search of a parked car as reasonable, since the police could not know when the suspect might move it. The Carroll Doctrine was reaffirmed in 1970, when the Supreme Court held that a warrantless search of an automobile that resulted in the seizure of weapons and other evidence, but that was conducted many hours after the arrests of the suspects, was lawful.

case. At the level of police or prosecutorial investigation, a set of circumstances under investigation involving one or more persons; at subsequent steps in criminal proceedings, either a charging document alleging the commission of one or more crimes or a single defendant charged with one or more crimes; in juvenile or correctional proceedings, a person who is the object of agency action.

case law. Judicial precedent generated as a byproduct of the decisions that courts have made to resolve unique disputes, as distinguished from statutes and constitutions. Case law concerns concrete facts; statutes and constitutions are written in the abstract.

caseload. (1) The total number of clients registered with a correctional agency or agent on a given date or during a specified period, often divided into active supervisory cases and inactive cases, thus distinguishing between clients with whom contact is regular and those with whom it is not. (2) The number of matters requiring judicial action at a certain time or acted upon in a court during a given period. A model court caseload statistical system was developed by the National Center for State Courts, Court Statistics Project (CSP) under Bureau of Justice Statistics sponsorship, to encourage development of fully comparable cross-jurisdictional caseload data.

Cassidy, Butch. *See* Parker, Robert

cast. (1) To mold; to take the impression of certain objects and markings by using a substance that will harden and retain its shape. Used in law enforcement to record

in physical form such evidence as footprints in soil, tire impressions, tool marks, bite marks, and so forth. Many casting materials are used, including Plaster of Paris for casting impressions in soil and a material called moulage for detail work on a rigid surface. Other methods include casting silicone, casting putty, and various dental casting materials. (2) The physical object or reproduction made by casting.

Castellano, Paul. (aka "Big Paul," "BP," "Howard Hughes") (1915–1985). A Mafia boss in New York City, Castellano succeeded Carlo Gambino as head of the Gambino crime family in 1976. During his nine years as Mafia head, Castellano made a few critical mistakes that preempted his assassination: he "disrespected" rivals by not attending key events; he did not interact with line soldiers, which his men interpreted as arrogance; and he promoted a brutish, unskilled soldier in lieu of other, more diplomatic ones. In 1984, he was indicted on R.I.C.O. and murder charges and subsequently arrested for racketeering, resulting in the Mafia Commission Trial of 1985. He was released on a $3 million bail bond, but his men believed he would testify for the FBI to avoid prison. While out on bail, Castellano and his bodyguard were murdered outside a Manhattan restaurant; the homicide was orchestrated by John Gotti, who became the next head of the Gambino family. *See also* Gambino, Carlo; Gotti, John; Mafia Commission Trial

castration. The removal or functional inhibition of testicles or ovaries. Castration can be accomplished surgically or through chemical means. While the term can be applied to males or females, it generally refers to the removal of testicles in a male. Castration drastically reduces a man's level of testosterone, a hormone that is associated with aggression.

castration, chemical. Through weekly injections of medroxyprogesterone acetate (MPA), a synthetic female hormone often sold under the name Depo-Provera, this procedure is intended to suppress the sex drive of male offenders. The practice received its first statutory approval in California, effective January 1, 1997. Since that time, many other jurisdictions have enacted similar laws. Since the effect of chemical castration is temporary, injections continue until authorities determine they are no longer necessary.

catamite. (1) A boy who is in a pederastic sexual relationship with a man. (2) A homosexual male prostitute or a kept male.

cause. The matter brought before a court for decision.

cause, challenge of jurors for. Each side in a trial—prosecution and defense—has the right, prescribed by law, to challenge prospective jurors (veniremen) for cause, such as prior convictions, unsound mind, kinship to one of the parties, bias or prejudice, and so forth. If the court agrees with the challenge, the prospective juror will not be allowed to serve.

caveat. A formal notice given by an interested party to a court or judge, warning against the performance of certain judicial acts.

caveat emptor (Lat., lit. "let the buyer beware"). A formula that, under certain legally qualified conditions, enables sellers to decline legal responsibility for the quality or quantity of their wares. It does not, however, apply to the question of the title of property. The common law doctrine that the buyer is responsible for assessing the quality of a purchase before the transaction is completed.

cease-and-desist order. An order, issued by a judge or an administrative agency to an individual, firm, or corporation, requiring that a particular activity, fiscal or business practice be discontinued, and remaining in effect until reversed by the court that decides the resulting lawsuit. The order is commonly used by agencies charged with the regulation of business, such as the Federal Trade Commission or a state public utilities or railway commission.

celerity. Speed or swiftness; in criminal justice it refers to the apprehension, trial, and punishment of an offender. The advocates of the concept of deterrence regard celerity as a major factor in the effectiveness of punishment. *See also* deterrence

cell. (1) In jails or prison, a unit of confinement which generally includes a cot or sleeping area, sink and toilet. The term *cell* implies sufficient space for one or two inmate occupants; larger units of confinement are generally called dormitories. (2) The smallest unit within a guerrilla or terrorist group, generally consisting of two to five people committed to a common terrorist cause.

censorship. The act of suppressing or controlling books, plays, films, or other media content or the ideas, values, and beliefs held by certain groups, on the grounds that the contents or ideas are morally, politically, militarily, or otherwise objectionable. Such control may be imposed internally, by the groups producing the information, or externally by governments, regulatory bodies, or other organizations. Many legal codes of censorship represent the formal embodiment of customs or mores. Such codes may express the values of only one segment of a society, however, and may thereby infringe the rights of other segments. Thus censorship remains a controversial topic.

censure. The formal resolution of a legislative, administrative, or other body to reprimand an administrative officer or one of its own members for specific conduct.

census tract. A relatively small, permanent, geographic area, having a population between 1,200 and 8,000. They are designed to be homogeneous with respect to population characteristics, economic status, and living conditions, and they do not cross county boundaries. Census tracts are delineated for statistical and local administrative purposes. Many police departments have realigned their "beats," or reporting districts, to conform with census-tract boundaries, allowing for demographic crime analysis.

Centennial Olympic Park bombing. A terrorist bombing in Atlanta, Georgia, United States, during the 1996 Summer Olympics.

The bomb was detonated on July 27, 1996, resulting in two deaths and 111 injuries. Richard Jewell, a security guard who discovered the bomb and attempted to move spectators away from the device before detonation, was heralded as a hero, then a possible suspect. Jewell was subsequently exonerated. In 1997, the bombings of two abortion clinics and lesbian nightclub led investigators to Eric Robert Rudolph. Rudolph, a fugitive for five years, was arrested in 2003. He was convicted of all four bombings and is currently serving four consecutive life sentences in the federal supermaximum security prison near Florence, Colorado. *See also* domestic terrorism; Rudolph, Eric Robert

Center for Criminal Justice Training and Research. Connected with the College of Health and Human Services, California State University at Long Beach, provides California Commission on Peace Officer Standards and Training (P.O.S.T.) certified training. Address: 1250 Bellflower Blvd., Long Beach, CA 90840. Web: http://www.csulb. edu/colleges/chhs/centers/cj/index.htm.

Center for Public Safety. Established as the Traffic Institute at Northwestern University in 1936, the center was renamed the Center for Public Safety in recognition of its expanding scope, which includes crash investigation, police operations, police management, transportation engineering and DUI courses. The center also provides research and technical assistance to police agencies nationwide. Address: Northwestern University Center for Public Safety, 1801 Maple Avenue, Evanston, IL 60208; Web: http:// nucps.northwestern.edu/.

Center for Research in Criminology. Founded by Indiana University of Pennsylvania in 1983. The goals of the center include the advancement of criminology and criminal justice as both a discipline and a system. The center actively participates in research and provides consultants for national, state, and local criminal justice agencies. Address: Criminology Department, Wilson Hall, Room 200, 411 North Walk, Indiana, PA 15705.

Center for Studies in Criminal Justice (CSCJ). Founded in 1965. Address: University of Chicago Law School, 1111 E. 60th Street, Chicago, IL 60637.

Center for Substance Abuse Prevention (CSAP). A unit of the Substance Abuse and Mental Health Services Administration (SAMHSA) within the United States Department of Health and Human Services, CSAP is designed to "develop comprehensive prevention systems that create healthy communities," including "supportive work and school environments, drug-and crime-free neighborhoods, and positive connections with friends and family." http://www.prevention.samhsa.gov/.

Center for Substance Abuse Treatment (CSAT). A unit of the Substance Abuse and Mental Health Services Administration (SAMHSA), within the U.S. Department of Health and Human Services (HHS). According to its Web site, CSAT "promotes the quality and availability of community-based substance abuse treatment services" and aims to "improve and expand existing substance abuse treatment services." Web: http://csat. samhsa.gov/.

Center for the Study of Law and Society. Founded in 1961 by the University of California at Berkeley, the center is "where analysis of legal institutions and legal change is encouraged." Address: 2240 Piedmont Avenue, University of California, Berkeley, CA 94720-2150. Web: http://www.law. berkeley.edu/csls.htm.

Center for Women Policy Studies. Founded in 1972 as the nation's first feminist policy institution, the center promotes women's human rights and equality. Address: 1776 Massachusetts Ave., NW, Suite 450, Washington, DC 20036. Web: http://www.center-womenpolicy.org/.

Centers for Disease Control and Prevention (CDC). An agency of the U.S. Department of Health and Human Services, its mission to collaborate to create the expertise, information, and tools that people and communities need to protect their health—through health promotion, prevention of disease, injury and disability, and preparedness for new health threats. Address: 1600 Clifton Rd. Atlanta, GA 30333, USA. Web: http://www.cdc.gov/.

Central Intelligence Agency (CIA). An agency, created by the National Security Act of 1947, the CIA is charged with "collecting intelligence through human sources and by other appropriate means, except that he shall have no police, subpoena, or law enforcement powers or internal security functions; correlating and evaluating intelligence related to the national security and providing appropriate dissemination of such intelligence; providing overall direction for and coordination of the collection of national intelligence outside the United States through human sources by elements of the intelligence community authorized to undertake such collection and, in coordination with other departments, agencies, or elements of the United States government that are authorized to undertake such collection, ensuring that the most effective use is made of resources and that appropriate account is taken of the risks to the United States and those involved in such collection; and Performing such other functions and duties related to intelligence affecting the national security as the President or the Director of National Intelligence may direct." The CIA training school is believed to be located at Camp Peary near Williamsburg, VA (sometimes called "The Farm"). Address: CIA, Office of the Public Affairs, Washington, DC 20505. Web: https://www.cia.gov/.

central tendency. A variety of statistical terms referring to the most common or representative value in a distribution. Three measure of central tendency are mean, median, and mode.

central station alarm system. An alarm system or group of systems, the activities of which are transmitted to, recorded in, maintained by, and supervised from a central station. This differs from proprietary alarm systems in that the central station is owned and operated independently of the subscriber.

Centre of Criminology Library. Founded in 1963 by the University of Toronto, the centre is a comprehensive library devoted to criminology in all its aspects. The resources of this library are available to interested persons outside the university in any area of the administration of criminal justice. Located at the University of Toronto, 14 Queens Park Crescent West, Toronto, Ontario, M5S 3K9, Canada. Web: http://www.criminology.utoronto.ca/lib/.

Certificate of Confidentiality. Certificate issued by the United States National Institutes of Health (NIH) to "protect identifiable research information from forced disclosure." A Certificate of Confidentiality provides subpoena protection for research, allowing researchers to refuse disclosure of identifiable information from subject "in any civil, criminal, administrative, legislative, or other proceeding, whether at the federal, state, or local level." For more information, visit: http://grants.nih.gov/grants/policy/coc/index.htm.

certificate plan. A system of legal aid in the province of Ontario, Canada, whereby an eligible defendant is issued a certificate that entitles him or her to choose private counsel, whose fee will be paid in whole or in part out of public funds.

certification. A process in which a lower court requests a higher court to decide certain questions in a given case, pending final decision by the lower court.

certified copy. A copy to which is added a certificate, with signature and official seal, of the public officer authorized to certify it.

Certified Fraud Examiner (CFE) A credential that denotes expertise in fraud prevention, detection, and deterrence. *See also* Association of Certified Fraud Examiners *certiorari* (Lat., lit. "to be more fully informed"). (1) An original writ or action whereby a case is removed from a lower to a higher court for review. The record of the proceedings is then transmitted to the superior court. (2) A discretionary appellate jurisdiction that is invoked by a petition, which the appellate court may grant or deny; a dominant avenue to the Supreme Court. *See also* rule of four

chain gang. A group of prisoners bound together by a chain, generally for the purpose of preventing escape while forced to do agricultural or other manual labor. Typically, inmates are shackled at the ankle with three-pound leg irons and bound together by eight-foot lengths of chain. The practice fell out of favor nationwide, with Georgia being the last state to abolish chain gangs around 1955. In 1995, Alabama became the first American penal institution to use chain gangs in more than 30 years, and many others followed suit. The practice ended within a year in all states except Arizona. Arizona soon followed suit; Arizona currently has chain gangs for men and woman, and has the world's first juvenile volunteer chain gang, in which inmates on the chain gang earn high school credit toward a diploma. *See also* Arpaio, Joe

chain of command. A supervisory hierarchy; the levels of personnel from the top to the bottom. It is the route taken for formal communications. In theory, this system, adopted originally from the military, supports the principles of unity of command, span of control, and regulated communication channels. In large organizations it is cumbersome and time-consuming and is usually rectified by decentralization.

chain of custody. A formal, written process recording the persons having custody of evidence from initial point of collection to final disposition. The record also reflects the dates and reasons evidence is transferred from one location or person to another.

challenge of jurors. Action, on the part of either prosecution or defense in a trial by jury, against the prospective jurors (veniremen) to prevent them from serving. There are two kinds: (a) peremptory—no reasons must be given for objecting to the prospective juror, but the number of peremptory challenges is limited by law, and (b) challenge for cause—the reason for objecting to someone as a juror must be given (such as prior conviction, kinship to parties, bias or prejudice), but no limit is placed on the number to be so challenged. *See also* cause, challenge of jurors for; peremptory challenge

chambers. The official private office or quarters of a judge; the office of the judge when he or she is not in the courtroom.

champerty. Participating in a lawsuit in the name of another person but at one's own expense, with the goal of receiving as compensation a certain share of the proceeds of the suit. In common law, champerty generally includes an enticement for frivolous action and is therefore illegal. The practice should not be confused with a contingency fee arrangement.

chancery procedure. Formerly the procedure in chancery courts where the king's representative (the chancellor) presided over cases involving certain persons, usually women or children, who were unable under existing laws to protect themselves or for whom substantial inequity existed. Today such a procedure has been adopted by juvenile courts in assuming the guardianship of delinquent children and a protective interest in their welfare.

change of venue. The movement of a case from the jurisdiction of one court to that of another that has the same subject-matter jurisdictional authority, but is in a different geographic location. The most frequent reason for a change of venue is a judicial determination that an impartial jury cannot be found within a particular geographic jurisdiction, usually because of widely publicized prejudicial statements concerning the events that are the basis for the case.

Chaplains, International Conference of Police. An organization providing assistance to members of the ministry in law enforcement agencies. Address: P.O. Box 5590, Destin, FL 32540-5590 Web: http://www.icpc4cops.org/.

Chapman, Duane Lee "Dog" (1953–). Born in Denver, Colorado, Chapman is a bounty hunter and star of the reality series "Dog the Bounty Hunter." Chapman was an amateur boxer and member of an outlaw motorcycle gang when he was charged with murder in 1977. He was convicted, sentenced to five years in prison, and served 18 months for the crime. Chapman is probably best known for his 2003 apprehension of Andrew Luster, a fugitive convicted of 86 counts of rape in the United States. Chapman tracked Luster to Mexico and captured him, for the purpose of returning him to the United States to serve his sentence. However, the Mexican government charged Chapman with kidnapping, which ignited a legal battle over his extradition. Mexico dropped charges in 2007, citing an expiration of the statute of limitations. Chapman currently lives in Hawaii with his business partner (and fifth wife) Beth and their children.

Chapman, Mark David (1955–). Mark Chapman was a devoted Beatles fan in the 1960s who became so fixated on John Lennon, he came to believe he actually was Lennon. On December 6, 1980, Chapman traveled to New York City, waiting outside Lennon's apartment for days, and killed him. Chapman pled guilty to the murder against the advice of his attorney, and was sentenced to 20 years to life in 1981. He currently remains incarcerated, having been denied parole five times: 2000, 2002, 2004, 2006, and 2008. His next parole hearing is scheduled for August 2010. While the motive for the slaying remains unknown, some theorize that Chapman became so convinced he was Lennon, the real Lennon must be eliminated.

Others theorize that Lennon's comment that the Beatles were "more popular than Jesus" enraged the zealot Chapman and convinced him Lennon was the anti-Christ. *See also* stalking; insanity

character. The set of qualities or features that distinguish individuals from each other. In criminal justice, this generally refers to moral or ethical strength, or lack thereof. Evidence of a person's character is generally admissible in the following cases: (a) the fact that the defendant has a good reputation for the trait of character involved in the crime charged may be shown, but the state cannot show that he or she has a bad character, unless that character is itself a fact in issue or evidence has been given that he or she has a good character; (b) the character of the deceased as a violent and dangerous person may be shown in prosecutions for homicide, on the question of whether the defendant acted in self-defense; the term "character" as used in the rules above means reputation as distinguished from disposition; (c) a witness may be impeached by proof of bad character for truth and veracity, and a witness who has been impeached may be rehabilitated to a degree by proof that his or her reputation for truth and veracity is good; and (d) in crimes where character is an element.

charge. An allegation that a specified person or group has committed a specific offense, which is recorded in a functional document, such as a record of an arrest, a complaint, an indictment, or a judgment of conviction.

charging document. A formal, written accusation submitted to a court, alleging that a specified person or group has committed one or more specific offenses.

charity schemes. Fraudulent telemarketers have often exploited the desire of honest citizens to help worthy causes by devising schemes that purport to raise money for charities. Such fraudulent schemes solicit money, for example, under the guise of helping victims of the Hurricane Katrina and family members of firefighters killed in the September 11 attacks. *See also* telemarketing fraud

Chase, Salmon Portland. (1808–1873). American statesman; U.S. senator from Ohio (1849–1855, 1861); Governor of Ohio (1856–1860); U.S. secretary of the treasury (1861–1864); responsible for national bank system (estab. 1863); Chief Justice of Supreme Court (1864–1873). He was an antislavery leader. As a supreme court justice, his dissenting opinion in the Slaughterhouse Cases subsequently became the accepted position of the courts as to the restrictive force of the Fourteenth Amendment. Presided over the impeachment trial of President Andrew Johnson. Chase earnestly sought the presidency four times but was never nominated.

Chase, Samuel. (1741–1811). American Revolutionary patriot, signer of the Declaration of Independence, associate justice of the U.S. Supreme Court (1796–1811). Impeached in 1804 on charge of political partiality but was acquitted.

chattel. Item, article, or piece of personal property that can theoretically be transferred to another person. In common law, a slave.

chattel mortgage. A security for the payment of a debt on personal property; sometimes called a secured transaction.

cheating. A fraudulent, financial injury to another person by some token, device, or practice calculated to deceive.

cheating at common law. The fraudulent obtaining of another's property by means of some false symbol or token that, when not false, is commonly accepted by the public for what it purports to represent; if the value of what was obtained is below a certain amount, cheating is a misdemeanor; above that amount it is a felony.

cheating by false pretense. Not a crime at common law but generally made so by statute, this term means knowingly and designedly obtaining the property of another with intent to defraud. The pretense must be (a) a false representation as to some part of existing fact or circumstance and not a mere expression of opinion or a promise; (b) knowingly false; (c) made with intent to defraud; (d) in some cases calculated to defraud; and (e) believed by the cheated party so that he or she gives up the property.

check fraud. Issuing or passing a check, draft, or money order that is legal as a formal document and signed by the legal account holder, but with the foreknowledge that the bank or depository will refuse to honor it because of insufficient funds or a closed account.

Chemical Transportation Emergency Center (CHEMTREC). Operated by the Manufacturing Chemists Association, provides information about hazardous chemicals involved in accidents. Web: http://www. chemtrec.com/Chemtrec/.

Cherry Hill. Nickname of the Philadelphia prison opened in 1829 on the site of an old cherry orchard. This historic Eastern Penitentiary was designed as a solitary-confinement facility.

Chicago Area Project. Begun in the early 1930s by Clifford R. Shaw of the Chicago School of Sociology, this was an influential crime study. Researchers proceeded on the assumption that crime was high in particular urban areas because those neighborhoods lacked cohesiveness, with a subsequent lack of concern for the welfare of the children living there. The project's goal was to develop self-help concepts to enhance mutual responsibility, neighborliness, and neighborhood pride. The project drew the attention of juvenile workers throughout the country and was copied by numerous other cities, including New York and Minneapolis. In 1959 the Illinois Youth Commission used the model to establish programs throughout the state. By the mid-1970s, similar programs existed in many American communities.

Chicago Boys' Court. This court was established in 1914 as the first special court for minor boys, aged 17 through 20, who were over the age for juvenile court jurisdiction.

Chicago Seven, the. (also called **Conspiracy Seven**) The group of David T. Dellinger, Thomas E. Hayden, Rennard C. Davis, Abbie Hoffman, Jerry C. Rubin, Lee Weiner, and John R. Froines, who were tried on the charge of crossing state lines to incite riots in 1968 at the time of the Democratic National Convention. (An eighth defendant, Bobby Seale—who cofounded the Black Panther Party For Self Defense with Huey Newton in 1966—was also charged, but his trial was severed, lowering the number of defendants from eight to seven in the notorious trial). On February 18, 1970, the first five were found guilty. All seven and two of their attorneys were sentenced on contempt of court due to their actions during the trial. All seven defendants were found guilty of the original changes, but all convictions were overturned on appeal due to judicial bias, and the defendants were not retried. The film *Chicago 8,* released in 2010, is based on the trial.

chicanery. Stratagem; trickery; sharp practice.

chief justice (federal). The official head of the United States court system. The chief justice of the Supreme Court of the United States, the highest judicial officer in the country, is chief administrative officer for the federal courts. The chief justice presides over the Senate when the president or vice president is impeached. The following have held this office: John Jay, 1789–1795; John Rutledge, 1795–1796; Oliver Ellsworth, 1796–1800; John Marshall, 1801–1835; Roger B. Taney, 1835–1864; Salmon P. Chase, 1864–1873; Morrison R. Waite, 1874–1888; Melville W. Fuller, 1888–1910; Edward D. White, 1910–1921; William Howard Taft, 1921–1930; Charles E. Hughes, 1930–1941; Harlan F. Stone, 1941–1946; Fred M. Vinson, 1946–1953; Earl Warren, 1953–1968; Warren Burger, 1969–1986; William Rehnquist, 1986–2005; and John Roberts, Jr., 2005–.

chief justice (state). The official head of the highest court of the state. The first woman to be appointed as state chief justice was Rose Elizabeth Bird of California in 1977.

chief of police. A law enforcement officer who is the appointed or elected head of a municipal police department, department of public safety, or special authority or district police unit. Chief of police usually refers to the head of a local, municipal police department, but the title is also used for the heads of agencies organized to serve other jurisdictions. Director or superintendent may be the title for the head of a public safety department or division. Commissioner usually refers to one of several persons sitting on a board or commission intended to direct police agency policy.

child. A person under the age of puberty. According to the United Nations, however, a child is "a human being below the age of 18 years unless under the law applicable to the child, majority is attained earlier." In law, a person under the age of 7 years is usually not capable of committing crime; those aged 8–adulthood believed to have committed a crime are generally adjudicated in juvenile court.

child abuse. (child maltreatment) As recently as the nineteenth century, American law regarded children solely as chattels belonging to the parents. Not until 1874 did abused children receive legal protection, and then only when the American Society for the Prevention of Cruelty to Animals argued in court that a child, Mary Ellen, was covered under laws barring the barbaric treatment of animals. The Center for Disease Control and Prevention (CDC) defines child abuse as "Words or overt actions that cause harm, potential harm, or threat of harm to a child. Acts of commission are deliberate and intentional; however, harm to a child may or may not be the intended consequence. Intentionality only applies to the caregivers' acts—not the consequences of those acts. For example, a caregiver may intend to hit a child as punishment (i.e., hitting the child is not accidental or unintentional) but not intend to cause the child to have a concussion. The following types of maltreatment involve acts of commission: physical abuse, sexual abuse, and psychological abuse." Child abuse may bring the child under the protection of the juvenile court and result in criminal penalties for the perpetrator. The U.S. Department of Health and Human Services estimates approximately 794,000 victims of child maltreatment in 2007, although many cases go undetected. *See also* Childhelp USA/International; Child Abuse and Neglect Information, National Center for; Child Welfare Information Gateway

Child Abuse and Neglect, National Clearinghouse on (NCCAN). Founded in 1975 as the National Center for Child Abuse and Neglect by the U.S. Department of Health and Human Services, NCCAN is a clearinghouse that tracks state laws and case law regarding child welfare; collects and provides information on child maltreatment and child protective services in the United States; and publishes an annual summary of Child Abuse and Neglect. The organization became the Child Welfare Information Gateway. Address: Child Welfare Information Gateway Children's Bureau/ACYF, 1250 Maryland Avenue, SW, Eighth Floor, Washington, DC 20024 Web: http://www.childwelfare.gov/.

Childhelp USA/International. Founded in 1959 by Sara O'Meara and Yvonne Fedderson, Childhelp is a leading national nonprofit organization dedicated to helping victims of child abuse and neglect. Childhelp's approach focuses on prevention, intervention and treatment National headquarters are located at 15757 N. 78th Street, Suite B, Scottsdale, Arizona 85260; telephone: (480) 922-8212 or 1-800-4-A-CHILD (1-800-422-4453) (The National Child Abuse Hotline). Web: http://www.childhelp.org/.

child delinquency law, first state. Passed on April 28, 1909, by Colorado, this law defined as guilty "persons who shall encourage, cause or contribute to the delinquency or neglect of a child."

child maltreatment. Defined by the Center for Disease and Prevention as "any act or series of acts of commission or omission by a parent or other caregiver that results in harm, potential for harm, or threat of harm to a child." Child maltreatment may bring the child under the protection of the juvenile court and result in criminal penalties for the perpetrator.

child molester. One who engages in sexual activity with a child. This term is used when lascivious interest in children is acted upon, and is thus differentiated from the term pedophile. *See also* pedophile, pedophilia

child neglect. The Center for Disease Control and Prevention defines child neglect as "The failure to provide for a child's basic physical, emotional, or educational needs or to protect a child from harm or potential harm. Like acts of commission, harm to a child may or may not be the intended consequence. The following types of maltreatment involve acts of omission: (1) failure to provide, including physical neglect, emotional neglect, medical/dental neglect, and educational neglect; and (2) failure to supervise, including inadequate supervision and exposure to violent environments." Such neglect may bring the child under protection of the juvenile court and result in criminal penalties for the abuser.

child support. Judicially mandated obligations owed by absent parents for the maintenance of minor children. The U.S. Department of Health and Human Services (DHHS) operates the Administration for Children and Families (ACF) which administers various programs targeting children, including assistance with welfare and child support enforcement. Address: 370 L'Enfant Promenade SW, Washington, DC 20447. Web: http://www.acf.hhs.gov/.

Child Welfare Information Gateway. Operated under the U.S. Department of Health and Human Services, compiles information pertaining to child health and welfare. Address: Child Welfare Information Gateway, Children's Bureau/ACYF, 1250 Maryland Avenue, SW, Eighth Floor, Washington, DC 20024. Web: http://www.childwelfare.gov/.

children's courts. Special courts established to solve the unusual legal and judicial problems of juvenile delinquency. Although a considerable body of protective legislation for the administration of juvenile crime was enacted in the Jacksonian period, it was not until the late nineteenth century that special children's tribunals were created to handle such cases. It had come to be accepted that juvenile lawbreakers were to be considered apart from adult criminals and subject to the special guardianship and administration of children's courts. A system of jurisprudence developed that emphasized informal procedures, separate hearings, psychiatric care, and probation and parole provisions for youth.

Children's Defense Fund. A private agency founded in 1973 that serves as an advocate for children's rights by researching the manner in which children are handled by social and justice agencies and by increasing public awareness about children's problems and needs. Address: 25 E Street, N.W., Washington, DC 20001. Web: http://www.childrens-defense.org/.

child welfare boards. A panel of local citizens elected by a Swedish community, who have the responsibility of investigating and adjudicating matters involving juveniles; these boards are similar to the juvenile courts of other Western societies.

choline. A water soluble, B-complex nutrient involved in the production of neurotransmitters regulating mood, appetite, behavior, memory, concentration, cognitive performance and alertness. Blood levels of choline typically decrease during prolonged periods of exercise or physical exertion. This nutrient is most effective in phosphatidyl choline form.

Chore Boy. Brand name for a copper cleaning pad, colloquial term often referring to its use as a filter to smoke illegal drugs, such as methamphetamine and cocaine. Pieces of the pad are broken off for this purpose.

chose **in action**. (Fr. *chose*, lit., thing). An issue in action; the right to receive or recover a large debt or damages through action at law.

Christopher Commission Report. The 226-page report issued by a panel chaired by Warren Christopher, secretary of state in the Clinton administration, to investigate the causes of the 1992 Los Angeles riots. Officially called the Independent Commission on the Los Angeles Police Department, the panel sought to examine all aspects of the law enforcement structure in LA that might cause or contribute to the use of excessive force. The report summary said, "The Report is unanimous. The [Rodney] King beating raised fundamental questions about the LAPD including: the apparent failure to control or discipline officers with repeated complaints of excessive force; concerns about the LAPD's 'culture' and officers' attitudes towards racial and other minorities; the difficulties the public encounters in attempting to make complaints against LAPD officers; and the role of the LAPD leadership and civilian oversight authorities in addressing or contributing to these problems. These and related questions and concerns form the basis for the Commission's work." *See also* King, Rodney

chromatograph. An instrument used in a crime laboratory to analyze gaseous substances or compounds that can be readily converted into gases.

chromatography. A set of laboratory techniques used for separation of mixtures into gases.

chromosomal aberration. Irregularities in the number or structure of chromosomes, often responsible for genetic disorders. In criminal justice, various theories have posited that such abnormalities form the basis of criminal behavior. For example, it was widely believed in the 1960s that males with an extra Y chromosome (XYY) have histories of violent and antisocial behavior. Most geneticists today doubt that the available evidence establishes a cause-and-effect relationship between such defects and deviant behavior. *See also* XXY syndrome, XYY syndrome

Church of Satan. Founded on April 30, 1966 (Walpurgis Night), by Anton Szandor

La Vey, who is the author of the 272-page *The Satanic Bible* (Avon Books, December 1969) and a former San Francisco police photographer and criminology student. The legally recognized church is focused in its Central Grotto (congregation) in San Francisco. The Temple Set was founded by Michael A. Aquino, who broke away from the Church of Satan in 1975. Aquino defines Set as another name for Satan, coming from the hieroglyphic Set-hen, the god's formal title.

CIA. *See* Central Intelligence Agency

Cipro. common name for ciprofloxacin an antibiotic in the fluoroquinolone family. Cipro is antibiotics used to treat anthrax.

circuit. A division of the state or county appointed for a judge to visit for the trial of cases.

circuit, class A. A type of four-wire alarm circuit used to detect an alarm or line fault. The circuit allows reporting of an alarm condition even when a trouble condition has occurred. Two conductors run from the alarm panel to the sensor, and two return. A single break does not prevent the reception of an alarm signal, but does cause a trouble condition.

circuit, class B. (1) A four-wire system in which two conductors travel from an alarm panel, connect with one or more alarm sensors, and return to the panel. One broken conductor prevents reception of an alarm signal from any point beyond the break, causing a trouble condition. (2) A two-wire system in which only one conductor travels from the panel to the sensors and back again. A single break prevents all alarm transmissions and causes a trouble condition at the panel.

circuit court. One of the lower constitutional courts created by the Judiciary Act of 1789. For much of U.S. history, these courts were the principal trial courts in the federal judicial system, with jurisdiction over federal crimes and diversity jurisdiction. There was no intermediate appellate court, and appeals went directly to the Supreme Court. The circuit courts also had appellate jurisdiction over the district courts, and in 1875, original federal-question jurisdiction was given to circuit courts by Congress. In 1891 Congress created the circuit courts of appeal, now called simply courts of appeal, to which the appellate jurisdiction of the circuit courts was given. The Judicial Code of 1911 abolished the circuit courts and gave their original jurisdiction to the district courts. There are two federal and 12 regional circuit courts of appeals. *See* Table 9. Map of United States Courts of Appeals and District Courts, page 78

circumstantial evidence. Evidence from which a fact can be reasonably inferred, although not directly proven.

citation to appear. A written order, issued by a law enforcement officer, directing an alleged offender to appear in a specific court at a specified time to answer a criminal charge and not permitting forfeit of bail as an alternative to court appearance.

cite. (1) To summon. (2) To read or refer to (legal) authorities, in support of a position.

citizen complaints. Oral or written notice of displeasure, often citing abuse or misconduct, presented by a member of the public against law enforcement or government official. Complaints by citizens against police officers should, ideally, be made a matter of record and promptly referred to the officers' immediate superiors. Complainants should be assured that an investigation and a report of the complaint will be made and that they will be informed as to the final disposition of the matter. The complaint dispositions generally fall into one of four categories: (a) sustained, the act did occur; (b) not sustained, the act might have happened but cannot be proven; (c) exonerated, the act did occur, but the officer was justified; and (d) unfounded, the act never occurred. Most law enforcement agencies have official policies for handling and resolving citizen complaints, and some agencies have citizen boards overseeing investigation and resolution of such matters. *See also* civilian review boards

TABLE 9   MAP OF UNITED STATES COURTS OF APPEALS AND DISTRICT COURTS

Geographic Boundaries
of United Courts of Apples and United States District Courts

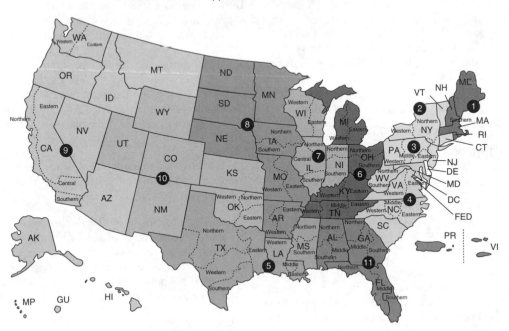

Source: Administrative Office of the U.S. Courts

citizen's arrest. An arrest by a citizen who is not a law enforcement officer for a felony, without a warrant. A citizen is not authorized to make an arrest by means of a warrant. In some common-law states (if not changed by statute), an arrest for a breach of the peace committed in his or her presence can be made by a citizen.

city court. A court that tries people accused of violating municipal ordinances, and which has jurisdiction over minor civil or criminal cases or both.

civil. Distinguished from criminal. Pertaining to (a) a legal dispute that is noncriminal in nature; (b) the personal or private rights of an individual; or (c) legal action in court to enforce private or personal rights. (A suit for personal injury is a civil action.)

Civil Asset Forfeiture Reform Act (CAFRA). Passed by Congress and signed by President Clinton, the law became effective on August 23, 2000. The purpose of CAFRA is to address several criticism of asset forfeiture subsequent to criminal conviction in the United States. Among other changes, CAFRA permits the United States to "disallow" claims of interest in property in a civil forfeiture case by people who flee the United States to avoid criminal prosecution. Under CAFRA, the government must prove, by a preponderance of evidence, that property should be forfeited. The government *must* give the owner 60 days' notice of pending seizure, although extensions are possible. Under CAFRA, owners must file a claim to potentially forfeited property within 30 days, and owners have five years to challenge the forfeiture. In the event an owner/claimant was not convicted of the crime resulting in forfeiture, compensation is available. If the owner establishes that s/he is indigent, and if the forfeited property is a primary residence, court-appointed counsel if available. Non-indigent owners may be entitled to court and litigation costs if they "substantially prevail" in the civil forfeiture action. Finally, CAFRA creates an "innocent owner defense" applicable to all federal civil asset forfeiture statutes.

civil commitment. The action of a judicial officer or administrative body ordering a person to be placed in an institution or program, usually one administered by a health service, for custody, treatment, or protection.

civil case. A judicial proceeding to enforce a private right or to obtain compensation for its violation; distinguished from a criminal case.

civil commotion. A serious and prolonged disturbance of the peace, but less severe than an insurrection.

civil/criminal courts. Civil courts are established for the adjudication of private wrongs. Criminal courts are charged with the administration of the criminal laws under which public offenders are tried.

civil death. Denial of all, or almost all civil rights, such as an individual's right to vote, to hold public office, and to enter into contracts, usually following felony conviction In medieval times, civil death led to actual death, as there were generally no consequences for injuring such a person.

civil disabilities. Rights or privileges denied a person as a result of conviction or a guilty plea, in addition to or other than the imposed legal penalty. *See also* felony disenfranchisement

civil disobedience. Nonviolent action, such as demonstrating or picketing, against a law, on the basis that the law is morally wrong or unjust, and acceptance of the penalty for disobeying it. In a sense, civil disobedience involves adherence to a higher law than the current written code when a conflict exists between the two. In using this technique, the demonstrator hopes to appeal to the conscience of the community by serving a seemingly unjust jail sentence. The term was used by Henry David Thoreau, in his famous 1849 essay "Civil Disobedience," to describe his refusal to pay taxes because of his objections to slavery and war. Civil disobedience was used by Mohandas K. Gandhi in his fight against British rule in India and also was employed effectively during the United States civil rights movement in the 1960s under the leadership of such men as Dr. Martin Luther King, Jr.

civil disorders. Also called civil unrest, civil disturbance, or urban riot, refers to disturbance caused by a group of people, often as a protest or in response to social-political issues. For example, Cincinnati, OH April 9–11, 2001. This three-day riot of looting, beatings and arson attacks in the downtown area started two days after a white officer shot an unarmed black male (Timothy Thomas, 19) fleeing arrest on foot.

Civil Disorders, National Advisory Commission on. Known as the Kerner Commission, established in 1967 to study the increasing number of civil disorders and race riots in the nation during the 1960s. Under the chairmanship of former Ohio governor Otto Kerner, the commission saw the nation as moving toward "two societies, separate and unequal." An attempt by vice chairman Mayor John V. Lindsay of New York and Senator Fred Harris of Oklahoma to reconvene the body for further study failed, but a follow-up report was issued in 1969 by the Urban Coalition and Urban America, Inc. The findings of the Kerner Commission related to those of the Eisenhower commission on the causes and prevention of violence and to the Scranton commission on campus unrest. All three panels saw the country becoming increasingly polarized as a result of the prolonged Vietnam War and the domestic inequalities inherent in a society that was described as racist, whether consciously or unconsciously. In 1998, the Eisenhower Foundation sponsored two reports, The Millennium Breach and Locked in the Poorhouse to reevaluate issues raised in the Kerner report. One stated, in part, "there is more poverty in America, it is deeper, blacker and browner than before, and it is more concentrated in the cities, which have become America's poorhouses."

As a result of these reports, federal organizations such as the Minority Business Development Agency were created to combat the divisiveness of American society.

civil disturbances Also called urban riots or civil disorder, refers to disorder caused by a group of people, often as a protest or in response to social political issues. A table of U.S. urban riots is provided on Table 10. *See also* Civil Disorders, National Advisory Commission on; King, Rodney; McDuffle; Arthur; Overtown; urban riots.

civilianization. The process in police departments of replacing sworn peace officers with civilians to handle such non-law enforcement functions as dispatch, parking, training, budget, and planning/forecasting. Civilianization is a relatively recent innovation, with the general ratio now being 30 percent civilians

TABLE 10 URBAN RIOTS IN THE UNITED STATES

Location	Date	Cost	Casualties
East St. Louis, Illinois	July 1917	No monetary value, 244 buildings destroyed	At least 1 dead
Chicago, Illinois	July 27–August 2, 1917	Unknown	38 dead, 537 injured
Tulsa, Oklahoma	May 31, 1921	$1.8 million	Estimated dead at 300, 800 injured
Harlem, New York, New York	March 19, 1935	$2 million	3 dead, 100 wounded
Rochester, New York	July 24, 1964	Unknown	4 dead, 350 injured
Philadelphia, Pennsylvania	August 28–20, 1964	Unknown	341 injured
Los Angeles, California (Watts)	August 11–17, 1965	$40 million	34 dead, 1,032 injured
Cleveland, Ohio	July 18–July23, 1966	Unknown	4 dead, 30 injured
Newark, New York	July 12–July 17, 1967	More than $10 million	26 dead, 725 injured
Plainfield, New Jersey	July 14, 1967	Unknown	1 dead
Detroit, Michigan	July 23–27, 1967	$80 million	43 dead, 467 injured
Chicago, Illinois	April 4, 1968	$10 million	11 dead, 500+ injured
Washington, D.C.	April 4, 1968	$27 million	12 dead, 1,097 injured
Baltimore, Maryland	April 4, 1968	$ 12 million	7 dead
Miami, Florida	May 17–20, 1980	Unknown	15 dead, 188 injured
Los Angeles, California	April 29–May 4, 1992	$1 billion	53 dead, 2,383 injured
Cincinnati, Ohio	April 9–11, 2001	$3.6 million	1 dead

Compiled by Richard Porter, CSULB.

to 70 percent sworn peace officers. *See also* community service officer

Civilian Oversight of Law Enforcement, National Association for (NACOLE). A voluntary, nonprofit organization that brings together individuals and agencies working to establish or improve oversight of police officers in the United States. Address: 638 E. Vermont St., Indianapolis, IN 46202Web: http://www.nacole.org/.

civilian review boards. Advisory groups of citizens from outside the police department who are responsible for investigating charges of misconduct by municipal employees, including police officers. Such oversight boards or commissions may be established by state law, municipal charter, charter amendment, referendum resulting in ordinance, ordinance, or police order. A few civilian review boards have subpoena power, but most only conduct investigations and recommend disciplinary actions. The idea of review boards was initially formally opposed by such vested-interest groups as the International Association of Chiefs of Police, the International Conference of Police Associations, and the Fraternal Order of Police. The first review board was established in Philadelphia in October 1958. New York City created its Civilian Complaint Review Board in July 1966. Within four months, the New York Patrolmen's Benevolent Association had persuaded voters to abolish the review board, and the Philadelphia board was similarly disbanded in 1967. Subsequently, however, questionable police practices created sufficient pressure to revive the civilian oversight movement. Most law enforcement agencies have some form of civilian review boards, whether active or on call. *See also* Civilian Oversight of Law Enforcement, International Association for; White Night

civil law. This term originally referred to the system of jurisprudence developed in the Roman Empire and now usually refers to the legal system descended from Roman law and prevailing in most of continental Europe. In this system of law, cases are decided *a priori,* applying highly abstract legal concepts known as codes. In this sense, civil law is opposed to common law. The Western world generally adheres to one or the other of these two legal systems. The term civil law is also used to distinguish the law of a political entity from international law and natural law, but municipal law is a more appropriate term in this context. In other contexts, civil law has been distinguished from criminal law, canon law, and admiralty law.

civil liability. A complaint filed in an appropriate court by an individual seeking to recover damages, which includes the reason for the suit (cause of causes) and the amount of damages sought. The right of civil or private redress stems from the common law of torts. It first appeared in U.S. federal law in Section 1 of the Civil Rights Act of 1871, which has now been codified as 42 U.S.C. 1983. *See also* vicarious liability

civil liberties. Basic individual rights guaranteed in the U.S. Bill of Rights. They include freedom of speech, religion, and the press; the right to trial by jury; protection against unreasonable searches and seizures; protection from being forced to testify against oneself in a criminal trial; and protection from being deprived of life, liberty, and property without due process of law. It was argued at the Constitutional Convention that the Bill of Rights (the first 10 amendments) were unnecessary because the federal government had no power whatsoever to abridge civil liberties. However, others at the Constitutional Convention, such as James Madison, favored the amendments in order to separate "the well-meaning from the designing opponents of the Constitution." During several periods in American history, there have been serious infringements of citizens' civil liberties. Examples are the Civil War, World War I, the notorious "Red Scare" Palmer raids of 1920, the treatment of Americans of Japanese descent during World War II, and racial prejudice. However, the Supreme Court has generally supported such liberties. Perhaps some of the most far-reaching civil liberties decisions were handed down during the Warren Court; these included several on school desegregation and the one-man-one-vote ruling. Civil liberties have been legislated by specific statutes, as in the Civil Rights Acts of the 1960s that outlawed discrimination in public accommodations, employment, and schools. Civil liberties are intended to guarantee equality of all individuals before the law. As set forth in the Bill of Rights, they are an embodiment of natural law principles. But the Bill of Rights also implies the responsibility of society to preserve individual liberties against infringement by the government and its agencies, while those very liberties protect the mass media, political leaders, courts, and a vigilant public. Organizations such as the American Civil Liberties Union offer legal counsel in selected constitutional cases.

civil process. Official orders and documents issued by, or under the authority of, a court when handling civil matters such as summonses, subpoenas, injunctions, eviction orders, and so forth.

civil rights. Those liberties possessed by the individual as a member of the state, especially those guaranteed against encroachment by the government. In this latter sense, civil rights are enumerated in the bills of rights of federal and state constitutions and include both substantive rights, such as freedom of speech, press, assembly, or religion, and procedural rights, such as protection against unreasonable searches and seizures or against punishment without a fair trial. The most important civil right is embodied in those clauses in state and federal constitutions that prohibit government from depriving anyone of life, liberty, or property without due process of law. Twice found in the Constitution, such clauses impose limitations on the states as well as on Congress. Of somewhat less importance is the equal protection clause of the Fourteenth Amendment, which limits state action. By its interpretation of these clauses, the Supreme Court largely determines the scope of civil rights

in America. Recently, interest in civil rights has been directed toward legislation by Congress and state legislatures to secure certain liberties of the individual against encroachment by other individuals and groups, and to prohibit such individuals and groups from discrimination on the basis of race, color, religion, or membership in labor unions. On April 26, 1996, Len Davis, a former New Orleans policeman who in October 1994 ordered a woman murdered the day after she filed a brutality complaint against him, was given the death penalty by a federal jury. Davis is the first person sentenced to death in a civil rights case.

Civil Rights Acts (CRAs). Congress passed seven civil rights acts during Reconstruction to guarantee the rights of freed slaves and to implement the Thirteenth, Fourteenth, and Fifteenth Amendments to the Constitution. Despite this far-reaching egalitarian legislation, social and political equality remained far out of reach. Those provisions that were not declared unconstitutional in the next two decades by the Supreme Court were rendered ineffectual via narrow rulings handed down by judges responding to broad sentiment against legislating equality between the races. An additional twelve civil rights acts have subsequently passed to address racial equality. These are detailed in Table 11. Civil Rights Acts in the United States, page 83

Civil Rights, Commission on. An independent, bipartisan federal agency set up in 1957. The organization is charged with investigating complaints alleging that citizens are being deprived of their right to vote by reason of their race, color, religion, sex, age, disability, or national origin, or by reason of fraudulent practices. They also study and collect information relating to discrimination or a denial of equal protection of the laws under the Constitution because of race, color, religion, sex, age, disability, or national origin, or in the administration of justice. The commission appraises federal laws and policies with respect to discrimination or denial of equal protection of the laws

TABLE 11   CIVIL RIGHTS ACTS IN THE UNITED STATES

Civil Rights Act Date Passed	Purpose	Notable Judicial Debate
April 9, 1866	Extended citizenship to those born in United States; gave blacks equality.	Debate ended with 14th amendment.
April 21, 1855 and March 2, 1867	Implemented 13th amendment; eliminated peonage and illegalized bringing people into slavery.	None.
May 31, 1870	Criminal sanctions for interfering with suffrage.	Sections 3, 4, and 16 disallowed by Supreme Court.
February 28, 1871	Appointment of supervisors and marshals to oversee congressional elections.	None.
April 20, 1872	Anyone using law or custom to the detriment of another's Constitutional rights is subject to federal punishment.	Section 2 declared unconstitutional.
March 1, 1875	All people entitled to "the full and equal enjoyment of the accommodations, advantages, facilities and privileges of inns, public conveyances on land or water, theaters and other places of public amusement."	Nullified by Civil Rights Cases of 1883.
1957	Established the Civil Rights Commission; added assistant attorney general to oversee Civil Rights Division; qualified all people for jury duty.	None.
1960	Set penalties for obstructing federal court order; made it necessary to maintain all election records for 22 months; appointed voting referees.	None.
1964	Forbade discrimination; extended duties and rights of Civil Rights Commission.	In line with 14th amendment due process clause.
1968	Protects civil rights workers; forbids housing discrimination; provides penalties for those who attempt to interfere with individual rights.	None.
1991	Modifies procedural and substantive rights provided by federal law in discrimination cases; also limits the amount that can be rewarded.	None.

Compiled by Richard Porter, CSULB.

because of race, color, religion, sex, age, disability, or national origin, or in the administration of justice. The organization serves as a national clearinghouse for information in respect to discrimination or denial of equal protection of the laws because of race, color, religion, sex, age, disability, or national origin. Address: U.S. Commission on Civil Rights, 624 Ninth Street, NW, Washington, DC 20425, Web: http://www.usccr.gov/.

Civil Rights Division. Under the Department of Justice, the Civil Rights Division is charged with upholding the civil and constitutional rights of all Americans, particularly some of the most vulnerable members of our society. The Division enforces federal statutes designed to protect the civil rights of all individuals and prohibit discrimination on the basis of race, color, sex, disability, religion, and national origin. Web: http://www.justice.gov/crt/.

civil rights enforcement. Violations of civil rights are addressed at the federal level by the Department of Justice, Civil Rights Division. *See* Civil Rights Division

Civil Rights Institute. Established in fall 1992 in Birmingham, AL, the institute is located at 520 16th St. North; admission is free. Of particular interest to scholars of criminal justice is the exhibit section "Movements," which includes a life-sized replica of a burned-out Greyhound bus and video footage of freedom riders, police officers wielding fire hoses against demonstrators, sit-ins, and packed jails. Web: http://www.bcri.org/index.html.

Civil Rights of Institutionalized Persons Act (CRIPA). A federal law (42 U.S. Code 1997) that gives the Justice Department, Civil Rights Division, the authority to sue correctional facilities on behalf of inmates, to protect their civil rights, and encourages the development of inmate grievance procedures and programs.

Civil Rights—Special Litigation. An office under the Department of Justice that is responsible for protecting rights secured under Title VI of the CRA of 1964 requiring nondiscrimination against persons confined in state and local prisons and jails. Address: Special Litigation Section, 950 Pennsylvania Ave., N.W, PHB, Washington, DC 20530. Web: http://www.justice.gov/crt/split/.

civil service. The term applied to the body of employees working for a government. In the United States, employees of business enterprises operated by federal, state, or local governments are included; elected officials, judges, and the military are excluded.

civil suit. Legal process before a court to recover property, maintain a right or privilege, or satisfy a claim. *See also* civil law; civil process

clandestine. Describing actions that are concealed or secret. *See also sub rosa*

Clandestine Laboratory Enforcement Program (CLEP). Under the California Department of Justice, this agency within the Bureau of Narcotic Enforcement (BNE) investigates illegal drug-manufacturing operations statewide. The agency sponsored the Crank-Up Task Force in 1987 and established the California Methamphetamine Strategy (CALMS) in 1998, which spearheads a comprehensive attack on methamphetamine production and distribution in the state. According to the state Web site, "CALMS teams have conducted over 1,900 investigations, made nearly 2,400 arrests and seized over 27,000 pounds of methamphetamine" since inception. Address: Controlled Chemical Substance Program P.O. Box 161089, Sacramento, CA 95816-1089. Web: http://ag.ca.gov/bne/clanlab.php.

class action. A legal effort made by a group of persons on behalf of themselves and all others similarly situated or injured. Although the process has existed for some time, class action has only become prominent in the last four decades. It has proven a very useful device for the enforcement of liabilities when the interest of any one person is too small to render a suit economically viable. A court will usually award lawyers' fees out of the aggregate judgment on behalf of the class.

classification of crimes. Crimes in common law are divided into treason, felonies, and misdemeanors. Some jurisdictions have a fourth classification of minor or petty offenses, less than misdemeanors, sometimes described either as those of which magistrates have had exclusive summary jurisdiction or as police regulations.

classifications of prisoners. The process, sometimes referred to as diagnostic classification, through which a new prisoner is categorized according to educational, vocational, treatment, and security needs for proper placement in facilities by security level or treatment program.

Clayton Act (1914). Federal legislation enacted to exempt labor organizations and their legitimate concerted activities from the provisions of the Sherman Antitrust Act and to narrow the jurisdiction of the federal courts in labor disputes. *See also* antitrust cases

clearance. The step in police-level reporting in which a known occurrence of an offense is followed by an arrest or other decision that indicates a solved crime. In Uniform Crime Report (UCR) vocabulary, a known offense is "cleared" or "solved" by two means: (1) clearance by arrest, including an arrest, official charging, or prosecution; and (2) exceptional means, such as when a suspect has been identified and located and an arrest is justified, but action is prevented by circumstances outside law enforcement control (e.g., the suspect is dead, the suspect is already in custody, or the victim of the offense has refused cooperation in prosecution. *See also* clearance rate

clearance rate. The number of offenses cleared, divided by the number of offenses known to police. Although a "clearance by arrest" or by "exceptional means" may have been recorded for UCR purposes, active investigation will continue, for example, where a crime has been cleared by the arrest of one suspect but a second suspect is still being sought. Conversely, the closing of a police case may or may not indicate a "clearance." Where, for example, investigation of all available leads has not resulted in the identification of a suspect, a case not cleared may be filed inactive or closed pending new information.

clear and present danger. A court test used in determining the limits of free expression guaranteed in the First Amendment. This yardstick was first formulated by Justice Oliver Wendell Holmes in the Supreme Court's 1919 decision in *Schenck v. United States,* in which Holmes said that speech could be punished if there were a serious and imminent danger that such speech would result in illegal action. The clear-and-present-danger test is applied in times of crisis. Other tests of the right to free expression include the more limiting dangerous-tendency test (of speech that has a tendency to bring about dangerous results), the preferred-position test (a more rigorous standard of review required because of the importance of the right of free speech), and the sliding-scale test (involving careful examination of the facts of each individual case). *See also* dangerous-tendency test

clemency. The doctrine under which executive or legislative action reduces the severity of or waives legal punishment of one or more individuals, or an individual is exempted from prosecution for certain actions. Grounds for clemency are such mitigating circumstances as postconviction evidence of a prisoner's innocence; a prisoner's dubious guilt, illness, reformation, services to the state, or turning state's evidence; reasons of the state such as the need to restore civil rights; and corrections of unduly severe sentences or injustices stemming from imperfections in penal law or the application of it. The chief forms of clemency are pardons (full and conditional), amnesties, commutations, reduced sentences, reprieves, and remissions of fines and forfeitures.

Cleveland steamer. Colloquial term for a form of coprophilia, where one defecates on their partner's chest, then rocks back and forth imitating the motion of a steamroller. In 2002, the Federal Communications Commission (FCC) issued a fine of $27,000 to a Detroit radio station for describing the term (among other paraphilias) on the air. *See also* coprophagia, coprophilia

Clink. Originally a London prison that dominated the south bank of the Thames near London Bridge, where it was a well-known landmark in the days of Hogarth and Dickens. Not only a generic name for all prisons, but also for the brothels and the Southwark

Fair depicted by Hogarth; now only its name survives at its site on Clink Street.

closed shop. A labor agreement by which an employer may hire only people who are continuing union members. The closed shop is illegal under the Taft-Hartley Act of 1947.

CN (chloroacetophenone). The chlorinated form of acetophenone, a lachrymator (tear causing) chemical most commonly used in tear gas and in aerosol irritant projectors. The chemical name is chloroacetophenone.

Coast Guard jurisdiction. Commissioned, warrant, and petty officers of the Coast Guard are empowered to make inquiries, examinations, inspections, searches, seizures, and arrests upon the high seas and the navigable waters of the United States, its territories, and possessions. Such power does not apply to inland waters, except for the Great Lakes and its connecting waters.

cobalt thiocyanate test. (or **Scott test**) a screening test for the presence of cocaine.

cocaine. A drug that occurs naturally in the leaves of the coca plant, *Erythroxylon coca,* which is native to Colombia, Peru, and Bolivia. Cocaine was originally thought to be nonaddictive, but today it is widely recognized as a very potent addictive substance that can cause both physical and psychological dependence. Euphoric excitement is produced when cocaine is sniffed. Delusions and hallucinations are common with large doses. Cocaine was widely used as a local anesthetic but has been replaced by a synthetic, Novocaine. First purified by German chemist Albert Neimann in the nineteenth century, cocaine was used as a central nervous system stimulant, appetite suppressant, and local anesthetic. Freud recommended it as a cure for depression, alcoholism, and morphine addiction, and the general public made it a fashionable social pastime. A 1902 survey indicated that the nonprescription use of cocaine accounted for 92 percent of its total use in the United States. Until it was legally restricted in 1914, cocaine was regularly added to tonics and such beverages as

Coca Cola. Medical acceptance of the drug declined as its detrimental effects became obvious and nonaddicting medications became available. An estimated 27 million Americans have tried or are current users of cocaine. However, current users (those who have taken the drug in the last month) declined by 71 percent between 1985 and 2001. Nevertheless, it is still the second-most popular illicit drug, after marijuana, among adolescents and young adults. Cocaine is a $35 billion industry, now exceeding coffee as Colombia's number-one export. Bolivia is the second-biggest producer of coca leaf in South America, behind Peru. The Bolivians cultivate between 25,000 and 40,000 metric tons of leaves each year, enough to produce 50 to 80 tons of cocaine.

cocaine, crack. The product created when powdered cocaine is dissolved in water, combined with baking soda, and heated until the water evaporates, leaving crack rocks. One lb. of powdered cocaine produces 0.9 lbs. of crack. It appears as small, colored rocks or chips that vary in size, shape, color, and consistency, but are usually yellowish or beige with a waxy look resembling that of soap chips. Crack cocaine has been shown to be very addictive, causing both physical dependence and psychological addiction.

code. (1) A body of law covering one general subject, established by the legislative authority of the state. (2) (in Roman-law countries) A systematic statement of the body of the law enacted or promulgated by the highest authority of the state, on which all judicial decisions must be based. (3) (in the United States) A private or official compilation of all permanent laws in force, consolidated and classified according to subject matter. Such compilations of national laws are the *Revised Statutes of the United States,* first enacted in 1874, and *A Code of the Laws of the United States.* Many states have published official codes of all laws in force, including the common law and statutes as judicially interpreted, which have been compiled by code commissions and enacted by the legislatures. American codes lack the permanence and authority of European codes because of the volume of new statutes and of judicial decisions, each of which, under common-law principles, constitutes a precedent for the decisions of later cases.

Code, International. A code of words used in law enforcement to clarify letters of the alphabet when spelling orally, as by telephone or radio. The code words are: A = Alpha, B = Bravo, C = Charlie, D = Delta, E = Echo, F = Foxtrot, G = Gold, H = Hotel, I = India, J = Juliette, K = Kilo, L = Lima, M = Mike, N = November, O = Oscar, P = Papa, Q = Quebec, R = Romeo, S = Sierra, T = Tango, U = Uniform, V = Victor, W = Whiskey, X = X-ray, Y = Yankee, Z = Zulu.

Code, Napoleonic. The codification of French private, substantive law prepared at the urging of Napoleon Bonaparte. It became widely accepted as a model among Latin peoples.

code of ethics. Written rules, regulations, and/or standards of conduct for members of groups engaged in given professions or occupations. The Law Enforcement Code of Ethics was first developed by the California Peace Officers' Association and the Peace Officers' Research Association of California in 1956 and adopted by the IACP at its 1957 conference. *See* Table 12. American Correctional Association Code of Ethics, page. 88; *see also* Table 13. Law Enforcement Code of Ethics, page 89

Code of Hammurabi. Babylonian laws, written around 1790 B.C., generally regarded by historians as a moderate and humanitarian code for its period; one of the oldest codes of law.

codefendants. More than one person charged jointly for the same crime.

codeine. Methylmorphine, a sedative and pain-relieving agent produced by the poppy plant, *Papaver somniferum*. Codeine, along with the structurally similar morphine, hydrocodone, hydromorphone, oxycodone,

oxymorphone, is an opoid. Codeine is a relatively weak analgesic, and is roughly one-sixth to one-tenth as potent as morphine.

Codependents Anonymous. Self-help group whose common purpose is to develop healthy relationships. Address: P.O. Box 33577, Phoenix, AZ 85067-3577. Web: http://www.codependents.org/.

codicil. Any provision appended to a will after its original preparation, which adds to, takes from, or alters its earlier content.

CODIS. *See* Combined DNA Index System

Coed killer. *See* Kemper, Ed

coequal staffing. A human resources issue, which pertains to comparable pay and benefits for those employed in jail facilities compared to those performing similar tasks in law enforcement departments

coercion. (1) The use of force to compel performance of an action. (2) The application of sanctions or the use of force by government to compel observance of law or public policy.

cognomen. A family name; a surname; the third name of an Ancient Roman citizen.

cohabitation. Living together as husband and wife, as in an emotionally and sexually intimate relationship, especially when not legally married. Legally, a couple must share a residence all or most of the time to be cohabiting; occasional intercourse does not constitute cohabitation. Cohabitation is still a misdemeanor in Mississippi, Virginia, West Virginia, Florida, and Michigan, although these laws are generally not enforced and are generally found unconstitutional when challenged.

cohort. In statistics, a group of individuals having one or more defining characteristic in common in a demographic study; they generally share a common experience at a common time. The landmark study *Delinquency in a Birth Cohort,* authored in 1972 by Marvin Wolfgang and his associates at the University of Pennsylvania and replicated in 1985, is a

text continues on page 89

TABLE 12   AMERICAN CORRECTIONAL ASSOCIATION CODE OF ETHICS

Preamble

The American Correctional Association expects of its members unfailing honesty, respect for the dignity and individuality of human beings and a commitment to professional and compassionate service. To this end, we subscribe to the following principles.

Members shall respect and protect the civil and legal rights of all individuals.

Members shall treat every professional situation with concern for the welfare of the individuals involved and with no intent to personal gain.

Members shall maintain relationships with colleagues to promote mutual respect within the profession and improve the quality of service.

Members shall make public criticism of their colleagues or their agencies only when warranted, verifiable, and constructive.

Members shall respect the importance of all disciplines within the criminal justice system and work to improve cooperation with each segment.

Members shall honor the public's right to information and share information with the public to the extent permitted by law subject to individual's right to privacy.

Members shall respect and protect the right of the public to be safeguarded from criminal activity.

Members shall refrain from using their positions to secure personal privileges or advantages.

Members shall refrain from allowing personal interest to impair objectivity in the performance of duty while acting in an official capacity.

Members shall refrain from entering into any formal or informal activity or agreement which presents a conflict of interest or is inconsistent with the conscientious performance of duties.

Members shall refrain from accepting any gifts, service, or favor that is or appears to be improper or implies an obligation inconsistent with the free and objective exercise of professional duties.

Members shall clearly differentiate between personal views/statements and views/statements/positions made on behalf of the agency or Association.

Members shall report to appropriate authorities any corrupt or unethical behaviors in which there is sufficient evidence to justify review.

Members shall refrain from discriminating against any individual because of race, gender, creed, national origin, religious affiliation, age, disability, or any other type of prohibited discrimination.

Members shall preserve the integrity of private information; they shall refrain from seeking information on individuals beyond that which is necessary to implement responsibilities and perform their duties; members shall refrain from revealing nonpublic information unless expressly authorized to do so.

Members shall make all appointments, promotions, and dismissals in accordance with established civil service rules, applicable contract agreements, and individual merit, rather than furtherance of personal interests.

Members shall respect, promote, and contribute to a work place that is safe, healthy, and free of harassment in any form.

Adopted August 1975 at the 105th Congress of Correction
Revised August 1990 at the 120th Congress of Correction
Revised August 1994 at the 124th Congress of Correction

TABLE 13   LAW ENFORCEMENT CODE OF ETHICS

As a Law Enforcement Officer, my fundamental duty is to serve mankind; to safeguard lives and property; to protect the innocent against deception, the weak against oppression or intimidation, and the peaceful against violence or disorder; and to respect the Constitutional rights of all persons to liberty, equality and justice.

I will keep my private life unsullied as an example to all; maintain courageous calm in the face of danger, scorn or ridicule; develop self-restraint; and be constantly mindful of the welfare of others. Honest in thought and deed in both my personal and official life, I will be exemplary in obeying the laws of the land and the regulations of my department. Whatever I see or hear of a confidential nature or that is confided to me in my official capacity will be kept ever secret unless revelation is necessary in the performance of my duty.

I will never act officiously or permit personal feelings, prejudices, animosities or friendships to influence my decisions. With no compromise for crime and with relentless prosecution of criminal, I will enforce the law courteously and appropriately without fear or favor, malice or ill will, never employing unnecessary force or violence and never accepting gratuities.

I recognize the badge of my office as a symbol of public faith, and I accept it as a public trust to be held so long as I am true to the ethics of the police service. I will constantly strive to achieve these objectives and ideals, dedicating myself before God to my chosen profession . . . law enforcement.

Adopted by the Executive Committee of the International Association of Chiefs of Police on October 16, 2001, by IACP. Previous versions of the code were adopted October 17, 1989, during its 96th Annual Conference in Louisville, Kentucky to replace the 1957 Code of Ethics adopted at the 64th Annual IACP Conference.

---

landmark piece of criminal justice research and has become a major influence in crime control methods. The authors discovered that a small group of delinquents are responsible for a majority of all crimes and for about two thirds of all violent crimes.

Cointelpro. Abbreviated from counter intelligence program. An FBI counterintelligence program (1956–1971) that emphasized harassment of suspected subversives. The covert, and often illegal, activities of this program were brought to light by the 1967 Freedom of Information Act.

cold blood. Term used to describe crimes committed in the absence of a fit of anger; homicide cases in which the murderer experienced no strong emotion or violent passion; without emotion or remorse.

collateral bond. Arrangement in which the defendant must post property valued at the full bail amount in order to secure release from custody pending trial. *See* Table 3, Types of Pretrial Release, page 36

collateral consequence. Any penalty that may result from a guilty plea or a conviction, in addition to the preordered punishment. Traditional examples include deportation, disenfranchisement, disbarment, or loss of license to practice certain professions. More recently, this term also encompasses the displacement of children and impact of incarceration to families and communities.

collateral facts. Facts not directly connected with the matter in dispute.

collateral security. A bond or deposit in addition to the principal or original security.

collective bargaining. A process of setting ages, hours, and working conditions for employees by means of structured meetings involving affected employees, acting through their unions or associations, and their managers, or employers. The term thus includes both contract negotiation and ongoing administration of the provisions of existing labor contracts. Several states have enacted legislation enabling police unions or associations to "meet and confer, in good faith" with city or county officials regarding "wages and conditions of employment." All law enforcement and correctional personnel at virtually any rank have union/association representation. Since most law enforcement agencies bargain collectively, they have established memorandums of understanding to delineate the process of contract negotiation and define that issues will be decided through this process. *See also* arbitration; conciliation; mediation; public sector unions

collusion. An agreement between two or more persons for a fraudulent purpose; an agreement between two or more persons to defraud a third person of his or her rights or to obtain an object forbidden by law.

colony, penal. A remote area, generally a distant island outside a nation's borders, or occasionally a remote part of a nation, where criminals are sent upon conviction of crimes, usually those within special categories. In effect, sentence to a penal colony involves virtual banishment or exile. England used colonial America and parts of Australia as penal colonies in the 1700s.

color of authority. An apparent prima facie right or authority; the presumption of authority, which justifies the actions of an officer and that is derived from a badge, certificate, or writ which is apparently legal; legitimacy through role as government agent; authority derived from election or appointment.

Colt, Samuel. American inventor (1814–1862) famous for the invention of the six-shooter revolver, accepted by the U.S. Army in 1847 but first patented in 1836. The revolver was ideal for mounted warfare, and the Colt became the standard weapon on the Great Plains. Colt's revolver sometimes overshadows his great contribution to the

technique of the mass production of large quantities of complex components.

Columbine Massacre. On April 20, 1999, in the Colorado Columbine High School, students Eric Harris and Dylan Klebold shot and killed twelve people. Both assailants committed suicide inside the school building.

Combined DNA Index System (CODIS). Launched in 1990, CODIS is the FBI database of genetic DNA material used nationwide. According to the FBI, CODIS is currently used by over 170 public law enforcement laboratories nationwide and more than 40 international law enforcement laboratories. CODIS contains several indexes, including: Convicted Offender—contains profiles of individuals convicted of a crime; Forensic—contains DNA profiles developed from crime scene evidence such as semen stain or blood; Arrestees—contains profiles of arrested persons (if state law permits the collection of arrestee samples); Missing Persons—contains DNA reference profiles from missing persons; Unidentified Human Remains—contains DNA profiles developed from unidentified human remains; and Biological Relatives of Missing Persons—contains both nuclear and mitochondrial DNA profiles voluntarily contributed from relatives of missing persons. According to the FBI, CODIS assisted in nearly 81,000 investigations in 2008. For further information on CODIS, visit: http://www.fbi.gov/hq/lab/html/codis1.htm.

comity. Reciprocal courteous behavior: used primarily in the phrases "judicial comity" and "comity of nations". Judicial comity refers to the principle that the courts of one state or jurisdiction should give full effect to the laws and judicial decisions of another state. Comity of nations refers to the recognition granted by one nation, out of courtesy or convenience, to the laws of another nation, even though such recognition is not required by international law.

command. To direct with authority. In accordance with statutory requirements, a warrant must command an officer or officers to search for personal property, seize it, and create an inventory of the property. The warrant is void if it does not command the officer to present both property and inventory to the judge who issued the warrant, or to another other judge or court that has some official responsibility in the case.

commercial law. This branch of law embraces those statutes relating both to the rights of property and to the relations of persons engaged in business and commerce.

Commercial Litigation Branch. This DOJ office represents the United States before foreign tribunals in civil cases brought by and against the United States. It represents the government in domestic cases involving questions of international and foreign law. Address: Commercial Litigation Branch, Civil Division, DOJ, 550 11th Street, NW, Room 1234, Washington, DC 20530; Web: http://www.justice.gov/civil/Foreign%20 Litigation.htm.

commission. (1) A warrant, usually issued by the chief executive, which confers the powers and privileges of an office upon a person newly appointed to it. (2) A body of three or more officials who collectively discharge the duties of an administrative agency.

commissioner. A member of certain independent federal agencies, certain state boards, a principal county board, or the governing board of a city under the commission form of government.

Commissioner of Deeds. An officer authorized to administer oaths in all cases where no special provision is made by law.

commission of inquiry. A board composed of members of the legislature, administrative officials, nonofficial members, or a combination of two or more of these groups, appointed to investigate and report on a particular problem.

commission on interstate cooperation. The first interstate commission to establish cooperative law enforcement procedures in U.S.

history was the New Jersey Commission on Interstate Cooperation, created by a joint resolution passed on March 12, 1935. The commission was responsible for developing cooperation among states on various problems in the areas of crime control, motor vehicles, conflicting taxation, agriculture, and other matters. Today, most jurisdictions have a such a commission

commitment. The action of a judicial officer ordering that a person subject to judicial proceedings be placed in a particular kind of confinement or residential facility for a specific reason authorized by law; also the result of the action, that is, the individual's admission to the facility.

Commodities Futures Trade Commission (CFTC). Created by congress in 1974, the CFTC regulate commodity futures and option markets in the United States. Address: Commodity Futures Trading Commission, Three Lafayette Centre, 1155 21st Street, NW, Washington, DC 20581. Web: http:// www.cftc.gov/.

common law. In its broadest sense, the original English legal system that has been adopted, in varying degrees, by most English-speaking countries. It is a system of judge-made law, although its principles theoretically derive from general usage and immemorial custom, which the judge only applies. Common law is often called "unwritten law," even though one looks to printed reports of decided cases to deduce its principles. No comprehensive listing of its legal rules is available, unlike civil law's codes. Because the legal rules depend on the nuances of the particular situation, decisions on cases are reached by reasoning inductively, comparing the cases' facts with those of previously decided cases. Within this legal system, the term common law is used to distinguish both judge-made law from statutory law and the system of rigorously applied legal principles from the system of flexible, equitable remedies. After 900 years, the common law endures as a great collective achievement.

Today the family of common law takes its place beside two other major families of law, the Romano-Germanic and the socialist. *See also* Common Law of England

Common Law of England. A type of law that emerged from the way the government of England was centralized and specialized after the Norman Conquest in 1066. In the course of unifying England, the Normans and their successors were faced with the problem of gaining universal jurisdiction for the royal courts. This was by no means an easy task. The Anglo-Saxon courts were local in nature, and customs varied from shire to shire. Elements of canon, Roman, and Germanic law can be found in the common law, which gradually emerged from administrative efforts to centralize legal processes.

common-law marriage. A marriage in which the partners have simply accepted each other as husband and wife, with no license, formal ceremony, blood test, or official witnesses. The term derives from historical roots: when marriages were neither religious nor civil but were arranged between two families, they were part of the unwritten or common law. Common-law marriage can still be contracted in some states, but cannot be contracted in the majority of states. However, all states recognize common-law marriages which are lawfully contracted within the jurisdictions where it is still permitted.

common scold. In common law, a common scold was a quarrelsome woman who broke the peace by arguing with her husband or neighbors. *See also* ducking stool

communication. Violations of federal communications law, such as for unlawful wiretapping and interception.

Community Anti-Drug Coalitions of America. (CADCA). Founded in 1992, an advocacy organization offering information and technical assistance for developing and implementing strategic plans and public policy initiatives. The organization is affiliated with the National Association of Drug Court Professionals. Address: 625 Slaters Lane, Suite 300, Alexandria, VA 22314. Web: http://www.cadca.org/.

community-based corrections. Includes any form of correctional treatment, such as halfway houses, probation or parole, that deals with the offender within, as opposed to outside, society (in contrast with incarceration or institutionalization).

community-based policing. A style of local law enforcement emphasizing the idea that the public should play a more active and coordinated role in crime control and prevention. Imposes a police responsibility to devise new and innovative ways of associating the public with law enforcement and the maintenance of order. Community-based policing involves collaboration partnerships between the community, government and police; proactive problem solving; and community engagement to address the causes of crime, fear of crime and community quality of life issues. The four major elements are: (1) organize community-based crime prevention; (2) reorient patrol activities to emphasize nonemergency servicing; (3) increase accountability to local communities; and (4) decentralize command. *See also* community-oriented policing; neighborhood watch

community confinement. Criminal sentence for a term of custody in the community, generally in a specific facility such as a residential treatment center, halfway house, or mental health center. Persons sentenced to such are generally expected to comply with the rules and regulations of the facility, as well as court ordered conditions. This often includes treatment, educational/vocational training, and employment.

Community Effort to Combat Auto Theft (CECAT). A multiagency task force coordinated by the Los Angeles Police Department in the 1980s focused on international auto theft operations. *See also* Operation Guatemalan Auto Theft Enforcement; vehicle theft

community-oriented policing (COP). A continuing organizational philosophy, management style, and cooperative community strategy to enhance local crime prevention and control. COP is a form of policing oriented toward the public, or police forces' clients, and designed to provide communities with responsive, ethical, high-quality police service. COP involves a commitment to attitudinal change at all levels of local law enforcement and an ongoing partnership among the police force, the local government, and the community. COP law enforcement tactics might include foot patrols, storefront police stations, bilingual crime hotlines and prevention newsletters, open communication, external review boards, multiethnic recruitment, and cultural-awareness training for police officers. Although some communities interpret COP to include addressing the causes of crime, police forces generally do not have the resources to alleviate social pressures believed to cause crime. Community relations, team policing, and problem-oriented policing were all earlier methods leading up to COP. COP also shares many features with total quality management (TQM). In 1994 the U.S. Department of Justice created the Office of Community Oriented Policing Services to help advance the practice of community policing across the United States Address: 1100 Vermont Ave., NW, Washington, DC 20530. Web: http://www.cops.usdoj.gov/. *See also* National Center for Community Policing; total quality management

community policing. According to the U. S. Department of Justice, "Community policing is a philosophy that promotes organizational strategies, which support the systematic use of partnerships and problem-solving techniques, to proactively address the immediate conditions that give rise to public safety issues such as crime, social disorder, and fear of crime." Community policing includes three key components: community partnerships, organizational transformation, and problem solving.

Community Policing Consortium (CPC). This initiative includes five leading U.S. policing organizations: the International Association of Chiefs of Police, the National Organization of Black Law Enforcement Executives, the National Sheriffs' Association, the Police Executive Research Forum, and the Police Foundation. CPC is funded by the U.S. Department of Justice, Bureau of Justice Assistance, and provides information and assistance to community-oriented policing efforts. The CPC publishes *Community Policing Exchange,* a free bimonthly newsletter. Address: 1726 M St. N.W., Suite 801, Washington, DC, 20036 Web: http://www.communitypolicing.org/.

community property. Property acquired during a marriage by either husband or wife or both, except property that is acquired separately by either spouse. In community property states, all property acquired during the marriage by either party, except for gifts or inheritances, is owned jointly by both spouses. Community property is divided equally between the spouses (or their heirs) upon divorce, annulment, or death.

community relations. A concept involving local residents and police in a partnership to resolve mutual concerns. Generally, police-community relations (PCR) consist of public relations, community service, community participation, and crime prevention. PCR has much to do with attitudes, both those of the police toward themselves and the community and those of the community toward themselves and the police. Open communication, honesty, fairness, and equality are essential elements. Although some police departments have a special section/division under the chief of police to develop, implement, maintain, and evaluate such programs, ideally every member of a department should feel a part of such an effort.

Community Resources Against Street Hoodlums (CRASH). A specialized unit of LAPD charged with investigating gang and narcotics crime in Los Angeles from 1978–2000, closed following the Rampart Scandal. *See also* Rampart Scandal

Community Relations Service (CRS). Created by the Civil Rights Act of 1964, the CRS is an agency of the U. S. Department of Justice. CRS sees its primary duty as "peacemaker" for community conflicts and tensions arising from differences of race, color, and national origin. Headquartered at: 600 E. Street, N.W., Suite 6000, Washington, DC 20530. Web: http://www.justice.gov/crs/.

community service dispositions. A correctional practice in which, in lieu of or in addition to time in jail or on probation, an offender must perform service to the community in the form of public works or volunteer activity at hospitals or other agencies or institutions.

community service officer. A nonsworn officer who handles nonemergency situations for a police department. CSOs generally provide support to law enforcement in the form of crime prevention, investigation, nonemergency response, and in capacities where full police powers are unnecessary.

community standard. Local norms of acceptable conduct. This phrase was used by the U.S. Supreme Court in its 1973 *Miller* decision in defining material as pornographic and subject to criminal sanctions if patently offensive in a given geographic or local area. *See also* pornography

commutation. see commutation of sentence.

commutation laws. *See* good-time

commutation of sentence. A reduction of a sentence originally prescribed by a court, generally by executive order (governor for state crimes, President for federal crimes).

comparison microscope. A device comprised of two microscopes connected by an optical bridge. Both images are magnified and brought into focus in a single or double eyepiece with prisms, which allows side-by-side comparison of two specimens This instrument is usually found in a crime laboratory and used to examine, among other things, markings on two bullets to determine if they were both fired from the same weapon.

competency. (1) Capability, such as power, jurisdiction, or the ability to serve as a witness; (2) evidence, written or otherwise, that is appropriate for presentation. (3) more commonly, this term refers to the defendant's ability to understand and participate in a court process. Various U.S. Supreme Court cases have addressed the issue of competence. In *Dusky v. United States* 362 U.S. 402 (1960), the court addressed competence to proceed to trial, defined as a defendant's ability to both understand the charges and aid his attorney in his own defense. In *Ford v. Wainwright,* 477 U.S. 399 (1986), the court addressed competence for execution, ruling that an insane defendant could not be executed; in such cases, treatment must be provided to aid the inmate in gaining competency in order to carry out the execution. In *Godinez v. Moran,* 509 U.S. 389 (1993), the court held that the standard for competence in pleading guilty or waiving counsel was equivalent to the standard for proceeding to trial as established in *Dusky.* Additional cases addressing criminal competency are provided in Table 14. Criminal Competencies in the United States, 2010, page 95.

competent evidence. Any evidence declared admissible by law, or, more specifically, the type of evidence that the nature of a given case requires as proof.

complainantless crime. A type of crime that typically involves a "willing victim," such as gambling, drug use and addiction, or prostitution. One result of such victimless crimes is that no one complains to the police about the illegal activity. *See also* consensual transaction; victimless crime

complaint. (1) In general criminal justice usage, any accusation that a person has committed an offense, received by or originating from a law enforcement or prosecutorial agency or received by a court. (2) In judicial process usage, a formal document submitted to the court by a prosecutor, law enforcement officer, or other person, alleging that a specified person has committed a specified offense and requesting prosecution.

Complex Systems Science (CSS). A research tool that attempts to utilize information that is disregarded by linear analysis.

TABLE 14 CRIMINAL COMPETENCIES IN THE UNITED STATES, 2010

The Competency	What This Means	Legislation
The Competency to Consent to Search and Seizure	The individual is protected from unwarranted and unnecessary search and seizure.	*Mapp v. Ohio, Katz v. United States, Florida v. Rodriguez,* 4th amendment
Competency to Stand Trial	The defendant must have sufficient mental faculties to consult with his/her lawyer with rational understanding.	*Dusky v. United States, Panetti v. Quarterman*
Competency to Waive Right to Competency		*United States v. Morin*
Competency to Confess	The suspect must know his/her rights and the confession cannot be extracted by coercion.	*Brown v. Mississippi, Miranda v. Arizona, Colorado v. Connelly*
Competency to Plead Guilty	Defendant must have sufficient mental faculties to consult with his/her lawyer with rational understanding.	*Selling v. Eyman, Godinez v. Moran, Godinez & Warden v. Moran*
Competency to Refuse an Insanity Defense	A judge cannot impose an insanity defense over the defendant's objections.	*Whalem v. United States, Frendak v. United States*
Competency to Testify	Witness must meet mental competency and credibility requirements.	Federal Rules of Evidence 601 and 508
Competency to be Sentenced and Executed	In order to be sentenced to death the convicted must be competent enough to realize his/her actions were illegal. Person cannot be insane or profoundly retarded.	*Saddler v. United States, Chavez v. United States, Ford v. Wainright, Penry v. Lynaugh*
Competency to Refuse Treatment	Individuals cannot be forcibly medicated in order to make them competent for execution.	*Perry v. Louisiana*

Compiled by Richard Porter, CSULB.

complicity. Any conduct, on the part of a person other than the chief actor in the commission of a crime, by which that person intentionally or knowingly serves to further the intent to commit the crime, aids in the commission of the crime, or assists the person who has committed the crime to avoid prosecution or escape from justice.

compounding a criminal offense. Unlawful agreement by a person to avoid or stop prosecution, or assistance in prosecution, in return for payment of money or anything else of value.

Comprehensive Crime Control Act of 1984. A major revision of Title 18 U.S. Code, the Omnibus Crime Control and Safe Streets Act of 1968, and of other federal statutes (codes) and acts containing definitions, penalties, and enforcement provisions related to crime control, including a mandatory penalty for the use of a firearm during a federal crime of violence. The 1984 act established the United States Sentencing Commission, the Bail Reform Act, the Insanity Defense Reform Act, the Sentencing Reform Act, the Comprehensive Forfeiture Act, the Controlled Substances Penalties Amendments Act, the Justice Assistance Act, an Office of Juvenile Justice and Delinquency Prevention, the Missing Children Act, the National Narcotics Act, the Victims of Crime Act, the Trademark Counterfeiting Act, the Credit Card Fraud Act, the Armed Career Criminal Act, the Act for the Prevention and Punishment of the Crime of Hostage-Taking, the Counterfeit Access Device and Computer Fraud and Abuse Act, and the President's Emergency Food Assistance Act. For further information or copies of provisions, contact the Bureau of Justice Assistance, Office of Justice Programs, 810 Seventh Street NW., 4th Floor, Washington, DC 20531. Web: http://www.ojp.usdoj.gov/BJA/.

Comprehensive Drug Abuse Prevention and Control Act (1970). Requires security and strict record keeping for certain kinds of drugs, created "schedules" for classifying drugs, empowered the government to use civil forfeiture against property used or acquired in violation of federal drug laws.

CompStat. A portmanteau combining the words comparative statistics (sometimes computer statistics). CompStat references a proactive and outcome-oriented approach to organizing and managing policing operations and is used in many law enforcement agencies in the United States and internationally.

compulsion. An abnormal urge or irresistible impulse to commit an act without the rational desire to do so. Compulsion is seen as an underlying, unconscious motive that the individual cannot control.

compurgation. A primitive form of defense against an accusation of crime, often referenced in medieval law, whereby the accused tried to establish innocence by bringing into court a sufficient number of persons who by oath testified to their belief in the innocence of the defendant. It is commonly assumed that the jury system evolved from this procedure.

Computer-Aided Dispatch (CAD). Also called computer-assisted dispatch. Electronic data processing system that assists the dispatcher by performing repetitive tasks when there is a large volume of emergency calls. It is generally used by emergency communications dispatchers and 911 operators in centralized, public-safety call centers in most U.S. jurisdictions. The system includes various modules and services, such as call input, dispatch, notes, field unit status, tracking, and resolution. Various interfaces allow verification of the address of the call and history of the location prior to the arrival of the officer.

computer crime. Also called cybercrime. A type of crime that uses the Internet or computers to carry out the offense. Early examples of computer crime include those under the general term "hacking," gaining illegal access to secure networks, and fraud through "phishing scams," such as unsolicited emails designed to trick the recipient into disclosing banking information. Today, computer crimes are generally of two types: (1) crimes targeting networks, systems, and hardware; and (2) crimes facilitated by computers, but with an independent target. Modern examples of crimes targeting networks include spam, malware, and viruses, which generally execute programs designed to disable or destroy systems when opened. A wide variety of crimes have evolved with global access to computers and the Internet. Such crimes that use computers and the Internet to carry out crimes directed at an independent target include fraud, identity theft, harassment, cyber bullying, and cyber stalking. These are examples of crimes that are relatively new and only possible via the Internet. However, various activities that are crimes independent of computer use have also been facilitated by the Internet. Such examples include dissemination of child pornography on the Internet, and the use of the Internet for drug manufacture and trafficking. Cyber terrorism, an act of terrorism committed through the Internet or computer resources, is another such example.

Computer Crime Information. The Bureau of Justice offers publications such as *Electronic Fund Transfer Systems* and *Crime and Computer Security Techniques. Computer Security Handbook, the Practitioner's Bible* and *Computer Security, the Newsletter for Computer Professionals* are published by Computer Security Institute, 43 Boston Post Rd., Northborough, MA 01532. The *Handbook* contains a listing of computer security newsletters, magazines, and journals; computer security special interest groups; and associations with computer security subgroups.

Computer Emergency Readiness Team (CERT). US-CERT is the operational arm of the National Cyber Security Division (NCSD) at the Department of Homeland Security (DHS). It is a public-private partnership, established by DHS, to serve as the federal government's cornerstone for cyber security coordination and preparedness. Address: Department of Homeland Security, Attn: NPPD/CS&C/NCSD/US-CERT, 245 Murray Lane SW, Bldg 410, Washington, DC 20598. Web: http://www.us-cert.gov/.

Computer Online Forensic Evidence Extractor (COFEE). Computer forensic software developed by Microsoft, COFEE is a USB port device that provides law enforcement with the ability to extract forensic data from Windows-based computers, including data from hard drives that have been deleted or erased. *See also* DECAF

Computer Security Institute. Founded in 1975, this is an educational membership organization for information security professionals. The organization publishes the *CSI Computer Crime and Security Survey.* Web: http://gocsi.com/.

conciliation. Bring opposing sides together in a compromise. This process originated in French civil law—there is no such process in common law—and that requires disputing parties to appear before a judge, who tries to persuade them to settle their differences and thus avoid further court proceedings. A "pre-trial conference" can be held at the court's discretion, but involving the lawyers rather than their clients, and for the purpose of simplifying, but not settling, the case. Conciliation is frequently used by U.S. courts in certain civil proceedings, such as labor disputes. In the context of labor disputes, it is generally an informal type of third-party intervention into collective bargaining over new contract terms, when the bargaining has broken down or threatens to do so. The conciliator attempts to bring the parties together and restore constructive dialog and bargaining. Conciliation is a voluntary and nonbinding process. If conciliation fails, mediation may be mandated for the disputing parties. *See also* arbitration; collective bargaining; mediation

conclusive evidence. That which is incontrovertible, either because the law does not permit it to be contradicted or because it is so strong and convincing as to overbear all proof to the contrary and establish the proposition in question beyond any reasonable doubt.

concomitant. At the same time. In criminal justice, this term generally means a mix of two or more drugs

concubinage. Informal marriage; cohabitation.

concurrent. To operate or run at the same time.

concurrent jurisdiction. A situation when more than one court is entitled to consider the same case, which often occurs in the United States because of its federal structure. The Constitution does not prohibit state courts from hearing suits involving federal questions, although Congress does so in specific instances such as national security cases and seditions. Article III of the Constitution grants federal courts jurisdiction where there is a diversity of citizenship. Where concurrent jurisdiction exists, a person can often choose whether to begin the suit in state or federal court.

concurrent sentence. When used in reference to sentences imposed upon someone convicted of crime, it means the person serves all sentences simultaneously. A concurrent sentence is composed of two or more sentences being served at the same time and imposed at the same time after conviction for more than one offense; or, a new sentence imposed upon a person already under sentence(s) for a previous offense(s), to be served at the same time as one or more of the previous sentences. If anyone should be sentenced on two charges and receive five-year sentences on each charge, to run concurrently, he or she has satisfied both after five years' imprisonment. Concurrent sentences are served at the same time; consecutive sentences are served one after the other. *See also* consecutive sentence

concurrent writs. Several writs running at the same time for the same purpose. Examples are writs in several locations for the arrest of a person whose whereabouts are unknown or writs to be served on several persons, such as codefendants.

condemn. (1) To find a person guilty or impose sentence on someone convicted of a crime; (2) to judge a property or facility unfit or unsafe; or (3) to set a property or facility apart for public use.

condemnation. (1) The judgment by which property seized for violation of revenue or other laws is declared forfeited to the state. (2) The determination of a court that a ship is unfit for service or was properly seized and held as a prize.

conditional pardon. Any pardon to which one or more conditions or qualifications are attached; conditional release. The release, by executive decision, from a federal or state correctional facility, of a prisoner who has not served his or her full sentence and whose freedom is contingent upon obeying specified rules of behavior.

conditional release. Release from incarceration contingent upon some combination of

guarantees that the offender will comply with court orders or the instructions of the parole agent or probation officer.

conditions of criminality. To render a person criminally responsible for the commission of a common law crime, that person must (a) be of sufficient age, (b) have sufficient mental capacity, (c) act voluntarily, and (d) have criminal intent.

confabulation. Spontaneous reporting of false memories; the relating of events or experiences as though they actually occurred, when in fact they are imaginary, a trait sometimes found in persons with mental illness.

confession. A statement, usually recorded, by a person who admits violation of the law; an admission of criminal activity. A confession must be given voluntarily, without force, threats, promises, or coercion being used by the officer receiving it. Under the Miranda ruling (*Miranda v. Arizona* 384 U.S. 436 (1966)), persons being interviewed must be warned of their constitutional rights, and suspects must understand and waive such rights before any incriminating statements they make in response to questions can be admitted into evidence.

confidence game. (also called confidence trick). A name for false representation to obtain money or any other thing of value, where deception is accomplished through the trust placed by the victim in the character of the offender. The term is not used in statutes. "Swindle" is sometimes used as a synonym for confidence game, but a distinction is often made. A swindle is an intentional false representation to obtain money or any other thing of value, whereas deception is accomplished through the victim's belief in the validity of some statement or object presented by the offender. Trust in a person, as opposed to belief in a statement or object, distinguishes a confidence game from a swindle.

confidential communications. Statements, made by one person to another when their relationship requires mutual truth and confidence, that the receiving person cannot be compelled to disclose. Examples include the statements made between spouses, by a client to his or her attorney, or (to a lesser extent) by patient to doctor or parishioner to priest. *See also* privileged communication

confinement. Physical restriction of a person to a clearly defined area, from which (a) he or she is lawfully forbidden to depart and (b) departure is usually constrained by architectural barriers and/or guards or other custodians. The term generally refers to the use of jails and prisons.

confinement, congregate. A method of imprisonment characterizing the early jails of Europe and of the U.S. before the reforms introduced into the Walnut Street Jail of Philadelphia in 1790. Before these reforms, the prisoners were allowed to associate with each other day and night. Owing to serious abuses, the Walnut Street Jail began keeping more hardened inmates in separate cells without work, while allowing the others to live in dormitories and work together in common workshops. Later the term was applied to the Auburn, NY, system to contrast it with the Pennsylvania, or separate, system.

confinement, solitary. A severe measure of prison discipline used in most prisons, it involves placing the prisoner in a special cell with limited access to light, recreation, programming, or amenities. Often, only a board or the floor is provided for sleep, with minimal rations of food. Historically, such confinement was characterized by removal of all stimuli, including light and contact with personnel, and prisoner could be chained to restrict his movements. Such measures are becoming less common as lawsuits have established minimum humane conditions of confinement, and as prison discipline becomes better understood.

confiscation. Government seizure of private property without compensation to the owner. This is often a consequence of conviction for crime, or because possession of the property was contrary to law, or because it was being used for an unlawful purpose. *See also* forfeiture

conflict model. A theory that views law as emerging from conflict between interest groups with differing degrees of power.

conflict model of legislation. The view that a society's laws represent the interests of its most powerful groups.

conflict of interest. In law enforcement, the situation that arises when an officer, in the discharge of his public duties, has to administer, decide, or vote on some matter in which he, or a member of his family, has a private financial interest. Anticipating such a situation, high public officials, upon being elected or appointed, sometimes divest themselves of stock or other forms of ownership in private companies or place their property in the hands of trustees. Very little legislation regulating conflict of interest has been enacted.

conflict of laws. Differing provisions of two or more laws, any or all of which can be interpreted to apply to a given case.

conflict resolution. Means by which individuals or groups with competing goals find ways of eliminating their disagreements. Conflicts can be resolved through war, negotiation, compromise, arbitration, and so forth.

confrontation. A meeting arranged between a witness and an accused for such purposes as identification, or to determine what objections the accused has to the witness.

conjugal visitation. A program in which prison inmates and their spouses are permitted to spend time together in private quarters on prison grounds, during which they may engage in sexual relations. It has been promoted as a means of reducing rape in prison, as well as of raising inmate morale and maintaining family ties. Currently, most states and the federal system prohibit conjugal visits. However, such visits are permitted in California and a few other states. *See also* family visit

connivance. (1) Guilty knowledge of, or assistance in, a crime; tacit consent to the commission of an illegal act by another; ignoring the wrongdoing of an associate, despite your knowledge that such behavior should be stopped. (2) Historically, the consent, express or implied, by one spouse to the adultery of the other.

conscience. Representing the internalization of the rules of society, conscience is experienced through feelings of anxiety and guilt that accompany anticipated or actual transgression. The two major theories of its origins are the psychoanalytic view and the behavioristic view. Self-regulation of behavior—particularly resisting temptation—is determined in large measure by conscience.

conscientious objector. One who, for reasons of conscience, refuses to participate in war or combat. In the United States, the period since World War I has seen the progressive broadening of the term to include not only members of organized religions opposed to war, as was the case in 1917, but also anyone whose "religious training and belief" need not necessarily imply belief in a Supreme Being in the conventional sense. The courts have so far refused, however, to allow "selective conscientious objection," or objection to a particular war as immoral or unjust.

consecutive sentence. A sentence that is one of two or more sentences imposed simultaneously after conviction for more than one offense, and which is served in sequence with the other sentences; or, a new sentence for a new conviction, imposed upon a person already under sentence(s) for a previous offense(s), which increases the maximum time the offender may be confined or under supervision. Consecutive sentences are served one after the other; concurrent sentences are served at the same time. If anyone should be sentenced on two charges and receive five-year sentences on each charge, to run consecutively, he or she has satisfied both after 10 years' imprisonment. *See also* concurrent sentence

consensual transaction. A mutually agreed upon exchange of goods and services that often characterizes victimless or complaintless crimes such as drugs, gambling, or prostitution.

consensus model of legislation. The view that a society's laws are based on agreement among diverse groups about basic values. *See also* conflict model

consent decree. A judgment of a court that is agreed to by all parties involved in the litigation. Although it is not a judicial sentence, it is a solemn contract among the parties and, in effect, their admission that the decree is a just determination of their rights upon the real and proven facts of the case. Consent decrees are especially common in the U.S. prison system, as many states operate prisons under decrees regarding such prison conditions as overcrowding, unsatisfactory food, and uneven disciplinary procedures. *See also* decree, special master

consent, implied. Consent that is not expressly given but that is inferred from actions or is prescribed by law. Several states have laws, for example, that provide that when the operator of a motor vehicle obtains a driver's license, he waives his right to object to an intoxication test if he should at a later date be charged with driving while intoxicated. This type of statute is generally referred to as an implied consent law.

consenting adult laws. In its 1986 *Bowers v. Hardwick* decision, the U.S. Supreme Court upheld the right of states to regulate adult consensual sexual behavior. The court overturned *Bowers* in *Lawrence v. Texas* (2003), holding that such laws are unconstitutional. Today, the argument is generally directed towards drug use and prostitution, which usually involve consenting adult parties, and which are still illegal in most jurisdictions.

consent of the victim. Any voluntary agreement of a victim to an offending party's action that the victim knowingly gives. Victim consent can be a criminal defense, provided that: (a) the victim was capable of giving consent; (b) the offense was "consentable" (murder and statutory rape are not considered consentable crimes); (c) consent was not obtained by fraud; and (d) the person giving consent had authority to do so. Recent research has examined contradictions of consent laws, pointing out, for example, that consent legalizes aggravated assault in some contexts (e.g., boxing match) but not others (e.g., sadomasochistic sexual practices).

consent search. Voluntary consent of the legal owner of premises or property for it to be searched. A person, place, or piece of property may be lawfully searched by an officer of the law if the owner gives his free and voluntary consent. However, owners may not always have the legal right of possession to all their property. For example, a hotel owner cannot consent to a search of a room currently occupied by a hotel guest. In that case, the guest, as the legal possessor of the room, must consent to a search.

conservative. A term used to describe a political or social position that holds that individuals act with free choice, based on free will, so that each person is seen to be responsible for his or her own actions or inactions. In the conservative view, crime is basically the result of moral failure rather than of political or social factors. This view emphasizes punitive punishment as a crime deterrent. Conservatives thus generally support more prisons, stiffer penalties, and the imposition of capital punishment.

consolateur. A manual or electric dildo, or penis-shaped tool used in erotic play.

consolidated laws. A compilation of all the laws of a state that are in force, arranged according to subject matter. *See also* code

conspiracy. A combination or agreement between two or more persons to commit an unlawful act, whether that act be the final object of the combination, or only a means to the final end, and whether that act be a crime, or an act hurtful to the public, a class of persons, or an individual. The offense is usually divided into three categories: (a) an act where the end to be attained is in itself a crime; (b) an act where the object is lawful, but the means by which it is to be attained are unlawful; (c) an act where the object is to do an injury to a third person or a group, even though if the wrong were inflicted by

a single individual it would be a civil wrong rather than a crime. An overt act is generally necessary. Conspiracies are misdemeanors, unless made felonies by statute.

constitution. A set of rules outlining the structure, procedures, powers, duties and functions of government. The fundamental law of a state, consisting of: (a) the basic political principles that ought to be followed in conducting the government; (b) the organization of government; (c) the vesting of powers in the principal officers and agencies; (d) the limitations on the extent of, and methods of exercising, these powers; and (e) the relationship between the government and the people who live under it. The constitution may be simply an uncollected body of legislative acts, judicial decisions, and political precedents and customs, like that of the United Kingdom. At the other extreme, a constitution may be a single document drafted and promulgated at a definite date by an authority of higher competence than that which makes ordinary laws, like constitutions in the United States. It may be endorsed by the courts as superior to statutes that conflict with it, as in the United States and a few other countries, or its preservation may be entrusted to political authorities. In the latter case, which is still the usual one in Europe, a written constitution stands as a convenient standard by which the people may judge the conduct of their government and the degree of its respect for their liberties. Constitutions are sometimes classified as (a) written or unwritten, according to whether or not their written material is presented in consolidated and systematic form; or (b) as flexible or rigid, according to whether they can be amended by legislative enactment or require a more complicated procedure of proposal and ratification by different authorities. *See also* state constitutions

constitutional court. (1) A court created by or authorized under a specific constitution. (2) A court in the U.S. federal judicial system, established under Article III of the Constitution, whose judges are entitled to tenure during good behavior and to salaries that cannot be decreased. The U.S. Supreme Court of Appeals and district courts were created as constitutional courts, and the same rank was accorded by Congress in 1946 to the Court of Claims, the Court of Customs and Patent Appeals, and, in 1956, to the Customs Court, all three of which previously had been legislative courts.

constitutionalism. The doctrine that the power to govern should be limited by definite and enforceable principles of political organization and procedural regularity embodied in the fundamental law or custom, so that basic constitutional rights of individuals and groups will not be infringed.

constitutional law. The body of legal rules and principles, usually formulated in a written constitution, which define the nature and limits of governmental power, as well as the rights and duties of individuals in relation to the state and its governing organs, and which are interpreted and extended by courts of final jurisdiction exercising the power of judicial review.

constitutional rights. The rights of citizens as guaranteed by the United States Constitution. *See also* bill of rights

constructive contempt. A contempt, committed out of the presence of the court, which does not involve a failure to appear in court or other official judicial body as ordered by the court. *See also* contempt of court

Consumer Bill of Rights. In 1962, President John F. Kennedy presented a speech to the United States Congress in which he outlined basic consumer rights, which later formed the basis of the Consumer Bill of Rights. These include: (1) The Right to Be Safe—consumers should be protected against injuries caused by products when used as intended; (2) The Right to Choose Freely—consumers should have a variety of options provided by different companies from which to choose; (3) The Right to Be Heard—consumers can voice complaints and concerns about a product; (4) The Right to Be Informed—businesses should provide consumers with enough information to make

informed product choices; (5) The Right to Education—consumers should have access to programs and information to make better decisions in the marketplace; (6) The Right to Service—consumers should be treated with courtesy and respect, and have the right to refuse services.

consumer fraud. Deception of the public with respect to the cost, quality, purity, safety, durability, performance, effectiveness, dependability, availability, or adequacy of choice relating to goods or services offered or furnished and with respect to credit or other matters relating to terms of sales. Deliberately deceptive practices employed during operation of seemingly legitimate commercial transactions, resulting in consumer financial loss. As a generic term, consumer fraud indicates the focus of crime prevention or law enforcement activities associated with consumer affairs agencies. Particular instances of consumer fraud are prosecuted as types of fraud designated in statutes under a variety of names. In the United States, the Federal Trade Commission (FTC) tracks consumer fraud. Consumers reported $680 million in fraud losses in 2005. Internet-related complaints accounted for nearly half of all reported fraud complaints, with identity theft as the most common complaint filed with FTC.

Consumer Product Safety Commission (CPSC). Created by the Consumer Product Safety Act of 1972, CPSC has jurisdiction over commercial products, enabling it to establish performance standards, product testing, warning labels, and to force product recalls. The agency is charged with "protecting the public from unreasonable risks of serious injury or death from thousands of types of consumer products under the agency's jurisdiction. The CPSC is committed to protecting consumers and families from products that pose a fire, electrical, chemical, or mechanical hazard or can injure children." Address: U.S. Consumer Product Safety Commission, 4330 East West Highway, Bethesda, MD 20814. Web: http://www.cpsc.gov/.

consumer protection. Local, state, and federal laws and regulations governing various aspects of business. Examples of federal consumer protection laws are the Sherman and Clayton Antitrust Acts, the Food and Drug Act, and the Truth in Lending Act. In addition, administrative laws and regulations are established by agencies such as the Federal Trade Commission and the Pure Food and Drug Administration, which are charged specifically with regulating commercial activities. The Federal Trade Commission has developed a specialized agency, the Bureau of Consumer Protection, which works to "prevent fraud, deception, and unfair business practices in the marketplace." Industry's efforts to protect consumers are exercised via trade associations, chambers of commerce, and better business bureaus through the adoption of codes of conduct and product standards. Consumer advocates study industry practices and product performance to determine abuses against which the consumer should be protected. Their chief weapon is carefully documented publicity that is adverse to a company or a product. Consumer movements are sometimes formalized: delegates meet and attempt to exert pressure for legislation to protect the consumer.

consumers' rights movement. Action begun by public groups and individuals in the 1960s and 1970s to secure standards of safety and honesty in the public marketplace. The movement in its current form was begun with the publication of Ralph Nader's *Unsafe at Any Speed* (1965), a critique of the Corvair automobile. The disclosures in Nader's report struck a spark, and the public began to demand legislation to protect their rights as consumers. Congress responded with such legislation as the Fair Packaging and Labeling Act of 1966, the Toy Safety Act of 1969, and the Poison Prevention Packaging Act of 1970. In 1972 the Consumer Product Safety Commission was created.

contact surveillance. A practice more often employed in the 1970s and 1980s, the use of tracer preparations which adhere to the hands, other body areas, or clothing of a suspect when he or she comes in contact with it.

containment theory. Theory of criminality, especially juvenile delinquency, which postulates that delinquency and crime occur to the extent that a breakdown occurs in "inner" and "outer" constraining or restraining forces of society. Inner restraints consist of moral, religious, and ethical values, while outer restraints derive from family, educators, and other authority figures.

contemporaneous. Occurring at the same time as something else. In an arrest, it is something that happens at the time of the arrest or soon thereafter and is part of a continuous, uninterrupted lawful investigation.

contempt of Congress. The refusal to answer pertinent questions before a congressional committee when summoned, or to otherwise obstruct the work of the United States Congress, its committees, or subcommittees. Contempt of Congress is a misdemeanor, punishable by a fine of at least $100 (up to $100,000) and imprisonment from 1 to 12 months. To cite a person for contempt, the committee concerned must introduce a resolution into the House or Senate. A simple majority is needed for approval, and, if approved, the matter is referred to a U.S. attorney for presentation to a grand jury and prosecution in a federal court. Contempt of Congress was first ruled a criminal offense in 1857.

contempt of court. Intentionally obstructing a court in the administration of justice, acting in a way calculated to lessen its authority or dignity, or failing to obey its lawful orders. The term applies to disobedience of a court order, disruptive acts, and the use of objectionable language in a courtroom. One need not be a party to an action pending before a court to be held in contempt. Contempts are classified in two ways: civil or criminal and direct or constructive. Direct contempt is committed in the presence of the court; constructive contempt is committed elsewhere. Civil contempt is a failure to do something ordered for the benefit of one's adversary, while criminal contempt is a failure to act as ordered for the court's benefit.

contingency fee. A fee charged for a lawyer's services, contingent upon a successful outcome. The fee is paid only if the attorney secures a successful or favorable settlement, generally calculated as a percentage of the client's total recovery. The American Bar Association discourages the use of contingency fee arrangements in family law and criminal actions; thus, such arrangements are prohibited in most states. However, contingency fee arrangements are common practice in personal injury and other types of civil litigation.

continuance. Adjournment or postponement of a case or action before a court, either to a later date or indefinitely.

continuing criminal enterprise. The Bureau of Justice Statistics defines this as "a felony committed as part of an ongoing series of violations, which is undertaken by a person in concert with five or more other persons with respect to whom such person occupies a position of organizer, a supervisory position, or any other position of management, and from whom which such person obtains substantial income or resources."

continuous crime. A crime consisting of continuous violations, such as possession of stolen property or carrying a concealed weapon. The statute of limitations does not begin to operate on such a crime until the person discontinues the acts constituting the violation.

contraband. Goods, the possession of which is illegal, especially smuggled goods.

contraband, possession in prison. An inmate's possession of drugs, weapons, or currency is prohibited in all U.S. prisons and jails. Punishments are prescribed in Title 18, U.S. Code provides punishment for federal prison inmates found to possess, or anyone who provides or attempts to provide an inmate with contraband, including fines and imprisonment up to 20 years, depending on the nature of the violation. Title 18 identifies the following contraband for federal prisons: (a) a firearm, ammunition, or destructive device; (b) any other weapon or object that may be used as a weapon or as a means of facilitating escape; (c) a narcotic drug as defined in the Controlled Substances Act; (d) a controlled substance other than a narcotic drug or alcoholic beverage; or (e) United States or foreign currency.

contract. A legally enforceable agreement between two or more parties, under the terms of which, for valid consideration, the parties agree to perform, or refrain from performing, some act. Most commonly, a contract is written. However, verbal contracts are also enforceable provided the parties had a shared understanding or a "meeting of the minds."

contract law enforcement. A form of regional law enforcement in which small communities contract with their county or an adjacent city for police services.

contract system. A system of prison labor in which an employer contracts for the use of prisoners at or near the prison, which continues to provide inmates with food, clothing, and general supervision. The system began at the end of the eighteenth century and for a time was the most popular form of prison labor. Opposition of labor unions and private manufacturers, which objected to the unfair competition provided with cheap inmate labor costs, and the abuses caused by unscrupulous prison officials led to the rapid decline of the system. Few prisoners are employed under this system. More commonly, inmate labor is used to manufacture goods used by the state. *See also* Federal Prison Industries

contractual rights. Property or other rights secured under a contract. The courts afford protection for such rights, so that an injured party to a contract can sue for damages any other party to the contract who has failed to fulfill his or her covenanted obligations. Another legal remedy is a writ of specific performance, to secure the fulfillment of contractual rights. Contracts, and rights thereunder, are protected by the contract clause of the Constitution, as well as by its due process clauses against impairment by state legislatures. However, contractual rights are safeguarded no more than other rights against the exercise of a state's prerogatives of eminent domain, taxation, and police power.

contravention. (1) A process of social interaction, midway between competition and conflict, consisting of a wide range of activities, from mere withholding of cooperation to reproaching, disparaging, thwarting, betraying, or conniving against another, but always falling short of the use or the threat of violence. (2) In the French penal code, offenses are divided into crimes, delits, and contraventions in the order of their diminishing seriousness. This classification does not correspond exactly with that of the English common law—treason, felony, and misdemeanor. Under French law contraventions are violations of police regulations.

contributing to the delinquency of a minor. The offense committed by an adult who in any manner causes, encourages, or aids a juvenile to commit a crime or status offense. *See also* status offense

contributory negligence. A common law rule that any lack of care on the part of an injured employee relieves the employer of liability for damages. It has been modified by statute in most states in favor of the rule of comparative negligence, by which the employer is relieved of responsibility only in proportion to the relative negligence of himself and the employee.

Controlled Substances Act. Title II of the Comprehensive Drug Abuse and Control Act of 1970. It brought together under one law most of the drug controls that had been created since the Harrison Act in 1914; categorized certain substances into five "schedules"; and defined the offenses and penalties associated with the illegal manufacturing, distributing, and dispensing of any drug in each schedule. The act was amended by the Comprehensive Crime Control Act of 1984, which redefined the schedules and provided penalties for distribution in or near schools. The act also established the Dangerous Drug

Diversion Control Act of 1984. *See also* narcotic drugs

contumacious. Willful or obstinate disobedience to a court or other authority; insubordination.

conversion. In law, taking the property of another and using it for one's own benefit, or changing property from real property to personal, or the reverse.

conveyance. A written instrument transferring property, or title to property, from one person to another.

convict. (1) To find guilty. (2) A person found guilty of a crime or misdemeanor. (3) Any person confined to a state or federal prison under sentence of more than a year for the commission of crime. The term does not apply to persons confined in city and county jails.

convict code. A value system among prison inmates that is heavily influenced by the thieves' code, which includes these precepts: Do your own time, never snitch on another prisoner, maintain dignity and respect, help other convicts, leave the majority of other prisoners alone, and show no weakness.

conviction. The judgment of a court, based on the verdict of a jury or judicial officer or on the guilty or *nolo contendere* plea of a defendant, that the latter is guilty of the offense(s) with which he or she has been charged.

convict labor. Work performed by inmates of penal institutions, either under contract with private parties or directly for the state, the products of which were forbidden in interstate commerce by an act of Congress effective in 1934. *See also* contract system

Cooper, D. B. The man who boarded a Northwest Orient Airlines jet on November 24, 1971, and then hijacked it. After receiving $200,000 in ransom and four parachutes, Cooper jumped from the jet over a rural area of Washington state. Some argue the hijacker did not survive the jump: Expert meteorologists and skydivers indicated that when the skyjacker hit the freezing air at 200 miles per hour, his eyes would have been immediately blackened, his clothing torn off, his body thrown into a severe tumble, and that he would have been unable to open his parachute. Others argue that the hijacker used a "dummy parachute" as his primary escape, resulting in his certain death. To date, the suspect has not be identified, nor remains found; however, in 1980, 8-year old Brian Ingram found $5,880 of the ransom money (verified by serial number) on the banks of a river outside Vancouver, Washington. Out of nearly one thousand possible suspects reported to the FBI, the only remaining viable suspect is William Gossett, a college instructor from Utah who died in 2003. Before his death, Gossett reportedly confessed to his two sons, a lawyer, and a judge that he was the infamous hijacker, and that the ransom is stored in a safe deposit box in Vancouver, B.C.

coprolalia. Medical term for uncontrolled, involuntary use of obscene language. Sudden overuse by an individual may be a symptom of mental illness, and compulsive use may occur involuntarily in victims of Gilles de la Tourette syndrome.

corprophagia. Consumption of feces, most commonly by dogs or other animals. Can also refer to human consumption of feces. This term is devoid of sexual arousal, as opposed to coprophilia, which is sexual pleasure derived from feces (although not necessarily eaten). *See also* coprophilia, Cleveland steamer

coprophilia (also called scatophilia or scat). Paraphilia involving sexual pleasure from feces. *See also* corprophagia, Cleveland steamer

coprophobia. The abnormal, persistent fear of excreting or of excreta.

copulatio analis. Sexual activity involving insertion of the penis into the anus. Historically called pederasty, or anal sodomy.

copycat syndrome. The tendency of individuals to commit criminal acts that imitate those of others, either compulsively or to avoid detection. The so-called copycat effect is also thought to lead to multiple suicides in a given community after one individual has killed him- or herself. *See also* Werther effect

copyright. A legal protection afforded to "original works of authorship," such as writing, music, and art. The 1976 United States Copyright Act declares that a work written, or fixed in some tangible form, is protected by statutory copyright. The term of copyright continues from the moment of creation in a fixed tangible manner for 50 years after the author's death. Unpublished works created before January 1, 1978, enjoy the same copyright as those created after this date. Formerly, works were copyrighted for terms of 28 years; therefore the Copyright Act stipulates that the work of a deceased author whose work was copyrighted after September 19, 1906, and was copyrighted again after September 19, 1962, or was in its final year of copyright protection in 1977, is automatically protected further so that the total length of copyright protection (including its renewal period) will not exceed 75 years. A copyright held by a living author, prior to January 1, 1978, in its first 28-year term must be renewed in its 27th year of copyright (unlike new works under the 1976 Copyright Act, which require no renewal), but its renewal term will be for 47 years, thus bringing the total copyright protection to 75 years. This renewal is not automatic but must be applied for. A work that has been copyrighted for its initial term and has not been renewed and has thus fallen into the public domain cannot be afforded any further copyright protection.

Corallo, Anthony "Tony Ducks." (1913–2000) Boss of the Lucchese crime family, convicted and sentenced to 100 years in prison in 1985. Corallo died in federal prison in 2000. *See also* Mafia; Mafia Commission Trial

corneali complex. The incestuous desire of a mother for her son.

coroner. From the Latin *coronae*, or of the crown, an official who performs specified duties in investigating cases of death where there are questionable circumstances or where the deceased was unattended by a physician at the time of death. This office of coroner originated in England in the twelfth century and has been adopted in most of the United States. Usually there is one elected coroner in each county. In some states the coroner has been replaced by a medical examiner.

corporal punishment. Deliberate infliction of pain or physical punishment as a consequence for offense; commonly called "spanking." Corporal punishment of minors by their parents is permitted in all 50 states. Corporal punishment in schools, commonly called "paddling," is permitted in a few states and is most commonly associated with parochial school discipline. By the twentieth century, judicial corporal punishment, or state-sponsored flogging of criminals, had been abolished. The pillory, an upright wooden frame used to confine offenders and allow the public to pelt them, has been virtually extinct in the United States for more than 150 years.

corporate crime. Illegal act(s) committed by a corporate body or by executives and managers acting on behalf of a corporation. Such acts include consumer fraud, insider trading and antitrust violations, environmental damage, violation of health and safety laws, and labor exploitation. In 2007, the UK passed legislation creating the offense of corporate manslaughter. *See also* white-collar crime

corporate manslaughter. In some jurisdictions, notably England, Wales, Northern Ireland, and Scotland, a corporation can be criminally prosecuted for manslaughter.

Corporation for National and Community Service (CNCS). Formed in 1993, CNCS merged the offices of ACTION and the Commission on National and Community Service to connect Americans with opportunities to give back to their communities. NCSC coordinates various voluntary service programs within the federal government, including SeniorCorps, AmeriCorps,

Volunteers in Service to America (AmeriCorps VISTA), National Civilian Community Corps (AmeriCorps NCCC), and Learn and Serve America, Through these programs, NCSC also administers the Foster Grandparents Program, Senior Companions, and the Retired Senior Volunteers Program (RSVP), Address: 1201 New York Avenue, NW, Washington, DC 20525. Web: http://www.nationalservice.gov/.

corpus delicti (Lat., lit, body of the crime). The facts constituting or proving a crime, composed of (a) the act and (b) the criminal agency producing it. In a homicide case, it must be shown that a human was killed and that the killing was done by another human being. A suicide or accidental death does not satisfy the proof of *corpus delicti*. Loosely, the term also means the victim's body in a murder case.

corrections. A generic term that includes all governmental agencies, facilities, programs, procedures, personnel, services and techniques concerned with the intake, custody, confinement, supervision, treatment, or presentencing or predisposition investigation of alleged or adjudicated adult offenders, juveniles, delinquents, or status offenders. *See also* National Institute of Corrections; status offense

correctional agency. A federal, state, or local criminal or juvenile justice agency, under a single administrative authority, of which the principal functions are the intake, screening, supervision, custody, confinement, treatment, or presentencing or predisposition investigation of alleged or adjudicated adult offenders, youthful offenders, delinquents, or status offenders.

Correctional Association, American. Founded in 1945, the group's goals are to increase the effectiveness, expertise, and skills of educators and administrators providing services to adult and juvenile students in correctional settings, and to improve the quality of educational programs and services. Address: 206 N. Washington Street, Alexandria, VA 22314; Web: http://www.aca.org/.

correctional client. A person, generally an inmate, probationer, or parolee, who has been convicted of a crime and sentenced to correctional treatment.

correctional day program. A publicly financed and operated, nonresidential educational or treatment program in which persons required by a judicial officer must participate. Typically, offenders report to the program each day for educational services, treatment, drug testing, vocational assistance, or other rehabilitative intervention.

correctional facility. A building or part thereof, set of buildings, or area enclosing a set of buildings or structures operated by a governmental agency for the physical custody, or custody and treatment, of persons sentenced or subject to criminal proceedings.

Correctional Services of Canada. The agency of the Canadian federal government that has responsibility for providing correctional services to all offenders sentenced to serve two or more years in a correctional institution. National headquarters at: 340 Laurier Avenue West, Ottawa, Ontario, K1A 0P9. Web: http://www.csc-scc.gc.ca/.

corrections statistics, history of. In 1850 the federal government, in cooperation with the states as a part of the Seventh Decennial Census, initiated a count of prisoners in 32 states and the territories of Minnesota, New Mexico, Oregon, and Utah. Between 1850 and 1870, U.S. marshals administered the census of prisoners as part of a special schedule of social statistics. The 1880 report indicated there were 61 state prisoners per 100,000 residents. By 1890 Nevada had the highest per capita rate among the states, 203, and Wyoming had the lowest at 16; New York had 136 prisoners per 100,000, and California had 169. In 1910 the introduction of the indeterminate sentence was described in prisoner statistics: 21 percent of state prisoners on January 1 had received such sentences. The 1923 report showed that more than half of the prison admissions were under indeterminate sentences, and observed that such sentences resulted in wide ranges between minimum and maximum sentences and disparities in setting release dates. In 1926 the Bureau of the Census began the annual collection of prisoner statistics, and that year's report described the goal of the collection of data: "to show the application of penal policies for various classes of offenders and in different parts of the country." That first annual report in 1926 provided information by jurisdiction on admissions, releases, sentences and time served, inmates under sentence of death, recidivism, and crowding. In 1950 data collection was transferred from the Bureau of the Census to the Bureau of Prisons in the Department of Justice, and in 1971 to the predecessor agency of the Bureau of Justice Statistics (BJS), the National Criminal Justice Information and Statistics Service of the Law Enforcement Assistance Administration (LEAA). LEAA added the statistical series on local jails (1970), parole (1976), and probation (1979). In 1979 the first annual report on parole and probation appeared, published by BJS. BJS remains the primary organization responsible for disseminating crime statistics in the U.S.

corrupt. (1) Evil, depraved; debased. (2) in criminal justice, the practice of taking bribes; dishonest. *See also* Operation Greylord

Corrupt Practices Acts. State and federal statutes aimed at eliminating campaign and election abuses. The basis of modern federal legislation is the act of 1910, amended in 1911 and 1925, the scope of which was widened with the Federal Election Campaign Act of 1971.

corruption. In the broadest sense, any illegal act by a sworn peace officer, including all violations of fiduciary trust and the professional codes of conduct and ethics. Specific examples include taking bribes, selling favors, accepting gifts, and committing, aiding, or abetting criminal behavior.

corruption of blood. The legal consequence, under common law, of conviction of treason or felony, according to which the person so convicted could neither possess nor transmit by inheritance any property, rank, or title.

Costello, Frank (1891–1973). Called the "Prime Minister" of the New York Mafia in the 1920s, this Italian-born immigrant was soldier, consigliere, and boss of the Genovese crime family. This criminal empire spanned the nation and engaged in bootlegging, bribery, extortion, gambling, robbery, theft, narcotics, and murder. Costello was called to testify before a senate hearing in 1951, and his defiant attitude during testimony yielded charges for contempt of court and tax evasion, for which he served prison time. Costello survived an assassination attempt following his release from prison in 1957. He retired from crime in the mid 1960s and died of heart attack in 1973. In 1974, Costello's mausoleum was bombed, in retaliation for an old feud. *See also* Luciano, Lucky; mafia; Siegel, Bugsy

coulrophobia. The abnormal or exaggerated fear of clowns.

Council of State Governments. Founded in 1933, the council operates the States Information Center "to assist state officials with up-to-date research pertaining to problems within state government jurisdictions." Address: 2760 Research Park Drive, P.O. Box 11910, Lexington, KY 40578; Web: http://www.csg.org/.

counsel. Legal assistance from one trained in law; an attorney.

count. *See* charge

count, prisoner. (1) In published summary data, usually the number of inmates present in a given facility or facility system on a regular, specified day of the year, month, or quarter. (2) In management usage, the daily, weekly, or other periodic tally of inmates present in a particular facility.

counterfeiting. The manufacture or attempted manufacture of a copy or imitation of a negotiable instrument with value set by law or convention, or the possession of such a copy without authorization, with the intent to defraud by claiming the genuineness of the copy. In statutes, counterfeiting is included with the definition of forgery. Where a distinction is made, it rests on the fact that counterfeiting presupposes the prior existence of an officially issued item of value that provides a model for the perpetrator. Examples include currency, coins, postage stamps, ration stamps, food stamps (under the jurisdiction of the U.S. Department of Agriculture), bearer bonds, and so forth. This preexisting model is absent in a forgery.

counterfeiting, trademark. The Trademark Counterfeiting Act of 1984 provides that (a) whoever intentionally traffics or attempts to traffic in goods or services and knowingly uses a counterfeit mark on or in connection with such goods or services shall, if an individual, be fined not more than $250,000 or imprisoned not more than five years or both, and, if other than an individual, be fined not more than $1 million; and in the case of a second offense for an individual, be fined not more than $1 million or imprisoned not more than 15 years or both, and, if other than an individual, be fined not more than $5 million; and (b) upon a determination by a preponderance of the evidence that any articles in the possession of a defendant in a prosecution under this section bear counterfeit marks, the United States may obtain an order for the destruction of such articles. In a prosecution, the defendant shall have the burden of proof, by a preponderance of the evidence, of any such affirmative defense. The term *counterfeit mark* means a spurious mark—one that is identical with, or substantially indistinguishable from, a mark registered for those goods or services on the principal register in the U.S. Patent and Trademark Office and in use, whether or not the defendant knew such mark was so registered, and the use of which is likely to cause confusion, to cause mistake, or to deceive. In addition, defendants are prosecuted under the Lanham Act, which provides for the registration and protection of trademarks used in commerce, carries out the provisions of certain international conventions, and has other purposes, as approved on July 5, 1946.

counter methods. Techniques employed to reduce exposure of information due to counter surveillance. Such methods can include physical distribution of counter surveillance device, use of electronic equipment to disable listening devices ("bugs"), leaving the unsecure area, or using the counter surveillance device to provide misdirection or misinformation.

counter surveillance. Efforts by police officers, investigators, and others to determine if anyone is monitoring their activities, for example, "sweeping for bugs." If such monitoring is found, counter measures are generally employed to reduce the exposure of information. The term counter surveillance can be used in regards to police departments detecting surveillance by nonauthorized personnel (unauthorized listening to police scanners), and by criminals detecting police surveillance (finding police bugs or wiretaps).

county. A geographical and political division of the state, in all states except Louisiana, where a county is termed a parish.

county court. A body, formerly composed of all the justices of the peace within a county, which was both the chief county administrative board and a court lower than the circuit court. At present it may have purely administrative or judicial functions or combinations of both, depending on the laws of particular states.

county judges—criminal court. A criminal court of general jurisdiction in Canada which sits without a jury to hear indictable offenses.

coup d'état. A sudden, forcible seizure of power by a political faction. Statisticians contend that Bolivia, since it became a sovereign country in 1825, has had 189 coups d'état.

court. Agency or unit of the judicial branch of government, authorized or established by statute or constitution and consisting of one or more judicial officers, which has the authority to decide upon cases, controversies in law, and disputed matters of fact brought before it. Court, judge, and bench are used interchangeably in many contexts; often the court means the judge or the judicial officer. The term includes: (a) trial court, of which the primary function is to hear and decide cases; (b) court of limited (special) jurisdiction, a trial court having original jurisdiction over only that subject matter specifically assigned to it by law (these courts go by such names as municipal court, justice court, magistrate court, family court, probate court, and traffic court); (c) court of general jurisdiction, a trial court having original jurisdiction over all subject matter not specifically assigned to a court of limited jurisdiction (these courts are frequently given jurisdiction over certain kinds of appeal matters and are usually called superior courts, district courts, or circuit courts); (d) appellate court, of which the primary function is to review the judgments of other courts and administrative agencies; (e) intermediate appellate court, of which the primary function is to review the judgments of trial courts and the decisions of administrative agencies and whose decisions are in turn usually reviewable by a higher appellate court in the same state; and (f) court of last resort, an appellate court having final jurisdiction over appeals within a given state.

court administrator. The official responsible for supervising and performing administrative tasks for a given court(s).

court, adolescent. An experimental court designed to deal with persons between the ages of 16 and 18 or 21, when moral responsibility seems to have matured. Its procedure follows the same informal pattern as the juvenile court, and probation and other protective services are used extensively. Chicago and New York City have experimented with this type of court, but opinions differ as to its value.

court calendar. The court schedule; the list of events comprising the daily or weekly work of a court, including the assignment of the time and place for each hearing or other item of business or the list of matters which will be reviewed in a given court term.

court, canonical. The ecclesiastical court of the Middle Ages, to which both criminal cases and those involving domestic and marital law were referred.

court clerk. An elected or appointed court officer responsible for maintaining the written records of the court and for supervising or performing the clerical tasks necessary for conducting judicial business; also, any employee of a court whose principal duty is to assist the court clerk.

court, criminal. A court where criminal, as opposed to civil, cases are tried.

court decision. In popular usage, any official determination made by a judicial officer; in special judicial usages, any of several specific kinds of determinations made by particular courts. A decision may be called a judgment, decree, finding, court order, or opinion.

Court Delay Reduction Program. A number of efforts to reduce both criminal and civil court delays through the exercise of rulemaking powers and statewide case reporting systems.

court disposition. The judicial decision terminating proceedings in a case before judgment is reached; the judgment. The data representing the outcome of judicial proceedings and the manner in which it was reached.

court, domestic relations. Also called Family Court. A court having jurisdiction over cases involving divorce, dissolution, annulment, child custody and support, child abuse and dependency, and juvenile court. The general philosophy of such courts in dealing with delinquency is that the family is a unit and that the problem is frequently a familial rather than an individual one. Domestic relations courts exist only in our larger cities, where sufficient cases arise to warrant a separate court.

Court Employment Project. Founded in 1967, and also called the Manhattan Court Employment Project until 1970. It provided counseling, education, employment, and legal and vocational services to young offenders (ages 14–21) involved with the New York City Criminal and Supreme courts.

Court for the Correction of Errors. An early form of appeals court, it was the court of last resort in New York until the state's 1846 constitution, which replaced the court with the New York Court of Appeals.

courthouse. The building at the county seat that houses the principal offices of county government and provides for courts.

court, inferior. A court of primary and/or limited jurisdiction that tries cases of a minor nature. It is generally not a court of record; that is, no record of its proceedings is made unless one is specifically requested by the parties. Inferior courts usually try misdemeanor cases and hold preliminary hearings or examinations. Also called lower courts, they act as committing agencies for higher courts. Examples of inferior courts include justice of the peace, police courts, mayor's court, and municipal or city courts.

court, juvenile. A court dealing with youthful offenders or juvenile dependents and with adults who contribute to the delinquency of children. Depending on the state, the jurisdiction of such courts is limited to children under 16, under 18, or in some cases, young persons under 21. In general, juvenile offenses are transferred to the regular criminal court. However, minor juvenile offenders, sometimes called juvenile delinquents, are considered wards of the court and are presumed to be treated as children needing help rather than as guilty persons requiring punishment. Hearings are usually private and there is generally no trial, although a number of states paradoxically allow a trial if demanded by the child's parents However, there are no jury trials in juvenile court. *See* Table 15. Comparison of Adult and Juvenile Court Terms, page 112

TABLE 15   COMPARISON OF ADULT AND JUVENILE COURT TERMS

Adult Court Term	Juvenile Court Term
Arrested	Detained
Charged	Referred to court
Indicted	Petitioned
Defendant	Respondent (sometimes called a "ward")
Trial	Hearing
Verdict	Finding
Conviction	Adjudication (positive finding, affirmative finding)
Sentence	Disposition
Probation	Probation
Incarcerated	Placement
Jail	Juvenile hall
Prison	Youth authority, training center, youth camp (varies by jurisdiction)
Parole	Aftercare

court, magistrate's. In most cities, the lowest court of original jurisdiction in criminal cases. Suspects apprehended by the police are first arraigned in magistrate's court, where evidence is examined. If, in the mind of the magistrate, the evidence is sufficient, the suspect is bound over to the grand jury or some other specialized court, and bail is set to ensure the suspect's appearance at trial. If the offense is a minor one, such as violation of a city ordinance, the magistrate may have the power to make a judgment and set the penalty.

court-martial. A tribunal in each branch of the armed services, composed of officers and enlisted persons, that tries armed forces personnel or others accused of violating military law under the provisions of the Uniform Code of Military Justice. A general court-martial may try any offense; special and summary courts-martial have limited jurisdiction. In the American armed services, a court-martial verdict may, in some instances, be appealed to the U.S. Court of Military Appeals, which is composed of civilian judges, but not to the civil courts. The first U.S. court-martial was held on August 24, 1676, in Newport, RI. The first court-martial trial at which enlisted men were allowed to sit as members was convened on February 3, 1949, at Fort Bragg, NC, and consisted of four sergeants and five officers.

Court of Assizes. (1) Historically, a periodic traveling court. (2) The highest court of original criminal jurisdiction in France and the only court in which a jury considers the case against the accused and assists in rendering a verdict. (3) A temporary court in Belgium that is charged with hearing criminal cases. (4) A temporary criminal court of England and Wales, abolished with the Courts Act of 1971.

court of chancery. A court of equity. Formerly existed in England and still exists in some U.S. states. *See also* equity jurisdiction

court of common pleas. A court of original jurisdiction for trials according to common law.

court of equity. A court that administers justice according to the principles of equity. *See also* court of chancery

court of errors and appeals. An early form of appeals court, it was the court of last resort in New Jersey until the state's 1947 constitution, which replaced the court with the New Jersey Supreme Court

court of general sessions. In certain states, a court of general original jurisdiction.

court of primary jurisdiction. A court that has authority to hear (try) cases at the point of origin.

Court of Queen's Bench. The highest court of general jurisdiction in Alberta Canada, which sits with a jury.

court of record. A court in which a complete and permanent record of all proceedings or specified types of proceedings are kept. Felony trial courts are courts of record. Trial proceedings are supposed to be recorded verbatim. The record, usually in the form of a stenotype representation but sometimes stored on audiotape, is not necessarily transcribed. The court reporter may store such material in its original form, which will not be converted into a typed transcript unless the record pertaining to a case is requested.

Court of Star Chamber. An English court originally created to prevent the obstruction of justice in the lower courts. Its powers were expanded to an unreasonable degree, and it was finally abolished.

court order. A mandate, command, or direction issued by a judicial officer in the exercise of his or her judicial authority.

court-ordered release from prison. A provisional exit, by judicial authority and from a prison facility, of a prisoner who has not served his or her full sentence and whose freedom is conditional upon an appeal, a special writ, or other legal proceeding.

court packing. A term first used to describe President Franklin Roosevelt's plan to alter the composition of the Supreme Court. Roosevelt attempted to gain the authority to appoint up to six additional justices.

court probation. A criminal court requirement that a defendant or offender fulfill specified conditions or behavior in lieu of a jail sentence, but without being assigned to a probation agency's supervisory caseload.

court report. A social study of an individual offender containing recommendations for his or her treatment, assessment of family status and functioning, educational and vocational assessment, medical and mental health status (including, for example, addiction, depression), treatment needs, and plans for the future.

court reporter. A person present during judicial proceedings who records all testimony and other oral statements.

courtroom disruptions. Misconduct that disrupts the orderly proceedings of the court.

The Supreme Court has ruled that a judge may take one or more of three steps to ensure orderly conduct in court: (a) warn the defendant (if he or she is disruptive) and then exclude him or her from the courtroom and proceed with the trial, (b) bind and gag the defendant and (c) cite him or her for contempt of court.

Court Statistics Project (CSP). The CSP collects and analyzes data relating to the work of state courts in the United States Address: National Center for State Courts, 300 Newport Avenue Williamsburg, VA 23185-4147. Web: http://www.ncsconline. org/D_Research/csp/CSP_Main_Page.html.

courts, federal. The courts established or provided for by Article III of the Constitution or established by Congress under its delegated powers. As defined by the Supreme Court, these include the constitutional courts—the Supreme Court, the Courts of Appeals, and district courts—as well as the special or legislative courts. *See* Table 16. Navigating the Federal Court System, page 114

Courts of Appeals. One of the systems of appellate courts in the United States. Congress created courts of appeals because the Constitution itself created only one court, the Supreme Court. Nevertheless, courts of appeals are called constitutional courts because they exercise part of the judicial power of Article III of the Constitution. Courts of appeals have appellate jurisdiction over most administrative agencies and the final decisions of district courts, except in the few cases where there is a right of direct appeal to the Supreme Court. Appeal from district court decisions is a matter of right, as these courts do not have any original jurisdiction. Since the availability of Supreme Court review is limited, the courts of appeals function as courts of last resort in most instances. There are 13 courts of appeals, one for each judicial circuit and one federal, and cases there are heard before three judges. See Table 9. Map of United States Courts of Appeal and District Courts, page 78

TABLE 16 NAVIGATING THE FEDERAL COURT SYSTEM

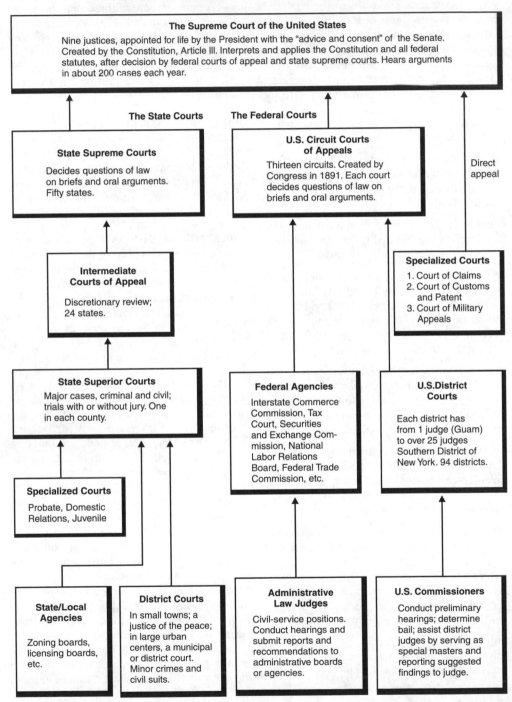

The Supreme Court of the United States

Nine justices, appointed for life by the President with the "advice and consent" of the Senate. Created by the Constitution, Article III. Interprets and applies the Constitution and all federal statutes, after decision by federal courts of appeal and state supreme courts. Hears arguments in about 200 cases each year.

The State Courts

The Federal Courts

State Supreme Courts

Decides questions of law on briefs and oral arguments. Fifty states.

U.S. Circuit Courts of Appeals

Thirteen circuits. Created by Congress in 1891. Each court decides questions of law on briefs and oral arguments.

Direct appeal

Intermediate Courts of Appeal

Discretionary review; 24 states.

Specialized Courts

1. Court of Claims
2. Court of Customs and Patent
3. Court of Military Appeals

State Superior Courts

Major cases, criminal and civil; trials with or without jury. One in each county.

Federal Agencies

Interstate Commerce Commission, Tax Court, Securities and Exchange Commission, National Labor Relations Board, Federal Trade Commission, etc.

U.S. District Courts

Each district has from 1 judge (Guam) to over 25 judges Southern District of New York. 94 districts.

Specialized Courts

Probate, Domestic Relations, Juvenile

State/Local Agencies

Zoning boards, licensing boards, etc.

District Courts

In small towns; a justice of the peace; in large urban centers, a municipal or district court. Minor crimes and civil suits.

Administrative Law Judges

Civil-service positions. Conduct hearings and submit reports and recommendations to administrative boards or agencies.

U.S. Commissioners

Conduct preliminary hearings; determine bail; assist district judges by serving as special masters and reporting suggested findings to judge.

court, specialized. A court that has jurisdiction over special types of criminal or civil suits, such as a morals court, juvenile court, or appellate court.

courts, state. The various judicial systems in the 50 states, authorized under the Tenth Amendment of the Constitution and established by the state constitutions or state legislation. Three features are common to the organization of all state court systems. Each state has a high court of appeals (usually a Supreme Court); a level of courts of original and general jurisdiction commonly called district or county courts; and, at the bottom, a tier of justice of the peace courts, including municipal, police, and magistrate courts for the trial of minor civil and criminal cases. Some states have an additional group of intermediate courts of appeal. All states have various specialized courts for the administration of estates, wills, domestic relations and children's problems, juvenile delinquency, and small claims.

Court, Supreme. The court of last resort; the highest court found in the federal system and in each state.

Court, Tax. The federal forum in which a taxpayer may contest a tax deficiency (tax due) asserted by the Internal Revenue Service. The Tax Court hears only contests involving deficiencies. A taxpayer who feels he or she has overpaid may sue the government for a refund in either the Court of Claims or the district court, but not in the Tax Court.

covenant. A binding legal agreement or promise.

covert. (1) Hidden or secret, as opposed to overt. (2) Sheltered. (2) In common law, a covert woman is under the protection of her husband.

coverture. (1) A legal doctrine in which the rights of a married woman are subsumed by her husband; the separate legal rights of a woman disappeared upon marriage. (2) The state of being concealed, obscured, hidden, or disguised.

CPR (cardiopulmonary resuscitation). The reestablishment of heart and lung functions following cardiac arrest, cardiovascular collapse, electric shock, drowning, respiratory arrest, or other causes; the manual basic life support provided until advance support is available; a combination of artificial respiration (rescue breathing) and artificial circulation (external cardiac compression.) ABC is the acronym for basic CPR steps: Airway, Breathing, Circulation (D for Defibrillation has since been added to the steps).

Crank-Up Task Force. A 1987 California program created within the Department of Justice as part of the Clandestine Laboratory Enforcement Program with responsibility for establishing, conducting, supporting, and coordinating groups of state and local law enforcement agencies to investigate, seize, and clean up secret laboratories used to manufacture methamphetamine.

Credit-Card, Credit-Repair and Loan Schemes. These schemes victimize consumers with bad credit, offering credit cards for a fee. The victim pays the fee, but does not receive a credit card. In credit-repair schemes, victims pay a fee to have bankruptcies and negative items removed from their credit report; the victim pays the fee, but the credit is not repaired. The scheme for advance-fee loans is similar, wherein victims pay an up-front fee to get a loan, but their loan is never approved. *See also* telemarketing fraud

credit card fraud. A general term for theft committed through the use of an illegally obtained credit card. It is often associated with Identity theft.

Credit, Equal Opportunity Act. According to the Federal Trade Commission (FTC), the Equal Credit Opportunity Act (1974) "prohibits credit discrimination on the basis of race, color, religion, national origin, sex, marital status, age," or due to receipt of public assistance. *See* Fair Housing and Equal Credit Opportunity

Credit Fraud Act of 1984. The purpose of the act is to reduce hacking and address "protected computers," such as those of banks and those affecting interstate commerce. This act was subsequently amended in 1986, 1988, 1989, 1990, 1994, 1996. It was amended in 2001 by the USA PATRIOT Act.

crime. An act committed or omitted in violation of a law forbidding or commanding it, for which the possible penalties upon conviction for an adult include incarceration, for which a corporation can be penalized by fine or forfeit, or for which a juvenile can be adjudged delinquent or transferred to criminal court for prosecution. Crimes are defined as offenses against the state and are to be distinguished from violations of the civil law that involve harm done to individuals—such as torts—for which the state demands restitution rather than punishment. An antisocial act is not a crime unless it is prohibited by criminal law and coupled with a specified punishment. Criminal law generally requires proof of both *mens rea,* or a criminal intent or a wrongful purpose, and of the commission of an overt criminal act. Criminal law commonly classifies violations into (a) crimes against property, (b) crimes against the person, and (3) crimes against public safety and morals. *See also* Crime Index

crime analysis. A system using regularly collected information on reported crimes and criminal offenders for crime prevention, suppression, and the apprehension of criminal offenders. Crime analysis supports police operations particularly in strategic planning, personnel deployment, and investigation assistance.

crime, business. *See* white-collar crime

crime, capital. An offense where the punishment may be death, regardless of whether or not the death penalty is actually inflicted. It remains so even where juries are given the option of imposing life imprisonment instead of death as the penalty. Capital crimes are usually not bailable. The number of offenses regarded as capital has been sharply reduced in modern times. *See also* punishment, capital

Crime Clock. A term used in the FBI's Uniform Crime Report (UCR), published annually, which represents the ratio of crime to fixed time intervals. An example from the 2008 UCR is: "One murder [is committed in the U.S.] every 32 minutes," which is much improved over the 1992 clock, in which one murder is committed every 22 minutes. UCR readers are cautioned in the report that the Crime Clock should not be interpreted to imply any regularity in the commission of crimes. *See* Table 17. Crime Clock, 2007, on page 117. *See also* Crime Index

crime commission model. Introduced by the President's Commission on Law Enforcement and the Administration of Justice, the Crime Commission Model applied the systems approach to the process of criminal justice. It provided a conceptual framework, and focused on the flow of cases between agencies. The main shortcoming is that it portrays a single justice system, handling all cases the same. *See* President's Crime Commission and wedding cake model

crime, companionate. A crime committed jointly by two, or occasionally more than two, persons against a third party. Companionate crime, as differentiated from organized crime, is occasional and generally involves only one offense. Organized crime is consistent and habitual behavior. Companionate crime generally involves a victim and is thus unlike such potentially illegal behavior as prostitution, drug trafficking, or gambling. The above offenses are generally (also called victimless offenses) often associated with organized crime.

crime control model. A perspective on the criminal justice process based on the proposition that the most important function of criminal justice is the repression of crime The crime control model repression of the criminal conduct is core. This is contrasted by the due process model, which emphasizes equal treatment of the defendant. *See also* due process model

TABLE 17   CRIME CLOCK, 2007

CRIME CLOCK STATISTICS

Violent Crime	22.8 seconds
One Murder every	32.3 minutes
One Forcible Rape every	5.9 minutes
One Robbery every	1.2 minutes
One Aggravated Assault Every	37.8 seconds
Property Crime	3.2 seconds
One Burglary every	14.2 seconds
One Larceny-theft every	4.8 seconds
One Motor Vehicle Theft every	33.0 seconds

The Crime Clock should be viewed with care. The most aggregate representation of UCR data, it conveys the annual reported crime experience by showing a relative frequency of occurrence of Part I offenses. It should not be taken to imply a regularity in the commission of crime. The Crime Clock represents the annual ratio of crime to fixed time intervals.

Source: Federal Bureau of Investigation (2009), Crime in the United States.

crime displacement. Term describing what happens when law enforcement or prevention efforts cause a particular criminal activity simply to shift to another location. For example, police will often crack down on prostitution in particular neighborhoods because of citizen complaints. The prostitutes then move their business to another location until enforcement returns to previous levels.

crime, etiology of. The study of the causes of criminal behavior, generally by the case study or clinical method, usually proceeding from the study of individual cases. This method can be contrasted with the isolation of factors connected with crime in general, by statistical or observational methods, which is the study of general causes.

crime gradient. A concept adopted by some criminologists in the study of the ecological distribution of crime. It designates the profile of a curve based on the crime rates of consecutive geographic areas located along a straight line.

Crime Index. A set of data compiled by the Federal Bureau of Investigation that indicates the volume, fluctuation, and distribution of crimes reported to local law enforcement agencies, for the United States as a whole and for its geographical subdivisions, based on counts of reported occurrences of the FBI's annual Uniform Crime Report's index crimes. These index crimes are: homicide and nonnegligent manslaughter, robbery, forcible rape, aggravated assault, burglary, larceny/theft, motor vehicle theft, and arson. *See also* National Crime Victimization Survey. In national UCRs, the crime rate is the number of Crime Index offenses known to police, per 100,000 population. In some state-level publications, crime rates are based on a different population unit, typically 1,000 persons.

crime insurance, federal. A government subsidized risk pool allowing residents and business owners to purchase burglary and robbery insurance in cities where this coverage is difficult to obtain or not affordable in the private market.

crime, multiple causes of. As opposed to the concept of a single cause of crime, such as congenital predisposition, mental retardation, or poverty, the multiple-causes approach posits several or many factors operating cumulatively to produce crime.

crime of passion. An unpremeditated murder or assault committed under circumstances of great anger, jealousy, or other emotional stress.

crime of violence, mandatory penalty for use of a firearm in. *See* Comprehensive Crime Control Act of 1984

crime pact, first interstate. Effected between New York and New Jersey and signed September 16, 1833, in New York City, the agreement to cooperate in certain aspects of crime prevention and control was ratified by Congress on June 28, 1834.

crime prevention. A significant effort in criminal justice that aims to reduce criminal victimization, by deterring crime and criminals. Such efforts often involve three prongs: (1) efforts at "target hardening," including increased public awareness of opportunistic criminal activity and profiles of typical crime victims; (2) efforts to reduce opportunities for crime, such as by establishing neighborhood watch programs; and (3) deterring offenders through rapid response to crimes in progress and strengthening of criminal penalties. These tactics illustrate the three basic strategies of crime prevention from a routine activities approach. *See also* Routine Activities

Crime Prevention Council, National. Aims to help keep citizens, families, and communities safe from crime by producing "tools that communities can use to learn crime prevention strategies, engage community members, and coordinate with local agencies." Address: 2345 Crystal Suite 500, Arlington, VA 22202. Web: http://www.ncpc.org/.

crime prevention, special procedures for. A number of special legal procedures have been created to control crime that avoid the use of trial by jury. One is the abatement of nuisances, including houses of prostitution, illegal gambling parlors, areas in which gang members congregate, and buildings used to manufacture controlled substances. *See also* abatement; forfeiture; Racketeer Influenced and Corrupt Organizations

crime score. A number assigned from an established scale, signifying the seriousness of a given offense with respect to the extent of personal injury or damage to property it caused.

crime statistics, United States. A compilation based on law enforcement information furnished by nationwide local agencies. It is prepared and published annually by the FBI under the title *Crime in the United States*.

Crime Stoppers. The first Crime Stoppers program was established by an Albuquerque police officer in 1976. It offered cash (to overcome apathy) and anonymity (to overcome fear of retaliation) to any citizen willing to provide police with information on criminal conduct that could lead to conviction of criminals. According to Crime Stoppers USA, local crime stopper programs nationwide led to a total of 517,039 arrests, 854,193 cleared cases, $77,984,667 rewards paid, and $2,959,015,075 in drugs seized. Web: http://www.crimestopusa.com/.

crime, violent. (1) Any offense that has as an element the use, attempted use, or threatened use of physical force against the person or property of another. (2) Any other offense that is a felony and that, by its nature, involves a substantial threat of physical force against the person or property of another. *See also* racketeering

crimes against family members of federal officials. According to federal law (18 U.S.C. §115), it is a crime to attempt, conspire or complete an assault, kidnap, or murder "a member of the immediate family of a United States official, a United States judge, a federal law enforcement officer," or any other "officer or employee who is engaged in or on account of the performance of official duties, or any person assisting such an officer or employee in the performance of such duties."

crimes against the state. Acts that are directed against the interests of the sovereignty rather than the individual. In the United States, few crimes are included in this category, and rarely is anyone prosecuted for an act against the government other than for disorderly conduct.

crimes without complaints. Another term for victimless crimes, or crimes that provide goods and/or services that are in demand but are illegal, such as gambling, narcotics, and prostitution. The police themselves typically serve as complainants in such crimes, since citizens are usually not willing to accept this role.

criminal. Broadly, a person who has committed a crime; but legally and statistically, only a person who has been convicted of a crime. The attempt to limit the concept of "criminal" to persons who have committed serious crimes or those whose motives are distinctly evil involves value judgments that have no scientific basis and is therefore at odds with modern criminal justice.

criminal action. The accusation, trial, and punishment of a person charged with a public offense. Cases may be prosecuted by the state, either as a party itself or at the request of an individual to prevent a crime against his or her person or property.

criminal anthropology. A criminological theory of Cesare Lombroso, postulating that there are discernible and identifiable criminal types. *See also* anthropology; Lombroso, Cesare

Criminal Appeals Act. An act of Congress that allows the United States to appeal to the Supreme Court in a criminal case when a lower court, without having placed the defendant in jeopardy, has held that a federal statute is unconstitutional.

criminal biology. The scientific study of the relation of hereditary traits linked to criminal behavior. Historically, this involved the study of innate tendencies to commit crime in general or crimes of any particular type.

Various contemporary researchers have studied socio-biological bases of crime, including mapping brain function in convicted criminals. *See also* Raines, Adrian

criminal case. A case initiated in a court by the filing of a charging document containing one or more criminal accusations against one or more identified persons.

criminal charge. A criminal accusation, through a written complaint, an indictment, or information, which is then acted upon by a prosecutor.

criminal conversation. An obsolete phrase in modern times, this term was historically used to denote adultery or illegal sexual relations involving a married person and a partner other than his or her spouse.

criminal history. The official record of a person's arrests, convictions, and sentences.

criminal homicide. The causing of the death of another person without legal justification or excuse.

criminal identification. The recording of significant physical characteristics, especially photographs and fingerprints, of individual criminals for rapid and permanent identification.

criminal intent. The intent to commit an act, the results of which are a crime or violation of the law. There is general intent and specific intent. Some statutes require the existence of specific intent; some, only general intent. If no intent is set forth in the description of a particular crime by law, then the commission of the act is sufficient for charging, and intent need not be proven.

criminal justice. In the strictest sense, the criminal (penal) law, the law of criminal procedure, and that array of procedures and activities having to do with the enforcement of this body of law. Any activity, practice, system, or institution aimed at crime prevention, control, or reduction; the enforcement of the criminal law; or the management and rehabilitation of offenders.

criminal justice agency. Any court with criminal jurisdiction and any government agency or identifiable subunit that defends indigents or has as its principal duty(s) the performance of criminal justice functions (prevention, detection, and investigation of crime; the apprehension, detention, and prosecution of alleged offenders; the confinement, rehabilitation or official correctional supervision of accused or convicted persons; or the administrative or technical support of these functions) as authorized and required by statute or executive order.

Criminal Justice Association, National. Founded in 1971, this coordinating effort focuses on innovations in the criminal justice system. Address: 720 7th Street, NW, Third Floor, Washington, DC 20001-3716. Web: http://www.ncja.org//AM/.

Criminal Justice Center. Founded in 1965 by Sam Houston State University, the center is an educational agency designed to serve institutions and practitioners. Maintains a reference library (50,000 books, reports, and documents). The center also operates the National Employment Listing Service (NELS), established in 1976, which provides nationwide up-to-date information about available positions in criminal justice and social services. Publishes NELS Bulletin (monthly). Address: Criminal Justice Center, Sam Houston University, P.O. Box 2296, Huntsville, TX 77341.

Criminal Justice, National Council on Crime and Delinquency (NCDD) Library. Housed at Rutgers University since 1984; has extensive material related to crime and criminal justice. Address: Rutgers University, 185 University Avenue, Newark, NJ 07102; Web: http://catalogs.rutgers.edu/generated/scj/pg1570.html.

criminal law. A branch of law dealing with crimes and their punishments. A crime is an act considered an offense against public authority or a violation of a public duty. Crimes are usually classified as *mala in se*—immoral and wrong in themselves—or *mala prohibita*—illegal only because proscribed by statute. Crimes are also graded according to their gravity as misdemeanors or felony offenses. Procedural rules relating to proof of crime and defining and prescribing penalties for crimes are referred to as criminal, or substantive criminal, law. Criminal law is both common and statutory, although the former aspect has been of decreasing importance in the United States.

criminally insane. The term for the state of mental incompetence that accompanies or induces the commission of a crime and prevents the criminal from knowing the criminal nature of the act committed. There are various rules applied to the finding of criminal insanity, which vary by jurisdiction. Most notably (see also): M'Naghten Rule, Irresistible Impulse, Durham/New Hampshire Test, American Law Institute Model, Brawner Rule, Substantial Capacity Test, Temporary Insanity. *See also* Insanity Defense Reform Act of 1984

criminal mischief (malicious mischief). Intentionally destroying or damaging, or attempting to destroy or damage, the property of another without his consent, usually by a means other than burning.

criminal offense. An offense against a state, including both crimes and misdemeanors. The term has been defined by statute as consisting of (a) a violation of a public law, in the commission of which there shall be a union or joint operation of act and intention, or criminal negligence, and (b) any offense, misdemeanor, or felony, for which any punishment by imprisonment or fine or both may by law be inflicted.

criminal organization. The structure of relationships between persons and groups that makes the commission of crime possible and facilitates avoidance of the legal penalties. This structure may be loose, informal, and decentralized, or it may be explicitly institutionalized and centralized. Also, any group of persons who systematically devote themselves, as a collective unit, to the commission of crime. *See also* organized crime

TABLE 18   SEQUENCE OF EVENTS IN THE CRIMINAL JUSTICE SYSTEM

CRIMINAL JUSTICE

What is the sequence of events in the criminal justice system?

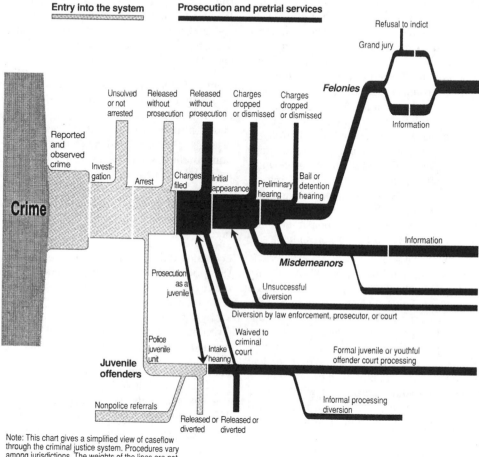

Note: This chart gives a simplified view of caseflow through the criminal justice system. Procedures vary among jurisdictions. The weights of the lines are not intended to show actual size of caseloads.

criminal, pathological. An antiquated term referring to a criminal who deviates from the mental norm. Associated terms, many of which are no longer in use, include: mental defective or feeble-minded, psychotic or insane, psychopathic, and neurotic. The term is often used to describe those who behave amorally, asocially, and irresponsibly.

criminal procedure. The legal methods used in the apprehension, trial, prosecution, and sentencing of criminals.

criminal proceedings. The regular and orderly steps, as directed or authorized by statute or court of law, taken to determine whether an adult accused of a crime is guilty or not guilty.

criminal responsibility. Criminal liability for an offense. To be so liable, the person committing the act must do so of his or her own free will and volition, have the capacity to distinguish right from wrong, and have the ability to foresee the evil consequences of the act. The presence of these conditions constitutes responsibility and, hence, liability and punishability. On the other hand, certain circumstances may negate responsibility. These are principally: (a) Infancy. Under the common law, children under 7 years of age are not regarded as being responsible. A similar presumption generally applies to children between 7 and 14 years. In most states, statutory provisions give juvenile courts jurisdiction over the criminal or delinquent acts of children beyond the age of 14; in some instances, jurisdiction is waived to adult court. (b) Insanity. The provisions for insanity are defined by statute and are generally interpreted by the courts to mean that a person is incapable of making moral distinctions between right and wrong or of knowing the evil consequences of his acts. (c) Intoxication. Ordinarily, intoxication provides no exemption from criminal liability, though it may reduce the degree of responsibility and, hence, lessen the severity of punishment. *See also* culpability; juvenile waiver; insanity

criminal saturation, law of. A theory developed by the Italian criminologist Enrico Fern, which holds that each society has the number of criminals that the particular conditions in that society produce. "As a given volume of water at a definite temperature will dissolve a fixed quantity of chemical substance and not an atom more or less; so in a given social environment with definite individual and physical conditions, a fixed number of crimes, no more and no less, can be committed."

criminal statistics. The tabulated, numerical data found in the official reports of agencies that deal with the apprehension, prevention, and treatment of offenders of the criminal law. The unit of tabulation may be the case, the offender, or the offense. A common classification of criminal statistics distinguishes among police, judicial, and correctional (institutional) statistics. In the United States the term is generally inclusive; on the continent of Europe, it is ordinarily used to designate only the tabulations based on the characteristics of the offender, as distinguished from statistics of criminal justice, or correctional institutions.

criminal syndicalism. A legal phrase of American law to describe the advocating of the unlawful destruction of property or an unlawful change in its ownership; a doctrine and practice attributed to the Industrial Workers of the World, a labor organization, and embodied in many state statutes aimed to curb such activities, adopted between 1917 and 1924.

criminal tendencies. An antiquated term referring to classifiable behavioral tendencies that, if not recognized or checked, may end in ultimate commission of a criminal act or acts; behavioral tendencies that under certain conditions can be expected to develop into a delinquent or criminal pattern; tendencies toward criminal behavior. Such references are generally not used in modern courts, although they often exist in public perception.

criminal tribes. Tribes with a culture that sanctions behavior toward nonmembers of the tribe that is prohibited by the laws of the state to which the tribe belongs. Term generally applies to British law, as outlined in Criminal Tribes Acts of 1876 and 1911 and applied in the British Indies around that time.

criminal typologies. American criminologist Stephen Schafer's life-trend classification of criminals. According to Schafer's 1970 typology, types of criminals include abnormal, convictional, habitual, occasional, and professional. This typology is not in modern usage.

criminal, white-collar. An employee or professional who violates the criminal law in the course of his/her occupational or professional activities. The state, insofar as it reacts against white-collar crimes, generally does so through bureaus and commissions rather than through the police and the criminal courts. However, criminal prosecution does occur in some cases. For example, in 2009, an FBI investigation coined "Florida's Mortgage Fraud Surge," resulted in 105 criminal indictments against white-collar criminals in that state.

TABLE 19 PROCESSING AND DISPOSITIONS IN CRIMINAL JUSTICE

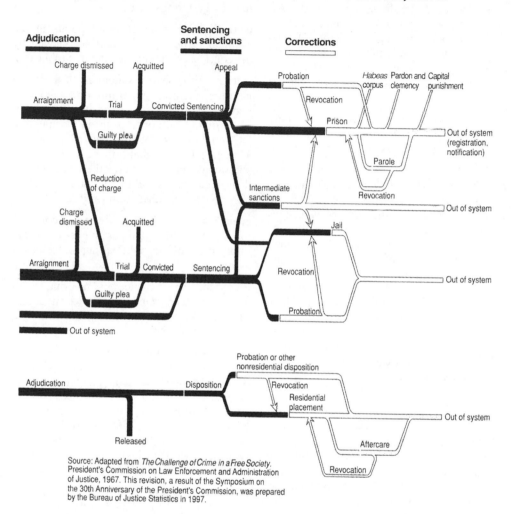

Source: Adapted from *The Challenge of Crime in a Free Society*. President's Commission on Law Enforcement and Administration of Justice, 1967. This revision, a result of the Symposium on the 30th Anniversary of the President's Commission, was prepared by the Bureau of Justice Statistics in 1997.

criminalist. A scientist trained to perform crime laboratory functions and relate the findings to criminal investigations.

criminalistics. The science of crime detection, involving the application of chemistry, physics, physiology, psychology, and other sciences.

Criminalistics Laboratory Information System. A computerized database composed of a general Rifling Characteristics File that is used to identify the manufacturer and type of weapon that may have been used to fire a bullet or cartridge.

criminate. To accuse of a crime.

criminogenic. Refers to those features of a culture or environment that are believed to produce crime.

criminogenic needs. A set of changeable deficiencies associated with criminal activity. Multiple studies have identified a consistent set of such criminogenic factors which, when addressed, may reduce recidivism.

These include: antisocial/procriminal attitudes, values, and beliefs; procriminal associates; temperament and personality factors, such as impulsivity, anger; a history of antisocial behavior; family factors such as family criminality, addiction, and violence; and low levels of educational, vocational or financial achievement.

criminologist. One whose professional study encompasses all facets of crime, criminals, and the justice process or system. *See also* criminology

criminology. The study of crime and corrections and the operation of the system of criminal justice. Criminology had its origins in the Enlightenment of the eighteenth century, when such men as Cesare Beccaria and Jeremy Bentham explored ways of making criminal law a more just and humane instrument of the state. The nineteenth century saw the rise of the positivist school, which stressed the need for a scientific understanding of the causes of crime and its control. In the United States since 1900, criminology has been largely in the domain of the social sciences. *See also* Beccaria, Cesare; Bentham, Jeremy

Crips. An African American gang founded in Los Angeles around 1969 by Raymond Washington and Stanley "Tookie" Williams. The Crips gang is one of the largest and most violent street gangs in the United States, with an estimated 30,000 to 35,000 members according to the Department of Justice. The gang is known for wearing the color blue (contrasted with the color red associated with the Bloods); however, this practice has waned. The Crips have an historically bitter rivalry with the Bloods. *See also* Bloods

crisis intervention center. A service designed to give immediate help to people with serious emotional problems. Examples are suicide prevention centers and suicide hot lines.

crisis intervention units. Special programs for peace officers who frequently deal with domestic disturbances. These officers undergo extensive training in the study of psychology, body language, conflict resolution, and referral services.

critical stage. One or more points in the criminal justice process that are viewed by the court as crucial to the outcome of a case.

criticize. To make a statement of a critical nature concerning something or someone. It may be constructive or destructive criticism. The Circuit Court of Appeals, in Washington, DC, on June 19, 1970, ruled in the case of *Minard v. Mitchell* that officers have the constitutional right to criticize the operations of their departments and that no punitive action may be taken against them for it.

crony. A close friend, associate, or companion. It is sometimes a pejorative term, used to imply partiality in political appointments or associations.

cronyism. The practice of favoring one's close friends, especially in political situations. This includes hiring, promotions, assignments, and cover-ups.

cross-border schemes. A number of telemarketing fraud schemes in which the calls originate in one country and target victims in another country. This method of fraud adds a layer of protection to the offender, as fraud involving multiple countries involves complicated legal jurisdiction issues; such fraud is difficult to investigate and prosecute. *See also* telemarketing fraud

cross-examination. The questioning of a witness called by the opposing party.

cross-projection. A method of sketching the details of a room in which the walls and the ceiling are shown or drawn as if they were on the same plane as the floor. This method gives a clear understanding of a crime scene, especially if evidence is found on the walls or ceiling.

crosswalk. Any portion of a roadway distinctly indicated for pedestrian crossing by lines or other markings on the road surface.

crowdsourcing. A portmanteau of "crowd" and "outsourcing." The term refers to leveraging mass collaboration, or harnessing the skills and enthusiasm of those outside an organization to volunteer their time in an effort towards achieving a common goal.

Crowley, Aleister. (1875–1947) (also known as Frater Perdurabo and The Great Beast). Born Edward Alexander Crowley in 1875, the year of the death of Eliphas Levi, who wrote several books on occultism. Crowley believed he was a reincarnation of Levi. Many called Crowley the beast or the Antichrist, and he was thought to have made human sacrifices. In 1898 he joined the OTO (*Odro Templi Orientis*) cult, also known as the Order of the Golden Dawn. He founded the Argenteum Astrum (Silver Star) in 1904. Crowley's most famous book was *Magick in Theory and Practice,* published in 1919. He died in 1947.

crown attorney. The term for a prosecutor in Canada.

cruel and unusual punishment. Prohibited by the Eighth Amendment to the Constitution, which states, "Excessive bail shall not be required, nor excessive fines imposed, nor cruel and unusual punishments inflicted." At the time of the original congressional debate over the Bill of Rights, some delegates objected that the provisions of the Eighth Amendment were vaguely defined; in practice, the courts have determined the amendment's applications and limitations. The Supreme Court has held that Eighth Amendment guarantees apply to the states by the due process clause of the Fourteenth Amendment.

cryptographer. One who solves or deciphers cryptograms or decodes any secret communications.

CS. A chemical agent used as tear gas, which is widely believed to be nontoxic. CS gas is commonly used as a riot control agent in the United States, most notably during the FBI raid at Waco, Texas in 1993, and the Pittsburgh riots in 2009. The use of CS gas is banned by the United Nations' Chemical Weapons Convention of 1997, which the United States adopted. However, this document pertains to the use of CS gas internationally; the United States can (and does) use CS gas against its own citizens on its own soil. Chemical name is orthochlorbenzalmalononitrile.

culpable (Lat., *culpa,* lit. "blame"). At fault or responsible, but not necessarily criminal.

culpability. (1) Blameworthiness, responsibility in some sense for an event or situation deserving of moral blame. (2) In Model Penal Code usage, a state of mind on the part of one who is committing an act that makes him or her potentially subject to prosecution for that act.

culprit. One who has violated the law but has not been convicted. He or she may still be sought for, or may have been legally charged with, the crime but not tried.

cults. A pejorative term referring to social or organizational groups formed to conduct ritual, magical, or unconventional religious practices; generally, cults are reputed to have rigid belief structures that require unwavering adherence, and are often thought to employ some degree of mind control, coercion, or brainwashing of members. Cults vary according to their membership, belief systems, and types of ritual practices. Such groups often believe in a sacred wisdom accessible only to a select few. *See* Table 20. Notable Cults in Criminal Justice, page 126

cunnilingus. Oral contact with the female genitals for sexual gratification of one or both partners. *See also* fellatio

curative statute. A law, retrospective in effect, which is designed to remedy some legal defect in previous transactions and to validate them.

curfew violation. The offense of being found in a public place after a specified hour of the evening, usually established in a local ordinance and applying only to persons under a specified age, but sometimes imposed on all residents during civil disturbances.

TABLE 20   NOTABLE CULTS IN CRIMINAL JUSTICE

Date	Leader	Name of Cult	Location	Estimated Membership	Result
Late 1960s	Charles Manson	Manson Family	Los Angeles, California	>100	At least 6 murders
November 18, 1978	Jim Jones	People's Temple	Guyana	913	Mass suicide
May 13, 1985	John Africa	MOVE	Philadelphia, Pennsylvania	Unknown	11 dead in shootout with police
1987–Present (continued conflicts)	Joseph Kony	Lord's Resistance Army	Northern Uganda	500–100,000	> 500 dead
February 28, 1993	David Koresh	Branch Davidian	Waco, Texas	95	86 killed in shootout with police and subsequent fire
October 1994	Joseph Di Mambro and Luc Jouret	Order of the Solar Temple	Geneva France	Unknown	53 dead in murder/ suicide ritual
March 20, 1995	Shoko Asahara	Aum Supreme Truth	Japan	9,000 in Japan 40, 000 worldwide	Sarin gas attack in subway killed 12 and injured 980. Still active
December 23, 1995	Joseph Di Mambro and Luc Jouret	Order of the Solar Temple	Southeast France	Unknown	16 dead in murder/suicide
March 23, 1997	Joseph Di Mambro and Luc Jouret	Order of the Solar Temple	Quebec, Canada	Unknown	5 dead in group suicide
March 26, 1997	Marshall Applewhite, Bonnie Nettles	Heaven's Gate	San Diego, California	Unknown	39 dead in mass suicide
March 17, 2000	Credonia Mwerinde, Joseph Kibweteere, and Bee Tait	Movement for the Restoration of the Ten Commandments of God	Uganda	Unknown	778 dead in mass murder/ suicide
June 19, 2002	Ruben Ecleo Jr.	Philippine Benevolent Missionaries Association	Philippine Island of Dinagat	1,000,000	At least 23 dead in confrontations with police

Compiled by Richard Porter, CSULB

curtilage. The grounds inside a wall sur-rounding a house or building.

custodial care. The care afforded in institu-tions to socially or physically incapacitated persons who need close supervision or assis-tance in performing basic tasks.

custodial officer. One charged with the keep, safety, and/or detention of persons in a prison, jail, or hospital.

custody. Legal or physical control of a per-son or thing; legal, supervisory, or physical responsibility for a person or thing.

custody, close. Constant supervision of a prisoner on the assumption that he or she will not only escape if the opportunity is offered, but will also make the opportunity.

custody, maximum. Care in the type of prison that provides the maximum security—high walls, tool-proof bars, numerous armed guards, rigid discipline, technologically sophisticated measure to prevent escape and so forth—for the most hardened prisoners.

custody, medium. Care for prisoners in an institution with a type of physical plant less strongly built and equipped than a maximum-custody facility. Intended to house less hard-ened and dangerous criminals and to give them more freedom of movement and greater self-direction.

custody, minimum. Care of prisoners in an institution built, equipped, and guarded with the least possible restraint required to keep them safely and to allow the greatest pos-sible freedom. Such an institution is exempli-fied by some of the prison camps and farms, reformatories, or honor dormitories within a prison facility.

custody, protective. Detention by the police of persons essential to the prosecution of jus-tice, presumably in order to prevent reprisals against them by criminal elements for their part in furthering the investigation of a crime. In prisons, inmates can also be assigned to protective custody if their safety is endan-gered in the general population, as is often the case with child molesters, former police

officers, snitches, gang drop-outs, high pro-file inmates, or notorious criminals.

custom laws. The U.S. Bureau of Justice Statistics defines customs laws as "viola-tions regarding taxes which are payable upon goods and merchandise imported or exported. Includes the duties, toll, tribute, or tariff payable."

Customs and Patent Appeals, Court of. This specialized court was created by Con-gress and given appellate jurisdiction over decisions of the Customs Court, Patent Office, and Tariff Commission. The court operated from 1909 to 1982, when the court was abolished and jurisdiction was trans-ferred to the United States Court of Appeals for the Federal Circuit.

Customs Court. This court had exclusive jurisdiction to review decisions of customs collectors on questions affecting imports and import duties. Formerly called the Board of General Appraisers, the Court's name was changed by Congress in 1926, but no change was made in its functions, which are quasi-judicial and quite similar to those usually performed by an administrative agency. The court was abolished in 1980, with jurisdic-tion transferred to the U.S. Court of Interna-tional Trade

cyber bullying. The National Crime Preven-tion Council defines cyber bullying as use of "the Internet, cell phones or other devices are used to send or post text or images intended to hurt or embarrass another person." The tar-get of cyber bulling is generally an adult or child, but not an organization. This is distinct from cyber stalking, which is often used to describe this behavior perpetrated by adults toward adults (excludes child victims). *See also* cyber stalking; Drew, Lori

cyber bully mom. In this first-ever cyber bully case, 47-year old defendant Lori Drew was charged in federal court with four counts related to her alleged cyber bullying against 13-year old victim Megan Meier. According to trial and public records, Drew's daughter was a friend of Meier in seventh grade, but

Meier changed schools the following year and indicated she did not want the friendship to continue. Concerned that Meier was spreading rumors about her daughter, Drew opened a fictitious MySpace account for a fictitious 16-year old boy, "Josh Evans" for the purpose of finding out what Meier was saying about Drew's daughter. Over the course of one month, Drew used the fictitious Evans account to flirt with Meier. During this time Drew was aware that Meier was taking antidepression medication. Drew (Evans) eventually told Meier the world would be a better place without her. Accounts linked to Evans began to harass Meier. Within 15 minutes of this exchange, Meier's mother discovered Meier, who hanged herself in her bedroom. A jury found Drew guilty of one misdemeanor, acquitted Drew of three counts, and was deadlocked on one conspiracy count. A judge later overturned the conviction, and no further proceedings occurred. The Meiers, who have since filed for divorce, have not sought a civil suit, although they expressed a desire to have laws in place to prevent such. *See also* Drew, Lori; cyber bully

cyber stalking. Use of Internet, cellular, or other device to hurt, embarrass, or harass an adult. *See also* cyber bullying

cyber terrorism. An act of terrorism committed through the Internet or computer resources. Often, this involves attacks on computer networks or systems, generally by hackers working with or for terrorist groups. Examples include denial of service attacks, inserting viruses, or stealing data.

cyber terrorist. One who intimidates or coerces a government or organization to achieve political or social objectives, when such threats are facilitated via a computer or the Internet, or when such large-scale threats are aimed at computers, networks, and classified information.

Czolgosz, Leon. The American anarchist (1873–1901) who shot and killed President William McKinley in Buffalo on September 6, 1901. He felt that the president was "an enemy of the good working class" and must be executed. He was convicted and sentenced to death on September 24, 1901, in a trial that took less than nine hours. He was electrocuted in New York's Auburn Prison just five weeks later, on October 29, 1901.

D

dactyloscopy. (1) Fingerprints as a means of identification. (2) The study of fingerprints and their use as a means of identification.

Dahmer, Jeffrey Lionel (1960–1994). Born in Wisconsin and raised in Ohio, Dahmer became fascinated with dead animals in his adolescence and was a self-reported alcoholic by his late teens. After high school, Dahmer's parents divorced, and Dahmer spent two years in the Army. He was discharged due to alcoholism. He was convicted of sex offenses in 1982 and 1986, and began killing in 1988. He is notorious for soliciting male prostitutes or luring young boys into his apartment, where he would have sex with them, murder them, and eat the remains. At one point, he attempted to create sexual zombies by drilling a hole in his live victim's skull and filling it with scalding water or hydrochloric acid. In early 1991, two women called 911 after finding a disoriented, bleeding, and naked boy. The police returned the boy to Dahmer, who claimed the boy was his 19-year-old lover. Dahmer subsequently killed the boy. That summer, a second victim escaped and found police, who saw photographs of dismembered bodies and noticed the smell of decomposition in Dahmer's apartment. Dahmer pled not guilty by reason of insanity but was found sane and guilty of fifteen counts of murder in Wisconsin, one count of murder in Ohio, and sentenced to consecutive life terms. Dahmer was murdered by another inmate in 1994. *See also* cannibalism, sex offender

damages. Compensation that the law will award for injury done.

dangerous-tendency test. A court test used in determining the limits of free expression guaranteed in the First Amendment. In *Gitlow v. New York* (1925) the Supreme Court rejected Oliver Wendell Holmes's clear-and-present-danger test for interfering with freedom of speech, as enunciated in *Schenck v. United States* and *Abrams v. United States,* both 1919 decisions, in favor of a bad- or dangerous-tendency test. According to this standard, states can curtail free speech by making a rational connection between the speech and the evil sought to be prevented. More limiting than the clear-and-present-danger test, the dangerous-tendency test makes punishable, by the government, those responsible for publications and speeches that, even though they create no immediate danger, have a "tendency" to bring about results dangerous to public safety—corrupting public morals, inciting to crime, or disturbing the public peace. In *Dennis v. United States,* a 1951 Supreme Court case involving the Communist Party in the United States, the Court attempted to reconcile the two tests by a yardstick measuring the gravity of an evil against the probability of its occurring.

dangerous weapon. A device or instrument capable of inflicting great bodily harm or death.

DARE. Drug Abuse Resistance Education is a program, originated in 1983 by the Los Angeles Police Department, under which uniformed police officers visit elementary and middle school classrooms throughout the United States. The curriculum uses police officer-led series of classroom lessons that teaches children from kindergarten through 12th grade how to resist peer pressure and live productive drug- and violence-free lives. Address: D.A.R.E. America, P.O. Box 512090, Los Angeles, CA 90051-0090; Web: http://www.dare.com/home/.

darkness. Anytime from one-half hour after sunset to one-half hour before sunrise and any other time when visibility is not sufficient to render clearly discernible any person or vehicle on a road at a distance of 1,000 feet.

Darrow, Clarence (Seward). (1857–1938) Celebrated defense attorney. Born in Kinsman, OH, in 1857, he studied law for one year at the University of Michigan and was admitted to the Ohio bar in 1878. His early career was as a law partner of Illinois governor John P. Altgeld. In 1894, however, his defense of Eugene V. Debs and the American Railway Union launched him on a vocation as defender of unpopular causes and minority rights. As a labor lawyer, he represented, among others, the coal miners in the anthracite strike of 1902 and William Haywood and other Wobblies for their alleged murder of a former Idaho governor. An ardent opponent of capital punishment, he secured life imprisonment for Richard Loeb and Nathan Leopold in the infamous thrill-slaying of a Chicago youth. In the Scopes trial of 1925, he engaged in a famous clash with William Jennings Bryan over the right of Tennessee to forbid the teaching of evolution in the public schools. The following year he defended 11 blacks accused of the murder of a Detroit Ku Klux Klansman. A lifelong Democrat, Darrow was chosen by Franklin D. Roosevelt in 1934 to head a commission to study the operations of the National Recovery Administration. He died in 1938.

data, tier I. Sometimes called "basic availability," which consists of a server room. This is the fastest, cheapest, and easiest to implement, but it is susceptible to disruption.

data, tier II. Includes redundant site infrastructure. Less susceptible to disruption than tier I, but more costly to implement.

data, tier III. This system of concurrently maintainable site infrastructure is less susceptible to disruption than tier I, but more costly to implement

data, tier IV. Used primarily for mission critical computer systems, this system is the least susceptible to disruption. However, it is also the most costly and takes the longest to implement.

Data Encryption Standard (DES). Adopted by the National Institute of Standards and Technology, DES refers to a series of algorithms for secure transmission. Currently, NIST lists three approved algorithms for encryption: Advanced Encryption Standard (AES), Triple-DES, and Skipjack.

date rape drug. *See* gamma hydroxy butyrate (GHB)

Daubert standard. A rule of evidence governing admissibility of expert witnesses' testimony, established in *Daubert v. Merrell Dow Pharmaceuticals, Inc.,* 43 F.3d 1311 (9th Cir. 1995). The Daubert standard requires: scientific expert testimony must proceed from scientific knowledge; expert testimony must be relevant and rest on a reliable foundation; and must be of sound scientific methodology. *See also* Frye standard

Daugherty, Harry M. (1860–1941). The U.S. attorney general from 1921 to 1924, Daugherty was accused of taking part in the scandal concerning the oil lands at Teapot Dome. The case was dismissed.

Davis, Allen Lee ("Tiny," 1944–1999). A Florida felon who, while on parole for robbery, brutally murdered a pregnant woman and her two young daughters. Davis was sentenced to death for the crimes, carried out on July 8, 1999 by electrocution in "Old Sparky" (nickname for Florida's electric chair). Davis' execution drew national attention, as he bled from his eyes, nose, and ears during the electrocution, and he suffered burns to his head, leg, and genitals. Witnesses also testified that he moaned out loud, presumably in pain, during the procedure. The incident, which was not the first problematic electrocution in Florida, prompted court review of execution via electrocution as possible cruel and unusual punishment, which is unconstitutional. The Florida Supreme Court later ruled that Davis died a painless death; the method continues in Florida as of 2010. *See also* electrocution

Davis, David. (1815–1886). Associate justice of the Supreme Court (1862–1877). His decision in *Ex parte Milligan* (1866), denouncing arbitrary military power, became a bulwark of civil liberty in the United States Davis helped manage Lincoln's campaign for presidency.

daytime. In law enforcement, the general criterion for distinguishing daytime is that there is enough natural light to recognize a person's features at a distance of 10 yards. This becomes important in connection with searches where the law and the search warrant specify search during the daytime. Some courts adopt the so-called "burglary test" of the ability to recognize a person's features, holding that, when recognition is possible, a daytime warrant may be executed even though it is after sundown. Other courts, to set a clear and easily ascertainable period, limit the definition of daytime to the period between the rising and the setting of the sun; under this rule a service of a daytime warrant after sunset is invalid.

DC sniper. *See* Beltway sniper attacks

dead body. A corpse. The body of a human being deprived of life but not yet disintegrated. The legal definition of corpse covers all deceased human beings except stillborn infants.

dead letter. Term used to describe statutes that have become obsolete through long disuse.

deadly force. On March 27, 1985, in *Tennessee v. Garner,* the U.S. Supreme Court established guidelines for police use of deadly force, deciding that a Tennessee statute was unconstitutional insofar as it authorized the use of deadly force against fleeing suspects who are unarmed and pose no threat to the officer or third parties. As taking a life is considered a seizure subject to Fourth Amendment protections, any use of deadly force must be reasonable under the circumstances. The Court, like the Sixth Circuit, prefer the guidelines of the Model Penal Code, restricting the use of deadly force by the police to serious felonies and situations. Today, police agencies limit the use of deadly force to life-threatening situations only.

deadly weapon. An instrument designed to inflict serious bodily injury or death or capable of being used for such a purpose.

dead, presumed. *See* Enoch Arden law

death. Condition of being dead; permanent cessation of the functions of the vital organs. With the advent of vital-organ transplants by surgery, determining the definition of death has become a very controversial legal question.

death penalty. *See* punishment, capital

death penalty rulings by the U.S. Supreme Court. The following selected cases reflect recent court decisions regarding the death penalty in the United States.

Furman v Georgia 408 U.S. 238 (1972). USSC ruled the death penalty was often arbitrarily imposed, and appeared to disproportionally impact persons based on race, not heinousness of crime

Georgia v Gregg 428 U.S. 153 (1976). USSC reinstated the death penalty when objective criteria are used in determining sentence.

Coker v. Georgia, 433 U.S. 584 (1977). The Court declared that the death penalty was unconstitutionally excessive for rape of a woman, if death did not occur.

Ford v. Wainwright, 477 U.S. 399 (1986). The USSC banned the execution of insane persons and required an adversarial process for determining mental competency

Penry v Lynaugh 492 U.S. 302 (1989). The USSC allows the execution of "mentally retarded" persons.

Atkins v Virginia 536 U.S. 304 (2002), The USSC declares the execution of mentally retarded persons unconstitutional.

Roper v Simmons 543 U.S. 551 (2005). The USSC declares the execution of persons who are under age 18 at the time of the crime unconstitutional.

Baze v. Rees, 553 U.S. 35 (2008). The USSC authorizes the use of lethal injection as an approved method of execution, despite petitioner claims that it violates constitutional protections against "cruel and unusual punishment" when administered incorrectly.

Kennedy v. Louisiana, 554 U.S. an alternative would be 129 S. Ct. 1 (2008). The USSC invalidated a Louisiana law that allows the execution of persons convicted of child rape, arguing that the execution for a crime that leaves the victim alive is not proportional.

Death Penalty Focus of California. Founded in 1988, a nonprofit advocacy organization dedicated to the abolition of capital punishment. The organization focuses on "public education; grassroots and political organizing; original research; media outreach; local, state, and nationwide coalition building; and the education of religious, legislative and civic leaders about the death penalty and its alternatives." Address: 870 Market Street, Suite 859, San Francisco, CA 94102; Web: http://www.deathpenalty.org/.

Death Penalty Information Center. Founded in 1990, a nonprofit organization serving the media and the public with analysis and information on issues concerning capital punishment. Address: 1015 18th St. NW, #704, Washington, DC 20036; Web: http://www.deathpenaltyinfo.org/.

Death Penalty, National Coalition Against the (NCADP). An organization that provides resources and an information center to aid in the abolition of the death penalty, coordination of local efforts, and a united voice against executions. NCADP publishes *Lifelines* (quarterly newsletter). Address: 1705 DeSales Street, NW, Fifth Floor Washington DC, 20036. Web: http://www.ncadp.org/.

Death Penalty, Oregonians for Alternatives to the. A nonprofit advocacy group focused on research and education on the effectiveness of the death penalty and its alternatives. Address: PO Box 361, Portland, OR 97207-0361. Web: http://www.oadp.org/.

Death Penalty, Washington Coalition to Abolish the. A grassroots, nonprofit organization dedicated to the abolition of the death penalty. Address: P.O. Box 3045, Seattle, WA 98114-3045. Web: http://www.abolishdeath penalty.org/.

Death Row, U.S.A. A monthly newsletter listing data current statistics and national data

TABLE 21   EXECUTIONS IN THE UNITED STATES

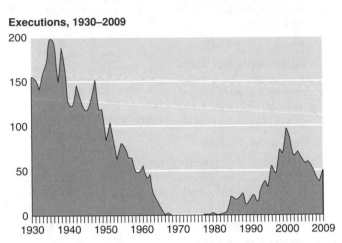

Executions, 1930–2009

Source: Bureau of Justice Statistics, Capital Punishment, 2008—Statistical

on the death penalty. Published by NAACP Legal Defense and Educational Fund, Inc., Suite 1600, 99 Hudson Street, New York, NY 10013. Web: http://www.naacpldf.org/.

death warrant. A written order issued by the legally authorized executive official (usually the governor), setting the place and time for executing an individual sentenced to death by the court.

Death with dignity. Political movement that supports the right to die, particularly for persons with incurable, debilitating, or fatal diseases. For more information, visit: http://www.deathwithdignity.org/aboutus/. *See also* euthanasia

Debs, Eugene V. American Socialist leader (1855–1926). Advocate of industrial unionism and a pacifist; imprisoned in 1895 for violating injunction in strike at Pullman, IL, and in 1918 under Espionage Act. He was pardoned by President Harding. Debs was a Presidential candidate four times: 1904, 1908, 1912, and 1920. Widely revered as martyr for his principles, he was nominated for a Nobel Peace Prize in 1924.

Debtors Anonymous. Self-help group. Address: General Service Office, P.O. Box 920888, Needham, MA 02492-0009. Web: http://www.debtorsanonymous.org/.

DECAF. Detect and Eliminate Computer Assisted Forensics (DECAF). DECAF is a program or software used by hackers designed to counteract the COFEE computer forensic software program. *See also* COFEE

decedent. One who has died, especially one recently dead.

deceptive advertising. Advertising that misleads the consumer in some material respect about a product offered for sale. This current legal definition, supplanting the earlier view that deceptive advertising is that which misleads the consumer in any particular, recognizes that, while some exaggeration or "puffing" of claims for a product is inevitable, the consumer is entitled to protection against substantial misstatement or intent to deceive. Deceptive advertising is prohibited by the Wheeler-Lea Act of 1938.

decision. A court order, decree, or judgment on a question of law or fact. It is distinguished from an opinion, which forms the basis of the decision.

decision tree concept, management. A graphic technique for assessing decision alternatives. Decisional alternatives are displayed in the form of a tree with nodes and branches. Each branch represents an alternative course of action/decision, leading to a node (event).

declaration. A statement.

declaration of intention. A necessary step in the procedure an alien follows to become an American citizen. In this step, he or she renounces allegiance to a native country and expresses the intention of becoming a citizen of the United States.

declarations of persons other than defendant. In court, such declarations cannot be proven unless they are (a) part of the *res gestae,* (b) admissible as dying declarations, (c) admissible as declarations by authority of the defendant, or (d) admissible as evidence given in a former proceeding.

declaratory judgment. A binding judicial declaration of rights, duties, or obligations in a dispute over the rights of parties under a statute, contract, will, or other document, without further action to grant relief. It is not necessary to show either that any wrong has been done, as in action for damages, or that any is immediately threatened, as in injunction proceedings. In most states and territories, and in federal courts since 1934, declaratory judgment has been made available by statute as a means of ascertaining the rights of parties without expensive litigation, though the courts tend to construe these statutes narrowly.

declaratory statute. A statute designed to remove doubts as to the meaning of the law on some particular subject.

declination. The U.S. Bureau of Justice defines declination as the prosecutorial decision not to file a case received for investigation/ prosecution.

decoy. (1) One whose role is to lure someone into a situation where he or she may be the victim of a crime; one who assumes the role of diverting attention away from another. (2) To lure.

decree. A judgment of a court or admiralty, or of another agency or individual answering for most purposes to the judgment of a court of common law. An order by an authority which has the force of law.

decree in equity. A sentence or order of the court, pronounced following a hearing and understanding of all the points at issue and determining the rights of all parties to the suit according to equity and good conscience. A decree is a declaration of a court that announces the legal consequences of the facts found.

decriminalization. The process of removing some form of conduct, previously defined as criminal, from the jurisdiction of criminal justice agencies. Several states have, for example, reduced criminal sanctions from a felony/misdemeanor to an infraction for the possession of small amounts (less than one ounce) of marijuana.

dedicated line. A permanent communications link devoted to a specific application. Generally not referencing one specific cable or line, the term refers to an expectation of constant availability in communications using the dedicated line.

dedicated security mode. An automated data processing system, its peripherals, and remotes that are exclusively used and controlled by specific users or groups of users to process a particular type and category of sensitive material. System users must have a need-to-know for all material in the system.

deduction. A form of logical inference in which particular conclusions are drawn from general principles. The classic deductive argument is the syllogism, which consists of three parts: a major premise, a minor premise, and a conclusion. A well-known example of a syllogism is: All men are mortal; Socrates is a man; therefore, Socrates is mortal. An argument that is valid according to the rules of deductive logic need not be true in the factual sense. A deductive argument is considered sound only when the premises are factually true and the derived conclusions are valid.

deep throat. Pseudonym given to the unnamed informant involved in the Watergate break-in of 1972. Deep throat provided Washington Post reporters Robert Woodward and Carl Bernstein with critical information about the break-in, leading to implications within the Nixon Presidency and ultimately, Nixon's resignation. After more than 30 years of anonymity, William Mark Felt, Sr., admitted to being Deep Throat in 2005, and his identity was confirmed by Woodward and Bernstein.

deface. To disfigure, mar, or alter the face or surface of something; to obliterate, alter, or destroy such things as inscriptions, writings, and so forth.

de facto (Lat.). (1) Actually; in fact. (2) Pertaining to a condition of affairs that actually exists. *See also de jure*

defamation. Intentional causing, or attempting to cause, damage to the reputation of another by communicating false or distorted information about his or her actions, motives, or character. Defamation is not a criminal offense in all jurisdictions; it can, however, always be a cause of action in a civil suit.

defame. To make slanderous statements about someone; to maliciously publish or express to any person, other than the one defamed, anything that tends to expose (a) any person to hatred, contempt, or ridicule or (b) the memory of one deceased to such things; to injure the good name or reputation of another.

default. (1) Failure to appear in court at an appointed or particular time. (2) Failure to pay a debt or obligation when it is due.

defendant. A person formally accused of an offense(s) by the filing in court of a charging document.

defendant dispositions. The class of prosecutorial or judicial actions that terminate, or provisionally halt, proceedings regarding a given defendant in a criminal case after charges have been filed in court. Dispositions are: no true bill, *nolle prosequi;* dismissal; transfer to juvenile court; adjudication withheld (with referral to probation or other criminal justice agency, with referral to noncriminal-justice agency, or with no referral); incompetent to stand trial; civil commitment;

acquittal; not guilty by reason of insanity; sentencing postponed; suspended sentence (unconditionally suspended sentence or conditionally suspended sentence); balance of sentence suspended or sentenced to time served; grant of probation (court probation or supervised probation); restitution, fine, forfeit, or court costs; residential commitment; jail commitment; and prison commitment (definite term, minimum-maximum term, life term, or death sentence).

defense. (1) The party (or his or her attorney) against whom a civil or criminal action in court is brought. Under the adversary system used in our courts, the two parties in a criminal action are the prosecution and the defense. (2) That which is offered or pleaded in denial of the charge against the accused. *See also* consent of the victim; duress; entrapment; insanity; justification; mistake of fact; mistake of law

defense attorney. The lawyer representing the defendant in a criminal action.

defense counsel. Counsel for the defendant; an attorney who represents and aids the defendant. The courts have held in recent years that a defendant has the right to counsel, either employed by the defendant or appointed by the court, to represent him or her at each critical stage of the prosecutive procedure, as guaranteed by the Sixth Amendment of the U.S. Constitution.

defense of accused person. It is a universal principle of criminal law in the United States that a person accused of crime is entitled to be advised by a lawyer and to be represented by one at all critical stages of criminal proceedings, including custodial interrogation, post-indictment lineups, preliminary hearings, arraignment, trial, sentencing, and the first appeal of conviction (not in appellate courts). This means counsel is provided without cost for a defendant who is too poor to employ a lawyer. In most states, such counsel is appointed by the judge in the court where the defendant is standing trial. Some jurisdictions have an officer, known as a public defender, who represents indigent defendants.

Defense Intelligence Agency (DIA). The Defense Intelligence Agency is a Department of Defense combat support agency headquartered at the Pentagon, Washington, DC. Mission of DIS is to "plan, manage, and execute intelligence operations during peacetime, crisis, and war."Address: DOD, The Pentagon, Washington, DC 20301; Web: http://www.dia.mil/.

Defense Investigative Service (DIS). Agency within the U.S. Department of Defense from 1972–1999. Became Defense Security Service in 1999.

Defense Logistics Agency. (DLA). Agency within the U.S. Department of Defense established in 1961 that provides "logistics combat support agency, providing worldwide logistics support in both peacetime and wartime to the military services as well as several civilian agencies and foreign countries." Address: Andrew T. McNamara Building, 8725 John J. Kingman Road. Fort Belvoir, VA 22060-6221; Web: http://www.dla.mil/.

Defense Security Service (DSS). Agency that operates within the U.S. Department of Defense and provides "security investigations, supervising industrial security, and performing security education and awareness training." The agency does not have police powers and is not staffed by sworn law enforcement officers. Predecessor agency was Defense Investigative Service (1971–1999). Address: 2780 Airport Drive, Ste 400 Columbus, OH 43219-2268; Web: https://www.dss.mil/GW/ShowBinary/DSS/index.html.

defensible space. (1) A theory developed by Oscar Newman suggesting that proper physical design of housing encourages residents to extend their social control from their homes and apartments into surrounding common areas. Residents change what had been perceived as semipublic or public territory into monitored private territory. Collective care and attention to the common areas results in a form of social control and discourages crime. (2) Protective devices such as guards, alarms, locks, lights, barriers, and animals, to discourage or thwart unauthorized entry, sometimes referred to as "hardening the target." *See also* broken window syndrome; Newman, Oscar

deferred sentencing. A system, provided by law in some states, in which sentencing is postponed for a specified period of time following conviction. Generally in cases with low recidivism risk. If the defendant complies with court ordered provisions (generally to remain crime-free), the conviction is often vacated. However, if the defendant is arrested or comes before the court during the deferment period, the court may impose sentence. *See also* suspended sentence

deficiency judgment. A creditor's claim against a debtor for that part of a judgment debt not satisfied by the sale of the mortgaged property. Example: A owes B $1,000 secured by a mortgage on property belonging to A. A default in payment of the debt. B obtains a judgment and forecloses, and the mortgaged property is sold according to law for $900. The difference—$100—is still owed by A and is covered by a deficiency judgment.

definite sentence. A sentence that includes a specific period of imprisonment.

definition of crime. An act injurious to the public, forbidden by law, and punishable by the state by fine, imprisonment, or both, through a judicial proceeding brought by the state.

defounding. The process of statistically lowering unsolved felonies to misdemeanors. *See also* unfounding

defraud. To cheat or deprive another.

degree. In criminal law, the ranking of crimes according to seriousness.

Dei gratia (Lat.). By the grace of God.

deindividuation. The process by which a person in a group loses responsibility as an identifiable individual. This loss can account for the uncharacteristically bold group actions of usually restrained individuals, as in mob behavior.

deinstitutionalization. In criminal justice, moving special populations such as juveniles or the mentally ill out of secure-care facilities, detention centers, or jails and into community-based programs or to the community.

de jure. (1) By right, according to law. (2) Pertaining to a situation that is based on law, or right, or previous action. *See also de facto*

deliberately. Intentionally, "in cold blood."

deliberation. The action of a jury to determine the guilt or innocence, or the sentence, of a defendant.

delinquency. In its broadest sense, delinquency is defined as (a) juvenile actions or conduct in violation of criminal law; (b) juvenile status offenses (a variety of acts and behaviors that are not illegal if committed by adults); and (c) other juvenile misbehavior.

delinquency law, first state. *See* child delinquency law, first state

delinquent. (1) In American penology the term *delinquent* usually refers to the juvenile offender whose misconduct is a violation of the law. Such conduct is generally considered less offensive than an adult's misconduct because of the child's age and/or the lack of seriousness of the offense; (2) a pejorative term used to describe a adolescent or young adult who engages in nuisance or malfeasant behavior that elicits aggravation, but which is not necessarily illegal.

delinquent, defective. An antiquated term referring to a juvenile or an offender who commits relatively non-serious offenses, who has some defect in his or her physical or mental faculties. The historical use of the term generally refers to delinquents who were labeled "feeble-minded" or "mentally incompetent" and were hence incapable of assuming responsibility for their conduct.

delirium tremens. A severe reaction to the withdrawal of alcohol, which can occur during alcohol detoxification in chronic alcoholics. The following symptoms may be observed: body tremors, irritability, confusion, disorientation, diminished attention span, stupor, delirium, hallucinations, seizures, nausea, vomiting, fever, stomach pain, chest pain. Although rare, it can also lead to death. The onset of symptoms generally occur around 72 hours after last drink, but onset can also begin as late as 7–10 days after last drink.

delit. A grade of crime. American criminal law has followed the English common law in dividing crimes into treason, felonies, and misdemeanors. The Continental European Codes use a different, although roughly comparable, classification. In the French *Code Penal,* crimes are classified as *crimes* (felonies), *delits* (indictable misdemeanors), and *contraventions* (violations of police regulations). The Italian *Codice Penale* uses *delitti* for felonies and *contravenzioni* for misdemeanors. The German *Strafgesetzbuch* employs *verbrechen* (felonies), *vergehen* (the French *delits* and American misdemeanor), and *ubertretung* (violation of police regulations).

DeLorean, John (1925–2005). American automobile engineer and chairman of DeLorean Motor Corporation (1975–1982). DeLorean was charged with drug trafficking in 1982, which resulted in acquittal when he successfully argued entrapment, as the government reportedly used his financial desperation, caused by his failing automobile business, to induce him to commit a crime he was otherwise unlikely to commit. He 1984 acquittal followed two years behind his corporate bankruptcy in 1982. *See also* entrapment

Delphi method. A decision-making method often used in business that uses forecasts from a structured group of experts in multiple iterations of forecasting to arrive at the most accurate prediction.

delusion. A false belief that persists in the face of evidence that it is irrational. Such beliefs are often symptoms of mental illness. A paranoid patient, for example, may have delusions of grandeur, being convinced that he or she is the Messiah or the secret power in the government. Also found in paranoid schizophrenia are delusions of persecution, such as an elaborately detailed belief that hidden enemies have been plotting against the patient for years. Delusions of extreme worthlessness, sin, and guilt are found in depressed patients.

dementia. A group of symptoms caused by changes in brain function often associated with aging, and most commonly due to Alzheimer's disease. According to the National Institute on Aging, symptoms of dementia include "asking the same questions repeatedly; becoming lost in familiar places; being unable to follow directions; getting disoriented about time, people, and places; and neglecting personal safety, hygiene, and nutrition."

demise. (1) The transfer or conveyance of an estate to another. (2) Termination. The cessation of activity or existence.

democracy. A form of government in which the nation's (or state's) power resides in the people. If all the people participate directly, it is a pure democracy. If the people elect representatives to speak for them, as in the United States, it is a representative democracy.

demography. The statistical study of human populations, including size, composition, distribution, and patterns of change. *See also* census tract; Metropolitan Statistical Areas

demonstration. (1) A nonviolent group display expressing opinion or protest regarding a political, social or other cause, generally manifested by parades, meetings, exhibiting placards, shouting, speeches, sit-down actions, and so forth. (2) A military attack or show of force, often to distract the enemy.

demonstrative evidence. Evidence that speaks for itself, such as real or physical evidence. Evidence that a jury can see and use in arriving at a conclusion without needing it

explained. A gun in a murder case would be an example.

demur. To object or take exception.

demurrage. (1) Detention of a vessel or vehicle beyond the time allowed for loading or unloading. (2) Payment for such detention.

demurrer. Plea for the dismissal of a suit on the grounds that, even if true, the statements of the opposition are insufficient to sustain the claim.

de novo (Lat.). As new; anew; all over again. When an appellate court reviews a case of a lower court that is not a court of record, the case is heard *de novo;* that is, it is tried again in its entirety.

deoxyribonucleic acid (DNA). Deoxyribo nucleic acid is an essential component of all living matter and the basic chromosomal material transmitting the hereditary pattern. Investigators can identify suspects by comparing their unique individual genetic codes with the code found in samples of hair, blood, skin, and semen left at crime scenes. *See also* DNA analysis

Department of Criminology and Criminal Justice. Founded in 1961 as the Center for the Study of Crime, Delinquency and Corrections by the College of Human Resources, Southern Illinois University, the department is responsible for instruction and research in the field of criminal justice. Address: College of Human Resources, Southern Illinois University at Carbondale, Carbondale, IL 62901.

Department of Homeland Security (DHS). Established in 2004, the mission of the United States Department of Homeland Security is "to secure the nation from the many threats we face." The DHS covers five primary areas, including: antiterrorism; border security; immigration enforcement; disaster readiness, response and recovery; unifying such efforts in a central department. Address: Department of Homeland Security, U.S. Department of Homeland Security, Washington, DC 20528; Web: http://www.dhs.gov/index.shtm.

Department of Justice (DOJ). The legal department of the federal government, created by law on June 22, 1870, which expanded the office of the attorney general. The DOJ furnishes legal advice and opinions to the president and heads of other federal departments and represents the government in legal matters concerning taxes, lands, monopolies and trusts, immigration and naturalization, civil rights, internal security, and other civil and criminal proceedings. The department directs and supervises the work of the Federal Bureau of Investigation, the U.S. marshals and district attorneys, the federal penal institutions, the pardon attorney, and the Parole Board and conducts all suits in the Supreme Court in which the United States is a party. To enforce the law and defend the interests of the United States according to the law; to ensure public safety against threats foreign and domestic; to provide federal leadership in preventing and controlling crime; to seek just punishment for those guilty of unlawful behavior; and to ensure fair and impartial administration of justice for all Americans. The Border Patrol Academy of the DOJ is located at Artesia, NM. Address: U.S. Department of Justice, 950 Pennsylvania Avenue, NW, Washington, DC 20530-0001; Web http://www.justice.gov.

Department of the Treasury. A department of the federal government, created on September 2, 1789, which superintends and manages national finances and is especially charged with improvement of public revenues and public credit. The Treasury Department is the executive agency responsible for promoting economic prosperity and ensuring the financial security of the United States It analyzes taxing policies, collects customs duties and internal revenue taxes, is responsible for borrowing, paying off, and refunding long- and short-term debts, continually studies the flow of lending, enforces export controls, registers and licenses vessels engaged in foreign and domestic commerce, administers the narcotics laws, coins money, prints paper money and postage and other stamps, suppresses counterfeiting and violations of the revenue laws, investigates thefts of government property, and, through its Secret Service division, protects the person of the president. Address: 1500 Pennsylvania Avenue, NW Washington, DC 20220; Web: http://www.ustreas.gov/.

departure. Term used in reference to a deviation from expected sentence, as defined or expressed in statute. In many jurisdictions, departure from a statutorily defined sentence requires judicial explanation of why such a sentence is necessary in the case at hand.

dependency. The state of being dependent upon another person or entity for proper care and support. One who is unable to provide for their own care and support and must look to another for care. In criminal justice, this generally pertains to a dependent child who is under the care of the juvenile or family court. This term can also reference a geographic region that is under the jurisdiction of another, such as Puerto Rico to the United States.

dependent child. A minor who has been declared, generally by a court ruling, to be under the jurisdiction of the juvenile court.

deponent. (1) One who makes a deposition. (2) One who testifies or swears to the veracity of certain facts; an affiant.

Depo-Provera. brand name for medroxyprogesterone acetate (DMPA). In females, Depo-Provera is a contraceptive injection, preventing pregnancy for about three months per administration. It is also used as a "chemical castration" drug for male sex offenders, as it greatly reduces sexual response in men

deport. To banish; to return a person to the country from which he came.

deportation. Forcible expulsion or removal of a person from his or her territory or country of residence. As a form of punishment, deportation appears in history from very ancient times. In the United States several laws concerning deportation have been enacted since the Alien Act (1798), later repealed, which gave the president power to deport any alien judged dangerous. Only aliens can be deported; American citizens cannot be expelled from the United States. Sometimes called "Treaty Transfer" in federal court. *See also* United States Citizenship and Immigration Service

deposit bond. Requirement that a defendant post a fraction of the total bail in order to secure release.

deposition. Sworn testimony obtained outside, rather than in, court. Generally recorded in written form for use in court at a later time.

depression era gangsters. *See* Dillinger, John; Floyd, Charles; Kelly, George, and Nelson, George

deputy. A substitute; a person duly authorized by an officer to exercise some or all of the officer's duties in his or her stead.

deputy sheriff. One appointed to act in the place and stead of the sheriff in his or her official duties. A general deputy or "undersheriff" is one who, by virtue of his or her appointment, has authority to execute all the ordinary duties of the office of sheriff and who executes process without any special authority from his or her principal. A special deputy, who is an officer *pro hac vice,* is one appointed for a special occasion or service, such as keeping the peace when a riot or tumult is expected or in progress. He or she acts under a specific, and not a general, appointment and authority.

deringer; derringer. A small pocket pistol, originally made by Henry Deringer of Philadelphia, but copied by many others.

derivative evidence. Evidence obtained as the result of information gained through a previous act or statement, such as a search of premises that furnished leads on the basis of which the later evidence was found. The same would hold where a statement or confession is the basis for obtaining the derivative evidence. If the first acts are illegal, then the derivative evidence falls into "the fruit of the poisonous tree" category and is inadmissible. *See also* fruit of the poisonous tree

DeSalvo, Albert Henry (The Boston Strangler). (1931–1973). Born the son of a violent alcoholic, DeSalvo was raised in severe violence, witnessing his father beat his mother and being forced to watch his drunk father have sex with prostitutes. He began torturing animals by age 9. He and his sister were sold into slavery to a farmer; they escaped and returned home, after which time DeSalvo began to torture animals, steal, and commit robbery. His first serious arrest (for robbery and battery) occurred when he was just 12 years old. He was arrested multiple times before he joined the army. DeSalvo is suspected of beginning his killing spree around age 30. Between 1962–1964, at least 13 women were raped and murdered in Boston, the crimes attributed to the "Boston Strangler." DeSalvo was arrested and convicted of rape and robbery in 1967 and sentenced to life in prison. During his trial, he confessed to the Boston Strangler murders, although he was never charged. DeSalvo was murdered in prison in 1973.

descriptive statistics. Measures used to summarize the observations in a sample. Because hundreds of individual measurements are impossible to comprehend, statistics are used to reduce and summarize data into more manageable and interpretable forms. Descriptive statistics are often displayed in a frequency distribution. Researchers often use statistics to describe what the typical observation in a sample looks like (for example, some measure of central tendency such as mean, median, or mode), as well as a measure of how much variability exists around this typical observation (a measure of dispersion such as range, variation, or standard deviation). For example, a researcher might describe a sample by saying that the average respondent is 32 years old, but that persons in the sample range are in age from 18 to 73. In addition to describing individual variables in a summary way, the researcher often will also describe relationships between and among variables with other statistics, such as the correlation coefficient. *See also* inferential statistics

desecration. The defacing, damaging, or mistreatment of a public structure, monument, or place of worship or burial.

desegregation. The process of abolishing racial segregation, most commonly in reference to the United States desegregation of the 1950s and 1960s. In *Brown v. Board of Education of Topeka* (1954) Chief Justice Earl Warren of the Supreme Court read the unanimous opinion of the Court, which declared that segregation of children in public schools solely on the basis of race, even though physical facilities and other "tangible" factors are equal, deprives such children of equal educational opportunities. In 1955, the Court decreed that the implementation of its earlier decision was to be assumed by the lower federal courts, which were to supervise and enforce desegregation within a reasonable time. In *Bolling v. Sharpe* (1954), the Court also ruled unanimously that segregation deprives children of due process of law under the Fifth Amendment.

desertion. (1) Also called abandonment, the willful abandonment of one spouse by the other without legal cause or intention of returning. In constructive desertion, the misconduct of one spouse forces the end of cohabitation. In most of the United States, desertion of one to two years' duration is grounds for divorce; (2) in military terms, desertion is abandonment of a military post without authorization from superiors. *See also* Absence Without Leave

designer drugs. Drugs whose molecules are altered to make them legal and more potent; substances designed to be undetectable by traditional methods of testing. Drug laws define illegal drugs by their exact molecular structure, so it is possible for a chemist to evade the law by making minor changes in these structures. If an analog is identified, but is not on the controlled substance list, it is not illegal.

detain. To stop someone and prevent his or her freedom of movement or action for a short period of time; to interfere with one's freedom of movement or actions.

detainee. Usually, a person held in local, very short-term confinement while awaiting consideration for pretrial release or first appearance for arraignment.

detainer. In corrections, an official notice from a governmental to a correctional agency, requesting that a person wanted by the government but subject to the prison's jurisdiction not be released or discharged without notification, and without giving the government an opportunity to respond.

detective. Usually a sworn law enforcement officer engaged in investigating criminal matters. Such officers are generally plainclothed, as opposed to uniformed. Also, term can reference a privately employed detective investigating civil and criminal matters.

detector. A sensor such as those used to alert occupants of a dwelling, owners of a business, or officials to a specified event. Such events can include intrusion, equipment malfunction or failure, rate of temperature rise, smoke, carbon monoxide, or fire.

Detector Dogs, U.S. Customs and Border Patrol. Name given to canines working within the U.S. Customs and Border Patrol. The detector dogs screen for prohibited contraband such as narcotics, explosives, and weapons at U.S. border crossings. http://www.cbp.gov/xp/cgov/border_security/port_activities/canines/.

detention. The legally authorized confinement of a person subject to criminal or juvenile court proceedings until commitment to a correctional facility or release. Detention describes the custodial status (reason for custody) of persons held in confinement after arrest or while awaiting the completion of judicial proceedings. Release from detention can occur either prior to trial or after trial or adjudication, as a result of a dismissal of the case, an acquittal, or a sentencing disposition that does not require confinement.

detention center. The locked ("secure") facility in which juveniles are detained.

detention hearing. A juvenile court hearing on the issue of limiting a parent's or guardian's custody of a minor by determining where the child is to be housed.

detention, preventive. The incarceration of an unconvicted person, without bail, on the grounds that the person poses a danger to society. Generally, this occurs when the person is accused of a serious felony, and incarceration during trial ensures public safety. In 2009, President Obama proposed plans for indefinite preventive detention of persons suspected of terrorist activity. *See* preventive pretrial detention

detention, protective. Based on a policy of social defense or protection, some countries and states have attempted to keep selected offenders, in custody for an indefinite or life period after they would qualify for release if they were ordinary offenders. Most commonly, such statues are proposed for the confinement of habitual offenders in prison; such an extended stay is often accomplished by delaying parole or by the use of third- and fourth-time offender acts, under which a prisoner may be detained for periods up to life.

deter. To prevent a person from an act by threat, warning, or, as in imprisonment, example.

deterrence. A theory that swift, certain, and severe punishment will discourage specific wrongdoers and others generally from similar illegal acts. There are two types of deterrence: general and specific. General deterrence refers to setting examples that discourage criminal behavior in the population at large, but specific deterrence is directed at a single individual by incarcerating or supervising him or her.

detox, detoxification. (1) Removal of toxins from the body. (2) In criminal justice, detox generally refers to the processes of managing withdrawal symptoms in addicted persons when they stop injecting the substance of addiction.

detoxification center. A public or private facility for the short-term medical treatment of either acutely intoxicated persons or chronic drug or alcohol abusers. Such a center often functions as an alternative to jail for persons who have been taken into custody.

developmental disability. Various terms such as mental deficiency, feeblemindedness, amentia, mental subnormality, imbecile, mental defectiveness, and mental retardation have historically been used in court to describe a state of developmental disability. Developmental disability is a broad category of conditions characterized by impaired cognitive function and deficits in adaptive behavior, with onset before age 18. Although this category includes persons with autistic spectrum disorders, epilepsy, and cerebral palsy, it is the term best suited for use in the criminal justice system, as it is devoid of pejorative connotation characterized in other terminology. The Diagnostic and Statistical Manual of Mental Disorders-IV-TR, includes a range of disability, generally classified by Intelligence Quotient (IQ): IQ 70–84 is considered "borderline intellectual functioning, IQ 50–69 is mild mental retardation, 35–49 is moderate mental retardation, 20–34 is severe mental retardation, and below 20 is profound mental retardation. Each of these levels corresponds to decreasing ability to perform basic tasks of self-care and sufficiency, as well as different levels of criminal liability. Generally, persons with IQ below 70 are not prosecuted for criminal acts, as they generally lack the intent required by codes. However, this is a general standard promoted by experts in the field and does not preempt statute. It is also a somewhat dynamic area of law. For example, the U.S.S.C. allowed the execution of persons with "mental retardation" in *Penry v. Lynaugh (1989)*. In *Atkins v. Virginia (2002)*, however, the Court declared the execution of the "mentally retarded" as a cruel and unusual punishment in violation of the Eighth Amendment's ban, citing national consensus about the inappropriateness of executing persons with developmental disabilities. Developmental disability is markedly different from mental illness. *See also* mental illness

deviance. Behavior that is contrary to the standards of conduct or social expectation of a given group or society. Deviance has alternately been described as being pathological, or having roots in social disorganization. *See also* anomie; Merton, Robert

devise. To give or bequeath by will.

devisee. Person or organization to whom a devise or bequest is made.

diagnosis or classification center. A functional unit within a correctional or medical facility, or a separate facility, which contains persons held in custody for the purpose of determining whether criminal proceedings should continue or whether sentencing, treatment, or disposition to a correctional facility or program is appropriate for a committed offender. Persons may be sent to these centers either before or after court disposition of the case. Parolees returned to prison for alleged or confirmed parole violations may also be placed in diagnostic facilities for study and/ or reclassification. Many state prison systems employ a classification center, also called a reception center, to intake new inmates and assign them to appropriate institutions. *See also* reception center

diagnostic commitment. The action of a court ordering a person subject to criminal or juvenile proceedings to be temporarily placed in a confinement facility for study and evaluation of his or her personal history and characteristics, usually as a preliminary to a sentencing or other disposition of the case. This kind of commitment, usually a provisional one that is followed by a final defendant disposition, may occur before judgment and thus be unrelated to any determination of guilt. Diagnostic commitments

have various purposes. A court may commit a person for study and observation to determine whether he or she is competent to be tried and, if found incompetent or not guilty by reason of insanity, whether the person is a danger to self or others. There is also the diagnostic commitment to advise the court as to what kind of correctional program, if any, is most suitable for a person convicted of a crime or adjudged to be a delinquent or status offender. This kind of determination is often made for presentation to the court in a presentence (adult) or predisposition (juvenile) report.

Diagnostic and Statistical Manual (DSM). Published by the American Psychiatric Association, the DSM lists symptoms and diagnostic criteria for mental health disorders. Recognized by the APA. It is important to note that this manual is fluid, with various editions adding and omitting disorders. For example, homosexuality was listed as a sexual deviation until it was removed from the DSM-II in 1973; post-traumatic stress disorder was added to the DSM-III in 1980, although the diagnostic criteria has changed in each subsequent edition of the DSM.

dialed number recorders. (1) Devices, also called traps and tracers, used by telephone companies in cooperation with law enforcement agencies to determine either (a) what numbers are being called from a particular phone or (b) what phones are being used to call a particular number. When used in situation (a), the dialed number recorder is attached to the suspect's phone line in a legal wiretap for which the law enforcement agency has obtained a warrant. Situation (b) is the result of a consumer's complaint to local law enforcement that he or she is receiving harassing phone calls; the trap is then placed on the victim's phone line to help determine the source of the calls; (2) private, noncommercial installation and use of a device to record both sides of a telephone conversation. Such use is accomplished through purchase of devices sold for this purpose, readily available at most electronic stores. Such devices generally come with disclaimers stating it is the users responsibility to ensure compliance with the Federal Wiretap Act of 1968. *See also* harassing calls; pen register

Diana Screen. A computer-based screening instrument developed by Abel Screening, Inc. which aims to reduce the risk of placing persons who present sexual risks to children and teenagers into positions of trust. Intended for use as a screening instrument for volunteer organizations, churches, day care centers, etc., this system is often used in conjunction with, not as a substitute for, criminal background screening.

dichotomy. (1) A division into two parts or lines. In charting the organizational structure (chain of command) of a police agency from the chief downward, there is a dichotomy when "line" and "staff" are shown; (2) a division into contradictory or opposing parts.

dictum. (1) Formal statement made by a judge. (2) A statement or opinion by the judge on some legal point other than the principal issue of the case.

dies non (Lat.). A day on which the courts do not transact any business, such as a Sunday or legal holiday.

diethyltryptamine. A relatively uncommon psychedelic drug found in many South American snuffs, such as yopo (prepared from the beans of the tree *Piptadenia peregrina*); the street name is DET.

differential association. A prominent sociological theory of crime causation, first published in 1939 by Edwin H. Sutherland. The concept of crime as "learned behavior" was formulated by Gabriel Tarde, a French jurist, who in 1890 published his ideas in his *Laws of Imitation.* Sutherland began with this concept; his theory consisted of seven basic correlates (later expanded to nine) explaining the process by which a particular person comes to engage in criminal behavior. Differential association asserts that criminal behavior is learned, and not the result of any concrete condition such as poverty or mental deficiency. This principle forms the crux of a general theory of crime designed to encompass white-collar and professional crime, as well as crime ordinarily related to social disorganization.

differential opportunity. A criminological theory explaining delinquent and criminal behavior, which emphasizes the access or lack of access people have to both legal and illegal ways of meeting their individual goals.

differential pressure sensor. A sensor used for perimeter protection that responds to the difference between the hydraulic pressures in two liquid-filled tubes buried just below the surface of the earth around the perimeter of the protected area. The pressure difference can indicate an intruder walking or driving over the buried tubes.

dilatory. Term that in law describes activity for the purpose of causing a delay or to gain time or postpone a decision.

dilatory exceptions. Those exceptions and motions filed for the purpose of retarding progress of the case but which do not tend to defeat the charges.

Dillinger, John Herbert (1903–1934). Dillinger was a nefarious bank robber and murdered during the Great Depression, suspected in dozens of bank robberies and multiple murders of police officers. In 1929, Dillinger was sentenced to 10 years for theft of $20 in 1929; Dillinger reportedly met multiple criminal associates and planned future crimes before his parole in 1933. He was apprehended twice for additional robberies between 1933–1934, although he escaped both times. He died in Chicago in 1934, during a police shoot-out in a movie theater. *See also* depression era gangsters

dimorphism. Possessing both male and female reproductive organs, sexual characteristics, or responses.

diphenylaminechloroarsine. (DM) A solid material that is dispersed by heat to produce an aerosol causing skin and eye irritation, chest distress, and nausea. In popular usage, "adamsite," used as a riot control gas, causes severe sneezing and vomiting; it is relatively nontoxic.

diphenylchloroarsine (DA). This mob- and riot control gas has a very rapid rate of action. Effects are felt within two or three minutes after one minute of exposure. It causes irritation of the eyes and mucous membranes, viscous discharge from the nose similar to that caused by a cold, sneezing and coughing, severe headache, acute pain and tightness in the chest, and nausea and vomiting. In moderate concentrations the effects last about 30 minutes after an individual leaves the contaminated atmosphere. At higher concentrations the effects may last up to several hours. Initially used in trench warfare of World War I, this substance is rarely used in the United States today.

diphenylcyanoarsine (DC). This mob- and riot-control gas has a very rapid rate of action. It causes the same symptoms as DA, but is more toxic.

diplomatic immunity. The law relating to diplomatic immunity is found in the Vienna Convention on Diplomatic Relations, which went into effect as part of U.S. federal law in 1972. Diplomats are exempt from local jurisdiction. They are free from arrest; trial in local courts; and police, fiscal, and ecclesiastical jurisdiction. Diplomats cannot be required to give evidence. They are entitled to freedom of communication. The diplomatic pouch is inviolate. Immunity extends to diplomats' families, documents, homes, and other personal belongings. Diplomatic immunity is based on common practice and is reciprocal. Because a diplomat cannot be tried in local courts, a host country may ask the diplomat's government to recall the offending official and to punish him or her. If diplomats commit serious crimes, they can be expelled from their host countries. They are expected to give due regard to local laws and regulations for the maintenance of public order and safety, and they may not interfere in domestic matters; if they do, they can be recalled.

dipsomania. Alcoholism; historical term describing an uncontrollable desire for intoxicating drinks; an irresistible impulse to indulge in intoxication, either by alcohol or other drugs.

direct action. Intimidation or violence (as a sit-in, street demonstration, or riot) in order to overawe the authorities, seize power, or obtain some other political objective.

direct contempt of court. Any contempt committed in the presence of the court, or the failure to comply with a summons, subpoena, or order to appear in court. *See also* contempt of court

direct evidence. Testimony or other proof that expressly or straightforwardly proves the existence of fact.

direct examination. Initial examination of witnesses by the side or party who calls them.

directed verdict. A verdict pronounced by a judge, or the order of a judge to a jury, for acquittal. Directed verdict is given during the trial of a criminal case in which the evidence presented by the prosecution clearly fails to show the guilt of the accused.

disability. (1) The Americans with Disability Act (ADA) defines a disability as "a physical or mental impairment that substantially limits a major life activity." The 2008 amendment to the ADA added examples of "major life activities" including such factors as "caring for oneself, performing manual tasks, seeing, hearing, eating, sleeping, walking, standing, lifting, bending, speaking, breathing, learning, reading, concentrating, thinking, communicating, and working." According to the World Health Organization, "Disabilities is an umbrella term, covering impairments, activity limitations, and participation restrictions. An impairment is a problem in body function or structure; an activity limitation is a difficulty encountered by an individual in executing a task or action; while a participation restriction is a problem experienced by an individual in involvement in life situations. Thus disability is a complex phenomenon, reflecting an interaction between features of a person's body and features of the society in which he or she lives." (2) Lack of legal qualifications to hold office, such as want of sufficient age or period of residence, the holding of an incompatible office, foreign citizenship, or, for the U.S. presidency, foreign birth.

Disaster Squad. In August of 1940, the FBI created a Disaster Squad to assist civilian authorities in identifying persons who died in a Virginia plane crash. FBI personnel were among the victims. The FBI's Disaster Squad identifies, through fingerprints, the victims of disasters. Its services are available, upon the request of local law enforcement and government agencies or transportation companies, following a catastrophe where the identification of victims is a problem. The squad also assists in identifying Americans in disasters abroad, but only at the specific invitation of the country involved. Address: FBI Disaster Squad, Identification Division, FBI, DOJ, 935 Pennsylvania Avenue Northwest, Washington, DC 20535-0001. Web: http://www.fbi.gov/hq/lab/disaster/disaster.htm.

discharge. To release a person from confinement, supervision, or a legal status imposing an obligation on him or her.

disciplinary punishment. Punishment to ensure compliance with the rules of a correctional facility.

disclaimer. A denial; disavowal.

discretion. An authority conferred by law on an official or an agency to act in certain conditions or situations in accordance with the named official's or agency's considered judgment and conscience.

discrimination. Unfavorable treatment of groups of people based on their class or category, such as race or religion; a form of control that keeps such groups socially distant from one another. This separation is accomplished through informal and formal institutionalized practices that attribute inferiority on the basis of notions that frequently have little or nothing to do with the real behavior of those who are discriminated against.

disfranchisement. (1) State action depriving a designated class or an individual of the privilege of voting, by imposition of new requirements such as a literacy test, as a consequence of conviction for felony or bribery, or by the neglect or refusal of election officers to register otherwise qualified voters. (2) Any act of discrimination or intimidation that has the practical effect of preventing exercise of suffrage; usually used colloquially.

disinter. To remove from the grave; exhume.

dismissal. (1) In judicial proceedings, generally, the disposal of an action, suit, motion, or the like without trial of the issues; the termination of the adjudication of a case before the case reaches judgment. (2) The decision by a court to terminate adjudication of all outstanding charges in a criminal case, or against a given defendant in a criminal case, thus terminating court action and, permanently or provisionally, court jurisdiction over the defendant in relation to those charges. This second definition and usage are more common than the first.

dismissal for want of prosecution. The judicial termination of a case against a defendant, occurring after the filing of a charging document but before the beginning of a trial, on grounds that the prosecuting party has withdrawn or is unable to proceed with the suit.

dismissal in the interest of justice. The judicial termination of a case against a defendant on the grounds that the ends of justice would not be served by continuing prosecution.

disorder. Riotous behavior; confusion of actions; disturbance of the peace.

disorderly conduct. A general term signifying any behavior that is contrary to law and, more particularly, that tends to disturb the public peace or decorum, scandalize the community, or shock the public sense of morality. Generally, disorderly conduct includes acts such as public drunkenness and disturbing the peace. State statutes often define behaviors that constitute disorderly conduct.

disorderly house. A house in which people live, or to which they resort, for purposes injurious to public morals, health, convenience, or safety. This term generally refers to houses of prostitution, illegal gambling or gaming casino, and locations where illegal drugs are sold.

disorderly person. One guilty of disorderly conduct.

disposition. The action by a criminal or juvenile justice agency that signifies either that a portion of the justice process is complete and jurisdiction is terminated or transferred to another agency or that a decision has been reached on one aspect of a case and a different aspect, requiring a different kind of decision, is now under consideration.

disposition hearing. A hearing in juvenile courts, conducted after an adjudicatory hearing and the subsequent receipt of the report of any predisposition investigation, to determine the most appropriate form of custody and/or treatment for a juvenile who has been adjudged a delinquent, a status offender, or a dependent. The possible dispositions of juveniles over whom a court has assumed jurisdiction range from placement, on probation or in a foster home, to confinement.

disqualification. Depriving someone from participating in a proceeding, due to a condition or some irregularity. A juror, because of prejudice or bias, may be disqualified from serving on a jury. Judges may disqualify themselves from conducting a trial because of a personal relationship to one or more of the parties or because of bias or prejudice.

dissent. (1) The opinion of a judge or judges, on a multi-judge court, presenting a view in opposition to all or part of the majority holding in the case being decided. (2) The expression of a judge who does not agree with the verdict of the majority of the court.

dissident. (1) Differing; not in accord with existing policy, rules, or laws; opposing; dissenting. (2) One who disagrees with existing laws, rules, or governmental actions.

dissolve. To annul or set aside an order such as an injunction.

distress. (1) To cause anxiety, strain, or worry; (2) The seizing of property from a wrongdoer to give an injured party in compensation for the wrong done, generally without legal authority or process for such seizure.

distribution. Delivery of a controlled substance other than by administration or dispensing.

district attorney. A locally elected official who represents the state in bringing indictments and prosecuting criminal cases; the prosecuting attorney or state's attorney. *See also* United States Attorneys

District Court, U.S. In the federal court system, the court of original criminal jurisdiction and a court of record; one such court is located in each federal judicial district and has jurisdiction over matters of that district. Several states have district courts that are courts of original jurisdiction. The district over which they have jurisdiction may be composed of one or more counties. They are similar to county courts in other states.

District of Columbia Preventive Detention Law. A 1970 bill in Washington, DC, that authorized pretrial preventive detention of offenders for 60 days on the basis of a judge's prediction of dangerousness.

distringas **writ**. A writ issued to a sheriff to seize the property of a defendant and/or the defendant, so that the person or evidence will be available when the suit proceeds.

disturbance of public meeting. In common law it is a misdemeanor to disturb a group of people convening for any lawful purpose, particularly for a distinctly moral or benevolent purpose.

disturbing the peace. Unlawful interruption of the peace, quiet, or order of a community, including offenses called disorderly conduct, vagrancy, loitering, unlawful assembly, and riot.

diversion. (1) In the broadest usage, any procedure that substitutes: (a) nonentry for official entry into the justice process; (b) the suspension of criminal or juvenile proceedings for continuation; (c) lesser supervision or referral to a nonjustice agency or no supervision for conventional supervision; or (d) any kind of nonconfinement status for confinement. (2) In criminal justice usage, the official suspension of criminal or juvenile proceedings against an alleged offender at any point after a recorded justice system intake but before the entering of a judgment and a decision either to refer the person to a treatment or care program administered by a nonjustice or private agency or not to make a referral.

diversity jurisdiction. That aspect of the jurisdiction of the federal courts that applies to suits between residents of different states.

Division of Investigation Act. Law passed by Congress on June 18, 1934, empowering certain members of the Division of Investigation of the Department of Justice to serve warrants and subpoenas issued under the authority of the United States; to make seizures under warrant; and to make arrests without warrant for felonies committed, if the person making the arrest has reasonable grounds to believe that the person being arrested is guilty of a felony and where the person is likely to escape before a warrant can be obtained. Prior to this, agents of the DOJ could only make citizen's arrests. *See also* Federal Bureau of Investigation, history of

divorce. The dissolution, or partial suspension by law, of a marital relationship.

divorce, no-fault. A legal option to dissolve a marriage, in which neither party is required to charge the other with a violation of the marital contract. Instead, one or both parties can declare they wish to divorce because of irreconcilable differences. In 1970, California was the first state to adopt a no-fault divorce law.

DNA. *See* deoxyribo nucleic acid

DNA analysis. There are at least six types of DNA analysis: the Restriction Fragment Length Polymorphism (RFLP) test; Polymerase Chain Reaction (PCR); PCR-based Short Tandem Repeat (STR) method; Amplified Fragment Length Polymorphism (AmbFLP) method; Short Tandem Repeat on the Y-chromosome (Y-STR); and mitochondrial DNA (mtDNA). While paternity and family relationship analysis are applications of DNA testing, they employ one of the methods above and are not a distinct test. The FBI currently uses the PCR-based Short Tandem Repeat (STR) typing" method. *See also* Restriction Fragment Length Polymorphism (RFLP) test; Polymerase Chain Reaction (PCR); PCR-based Short Tandem Repeat (STR) method; Amplified Fragment Length Polymorphism (AmbFLP) method; Short Tandem Repeat on the Y-chromosome (Y-STR); and mitochondrial DNA (mtDNA)

docket. A formal record of court proceedings.

document. An official paper, deed, manuscript, or any other written or inscribed instrument that has informational or evidentiary value.

documentary evidence. Evidence supplied by papers, books, or other written material.

document, class A. An identification document regarded as generally reliable. Examples include passports and armed forces identification cards.

document, class B. An identification document regarded as often reliable. Examples include photo-bearing drivers' licenses and photo-bearing employee cards issued by national firms.

document, class C. An identification document regarded as doubtfully reliable. This type of document will usually not contain a photo, serial number, or other means of verification.

document, class D. An identification document regarded as unreliable. This type of document can be obtained without proving identity, as in the case of a Social Security card.

document examiner. One who is an expert in the field of handwriting, handprinting, typewriting, inks, printing, and so forth.

Document Examiners, National Association of (NADE). Founded in 1979, as association of private forensic handwriting or document examiners. Publishes *The Communique* (quarterly newsletter) and *The Journal of the National Association of Document Examiners*. Web: http://documentexaminers. org/.

Doe, Jane. A fictitious name used to identify a female party in a legal action whose true name is unknown or who wishes to remain anonymous. Additional unknown or anonymous parties are sometimes known as Jane Roe. Doe is also used as a placeholder for an unknown female, such as an unidentified female corpse, or used to signify a typical female. *See also* Doe, John

Doe, John. A fictitious name used to identify a male party in a legal action whose true name is unknown or who wishes to remain anonymous. Additional unknown or anonymous parties are sometimes known as Richard Roe. Doe is also used as a placeholder for an unknown male, such as an unidentified male corpse, or used to signify a typical male. *See also* Doe, Jane

Dog, the Bounty Hunter. Reality television show based on the experiences of Duane Lee Chapman and his associates, who operate a bounty hunting business in Honolulu, Hawaii. *See* Chapman, Duane Lee

Dog Association, North American Police Work. Founded in 1977. Address: 4222 Manchester Avenue, Perry Ohio 44081. Web: http://www.napwda.com/.

Dogging. A colloquial expression used to describe the practice of engaging in sexual intercourse in a public, or semipublic location. Most commonly, such activities occur in parked cars in secluded locations. Persons caught engaging in public sex acts can be criminally prosecuted. *See also* exhibitionism, sex offender

domestic battering. Includes physical abuse between individuals who have an intimate relationship. Although wives are the most frequent victims, the term includes husbands and unmarried individuals. *See also* battered person syndrome, domestic violence; intimate partner violence

domestic relations court. A judicial branch, usually part of a system of municipal courts, the jurisdiction of which extends typically to matters concerned with family support and the care of children. The first domestic relations court was established in Buffalo, NY, in 1909 by Simon Augustine Nash, Judge of Police Court, who privately heard domestic relations cases in his chambers instead of in open court. Chapter 570, Laws of New York State, approved on May 29, 1909, established the City Court of Buffalo; the domestic relations division was opened January 1, 1910.

domestic terrorism. According to the USA PATRIOT Act, domestic terrorism are acts that "(A) involve acts dangerous to human life that are a violation of the criminal laws of the United States or of any State; (B) appear to be intended— (i) to intimidate or coerce a civilian population; (ii) to influence the policy of a government by intimidation or coercion; or (iii) to affect the conduct of a government by mass destruction, assassination, or kidnapping; and (C) occur primarily within the territorial jurisdiction of the United States." *See also* Bombing of Los Angeles Times building, Wall Street bombing, Unabomber attacks, Oklahoma City bombing, Centennial Olympic Park bombing, September 11 attacks, World Trade Center attack, anthrax attacks, Holocaust Memorial Museum shooting, IRS building suicide crash, shoe bomber, underwear bomber

domestic violence. Pattern of abusive behavior which includes physical violence, emotional abuse, sexual assault, or economic coercion, perpetrated by one or both partners in an intimate relationship. Can also refer to such acts against a member of one's family or household, including spouses, ex-spouses, parents, children, persons otherwise related by blood, persons living in the household, or persons formerly living there. According to the Bureau of Justice Statistics, there were approximately 627,400 nonfatal intimate partner victimizations in 2004, with violence occurring three times as often against women than men. Approximately one-third of these offenses were serious violent crimes such as rapes, sexual assaults, robberies, and aggravated assaults involving serious injuries, weapons or sexual offenses. Persons who have been convicted in any court of a qualifying misdemeanor crime of domestic violence (MCDV) generally are prohibited under federal law from possessing any firearm or ammunition in or affecting commerce (or shipping or transporting any firearm or ammunition in interstate or foreign commerce, or receiving any such firearm or ammunition). This prohibition also applies to federal, state, and local governmental employees in both their official and private capacities. Violation of this prohibition is a federal offense punishable by up to 10 years' imprisonment. Many states also have laws prohibiting the possession of a firearm by anyone, including law enforcement officers, convicted of a domestic violence offense. *See also* intimate partner violence

domicile. The permanent place of residence of persons, or the place to which they intend to return even though they may actually reside elsewhere. The legal domicile of a person is important since it, rather than the actual residence, often controls the jurisdiction of the taxing authorities and determines where a person may exercise the privilege of voting and other legal rights.

Doolin–Dalton Gang. *See* Wild Bunch

double jeopardy. Putting a person on trial for an offense for which he or she has previously been indicted and a jury empanelled and sworn to try him or her, provided that the jury did not disagree or was discharged because of the illness of a juror or other sufficient reason. It is prohibited by the Fifth Amendment, which provides in part, "Nor shall any person be subject for the same offense to be twice put in jeopardy of life or limb." The purpose of the prohibition is to prevent repeated harassment of an accused person and reduce the danger of convicting an innocent one. Double jeopardy does not apply when a convicted person appeals to a higher court or when state and federal governments prosecute separately for different offenses arising from the same act. Under state statutes, pleas of not guilty on double jeopardy grounds can be of two types: either *autrefois* acquit (formerly acquitted) or *autrefois* convict (formerly convicted) of the identical charge involving the same set of facts on a previous occasion before a court of competent jurisdiction.

doubt, reasonable. The state of mind of jurors in which, after the comparison and consideration of all the evidence, they cannot say that they feel an abiding conviction, a moral certainty, of the truth of a criminal charge against a defendant. Reasonable doubt, which is the standard of proof in most criminal cases, does not presuppose all doubt; there can still be some degree of doubt, but that doubt would not impact a reasonable person's belief that the defendant is guilty.

Draft Riots. For five days in July 1863, gangs laid siege to New York City. Their goal was to disrupt the process of the newly established draft. Rioters attacked the police and prominent politicians, looted stores, burned buildings, and destroyed railroad cars and telegraph lines. More than 100 people died.

dram law. A liquor law providing that person(s) serving someone who is intoxicated or contributing to the intoxication of another may be liable for subsequent injury or damage caused by the intoxicated person. Such state laws open public bars and, in some cases, private individuals, to liability suits. Many states in the United States have enacted dram laws, although the provisions for such laws vary by jurisdiction.

Dreyfus, Alfred. A young Jewish captain in the French army who was framed on a charge of passing secrets to the Germans. He was convicted in a closed-door court martial and sent to Devil's Island with a sentence of life in prison. The so-called Dreyfus Affair occurred during a period of intense nationalism and anti-Semitism in France. When the Army command realized that its case was weak, it manufactured evidence, reasoning that the honor of the army was more important than one man's life and career.

Timeline of Alfred Dreyfus:

October 10, 1894: The French minister of war accuses Capt. Dreyfus of being the author of a document sent to the Germans.

October 15: Dreyfus is arrested, and the army decides that his handwriting is similar to that in the document.

December 12: He is sentenced to life in prison.

January 5, 1895: He is stripped of his military rank in the courtyard of the Ecole Militaire.

March 1895–June 1899: Dreyfus is imprisoned on Devil's Island.

January 13, 1898: Émile Zola publishes "J'Accuse," telling Dreyfus's story, in the newspaper *L'Aurore.*

June 3, 1899: Dreyfus's military court sentence is annulled.

September 9, 1899: The War Council again convicts him, sentencing him to 10 years in prison.

July 12, 1906: The Supreme Court of Appeals annuls this sentence.

July 13: He is reintegrated into the army with the rank of commander. Dreyfus returned to active duty, fought beside his son in World War I, and was later awarded the French Legion of Honor medal.

July 12, 1935: Alfred Dreyfus dies in Paris at the age of 35. His death occurred on the twenty-ninth anniversary of the day the Supreme Court annulled his sentence.

driver. A person who operates or is in physical control of a vehicle.

driver and pedestrian education. The National Highway Traffic Safety Administration (NHTSA) of the Department of Transportation (DOT) provides information to states and local communities on various topics related to driver education and pedestrian safety. Research is also conducted on unsafe driving, vehicle occupant restraints, alcohol, pedestrians, and young drivers. Address: NHTSA Headquarters, 1200 New Jersey Avenue, SE, West Building, Washington, DC 20590; Web: http://www.nhtsa.dot.gov/.

driving records. The National Driver Register is a computerized database maintained by the National Highway Traffic Safety Administration (NHTSA) within the Department of Transportation (DOT). According to the NHTSA Web site, "the database contains information about drivers who have had their licenses revoked or suspended, or who have been convicted of serious traffic violations such as driving while impaired by alcohol or drugs. State motor vehicle agencies provide NDR with the names of individuals who have lost their privilege or who have been convicted of a serious traffic violation. When a person applies for a driver's license the state checks to see if the name is on the NDR file. If a person has been reported to the NDR as a problem driver, the license may be denied." Address: NHTSA Headquarters 1200 New Jersey Avenue, SE, West Building, Washington, DC 20590; Web: http://www.nhtsa.dot.gov/.

driving under the influence (DUI). (sometimes called driving while intoxicated). Unlawful operation of any motor vehicle while under the influence of alcohol or a controlled substance(s) or drug. While such laws are generally directed at the operation of automobiles, they include any motor vehicle, including motorcycles, mopeds, boats, jet skis, snow vehicles, assisted mobility devices, and aircrafts. In some states, DUI laws extend to other forms of transportation, including bicycles and horses. In 2007, an estimated 11,773 people died in drunk driving related accidents.

Driving under the Influence Cost Recovery Program. Program in effect in many states providing that any person under the influence of alcohol or a controlled substance whose negligent operation of a motor vehicle causes any incident leading to an emergency response is responsible for the costs associated with the response.

driving while intoxicated (DWI). *See* driving under the influence

Dr. Snow. *See* Lavin, Larry. (also called "Dr. Snow"). First indicted in 1984, this drug dealer's real name is Larry Lavin, then a 26-year-old dentist. The case involved a 60-kilogram-per-year cocaine distribution network headquartered in Philadelphia and headed by Lavin. By the time he was indicted under the "drug kingpin" statute, he had personally reaped an estimated $6 million from his drug operations. In 1986, Lavin was sentenced to 22 years after pleading guilty to five counts of drug conspiracy, and also received a 20-year sentence for tax evasion. He has since completed his term and was released from prison.

drug. Any substance that alters normal body functions when consumed. While this term can refer to over the counter medications, prescription medications, and herbal remedies, the use of this term in criminal justice generally denotes an illicit drug used for recreational purpose. This term is derived from the fourteenth-century French word *drogue,* meaning a dry substance. Most pharmaceuticals during that period were prepared from dried herbs. The National Clearinghouse for Alcohol and Drug Information includes the following types of drugs on their Web site: Acid/ LSD, Alcohol, Amphetamines, Analgesics,

Barbiturates, Buprenorphine, Club Drugs, Cocaine, Crack Cocaine, Depressants, Designer Drugs, Dextromethorphan (DXM), Ecstasy, Gamma Hydroxy Butyrate (GHB), Hallucinogens, Heroin/Morphine, Inhalants, Ketamine, Lysergic Acid Diethylamide (LSD), Marijuana, Methadone, Methamphetamines, Nicotine, Nitrous Oxide, Opiates/ Narcotics, Phencyclidine (PCP), Prescription Drugs, Prescription Medications, Psychedelics, Rohypnol, Steroids, Stimulants, Tobacco, and Vicodin. *See also* addiction; amphetamine; anabolic steroids; cocaine; cocaine, crack; gateway drugs; heroin; inhalants; marijuana; methadone; methaqualone; methylphenidate; morphine; nicotine; opium; peyote; phenecyclidine; salvia divinorum; and Valium and Librium

drug abuse. The pattern of continued use of a medication outside of prescribed or conventional uses in a manner that results in adverse consequences. The National Clearinghouse for Alcohol and Drug Information collects and disseminates information on drug abuse and produces information on drugs, drug abuse, and prevention. Web: http://ncadi.samhsa.gov/. *See also* addiction; drug misuse. *See* Table 22. Common Drugs of Abuse, page 152

Drug Abuse Epidemiology Data Center. *See* Division of Epidemiology, Services and Prevention Research (DESPR) Division of Epidemiology, Services and Prevention Research (DESPR)The research division of the National Institute on

Drug Abuse, U.S. Department of Health, Education, and Welfare. According to the organization's Web site, DESPR is NIDA's Division of Epidemiology, Services and Prevention Research (DESPR) which promotes integrated approaches the continuum of problems related to drug use. Address: Division of Epidemiology, Services and Prevention Research, National Institute on Drug Abuse, 6001 Executive Boulevard, Room 5153, MSC 9589, Bethesda, Maryland 20892-9589; Web: http://www.nida.nih.gov/about/organization/DESPR/.

text continues on page 154

TABLE 22   COMMON DRUGS OF ABUSE

Substance Category:	Substance Name:	Street Names / Examples:	DEA Schedule:	Administration:
Cannabinoids	Hashish	Boom, chronic, hash, hash oil, hemp	I	Swallowed, smoked
	Marijuana	Blunt, dope, ganja, grass, herb, Mary Jane, pot, reefer, skunk, weed	I	Swallowed, smoked
Depressants	Barbiturates	Barbs, reds, red birds, phennies, tooies, yellow, yellow jackets/*Amytal, Nembutal, Seconal, Phenobarbital*	II, III, V	Injected, swallowed
	Benzodiaze-pines	Candy, downers, sleep-ing pills, tranks/*Activan, Halcion, Librium, Valium, Xanax*	IV	Swallowed, injected
	Flunitrazepam	Forget-me pill, Mexican Valium, R2, Roche, roofies, roofinol, rope, rophies /*Rohypnol*	IV	Swallowed, snorted
	GHB	G, Georgia home boy, grievous bodily harm, liquid ecstasy/*Gamma-hydroxybutyrate*	I	Swallowed
	Methaqualone	Ludes, mandrex, quad, quay/*Quaalude, Sopor, Parest*	I	Injected, swallowed
Dissociative Anesthetics	Ketamine	Cat Valiums, K, Special K, vitamin K/*Ketalar SV*	III	Infected, snorted, smoked
	PCP and analogs	Angel dust, boat, hog, love boat, peace pill/*phencyclidine*	I, II	Injected, swal-lowed, smoked
Hallucinogens	LSD	Acid, blotter, boomers, cubes, microdot, yellow sunshines/*lysergic acid diethylamide*	I	Swallowed, absorbed through mouth tissues
	Mescaline	Buttons, cactus, mesc, peyote	I	Swallowed, smoked
	Psilocybin	Magic mushroom, purple passion, shrooms	I	Swallowed

(continued)

Substance Category:	Substance Name:	Street Names / *Examples*:	DEA Schedule:	Administration:
Opioids and Morphine Derivatives	Codeine	Captain Cody, Cody, schoolboy (with glutethimide), doors and fours, loads, pancakes and syrup/*Empirin with Codeine, Fiorinal with Codeine, Robitussin A-C, Tylenol with Codeine.*	II, III, IV, V	Injected, swallowed
	Fentanyl and fentanyl analogs	Apache, China girl, China white, dance fever, friend, goodfella, jackpot, murder 8, TNT, Tango and Cash/*Actiq, Duragesic, Sublimaze*	I, II	Injected, smoked, snorted
	Heroin	Brown sugar, dope, H, horse, junk, skag, skunk, smack, white horse/*Diacetylmorphine*	I	Injected, smoked, snorted
	Morphine	M, Miss Emma, monkey, white stuff/*Roxanol, Duramorph*	II, III	Injected, swallowed, smoked
	Opium	Big O, black stuff, block, gum, hop/*Laudanum, paregoric*	II, III, V	Swallowed, smoked
	Oxycodone HCL	O.C., killer/*OxyContin*	II	Swallowed, snorted, injected
	Hydrocodone bitartrate, acetaminophen	Vike, Watson-387/*Vicodin*	II	Swallowed
Stimulants	Amphetamine	Bennies, black beauties, crosses, hearts, LA turnaround, speed, truck drivers, uppers/ *Biphetamine, Dexedrine*	II	Injected, swallowed, smoked, snorted
	Cocaine	Blow, bump, C, candy, Charlie, coke, crack, flake, rock, snow, toot	II	Injected, smoked, snorted
	MDMA (methylenedioxymethamphetamine)	Adam, clarity, ecstasy, Eve, lover's speed, peace, STP, X, XTC	I	Swallowed

(continued)

Substance Category:	Substance Name:	Street Names / Examples:	DEA Schedule:	Administration:
	Metham-phetamine	Chalk, crank, crystal, fire, glass, go fast, ice, meth, speed/*Desoxyn*	II	Injected, swallowed, smoked, snorted
	Methylphenidate (safe and effective for treatment of ADHD)	JIF, MPH, R-ball, Skippy, the smart drug, vitamin R/*Ritalin*	II	Injected, swallowed, snorted
	Nicotine	Cigarettes, cigars, smoke-less tobacco, snuff, spit tobacco, bids, chew	Not scheduled	Smoked, snorted, taken in snuff and spit tobacco
Other Compounds:	Anabolic steroids	Roids, juice/*Anadrol, Oxandrin, Durabolin, Depo-Testosterone, Equipoise*	III	Injected, swallowed, applied to skin
	Dextromethorphan (DXM)	Found in some cough and cold medications; Robotripping, Robo, Triple C	Not scheduled	Swallowed
	Inhalants	Solvents (paint thinners, gasoline, glues), gases (butane, propane, aerosol propellants, nitrous oxide), nitrates (isoamyl, isobutyl, cyclohexyl): laughing gas, poppers, snappers, whippets	Not scheduled	Inhaled through nose or mouth

Source: National Institute on Drug Abuse. Compiled by Jennifer Doyle, CSULB.

drug abuse violations. Offenses relating to growing, manufacturing, making, possessing, using, selling, or distributing narcotic and dangerous nonnarcotic drugs. *See also* drug law violations; designer drugs

Drug Abuse Warning Network (DAWN). Begun in 1972 and funded by the National Institute on Drug Abuse, this network identifies and evaluates the scope and magnitude of drug abuse in the United States using information about drug-related visits to hospital emergency rooms and drug related deaths investigated by medical examiner facilities. DAWN identifies drugs currently being abused, determines existing patterns and profiles of abuse/abuser, monitors systemwide abuse trends, detects new abuse entities and polydrug combinations, provides data for the assessment of health hazards and abuse potential of drug substances, and provides data needed for rational control and scheduling of drugs of abuse. Address: P.O. Box 2345, Rockville, MD 20847-2345. Web: https://dawninfo.samhsa.gov/.

drug addiction. In 2001, the American Academy of Pain Medicine, the American Pain Society, and the American Society of Addiction Medicine defined drug addiction as "a primary, chronic, neurobiologic disease, with genetic, psychosocial, and environmental factors influencing its development and manifestations. It is characterized by behaviors that include one or more of the following: impaired control over drug use, compulsive use, continued use despite harm, and craving." *See also* addiction, drug use, substance dependence

drug and alcohol abuse in the military. The Office of Drug Abuse has identification, treatment, and educational programs on drug and alcohol abuse. It provides quarterly reports that include data on the number of people identified, rejected, discharged, tried, and court-martialed by the military. Address: Office for Drug and Alcohol Abuse Prevention, Health Affairs, Department of Defense, The Pentagon, Room 3D171, Washington, DC 20301.

drug czar. A popular designation for the director of the White House Office on National Drug Policy, which was created by then vice president George Bush in 1988 to coordinate the 50 U.S. agencies charged with suppressing illegal drugs and their use. The first such director was William Bennett, who served from 1989 to 1990. Next was Robert Martinez, also appointed by Bush, who served from 1990 to 1991; John Walters was acting director from 1991 to 1993; next was Lee Brown, appointed by President William Clinton, who served from March 8, 1993, to November 1994; the fourth director was Barry McCaffrey, a retired four-star general of Gulf War fame, who was appointed by President Clinton and took office in March 1995. John Walters, acting director from 1991 to 1993, was appointed director by President George W. Bush on December 7, 2001. Walters is credited with the launching of an award-winning campaign linking drug trafficking and terrorism. Most recently, Gil Kerlikowske was appointed by President Barack Obama on May 7, 2009.

Drug Dealer Liability Act. A statute providing a civil damages to people injured as a result of the use of a controlled substance. Such victims can include the parents of a drug

user, employers, insurers, governmental agencies, and others who pay for drug treatment programs, as well as infants injured as a result of exposure to controlled substances in utero. Many states in the United States have similar laws, the provisions of which vary by statute.

drug detection. Law enforcement has relied upon several methods in detecting or searching for illegal drugs. They include informants; drug-sniffing dogs; visual and enhanced visual observation (binoculars); and low-flying aircraft and helicopters. However, in June 2001, the Supreme Court (*Kyllo vs. U.S. 99-8508*) ruled that the use of thermal imaging to detect heat from a home violated the 4th Amendment. A thermal imager operates like a video camera, except that it shows white heat spots. This decision dealt only with a private residence, not a car or a work site.

drug education materials. Drug education materials are available free of charge to civic, educational, private, and religious groups through the National Institute on Drug Abuse (NIDA). Address: National Institute on Drug Abuse, National Institutes of Health, 6001 Executive Boulevard, Room 5213, Bethesda, MD 20892-9561, Web: http://www.nida.nih.gov/.

Drug Enforcement Administration (DEA). According to its Web site, the mission of the DEA, which was founded in 1973 under the U.S. Department of Justice, is to "enforce the controlled substances laws and regulations of the United States and bring to the criminal and civil justice system of the United States, or any other competent jurisdiction, those organizations and principal members of organizations, involved in the growing, manufacture, or distribution of controlled substances appearing in or destined for illicit traffic in the United States; and to recommend and support nonenforcement programs aimed at reducing the availability of illicit controlled substances on the domestic and international markets." Address: Drug Enforcement Administration, Mailstop: AES, 8701 Morrissette Drive, Springfield, VA 22152; Web: http://www.justice.gov/dea/index.htm.

drug enforcement research. The DEA conducts research related to its law enforcement, intelligence, and regulatory functions, including research on drug analysis for prosecution of illicit drug violators and covert surveillance systems. It also provides support to other enforcement agencies in the form of systems studies for voice-privacy requirements and regional communication networks. Contact: Office of Science and Technology, DEA, 8701 Morrissette Drive, Springfield, VA 22152.

drug enforcement training. Provided by the DEA, the program provides basic and advanced training in drug law enforcement skills for DEA and other federal, state, local, and foreign officials. The National Training Institute also provides both basic and advanced training in drug law enforcement and related skills to forensic chemists, intelligence analysts, and the foreign drug law enforcement community. Address: DEA Office of Training, P.O. Box 1475 Quantico, Virginia 22124-1475. Phone: (703) 632-5000. Web: http://www.justice.gov/dea/programs/training.htm.

drug law violations. The unlawful sale, purchase, distribution, manufacture, cultivation, transport, possession, or use of a controlled or prohibited drug or the attempt to commit these acts. The number of drug arrests tripled from 471,000 in 1980 to 1,247,000 in 1989; it rose to 1,702,537 in 2008. *See also* drug monitoring, voice identification

drug misuse. The use of any drug (legal or illegal) for a medical or recreational purpose when alternatives are available, practical, or warranted; drug use endangering either the user or others with whom he or she may interact.

drug monitoring. Several devices have been developed to monitor individuals' drug use. Common methods include urine testing, often conducted at drug treatment programs using commercially available test strips and the sweat patch, which collects evidence of drug use in perspiration. Drug testing can also be conducted via the use of hair samples, which provide an estimate of the type of drug(s) ingested and the approximate time of ingestion, and blood samples. *See also* sweat patch, urine testing, hair testing, and saliva testing. *See also* sweat patch voice identification

drug offense. The Bureau of Justice defines drug offense as those that involve manufacturing, importing, exporting, distribution or dispensing of a controlled substance, or the possession of a controlled substance "with intent to manufacture, import, export, distribute or dispense." This includes fraudulent prescriptions.

drug references and resource. *See* American Probation and Parole Association; American Bar Association; Bureau of Justice Assistance; Center for Substance Abuse Prevention; Center for Substance Abuse Treatment; Community Anti-drug Coalitions of America; Community Policing Consortium; Drug Abuse, U.S. Department of Health, Education, and Welfare; Drug Abuse Warning Network (DAWN); Drug Strategies; Join Together Online; National Alliance for Model State Drug Laws; National Association of Drug Court Professionals; National Association of State Alcohol and Drug Abuse Directors; National Center for State Courts; National Clearinghouse for Alcohol and Drug Information National Conference of State Legislatures; National Crime Prevention Council; National Criminal Justice Reference Service; National Institute on Drug Abuse; National Institute of Justice; National Judicial College; National League of Cities; Office of National Drug Control Policy; Sentencing Project, The; Therapeutic Communities of America; Substance Abuse and Mental Health Administration; United States Conference of Mayors; Western States Information Network; Youth Crime Watch of America.

drug registration. Every person who manufacturers, distributes, or dispenses any drug covered under the Controlled Substance Act or who proposes to do so must register annually with the registration branch of the DEA. A The DEA has more than 540,000 registrants, whom it monitors and periodically investigates to ensure that they are accountable for the controlled substances handled. Drug Enforcement Administration, Registration Section/ODR, P.O. Box 2639, Springfield, VA 22152-2639; Web: http://www. deadiversion.usdoj.gov/drugreg/process.htm. *See also* Table 23. Schedule of Controlled Substances, page 158

drug reporting systems. Two computerized systems are maintained by the DEA for controlled substances: Automation of Reports and Consolidated Orders System (ASCOS)—a comprehensive drug-tracking system that enables DEA to monitor the flow of selected drugs from points of import or manufacture to points of sale, export, or distribution; and Controlled Substance Ordering System (CSOD)—allows for secure electronic controlled substances orders without additional documentation for registered purchasers. Contact: DEA, 8701 Morrissette Drive, Springfield, VA 22152; Web: http://www.deadiversion.usdoj.gov/.

Drug Seizure System, Federal-wide (FDSS). This network reflects the combined drug seizure efforts of the DEA, FBI, and U.S. Customs Service within the jurisdiction of the United States, and U.S. Border Patrol, as well as maritime seizures by the U.S. Coast Guard. FDSS eliminates duplicate reporting of a seizure involving more than one federal agency. According to the Bureau of Justice Statistics, which publishes FDSS data compiled from the DEA, 2.9 million pounds of drugs were seized in 2003.

drug situation indicators. A retail and wholesale heroin price/purity index is available based on data from the analysis of drug-evidence samples submitted to the Drug Abuse Warning Network (DAWN). Reports are available on drug-related emergency room admissions and deaths in selected Standard Metropolitan Statistical Areas using DAWN data. Also, all legal drug handlers are registered with DEA and are required to report thefts or losses of controlled substances. Stolen supplies of controlled drugs

comprise a substantial portion of the supply of certain substances in the illicit drug distribution network. DEA uses these data to evaluate trends in the overall heroin situation.

Drug Strategies. A national organization established in 1992 whose mission is to find more effective drug abuse prevention, education, and treatment programs in the United States. Address: 1616 P Street, N.W. Suite 220, Washington, DC 20036. Phone: (202)289-9070. Web: http://www.drugstrategies.com/.

drugs, synthetic. *See* designer drugs

drug testing, technologies for. The technologies of testing for use of illicit drugs most often used are immunoassay and chromatography. In both tests, the hair is first treated to extract and concentrate the drug-related materials in a solution, which is then chemically analyzed in much the same way as a urine sample would be. Immunoassay testing uses antibodies to detect the presence or absence of drugs in a urine sample or a solution made from hair. An antibody is a protein that reacts only in the presence of a specific substance (the antigen) or group of chemically similar substances. In testing for drugs, a label or "tag," which can be identified and measured after the reaction of the antigen with the antibody, is mixed with the substance being used in the test (the tagged antigen). Commonly used tags include radioactive materials (as in radioimmunoassay tests—RIA and RIAH), enzymes (as in an enzyme-multiplied immunoassay test), or fluorescent materials that glow (as in fluorescent polarization immunoassay tests—FPIA). The tagged antigen, the dissolved hair shaft that may contain drugs (untagged antigens), and the antibodies are mixed. Mixing causes the tagged and untagged antigens to compete to react and bond with the antibodies. The amount of unbonded tag that remains is then compared with a known quantity of the drugs being tested for. If the amount in the sample specimen is higher than or equal to the known quantity, the test is considered positive; if lower, it is considered negative.

text continues on page 159

TABLE 23   SCHEDULE OF CONTROLLED SUBSTANCES

Schedule:	Medical Use:	Abuse / Dependence:	Examples:
I	Drug/substance has no currently accepted medical use in treatment in the U.S.	Drug/substance has a high potential for abuse.	Heroin, lysergic acid diethylamide (LSD), marijuana, and methaqualone
II	Drug/substance has a currently accepted medical use with severe restrictions.	Drug/substance has a high potential for abuse. Abuse drug/substance of the drug may lead to severe psychological and/or physical dependence.	Morphine, phencyclidine (PCP), cocaine, methadone, and methamphetamine
III	Drug/substance has a currently accepted medical use in treatment in the U.S.	Drug/substance has less potential for abuse than the drugs/substances in Schedules I and II. Abuse of the drug/substance may lead to moderate or low physical dependence or high psychological dependence.	Anabolic steroids, codeine and hydrocodone with aspirin or Tylenol®, and some barbiturates
IV	Drug/substance has a currently accepted medical use in treatment in the U.S.	Drug/substance has a low potential for abuse relative to the drugs/substances in Schedule III. Abuse of the drug/substance may lead to limited physical dependence or psychological dependence relative to the drugs/substances in Schedule III.	Darvon®, Talwin®, Equanil®, Valium®, and Xanax®
V	Drug/substance has a currently accepted medical use in treatment in the U.S.	Drug/substance has low potential for abuse relative to the drugs/substances in Schedule IV. Abuse of the drug/substance may lead to limited physical/ psychological dependence relative to the drugs/substances in Schedule IV.	Cough medicines with codeine

Source: Drug Enforcement Administration. Compiled by Jennifer Doyle, CSULB.

drug types. Subclassifications of drugs vary. The Uniform Crime Reports collects data on arrests for drug abuse violations using four drug-type categories: (1) heroin or cocaine and their derivatives; (2) marijuana; (3) synthetic or manufactured drugs; and (4) other dangerous nonnarcotic drugs. *See also* designer drugs

Drug Use Forecasting (DUF) Program. The DUF was a federal program, established in 1987 to assist law enforcement agencies in developing programs to combat drug abuse and to expand drug treatment by identifying drug use levels among arrestees, determining what drugs are used in specific jurisdictions, and tracking changes in drug use patterns. The DUF program used a nonexperimental survey of drug use among adult male and female arrestees to assess self-reported drug use, which was then matched with a urine sample, The DUF program continued through 1997, producing annual reports on drug use among arrestees. The DUF instrument was modified for part of the 1995 data and all of the 1996–1999 data to include questions about specific drug use. Juvenile data were added in 1991. The Arrestee Drug Abuse Monitoring Program (ADAM) absorbed the DUF program in 2000, using an expanded adult instrument for both the male and female data, and incorporating a juvenile component. *See* Arrestee Drug Abuse Monitoring Program.

drunkard. One who is habitually drunk; historically, a "common drunkard" was sometimes legally defined as a person who has been convicted of drunkenness a certain number of times over a specific period of time.

drunkenness. Voluntary intoxication in a public place is a misdemeanor in most jurisdictions. Although the mere drinking of alcohol is not illegal, appearing in a public place under the influence of alcohol to such an extent that persons endanger themselves, others, or property is classified as an offense in most jurisdictions. In several states, public drunkenness has been decriminalized.

Voluntary drunkenness is not grounds for exemption from criminal responsibility except: (a) where the act is committed while laboring under insanity or delirium tremens resulting from intoxication; (b) where a specific intent is essential to constitute a crime, and intoxication may negate such intent; and (c) where provocation for the act is shown, the fact of intoxication may be material.

dual citizenship. (1) Concurrent status of citizenship in more than one country or state; such persons are subject to the regulations of both countries (2) simultaneous citizenship of the United States and of a state. The Fourteenth Amendment to the Constitution says, "All persons born or naturalized in the United States, and subject to the jurisdiction thereof, are citizens of the United States and of the State wherein they reside."

dual and successive prosecution policy (also called petite policy). Federal prosecutorial guidelines used to determined whether to bring federal prosecution based on the same act(s) or acts involved in a prior criminal proceeding.

duces tecum (Lat., lit. "bring with you"). A writ that requires a party who is summoned to appear in court to bring with him or her some document or tangible piece of evidence to be used or inspected.

ducking stool. A stool or chair in which "common scolds" (a female public nuisance) were tied and then plunged into water. It is mentioned in the Domesday Book and was extensively used throughout England from the fifteenth to the beginning of the eighteenth century. The last recorded instance of its use was in England in 1809. *See also* common scold

due process model. A philosophy of criminal justice based on the assumption that an individual is presumed innocent until proven guilty and that individuals ought to be protected from arbitrary power of the state. *See also* crime control model

due process of law. A clause in the Fifth and the Fourteenth Amendments ensuring that laws are reasonable and that they are applied in a fair and equal manner. Essentially, due process guarantees that persons have a right to be fairly heard before they can be deprived of life, liberty, or property. Due process of law restricts the lawmaking powers of the government by banning laws and executive orders that are arbitrary or unreasonable. Due process of law was codified in 1215 in Article 29 of the Magna Carta and appears in an Edward III statute of 1354. Because of the protection afforded in the Bill of Rights against strictures of the federal government, the due process clause of the Fifth Amendment, which applies only to the federal government, is not as important in actual practice as the Fourteenth Amendment's clause, which applies to the states. In fact, this clause has been basic in enforcing the freedoms cherished by Americans; it has been the source of more constitutional law than any other language in the Constitution. The Fourteenth Amendment was passed in 1868 in hopes of applying the Bill of Rights to the states, because, until then, it restricted only the federal government. The first major decision on due process did not come until 1925, when the Supreme Court ruled that the free speech provision of the First Amendment should be brought within the scope of the Fourteenth Amendment and so bind the states. By 1937, all the rights of the First Amendment were covered by the due process clause. In that year Supreme Court Justice Benjamin Cardozo held that all Bill of Rights provisions essential to liberty and justice be included under the protections of due process. The provisions of the Bill of Rights that have been included within the due process clause are protection against unreasonable searches and seizures (Fourth Amendment); protection against self-incrimination (Fifth Amendment); the right to have counsel, confront hostile witnesses, and receive a jury trial in criminal cases (Sixth Amendment); and the prohibition of cruel and unusual punishment (Eighth Amendment).

dueling. The fighting of two persons at an appointed time and place, based on a preceding quarrel. It is a misdemeanor in common law to challenge another to fight a duel, be the bearer of such a challenge, or provoke another to send a challenge. To constitute the crime, no actual fighting is necessary. If the duel takes place and one of the parties is killed, the other is guilty of murder, and all who are present abetting the crime are guilty as principals in the second degree. It is immaterial that the duel is to take place in another state.

dumdum; dum dum bullet. A bullet that flattens excessively on contact; an expanding bullet such as a hollow point bullet, designed to produce a large diameter wound. The name derives from Dum Dum, India, where such bullets were first manufactured. The use of this type of bullet is prohibited under international law.

dumpster diving. The practice of digging or foraging through trash receptacles for items of value, such as food and shelter items (e.g., by homeless persons) or to unlawfully acquire personally identifying information (e.g., for the purpose of fraud or identity theft).

Duquenois reaction. A chemical test for identifying marijuana.

Duquenois reagent. Compound used in a screening test for the presence of marijuana.

duress. Unlawful constraint or influence used to force an individual to commit some act that he or she otherwise would not commit; compulsion; coercion.

duress alarm device. A device that produces either a silent or a local alarm under a condition of personal stress such as holdup, fire, illness, or other panic or emergency. The device is normally manually operated and may be either fixed or portable.

Durham rule. A legal precedent of 1954 that altered the concept of *mens rea* by providing for a much broader test of mental illness as a legal defense, stipulating that "an accused is not criminally responsible if his unlawful act was the product of mental disease or defect."

In Durham v. U.S. (214 F.2d 862), the U.S. Court of Appeals in the District of Columbia established that a defendant is entitled to acquittal if the crime was the *product of* mental illness. *See also* insanity

DWI. Driving while intoxicated. *See* driving under the influence

dyathanasia. The passive form of "mercy killing." It generally involves the discontinuing of extraordinary means of sustaining life, so that the patient expires. *See also* euthanasia; mercy killing

Dyer Act. The federal law established in 1919, which deals with the interstate transportation of stolen motor vehicles; more commonly referred to as the Interstate Transfer of Stolen Motor Vehicles (ITSMV).

dyes. The use of chemical inks or dyes, such as Methylene-blue, which is difficult to wash away, is used in criminal justice as a theft deterrent method; it is also used to apprehend suspects. Dye is placed in intimate contact with an article or substance likely to be removed or stolen. When disturbed, the article stains the suspect's hand(s) a bluish color. Other materials, such as nitrate of silver, when subjected to light will darken an invisible stain and make it visible. Naphthionate of sodium powder, which is fluorescent, will luminesce under an ultraviolet light. *See also* carbofuchsin

dying declaration. A statement made just before death, or one made by a person who believes that he or she is about to die. The declaration must be a statement of fact as to how the person was injured, and it must appear that the deceased expected to die and was without hope of recovery. Such a statement is admissible evidence only in homicide cases.

E

Earth Liberation Front (ELF). (members are sometimes called "Elves"). Founded in the United Kingdom in 1992, this organization engages in guerilla warfare in protest to environmental destruction. The most notable demonstrations included the torching of SUVs in 2001, the burning of a new condominium complex in San Diego in 2003, and the bombings of several multimillion dollar homes in Seattle in 2008. The Federal Bureau of Investigation named ELF the top domestic terrorism threat in March of 2001. *See also* ecotage; eco-terrorism

Eastman Gang. An Irish-organized gang that dominated the Bowery and East River areas of New York City around the turn of the century. It lost power after its leader, Edward Monk Eastman, went to jail on a robbery and assault charge.

eavesdropping. Interception of oral communications in a surreptitious effort to hear/record conversation, without knowledge of at least one of the persons speaking. When hidden electronic equipment is used, the process is called "bugging," the equipment is a "bug," and the premises are "bugged."

eBomb (or e-bomb). An electromagnetic bomb that produces a brief pulse of energy, impacting electronic circuitry. An e-bomb can disable electronics systems (computers, radios, and transportation systems, etc.) or completely destroy circuitry, causing mass disruption of infrastructure.

ecology. Study of the distribution of people and their activities in time and space; used in the study of criminology in relationship to environmental circumstances that precede criminal behavior or in which the behavior occurs.

ecotage. A contraction of ecology and sabotage, this term refers to civil disobedience employing violent and nonviolent disruptive actions by radical environmentalists, either to impede depletion/commercial use of natural resources or to destroy existing facilities. Logging efforts have been affected by disabling equipment (sand in gas tanks), inserting plastic or steel spikes in trees, and/or direct physical confrontation. "Earth First!" a Tucson, AZ-based ecotage organization founded in 1980, was infiltrated and investigated by the FBI's domestic counter-terrorism squad in the period from 1987 to 1990. The most notorious ecotage organization is Earth Liberation Front, which is believed to be responsible for arsons in Vail, Colorado in 1998, logging fires in Oregon in 1999, firebombs at the University of Washington in 2001, burning of a condominium complex under construction in San Diego in 2003, and the burning of SUVs and Hummers in Los Angeles in 2003. *See also* Earth Liberation Front, eco-terrorism

eco-terrorism. Acts of intentional sabotage with the goal of hindering activities that are considered damaging to the environment. Eco-terrorism is a movement in the United States and Canada that purports to defend the environment and oppose urbanization by setting fires in or attempting to destroy such widely diversified targets as development projects, sport utility vehicles, ski lifts, genetic engineering laboratories, and logging operations. One prominent group is the Earth Liberation Front (ELF), which is suspected of being involved in the arson fire that destroyed an apartment construction project in San Diego in August 2003. The fire caused $20 million in damages and was so intense that it blew out glass panes and melted window shades in residences blocks away. Less than a month later, dozens of sport utility vehicles were vandalized or burned in several simultaneous attacks at auto dealerships in the San Gabriel Valley, east of Los Angeles. *See also* ecotage; Earth Liberation Front

Ecstasy (MDMA). A synthetic methamphetamine compound with both psychedelic and stimulant effects. According to the National Institute on Drug Abuse, effects generally include: increased heart rate, blood pressure, and metabolism; feelings of exhilaration, energy, and increased mental alertness; rapid or irregular heart beat; reduced appetite, weight loss, nervousness, and insomnia; mild hallucinogenic effects; increased tactile sensitivity; empathic feelings In higher levels, associated with impaired memory and

learning; hyperthermia; heart failure, cardiac toxicity, renal failure, and liver toxicity. MDMA was used clinically until 1988, when it was reclassified as a controlled substance. Under the street name Ecstasy, it is most often found in tablet or capsule form.

Edmunds Act (also called the Edmunds Anti-Poligamy Act of 1882). Passed by Congress in 1882, this law provided for the regulation and restriction of Mormon polygamy in Utah. Under the law, Mormons were, to a great degree, excluded from holding local office, and many were indicted and punished for polygamous practices. Act was named for U.S. Senator George Edmunds of Vermont, a strong supporter of the bill. *See also* polygamy, Edmunds-Tucker Act of 1887

Edmunds-Tucker Act of 1887. Cosponsored by U.S. Senators George Edmunds and John Tucker, the act dissolved the Church of Latter Day Saints (Mormonism) and authorized the confiscation of church assets. The act was repealed in 1978. *See also* Edmunds Act

effigy. The image or representation of a person.

e.g., *Exempli gratia* (Lat., lit.). For the sake of the example.

Egan's Rats. A criminal gang in St. Louis between 1890–1924 organized by Thomas "Snake" Kinney and Tom "Jellyroll" Egan. Members of the gang were suspect in the St. Valentine's Day Massacre. It eventually became an Irish-organized crime gang that was associated with St. Louis's modern-day Cosa Nostra. *See also* St. Valentine's Day Massacre

egress. The means of exit from a building or other enclosure; the right of a person to leave a property.

election law (federal), corrupt practices. The first such law was passed on January 26, 1907, prohibiting corporations from contributing campaign funds in national elections of president, vice president, senators, and representatives. An act passed on March 4, 1909, and effective on January 1, 1910, further prohibited national banks and corporations from contributing campaign funds in connection with any election to any political office. In January of 2010, the U.S. Supreme Court overturned a federal law that prohibited the use of private funds contributed by businesses and labor unions for the purpose of political advertising. The ruling is expected to be followed by additional laws restricting the campaign contributions by lobbyists.

election law, first. Passed on May 22, 1649, by the General Court in Warwick, RI, it provided that "no one should bring in any votes that he did not receive from the voters' own hands, and that all votes should be filed by the Recorder in the presence of the Assembly." A committee of four freemen was authorized to determine violations of the law and "to examine parties and to present to this court what they find in the case."

electrified fences. Security devices used at prisons that carry several thousand volts and more than the 70 milliamperes necessary to cause death. Such fences are usually placed second in a group of three, and are in use, for example, at many California prisons.

electrocution. In this method of execution, the prisoner is strapped into a wooden chair and electrodes are attached to the individual's calf and head. A sponge rests on the prisoner's shaved head, beneath a leather and metal headset strapped and bolted into place. Soaked in liquid, the sponge conveys the 2,000 volts and 14 amps of current into the prisoner's skull. Electric current passes through the electrodes in a cycle designed to interrupt the heart's normal electrical pattern and cause it to stop beating, Blood circulation stops, consciousness is lost, brain damage is massive, and death results in about four minutes. Electrocution is still permitted in the following nine states, all of which offer more than one method of execution: Alabama, Arkansas, Florida, Illinois, Kentucky, Oklahoma, South Carolina, Tennessee, and Virginia. Some states offer alternatives. In 1999, the Florida Supreme Court upheld electrocution following "irregularities" in the execution of Allen Lee Davis and others. The Nebraska Supreme Court declared electrocution to be "cruel and unusual punishment" in 2008. The most recent use of electrocution was condemned inmate Paul Warner Powell, on March 18, 2010. *See also* Davis, Tiny; execution, methods of; lethal injection; lethal gas; hanging; and firing squad. *See* Table 19. Methods of Execution in the United States, page 173

electroencephalogram (EEG). A physiological test that measures electrical activity in the scalp as an indicator for neurological activity in the brain. Criminological research using EEGs has explored the relationship between schizophrenia, psychopathy, and homicide.

Electronic Communications Privacy Act of 1986. Designed to restrict unauthorized government access to telephone calls and computer activity, the Act amended the Federal Wiretap Act of 1968 by listing enhanced protections against access and disclosure of electronically stored communications such as email. *See also* Federal Wiretap Act of 1968

electronic monitoring (EM). The process of tracking those under correctional supervision through the use of electronic tracking systems, including Global Positioning Satellite (GPS) technology. EM equipment receives information about monitored offenders and transmits it over telephone lines to a monitoring agency computer. There are two basic types: continuously signaling devices that constantly monitor the offender's presence at a particular location, and programmed contact devices that contact the offender periodically to verify presence. The continuously signaling device has three major parts: a transmitter (attached to the offender), a receiver-dialer, and a central computer. Programmed contact devices use a computer programmed to telephone the offender during the monitored hours, either randomly or at specified times. The first EM program was begun in Palm Beach, FL, in December 1984. All states now use EM programs to supervise offenders. In 2002, 20 companies were manufacturers of EM equipment. EM systems are often used as a condition of bail, in cases of domestic violence, and with high risk sex offenders. *See also* house arrest; net-widening; GPS tracking unit

Electronic Suspected Child Abuse Report (ESCAR). Online method of submitting suspected child abuse reports to facilitate child abuse investigations.

electrophoresis. The process of dispersing particles in a gelatinous or fluid medium using a uniform electric field. In forensics, electrophoresis is used blood protein analysis and DNA analysis.

element of the offense. Any conduct, circumstance, condition, or state of mind which, in combination with other conduct, circumstances, conditions, or states of mind, constitutes an unlawful act. *See also corpus delicti*

eligible for parole. The status of a person who has been committed to the jurisdiction of a federal or state prison system and is usually confined in an institution, and who, by a combination of such factors as sentence effective date, statutory provisions concerning length of sentence to be served in confinement, time credit deductions, and individual sentence, can legally be considered for release from prison to parole.

Elmira Reformatory. The first reformatory built in the United States, it used classification of prisoners, education, vocational training, and indeterminate sentencing.

emancipation. Being freed or set at liberty by (one's) parents, guardian, or master; the acquisition of political rights by a disenfranchised group.

embargo. (1) An edict of a government prohibiting the departure or entry of ships; (2) any prohibition imposed by law on commerce.

embezzlement. The misappropriation, misapplication, or illegal disposal of legally entrusted property by the person(s) to whom it was entrusted, with intent to defraud the legal owner or intended beneficiary. In some state codes embezzlement is treated as a form of larceny, that is, theft by taking; in others, as fraud, that is, theft by deception. In Uniform Crime Reports it is described as offenses of "misappropriation or misapplication of money or property entrusted to one's care, custody, or control."

embracery. Any attempt to influence a jury corruptly by promises, persuasions, entreaties, entertainments, and so forth.

embryo. A human fetus from conception through about 10-weeks' gestation.

emergency strikes. Work stoppages that are especially harmful to the public interest. Most strikes impose an inconvenience on consumers, and they often lead to serious economic damage. But economic harm alone does not create an emergency. Only if a strike seriously jeopardizes the public's safety and well-being does it become an "emergency strike." Such strikes may occur in the public sector, for example, by refusals to work by firemen, policemen, sanitation workers, or nurses, and in the private sector by food- or fuel-delivery personnel. Strikes by public school teachers or auto and steel workers generally would not constitute emergencies. *See also* strike; job action

emetophobia. The fear of vomit and vomiting.

eminent domain. The right of a government to take private property for public use. The private owner must be given reasonable compensation for the property, and the government's action must be in accord with the due process of law as outlined in the Fifth and Fourteenth Amendments.

Emotionally Intelligent Justice. Efforts to evaluate and administer punishments in a way that will not further harm victims and society.

empathy. Broadly defined, the ability to appreciate another's feelings by putting oneself in the other's position and experiencing those feelings. Empathy can be felt by people who have experienced similar situations, who are intimate with one other, or who have special training in interpersonal skills. In empathy training, for example, police officers have posed or role-played as pickets, homeless persons, prisoners, live-in guests of minority families, and participant-observers in probation or social work.

empirical. Based on experience and observation; based on established facts.

Empirical Legal Studies. The application of empirical, social scientific research methods to questions of law, legal procedure, and legal theory. This is a relatively new but growing method of legal research, as evidenced in the 2004 launch of the *Journal of Empirical Legal Studies,* now a highly ranked journal, by Cornell Law School and the Society for Empirical Legal Studies.

employee assistance programs (EAPs). Generally provided by employers to help workers with alcohol and other drug abuse problems, EAPs also provide counseling for financial, marital, childrearing, or any other personal or psychological problems that management or human resources feels may be interfering with an individual's productivity. Some EAPs help with career development, weight control, smoking cessation, and a variety of other topics.

empowerment. In business management, giving employees the authority to make decisions within their realm of work operations or scope of employment.

en banc. A French phrase meaning full bench, the term refers to sessions in which the full membership of a court participates. In the United States, federal districts are single-judge courts; cases in Courts of Appeal are normally heard by a three-judge panel, but important cases may be heard *en banc;* and all cases heard by the Supreme Court are decided *en banc*. The Constitution refers to "one Supreme Court," and the Court has interpreted this to mean that the entire membership should participate as a full bench in each case.

EnCase Software. Computer Forensics software used by law enforcement agencies to extract data on hard drives that have been deleted or erased. *See also* COFEE

enforcement. An action or process to compel observance of law or the requirements of public policy.

Enforcement Acts. Three laws passed in 1870 and 1871 to enforce the Fourteenth and Fifteenth amendments. The first (May 31, 1870) forbade the use of force, threats of violence, bribery, registration trickery, or economic coercion as tools to prevent eligible voters from exercising their right to vote, and set heavy penalties for violations. The law also provided for strict federal supervision of congressional elections, a clause tightened by the second Enforcement Act (February 28, 1871). Congress passed the third act on April 20, 1871, to suppress the Ku Klux Klan and similar Southern organizations. It provided severe penalties for those guilty of terrorist activities and authorized the president to suspend the privilege of the writ of *habeas corpus* and to call out the army and militia to put down such violence.

English common law. The basis of the English common law is immemorial usage and custom, not legislative enactment. For this reason it is often called the "unwritten law." The generic term *common law* has been well-defined as "those maxims, principles, and forms of judicial proceedings, which have no written law to prescribe or warrant them, but which, founded on the laws of nature and the dictates of reason, have, by usage and custom, become interwoven with the written laws; and, by such incorporation, form a part of the municipal code of each state or nation."

Enoch Arden law. A statute granting permission to remarry without fear of legal penalty of polygamy to a person whose spouse has been absent, usually for seven successive years (in New York, five), and is presumed dead.

entail. A principle of law originating in medieval England that provided that, upon the death of the owner of an estate, the entire estate was bequeathed to his heir and subsequently to an established line of legatees. The system was imported into the British colonies, where it was met with great resistance because of its undemocratic features. Virginia took the lead in abolishing entail in 1776 and was followed by other states. By the Jeffersonian period, entail had disappeared from the United States.

enterprise. Any individual, partnership, corporation, association, or other legal entity; any union or group of individuals associated in fact although not a legal entity.

entrapment. Inducing an individual to commit a crime he or she did not contemplate, for the sole purpose of instituting a criminal prosecution against the offender. This is a defense to criminal responsibility that arises from improper acts committed against an accused by another, usually an undercover agent. Inducement is the key word; when police encouragement plays upon the weaknesses of innocent persons and beguiles them into committing crimes they normally would not attempt, it can be deemed improper as entrapment and the evidence barred under the exclusionary rule. *See also* DeLorean, John

entry. Entering a building by going inside; achieved when any part of the body or any instrument or weapon held by hand enters a building.

enuresis. Bed-wetting is common in childhood, and most children grow out of enuresis with time. Enuresis is also one of three elements in the MacDonald Triad, suggesting precursors for sociopathy. *See also* Mac Donald Triad

environmental crimes. A violation of environmental law, including, for example, pollution and toxic waste disposal. Such acts are civilly litigated and criminally prosecuted by the Environment and Natural Resources Division of the Department of Justice.

Environmental and Natural Resources Division, U.S. Department of Justice. Formed in 1983, the environmental crimes section of the Department of Justice's Environment and Natural Resources Division handles environmental and natural resources litigation. The agency is charged with the Prevention and Clean Up of Pollution through enforcement of environmental laws including: "the Clean Air Act to reduce air pollution; the Clean Water Act to reduce water pollution and protect wetlands; the Resource Conservation and Recovery Act to ensure that hazardous wastes are properly stored, transported, and disposed; the Comprehensive Environmental Response, Compensation and Liability Act (or "Superfund"), which requires those who are responsible for hazardous waste sites to pay for their clean up; the Safe Drinking Water Act and the Lead Hazard Reduction Act, which directly protect the health of Americans." Under 1990 amendments to the Clean Air Act, the government can bring criminal as well as civil suits against violators. The largest civil penalty ($15 million) under the act was assessed against Texas Eastern Natural Gas Pipeline in 1987. The second-largest was an $11.1 million penalty in 1993 against Louisiana-Pacific Corporation for Clean Air Act violations at 14 of its plants. On March 24, 1989, the tanker *Exxon Valdez* ran aground and spilled more than 10 million gallons of oil into Alaska's Prince William Sound. Two years later, Exxon Corporation settled government claims arising from the nation's worst oil spill by agreeing to pay a record $100 million fine for four environmental crimes and to spend an additional $900 million to complete a cleanup of Alaska's coast. Exxon had already spent $2.5 billion on cleanup efforts. The fine was 20 times larger than the prior record, $5 million paid by Allied Chemical in 1976 for dumping chemicals into Virginia's James River. On May 1, 1991, Pfizer, Inc., paid a $3.1 million fine for dumping pollutants into the Delaware River between 1981 and 1987. This civil settlement covered violations at a Pfizer iron ore plant in Easton, PA, about 50 miles north of Philadelphia. Pfizer admitted no liability in agreeing to the settlement, a record civil penalty under the federal Water Pollution Control Act. In 1999, Royal Caribbean Cruises Ltd. (RCCL) pled guilty to 21 felony counts for dumping waste oil and hazardous chemicals into the waters near in Miami, New York City, Los Angeles, Anchorage, St. Thomas, U.S. Virgin Islands, and San Juan, Puerto Rico. RCCL paid an $18 million fine. In [*U*] *United States v. Elias* (D. Idaho), Elias ordered two employees to clean a tank containing cyanide waste with no protection, then lied to emergency responders when an employee, became unconscious (the employee sustained permanent brain damage from cyanide poisoning). Elias was convicted of knowing endangerment under RCRA and sentenced to 17 years in prison and ordered to pay $6 million in fines/restitution. In 2000, Central Industries, et al. (S.D. Miss.). pleaded guilty in November 2000 to 26 felony violations of the Clean Water Act associated with the illegal dumping of 500,000 gallons of wastewater per day into the drinking water of Jackson, Mississippi. The corporation was ordered to pay $14 million in fines/restitution, and three corporate officials were also convicted. Address: U.S. Department of Justice, Environment and Natural Resources Division, Law and Policy Section, P.O. Box 4390, Ben Franklin Station, Washington, DC 20044-4390; Web: http://www.justice.gov/enrd/index.html.

Environmental criminology. The study of the causes and consequences of crime as a function of place. Environmental criminology was "born" in the Chicago School, when researchers developed a concentric zone theory to explain crime. Current applications include computerized crime mapping systems, the use of geographic profiling, and crime prevention through environmental design (CPTED).

environmental offense. According to the Bureau of Justice, this is a violation of federal law enacted to protect the environment.

Environmental Protection Agency (EPA). An independent agency in the executive branch, established in 1970 to permit coordinated federal protection of the environment by the systematic control of pollution. Former President George Bush elevated it to cabinet rank in 1990. EPA is responsible for implementing regulations for environmental law, for assistance to organizations wishing to comply with environmental law, and in enforcement of environmental law. Address: Environmental Protection Agency, Ariel Rios Building, 1200 Pennsylvania Avenue, N.W. Washington, DC 20460. Phone: (202) 272-0167; Web: http://www.epa.gov/.

ephedrine. Structurally related to the stimulant methamphetamine, this drug is a primary ingredient in over-the-counter cold and allergy remedies. "Ripped Fuel" is the trade name of a drug made from the Chinese herb *ma huang,* which contains 2.5 times more ephedrine than pseudoephedrine (Sudafed) and has been used for centuries to treat allergic reactions, including asthma.

episodic criminal. A person who commits a crime under extreme emotional stress, as the single exception to an otherwise lawful life; for example, an individual who kills in the heat of passion.

Equal Employment Opportunity Commission, U.S. (EEOC). The lead federal government civil rights agency, created in 1964 by Congress under Title VII of the Civil Rights Act of 1964. EEOC has primary responsibility for Title VII enforcement pertaining to "federal laws that make it illegal to discriminate against a job applicant or an employee because of the person's race, color, religion, sex (including pregnancy), national origin, age (40 or older), disability or genetic information." Web: http://www.eeoc.gov/. *See also* sexual harassment

equal protection. Guaranteed by Section I of the Fourteenth Amendment, equal protection means that no citizen of any state may be discriminated against by any act or condition. Areas in which equal protection have often been abused include jury selection, voting, use of public facilities, transportation, housing, education, and women's rights. Attempts to eliminate discrimination on the grounds of race, religion, political beliefs, and sex have taken the form of civil rights legislation in Congress and favorable Supreme Court decisions. The equal protection provision, adopted in 1868, was at first interpreted as forbidding a state government to discriminate against any person within its jurisdiction. In 1954 the Supreme Court expanded this interpretation by making it the states' responsibility to remove discriminatory conditions wherever they exist. The Court strengthened its position in 1964 by declaring that, if a state did not do everything it could to eliminate discrimination, action would be enforced by Court decree.

equipment for law enforcement, testing. *See* law enforcement equipment

equitable action. One founded on an equity or in a court of equity; an action arising, not immediately from the contract in suit, but from an equity in favor of a third person, not a party to it, but for whose benefit certain stipulations or promises were made.

equitable right. A right enforceable in a court of equity.

equity jurisdiction. The jurisdiction belonging to a court of equity; all cases, controversies, and occasions that form proper subjects for the exercise of the powers of a chancery court.

equity of redemption. (1) The interest that a mortgagor retains in the property mortgaged. (2) The right of the mortgagor of an estate to redeem the same, after it has been forfeited at law by a breach of the condition of the mortgage, by paying the amount of debt, interests, and costs.

equivocate. (1) To conceal the truth. (2) To use ambiguous words.

ergonomics. The study of human capability and psychology in relation to the employee's working environment and equipment. Also known as human engineering, human factors engineering, or engineering psychology. Ergonomics is based on the premise that tools individuals use and the environment they work in should be matched with their capabilities and limitations, rather than the reverse where people are forced to adapt to the physical environment.

erotic asphyxiation. The intentional restriction of oxygen to the brain for sexual arousal.

error in fact. In a judicial proceeding, an error not known to the court that may, depending on its seriousness, make a judgment void or voidable.

error in law. An error by the court in applying a law to a particular case on trial, such as allowing evidence that has been established as incompetent, or charging a jury erroneously with respect to the law of the case.

escape. The unlawful departure from official custody of a lawfully confined person. Escapes are either voluntary or negligent. Voluntary escape occurs when the keeper voluntarily concedes to the prisoner any liberty not authorized by law; negligent escape occurs when the prisoner contrives to leave a place of confinement, either by forcing his or her way out or by any other means, without the knowledge or consent of the keeper. Prison breach is the breaking and leaving of confinement. Rescue is the forcible taking of a prisoner from lawful custody by anyone who knows that the person is in custody. The longest recorded escape by a prisoner who was eventually recaptured was that of Leonard T. Fristoe, 77, who escaped from Nevada State Prison on December 15, 1923, and was turned in by his son on November 15, 1969, at Compton, CA. He had 46 years of freedom under the name of Claude R. Willis. He had killed two sheriff's deputies in 1920.

Escobedo, Danny. The Supreme Court's 1964 *Escobedo v. Illinois* decision overturned Escobedo's murder conviction on the grounds that his constitutional rights had been violated when police refused him access to an attorney before he confessed to the slaying of his brother-in-law. The construction of the legal bridge that led to the 1966 *Miranda v. Arizona* decision had its beginning in

Gideon v. Wainwright (1963), and was completed in *Escobedo*. Within two years of the Supreme Court's decision, Escobedo himself was making regular appearances before Chicago magistrates due to arrests on various charges of disorderly conduct, burglary, weapons violations, and drug sales. On the drug and burglary charges, he was convicted and received concurrent sentences of 22 and 20 years. Subsequent appeals failed to bring about his release.

espionage. The act of covertly obtaining a military secret for a foreign government in time of war or peace. Most countries have organizations engaged in espionage activities even in peacetime. Organizations such as the CIA or the (former Soviet) KGB have been viewed as instruments for subversion, manipulation, violence, and secret intervention in the affairs of other countries.

Espionage Act. A 1917 bill limiting civil liberties, passed as United States entry into World War I brought a wave of popular war hysteria and fear. The Espionage Act allowed up to 20 years' imprisonment for disloyalty or opposition to the draft. The Sedition Act of 1918 extended the charges to published writings. These federal laws were copied by the states, with some excesses. Almost 2,000 cases were tried under the acts, but many pardons were granted after war fears had subsided.

espionage, industrial. Agents or paid representatives of one company or industry who obtain secret information about another. This often includes theft of trade secrets and may be accomplished by placing an agent in another company as an undercover employee.

Estes Scandal. The rigging of cotton-acreage allotments and contracts for storing government agricultural surpluses by Billie Sol Estes, a Texas manipulator. His indictment in 1962 was followed by the resignation of two federal officials, Republican charges of corruption, and his own conviction for swindling. The conviction was later set aside by the Supreme Court in 1965 because at the preliminary hearing, and to a lesser degree at

the trial, the bright lights, numerous strands of television cable, and activities of representatives of news media, which were excessive in relation to the public's interest in the news, had prevented a sober search for the truth and so had denied Estes a fair trial.

estoppel. An impediment or bar that precludes a person from alleging or denying a fact in consequence of his or her own previous act or in consequence to ones on previous assertion of fact; prevents denial of what has been established as fact.

ethics. Standards of moral and official conduct; a system of morals; set of rules drawn from the science of human duty. *See also* canons of police ethics; code of ethics

Ethics in Government Act. Established in 1978, this law required financial disclosure by top government officials and applied similar disclosure rules to high-ranking executive and judicial officials as had previously been applied to members of Congress in codes of ethics adopted in 1977.

ethnography. A qualitative research method that aims to describe the culture of those studied through field observation.

eugenics. A paradigm popular in the early 1900s, eugenics is the study of selective breeding in humans. Eugenics aimed to improve the human species through selective breeding to propagate desired human traits and eliminate undesired traits such as mental illness, development disability, low IQ, and physical disabilities. In extreme forms, proponents of eugenics consider forced reproductive sterilization and even extermination of "unfit" specimens. Eugenics lost favor in the 1930s due to the use of eugenics practices in Nazi Germany. *See also* Jukes and Kallikaks

euthanasia. The act of painlessly ending the life of a person suffering from an incurable and distressing disease, committed as an act of mercy. The theory or practice of permitting physicians or other socially authorized persons to give a lethal dose of medicine to persons painfully and incurably ill. At present this theory is opposed to the law and the medical code of ethics; but a sample poll has shown that some 46 percent of the people giving opinions favored euthanasia under government supervision. The state of Oregon passed the first U.S. euthanasia law in 1994; Washington is the only other state with a similar law, enacted in 2008. Euthanasia is illegal in all other states. On April 10, 2001, after 30 years of lobbying, the Netherlands became the first country to legalize euthanasia. *See also* dyathanasia; Kevorkian, Dr. Jack; medicide; mercy killing

evidence. All means of giving information to courts trying cases involving factual disputes, including testimony, documents, and physical objects. In the common law system, the law of evidence principally determines when to admit or exclude evidence items, not how much weight to give them. Juries or judges trying facts determine the weight, using their own experience and common sense as guides. Parties' attorneys obtain, select, and present evidence (the adversary system). In constitutional aspects of criminal cases, courts have in recent years greatly restricted evidence admissibility and created a criminal law revolution, which is now beginning to recede. In other respects, the trend is toward broader admissibility, with greater reliance on trial judges' discretion.

Evidence Terms

Direct evidence establishes a fact without the need for inferences or presumptions.

Circumstantial evidence proves facts that may support an inference or presumption of the disputed fact.

Prima facie evidence suffices to prove a fact until there is rebuttal evidence.

Relevancy. Only relevant evidence, which logically tends to prove or disprove a disputed fact, may be admitted. Many exclusionary rules may bar even relevant evidence, however.

Competency. At one time, parties could not testify in their own lawsuits, nor could

witnesses with direct interests in the case; neither convicted felons nor spouses could testify for or against each other in civil or criminal cases. Statutes have since abolished all but one of these restrictions—the one barring survivors, and persons interested in the outcome, from testifying to personal transactions or communications with someone deceased when suing his or her estate. Some variant states either accept survivors' testimony (but require corroboration to support judgments) or accept both survivors' testimony and decedents' written or oral statements on the subject.

Hearsay. Witnesses ordinarily give oral testimony telling what they have themselves seen, heard, or done. Witnesses' evidence of third parties' statements about things seen, heard, or done are hearsay if used to prove those facts. Documents containing such statements are also hearsay. Such evidence is ordinarily excluded, because the declarants were usually not under oath and not cross-examinable. If all hearsay were barred absolutely, however, needed and trustworthy evidence of persons unavailable as witnesses would often be completely lost; hence, numerous hearsay exceptions have developed.

Opinions. Witnesses ordinarily testify to facts; opinions or conclusions are excluded. The fact-triers should form opinions and conclusions, but if special training or experience is needed for a reliable opinion (for example, on scientific or technical subjects), experts' opinions are admissible if they can assist fact-triers.

Character. Those accused in criminal cases may prove their good character to imply unlikelihood of their having committed the crime charged. If they do so, prosecutions may afterward show their bad character. In civil and criminal cases, witnesses' credibility may be attacked by proving their bad character for truthfulness or honesty or their prior criminal conviction; only subsequently may their good character be shown. The general rule in criminal cases is that proof of other crimes by the accused should not be received, but many exceptions allow admission when relevant to show more than simply the defendant's criminality.

Privilege. Though excluding relevant evidence thereby, the law protects against compelled disclosure of confidential communications between spouses, attorney and client, and frequently between physician and patient, or clergy and penitent. Similar privileges exist for state secrets, government informants, and, infrequently, accountants and journalists.

Writings. Documents are inadmissible without proof or concession of genuineness (authentication). All exclusionary evidence rules and some special doctrines apply to documents. The best-evidence rule demands that original documents prove their own contents; secondary evidence (copies or testimony) is inadmissible unless the original's unavailability is properly explained.

Scientific Evidence. Expanding scientific knowledge and techniques keep enlarging this field. It now includes fingerprints, testing of questioned documents, ballistics, blood grouping, drunkenness tests, carbon dating, radar, lie detection, radiation recordings, medicine, engineering, physics, chemistry, and so on.

Judicial Notice. Courts consider evidence unnecessary to establish certain obvious facts, like weights- and-measures tables or historical dates. State courts also judicially notice the federal and their own constitutions, statutes, and laws but not those of sister states or foreign countries (except as widely adopted statutes permit). Federal courts judicially notice federal and state provisions.

Burden of Proof. In trials, parties having the burden of proof lose their cases unless, on their whole claim or defense, they persuade the fact-triers that the facts they allege are true. Parties having the burden of producing evidence must produce some, or additional, evidence supporting their allegations on controverted facts or else have those allegations determined adversely. The burden of proof is fixed at the trial's start and continues unchanged, but the burden of evidence may shift between parties on different matters during trial. *See also* International Association for Property and Evidence, Inc.

evidence aliunde. *See* extraneous evidence

evidence, associative. The establishment of a link between the accused and the crime scene by information obtained from physical evidence found at the crime scene and physical evidence found on the accused or in places traceable to him or her.

evidence, corroborating. Evidence that strengthens or supports other evidence.

evidence, derivative. *See* derivative evidence

evidence given in former proceeding. This is admissible, for the purpose of proving statements made in a later stage of the same proceeding, under the following circumstances: when the witness (a) is dead; (b) is insane; (c) is out of the jurisdiction; (d) cannot be found within the jurisdiction; and (e) could have been, or was, cross-examined earlier by the person against whom the evidence is to be given.

evidence, material. Material evidence must relate to the facts at issue and must also be important enough to warrant its use. Materiality of evidence describes its importance.

Evidence Photographers International Council (EPIC). Founded in 1967, EPIC is a nonprofit educational and scientific organization dedicated to the advancement of forensic photography and videography in civil evidence & law enforcement. Address: 229 Peachtree St. NE, #2200, Atlanta, GA 30303. Phone: (866) 868-3742; Web: http://www.evidencephotographers.com/index.html.

evidence, prejudicial. Evidence that is so shocking to the senses of jurors that it may unduly sway their attitude toward one of the parties in a criminal trial; inflammatory evidence.

evidence rule, best. *See* best evidence rule

evidence wrongfully obtained. The fact that articles or admissions were wrongfully obtained from the defendant does not necessarily render them inadmissible as evidence. *See* exclusionary rule, fruit of the poisonous tree, inevitable discovery

evidentiary items. Items connected with a crime, not including contraband, profits from, or weapons or other instruments used in the crime. *See also* mere evidence

examination. The preliminary hearing before the magistrate of the evidence against a person accused of a crime.

examination; cross-examination. Witnesses in open court must first be directly examined by the party that called them; they may then be cross-examined and then reexamined. Both examination and cross-examination must relate to facts at issue or relevant to the case, and in most states the cross-examination must be confined to the facts to which the witness testified on his or her direct examination. The reexamination must be directed to the explanation of matters referred to in cross-examination, and, if new matter is, by permission of court, introduced in reexamination, the opposing party may further cross-examine on the new matter.

examining trial. *See* preliminary hearing

exception. Formal notification to the court during a trial that one party objects to or has reservations about the court's ruling on a request or objection made by the other party to the suit.

exclusion. Rule of evidence that holds that illegally obtained evidence is generally inadmissible in criminal trial.

exclusionary rule. Legal prohibitions against government prosecution using evidence illegally obtained, such as by illegal search and seizure. Prior to the 1961 *Mapp v. Ohio* decision, several states, by law, had exclusionary rules that precluded the use of such evidence. After *Mapp*, all states were prohibited from its use.

exculpate. To exonerate; to clear of blame or guilt; to prove innocent.

ex delicto (Lat., lit.). From the crime.

execution. (1) A judicial writ directing an officer to carry out the judgment of a court of law. (2) Enforcement of a judgment, especially of the death penalty, following conviction of a capital crime and sentence by a court of law. (3) Rendering valid a legal document by signing and delivering it. *See also* punishment, capital

execution and return of warrant. A search warrant is executed by limiting the search and the authority of the officer in such search named to conduct it, as to the place to be searched and the time and manner of the execution of the warrant; hence, a warrant cannot be extended beyond the privileges granted in its issuance.

execution, methods of. Five methods of execution are currently legal in the United States. These include (see also): Lethal Injection, Electrocution, Lethal Gas, Hanging, and Firing Squad. *See* Table 24. Execution Methods in the United States, page 173

execution of a warrant. (a) A warrant can only be executed by the officer to whom it is directed, either by name or by description of his or her office; (b) it cannot confer authority to execute it on one officer, where a statute provides for its execution by another; (c) unless a statute so allows, it cannot be executed outside the jurisdiction of the issuing magistrate or court; (d) where the warrant is necessary, it must be in the possession of the officer at the time of search or arrest; and (e) it must be returned after the search or arrest.

executive branch. The part of the government that applies the law. In a separation of powers system, there is an attempt to distinguish the functions of rule initiation, rule application, and rule interpretation, and to assign the primary responsibility for each function to the legislative, executive, and judicial branches respectively, although there is much sharing of functions among

TABLE 24   EXECUTION METHODS IN THE UNITED STATES, BY STATE, 2010

Alabama [a,b]	Idaho [a,e]	Missouri [a,c]	Pennsylvania [a]
Alaska [f]	Illinois [a,b]	Montana [a]	Rhode Island [f]
Arizona [a,c]	Indiana [a]	Nebraska [b]	South Carolina [a,b]
Arkansas [a,b]	Iowa [f]	Nevada [a]	South Dakota [a]
California [a,c]	Kansas [a]	New Hampshire [a,d]	Tennessee [a,b]
Colorado [a]	Kentucky [a, b]	New Jersey [f]	Texas [a]
Connecticut [d]	Louisiana [a]	New Mexico [a]	Utah [a,e]
Delaware [a,d]	Maine [f]	New York [a]	Vermont [f]
District of Columbia [f]	Maryland [a]	North Carolina [a]	Virginia [a,b]
Federal System [a]	Massachusetts [f]	North Dakota [f]	Washington [a,d]
Florida [a,b]	Michigan [f]	Ohio [a]	West Virginia [f]
Georgia [a]	Minnesota [f]	Oklahoma [a,b,e]	Wisconsin [f]
Hawaii [f]	Mississippi [a]	Oregon [a]	Wyoming [a,c]

a. Lethal Injection
b. Electrocution
c. Lethal gas
d. Hanging
e. Firing squad
f. No executions in state

NOTE: More than one method is authorized in some jurisdictions.

Source: U.S. Department of Justice, Bureau of Justice Statistics.

branches. Law enforcement is under the executive branch of government.

executive clemency. Authority and power given to certain executive authorities of the government, such as a governor, to set aside a court judgment of sentence. This power is granted by law, usually under provisions of the Constitution.

executive order. A presidential directive that becomes law. Executive orders issued by the president or by administrative agencies must all be published in the *Federal Register.*

executive privilege. An accepted practice that prevents congressional committees from interrogating executive officials without the express consent of the president. A reference case is *United States v. Nixon.*

executor (m.), executrix (f.). An individual appointed in a will to carry out its provisions.

executory process. Proceedings in which, by previous agreement of the parties involved, mortgaged property may be seized and sold without going through the procedure of citing the mortgage debtor into court and obtaining a judgment against him or her. It is an expeditious way of foreclosure and sale of property on which a mortgage or privilege exists.

exemplar. A known specimen of evidence to be used by experts for comparison with other (questioned) evidence.

Exemplary Rehabilitation Certificates. Awarded by the Secretary of Labor to servicemen separated from the armed forces under conditions other than honorable, if it is established that they have rehabilitated themselves. This certificate provides tangible evidence of rehabilitation since discharge, to present to a prospective employer.

The certificate does not in any way change the nature of original discharge or alter ex-servicemen's eligibility for veterans benefits. The Act was repealed in 1982 (U.S. Code Title 29, Chapter 13).

ex facie (Lat., lit. "from the face"). Apparently; evidently. A term applied to what appears on the face of a writing.

exhibit. An item of evidence; an item obtained in an investigation, particularly one that is to be used as evidence; a physical object offered in evidence during a trial.

exhibitionism. Displaying one's naked sex organs, including bare breasts for women and genitals (or buttocks) for either sex, in a situation or way in which they are not usually exposed. Exhibitionism generally implies such exposure is intended for the sexual gratification of the person exposing his/her sex organs, although the term generally connotes a male exposing his genitals to an unsuspecting victim. Such exposure is grounds for criminal prosecution, particularly when the act occurs against a stranger, a child, or in places where children congregate, such as a public park or beach. In serious cases, the exhibitionist is subject to criminal penalties including incarceration, sex offender treatment, and lifetime sex offender registration. *See also* flashing, mooning, anasyrma, reflectoporn, streaking, sex offender

exhibitionist. One who engages in exhibitionism. A person who has a compulsion to show his or her genitals or other body parts in inappropriate circumstances, usually to members of the opposite sex.

exhumation. Disinterment; removing from the earth something that has been buried, especially a human corpse.

exitus. Death.

ex officio (Lat.). By virtue of the office.

exonerate. To prove not guilty; to acquit; to clear of blame or fault.

exonerate bail. To release a surety on a bail bond.

ex parte. A hearing or examination in the presence of only one of the parties to a case, such as a writ of *habeas corpus.*

expatriation. The act of voluntarily leaving, or abandoning allegiance to, one's country.

expert testimony. When there is a question on an aspect of science or other specialized fields, the opinions on that point of persons particularly skilled in that field may be given in court. Expert testimony can be offered on any subject that requires a course of special study or experience in order to form an opinion. The opinions of experts on matters of common knowledge are not admissible, for the jury is as able to judge such facts as experts would be. Where witnesses have expertise in a trade or science beyond that of the average person, they may give their opinions, so that the jury may have this knowledge in arriving at a verdict.

expiation. (1) A spiritual or religious act of atonement intended to change or cleanse the person. (2) A theory of the purpose of punishment for crime based originally upon the belief that crime aroused the anger of the gods against the whole community, and that the only way to mollify that anger was to destroy the offender. More recently, the term has been widened in its meaning to include punishing the offender. Used in this way, expiation is virtually synonymous with retribution.

expiration of sentence. The termination of the period of time during which an offender has been required to be under the jurisdiction of a state prison or parole agency as the penalty for an offense. A method of prison release in which the inmate serves the entire sentence imposed, without benefit of a reduction in time as generally afforded with "good time" credits; release in this manner generally occurs when inmates engage in a continual pattern of problem behavior in prison, such as fighting or refusing to follow instructions, leading to the expiration of sentence. This is an unintended consequence of determinate sentencing laws, which provide offenders with an automatic release date regardless of treatment progress or conduct in prison.

exploitation. Unmitigated consumption; to use for the greatest possible selfish advantage. In criminal justice, this term generally applies to unequal social relations resulting in the acquisition of a valued commodity by a dominant individual or group. For example, labor, sexual favors, or natural resources have been exploited by historically powerful elites. Some attribute exploitive tendencies to religious institutions, patriarchy, economic systems, and racist institutions. The term is often used by those individuals who no longer accept the legitimacy of their inferior status in society or in reference to those who are unaware of their status or are unable to stop their continued misuse by more powerful groups (e.g., exploitation of prostitutes, drug addicts, homeless persons, etc.).

explosive bullet. A bullet that contains an explosive that is detonated on contact with its target or via a time fuse. Such bullets were banned for small arms by international agreement in 1868.

explosive D. So named from the initial of Col. B.W. Dunn, its inventor, this explosive is also called dunnite. It consists mainly of ammonium picrate and is used in some armor piercing projectiles because of its comparative insensitivity to shock and friction.

explosive-ordnance disposal unit. (Sometimes called "bomb squads"). Personnel with special training and equipment who render explosive ordnance (such as bombs, mines, projectiles, and booby traps) safe, make intelligence reports on such ordnance, and supervise its safe removal.

explosives classifications. Established by the U.S. Dept. of Transportation as specified in the U.S. Code of Federal Regulations (49 CFR), Class 1 explosives are divided into six types: Division 1.1 explosives are materials that pose a mass explosion hazard, which affects all or most of the entire explosive simultaneously; Division 1.2 explosives have a projection hazard but not a mass explosion hazard as defined in division 1.1; Division 1.3 explosives pose a fire hazard and also pose either a minor blast hazard or minor projection hazard; Division 1.4 explosives present a minor explosion hazard, with no significant blast or minor projection hazard, such that any explosion is generally contained within the package; Division 1.5 explosives consist of blasting agents that are insensitive and thus pose little risk of detonation or fire during normal transport; and Division 1.6 explosives include extremely insensitive detonating agents with little likelihood of accidental fire or explosion during normal transportation.

ex post facto law. A law retroactively making illegal a certain behavior, increasing punishment for it, or removing lawful protection from it. A basic principle recognized by civilized countries is that of *nulla poena sine lege* (Lat., no punishment without law). Article I of the Constitution forbids Congress and the states to pass any ex post facto law. The Supreme Court used this prohibition to strike down the test-oath laws after the Civil War; civil cases are not, however, affected by this protection.

expropriation. Action by the state, under its sovereign power, to take over property for the use of the people (public use). *See also* eminent domain

expunge. To erase or destroy information in files, computers, or other depositories. A criminal conviction can often be expunged or erased from official record, resulting in the removal of a criminal conviction from one's "rap sheet." Such action is generally initiated by the defendant, who petitions the court subsequent to conviction and generally provides evidence of law-abiding activities and a desistance from crime. If granted, the court issues an order of expungement, which the defendant (or attorney) must file with appropriate agencies in order to remove the specified conviction from criminal database(s). Provisions for expungement are generally specified in state statutes and often require a duration of 5 to 10 years since conviction before expungement is possible.

ex rel (Lat., lit. "by or on the information of"). In titles of cases, it designates the individual for whom the government or public official is acting.

exsanguination. Death by hypovolemia, or total blood loss; bleeding to death.

extenuating circumstances. Particular characteristics of an offender, situation, or offense that partially or entirely excuse the offender or serve to reduce the gravity of the act.

exterior ballistics. The branch of ballistics that deals with the motion of a projectile while in flight.

extortion. Unlawfully obtaining or attempting to obtain something of value from another by compelling the other person to deliver it by the threat of eventual physical injury or other harm to that person, his or her property, or a third person. Extortion differs from robbery in that in robbery, there is an immediate confrontation between offender and victim, and the threatened injury is physical and imminent. Extortion is usually categorized as a type of theft offense in penal codes. Blackmail is the popular name for the kind of extortion where the threat is not physical but relates to exposing some secret fact (whether true or alleged) that would do harm to a person's circumstances or damage his or her reputation.

extortion by means of telephone. An act passed by Congress on May 18, 1934, applied the powers of the federal government, under the commerce clause of the Constitution, to extortion by means of telephone, telegraph, radio, oral message, or otherwise.

extradition. The surrender, by one state to another, of an individual accused or convicted of an offense in the second state. (1) Interstate extradition. The Constitution, several acts of Congress, and the statutes of several states provide that a person charged with a crime in one state who flees from that state into another may be returned to the former. In order to be extradited, the person: (a) must be judicially charged with a crime in the demanding state; (b) must not be charged with a crime against the state to which he or she has fled; and (c) must have been in the demanding state in order to have "fled from justice." (2) International extradition. By treaties between the United States and most foreign countries, provision is made for the extradition of fugitives from justice in specified cases. The states cannot act in this matter. Countries without the death penalty often do not honor extradition in capital cases. *See also* Polanski, Roman

extrajudicial. Out of the ordinary course of law. For example, an extrajudicial statement is one made outside of court.

extralegal. Outside or beyond the scope of law.

extraneous. Not germane or relevant to the matter at hand.

extraneous evidence. In reference to any document, a type of evidence that is not derived from anything in the document itself.

Extraordinary Rendition. A covert practice of transporting foreign suspects to remote locations, often in third countries, for detention and interrogation.

extraterritorial operation, of laws. In general, the laws of a country are not effective beyond its territorial limits, on the theory that crime is essentially local and is determined by the law that defines or prohibits it. However, mere physical presence, citizenship, or residence within a state is not always essential to rendering someone subject to its laws and its prosecution. Among the exceptions to the general rule are cases in which a person, being at the time in one state or country, commits a crime that takes effect in another.

extremist group. A group or organization, the avowed purpose of which is to bring about some change in government functions and in society by radical, disorderly, and/or violent methods.

extrinsic evidence. External evidence; facts other than those contained in the body of an agreement, document, or other object.

F

Facial Recognition Software. computer software that enables authorities to identify specific faces out of a crowd, particularly those wanted for criminal activity or suspected of terrorism.

facsimile. An exact copy.

fact. A thing done; an actual occurrence.

fact finder (trier of fact). The individual or group with the obligation and authority to determine the facts (as distinct from the law) in a case. In a jury trial, the jury is the fact finder and is charged with accepting the law as given to it by the judge.

fact-finding. A form of third-party intervention in collective bargaining impasses. In public interest disputes, fact-finding by a government-designated board may cut through claims and allegations to the facts. The results of fact-finding may provide an incentive for the parties to settle. *See also* collective bargaining

failure to appear. Willful absence from a court appearance.

fair comment. A term used in defamation cases (libel or slander), pertaining to statements made by a writer in an honest belief of their truth, although they in fact are not true.

Fair Housing and Equal Credit Opportunity. Title VIII of the Civil Rights Act of 1968 as amended by the Fair Housing Amendments Act of 1988 is designed to ensure freedom from discrimination in the sale, rental, and financing of housing. A private suit alleging discrimination may be filed in the appropriate federal or state court. The Attorney General is authorized to bring civil actions in federal courts when there is reasonable cause to believe that any person or group of persons is engaged in a pattern or practice of discrimination or any group has been denied equal rights in a case of general public importance. The Equal Credit Opportunity Act is designed to prohibit discrimination in all aspects of credit transactions. Persons who believe they are victims of such discrimination may file complaints with one of the appropriate federal regulatory agencies or may bring the information to the attention of the Attorney General. In addition, an aggrieved person may institute suit in federal court. For further information, contact: U.S. Department of Housing and Urban Development, 451 7th Street S.W., Washington, DC 20410; Web: http://www.hud.gov/offices/fheo/FHLaws/yourrights.cfm. Phone: (202) 514-4713.

fair trade laws. State laws passed under the authorization of the Miller-Tydings Act for the purpose of allowing manufacturers of branded products to establish minimum resale prices.

fait accompli. (Fr.). An action that is regarded as completed and therefore not subject to further negotiation.

faith-based. Term refers to an organization that is religious in nature, and that generally offers low- or no-cost services to persons under correctional supervision. Examples include prison ministries, and religious-based drug treatment programs. *See also* Prison Fellowship Ministries; Prison Ministry International

FALN (*Fuerzas Armadas de Liberación Nacional Puertorriqueña*). *See* Puerto Rican Armed Forces of National Liberation.

false arrest. Unlawful physical restraint of an individual's liberty; such restrictions may occur in prisons, jails, or other maximum security facilities.

False Claims Act. (also called the "Lincoln law"). This federal law traces its roots to the Civil War, but it was little used until 1986, when it was strengthened to attract more whistle-blowers, by enabling them to share up to 30 percent of any damage claim paid to the government. By 2008, $22 billion had been recovered by the government on whistle-blower suits since the law was modified.

false impersonation. Also called person-ation. To impersonate another falsely and to demand or obtain something of value for oneself or someone else is a federal and state violation.

false imprisonment. (1) Detention under false or assumed authority or because of a miscarriage of judicial procedure. (2) Any unlawful restraint of a person's liberty. Isa-dore Zimmerman (1917–1983) of New York spent 24 years in prison before his conviction for murdering a police officer was overturned because of new evidence. On his release at age 66, he was awarded $1 million, which is equivalent to $42,000 for each year he spent in prison. But, after legal fees and expenses, he ended up with only 60 percent of the money. He decided not to appeal the award, and died a little more than a year later. *See also* wrongful conviction

false negative. Occurs when an event is not predicted, but it does occur. For example, an offender is deemed unlikely to recidivate, and is therefore a good parole risk, yet he commits another crime upon release.

false positive. Occurs when an event is pre-dicted to occur, but it does not. For example, an offender is deemed a high recidivism risk, yet he does not commit further criminal activity.

false pretenses. False representations and/or statements made with fraudulent design to obtain money, goods, wares, or merchan-dise with intent to defraud. The distinction between larceny and false pretenses is that in larceny, the owner of something has no intention to part with it, while in false pre-tenses, the owner does intend to part with the property, but it is obtained from him or her by fraud.

Family Court. Sometimes called domestic relations court, family court is a court with jurisdiction over family matters, including such issues as divorce, dissolution, annul-ment, child custody, child support, alimony, visitation, emancipation of minors, child abuse and neglect, and juvenile offenses. *See also* domestic relations court

family visit. Designation used in some juris-dictions to replace the term *conjugal visit*. A family visit is an extended visit between an inmate and his/family, including spouse and children. Such visits occur on prison grounds, in special units like apartments designed for this purpose. Although provisions vary by state, family visits are generally limited to less-serious, less-violent offenders, and the visiting family must pass a background clearance and submit to extended security precautions, including the search of prop-erty (food, linens) several weeks in advance of the visit. The U.S. federal prison system does not permit family visits, but a few states allow them. In 2007, California became the first state to allow same-sex conjugal visits to comply with state law permitting same sex marriages. *See also* conjugal visit

Families with Service Needs. A designa-tion proposed by the Task Force on Juve-nile Justice and Delinquency Prevention, in which both status offenders and their families would come under the authority and jurisdic-tion of the juvenile court.

fascism. An autocratic form of central-ized government that represses opposition and rigidly controls finance, commerce, and industry. It can become a dictatorship.

FBI. *See* Federal Bureau of Investigation

FBI Academy. Founded in 1935, the acad-emy offers a variety of programs at its 385-acre academy located in Quantico, Virginia. In addition to the training for new FBI agents, the FBI Academy also serves as an interna-tional training center providing the following resources to other law enforcement agencies (and in some cases, private citizens): Citi-zens' Academy, Driving Skills (TEVOC), Firearms Training, Survival Skills (LETSS), Overseas Survival Awareness, Center for Intelligence Training, International Training,

Leadership Development Institute (NEI, LEEDs, etc.), Counter-Terrorism Training and Resources for Law Enforcement (includes non-FBI), FBI Laboratory Specialized Training, Fingerprint and Criminal History Record Training, Hazardous Devices School, and Large Vehicle Bomb Post-Blast Crime Scene School. Address: FBI Academy, Quantico, VA 22135; Web: http://www.fbi.gov/hq/td/academy/academy.htm.

FBI field training. Courses available from FBI instructors range from basic recruit training to specialized instruction in such areas as fingerprinting, legal topics, police-community relations, hostage negotiation, white-collar crime, organized crime, computer fraud, management techniques, and so forth. FBI training assistance is available in complete programs of instruction or as supplemental courses to already-existing, local police training sessions. For further information, contact: Federal Bureau of Investigation, J. Edgar Hoover Building, 935 Pennsylvania Avenue, NW Washington, DC 20535-0001. Phone: (202) 324-3000; Web: http://www.fbi.gov/howto.htm.

FBI Laboratory. Facilities are available to duly constituted municipal, county, state, and federal law enforcement agencies in the United States and its territorial possessions. Submitted evidence is examined, and the laboratory also furnishes the experts necessary to testify in connection with the results of these examinations. These examinations are made only if the evidence is connected with an official investigation of a criminal matter (for federal agencies, both criminal and civil matters) and if the laboratory report will be used only for official purposes related to the investigation or a subsequent prosecution. The FBI will not accept cases from other crime laboratories that have the capability of conducting the requested examinations. This laboratory is divided into five major sections: Forensic Analysis; Scientific Analysis; Operational Response; Forensic Science; and Evidence Control. Address: FBI Laboratory, 2501 Investigation Parkway, Quantico,

Virginia 22135; Web: http://www.fbi.gov/hq/lab/labhome.htm.

feasance. A doing; the doing of an act; a performance. *See also* malfeasance; misfeasance; nonfeasance

Federal Air Marshal Service (FAMS). FAMS is the primary law enforcement body within the Transportation Security Administration (TSA), which operated under the U.S. Department of Homeland Security (DHS). FAMS deploys marshals on flights around the world and in the United States, with a primary mission of protecting air passengers and crew. Address: Transportation Security Administration, 601 South 12th Street. Arlington, VA 20598; Web: http://www.tsa.gov/lawenforcement/index.shtm.

Federal Alcohol Control Board. An agency created by Congress in 1933 for the purpose of regulating the branding and grading of alcoholic beverages and for dealing generally with the new problems of interstate liquor traffic raised by the Twenty-first Amendment. It was authorized to establish proper business standards for the liquor industry and to foster fair trade methods in the interests of producers and consumers. The agency was later reorganized into the Federal Alcohol Administration, then into the Bureau of Alcohol, Tobacco and Firearms (ATF). The Homeland Security Act of 2002 bifurcated the ATF into the Alcohol and Tobacco Tax and Trade Bureau (TTB) under the Department of the Treasury and the Bureau of Alcohol, Tobacco, Firearms and Explosives (ATF) under the Department of Justice. The TTP performs regulatory functions similar to those of the original Federal Alcohol Control Board, while the ATF maintains law enforcement functions. *See also* Alcohol and Tobacco Tax and Trade Bureau; Bureau of Alcohol, Tobacco, Firearms and Explosives

federal anti-lynch laws. *See* anti-lynch bills

Federal Assault Weapons Ban of 1994 (AWB, also called Public Safety and Recreational Firearms Use Protection Act). Among other things, this 1994 law bans the sale of semi-automatic "assault weapons" to civilians. This Act had a 10-year duration and expired in 2004. Efforts to renew this Act have not been successful as of 2010. *See also* Brady Handgun Violence Prevention Act; Bureau of Alcohol, Tobacco, Firearms and Explosives (ATF); Federal Assault Weapons Ban of 1994; Federal Firearms Act of 1938; Firearm Owners' Protection Act of 1986; Gun Control Act of 1968; National Firearms Act of 1934; Omnibus Crime Control and Safe Streets Act of 1968; Violent Crime Control and Law Enforcement Act of 1994

Federal Aviation Act. A law enacted by Congress in 1968. Paragraph 902 of the act makes it a crime for persons with a concealed weapon to board an aircraft operated by an air carrier; such provisions were expanded further under the USA PATRIOT Act. Many law enforcement officers, (such as municipal, state, and federal) are exempted.

Federal Aviation Administration (FAA). Formerly the Federal Aviation Agency, it is an arm of the U.S. Department of Transportation. The FAA is responsible for the safety of civil aviation. The Federal Aviation Act of 1958 created the agency under the name Federal Aviation Agency; the FAA adopted the present name in 1967 when they became part of the Department of Transportation. The FAA is charged with: regulating civil aviation to promote safety; encouraging and developing civil aeronautics, including new aviation technology; developing and operating a system of air traffic control and navigation for both civil and military aircraft; researching and developing the National Airspace System and civil aeronautics; developing and carrying out programs to control aircraft noise and other environmental effects of civil aviation; and regulating U.S. commercial space transportation. Address: Federal Aviation Administration, Department of Transportation, 800 Independence Avenue, SW, Room 707, Washington, DC 20591. Phone: (866) 835-5322. Web: http://www.faa.gov/.

Federal Bureau of Investigation. Established in 1908, the FBI is the investigative arm of the Department of Justice. It investigates all violations of federal law except those specifically assigned to some other agency by legislative action (e.g., counterfeiting and internal revenue, postal, and customs violations). This agency is primarily concerned with enforcement of the laws that involve interstate crimes, such as transportation of stolen vehicles across state lines (the Dyer Act) or flight from one state to another to avoid prosecution for a felony (the Fugitive Felon Act); crimes involving federal institutions, such as robbery of a federally insured bank (the National Bank Robbery Act); or crimes on federal property (such as a military reservation). The powers of the FBI expand as Congress enacts additional federal criminal laws, such as the National Stolen Property Act (dealing with interstate shipment of stolen goods), the Federal Kidnapping Act, the Hobbs Act (extortion), the White Slavery Act (prostitution), and federal interstate gambling and civil rights laws. The FBI's Identification Division houses the largest fingerprint repository in the world. Address: J. Edgar Hoover Building, 935 Pennsylvania Avenue, NW Washington, DC 20535-0001. Phone: (202) 324-3000; Web: http://www.fbi.gov/.

Federal Bureau of Investigation, history of. In June/July of 1908, Attorney General Charles Bonaparte ordered creation of special agent force, and assigned them to report to the U.S. chief examiner. While the agency performed many law enforcement functions, agents were not authorized to make arrests or carry firearms, instead calling on U.S. marshals or local police for these functions. This organization was named the Bureau of Investigation (BOI) in 1909. In 1932, the agency was renamed the U.S. BOI; it was renamed the Division of Investigation (DOI) the same year. In 1934, U.S. Congress passed a series of crime bills, including the Division of Investigation Act, which gave DOI Special Agents the power of arrest and the authority to carry firearms. In 1935, the agency was officially renamed the Federal Bureau of Investigations, its current name.

Federal Bureau of Prisons. (FBP) Established in 1930 for confinement of federal inmates. The bureau "protects society through the care and custody of those persons convicted by the courts to serve a period of time incarcerated in a federal penal institution." Currently, FBP has 115 institutions that provide for the custody of about 209,000 federal offenders. Address: 320 First St., NW, Washington, DC 20534; Web: http://www.bop.gov/.

Federal Bureau of Prisons, history of. During the first century of American independence, there were virtually no federal prison facilities. Most federal offenders were incarcerated in state prisons and county jails. After the Civil War, the federal inmate population began to rise. Congress enacted legislation in 1891 to construct three federal penitentiaries. In the 1920s, a women's reformatory, a youth facility, and a detention center were added to the federal system. By the late 1920s, new federal laws such as the Volstead Act (Prohibition) had caused severe overcrowding in the few existing facilities. A special committee of the House of Representatives on federal penal and reformatory institutions met in January 1929, responding to overcrowding, political concerns, and lax management. On May 14, 1930, President Herbert Hoover signed legislation establishing the Federal Bureau of Prisons within the Department of Justice to manage and regulate all federal prisons, authorized the building of new prisons, created a new Board of Parole, and provided prisoner medical treatment by the U.S. Public Health Service. The first director of the Bureau of Prisons was Sanford Bates. The bureau built or acquired several new facilities, ranging from minimum security prison camps, to the maximum security penitentiary at Alcatraz, to a large hospital for federal prisoners in Springfield, MO. In 1934 the Federal Prisons Industries, Inc. (UNICOR) was established. The bureau works closely with the National Institute

of Corrections, founded in 1974 to provide advisory and technical support to state and local agencies. In 1992 the bureau supported a prison population of 63,483, served by 23,000 staff members at 68 institutions, with 27 more facilities under construction. Currently, FBP has 115 institutions that provide for the custody of about 209,000 federal offenders. *See also* Bates, Sanford

Federal Communications Commission (FCC). An independent federal agency that regulates interstate communications and their facilities, including telephone, telegraph, cable, radio, and television. Address: 445 12th Street SW, Washington, DC 20554. Phone: (888)225-5322. Web: http://www.fcc.gov/.

Federal Deposit Insurance Corporation (FDIC). A federally created corporation established under the Banking Act of 1933 to provide insurance for deposits in member banks. Banks insured by FDIC are under federal jurisdiction where crimes are involved related to banking. Thus such crimes as bank robbery, embezzlement, and theft are federal criminal violations. Address: 550 17th Street, NW, Washington, DC 20429. Phone: (877) 275-3342. Web: http://www.fdic.gov/.

Federal Emergency Management Agency (FEMA). FEMA founded the Arson Resource Center in 1983 to "inform the public about arson" and offer reference service to the general public on arson and related areas of interest. FEMA also founded the National Emergency Training Center Learning Resource Center in 1976. The center's goal is to support the staff and student activities of the National Emergency Training Center. Major subject areas are fire-related fields, management, and education. Address: 16825 South Seton Avenue, Emmitsburg, MD 21727. FEMA's headquarters is at 500 C Street, SW, Washington, DC 20472. Phone: (202) 646-2500. Web: http://www.fema.gov/.

Federal Firearms Act (1938). A law of Congress, enacted June 30, 1938, aimed at reducing the possession of firearms by criminals. The Act forbids any unlicensed person to ship firearms or ammunition in interstate commerce and subjects such shipments to numerous restrictions. Criminals are banned from sending or receiving weapons under this Act, and firearms without serials numbers are banned from commerce. *See also* Brady Handgun Violence Prevention Act; Bureau of Alcohol, Tobacco, Firearms and Explosives (ATF); Federal Assault Weapons Ban of 1994; Firearm Owners' Protection Act of 1986; Gun Control Act of 1968; National Firearms Act of 1934; Omnibus Crime Control and Safe Streets Act of 1968; Violent Crime Control and Law Enforcement Act of 1994

Federal Judicial Center. Investigative organization empowered by Congress in 1967 to improve the administration of the court system and to develop judicial training programs. The center, located in Washington, DC, was created in 1967 after much public debate about crowded and poorly managed court calendars. Address: Federal Judicial Center, Thurgood Marshall Federal Judiciary Building, 1 Columbus Circle NE, Washington DC 20002-8003. Web: http://www.fjc.gov/.

Federal Kidnapping Law. *See* kidnapping; Lindbergh Law

Federal Law Enforcement Training Center (FLETC). This interagency facility was established in 1970 under the Department of the Treasury, it now operates under the Department of Homeland Security. The main center is a 1,500-acre site near Brunswick, GA. Other facilities are located in Artesia, NM, and Charleston, SC. Organization provides basic police and criminal investigator training for officers and agents of the participating federal organizations, as well as advanced and specialized training that is common to two or more organizations. Its programs include: criminal investigation programs and police programs, criminology skills, investigative techniques, legal courses, communications skills, ethics, and firearms training. Address: Federal Law Enforcement

Training Center, Department of the Treasury, Glynco Facility, Brunswick, GA 31524. Web: http://www.fletc.gov/.

Federal Motor Vehicle Safety Standards. Mandatory vehicle performance, design features, and objectives established by the National Highway Traffic Safety Administration of the Department of Transportation to enhance vehicle and occupant safety.

Federal Prison Industries, Inc. (FPI, also known as UNICOR). UNICOR is the trade name under which Federal Prison Industries does most of its business. Government corporation established by Congress on June 23, 1934, to employ and provide job skills and training to inmates confined within the Federal Bureau of Prisons. UNICOR keeps inmates constructively occupied by using inmate labor to produce goods and services for sale to the federal government. According to FPI, UNICOR is "first and foremost, a correctional program" dedicated to prepare inmates for release and secondarily a business. All UNICOR sales are to federal government agencies, including: Department of Defense, Department of Homeland Security, General Services Administration, Federal Bureau of Prisons, Social Security Administration, Department of Justice, United States Postal Service, Department of Transportation, Department of the Treasury, Department of Agriculture, and Department of Veterans Affairs. They do not sell goods to the general public. Address: Federal Prison Industries, 400 First Street, NW, Washington, DC 20534. Web: www.unicor.gov.

Federal Programs Branch. This branch of the Department of Justice employs more than 100 attorneys who handle litigation against federal agencies, cabinet officers, and other officials. It handles enforcement and litigation aimed at remedying statutory or regulatory violations, the defense of employment policies and personnel actions, and litigation relating to the disposition and availability of government records. Address: Federal Programs Branch, Civil Division, DOJ, 950 Pennsylvania Ave. NW, Washington DC

20530-00001. http://www.justice.gov/civil/ Federal%20Programs.htm.

federal question. Any case with a major issue involving the Constitution or statutes. The jurisdiction of the federal courts is partly controlled by the existence of a federal question.

Federal Register. A U.S. government publication that prints presidential proclamations, reorganization plans, and executive orders. Notices of proposed rules and regulations and administrative orders of public agencies are also published in the *Register:* The Federal Register Act of 1935 requires the publication of presidential proclamations, and the Administrative Procedure Act of 1946 requires compliance by public agencies. Because of the continuing increase in subject matter, the *Federal Register* is an extremely important and widely read publication. Before its existence, citizens and business interests had no way of knowing what new rules applied to them. The publication gives all interested parties the opportunity to be heard prior to the enforcement of any rules and regulations. It is published five times a week, and the documents are codified in the Code of Federal Regulations. Available through the U.S. Government Printing Offices and online at: http://www.gpoaccess. gov/nara/index.html.

Federal Reserve banknotes. The serial numbers on all U.S. currency, also called Federal Reserve banknotes, are preceded by a letter designating which one of the 12 Federal Reserve districts issued the bill.

federal security level designations. The Federal Bureau of Prisons has designated the following classifications for use in federal institutions: Minimum, Low, Medium, High, and Administrative.

Federal Tort Claims Act. Title IV of the Legislative Reorganization Act of 1946, revised in 1948, permits private parties to sue the United States and authorized federal district courts to render judgments on claims against the United States because of property damages, personal injury, or death caused by the negligence of a government employee. The heads of federal agencies were required to submit annual reports to Congress of all claims made under the law. The U.S. government was made liable with respect to claims (including costs) tried in the district courts. Employees of the government, however, were exempted from any action by claimants in the event of district court action. The decisions of the district courts were made reviewable on appeal in the courts of appeals or in the U.S. Court of Claims. The attorney general was authorized to arbitrate, compromise, or settle any claim after its institution, with the consent of the court.

Federal Trade Commission. A powerful, five-member, independent, bipartisan commission established in 1914, the FTC exercises extensive quasi-judicial and quasi-legislative functions in enforcing most of the nations laws related to industrial practices, pricing, food and drug purity, labeling and packaging, telemarketing, and fair credit. The FTC's main objective is to maintain the free enterprise system by preventing unfettered monopoly or corruption by unfair and deceptive trade practices. Much of its work is in guiding industry to voluntary compliance, but the FTC can institute legal cease-and-desist proceedings and impose penalties subject to court appeal. The members, including the chairman, are appointed by the president with senatorial consent. Address: 600 Pennsylvania Avenue, NW, Washington, DC 20580, (202) 326-2222 Web: http://www. ftc.gov/.

Federal Wiretap Act of 1968. Federal legislation that makes it illegal to intercept or disclose intercepted telephone communications, unless so ordered or authorized by a court. *See also* Omnibus Crime Control and Safe Streets Act of 1968

feeblemindedness. Historical term used to describe developmental disabilities. *See* developmental disability

feigned accomplice. An individual who pretends to act with others in the planning or commission of a crime for the purpose of discovering their plans or compiling evidence against them.

fellatio. Oral contact with the male genitals for sexual gratification of one or both partners. *See also* cunnilingus

felon. A term derived from the legal classification of crimes as felonies and misdemeanors. The former category includes those crimes regarded as the more serious or heinous, which usually involve as punishment either confinement in a state or federal prison or death. A felon is therefore one who commits a felony or who habitually commits felonies.

felonious. (1) Malignant, malicious. (2) Done with intent to commit a crime.

felony. A criminal offense punishable by death or incarceration of at least one year in a prison facility.

felony disenfranchisement. Term used to describe the practice of prohibiting people from voting (known as disenfranchisement) based on the fact that they have been convicted of a felony; disenfranchisement disproportionately impacts African Americans. In *Richardson v. Ramirez,* the United States Supreme Court upheld the constitutionality of felon disenfranchisement statutes, finding that the practice did not deny equal protection to disenfranchised voters. If passed, the Democracy Restoration Act of 2009 (congressional testimony is in progress as of March 2010), would restore voting rights to millions of Americans with past felony convictions.

felony murder rule. The rule stating that an accidental killing that occurs during the commission of a felony may be prosecuted as murder.

Female Offender Programs, Bureau of Prisons. This office monitors programs for female inmates, including programs to meet their physical, social, and psychological needs. Address: Correctional Programs Division, Bureau of Prisons, DOJ, 320 1st Street, NW, Room 534, Washington, DC 20534. http://www.bop.gov/inmate_programs/female.jsp.

femicide. The killing of a woman.

fence. (1) A receiver and seller of stolen property who either pursues this line of work exclusively, or, more often, in connection with a legitimate business. (2) The establishment in which such a person does business.

fencing. The act of receiving stolen goods; the receipt, handling, and sale of stolen goods as a business and occupation.

fetal alcohol syndrome (FAS). A complex set of congenital anomalies seen in newborns of women who ingest alcohol, which can easily cross the placenta during pregnancy. Defects in infants can include premature birth, underweight at birth, growth deficiency, craniofacial abnormalities, central nervous system damage, microcephaly (small head) and functional impairments such as learning disabilities, hyperactivity, poor impulse control, low IQ, and impaired executive function, communication, memory, and mental retardation.

feticide. Destroying a fetus; criminal abortion.

fetishism. The attribution of power or value to an object beyond the norm. Fetishism may or may not be of a sexual nature. When sexual, the term refers to sexual gratification obtained through the medium of an inanimate object. Common fetish objects are women's lingerie and footwear and garments made entirely of rubber, leather, or fur. *See also* sexual fetish

fetus. An unborn animal or human in the womb. In humans, the developing child is referred to as a fetus from the end of the third month until birth.

fiction. Legally, the assumption of a thing as being factual, regardless of its truthfulness.

fiduciary. Referring to one authorized to act for another. Fiduciary trust is the power given to the police by the public to act in its interests.

field interview. Generally, any contact between a private citizen and a law enforcement officer acting in his or her official capacity, whether or not relating to suspicion or criminal activity.

55-mph speed limit. Once a federal law governing drivers nationwide, this statute was repealed in December 1995, returning to the states the right to set their own speed limits.

filing. (1) In recommended general court terminology, the initiation of a case in court by formal submission of a document alleging the facts of a matter and requesting relief. (2) In recommended criminal justice statistical terminology, the initiation of a criminal case in a court by formal submission of a charging document, alleging that one or more named persons have committed one or more specified criminal offenses.

final. A term used in classifying fingerprints according to the Henry system. In the Henry classification formula, it appears at the extreme right on the classification line and above the line. It is determined by ridge counts in the little finger. The right hand is used if it has a loop; if not, the left is used if it has a loop. If neither has a loop but each has a whorl, a ridge count between delta and core is made in the right hand. *See also* Henry system

financial conditions. Release from custody pending trial on the basis of financial bail, including deposit bond, surety bond, or collateral bond. *See* Table 3. Types of Pretrial Release, page 36

finding. A conclusion of fact certified after inquiry by a judicial or other body.

fine. The penalty imposed upon a convicted person by a court, requiring that he or she pay a specified sum of money to the court.

fingerprint classification. A system of classifying fingerprints according to the patterns of the friction ridges on the fingertips used through the 1990s. The most common systems were the Roscher system, used in Japan

and Germany, the Juan Vucetich system, used in South America, and the Henry Classification System, used in India, the United States, and England. *See also* fingerprint patterns, Henry classification, Juan Vucetich system, Roscher system

fingerprint conviction, first. Obtained by the New York Police Department, which arrested Caesar Cella, alias Charles Crispi, for burglary on March 8, 1911. Latent fingerprints found at the scene of the crime were introduced as evidence. He was convicted and sentenced to the NY County Penitentiary by Judge Otto Alfred Rosalsky in General Sessions Court, New York City, on May 19, 1911.

fingerprint Identification. The FBI operates a law enforcement assistance service that provides criminal identification by means of fingerprints, determination of the number of previously reported arrests and convictions, fingerprint identification of victims of major disasters (*see* Disaster Squad), and processing of submitted evidence for latent fingerprint impression. Information must be used for official purposes only and is not furnished for public dissemination. The CAL-ID Automated Fingerprint System, implemented in 1985, used imaging and database technology to store over 7 million fingerprint images representing over 1 million individuals through the mid-1990s. In 1999, the FBI transitioned to the Integrated Automated Fingerprint Identification System (IAFIS), which contains fingerprints of 55 million subjects. For further information, contact: Criminal Justice Information Services, FBI, DOJ, Washington, DC 20537.

fingerprint, latent. A chance fingerprint left accidentally or otherwise on a surface.

fingerprint patterns. The configuration of the friction ridges on the fingers is called a pattern. There are basically three patterns: arches, loops, and whorls. An arch is where the ridges come in from one side, do not recurve, and go out the other side. The ridges make an upward thrust at or near the center of the pattern, also called the core. There are two kinds: the plain arch, where the upthrust is smooth and gradual, and the tented arch, where the upward thrust is sharp. A loop has ridge lines that enter from either side, recurve, touch or pass an imaginary line between the delta, or pattern of radiation outward from the center, and the core, and pass out on the side from which the ridge or ridges entered. A plain whorl has one or more ridges that make a complete circuit. It has two deltas, between which, when an imaginary line is drawn, at least one recurving ridge is cut or touched. These basic patterns are subdivided as follows: Arch: plain arch; tented arch. Loop: radial loop; lateral loop; ulnar loop; central pocket loop; twin loop. Whorl: plain whorl. In addition to the three basic types of fingerprints, there is a catchall or nondescript pattern called accidentals.

fingerprints. Also referred to as dactyloscopy, the prints or impressions produced by the friction ridges of the inner surface of the fingertips. The impressions may be left accidentally or otherwise on objects touched by the fingers or may be taken by two methods: (a) rolled—the fingertips are rolled on a freshly inked surface and then rolled on a white paper; (b) plain—the fingertip is pressed on an inked surface without rolling and the print is made on a light-colored surface. John Vucetichi, born in 1858, is considered the "father of fingerprinting." His system generally followed the Galton-Henry system. The first state prison to take fingerprints of its prisoners was Sing Sing Prison in Ossining, NY, which commenced taking impressions on March 3, 1903. *See also* Galton, Francis; Henry system

fingerprint system, first police department to adopt. The St. Louis (MO) Metropolitan Police Department, on October 28, 1904, adopted the Henry method to fingerprint persons arrested on serious charges. John M. Shea was the first to qualify as a fingerprint expert connected with any police service. He joined the department on May 1, 1899, and was appointed Superintendent of the

Bertillon System on September 14, 1903. He remained in office until his death on July 17, 1926. *See also* Bertillon method; Henry system

fire. A state, process, or instances of combustion in which fuel or other material is ignited and combined with oxygen, giving off light, heat, and flame.

firearm. (1) In a general sense, a gun. (2) Specifically, a small arm, such as a pistol or rifle, designed to be carried by an individual. Although it cannot be accepted as proven, the best opinion is that the earliest guns were constructed in North Africa, possibly by Arabs, around 1250. The earliest representation of an English gun is contained in an illustrated manuscript dated 1326 at Oxford University, England.

Firearm Act, Federal. The 1934 National Firearms Act regulated possession of submachine guns, silencers, and several other weapons. In 1938 the Federal Firearms Act was passed, requiring the licensing of firearms manufacturers and dealers. As a result, all new weapons sold legally in the United States since 1938 have been registered and can be traced. The most important federal action was the passage of the Gun Control Act of 1968, as it prohibited interstate retailing of all firearms. Its purpose was to prevent individuals who cannot legally own a gun from ordering guns by mail under false names. *See also* Brady Handgun Violence Prevention Act; Bureau of Alcohol, Tobacco, Firearms and Explosives (ATF); Federal Assault Weapons Ban of 1994; Firearm Owners' Protection Act of 1986; Gun Control Act of 1968; National Firearms Act of 1934; Omnibus Crime Control and Safe Streets Act of 1968; Violent Crime Control and Law Enforcement Act of 1994

firearms acts. *See* Brady Handgun Violence Prevention Act; Bureau of Alcohol, Tobacco, Firearms and Explosives (ATF); Federal Assault Weapons Ban of 1994; Federal Firearms Act of 1938; Firearm Owners' Protection Act of 1986; Gun Control Act of 1968;

National Firearms Act of 1934; Omnibus Crime Control and Safe Streets Act of 1968; Violent Crime Control and Law Enforcement Act of 1994

Firearm Owners' Protection Act of 1986. Passed in 1986, this act modified many provisions of the 1968 Gun Control Act in response to a Congressional report indicating that many prosecutions under the 1968 Gun Control Act violated constitutional protections. This act eased laws governing interstate sale of weapons and ammunition, and loosened tracking of ammunition sales nationwide. The law also banned the sale of machine guns manufactured after 1986 to civilians. *See also* Brady Handgun Violence Prevention Act; Bureau of Alcohol, Tobacco, Firearms and Explosives (ATF); Federal Assault Weapons Ban of 1994; Federal Firearms Act of 1938; Firearm Owners' Protection Act of 1986; Gun Control Act of 1968; National Firearms Act of 1934; Omnibus Crime Control and Safe Streets Act of 1968; Violent Crime Control and Law Enforcement Act of 1994

Fireman's Rule. Used as a basis for court decisions as early as 1892, this criterion reflects an effort by courts to reconcile the unique activities of policemen and firemen with the general rule of allowing injured employees to maintain traditional tort actions against third parties for virtually all negligently inflicted injuries. The traditional Fireman's Rule denies a fireman's or policeman's cause of action against any individual whose only negligence was to cause a situation for which the officer was summoned and subsequently injured. Historically underlying the rule are the notions: (a) that firemen and policemen are mere "licensees" in the eyes of the law, and little or no duty is owed them by owners or occupiers of land; (b) that the occupation of policeman and fireman is inherently dangerous, and thus those accepting the position assume the risk of being injured by negligent conduct; (c) that policemen and firemen are compensated for the risks they face; and (d) that public policy demands application

of the rule. Despite complaints that it is an anachronism, the rule continues to be followed by most state courts. Once restricted to acts of negligence, it has been expanded in recent years to include willful, wanton, reckless, and, in some circumstances, intentional conduct, as later interpretations of the risk principles were adopted. The rule remains an important barrier to recovery for injuries policemen receive in the line of duty.

fires, classification. Fires can be grouped into five basic types: Class A: Fires involving ordinary combustible materials (wood, cloth, paper, rubber, and many plastics) requiring the heat-absorbing (cooling) effects of water, water solutions, or the coating effects of certain dry chemicals that retard combustion. Class B: Fires involving flammable or combustible liquids, flammable gases, greases, and similar materials where extinguishment is most readily secured by excluding air (oxygen), inhibiting the release of combustible vapors, or interrupting the combustion chain reaction. Class C: Fires involving energized electrical equipment where safety to the operator requires the use of electrically nonconductive extinguishing agents. Class D: Fires involving certain combustible metals (magnesium, sodium, titanium, zirconium, potassium) requiring a heat-absorbing extinguishing medium not reactive with the burning metals. Class K: Fires involving combustible cooking elements, such as grease and oil. *See also* burns

fires, historic.

The Great Chicago Fire. During October 8–10, 1871, wiped out 3 square miles of the city, killing 120 people, destroying 12,000 buildings, and causing approximately $200 million in damages.

Iroquois Theater, Chicago. On December 30, 1903, the theater caught fire after an overheated spotlight ignited stage riggings; 602 people died.

Triangle Shirtwaist Co., New York. On March 25, 1911, this sweatshop in lower Manhattan, in which 500 immigrants worked on the eighth and ninth floors of a 10-story building, became an inferno when a rag bin caught fire. Exits were blocked and fire hoses were rotted, resulting in 146 deaths.

Coconut Grove, Boston. On November 28, 1942, a small fire in the basement raced through the nightclub, resulting in 491 dead. Approximately 200 died from smoke, fire, and trampling.

MGM Grand Hotel Fire, Las Vegas. On November 21, 1980, a fire caused by a short circuit started in the wall and ceiling of a delicatessen and spread through the lobby. Toxic fumes and dense smoke poured through the air-conditioning ducts and elevator shafts, killing 85 people.

First Interstate Building, Los Angeles. On May 4, 1988, a fire in the 62-story building gutted four floors, killing one person and injuring 40 more. This fire caused over $450 million in damages, and the cause was never determined.

One Meridian Plaza, Philadelphia. On February 23, 1991, three firefighters died battling the flames on the 22nd floor. It raged out of control for 19 hours, causing $100 million in damage.

Oakland Hills. Between October 19–23, 1991, fire raged the hills surrounding Oakland, California, killing 25 people and injuring 150 others. In all, 1,520 acres were destroyed, including nearly 4,000 residences and resulting in $1.5 billion in total losses.

Cedar Fire. In 2003, the largest wildfire in California history burned 280,278 acres and 2,232 homes and had killed 15 people.

California Wildfires. In October 2007, a series of 17 wildfires plagued Southern California, destroying 1,500 homes and 500,000 acres, and requiring deployment of 2,400 National Guard troops. The fires, which raged for 19 days between Santa Barbara and the Mexican border, resulted in nine deaths, 85 injuries, deployment of 2,400 troops and evacuation of 950,000 people. The fires were also visible from space.

firing pin impressions. Marks made on the base of a cartridge case or shotgun shell by the firing pin. Such impressions are used by crime laboratories in determining whether a certain cartridge or shell was fired in a specific weapon.

firing squad. Execution by firing squad generally includes the use of five executioners armed with firearms, with at least one blank round in one of the guns. The condemned is generally restrained and hooded, and the shots are aimed at the chest (not head) and fired from a distance of 20–30 feet. John Albert Taylor's 1996 execution in Utah is the only example of death by firing squad in recent history. Only two states, Oklahoma and Utah, can still execute condemned persons by firing squad. While lethal injection is the primary method in these states, condemned persons can be executed in Oklahoma if both lethal injection and electrocution are declared unconstitutional. In Utah, persons condemned to die before 2004 can select their method of execution. *See also* execution, methods of; lethal injection; electrocution; lethal gas; and hanging. *See* Table 24. Execution Methods in the United States, by State, 2010, page 173

first release. Term used to reference an inmate's discharge from their initial prison term. This excludes discharge of offenders who are subsequently returned to custody.

fiscal year. A 12-month financial reporting period for a company or agency that often does not coincide with the calendar year. Government agencies, for example, often have fiscal years running from July 1 to June 30, while retail firms' fiscal years are usually February 1 through January 31.

fisting. To insert the fist into the rectum or vagina of (another) for the purpose of sexual stimulation.

flag, U.S. The word flag comes from the Anglo-Saxon *fleogan,* meaning "to fly in the wind." Flag scholars are vexillologists. The following abbreviated rules are excerpted from the Flag Code of the United States: It is the universal custom to display the flag only from sunrise to sunset on buildings and on a stationary flagpole in the open. However, when a patriotic effect is desired, the flag may be displayed 24 hours a day if properly illuminated during the hours of darkness. When flags of states, cities, or localities, or pennants of societies are flown on the same halyard with the U.S. flag, the latter should always be at the peak. When the flags are flown from adjacent staffs, the U.S. flag should be hoisted first and lowered last. No such flag or pennant may be placed above or to the right of the U.S. flag. When flags of two or more nations are displayed, they are to be flown from separate staffs of the same height. The flags should be of approximately equal size. International usage forbids the display of the flag of one nation above that of another nation in time of peace. The flag should be raised quickly, but lowered ceremoniously. Never allow the flag to touch the ground when it is being raised or lowered for the day. Local American Legion Centers provide for the destruction of soiled or damaged flags (http://legion.org/flag/ceremony). For a free catalog about flags, call the All Nations Flag Co.; (800) 533-FLAG.

flare, fuzee. A flare having a spike at the bottom and a cap at the top; positioned on or next to roadways and ignited to warn motorists of hazards.

flasher. One who engages in flashing.

flashing. Displaying ones naked sex organs, including bare breasts for women and genitals (or buttocks) for either sex, to another person or in a public place. Generally, flashing denotes a brief exposure that the viewer does not expect, although it can also occur for a prolonged duration and the observer may expect it. In criminal justice, the term connotes a male who habitually exposes his genitals to an unsuspecting victim. In most jurisdictions, intentional exposure of one's sex organs in this manner is illegal, particularly when the exposure is to an unknown person or a child. In serious cases, the flasher is subject to criminal penalties that can include incarceration, sex offender treatment, and lifetime sex offender registration.

A less frequently prosecuted form of flashing often occurs at Mardi Gras celebrations, typically when women expose their bare breasts (sometimes in exchange for beaded necklaces); however, such acts are potentially prosecuted. *See also* exhibitionism, sex offender

Fleiss, Heidi (1965–, known as the "Hollywood Madam"). Fleiss worked as a prostitute and managed a prostitution ring for "Madam Alex" from 1987–1990. From 1990–1993, she ran one of the most profitable prostitution rings in modern history, boasting that she earned a million dollars in her first four months as a madam. She was arrested in 1993 for multiple counts of pandering, conspiracy, money laundering, and tax evasion. Her state pandering conviction was vacated due to juror misconduct, as jurors engaged in "vote swapping." In 1996, Fleiss was sentenced to 37 months in federal prison for income tax evasion and money laundering. Fleiss was convicted of state pandering charges in her 1997 retrial, ordered to run concurrent with her federal sentence. Released in 1999, Fleiss is currently engaged to Dennis Hof, owner of the Moonlite Bunny Ranch, a legal brothel in Nevada.

flight. The act of an accused in escaping or fleeing from justice, especially if he or she has been notified as to an officer's intention of arresting him or her. Flight is presumptive evidence of guilt if supported by evidence of the motivation that prompted it.

Florida State University College of Criminology and Criminal Justice. Established in 1955, it conducts academic research and teaching in criminology and criminal justice. Address: FSU, College of Criminology and Criminal Justice, Hecht House, 634 W. Call Street, Tallahassee, Florida 32306-1127, Phone: 850-644-4050; Web: http://www.criminology.fsu.edu/.

Floyd, Charles Arthur ("Pretty Boy," AKA Jack Hamilton) (1901–1934). Born in Oklahoma in 1901, Floyd's criminal career began with the theft of $3.50 from a post office. He subsequently spent five years in prison for payroll robbery and was released in 1929, vowing never return to prison. Over the next five years, Floyd committed multiple bank robberies and homicides. Between 1925 and his death by FBI agents on October 22, 1934, he was credited with eight robberies and 13 murders in the Midwestern states. Six of the murders occurred in the Kansas City Massacre, in which "Pretty Boy" was claimed to have been a machine gunner. *See also* depression era gangsters; Nelson, George; Dillinger, John

Food and Drug Administration. A law enforcement agency established in 1907 in the U.S. Department of Health and Human Services (formerly the Public Health Service, formerly Department of Health, Education, and Welfare). The major responsibilities of FDA are directed toward protecting public health by ensuring that foods are safe and pure, drugs are safe and effective, cosmetics are harmless, and products are honestly and informatively labeled and packaged. These responsibilities are carried out by six product centers (Center for Biologics Evaluation and Research, Center for Devices and Radiological Health, Center for Drug Evaluation and Research, Center for Food Safety and Applied Nutrition, Center for Tobacco Products, Center for Veterinary Medicine), one research center (National Center for Toxicological Research), and two offices (Office of Regulatory Affairs, Office of the Commissioner). Address: Food and Drug Administration, 10903 New Hampshire Ave., Silver Spring, MD 20993-0002. Web: http://www.fda.gov/.

food and drug violations. The Bureau of Justice defines this as any violation of the Federal Food, Drug and Cosmetic Act related to the sanitary transport of animals, or mishandling food or drug, and attempt to distribute adulterated food.

food stamps. The U.S. Department of Agriculture is charged with the investigation of counterfeiting or misuse of food stamps, also called Supplemental Nutritional Assistance Program (SNAP). Address: USDA Food and Nutrition Service, 3101 Park Center Drive. Alexandria, Virginia 22302.

footcandle. A unit of measure for the intensity of illumination thrown onto a surface one foot away from the light source.

foot fetish. *See* podophilia

foot rail. A holdup alarm device, often used at cashiers' windows, in which the operator places a foot under the rail and lifts it to give an alarm signal.

force, reasonable. The amount or degree of force that can be reasonably used by persons in protecting themselves or others; the force that can be used by law enforcement officials in the conduct of their duties as authorized by law. The general rule is that an officer can use force no greater than that which is necessary. To effect an arrest, an officer may use reasonable force to overcome resistance.

forcible entry. To enter onto the lands or other property of another by the use of force or fear and without the free consent of the owner or possessor of such property.

forcible rape. Sexual intercourse or attempted sexual intercourse with a female against her will by force or threat of force. In most states forcible rape now covers both male and female victims.

foreclosure. Act of barring a mortgagor's fight to redeem mortgaged property; act of foreclosing a mortgage. *See also* homestead

Foreign Claims Settlement Commission (FCSC). This quasi-judicial DOJ agency determines claims of U.S. nationals against foreign governments for losses and injuries sustained by them. Address: Foreign Claims Settlement Commission of the United States, DOJ, 600 E St., NW, Suite 6002, Washington, DC 20579; Web: http://www.justice.gov/fcsc/.

forensic. Related to courts of law.

forensic accounting. An accounting specialty that focuses on the communicating complex fiscal information in a legal setting. Sometimes called forensic auditors, persons employed in this field assist the court in calculating and quantifying fiscal loss in bankruptcy, economic damages in civil cases, and gathering evidence about true sources (and location of) hidden funds in fraud and money laundering cases. They are also used in family court to help determine appropriate division of property, alimony and child support.

forensic anthropology. A field of study that applies the science of the human species (anthropology) and skeleton (osteology) in the legal system. Persons employed in this capacity often conduct examinations in cases where the victim's remains are in advanced decomposition.

forensic archaeology. The field of study that applies the science, technology, and methodology of archaeological "digs" in the legal system. Persons employed in this capacity assist in locating evidence from old crime scenes where evidence is gathered using archaeological expertise. Such involvement includes, for example, locating and excavating: buried human remains, buried small items of probative value, and potential single and mass gravesites.

forensic entomology. The field of study that applies the study of insect biology in the legal system. Persons employed in this capacity often conduct examinations in cases with early decomposition, using their knowledge of insects to help establish time of death and also presence of various biological and chemical substances in evidence.

forensic medicine. Also called forensic science; the subdiscipline in medicine that establishes facts within the legal system. This is an area related to legal medicine and applies anatomy, pathology, toxicology, chemistry, botany, and other fields of science in expert testimony in court cases or hearings. Perhaps the most celebrated case of forensic medicine is the Warren Commission investigation of the assassination of President John F. Kennedy.

forensic odontology. Investigative branch of dentistry often used to identify cadavers and bite marks, as no two bite marks are identical. Professionals employed in this capacity often conduct competency evaluations and testify as expert witnesses in criminal matters where mental health is at issue.

forensic pathology. A branch of medicine specializing in pathology. Those employed in this capacity generally conduct examinations to determine the cause of death in suspected homicide cases and who is in a position to testify to those findings in a court of law. This specialty area of medicine includes pathology examinations of persons who have been injured or who are suffering from disease, and these findings are also usable in legal proceedings.

forensic psychiatry. A branch of medicine focusing on the study and treatment of mental disorders (psychiatry) in the legal system. Persons employed in this capacity often conduct evaluations for competence to stand trial, insanity, and sometimes serve as expert witnesses in matters of recidivism risk and sentencing.

forensic psychology. The field that applies the study of human behavior to the legal system. Persons employed in this capacity often conduct competency evaluations and serve as expert witnesses, as forensic psychiatrists do. In addition, forensic psychologists are sometimes also concerned with human perception and memory as these factors intersect with court. For example, forensic psychologists often conduct research about the accuracy of eyewitness testimony, often testifying as an expert about such issues in court.

forensic science. Science as applied and used in judicial matters.

Forensic Science, American Academy of (AAFS). Founded in 1948, AAFS is a professional organization that aims to promote the application of science to the legal system. Publishes Journal of Forensic Sciences. Address: 410 North 21st Street, Colorado Springs, CO 80904. Web: http://www.aafs.org/.

Forensic Sciences Foundation. Founded in 1969. Publishes *Forensic Serology News* (quarterly) and *News and Views in Forensic Toxicology* (quarterly). Address: 410 North 21st, Colorado Springs, CO 80904. Telephone: (719) 636-1100; Web: http://www.forensicsciencesfoundation.org/.

Forensic Science Technology Center, National (NFSTC). Founded in 1995, a nonprofit organization whose mission is "supporting the justice community in ensuring the public safety by assisting the forensic sciences in the achievement of the highest level of quality services." Address: 7881 114th Avenue North, Largo, Florida 33773; Web: http://www.nfstc.org/.

forensic serology. The examination of certain evidence materials (swabs, cuttings, or items) to determine if those items contain human blood or other body fluids.

Forensic Toxicologists, Society of. Founded in 1970. Publishes *Journal of Analytic Toxicology, Forensic Toxicology Laboratory Guidelines, Tox Talk* (quarterly newsletter). Address: One MacDonald Center, 1 N. MacDonald Street, Suite 15, Mesa, AZ 85201. Telephone: 1-888-866-7638.; Web: http://www.soft-tox.org/.

forensic trace. Use of microscopy to examine biological evidence such as hair or particles of tissue not evident to the naked eye, but which could have sufficient material for DNA analysis. Analysis can also include nonbiological evidence such as fibers and other particulate matter of evidentiary value.

Forest Service. Established in 1905, the service is a division of the U.S. Department of Agriculture responsible for managing the more than 150 national forests and 19 national grasslands, protecting them from disease, insect pests, and wildfire. Forest rangers have been given limited peace officer authority to enforce standards of compliance within these protected areas. Address: Office of Communication, Mailstop: 1111, 1400 Independence Ave., SW, Washington, DC 20250. Telephone: (800) 832-1355; Web: http://www.fs.fed.us/.

forfeiture. The act of surrendering assets, such as property or cash, as a form of civil or criminal penalty for the illegal use of the property in question, or as a sanction for the commission of a crime. *See also* Civil Asset Forfeiture Reform Act of 2000; confiscation; Racketeer Influenced and Corrupt Organizations (RICO); Resolution Trust Corp.

forfeiture, civil. A proceeding against property used in criminal activity, which was first authorized by the First Congress in allowing the forfeiture of vessels that smuggled contraband into the United States. Property subject to civil forfeiture often includes vehicles used to transport contraband, equipment used to manufacture illegal drugs, cash used in illegal transactions, and property purchased with criminal proceeds. The government is required to notify registered owners and post notice of the proceedings so that any party who has an interest in the property may contest the forfeiture. If no one claims the property, it is forfeited administratively. If a claim is made, the case must be heard in a civil court, where no finding of criminal guilt is required. *See also* Civil Asset Forfeiture Reform Act of 2000; forfeiture, criminal; Resolution Trust Corp.

forfeiture, criminal. Criminal forfeiture was first authorized in 1970 as part of the criminal action taken against defendants accused of racketeering, drug trafficking, or money laundering. The forfeiture is a sanction imposed upon conviction that requires the defendant to forfeit various property rights and interests related to the violation. *See also* Civil Asset Forfeiture Reform Act of 2000; forfeiture, civil; Resolution Trust Corp.; Racketeer Influenced and Corrupt Organizations

forgery. The creation or alteration of a written or printed document that, if validly executed, would constitute a record of a legally binding transaction, with the intent to defraud by affirming it to be the act of an unknowing second person; also, the creation of an art object with intent to misrepresent the identity of the creator. The greatest recorded forgery was the German Third Reich government's operation, code named "Bernhard" engineered by S.S. Sturmbannfuhrer Alfred Naujocks in 1940–1941. It involved about $300 million in Bank of England notes.

forgery and counterfeiting. In Uniform Crime Reports terminology, the name used to record and report arrests for offenses of making, manufacturing, altering, possessing, selling, or distributing, or attempting to make, manufacture, alter, sell, distribute, or receive "anything false in the semblance of that which is true."

Fort Hood Shooter. *See* Hasan, Nidal Malik

Fort Hood Shooting. Name given to mass shooting at Fort Hood military base in Texas. On November 5, 2009, an armed shooter opened fire against military and civilian personnel, leaving 13 dead and 32 wounded. The perpetrator, later identified as Army psychiatrist Nidal Hasan, was shot by military police. Hasan is awaiting court-martial as of 2010. *See also* Hasan, Nidal Malik

Fortune Society. Founded in 1967, the society's mission is to "support successful reentry from prison and promote alternatives to incarceration, thus strengthening the fabric of our communities." The society sends teams of speakers to schools, churches, and civic groups and provides witnesses and testimony before city, state, and federal legislators. Publishes *Fortune News* (newsletter). Address: The Fortune Society 29-76 Northern Blvd., Long Island City, NY 11101. Telephone: (212) 691-7554; Web: http://www.fortunesociety.org.

Fosdick, Raymond Blaine. Lawyer, public servant, and author (1883–1972), Fosdick was born in Buffalo, NY, earning his BA in 1905 and his MA in 1906. He received his law degree from New York Law School in 1908 and worked for New York City mayor George B. McClellan. Through the Rockefeller Bureau of Social Hygiene, John D. Rockefeller, Jr., gave Fosdick a study grant, as a result of which he wrote *European Police Systems,* published in 1915. The following year he rode with "Black Jack" Pershing against Pancho Villa in Mexico. In 1917 he observed military training methods in England, Canada, and France, publishing his findings in *Keeping Our Fighters Fit.* After World War I Fosdick was U.S. representative to the League of Nations. In *American Police Systems,* published in 1920, he declared them inferior to their European counterparts. This book was followed in 1922 by *Criminal Justice in Cleveland,* which termed that city's police department lethargic, inadequate, ragged, and lacking intelligence. In 1933, he published *Toward Liquor Control,* coauthored with Arthur Scott. In all, Fosdick wrote 14 books, received the Distinguished Service Medal and two doctorates, was given the rank of commander of the French Foreign Legion, and earned many other honors.

foster family. A temporary substitute family for a child whose parents cannot provide him or her with adequate care at home situation because of such factors as economic hardship, death of a parent, illness, incarceration, family breakdown, or psychological problems. The child's expenses are generally paid by a private or public agency that has legal custody.

foster grandparents program. Operated through Senior Corps, a division of the Corporation for National and Community Service, the Foster Grandparents Program is a volunteer organization for persons 55 and older who want to serve as role models, mentors, and friends to at-risk youth. Foster grandparents help children learn to read, provide one-on-one tutoring, and guide children at a critical time in their lives by providing comfort and love. For general information, contact: Senior Corps, 1201 New York Avenue, NW, Washington, DC 20525. http://www.seniorcorps.gov/about/programs/fg.asp.

frangible bullet. A reduced-hazard bullet, frangible bullets are made of brittle plastic or other nonmetallic material used for firing practice which, upon striking a target, breaks into powder or small fragments without penetrating. Frangible bullets are usually designed to leave a mark at the point of impact.

frangible grenade. An improvised incendiary hand grenade consisting of a glass container filled with a flammable liquid, with an igniter attached. It breaks and ignites upon striking a resistant target. Sometimes called a "Molotov cocktail."

Frank J. Remington Center. Established by the University of Wisconsin Law School as a "learning center" in the area of criminal justice. Address: Frank J. Remington Center, University of Wisconsin Law School, 975 Bascom Mall, Madison, WI 53706-1399; Web: http://law.wisc.edu/fjr/.

Frankfurter, Felix. Frankfurter (1882–1965) was an associate justice of the Supreme Court, presidential adviser, and a leading liberal known as a champion of judicial restraint. An emigrant from Austria, he graduated from Harvard Law School with highest honors. In 1914 he joined the school's faculty and remained a classroom teacher for a quarter-century. After World War I, Frankfurter became a legal adviser at the Paris Peace Conference. He also helped to found the American Civil Liberties Union and *The New Republic;* he tried to obtain a new trial for Sacco and Vanzetti. In 1939 Frankfurter, an intimate adviser of President Roosevelt, was made an associate justice of the Supreme Court. Many of his opinions reflect his belief that government by judges is a poor substitute for government by the people.

frankpledge. In old English law, a system whereby the members of a tithing (group who supported their organization or church with 10 percent of their earnings) had corporate responsibility for the behavior of all members over 14 years old.

Fraternal Order of Police. Founded in 1915, this is the oldest and largest of the major police organizations, with 325,000 members. According to their Web site, the group is "committed to improving the working conditions of law enforcement officers and the safety of those we serve through education, legislation, information, community involvement, and employee representation." Address: 701 Marriott Drive, Nashville TN 37214; http://www.grandlodgefop.org/.

fratricide. The act of killing or murdering one's brother or sister.

fraud. The use of deception or false pretenses to obtain money or other things of value. Forgery, counterfeiting, and embezzlement can be considered types of fraud; however, these crimes are prosecuted as distinct types.

fraud, charity. The use of deception to obtain money or other items of value from people who believe they are donating to a legitimate, tax-exempt charitable organization. Various organizations can assist law enforcement personnel or consumers by providing information on the operations of charitable organizations and whether they appear to be legitimate, based on complaints and/or filed financial statements: local Better Business Bureaus (check phone directories); Council of Better Business Bureaus, Charities Division, 4200 Wilson Blvd., Suite 800, Arlington, VA 22203.

fraud examiner, certified (CFE). A credential that denotes expertise in fraud prevention, detection, and deterrence. CPEs are specialists in the detection and/or deterrence of a wide variety of fraudulent conduct, from identifying employees or executives who misappropriate company assets to assisting investors who are defrauded in the course of commercial transactions. Responsibilities include resolving aggregations of fraud by obtaining evidence, taking statements and writing reports, and testifying to findings in court. Many members are law enforcement personnel, while others are certified public accountants. see also Association of Certified Fraud Examiners, http://www.acfe.com/.

fraud, health care. The National Healthcare Anti-Fraud Association estimates (NHCAA),

$68 billion is lost to health care fraud each year, with approximately 60 percent of individual fraud victims being elderly. According to the NHCAA the most common types of health care fraud are billing for nonrendered services; billing for more expensive services than provided; performing medically unnecessary services; misrepresenting noncovered treatments; falsifying diagnoses to justify unnecessary tests, surgeries or procedures; unbundling—billing each step of a procedure; billing a patient more than the copay; accepting kickbacks for patient referrals; waiving patient copays or deductibles and overbilling the insurance. Health care fraud as a federal crime with a federal prison term of 10 years, 20 years, or even life imprisonment if a patient died as a result of health care fraud. Financial penalties also apply [*United States Code, Title 18, Section 1347.*] Before buying products represented as preventives, treatments, or cures, but not prescribed by your doctor, check with **Cancer:** (800) 422-6237, a toll-free line at the National Cancer Institute; **Arthritis:** (800) 283-7800, the Arthritis Foundation's Information Line; **To report suspected fraud:** (800) 447-8477 U.S. Department of Health and Human Services, Office of the Inspector General. *See also* U.S. Department of Health and Human Services, Office of the Inspector General; National Council Against Health Fraud; National Healthcare Anti-Fraud Association

fraud, investment. Enticing unsuspecting investors to part with their money based on deceptive means, which often include promise of large investment returns and frequently resulting in loss. Such practices are in violation of Securities Exchange Commission (SEC), Commodities Futures Trading Commission (CFTC) and Federal Trade Commission (FTC) regulations. According to the FCC, consumers also invest large sums in less traditional offerings, including investments in tangibles (such as rare coins and art), oil and gas lottery application services, and telecommunications. In investment cases brought by the FTC in 1996, scam artists consistently took thousands of dollars from consumers. Investment fraud constitutes half of all consumer fraud, with an average loss of over $15,000 per consumer. The North American Securities Administrators Association (NASAA) lists the most common types of investment fraud as: Ponzi schemes, unlicensed individuals selling securities, unregistered investment products, unsecured promissory notes, senior investment fraud, high-yield investments, Internet fraud, affinity fraud, variable annuity sales practices, and oil & gas scams. *See also* Federal Trade Commission, North American Securities Administration Association, Securities Exchange Commission, and Commodities Futures Trade Commission (CFTC)

fraud offenses. The type of crime comprising offenses sharing the elements of practice of deceit or intentional misrepresentation of fact, with the intent of unlawfully depriving a person of his or her property or legal rights. *See also* fraud penalties, most severe

fraud penalties, most severe. The most several fraud penalties nationwide include:

On June 3, 1985, financier Jake Butcher was sentenced to 20 years in prison for his theft of $20 million from depositors. Butcher was chairman of a $1.5 billion-financial empire in Tennessee and Kentucky that began to crumble with the 1983 failure of his United American Bank of Knoxville, then the third largest commercial bank failure since the Depression. The Department of Justice indicated this was the most severe sentence given to date for a person convicted of a white-collar crime. The longest sentence for a single antitrust violation was 48 months, imposed in 2009 against Peter Baci, a shipping executive who conspired to suppress and eliminate competition in the coastal water freight transportation

The nation's second-largest law firm—Jones, Day, Reavis & Pogue—agreed (without admitting guilt) on April 19, 1993, to pay a record $51 million to savings and loan regulators for its role in the 1989 collapse of Lincoln Savings & Loan. In a lawsuit, the

Resolution Trust Corporation had accused Jones, Day of helping Charles H. Keating, Jr., to keep control of the Irvine, CA-based financial institution even though the firm knew that Keating was looting it. The failure of Lincoln Savings cost taxpayers $2.6 billion. Keating received a 10-year prison term for his December 1991 state securities fraud conviction. Ernst & Young, the nation's largest accounting firm, paid $463 million to regulators who had alleged the firm failed to warn about disastrous problems at major thrifts nationwide. *See also* Resolution Trust Corp.

In 2007, DOJ imposed fines of $300 million dollars each against Korean Airlines, for conspiracy to fix international cargo rates and passenger fares, and British Airways, for conspiracy to fix international cargo rates and passenger fuel surcharges. To date, the largest fine remains the $500 million fine imposed against F. Hoffmann-La Roche, a Swiss healthcare company, for vitamin price-fixing.

fraud, postal. The U.S. Postal Service investigates and pursues complaints regarding bogus mail-order investments and other businesses that use, advertise, or sell through the mail. This includes telephone solicitors and newspaper ads, because money sent in response to such ads is usually mailed. Contact your local postmaster or postal inspector.

Fraud Section, Department of Justice. The Fraud Section of DOJ directs and coordinates the federal effort against economic crime. The section investigates and prosecutes white collar crime cases throughout the country. Address: U.S. DOJ, Criminal Division/Fraud Section, 10 th & Constitution Ave., NW, Bond Building, 4 th Floor, Washington, DC 20530. Telephone (202) 514-7023. http://www.justice.gov/criminal/fraud/.

fraud, telemarketing. The U.S. Department of Justice defines telemarketing fraud as "any scheme to defraud in which the persons carrying out the scheme use the telephone as their primary means of communicating with prospective victims and trying to persuade them to send money to the scheme." The most common types of telemarketing fraud include: Charity Schemes; Credit-Card, Credit-Repair and Loan Schemes; Cross-Border Schemes; Internet-Related Schemes; Investment and Business-Opportunity Schemes; Lottery Schemes; Magazine-Promotion Schemes; Office-Supply Schemes; Prize-Promotion Schemes; "Recovery-Room" Schemes and "Rip-and-Tear" Schemes. *See also* Alliance Against Fraud in Telemarketing

fraud, toll. The offense category considered the most costly for telephone companies and their customers. Two types of toll fraud predominate: (a) theft of telephone credit card numbers; and (b) theft of business toll codes. Stealing credit card numbers is a multimillion-dollar business involving, among other techniques, binoculars used near busy coin phones to record people's dialing sequences as they charge calls to their cards. In stealing corporate billing codes, thieves tap into a firm's telecommunications switching equipment, use an automatic dialer to try all four-digit codes until it finds the right ones, then sell the codes. Although telephone companies use automated call-tracking equipment to alert staff when a particular credit card or corporate toll code is being used in a heavy and unusual manner, thieves can make thousands of dollars worth of toll calls in the few hours before phone company staff is alerted. Many offenders are prosecuted each year, but most toll fraud must be written off as an expense to phone companies and their customers.

fraudulent retaliation. The use of deception to gain access to, or information about, the resources of a wrongdoer, with the express purpose of using that information to retaliate against said person for the wrong they caused.

freedom of assembly. One of the fundamental rights guaranteed the individual under the First Amendment. Like other rights in the Constitution, the right of assembly is not absolute or unlimited. In interpreting the extent of these freedoms, the courts have ruled that, although a meeting cannot be prohibited for advocating unpopular views, the right to assemble is subject to reasonable police regulation to ensure general safety and the maintenance of peace and order.

Freedom of Information Act. A 1967 bill designed to give the public greater access to government records. The act, signed by President Lyndon Johnson, superseded the Disclosure of Information Act (1966). The new act permits exemptions only in nine specific areas. Among these are national defense, confidential financial information, and law enforcement files and certain personnel files, in addition to information whose disclosure has been prohibited by statute. The U.S. Department of Justice's Office of Information Law and Policy carries out the DOJ's responsibilities under the act to encourage agency compliance. It also advises other departments and agencies on questions of policy, interpretation, and application of the act. Contact: FOIA/PA Mail Referral Unit, Department of Justice, Room 115, LOC, Washington, DC 20530-0001.

freedom of religion. One of the basic liberties guaranteed by the First Amendment, which states that "Congress shall make no law respecting an establishment of religion, or prohibiting the free exercise thereof."

freedom of speech and press. Basic liberties guaranteed by the First Amendment, which prohibits Congress from abridging them; these are also included among the fundamental rights protected from infringement by the states by the Fourteenth Amendment. In 1978 the confidentiality of news files was lost when it was ruled that a news office could be searched by the police with a search warrant.

free exercise clause. This part of the establishment clause is another name for the First Amendment provision for freedom of religion. It prevents compulsion by law of the acceptance of any creed or the practice of any form of worship. Conversely, it safeguards the free exercise of any chosen form of religion. However, the free exercise clause does not embrace actions that are in violation of social duties or subversive in nature. This interpretation enabled the Supreme Court to uphold Congress's ban on polygamy and, on the other hand, to strike down Wisconsin's law compelling Amish parents to send their children to secondary school.

free venture program. Started by the federal government to encourage the development of job opportunities for state prison inmates, free venture programs use business principles and practices in an attempt to make prison industries profitable and provide transferable work skills.

freeway. A highway to which owners of abutting land have no or only very limited rights of easement or access from their land.

Freeway Killer. *See* Kearney, Patrick Wayne

freeway patrol. The law enforcement function concerned with the management and surveillance of traffic on a freeway. This function may include rendering assistance, accident investigation, traffic direction, and traffic law enforcement. It may be accomplished with automobile, motorcycle, or aircraft patrol. Sometimes referred to as the highway patrol or state police.

Freeway Strangler. *See* Bonin, William

French Connection. A drug-smuggling operation, the investigation of which began one evening early in 1962. While drinking in a New York nightclub, detectives Eddie Egan and Sonny Grosso, both of the narcotics division, observed a man flashing large sums of money. They followed him and found that he was the proprietor of a small newsstand. What evolved from Egan and Grosso's simple observations was a joint federal–New York Police Department investigation that uncovered a major heroin-importing circuit operating out of Marseilles, France. Raw opium was being transported from Turkey and the Far East to Marseilles, where it was being refined into water-soluble heroin. From there it was being exported to the United States. The Connection was broken, arrests were made, and almost 97 pounds of heroin—valued at $32 million—were confiscated. Sometime between 1962 and 1972, 81 pounds of these narcotics disappeared from the property clerk's office. To this day, the loss remains a mystery.

frequency distribution. A method for organizing and presenting statistical data. The initial procedure consists simply of counting the number of times each item under study occurs. A standard step is to tabulate the number of individuals receiving each possible score, from low to high. Observing the distribution of scores is a step in analyzing test results. For example, when scores on an achievement test given to all students in a school system cluster toward the lower end of the range, several different factors might be accountable: design errors in the test or its scoring, students' lack of motivation, or ineffective teaching. Normal frequency is an ideal situation in which half the scores fall above the midpoint and half below. When this occurs, the mean, the median, and the mode of the results are all the same.

fresh fish. Colloquial term used by prison inmates in reference to new inmates

friction, coefficient of. The amount of friction on a roadway surface, determined in calculating the speed of a vehicle as shown by skid marks. Speed and weight of the vehicle are factors, as well as the surface that the vehicle was traveling upon. The coefficient of friction is also referred to as the drag factor.

friction ridges. The ridges of the skin on the palms and palmar side of the fingers. Similar ridges are found on the sole of the foot and lower side of the toes. The prime function of the ridges is to afford friction with surfaces and objects touched by these parts of the body. These ridges are the means by which fingerprints are formed.

Friends Outside. Founded in 1955, this nonprofit organization's purposes are to: aid prisoners and their families in dealing with traumas and limitations imposed by separation; assist officials in improving conditions of confinement and promote alternatives to confinement; aid ex-offenders in transition; develop public awareness of problems caused by incarceration; and seek volunteers. Publishes a monthly newsletter. Address: P.O. Box 4085, Stockton, CA 95204. Telephone: (209) 955-0701; Web: http://www.friends outside.org/.

fringe benefits. Sometimes referred to as collateral entitlements, employee benefits are a labor cost to employers incurred in providing compensation above and beyond wages and salaries. Benefits usually include time off with pay (holidays, vacations, sick leave); retirement pensions (deferred payments); life, medical, and hospitalization insurance; and special incentive pay increases for educational achievement, outstanding performance, or profit sharing. Along with wages and salaries, fringe benefits are usually the topic of collective bargaining.

frisk. A precautionary, superficial search of the outer clothing and property (purse or briefcase) in the immediate possession of a suspect to ensure the suspect is not holding a weapon or illegal/dangerous object. A frisk is usually less intrusive than the full search permitted in a lawful arrest or detention.

Fromme, Alice (Squeaky) (1952–). A member of the Manson Family, Fromme was convicted of contempt of court and obstruction during the Manson prosecution for the Tate and LaBianca murders in 1969. Fromme herself was not charged with the murders. In 1975, she attempted to meet with President Ford at the California Capitol building to kill him. She was apprehended, with an unloaded gun, seeking entrance to the building. She was convicted of the attempted assassination of President Ford and sentenced to life imprisonment. Fromme escaped from prison in1987 (for two days) and received additional time. She was paroled in 2009.

fruit of the poisonous tree. A term used by the courts to denote evidence tainted as the result of its being derived from evidence obtained illegally or in such fashion that it was inadmissible. If certain evidence was obtained as the result of an illegal search and, based upon information secured by that search, other evidence was located elsewhere, the latter evidence is also inadmissible even though properly obtained.

fruits of a crime. Any material objects obtained through criminal acts.

Frye Test. (also called Frye Standard) A legal benchmark that determines the admissibility of scientific evidence in trial. The Frye standard, established in *Frye v. United States,* 293 F. 1013 (DC Cir. 1923), requires evidence to be generally accepted as reliable in the relevant scientific community. In most jurisdictions, Frye was replaced with the Daubert standard in 1993. *See also* Daubert standard

fugitive. (1) One who flees (or cannot be located by law enforcement officers) to avoid arrest, incarceration, or questioning concerning an alleged violation of the law. (2) One wanted for a crime who goes outside the state or the territorial jurisdiction of a court.

Fugitive Felon Acts. Acts of Congress, in 1932 and 1934, that make it a federal offense to travel in interstate or foreign commerce in order to avoid: (a) prosecution; (b) confinement after conviction; or (c) giving testimony, where under the laws of the state, the offense charged is a felony (or in NJ, a high misdemeanor). Under these acts, Fugitive Felons are ineligible to receive certain state and federal benefits such as social security, food stamps, Temporary Aid for Needy Families (TANF, also called welfare), public housing, and veterans benefits.

fugitive from justice. (1) A person who has fled from a state, in which he is accused of having committed a crime, in order to avoid arrest and punishment. (2) A person who has fled from a state in order to avoid giving testimony in a criminal prosecution. *See also* extradition

fugitive slave laws. Statutes passed by Congress from 1798 to 1850, these laws covered the return of slaves who escaped from one state and were found in another state or territory.

fugitive warrant. An arrest warrant issued for a person wanted for a violation of the criminal law in another state or jurisdiction; a warrant for a fugitive from justice.

full-time temporary release. The authorized temporary absence of a prisoner from a confinement facility, for a period of 24 hours or more, for purposes relating to such matters as the prisoner's employment, education, or personal or family welfare. *See also* furlough

functional authority. The authority to complete a task by virtue of expertise or ability, rather than of power vested by rank.

functional specialization. All functions of a criminal justice agency may be classified as line, auxiliary, or administrative. Operations that a police department is primarily created to perform are called line, primary, or operational duties. Functional specialization further connotes authority and duties based on knowledge and experience rather than rank.

fundamental fairness. The basic principle that crime prevention and control methods must be democratic and fair.

fundamental law. (1) A constitution; statutes or laws that are intrinsically superior to the ordinary law of a state or that the courts regard as law of superior obligation; (2) natural law, which is sometimes deemed to be morally, if not juridically, superior to positive law.

furlough. Overnight, or longer, leave granted to the inmate of a correctional facility. *See also* Horton, William

G

GAAP. An acronym from the phrase "generally accepted accounting principles," the guidelines used by comptrollers and auditors to ensure that financial records are kept properly and in a manner that can be understood by any accountant.

Gacy, John Wayne, Jr. (1942–1994). Born in Chicago, Illinois, Gacy was a high school drop-out who attended business college until he began managing a fast food restaurant owned by his in-laws. From the mid-1960s until his arrest, he entertained children and neighbors by dressing up as "Pogo the Clown" at neighborhood gatherings, a proclivity that earned him the nickname "Killer Clown" in later years. In 1967, two teenage boys accused Gacy of sexual assault, and he was subsequently sentenced to 10 years for sodomy. He was paroled after only 18 months. Despite a series of arrests for sexual assault, he was discharged from parole in 1971. Gacy began killing in 1972, targeting teenaged males for rape and murder. In all, he is believed to be responsible for at least 33 rapes and murders, disposing of 29 corpses on his own property before he was apprehended in 1978. Gacy pled not guilty by reason of insanity, his defense arguing both temporary insanity and sociopathy. Gacy was found guilty at trial, and was sentenced to death in 1980. He was executed by lethal injection on May 10, 1994. *See also* serial killer, sociopathy, insanity

gag law. Any law abridging freedom of speech, the press, or the right of petition.

Galleani, Luigi (1861–1931). An anarchist, insurrectionist, and communist thought to have inspired the anarchist bombings in the United States between 1914–1930. Born in Italy, Galleani moved to France, Switzerland, Egypt, Canada, and England before coming to the United States in 1901. He developed and propagated his anarchist ideas in these countries, many of which arrested or expelled him for conspiracy and inciting anarchy. In the United States, he was defiant of government and practiced violent anarchy, encouraging his followers to use bombs. He published a bomb-making guide *La Salute è in voi!* (*Health is in You!*) in 1908. The anarchist bombings throughout the 1910s in the United States, are thought to have been inspired by his followers, who were called Galleanist anarchists. He was deported back to Italy in 1919, which inspired increased anarchist bombings in the United States. Galleani died in Italy in 1931.

Galleanist anarchists. Follower of Luigi Galleani, thought to be responsible for a wave of U.S. bombings between 1914–1930. *See also* anarchist bombings; Galleani, Luigi; Sacco; Vanzetti

Gallup poll. A well-known series of public opinion surveys, Gallup polls since 1950 have been based on a representative, independent sample of interviewees. The United States, through categories based on size of communities, population densities, and geographical locations, is divided into approximate blocks of population, with equal probability of selection. A random starting place is selected, and interviewers follow a predetermined pattern until their interview quota is filled. Within each household, the interviewer asks to speak to the youngest man, 18 or older. If no men are home, then the interviewer asks for the oldest woman over 18 years of age. Interviews are conducted at different times of the day and week in order to get a better sample. This procedure is designed to "produce an approximation of the adult civilian population living in the United States, except for those persons in institutions, such as hospitals and prisons." Gallup measures and tracks public opinion on current political, social, and economic issues. The organization was founded on the philosophy of Dr. Georg Gallup in the mid-1930s, with a guiding principle of independence from sponsorship or special interest groups, which provides the hallmark objectivity of Gallup. In 2005, Gallup expanded the scope of polling to include worldwide surveys of respondents in more than 140 countries. *See also* Harris poll

Galton, Francis. An English scientist and criminologist (1812–1911), and cousin of Charles Darwin, Galton was a pioneer in the field of fingerprint science. Although he didn't develop a workable classification system, his work greatly aided Sir Edward

Henry in his developments in this area of criminology. *See also* Henry system

galvanometer. An instrument used for measuring small amounts of electricity. Used in some types of electrocardiographs (ECG), electroencephalographs (EEG) and polygraphs (lie detectors). *See also* electroencephalograph; polygraph

Gambino, Carlo (1902–1976). Head of the Gambino crime family in New York. Gambino lived a humble and low-key life, despite his illicit activities that included drugs, racketeering, prostitution, extortion, and murder. He died of a heart attack at age 74 and was succeeded by Paul Castellano. *See also* Castellano, Paul

Gamblers Anonymous. Self-help group founded in September 1957, reportedly the fourth such group patterned after Alcoholics Anonymous and based on a 12-step recovery model. Now includes some 800 local chapters. Address: P.O. Box 17173, Los Angeles, CA 90017. Families and friends of compulsive gamblers can join Gam-Anon Family Groups. Address: P.O. Box 157, Whitestone, NY 11357.

gambling. Staking or wagering of money or anything of value on a game of chance or an uncertain event. Gambling is the category used to record and report arrests for offenses relating to promoting, permitting, or engaging in gambling. The UCR reports a breakdown by type of gambling as follows: (a) bookmaking (horse and sports betting); (b) numbers and lottery; and (c) all others. The state of Nevada, which legalized gambling in 1931, cites gambling as a major source of income. In 1963 New Hampshire became the first state to adopt a legal lottery. In 1977 North Dakota legalized bingo and a lottery and in 1981 legalized blackjack gambling in bars, restaurants, and motels. In 1978 legal gambling casinos opened in Atlantic City, NJ. Federal law in 1988 allowed Native Americans extensive rights to run their own gaming on Indian reservations. On April 1, 1991, the Diamond Lady, the nation's first

legal riverboat casino, was launched at Davenport, Iowa. In 1974, Americans spent $17 billion on gambling activities; by 1992, the figure had risen to $330 billion, growing to $630 billion in 1998 and $910 billion in 2006 spent in legal activities (revenue from gambling is estimated at $92.27 billion in 2007 after winnings are paid). The FBI estimates that $40 billion or more is wagered illegally each year. State-sanctioned casino gambling accounts for more than 40 percent of all gaming revenues, followed by gaming on Indian reservations, state-run lotteries, and horse racing. Utah and Hawaii are the only two states that have no legal gambling. In 2010, 43 states had lotteries. *See also* gaming

gaming. An agreement between two or more persons to play together at a game of chance for a stake or wager that is to become the property of the winner and to which all contribute. The words *gaming* and *gambling* in statutes are similar in meaning. To constitute gambling, winner must either pay a consideration for the chance to win or, without paying anything in advance, stand a chance to lose or win. Gaming is properly the act or engagement of the players; if bystanders or other third persons put up a stake or wager among themselves, which will go to one or the other according to the result of the game, this is more correctly termed betting. *See also* gambling

gamma hydroxy butyrate (GHB). Sometimes called a "roofie," GHB is often called the "date rape drug" because it is used to render women helpless against sexual aggression. GHB is an odorless and tasteless depressant that can cause euphoria, but in large doses leads to breathing problems, seizures, coma, and death. There is no antidote for overdoses. GHB can be either a liquid or a powder. GHB is classified as Schedule I depressant; a derivative drug, *Xyrem,* is a Schedule III drug prescribed to reduce sleepiness in narcolepsy patients.

Gang Crime Research Center, National. Formed in 1990 to research gangs and gang members, disseminate information, and provide training and consulting services. Address: P.O. Box 990, Peoptone, IL 60468-0990. Web: www.ngcrc.com. *See also* GANG JOURNAL: AN INTERDISCIPLINARY RESEARCH QUARTERLY in Appendix D

Gantt chart. Developed during World War I by Henry L. Gantt, it is a planning and control instrument that graphically presents work planned and work accomplished in relation to each task and in relation to time.

Gardner, Erle Stanley. A California lawyer (1889–1970), Gardner received his notoriety through his famous Perry Mason novels. The character of Mason later inspired several movies, radio and television series, and over 100 books, that made Gardner an extremely wealthy man. He also started "The Court of Last Resort," an organization which aided persons believed to have been wrongfully convicted.

garnish. To use a legal civil action brought by a creditor, whereby the debtor's money is impounded or attached while in the hands of a third party. The garnishee is instructed not to deliver the money or property to the defendant debtor until the lawsuit is concluded.

garnishment. A form of attachment that has as its object the appropriation of money or credits in the hands of a third person.

garrote. To strangle and execute a person by any of several handheld means, such as a chain, fishing line, rope, scarf, string, or wire; the implement or apparatus used to accomplish the strangulation.

gas chromatography (GC). An analytical technique used to separate the individual components of a sample, which is dissolved in a suitable solvent and injected into an instrument which separates sample components.

gas chromatography/mass spectometry (GC/MS). GC/MS is a process in which a nonreactive gas (one that will not react chemically with the substance being tested) is used in a detector (the mass spectrometer) to identify drugs or unknown substances and the

amount of each. Each drug has a specific mass spectrum "signature" that eases identification.

gatekeeping. Counting heads; keeping records, as of prisoners; controlling access to or exit from any system, organization, or facility.

gateway drugs. A term for the substances usually tried initially by inexperienced drug users, including inhalants, nicotine, alcohol, and marijuana, so-called because it is theorized that users move on to stronger and more controlled substances after they have passed through the "gateway."

Gatling, Richard Jordan. American inventor (1818–1903) of the Gatling multiple-firing gun, precursor of the machine gun. His name gave rise to the slang word *gat*.

gauge. The unit of bore measurement for shotguns. Originally it referred to the number of solid lead balls of bore diameter that could be cast from one pound of lead; the larger the bore, the lower the number.

gay. (1) The term gay was synonymous with happy and carefree through the mid-twentieth century. (2) From the early nineteenth century to the present day, the term day is a colloquial term to describe homosexual males and to a lesser extent homosexual females (lesbians). The Golden State Peace Officer's Association is a California-based association for gay and lesbian peace officers, as is the Gay Officers Action League of New York City. In modern usage, gay also refers to people, places, acts, and culture associated with homosexuality. (3) From the start of the twentieth century, the term was used by the millennium generation as a pejorative to describe anything that is disliked. For example, the term "that's so gay" means "that's absurd or stupid." There is debate about whether or not the term retains derisive reference to homosexuality when used in this way. *See also* ACT-UP; Stonewall Riot; White Night

gay marriage. *See* same sex marriage

GED (general equivalency diploma). A certificate of secondary educational, or high school, completion that is awarded when an individual has passed standard examinations.

Usually used in place of traditional diplomas for individuals who did not finish high school but gained the needed knowledge in other ways.

Gein, Edward "Ed" Theodore (1906–1984). Born in Wisconsin, Gein was raised in isolation by an abusive alcoholic father and a mother who told him that all women were prostitutes and instruments of Satan. Gein was suspected of killing his older brother in 1994, but no charges were brought. In 1957, police found remains of a missing woman in Gein's shed. Her body was decapitated, hung upside down, and mutilated by "field dressing," a process of removing internal organs from deer and game after a successful hunt. Further search of Gein's property revealed: four human noses; nine human skin masks; 10 mutilated female heads; two heads in bags; genitals from nine women in a box; three chairs upholstered in human skin; and a pair of human lips used as the weight on the drawsting of a windowshade. Gein admitted to robbing as many as nine graves to obtain parts that resembled his mother for the purpose of making a "woman suit" to wear. Gein was charged with a single murder, but was sent to a hospital for the criminally insane for more than 10 years. In 1968, he was sane enough for trial and was found "guilty but insane." Gein was returned to the mental hospital, where he died of heart failure in 1984. Gein is believed to be the real-life inspiration for fictional characters Norman Bates (*Psycho*) and Jame Gumb (*Silence of the Lambs*). *See also* serial killer, insanity

gendarme. A member of an armed police organization, such as in France; a member of the Gendarmerie Nationale, the national police force in France. The term is sometimes used incorrectly in reference to any French police officer.

Gendarmerie Nationale. A military force in France under the control of the minister of the armed forces, utilized primarily for policing rural areas.

Gender-Neutral needs scale. An assessment of criminogenic risks and unmet treatment needs, commonly used in prison classification, programming, parole, and community treatment, which can be used for both male and female clients. Gender-neutral scales were developed in response to most traditional risk/needs assessments, which are generally normed using primarily male samples. A gender-neutral needs scale is normed for both male and female clients. Such scales sometimes include separate versions targeting male and female clients.

general adaptation syndrome (GAS). A response to stress involving the mobilization of all an individual's biological and psychological resources. Austrian-Canadian physician Hans Selye, born in 1907, first described the GAS, which consists of three stages: (1) *alarm:* the person responds to stress as if it were an emergency, releasing adrenalin, increasing blood pressure and heart rate, and becoming more alert; as stress continues, the person develops (2) *resistance* to it, often pretending to relax while actually remaining tense; if under stress for an extended period of time, the person may enter (3) a state of *exhaustion,* in which the physical and mental resources are depleted. This may lead ultimately to a mental breakdown or even, in extreme cases, to death. *See also* stress

general appearance file. A file maintained by law enforcement agencies for photographs and descriptions of persons known to engage habitually in certain types of crime.

general deterrence. A strategy in which the punishment against one specific deviant serves as a generic example to prevent others from following. *See also* deterrence; specific deterrence

general intent. Conscious wrongdoing whose motive is inferred, unless expressly denied, as a method of legal proof.

general law. A statute expressed in general terms and affecting all places, persons, or things within the territory over which a legislature has power to act, but which may include reasonable classifications or categories, provided that all places, persons, or things within each category are treated alike—as distinguished from local legislation and special legislation.

general verdict. A verdict of either guilty or not guilty.

genetic algorithms. A data mining technique that assists in DNA analysis, genetic profiling, decryption, and several counterterrorism applications.

Genovese, Kitty. (1935–1964) Born Catherine Susan Genovese, "Kitty" Genovese was stabbed to death outside her apartment building in New York City. On March 14, 1964, at 3:20 A.M., 28-year-old Kitty Genovese returned home from work and parked her car 150 feet from her apartment at 82-70 Austin St. (Kew Gardens) in Queens County, NY, a borough of New York City. A man came out of the shadows, stabbed her, and began to sexually assault her. She screamed and lights came on in the apartment houses along Austin St. For the next 25 minutes, the attacker stalked, assaulted, and stabbed Ms. Genovese until she eventually died just before 3:50 A.M. Although 37 witnesses heard her screams for help and watched the assault, the first call to the police did not occur until some minutes after her death. Her attack gained national attention and prompted social psychological research into what is now called the "bystander effect." This incident is often used to typify *anomie* as a component of contemporary urban crime. *See also* anomie

Genovese, Vito (1897–1969) (Don Vitone). Born in Naples, Italy, Genovese immigrated to New York and became involved in bootlegging and extortion. He held key positions in La Cosa Nostra, including underboss of Genovese crime family until he fled to Italy (1937–1994) to avoid murder charges. He returned to New York in 1944, rose to "Boss" in 1957, and was convicted of heroin trafficking in 1959. While incarcerated, he reportedly remained Boss of the Genovese crime family until his death by heart attack in 1969 in a federal prison hospital. *See also* Costello, Frank; Luciano, Charles Lucky; mafia

geographic base files. Geographically coded database covering, for example, calls for service, field-interrogation/interview cards, offense/incident records, moving violation citations, and arrest records. The data lend themselves to computer-assisted dispatch, crime-trend analysis, planning, research, and resource allocation. Some agencies have geographic (geo-coded) reporting districts configured to census tracts. *See also* census tract; demography; metropolitan statistical areas

Germanic law. The law of the Teutonic, or Germanic, tribes refers to a family of customary laws in which there were wide variations. Nordic customary laws and the laws of the German barbarians who conquered the Roman Empire in the West are generally included in this category. Although the Germanic tribes are associated with primitive elements of law and the code of bravery, their oral-law tradition contained many elements that would be regarded as democratic. A public assembly or representative body called the Ting acted as the protector of rights of the people. The word *law* is a Norse word, and the concept that no man is above the law is associated with the law speakers of the Germanic tribes. The concept of damages to prevent violent retribution was also an early kind of tort sometimes recommended by the law speakers. The seafaring expeditions of the Vikings in the ninth and tenth centuries did much to promote Germanic customs, and Canute's settlement in England was known for the fairness and impartial application of its laws. Romano-Germanic law stands today as one the three main families of laws.

gestational uroxicide. Term coined by Lizarraga meaning killing of one's pregnant wife. *See also* Peterson, Scott

Gideon, Clarence Earl. Charged with breaking and entering of the Bay Harbor Pool Room in Panama City, FL, with the intent of committing a misdemeanor—a case of petty larceny which, under Florida law, is considered a felony. On August 4, 1961, he was tried, served as his own defense, was found guilty, and sentenced to serve five years in state prison. On January 8, 1962, the U.S. Supreme Court received a large envelope from Gideon containing his petition *in forma pauperis*—in the form of a poor man. Certiorari was granted and the Court assigned Washington, DC, attorney Abe Fortas to argue Gideon's claim. Fortas contended that counsel in a criminal trial is a fundamental right of due process enforced on the states by the Fourteenth Amendment. The Court's decision was unanimous, overturning Gideon's conviction in the landmark case *Gideon v. Wainwright,* 372 U.S. 335 (1963). In the USSC decision, Justice Black wrote: "Any person hailed into court, who is too poor to hire a lawyer, cannot be assured a fair trial unless counsel is provided for him. This seems to be an obvious truth." This ruling on March 18, 1963, after Gideon had served almost two years in prison, entitled him to a new trial. He was retried, represented by counsel, and acquitted. Gideon died in 1972. Abe Fortas, who later served as a Supreme Court justice, died in 1982. *See also* Table 50. United States Supreme Court Justices, pages 464–470

gift *causa mortis*. A gift of personal property made by a party in the expectation that his or her death is imminent.

gift *inter vivos*. A gift from one living person to another.

global positioning satellite. *See* GPS tracking

going native. A term used to describe the unexpected adoption of and adherence to cultural norms and practices by a person immersed in the field. Ethnographers and field researchers can "go native," as can undercover law enforcement personnel when immersed in field research for a prolonged period of time.

golden shower. The act of urinating on another person, often for sexual gratification. *See also* urolagnia, urophilia

good faith. With good intention; true and trustworthy, especially in the performance of an obligation or a vow. An honest intention of carrying out a duty without taking any undue advantage.

good Samaritan. A person other than a peace officer who is not directly involved in an incident/situation but steps in to prevent injury, aid a victim, or apprehend an offender; usually a bystander or passerby. *See also* victim compensation

good Samaritan law. Category of laws that protect from liability any bystander who comes to the aid of others during an emergency. Such laws are designed to reduce bystander inaction in life-threatening emergency. While provisions vary by jurisdiction, most such laws do not require a bystander to render aid, unless the bystander is a caretaker for the injured party (such as a parent) or is responsible for the injury. Generally, however, once a bystander renders aid, s/he is responsible to maintaining aid until relieved by bystander of equal/greater competence or authorities.

goods and chattels. Personal property of every kind, as distinguished from real property.

good-time. The amount of time deducted from time to be served in prison on a given sentence(s) and/or under correction agency jurisdiction, awarded at some point after a prisoner's admission to prison and contingent upon good behavior and/or awarded automatically by application of a statute or regulation. Application of an automatic good-time rule usually reduces the offender's maximum potential term in confinement and/or under correctional jurisdiction, though in many states it reduces the minimum term, and thus the parole eligibility date is affected. Some states have no "good-time" provisions. Good-time can be lost by misbehavior, unless awarded under a statute or regulation providing otherwise. Fixed good-time is called vested good-time.

Goring, Charles Buckman. A British research scientist and prison physician (1870–1919), Goring published a statistical study of 3,000 male convicts entitled *The English Convict,* in which he claimed criminal tendencies are related to mental deficiencies and psychological factors rather than to physical characteristics as theorized by Cesare Lombroso.

Gotti, John (the Dapper Don, the Teflon Don). (1940–2002). John Gotti was the boss of the Gambino crime family following the murder of head Paul Castellano, which Gotti reportedly orchestrated in 1985 to assume power. Gotti was dubbed "the Teflon Don" due to the fact that various criminal charges against him rarely stuck during his career (most cases ended in acquittal or a hung jury). He was also called "the Dapper Don" due to his penchant for expensive clothing. By the early 1990s, Gotti was under federal surveillance, which included the tracking of weekly meetings with his "capos" at a local restaurant. The intelligence gathered resulted in indictment, and Gotti was convicted in 1992 of 13 murders, conspiracy to commit murder, racketeering, obstruction of justice, illegal gambling, extortion, tax evasion, and loan sharking, based in large part on his own recorded statements. Gotti was sentenced to life in prison and died from cancer in 2002. *See also* Castello, Paul; Gravano, Sammy

government agency. A subdivision of the executive, legislative, judicial, or other branch of a government, including a department, independent establishment, commission, administration, authority, board, and bureau; or a corporation or other legal entity established by, and subject to control by, a government or governments for execution of a governmental or intergovernmental program.

GPS tracking. An electronic device that uses the triangulation of global positioning satellite to track the location and movements of a person or object. In criminal justice, GPS tracking is most commonly used as a form of community supervision for high risk sex offenders and persons convicted of domestic violence. GPS tracking is also used in criminal justice to track vehicles.

graffiti. *See* vandalism

graft. Money or valuable privileges gained at the expense of the public or the public interest, usually by officeholders, employees, or persons who possess political influence, and obtained through actions ranging from theft to morally reprehensible acts for which there is no legal penalty.

graft, honest. A term coined by the famous Tammany Hall chieftain George Washington Plunkitt to identify the profit secured by politicians in making use of their foreknowledge of public building projects and improvements. Dishonest graft is payment for nonexistent jobs and services to persons who return a portion of the payment to the politicians who made it. *See also* Tweed, William Marcy

Graham, Jack Gilbert. Mass murderer who constructed a bomb, which he placed in his mother's luggage, set to detonate 10 minutes after her plane departed from Denver's Stapleton Airport bound for Seattle. On the early evening of November 1, 1955, United Airlines flight 629 was blown apart over a beet farm near Longmount, CO, killing all 44 passengers and crew members aboard. Graham was convicted in a Colorado trial in the first officially state sanction use of television cameras to broadcast criminal trials. He was executed by lethal gas on January 11, 1957.

grain. The unit of measurement used to express the weight of a powder charge or a bullet; 437.5 grains equal 1 oz. avoirdupois, and 7,000 grains equal 1 lb.

grandfather clause. (1) Found initially in the Motor Carrier Act of 1935 and often included in legislation that provides for regulatory control of an industry. Such a clause attempts to preserve the rights of firms in operation before enactment of a law by exempting these firms from certain provisions of that law. Grandfather provisions have also been included in protecting existing employees from change(s) made affecting all new hires. (2) General term that refers to an exception to law that allows the old provisions to apply in certain situations. For example, states raising the drinking age from 18 to 21 years often include a grandfather clause permitting those who were of legal drinking age before the change to legally consume alcoholic beverages after the change.

grand jury. The grand jury system originated in England in 1166, when King Henry II required knights and other freemen drawn from rural neighborhoods to file with the court accusations of murder, robbery, larceny, and harboring of known criminals. In time, as the common law developed, the English grand jury came to consist of not fewer than 12 nor more than 23 jurors. Not only did they tender criminal accusations, but they considered them from outsiders as well. The jurors heard witnesses and, if convinced that there were grounds for trial, returned an indictment. Historically, the purposes of the grand jury were to serve as an investigatory body and to act as a buffer between the state and its citizens in order to prevent the Crown from unfairly invoking the criminal process against its enemies. The grand jury was incorporated into the Fifth Amendment of the U.S. Constitution, which provides that "no person shall be held to answer for a capital or otherwise infamous crime, unless on a presentment or indictment of a grand jury." The grand jury has remained unchanged; it is defined as a body of persons who have been selected according to law and sworn to hear the evidence against accused persons and determine whether there is sufficient evidence to bring those persons to trial, to investigate criminal activity generally, and to investigate the conduct of public agencies and officials. It is called a grand jury because it comprises a greater number of jurors than the ordinary trial, or petit, jury. The composition of not less than 12 nor more than 23 members is still the rule in many of the states, though in some the number is otherwise fixed by statute.

grand jury, charging. A grand jury that must decide whether or not to ratify the prosecutor's request for a formal charge against a defendant.

grand jury, investigatory. The grand jury for a court with the authority to conduct investigations into possible crimes.

grand larceny. Larceny of property where the value of the property stolen exceeds the amount fixed by statute in the different states. Often includes larceny from the person and larceny of specific kinds of property. *See also* larceny

grant of probation. A court action requiring that a person fulfill certain conditions of behavior for a specified period of time; often includes assignment to a probation agency for supervision in lieu of either prosecution, judgment, or, after conviction, usually a sentence to confinement.

graphology. Handwriting analysis. Psychologists are interested in this subject because of the hypothesis that handwriting is a projection of personality. Forensic graphology, the study of handwriting to determine who wrote what, is another specialty.

gratuity. A gift or present.

Gravano, Salvatore "Sammy the Bull" (1945–) Gravano was John Gotti's underboss in the Gambino crime family from 1985 until he entered into a plea bargain with the FBI in 1991. Gravano allegedly helped John Gotti plan the assassination of Paul Castellano, Gambino crime boss, in 1985. In 1991, Gravano agreed to testify against crime boss John Gotti in exchange for lenient sentencing. Due to Gravano's testimony, which included a first-hand account of racketeering, aggravated assault, and murder, John Gotti was sentenced to life imprisonment. Gravano was convicted of racketeering charge and sentenced to five years. Following his release from prison, Gravano entered the U.S. Witness Protection Program, but he left the program in 1995 and lived a very public life giving newspaper and television interviews and collaborating on an autobiography (*Underboss*). He began distributing ecstasy around 1998, was convicted of distribution of MDMA in 2002, and was sentenced to 19 years in prison. He remains incarcerated today and is the highest-ranking mafia member to testify against the mob. *See also* Castellano, Paul; Gotti, John; mafia

grave wax. *See* adipocere

gray matter. Part of the human central nervous system comprised of neuron cell bodies, glial cells (providing nutrients and protection) and capillaries (for blood exchange). Brain activity occurs in gray matter, as opposed to white matter, which primarily contains axons (or nerve tracts), and myelin (a fat-based insulator).

Greek law. Greek contributions to Western thought about law come from the ideas of great philosophers such as Socrates, Plato, and Aristotle. From these men emerged notions of justice that profoundly influenced legal reasoning. The Greeks distinguished, for example, between natural law and positive law. The Socratic method, the use of questions to establish a proposition, is still used in the case method of training lawyers in the United States. The need for equity, a principle to temper the harshness of the law and ensure justice, was recognized by Aristotle; and the principle of equity, continuing in the English courts of chancery, provided one of the founding principles of modern juvenile justice. Another idea to emerge from Greek philosophical thought was Aristotle's Stoic concept of the reasonably prudent man. *See also* Roman legal system

Green Haven Prison. New York's Green Haven Correctional Facility (called Green Haven Prison until 1970) was built as a military prison during World War II and acquired by New York in 1949. It was designed to be an escape-proof institution. Its outer wall of reinforced concrete is 30 feet high, almost 3 feet thick, and is said to go 30 feet below ground. Its 12 towers, reaching to 40 feet above the ground, are evenly positioned along the mile-long wall around the perimeter of the prison. No one has ever managed to escape over the wall at Green Haven.

Green River Killer. *See* Ridgway, Gary

Green River laws. Laws that prohibit door-to-door selling.

Green River Task Force. Group of law enforcement personnel assembled to investigate what was considered the nation's largest unsolved serial murder cases. The remains of 41 of 49 women reported missing from January 1982 through March 1984 have been found in and around Seattle, WA. At one time the task force involved 56 agents of local, state, and federal law enforcement. Gary Ridgway confessed to killing 48 women over a two-decade period. He pled guilty on November 5, 2003 and was convicted, receiving consecutive life sentences for each murder.

grid search. A technique for searching crime scenes, usually outdoors, in which an area previously searched by the strip method is again searched after being divided into lanes or zones running at right angles to the plots used in the strip search.

grievance. A grievance is any complaint concerning the interpretation or application of a memorandum of understanding, rules or regulations governing practices or conditions that departmental management has the ability to remedy. The use of grievance is generally used within state agencies, for example, initiated by police officers pertaining to unacceptable working conditions, or initiated by inmates pertaining to unsatisfactory classification decisions.

Grim Sleeper murders. The Grim Sleeper is an unidentified serial killer responsible for at least 13 murders in the Los Angeles area since 1985. In 2007, the most recent murder victim was linked through DNA to 12 unsolved homicides in the area dating back 22 years. The LAPD "800 Task Force" was formed in response, although no suspects have yet been identified. Los Angeles is offering a $500,000 reward for information leading to the capture of the serial killer, who has also been feature on *America's Most Wanted*. In February, 2009, LAPD Chief Bratton confirmed the serial killer, dubbed the "Grim Sleeper" by *L.A. Weekly. See also* serial killer

groove diameter. The diameter of a bore of a gun as measured from the bottom of one groove to the bottom of the opposite groove.

grooves. The spiral depressions in the rifling of a gun. They impart a spinning motion to a projectile, which stabilizes it in flight.

gross negligence. Serious carelessness; a reckless action taken without regard to life, limb, and/or property; conscious and voluntary disregard for the safety and well-being of others.

Group A Offenses. Offense types included in the more serious "Group A" crimes recorded by the National Incident Based Reporting System; Group B crimes are less serious. Group A offenses include the following 22 crime types: Arson, Assault Offenses (Aggravated, Simple, Intimidation), Bribery, Burglary/Breaking and Entering, Counterfeiting/Forgery, Destruction/Damage/ Vandalism of Property, Drug/Narcotic Offenses (including drug equipment violations), Embezzlement, Extortion/Blackmail, Fraud Offenses (false pretenses/swindle/ confidence game, credit card and ATM fraud, impersonation, welfare and wire fraud— excludes counterfeiting/forgery and bad checks), Gambling Offenses (betting, wagering, operating/promoting/assisting gambling, gambling equipment violations, sports tampering), Homicide Offenses (murder and nonnegligent manslaughter, negligent manslaughter, justifiable homicide), Kidnapping/ Abduction, Larceny/Theft Offenses (pocket picking, purse snatching, shoplifting, theft and all other larceny), Motor Vehicle Theft, Pornography/Obscene Material, Prostitution Offenses (prostitution, assisting or promoting prostitution), Robbery, Sex Offenses— Forcible (forcible rape, forcible sodomy, sexual assault with an object, forcible fondling), Sex Offenses—Nonforcible (incest, statutory rape—excludes prostitution), Stolen Property Offenses, and Weapon Law Violations. *See also* Group B Offenses, Index Crimes, National Incident Based Reporting System

Group B Offenses. Offense types included in the less serious "Group B" crimes recorded by the National Incident Based Reporting System; Group A types are generally more serious crimes similar to the UCR Index Crimes. Group B crimes include the following 11 categories: Bad Checks, Curfew/Loitering/Vagrancy Violations, Disorderly Conduct, Driving Under the Influence, Drunkenness (excludes driving under the influence), Family Offenses–Nonviolent (e.g., Abandonment, Desertion, Neglect, Nonsupport), Liquor Law Violations, Peeping Tom, Runaway (persons under 18—not a crime), Trespass of Real Property, and All Other Offenses. *See also* Group A Offenses, Index Crimes, National Incident Based Reporting System

Guantánamo Bay (also called "Gitmo"). Location of United States Naval base in Cuba, and subject of world-wide attention regarding the conditions of confinement for persons housed there under the category "enemy combatants." Conditions at the facility reported include various practices prohibited by the Geneva Convention, including sleep deprivation, prolonged constraint and waterboarding to prompt confessions. Amnesty International, as well as other human-rights organizations, has been highly critical of conditions, and the USSC ruled that prisoners housed here were entitled to constitutional protections in *Boumediene v. Bush* (2008). As of January, 2009, 245 persons remain detained there, although in December of 2009, President Obama expressed his intent to transfer inmates to the Thompson Correctional Center in Illinois.

guaranty. A promise or undertaking by one person to answer for the payment of some debt or performance of some contract in case of default by another person.

guardian. One who has legal responsibility for the care and management of the person, estate, or both, of an infant or other incompetent person.

guardian *ad litem*. A guardian appointed for the purpose of a lawsuit.

Guardian Angels. New York City's Guardian Angels were founded by Brooklyn-born Curtis Sliwa, the son of a second-generation Polish-American merchant. To protect the riders on the No. 4 subway, which was known as the muggers' express, he organized a group of his friends called The Magnificent Thirteen, and, on February 13, 1979, they went on their first subway patrol. They quickly expanded into the Guardian Angels, a group of unarmed but streetwise youths, self-appointed peacekeepers who patrol the city's buses, subways, and streets. Dressed in white T-shirts and red berets, the 700-plus force has had a reassuring effect on many New Yorkers. By 1982, the Guardian Angels had expanded their operations to more than 40 communities across the country, yet only the cities of New York, Boston, Los Angeles, Miami, and Baltimore have given them official recognition. Numerous cities in Europe, Asia, and South America had requested Sliwa's help in starting similar groups. In May, 1985, he took his group to the U.S.-Mexican border at Tijuana to assist in the protection of illegal aliens. Published the book *Street Smarts: The Guardian Angels Guide to Safe Living.* Address: The Alliance of Guardian Angels, 982 East 89 th St., Brooklyn, NY 11236. Telephone: (212) 860-5575.

guillotine. A machine, invented during the French Revolution, with two upright posts surmounted by a crossbeam grooved so that a weighted and oblique-shaped knife blade falls swiftly and with force when the cord by which it is suspended is released. This method of execution by decapitation was the official method of execution until France abolished the death penalty in 1981.

Guilty but Insane. Also called **"Guilty but Mentally Ill."** This is an alternative to "not guilty by reason of insanity," under this type of conviction, the defendant is found legally responsible for their crime but is generally confined to facility for mentally ill offenders.

guilt by association. The idea, which has sometimes been embodied in statutes, that a person's guilt is prima facie determined by membership in an organization stigmatized as criminal or subversive, regardless of the person's knowledge of the aims and activities of the organization or of his or her own active involvement.

gun. In general, a piece of ordnance consisting essentially of a tube or barrel and used for throwing projectiles by force, usually that of an explosive but sometimes that of compressed gas, a spring, and so forth. The general term embraces such weapons as howitzers, mortars, cannons, firearms, rifles, shotguns, carbines, pistols, and revolvers. *See also* firearm

Gun Control Act of 1968. Provides nationwide firearms regulation, including prohibiting interstate sale of firearms except by licensed manufacturers and dealers. *See also* Brady Handgun Violence Prevention Act; Bureau of Alcohol, Tobacco, Firearms and Explosives (ATF); Federal Assault Weapons Ban of 1994; Federal Firearms Act of 1938; Firearm Owners' Protection Act of 1986; National Firearms Act of 1934; Omnibus Crime Control and Safe Streets Act of 1968; Violent Crime Control and Law Enforcement Act of 1994

gun control laws. Federal, state, and local laws that regulate the importation, manufacturing, distribution, sale, purchase, or possession of firearms. The Bureau of Alcohol, Tobacco, Firearms and Explosives of the U.S. Department of Justice has jurisdiction over the federal laws. Efforts to pass gun control measures are often referred to as Brady legislation, after former President Ronald Reagan's press secretary, James Brady, who was shot and crippled in the March 1981 assassination attempt on Reagan. The United States has about 20,000 gun control laws, the vast majority of which are state or local ordinances. *See also* Firearm Act, Federal

gunshot residue (GSR). Comprised primarily of explosive primer, propellant, bullet, cartridge and firearm. Examination of gunshot residue is conducted with the use of scanning electronic microscope and the use of Chromatography, Capillary Electrophoresis, and Mass Spectrometry.

H

habeas corpus (Lat., lit. "you should have the body"). The British Parliament formalized the concept with the Habeas Corpus Act of 1679, and Americans wrote it into the U.S. Constitution. Article III, Section 9, reads, "The privilege of the writ of habeas corpus shall not be suspended, unless when in a case of rebellion or invasion the public safety may require it." The writ is a legal device to challenge the detention of a person taken into custody. An individual in custody may demand an evidentiary hearing before a judge to examine the legality of the detention. The writ is purely procedural: it guarantees only a right to a hearing. It has no bearing on the substance of the issue or charge.

habitual criminal laws. Many American states and other countries have passed laws that provide increased penalties for offenders with previous criminal records. The provision for the increased penalty is either permissive or mandatory. The habitual criminal law is invoked after conviction of a second, third, or fourth felony. The advocates of such laws believe the increased severity of the penalty will eliminate or considerably reduce serious crime. *See also* Baumes's laws, recidivism statutes; three strikes

habitual offender. A person sentenced under the provisions of a statute declaring that persons convicted of a given offense, and shown to have previously been convicted of another specified offense(s), shall receive a more severe penalty than that for the current offense alone. In certain states, under habitual offender acts or so-called Baumes's laws, persons convicted of a certain number of felonies, usually four, are sentenced to imprisonment for life. *See also* Baumes's laws, recidivism statutes; three strikes

habitual offender laws. *See* recidivism statutes

habitual offender statutes. *See* recidivism statutes

habituation. A psychological dependence upon a substance such as marijuana or tobacco. Withdrawal from these substances can be both physiological and psychological in nature.

hacker. A hacker is a skilled computer user. The term originally denoted a skilled programmer, particularly one skilled in machine code and with a good knowledge of the machine and its operating system. The name arose from the fact that a good programmer could always hack an unsatisfactory system around until it worked. The term later came to denote a user whose main interest is in defeating password systems. The term has thus acquired a pejorative sense, with the meaning of one who deliberately and sometimes criminally interferes with data available through telephone lines.

hacking. Bypassing security mechanisms of computer and network systems without authorization, generally for the purpose of theft, destruction of information, disabling of systems, or an illegal purpose.

hair testing. A type of drug detection technique that analyzes the hair follicle to determine drug usage. Results of such analyses generally include types of substances ingested and approximate dates of last usage, based on typical hair growth of one-half inch per month. *See also* drug monitoring, saliva drug testing, sweat patch, urine drug testing

halfway house. A term originally given to guidance centers for offenders who are halfway out of prisons, on probation or parole. Today, the term may mean a center to help mental patients readjust to living outside a hospital after discharge, or any therapeutic community for people continuing to recover from drug, alcohol, or other problems after discharge from an in-patient facility. The Isaac T. Hooper Home, the first halfway house in the United States, was opened by the Society of Friends (Quakers) in New York City in 1845.

Haloperidol. A nonnarcotic, nonaddicting drug prescribed for the treatment of psychosis (especially Schizophrenia), neurologic disorders (e.g., Tourette's syndrome), nausea following surgery or chemotherapy, and as an adjunctive treatment for chronic pain. It is also used for treating and controlling withdrawal symptoms associated with alcohol, heroin, and methadone addiction. Among its more controversial uses, Haloperidol has also been used by the former Soviet Union against dissidents; the U.S. Immigrations and Customs Enforcement (ICE) agency regularly used Haloperidol as a sedative on aliens being deported between 2002–2008, although this practice now requires medical monitoring and court order as a result of several lawsuits.

Hand, Learned (1872–1961). Considered one of the greatest jurists of his day, Hand served over 50 years on the bench as a federal judge. His final post (1924 to 1951) was as chief judge of the Federal Court of Appeals for the Second Circuit.

handicapped parking. On April 10, 1991, the U.S. Department of Transportation established the Informed System for Handicapped Parking. All state license plates issued to people with handicaps must include a three-inch-square image of the international symbol of access—a stick-figure profile of a wheelchair user. States are also required to make available placards of uniform size and color, to be hung from a car's rear view mirror, which clearly display the same symbol. Disabled drivers are entitled to more than one copy of the placard so that it can also be displayed in rental cars. For those with temporary disabilities, a temporary placard is available, with a doctor's authorization, granting disability parking status for up to six months. The temporary placards are red (placards for permanent disability are blue), and list the issuing state and date of expiration. The dates of state implementation of these regulations are decided by individual state legislatures.

hanging. A method of capital punishment devised in ancient times and currently in use in many countries. Originally, death came about by strangling, but the method was later modified by incorporating a several foot drop, which is designed to break the neck and cause instantaneous death. In this method of execution, the prisoner stands atop a trap door and a rope is placed around his or her neck. A formula based on the prisoner's weight and height determines the distance of the drop and the rope's thickness. The trap door opens and the prisoner falls. The rope tightens on the person's throat, often breaking the neck and causing paralysis. Simultaneously, the rope's pressure prevents breathing, causing oxygen deprivation and death in about four minutes. Although lethal injection is the primary method of execution in most states that permit capital punishment, hanging is also permitted in: Delaware, New Hampshire and Washington. The last U.S. execution by hanging was the execution of Billy Bailey in 1996, in the state of Delaware. *See also* execution, methods of; lethal injection; electrocution; lethal gas; firing squad, and Parker, Isaac C. *See* Table 24. Execution Methods in the United States, by State, 2010, page 173

Hanssen, Robert Philip (1944–). Born in Chicago, Illinois, Hanssen was an FBI agent from 1976–2001 and a Soviet (later Russian) spy from 1979–2001. Described by the FBI as "possibly the worst intelligence disaster in U.S. history," delivery of Hanssen's secrets to Russia (for which he was paid $1.4 million) resulted in the execution of at least two U.S. spies overseas. Hanssen pled guilty to 15 counts of espionage in 2001 to avoid the death penalty. He is currently serving a sentence of life without parole, under 23 hours of solitary confinement daily in the federal supermaximum security prison in Florence, Colorado.

harassing calls. Telephone calls, also called nuisance calls, placed repetitively to annoy or frighten a family or individual. Using the telephone in this manner is a criminal offense, and victims can prosecute if calls are frequent and harassing enough to warrant action. Working with local law enforcement personnel, with whom the victim must lodge a complaint, telephone companies can tap the victim's line to determine the source of the calls. *See also* dialed number recorders; pen register

harbor master. An administrator/officer charged with enforcing state harbor laws in addition to city ordinances, rules, and regulations.

Harlan, John Marshall I (1833–1911). Associate justice of the Supreme Court from 1877–1911 noted for his dissents in decisions upholding racial discrimination and segregation. Although he once supported slavery and strict enforcement of fugitive slave laws, his revulsion at terrorism helped to convert him to a pro-civil rights position. His support for Rutherford B. Hayes led to Harlan's appointment to the Supreme Court in 1877. He was the Court's outstanding liberal justice during his tenure and the only dissenter in the Civil Rights Cases (1883) and in *Plessy v. Ferguson* (1896), which established the separate-but-equal principle. Harlan built his legal philosophy on a reverence for the Constitution. Aside from civil rights questions, he was against weakening antitrust legislation. His grandson, John Marshall Harlan II, was a U.S. Supreme Court Justice from 1955–1971.

Harlan, John Marshall II (1899–1971). Associate justice of the Supreme Court from 1955–1971, noted as the conservative conscience of an activist Court and for his strict adherence to prior judicial decisions. He was named for his grandfather, John Marshall Harlan I, a U. S. Supreme Court Justice from 1877–1911. Harlan dissented from the liberal philosophy of his colleagues, although siding with the majority on civil rights issues. He also believed that the federal judiciary should not become involved in state and local problems. His conservative philosophy was influential at a time when the majority would have been willing to assert judicial power over other branches of government.

Harris, Eric (1981–1999). Born in Kansas, Harris moved with his family to Colorado in 1996. In 1999, Harris and Dylan Klebold, both high school seniors, shot and killed

13 people and injured 24 more at Columbine High School. Harris and Klebold killed themselves during the massacre. *See also* Columbine Massacre; Klebold, Dylan; Virginia Tech Massacre

Harrison Narcotics Act. A federal act that requires all persons who deal in narcotics to register with the director of Internal Revenue. The purpose of the act is to regulate the traffic in narcotics for medical and scientific purposes only.

Harris poll. These well-known surveys are based on Bureau of Census information about state and metropolitan populations. Interviews are conducted at different locations throughout the country, with multiple households contacted in each location. Although the sample is relatively small, it is representative of the civilian population of the United States, excluding Alaska and Hawaii and those in prisons, hospitals, and religious and educational institutions. *See also* Gallup poll

Hasan, Nidal Malik (1970–). Born in Virginia in 1970, Hasan was an Army psychiatrist stationed at Fort Hood Army base in Texas when he opened fire on military and civilian employees on November 5, 2009. In all, Hasan is believed to have killed 13 people (one of whom was pregnant) and injured 32 others. Hasan was shot by military police about 10 minutes into the rampage. While he survived the shooting, he is now reportedly paralyzed. He is in military custody awaiting court martial as of 2010. While many believe Hasan acted alone, others believe it was an act of terrorism, as the shooting following confirmed communication between Hasan and Imam Anwar al-Awlaki, a U.S. citizen and known al-Qaeda supporter who is officially on the CIA approved target list due to suspected terrorist activities. *See also* Fort Hood Shooting

hashish. An extract of the hemp plant (*cannabis sativa*) with a higher concentration of THC than marijuana. It may be inhaled, chewed, or smoked in order to produce a type of exhilaration accompanied by the disorganization of the central nervous system.

Hatch Act of 1939. A law of Congress enacted "to prevent pernicious political activities." It forbids anyone to intimidate, threaten, or coerce any person in order to influence his vote for a federal office. It further prohibits promise of employment or other advantage for political support and makes illegal the soliciting of political contributions by relief workers and federal executive or administrative employees. The latter were also prohibited from engaging in political management or in political campaigns. Exempted from its provisions were certain policy-determining officials. The amendment of 1940 attempted to regulate campaign contributions and expenditures. The act and its amendment, however, have proven unsuccessful. Expenditures and contributions by individual committees and persons have raised the amounts far beyond those laid down in the law, which is also known as the Federal Corrupt Practices Act of 1939. Presently, the federal government has not revised either act.

hate crimes. Statistical category of offenses against minorities included in the annual FBI Uniform Crime Reports. Data include offenses related to victims' race, religion, sexual orientation, and ethnicity. The Federal Civil Rights Law of 1969 established federal prosecution for any person who "willingly injures, intimidates or interferes with another person, or attempts to do so, by force because of the other person's race, color, religion or national origin" In June 1993 the U.S. Supreme Court upheld hate crime laws in 26 states that permit judges to impose longer sentences on those whose crimes grow out of their biases. The Violent Crime Control and Law Enforcement Act of 1994 expanded the definition to include women and persons with disabilities and provided sentencing enhancements for hate crimes. In this statute, hate crimes are those in which "the defendant intentionally selects a victim, or in the case of a property crime, the property that is the object of the crime, because of the actual or perceived race, color, religion, national origin, ethnicity, gender, disability, or sexual orientation of any person." In 2009, President Obama signed the Matthew Shepard and James Byrd, Jr. Hate Crimes Prevention Act, expanded the federal law to include crimes motivated by victim's actual or perceived gender, sexual orientation, gender identity, or disability; the law also removed the requirement that victims must be engaged in federally protected activity for an act to fall under federal jurisdiction. Three hate crime acts also govern the collection and dissemination of hate crime statistics: the Hate Crime Statistical Act of 1990, the Violent Crime Control and Law Enforcement Act of 1994, and the Campus Hate Crimes Right to Know Act of 1997. Hate crime victimization reached its peak in 2001 (most likely due to retaliatory violence following the September 11 attacks); the FBI reports 9,691 hate crime victims in 2008, based on Uniform Crime Report statistics, which may underestimate actual victimization. (H.R. 2647; 18 U.S.C. Sections 241, 242, 245, 247; 28 U.S.C. § 994; and 42 U.S.C. Section 3631). *See also* xenophobe

hate crime incident. A "hate incident" is not a crime and cannot be prosecuted because it lacks the element of damage to property, the element of harm or immediate threat of harm, and the element of violence or the immediate threat of violence. Examples could include hostile or hateful speech, or other disrespectful or discriminatory behavior, which although motivated by bias, is not illegal. The First Amendment of the Constitution protects free speech.

Hauptmann, Bruno Richard (1899–1936). A German immigrant who had been convicted of burglary and armed robbery, he entered the United States illegally in 1923. He allegedly kidnapped and murdered the one-year old son of Colonel Charles Lindbergh, a national hero. He was convicted and, on April 3, 1936, was electrocuted at the state prison in New Jersey. Some experts argue that Hauptmann was an innocent man—the scapegoat for police frustrations and the national public fervor surrounding the need to convict someone of the horrendous crime that shocked the nation. *See also* Lindbergh Law

Hawes-Cooper Act. A law enacted by the Congress and approved by the president on January 19, 1929, it became operative after five years. It provided that all prison-made goods entering into interstate commerce are subject to the laws of any state or territory of the United States to the same extent and in the same manner as prison-made goods manufactured in that state or territory. It was aimed at regulating the contract, piece-price, and public-account systems of prison labor.

Hawthorne effect. A transitory increase in worker productivity resulting from an expression of management's interest in work group activities. The phenomenon was first recognized in morale-enhancing activities of Elton Mayo and a Harvard University research team during industrial experiments at Western Electric's Hawthorne, IL, plant during the 1920s and 1930s. Recent views hold that a negative Hawthorne effect—decreased productivity because of a perception of lack of management interest—occurs more often than a positive one.

Hawthorne studies. A classic series of experiments conducted at the Hawthorne plant of Western Electric in Chicago from 1924 until 1932. The most famous involved the relay assembly test room, the mica-splitting test room, and the bank-wiring observation room. The research was originally conducted to determine the relationship between working conditions and employee productivity and satisfaction. The major finding was that human factors—perceptions of management interest in workers—were more significant than environmental factors as determinants of productivity and satisfaction. Informal work groups and interactions among employees play a key role in the organization, it was found. This discovery led

to the development of the human relations approach to the study of organizations.

Haymarket Massacre. A bombing and shooting incident on May 4, 1886. On May 3, striking workers at the McCormick Reaper works in Chicago attacked strikebreakers; police used guns and clubs to disperse the strikers. August Spies, editor of a German-language anarchist newspaper, called a protest meeting for Haymarket Square the following day. As that meeting was breaking up, a police officer leading 180 men ordered the crowd to disperse. A bomb was thrown among the police, and both sides opened fire with pistols. Seven policemen died, 60 or more were wounded, and a number of civilians were killed or wounded. Police arrested a number of prominent Chicago anarchists, including Spies, Albert Parsons (editor of an English-language newspaper), and Samuel Fielden (a teamster and anarchist leader). Of the seven men sentenced to be hanged, four were hanged, one committed suicide, and two had their sentences commuted. In 1892, Illinois governor John Peter Altgeld released the imprisoned survivors, claiming both judge and jury had shown extreme prejudice. The incident served to couple the labor movement to anarchic violence in the public mind.

hearing. A proceeding in which arguments, witnesses, or evidence are heard by a judicial officer or administrative body.

hearsay. Evidence that a witness has learned through others. It is generally inadmissible in court.

Hearst, Patricia Campbell (Patty, Tania) (1955–). Heiress granddaughter of publisher William Randolph Hearst, Patricia was kidnapped on February 5, 1974, in Berkeley, CA, by the Symbionese Liberation Army. This was the first U.S. political kidnapping. She became the object of an intensive manhunt. On May 16, 1974, SLA members and Hearst used a red 1970 Volkswagen van in a gunfire-filled getaway after a shoplifting incident in Inglewood, CA. When the police found the vehicle, they also discovered a gun nearby—registered to Emily Harris—and a parking ticket inside the van that led them to the SLA's hideout. A day later, six members of the terrorist group died in a two-hour shoot-out with 500 local and federal officers in south central Los Angeles. FBI agents captured Hearst in San Francisco on September 18, 1975, with others. She was indicted for bank robbery, and despite her attorney's (F. Lee Bailey) claim that she was coerced, intimidated, and brainwashed into participating in the bank robbery, a San Francisco jury convicted her on March 20, 1976. Her prison term was commuted by President Carter, resulting in her release from prison in February of 1979. She was granted a full pardon by President Clinton in 2001. *See also* Stockholm Syndrome

hebephile. Term for a pedophile who is drawn to young people during the period of puberty and adolescence. *See also* pedophile

heir at law. One entitled by law to inherit by descent the real estate of a decedent.

Hell's Angels Motorcycle Club. *See* motorcyclists, outlaw

Hemastix. chemical reagent strips used as a presumptive test for the presence of blood in a sample.

hematoporphyrin test. A chemical confirmation test for the presence of blood.

Hennard, George, Jr. On October 17, 1991, 35-year-old George Hennard drove his 1987 Ford Ranger XLT pickup through a Luby's cafeteria window in Killen, TX, and methodically shot and killed 22 people (14 women and eight men) and wounded 23 others, using a 9 mm Glock 17 and a Ruger P89, both semiautomatic pistols, before taking his own life. This tragedy is considered the worst one-man shooting massacre in U.S. history. *See also* Huberty, James

Henry System. A system of fingerprint classification devised by Sir Edward Richard Henry in 1901 in India and used in most English speaking countries until the 1990s.

The Henry system classifies the distinctive information found on the bulbs of the fingers and thumbs into a numerical and alphabetic formula having six major divisions: Primary, secondary, major, subsecondary, final, and key. The system divides prints into four main types—arches, loops, whorls, and composites and results in a fractional numerical score between 1/1, indicating no whorl patterns on any finger print, and 32/32, indicating whorl patterns on all fingers. *See also* Roscher system, Juan Vucetich system, fingerprint patterns

hero-homicide complex. A phenomenon wherein emergency personnel kill vulnerable persons (patients) in an effort to demonstrate their heroism or medical skill. Is such cases, the person is generally seeking recognition without an intent to kill, although some victims died despite efforts to save them. For example, Kristen Gilbert was convicted of four such homicides in 2001. Person meeting this profile are sometimes called "angel of death."

heroin. One of the opium family isolated in the search for nonhabit-forming anesthetics to take the place of morphine. Heroin is a trademark name which has become identified with a white crystalline form of morphine derivative. It is definitely habit-forming and has become one of the most widely used of all narcotics. It produces a quiet, pleasant, dreamlike slumber. In February 1989 an investigation, code-named Operation White Mare, seized 838 pounds of heroin valued at $1 billion and $3 million cash in New York City. In June 1991 U.S. Customs agents seized 1,080 pounds of China White (pure heroin) in a Hayward, CA, warehouse near San Francisco, with a street value of between $2.7 and $4 billion. By comparison, about 200 pounds of heroin were seized from the French Connection ring, broken in 1971. It is estimated that U.S. addicts consume four to six tons of heroin a year. *See also* French Connection

Herzberg's motivation-maintenance theory. Frederick Herzberg postulated, based on his

1950s study *The Motivation to Work,* that there exists a set of extrinsic job conditions that, when not present, result in dissatisfaction among employees. However, the presence of these conditions does not necessarily motivate employees. Potential dissatisfiers (maintenance factors) are: job security; salary; working conditions; status; company policies; quality of technical supervision; quality of interpersonal relations among peers, supervisors, and subordinates; and fringe benefits. There also exists a set of intrinsic job conditions, termed motivators or satisfiers, that include achievement, recognition, work itself, responsibility, advancement, personal growth and development. *See also* motivation

high crimes and misdemeanors. Offenses against law sufficiently grave to warrant impeachment by the House of Representatives.

higher law doctrine. (1) The concept of a law of nature intrinsically superior to positive law. (2) A declaration that "there is a higher law than the Constitution," made by Senator William H. Seward of New York, an abolitionist spokesman, on March 11, 1850, during the debates on the Compromise of 1850.

Highfields. *See* New Jersey Experimental Project for the Treatment of Youthful Offenders

high misdemeanor. In some states, crimes are classified as misdemeanors and high misdemeanors, the latter carrying heavier penalties.

High School Senior Survey on Drug Abuse. *See* Monitoring the Future. *See also* Drug Abuse Warning Network

high seas law enforcement. The U.S. Coast Guard enforces, within the territorial waters, contiguous zones, and special interest areas of the high seas, federal laws and international agreements, except those related to pollution, traffic control, and port and vessel safety. This activity also includes the detection of illegal fishing and other illegal activity. Address: Operational Law Enforcement Division, Office of Operations, Coast Guard,

DOT, 2100 2nd Street, SW, Room 3108, Washington, DC 20593.

highway. A way publicly maintained and open to the use of the public for purposes of vehicular travel. The term includes street.

highway patrol. A special state force, known by various names, which enforces motor vehicle and other laws in those states that have not established a state constabulary invested with general law-enforcement powers.

highway statistics. Statistics are available on such topics as: the number of motor vehicles by state; the amount of fuel consumed by state; the number of drivers' licenses issued by age, sex, and state; state finances; and vehicle miles traveled. Contact: U.S. Department of Transportation, Federal Highway Administration, 1200 New Jersey Ave SE, Washington, DC 20590, Phone: 202-366-4000; Web: www.fhwa.dot.gov

high-yield investments. A common type of investment fraud involves the sale of worthless investments, which the con artist deceptively represents as risk free or very high yield instrument. *See also:* fraud, investment

hijack alert system. A system created by trucking concerns, trucking associations, and law enforcement agencies whereby a theft or hijack is immediately reported to designated law enforcement agencies and to a designated trucking association. The latter, per a prearranged schedule, notifies certain strategically located trucking companies who, in turn, notify others until all truckers in a given area are notified. Truck drivers and others search for and report locations of the stolen equipment.

hijacking. Taking control of a vehicle by the use or threatened use of force or by intimidation; taking a vehicle by stealth, without the use or threatened use of force, in order to steal its cargo. Hijacking is a popular name for behavior that can constitute any of several statutory offenses. Where an occupant of the vehicle is forced to accompany a perpetrator, chargeable offense can be kidnapping or false imprisonment. Where a vehicle is taken by force, with intent to permanently deprive the owner of the vehicle or any of its parts or contents, the chargeable offense can be robbery. Where a vehicle is taken by stealth, the chargeable offense is usually larceny, but such an incident is usually recorded in a separate category of motor vehicle theft. *See also* September 11 attacks; skyjacking

Hillside Strangler. *See* Bianchi, Kenneth and Buono, Angelo

Hinckley, John Warnock, Jr. (1955–). In 1976, Hinkley became obsessed with actress Jodie Foster. He moved to Connecticut to be near Foster, who was a student at Yale, and began to stalk her. Hinkley sent dozens of cards and letters but was unsuccessful in his attempts to meet Foster. On March 30, 1981, Hinkley fired six shots in an attempted assassination of President Ronald Reagan, which was designed to impress Foster. The shots wounded President Reagan, a police officer, a secret service agent, and left Press Secretary James Brady permanently paralyzed. Hinkley was found not guilty by reason of insanity, sparking tremendous debate and legal maneuvering about the insanity defense nationwide. As of 2010, Hinkley remains confined to a mental hospital, although he is permitted regular passes to visit his mother in the community. *See also* assassination; Brady, James; insanity; stalking

Hiss, Alger (1904–1996). Born in Baltimore, Maryland, Hiss was an American attorney who worked for the U.S. Justice Department, Department of State, and was secretary-general of the United Nations charter meetings. He was accused of espionage by the House Un-American Activities Committee in 1948 and convicted of perjury in 1950. He served 44 months in prison as a result; he was readmitted to the Massachusetts bar in 1975 despite his criminal conviction and federal prison term. Hiss staunchly maintained his innocence until his death in 1996. To this day, experts remain divided as to Hiss' guilt or innocence as a Soviet spy. *See also* House Un-American Activities Committee

hit and run. Unlawful departure by a driver from the scene of a motor vehicle accident in which he or she was involved and that resulted in injury to a person or damage to the property of another.

hitman. Colloquial term for a hired assassin or professional killer, sometimes called a "Black Hand."

HITMAN. *See* Homicide Information Tracing Management Automation Network

HITS. *See* Homicide Investigation Tracking System

Hobbs Act. An act of Congress passed on July 3, 1947, designed to curb labor racketeering, which imposes penalties on persons found guilty of robbery or extortion when these acts have the effect of obstructing, delaying, or otherwise affecting interstate commerce.

Hoffa, James Riddle (Jimmy). (1913–1977?) Born in 1913, Hoffa succeeded Dave Beck as Teamsters Union president in 1957, when Beck was jailed for stealing union funds. As a result of Senate hearings, the Teamsters were expelled from the AFL-CIO. In 1964, Hoffa was convicted of jury tampering at the conclusion of a trial begun two years earlier. He was imprisoned in 1967 to serve an eight-year sentence. Released from prison, he disappeared in 1977, and although his body was never found, he was presumed murdered. His son, James Hoffa, currently serves as Teamster Union president.

Hollywood Madam. *See* Fleiss, Heidi

Holmes, Oliver Wendell, Jr. (1841–1935). Associate Justice of the Supreme Court from 1902–1932. Known as the "great dissenter," he was appointed by President Theodore Roosevelt and eventually ranked with John Marshall as one of the two greatest justices ever to sit on the Court. A veteran of the Civil War, he graduated from Harvard Law School in 1866, published *The Common Law* in 1881, and was appointed to the school's faculty in 1882. Within months, however, he had accepted a justiceship on the Massachusetts

Supreme Judicial Court and served almost 20 years, the last three as chief justice. Holmes became the most outspoken advocate of judicial self-restraint. He believed the Constitution allowed wide latitude for social experimentation by the states and by Congress. Holmes began the Supreme Court's initial involvement with freedom of speech and the meaning of the First Amendment. He formulated the famous rule that an utterance could be punished only if there was a "clear and present danger" that it would lead to an evil that Congress or the states could legitimately try to prevent.

Holocaust Memorial Museum shooting. On June 10, 2009, a gunman shot and killed a security guard at the U.S. Holocaust Memorial Museum in Washington, DC Authorities apprehended 88-year-old suspect James Wenneker von Brunn, reportedly a white supremacist who denied the Holocaust occurred, at the scene. Von Brunn was incarcerated pending trial, but he died on January 6, 2010 while in custody. Authorities believed he acted alone in the shooting. *See also* domestic terrorism; von Brunn, James Wenneker

holograph. A handwritten will, or any document completely in the handwriting of the person who has signed it.

home rule. The power of a local government, usually a city, to manage its own affairs and to draft or change its charter. Under home rule of municipalities, the state legislatures voluntarily renounce their power and authorize the cities to manage their affairs, subject only to broad state statutes. More than half of U.S. states allow varying degrees of freedom to their cities.

Homeland Security Act of 2002. Passed in response to the September 11 attacks, the act established the Department of Homeland Security. *See* Homeland Security, Department of

Homeland Security, Department of. Originally created as the White House Office of Homeland Security in the wake of the

September 11 terrorist attacks on the World Trade Center and the Pentagon, the agency was elevated to cabinet-level status by Congress in March 2003. The new Department of Homeland Security (DHS) brings together over 40 agencies, departments or offices in an effort to coordinate antiterrorism activities in the United States. The Secret Service, Coast Guard, Border Patrol, and Citizenship and Immigration Service are examples of major agencies transferred to the new department. In addition, the Bureau of Alcohol, Tobacco, and Firearms (BATF) was moved from the Treasury Department to the Department of Justice. The DHS is organized into four major directorates: Border and Transportation Security, Emergency Preparedness and Response, Science and Technology, and Information Analysis and Infrastructure Protection, plus the traditional functions of the U.S. Secret Service, Coast Guard, and Animal and Plant border inspections. When originally created, the DHS had over 177,000 employees, making it the third largest department in the federal government, with a budget of over $37 billion. The first Secretary of Homeland Security was Tom Ridge, former governor of Pennsylvania.

homestead. A filing process that protects property against most debts. Among the debts that are not affected by a declaration of homestead are taxes, mortgages, mechanics' liens, child support, alimony, and court judgments recorded before the declaration is filed. The homestead procedure varies from state to state, but generally it protects the first $30,000 of equity if the owner is single; $45,000, if married; and $55,000, if age 65 or disabled.

Homestead Massacre. A fight between strikers and company guards on July 6, 1892. Shooting occurred when Carnegie Steel Company's head manager, Henry Clay Frick, ordered 300 Pinkerton guards sent in to protect strikebreakers at the plant in Homestead, PA. When striking workers forcibly resisted the arrival of the Pinkertons, 10 guards and strikers were killed. The state militia was sent in to maintain order and, incidentally, protect strikebreakers. Both the strike and the union were broken, and the steel industry remained unorganized until the 1930s.

homicide. Any willful killing, including murder and nonnegligent manslaughter.

homicide, excusable. A killing under such circumstances of accident or misfortune that the party is relieved from the penalty attached to the commission of a felonious homicide.

homicide, felonious. A killing committed under such circumstances as to make it punishable as a felony.

homicide investigation, computerized. The use of specialized databases and software to assist in the apprehension of homicide cases.

Homicide Information Tracing Management Automation Network (HITMAN). Developed in 1985 by Lt. Hocking and Officer Willis of the Los Angeles Police Department. The system can scan Los Angeles homicides since 1983 (with plans to include files back to 1978) and can be asked nearly 100 different questions about each death.

Homicide Investigation Tracking System (HITS). A database in Washington state for linking violent crimes through signature analysis.

homicide, justifiable. A killing committed with full intent but under such circumstances of duty as to render the act proper, such as in cases of self-defense, defense of property, or an officer lawfully enforcing the law.

homophobia. Fear of homosexuals; range of negative attitudes towards homosexuality, including prejudice, hatred, and irrational fear. Homophobia is sometimes accompanied by hostility, discrimination and violence. *See also* hate crimes

homosexual. Person(s) attracted sexually to members of one's own sex. In 1989 Denmark was the first country to allow same sex marriages. France and Norway soon followed. Germany approved same sex marriages in August, 2001. As of 2009, six U.S. states

permit same-sex marriage: Massachusetts (2004); Connecticut (2008); Iowa (2009); Vermont (2009); New Hampshire (2010); and Washington, DC (2010). California passed same sex marriage on June 16, 2008; however, the passage of Proposition 8 on November 5, 2008, prevents the issuance of same sex marriage licenses in the state. *See* ACT-UP; gay; same sex marriage; Stonewall Riot; White Night

Hoover Commissions. The Commission on the Reorganization of the Executive Branch, operating from 1947 to 1949 and from 1953 to 1955 were the third and fourth of a series of commissions to study paralysis, waste, and corruption in the bureaucracy. Named chairman twice because of his eminence as a past president and his record of incorruptible public service, Herbert Hoover was particularly concerned with duplication of responsibilities and inefficiency. *See also* Little Hoover Commission

Hoover, J(ohn) Edgar. American public official (1895–1972) who served as first director of the FBI, holding that position for 48 years. Hoover was born in Washington, DC. After receiving a law degree, he began work at the Department of Justice. Within two years, he was named special assistant to Attorney General Palmer. He became the director of the FBI in 1924. Hoover turned the FBI into a symbol of law enforcement, established the world's largest fingerprint file, and created the FBI National Academy. From the late 1940s, he was known for his uncompromising attitude toward suspected communists and subversives; both the FBI and Hoover came under fire for exceeding their authority. He continued in office, however, until his death. His books include *Masters of Deceit* (1958) and *On Communism* (1969).

horses in law enforcement. *See* National Mounted Police Services; Services Organization, Mounted

hospice. An institution and a philosophy that offer an alternative to traditional hospital care for terminally ill patients. In a hospice, it is understood that no heroic effort will be made to prolong the patient's life, but that treatment to relieve pain will be provided. The hospice movement began in Great Britain, where St. Christopher's Hospice in London is considered a model. *See also* AIDS; euthanasia

Horton, William (1975–, Willie). Born on October 26, 1974, Horton is the convicted murderer who inadvertently assisted in the 1988 Presidential election of George H. W. Bush. Horton was convicted of robbing and murdering a gas station attendant in Massachusetts in 1974 and was sentenced to life without parole. In June of 1986, he was released on a Massachusetts weekend furlough program, and he did not return. In April of 1987, he brutally raped a woman after beating, stabbing, and tying up her fiancée in Maryland; he was caught in October and sentenced for two additional life terms for assault and rape in Maryland. Massachusetts Governor George Dukakis, the 1988 democratic Presidential nominee, supported the furlough program for rehabilitation and vetoed a bill that would have stopped furloughs for first-degree murderers in Massachusetts. The Horton story gained national attention in various media outlets, including Bush campaign adds, and is believed to be the incident that tipped public support from Dukakis to Bush, leading to the 1988 Bush victory. As of 2010, Horton remains incarcerated in the maximum security prison in Jessup, Maryland.

hostage. A person held as a pledge that certain terms or agreements will be kept. The taking of hostages is forbidden under the Geneva Convention of 1949.

hostage-taking. *See* terrorism

hot pursuit. A principle of international law justifying pursuit and arrest of vessels that have infringed the laws of a state, provided such pursuit begins within the territorial waters of the offended state and is continued without interruption. The right of pursuit ceases when the vessel reaches the territorial waters of another state.

hours of work. A major concern of labor as far back as 1840, when efforts were made to limit the number of hours that women and children could be allowed to work. In the early 1890s, wage earners averaged from 54 to 60 hours a week, and it took a quarter-century to enact child labor laws. In the early 1930s, state governments began to enact protective labor legislation in regard to working hours, and in 1938 Congress passed the Fair Labor Standards Act that established the 40-hour work week. From this emerged the concept of overtime pay. Many law enforcement agencies have adopted 10-hour, four-day (10 plan) work schedules. The 12-hour plan (a three-day work week) is gaining acceptance, while others maintain the five-day, eight-hour format or some variation. All work hour models may be either fixed or featuring rotating or overlapping shifts.

house arrest. Monitored restriction to one's residence. St. Paul the Apostle was placed under house arrest, as was Galileo in the 1600s, and, in 1917, the last czar of Russia, Nicholas II, and his family. In contemporary America, it was first used in Wisconsin in 1913 but did not receive much national support until the 1950s. House arrest is generally used for juvenile offenders and minor, first-time offenders. It is often accompanied by additional terms of supervision, including probation, electronic monitoring, and GPS tracking.

housebreaking. Breaking open and entering a house with felonious intent

Household Survey. *See* National Survey on Drug Abuse

house of correction. English institution established in the sixteenth century for vagabonds, prostitutes, rogues, and the unemployed. In the United States, it is a place of confinement for short-term offenders whose violations of the law are of a minor nature.

House Un-American Activities Committee (HUAC). A subcommittee of the United

States House of Representatives formed in 1938 to investigate persons and organizations believed to be a threats to national security. Targets of this committee included persons and organizations associated with Germans (especially after World War I), communists (especially after World War II), Nazis (World War II), Japanese-Americans (World War II), Klu Klux Klan, and trade unions. In the late 1940s, several Hollywood figures (including actors, directors, writers, etc.) were targeted by this committee due to alleged communist ideas, leading to the blacklisting of more than 300 Americans employed in the entertainment industry. Precursor committees include the Overman Committee (1918), the Fish Committee (1930), and the Special Committee on Un-American Activities (1934–1938). The House Un-American Activities Committee was ad hoc between 1938–1944, and was transformed into an ongoing House subcommittee from 1945–1969. It was renamed the House Committee on Internal Security from 1969 until it was abolished in 1975. *See also* Blacklist; Hiss, Alger

Huberty, James Oliver. An unemployed security guard, who on July 18, 1984, at a McDonald's fast-food establishment located in San Ysidro, CA, shot and killed 21 persons. The oldest victim was 74 years of age; the youngest eight months. Huberty was killed by a SWAT sharpshooter on the post office roof 113 feet away. *See also* Hennard, George, Jr.

hue. To sound an alarm by shouting. Colonial citizens would chase a criminal with shouts and cries.

huffing. Colloquial term used to describe the inhalation of gasses, aerosols, drugs, certain school supplies (white-out, permanent markers, etc.) and chemicals to achieve an intoxicating effect. Often, people who engage in this practice tend to be juveniles, incarcerated persons, and those with limited access to other forms of illicit drugs commonly used for recreational purposes. This method of intoxication can lead to hypoxia (lack of oxygen), cardiac failure, central nervous system damage and death. The National Institute on Drug Abuse estimates 2 million Americans age 12 and older had abused inhalants in 2008. *See also* inhalants

Human Growth Hormone (HGH). A protein based, poly-peptide hormone produced by the pituitary gland that stimulates cell growth and reproduction. *See also* anabolic steroid

human relations. An understanding of why people act in a certain manner, how they get along together in a group setting, and the characteristics of persons and groups. *See also* community relations; Hawthorne studies

hung jury. A jury that, after long deliberation, is so irreconcilably divided in opinion that it is unable to reach any verdict. A hung jury can lead to the termination of a trial before verdict and judgment when the court is satisfied that the jury is unlikely to agree upon a verdict within any reasonable period of time. Termination of a trial because of a hung jury usually results in retrial on the original charges but is occasionally followed by a dismissal of the charges.

hydrodynamics of blood drops and splashes. The patterns, shapes, and sizes of blood drops and splashes produced by factors such as distance of fall and direction and speed of the body from which they emanated.

hydroplaning. A condition in which the tire tread of a moving vehicle loses contact with the road surface, and thus loses traction, due to a film of water on the road surface.

hydrostatic shock. Injury caused by the hydraulic effects of sudden impact (such as with a bullet) to fluid filled tissue. This bodily shock wave, which travels close to the speed of sound, is created when fluid-filled body tissue is suddenly displaced by a bullet or other projectile. Research documents the risk of death or injury stemming from hydrostatic shock in gunshot victims. A bullet can create a hydrostatic wave in the body, much like ripples in a pond, sending the force of the impact to the neurological system and causing, for example, brain hemorrhaging, spinal injury, damage to heart, lungs and other organs.

hypothecation. A right that creditors have to the property of their debtors, through which they can have the property sold. In general terms, hypothecation means simply to place something of value in "hock."

hypothesis. A stated belief or theory, often one that can be tested; a predictive statement about the real world. For example, one might hypothesize that mean family incomes are different in Los Angeles and in Atlanta. Statistical inference can be used to test such a hypothesis to determine whether any observed difference is reasonably attributable to chance. The testing procedure begins with a null hypothesis and an alternative hypothesis. For example, the null hypothesis is that the true mean incomes are equal, and the alternative is that they are not equal. When we reject the null hypothesis, we accept the alternative.

hypothetical question. A form of question, put to expert witnesses after their competency has been established, containing a recital of facts assumed to have been proved, or proof of which is offered in the case, and requiring the opinion of the witness.

hysteria. Once a psychological condition, diagnosed exclusively in women, marked by symptoms ranging from nervous instability to fits of causeless crying and laughing. In modern times, it is a colloquial expression used to describe overwhelming feeling of intense emotion, such as fear or desperation; sometimes also used to described uncontrollable laughter or extremely humorous events.

I

iatregenic illness. An adverse mental or physical condition caused by the effects of treatment by a physician or surgeon. The term implies that it could have been avoided by judicious care on the part of the physician.

IED. *See* Improvised Explosive Device

ICE. *See* U.S. Immigration and Customs Enforcement

Ice. A crystallized form of methamphetamine that is smoked, with effects lasting up to 24 hours.

identification. A photograph showing the head and shoulders, both front and side views, of a person.

identification number. The number assigned to a person whose fingerprints are on file in an identification bureau of a police agency. The record of this person, showing all arrests, convictions, and dispositions of cases, is shown under this number.

identification order. The official wanted notice of the FBI, issued for persons wanted for crime violation. Each is numbered (in sequence), dated, and has the following information: the criminal charge, name, and aliases of the subject; subject's fingerprints; description and photograph; criminal record, information of caution concerning the subject; and request that the FBI be notified of any information concerning the subject. These notices are widely distributed to law enforcement agencies, post offices, and government agencies having frequent contact with the public.

identification record. Criminal record. The record of an individual, as maintained in the identification bureau of a law enforcement agency, which generally contains the person's fingerprints. The record also details the arrests, convictions, and dispositions of the individual.

identify. (1) To recognize a person or thing as being the same as a particular person or thing. (2) In the area of physical evidence, to place markings on evidence or place it in marked containers so it can be positively recognized at a later time.

Identi-Kit. A concept invented by a former Los Angeles law enforcement officer, this early Identi-Kit was a device consists of 536 photographic transparencies, enabling investigators to assemble a human face from overlaid combinations of facial features (eyes, beards, hairline, lips, moustache, glasses, etc.). The components are on easy-to-assemble 4 × 5-inch film. In modern times, Identi-Kit uses facial composite software to create photo realistic facial composite sketches.

identity theft. The act of obtaining the personal information of another, without their knowledge or consent, for the purpose of committing fraud or other crimes. Identity theft can include the acquisition and use of a person's identification and financial information to open bank accounts and credit cards in that person's name and make fraudulent purchases using the person's credit. The number of identity theft cases has skyrocketed in recent years, with reported cases rising from 86,000 in 2001 to over 700,000 in 2009. Several states have revised laws such that the statute of limitations for identity theft begins when the crime is uncovered, rather than when the crime occurred, as many cases are not discovered for months or years after they occur.

I except. Phrase used in court to register an objection to a ruling, so that the record may show that the exceptor is dissatisfied with the ruling and probably intends to appeal.

ignorance or mistake of fact, common law. In common law, ignorance or mistake of fact, as a rule, exempts a person from criminal liability, if the act done would be lawful were the facts as the actor believes, provided that the ignorance or mistake is not voluntary or due to negligence.

ignorance or mistake of fact, statutory offenses. Where an offense is defined by statute, whether or not ignorance or mistake of fact exempts a person doing a prohibited act from liability, as at common law, depends upon the language and construction of the statute. Unless the intention is clearly expressed, it must be determined by a construction of the statute, in view of the nature of the offense and the evils to be remedied, and of other matters making the one

construction or the other reasonable, whether it was the intention to make knowledge of the facts an essential element of the offense.

ignorance of the law is no excuse. The principle, probably originating in Roman law, that a wrongdoer is not freed from criminal responsibility because of lack of awareness that the act was in violation of the law.

illegal detention. The unlawful detention of a person when there is not sufficient cause to believe the person has committed a crime for which he or she could be arrested. Under such conditions courts have ruled that a confession, even though given voluntarily, is not admissible in evidence.

Illinois plan. *See* bail

immediate family member. Spouse, parent, brother or sister, child, or person to whom the person stands *in loco parentis;* or any other person living in the household and related by blood or marriage.

Immigration and Naturalization Service. *See* United States Citizenship and Immigration Service

immigration laws. Certain groups of persons, such felons, contract laborers, and others, are excluded by the immigration laws from entrance to the United States. Aliens who enter illegally and are apprehended are immediately returned to the country from which they came at the expense of the carrier that brought them. Aliens may be deported at any time upon proof of their advocating the destruction of property or overthrow of the government or if they (a) are convicted of a crime and sentenced to prison for moral turpitude; (b) become public charges because of some cause that antedates their entrance into the United States; or (c) are found to be connected with illegal traffic in women and children. When there is reason to believe that an individual has gained illegal entry into the United States, it is the duty of a local police officer to refer the facts to the U.S. immigration officers. When a case is accepted by the federal authorities, the responsibility of the police department ceases. If there happens to be a coincidence of violation of federal and state law, the merits of the case are considered by both local and federal officials to determine in whose jurisdiction action shall be instituted. The Immigration Reform Control Act of 1986 stated that any illegal immigrants who could prove they worked and lived in the United States prior to January 1, 1982, could apply for amnesty. In 2002 the U.S. government allowed about 1 million immigrants into the country. The U.S. Citizenship and Immigration Service provides information on laws, regulations and interpretations controlling immigration in the United States. *See also* U.S. Citizenship and Immigration Service; U.S. Department of Homeland Security; U.S. Immigration and Customs Enforcement

immunity. (1) Exemption of a person from a duty, obligation, service, or penalty (as presidential or diplomatic immunity from judicial process) that is imposed by law on all others not similarly situated. (2) Exemption from prosecution, which is sometimes promised by a prosecutor to a person accused of crime who agrees to "turn state's evidence," or testify again codefendants on behalf of the prosecution.

Immunity Act. A 1954 measure that forces witnesses appearing in national security cases to testify by granting them immunity from prosecution for self-incriminatory testimony. If granted immunity, witnesses must testify or face jail terms. Introduced at the height of the communist scare, the bill was aimed at witnesses who refused to testify under the provisions of the Fifth Amendment. The law allows either the House or the Senate, by majority vote, to grant immunity in national security cases if an order has first been obtained from a U.S. district court judge. The attorney general must be notified in advance and given the chance to present any objections he or she might have. Congressional committees, by a two-thirds vote, may also grant immunity, as may U.S. district courts to witnesses coming before either them or grand juries.

immunity bath. The exemption from prosecution of an excessive number of accused persons or principal defendants; the term originated in 1906 when 16 defendants, alleged to have been implicated in a beef trust, were exempted from prosecution because they had aided the government in obtaining evidence against other defendants.

impanel. The process of selecting the jury that is to try a case.

impeach. (1) To accuse, to discredit, or to censure. (2) To remove a public official from office, for reasons of misconduct or illegal activity, by prescribed methods. *See also* impeachment

impeaching credit of witness. The credit of a witness may be impeached either by the adverse party or by the evidence of persons from his or her own community who will swear (a) that they know the general reputation of the witness for truth and veracity; (b) that this reputation is bad; and (c) that they would not believe him or her on oath. In some states, the inquiry may be about the witness's general moral character. In most states, impeaching witnesses may be asked whether they would believe the other witness on oath; but in a few states this question cannot be asked. In all states, the inquiry is confined to general reputation, and specific acts by the witness sought to be impeached cannot be shown. The impeaching witness may be cross-examined and may also be impeached in the manner stated above. Impeaching witnesses cannot, in their examination in chief, give reasons for their belief; but they may be asked their reasons on cross-examination. The party introducing such witnesses cannot thus impeach them, unless they have testified adversely to the party calling them and the party had reason to expect favorable testimony, but a party is not precluded by the testimony of a witness introduced by the former from introducing other witnesses who will testify to the contrary.

impeachment. As authorized by Article I of the Constitution, impeachment is action by the House and Senate to remove the President, Vice President, or civil officer of the United Sates from office for crimes of "treason, bribery, or other high crimes and misdemeanors." Alexander Hamilton defined impeachment as a "method of national inquest into the conduct of public men." The procedure dates from fourteenth-century England and was adopted by the colonial government. Impeachment proceedings are initiated in the House of Representatives; if impeachment is approved by the House, the Senate tries the case. If the Senate convicts, the penalty is removal from office and disqualification from holding further office. There is no appeal. Impeachment proceedings have been initiated 51 times in the House, but only 13 cases have reached the Senate. Of these 13 cases, four ended in impeachment, seven in acquittal, and two in dismissal. Nine of these cases involved federal judges, who hold lifetime appointments to the bench and can be removed only by impeachment. Charges have ranged from loose morals and insanity to tyranny and advocating secession. The highest-ranking officials to be impeached by the House were Supreme Court Justice Samuel Chase—in 1805 for harsh and partisan conduct on the bench—President Andrew Johnson—in 1868 for violation of the Tenure of Office Act, and President Bill Clinton—in 1998 for loose morals and alleged perjury. All three, however, were acquitted by the Senate.

impersonating an officer. Pretending to be a peace officer, an officer of the armed services, or an official of a federal, state, or local law enforcement agency, usually by wearing a uniform, displaying an identification card or badge, or falsely identifying oneself as an officer.

importation model. A penology theory based on the concept that inmate subculture arises jointly from internal prison experiences and from external patterns of behavior that the offenders bring to prison.

imprisonment. A sentence imposed upon the conviction of a crime; the deprivation of liberty in a penal institution.

imprisonment for debt. Detention on civil process for debt. Formerly a universal practice. Since 1823, when Kentucky abolished it, prohibited or restricted by state constitutional provisions. Where it exists, it is usually applied for criminal misconduct related to debt, such as against absconding debtors, those who willfully fail to comply with an order of child support, or those who have deliberately entered into a contract without the means of fulfilling their obligations.

Improvised Explosive Device (IED). Improvised explosive devices are homemade or makeshift bombs, which are constructed and/or deployed in an unconventional way. Such devices can be assembled with conventional explosives or spare munitions, and they are often used in guerilla warfare.

impulse. Tendency to act without voluntary direction or reflection; a tendency to act that does not appear to be traceable to stimulation.

impunity. Exemption from punishment or penalty.

inadmissible. Not proper to be admitted; not allowed.

inalienable rights. Rights that inhere in a person and are incapable of being transferred. Such rights have been claimed under natural law.

in articulo mortis (Lat., lit.). At the point of death.

in camera (Lat., lit, in a room). A case heard when the doors of the court are closed and only persons concerned in the case are admitted; generally applies in highly confidential or delicate evidenciary matters.

incapable. Legally unable to do something. By law certain persons are considered incapable of violating the criminal law. Among these are children under certain ages, persons with developmental disabilities or certain forms of mental illness, and those who act through mistake of fact or in ignorance.

incapacitate. In general, to deprive an individual of ability, qualification, or strength; in criminal justice the term often means to deprive an offender of freedom and/or legal power, such as through imprisonment.

incapacitation. One of the four purposes of punishment; depriving an offender of the ability or opportunity to commit further crimes, often by incarceration. *See also* punishment, purposes of; deterrence rehabilitation; retribution

incarceration. Confinement or imprisonment in a penal institution.

incendiary. Tending to cause fire; in law, a person guilty of the crime of arson, or the burning of a building.

incest. Sexual intercourse, either with or without marriage, between persons too nearly related by blood to be entitled to marry. In Uniform Crime Reports, incest is included either by name in sex offenses or as "marriage within prohibited degrees."

Incest Anonymous. Either of two support groups for victims of incest. Survivors of Incest Anonymous, Address: World Service Office P.O. Box 190 Benson, MD 21028-9998. Web: http://incestanonymous.org/.

inchoate offense. Also called anticipatory offense, a violation consisting of an action or conduct that is a step toward the intended commission of another offense. *See also* attempt to commit a crime; conspiracy

incidence of crime. Criminality measured in a given population over a definite time span, as during a single day, month, or year. *See also* crime clock

incite. To impel another to particular action; to urge onward, to instigate. In criminal law, to persuade or move another to commit a crime.

included offense, lesser. An offense that is made up of elements that are a subset of the elements of another offense having a greater statutory penalty, and the occurrence of which is established by the same evidence or by some portion of the evidence that has been offered to establish the occurrence of the greater offense.

incompetent evidence. Evidence that is not admissible under the established rules of evidence; evidence that the law does not permit to be presented at all, or in relation to a particular matter, due to lack of authenticity or to some defect in the witness, the document, or the nature of the evidence itself.

incompetent to stand trial. The finding by a court that a defendant is mentally incapable of understanding the nature of the charges and proceedings against him or her, of consulting with an attorney, and of aiding in his or her own defense.

incorrigibility. The unmanageable or uncontrollable behavior of a child or minor, which is generally classified as an act constituting juvenile delinquency; such behavior hence demands that the child be made a ward of the juvenile court; see also status offense.

incriminate. To reflect guilt; to impute guilt or violation of the law; to imply illegal activity or guilt; tend to show guilt; to charge with a crime or a fault.

incrimination. The disclosure of facts that render one liable to criminal prosecution. An accused person cannot be compelled to be a witness against him- or herself in criminal cases, but the accused may waive the privilege and take the stand voluntarily. Witnesses are immune from being required to incriminate themselves in any proceeding, including a congressional investigation, but they may not withhold facts that merely impair their reputations, not even incriminating facts if they have been promised immunity from prosecution under the law. *See also* Immunity Act; search and seizure, unreasonable

inculpate. To imply guilt or wrongdoing; to accuse of crime; to involve in illegal or wrongful activity.

inculpatory. In the law of evidence, facts or opinions showing involvement in criminal activity; tending to establish, indicating, or reflecting guilt; incriminating.

inculpatory evidence. Evidence without which a particular fact cannot be proved.

incumbrance. A claim, lien, or liability attached to a piece of property.

indecent exposure. Unlawful intentional, knowing, or reckless exposing to view of the genitals or anus, or a woman's breasts, in a place where another person may be present who is likely to be offended or alarmed by such an act. Some states specify that the act must be performed in a "lewd or lascivious manner." *See also* exhibitionism

indefinite sentence. A system, not used in the United States, in which a person is sentenced without minimum or maximum limitations, with the length of time in prison determined by his or her behavior and other factors. *See also* indeterminate sentence

in delicto (Lat.). At fault.

indemnification. Compensation for loss or damage sustained because of improper or illegal action by a public authority.

indeterminate sentence. A type of sentence to imprisonment in which the commitment, instead of being for a specified single time, such as three years, is for a range of time, such as two to five years or five years maximum and zero minimum. Release is determined by a discretionary body, such as a parole board, which evaluates the inmate's behavior in prison, efforts at rehabilitation, and other factors. *See* also determinate sentence.

Index Crimes. Those crimes used by the FBI to measure the incidence of crime in the United States. The statistics appear in the Uniform Crime Reports.

Index Offenses. The eight types of Part I offenses reported by the FBI in the annual Uniform Crime Reports: homicide, robbery, forcible rape, aggravated assault, burglary, larceny/theft, motor vehicle theft, and arson.

indictment. A formal, written accusation submitted to the court by a grand jury, alleging that a specified person(s) has committed a specified offense(s), usually a felony. Since to indict means to accuse, indictment is sometimes used to mean any accusation

of wrongdoing. *See also* charging document; filing; information; presentment

indigent. Poor; destitute; unable to afford legal counsel.

indirect evidence. Evidence that does not actually prove the facts but from which they may be presumed or inferred. *See also* circumstantial evidence

individualized treatment. A philosophy of corrections stating that each individual is different in the causes of his or her criminality and in the particular manifestation thereof; consequently, corrections should look at the individual's unique cluster of traits and devise a treatment program based on needs and deficiencies. *See also* criminogenic needs

industrial espionage. *See* espionage, industrial

industrial school. Reform school; institution for delinquent or neglected youth. Industrial schools were established in the United Kingdom in 1866 and spread to other European countries.

Industrial Security Organization. *See* American Society for Industrial Security

inebriate. (1) To make one drunk; to intoxicate. (2) One who is often drunk.

inevitable discovery. Legal doctrine that holds that certain evidence that would generally be excluded under the exclusionary rule can be admitted as evidence, if such evidence is likely to have been discovered during routine investigation. Principle was established in *Nix v. Williams,* 467 U. S. 431 (1984)

in extremis (Lat.). At the point of death.

in facto (Lat.). In fact; in deed.

infamous crime. Crime punishable by imprisonment in a state penitentiary.

infamous punishment. Punishment by imprisonment or imprisonment at hard labor, particularly if in a penitentiary or state prison; sometimes, imprisonment at hard labor regardless of the location or type of facility.

infancy. In criminal law, the case where the accused has not arrived at such an age as to be able to distinguish between right and wrong, usually between age 7–12.

infanticide. Murder of an infant immediately after its birth. *See also* safe surrender law

infantophilia. Also called nephiophilia, a paraphilia indicating a sexual interest in very young children, primarily toddlers and infants aged 0–3 years old. *See also* pedophilia

inference. A method of reaching a conclusion based on applying known facts to estimate an unknowable fact, such as estimating total population based on experimental or sample numbers. To estimate total nonreported incidents of burglary of nonwhite families in Denver, for example, researchers could select a sample of a few such families and infer the mean for the total population from the sample mean. Polling every family in Denver to arrive at a true number would be impractical, even if it were possible.

inferential statistics. The techniques used to state the probability that any obtained sample statistic varies from some hypothesized population parameter by some specified amount, and to make estimates about the numerical value of a population parameter, given an obtained sample statistic but with a specifiable degree of confidence. The former branch of inferential statistics is called hypothesis testing and the latter, estimation. *See also* descriptive statistics

inferiority complex. A term coined by Austrian psychiatrist Alfred Adler (1870–1937) to describe an individual's (generally unconscious) sense that he or she is not equal in competence to other people and is inadequate to meet the demands of the environment. Psychologically, an individual might attempt to compensate for feelings of inferiority by concealing them through feats of courage and achievement. In extreme cases, efforts to compensate may result in aggressive or antisocial behavior.

infibulation. Torture of the genitals.

in flagrante delicto (Lat.). During the commission of a crime; colloquially, caught in the act.

influence. An exercise of power in which one person convinces another to behave in accordance with the first one's preferences.

informant. (1) A person, who, wittingly or unwittingly, provides information to an agent, a clandestine service, or the police. (2) In crime reporting, a person who has provided specific information and is cited as a source.

in forma pauperis. (Lat., lit. "In the form of a pauper") or as a poor person. Under U.S. law, an indigent or person with insufficient means can bring legal action without paying required fees for counsel, writs, transcripts, subpoenas, and the like.

information. (1) A formal, written accusation submitted to the court by a prosecutor, alleging that a specified person(s) has committed a specified offense(s). (2) Intelligence, or unevaluated material of every description, including that derived from observations, reports, rumors, imagery, and other sources which, when processed, may produce intelligence.

information highway. A term coined by Vice President Al Gore, the information highway, the Internet, an electronic communications network that easily connects all users to one another and provides every type of electronic service possible, including shopping, banking, education, medical diagnosis, video conferencing, and game playing.

infraction. (1) A violation of state statute or local ordinance punishable by a fine or other penalty but not by incarceration, unless it is a specified, unusually limited term. (2) In corrections, a statutory offense or a violation of prison or jail administrative regulations committed by an offender while incarcerated or in a temporary-release program such as work release or furlough.

infrared light. A light having a wavelength greater than the visible red. It is in the region of 8,000 to 9,000 angstroms, and is used to read writings that have been erased or obliterated and those that are not visible to the naked eye because of a dark background. It is at the opposite end of the spectrum from ultraviolet light.

infrared (IR) motion detector. A sensor that detects changes in the infrared light radiation from parts of a protected area. Presence of an intruder in the area changes the infrared light intensity from that direction.

Infrared Spectrometry. Used for the identification of controlled substances. This technique involves passing infrared radiation ("light") through the unknown sample, which absorb the infrared radiation in a series of valleys and peaks called an *infrared spectrum*. Each compound gives a highly specific infrared spectrum comparison of unknown samples to known standards enables identification of unknown compounds in criminalistics.

inhalants. Chemicals whose vapors cause an intoxicating effect when they are inhaled, acting as central nervous system depressants. Such household products as varnish, paint thinner, and model airplane glue are sources; as are fuels such as gasoline, kerosene, and lighter fluid; along with such chemical gases as nitrous oxide, Freon, and butane. Boys aged 12 to 15 are the most common users. *See also* huffing

initial appearance. The first appearance of an accused person in the first court having jurisdiction over his or her case.

injunction. An order issued by a court of equity commanding a person (a) to do an act or (b) to refrain from doing an act that would injure another by violating his or her personal or property rights. A mandatory injunction commands the specific performance of an act; a preventive injunction orders a person to desist from an act already commenced or contemplated; a preliminary or interlocutory injunction may be issued when a danger is immediately threatened and there is inadequate opportunity for a court to determine finally the rights of the parties; and a permanent injunction is the final decree of the court. The violation of an injunction is a contempt of court and may be punished by fine or imprisonment.

in loco parentis. (Lat., lit. "In the place of a parent").

inmate. One who is confined in a correctional facility.

Innocence Project, The. Founded in 1992 by Barry C. Scheck and Peter J. Neufeld at the Benjamin N. Cardozo School of Law, the Innocence Project is a national organization dedicated to exonerating wrongfully convicted persons. The organization assists prisoners who could be proven innocent through DNA testing. According to the organization's Web site, they have achieved exonerations for 258 people in the United States since 1992, including 17 persons under sentence of death for crimes they did not commit. Address: Innocence Project, 100 Fifth Avenue, 3rd Floor, New York, NY 10011, Web: http://www.innocenceproject.org/.

inquest. A legal inquiry to establish some question of fact; specifically, an inquiry by a coroner and jury into a person's death where accident, foul play, or violence is suspected as the cause.

inquisitorial system. The system of criminal prosecution prevailing in most of continental Europe, Japan, and other countries, in contrast to the English and American adversary system. In the inquisitorial system, a judicial officer has the responsibility to investigate and examine. Adjudication is not limited to the facts given in proof by the parties. *See also* adversary system

in re (Lat.). In the matter of, concerning; used to label a judicial proceeding in which there are no adversaries.

In re Gault. A Supreme Court case (387 U.S. 1967) concerning the basic right of children to be assured of fair treatment in juvenile courts. A 15-year-old, Gault had been sentenced by a juvenile court to up to six years' imprisonment for making lewd and indecent remarks on the telephone. When committed by an adult, this offense usually carried a maximum sentence of two months. Gault was taken into custody from his home, no notice or other advice of his arrest was left for his working parents, and the many other elements of due process granted to adults were not observed—a typical incident in juvenile courts at the time. In the opinion of the Court, a juvenile court must adhere to the due process requirements of notice, advice of the right to counsel, advice of the right to remain silent and avoid self-incrimination, offer of the right to confront accusers, and proper procurement of confessions.

in rem (Lat.). Against a thing; a legal proceeding instituted to obtain decrees or judgments against property.

insanity. Antiquated or colloquial term used to reference mental illness which impairs one's ability to appreciate or conform to societal norms. The term mental illness is preferred in modern usage, although the term *insanity* is used in criminal justice in reference to legal defenses that mitigate or excuse criminal malfeasance. *See also* insanity defense, mental illness

insanity defense. In the United States, insanity defense is an affirmative defense (the accused admits the act) but relies upon insanity status to mitigate or excuse criminal liability. While criteria and provisions vary by statue, types of insanity defenses used in the United States include (*See also*): M'Naghten Rule; irresistible impulse; Durham rule; American Law Institute Model; Brawner rule; substantial capacity test; and temporary insanity. *See also* Insanity Defense Reform Act of 1984 (U.S.); Table 25. Types of Insanity Defense in the United States, page 232

Insanity Defense Reform Act of 1984. Federal law under which it is an affirmative defense to a prosecution under any other federal statute that, at the time of the commission the acts constituting the offense, the defendant, as a result of a severe mental disease or defect, was unable to appreciate the nature and quality of the wrongfulness of his or her acts. Mental disease or defect does not otherwise constitute a defense. The defendant has the burden proving the defense of insanity by clear and convincing evidence.

insanity plea. An admission of guilt with the contention that the commission of the crime is not culpable in the eyes of the court because of the insanity of the defendant at the time he or she committed the act. More typically, dual plea of not guilty and not guilty by reason of insanity is entered, which implies, "The burden is on the government to prove I did the act upon which the charge is based, and, even if the government proves that at trial, I still claim that I am not culpable because I was legally insane at the time." One of the most famous insanity pleadings was entered by John W. Hinckley, Jr., when he was tried for the assassination attempt on President Ronald Reagan in 1981. *See also* Insanity Defense Reform Act of 1984

inspectional services. Historically, the specialized bureau in a traditionally organized police department responsible for internal affairs, field inspections, supervision of the morals division, and intelligence-gathering activities. In modern day, the term *inspectional services* is generally used in reference to building code and fire regulation inspections, often performed by building code inspectors or fire department officials.

instanter. Immediately; forthwith; without delay. Courts issue subpoenas or other orders specifying that they are returnable instanter, meaning the person upon whom papers are served should perform, as ordered, immediately.

Institute for Criminal Justice Ethics. A nonprofit, university-based center established to foster greater concern for ethical issues among practitioners and scholars in the criminal justice field. Address: The Institute for Criminal Justice Ethics, John Jay

text continues on page 234

TABLE 25 TYPES OF INSANITY DEFENSE IN THE UNITED STATES

Insanity Defense	Definition	Creation	How it Mitigates	Jurisdictions
American Law Institute Model	"A person is not responsible for criminal conduct if at the time of such conduct as a result of mental disease or defect he lacks substantial capacity either to appreciate the criminality of his conduct or to conform his conduct to the requirements of the law."	Model Penal Code in 1962	Asks whether or not defendants have the capacity to appreciate the criminality of their actions.	Still used by 18 separate states.
Brawner Rule	The presence of a mental disease or defect (specifically excluding personality disorders and diminished capacity conditions) and where either: (1) a substantial capacity to appreciate the wrongfulness of the act exists; or (2) an inability to conform or control one's behavior to the requirements of the law exists.	*United States v. Brawner* (1972)	Defendants must know what they did was wrong and be able to conform to the law in order to be deemed sane.	Superseded in 1984 by Congressional act.
Durham/ New Hampshire Test	Defendant is entitled to acquittal if his/her mental illness was the cause of the crime.	*Durham v. United States* (1954)	Provides lenient standard for insanity defense.	Was used in District of Columbia.
Irresistible Impulse	A test applied in a criminal prosecution to determine whether a person accused of a crime was compelled by a mental disease to commit it and therefore cannot be held criminally responsible for her or his actions	*Parsons v. State* (1887), Supreme Court of Alabama	Allows for recognizing of cognitive impairment among the accused.	Abolished by Insanity Defense Reform Act of 1984.
M'Naghten Rule	Available if, at the time of the offense, the accused was insane, had a disease of the mind such that he was unable to know that his act was wrong.	M'Naghten thought Peel wanted to be killed in 1843.	Allows for insanity defense if the defendant did not realize the act was wrong.	As of 1998 a version of this was still used in 25 states.

(continued)

Insanity Defense	Definition	Creation	How it Mitigates	Jurisdictions
Substantial Capacity Test	Allows for acquittal if crime was committed by reason of mental defect or disease.	Established by American Law Institute.	Person must know what he/she is doing is wrong.	Partially used in several jurisdictions.
Temporary Insanity	"A defense asserted by an accused in a criminal prosecution to avoid liability for the commission of a crime because, at the time of the crime, the person did not appreciate the nature or quality or wrongfulness of the acts."	First used by Congressman Daniel Sickles in 1859.	A sane person can be temporarily insane, and this can be the reason for acquittal.	Several jurisdictions throughout the country have some form of temporary insanity.
Insanity Defense Reform Act of 1984	Toughened standards for having a successful defense by reason of insanity.	Came about following the acquittal of John Hinckley following his assassination attempt of President Ronald Reagan.	1. Burden of proof on the defendant to establish the defense by clear and convincing evidence; 2. Limited the scope of expert testimony; 3. Eliminated diminished capacity; 4. Created a special verdict of "not guilty by reason of insanity," which triggers a commitment proceeding; and 5. Provided federal commitment of persons who become insane after having been found guilty or while serving a federal prison sentence.	Used as the standard in all federal cases.

*** Most jurisdictions use a combination of the established rules for defense by reason of insanity.

Compiled by Richard Porter, CSULB.

College of Criminal Justice, 555 West 57th Street, Suite 607, New York, NY 10019-1029. Web: http://www.lib.jjay.cuny.edu/cje/html/institute.html.

Institute for Court Management. Founded in 1971 and cosponsored by the National Center for State Courts, the American Bar Association, the American Judicature Society, and the Institute of Judicial Administration. Lists two major objectives: (a) Education: training and certification of court administrators, continuing education for certified court administrators, and short-term institutes on court management subjects for judges, clerks, court administrator staff, court planners, probationers, and related personnel; (b) Research: extensive and short-term studies of courts and related justice system agencies. Publishes the *Justice System Journal* 3/year. Address: 300 Newport Avenue, Willamsburg, VA 23187-8798. Phone: (800) 616-6164. Web: http://www.ncsconline.org/D_ICM/icmindex.html.

Institute of Governmental Studies Library. Founded in 1920 by the University of California at Berkeley, the aim of the library is to collect materials concerning all aspects of criminal justice. These materials are then made available to university students, faculty, research staff, and other professionals in the field through interlibrary loan. Publishes *Public Affairs Report* monthly. Address: 109 Moses Hall, #2370, University of California, Berkeley, CA 94720. Phone: (510) 642-1474. Web: http://www.igs.berkeley.edu/library/.

Institute of Judicial Administration. Founded in 1952 by the New York University School of Law, the institute counts among its major objectives the abilities to promote court modernization; conduct studies of structure, operation, and manpower of courts; provide education programs for appellate and trial judges and court administrators; coordinate efforts of bar associations and judicial councils; and publish results of research in the field of judicial administration. Publishes *IJA Report* (quarterly newsletter). Address:

40 Washington Square South, New York, NY 10012. Web: http://www.law.nyu.edu/centers/judicial/index.htm.

institutional capacity. The officially stated number of inmates that a confinement or residential facility is or was originally intended to house.

institutionalized personality. A nonclinical term that refers to an individual who has become so accustomed to existence in an institution that readjustment to life outside the institution is difficult.

insubordination. Defiance; resistance to authority; disobedience; willful failure to obey orders; open refusal to obey orders. Generally a basis of disciplinary action in a law enforcement agency.

insufficient evidence. Evidence that is not enough to constitute proof at the level required at a given point in the proceedings.

Insurance Crime Bureau, National (NICB). In January 1992 the insurance industry established the NICB to combat insurance abuse, especially automobile insurance fraud. The bureau consolidated the previous operations of the National Automobile Theft Bureau and the Insurance Crime Prevention Institute. Address: 1111 E. Touhy Ave., Ste. 400, Des Plaines, IL 60018. Phone: (800) 447-6282. Web: https://www.nicb.org//.

insurgency. A condition, which falls short of civil war, resulting from a revolt or insurrection against a constituted government.

insurrection. A rebellion or uprising of citizens or subjects in resistance to their government. It consists of any group resistance to the lawful authority of the state.

intake. The process by which a juvenile referral is received by personnel of a probation agency, juvenile court, or special intake unit; and a decision is made to close the case at intake, refer the juvenile to another agency, place him or her under some kind of care or supervision, or file a petition in a juvenile court.

Integrated Automated Fingerprint Identification System (IAFIS) is a national automated fingerprint identification and criminal history system maintained by the Federal Bureau of Investigation (FBI). IAFIS provides automated fingerprint search capabilities, latent searching capability, electronic image storage, and electronic exchange of fingerprints and responses. IAFIS maintains the largest biometric database in the world, containing the fingerprints and potential corresponding criminal history information for more than 55 million subjects.

Integrative Triple R Theory. Proposed by Gideon and Sung (2010), this theory focuses on rehabilitation, reentry, and rehabilitation.

intelligence. A function of law enforcement agencies concerned with the acquisition of information related to crime.

Intelligence Analysts, International Association of Law Enforcement. Founded in 1981, a nonprofit organization that promotes professionalism standards in law enforcement intelligence analysis. Address: PO Box 13857 Richmond, VA 23225.

Intelligence Association, National Military. Founded in 1974, a joint military intelligence professional association. Publishes *American Intelligence Journal* (quarterly) and a newsletter. Address: 256 Morris Creek Road Cullen, Virginia 23934. Phone: (434) 542-5929. Web: http://www.nmia.org/.

intelligence estimate. An appraisal of the elements of information about a specific situation or condition, with a view to determining the courses of action open to the other side or potential adversary and the probable order of their adoption.

Intelligence Officers, Association of Former. Founded in 1975. Publishes *INTELLIGENCER: Journal of U.S. Intelligence Studies* and *Periscope* (bimonthly newsletter). Address: 6723 Whittier Avenue, Suite 303A, McLean, VA 22101. Phone: (703) 790-0320. http://www.afio.com/.

Intensive case management (ICS). Type of probation or parole supervision that provides targeted programs for mentally ill offenders to help reduce recidivism.

Intensive supervision probation. A type of community corrections (generally probation) supervision that uses low offender-to-agent ratios, frequent contacts, and strict reporting requirements to ensure compliance to terms of supervision. ISP is generally used for high risk offenders, and research suggests ISP supervision results in high rates of technical violation.

intent. (1) The state of mind or attitude with which an act is carried out; the design, resolve, or determination with which a person acts to achieve a certain result. (2) Mere intent to commit a crime is not a criminal violation; an overt act must accompany or follow the intent. Most crimes require intent as an essential element; however, some do not have this requirement, particularly those that are less serious and do not involve moral turpitude. Some crimes, such as theft, require specific intent; others require only general intent; and in still others, constructive intent is sufficient. In cases of culpable negligence and in minor offenses such as traffic violations, no intent is required. *See also* intent, constructive

intent, constructive. Legal term for the situation in which a person intends to commit an illegal act and, in attempting to carry it out, injures someone. For example, if A intends to shoot and kill B but, in shooting at B, hits and kills C, the shooter by law is held to have intended to do what happened. Also called transfer of intent. *See also* intent

intent in cases of negligence. In crimes involving either neglect to observe proper care in performing an act or culpable failure to perform a duty, criminal intent is the state of mind that necessarily accompanies the negligent act or culpable omission. The question of criminal negligence most frequently arises in connection with manslaughter, nuisance, or escape.

intent, specific. There are certain crimes of which a specific intent to accomplish a particular purpose is an essential element and for which there can be no conviction upon proof of mere general malice or criminal intent. In these cases it is necessary for the state to prove the specific intent, either by direct or circumstantial evidence. *See also* intent, constructive; criminal intent

interactionist theory. A key sociological perspective in criminology that focuses on the way in which crime is generated by social control agencies as they attach stigmatizing labels to individual offenders, who often act out or live up to the criminal identity that flows from labels, and who subsequently devote themselves to criminal careers. *See also* labeling theory

inter alia (Lat.). Among other things.

interception of prisoners' mail. The constitutional guarantee of the right of privacy does not apply to the interception of a prisoner's mail by the jailer or warden, nor does it prohibit the turning over of such a letter to a prosecuting attorney, for use against the convict, by the warden who had a right to peruse the convict's mail.

interdict. To prevent or forbid.

interdiction. Prevention of movement through rigid enforcement. The U.S. Coast Guard, for example, interdicts drug trade.

interior ballistics. The science of the movement of projectiles within the bore of a gun, along with the combustion of powder, development of pressure, and other factors, to determine the effect of such factors as weight, size, shape, rifling, and others. Also called internal ballistics.

interlocutory. Temporary; not final. An interlocutory decree is a temporary court order pending the final determination of the case or matter.

interlocutory appeal. A request, made at some point before judgment in trial court proceedings, that a court having appellate jurisdiction review a prejudgment decision of the trial court before judgment is reached.

intermediate court. A court, known by various names, falling in a judicial hierarchy between the highest, or supreme, tribunal and the trial court. Its jurisdiction is usually appellate, but some states confer original jurisdiction in special cases such as election contests.

intermittent sentence. A sentence to periods of confinement interrupted by periods of freedom.

intern. (1) To shut up within a prescribed space. (2) A student of a certain profession working within that profession. Several colleges and universities offering criminal justice courses include internship in their respective programs.

Internal Revenue Service. Tax collector for the United States, endowed with discretionary powers in specific tax cases. A division of the Treasury Department, the IRS collects and deposits taxes, determines tax liability, certifies refunds, initially processes returns, investigates violations, and provides information to taxpayers. For a list of manuals and publications, contact IRS. Address: Department of the Treasury, 1111 Constitution Avenue, NW, Washington, DC 20224. http://www.irs.gov/.

International Association for Property and Evidence, Inc. Organization that conducts seminars and training. Located at 903 N. San Fernando Blvd., Suite 4, Burbank, CA 91504. Web: http://www.iape.org/.

International Association of Asian Crime Investigators (IAACI). Founded in 1987 by two Virginia police officers, James Badey of Arlington and Phil Hannum of Falls Church. Address: PO Box 1327, Marina, CA 93933; Web: http://www.iaaci.com/.

International Association of Chiefs of Police. Established in 1893, the association's objectives are to "advance the science and art of police service; to develop and disseminate improved administrative, technical, and operational practices and promote their use in police work; to foster police cooperation and the exchange of information and experience among police administrators throughout the world; to bring about recruitment and training of qualified persons; and to encourage adherence of all officers to high professional standards of performance and conduct." IACP has approximately 14,000 members representing 80 countries. Publishes *The Police Chief.* Address: 515 No. Washington St., Alexandria, VA 22314. Web: http://www.theiacp.org/.

International Association of Forensic Nursing. Established in 1993, this association aims "to provide leadership in forensic nursing practice by developing, promoting, and disseminating information internationally about forensic nursing science." Address: 1517 Ritchie Hwy, Ste 208, Arnold, MD 21012-2323; Web: http://www.iafn.org/.

International Brotherhood of Police Officers (IBPO). Organization founded in 1964 by officers in Rhode Island, combined with the National Association of Government Employees in 1969, and with the Service Employees International Union, an AFL-CIO affiliate, in 1982. It is the largest police union in the United States National headquarters is at 159 Burgin Parkway, Quincy, MA 02169, with fully staffed offices in other states. Web: http://www.ibpo.org/.

International Brotherhood of Teamsters. The largest labor union in the United States, the Teamsters represent small- to medium-sized police and sheriffs' departments in AK, CA, FL, IA, MA, MI, MN, NY, OK, SD, VA, and WI. Alleged ties between the Teamsters and organized crime, as well as internal corruption, led the AFL-CIO to expel the organization from its ranks in 1958. Address: International Brotherhood of Teamsters, Office of the General President, 25 Louisiana Avenue, N.W., Washington, DC 20001, Web: http://www.teamster.org/.

International City/County Management Association (ICMA). Founded in 1914,

ICMA limits its information services to municipal management officials or police executives. Technical assistance inquiries are limited to ICMA members. ICMA is a professional association of city/county managers. The criminal justice project of ICMA is aimed at increasing the expertise of municipal administrators when dealing with the law enforcement function. In 1938 the ICMA published *Municipal Police Administration,* the first in a series of volumes on police management. The book embodied the principles of administration critical to the reform movement of the era. It was later dubbed the Green Monster by officers using it to prepare for promotion examinations. Along with O. W. Wilson's *Police Administration,* published in 1950, the book is considered the classic police sourcebook. ICMA publishes *Target* (monthly newsletter, free upon request). Address: 777 North Capitol St. NE, Suite 500, Washington, DC 20002. Web: http://www.icma.org.

international code. A code adopted by many countries to facilitate sight communication between persons of different nations. The code uses some 26 flags, each standing for a letter of the Latin alphabet. They may be used in different combinations, each signifying a certain message, or used as letters to spell out a word or sentence. If flags are not used, the international Morse code is employed.

international cooperation. in criminal justice, this term refers to law enforcement agencies working and communicating together across language and time barriers to solve crime. It also includes extradition treaties and practices.

International Court of Justice. Successor to the League of Nations Permanent Court of Justice, established by the United Nations at the 1945 San Francisco Conference. Known now as the World Court, judicial organization of the United Nations (UN). The court's statute is a part of the UN charter, and all UN members are members of ICJ. Each member undertakes to abide by ICJ decisions in cases to which it is a party. The UN Security Council has the right to enforce decisions of the court. The court, seated at The Hague, has 15 judges, who are elected by absolute majorities in the General Assembly and the Security Council. The judges serve for nine-year periods. Nine judges form a quorum. Rulings are by majority vote and are final, without appeal. Only states can be parties in cases before the court, but a state can take up a case in which a national is involved. The court's jurisdiction includes all legal disputes that members refer to it and all matters provided for in the charter, treaties, and conventions. The court also gives advisory opinions to the General Assembly and the Security Council on request. Address: International Court of Justice, Peace Palace, Carnegieplein 2, 2517 KJ The Hague, The Netherlands. Web: http://www.icj-cij.org/.

International Criminal Police Organization. *See* Interpol

international extradition. By treaties between the United States and most foreign countries and by acts of Congress in accordance with the treaties, provision is made for the extradition of fugitives from justice in special cases. This is a matter in which the states cannot act. A person extradited for one crime cannot be tried for another. By weight of authority, a person can be tried and punished for a crime committed in this country, though he or she has been forcibly abducted from a foreign country. Some countries that do not have the death penalty refuse to extradite offenders back to the United States in cases where the state is seeking the death penalty.

International Guide to Missing Treasures (IGMT). A central index used by participating art dealers to record art thefts and disseminate reports and special bulletins to subscribers, legitimate art dealers, key persons in the art community, and law enforcement agencies.

international law. An inchoate body of rules, classified as laws of peace, war, or neutrality, that deal principally with relationships between governments of one state and subjects of another. Although various usages existed in the relations between peoples of earlier civilizations, modern international law is a product of the European nation-state system. In the past century, new rules have been decreed by states meeting in conferences and in organizations like the League of Nations and the United Nations and their auxiliary agencies, thereby adding written international law to customary law. Controversies over the existence of international law are due partly to the common misconception that international law defines interstate relations as they ought to be, and partly to the absence of a common superior to make it uniform and enforce it. The test of a rule of international law is its universal acceptance by the community of states and their obedience to its mandates.

International Law Enforcement Educators and Trainers Association. An organization "committed to the reduction of law enforcement risk through the enhancement of training for criminal justice practitioners." Address; 1972 Gail Lynne Drive, Burlington, WI 53105. Web: http://www.ileeta.org/.

International Maritime Organization (IMO). A organization of the United Nations, adopted in Geneva in 1948 and launched in 1959. According to their Web site, "IMO's main task has been to develop and maintain a comprehensive regulatory framework for shipping and its remit today includes safety, environmental concerns, legal matters, technical cooperation, maritime security and the efficiency of shipping." IMO tracks international piracy. Web: http://www.imo.org/.

International Narcotic Enforcement Officers Association. Established in 1960, the association "promotes and fosters mutual cooperation, discussion and interest in the worldwide problems of narcotic trafficking and drug abuse; enlists as members of this Association persons who are engaged in the field of narcotic enforcement in the United States of America, its states, territories and possessions, and in other nations; assists families of law enforcement officers killed in the line of duty; enlists the cooperation of international law enforcement agencies for the purpose of improving and enhancing efforts in narcotic enforcement; and promotes international cooperation and understanding in combating drug abuse." Address: P.O. Box 2938, Glenville, NY 12325. Web: http://www.ineoa.org/.

international police forces. Contingents of military forces of member states placed under United Nations control, as authorized by the UN Charter, for the purpose of preserving peace and preventing or resisting aggressive actions.

International Task Force on Euthanasia and Attempted Suicide. Organization aims to ensure "that a patient's right to receive care and compassion is not replaced by a doctor's right to prescribe poison or administer a lethal injection." Address: International Task Force on Euthanasia and Assisted Suicide, PO Box 760, Steubenville, OH 43952. Web: http://www.internationaltaskforce.org/index.htm.

International Union of Police Associations (IUPA). This organization traces its roots to the International Conference of Police Associations, which disbanded on December 4, 1978, over the issue of affiliating with organized labor. The IUPA represents the segment of the earlier group that remained with the AFL-CIO. It has locals throughout the United States and claims to represent over 200 law enforcement agencies. IUPA address: 1549 Ringling Blvd. Suite 600, Sarasota, FL 34236 Web: http://www.iupa.org/.

Internet fraud. The use of online "boiler rooms," instant messaging, and fake Web sites to lure investors into "pump-and-dump" stock schemes. *See also* fraud, investment

internet-related schemes. This type of fraud is often perpetrated via unsolicited spam e-mails offering businesses opportunities to hapless consumers. The consumer accepts the terms of the email, which can include business opportunities, work at home schemes, etc. As with other types of fraud, the victim gives money with the expectation of some return, which does not materialize. *See also* telemarketing fraud.

Interpol (International Criminal Police Organization). This organization was established in 1914 to facilitate cooperation in fighting international crime, and transferred its headquarters to Paris in 1938, where it became the International Criminal Police Organization. Interpol is a worldwide consortium of 188 countries, but its secretariat is staffed by French police officers. In each member country, a point of contact and coordination is established for the Interpol function. It coordinates and facilitates requests between foreign police organizations' law enforcement agencies for information regarding persons, vehicles, and goods that bear on criminal matters within their respective jurisdictions. Interpol exists as a catalyst to provide efficient police communications between the United States and other member countries and the General Secretariat Headquarters in Lyon, France. Investigations can cover criminal-history checks, license plate and drivers' license checks, International Wanted Circulars, weapons traces, and locating suspects. It keeps in daily contact with affiliates through its own network and provides assistance to national police within the terms of local laws. Interpol attempts to ensure and promote the widest possible mutual assistance among all police authorities within the limits of the laws existing in the different countries and in the spirit of the Universal Declaration of Human Rights, and to establish and develop all institutions likely to contribute effectively to the prevention and suppression of crime. It is a clearinghouse for international exchange of information, doing no investigation itself. The United States joined the group in 1958. For information, contact: National Central Bureau, Interpol, Department of Justice, 10th Street and Constitution Avenue, NW, Room 6649, Washington, DC 20530; Web: http://www.justice.gov/usncb/. Publishes *International Crime Police Review,* (monthly journal) and *International Crime Statistics* (every two years). Address: General Secretariat, 200, quai Charles de Gaulle, 69006 Lyon, France. Web: http://www.interpol.intdefault.asp. *See also* Table 26. Interpol Member Countries, 2010, page 241.

interrogation. To probe, with questions, persons believed involved in crime; to question in detail with the purpose of obtaining information relative to the involvement in crime of the person being questioned. *See also* Miranda rights

interrogatory. A question; sets of questions in writing intended to be proposed to a witness.

intersection. An area defined by lateral curb lines or lateral boundary lines of the roadways of two highways that join one another at approximately right angles.

interstate compact. An agreement between states, that, in criminal justice, involves transferring prisoners, parolees, or probationers from one jurisdiction to another, often in order to relieve overcrowding. The state with original jurisdiction retains legal authority to confine or release.

Interstate Commerce Commission. Former U.S. government agency, dismantled in 1995, whose responsibility was to regulate common carriers engaged in transportation.

interstate compact. An agreement between two or more states to transfer prisoners, parolees, or probationers from the physical or supervisory custody of one state to that of another, where the correctional agency that first acquired jurisdiction over a person usually retains the legal authority to confine or release him or her.

Interstate Compact for the Supervision of Parolees and Probationers. This agreement, first instituted in 1937 and entered into by all the states by 1951, allows for the supervision of a parolee or probationer in a state other than the state of conviction, provided that the parolee is a resident of that state, that his or her family lives there, or that the receiving state agrees to accept supervision. Extradition procedural requirements are waived under the compact.

Interstate extradition. Provision is made by the Constitution, the acts of Congress in pursuance thereof, and auxiliary statutes in the different states for the extradition of a person, charged in one state with a crime or misdemeanor, who flees from justice and is found in another state. Interstate extradition is also called rendition. To be extradited, a person must (a) be judicially charged with a crime in the demanding state, as by indictment or complaint, or (b) have been in the demanding state, in order to be seen as having fled from justice. It is enough that the person was in the demanding state, committed a crime there, and then left that state for any reason. A person may be extradited for any crime against the laws of the demanding state. By the weight of authority, a person may be tried for a crime other than that for which he or she was extradited, and forcible abduction from another state does not prevent this trial.

Interstate Transfer of Stolen Motor Vehicles (ITSMV). Federal law makes transportation of stolen vehicles across state lines a federal crime. *See also* Dyer Act

interval level of measurement. *See* scale, interval

intestate. Referring to anyone who died without making a will.

intimate partner abuse. Term used in place of "intimate partner violence" or "domestic violence" by Joanne Belknap (*Invisible Woman* Third Edition) as it incorporates the nonviolent types of abuse that can occur in intimate relationships.

intimate partner violence. Term used to describe violence by one or both partners in an intimate relationship, including spouses,

text continues on page 242

TABLE 26   INTERPOL MEMBER COUNTRIES, 2010

Afghanistan	Denmark	Lebanon	St Lucia
Albania	Djibouti	Lesotho	St Vincent &
Algeria	Dominica	Liberia	Grenadines
Andorra	Dominican Republic	Libya	Samoa
Angola	Ecuador	Liechtenstein	San Marino
Antigua & Barbuda	Egypt	Lithuania	Sao Tome & Principe
Argentina	El Salvador	Luxembourg	Saudi Arabia
Armenia	Equatorial Guinea	Madagascar	Senegal
Aruba	Eritrea	Malawi	Serbia
Australia	Estonia	Malaysia	Seychelles
Austria	Ethiopia	Maldives	Sierra Leone
Azerbaijan	Fiji	Mali	Singapore
Bahamas	Finland	Malta	Slovakia
Bahrain	Former Yugoslav	Marshall Islands	Slovenia
Bangladesh	Republic of	Mauritania	Somalia
Barbados	Macedonia	Mauritius	South Africa
Belarus	France	Mexico	Spain
Belgium	Gabon	Moldova	Sri Lanka
Belize	Gambia	Monaco	Sudan
Benin	Georgia	Mongolia	Suriname
Bhutan	Germany	Montenegro	Swaziland
Bolivia	Ghana	Morocco	Sweden
Bosnia &	Greece	Mozambique	Switzerland
Herzegovina	Grenada	Myanmar	Syria
Botswana	Guatemala	Namibia	Tajikistan
Brazil	Guinea	Nauru	Tanzania
Brunei	Guinea Bissau	Nepal	Thailand
Bulgaria	Guyana	Netherlands	Timor-Leste
Burkina-Faso	Haiti	Netherlands	Togo
Burundi	Honduras	Antilles	Tonga
Cambodia	Hungary	New Zealand	Trinidad & Tobago
Cameroon	Iceland	Nicaragua	Tunisia
Canada	India	Niger	Turkey
Cape Verde	Indonesia	Nigeria	Turkmenistan
Central African	Iran	Norway	Uganda
Republic	Iraq	Oman	Ukraine
Chad	Ireland	Pakistan	United Arab
Chile	Israel	Panama	Emirates
China	Italy	Papua New Guinea	United Kingdom
Colombia	Jamaica	Paraguay	United States
Comoros	Japan	Peru	Uruguay
Congo	Jordan	Philippines	Uzbekistan
Congo (Democratic	Kazakhstan	Poland	Vatican City State
Rep.)	Kenya	Portugal	Venezuela
Costa Rica	Korea (Rep. of)	Qatar	Vietnam
Côte d'Ivoire	Kuwait	Romania	Yemen
Croatia	Kyrgyzstan	Russia	Zambia
Cuba	Laos	Rwanda	Zimbabwe
Cyprus	Latvia	St Kitts & Nevis	
Czech Republic			

Source: Interpol.

paramours, co-habitants, etc. *See also* domestic violence, battered person syndrome

in toto (Lat., lit.). In the whole; entirely.

intoxication. A broad and comprehensive term with many definitions: drunkenness; inebriety; inebriation; poisoning; the act of inebriating; the state of being inebriated; the act of intoxicating or making drunk; the state of being intoxicated or drunk; or the state produced by using too much of an alcoholic beverage or using opium, hashish, or the like. The recommended usage is: the offense of being in a public place while intoxicated through consumption of alcohol or intake of a controlled substance or drug.

Intoximeter. Trade name of a device to test the breath to determine the amount of alcohol in the blood.

intrinsic evidence. Evidence that is derived from a document and needs no explanation.

investigate. The term comes from the Latin word *vestigium,* meaning a footprint.

investigation, presentence. An official investigation, ordered by a judge or court subsequent to conviction or a plea of guilty, for the use of the judge or court in arriving at the sentence to be given to the offender.

Investigations, Defense Central Index of. A locator file maintained by the Defense Department. It identifies the location of files concerning past and present military members, DOD civilian employees, and contractors. *See also* Defense Supply Agency File

investigative power of Congress. The power to make inquiries and hold hearings is an essential aspect of the legislative power conferred on Congress by the Constitution. Investigations are conducted by committee rather than by Congress collectively. The congressional power to investigate is reinforced by the subpoena power—the power to compel the attendance of witnesses and the delivery of documents—and by the power to cite a reluctant or uncooperative witness for contempt. Some subjects of investigation have attracted considerable attention: the use

of security classifications to prevent publication of information, Watergate, Koreagate, ABSCAM, and inquiries into the alleged ties between the Teamsters and organized crime (President's Commission on Organized Crime, April 1985).

Investigators Association, Federal Criminals. Founded in 1953, the "mission of FCIA is to ensure that Federal Law Enforcement Professionals have the tools and the support network to meet the challenges of future criminal investigations while becoming more community oriented." Address: P.O. Box 23400, Washington, DC 20026. Web: http://www.fedcia.org/.

Investigators, Society of Professional. Founded in 1955. Publishes an annual bulletin. Address: 233 Broadway, Suite 2201, New York, NY 10279.

investigatory stage. That part of a police investigation during which suspicion has not yet been focused on a particular person or persons.

investment and business-opportunity schemes. These schemes involve the use of opportunities such as investments in rare coins, precious metals, ostrich farms, telecommunications systems, etc. The consumer makes the investment expecting the promised high-yield return, which does not materialize. *See also* telemarketing fraud

involuntary manslaughter. Unguardedly or undesignedly killing another while committing either an unlawful act, not felonious or tending to great bodily harm, or a lawful act without proper caution or requisite skill.

involuntary servitude. Slavery, peonage, or forced labor to fulfill a contract or debt. The Thirteenth Amendment prohibits involuntary servitude, except as a criminal punishment.

iodine. A chemical element of which the fumes are used to develop fingerprints on paper.

Iran Contra Scandal. Term given to a political scandal under President Ronald Reagan in 1985–86, involving the U.S. sale of weapons to Iran in a debacle that culminated in an arms-for-hostages trade. Two Washington officials, Oliver North and John Poindexter, were convicted of several criminal charges related to the scandal, although those were later vacated. In 1992, President George H. W. Bush pardoned six officials associated with the scandal.

iris scanning. A security feature in which unique, discernable patterns in the tissue surrounding eye's pupil are used for identification and to access high-security applications. Simple but not foolproof, the use of iris scanning has increased in the first part of the twenty-first century.

Irish system. A system of punishment, developed by Sir William Crofton, that provided for progressive stages in a prison term and for release under supervision before final termination of sentence.

irresistible impulse. As used in criminal law, the state of a person, due to his or her mental condition, who is driven by an urge to do certain acts that neither willpower nor reasoning is sufficient to prevent. *See also* insanity defense; M'Naghten Rule, Durham rule, American Law Institute Model; Brawner rule; substantial capacity test, and temporary insanity. *See also* Insanity Defense Reform Act of 1984 (U.S.); Table 25. Insanity Defense in the United States, pages 232-233

irritant gas. A nonlethal gas that causes irritation of the skin and a flow of tears. Any one of the family of tear gases used for training and riot control. *See also* tear gas

IRS building suicide crash. On February 18, 2010, a small aircraft flown by pilot Andrew Joseph Stack III crashed into an Austin, Texas office complex. The building housed an Internal Revenue (IRS) office. Stack was killed in the crash, along with an IRS manager; 13 others were injured. Stack posted a suicide note to his business Web page, in which he expressed his displeasure with the IRS and federal bailout. *See also* domestic terrorism

ISBN. The International Standard Book Number is an ordering and identifying code for book products. The first number designates the language the book is published in, for example, the zero is for English. The second set identifies the publisher, and the last set identifies the particular item. The very last number is a "check number," which mathematically makes certain that the previous numbers have been entered correctly.

issuance of arrest warrants. Authorization to issue an arrest warrant before indictment depends on filing a proper complaint before at appropriate magistrate, showing that a crime has been committed and that there is probably cause to suspect the accused. After indictment the usual practice is to issue a bench warrant. An arrest under an insufficient warrant is in effect an arrest without any warrant at all, and, if a warrant is necessary, such an arrest is illegal.

issuance of search warrants. In general, issuance is regulated by constitutional and statutory provisions to the effect that search warrants must (a) be issued by one authorized to do so, upon application made by a proper party in proper form; (b) show probable cause supported by oath of affirmation; and (c) sufficiently describe the place to be searched and the thing to be seized.

issue. (1) Children, progeny. (2) A single, certain, and material point, deduced from the pleadings of the parties, that is affirmed by one side and denied on the other; a fact put in controversy by the pleadings; in criminal law. A fact that must be proved to convict the accused or that is in controversy.

issue of fact. A question of fact to be determined by the jury.

issue of law. A point to be decided only by the court.

Ivan the Terrible (Ivan IV Vasilyevich) (1530–1584). Born Ivan IV Vasilyevuch in 1530, named Grand Prince in 1533, and crowned Tzar in 1547, Ivan the Terrible was a notorious Russian ruler who built the region from a small nation to an empire, of which he was the first Tsar (Czar). His name derives from an incorrect translation of his nickname, *Ivan Grozny,* which is better translated *Ivan the Fearsome* or *Ivan the Dangerous.* In the early years of his rein, Ivan expanded his empire to nearly 1 billion acres, improved commerce and trade routes, and codified various laws. He became unstable in his later years and was known for paranoia and fits of rage, possibly caused by episodic mental illness, which culminated in several sadistic conflicts and brutal wars with neighboring territories. He also built a secret police unit called the Oprichnik, charged with the torture and murder of internal enemies, often with the most violent and gruesome methods, and often for the sadistic viewing pleasure of Ivan or his son and heir, Ivan Ivanovich. In one notorious fit of rage in 1581, Ivan the Terrible beat his son's pregnant wife so severely she miscarried. When Ivanovich confronted his father, Ivan the Terrible beat his own son to death. Ivan died three years later, leaving his empire to his second (and possibly unfit) son, Fedor I of Russia.

Ivins, Bruce Edwards. (1946–2008). Born in Ohio to a pharmacist father and stay-at-home mother, Edwards was a national honor student who subsequently earned a B.S., M.S., and Ph.D. in microbiology from the University of Cincinnati. Her married and had two children. He was employed as a senior biodefense researcher at the United States Army Medical Research Institute of Infectious Diseases (USAMRIID), and received the Decoration for Exceptional Civilian Service in 2003 for helping design anthrax vaccines. In 2006, Ivins was identified as a key suspect in the 2001 anthrax attacks in the United States. Over the next two years of investigation, Ivins began treatment for depression and lost security access. He was committed for psychiatric evaluation on July 24, 2008. Edwards committed suicide a few days later, just as the FBI was preparing formal charges against him. Ivins remains the sole suspect in the attack. *See also* anthrax attacks; domestic terrorism

J

Jack the Ripper (dates of birth and death unknown). Pseudonym given to the unknown serial murderer of Whitechapel, London, England in 1888. Ripper targeted prostitutes from the Whitechapel area, a London slum, murdering and mutilating them. In all, the Ripper is believed responsible for at least five murders, although some scholars believe he is responsible for 11 Whitechapel homicides, and others posit even more. Evidence suggests the Ripper stopped killing after 1889, perhaps due to death, incarceration for an unrelated crime, or due to relocation. To date, the identity of the Ripper has never been confirmed, although several authorities on the murder have narrowed the list of possible suspects to a handful, including:

William Henry Bury, convicted of murder and mutilation of his wife in 1889;

Dr. Thomas Neill Cream, a convicted murderer who spontaneously yelled, "I am Jack the . . ." as he was executed in 1892;

Thomas Hayne Cutbush, Whitechapel man institutionalized for insanity secondary to neurosyphilis in 1892;

Montague John Druitt, an attorney and schoolteacher who committed suicide in 1888;

Nathan Kaminsky (AKA David Cohen, possibly the same man as Kosminski), a boot-maker who was institutionalized for insanity and reported died in an asylum in 1889 (although some reports indicate he escaped and was reinstitutionalized under the name Kosminski in 1891);

James Kelly, convicted of murdering his wife in 1883, and escaping from asylum in 1888;

Seweryn Antonowicz Klosowski, a Whitechapel barber who was executed in 1903 for the murders of three wives;

Aaron Kosminski, a Whitechapel resident who was institutionalized for insanity in 1891;

Painter *Walter Sickert;*

Francis Tumblety, an English physician who fled to the United States in 1888 to avoid prosecution for sodomy;

Prince Albert Victor, or one of his Masonic associates, who committed the murders to cover up the illegitimate pregnancy of Victor's Whitechapel lover;

Sir John Williams, royal physician and obstetrician; and

Sir William Withey Gull, royal physician believed to have committed the murders to prevent a scandalous pregnancy, with Masonic conspiracy links.

Jackson State University. On May 14, 1970, students gatherered at Jackson State University in Mississippi to protest both the Vietnam War and the National Guard shooting of Kent State students who were gathered in protest 10 days earlier. As in the Kent State demonstration, National Guard troops were called, and they opened fire, killing two students and wounding seven others. *See also* Kent State University

Jacob Wetterling Crimes Against Children and Sexually Violent Offender Registration Act (1994). Named for Jacob Wetterling, an 11-year old boy abducted from his neighborhood in 1989, this federal law requires states to implement and maintain both a sex offender registry and a registry of crimes against children registry. This act is sometimes called the federal Megan's Law. *See also* Megan's Law

jail. A confinement facility administered by an agency of local government, typically a law enforcement agency, intended for adults but sometimes also containing juveniles and persons detained pending adjudication and/or persons committed after adjudication, usually those committed on sentences of a year or less.

jail commitment. A sentence of commitment to the jurisdiction of a confinement facility for adults that is administered by an agency of local government and of which the custodial authority is usually limited to persons sentenced to a year or less of confinement.

jail time. Credit allowed in a prison sentence for time a defendant spent in jail awaiting trial or mandate on appeal.

James, Jesse Woodson (1847–1882). Born in Clay County, MO, in 1847, James was the famous leader of a western outlaw gang that included his brother Frank, Cole Younger, and others, and that specialized in bank and train robberies. He was killed by gang member Robert Ford for a $5,000 reward in 1882.

Jay, John. Born in New York City in 1745, Jay was the first chief justice of the United States, serving from 1790 to 1795. He was also the New York State delegate to the Continental Congress, 1774–1779; president of the congress, 1778–1779; one of the negotiators and signers of the treaty of peace with Britain, 1783; U.S. secretary of foreign affairs, 1784–1789; author of five essays in *The Federalist,* which urged ratification of the U.S. Constitution, 1787–1789; negotiator of Jay's Treaty, which settled outstanding disputes with Britain, 1794; and governor of New York, 1795–1801. He died in 1829.

Jellinek's Curve. A graphic that represents the progress of the disease of alcoholism, including 43 different steps. Two basic phases, that of Purely Symptomatic and Addictive, are divided into subphases that include pre-alcoholic, alcohol addiction, chronic, and crucial.

jeopardy. The danger of conviction and punishment that defendants in criminal actions incur when lawfully charged with crimes before a tribunal properly organized and competent to try them. When jeopardy begins may differ slightly among the states; often it is when the petit jury has been impaneled and sworn or, if trial is before a judge without a jury, when the first witness is sworn.

Jesse James Act. Because of Cole Younger, Butch Cassidy and the Sundance Kid, and the

Jesse James gangs, who preyed on mail trains during the 1860s, the federal government passed the Jesse James Act, which mandates a 25-year prison sentence for conviction of armed robbery of a postal facility. This is one of the earlier mandatory sentences still in effect and one of the harshest federal statutes for robbery. *See also* James, Jesse

Jessica's Law. A 2005 Florida law named for Jessica Lunsford, a nine-year-old girl who was raped and murdered by a previously convicted sex offender. Since passage of Florida's law in 2005, other states have replicated the provisions, also naming such laws "Jessica's Law." In addition to Megan's Law, Jessica's Law imposes further residential restrictions for convicted sex offenders. *See also* Megan's Law

Jim Crow laws. Beginning in the 1880s, a number of ordinances were passed in southern states and municipalities that legalized segregation of blacks and whites. The name Jim Crow is believed to have derived from a character in a minstrel song.

job action. An organized action taken by members of a police association (or other labor union) to exert pressure on city government. Job actions are generally a means of demonstration to coerce public officials to meet union demands after good faith collective bargaining or negotiations have broken down. The issues could include compensation, benefits, or conditions of employment. Job actions can take the form of strikes, "blue flu" (sick-outs), slowdowns, speedups, or a variety of other means.

Johari window. A theoretical model developed in 1955 for explaining the concept of an individual's interpersonal disclosure and feedback. The model consists of four quadrants: (1) public self (known by individual and others), (2) blind self (known by others but unknown by the individual); (3) private self (known only by the individual); and (4) unknown area (information that neither the individual nor others are aware of).

John Birch Society. A semisecret, conservative (some would say extremist) organization founded by Robert Welch, a Massachusetts manufacturer, in Indianapolis in 1958. It opposes communism (its announced purpose), impugns the motives of moderate and liberal leaders, and opposes all forms of internationalism; named for a Georgia fundamentalist missionary preacher who was killed by the Chinese Communists following World War II, thus becoming the first U.S. casualty of the cold war. The society is highly supportive of traditional police practices and lobbied against civilian control and civilian review boards. Welch turned over the chairmanship in 1975 to Lawrence P. McDonald (Congressman, D-GA). The aircraft carrying McDonald was shot down by a Soviet fighter plane over the Sea of Japan on August 31, 1983.

John Doe. A fictitious name often used when the true name of a deceased or defendant is unknown, or to indicate a person for the purpose of argument.

John Howard Association. Founded in 1901 and named after John Howard (1726–1790), an English prison reformer. The organization is devoted to prison reform and the prevention and control of crime and delinquency; provides professional consultation and survey services in crime and delinquency. Publishes a bimonthly newsletter. Address: 300 West Adams Street Suite 423, Chicago, IL 60606.

John Jay College of Criminal Justice Lloyd Sealy Library. Founded in 1962 by the City University of New York, the library serves the "informational needs of criminal justice students, researchers, and professionals from within and outside of its own academic setting." Address: 899 10th Ave., New York, NY 10019. http://www.lib.jjay.cuny.edu/.

joinder. (1) In the broadest usage, the combining of multiple defendants and/or charges for purposes of any legal step or proceeding. (2) In criminal proceedings, the naming of two or more defendants and/or the listing of two or more charges in a single charging document.

Join Together Online. This electronic resource was created for communities fighting drug abuse. For a small fee, users can access the latest information about substance abuse and find links to the major online criminal justice resources. Address: 580 Harrison Avenue, 3rd Floor, Boston, MA 02118. E-mail: info@jointogether.org. Web site: http://www.jointogether.org.

Joint Terrorism Task Force (JTTF). Units of highly trained local law enforcement and intelligence agents located throughout the country that focus on recognizing, combating, and preventing terrorist activities. JTTFs are comprised of local, state, and federal authorities. *See also* National Joint Terrorism Task Force

Jones, Reverend James "Jim" Warren (1931–1978). Religious leader who founded the People's Temple, a religious organization with members who developed a socialist commune in 1974 in Jonestown (named after Jones) in Guyana. The commune grew to nearly 1000 members, which spawned national attention due to concerns with possible brainwashing and cult activities. In 1978, a U.S. congressional and media delegation traveled to Jonestown to investigate allegations of human rights abuses raised. Delegation members and defectors were attacked, and a battled ensued at the airstrip, leaving Congressman Ryan and four others dead as an NBC cameraman filmed the massacre. Seven delegation members escaped. Later that day, the remaining 909 People's Temple residents, including 276 children, died by cyanide poising in an apparent mass suicide. *See also* cult; Jonestown; mass murder

Jonestown. City in Guyana named for Jim Jones, this term generally refers to the mass suicide of 909 members of the People's Temple, a religious commune in Jonestown led by Jim Jones. In 1978, a U.S. delegation of congress and reporters traveled to Jonestown amidst human rights concerns

raised by relatives of commune members. The visit resulted in a gun battle that left U.S. Congressman Leo Ryan and four others dead, while the remaining seven delegation members escaped with their lives. Later that day, 909 residents of Jonestown engaged in a mass suicide by drinking cyanide-laced grape punch. *See also* cult; Jones, James; mass murder

JTTF. *See* Joint Terrorism Task Force

Juan Vucetich system. A fingerprint classification system developed in the late 1800s and used throughout South America through the mid 1980s. *See also* fingerprint patterns, Henry classification, Roscher system

judge. An officer who presides over and administers the law in a court of justice.

Judge Advocate General. The chief legal officer of a branch of the military services who has, among other duties, supervision of military justice and of the proceedings of courts martial and military commissions.

judge-made law. (1) The common law as developed in form and content by judges or judicial decisions. (2) Judicial decisions based on tortured constructions of the Constitution, selecting unusual historical and legal precedents, or using unusual definitions of terms in "discovering" the law applying to a given case—used derogatorily.

judgment. (1) In the broadest usage, any decision or determination of a court. (2) The statement of the decision of a court, that the defendant is acquitted or convicted of the offense(s) charged.

judge *pro tem (pro tempore)*. A judge who sits in lieu of a regularly appointed or elected judge and who is appointed with full authority to hear all cases scheduled for, and exercise all functions of, the regular judge.

judicial notice. An act whereby a court, in conducting a trial or framing its decision, will, of its own motion and without the production of evidence, recognize the existence and truth of certain facts having a bearing on the controversy that are matters of general or common knowledge. Among such matters are the laws of the states, historical facts, the Constitution, and principal geographical features.

judicial officer. Any person authorized by statute, constitutional provision, or court rule to exercise those powers reserved to the judicial branch of the government.

judicial powers. The powers of the courts to interpret laws and constitutions, define the powers of the branches of government, distinguish between the powers of the national government and those of the states, maintain private rights against illegal public encroachment, and void legislative acts. These powers arise either out of constitutional grant or judicial interpretation of the rendering of decisions.

judicial process. The procedures taken by a court in deciding cases or resolving legal controversies.

judicial reprieve. Early form of judicial action that predated the modern-day suspended sentence. In order to give a defendant an opportunity to apply for a pardon from the crown, a judge could grant this temporary suspension of judgment or imposition of sentence.

judicial review. The judiciary's review of the actions and determinations of executive officials of a government. Judicial review is akin to appellate court review of the decisions of lower courts. The principle is an old one in common law. By 1776 the right of judicial review of administrative action had become well enough ingrained to be included in Article III of the Constitution. Although the right to judicial review is guaranteed, its scope is not infinite. In the interest of minimizing litigation and encouraging full utilization of the administrative process, a court will not review administrative actions until all available administrative remedies, such as appeals up the chain of command within an executive department, have been exhausted.

judicial system. Taken together, the federal, state, and municipal courts form a complex judicial system in the United States. The regular federal court structure is three-tiered: the Supreme Court, 12 courts of appeals, and 94 district courts. U.S district courts are the trial courts or courts of original jurisdiction. They can hear cases involving the Constitution, acts of Congress, or treaties with foreign countries; civil suits between citizens of different states, where the amount in controversy exceeds $10,000; cases involving admiralty or maritime jurisdiction; cases where the United States is a party; cases instituted by a state against residents of other states; cases between a state or its citizens and foreign countries or individuals; and cases between two or more states. Decisions of a district court may be appealed to the Supreme Court: (a) if a federal law is held unconstitutional; (b) if a decision in a criminal case goes against the United States; or (c) in certain cases having to do with particular congressional acts or independent agencies. Generally speaking, however, most appeals from district courts are lodged with the courts of appeals. Courts of appeals have appellate jurisdiction over cases from the district courts, the regulatory commissions, and the Tax Court of the United States. The U.S. Supreme Court is the court of last resort for the nation. It hears appeals from the courts of appeals, the district courts, and the highest state courts in cases where a federal question is raised. The Supreme Court can also hear appeals from the special federal courts but rarely does so. It has original jurisdiction when a state is a party and in cases involving ambassadors and ministers. The federal judicial system also contains a number of special courts: the Customs Court, the Court of Customs and Patent Appeals, the Court of Claims, the Court of Military Appeals, and the Tax Court. State judicial systems vary enormously, organizing their courts on three or four levels. At the bottom are magistrate courts and those courts have specifically limited jurisdiction. Magistrate courts are also known as police courts, justice of peace courts, county courts, and municipal courts.

Examples of courts of limited jurisdiction include family courts, probate courts, small claims courts, juvenile courts, and domestic relations courts. These courts hear criminal and civil cases, where the crime involved is normally a misdemeanor or the civil claim is quite small. The second-level courts are usually labeled circuit, superior, or district courts. In most states these courts possess both criminal and civil jurisdiction, although 16 states have separate courts for special kinds of jurisdictions. Most states have only three levels of courts, but 14 states have an intermediate level of appellate courts above the circuit, superior, or district courts but below the states' highest tribunal. All states have a court of last resort, usually termed the state supreme court. This tribunal makes final determinations of questions of law on appeal from the lower courts. If a federal question is involved, decision of a state supreme court may be appealed to the U.S. Supreme Court.

Judiciary Acts. The Judiciary Act of 1789 that established the framework of the American judicial system and helped extend the powers of the federal government. The act provided for a Supreme Court, composed of a chief justice and five associate justices; 13 district courts; three circuit courts, each made up of two supreme court justices and a district judge; and an attorney general. The act represented a compromise between two forces: one wanted a powerful judiciary to administer a uniform United States code of justice, and the other wanted existing state courts to enforce federal laws. Section 25 of the law strengthened federal powers by permitting the Supreme Court to judicially review the states' highest courts when they upheld state laws that conflicted with federal statutes—the Constitution did not explicitly grant the Court these powers. The Judiciary Act of 1801 was passed by the Federalists after they had lost control of the presidency and Congress in the election of 1800, but before the new government had taken office. The act clearly helped to maintain a Federalist judiciary, but it also introduced reforms that had become necessary in the 1790s. By this act the Supreme Court membership was to be reduced to five, a new set of circuit courts was to be created (with judgeships to be filled), and the number of district court judges was to be increased. This act led to last minute "midnight appointments" by President Adams and caused considerable bitterness among the Democratic-Republicans. In 1802 the new Democratic-Republican administration repealed the act of 1801. The Judicial Act of 1802 restored the Supreme Court membership to six and established a lower number of circuit courts.

Jukes and Kallikaks. Two families, the surnames of which are pseudonyms, discussed in the late 19th and early 20th century literature as evidence of genetic inheritance of certain undesirable social traits. The Jukes were said to have inherited criminality, while the Kallikaks were said to have inherited "feeble-mindedness." The case studies of the families were examples used to discuss eugenics. *See also* eugenics, Jukes family, Kallikaks family

Jukes family. The case name given to a New York State family with a notable record for delinquency and crime. A study published by R. L. Dugdale and A. H. Estabrook in 1875 reported that more than 2,100 men and women of "Jukes blood" had been traced. Of these, 171 were classed as criminals, 458 were behind their age groups in school, and hundreds of others were labeled paupers, intemperates, and harlots. Like the record of the Kallikak family, the story of the Jukes was taken as proof that heredity is a dominant factor in development. This conclusion has been challenged, however, on several grounds. The investigator based many of his classifications on opinion rather than objective evidence, and he did not allow for the influence of environment on the family members. *See also* Jukes and Kallikaks; Kallikaks family

jurat. A certificate evidencing the fact or statement that an affidavit was properly made before a duly authorized officer.

juridical. In accordance with law and with due process in the administration of justice;

pertaining to the office and functions of a judge.

juridical days. Days in which courts are in session.

jurisdiction. The territory, subject matter, or persons over which lawful authority may be exercised by a court or other justice agency, as determined by statute or constitution. There are four elements of jurisdiction. *Subject-matter jurisdiction* is the authority to consider a particular class of cases. Federal courts, for example, do not have the power to decide cases between citizens of the same state unless a federal question is involved. *Jurisdiction in rem* is jurisdiction over things, typically land. The third element of jurisdiction is the *power to grant the relief* requested. The most difficult element is *jurisdiction of the person*. In common law, jurisdiction over a person is synonymous with power over him or her: it is necessary and sufficient to "serve" the person within the territory over which the court has authority. Civil law, on the other hand, considers a person subject to the court's authority only if the relationship that is the subject of the dispute is within the territory of the court.

jurisdiction in general. Unless extended by statute, a state has jurisdiction only over those crimes committed within its territorial limits and those committed by its own citizens abroad. A crime must be prosecuted in the county in which it was committed, and it is generally held to have been committed in the county in which it was completed or achieved its goal. Thus, where a blow is struck in one county and a death ensues in another, the offense is generally held to have been committed in the latter; and when a person in one county commits a crime in another by means of an innocent agent, such as the post office, the latter county has jurisdiction. Several states have special statutes governing the subject of prosecuting homicides in the county where the body is found, giving jurisdiction to either county where the crime is committed partly in one county and partly in another, or to either state under similar circumstances.

jurisprudence. In the strict sense of the term, an act or a technique that comprises the systematized prediction of what the courts will do, with the practical aim of facilitating the work of counselors, judges, and other practitioners. Since there are as many different judicial techniques as there are systems of law and corresponding types of societies, jurisprudence has sometimes been characterized as social engineering according to particular social structures and needs. So arose a misleading enlargement of the term jurisprudence, which came to mean a discrete science as well as an art.

jurist. Expert, scholar, or writer in law.

jury. The American jury system is traceable to ninth-century France and was imported to England by William the Conqueror. In its earliest form, a jury was a group of the defendant's neighbors, who were expected to answer questions based on their own knowledge. Such jurors functioned as both witnesses and triers of fact. In colonial America, the jury was the champion of the popular cause. After the Revolution, the right to a trial by jury was guaranteed by the Constitution and by the separate state constitutions. An accused is entitled to a trial by jury whenever the case is originally brought into federal court and involves an offense for which the punishment may exceed six months' imprisonment and in which the defendant is prosecuted as an adult. The size of the federal jury is not constitutionally stipulated. A state jury of six persons sitting for a serious offense case has been approved by the Supreme Court in language that clearly indicates constitutional approval of a federal jury of less than 12. Only about 15 percent of all criminal prosecutions result in jury trials. Among those, however, are usually cases in which defendants may receive the most severe punishments. The jury for civil cases has been abolished in Great Britain, and there are pressures to abolish it in the United States. Jury use is time-consuming, and some members of the bench and bar do not believe that a group of laymen is capable of deciding the technical, complex issues raised in civil suits. However, empirical data based on several studies provide an essentially positive image of the jury's competence.

jury, grand. *See* grand jury

jury, hung. A trial jury that, after exhaustive deliberations, cannot agree on a unanimous verdict, necessitating a mistrial and a subsequent retrial. In cases and jurisdictions where unanimity is not required, a hung jury results when the necessary votes for acquittal or conviction cannot be obtained.

jury panel. The group of persons either summoned to appear in court as potential jurors for a particular trial or selected from the group of potential jurors to sit in the jury box, from which a second group, those acceptable to the prosecution and the defense, is finally chosen as the jury. *See also voir dire*

jury poll. A poll, conducted by a judicial officer or by the clerk of the court, after a jury has stated its verdict but before that verdict has been entered in the record of the court, asking each juror individually whether the stated verdict is his or her own verdict.

jury school, first. Opened on January 16, 1937, by federal judge William Clark, U.S. District Court, District of New Jersey, in the post office building at Newark, NJ, to acquaint citizens with courtroom procedures and duties of jurors in considering evidence. The first class was attended by 150 men and women.

jury sentencing. Upon a jury verdict of guilty, the recommendation or determination of a sentence by the jury.

jury wheel. A device for selecting by lot the names of jurors who are to be summoned to attend a particular court.

jus gentium (Lat.). A body of law developed by Roman jurists for the trial of cases between Roman citizens and foreigners or provincials subsequently held by medieval jurists to embody principles of right reason applicable all human relationships and invoked by Dutch jurist Hugo Grotius

(1583–1645) and others as authority for rules of international law.

just deserts. A philosophical approach to the administration of justice, which assumes the individuals freely choose to violate criminal laws and therefore the state has a right and duty to punish them according to the nature of their acts.

justice. (1) The title of a judge. (2) The purpose of a legal system. The principles of law applied to the facts of a case should produce justice. There are many conceptions of justice, however, because definitions differ according to types and aims of legal systems. For instance, justice might be equality for all citizens in one system but maintenance of a class system in another. Usually the ethics and morality of a particular society determine the values that make up its idea of justice. Aristotle suggested that justice is equality for equals. He wrote: "Injustice arises when equals are treated unequally and also when unequals are treated equally." Chaim Perelmen, in his *Idea of Justice* (1963), further defines justice as not being arbitrary, as justifying itself, and as flowing from a normative system. Although Aristotelian concepts of justice are based on reason, Platonic concepts usually see justice as a function of a super-human being, the actual realization of justice being beyond human experience.

Justice Fellowship. Founded in 1983 by Christians supporting criminal justice system reform based on biblical teachings of reconciliation, restitution, and restoration. The organization seeks to develop a system in which criminals are held responsible for their crimes, victims are compensated, and communities are protected from crime. Publishes *The Justice eReport* monthly. Address: 44180 Riverside Parkway, Lansdowne, VA 20176; Web: http://www.prisonfellowship.org/prison-fellowship-home.

Justice Management Institute, The. Nonprofit organization that provides special expertise in court management issues. Address: 1888 Sherman Street, Suite 410, Denver, CO 80203. http://www.jmijustice.org/Home/PublicWeb

justice model. A conservative approach, adopted in the United States in 1974, to the purposes of incarceration. The model's goals are: to legally and humanely control the offender, to provide adequate care and custody, to offer voluntary treatment, and to protect society This approach views confinement as punishment and does not place great emphasis on rehabilitation. *See also* medical model

justice of the peace. In 1326 Edward II created the office of justice of the peace, designed to assist the "shire-reeve" in his law enforcement function. Noblemen appointed by the Crown, the justices of the peace first policed the counties but soon gained judicial powers and, within a few years, supplanted the constable as the most powerful local law enforcement agent. Today the position is a subordinate magistrate, usually without formal legal training, empowered to try petty civil and criminal cases and, in some states, to conduct preliminary hearings for persons accused of a crime and to fix bail for appearance in court. Justices of the peace are usually elected within a minor civil division, although their jurisdiction normally extends throughout a county. Except in a few states, their compensation is derived from fees, with the result that, in many cases, judgment is for the plaintiff.

Justice Research and Statistics Association. Founded in 1974 and funded by the Bureau of Justice Statistics of the U.S. Department of Justice, the association works to aid in the development, collection, analysis, and use of criminal justice statistics to meet state, interstate, and national needs in the areas of criminal justice administration, management, and planning. CJSA maintains an automated database of State Statistical Analysis Center projects and a library of state statistical reports. Publishes a quarterly newsletter. Address: 777 N. Capitol St. NE, Suite 801, Washington, DC 20002. http://www.jrsa.org/.

justice, sporting theory of. The term applied to the contentious method of judicial procedure in criminal trials. In this method, characteristic of criminal procedure derived from Anglo-Saxon precedents, the prosecution presents all the damaging evidence and the defense all the favorable, while the function of the judge is to act as umpire to see that the game is played fairly, according to the rules of procedure laid down in the law and in court decisions.

Justice, U.S. Department of. A federal department responsible for enforcing federal laws and representing and advising the federal government in legal matters. The Justice Department was established in 1870 with the Attorney General as its head. The department also supervises federal penal institutions, investigates violations of federal laws, and supervises U.S. attorneys and marshals. The department is organized into offices, divisions, bureaus, and boards. The offices of the attorney general, the deputy attorney general, and the associate attorney general oversee the entire department. The Attorney General is the chief law officer of the federal government; the deputy and associate attorneys general act as chief liaisons with other departments, recommend nominations for judicial appointments, and advise on pending legislation. Other offices include that of the solicitor general, the legal counsel, and the pardon attorney. Agencies within the Department of Justice include: Antitrust Division; Asset Forfeiture Program; Office of the Attorney General; Bureau of Alcohol, Tobacco, Firearms and Explosives; Bureau of Justice Assistance; Bureau of Justice Statistics; Civil Division; Civil Rights Division; Community Capacity Development Office; Community Oriented Policing Services; Community Relations Service; Criminal Division; Diversion Control Program; Drug Enforcement Administration; Environment and Natural Resources Division; Executive Office for Immigration Review; Executive Office for U.S. Attorneys; Executive Office for U.S. Trustees; Federal Bureau of Investigation; Federal Bureau of Prisons; Foreign Claims Settlement Commission of the U.S.; INTERPOL (U.S. National Central Bureau);

Justice Management Division; National Criminal Justice Reference Service; National Drug Intelligence Center; National Institute of Corrections; National Institute of Justice; National Security Division; Office of the Associate Attorney General; Office of Attorney Recruitment & Management; Office of the Chief Information Officer; Office of the Deputy Attorney General; Office of Dispute Resolution; Office of the Federal Detention Trustee; Office of Information Policy; Office of the Inspector General; Office of the Intergovernmental and Public Liaison; Office of Justice Programs; Office of Juvenile Justice and Delinquency Prevention; Office of Legal Counsel; Office of Legal Policy; Office of Legislative Affairs; Office of the Pardon Attorney; Office of Privacy and Civil Liberties; Office of Professional Responsibility; Office of Public Affairs; Office of Sex Offender Sentencing, Monitoring, Apprehending, Registering, and Tracking; Office of the Solicitor General; Office of Special Counsel; Office of Tribal Justice; Office for Victims of Crime; Office on Violence Against Women; Professional Responsibility Advisory Office; Tax Division; U.S. Attorneys; U.S. Marshals Service; U.S. Parole Commission; and U.S. Trustee Program. Address: U.S. Department of Justice, 950 Pennsylvania Avenue, NW, Washington, DC, 20530-0001; Web: http://www.justice.gov/. *See* Table 27. Department of Justice Organizational Chart, page 254

justifiable homicide. *See* homicide, justifiable

justification. Any just course or excuse for the commission of an act that would otherwise be a crime.

juvenile. A person subject to juvenile court proceedings because the event or condition for which he or she is in court occurred before the person attained an age specified by statute. The age limit defining the legal categories juvenile and adult varies among states and also, with respect to specified crimes, within states. The generally applicable age limit within a given state is most often the 18th birthday. In statutes establishing criminal-trial-court jurisdiction over persons below the standard age for specified crimes (usually violent crimes such a murder or armed robbery), the age limit may be lowered to 16 or even less.

Juvenile and Family Court Judges, Inc., National Council of. Founded in 1937, with the goal of improving the juvenile justice system through publications, training, and research. Publishes *Juvenile and Family Court Journal; Juvenile and Family Law Digest* (monthly); Address: P.O. Box 8970, Reno, NV 89507. Web: http://www.ncjfcj.org/content/blogcategory/0/576/9/45/.

juvenile court. (1) The name for the class courts that have, as all or part of their authority, original jurisdiction over matters concerning persons statutorily defined as juveniles. (2) A specialized court, having jurisdiction in cases of delinquent, neglected, or dependent children, which seeks to determine the underlying causes of misconduct and provides reformation through education, healthful activities, or institutional supervision. Juvenile defendants are entitled to be assisted by counsel and to have all the procedural safeguards that are accorded to adult defendants at all stages of police and judicial proceedings against them. The first juvenile court was the Juvenile Court of Cook County, known as the Chicago Juvenile Court, authorized on April 21, 1899, and opened on July 1, 1899. *See also* Mack, Julian; Table 15: Comparison of Adult and Juvenile Court Terms, page 112

juvenile court judgment. A decision, terminating an adjudicatory hearing, that the juvenile is a delinquent, status offender, or dependent, or that the allegations in the petition are not sustained.

juvenile disposition. The decision of a juvenile court, concluding a disposition hearing, that an adjudicated juvenile be committed to a juvenile correctional facility; placed in a juvenile residence, shelter, or care and treatment program; required to meet certain standards of conduct; or released.

TABLE 27 DEPARTMENT OF JUSTICE ORGANIZATIONAL CHART

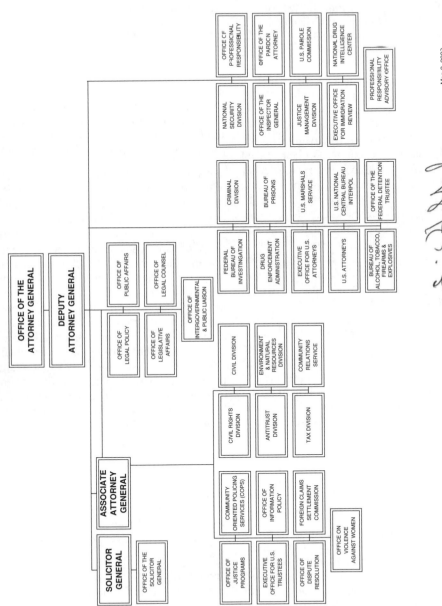

APPROVED BY: _____   DATE: _____ Mar. 2, 2009

ERIC H. HOLDER, JR.
ATTORNEY GENERAL

Source: U.S. Department of Justice.

juvenile facility. A building, section of a building, or area that is used for the custody and/or care and treatment of juveniles who have been either administratively determined to be in need of care or formally alleged or adjudged to be delinquents, status offenders, or dependents. These facilities are either short-term, long-term, open, or institutional. The individual juvenile facility types are: (a) training school, "a long-term specialized facility that provides strict confinement for its residents"; (b) ranch, forestry camp, and farm, "a long-term residential facility for persons whose behavior does not necessitate the strict confinement of a training school, often allowing them greater contact with the community"; (c) halfway house and group home, "a long-term facility in which residents are allowed extensive contact with the community, such as attending school or holding a job"; (d) detention center, "a short-term facility that provides temporary care in a physically restricting environment for juveniles in custody pending court disposition and, often, for juveniles who are adjudicated delinquent or are awaiting transfer to another jurisdiction"; (e) shelter, "a short-term facility that provides temporary care similar to that of a detention center, but in a physically unrestricting environment"; and (f) reception or diagnostic center, "a short-term facility that screens persons committed by the courts and assigns them to appropriate correctional facilities."

Juvenile Firesetter Intervention Program. Under FEMA, the U.S. Fire Administration offers courses to train fire education specialists, fire investigators, counselors, and law enforcement and juvenile authorities. The program is scheduled through state fire training offices. Address: Office of Planning and Education, Fire Administration, Federal Emergency Management Agency, 16825 South Seton Ave., Emmitsburg, MD 21727. http://www.usfa.dhs.gov/nfa/.

juvenile information source. The National Directory of Children and Youth Services contains lists of organizations and agencies that may be able to provide information on matters concerning juvenile justice. It is published by Dorland Health and is available for purchase at http://store.dorlandhealth.com/directories/2010-The-National-Directory-of-Children-Youth-&-Families-Services-2010_94.html.

juvenile justice agency. A government agency, or subunit thereof, of which the functions are the investigation, supervision, adjudication, care, or confinement of juvenile offenders and nonoffenders subject to the jurisdiction of a juvenile court; also, in some usages, a private agency providing care and treatment.

Juvenile Justice and Delinquency Prevention Act of 1974. Federal legislation, amended in 1977 and 1980, that provides funds to states and communities for prevention and treatment programs, emphasizes programs designed to deinstitutionalize status offenders, and provides funding for research on delinquency. This act was further revised with the Juvenile Justice, Runaway Youth, and Missing Children's Act Amendments of 1984. The act also established the Office of Juvenile Justice and Delinquency Prevention and the Missing Children's Assistance Act. In 2009, efforts to revive this Act resulted in the introduction of the Juvenile Justice and Delinquency Prevention Reauthorization Act of 2009. As of March, 2010, it was not yet approved, although it was placed on the legislative calendar in December of 2009.

Juvenile Justice, National Center for. Founded in 1973 as the research division of the National Council of Juvenile and Family Court Judges. Maintains library of databases, volumes on juvenile justice. Address: 3700 South Water Street Suite 200, Pittsburgh, Pa 15203. Web: http://www.ncjjservehttp.org/NCJJWebsite/main.html.

juvenile locators. The National Runaway Switchboard, operated by the Youth Development of Health and Human Services is dedicated to keeping America's runaway and at-risk youth safe and off the streets, informs youths what services are available to them and permits them to telephone their parents long distance without charge. The National Runaway Hotline permits youths to send messages to their parents without revealing their location. Its number is: **1-800-RUN-AWAY** (1-800-786-2929). Correspondence address: National Runaway Switchboard, 3080 N. Lincoln Ave., Chicago, IL 60657; http://www.1800runaway.org/.

juvenile offender. A person under 16, 18, or (in some states) 20 years of age who has been found guilty of committing offenses against the law.

juvenile petition. A document, filed in juvenile court, alleging that a juvenile is a delinquent, status offender, or a dependent, and asking that the court assume jurisdiction over the juvenile or that an alleged delinquent be transferred to criminal court for prosecution as an adult.

juvenile waiver. Practice of transferring juvenile cases to adult court. While provisions of juvenile waiver vary by jurisdiction, waivers usually occur in serious offenses (such as violent felonies), committed by older youth (ages 16–17), or in cases where a repeat juvenile offender continues to recidivate despite previous attempts at rehabilitation and treatment. In some jurisdictions, waiver is a judicial decision, in others, it is a filing decision made by the district attorney.

K

Kaczynski, Theodore John (the Unibomber) (1942–). American mathematician convicted of the Unibomber attacks in the United States. Born in Chicago, Illinois, Kaczynski was a gifted child. He attended Harvard and the University of Michigan, where he earned his Ph.D. in mathematics. He was employed briefly as an assistant professor of mathematics at the University of California, Berkeley for two years; after resigning his position, he moved to a remote cabin in Montana, where he became increasingly concerned with deforestation and wilderness encroachment. Kaczynski began sending bombs to universities and airlines in 1978, a practice that continued until his capture in 1996. In all, Kaczynski sent 16 bombs, killing three people and injuring 23 more. Kaczynski was captured after his brother, who recognized his handwriting and the content of his manifesto sent to newspapers, notified the FBI. Kaczynski pled guilty and was sentenced to life without parole. He is serving his sentence at the Administrative Maximum Facility, a federal super-maximum prison in Colorado. *See also* Unibomber attacks; domestic terrorism

Kagan, Elena (1960 to present). Born in New York City, Kagan graduated **summa cum laude** from Princeton University, received M. Phil. from Oxford University, and graduated *magna cum laude* from Harvard Law School. She was as a law clerk for Justice Thurgood Marshall. Kagan was a law professor at the University of Chicago Law School. She was also a professor at Harvard Law School where she served as dean from 2003–2009. In 2009, she became the 45th Solicitor General of the United States. President Obama nominated her as an Associate Justice of the Supreme Court, and she assumed that position on August 7, 2010.

Kallikaks family. Case name given to a New Jersey family chronicled in the 1912 book *"The Kallikak Family: A Study in the Heredity of Feeble-Mindedness"* by Henry Goddard. Goddard argued for the hereditary nature of "feeble-mindedness," including various conditions such as developmental disabilities, learning disabilities, and mental illness in today's terminology, by tracing the family lineage of a single girl in the New Jersey Home for the Education and Care of Feebleminded Children. Considered cutting edge in 1912, Goddard's methodology is considered extremely flawed in its lack of standardized training of research staff, many of whom pronounced a diagnosis of "feeble-mindedness" within a few minutes of meeting Kallikak relatives. Additionally, the effects of poverty and nutrition, major confounding variables, were not considered in his research. *See also* Jukes Family; Jukes and Kallikaks

Kansas City Experiment. A study conducted by the Police Foundation in 1972 and 1973 where three different levels of preventive police patrol were closely monitored and compared: "normal," "proactive," and "reactive." Normal patrol involved a single police car cruising the streets when not responding to calls; the proactive-patrol strategy involved increasing the levels of preventive patrol and police visibility by doubling or tripling the number of cruising cars; reactive patrol was characterized by the virtual elimination of cruising cars, with police entering the designated areas only in response to specific requests. At the conclusion of the study, no significant differences were found in any of the areas—regardless of the level of patrol. In effect this Kansas City experiment suggested that police patrol did not deter crime.

Kansas City Massacre. Shoot-out between law enforcement and gangsters in Kansas City, Missouri on June 17, 1933. Four lawmen and one fugitive died during the massacre, which occurred as outlaws successful retrieved convicted federal prisoner, Frank Nash. The massacre led to the passage of the Division of Investigation Act (1934), which allowed federal agents to carry firearms and execute arrests.

Kastle-Meyer test. A presumptive catalytic blood test, used to determine the presence of blood in a sample.

Kearney, Patrick Wayne (the "Freeway Killer," 1940–). American killer who is believed responsible for murders of 28 young men in the Los Angeles area between 1965–1977. Kearney generally picked up his victims at gay bars or while hitch-hiking. Kearney would shoot his victims, then mutilate and dismember their bodies, dumping their corpses along the freeway. He admitted 28 murders, he pled guilty to all 21 murders with which he was charged and received 21 consecutive life sentences. He remains incarcerated in a California prison. *See also* serial killer

Keating, Charles (1923–). Keating is best known as the head of Lincoln Savings and Loan Association, which went bankrupt in 1989 and ignited the Savings and Loan Crisis of the 1990s. Keating took advantage of loosened restrictions on Savings and Loan Associations (called S&Ls). Five U.S. senators (the Keating Five) argued for preferential treatment from regulators in 1987. Lincoln S&L engaged in risky investments, unsecured loans, preferential hiring of friends/relatives, and the institution failed in 1989. The failure of Lincoln Savings and Loan cost the federal government over $3 billion, left thousands of customers with worthless bonds, and led to the recession in the 1990s. Keating was convicted of fraud, racketeering, and conspiracy and served nearly five years in prison. His convictions were overturned in 1996; he subsequently pled guilty to lesser crimes (wire fraud and bankruptcy fraud counts), and was sentenced to time served. *See also* fraud offenses; Keating Five; Lincoln Savings and Loan; Savings and Loan Crisis

Keating Five. Five U.S. Senators accused of corruption in 1989 for improperly intervening in on behalf of Charles H. Keating, Jr., chairman of the Lincoln Savings and Loan Association in 1987. The five senators included: Alan Cranston, Dennis DeConcini, John Glenn (also a former astronaut), John McCain (lost Republication Presidential nominee in 2000; the 2008 Republican Presidential nominee), and Donald W. Riegle, Jr. *See also* fraud offenses; Keating, Charles; Lincoln Savings and Loan; Savings and Loan Crisis

Kelly, George "Machine Gun" (1895–1954). Notorious gangster of the depression era known for bootlegging in the depression and served three years federal imprisonment for smuggling alcohol onto an Indian Reservation in 1938. Kelly was also known for armed robbery, and the kidnap-for-ransom of an oil heir in 1933. George Kelly, along with his wife, were convicted and sentenced to life imprisonment for the kidnapping in the first-ever trial that permitted moving cameras in the courtroom. Kelly died of a heart attack in prison at the age of 59; his wife was released from prison in 1958. *See also* depression era gangsters

Kemper, Edmund E. Kemper III ("the Co ed Killer," 1948–). Kemper is an American serial killer who, between 1963–73, is believed to have murdered his grandparents (1963), six women in Santa Cruz area college campuses (1972–1973), and his mother and her friend (1973). After killing his college-student victims, Kemper had sex with the corpses and then mutilated the remains via dissection. Kemper attempted the insanity defense but was convicted of eight murders. He is serving a life sentence in California. *See also* necrophilia; serial killer

Kefauver Investigation. An inquiry into organized crime in interstate commerce by the Senate Crime Committee. The five-man committee was established on May 10, 1950, under the chairmanship of Senator Estes Kefauver, to investigate illegal operations, the influence of crime on political leaders, the use of criminal funds for business investments, and the bribery of police by criminal elements. By February 1951, the committee had interviewed 500 witnesses in New York and other large cities. These witnesses included public officers, political leaders, racketeers, and gamblers. In its first report, the committee declared that gambling involved over $20 billion annually. It recommended the establishment of a national crime commission, a federal ban on interstate transmission of bets and gambling information, a strengthening of federal law enforcement, and an improvement in federal tax laws to reach concealed profits from illegal deals. The committee highlighted the work of national crime syndicates, whose control over state and local politics rendered them immune from prosecution. In its final report on August 31, 1951, the committee declared that conditions in smaller cities were similar to those in large cities and recommended attacking crime at the local level.

Kent State University. On May 4, 1970, in response to a weekend of demonstrations that included arson and vandalism, Ohio National Guard troops opened fire on Kent State students who were protesting the U.S. invasion of Cambodia. Four students were killed and nine wounded. Ten days later, two students were killed and seven more wounded at Jackson State University in Mississippi in a student protest of the Vietnam War and National Guard shooting of Kent State students. State highway patrol officers and Jackson police ordered the students to disperse and the shooting began. *See also* Jackson State University

Kerner Commission. *See* Civil Disorders, National Advisory Commission on

Kevorkian, Dr. Jack. A controversial physician who, with his Mercitron machines, assisted willing patients to end their lives. In February 1993, the state of Michigan enacted legislation making assisted suicide a felony punishable by up to four years in prison and a $2,000 fine. Kevorkian was convicted of second degree murder in 1999 and sentenced to 10–25 years in prison. After serving eight years in prison, Kevorkian was released in June of 2006. As a condition of parole, he is prohibited from publicly discussing assisted suicide. *See also* euthanasia; medicide

key. A term used in fingerprint classification. It is obtained by counting the ridges in the first loop appearing in the set of fingerprints. The loop may be either ulnar or radial and in any finger except the little finger. The thumb may be used. *See also* fingerprint patterns

KEY/CREST program. Delaware-based substance abuse program that provides a continuum of care for substance abusing offenders. KEY, a prison-based therapeutic community, is the first phase of the program. CREST, the second phase, is a six-month, residential treatment program for offenders transitioning from prison to the community. The third component, aftercare, include weekly meetings for offenders who have transitioned back to community living.

Keyser Söze. Name of a fictional character depicted in the 1995 film, *The Usual Suspects,* Keyser Söze has become synonymous with a notorious criminal mastermind.

kidnapping, interstate. A federal crime defined by a law enacted in June 1936, referred to as the Lindbergh Law, as it was passed following the Lindbergh kidnapping case. The law makes it a crime to carry away persons against their will, transport them interstate, and hold them for ransom, reward, or otherwise. The law was later amended to create a presumption of interstate transportation after a victim has been kidnapped for 24 hours without release. *See also* Table 28. Infamous Kidnappings in the United States, this page

killers, serial. *See* serial murders

kilogram. Measure of weight. One kilogram = 2.2046 lb.; 1 gram = 1/28 oz.

King, Martin Luther, Jr. Civil rights leader (1929–1968) who won respect around the world for his nonviolent demonstrations and was awarded the Nobel Peace Prize in 1964.

text continues on page 260

TABLE 28   INFAMOUS KIDNAPPINGS IN THE UNITED STATES

Date	Victim	Perpetrator	Victim Outcome	Perpetrator Outcome
May 22, 1924	Robert Franks	Nathan Leopold and Richard Loeb	Murdered	Sentenced to life in prison.
March 1, 1932	Charles A. Lindbergh Jr.	Bruno Hauptman	Found dead May 12, 1932.	Executed by electrocution.
December 8, 1963	Frank Sinatra Jr.	Barry Keenan, Joe Amsler, John Irwin	Ransom paid and freed.	Sentenced to prison terms. All released within 5 years.
December 17, 1968	Barbara Jane Mackie	Gary Steven Krist, Ruth Eisemann-Schier	Ransom paid and found buried alive.	Convicted and released after serving shortened terms.
December 6, 1973	Victor E. Samuelson	Marxist People's Revolutionary Army	Record ransom paid and released.	Not caught.
December 15, 1973	J. Paul Getty III	Thought to be linked with 'Ndrangheta	Ransom paid and he was released.	Never caught.
February 4, 1974	Patty Hearst	Symbionese Liberation Army	Joined the SLA and was arrested.	William and Emily Harris convicted.
August 9, 1975	Samuel Bronfman	Mel Patrick Lynch and Dominic Byrne	NYPD found Bronfman and recovered ransom.	Convicted of extortion, but claimed Bronfman orchestrated the plan.
December 17, 1981	James L. Dozier	Red Brigade	Rescued	Entire cell was captured.
June 10, 1991	Jaycee Lee Dugard	Phillip Craig Garrido and Nancy Garrido	Rescued after 18 years of captivity.	Arrested and awaiting trial.
September 14, 2006	Andrew Luster	Duane, Tim, and Leland Chapman	Turned into police.	All charges dismissed.
October 2008	Julian King	William Balfour	Found dead.	Awaiting trial.

Compiled by Richard Porter, CSULB.

Born in Atlanta, GA, he drew national attention by leading a movement against segregation in buses. The 382-day Montgomery boycott in 1955/1956 was successful. Following this event, the Southern Christian Leadership Conference (SCLC) was formed to carry on the peaceful drive for the civil rights of black people. King became president of SCLC and continued leading sit-ins and other forms of protest against discrimination. He was arrested many times for violating state segregation laws. In August 1963, King was a leader of the March on Washington by as many as 250,000 supporters of equal rights. To this gathering he addressed his eloquent "I Have a Dream" speech. The efforts of King and his followers were a major force behind the passage by Congress of the Civil Rights Act of 1964, which has been called a Magna Carta for African Americans. In 1968 he went to Memphis, TN, and was assassinated there on April 4 by James Earl Ray. On October 22, 1984, Congress (Senate vote 78–22) designated the third Monday in January, beginning in 1986, as a national holiday in memory of Dr. King. *See also* Ray, James Earl

King, Rodney. The victim in a 1992 case in which an 81-second videotape by amateur photographer George Halliday showed Los Angeles police officers beating King, a motorist. Four officers were indicted, tried in Simi Valley, and acquitted. In the aftermath, the Los Angeles riot left 53 dead and upwards of $1 billion in property damage. Civil rights violations by the officers were filed in federal court, and on April 17, 1993, the verdict was reached and delivered. Officers Koon and Powell were found guilty, and Officers Wind and Briseno were found not guilty. *See also* civil disturbances; Christopher Commission Report; McDuffie, Arthur; Overtown; urban riots

kiting, check. A system of building up deposit balances in a number of banks by drawing on a series of banks where small accounts have been opened. The kiter endeavors to gradually increase the amounts of the deposits. It is a scheme or procedure to defraud and is illegal in many states

Klebold, Dylan (1999). Born and raised in Colorado, Klebold was one of two high school senior responsible for the massacre at Columbine High School on April 20, 1999. Along with friend Eric Harris, Klebold shot and killed 12 students, one teacher, and caused injuries to 24 others before ending his own life on the day of the killings. *See also* Columbine; Harris, Eric

kleptomania. Compulsive stealing, usually without any economic motive. Kleptomaniacs, unlike ordinary thieves or shoplifters, do not steal because they intend to use or sell the stolen items. Nor do they plan their crimes carefully to avoid being caught. Rather, they steal on impulse, and as a result they are easily and frequently caught. It is more common in women than men. According to some theories, kleptomania is traceable to emotional deprivation in infancy. The act of stealing is an expression of revenge directed against symbols of the parent.

Klinefelter's syndrome (XXY syndrome). A genetic condition in which males have an extra X sex chromosome. Klinefelter's is the most common sex chromosome disorder. Symptoms include small testicles and language delays, and deficits in executive functions. Associated with reduced fertility or infertility in adults with the condition. *See also* XYY syndrome

Knapp Commission. Officially called the *Commission to Investigate Alleged Police Corruption,* the Commission was a five-member panel formed in April 1970 to investigate corruption in the New York City Police Department. The commission was prompted by incidents surrounding Patrolman Frank Serpico. The commission's final report found widespread corruption in the New York City Police Department and identified two types of corrupt police officers: "Grass Eaters," who engage in petty corruption because of peer pressure; and "Meat Eaters," who actively pursue major corruption and pressure other officers. *See also* Serpico, Frank; Lexow Commission

known specimens. Items of physical evidence that are obtained from known sources. Handwriting specimens taken from, or known to be the writings of, a person are an example. A firearm taken from a person is a known specimen, contrasted with questioned specimens. Blood samples taken from known persons are known specimens. A crime laboratory, especially the FBI Laboratory, divides all specimens into known and questioned.

Koga method. A form of self-defense named for Robert K. Koga, a retired Los Angeles Police Department officer who began teaching his techniques in the 1960s. Koga draws heavily on the martial art aikido, and stresses minimal force during confrontations to reduce the likelihood of injury to officers and suspects. It also offers nontraditional ways, such as distraction, to achieve compliance. Address: The Koga Institute, 210 E. Fig St. Suite 103, Fallbrook, CA 92028. Web http://www.kogainst.com/index.html.

Krenwinkel, Patricia (1947–). Manson follower convicted of murder for the Tate and La Bianca murders in Los Angeles, California in 1969. Krenwinkel was sentenced to death, commuted in 1972 following a California Supreme Court decision (People v. Anderson). Krenwinkel remains incarcerated despite 11 attempts at parole. *See also* Manson, Charles

Ku Klux Klan. (1) An organization founded in Tennessee in 1866 to reassert white supremacy in the South. Disguised in white masks, robes, and conical hats, members of the Klan rode at night, terrorizing, whipping, and committing other acts of violence (including murder) against blacks who persisted in voting and acting contrary to a white-oriented society. After congress passed the Ku Klux Klan Act and the Force Act in 1871, the Klan adopted less violent means to accomplish its purpose. (2) The KKK is a general term referencing one of more than 150 ultra conservative hate groups in the United States claiming to protect the rights and interests of white Protestant Americans. This "subversive

or terrorist organization" often uses intimidation, violence, lynching, murder, and terrorism, often aimed at African Americans, Jews, and other non-white, non-Protestants. KKK is currently estimated to have 5,000–8,000 members in the United States, with a current focus towards issues of illegal immigration and same-sex marriage. In November of 2008, the Southern Poverty Law Center successfully brought a case against the Imperial Klans of America for beating a 16-year-old boy at a Kentucky fair. A jury awarded a total of $2.5 million in damages to the victim.

L

La Eme. *See* Mexican Mafia

labeling model in crime. A theoretical approach to deviant behavior, basically stating that applying formal definitions to an individual results in a negative self-concept that may subsequently provide motivation for further acts of deviance. *See also* labeling theory

labeling theory. Frank Tannenbaum in 1938 defined the beginning of a criminal career as the result of a "dramatization of evil,"—the point at which a child is singled out from the group and treated as a delinquent. By 1963, Howard Becker had further developed and renamed Tannenbaum's theory. Now called labeling, Becker's theory held that this interactionist concept could explain deviance in terms of societal reaction to acts of the individual. Labeling theory has come into prominence over the past several decades as a major approach to explaining the nature of deviance. The labeling theory stresses that social rules are not clear-cut and that they result in ambiguous evaluations of behavior. Deviance is also emphasized as a process in which deviant rules and self-conceptions are shaped. *See also* self-fulfilling prophecy

labor relations. The relations of employer and employee affecting the conditions of labor. As defined in federal and state labor relations acts, and interpreted by the courts, labor relations include matters dealing with wages, hours, tenure, security, hiring, discharge, union organization and activities, representation, and promotion.

labor union. A combination or association of workers in some trade or industry, or in several allied trades, that exists for the purpose of securing by concerted action the most favorable wages, hours, and conditions of labor, and otherwise improving workers' economic and social status.

laches. An unreasonable delay in pursuing a legal remedy, concurrent with resulting prejudice to the opposing party, whereby the individual who sought the legal remedy forfeits his or her right to do so.

lachrymator. A substance that causes severe weeping or tear production of the eyes. Such chemicals are used in tear gas.

La Cosa Nostra. Italian phrase, translated "this thing of ours," and colloquial term for Italian mafia in the United States. *See also* mafia

La Guardia Report. Short title for a 1938 study of marijuana ordered by New York mayor Fiorello La Guardia, conducted by the New York Academy of Medicine, with the assistance of the New York Police Department. Headed by George B. Wallace, the committee was composed of 31 eminent physicians, psychiatrists, clinical psychologists, pharmacologists, chemists, and sociologists. The study was in two parts: a clinical study of the effects of marijuana and a sociological study of marijuana users in New York City. The report refuted the stepping-stone hypothesis, and generally stressed that the sociological, psychological, and medical ills commonly attributed to marijuana are exaggerated.

Lanham Act of 1946. Federal statute that prohibits trademark infringement, trademark dilution, and false advertising. *See also* counterfeiting, trademark

Lansky, Meyer (1902–1983). Lansky was a prominent organized crime figure responsible for the rise of the mafia in the United States and was a close associate of Lucky Luciano. Lansky ran several successful bootlegging operations in the 1920s under prohibition, established organized crime presence in Cuba in the 1930s, and financed *The Flamingo* hotel in Las Vegas, run by Bugsy Siegel. Forbes named Lansky one of the wealthiest people in 1982, estimating his worth at over $100,000 million. He died of lung cancer in 1983, with almost no documented assets (which some attribute to his ability to hide funds). *See also* Luciano, Charles; Siegel, Bugsy; mafia.

larceny. Unlawful taking or attempted taking of property other than a motor vehicle from the possession of another, by stealth, without force and without deceit, with intent to permanently deprive the owner of the property. Larceny is a UCR reporting category under larceny-theft. The distinction between larceny as a felony or misdemeanor, or grand larceny versus petty larceny, is of a statutory nature, usually specified around $250, although this threshold varies by state. Grand larceny can range from as little as $5 if taken from a person in Virginia (or $250 if taken from property instead of a person in that state), to $1,000 in New York, to as much as $2,000 in PA; a value below these amounts constitutes a misdemeanor. The only exception is NC, where the law does not specify a dividing point.

laser. A term based on Light Amplification by Stimulated Emission Radiation, it is an electrical/optical device for producing a coherent parallel beam of light—that is, one in which the light waves are all in phase. Such a beam can be made much more precisely narrow and parallel than can one of ordinary light.

laundering money. Offenses defined as "all activities designed to conceal the existence, nature, and final disposition of funds gained through illicit activities." Money laundering per se did not become a federal crime until passage of the Money Laundering Control Act (MLCA) of 1986 (Pub. L. 99-570, 100 Stat. 3207-18). Until then, the main tools for combating money laundering were provided by the Bank Secrecy Act of 1970. The MLCA of 1986 created two new offenses related to money laundering and currency transaction reporting violations: (1) engaging in financial transactions and international transportations or transfers of funds or property derived from "specified unlawful activity," and (2) engaging in monetary transactions in excess of $10,000 with property derived from proceeds of specified unlawful activity. In addition, the Anti-Drug Abuse Act of 1986 prohibited the structuring of currency transactions to deliberately evade reporting requirements. Also, these offenses and certain violations of the currency reporting requirements are included acts under the Racketeer Influenced and Corrupt Organizations (RICO) statute. In 2008, the U.S.S.C. ruled in two cases that effectively reduced the scope of money laundering statutes. In *United States v. Santos,* 553 U. S. 507 (2008), the court opinion read: "criminal 'proceeds' strictures apply only to transactions involving criminal 'profits,' not criminal 'receipts,' and that there was no evidence that the transactions on which the convictions were based involved profits from respondents' illegal lottery operation;" this decision vacated several money laundering convictions. Likewise, in *Regalado Cuellar v. United States,* 553 U. S. 550 (2008), the USSC overturned the money laundering conviction of a man transporting $81,000, hidden under floorboards into Mexico. The court opinion read: "a conviction requires proof that the transportation's purpose, not merely its effect, was to conceal or disguise." The International Monetary Fund estimates the scope of money laundering at 2–5 percent of the worldwide global economy; others estimate between $300 and $500 billion annually. Combating money laundering is of growing importance given the ties between money laundering and terrorist financing. *See also* Bank Secrecy Act; Dr. Snow; Mafia;

Operation El Dorado; Operation Polar Cap; organized crime; Pizza Connection; Racketeer Influenced and Corrupt Organization; terrorist financing; Anti-Money Laundering/Combating Financing of Terrorism (AML/CFT)

law. (1) A general rule for the conduct of members of the community, either emanating from the governing authority by positive command or approved by it, and habitually enforced by some public authority by the imposition of sanctions or penalties for its violation. (2) The whole body of such rules, including constitutions, the common law, equity, statutes, judicial decisions, administrative orders, and ordinances, together with the principles of justice and right commonly applied in their enforcement.

law, administrative. Statutes, regulations, and orders that govern public agencies. Essentially these are rules governing the administrative operations of the government— public law as opposed to private law. Administrative law includes social insurance, legislative committee powers, and public authorities such as the Interstate Commerce Commission and the Federal Power Commission. There is no separate legal system of administrative law in the United States, as there is in European law systems, and matters of administrative law are considered by the Supreme Court. The existence of administrative law with legal standing gives the public some control over the administrative activities of the government. Illegitimate interference and abuse by public authorities can be checked, definite standards for public conduct established, and supervision of public authorities provided. Many believe that the increased administrative activities of the U.S. government and the resulting legal problems demand an established system of administrative law with qualified judges and courts. Administrative law has been referred to as the fourth branch of government.

law and order. A catch-phrase for the suppression of crime and violence, used particularly against civil rights activists and antiwar demonstrators during the 1960s and early 1970s. The term conveyed subtle racism where it was used by politicians to appeal to voters who opposed segregation in the South. Later the term was used by the federal government to justify the repression of antiwar demonstrators. Law and order was a particularly useful term for government officials because, with the high crime rate, race-connected riots, bombings, and street violence, few could argue against attempts to maintain law and order in the United States. Historically, the phrase was also heavily used as a convention slogan for the Harding-Coolidge ticket in 1920. Most contemporary politicians emphasize a strong law-and-order platform.

law and social control. Law imposes formal control on society by setting forth specific rules of conduct, planned sanctions to support these rules, and designated officials to make, interpret, and enforce the rules. The objective is conformity and stability in society. The emphasis on formalism in law makes the regulation of social relations seem more important than the social relations themselves. Nevertheless, formal social controls are considered necessary in modern society because of its complexity and anonymity.

law, blue. *See* blue laws

law book, first published. William Penn's *The Excellent Privilege of Liberty and Property Being the Birth-Right of the Freeborn Subjects of England,* an 83-page book, was printed by William Bradford and published in Philadelphia in 1687. It contained: "(a) the Magna Carta, with a learned comment upon it; (b) the confirmation of the Charters of the Liberties of England and of the Forrest, made in the 35th year of the reign of Edward I; (c) a statute made in the 34th year of the reign of Edward I, commonly called De Tallageo *non concedendo*, wherein all fundamental laws, liberties, and customs are confirmed, with a comment upon them; (d) an abstract of the patent granted by the king to William Penn and his heirs and assigns for the province of Pennsylvania; and (e) lastly, the charter of

liberties granted by the said William Penn to the freemen and inhabitants of the province of Pennsylvania and territories there unto annexed in America."

law, canon. A code governing the organization and operation of a church. The regulations of canon law apply the moral precepts of church doctrine to the daily lives of members.

law, common. Body of rules based on judicial decisions rather than legislation; it is the basis of the Anglo-American legal tradition. The common law judge relies on judicial decisions of the past in rendering rulings. Under the common law approach, the law can change gradually at the hands of the judges to meet changes in society. In the United States, the common law system is evident in the supremacy of the judiciary in determining the constitutionality of legislation. In contrast, the system of civil law prominent on the continent of Europe is based on Roman law and later codes of legislation.

Law, Elizabethan Poor. A law enacted by the English Parliament in 1603, summarizing and consolidating a variety of laws concerning poor relief passed during the preceding century. The law required the local community to assume responsibility for the care of its own poor, established the principle of destitution as a test of eligibility for assistance, and decreed that relief could be granted only in return for work in places provided for housing the poor. The principles of public assistance established by the Elizabethan Poor Law governed the administration of relief in England and the United States for over 300 years.

law enforcement. The generic name for the activities of the agencies responsible for maintaining public order and enforcing the law, particularly the activities of prevention, detection, and investigation of crime and the apprehension of criminals.

law enforcement agency. A federal, state, or local criminal justice agency or identifiable subunit whose principal functions are the prevention, detection, and investigation of crime and the apprehension of alleged offenders.

law enforcement assistance. Funds, equipment, training, intelligence information, and personnel.

Law Enforcement Assistance Administration (LEAA). An agency created by Title I of the Omnibus Crime Control and Safe Streets Act of 1968. In 1965, the Office of Law Enforcement Assistance (OLEA) was established within the U.S. Department of Justice to make funds available to states, localities, and private organizations to improve methods of law enforcement, court administration, and prison operations. It was the federal agency charged with channeling federal funds to states to assist local communities in combating crime and improving justice services. In 1969, LEAA assumed these functions and created state planning agencies, block and discretionary grants, and the National Institute of Law Enforcement and Criminal Justice. LEAA also supplied money for the training and education of criminal justice personnel through the Law Enforcement Education Program (LEEP). LEEP, throughout the 1970s, provided more than $40 million per year in loans for educational assistance to some 100,000 persons employed in, or preparing for, careers in criminal justice. Loans were forgiven at 25 percent each year the person was employed in the system. According to the Twentieth Century Fund Task Force, in spite of the billions of dollars spent, LEAA was deemed a failure and ceased operations in 1982. *See also* Comprehensive Crime Control Act of 1984

law enforcement community, federal. The term means the heads of the Federal Bureau of Investigation; Drug Enforcement Administration; Criminal Division of the Department of Justice; Internal Revenue Service; Customs Service; Immigration and Naturalization Service; United States Marshals Service; National Park Service; United States Postal Service; Secret Service; Coast Guard;

Bureau of Alcohol, Tobacco, Firearms and Explosives; Department of Homeland Security; and other federal agencies with specific statutory authority to investigate violations of federal criminal laws.

law enforcement emergency. A federal term meaning "an uncommon situation which is, or threatens to become, serious or of epidemic proportions, and in which state and local resources are inadequate to protect the lives and property of citizens or enforce the criminal law." The term does not include the perceived need for planning or other activities related to crowd control for general public safety projects or a situation requiring the enforcement of laws associated with scheduled public events, including political conventions and sports events.

law enforcement equipment. The National Bureau of Standards Library has a special division that investigates such products as surveillance cameras, vapor generators, radar, breath alcohol detection, and clothing worn by law enforcement officers. Address: Office of Law Enforcement Standards, 100 Bureau Drive, M/S 8102, Gaithersburg, MD 20899. Web site: www.eeel.nist.gov.

Law Enforcement Intelligence Units. Units within law enforcement agencies that focus on the collection of materials that are analyzed to produce information on criminal patterns, organizations, networks and activities to support law enforcement agencies in their fight against crime. *See also* Association of Law Enforcement Intelligence Units

law enforcement officer. (1) In some usages, any government employee who is an officer sworn to carry out law enforcement duties, whether or not employed by an agency or identifiable subunit that primarily performs law enforcement functions. (2) An employee of a law enforcement agency who is an officer sworn to carry out law enforcement duties. Examples of federal law enforcement officers include agents of the Federal Bureau of Investigation; the Bureau of Alcohol, Tobacco, Firearms and Explosives; the U.S. Marshall Service, and the investigative staff of federal organized crime units and tax law enforcement units. State law enforcement officer examples include: state, police officers, state highway patrol officers and state park police and campus police officers who are employees of state universities and state colleges. Local law enforcement officer examples include: sheriffs, deputy sheriffs, chiefs of police, city police officers, sworn personnel of law enforcement subunits of port and transit authorities, and campus police officers who are employees of local city and community college districts. Private campus police are generally excluded.

Law Enforcement Officers Killed and Assaulted (LEOKA). The FBI annually compiles data concerning the felonious and accidental line-of-duty deaths and assaults of law enforcement officers and presents these statistics in *Law Enforcement Officers Killed and Assaulted* (LEOKA). Tabular presentations include weapons used, use of body armor, and circumstances surrounding murders and assaults of officers. Web: http://www.fbi.gov/ucr/killed/2008/. *See* Table 29. Law Enforcement Officers Feloniously Killed, page 267

Law Enforcement Officers Memorial, National. The memorial was dedicated by President George Bush in Washington, DC, on October 15, 1991, after seven years of planning. It was built with $10.5 million in private contributions. Inscribed on its two curved marble walls—304 feet long and 3½ feet high—are the 12,561 names of U.S. law enforcement officers who have died in the line of duty since 1794. Statues of lions guard each end, and the site is brimming with trees, grass, and flowers.

Law Enforcement Research Publications. This office of the National Institute of Justice (DOJ) is responsible for the publication and distribution of institute research and evaluation findings and programs. It also oversees the operations of the National Criminal Justice Reference Services. Address: National Institute of Justice, DOJ, 810 Seventh Street NW, Washington, DC 20531. Web site: www.ojp.usdoj.gov/nij/.

Law Enforcement Training Network (LETN). Established in 1989, LETN is a 24-hour exclusive satellite television network for law enforcement. Programs feature training, daily news, documentaries, and police events. Address: 4101 International Parkway, Carrollton, TX 75007. Web site: www.letn.com/.

law, natural. An abstract concept of law based on the relation among God, man, and nature. An ideal higher than positive or man-made law, it forms the basis of justice in the ethical sense. It embodies such ideas as the existence of a universal order governing all people and the inalienable rights of the individual. John Locke used natural law principles in setting forth the basic rights of the individual in his social contract theories, and natural law ideas were influential in the framing of the Constitution of the United States.

law of effect. A fundamental concept in learning theory holding that, all other things being equal, a person will more readily learn those habits leading to satisfaction and will not learn (or will learn with greater difficulty) those habits leading to dissatisfaction.

law of nations. Called international law and sometimes public law, it includes those rules that define and regulate the conduct of nations in their interaction with each other. It consists of: (a) a code of what may be called natural law, dictated by the sentiment that nations should cooperate with each other; (b) a system of unwritten law, depending upon principles of comity or international courtesy; and (c) a code of positive law, derived from ancient codes, treaties, judicial decisions, state papers, and the opinions of great writers upon the subject whose experience as statesmen gives their words authority.

law of the sea. The UN Conference on the Law of the Sea (1973–1982) addressed international issues such as navigation, overflight, conservation and management of fisheries' resources, protection of the marine environment, exploitation of oil and gas in the continental shelf, marine scientific research, and a system of compulsory dispute settlement. An

TABLE 29 LAW ENFORCEMENT OFFICERS FELONIOUSLY KILLED Population Group/Agency Type of Victim Officer's Agency, 1999–2008											
Population Group/Agency Type	Total	1999	2000	2001[1]	2002	2003	2004	2005	2006	2007	2008
Number of victim officers	530	42	51	70	56	52	57	55	48	58	41
Group I (cities 250,000 and over)	103	8	8	13	6	9	15	12	8	12	12
Group II (cities 100,000–249,999)	48	1	4	7	6	4	6	6	4	9	1
Group III (cities 50,000–99,999)	25	1	1	1	3	3	4	4	2	5	1
Group IV (cities 25,000–49,999)	24	3	0	1	1	5	2	2	3	2	5
Group V (cities 10,000–24,999)	34	2	3	6	5	2	5	2	3	3	3
Group VI (cities under 10,000)	60	8	9	7	6	5	7	10	3	5	0
Metropolitan counties	101	5	11	15	11	10	8	6	15	11	9
Nonmetropolitan counties	63	8	10	9	8	9	4	4	3	4	4
State agencies	42	5	3	4	4	5	3	5	4	6	3
Federal agencies	10	1	0	1	2	0	0	2	1	0	3
Puerto Rico and Other Outlying Areas	20	0	2	6	4	0	3	2	2	1	0

About 72 deaths on September 11, 2001 not included in table.

Source: Federal Bureau of Investigation, *Law Enforcement Officers Killed and Assaulted.*

impressive collection of reports of the UN Law of the Sea are archived at the Bodleian Library at Oxford University: http://www.bodleian.ox.ac.uk/.

law of the situation. A management concept suggesting that one person should not give orders to another person, but both should agree to take their action cues from the situation at hand.

law, poor. An antiquated name still frequently applied to the body of laws governing the administration of public assistance. The name dates from sixteenth-century England and is best known in relation to the

Elizabethan Poor Law of 1603. The name was borrowed by the colonies and continued in use to designate various state laws dealing with relief of poor and dependent persons. Public welfare and public assistance are terms that are gradually replacing the term *poor law*. In a wider sense, poor law is synonymous with a degrading and short-sighted system of poor relief based on severe laws of settlement, pauper oaths, standards of relief below that of the poorest-paid common laborer, and relief in kind.

law reform. Adjustment of legislation to changing social conditions. Reform is called for when a law is not incorporated into the culture of the society and is thus not enforceable. Law reform can take place in the courts, through lawyers, or in legislatures. The courts can initiate basic change by reinterpreting the Constitution or by making decisions that lay the groundwork for legislation. For example, various Supreme Court decisions on civil equality culminated in the Civil Rights Act of 1965. Citizens can also institute law reform through the courts by bringing representative suits—actions against local authorities on behalf of a group—to produce a declaratory judgment. Lawyers play a significant role in law reform through the law revision committees set up by bar associations. Legislative law reform, which generally is slower than court reform, takes place on the state and federal levels.

laws. (1) a system of rules enforced through institutions. (2) The individual items within the broad field of law, natural or manmade. Scientific laws are particular statements of generalized truths, especially those having to do with causative sequence. Juristic laws are the items on the statute books of states; in ordinary usage, the current statutes of any particular state. These fall into three main categories: (a) general laws, which apply to all citizens or persons or to all persons within legally recognized groups or classes; (b) special laws, enacted for particular purposes; and (c) private laws, passed for the benefit of particular individuals. Scientific laws are divisible into (a) quantitative laws, which are

principles or generalizations explaining the aspects of quantity; and (b) qualitative laws, which are principles or generalizations explaining the aspects of quality.

laws, compilation of colonial, first. *"The Book of the General Lawes and Libertyes,* concerning the inhabitants of Massachusetts, collected out of the records of the General Court for the several years wherein they were made and established and now revised by the same Court and disposed into an Alphabetical order and published by the same Authorities in the General Court held at Boston the fourteenth of the first month Anno 1647."* The work was published in Cambridge, MA, in 1648 and sold by Hezekiah Usher in Boston.

laws, compilation of United States, first. Codifying the laws in force was *The Public Statutes at Large of the United States of America,* from the organization of the government in 1789 to March 3, 1845, arranged in chronological order with references to the matter of each act and to subsequent acts on the same subject and with notes on the decisions of the courts of the United States construing those acts and upon the subjects of the laws, with an index to the contents of each volume.

laws, sumptuary. Laws designed to regulate people's expenditures for food, clothing, and other consumable goods, especially luxuries; to restrict or forbid the use of certain goods. The method usually used today to exercise this type of control is taxation.

LCN. *See* low copy number

LD50 (lethal dose 50 percent). Nomenclature for "median lethal dose." The median lethal dose of a substance is the dose required to kill 50 percent of the subjects in a tested population. For example, the LD50 for ethanol (alcohol) is about 7,060 mg/kg in humans; LD50 for VX nerve agent is about 0.0023 mg/kg for humans; the LD50 for botox is 0.000001 mg/kg.

leading question. A question asked of a witness during a trial or court proceeding that suggests, and thus may elicit, an answer that might otherwise not be offered by the witness. Leading questions, while not ordinarily allowed, are permissible under certain conditions.

learning theory. An explanation of crime and delinquency postulating that criminal behavior, like legal and normative behavior, is learned. Such learning may be acquired from those already engaged in illegal activity, as in differential association theory; learning may be reinforced through rewards and punishments. *See also* differential association

learning, three schools of. (1) Classical conditioning; (2) operant conditioning; and (3) cognitive learning theory. (1) and (2) focus on the stimulus-response connection as the basic unit of analysis in the learning process; (3) suggests that conditioning and learning are one and the same.

leftists, political. Those people in the political spectrum who seek radical, innovative changes towards a more egalitarian society. Today, socialism is the dominant leftist position. The term derives from the seating arrangements in the French *Assemblee Nationale* in 1789, where radical Jacobin or Montagnard members sat on the presiding officer's left.

legal aid. Any number of programs designed to provide legal and quasi-legal assistance to persons who cannot afford to hire their own attorneys. The term is frequently used to include only legal assistance of a civil—as opposed to a criminal—nature, particularly since 1963, when *Gideon v. Wainwright* required a publicly appointed defense counsel in criminal cases (*See also* Gideon, Clarence). A large number of organizations, both privately and publicly sponsored, have been established to render this type of legal service. One of the oldest is the Legal Aid Society. In addition, the federal government sponsors the Legal Services Corporation, with headquarters in Washington, DC. One of the most promising developments is union-sponsored legal insurance, which keeps a law firm on retainer, for a fixed annual fee, to handle union members' problems without additional charge.

legal assistants. *See* paralegals

legal counsel for police. Attorneys who work for, and are employed by, law enforcement agencies as legal counselors, advisers, or house counsel.

Legal Counsel for the Elderly. Various organizations provide direct, free legal services to persons aged 55 and older. Information about such services is available through the American Association of Retired Persons (AARP): http://www.aarp.org/aarp/lce/ and the Legal Counsel for the Elderly, operated out of the University of Alabama Law School: http://www.uaelderlaw.org/.

legal ethics. Customs among those in the legal profession involving their responsibilities toward each other, the courts, and their clients. *See also* code of ethics

legal evidence. A broad, general term meaning all admissible evidence, including both oral and documentary, but with a further implication that it must be of such a character as to reasonably and substantially prove the point, not merely to raise a suspicion or conjecture.

legal fiction. A condition assumed to be true in law, regardless of its actual truth or falsity—sometimes used by judges so that a new subject, for which no rules of law have been formulated, may be embraced within existing rules.

Legal Investigators, National Association of. Founded in 1967. Publishes *Legal Investigator* (quarterly). Address: 235 N. Pine Street, Lansing, MI 48933. http://www.nalionline.org/.

legal malpractice. Sometimes called "ineffective counsel," the negligence of an attorney who makes a gross error no reasonable attorney would make, which causes harm to the client that would not have occurred but for the attorney's negligent act. *See also* malpractice

legal opinions. The legal opinions of the Department of Justice are published by the Office of Legal Counsel and are made available through the Superintendent of Documents, Government Printing Office, 732 North Capitol Street, NW, Washington, DC 20401. For further information, contact: Office of Legal Counsel, DOJ, United States Department of Justice, 950 Pennsylvania Avenue, NW, Washington, DC 20530. Web site: www.justice.gov/olc/.

legal person (sometimes called legal personality). The legal status accorded a corporation or other artificial person that entitles it to hold and administer property, to sue in the courts, and to enjoy many of the rights and assume many of the liabilities of an actual person.

legal provocation. Provocation that can be used as a legal defense for an act.

legal realism. A pragmatic approach concerned with the actual working of the rules of law. It centers on identifying the discrepancy between the form of law and the reality of law (or the letter and the spirit) that occurs when laws do not keep up with the changes in society. The basis of legal realism is the scientific method; psychology, sociology, criminology, economics, and statistics are among the disciplines that are incorporated into this method to study the social factors that create the law and its social results.

Legal Services for Children (LSC). Comprehensive, cost-free law firm devoted exclusively to protecting the legal rights of teens, children, and infants who are residents of San Francisco, CA, and other Bay Area counties. Supported by social workers, social work student interns, law students, and support staff. LSC is the first organization of its kind in the nation. Address: 1254 Market Street, 3rd Floor, San Francisco, CA 94102. Web site: http://www.lsc-sf.org/.

legislation. Laws of general application, enacted by a law-making body.

legislative power. The power to make law, generally the power to make policy. In the Constitution, this power is delegated to Congress in Article I. Under the separation-of-powers principle, legislative powers are theoretically exercised only by the legislature. In fact, the president exercises considerable legislative powers, and the Supreme Court's power of judicial review may be considered a legislative power as well.

legitimacy. The belief of a citizenry that a government has the right to rule and that a citizen ought to obey the rules and laws of that government. An illegitimate government must rule either by coercion or by providing material rewards. A legitimate government, on the other hand, should be able to withstand crises, such as economic depressions, when people may feel their needs are not being met and that laws are restrictive. A government can increase its legitimacy by appealing to such symbols as the flag or a constitution. In the United States, elections are probably the most important device for legitimating a government.

Leopold and Loeb. Two men convicted of killing 14-year-old Robert Franks in 1924. Leopold and Loeb committed what they felt would be a "perfect crime"—the kidnapping, ransoming, and killing of a young victim, 14-year-old Bobby Franks. Leopold and Loeb abducted Franks, a relative of Loeb, into a rental car, killed him, poured hydrochloric acid on their victim to prevent identification, and dumped the body in a ravine near railroad tracks. They mailed a ransom note, but the boy's body was found before they could collect. Leopold and Loeb, who were represented by Clarence Darrow, pled guilty to murder in an effort to avoid the death penalty; they were sentenced to life plus 99 years in prison. *See also* Leopold, Nathan Freudenthal, Jr., and Loeb, Richard Albert.

Leopold, Nathan Freudenthal, Jr. (1904–1971) Leopold was extremely intelligent, with an IQ reported to be 210. A graduate of the University of Chicago, law student, and the son of a multimillionaire shipping magnate, Leopold was only 19 years old when he and friend Richard Albert Loeb kidnapped and murdered 14-year-old Bobby Franks for the sole purpose of committing a perfect crime. Represented by Clarence Darrow, the two pled guilty to avoid the death penalty. They were sentenced to life plus 99 years. While incarcerated, Leopold was voluntarily infected with malaria as part of the Stateville Penitentiary Malaria Study. Leopold was paroled in 1958, after 33 years in prison and published a book entitled, *Life Plus 99 Years*. He died of a heart attack in 1971 and donated his organs. *See also* Darrow, Clarence; Loeb, Richard Albert; Leopold and Loeb

less lethal weapon. Weapons that are unlikely to cause death when properly used, but which can cause death in some circumstances. Examples include: rubber, plastic, bean bag, or paint bullets; flashbang, stun and sting grenades with rubber shrapnel; and tasers. Less lethal weapons generally include a higher level of force than those categorized as nonlethal weapons, which include, for example, electromagnetic weapons, water cannons, air guns, and gasses (such as tear gas and skunk spray). *See also* nonlethal force; less lethal weapon; TASER. *See also* nonlethal weapon

lesser included offense. A separate offense, all of the elements of which are alleged, among other elements, in an offense charged in an indictment.

lethal chamber. A room or place, within or adjacent to a prison or jail, where prisoners convicted of capital crimes are put to death.

lethal gas. A method of execution in which the prisoner is strapped into one of two seats in the 7½-foot-wide chamber (e.g., San Quentin Prison, CA). Beneath each chair is an empty ceramic reservoir. Suspended above the reservoir are sodium cyanide granules wrapped in foot-square pieces of cheesecloth. At the warden's signal, a valve is turned, releasing distilled water and sulfuric acid into the reservoirs. At a second signal, a switch is thrown and the cyanide granules are lowered into the acid. The prisoner inhales the rising lethal gas. Damaging all tissue it contacts, the gas reaches the lungs. In the lungs, blood is passing through capillaries surrounding the alveoli—tiny, grape-like structures where gas exchange takes place.

Normally, the red blood cells drop off carbon dioxide here and pick up oxygen. But cyanide gas binds more readily to blood cells than does oxygen. So the cells travel away to the body's tissues carrying cyanide, rather than their essential cargo of oxygen. As brain tissues begin to die from lack of oxygen and the cyanide's toxicity, the prisoner loses consciousness. Several minutes later, the heartbeat stops. Almost immediately breathing fails and the prisoner dies. The reservoirs are then drained. Caustic soda and water are flushed through the pipes and reservoirs. An exhaust fan sucks the gas up a copper pipe that rises 20 feet above the prison roof. In about 30 minutes, the chamber is opened and the body is removed. Although not used since 1999 (Walter La Grand, Arizona), four states currently authorize this method of execution. Lethal injection remains the primary method, but lethal gas is permitted in Arizona, California, Missouri, Wyoming. *See also* execution, methods of; lethal injection; electrocution; hanging; and firing squad. *See* Table 24. Execution Methods in the United States, by State, 2010, page 173

lethal injection. Lethal injection is a method of execution in which the prisoner is strapped to a gurney (table) and a combination of drugs is dripped from a bottle into veins in both arms. One drug, potassium, interferes with the heart's normal electrical pattern and makes it stop beating. Another drug paralyzes the body's muscles and makes breathing stop. The resultant oxygen loss causes brain damage and death results in about four minutes. Lethal injection is the most common method of execution in the United States and is in use by the following 37 jurisdictions: Alabama, Arizona, Arkansas, California, Colorado, Connecticut, Delaware, Florida, Georgia, Idaho, Illinois, Indiana, Kansas, Kentucky, Louisiana, Maryland, Mississippi, Missouri, Montana, Nevada, New Hampshire, New Mexico, New York, North Carolina, Ohio, Oklahoma, Oregon, Pennsylvania, South Carolina, South Dakota, Tennessee, Texas, Utah, Virginia, Washington, Wyoming, and the federal system. In *Baze v Rees* 553 U.S.

35 (2008), the U.S. Supreme Court considered the use of lethal injection, which was argued to be an Eighth Amendment violation of cruel and unusual punishment due to concerns that incorrect administration results in a inmate paralysis during an agonizing death due to asphyxiation. *See also* execution, methods of; electrocution; lethal gas; hanging; and firing squad. *See* Table 24. Execution Methods in the United States, by State, 2010, page 173

LETN. *See* Law Enforcement Training Network

Letourneau, Mary Kay. (1962–). Born Mary Katherine Schmitz, became Letourneau upon marriage (since divorced from Mr. Letourneau); her current legal name is Mary Kay Fualaau. Letourneau was the married mother of four and a teacher when she was convicted of the statutory rape of a 13-year old boy, one of her students, in 1997. Letourneau was the boy's teacher in second grade, although the sexual relationship did not begin until he was a sixth grader in her 5th–6th grade combination class. Letourneau became pregnant when her victim was 13 and she was 35. The affair reportedly became known when Letourneau's husband read letters between his wife and the boy; police were subsequently notified. Letourneau was arrested on February 26, 1997. She gave birth to a daughter in June of 1997, was convicted, and was given a suspended sentence of 89 months in August of the same year. Under the terms of her suspended sentence, she was ordered to serve six months in jail, attend a three-year sex offender program, and stay away from the victim. She was released from custody in January 1, 1998; she was arrested again on February 3, 1998, when police found her in a car with the victim, a large sum of cash, baby clothes, and a passport. Her probation was revoked and the 89-month suspended sentence was subsequently imposed. Letourneau gave birth to a second child fathered by her victim, delivered in October of 1998, while she was incarcerated. In 1999, she and her husband divorced, and he moved to another state with their children. Letourneau was released from prison August 4, 2004. Within days, the victim, who was then aged 21, petitioned the court to lift the no-contact order issued in 1997; the order was lifted August 7, 2004. Letourneau and Vili Fualaau, the victim, were married on May 20, 2005. The couple occasionally host "Hot for Teacher" night at clubs in the Seattle area. *See also* pedophile

LETS. The national Law Enforcement Teletype System, a noncommercial, cooperative interstate system of information exchange between law enforcement agencies in the mid-1960s through 1980s. The system used common carrier landline circuits.

leuco-malachite test. A preliminary test for the presence of blood. A positive result is not conclusive, but a negative result indicates blood is not the substance being tested.

lewd and lascivious conduct. A statutory, term describing criminal sexual behavior such as gross, wanton, and public indecency; a sexual act that the actor knows will be observed by someone; a sexual act that would offend most people if detected. Often acts under this category include child victim and contain acts that are lustful, or intended to excite a sexual desire. However, crimes in this category generally do not include penetration, which is usually prosecuted as rape.

lex talionis (Lat., lit.). Law of the claw. (1) Law of retaliation, such as "an eye for an eye and a tooth for a tooth." (2) In modern times, also the acts of one nation in retaliation for the acts of another, which may include amicable retaliatory acts.

Lexow Commission. A committee appointed by the New York State legislature in 1894 to investigate complaints of corruption in the New York City Police Department. The Committee's findings were an important stimulus toward the first major efforts to reform urban police in the United States. *See also* Knapp Commission

libel and slander. Printed and spoken defamation of character, respectively, of a person or an institution. The laws of libel and slander concern the abuse of free expression guaranteed in the First Amendment. Usually civil offenses, libel and slander may be criminal. In a slander action, it is usually necessary to prove specific damages caused by the spoken words to recover, but in a case of libel, the damage is assumed to have occurred by publication. A slander conviction carries a small fine and a reprimand by the judge, but the more serious libel conviction carries greater penalties. Members of Congress, judges, executive officials of the federal government, and state officials are immune from defamation action in the performance of their duties.

liberals, political. Liberalism is an ideology or philosophy that advocates social reforms designed to increase equality among citizens and greater democratic participation in governance. Liberals generally support the use of governmental power to aid disadvantaged people and groups; take the position that much criminal activity has roots in the social fabric; emphasize alternative sentencing, environmental issues, education, due process, and individual rights; and oppose the death penalty. Liberals are often regarded as proactive, academic, and open-minded; however, they are also sometimes criticized as socialistic.

Librium. Brand name for the generic drug Chlordiazepoxide, a sedative/hypnotic drug in the benzodiazepine family. This medication is used in the short-term treatment of anxiety; it is also used to mitigate the effects of acute alcohol withdrawal syndrome during detoxification.

license. Permission by public authority to perform a certain act, such as driving a car, or to engage in a business or profession; often granted only after the passing of a qualifying examination, the payment of a fee, or both, and revocable if either the terms of the license or the laws or regulations concerning the conduct of the business or profession are violated. Licensing is an administrative device for expediting maintenance of legally stipulated professional or vocational standards or for correction of violations, without the necessity of bringing prosecutions in the courts. The licensee may, however, appeal to the courts to overturn a ruling of the enforcement officers.

lie detector. Often called the polygraph, a device designed for the measurement of many biological responses that are under autonomic control. These biological responses include the EEG (brain waves), heart rate, blood pressure, blood flow, respiration, and skin resistance (galvanic skin response). The courts generally have not allowed lie detector findings to be presented as evidence during a trial, and findings can never be used without the consent of the person tested. Lie detectors are also used by government security agencies and by private personnel departments for such purposes as screening job applicants and investigating leaks of information and thefts of money or goods. Some states allow the use of the device to screen prospective police applicants but prohibit the use of polygraph tests on unwilling police officers undergoing internal affairs investigation(s) that could lead to some form of punishment.

life course theory. Developed in the 1950s, the life course theory studies social, economic, and environmental factors in a person's history to explain their later life events.

life cycle theory. A theory of leadership that was renamed situational leadership in the 1970s. *See* Situational Leadership Theory

Likert Scale. A psychometric rating scale used in surveys and questionnaires. The Likert Scale presents a respondent with a statement calling for a reaction/opinion in one of five or more possible responses. The statement, for example, might be "Drug offenders should receive mandatory treatment." The responses to choose from might be (1) strongly agree, (2) agree, (3) somewhat agree, (4) not sure, (5) somewhat disagree, (6) disagree, (7) strongly disagree.

limbic structures. Brain structures including the amygdala, thalamus, and hippocampus, the limbic system is responsible for regulating emotion and emotional memory. This system is the crux of the human brain's pleasure center, and thus, feelings of sexual arousal and the "high" associated with recreational drugs are also generated here.

limit line. A solid white line not less than 12 nor more than 24 inches wide, extending across a roadway to indicate the point at which traffic is required to stop in compliance with laws.

limitations of actions. The period of time after a crime is committed during which an indictment must be presented.

Lincoln law. *See* False Claims Act

Lincoln Savings and Loan. A Savings and Loan Corporation located in Irvine, CA, which was purchased by Charles Keating in 1984. Due to deregulation of Savings and Loans in the 1980s, Keating's management strategy included high risk investments, which resulted in the collapse of the financial institution in 1989. The federal government bailed out the institution, covering most debts and investors principle in the amount of $3 billion. Keating was subsequently imprisoned for fraud. *See also* Keating Five; Keating, Charles; Savings and Loan Crisis

Lindbergh Law ("Little Lindbergh Law"). An act of Congress on May 18, 1934, named for American aviator Charles A. Lindbergh (1902–1974), whose baby son was kidnapped. The law forbids, under penalties of death or imprisonment, the transportation in interstate or foreign commerce of any person who has been kidnapped and held for ransom. Failure to release a person within seven days after he or she has been kidnapped creates the presumption of interstate or foreign transport. *See also* kidnapping; Hauptman, Bruno

line. In public administration, that portion of the civil service, from highest officials to office employees and field force, that has the responsibility for carrying out the basic functions for which an administrative department is established—distinguished from staff (planning) and housekeeping (auxiliary) functions.

linear design. In penology, a type of jail architecture in which inmate cells are situated along corridors, which requires staff to walk the corridors in order to monitor conditions. This outdated form is also called traditional jail design.

line supervision. Sergeants, in most traditional police departments, are considered first-line supervisors. As such, they serve as links between line and staff employees.

line-up, police. A procedure of placing crime suspects with others, not believed implicated in the crime, in a line or other position so that witnesses can view them for the purpose of making possible identifications. Since 1967, in the case of *U.S. v. Wade,* the Supreme Court has required that an attorney for the accused be present during the line-up.

link network diagrams. Models that provide intelligence analysts with a visual representation of associations between persons and/or organizations. The technique may also be adapted to show associations between telephone numbers, car license plate numbers, and so forth. *See also* Program Evaluation and Review Technique

liquor laws. The crime category used to report offenses relating to the manufacture, sale, distribution, transportation, possession, and use of alcoholic beverages, except public drunkenness and driving under the influence.

litigation. A judicial controversy; a contest in a court of justice for the purpose of enforcing a right; any controversy that must be decided upon evidence.

Little Hoover Commission. An independent state oversight agency created in California in 1962 to evaluate state government operations and "promote efficiency, economy and improved service." The commission is comprised of nine citizen members (five appointed by the governor and four appointed by the legislature), two senators, and two members of the assembly. Subject areas include: Education; Energy, Environment & Resources; General Government; Health & Human Services; Infrastructure; and Public Safety. Within the Public Safety domain, they have published reports on California prisons, parole, and juvenile facilities. Address: 925 L Street, Suite 805, Sacramento, CA 95814; Web: http://www.lhc.ca.gov/.

Little Lindbergh Law. *See* Lindbergh Law

Little Rock riots. Disorders attending efforts to desegregate the Little Rock, AR, schools under a court order that, in September, 1957, led President Dwight Eisenhower to send troops to the city to compel a reluctant Governor Orval Faubus and citizenry to permit black children to attend public schools previously reserved for whites.

Livescan. Electronic technology used by law enforcement and government agencies to electronically capture finger and palm prints. Livescan eliminates the use of ink and paper, allows prints to be stored electronically for future comparison, and considerably shortens the time required for background investigations.

livestock, theft. The use of farm animals or equipment without the permission of the owner, with the intent to deprive the owner of the animals or equipment. The specific provisions of livestock theft vary by state. However, the United States Code (18USC) defines theft of livestock as: "Whoever obtains or uses the property of another which has a value of $10,000 or more in connection with the marketing of livestock in interstate or foreign commerce with intent to deprive the other of a right to the property or a benefit of the property or to appropriate the property to his own use or the use of another shall be fined under this title or imprisoned not more than five years, or both."

lividity, postmortem. A condition caused by the pooling of blood in a dead body. The blood flows by gravity to the lower parts of the body and causes a peculiar discoloration—

usually bluish-red. The condition appears about three hours after death. Due to pressure on the parts of the body touching the surface on which it rests, those parts do not assume the discoloration. If the body is moved after lividity has developed, the change of position will be indicated by lividity. Postmortem lividity generally becomes fixed after 6–9 hours; however, some suggest postmortem lividity is an inaccurate measure to determine time of death when a body is exposed to extreme temperatures (cold).

Livingston, Edward (1764–1836). A noted American penologist, considered to have been the first legal genius of modern times. Livingston wrote a system of criminal jurisprudence for the state of Louisiana and subsequently served as Secretary of State and minister to France under President Andrew Jackson.

Livor mortis. *See* lividity, postmortem

loan shark. One who loans money at a very high—usually an unlawful—interest rate. *See also* usury

loan sharking. The practice of loaning money at very high interest rates. The practice is associated with organized crime.

local union. An organization of workers that exists independently of any employer, based on other mutual interests. Through authorized agents, a local negotiates with employers the terms of the employees' work agreement, handles grievances, and helps to influence wages.

Locke, John (1632–1704). An English philosopher, Locke supposed that people came to an agreement, or a social contract, with one another to surrender their individual rights of judging and punishing, not to a king, but to the community as a whole. He also advocated that, should the sovereign government violate any of the laws, the community has the right to withdraw from that authority.

Loeb, Richard Albert (1905–1936). Richard A. Loeb was a University of Michigan graduate and the son of Sears, Roebuck vice president Albert A. Loeb. He was 18 years old when he and Nathan Leopold planned what they believed would be the "perfect crime:" the kidnapping, ransom, and murder of Loeb's 14-year old neighbor and relative, Bobby Frank. The two pled guilty to avoid execution and were sentenced to life plus 99 years in prison. Loeb was attacked by another inmate in the shower in 1936, and died from stab wounds. The attacker claimed the attack was self-defense, as Loeb tried to sexually assault him. *See also* Leopold and Loeb; Leopold, Nathan Freudenthal; Darrow, Clarence

logistics. The area of activity in a police operation pertaining to both supplies, equipment, and facilities and to the maintenance and support of personnel.

LOJACK Auto Recovery System, manufactured in Massachusetts, was introduced as a Department of Justice model program in Los Angeles County in June 1990, with 41 agencies participating. It has grown nationally and worldwide. Today, this "provider of wireless tracking and recovery systems for mobile assets," boasts a 90 percent recovery rate for 250,000 stolen vehicles (valued at $5 billion) globally. According to the Web site, "LoJack installs its Police Tracking Computers (PTCs) in law enforcement vehicles, helicopters and fixed-wing aircraft for optimal tracking and recovery of stolen assets. LoJack's software and databases are directly integrated into each state's crime computers, providing another connection to law enforcement." http://www.lojack.com/.

Lombroso, Cesare (1835–1909). Italian criminologist and professor of psychiatry, and later of criminal anthropology, at the University of Turin. Lombroso is considered a father of modern criminology and the original spokesman for the positivist viewpoint. In his book *The Criminal Man,* Lombroso maintained that the criminal type can be identified by a number of different physical characteristics. He believed that the victim should be compensated by the criminal and that society should be protected from

"degenerate" and "atavistic" criminal types. He also advocated the use of indeterminate sentences, but favored the death penalty as a last resort. Contemporary sociologists have criticized his restricted notion of crime and criminal behavior, claiming that, because he focused primarily on the perpetrators of violent crimes against the person, he failed to develop a meaningful theory that would also explain why intelligent people of "normal" appearance and affluent status happen to engage—sometimes routinely—in property crimes, which often require complex legal, business, or organizational skills.

Longabaugh, Harry (Sundance Kid, 1867–1908?). Longabaugh was an outlaw member of Butch Cassidy's "wild bunch" in the wild west circa 1896–1908. The gang was notorious for successful robberies, which were generally (but not always) nonviolent. Longabaugh is believed to have moved to Bolivia around 1908 to avoid capture in America. Some reports suggest he died in Bolivia in 1908, while others believe he returned to the United States and died in Utah around 1936. *See also* Cassidy, Butch

Los Angeles County Professional Peace Officers Association. publishes *Star & Shield* (monthly). Address: 188 E. Arrow Highway, San Dimas, CA 91773. Web: http://www.ppoa.com/.

lottery schemes. These telemarketing schemes involve the promise of investment in out-of-state and foreign lotteries, which are prohibited by federal law. The victim pays money for such investments and receives no returns. When victims attempt to report the fraud, they learn such activities are illegal. *See also* telemarketing fraud

low copy number (LCN). Developed around 1999, LCN is a somewhat controversial DNA profiling technique that uses a very small amount of tissue evidence or a fingerprint from which to "copy" additional material for DNA analysis. According to the FBI, this method is unreliable and should not be used as evidence in court.

LSD. *See* lysergic acid diethylamide

Luciano, Charles (Lucky). (1897–1962). An Italian-American gangster known for his success during prohibition and establishment of La Cosa Nostra in the United States. Luciano is believed to be the first boss of the Genovese crime family, and, along with associate and friend Meyer Lansky, is believed to have established an organized board of mafia heads called the Mafia Commission in the 1930. Although sentenced to 30–50 years for running a prostitution ring in 1936, Luciano continued to run his organization from prison. He was released and deported to Italy in 1946, and died in a Naples airport in 1962. *See also* Costello, Frank; Lansky, Meyer; mafia; Siegel, Bugsy

lynch. To practice the custom of enforcing certain mores by death or of punishing violations of certain fundamental regional mores without due process of law. The avenging group is composed of at least two persons. Following these customs is commonly referred to as operating under lynch law.

lynching. In American history, two types of lynching were common. In frontier areas, with few courts and jails, vigilantes frequently took the law into their own hands and punished (often by death) those accused of crimes. In the South, especially after the Civil War, mobs lynched African Americans in the name of white supremacy. Although the practice dates from the eighteenth century, no statistics were kept before 1882. Since then, about 5,000 people, 80 percent of them black, have been lynched in the U.S. Ninety percent of these lynchings were in the South, with the remainder in bordering states, and most took place in poor rural areas. Frequently, victims suffered torture and mutilation before being hanged, shot, or burned. Members of lynch mobs were almost never punished. The alleged crimes committed by lynching victims were homicide (38 percent), rape (23 percent), theft (7 percent), felonious assault (6 percent), and "insults to whites" (2 percent). About one-quarter were for miscellaneous offenses, such as an African American person's bringing suit or testifying against a Caucasian in court, using "offensive" language, boasting, or refusing to pay a debt. Since 1940, lynching has virtually disappeared, but not entirely. In 1981, Alabama KKK members murdered Michael Donald in retaliation for an unrelated case in which a black man was acquitted of murdering a police officer. The perpetrators were convicted and a $7 million judgment was awarded, bankrupting the subgroup of KKK members. In 1998, three Texas KKK members murdered James Byrd, Jr., a 49-year-old father of three. They randomly selected him, offered him a ride home, and dragged him behind their truck, killing him. Two perpetrators were sentenced to death; one was sentenced to life imprisonment. The U.S. Senate issued a formal apology in 2005, citing failure to enact a Federal anti-lynch law. *See also* anti-lynch bills

lysergic acid diethylamide (LSD). Derived from lysergic acid, which comes from ergot, a fungus growth on rye. One ounce of LSD is enough to provide 300,000 average doses, each of which is a tiny speck whose effect lasts from 8 to 12 hours. LSD is considered a semisynthetic psychedelic drug. LSD and other hallucinations cause extreme distortions in a person's perception of reality: people see images, hear sounds, and feel sensations which are not real. The effects can be frightening and sometimes result in panic, despair, or fear of insanity and death. LSD users can also experience flashbacks; persistent flashbacks causing social or occupational impairment is called hallucinogen-induced persisting perceptual disorder (HPPD). While LSD is not an addictive drug, some users experience tolerance and ingest higher doses to obtain the same "high."

M

Ma Barker. *See* Barker, Arizona Donnie Clark

MacDonald, Dr. Jeffery Robert. Former Green Beret captain and practicing physician convicted in 1979 of the highly controversial

1970 slaying of his pregnant wife and two daughters in their home near the Fort Bragg, NC, Army base. He is serving a life sentence in the federal prison in Cumberland, Maryland. In June 1985, the National Association of Criminal Defense Lawyers filed a brief in Richmond, VA, contending he was wrongfully convicted. Dennis Eisman, a Philadelphia lawyer who served as co-counsel during the army hearings that initially cleared MacDonald, assisted in the preparation of the friend-of-the-court brief. MacDonald's defense subsequently argued that exculpatory evidence was suppressed and sought DNA examination to exonerate MacDonald. The DNA analysis indicates all but three hairs are that of MacDonald; three unknown hairs (found on the bed sheet, the wife's leg, and daughter's fingernail) did not match any MacDonald family member or known suspects. Last denied parole May 10, 2005 still maintains he is "factually innocent." MacDonald's next scheduled hearing will be in May 2020.

MacDonald Triad. Theory posited by Yarnell, MacDonald, and others positing that the convergence of three behaviors in childhood—enuresis (bedwetting), arson, and zoosadism (animal torture)—are precursors to sociopathy in adulthood.

Mace. Trade name for an aerosol irritant projector used to stun an attacker or subdue protesters. *See also* pepper spray

Mack, Julian W. (1866–1943). A federal judge for 30 years, Mack ranks as one of the foremost innovators of juvenile justice. Born in San Francisco, he received his law degree at Harvard and went into practice in Chicago in 1890. He was elected to a judgeship for the Circuit Court of Cook County, IL, in 1903; between 1904 and 1907, he presided over Chicago's Juvenile Court, the first in the world. This court was established by the Illinois legislature in 1899. Under Mack, the court dealt with neglected and abused children, runaways, school dropouts, and juveniles who committed crimes. Mack supported the founding of the National

Probation Officers Association. In 1907 he was promoted to the Illinois Appeals Court, and in 1911 he was appointed by President William H. Taft to a seat on the U.S. Court of Appeals for the Seventh Circuit, from which he retired in 1941.

Machine Gun Kelly. *See* Kelly, George

Macro-micro link. Theoretical attempt to incorporate both macro (big picture) and micro (lower level, individual factors) to explain crime.

madam. A female procurer, pimp, or panderer. *See also* Fleiss, Heidi

MADD. *See* Mothers Against Drunk Driving

Mafia. The largest syndicate of organized crime is the Mafia (*Morte Alla Francia Italia Anela*—Death to France Is Italy's Cry—an acronym devised when the secret society was first organized in the 1860s to combat French forces). The organization is also referred to as La Cosa Nostra ("our thing"). It is a group of organized and generally violent criminals, supposed to have originated in Sicily as an unofficial police system on large estates to protect the owners during the period of disorganization following the Napoleonic invasion, and to have become a distinctly criminal organization when it turned against the owners and became an independent secret group. Its behavior includes tests for admission and an oath not to refer any controversy to legal authorities. The group is said to have started in the United States in New Orleans in 1869, and some believe it has infiltrated the executive, judiciary, and legislative branches of the U.S. government.

Mafia, notable events in the United States. In 1929, the St. Valentine's Day massacre in Chicago launched great public concern about growing mob violence during prohibition. The Massacre occurred on February 14, 1929, after a culmination of events related to competition between Al Capone's group of South Side Italian gangsters and North Side Irish gangsters led by Bugs Moran. The Massacre resulted in seven deaths. The single largest Mafia killing was

Sept. 11–13, 1931, when Salvatore Maranzano II and 40 allies were slaughtered. The greatest breaches of members' vow of silence were by Joseph Valachi in 1963 and by Tommaso Buschetta in 1984.

Between 1964–1969, the Mafia engaged in a five-year conflict dubbed the "Banana War," named for Joseph "Banana" Bonanno. Bonanno, an aging Don, planned the coordinated assassination of the Dons of several other mafia families, including Carlo Gambino, Tommy Lucchese, Stefano Magaddino and Frank DeSimone. Bonanno himself was kidnapped and released on his promise to retire. Bonnano had a heart attack in 1969, and subsequently moved to Arizona, ending the conflict.

On February 26, 1985, nine racketeering indictments were returned on 15 counts on the so-called Boss of Bosses, Paul "Big Paul" Castellano of the Gambino family; Anthony "Fat Tony" Salerno of the Genovese family; Anthony "Tony Ducks" Corallo of the Lucchese family; Philip "Rusty" Rastelli of the Bonanno family; Gennaro "Gerry Lang" Langella of the Colombo family; plus four of their top lieutenants. Police said that the charges—extortion, a pattern of racketeering, and conspiracies to commit more than six murders, including the 1979 slaying of Mafia underboss Carmine Galante at a restaurant table—were designed to keep the crime lords in court, if not in prison, for many years to come. Officials did not expect their arrests of the bosses to end Mafia-type crime. Drugs, loan sharking, extortion, gambling, and prostitution are too lucrative to extinguish given the size of the organization; there are an estimated 3,000 to 5,000 individual members in 25 "families" federated under "The Commission" with an estimated 17,000 confederates.

The federal government, in an attempt to combat organized crime, has placed nearly every major financial institution under scrutiny. During 1984, the Pan American International Bank in Las Vegas pleaded guilty to conspiracy not to file required currency reports on transactions totaling more than $100,000. Six men were indicted in December 1984 for allegedly buying and using the Sunshine State Bank of Miami to launder the profits from a marijuana-smuggling ring. The Global Union Bank of New York City was fined $63,750 and the Rockland Trust Company of Rockland, MA, was fined $50,000—both for not reporting large cash deposits. The Bank of Boston admitted not reporting $1.2 billion in international cash transactions, most with Swiss banks, over a four-year period ending September 1984. It was fined the maximum, $500,000. The government, from 1976 to 1985, fined 24 banks nearly 1.8 million for failing to report large cash transactions.

In the Mafia Commission Trial, 11 high-ranking mafia members were federally prosecuted for racketeering, extortion and murder. *See* Mafia Commission Trial

In a 1991 plea agreement, Sammy "the bull" Gravano testified against mod boss John Gotti. Gravano was the underboss, second in command of the Gambino Crime family operated by John Gotti. Gotti was subsequently convicted of murder, conspiracy, loan sharking, racketeering, obstruction of justice, illegal gambling, and tax evasion and sentenced to life in prison. Gravano remains the highest-ranking mafia member to testify against the mob

Mafia Commission Trial (1985–1986). New York State Attorney General Rudy Giuliani used evidence obtained by the FBI to indict 11 Mafia members under the Racketeer Influenced and Corrupt Organizations Act (RICO) for extortion, racketeering, and murder. This struck a blow against "The Commission," a group of Mafia organizations that resolved disputes among its members and discuss strategy. The defendants included: Paul "Big Paul" Castellano, Boss of the Gambino crime family; Anthony "Fat Tony" Salerno, Boss of the Genovese crime family; Carmine "Junior" Persico, Boss of the Colombo crime family; Anthony "Tony Ducks" Corallo, Boss of the Lucchese crime family; Philip "Rusty" Rastelli, Boss of the Bonanno crime family; and six subordinates: Aniello Dellacroce, Gambino Underboss; Gennaro Langella, Colombo Underboss;

Salvatore Santoro, Lucchese Underboss; Christopher Furnari, Lucchese Consigliere; Ralph Scopo, Colombo soldier, and Anthony Indelicato, Bonanno soldier. Of the 11 defendants, one (Rastelli) obtained a separate trial, one (Dellacroce) died of cancer, and one (Castellano) was murdered while out on bail, reportedly by John Gotti, who replaced Castellano as head of the Gambino family. All eight remaining defendants were convicted and sentenced to prison in 1987. As of 2010, four of those convicted are deceased. Three (Fernari, Persico, and Langella) remain in federal prison, and Indelicato is on parole.

magazine-promotion schemes. In these schemes, the telemarketer tells the victim s/he has won a valuable prize. Victims pay hundreds to thousands of dollars in magazine subscriptions to claim their prize, which never materializes. *See also* telemarketing fraud

magistrate. (1) A public official. (2) A local official exercising jurisdiction of a summary judicial nature over offenses against municipal ordinances or minor criminal cases.

magistrature assise (Fr.). The title of the judge in a French court.

magistrature debout (Fr.). The title of the prosecutor in a French court.

Magna Carta (Lat., lit, great charter). An important thirteenth-century English document that granted rights and privileges to some citizens. It influenced the first 10 amendments to the U.S. Constitution, the Bill of Rights. The Magna Carta originally granted freedoms to barons and the church. It did, however, extend several rights to the common man. Pressured by his rebellious barons, King John issued the charter at Runnymede on June 15, 1215. It has, by liberal interpretations through the centuries, come to be thought of as the basis for constitutional government and as an impartial judicial system in English-speaking countries.

magnetic ink character recognition. A computer technology developed by the American Bankers' Association (ABA) as a machine language that facilitates the processing of checks, drafts, and similar documents required to be processed through the Federal Reserve System. Special numeric MICR groupings, called "fields," are printed in magnetic ink on the check or other instruments. The numbers identify the Federal Reserve routing code, ABA transit number, account number, and the amount.

magnetic resonance imaging (MRI). A medical imaging technique that relies upon magnetic fields to align hydrogen atoms in the body, producing a view of complex structures not otherwise visible. In criminal justice, the use of MRI is often associated with brain imagining.

mail fraud. According to the U.S. Code, a person is not allowed to place in a post office or other authorized depository any scheme or artifice to defraud or obtain money or property by means of false pretenses. There are many types of mail-fraud schemes, including chain letters, pyramid schemes, investment swindles, land sale frauds, work-at-home schemes, medical quackery, fake contests, and charity rackets. Consumers who suspect they have been victims should contact the nearest postmaster or postal inspector or write to: Criminal Investigation Service Center, ATTN: Mail Fraud, 222 S. Riverside Plaza, Suite 1250, Chicago, IL, 60606-6100. Web site: https://postalinspectors.uspis.gov/investigations/MailFraud/MailFraud.aspx.

maim. To willfully inflict upon another an injury that disfigures by mutilation, destroys any limb or organ, or seriously diminishes physical vigor.

maintenance. Offense in which a person unlawfully interferes with a lawsuit in which he or she has no interest, by helping the prosecution or defense, with money, for example.

majority. (1) The greater number; more than half. (2) The condition of being of full or adult age.

maladministration. Corruption in public affairs.

mala in se (Lat., lit. bad in itself). Crimes have been divided, according to their nature, into crimes *mala in se* and crimes *mala prohibita*. The former comprise those acts that are immoral or wrong in themselves, such as murder, rape, arson, burglary, larceny, breach of the peace, forgery, and the like. *See also mala prohibita*

mala fides (Lat.). Bad faith, as opposed to bona fides, or good faith.

mala prohibita (Lat.). Term for crimes that are made illegal by legislation, as opposed to acts that are crimes because they are considered evil in and of themselves, or *mala in se*. Examples include prostitution, underage drinking, unlicensed gambling, etc. *See also mala in se*

Malcolm X.(1925–1965) A Muslim minister and human rights activist known for his outspoken criticism of racism in the U.S. He remains a controversial figure, whose detractors characterize him as a violent, racist, black supremacist; others believe he was a influential martyr and one of the greatest African Americans in U.S. history. A leader of the black-consciousness movement. He was born Malcolm Little in Omaha, NE, in 1925, and later lived in MI, MA, and NY. While serving a prison term in 1946, he joined the Black Muslims and took the name Malcolm X. After he was paroled, he had great success in expanding the number of temples and lecturing to many audiences. Conflicts developed, however, between Malcolm X and Elijah Muhammand, leader of the Black Muslims. In 1964 Malcolm X broke away to form his own black nationalist movement, the Organization of Afro-American Unity. In the same year he made a pilgrimage to Mecca. He was assassinated by black gunmen as he was about to make a speech to followers in the Audubon Ballroom in New York City on February 21, 1965. The perpetrators, Talmadge (HayerMujahid Halim), Norman Butler (now Muhammad Abdul Aziz) and Thomas Johnson (Khalil Islam) were convicted and sentenced for the murder; they were paroled in 2010, 1985, and 1987, respectively.

malfeasance. Commitment of an act forbidden by the moral code or by contract; committing an act that one has no right to do and against which a court action may be instituted. Malfeasance has come to be commonly used in referring to the misconduct of public officials. *See also* misfeasance

malice. Intent to commit a wrong or hurtful act with no reason or legal justification.

malice aforethought. Prior determination, and often planning, to commit a criminal act.

malice, express. Actual, overt, or specific malice.

malice, general. Wickedness; tendency toward wrongdoing.

malice, implied. Malice suggested by the actions of the subject.

malice, legal. Intention or purposefulness to commit a crime, in law.

malicious act. An unlawful act done through malice.

malicious arrest. An arrest made without probable cause.

malicious mischief. A crime consisting of willful damage to, or destruction of, personal property of another and motivated by ill will or resentment toward its owner or possessor.

malicious prosecution. A judicial proceeding instigated by the prosecutor without probable cause to sustain it.

malign. Slander; to make harmful and untrue statements about another. *See also* libel

malpractice. Negligent acts by a professional, who has a duty to provide reasonable care according to accepted professional practices, resulting in harm or injury to client. *See also* fraud offenses; legal malpractice; medical malpractice

maltreatment. Improper or unskilled treatment or abuse, given willfully or arising from ignorance, neglect, or malicious intent.

Malvo, Lee Boyd.(1985–). Born in Jamiaca, Malvo immigrated illegally to the United States in 2001 in the care of John Allen Muhammad, a family friend. Malvo was convicted with Muhammad in the Beltway sniper attacks, which terrorized the Washington, DC/Virginia area in the fall of 2002. Between September 5–October 23, 2002,

Malvo, who was 17 at the time, and Muhammad killed 10 people and wounded three others along Interstate 95. The two were apprehended on October 24 of the same year. Malvo initially pled not guilty by reason of insanity, claiming he was under Muhammad's complete control. A Virginia jury found him guilty of murder in his first trial and he was sentenced to life without parole. In October of 2004, his gave an "Alford plea" for one additional Virginia murder, an attempted murder, and weapons charges and received a consecutive life sentence plus eight years. In October of 2006, Malvo was charged for crimes committed in Maryland. During the Maryland trial, Malvo disclosed the full plan, which included their intent to kill six white people a day for 30 days, then shoot a pregnant woman in the stomach, shoot a police officer and detonate bombs at the funeral, extort money from the United States, and use funds to recruit other orphaned boys to shoot white people in the United States. In the fall of 2006, Malvo pled guilty to six additional murders and was sentenced to six consecutive life sentences in Maryland. He is currently confined in the Red Onion State Prison in Virginia. *See also* Alford plea; Beltway sniper attacks; Muhammad, John Allen

Malware. (also called malicious software). Hostile, intrusive, or annoying software or program code designed to infiltrate a computer system without the owner's consent.

manacles. Restraining devices such as handcuffs or leg irons.

management functions. The following tasks are usually seen as functions of management: planning, organizing, staffing, directing, coordinating, reporting, and budgeting. A common acronym for these functions is POSDCORB.

managerial style grid. An organizational development or personnel measurement tool that evaluates a manager in terms of how he or she balances the needs of production with employee needs. The grid has 81 blocks: 9 blocks on the horizontal axis represent concern for production, and 9 blocks on the vertical axis represent concern for people. According to the grid, a manager who favors productivity over people is said to "9–1" his or her decisions.

mandate. An order or command; a directive of a superior court, or its judge, to a lower one.

mandate law. A law that imposes a duty upon some public official, agency, or local government body and requires that it be executed without exercise of discretion and in accordance with the express terms of the law.

mandatory sentences. A statutory requirement that a certain penalty shall be set and carried out in all cases upon conviction for a specified offense or series of offenses. Since the mid-1970s, nearly all states have passed some form of mandatory sentencing legislation. In California, the prison population explosion is due in part to laws requiring judges to imprison all those who commit violent felonies. However, in *Begay v. United States* 553 U.S. 137 (2008) the Supreme Court considered the interpretation of "violent offender" set forth in Armed Career Criminal Act (ACCA), which provides a 15 year mandatory sentence for offenders with three violent felonies. The Court ruled that a drunk-driving offense differs substantially from other violent offenses covered in the statute, therefore a mandatory 15 year sentence as required by the Armed Career Criminal Act does not apply to drunk driving. *See also* crime of violence, mandatory penalty

mandatory supervised release. A conditional release from prison required by statute when an inmate has been confined for a period equal to his or her full sentence minus statutory good time, if any.

Manhattan Bail Project. A 1961 experimental release-on-recognizance (ROR) project funded by the Vera Foundation, this project provided empirical support for ROR bail in the U.S. The results of the study show that from October 16, 1961, through April 8, 1964, out of 13,000 total defendants, 10,000 were interviewed for the program, 4,000 were recommended, 2,195 were paroled, and 3,000 were not eligible, based on their offenses. Only 15 defendants failed to show up in court, a default rate of less than 7/10 of 1 percent. This project became the model for nationwide programs, such as the Philadelphia Common Pleas and Municipal Court ROR Program and the San Francisco ROR Program, whose results from August 1, 1964, to July 31, 1968, revealed that 6,377 persons were released on their promise to appear, ninety percent returned for trial and only one percent evaded justice altogether. *See also* citation to appear

Mann Act. A law passed in 1910 through the efforts of James Robert Mann. Also known as the White Slave Traffic Act, it was passed after various lurid revelations of the growth of prostitution in the United States and in response to fears about the importing of European women for U.S. brothels. Nations had begun to cooperate against prostitution after an international congress on the problem was held in London in 1899. The act, upheld by the Supreme Court in 1913, forbade the transportation of women across state lines for immoral purposes and was so worded because of the federal government's authority over interstate commerce under the commerce clause of the Constitution. The prohibition of prostitution within the states is an exercise of the states' police powers, reserved to them in the Tenth Amendment of the Constitution. At the state level, every government except Nevada has outlawed houses of prostitution.

manslaughter. Homicide resulting from culpable recklessness or negligence.

Manson, Charles (1934–). On August 8, 1969, five people entered the Beverly Hills home of Polish film director Roman Polanski and shot or stabbed to death five guests, including Polanski's actress wife, Sharon Tate, who was pregnant. The next night, the same killers entered the home of grocery-chain owner Leo LaBianca and murdered him and his wife. Manson did not participate in the killings, but he was charged with

ordering his followers, the "Manson family" to commit them. In 1971 Manson and four others (Susan Atkins, Patricia Krenwinkel, Leslie Van Houten, Charles Denton Watson) were found guilty of the murders and sentenced to death. The sentences were reduced to life imprisonment when the 1972 ruling in *California v. Anderson* (1972) effectively banned capital punishment until the passage of Proposition 17 (passed in 1972); this also coincided with the USSC decision in *Furman v Georgia* (1972). Manson is currently incarcerated at Corcoran State Prison. *See also* capital punishment; Atkins, Susan; Krenwinkel, Patricia; VanHouten, Leslie; Watkins, Tex; Tate, Sharon; Polanski, Roman

Mapp, Dollree. The defendant in the landmark 1961 Supreme Court decision *Mapp v. Ohio,* which extended the exclusionary rule to the states. Mapp's conviction for illegal possession of obscene materials was overturned on the grounds of illegal search and seizure. On November 2, 1970, she was arrested by the New York Police Department on suspicion of dealing in stolen property. The detectives, without a search warrant, found 50,000 envelopes of heroin and stolen property valued at over $100,000 in her home. On April 23, 1971, she was convicted of the felonious possession of dangerous drugs and sentenced to a term of 20 years to life. On December 31, 1980, New York Governor Hugh Carey commuted her sentence, making her eligible for parole the next day.

marijuana; marihuana. Drug from the leaves and flowering top of the plant *Cannabis sativa*. When these parts of the female plant are smoked or ingested, they produce an intoxicating effect characterized by relaxed mood (although paranoia is also reported), distorted perceptions, impaired coordination, difficulty in thinking, and increased appetite. Side effects can include memory problems; difficulty with problem solving; and increased heart rate. Many states have reduced the criminal penalties for individual use and possession of marijuana. The first legal use of marijuana for medicinal purpose was smoked by Bonnie Adlman, a patient at North Shore Hospital in Manhasset, New York; Marijuana use was allowed under a 1981 New York law to combat the nausea that follows chemotherapy treatment given to cancer patients. Since then, 14 states have enacted laws legalizing marijuana for medical use, and its recreational use is widespread (although technically illegal). Today, marijuana is the most commonly abused illicit drug. *See also* medical marijuana

Marine Resources. This Department of Justice office handles litigation relating to mineral and biological resources of the adjacent seas and seabed. It is responsible for cases involving the determination of the coastline and other maritime boundaries of the United States and those dealing with the rights of the United States in submerged lands, particularly as those rights involve increasingly valuable oil and gas resources. The office also has the responsibility for litigation concerning the conservation and management of the living resources of the adjacent seas and the more than 70 species of fish in the 200-mile fishing zone. Address: Wildlife and Marine Resources Section, Environment and Natural Resources Division, DOJ, 950 Pennsylvania Avenue, NW, Washington, DC 20530-0001. Web site: http://www.justice.gov/enrd/index. html. *See also* Table 27. Department of Justice Organizational Chart, page 254

Marquis reagent test. A presumptive test to identify alkaloids and other compounds. It is the primary presumptive test used in Ecstasy testing. It can also be used to test for such illegal substances as cocaine, opiates (e.g., methadone, heroin), and phenethylamines (e.g., methamphetamine, amphetamine).

marriage, consanguineous. Unions between people who are considered too closely related by birth, such as first cousins. Most states prohibit such marriages.

marshal. (1) An appointed officer in each judicial district of the United States who executes the processes of the court and has law enforcement authority similar to that of a sheriff. (2) An officer sometimes attached to a magistrate's court.

marshal, U.S. An official of the federal judicial system whose functions are the following: make arrests of persons charged with federal criminal violations, transport federal prisoners and ensure their incarceration pending trial, maintain order in the federal courts, carry out orders of the federal courts, and serve processes in the federal judicial district in which appointed. Duties correspond to those of a sheriff of a county in many respects.

Marshall, John (1755–1835). Fourth chief justice of the Supreme Court, called the Great Chief Justice by Justice Benjamin Cardozo, a title that is hardly ever questioned. Appointed in the last days of President John Adams's administration in 1801, Marshall battled with a series of presidents, nearly all of whom were vigorously opposed to his Federalist interpretation of the Constitution. Although there are some disagreements, it is generally acknowledged that Marshall strengthened both the Supreme Court and the Constitution. During his 34 years as chief justice, he maintained dominance over those justices appointed by presidents opposed to his policies. Marshall helped structure a distribution of the powers of government that has lasted to the present. He died in office, still battling his adversaries in the other branches of government.

martial law. Refers to control of civilian populations by a military commander. Commanders are permitted to exercise this control because there is no power sufficient to stop them or to control the situation during war, insurrection, or violence. Martial law replaces all civilian laws, authorities, and courts. It is an exercise of military power that is totally arbitrary and unfettered: the commander is legislator, judge, and executioner.

martymachlia. A paraphilia involving compulsive exhibitionism, generally including sexual gratification obtained by having other's watch one's completion of a sexual act. *See also* exhibitionism, sex offender

Mashups. Colloquial term used to describe the merging of applications and software, or the combination of multiple tools to create improved Web services.

Maslow's hierarchy of needs. American sociologist Abraham Maslow separated human needs into higher and lower levels. Physiological (hunger, thirst, shelter, sex, and other bodily needs) and safety (security and protection from physical and emotional harm) were described as lower-order needs, and belongingness (affection, belonging, acceptance, and friendship), esteem (self-respect, autonomy, achievement, status recognition), and self-actualization (the drive to fulfill one's potential and self-fulfillment) as higher-order needs. As each need is satisfied, the next level becomes dominant. *See also* Herzberg's motivation-maintenance theory; motivation

mass murder. *See* murder, mass

massacre. The wanton killing of a large number, especially of unresisting human beings or animals. *See* Columbine; Rosewood Massacre

mass spectrometry (MS). Highly specific analysis used for identification of controlled substances; often used in combination with gas chromatography and referred to as gas chromatography/mass spectrometry (GC/MS).

masters/special masters. Court-appointed overseers to ensure that the provisions of decree orders are followed. Masters are usually found in prisons.

material evidence. *See* evidence, material

material fact. A fact necessary to the support of a case or defense.

material witness. One who possesses information of value in the trial of a criminal case. Appropriate magistrates may force such witnesses to post bond to ensure their appearance in court. In lieu of bond being posted, witnesses may be detained. The defense also has rights to ensure the testimony of material witnesses if circumstances suggest they may be unavailable at the time of the hearing or trial.

mathematical theory. Attempts to translate verbal statements of social relationships into mathematical terms in order to introduce greater precision and scientific rigor into sociology and/or criminology.

matic. An alarm system that employs a holdup alarm device, such as a money clip in a cash drawer, in which the signal transmission is initiated solely by the action of the intruder.

matricide. The killing or murder of a mother.

Mattachine Society. Organization founded in 1950 by Henry Hay to defend the rights of homosexuals. The organization grew through the mid-1950s but began to decline in 1961 as the organization splintered into smaller subgroups.

maximum sentence. (1) In legal usage, the maximum penalty provided by law for a given offense, usually stated as a maximum term of imprisonment or a maximum fine. (2) In correctional usage, any of several periods (expressed in days, months, or years) that may vary according to whether they were calculated at the point of sentencing or at a later point in the correctional process and according to whether the period referred to is the term of confinement or the total time under correctional jurisdiction.

mayhem. Intentional infliction of injury on another that causes the removal of, disfigures, renders useless, or impairs the function of any limb or organ of the body. In Uniform Crime Reports mayhem is classified as aggravated assault.

McAdoo, William. Lawyer and public official (1853–1930) born in Ireland. Practiced law in New Jersey; member, U.S. House of Representatives (1883–91); appointed by President Grover Cleveland as assistant secretary of the Navy; practiced law in New York City; police commissioner (1905–06); chief magistrate (1910–30); largely responsible for a complete reorganization and reform in the New York City Magistrate's Courts.

McCarthyism. A tendency to brand all except extreme right-wing ideas as communistic, of indiscriminately leveling false charges of treason, of making new charges instead of furnishing facts, and of attacking the motives of those who question the authenticity of statements. The term arose from the specious charges of Senator Joseph R. McCarthy of Wisconsin, who undermined public confidence in many public officials and private persons until finally censured by the Senate on December 2, 1954.

McDonald's massacre. A 1984 killing spree at a McDonald's Restaurant outside San Diego by James Huberty. For no apparent reason, Huberty entered the restaurant and fired multiple weapons, killing 21 people and injuring 19 others. Huberty was also killed. *See also* Huberty, James

McDuffle, Arthur. At 1:59 A.M. on December 17, 1979, in Miami, FL, a lone black male was said to have crashed his motorcycle while evading police at speeds up to 100 miles per hour. He died four days later of head injuries. The victim had been Arthur McDuffle, a 33-year-old insurance salesman and ex-marine. A reconstruction of the case suggested that McDuffle may indeed have tried to elude the police. When he finally slowed down, however, the police pulled him from his vehicle; one officer held him while the others "taught him a lesson." Indicted for manslaughter in the case were four white Miami patrolmen. On May 17, 1980, the officers were acquitted by an all-white jury, causing the worst outbreak of racial violence the country had seen since 1967. After three days, 15 persons were dead, and the city and its suburbs had suffered a financial toll of some $200 million. *See also* civil disturbances

McGregor, Douglas. *See* Theory X and Theory Y

McGruff. In October 1979 the National Crime Prevention Council began a national media campaign to educate the public about its responsibility for preventing crime. McGruff, a cartoon dog, was adopted as the campaign symbol for crime prevention, urging the public to "take a bite out of crime."

McLeod case. An international incident resulting from an arrest of Alexander McLeod, a Canadian deputy sheriff, in New York in 1840 on charges of murder and arson at the time of the destruction of the ship *Caroline*. State authorities refused to release him on demand of the British government, supported by U.S. authorities. He was tried and acquitted. To address such contingencies, Congress empowered federal courts to issue writs of *habeas corpus* for aliens held by state courts.

McNaughton rule. *See* M'Naghten rile

measurement, levels of. A set of rules by which numbers are assigned to the different outcomes a group of variables can exhibit. A particular measurement scale is a statement of the rules of correspondence between outcome of the phenomenon under study and the actual numbers of the measuring instrument. Four basic types of measurement scales are commonly used in criminological research: nominal, ordinal, interval, and ratio. The first two are classified as discrete measures and the second two as continuous measures. *See also* scale, interval; scale, ordinal; scale, nominal; scale, ratio; statistics

mechanic's lien. A legal recourse for a contractor to obtain money owed by attaching the debtor's property or equipment.

median lethal dose. Dose of a substance that typically kills 50 percent of subjects in a known population. *See also* LD50

mediation. Nonbinding third-party intervention in the collective bargaining process, particularly during a strike considered a public emergency and often used in child custody disputes. Unlike an arbitrator, who renders a decision after hearing the positions of labor and management, a mediator endeavors mainly to keep the bargaining from breaking down and to seek paths to an agreement. By clarifying the issues, defining and containing areas of disagreement, offering suggestions, and serving as an intermediary, a mediator can contribute substantially to a settlement.

medical examiner. A qualified physician appointed to examine or perform autopsies on the bodies of persons whose cause of death are unknown, or who met violent deaths, and to investigate the causes and circumstances of death. In some states this position has supplanted that of the coroner.

medical jurisprudence. The science consisting of the application of medical and surgical knowledge and skill to the principles and administration of the law. It comprises all medical subjects that have a legal aspect.

medical malpractice. The negligent treatment of disease or injury through ignorance, carelessness, or criminal intent. *See also* malpractice

medical marijuana. Refers to the use of Cannabis (*marijuana*) as a physician-recommended treatment or therapy. Cannabis has well-documented medical benefits, including: reducing nausea and increasing hunger in cancer and AIDS patient; relieving inner eye pressure in treatment of glaucoma; and as a pain reliever. Other medicinal uses, although not well established, include reduction of symptoms in patients with depression and multiple sclerosis. To date, 14 states permit the legal dispensing of marijuana with a doctor's recommendation, including: Alaska, California, Colorado, Hawaii, Maine, Michigan, Montana, Nevada, New Jersey, New Mexico, Oregon, Rhode Island, Vermont and Washington state. California, one of six states that authorize marijuana dispensaries, generated $2 billion in medical marijuana sales, resulting in $100 million in state tax revenue in 2008. While 14 states have approved the use of medical marijuana, the U.S. Food and Drug Administration maintains that marijuana has no documented medical value, and marijuana is still illegal according to federal law. In 2009, the U.S. Deputy Attorney General issued an internal memorandum cautioning against DEA prosecutions for medical

marijuana, when such is in compliance with state law. Likewise, President Obama indicated his intent to address federal law pertaining to medical marijuana use. However, the DEA performed at least three raids on licensed medical marijuana facilities in Colorado in early 2010. On January 27, 2010, Full Spectrum Laboratories, a medical marijuana testing facility, was raided while executives were testifying at the state capital on medical marijuana. On February 11, 2010, Colorado Springs laboratory Genovations was likewise raided. These raids occurred following each lab's submission of an analytic laboratory license to the DEA, in accordance with federal law. On February 12, the DEA raided the Highlands Ranch home of Chris Bartkowicz, a licensed medical marijuana caregiver, and arrested him. This raid occurred the day after an interview of Bartkowicz aired on television.

medical model. A perspective of certain offenders as sick and in need of treatment; based on the analogy of criminal behavior and disease. The medical model supports rehabilitation as the goal of penalties, and believes criminal behavior can be cured. Beginning in the 1930s, this model was increasingly overshadowed by the justice model, which was adopted in 1974. *See also* justice model

medicide. A legal term used to denote the medical termination of life. The Supreme Court ruled in 1990 that Nancy Cruzan's parents could be permitted to remove the feeding tube keeping their comatose daughter alive, without risking homicide charges. In 2005, the Florida Sixth Circuit Court ruled that Terri Schiavo, who had been in a persistent vegetative state since 1990, would not wish to have continued life-prolonging measures. This was a very controversial case initiated by the husband (who initiated the action, transferring his authority as guardian to the court), Schiavo's parents (who insisted that she was alert), medical experts, the media, and emergency legislation signed by President George W. Bush to sustain Schiavo's life. The U.S.S.C. denied certiorari (refusing to hear the case), leaving the Sixth Circuit ruling in effect. Schiavo was removed from life support on March 18, 2005, and died on March 31. *See also* euthanasia; Kevorkian, Dr. Jack; mercy killing

Megan's Law. Overarching term for laws that require public notification of sex offenders within a given jurisdiction. Named after 7-year-old Megan Kanka of Hamilton Township, NJ, who was murdered in 1994. A convicted sex offender who lived across the street from the Kanka family was accused of the crime. In response to her parents' outrage that no one had warned them about their neighbor's past, New Jersey passed a law mandating notification to a community when a convicted sex offender moves in, with different levels of notification required for different levels of offense. On July 1, 1996, a NJ federal district judge upheld the central aspects of Megan's Law. A 1994 federal version of this law, the Jacob Wetterling Crimes Against Children and Sexually Violent Offender Registration Act of 1994, included provisions allowing for, but not requiring, similar notifications when a known sex offender is released from prison. Today, most states have some form of Megan's Law, although specific provisions vary by statute. *See also* Jacob Wetterling Crimes Against Children and Sexually Violent Offender Registration Act; sex offender registration

meeting of the minds. Legal concept that defines a contract. Although contracts are most easily enforced when written, a verbal contract is enforceable if the two parties reached a "meeting of the minds."

memorandum of understanding. An official document created in collective bargaining, usually agreed upon by parties involved, clearly delineating the role, tasks, and responsibilities of management and of labor. MOUs are the guiding force in personnel matters and are often bargained or mediated.

Menendez, Joseph Lyle and Erik. Two brothers who acknowledged the murder of their wealthy parents at the family home in California. Their first trials, in 1994 before two different juries, both resulted in deadlocks, also called a hung jury. Their second trial, before the same jury in 1995, led to a unanimous verdict of guilt. *See also* hung jury, patricide

mens rea (Lat.). One of the two elements of every crime, which are the criminal act or omission and the mental element or criminal intent, the *mens rea*. The latter is the state of mind that accompanies the particular act defined as criminal. Hence, the *mens rea* of each crime will be different. For instance, in the crime of receiving stolen goods, it means knowledge that the goods were stolen; in the case of murder, malice aforethought; in the case of theft, an intention to steal.

mental element in crime. Criminal intent. Every common law crime consists of two elements, the criminal act, or omission, and the mental element, commonly called criminal intent.

mental illness. Clinically, a mental illness includes a variety of disorders articulated in the Diagnostic and Statistical Manual of Mental Disorders, published by the American Psychiatric Association. Such disorders can include relatively mild conditions such as seasonal dysthymia, to more severe conditions such as schizophrenia and antisocial personality disorder. In criminal justice, some mental illnesses can mitigate or excuse criminal behavior. *See also* insanity, insanity defense

mercy killing. An ethically controversial action involving the removal of a terminally ill patient from life-support systems. The motive in such a case is not generally considered a sufficient defense in a homicide charge. *See also* dyathanasia; euthanasia; Kevorkian, Dr. Jack

mere evidence. Evidence that will aid in the proof of the commission of a crime but that does not fall into the evidentiary categories of contraband or profits of the crime.

merger of offenses. A legal procedure occurring when the same criminal act constitutes both felony and misdemeanor or where one crime culminates in another.

merit system. The method of appointing members of the civil service by open competitive examination. Although temporarily instituted by President Ulysses Grant in 1876, the permanent merit system was not established until the passage of the Pendleton Act in 1883. In 1789, the entire civil service was politically appointed. After passage of the Pendleton Act, 13 percent of civil service workers were appointed on a merit basis; by 1932 the figure had risen to 80 percent. President Harry Truman declared that 93 percent of the federal service at the time of his term in office was on a merit basis. Individual merit systems have been put into effect by some independent bodies, including the Federal Bureau of Investigation. A merit examination may be written, or, as in recent developments, it may take the form of a performance, oral, or interview examination. The merit system has spread widely to state and municipal governments, and has been adopted by private industry.

mental defectiveness. Historical term used to describe developmental disabilities. *See* developmental disability

mental deficiency. Historical term used to describe developmental disabilities. *See* developmental disability

mental retardation. Historical term used to describe developmental disabilities. This term has fallen out of favor due to use of the term "retarded" as a pejorative. *See* developmental disability

mental subnormality. Historical term used to describe developmental disabilities. *See* developmental disability

Merton, Robert K. (1910–2003) American sociologist who applied the concept and theory of anomie to crime and deviance. He used the term *anomie* to describe the condition of normlessness that occurs when the

means of achieving success available to people are insufficient for them to achieve what society has deemed success. Individuals who perceive that they cannot succeed conventionally will resort to illegitimate or illegal ways of doing so, Merton believed, and he termed such behavior innovation. *See also* anomie

mesne process. As distinguished from final process, this term is used for any writ issued between the beginning of a case and its conclusion. Mesne, in this context, may be defined as intermediate; intervening; the middle between two extremes.

Mesopotamian laws and codes. The earliest signs of well-developed written law codes emerged from early cultures in Mesopotamia, the land bordered by the Tigris and Euphrates rivers. Although early Sumerian codes no doubt existed as far back as B.C. 3000, the Babylonian Code of Hammurabi—discovered by the French in 1902—is the most famous of the Mesopotamian codes to survive in its entirety. Certain of its legal phrases indicate that the Code of Hammurabi (circa B.C. 1760) was based on prior codes.

meta-analysis. The use of various statistical methods to synthesize the results of several studies focused on a similar hypothesis. Meta-analysis often includes examination of effect size across multiple studies, particularly in situations where small sample size reduces statistical power in each of the individual studies, resulting in a larger effect size when those studies are combined.

methadone (Dolophine). A synthetically produced opiate narcotic. Since its discovery, methadone has been tested and used as a medication for treating narcotic withdrawal and dependence. Heroin and other narcotics induce excess amounts of dopamine in the body by occupying the opiod receptor in the brain. Methadone blocks this receptor to prevent withdrawal while stabilizing the addictive craving.

methadone maintenance. A means of treating addiction to narcotic- or opium-derived drugs, begun experimentally in 1964 at Rockefeller University Hospital in New York. The addict is given methadone, a synthetic opiate, in an amount (usually 100 milligrams per day) sufficient to satisfy his or her craving for heroin. Once stabilized under hospital observation, the addict can be treated on an outpatient basis, returning to the clinic or hospital each day for methadone.

methamphetamine. The second most commonly abused illicit drug in the United States. It is a potent type of amphetamine, and has a high potential for abuse as well as both psychological and physical dependence. As an amphetamine, it is a central nervous system stimulant that works to increase dopamine throughout the body. While it was once medically prescribed, today methamphetamine is illegally manufactured in laboratories using common household chemicals. *See also* amphetamine.

See Table 30. Methamphetamine Labs in the United States, 2008, this page

methaqualone. A synthetic, white, crystal powder processed into tablets or capsules, this addictive central nervous system depressant has been associated with the trade product Quaalude, which is no longer manufactured. Abusers of this drug get high by fighting sleep to experience impaired coordination, lowered inhibitions, and greater sociability. Methaqualone is classified as a sedative-hypnotic and is sometimes prescribed by physicians to relieve anxiety or as a sleep aid.

methodology. The logic of scientific procedure; a system of principles, rules, and techniques of regulating a scientific discipline or inquiry. In criminology, methodology is the logical and theoretical basis for the acceptance of research results by the academic community.

TABLE 30   METHAMPHETAMINE LABS IN THE UNITED STATES, 2008

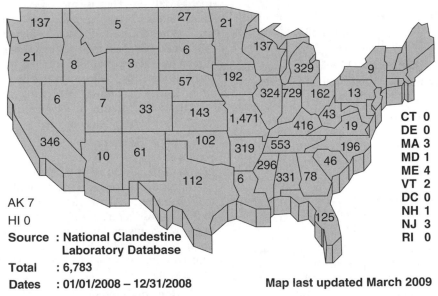

Total of All Clandestine Meth Laboratory Incidents Including Labs, Dumpsites, Chem/Glass/Equipment Calender Year 2008

AK 7
HI 0
Source : National Clandestine Laboratory Database
Total : 6,783
Dates : 01/01/2008 – 12/31/2008

CT 0
DE 0
MA 3
MD 1
ME 4
VT 2
DC 0
NH 1
NJ 3
RI 0

Map last updated March 2009

Source: National Clandestine Laboratory Database.

methylphenidate (Ritalin). A central nervous system stimulant chemically and pharmacologically related to amphetamines. Often prescribed for victims of narcolepsy, or the tendency to fall suddenly and deeply asleep at inappropriate times. Also commonly prescribed for victims of Attention Deficit Disorder and Attention Deficit Hyperactivity Disorder. Today, Ritalin and other prescription medications like Adderall are commonly abused as performance enhancers, to increase focus and alertness. Ritalin is also abused in dieting, since stimulants are known to decrease appetite.

metropolitan statistical areas. A Census Bureau method of measuring population, formerly called standard metropolitan statistical areas (SMSAs). According to the Executive Office of the President, Office of Management and Budget, a Metropolitan Statistical Area has "at least one urbanized area of 50,000 or more population, plus adjacent territory that has a high degree of social and economic integration with the core as measured by commuting ties." A Micropolitan Statistical Area has "at least one urban cluster of at least 10,000 but less than 50,000 population, plus adjacent territory that has a high degree of social and economic integration with the core as measured by commuting ties." As of November 20, 2008, there were 366 Metropolitan and 574 Micropolitan statistical areas in the United States. These designations provide the population aggregates of metropolitan centers to show density, growth and decline, population shifts, and other demographic data, including such variables as age, economics (poverty levels), mobility, occupations, sex, ethnic distributions, transportation, and household data. The chief reason the Constitution provided for a census of the population every 10 years was to give a basis for apportionment of representatives among the states. This apportionment largely determines the number of electoral votes allotted to each state. The number of representatives of each state in Congress is determined by the state's population, but each state is entitled to one representative regardless of population. A congressional apportionment has been made after each decennial census except that of 1920. *See also* census tract, Micropolitan Statistical Area

Mexican American Legal Defense and Education Fund (MALDEF). Founded in 1968 by Pedro "Pete" Tijerina of San Antonio, Texas. MALDEF was created by a $2.2 million Ford Foundation grant. It is based in Los Angeles with offices in San Antonio, Atlanta, Chicago, Houston, Sacramento, and Washington. Its services include advocacy, community education and outreach, leadership development, and higher education scholarships. Web: http://www.maldef.org/.

Mexican Mafia. Also known as La Eme (Spanish for the letter M), the Mexican Mafia is a powerful criminal organization founded in the 1950s and is notorious for its strong presence in the California Prison system. The early members of the gang organized while incarcerated at Deuel Vocational Institution, a state prison, and recruited gang members from Los Angeles. The organization was founded to protect members from assault by other inmates as well as corrections officers. The gang increased in violence to provide a veil of protection to incarcerated members and to secure a stronghold in black market activities, including weapons and drugs. The gang spread to multiple prisons in California, as well as to prisons in Arizona, New Mexico, and Texas. As a loosely organized criminal enterprise, the Mexican Mafia is believed to engage in extortion, assault, drug trafficking, murder, and contract killings both inside and outside the prison system. Various members of the Mexican Mafia were imprisoned through the 1990s, although generally for single incidences of criminal activity. However, the Department of Justice indicted dozens of members in 1995, and also in 2006, under the federal Racketeer Influenced and Corrupt Organizations (RICO)Act, leading to multiple prison terms; however, members allegedly knew how to "work the system," often using subpoena power as a mechanism by which senior members at multiple institutions could gather to discuss gang business. When several key informants were killed in this way, prison officials tightened security, but the gang continues to evolve its methods of continuing its criminal enterprise. The organization, which uses a black hand or eagle/snake symbol, has a reported alliance with the Aryan Brotherhood and maintains a rivalry with Nuestra Familia and the Black Guerilla Family.

Miami riots. *See* civil disturbances; McDuffle, Arthur

microchemistry. The field of chemistry involving testing and analysis of minute quantities of substances.

microcrystalline microscopic analysis. A chemical test for the presence of GHB. Given the notorious use of GHB as a date rape drug, often slipped into a victim's drink, some scholars have extended the application of this test to presence of GHB in beverages. However, this application is not well established.

Micropolitan Statistical Area. The term Micropolitan Statistical Area encompasses a new set of statistical areas established in 2003. This is a Census Bureau method of measuring population to show density, growth and decline, population shifts, and other demographic data, including such variables as age, economics (poverty levels), mobility, occupations, sex, ethnic distributions, transportation, and household data. According to the Executive Office of the President, Office of Management and Budget, a Micropolitan Statistical Area has "at least one urban cluster of at least 10,000 but less than 50,000 population, plus adjacent territory that has a high degree of social and economic integration with the core as measured by commuting ties." A Metropolitan Statistical Area has "at least one urbanized area of 50,000 or more population, plus adjacent territory that has a high degree of social and economic integration with the core as measured by commuting ties." As of November 20, 2008, there were 366 Metropolitan

and 574 Micropolitan statistical areas in the United States. Taking a census of the population every 10 years provides the basis for apportionment of representatives among the states, including the number of electoral votes allotted to each state and the number of representatives of each state in Congress. *See also* census tract, Metropolitan Statistical Area

microscope, comparison. A microscope that has two objectives or lens systems converging into a single field of vision. Two separate objects can be seen simultaneously and thus compared. Used in crime laboratories to determine if the markings on two bullets match, which would prove they were fired with the same weapon.

microscopy. Investigation with the use of a microscope.

Midwest Research Institute (MRI). Founded in 1944, MRI has performed contract research for criminal justice agencies since 1968. Its Justice Group was formed to provide assistance in the areas of management and operations. Address: 425 Volker Blvd., Kansas City, MO 64110. Web site: www.mriresearch.org/.

milieu management. A technique of treating deviant behavior that involves the group therapy approach. Therapeutic communities are developed in which inmates and free employees with law-abiding ideals live together and share management responsibilities. Inmates and employees jointly develop the therapeutic program to be used by the community. This approach is somewhat confrontational.

military law. Any system of rules and regulations governing military forces. Both the president—by virtue of authority as commander in chief—and Congress may make military law. It also includes certain customary usages that might be called military common law. Military justice is administered by court-martial with no concern for the judicial power or civil law of the United States.

Courts-martial are convened for the duration of a particular case. The regulations governing military justice in the United States are set forth in the Uniform Code of Military Justice (1951) and the Manual for Courts-Martial (MCM) (2008).

military police. The police force of an army, charged with maintaining law, order, and security. These include the Military Police Corps/Provost Marshal (Army); Provost Marshal's Office (Marine Corps); Masters-at-Arms branch (Navy); and Air Force Security Forces, formerly the Security Police (Air Force).

military prisons. Institutions designed to hold members of the armed forces who have been convicted of violations of the Uniform Code of Military Justice. The term also includes stockades, guardhouses, penitentiaries, and rehabilitation centers.

militia. (1) All able-bodied male citizens and resident male aliens between the ages of 18 and 45, whether members of the organized militia (National Guard) or not. The states retain power to appoint officers, train their militias according to the discipline prescribed by Congress, and call them out for defense and the preservation of order in emergencies. The federal government may provide for their organization, arming, and discipline and may call them into the national service in time of war or other emergencies. (2) Colloquially, the National Guard.

Miller Tidings Fair Trade Act of 1937. An amendment to the Sherman Act that gives manufacturers control over pricing in order to prevent large stores from undercutting small stores and driving out competition. Provisions were expanded in the McGuire Act (1952).

Milton S. Eisenhower Foundation. Non-profit organization founded in 1981 with the goal to increase economic and psychological self-sufficiency and reduce crime in inner-city neighborhoods. Address: 1875 Connecticut Ave. NW, Suite 410, Washington, DC 20009. Web site: http://www.eisenhowerfoundation.org/.

Minnesota Multiphasic Personality Inventory-2-Restructured Form (MMPI-2-RF). A commonly used psychological test designed to measure important aspects of personality, including psychopathology. Originally developed in a clinical setting in 1939, the 2008 revision of this instrument consists of 338 statements covering a wide range of subject matter—from physical conditions to the morale and social attitudes of the individual being tested. The subject must respond with "true," "false," or "cannot say" to each statement. Results of the inventory yield the following 10 subscales: hypochondriasis (Hs), depression (D), hysteria (Hy), psychopathic deviate (Pd), masculinity/femininity (MF), paranoia (Pa), psychasthenia (Pt), schizophrenia (Sc), hypomania (Ma), and social introversion. The instrument also includes validity subscales designed to measure: nonresponding or inconsistent responding, over reporting or exaggerating psychological symptoms, underreporting or downplaying, and over reporting somatic symptoms. Several criminal justice agencies use this instrument in employment prescreening.

minor. A person who has not reached the age, usually between 18 and 21 years, at which the law recognizes adulthood, or a general contractual capacity.

minority. A sociological term used to describe a group of persons with similar demographic characteristics, and which does not represent the majority, most common, or most powerful group in the population. In criminal justice, the term minority generally connotes a racial minority, generally persons of African American decent. Minority groups are studied in criminal justice due to the disproportionate representation of certain groups in prison and on death row.

Minority Business Development Agency. An agency within the United States Department of Commerce that is "dedicated to advancing the establishment and growth of minority-owned firms in the United States." Address: U.S. Department of Commerce, Minority Business Development Agency, 1401 Constitution Avenue, NW, Washington, DC 20230 Web: http://www.mbda.gov/.

minute order. The official record of orders and findings made by a court.

minutes. Memoranda of what takes place in court, made by authority of the court.

Miranda, Ernesto (1941–1976). The accused in the 1966 prisoners' rights *Miranda v. Arizona* case. An eighth-grade dropout with an extensive criminal record, Miranda was retried on kidnapping and rape charges in February 1967, because while the Supreme Court overturned his original conviction, it had not vacated the indictment. During his second trial, Miranda's common-law wife, Twila Hoffman, testified that he had admitted kidnapping and raping the victim. Miranda was convicted and sentenced to a 20-to-30-year term in state prison and was paroled in 1972. Two years later he was arrested on a gun charge and for possession of drugs, but the cases were dismissed due to Fourth Amendment violations. In 1975, Miranda was returned for a brief period to Arizona State Prison for parole violation but released later that year. In early 1976, at age 34, Ernesto Miranda was slain in a Phoenix skid-row bar during a quarrel over a card game.

Miranda rights. Set of rights that a person accused or suspected of having committed a specific offense has during interrogation and of which he or she must be informed prior to questioning, as stated by the Supreme Court in deciding *Miranda v. Arizona* in 1966 and related cases. The process of informing persons of their Miranda rights is often called admonition or admonishment of rights, and the information is called the Miranda warning. Many jurisdictions now require a statement, signed by the person to be interrogated, that he or she has heard and understood these rights. An individual's decision to waive these rights and to give information, or the signed statement recording such a decision, is often

called admonition and waiver. Most jurisdictions require that police read the Miranda warning from a proscribed card, although the U.S.S.C. ruled in *Florida v. Powell* 130 S. Ct. 1195 (2010) that police can improvise *Miranda*. According to the Court, "different words were used in the advice Powell received, but they communicated the same essential message." *See* Table 31. Example Miranda Warning, page 295

misanthropic. Describing behavior or attitudes that are mistrustful or hostile to all others.

miscegenation laws. Statutes formerly on the books in several states, designed to prevent interracial marriages. In *Loving v. Virginia* (1967), the Supreme Court struck down such laws.

miscellaneous docket. The docket of the Supreme Court on which are listed all cases filed *in forma pauperis*.

misconduct in office. Negligent, improper, dishonorable, or unlawful behavior on the part of an individual holding a position of public trust, which may result in removal from office.

misdemeanor. An offense punishable by incarceration, usually in a local confinement facility, for a period of which the upper limit, typically a year or less, is prescribed by statute in a given jurisdiction. Also known as *delicta*.

misfeasance. Performance of a lawful act in an improper or illegal manner—distinguished from malfeasance, which is the performance of a wrong act, and nonfeasance, the omission or neglect of duty.

misnomer. A misleading description or misidentification of someone or something. Courts usually have the right to amend indictments by inserting an individual's correct name.

misogynist. Any person who hates females.

misprision. (1) The concealment of a crime, such as a felony, or treason. (2) In criminal law, a term used to signify any significant

TABLE 31 EXAMPLE MIRANDA WARNING	
Miranda Advisement	**Aviso De Miranda**
1. "You have the right to remain silent. Do you understand?"	1. "Usted tiene el derecho de no decir nada. Entientde?"
2. "Anything you say may be used against you in court. Do you understand that?"	2. "Lo que usted diga ahora se puede usar, en su contra en un tribunal. Entiende?"
3. "You have the right to an attorney before and during questioning. Do you understand?"	3. "Usted tiene el derecho a un abogado, antes y durante cualquier interrogatorio. Entiende?"
4. "If you cannot afford an attorney, one will be appointed for you before questioning, if you wish. Do you understand that?"	4. "Si usted no tiene dinero para pagar por un abogado, uno le sera nombrado antes cualquier interrogatorio, si usted lo desea. Entiende?"
(If expressed waiver desired: "can we talk about what happened?") 72–40	(If expressed waiver desired: "podemos hablar sobre lo que sucedio?") 72–40

Source: Irvine Police Department, California Department of Justice.

misdemeanor that doesn't have a specific legal name.

misprision of felony. The offense of concealing a felony committed by another, but without such previous interaction with or subsequent assistance to the felon as would make the concealing party an accessory before or after the fact.

misprision, negative. The concealment of something that ought to be revealed.

misprision, positive. The commission of something that ought not to be done.

misprision of treason. The knowledge and concealment of an act of treason or treasonable plot, without any assent or participation therein. If assent or participation is present, the party becomes a principal.

misrepresentation. Stating something as a fact while knowing it is untrue; making any deceiving or misleading statement.

missing children. In federal law, any individual less than 18 years of age whose whereabouts are unknown to legal custodians, if (a) the circumstances indicate that the individual may have been removed by another from the control of the legal custodian without consent or (b) the circumstances strongly indicate that the individual is being abused or sexually exploited.

Missing Children Acts. Several federal statutes have addressed the issue of missing children. The National Center for Missing and Exploited Children, which provides information and promotes coordinated services for missing and exploited children, maintains a listing of such laws. As of 2010, these include:

Uniform Child Custody Jurisdiction Act (UCCJA), 9 ULA at 123 (1968): creates guidelines to avoid jurisdictional conflict in matters of child custody.

Juvenile Justice and Delinquency Prevention Act (1974): provides technical assistance to public and private nonprofit juvenile-justice and delinquency-prevention programs.

Hague Convention on the Civil Aspects of International Child Abduction (1980): establishes procedures to ensure the prompt return of children wrongfully removed to or detained in a foreign country.

Parental Kidnapping Prevention Act (PKPA), 28 USC 1738 A (1980): assures that full faith and credit is given to child-custody determinations, authorizes states to enforce custody decisions made in other jurisdictions.

Missing Children Act, 28 USC 534 (1982): establishes procedures to collect and exchange information to assist in the identification of unidentified deceased or missing children.

Missing Children's Assistance Act, 42 USC 5771 (1984): establishes national toll-free telephone line to assist missing children.

International Child Abduction Remedies Act (1988): implements Hague Convention on International Child Abduction, authorizing U.S. courts to hear such cases.

National Child Search Assistance Act, 42 USC 5779-80 (1990): requires all law-enforcement agencies to post information about missing children younger than 18 into the Federal Bureau of Investigation's (FBI) National Crime Information Center (NCIC) database.

International Parental Kidnapping Crime Act (IPKCA), 18 USC 1204 (1993): removal of a child from the United States with the intent to obstruct the lawful exercise of parental rights is a felony.

Jacob Wetterling Crimes Against Children and Sexually Violent Offender Registration Act, 42 USC 14071 (1994): offenders convicted of sexually violent offenses or criminal offenses against child victims have 10-year registration requirements.

The Uniform Child Custody Jurisdiction and Enforcement Act (UCCJEA) (1997): replaces the Uniform Child Custody Jurisdiction Act and governs jurisdiction in interstate custody and visitation cases, requires interstate enforcement and nonmodification of sister-state custody orders, and authorizes public officials to play a role in civil child custody enforcement and cases involving the Hague Convention on the Civil Aspects of International Child Abduction.

Prosecutorial Remedies and Other Tools to End the Exploitation of Children Today Act (2003): PROTECT Act strengthens laws against child pornography; increases

in the base-offense level for kidnapping; mandatory 20-year sentence for an offender whose kidnapping victim is a nonfamily-member minor; attempt liability for international parental kidnapping. This act also codifies several related provisions, including Suzanne's Law, requires all law-enforcement agencies to post information about missing children younger than 21 into the FBI's NCIC database; America's Missing: Broadcast Emergency Response (AMBER) Alert provisions calling for the national coordination of state and local AMBER Alert programs; a Code ADAM program to establish procedures for locating a child who is missing in public building; and increasing the statute of limitations for child abduction.

Adam Walsh Child Protection and Safety Act (2006): mandates law enforcement entry of information about missing and abducted children into the National Crime Information Center (NCIC) database within two hours of notification. *See also* National Center for Missing and Exploited Children

missing children programs. A variety of public programs exist to aid in the recovery of missing children. Historically, these included the publication of missing children photos on milk cartons and grocery bags, but such practices have largely been replaced by Internet dissemination. The National Center for Missing and Exploited Children can be reached by calling (800) 843-5678. *See also* juvenile locators

missing persons. Policies governing the acceptance of reports of and search for missing persons vary. Generally, immediate attention is given if the missing person is below the age of 11 or elderly, mentally ill, or disabled; or if he or she might be suicidal or the victim of an accident or crime. Reports of these types of missing persons are usually accepted by telephone, with a formal report generated later. In other cases, generally a 24-hour period of absence must occur prior to investigation or completion of a formal report. The FBI will not look for a missing person but will notify an inquirer of any information received. For further information, contact FBI Headquarters in Washington, DC: Federal Bureau of Investigation, J. Edgar Hoover Building, 935 Pennsylvania Avenue, NW, Washington, DC 20535-0001, (202) 324-3000. Web site: http://www.fbi.gov/wanted/kidnap/kidmiss.htm.

Missing Person Locator. A service available to the public provided by the Salvation Army. To begin a search, the Missing Persons Inquiry Form should be completed as thoroughly as possible and submitted with a $25.00 non-refundable registration fee. The Salvation Army will maintain the privacy of a missing person who does not wish to be reunited, and will not conduct searches in legal matters, adoption cases, genealogical searches, persons under age 18, and persons missing less than six months. Address: Salvation Army Missing Persons Locator Service, 180 East Ocean Blvd Long Beach, CA 90802, Phone: 800-698-7728; Web: http://www.use.salvationarmy.org/use/www_use.nsf/vw-sublinks/185265C165A62EE085256EC30069DD66?openDocument. The missing persons form is available at: http://www.use-salvationarmy.org/Downloads/SA_MissingPersonsForm.pdf.

mission statement. An increasingly popular means of establishing with and for all employees of a company, agency, or department agreement on the basic and broad purposes of the organization as a whole. Goals and values may also be included in the policy statement or appended as substatements.

mistake of fact. Any erroneous conviction of fact or circumstance resulting in some act that would not otherwise have been undertaken. Mistake of fact becomes a defense when an individual commits a prohibited act in good faith and with a reasonable, though false, belief that certain facts are correct. The mistake must be honest and not the result of negligence or poor deliberation. Mistake of fact does not, however, excuse persons in "strict liability" cases, such as unlawful sex with a minor or selling alcohol to a minor.

mistake of law. Any want of knowledge or acquaintance with the laws of the land insofar as they apply to the act, relation, duty, or matter under consideration. Ignorance of the law is no excuse; simple ignorance of forbidden behavior is not usually an acceptable defense. In contrast, however, the Supreme Court ruled in *Lambert v. California* (1957) that ignorance of the law may be a defense, if the law has not been made reasonably well known.

mistrial. A trial that has been terminated and declared invalid by the court because of some circumstance that creates a substantial and uncorrectable prejudice to the conduct of a fair trial or that makes it impossible to continue the trial in accordance with prescribed procedures. Mistrials can occur if the jury is deadlocked or "hung" in its decision, meaning it cannot reach a verdict. When a mistrial is declared, the criminal prosecution generally restarts.

mitigation. Alleviation; abatement; making less rigorous.

mitochondrial DNA (mtDNA). (1) A type of DNA found in particular structures of the body and passed through the maternal line of descent. (2) mDNA is also a method of analysis generally used on degraded samples, as mitochondrial DNA is more abundant than nuclear DNA in a given sample. Specific regions of mitochondrial DNA are amplified for comparison. Mitochondrial DNA is maternally linked, making it a useful tool in maternal lineage and also for identifying human remains. *See also* Deoxyribo nucleic acid; DNA analysis; Restriction Fragment Length Polymorphism (RFLP) test; Polymerase Chain Reaction (PCR); PCR-based Short Tandem Repeat (STR) method; Amplified Fragment Length Polymorphism (Amb-FLP) method; and Short Tandem Repeat on the Y-chromosome (Y-STR)

mittimus. A court order directing a peace officer to take a person to jail.

M'Naghten Rule. A legal decision of 1843 that established the first clear precedent for acquittal based on the defense of insanity. Daniel M'Naghten killed the secretary to England's Sir Robert Peel, but claimed at his trial that at the time he committed the act, he had not been of sound state of mind. From this came the M'Naghten rule, the right-from-wrong test of criminal responsibility: "If the accused was possessed of sufficient understanding when he committed the criminal act to know what he was doing and to know that it was wrong, he is responsible therefore, but if he did not know the nature and quality of the act or did know what he was doing but did not know that it was wrong, he is not responsible." In 1954 the U.S. Court of Appeals for the District of Columbia broadened the M'Naghten test in favor of the Durham rule. *See also* Durham rule, insanity defense

mob. (1) A large crowd, particularly one that is violent and disorderly; (2) colloquial term used in reference to organized crime groups.

mobile command post. A vehicle, containing communications and other operations control equipment, that enables commanding officers to establish a temporary command post in the field.

mobile crime laboratory. A vehicle, usually a van, equipped with investigative instruments, equipment, and supplies. It can be moved to the site of an investigation for immediate analysis of materials and clues found at the scene of an incident.

mode. In statistical research, the most easily obtained measure of central tendency; the score that occurs most frequently in any study.

Model Penal Code. A generalized, modern codification of the principles considered basic to criminal law, published by the American Law Institute in 1962 and last updated in 1982.

Model Sentencing Act. A document, drawn up by the Advisory Council of Judges of the National Council on Crime and Delinquency (NCCD) in 1972, outlining a proposed model for sentencing.

modification of probation. A court-ordered change in the terms and conditions of a probation order, making them more, or less, restrictive.

modus operandi. A characteristic pattern of behavior repeated in a series of offenses that coincides with the pattern evidenced by a particular person or group of persons. It is based upon the theory that each professional criminal has a method of committing a crime peculiar to him- or herself. Devised by Major Atcherley of Yorkshire, England, it is used to supplement the fingerprint method. The Atcherley system is a modus operandi file recording offender/suspect peculiarities. Categories may include property, time, location, victim(s), method, and habits.

molding. *See* moulage

Molly Maguires (Mollies). Terrorist organization of Irish anthracite-coal miners that flourished in east-central Pennsylvania between 1843 and 1876. The Mollies allegedly operated by terrorism—assaulting, even murdering, persons they found offensive. Many of the crimes attributed to the Mollies involved coal-mine supervisory personnel. The group was eventually infiltrated by a Pinkerton detective, who discovered information that led to the arrest of men alleged to be Mollies. Beginning in 1876, 19 of these men were hanged and others imprisoned.

molotov cocktail. A fire bomb or hand grenade usually made with a breakable bottle containing a flammable liquid and with a rag wick protruding from the mouth of the bottle. It is used by lighting the wick and throwing the container against an object, causing the bottle to break and thus igniting the fuel.

Monitoring the Future. Since 1975, the National Institute on Drug Abuse has sponsored this research, which collects data from 50,000 students annually in public and private high schools. The research assesses the behaviors, attitudes, and values of American secondary school students, college students, and young adults. Primary uses of the data include assessing the prevalence and trends of drug use among seniors; better understanding the lifestyles and value systems associated with drug use; and monitoring how these attitudes shift over time. Web: http://monitoringthefuture.org/. *See also* Drug Abuse Warning Network

monogamy. (1) The practice of having one sexual partner at a time. (2) A marriage consisting of only two parties, generally one male and one female. *See also bigamy, polygamy*

mooning. The intentional exposure of one's naked buttocks, generally while bending over and pulling down the pants and underwear. Typically, mooning is a form of sophomoric humor or an insult, although it can be prosecuted. *See also* exhibitionism, flashing

moot court. A mock court used by criminal justice students to argue hypothetical cases.

moot question. A case that, because circumstances or conditions changed after the litigation was begun, is no longer liable for trial or subject to court jurisdiction.

moral. According to the standards of a society; ethical, good, honest, upright, and virtuous.

moral development. The study of moral development has concentrated on how individuals come to adopt the standards of right and wrong established in their cultures and how they resist the temptation to transgress the rules of acceptable conduct. The moral developmental theory stems largely from the work of Swiss child psychologist Jean Piaget (1896–1980).

moral evidence. *See* circumstantial evidence

moral turpitude. The quality of a crime that characterizes it as *malum in se,* that is, as inherently vicious and depraved or as offensive to public morals. Foreign citizens convicted of a crime involving moral turpitude are generally debarred from entry under U.S. immigration laws.

Moran, Thomas Bartholomew. When Moran died in 1971 at the Miami Rescue Mission, he was a vagrant and a derelict, and his pockets were empty. Moran had been a celebrated criminal whom many considered the dean of American pickpockets. His career began in 1906 when, at 14, he would pass through the crowded streets and stores of downtown Kansas City, opening women's purses and removing small change. Moran ultimately achieved the rank of "class cannon," a designation that typified him as a thief with skill and daring. The world-class pickpocket had even been aboard the *Titanic* when it left on its ill-fated maiden voyage, and he was one of the 705 survivors.

mores. Morals; manners.

morgue. A public depository or building for temporarily holding bodies for identification. The morgue was originally a building in Paris, France, where police inspected new prisoners to memorize their features. This is presumably why many newspapers use the term to indicate their archives of clips and photographs.

morphine. A habit-forming narcotic drug; the major sedative and pain-relieving drug found in opium, being approximately 10 percent of the crude opium exudate.

mortis causa (Lat.). In contemplation of death; by reason of death.

Mosaic code. The law of the Old Testament, particularly as expressed in the Ten Commandments, proscribing such actions as murder, adultery, stealing, and bearing false witness.

Mothers Against Drunk Driving (MADD). A nationally known organization to combat drunk driving; founded in May, 1980, by Candy Lightner following the death of her teenage daughter Cari. The motorist who killed Cari, Clarence Busch, pleaded innocent to his sixth drunk-driving charge in Sacramento Municipal Court in May, 1985, after spending 16 months in state prison. MADD is a citizens awareness group of approximately 600,000 members, which supports legislation for harsher sanctions against drunk drivers. MADD has grown to a $40 million-a-year corporation with 397 local chapters run by a 16-member board. Located at 511 E. John Carpenter Freeway, Suite 700, Irving, TX 75062. Similar programs include: SADD (Students Against Drunk Drivers), which was founded in 1983 in Marlboro, MA, by Robert Anastas, a teacher from Wayland High School in Wayland, MA, after two of his students were killed in a car crash (for the free SADD kit, send a long, stamped, self-addressed envelope to SADD, 255 Main Street, Marlborough, MA 01752. Other organizations include: RID (Remove Intoxicated Drivers); VODD (Virginians Opposing Drunk Drivers); DDADD (Drunk Drivers Against Drunk Driving). Web site: www.madd.org/. *See also* SADD

motion. An oral or written request made to a court at any time before, during, or after court proceedings, asking the court to make a specified finding, decision, or order.

motivation. The term for desired or actual movement toward an identified goal. Four major theories of human goals, drives, or needs are: (1) Abraham Maslow's hierarchy of needs, described in his *Toward a Psychology of Being;* (2) Clayton Alderfer's theory, central to his work with people in organizations, of three core need groups: existence, relatedness, and growth; (3) achievement, power, and affiliation; (4) Frederick Herzberg's motivation-maintenance theory. *See also* Herzberg's motivation-maintenance theory; Maslow's hierarchy of needs

motive. An impulse or emotion toward action. As distinguished from intent, motive is not an essential element of crime. An evil motive will not make an act a crime, nor will a good motive prevent an act from being a crime. Motive may, however, tend to show that an act was willful and done with criminal intent, or tend to incriminate or prove the guilt of the perpetrator.

motorcyclists, outlaw. A type of organization generally centered on cruiser motorcycles, such as Harley-Davidsons or choppers, whose members generally value principles of nonconformity (their basic motto is "FTW"—Fuck the World), and whose activities center around criminal behavior. Such activities include: narcotics manufacturing and distribution, prostitution, weapons-related violations, extortion, murder, arson-for-hire, pornography, protection rackets, loan sharking, interstate transportation of stolen property and stolen motor vehicles, insurance fraud, and obstruction of justice. The five main motorcycle groups currently are Hell's Angels, Outlaws, Pagans, Bandidos, and Sons of Silence. The Outlaws, also known as the American Outlaw Association, was founded in Chicago in 1959. The Pagans were established in 1959 in Prince Georges County, MD. The Bandidos, or Bandido Nation, came into being in 1966 in Houston. The Sons of Silence was formed in Commerce City, CO, in 1968. The five main gangs only allow white male membership, although all-black outlaw motorcycle gangs do exist.

motor vehicle. A vehicle that is self-propelled. The term does not include a self-propelled wheelchair, tricycle, or motorized quadricycle when operated by a person who, because of physical disability, is otherwise unable to move about as a pedestrian. However, courts have established that some assisted mobility devices, most notably power chairs, do constitute a motor vehicle, and operation of such while intoxicated can result in criminal prosecution under DUI statutes in some jurisdictions. *See also* DUI

motor vehicle research. National research is conducted on vehicles under 10,000 lbs., including cars, pickup trucks, and vans. Studies are made on automotive systems, occupant packaging (seating/restraints for driver and passengers), accident avoidance (tires, braking, towing), structures (fuel tanks, crash performance), technology assessment (advanced technology, diesels, emissions, new materials), economic assessment (cost of new technology, production engineering), experimental vehicles, downsizing, and fuel economy. For further information, contact: NHTSA Headquarters, Vehicle Research and Test Center, 1200 New Jersey Ave., SE, West

Building, Washington, DC, 20590. Web: http://www.nhtsa.dot.gov/portal/site/nhtsa/menuitem.081e92a06f83bfd24ec86e10dba046a0/.

motor vehicle safety standards. The National Highway Traffic Safety Administration (NHTSA) provides information and sets standards for air bags, seat belts, child restraint safety seats, motorcycle helmets, fuel system integrity, odometers, windshield defrosters, rearview mirrors, tire selection and rims, door locks, school bus rollover protection, seating systems, new pneumatic tires, and more. A publication covering this topic, *Federal Motor Vehicle Safety Standards and Regulations (2004)*, is available at: http://www.nhtsa.dot.gov/cars/rules/standards/FMVSS-Regs/NHTSA. Web site: http://www.nhtsa.dot.gov/.

motor vehicle theft. Unlawful taking, or attempted taking, of a self-propelled road vehicle owned by another, with the intent to deprive him or her of it permanently or temporarily.

Motor Vehicle Theft Act. An act of Congress on October 29, 1919, that made it a federal offense to transport across state boundary lines a motor vehicle known to have been stolen.

Motor Vehicle Theft Law Enforcement Act of 1984. This law requires car manufacturers, beginning with 1987 models, to mark 14 major components in "high-theft-risk" cars with a 17-character identification number, called a Vehicle Identification Number (VIN number). Major components include the engine, transmission, front fenders, hood, doors, and front and rear bumpers. In addition, replacement parts must bear the manufacturer's registered trademark, or some other unique marking if there is no trademark, and the letter R. The act is designed to combat the sale of parts of stolen vehicles by making components traceable.

moulage. A synonym for molding and casting in criminal investigation work, but the term in criminal justice usually means certain materials used in molding and casting, sold under trade names. Moulage is cast materials manufactured commercially and consisting of types (a) for making a negative mold and (b) for making the positive cast. This process will record fine detail.

MOVE (name is not an acronym). Radical group founded in Philadelphia by John Africa in 1972, the group supported a return to nature and vehemently opposed technology. The organization engaged in multiple confrontations with Philadelphia police between 1972–1980s, including a one year stand-off with police, which ended in a shoot-out. In 1985, the Philadelphia police department bombed the MOVE headquarters, killing 11 people, including five children. The city of Philadelphia paid $1.5 million to survivors. *See also* SWAT

move. (1) To make a motion, or formally ask for something. (2) To apply to a court for an order or a rule.

movement. In corrections, an admission to or a release from a status—prisoner, parolee, or probationer. A transfer between facilities does not, unless specifically noted, count as a movement for reporting purposes.

muckrakers. The name given to a group of early-twentieth-century writers, including Lincoln Steffens and Upton Sinclair, who exposed public corruption and attacked slums, juvenile delinquency, prostitution, and the social evils that produced them.

mug shot. A photograph showing the head and shoulders, both side and front views, of a criminal.

Muhammad, John Allen (1960–2009). Born in New Orleans, Louisiana as John Allen Williams, Muhammad enlisted in the Louisiana Army National Guard in 1978 and served in active duty in 1985, learning about mechanics and weaponry, and earning his Expert Rifleman's Badge. In 1987, Muhammad joined the Nation of Islam, although he remained in the military until his discharge in 1994. He moved to Antigua in 1999, where he met 14 year old Lee Malvo. Around 2001,

Williams returned to the United States, changed his surname to Muhammad, and provided care for 16-year-old Malvo, who immigrated illegally. Muhammad was convicted with Malvo in the Beltway sniper attacks, which terrorized the Washington, DC/Virginia area in the fall of 2002. Between September 5–October 23, 2002, Muhammad (aged 42 at the time) and Malvo (aged 17) killed 10 people and wounded three others along Interstate 95. The two were apprehended on October 24. In 2003, Muhammad was convicted of four felonies in Virginia: two counts of murder, conspiracy, and illegal firearm; he was sentenced to death in 2004. Muhammad was extradited to Maryland for crimes committed in that state. In Maryland, codefendant Malvo testified about the full plan, which included their intent to kill six white people a day for 30 days, then shoot a pregnant woman in the stomach, shoot a police officer and detonate bombs at the funeral, extort money from the United States, and use funds to recruit other orphaned boys to shoot white people in the United States. Malvo was convicted of six counts of murder and received six consecutive life sentences in Maryland and was returned to Virginia. Muhammad was executed in Virginia by lethal injection on November 10, 2009. *See also* Beltway sniper attacks; Malvo, Lee Boyd

mulet. (1) To punish by fine. (2) To deprive.

multicide. The killing of many individuals. *See also* murder, mass; murder spree; serial murders

multilevel modeling. Advanced statistical technique used to account for the interdependence amongst units with the sample.

multiple marginality. Conceptual framework that attempts to explain gang involvement by considering environmental, socioeconomic, cultural, and psychosocial factors.

municipal charter. A legislative enactment conferring governmental powers of the state upon its local agencies, generally cities.

municipal corporation. A public corporation established as a subdivision of a state for local governmental purposes.

municipal court. A minor court authorized by municipal charter or state law to enforce local ordinances and exercise the criminal and civil jurisdiction of the peace.

municipal home rule. A plan whereby a greater measure of political autonomy is allowed a city within the terms of a charter granted by the state legislature. In 1952 more than 16 states had embodied home-rule provisions in their constitutions. The home-rule charter is forbidden to contain provisions contrary to the Constitution, statutes, or treaties of the United States or to the constitution or laws of the state. The general clauses of a home-rule charter provide for the incorporation of the city, describe its framework of government, and determine its officers, elections, tenure, and similar details. They also prescribe the city's power over contracts, finances, and other purely municipal functions that remain within its jurisdiction. *See also* home rule

municipality. A local area of government in the United States. At various times it has taken the forms of parish, borough, town, township, village, county, and city governments. In the U.S. constitutional system, a municipality is a nonsovereign entity, its powers depending wholly upon state grant. Municipalities may be incorporated or unincorporated. In the former, a state charter provides a degree of autonomy with respect to purely local functions. In the latter, control is generally exercised by the state legislature, operating through a local government. The governments of municipalities vary but consist generally of a legislature in the form of a council, board of trustees or supervisors, or board of selectmen. If there is an executive, it is usually a mayor, although this office is customarily absent from a county. Other municipal offices include those in the court, police, sheriff's, clerk's, and legal sectors.

municipal law. The law of a state or nation, based on the power of the state; also sometimes called arbitrary law, or the power to command what is right and prohibit what is wrong. It is made by people, founded on convenience, and is dependent upon the authority of the legislative body enacting it. The term also designates the law applicable to municipalities. Municipal law is classified as: (a) criminal law and (b) civil law. Criminal law deals with those offenses against the individual or the community that the state recognizes as wrongs to society.

municipal officer. An officer belonging to a municipality—a city, town, or borough—rather than a county.

municipal ordinance. A law created by a municipal corporation to define the proper conduct of its affairs or its inhabitants.

municipal reform. The attempts to increase popular controls over municipal government for the purpose of weakening or eliminating political machines. Some of the developments in this direction include the use of municipal home rule for larger cities, proportional representation, the short ballot, the county executive plan, and the county-manager and city-manager systems.

murder and nonnegligent manslaughter. Intentionally causing the death of another without legal justification or excuse, and/or causing the death of another while committing, or attempting to commit, another crime. Murder appears as a proscription in both the Old and New Testaments, and its designation as a capital offense appears in an early chapter of Genesis. On June 14, 1985, a landmark decision was handed down by the Illinois Supreme Court, in which three corporate officers were found guilty of murder for the cyanide-poisoning death of a worker in a silver recovery plant they managed and operated in suburban Chicago. They were the first company officers to be charged with, and convicted of, murder for management actions and inactions that contributed to the death of a worker. On March 18, 1997, in Ventura, CA, 92-year-old Alfred Pohlmeier was the oldest defendant ever to be convicted in a second-degree murder case. At his sanity hearing, he was found to be legally insane and was ordered to undergo treatment.

Murder Inc. Name given to organized crime group believed to be founded by the Mafia in the 1930s to address high rates of violence, warfare, and murder, especially during the prohibition era. Murder Inc. was believed to be the mafia unit charged with carrying out "approved" assassinations of mafia members, and included notorious mafia figures Bugsy Siegel and Meyer Lansky. The group disbanded in the early 1940 following successful prosecution (and death sentences) for more than a dozen mafia hit men. *See also* Costello, Frank; Luciano, Charles; Genovese, Vito; Lansky, Meyer; mafia; Siegel, Bugsy

murder, mass. The killing of four or more victims at one location, within one event. *See also* cults; Hennard, George; Huberty, James; murder spree; National Center for the Analysis of Violent Crime. *See* Table 32. Infamous Mass Murders in the United States, pages 304 & 305.

murder spree. Defined as killings at two or more locations with little or no intervening time and as the result of a single event. For example, in February 1985 Daniel Remeta and two others robbed and killed the manager of a restaurant in Grainfield, KS. An hour later, Remeta shot a sheriff's deputy who was trying to flag down his car. The killer then fled to a nearby grain elevator, shot the manager, and killed two hostages before he was captured. *See also* Starkweather, Charles

museums, police. The New York City Police Museum features narcotics and police exhibits open to the public weekdays without charge; the reference library is available to law enforcement officers and college students; located at 100 Old Slip, New York, NY; Web: http://www.nycpolicemuseum.org/. The Royal Canadian Mounted Police Museum is open, without charge, daily from June 1 through November 15; located

text continues on page 305

TABLE 32	INFAMOUS MASS MURDERS IN THE UNITED STATES		
Year	State	Murderer	Death Toll
1949	New Jersey	Howard Unruh	Shot 13 neighbors.
1955	Colorado	John Graham	44 died via plane bomb.
1966	Illinois	Richard Speck	Stabbed/strangled 8 student nurses.
1966	Texas	Charles Whitman	Shot 16, mostly students.
1966	Arizona	Robert Smith	Shot 5 women in beauty salon.
1969	California	Susan Atkins, Linda Kasabian, Patricia Krenwinkle, Leslie Van-Houten, & Charles Watson	Stabbed 9 people for Charles Manson.
1974	Louisiana	Mark Essex	Shot 9, mostly police officers.
1975	Florida	Bill Ziegler	Shot 4 adults in a store.
1976	California	Edward Allaway	Killed 7 persons at university library.
1977	New York	Frederick Cowan	Shot 6 co-workers.
1978	Guyana	Jim Jones	Shot and enticed to suicide (by poison) 912 cult members, including children.
1983	Washington	Willie Mak & Benjamin Ng	Shot 13 people.
1984	California	James Huberty	Shot 21 persons at McDonald's.
1986	Oklahoma	Patrick Sherrill	Shot 14 co-workers.
1987	Florida	William Cruse	Shot 6 persons at mall.
1988	California	Richard Farley	Shot 7 persons at computer company.
1988	California	James Purdy	Shot 5 children in playground.
1988	North Carolina	Michael Hayes	Shot 4 neighbors.
1989	Kentucky	Joseph Wesbecker	Shot 8 co-workers.
1990	Florida	James Pough	Shot 13 persons at auto loan company.
1990	New York	Julio Gonzalez	Killed 87 people in nightclub fire (arson).
1991	New Jersey	Joseph Harris	Shot 4 people at post office.
1991	Texas	George Hennard	Shot 22 people at restaurant.
1991	Iowa	Gang Lu	Shot 5 college students and officials.
1995	California	Willie Woods	Shot 4 electrical company co-workers.
1995	Texas	James Simpson	Killed 5 persons at refinery inspection station.
1996	Mississippi	Kenneth Tornes	Firefighter killed 4 co-workers.
1997	South Carolina	Arthur H. Wise	Killed 4 co-workers on assembly line.
1997	California	Arturo Torres	Killed 4 co-workers at maintenance yard.

(continued)

Year	State	Murderer	Death Toll
1998	Connecticut	Matthew Beck	State lottery employee killed 4 executives.
1999	Georgia	Mark Barton	Killed 9 co-workers at brokerage firm.
1999	Alabama	Alan E. Miller	Truck driver killed 3 co-workers.
1999	Hawaii	Bryan Uyesugi	Copier repairman killed seven Xerox co-workers.
1999	Florida	Silvio Izquierdo-Leyva	Housekeeper shot 5 co-workers at hotel.
1999	Colorado	Eric Harris and Dylan Klebold	Killed 12 students and 1 teachers at Columbine High School.
2000	Texas	Robert Harris	Killed 5 persons at car wash.
2000	Massachusetts	Michael McDermott	Killed 7 co-workers.
2005	Minnesota	Jeffrey Weise	Shot 9 persons, mostly HS students.
2006	Pennsylvania	Charles Carl Roberts	Shot 5 school children.
2007	Virginia	Seung-Hui Cho	Killed 32 at Virginia Tech University.
2008	Illinois	Steven Kazmierczak	Killed 6 university students.
2009	Alabama	Michael McLendon	Killed 10 people by firearm and arson.
2009	New York	Jiverly Wong	Killed 13 persons.
2009	Texas	Nidal Hasan	Killed 13 persons at Fort Hood Army Base.
2010	Alabama	Amy Bishop	Killed 5 co-workers at University.

Note: Table excludes international, terrorist-perpetrated, or domestic-violence related acts of mass murder.

in Regina, Saskatchewan. *See also* Federal Bureau of Investigation, T. H. Pendergast California Parole Museum

mutiny. An uprising by sailors or soldiers against their commanders. Because of its need for discipline and obedience to authority, the military's most serious offense is mutiny. It has been defined in American military law to mean action by two or more who, with intent to usurp or override lawful military authority, in concert disobey orders, shirk their duty, or create any violence or disturbance. The maximum penalty for mutiny is death.

mutual agreement program. A program, providing a form of contract between a prisoner and state prison and parole officials, wherein the prisoner undertakes specified self-improvement programs in order to receive a definite parole date, and the agency promises to provide the necessary educational and social services.

mutual aid. In law enforcement, a contractual agreement among various contiguous agencies to provide back-up assistance to one another in emergency situations. Agencies could include the highway patrol, state police, county sheriff's department, and other local agencies. Beyond such contractual agreements, situations may demand the next higher level of imposing control, use of the state's National Guard troops, or, as a last resort, federal intervention. *See also* National Guard

mutual transfer. When two or more objects come in contact with one another, trace evidence from each may be left on the other. This is called mutual transfer. This is often the case when one vehicle is struck by another; each usually leaves some evidence on the other, such as an exchange of paint traces.

N

nalline test. Nalorphine or *N*-allyl-normor phineis an opiod antagonist that binds at opiate receptors in the brain. This test was developed in the early1950s for treatment in opium overdose. Around 1956, it was also used as a field screening test to determine whether or not a suspect was using opiate narcotics, such as heroin. In the Nalline test, the suspect is injected with Nalorphine. The chemical causes immediate withdrawal symptoms i addicts; it also causes the pupils to dilate. It has no appreciable effect on non-addicts, except pupil constriction. The practice has not been widely used in the United States since the early 1970s.

Napoleonic Code. The code of laws adopted in France by the regime of Napoleon Bonaparte in 1810 and revised in 1819. The code became the basis for the criminal code in most continental European and Latin American countries.

narcoterrorism. (1) Term coined in 1983 referencing terrorist-type attacks against anti-narcotics police. (2) Term used to describe the alliance between drug traffickers and political terrorists.

narcotic. Any drug or psychoative compound with effects similar to opiate-derived drugs. The Uniform Crime Reports category for the unlawful possession, sale, use, growing, and manufacturing of illicit drugs.

narcotic drugs. The term *narcotic drug* refers to the following, whether produced directly or indirectly by extraction from substances of vegetable origin, independently by chemical synthesis, or by a combination of the two: (a) opium, opiates, and their derivatives, including their isomers, esters, ethers, and salts, but not including the isoquinoline

alkaloids of opium; (b) poppy straw and concentrate of poppy straw; (c) coca leaves, except those and their extracts from which cocaine, ecgonine, and derivatives of ecgonine or their salts have been removed; (d) cocaine, its salts, isomers, and salts of isomers; (e) ecgonine, its derivatives, their salts, isomers, and salts of isomers; and (f) any compound, mixture, or preparation that contains any quantity of any of the substances referred to above. Common narcotics include heroin, morphine, Vicodin, Codeine, hydrocodone, and oxycodone.

narcotic prohibition act, first federal. The first federal narcotic regulation was enacted by Congress as part of the McKinley Tariff Act on October 1, 1890. This act provided for an internal revenue tax of $10 a pound on all smoking opium manufactured in the United States for smoking purposes and limited the manufacture, keeping of books, rendering of returns, and so forth. Section 1 of the federal act of February 9, 1909, read: "After the first day of April 1909, it shall be unlawful to import into the United States, opium in any form or any preparation or derivative thereof . . . other than smoking opium for medicinal purposes."

narcotic regulation, first state. Adopted on March 10, 1933, by Nevada.

narcotics and dangerous drugs training. The U.S. Drug Enforcement Agency (DEA) Office of Training provides training for state and local police officers in rural jurisdictions. According to the DEA, three programs are available, including: Drug Law Enforcement School for Patrol Officers (DLESP), the Drug Enforcement Training Program (DETP) Train-the-Trainer School, and the Drug Task Force Supervisors School (DTFSS). Address: DEA Office of Training, P.O. Box 1475, Quantico, Virginia 22124-1475. Web http://www.justice.gov/dea/pro grams/training/part15.html.

Narcotics Anonymous. A self-help organization founded in July 1953 and modeled after Alcoholics Anonymous. According to their Web site, Narcotics Anonymous is an international, community-based association of recovering drug addicts with more than 43,900 weekly meetings in over 127 countries worldwide. This is the third largest self-help group, after Alcoholics Anonymous and Al-Anon. Address: P.O. Box 9999, Van Nuys, CA 91409. Web site: http://www.na.org/.

narcotic tariff, first. The first federal law governing the importing of narcotics into the United States was the Tariff Act of August 30, 1842, which placed a levy of 75 cents a pound on opium. Prior to this act, opium was exempted from duty by the acts of July 14, 1832, and March 2, 1833.

Nation of Islam. (historically called The Black Muslim Nationalist Movement) was founded in Detroit in 1930 by Wallace D. Fard Muhammad, who was succeeded by Elijah Muhammad with the help of Malcolm X. The organization, headquartered in Chicago, IL maintains their own schools, stores, farms, and a newspaper, *Muhammad Speaks*. They believe they are descendants of an ancient lost tribe of Muslims, and they adhere to some orthodox Islamic beliefs. Louis Farrakhan has been the leader of the organization since 1978. *See also* Malcolm X

National Advisory Commission on Criminal Justice Standards and Goals. Appointed in 1971 by the administrator of the Law Enforcement Assistance Administration to formulate, for the first time, national criminal justice standards and goals for crime reduction and prevention at the state and local levels. In 1973 the Commission recommended guidelines covering all areas of police practices.

National Advisory Committee for Juvenile Justice and Delinquency Prevention and Treatment. Initiated in 1974 by the Juvenile Justice and Delinquency Prevention (JJDP) Act, NCACJJDPT was a 1970–1980 U.S. Department of Justice committee responsible for developing standards for the administration of juvenile justice. As of 2004, the Federal Advisory Committee on Juvenile Justice

(FACJJ) an annual report on juvenile justice issues. If enacted, the Juvenile Justice and Delinquency Prevention Reauthorization Act of 2009 (proposed, not yet passed) would reauthorize the committee to continue.

national agency check. A personnel security investigation consisting of a records review of national agencies, including the FBI and the Department of Justice (DOJ) Defense Central Index of Investigations.

national agency check and inquiry. Similar to a national agency check, this term is often used interchangeably. However, it is personnel security investigation combining a national agency check (as above) with additional background inquiries to law enforcement agencies, former employers and supervisors, references, and schools.

National Alliance for Model State Drug Laws (NAMSLD). A nonprofit organization created by Congress in 1995, NAMSLD is the successor organization to the President's Commission on Model State Drug Laws and strives to develop a uniform code for state drug laws. This resource center is dedicated to helping "governors, state legislators, attorneys general, drug and alcohol professionals, community leaders, the recovering community, and others striving for comprehensive and effective state drug and alcohol laws, policies, and programs." Address: 1414 Prince St., Suite 312, Alexandria, VA 22314. Web site: http://www.namsdl.org/home.htm.

National Archive of Criminal Justice Data. Sponsored by the Department of Justice, Bureau of Justice Statistics, National Institutes of Justice, Office of Juvenile Justice and Delinquency Prevention, and the Bureau of Justice Assistance, the mission of the National Archive "is to facilitate research in criminal justice and criminology, through the preservation, enhancement, and sharing of computerized data resources; through the production of original research based on archived data; and through specialized training workshops in quantitative analysis of crime and justice data." Address: Inter-University Consortium, for Political and Social Research, University of Michigan, Institute for Social Research, P.O. Box 1248, Ann Arbor, MI 48106. Web: http://www.icpsr.umich.edu/NACJD/.

National Association of Crime Victim Compensation Boards (NACVCB). Established in 1977, this association exchange of information and ideas through a nationwide network of victim compensation programs. Address: P.O. Box 16003, Alexandria, VA 22302; Web: http://www.nacvcb.org/.

National Association of Document Examiners. Founded in 1979, as association of private forensic handwriting or document examiners. Publishes *The Communique* (quarterly newsletter) and *The Journal of the National Association of Document Examiners*. Web: http://documentexaminers.org/.

National Association of Drug Court Professionals (NADCP). NADCP is a nonprofit corporation founded in 1994 under the auspices of Community Antidrug Coalitions of America and with the assistance of the first drug courts in the United States. The organization's membership includes judges, prosecutors, defense attorneys, and clinical professionals dedicated to a "common-sense approach to improving the justice system by using a combination of judicial monitoring and effective treatment to compel drug-using offenders to change their lives." Address: 4900 Seminary Road, Suite 320, Alexandria, Virginia 22311. http://www.nadcp.org/nadcp-home/.

National Association of Legal Assistants, Inc. (NALA). NALA, incorporated in April 1975, is the leading professional association for legal assistants, or paralegals, providing continuing education, professional development, and certification programs in the field. Begun by NALA in 1976, the Certified Legal Assistant (CLA) examination and program has become the national professional credential for legal assistants, ensuring uniformity of professional standards and permitting legal assistants to move among states without losing certification. Address: NALA, 1516 S. Boston Ave., Suite 200, Tulsa, OK 74119. Web site: http://www.nala.org.

National Association of Police Organizations (NAPO). According to their Web site, the National Association of Police Organizations is a coalition of police unions and associations from across the United States that serves to advance the interests of America's law enforcement officers through legislative and legal advocacy, political action, and education. NAPO represents more than 2,000 police units and associations. Address: 750 First St., NE, Suite 920, Washington, DC 20002. Web site: http://www.napo.org.

National Association of State Alcohol and Drug Abuse Directors (NASADAD). The NASADAD was founded in 1971 to serve State Drug Agency Directors. According to its Web site, the organization expanded in 1978 to include the Directors of State Alcoholism Agencies. Its purpose is to foster and support the development of effective alcohol and other drug abuse prevention and treatment programs in each state. Address: 808 17th St., NW, Suite 410, Washington, DC 20006. Web http://www.nasadad.org/.

National Audiovisual Center. Part of National Technical Information Service, an agency of the U.S. Department of Commerce, the center is the central distribution source of audiovisual programs produced by the U.S. government on fire, law enforcement, and emergency medical services. Address: Alexandria, VA 22312. http://www.ntis.gov/products/nac.aspx.

National Black Police Association. Established in 1972, NBPA is a nonprofit organization of African American Police Associations "dedicated to the promotion of justice, fairness, and effectiveness in law enforcement." The organization also advocates for minority police officers nationwide. Address: 30 Kennedy Street-NW, Suite 101, Washington, DC 20011Web: http://www.blackpolice.org/.

National Bureau of Standards. *See* National Institute of Standards and Technology

National Center for the Analysis of Violent Crime (NCAVC). A subdivision of the FBI's Behavioral Science Unit, which provides assistance to "federal, state, local, and foreign law enforcement agencies investigating unusual or repetitive violent crimes." The NCAVC operates with three distinct unit: Behavioral Analysis Unit (BAU); Child Abduction Serial Murder Investigative Resources Center (CASMIRC); and Violent Criminal Apprehension Program (VICAP). Address: Federal Bureau of Investigation, Critical Incident Response Group, FBI Academy, Quantico, VA 22135; Web: http://www.fbi.gov/hq/isd/cirg/ncavc.htm.

National Center for Community Policing. Hosts training sessions and conferences, and provides on-site technical assistance to police agencies, community groups, and civic officials. Address: School of Criminal Justice, Michigan State University; 560 Baker Hall, East Lansing, MI 48823. Web site: http://www.cj.msu.edu/~people/cp/.

National Center for Juvenile Justice. The private, nonprofit research division of the National Council of Juvenile and Family Court Judges (NCJFCJ). Founded in 1973, NCJJ conducts research on topics related directly and indirectly to the field of juvenile justice. Address: 3700 South Water Street Suite 200, Pittsburgh, Pa 15203; Web: http://www.ncjjservehttp.org/NCJJWebsite/.

National Center for Missing & Exploited Children (NCMEC). Established in 1984, the center is a private, nonprofit 501(c)(3) organization that provides "services nationwide for families and professionals in the prevention of abducted, endangered, and sexually exploited children" as established by congressional mandate (42 U.S.C. §§ 5771). According to their Web site, NCMEC provides a plethora of public services including (partial list) a clearinghouse for information on missing and exploited children; operates a 24-hour toll-free hotline, 1-800-THE-LOST

(1-800-843-5678), to receive reports of missing children; operates the CyberTipline, the '9-1-1 for the Internet,' for reporting Internet-related child sexual exploitation; provides information about services and federal programs for missing and exploited children; coordinates public and private programs that locate, recover, or reunite missing children with their families; provides technical assistance and forensic training to individuals and law enforcement; tracks attempted child abductions; facilitates the National Emergency Child Locator Center during national disasters; and deploys Team Adam, a rapid response and support system for child abduction and sexual exploitation." Address: National Center for Missing and Exploited Children, Charles B. Wang International Children's Building, 699 Prince Street, Alexandria, Virginia 22314-3175;Web: www.missingkids.com

National Center for State Courts. Provides technical assistance and funding for a wide variety of court programs and services. Address: 300 Newport Ave., Williamsburg, VA 23185. Web site: http://www.ncsc.org.

National Center for State Courts. An independent, nonprofit court improvement organization that serves as a clearinghouse for research information and comparative data to support improvement in judicial administration in state courts. Address: National Center for State Courts, 300 Newport Avenue, Williamsburg, VA 23185-4147. Web: http://www.ncsc.org/.

National Center for the Analysis of Violent Crime (NCAVC). The FBI's NCAVC provides special resources to local law enforcement agencies. Its behavioral science unit provides training and research in criminal profiling, a process to identify major offender personality and behavioral characteristics based on analyses of the crime or crimes committed. The NCAVC operates the Violent Criminal Apprehension Program (VCAP), a national clearinghouse for information about unsolved violent crimes, particularly murder. Local law enforcement agencies report unsolved violent crime data to the FBI, which analyzes the data, seeking to identify similarities with other unsolved crimes. If similarities exist, the participating agencies are notified to coordinate their investigations. Web site. http://www.fbi.gov/hq/isd/cirg/ncavc.htm.

National Clearinghouse for Alcohol and Drug Information. The information service of the Center for Substance Abuse Prevention, this organization offers bibliographies, free computer searches, treatment referrals, and other resources on alcohol, drugs, prevention, and education. The Clearinghouse is cosponsored by U.S. Department of Health and Human Services and Substances Abuse and Mental Health Administration (SAMHSA). Address: P.O. Box 2345, Rockville, MD 20847-2345. Web site: http://ncadi.samhsa.gov.

National College of District Attorneys. Established in 1970 by the University of Houston, the college is cosponsored by the American Bar Association, the National District Attorneys Association, the American College of Trial Lawyers, and the International Academy of Trial Lawyers. NCDA provides continuing legal education for prosecuting attorneys in all areas of criminal law. Address: University of South Carolina, 44 Canal Center Plaza, Suite 110, Alexandria, VA 22314. Web site: http://www.ndaa.org/ncda/ncda_home.php.

National Commission on Law Observance and Enforcement. A commission created by President Herbert Hoover in 1929, and composed of 10 attorneys and a woman college president. Its purpose was to study crime as a national problem. It was called the Wickersham Commission after its chairman, George W. Wickersham, former U.S. attorney general. It completed its last report, of a total of 12, in 1931.

National Commission on the Causes and Prevention of Violence. Created by President Lyndon B. Johnson on June 10, 1968, to investigate and make recommendations pertaining to causes and prevention of violence, with the cooperation of other executive departments and agencies; to report its findings and recommendations not later than June 10, 1969. Its term was extended by President Richard M. Nixon on May 23, 1969, for completion of its final report.

National Commission on Terrorist Attacks Upon the United States. Established in 2002 and closed in 2004, an independent, bipartisan commission chartered to examine and report on the circumstances surrounding the September 11, 2001, terrorist attacks in the United States. The commission also provides recommendations designed to guard against future attacks.

National Computerized Criminal History System. Inaugurated by and through the National Crime Information Center, U.S. Department of Justice, in 1971. *See* National Crime Information Center

National Conference of State Legislatures. Serving legislatures and staffs nationwide, this agency offers status reports on state legislation and analyses of public safety and drug-related issues. Address: 7700 East First Place, Denver, CO 80230. Web site: http://www.ncsl.org.

National Consumers League (NCL). Operates a Fraud Information Center that serves as a clearinghouse for information on consumer fraud; telephone (800) 876-7060. Web: http://www.natlconsumersleague.org/.

National Council Against Health Fraud. Private nonprofit, voluntary health agency that focuses upon health misinformation, fraud, and quackery as public health problems Contact: National Council Against Health Fraud, Victim Redress Taskforce, P.O. Box 1747, Allentown, PA 18105 http://www.ncahf.org/index.html.

National Council of Juvenile and Family Court Judges (NCJFCJ). Founded in 1937 NCJFCJ's mission is "to improve courts and systems practice and raise awareness of the core issues that touch the lives of many" children and families. Address: National Council of Juvenile and Family Court Judges, P.O. Box 8970, Reno, NV 89507; Web: http://www.ncjfcj.org/.

National Crime Commission (President's Commission on Law Enforcement and Administration of Justice). Established by President Lyndon B. Johnson on July 23, 1965, to study the whole field of criminal justice, making comments on its findings and recommendations. The study was divided into five task forces: Assessment of the Crime Problem, Police and Public Safety, Administration of Justice, Corrections, and Science and Technology. Its first report, "The Challenge of Crime in a Free Society" was released on February 18, 1967.

National Crime Coordinating Council. *See* Kefauver Investigation

National Crime Information Center (NCIC). Established on January 27, 1967, NCIC is the computerized FBI index of criminal history, fugitives, stolen properties, and missing persons, compiled from FBI, federal, state, local and foreign criminal justice agencies. It is available to federal, state, and local law enforcement and other criminal justice agencies on demand, 24 hours a day, 365 days a year. Address: National Crime Information Center, Criminal Justice Information Services (CJIS) Division, 1000 Custer Hollow Road, Clarksburg, West Virginia 26306. Web: http://www.fbi.gov/hq/cjisd/ncic.htm.

National Crime Prevention Council. Founded in 1982 to manage the National Citizens' Crime Prevention Campaign and McGruff the Crime Dog and to administer the Crime Prevention Coalition of America. Address: 2345 Crystal Drive, Suite 500, Arlington, VA 22202. Web site: http://www.ncpc.org. *See* Crime Prevention Council, National

National Crime Victimization Survey (NCVS). A statistical program instituted in 1972, which serves as a second source, along with the Crime Index, which is based on the FBI's Uniform Crime Reports (UCR) of incidents reported to the police, to gauge the national incidence of crime. NCVA data are collected by the Bureau of Census and provide information on the extent to which persons 12 years of age and older and households have been the victims of selected crimes.

National Criminal Justice Reference Service. Established in 1972, NCJRS is a federally funded resource offering justice and substance abuse information to support research, policy, and program development worldwide. Address: National Criminal Justice Reference Service (NCJRS), P.O. Box 6000, Rockville, MD 20849-6000 Web site: www.ncjrs.gov. *See* National Institute of Justice

National Directory of Expert Witnesses. Founded in 1978, expert witnesses and litigation consultants who serve attorneys, insurance companies, and government agencies. Address: P.O. Box 270529, San Diego, CA 92198. Web: www.national-experts.com

National District Attorneys Association (NDAA). Founded in 1950, NDAA is a professional organization representing criminal prosecutors. Subcommittees within the organization include: Audit, Crime Control, Ethics and Services, Finance, Juvenile Justice and Family Law, Legislation, Membership, Metropolitan Prosecutors, National, Nominating, Science and Technology Committee, Media and Communications, Corrections and Reentry, and Victims. Address: 44 Canal Center Plaza, Suite 110, Alexandria, VA 22314. Web site: http://www.ndaa.org/index.html.

National Drug Enforcement Board. The National Narcotics Act of 1984 established the NDEB. Its chairman is the attorney general, with the remaining members composed of the secretaries of state, treasury, defense, transportation, and health and human services; the directors of the Office of Management and Budget and of the Central Intelligence Agency; and other officials as

TABLE 33   PERCENT OF CRIME REPORTED TO POLICE, 2006

Type of Crime	Number of Victimizations	% Reported to Police	% Not Reported to Police	Most Common Reason for Not Reporting
All crime	25,183,350	40.6	58.2	---
Personal Crime	6,267,610	49.0	49.2	Private or personal matter
Violent crime	6,094,390	48.8	49.4	Private or personal matter
Rape	260,940	43.4	56.6	---
Robbery	712,610	56.8	41.9	Police inefficient, ineffective, or biased
Assault	5,120,840	48.0	50.1	Private or personal matter
Purse snatching/ pickpocketing	173,220	55.9	42.4	---
Property crime	18,915,740	37.8	61.2	Object recovered— offender unsuccessful
Household burglary	3,560,920	49.5	49.0	Object recovered— offender unsuccessful
Motor vehicle theft	992,260	80.9	18.8	Other reasons
Theft	14,362,570	31.9	67.1	Object recovered— offender unsuccessful

Sources: U.S. Department of Justice, Bureau of Justice Statistics, *Criminal Victimization in the United States, 2006 Statistical Tables,* NCJ 223436, Table 91 [Online].
U.S. Department of Justice, Bureau of Justice Statistics, *Criminal Victimization in the United States, 2006 Statistical Tables,* NCJ 223436, Table 102 [Online].

appointed by the president. The board was established to facilitate coordination of U.S. operations and policy on drug law enforcement. This board was replaced by the White House Office of National Drug Control Policy (ONDCP), established by the Anti-Drug Abuse Act of 1988. *See also* White House Office of National Drug Control Policy; Anti-Drug Abuse Act of 1988

National Drug Prosecution Center. This group was part of the American Prosecutors Research Institute, a nonprofit, public education and technical assistance affiliate of the National District Attorneys Association until the mid 1990s. The center's mission was to train prosecutors to investigate and prosecute drug cases more effectively, to identify and evaluate drug control and demand-reduction strategies, to provide technical assistance regarding task forces or anti-drug abuse programs, and to develop model legislation on drugs. *See also* National District Attorneys Association

National Federation of Paralegal Associations (NFPA). Organized by eight associations in 1974, NFPA by 1992 represented more than 50 member associations with total membership exceeding 17,500. Its mission statement describes NFPA as a nonprofit, professional organization of state and local paralegal associations throughout the United States that supports increased quality, efficiency, and accessibility in the delivery of legal services, with the paralegal profession as an integral partner in that delivery. Publishes *National Paralegal Reporter* quarterly. Address: P.O. Box 2016, Edmonds, WA, 98026. Web site: http://www.paralegals.org.

National Fire Academy. The academy trained over 120,000 students in 2009. Courses include Arson, Emergency Medical Services, Executive Development, Fire Prevention: Management, Fire Prevention: Public Education, Fire Prevention: Technical, Hazardous Materials, Incident Management, Management Science, Planning and Information Management, and Training Programs. Contact: NFA, Fire Administration, Federal Emergency Management Agency, U.S. Fire Administration, 16825 S. Seton Ave., Emmitsburg, MD 21727. Web site: http://www.usfa.dhs.gov/nfa.

National Firearms Act of 1934. An act passed by Congress on June 26, 1934, which restrained the importation and interstate transportation of sawed-off shotguns, machine guns, and silencers for any type of weapon. This act was aimed at "gangster weapons" used by depression-era criminals. Act also placed a tax on dealers of firearms. *See also* Brady Handgun Violence Prevention Act; Bureau of Alcohol, Tobacco, Firearms and Explosives (ATF); depression era gangsters; Federal Assault Weapons Ban of 1994; Federal Firearms Act of 1938; Firearm Owners' Protection Act of 1986; Gun Control Act of 1968; Omnibus Crime Control and Safe Streets Act of 1968; Violent Crime Control and Law Enforcement Act of 1994

National Fire Prevention and Control Administration Fire Reference Service. Created in 1974 by the U.S. Department of Commerce to "provide the fire prevention and control community with an extensive repository of fire-related information that can assist them in the performance of their duties." Agency functions were absorbed by the U.S. Fire Administration.

National Fire Protection Association (NFPA). Established in 1896, the goal of this nonprofit organization is "to reduce the worldwide burden of fire and other hazards on the quality of life by providing and advocating consensus codes and standards, research, training, and education." Publishes and updates codes and standards for fire safety necessary for the public interest, including correctional facilities. Address: 1401 K Street NW, Suite 500, Washington, DC 20005. Web: http://www.nfpa.org.

National Fraudulent Check File. Maintained by the FBI Laboratory, Questioned Documents Unit (QDU), this file serves as a "clearinghouse" for information on worthless checks. Checks sent in by law enforcement agencies are searched against reproductions of checks on file to determine if the writing, printing, check protector, and so forth are identified with that or other checks in the file. If an identification is made, a copy of the check is recorded for future reference.

National Futures Association (NFA). A self-regulatory organization for all registered individuals or brokerage firms selling commodity futures, such as sugar, gold, petroleum, soybeans, or foreign currencies. To report fraud, write NFA, 300 S. Riverside Plaza, #1800, Chicago, IL 60606. Telephone: (312) 781-1300; Web: http://www.nfa.futures.org/.

National Guard. Established in 1636 with the earliest colonial militias, including farmers, shopkeepers, and other citizens who defend their communities when need arises. The volunteer militia of the states, which in 1916 was organized as an auxiliary of the regular army, armed and trained by the federal government, and made subject to federal service in wartime or other emergencies on call of the president. At other times, the respective state contingents may be called out by the governor when, in his or her judgment, the regular police forces are unable to maintain order. 1-800-GO-GUARD. Web: http://www.nationalguard.com/.

National Healthcare Anti-Fraud Association. Founded in 1985 "to protect and serve the public interest by increasing awareness and improving the detection, investigation, civil and criminal prosecution and prevention of health care fraud." 1201 New York Avenue, NW, Suite 1120, Washington, DC 20005. Web: http://www.nhcaa.org.

National Highway Traffic Safety Administration (NHTSA). According to their Web site, NHTSA was established by the Highway Safety Act of 1970 to carry out safety programs previously administered by the National Highway Safety Bureau. Specifically, the agency directs the highway safety and consumer programs established by the National Traffic and Motor Vehicle Safety Act of 1966, the Highway Safety Act of 1966, the 1972 Motor Vehicle Information and Cost Savings Act, and succeeding amendments to these laws. Address: NHTSA Headquarters, 1200 New Jersey Avenue, SE, West Building, Washington, DC 20590. Web: http://www.nhtsa.dot.gov/.

National Household Survey on Drug Abuse. *See* National Survey on Drug Use and Health

national incident-based reporting system (NIBRS). In 1988 the FBI announced it had a new reporting plan in collecting crime data. In this system, a crime is viewed along with all of its components, including type of victim, type of weapon used, location of the crime, alcohol and/or drug influence, type of criminal activity, relationship of victim to offender, residence of victims and arrestees, and a description of property and its value. This system includes 22 crimes in Group A offenses, plus 11 crimes in Group B offenses, rather than the eight that constitute the FBI's UCR Part I crimes. *See also* Group A offenses, Group B offenses, Index Crimes

National Institute of Corrections. Gives technical assistance and provides training to state and local correctional programs. Grants finance projects in the institute's priority areas. The NIC Information Center functions as the base for information collection and dissemination on correctional programs, policies, practices, and standards. Address: 791 N. Chambers Rd., Aurora, CO 80011. Web site: http://www.nicic.org.

National Institute of Standards and Technology (NIST). Known as the National Bureau of Standards from 1901–1988, this is a nonregulatory agency within the U.S. Department of Commerce. The mission of the NIST is to "promote U.S. innovation and industrial competitiveness by advancing measurement science, standards, and technology in ways that enhance economic security and improve quality of life." Address: 100 Bureau Drive, Stop 1070, Gaithersburg, MD 20899-1070. Web: http://www.nist.gov/index.html.

National Institute on Alcohol Abuse and Alcoholism (NIAAA). A part of the National Institutes of Health, U.S. Department of Health and Human Services, the NIAAA provides leadership in the national effort to reduce alcohol-related problems and publishes *Alcohol Research and Health* (quarterly). Address: 5635 Fishers Lane, MSC 930, Bethesda, MD 20892-9304. Web: http://www.niaaa.nih.gov/.

National Institute of Justice. The National Institute of Justice/NCJRS—the National Criminal Justice Reference Service—is the centralized national clearinghouse serving the criminal justice community since 1972. NCJRS also operates the Juvenile Justice Clearinghouse for the National Institute for Juvenile Justice and Delinquency Prevention; the Dispute Resolution Information Center for the Federal Justice Research Program; and the Justice Statistics Clearinghouse for the Bureau of Justice Statistics. NCJRS maintains a steadily growing computerized database of more than 75,000 criminal justice documents, operates a public reading room, and offers complete information and referral services. Among the products and services provided by NCJRS are custom searches, topical searches and bibliographies, research service, audiovisual and document loans, conference support, selective dissemination of information, and distribution of documents in print or microfiche. A Visiting Fellowship Program is open to senior-level criminal justice professionals and researchers. Registered users of NCJRS receive *NIJ Reports* bimonthly. Address: 810 Seventh St., NW, Washington, DC 20531. Web site: http://www.ojp.usdoj.gov/nij/welcome.html.

National Institute on Drug Abuse (NIDA). A federal agency operated under the national Institutes of Health, NIDA "conducts research and disseminates findings to improve drug abuse and addiction prevention, treatment, and policy." Address: National Institute on Drug Abuse, National Institutes of Health, 6001 Executive Boulevard, Room 5213, Bethesda, MD 20892-9561; Web: http://www.nida.nih.gov/NIDAHome.html.

National Institute of Mental Health. One of the major operating divisions of the National Institutes of Health (NIH) in the U.S. Department of Health and Human Services. The institute has conducted or supported research on alcoholism, narcotics addiction, suicide, delinquency and crime, and problems of city living. NIMH began operations in 1949, authorized by the National Mental Health Act of 1946. Address: National Institute of Mental Health (NIMH), Science Writing, Press, and Dissemination Branch, 6001 Executive Boulevard, Room 8184, MSC 9663, Bethesda, MD 20892-9663. Web: http://www.nimh.nih.gov.

National Integrated Ballistic Information Network (NIBIN) In 1999, ATF established and began administration of the National Integrated Ballistic Information Network (NIBIN). Nationally interconnected, computer-assisted ballistics imaging system used by forensic firearms examiners to obtain computerized images of the unique marks made on bullets and/or cartridge cases when guns are fired. Through NIBIN, these images can then be compared rapidly with all other images in the system of about 220 federal, state, and local law enforcement laboratories. http://www.nibin.gov.

National Joint Terrorism Task Force (NJTTF). Established in 2002 by the Department of Justice, the National Joint Terrorism Task Force (NJTTF) is a coordinating agency that facilitates information sharing and the management of large-scale projects *See also* Joint Terrorism Task Force (JTTF)

National Judicial College. Offers courses for judges, including several that focus on substance abuse. Address: Judicial College Building/MS 358, University of Nevada, Reno, NV 89557. Web site: http://www.judges.org.

National Laboratory Response Network (LRN). Established in 1999, the LRN is a collaborative association between the U.S. Association of Public Health Laboratories and the U.S. Centers for Disease Control and Prevention (CDC). There are three levels of LRN laboratories: Sentinel, the lowest level of LRN lab, authorized to rule out certain biological agents and handle specimens for transfer to higher levels; Reference, more advanced LRN generally found at the state level; and National, the highest level of LRN lab, equipped to handle all bio-terrorism specimens, located at the CDC and U.S. Army Medical Research Institute of Infectious Diseases (USAMRIID). *See also* bio-terrorism

National Labor Relations Board. Independent, regulatory agency empowered under the Wagner Act (1935), the Taft-Hartley Act (1947), and the Landrum-Griffin Act (1959). The NLRB consists of five members appointed by the president for five years and a general counsel appointed for four years. The board performs quasi-judicial and quasi-legislative functions aimed at preventing and remedying unfair labor practices by employers or union organizations and at protecting fair union representation. The board maintains 31 regional and subregional offices. It is the agency most responsible for ending violent labor-management confrontations. Address: National Labor Relations Board, 1099 14th St. N.W., Washington, DC 20570-0001. Web: http://www.nlrb.gov/.

National League of Cities. Formerly the American Municipal Association, this is an organization of state leagues of municipalities. The local leagues provide consultant services on problems of municipal government, and some issue periodicals and other publications. A membership organization of local elected officials, the NLC has created an awards program to study and honor innovative local public safety initiatives with the National Institute of Justice. Address 1301 Pennsylvania Ave., NW, Suite 550, Washington, DC 20004. Web site: http://www.nlc.org.

National Legal Aid and Defenders Association. Founded in 1911, NLADA is an "advocate for front-line attorneys and other equal justice professionals—those who make a difference in the lives of low-income clients and their families and communities." NLADA performs two major functions: it provides products and services and contributes to public policy and legislative debates on equal justice." Address: 1140 Connecticut Ave. NW, Suite 900, Washington, DC 20036. Web site: http://www.nlada.org.

National Mounted Police Services, Inc. (NMPS). Organization established by Bill Richey to train officers for mounted policing. Address: 275 Kings Point Road, Kings Point, NY 11024. Telephone: 239-214-2062. Web site: http://www.mountedpolice.org/.

National Museum of Crime and Punishment. Located in a 25,000-square-foot facility, the National Museum of Crime and Punishment includes historical crime facts, exhibits, and artifacts, It also hosts the filming studios for America's Most Wanted. The museum has more than 100 interactive exhibits, including a simulated shooting range, high-speed police-chase, safe cracking, and computer hacking. The museum also has full-scale models of a crime scene (with fresh evidence), a booking station, police line-up, lie detector test, replica jail cell, and a CSI lab. This is a highly rated museum that Good Morning America called "a must-see for CSI fans." Address: National Museum of Crime & Punishment, 575 7th St. NW, Washington, DC 20004, 202-621-5550. Web: http://www.crimemuseum.org/.

National Narcotics Act of 1984. The purpose of this act is to ensure that (a) a national and international effort against illegal drugs are maintained; (b) the activities of the federal agencies involved are fully coordinated; and (c) a single, competent, and responsible high-level board of the U.S. government is charged with this coordination. The 1984 Act established the National Drug Enforcement Policy Board (NDEPB). In 1988, the National Narcotics Leadership Act, replacing the NDEPB with the Office of National Drug Control Policy. *See also* Office of National Drug Control Policy

National Narcotics Border Interdiction System (NNBIS). Established in 1983 by President Ronald Regan and headed by then Vice President George H. W. Bush, former head of the CIA, the NNBIS was a federal effort to combat drug smuggling and coordinated the activities of the CIA, military intelligence agencies, and domestic crime officials. In 1985, a Government Accounting Office (GAO) report evaluated the NNBIS and expressed concerns, namely that the NNBIS "has had difficulty acquiring tactical intelligence . . . has not played a coordinating role in most drug interdictions" and that "the organizational placement of NNBIS could limit the Board's ability to facilitate the coordination of drug interdiction." Subsequently, the NNBIS was disbanded, and many of the planning functions were distributed to High Intensity Drug Trafficking Area (HIDTA) organizations within the Office of National Drug Control Policy (ONDCP) in 1998.

National Narcotics Intelligence Consumers Committee. A federal interagency consortium to coordinate drug intelligence collection and produce estimates and periodic reports on the status of illicit drugs worldwide, including production and availability estimates for marijuana, cocaine, opiates, and synthetic drugs. Reports also cover drug-trafficking routes and methods and money trails. Around 1995, the committee was dissolved, with functions assumed under the National Survey on Drug Abuse. *See also* National Survey on Drug Abuse

National Organization for Women. A civil rights pressure group formed in 1966 to campaign for legislative and economic reforms to ensure equality for women; admits men as well as women. NOW's overriding goal is to bring about equality for all women, achieved through their efforts to "eliminate discrimination and harassment in the workplace, schools, the justice system, and all other sectors of society; secure abortion, birth control and reproductive rights for all women; end all forms of violence against women; eradicate racism, sexism and homophobia; and promote equality and justice in our society." Address: National Organization for Women, 1100 H Street NW, 3rd floor, Washington, DC 20005, http://www.now.org/.

National Runaway Switchboard. *See* juvenile locators

National Security Agency (NSA)/Central Security Service (CSS). Federal security agencies that are components of the Department of Defense (DOD). The NSA was established by a presidential directive as a separately organized agency within the DOD in 1952; the CSS was created in 1972 in accordance with a presidential memorandum. The NSA director is also chief of the CSS. The NSA/CSS is responsible for coordination, direction, and performance of technical functions in support of government activities to protect U.S. communications and to produce foreign intelligence data. For example, in the course of its work NSA can intercept and decipher electronic communications. http://www.nsa.gov/.

National Sheriffs' Association. Founded in 1942, NSA is a nonprofit organization dedicated to raising the level of professionalism among those in the criminal justice field. Address: The National Sheriffs' Association, 1450 Duke St., Alexandria, VA 22314-3490. Web: http://www.sheriffs.org/.

National Stolen Property Act. A federal law of May 22, 1934, to extend the provisions of the National Motor Vehicles Theft Act to other stolen property, such as securities, which includes any note, stock certificate, bond, debenture, check, draft, warrant, travelers check, letter of credit, warehouse receipt, negotiable bill of lading, or evidence of indebtedness. The law also covers money—U.S. or foreign legal tender or counterfeit. Any person violating this act may be punished in any district into or through which such property has been transported or removed.

National Survey on Drug Use and Health. Sometimes referred to as the National Household Survey on Drug Abuse, this research is funded by the National Institute on Drug Abuse and conducted by the Substance Abuse and Mental Health Services Administration (SAMHSA). The survey has been conducted every 2–3 years since 1972 and gathers information on the "prevalence, patterns, and consequences of alcohol, tobacco, and illegal drug use and abuse in the general U.S. civilian noninstitutionalized population, age 12 and older." These data are combined with those of the High School Senior Survey. *See also* Monitoring the Future; Drug Abuse Warning Network

Nation of Islam. The name given to the original Black Muslim movement in the United States by its founder, Elijah Muhammad. His son later changed the name to American Muslim Mission. The earlier name has been adopted by a splinter group under Louis Farrakhan.

naturalization. The conferring upon an alien of the rights and privileges of U.S. citizenship. This is achieved through federal laws administered by the Bureau of Immigration and Naturalization and the federal courts.

natural law. A set of principles and rules discovered by human reason that, it is supposed, would govern people in a state of nature (before formal law existed), or provide rational principles for the government of people in society. It has also been considered a valuable supplement to formal law in setting moral standards by which the conduct of governments may be judged. Natural law theories originated with Stoic philosophers and statesmen. In the eighteenth century, natural law was variously derived from reason, the Bible, and the fundamental principles of the common law. *See also* common law; positive law

natural rights. Those rights believed to be intrinsic to the individual before the creation of the state. They were developed in the political philosophies of John Milton, John Locke, and Jean Jacques Rousseau and modified in America by Thomas Jefferson, Samuel Adams, and Thomas Paine. In the early Revolutionary period, these rights were conceived of as part of the heritage of British constitutionalism, although Paine considered natural rights as independent of constitutions. As developed in the United States, natural rights included popular sovereignty, the right of revolution against tyranny, democracy, liberty, the pursuit of happiness, and property rights. Varying emphases on the importance of natural rights have played significant roles in U.S. history. Alexander Hamilton, for example, emphasized property rights. Jefferson and Paine emphasized personal civil rights. Later, South Carolina statesman John C. Calhoun (1782–1850) repudiated the entire doctrine of natural rights as unsound.

natus (Lat.). Born.

Naval Criminal Investigative Service. A law enforcement organization staffed mostly by civilians and responsible for providing investigative support in matters involving serious crimes committed by or against Navy personnel. The descendant of a small undercover unit formed in New York City in 1916, today's NIS was established in 1966 with the personnel resources of the old district intelligence offices of the Office of Naval Intelligence. With three major purposes, preventing terrorism, protecting National secrets and reducing crime, the NIS has 140

locations worldwide, including 16 regional offices. Headquartered at: Washington Navy Yard, 716 Sicard Street, S.E., Washington, DC 20388-5380. Web: http://www.ncis.navy. mil/.

Nazi war criminals. Those accused of these offenses during World War III: conspiracy to commit crimes alleged in other counts (such as murder, but also including conspiracy to detain or transport prisoners to concentration camps); crimes against peace; war crimes; or crimes against humanity. The overarching crime for the four specific offenses was the murder of 6 million Jews and the brutal conditions in the concentration camps, which amounted to slave labor. *See also* Nuremberg trials; Office of Special Investigations

N.B. (Lat., lit.). Abbreviation for *nota bene,* take note, or note well.

NCAVC. *See* National Center for the Analysis of Violent Crime

ne exeat (Lat., lit.). (In order) that he or she does not depart.

negligent. Culpably careless; doing something, or omitting to do something, which a person of ordinary prudence would not have done, or omitted to do. Negligent conduct may be defined as acting without the due care required by the circumstances. *See also* vicarious liability

negligent manslaughter (manslaughter by negligence). Causing the death of another by recklessness or gross negligence.

negotiable. Capable of being transferred to another by assignment or endorsement.

negotiable instrument. A written promise or request for the payment of a certain sum, such as a check or promissory note.

neighborhood (team) policing. Assigning a team of officers to police a specific geographic area on a 24-hour basis.

neighborhood watch. Procedure started in the United States in the early 1970s to foster community-based crime prevention. Neighborhood watch is a crime prevention strategy in which citizens help themselves prevent crime in their communities by identifying and reporting suspicious activity. This can be achieved through strategies such as promoting community social interaction, informal social controls and "watching out for each other," and active community patrols by concerned citizens *See also* radio watch; USA on Watch

Nelson, George "Baby Face" (1908–1934). Born with the name Lester Gills in Chicago in 1908, Nelson was a notorious gangster, bank robber, and murderer during the depression. Because of his multiple murders of FBI agents, J Edgar Hoover called Nelson "public enemy number one" in 1934. Nelson was shot and killed by federal agents in the Battle of Barrington on November 27, 1934. *See also* depression era gangsters

nemo (Lat.). No one.

neoclassicism. A trend in the history of criminology that flourished in Europe during the early nineteenth century. It modified the views of the classical school of criminology by introducing the concepts of diminished criminal responsibility and less severe punishment due to the age or mental condition of the offender.

nephiophilia. Also called infantophilia, a paraphilia indicating a sexual interest in very young children, primarily toddlers and infants aged 0–3 years old. *See also* pedophilia

nepotism. Favoritism granted to relatives without due regard for merit; family favoritism. Used to describe the employment of any immediate family member by his or her relative; especially, to hire close relatives regardless of their qualifications.

net-widening. A correctional concept suggesting that community control alternatives to incarceration, such as electronic monitoring and house arrest, are options that merely expand the number of people under sentence, or prisoner population, without a corresponding expansion of facilities.

network analysis. A relational-based approach to statistical analysis that provides leverage to answer questions that cannot be answered using nonrelational analyses.

neuropsychology. Discipline that studies the structures and functions of the brain as related to human behavior. Persons working in this field often conduct research on brain disorders and behavior, conduct evaluations in forensic settings, and engage in treatment in private practice.

Neutrality Laws. Acts of Congress that forbid the fitting out and equipping of armed vessels or the enlisting of troops for the aid of either of two belligerent powers who are at war with each other, but with whom the United States is at peace.

neutron activation analysis. A test using radioactive materials to detect the presence and quantities of chemical elements in a substance even when quantities are minute (trace elements). It is useful in crime laboratories for analyzing substances such as poisons, traces of contaminants, and residues on the hands of homicide suspects to determine if a handgun has been recently fired.

new court commitment. The readmission to prison of a person entering on one or more new sentences rather than on any prior sentence still in effect.

new-generation jail. Term used to describe attempts to modernize the structure and operations of jails, including approaches to inmate management and service delivery

New Jersey Experimental Project for the Treatment of Youthful Offenders. This project and facility, known as Highfields, was established in 1950. Its philosophy is that rehabilitation of offenders is facilitated by close interpersonal contact among the boys in small groups, and between the boys and the staff. The program operated on a four-month incarceration program for youthful offenders during the 1950s.

newly discovered evidence. Evidence of a new and material fact, or new evidence in relation to a fact at issue, discovered by a party to a cause after the rendition of a verdict or judgment therein.

Newman, Oscar. (1935–2004). Born Sept. 30, 1935, in Montreal, Canada Newman is best known for development of "defensible space theory." *See also* defensible space

new trial. Any trial in which issues of fact and law are examined that have already been the subject of an earlier trial.

next friend. Anyone who enters a legal case or conducts a suit on behalf of someone who is unable to bring the action for themselves, such as a minor person with developmental disabilities.

next of kin. Nearest in relationship according to the degrees of consanguinity.

nicotine. The poison contained in tobacco leaves. When tobacco products are smoked, dipped, or chewed, nicotine chemically attaches to receptors in the user's brain, which can cause either relaxation or arousal. Continued use leads to addiction, and smoking is the leading preventable cause of death in the United States. In fact, cigarette smoking alone is responsible for about one in five deaths in the United States. Tobacco use has been linked to various cancers, heart disease, and lung disease.

Nicotine Anonymous. Self-help group for those addicted to nicotine. Address: 419 Main Street, PMB# 370, Huntington Beach, CA 92648. Web site: http://www.nicotine-anonymous.org.

Niederhoffer, Arthur. A noted author (1917–1981) on police work, Niederhoffer graduated from Brooklyn College in 1937, earned his law degree from Brooklyn Law School, and was admitted to the bar in New York in 1940, joining the New York City Police Department that year. He was promoted to sergeant in 1951 and to lieutenant in 1956, earning that year an M.S. in sociology. His first book, written with another author, was *The Gang: A Study of Adolescent*

Behavior; published in 1958. He earned a Ph.D. from New York University in 1963, two years after retiring from the NYPD. Niederhoffer then became an instructor at the New York City Police Academy. Based on his doctoral dissertation, *The Mobile Force: A Study of Police Cynicism,* he devised a "cynicism scale," which has been widely replicated. Other books include *Behind the Shield: The Police in Urban Society* (1967), with Abraham Blumberg; *The Ambivalent Force: Perspectives on the Police* (1970), with Smith; *New Directions in Police-Community Relations,* (1974); and with his wife, Elaine, *The Police Family: From Station House to Ranch House* (1974). He became a professor of sociology at John Jay College of Criminal Justice and in 1980 was elected a fellow of the American Society of Criminology.

night court. A criminal court which, in certain cities, sits during the early evening hours for the immediate disposition of petty offenses and the granting or withholding of bail in more serious cases. The first night court was opened in New York City on September 1, 1907.

Night Stalker. *See* Richard Ramirez

nightstick. *See* baton

nihil (Lat.). Nothing; shortened to nil.

nihilism. (1) A political or social position involving total rejection of belief in laws. (2) Use of force and violence against authority or those representing such authority.

nine-one-one (911). The uniform national emergency telephone number established by AT&T and the (former) Bell System—by default, since all other 3-digit codes below that number had been assigned or were in use. The first digit, 9, distinguishes emergency calls in the nationwide switched telecommunications network from long-distance calls or attempts to reach an operator; when the 9 is followed by 1 + 1, the network has been programmed to route calls to appropriate fire, police, and ambulance personnel.

Almost all communities in the United States have 911 service. Typically, such calls are routed to a "Public Safety Answering Point" (PSAP), which automatically logs the origination location for the call and dispatches appropriate emergency services. The widespread use of cellular phones, which in many cases has replaced the use of land lines, complicates the process, as PSAPs cannot log the location of a cellular number as they can a land line; for example, the cellular billing address may not be the location from which the emergency call is placed. To address wireless 911 calls, the Federal Communications Commission (FCC) requires 911 calls made by wireless or mobile telephones to be relayed to a call center, regardless of whether the mobile phone user is a customer of the network being used. Within six minutes of receipt of mobile 911 calls, wireless network operators must identify the phone number and cell phone tower used in the call and provide the latitude and longitude of callers (within 300 meters) to the PSAP, within six minutes of a request by a PSAP.

Nineteen Eighty-three. Jargon for a section of federal civil rights law, which reads: "Every person who, under color of any state or territory, subjects, or causes to be subjected, any citizen of the U.S. or other person within the jurisdiction thereof to the deprivation of any rights, privileges, or immunities secured by the Constitution and laws, shall be liable to the party injured in an action at law, suit in equity, or other proper proceedings for redress." The name comes from the U.S. Code, in which this provision is Section 1983 of Title 42.

nisi prius court. A court in which trials of issues of fact are held before a jury and a single presiding judge.

No contest. The English translation of the *nolo contendere* plea, a plea of no contest is tantamount to a guilty plea without an admission of guilt. It is often used in plea bargaining when there is sufficient evidence for a guilty verdict, but the defendant wishes to assert his or her innocence. *See also nolo contendere* and Alford plea

"no knock" law. A law that empowers an officer to enter a home or other place, with a suitable court order, without knocking or announcing his or her identity, when to give warning would imperil the officer's safety or allow evidence to be easily and quickly destroyed.

nolle prosequi (Lat.). A prosecutor's decision not to initiate or continue prosecution.

nolo contendere (Lat., lit., I will not contest it). A plea in a criminal action having the same legal results as a plea of guilty. This plea is usually used in a criminal proceeding from which possible civil proceedings and liabilities might result. *See also* no contest, Alford plea

nominal damages. A trifling sum, awarded to a plaintiff who has sued for damages, that shows a breach of duty on the part of the defendant but no serious loss resulting therefrom.

nominal level of measurement. *See* scale, nominal

non compos mentis (Lat.). Meaning not of sound mind.

nonfeasance. Omission to do something; not doing what ought to be done. *See also* malfeasance; misfeasance

nonjuror. A person who declines to take an oath required in a proceeding.

nonlethal force. Also referred to as less than lethal force, this includes devices or agents used to induce compliance without substantial risk of permanent injury or death. Three general categories are: (1) electrical: TASER, stun gun; (2) chemical: tear gas, Mace; and (3) impact: water cannon, baton, rubber bullets, and shot-filled bean bags. *See also* Koga method; nonlethal weapon

nonlethal weapons. Weapons that generally do not cause death when properly used, such as electromagnetic weapons, water cannons, air guns, and gasses (such as tear gas and skunk spray); however, both the Air Force and Department of Defense agree that while non-lethal weapons generally will not cause death, they sometimes do. Thus, the term nonlethal weapon has largely been replaced by use of the term "less lethal weapons." Less-than-lethal weapons generally include a higher level of force than those categorized as non lethal weapons, such as the use of rubber or paint bullets and tasers. Although designed only to incapacitate, they may cause death under unusual circumstances or if inappropriately used. *See also* nonlethal force; less lethal weapon; TASER

non prosequitor (Lat., shortened to *non pros*). He or she does not prosecute.

nonsecretor. A person whose saliva and other bodily fluids do not contain blood group antigens. Hence, it is not possible to type the person's saliva and other bodily fluids, an important technique in criminal justice.

non sequitur (Lat., lit.). It does not follow.

nonsuit. A judgment given against a plaintiff for failure to establish a case.

nonrevocable parole. The status of parolees discharged from prison with low-risk criminal convictions, for whom parole is generally unsupervised.

nonviolence. A policy adopted by an adversarial group that refrains from the use of overt force, either as a matter of principle or expediency.

norm. A term for the common or average score or performance in a given group; the result that occurs most often. *See also* central tendency

normal curves. Bell-shaped symmetrical distributions of statistics characterized by symmetry (mirror image between the two halves); equivalent mean, median, and mode; and asymptopic tails (even the very far ends of the distribution fall above the horizontal axis). The precise shape of any such curve will depend on the mean and standard deviation used in the study. The standard normal curve has a mean of 0 and a standard deviation of 1; that is, a standard normal curve is one in which all the observations have been converted to standard scores. The symmetrical shape of the normal curve gives it certain useful properties for statistical research. For example, in a normal curve, 68 percent of all observations fall within one standard deviation, plus or minus, of the mean, 95 percent fall within two standard deviations, and 99 percent fall within three standard deviations. Thus, any observation varying from the mean by three standard deviations is atypical in a normal distribution. *See also* frequency distribution

normative power. The ability of any leader to obtain compliance from followers by using symbolic rewards.

North American Association of Wardens and Superintendents. A national group of correctional administrators. Address: P.O. Box 11037, Albany, NY,12211.

North American Securities Administrators Association (NASAA). An international investment protection agency. Telephone numbers for securities agencies in each state can be obtained by calling NASAA at (202) 737-0900. Address: 750 First Street, N.E., Suite 1140, Washington, DC 20002.

Northwestern University Traffic Institute. Begun in 1932 as a two-week training program for traffic officers, this organization eventually spawned the National Highway Traffic Safety Administration in 1966, which became a U.S. Department of Transportation Agency. The Traffic Institute itself was founded in 1936; early texts were *Evidence Handbook* and *The Traffic Accident Investigation Manual,* which was the first of its kind. First revised in 1981, it then adopted an "accident reconstruction" approach. The Traffic Institute was renamed the Center for

Public Safety . Along with the FBI Academy and the Southern Police Institute, it is one of the major law enforcement training centers in the United States. *See also* Center for Public Safety

notary public. A public officer authorized to authenticate and certify documents such as deeds, contracts, and affidavits with his or her signature and seal

not guilty by reason of insanity. This verdict excuses criminal responsibility due to mental illness. *See also* insanity, guilty by mentally ill

not-guilty plea. An answer given in criminal court in which the defendant asserts that s/he did not commit the crime charged. *See also* plea

notice. An advice, or written warning, in more or less formal format, intended to apprise persons of some proceeding in which their interests are involved or to inform them of some fact that it is their right to know and the duty of the notifying party to communicate.

Notorious B.I.G. *See* Wallace, Christopher

NRP. *See* nonrevocable parole

nuisance. Generally defined as any activity that interferes with the quality of life in a community, such as an establishment or practice that offends public morals or decency or menaces public health, safety, or order. Indications that a nuisance exists include any documented activity commonly associated with narcotics or vice violations. *See also* abatement

null. Of no legal or binding force.

null hypothesis. A statement that there is no relationship between two things being studied. Researchers expect to be able to reject null hypotheses if they prove their scientific hypotheses; that is, proof of one hypothesis nullifies its opposite.

nulla poena sine crimine (Lat.). No punishment without a crime.

numbers, obliterated. Serial or identification numbers on objects that have been removed or made unreadable by being hammered or punched. Thieves use this technique on such things as guns, motor vehicles, and other items of value that have identification numbers, thus making it difficult or impossible to identify the objects. Crime laboratories can restore such numbers in many instances by use of acid etching, the application of heat, or other methods.

Nuremberg trials. A series of trials conducted by an international military tribunal at Nuremberg, Germany, after World War II. The defendants were Nazi party and military officials and other persons intimately associated with the Hitler regime, who were accused of violations of the laws of war, crimes against humanity, and other international crimes, based on their involvement with the Holocaust. Judges for the trial included Great Britain, France, the Soviet Union, and the United States. Trials of the most serious offenders began November 21, 1945, and ended on September 30, 1946 (additional trials followed through October of 1946, but the first is generally known as the Nuremberg Trials). In all, 22 highly influential leaders of Nazi Germany were prosecuted for war crimes related to the murder of 6 million Jews during the war. All 22 defendants pled not guilty; three were acquitted and 18 were found guilty. Those convicted received sentences ranging from life imprisonment for seven defendants to death by hanging for the remaining eleven. *See also* Nazi War criminals

O

oath. A solemn appeal to God or the Supreme Being as to the truth of a statement. A false oath is punishable as perjury.

obit (Lat., lit.). He died.

obiter (Lat.). Something incidental in an opinion rather than the principal question.

obiter dictum (Lat.). A belief or opinion included by a judge in his or her decision in a case.

objectivity. A claim intended to ensure the legitimacy of a statement describing empirical reality; the quality of being observable or verifiable, especially scientific methods.

obligatory. Binding in law or conscience; requiring performance or forbearance of some act.

obscenity. First defined in law in *Miller v. California,* 1973, which carefully limited the scope of state statutes designed to regulate obscene material. Basic guidelines established were (a) whether the average person, applying contemporary community standards, would find that a work, taken as a whole, appeals to the prurient interest; (b) whether the work depicts or describes, in a patently offensive way, sexual conduct specifically defined by the applicable state law; and (c) whether the work, taken as a whole, lacks serious literary, artistic, political, or scientific value. Following *Miller,* the USSC affirmed states right to bar the showing of obscene films in a movie theatre restricted to consenting adults in *Paris Adult Theatre I v. Slaton* (1973). In *New York v. Ferber* (1982) the Court ruled child pornography is unprotected by the First Amendment; however, obscene material that appears to depict minors, but which actually uses adult actors, may be protected by the First Amendment according to the court's decision in *Ashcroft v. Free Speech Coalition* (2002).

OBSCIS. An acronym for Offender-Based State Corrections Information System, OBSCIS was a multistate program for the development of prisoner information systems for state correctional agencies. Data elements and basic OBSCIS code structure are presented in the OBSCIS Data Dictionary.

observation. The procedure by which a researcher gathers data. Whereas measurement is the assignment of numbers to the various outcomes that variables can exhibit, observation is the method of undertaking to measure a phenomenon. It may be direct, where a researcher actually observes behavior or individuals, or indirect, through the use of questionnaires, interviews, projective techniques, or physiological reactions. *See also* participant observation

obstruction of justice. All unlawful acts committed with intent to prevent or hinder the administration of justice, including law enforcement, judicial, and corrections functions.

OBTS. An abbreviation for Offender-Based Tracking System, OBTS refers to various methods to manage offender movement. In some jurisdictions, this term refers to a centralized database that houses criminal records for use by law enforcement, courts, parole agents, prison staff, and other justice professionals. In other jurisdictions, the term refers to the use of global positioning satellite (GPS) technology to track the physical location of offenders in the community.

occasional property crime. Those types and instances of burglary, larceny, forgery, and other thefts undertaken infrequently, irregularly, and often quite crudely. Offenders who engage in this level of property crime do not pursue it as a career. Edwin M. Lemet's study of "naive check forgers," undertaken many decades ago, clearly illustrates the factors associated with occasional property crime as a behavior system.

occult. *See* Crowley, Aleister; satanic cult

Occupational Safety and Health Administration (OSHA). A federal agency established by act of Congress in 1970. OSHA is responsible for developing standards of workplace safety, issuing regulations to protect workers, and enforcing these laws, regulations, and standards. OSHA is empowered to inspect workplaces and to issue citations and fines for noncompliance. Address: U.S. Department of Labor, Occupational Safety and Health Administration, 200 Constitution Ave., Washington, DC 20210. Web site: www.osha.gov.

o'clock. The position of points on a target or at a scene when compared to the face of a clock. As the target is viewed from the front, it is compared with a clock face held in front of the viewer. Three o'clock position is the right side of a horizontal line drawn through the center of the target; six o'clock is the bottom of the target and in line with a vertical line drawn through the center of the target.

odometer tampering. Federal law prohibits tampering with a vehicle's odometer (often misidentified as a speedometer, an odometer measures the distance traveled by a vehicle). No one, including the vehicle owner, is permitted to turn back or disconnect the odometer, unless performing repairs. When a broken odometer cannot be adjusted to reflect the true mileage, the odometer must be set at zero and a sticker indicating the true mileage before service and the date of service attached to the left door frame. Federal law also requires disclosure of the vehicle mileage upon transfer of ownership. Purchasers who suspect tampering should contact: Administrator, National Highway Traffic Safety Administration, Department of Transportation, Washington, DC; Consumer Affairs Section, Antitrust Division, DOJ, Washington, DC; or local or state law enforcement authorities.

offender. An adult who has been convicted of a crime.

offender groups, in federal prisons. Comprised of (1) Drug offenders: all individuals sentenced for violation of the federal narcotics laws according to the Federal Bureau of Prisons. This includes offenses pertaining to the use, manufacture, sale, and distribution of drugs or controlled substances. (2) Violent offenders: all individuals sentenced for the commission of violent crimes, which include assault, homicide, kidnapping, rape, robbery, injuries resulting from explosives, and threats against the president. (3) Property offenders: all individuals sentenced for the violation of property crimes, which include burglary, violation of customs laws, destruction of property, embezzlement, forgery,

larceny theft, lottery, mailing or otherwise transporting obscene material, robbery theft, and violations of the Interstate Commerce Act. (4) Other offenders: all individuals sentenced for offenses other than drug, violent, and property offenses.

offenders, sex. Sex offenders may be divided into two classes: persons committing *mala in se* crimes, or acts that are wrong in and of themselves, such as forcible rape; and those committing *mala prohibita* acts, which in themselves are not wrong or immoral, but have been declared unlawful. Examples of such acts include solicitation for prostitution and statutory rape (e.g., sex between consenting adolescents of similar age, performed in a jurisdiction where at least one of the parties does not meet the legal age of consent).

offense. (1) A felony, misdemeanor, or a less serious violation of the law of a state. (2) A breach of international law that Congress is authorized to punish.

offenses against the family and children. Offenses relating to desertion; abandonment, nonsupport, neglect, or abuse of spouse or child; nonpayment of alimony; or other similar acts. *See also* child support

Office of National Drug Control Policy. Agency that coordinates federal, state, and local efforts to control illegal drug use and devises national strategies to carry out anti-drug programs. Prepares the annual National Drug Control Strategy and accompanying budget. Address: P.O. Box 6000, Rockville, MD 20849-6000. Web site: http://www.white housedrugpolicy.gov.

Office of Sex Offender Sentencing, Monitoring, Apprehending, Registering, and Tracking (SMART) Authorized by the Adam Walsh Child Protection and Safety Act of 2006, *see also* Walsh, Adam. The SMART Office provides guidance in implementation and technical assistance related to the Child Protection and Safety Act. The mission of SMART is: "to protect the public by supporting the national implementation of a comprehensive sex offender registration and notification system." Address: SMART Office, 810 7th Street, NW, Washington, DC 20531; Web: http://www.ojp.usdoj.gov/smart/.

Office of Special Investigations. The Office of Special Investigations was originally established in 1979 to detect, identify, and take administrative action leading to denaturalization and/or deportation of Nazi war criminals. It provides historic research, investigations, and proceedings before both administrative bodies and U.S. courts. In December of 2004, the enactment of the Intelligence Reform and Terrorism Prevention Act (IRTPA) gave the OSI authority "for investigating and bringing legal actions in federal court to revoke the United States citizenship of any naturalized U.S. citizen who committed, ordered, incited, assisted, or otherwise participated abroad in genocide or, under color of foreign law, torture or extrajudicial killing." For further information, contact: OSI, Criminal Division, DOJ, 950 Pennsylvania Ave., Washington, DC 20530-0001. Web site: http://www.justice.gov/criminal/osi.

Office for Victims of Crime (OVC). Established by the 1984 Victims of Crime Act (VOCA), this Office of Justice Program under the Department of Justice oversees diverse programs that benefit victims of crime. According to their Web site, the "OVC provides substantial funding to state victim assistance and compensation programs—the lifeline services that help victims to heal." Address: Office for Victims of Crime, Office of Justice Programs, 810 7th Street, NW, Washington, DC 20531. Web site: http://www.ojp.usdoj.gov/ovc/. *See also* Victims of Crime Act

office-supply schemes. This type of telemarketing scheme is often directed at businesses. For example, telemarketers call a business and inform them that the price of their toner is scheduled to increase, enticing the victim to buy a large quantity of toner before the price change takes effect. The victim receives "graymarket" toner, which is not graded for use in copiers, at an exaggerated price and substantial cost in damaged equipment. *See also* fraud, telemarketing

oil and gas scams. A common type of investment fraud in which con artists promise quick profits in oil and gas ventures. *See also* fraud, investment

Oklahoma City bombing. On April 19, 1995, the Murrah Federal Building in Oklahoma City was bombed in the most catastrophic bombing on U.S. soil until the September 11 attacks. Casualties included 168 deaths, including 16 children from the America's Kids Day Care Center located at the blast site, and 680 injuries. Damage was sustained up to sixteen blocks away from the blast site, costing over $650 million to repair. Suspect Timothy McVey was arrested within 90 minutes of the bombing. At trial, McVeigh was found guilty on eleven counts of murder and conspiracy and was sentenced to death. He was executed on June 11, 2001, the first federal execution in nearly 40 years. A second suspect, Terry Nichols, was found guilty of conspiring to build a weapon of mass destruction and of eight counts of involuntary manslaughter at federal trial and sentenced to life without parole. Subsequently, he was prosecuted for 161 counts of murder by the State of Oklahoma and sentenced to 161 consecutive life terms. Michael Fortier, an accomplice who agreed to testify for the prosecution, was convicted and sentenced to twelve years in prison; he was released on January 20, 2006 and is currently in the United States Witness Protection Program. *See also* domestic terrorism

Old Sparky. Nickname for electric chairs in general, or an electric chair in one of the southern states that uses this method of execution: Alabama, Arkansas, and Florida.

oligarchy. Rule by a select few, especially by those at the top of an organizational hierarchy.

Olympic Park Bomber. *See* Rudolph, Eric Robert

Olympic Park Bombing. *See* Centennial Olympic Park bombing

ombudsman. In criminal justice, an individual who operates within the prison institution but is ideally independent of both the administration and the inmates. This individual acts as an intermediary between the prison inmates and the staff in airing grievances, investigating them, and so forth. The function is a tension-relieving device that allows inmates to feel they have an outlet for their complaints.

Omnibus Crime Control and Safe Streets Act of 1968. A series of acts passed by Congress to deal with the rise of crime in the United States. The acts established the Law Enforcement Assistance Administration (LEAA) to carry out a broad program of aid to the states and localities for crime control—with particular attention to street crime, riots, and organized crime. Other provisions of the acts and their subsequent amendments include a ban in federal court against evidence gained from wiretaps or listening devices; the regulation of firearm sales, transport, and possession; grants for the construction and renovation of correctional facilities, courtrooms, treatment centers, and so forth; and the establishment of the Bureau of Justice Statistics. This act was amended by the Comprehensive Crime Control Act of 1984. see also Federal Wiretap Statute, Brady Handgun Violence Prevention Act; Bureau of Alcohol, Tobacco, Firearms and Explosives (ATF); Federal Assault Weapons Ban of 1994; Federal Firearms Act of 1938; Firearm Owners' Protection Act of 1986; Gun Control Act of 1968; National Firearms Act of 1934; Omnibus Crime Control and Safe Streets Act of 1968; Violent Crime Control and Law Enforcement Act of 1994.

Onion Field, The. A nonfiction book authored by Joseph Wambaugh, depicting the murder of a Los Angeles policeman, Ian Campbell. Officers Campbell and Karl Hettinger, while on routine patrol, were kidnapped at gunpoint from Hollywood, CA, on the night of March 9, 1963, and driven 95 miles to an onion field 30 miles south of Bakersfield, CA, by Gregory Powell and Jimmy Lee Smith. Powell shot Campbell in the mouth and then four more times, as the officers stood with their hands over their heads. The killing reportedly occurred because Powell misinterpreted California's "Lindbergh Law" and believed he would face the death penalty for kidnapping the officers (under this law, kidnapping was a capital offence only if the victim was injured). Hettinger fled when a cloud obscured the moon. Powell and Smith twice were sentenced to death, but their sentences were reduced to life in prison with the possibility of parole in 1972, when the California state Supreme Court declared the death penalty law unconstitutional. Smith was paroled in 1982 but later returned to prison on a heroin charge. He was eventually released from prison and absconded from parole in December of 2006. He was apprehended in February of 2007 and charged with parole violation. He died of a heart attack in custody in April of 2007. The state parole board in 1977 found Powell suitable for release and affirmed the finding in 1978 and 1979. However, intense public and political pressure caused the board to withdraw Powell's parole date shortly before his scheduled release in June 1982. He remains incarcerated and was most recently denied parole on January 27, 2010. After the trials, Hettinger was ostracized by fellow officers and experienced marital strain. He committed a series of shoplifting offenses and was forced to resign from the LAPD. A psychiatrist reported this was due to an unconscious need to be punished. Hettinger was unemployed for a time, worked as a gardener in LA, and took a job as a greenhouse manager in Bakersfield some nine years after the killing. In 1977 he became an aide to Kern County (Bakersfield) Supervisor Harvey, a position he held for several terms. He died in 1994 of liver disease.

open court. (1) A court whose sessions may be attended by spectators. (2) A court that is in session for the transaction of judicial business.

opening statement. First statement made by prosecutors to the jury, in which they outline the case, pointing out the general proof that will be offered. The purpose is to give the jury a brief summary of the case, enabling it to understand the evidence.

Operation Armas Cruzadas, A program within the office of the U.S. Immigration and Customs Enforcement (ICE) established in 2008 to "comprehensively identify, disrupt and dismantle transborder weapons smuggling networks." The program works in conjunction with the U.S. Bureau of Alcohol, Tobacco, Firearms and Explosives (ATF) and the Mexican government to decrease the level of violence within Mexico, reduce weapons smuggling into the United States, and dismantle the criminal organizations responsible for these activities.

Operation El Dorado. A task force headquartered in New York and launched in 1992 by the U.S. Treasury Department to interdict illegal, drug-generated, bulk cash transfers. By 2002, the task force seized $425 million and arrested 1,500 individuals.

Operation Greylord. An unprecedented, four-year-long undercover investigation of the Cook County, IL, court system (the nation's largest unified court system), conducted by the Federal Bureau of Investigation and IRS Criminal Investigation Division. The inquiry resulted in indictments of 92 officials, including 17 judges, 48 lawyers, eight policemen, 10 deputy sheriffs, eight court officials, and one state legislator. In a series of trials that lasted nearly 10 years, nearly all defendants were convicted or pled guilty. In the trial of former Circuit Judge Murphy it was disclosed that he fixed more than 100 drunk-driving cases for $100 each. He was convicted of 24 counts and sentenced to 10 years in prison. A former narcotics court judge boasted in conversations recorded by the FBI that he could "make $1,000 a week fixing cases." This is believed to be the first time the FBI bugged the private chambers of a judge. Circuit Judge Devine received one-third of lawyers' legal fees in

a kickback scheme. He was convicted of 47 charges related to bribery and extortion and was sentenced to 15 years in prison. Judge Maloney, the last to be convicted when the trials concluded in 1994, was released from federal prison in March of 2008, maintaining his innocence. He died of kidney failure in October of the same year at the age of 83.

Operation Guatemalan Auto Theft Enforcement (GATE). This multiagency task force involves the states of Texas, New Mexico, Arizona, and California. A November 1995 operation resulted in the recovery of 31 vehicles and the arrest of seven suspects. *See also* Cargo CATS

Operation Identification. A citizen's burglary prevention program which involves engraving or otherwise marking property with a unique identification number that is intended to deter potential burglars and increase the probability of recovering stolen property. The National Sheriffs' Operation Identification Registry provides the computer storage service for individuals to register their property. This file is accessible to law enforcement agencies on a round-the-clock basis.

Operation Intercept. A program instituted on the U.S.-Mexican border on September 21, 1969, to cut off the flow of narcotics, marijuana, and dangerous drugs into the United States. The program was jointly undertaken by the U.S. Treasury and Justice departments, with the Bureau of Customs, Immigration and Naturalization Service, Bureau of Narcotics and Dangerous Drugs, Coast Guard, Navy, Federal Aviation Administration, and General Services Administration participating.

Operation Panama Express. An Organized Crime Drug Enforcement Task Force (OCDETF) operated from Tampa, Florida, which targets cocaine shipments from Colombia and other countries in South America. The operation is a collaborative effort of U.S. law enforcement agencies, including Drug Enforcement Administration,

Federal Bureau of Investigation, Immigration and Customs Enforcement (ICE), U.S. Attorney's Office, and U.S. Coast Guard. As of 2006, Operation Panama Express yielded the seizure of 350 metric tons (392 tons) of cocaine and 1,107 arrests. In September of 2008, the U.S. Coast Guard seized a submarine carrying seven tons of cocaine into the United States as part of Operation Panama Express. *See also* Organized Crime Drug Enforcement Task Force

Operation Polar Cap. In March 1989 federal agents seized three boxes of documents from the New York City branch of Continental Illinois Bank. The seizure was the culmination of a two-year investigation that broke up a Colombian Medellin Cartel money-laundering organization operating in Europe, South America, and the United States. Colombian cocaine manufactured by the Medellin Cartel was sold on the streets of New York. The cash from sales was packed in boxes, labeled as jewelry, and delivered by armored car to La Guardia Airport for shipment to Los Angeles. It was then delivered to nearby banks and deposited as if it were the proceeds of jewelry sales; later it was transferred by wire back to NY banks, which unsuspectingly wired it to accounts in other NY banks. Ultimately, the money was wire-transferred to banks in Colombia. During the first phase of the investigation, 127 persons were arrested. A federal grand jury in Atlanta returned indictments against two South American banks, charging their involvement in laundering more than $300 million in drug proceeds from the United States. On November 25, 1991, 50 people in five states were charged with operating a coast-to-coast ring. More than $10 million in cash and bank accounts was seized.

Operation Rescue. A militant pro-life group founded by Randall Terry that uses civil disobedience in its attempts to close abortion clinics. Major confrontations with the police have occurred in Wichita, Los Angeles, Pittsburgh, Milwaukee, south Miami, Philadelphia, Phoenix, and throughout New Jersey. After a dispute about the legal name Operation Rescue, there are now two similar organizations operating with a similar purpose: the original Operation Rescue changed its name to Operation Save America and expanded to protest homosexuality and pornography in addition to abortion (www.operationsaveamerica.org). The organization formerly known as Operation Rescue West or California Operation Rescue is now called Operation Rescue and is based in Kansas; this group maintains its focus on pro-life activities (www.operationrescue.org). The National Abortion Federation (Web: http://www.prochoice.org/) collects data regarding violence against abortion clinics.

Operation Resurrection. An undercover FBI investigation initiated in the late 1990s to target drug-trafficking and money-laundering by Colombia's Norte Valle Cartel, a criminal organization led by kingpin Diego Montoya-Sanchez estimated to supply 60 percent of the cocaine from Colombia to the United States. The Montoya-Sanchez drug-trafficking ring was believed to smuggle cocaine from Colombia to Ecuador to Mexico, then by land to Florida, New York, and Canada. Between 1990 and 2005, the organization is believed to have smuggled shipments between 1,000 and 6,000 kilos each, generally using maritime smuggling with various fishing and speed boats. Around 2003–2005, the organization experienced a violent turf war between Montoya-Sanchez and Wilber Varela, another kingpin, resulting in hundreds of murders, including civilian. Montoya-Sanchez was named one of FBIs 10 most wanted fugitives in 2004. Colombian officials arrested Montoya-Sanchez, found hiding in a creek bed, on September 10, 2007; he was extradited to the United States on December 12, 2008, where he pled guilty and was sentenced to 45 years in prison for racketeering, conspiring to import cocaine into the United States, and obstruction of justice by murder. As part of his 2009 plea agreement, Montoya-Sanchez admitted to using violence and murder against associates, including the murder of a coconspirator he suspected of being an FBI informant. The FBI and Colombian law enforcement investigation also led to the convictions of Montoya-Sanchez' cousin, Carlos Felipe Toro Sanchez, sentenced to 19 years in 2006, and the kingpin's two brothers: Juan Carlos Montoya-Sanchez, sentenced to 21 years in 2006, and Eugenio Montoya Sanchez, sentenced to 30 years in 2009. Three other coconspirators are awaiting extradition.

Operation Wire Cutter. An undercover investigation conducted by the Department of the Treasury, which investigated money laundering activities of Colombian peso brokers believed to have laundered money for several Colombian narcotics cartels. At the conclusion of the investigation in 2002, Treasury Investigators seized "over $8 million in cash, 400 kilos of cocaine, 100 kilos of marijuana, 6.5 kilos of heroin, nine firearms, and six vehicles."

operations. In criminal justice, the activity resulting from planning and controlling the current ongoing activities of a police force. This term may also refer to the office or communications center from which current operations are controlled.

opiate. Any natural or synthetic drug that exerts actions on the body similar to those induced by morphine, the major pain-relieving agent obtained from the opium poppy.

opiate narcotic. A drug that has both sedative and analgesic actions.

opinion. The official announcement of a decision of a court, together with the reason for that decision. An oral opinion is usually very brief. A full (or written) opinion is usually lengthy, presenting in detail the reasoning leading to the decision. A memorandum opinion (or memorandum decision) is also in writing but is a very brief statement of the reasons for a decision, without detailed explanation. A *per curiam* opinion is one issued by the court as a whole, without indication of individual authorship, while a signed opinion is one bearing the name of the individual judge who authored it, whether or not issued on behalf of the whole court. A majority opinion is that of the majority of the judges hearing the case; a dissenting (or minority) opinion is that of one or more judges who disagree with the decision of the majority; a concurring opinion states the reasoning of one or more judges who agree with the majority decision, but on different grounds.

opinion evidence. The fact that a person is of an opinion that a fact in issue, or relevant to the issue, does or does not exist is admissible only in exceptional cases. Generally, witnesses must testify to facts rather than stating their opinions or conclusions.

opium. The dried-out juice obtained from parts of the poppy *Papaver somniferum,* whose petals may be white, red, mauve, or purple. Nineteenth-century scientists isolated and intensified the poppy's strengths. Opium gum and poppy-straw concentrate hold the natural alkaloid morphine, still regarded as unsurpassed in treating severe pain. Heroin, chemically treated morphine, is now a worldwide problem as a street drug. Heroin is usually a powder, white or beige or chocolate brown, nearly always produced by criminals, primarily from poppies illicitly grown in remote corners of Asia or Mexico. Illegal fields of poppies alternate with wheat in Pakistan's Northwest Frontier Province. In 1979, when opium was declared illegal, 32,376 hectares (80,000 acres) were planted. In 1984, fewer than 2,500 hectares were said to remain. Federal authorities estimate they seize less than 10 percent of the heroin entering the U.S.—believed to be more than four metric tons each year.

O.R. Own recognizance. *See also* Manhattan Bail Project

oral evidence. Evidence given by the spoken word, as contrasted with documentary or real evidence. Sometimes referred to as parol evidence.

order. A communication, written, oral, or by signal, that conveys instructions from a superior to a subordinate. In a broad sense, the terms order and command are synonymous. However, an order implies discretion as to the details of execution, whereas a command does not.

order *nisi.* A conditional order.

order of recognizance or bail. In New York, an order setting bail or releasing a person on his own recognizance.

order to show cause. A court order calling on the opposing side to give a reason why a request of the petitioner should not be granted.

ordinal level of measurement. *See* scale, ordinal

ordinance. A law of an authorized subdivision of a state, such as a city or a county.

ordinary care. The degree of care exercised by ordinarily prudent persons.

ordnance. Weapons, ammunition, explosives, vehicles, and confrontation material collectively, together with the necessary maintenance and equipment.

Oregon boot. A device placed on the ankle and foot of a person to impede his or her walking or running. It has been used on convicts working outside of prison, such as on road gangs, and also in transferring prisoners. It consists generally of heavy metal contrivances, something like shoes or boots, that are joined by a chain of such length that a person can take only short steps.

organic law. The fundamental law or constitution.

organized crime. A complex pattern of activity that includes the commission of statutorily defined offenses, in particular the provision of illegal goods and services, but also carefully planned and coordinated instances of offenses by fraud, theft, and extortion groups, which are uniquely characterized by the planned use of both legitimate and criminal professional expertise and the use, for criminal purposes or organizational features, of legitimate business, including availability of large capital resources, disciplined management, division of labor, and focus upon maximum profit; also, the persons engaged in such a pattern of activity. Organized crime is not a statutory offense (a defined offense to which a penalty is attached). The Federal Omnibus Crime Control Act of 1970 defines organized crime for administrative purposes as: "the unlawful activities of the members of a highly organized, disciplined association engaged in supplying illegal goods and services, including but not limited to gambling, prostitution, loan-sharking, narcotics, labor racketeering, and other unlawful activities of members of such organizations." On July 28, 1984, then-President Reagan named a 20-member commission, headed by Judge Irving R. Kaufman, to analyze organized crime and recommend remedies. The President's Commission on Organized Crime (PCOC) defined the criminal group involved in organized crime as "a continuing, structured collectivity of persons who utilize criminality, violence, and a willingness to corrupt in order to gain and maintain power and profit." Characteristics are organizational continuity; hierarchical structure; restricted membership; criminality, violence, and power; legitimate business involvement; and use of specialists. *See also* laundering money; Mafia

Organized Crime Drug Enforcement Task Force (OCDETF). Created in 1982, a federal drug enforcement program under the Attorney General in the Department of Justice whose central mission "is to identify, disrupt, and dismantle the most serious drug trafficking and money laundering organizations and those primarily responsible for the nation's drug supply." The Task Force works in collaboration with state/local police departments and eleven federal agencies, including: Bureau of Alcohol, Tobacco, Firearms and Explosives; Bureau of Immigration and Customs Enforcement; DOJ Justice Criminal Division; Drug Enforcement Administration; Federal Bureau of Investigation; Internal Revenue Service; Tax Division;

U.S. Attorney's Office; U.S. Coast Guard; and U.S. Marshals Service. Using its force of 2,500 agents, the Task Force efforts have yielded 44,000 drug-related convictions and seizure of over $3.0 billion in assets, including cash, property, vehicles and equipment used in furtherance of the drug trade. Web: http://www.justice.gov/dea/programs/ocdetf. htm.

Organized Crime and Racketeering (OCR) Section. In 1951, the Kefauver Committee concluded that "there is a sinister criminal organization known as the Mafia operating throughout the country." The OCR office of the Department of Justice was established in 1954 to lead coordinated investigations of organized crime. By 1957 there were only 10 attorneys in OCR. In 1961 Attorney General Robert Kennedy took an active interest in the investigation and prosecution of organized crime figures. That year, only 49 such people were convicted, but by the time Kennedy left the DOJ in 1965, convictions had increased to 468. The Intelligence and Special Services Unit provides a comprehensive, central intelligence file devoted exclusively to organized crime. The OCR section develops and coordinates nationwide enforcement programs to suppress the illicit activities of organized criminal groups, including narcotics trafficking; loan-sharking; vice; and the illegal infiltrating of legitimate businesses, labor unions, and the political process. For further information, contact: Organized Crime and Racketeering Section, Criminal Division, DOJ, Criminal Division, 950 Pennsylvania Ave., Washington, DC 20530-0001. Web site: http://www.justice.gov/criminal/links/ocrs. html.

Organized Crime Control Act of 1970. Signed into law by President Nixon on October 15, 1970, the law broadens the fight against organized crime and charges the FBI with investigating bombings of, and bombing attempts on, any property of the federal government or that of any institution or organization receiving federal financial assistance.

Organized Crime, National Council on. Created by President Richard M. Nixon on June 4, 1970, for the purpose of controlling organized crime by coordinating efforts of the various federal agencies. Attorney General John N. Mitchell was named chairman. The council was composed of the postmaster general, the secretaries of labor and the treasury, and the heads of all federal investigative agencies.

organized deception of the public. Certain crimes against trust and ethics involving conspiracy by persons in high office to deceive the public concerning particular events. *See also* Teapot Dome Scandal; Tweed, William Marcy; Watergate affair

organoleptic. Testing or identification by means of the senses—commonly smell or taste.

original jurisdiction. The authority of a court to hear and determine a lawsuit when it is initiated.

orphanage. A facility, generally county or state funded, for children who become wards of the state due to abandonment or any form of abuse or neglect. The first orphanage in North America was founded by Ursuline nuns in 1792 after Indians massacred adult settlers in Natchez, Mississippi.

orphans' court. A court, so-called in PA and MD, that has jurisdiction over probate, administration of estates, and guardianship of minors. Called also surrogate's court in NJ. *See also* surrogate

Osborn, Albert Sherman. An American handwriting analyst (1858–1946) whose testimony was of substantial importance in the conviction of Bruno Hauptmann in the Lindbergh kidnapping case. *See also* kidnapping

ostracism. A form of punishment administered within a social or community group, in contrast with banishment. Neighborly help is forbidden, and even aid by the members of one's family is denied. Often it is accompanied by sneers and contemptuous attitudes or by complete indifference. Today the attitude of the public toward the ex–convict or the parolee is one of ostracism.

Oswald, Lee Harvey (1939–1963). Oswald is believed to be the assassin of President John F. Kenney, shot and killed in a motorcade in Dallas Texas on November 22, 1963. Oswald, who worked in the book depository from which Kennedy was shot, was found hiding in a theater within hours of the shooting. Oswald himself was shot and killed by Jack Ruby while being transported in police custody. Some maintain that Oswald did not kill Kennedy, but that Oswald was the scapegoat in a broader conspiracy involving organized crime and the U.S. government. *See also* Ruby, Jack

O.T.B. (OTB). Abbreviation for off-track betting. Legalized in New York City, where it started operations in April 1971. Now operated under government direction in many cities.

other crimes. When a person is being tried for one crime, the state cannot prove the commission by the accused of another crime in no way connected with the crime charged. But if the other crime was committed as part of the same transaction and tends to explain or qualify the fact in issue, it may be shown. The rule may also be stated thus: when it is legally permitted to prove a fact, such evidence cannot be excluded merely because it tends to prove a crime other than that for which the accused is on trial. Whenever the existence of any particular intention, knowledge, good or bad faith, malice, or other state of mind is in issue and the commission of another crime tends to prove its existence, the other crime may be shown.

overcriminalization. Enactment of legislation making marginal acts criminal and resulting in more criminal laws than can be enforced or are necessary for the protection of society and the safety of life and property.

Overseas Contingency Operation. Term used by the Obama administration in reference to ongoing military deployment initiated in the Bush "War on Terror." *See also* War on Terror

overt act. In criminal law, an act done to further a plan, conspiracy, or intent. In a criminal conspiracy case, mere planning is insufficient to constitute the crime; an overt act to further the plan must be done. The same applies in a criminal attempt case.

Overtown. A civil disturbance in 1989 that began when Miami police officer William Lozano shot the driver of a speeding motorcycle, which then crashed into a car, killing both drivers. Within an hour of this incident, residents of the city's Overtown neighborhood began pelting police officers and emergency workers with rocks and bottles. Three days of rioting followed. Lozano, claiming self-defense, was tried on two counts of manslaughter, convicted in December 1989, and sentenced to seven years in prison. An appeals court ordered a new trial in Orlando in 1991, ruling that the Miami jury was pressured into its decision by the possibility of more violence. A not-guilty verdict was reached on May 28, 1993, in the appeal. *See also* McDuffie, Arthur

own recognizance (OR). Pretrial release of a defendant based on his promise to refrain from criminal activity and appear for trial. OR release is generally given to persons will less serious criminal histories and charged with less serious offenses. *See also* bail, pretrial release. *See* Table 3. Types of Pretrial Release, page 36.

oyez. Means hear ye; a phrase often used to begin sessions in court.

P

paedophilia. *See* pedophilia

pandering. The activity of procuring another person for the purpose of prostitution. This term is generally used in the prosecution of pimps, although it is also charged in cases involving transportation of someone to an arranged location for the purpose of soliciting sex, or transportation of someone into the United States for the purpose of soliciting sex

pandering, notable cases. In 1985, the Los Angeles Police Department began arresting producers of hard core sex films under the state's pandering law, which carried a mandatory three-year prison term. Robert Harold Freedman, president of Hollywood Video Production Company, was convicted of five counts of pandering for hiring five actresses (each of whom testified against Freedman in court in exchange for leniency) in the production of a movie depicting explicit sex acts. The case was affirmed at appeal in 1987 by the District Court. In 1988, the California Supreme Court reversed the conviction, citing First Amendment (free speech) protections, writing "we are compelled to conclude the pandering statute was not intended to and does not apply to the conduct here involved and that defendant's convictions of pandering must be reversed." Similar cases have been reversed in Ohio (*People v. Dute* (2003). However, pandering has been upheld in the cases of "Hollywood Madam" Heidi Fleiss (1997) and *United States v. Williams* (2008), for pandering of child pornography. *See also* Fleiss, Heidi

panel. Schedule or roll containing the names of jurors summoned for service.

panhandle. (1) To approach people and beg, especially in a public place. (2) Colloquial term used to reference a geographical location in which the jurisdiction of one area has a fingerlike protrusion into the jurisdiction of another. For example, the Oklahoma Panhandle is the narrow strip of land on the far west of the state which lies between Kansas and Colorado on the north, Texas on the south, and New Mexico on the west.

panhandler. One who approaches people and begs, generally in public place.

Pan Opticon plan. Model for prison architecture developed by Jeremy Bentham in 1791. The model was circular, with all cells on the outside. It was thought that a guard stationed at the center of the circle could observe all the prisoners on the many-tiered circular structure. Although the idea proved much less efficient than expected and was not widely adopted, an example of this structure is still in use in Joliet, IL. *See* Table 34 on page 335. Pan Opticon Prison Diagram

paradigm. A collection of the major assumptions, concepts, and propositions in an area of business or research that suggests how organizational structure or operations should be approached. A paradigm resembles a model in that it serves to orient research and theorizing.

paraffin test. A technique of coating the hands of a person with melted paraffin. After the paraffin cools and hardens, the "glove" is removed by cutting with scissors and the inside surface is treated with a diphenylamine solution. If nitrates or nitrites are present a distinctive color is produced, thus indicating the presence of gun-powder residue. This test is not considered reliable due to the prevalence of nitrates and nitrites and is rarely used in modern times to detect gunshot residue. *See also* gunshot residue

paralegals. Legal assistants who assist attorneys in the delivery of legal services. Through formal education, training, and experience, paralegals gain knowledge of the legal system and substantive and procedural law. Paralegals may conduct interviews, investigations, and legal research, and perform limited functions in court, such as filing motions. They may not represent or give legal advice to clients. In the United States, paralegals are not licensed and have no degree requirements, although many paralegals earn a paralegal certificate in various accredited degree program (AA, BA level). In Canada, paralegals can earn licensure and are regulated in a similar manner to attorneys, which enables them to operate independently from attorneys in the Canadian legal system. *See also* National Association of Legal Assistants; National Federation of Paralegal Associations

TABLE 34   PAN OPTICON PRISON DIAGRAM

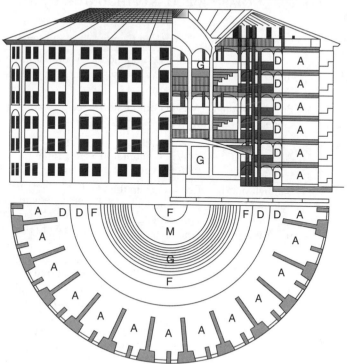

Designed by Jeremy Bentham circa 1787

paraphilia. Pejorative term referring to the sexual arousal to objects, situations, or individuals that are not part of normative stimulation. Such arousal generally causes distress or serious problems for the paraphiliac or persons associated with him or her.

paraphiliac. One who is sexually aroused to objects, situations, or individuals outside of normative stimulation.

parameter. (1) A measurable quantity whose magnitude can vary, depending on the areas or objects being compared, such as a predetermined length for a piece of string or for the cylinder capacity of a motor vehicle; similar to a benchmark. (2) A quantity in a mathematical calculation that may be assigned any arbitrary value.

pardon. There are two kinds of pardons of offenses: the absolute pardon, which fully restores to the individual all rights and privileges of a citizen, and the conditional pardon, which requires a condition to be met before the pardon is officially granted. Article II, Section 2, of the Constitution gives the president full pardon power ("executive clemency") in all cases involving federal infractions. In the Department of Justice there is an Office of the Pardon Attorney with responsibility for handling all administrative procedures concerning pardons. In most states, the governor has full pardoning power, although in some states he or she must share this power with the state senate or some other body. *See also* amnesty, clemency. *See* Table 35. Notable Pardons in the United States, pages 336–338

Pardon Attorney. This federal office receives all petitions for executive clemency; initiates the necessary investigations; and prepares recommendations of the attorney general to the president involving all forms of executive clemency, including pardon,

text continues on page 339

TABLE 35   NOTABLE PARDONS IN THE UNITED STATES

Date	President	Person Granted Pardon	Conviction Crime	Noteworthy Issues
1797	George Washington	Leaders of the Whiskey Rebellion	Acts in conjunction with the Whiskey Rebellion	Group pardon is also called amnesty. See also amnesty.
1857	James Buchanan	Brigham Young, Governor of Utah	Acts in conjunction with the Utah War	See also *amnesty*.
1865–1868	Andrew Johnson	All former confederates	Acts in conjunction with the Civil War	Four separate group pardons of former confederate officials and military personnel after the American Civil War. In the first three, specific persons were named. The last and most notable of these occurred on Christmas Day, 1868, in which Johnson gave unconditional amnesty to all former confederates. This occurred after the election of Ulysses S. Grant to succeed Johnson as president, but before Grant took office in March of 1869. See also *amnesty*.
		Samuel Mudd, Edmund Spangler, and Samuel Arnold	Conspiracy in the assassination of President Abraham Lincoln	
1971	Richard Nixon	Jimmy Hoffa	Bribery and fraud convictions in 1964	Hoffa went missing in 1975, presumed murdered. Nixon himself was pardoned in 1974.
1974	Gerald Ford	Robert E. Lee, general in the Confederate army	Acts in conjunction with the Civil War	Lee died in 1870. This is a posthumous pardon.
		Former President Richard Nixon	Misconduct related to Watergate scandal	See also *Watergate*.
1977	Jimmy Carter	All Vietnam-era draft dodgers	Avoiding draft	This is a group pardon (amnesty). Noteworthy, not only due to the public controversy it stirred, but also because this pardon was granted at the start of his presidential term rather than at the end. See also *amnesty*.

(continued)

Date	President	Person Granted Pardon	Conviction Crime	Noteworthy Issues
		Jefferson Finis Davis, Confederate President	Treason, acts in conjunction with the Civil War	Davis died in 1889. This is a posthumous pardon.
		G. Gordon Libby	Convicted of conspiracy, burglary, and illegal wiretapping related to the Watergate scandal	See also *Watergate*.
		Patty Hearst, heiress and alleged kidnap victim	Convicted of bank robbery	Sentence commuted, but Hearst not pardoned in 1977. Hearst subsequently pardoned by President Clinton in 1999.
1981	Ronald Reagan	W. Mark Felt, former Associate Director of the FBI	Civil rights violations	Felt was also known as "Deep Throat," the secret *Washington Post* informant during the Watergate scandal. See also *Watergate*.
1992	George H. W. Bush	Elliott Abrams	Convicted of unlawfully withholding information	Abrams, Clarride, Fiers, George, McFarlane, and Weinberger were White House staff in the Reagan Administration. All convictions were related to their involvement in the Iran-Contra Scandal. See also *Iran-Contra Scandal*.
		Duane Clarride	Convicted of perjury	
		Alan Fiers	Convicting of unlawfully withholding information	
		Clair George	Convicted of perjury, false statements, and obstruction	
		Robert McFarlane	Convicted of unlawfully withholding information	
		Caspar Weinberger	Convicted of perjury	
1993		Edwin L. Cox Jr.	Bank fraud	Edwin Cox Sr., father of the accused, subsequently donated at least $100,000 to the Bush Presidential Library.
1999	William Clinton	16 members of the Puerto Rican Armed Forces of National Liberation	Responsible for more than 100 bomb attacks in the U.S. between 1974–1983	See also *domestic terrorism; Puerto Rican Armed Forces of National Liberation*

(continued)

Date	President	Person Granted Pardon	Conviction Crime	Noteworthy Issues
		Patty Hearst, heiress and alleged kidnap victim	Convicted of bank robbery	Sentenced commuted in 1977 by President Jimmy Carter. See also *Hearst, Patty*
		Susan McDougal	Contempt of Court	McDougal and her husband were partners with President and Mrs. Clinton in the Whitewater real estate investment scandal. She refused to answer questions about whether President Clinton lied, and served 18 months for contempt as a result. See also *Whitewater Scandal.*
		Roger Clinton	Convicted of cocaine distribution	Roger Clinton is President Clinton's half-brother. Roger Clinton was arrested for drunk driving and disturbing the peace the month following his pardon.
2007	George W. Bush	Irve Lewis "Scooter" Libby	Convicted of perjury and obstruction of justice	Commuted sentence but did not give pardon for conviction connected to CIA leak that released the name of an undercover CIA operative.

Notable Gubernatorial Pardons

Date	President	Person Granted Pardon	Conviction Crime	Noteworthy Issues
1979	Ray Blanton, Governor of Tennessee	52 prisoners	Various	Governor removed from office and subsequently convicted of extortion, fraud, and conspiracy.
1986	Toney Anaya, Governor of New Mexico	All persons sentenced to death in New Mexico	Homicide	Death sentences commuted to life imprisonment.
2003	George Ryan, Governor of Illinois	All persons sentenced to death in Illinois	Homicide	Death sentences commuted to life imprisonment; this mass commutation raised awareness of capital punishment issues in the U.S., including wrongful conviction. Unrelated to these commutations, Governor Ryan was subsequently convicted of federal corruption charges. See also *wrongful conviction.*

commutation, reduction of sentence, remission of fine, and reprieve. For further information, contact: Office of the Pardon Attorney, DOJ, 500 First Street, NW, Suite 400, Washington, DC 20530. Web site: http://www.justice.gov/pardon/.

parens patrine (Lat., lit.). Father of his country; a doctrine under which a government supervises children and other persons who have been termed legally incapable. It often takes the form of supervision analogous to that of a parent.

parenteral. Introduced into the human body by some means other than through the intestines as a result of ingestion, such as by piercing the skin or mucous membrane with a needle, bite, cut, or abrasion.

parity pay. Generally, the same pay for the same job classification. Police associations and unions in collective bargaining survey surrounding and similar jurisdictions to ensure their members are compensated as well or better than their counterparts in other locations.

Park Police. The U.S. Park Police are part of the Department of the Interior, and most are assigned within the Washington, DC, metropolitan area. They have the same police powers as local police and act as hosts to park visitors. For further information, contact: 970 Ohio Drive SW, Washington, DC 20024. Web site: http://www.nps.gov/uspp/.

Park Rangers. The rangers of the National Park Service carry out conservation efforts to protect plant and animal life from fire, disease, and visitor abuse. They plan and conduct programs of public safety, including law enforcement and rescue work. For further information, contact: Ranger Activities and Protection Division, National Park Service, 1849 C Street NW, Washington, DC 20240.

Parker, Bonnie (1910–1934). Bonnie Parker was born in Rowena, TX, in 1910 and was an honor roll student despite her impoverished childhood. Parker met Clyde Barrow in early 1930 and began a stream of crimes in multiple states that gained them national attention, including bank robbery, murder,

and escape. Barrow and Parker were shot and killed by a posse in Louisiana. *See also* Barrow, Clyde

Parker, Isaac C. (1838–1896) On May 2, 1875, federal judge Parker arrived in Fort Smith to reestablish the federal court in the Western District of Arkansas. Eight days after his arrival, he opened his first term of court. Eighteen persons were brought before him charged with murder, 15 were convicted, and eight were sentenced to die. One was later shot during an escape attempt and another had his sentence commuted to life imprisonment. The mass hanging of the remaining six brought international attention to the court and its judge, who became known as "the hanging judge." In 21 years, Parker sentenced 168 persons to death, of whom 88 were actually hanged. He died in 1896 at the age of 58.

Parker, Robert (AKA "Butch Cassidy", 1866–1908?). Born Robert Parker, took the surname Cassidy after Mike Cassidy, a Western outlaw and neighbor who mentored Robert Parker. Cassidy, along with associate "the Sundance Kid," was a notorious bank and train robber in the late 1800s and early 1900s. To avoid U.S. capture, the pair reportedly traveled to South America where they continued robbing banks. The date and method of Parker's death are unknown, although most experts believe he died in Boliva around 1908. *See also* Sundance Kid

Parker, William H. (1902–1966). Born in Lead, SD, this law officer began his career with the Los Angeles Police Department in 1927, earned a law degree and became a member of the California bar in 1930, and was promoted to sergeant in 1931. Rising to the rank of inspector in 1940, he served in the army during World War II and participated in the reorganization of police forces in several German cities while overseas. After the war he returned to the LAPD, becoming deputy chief of internal affairs in 1949. He was named chief in 1950 and a year later, amid charges of vice-squad corruption, he disciplined more than 40 officers, freeing the department from political interference. He was admitted to the federal bar in 1956. The LAPD headquarters building was named the Parker Center in his memory.

parol evidence. Oral or verbal evidence; that which is given by word of mouth; the ordinary kind of evidence given by witnesses in court.

parole. A method of completing a prison sentence in the community rather than in confinement. The paroled offender can legally be recalled to prison to serve the remainder of his or her sentence if he or she does not comply with the conditions of parole. Parole has its roots in the English tradition. In 1617, the privy counsel of the English Parliament standardized the previously subjective practice of some English judges to spare the lives of condemned felons by exiling them to the newly created colonies of Australia and America. Alexander Maconochie and his disciple, Sir Walter Crofton, were early reformers. In the United States the first real parole system was begun in Philadelphia in 1822. The force behind American parole methods

was Zebulon Brockway. *See also* Table 36. Sample Conditions of Parole, pages 340–342

parole agency. A correctional agency that may or may not include a paroling authority, and whose principal functions are pre-release investigations, parole-plan preparation for prospective parolees, and the supervision of adults having parole or other conditional-release status.

parole board. An administrative board that by law has charge of granting paroles and of supervising parolees. Such boards usually follow laws governing who may be granted parole and the length of time parolees remain under its control. The concept was originally devised by Alexander Maconochie, called ticket-of-leave, and applied to prisoners transported to Norfolk Island as a method of improving discipline.

parole clinic. A facility that provides intensive aid to parolees who require continued mental health services and therapy after release. This facility is usually maintained by a governmental agency, such as a mental health or social service agency.

text continues on page 342

TABLE 36   SAMPLE CONDITIONS OF PAROLE

STATE OF CALIFORNIA   DEPARTMENT OF CORRECTIONS
NOTICE AND CONDITIONS OF PAROLE
CDC 1515 (Rev05/01)

You will be released on parole effective _____, 20_____ for a period of _____.
This parole is subject to the following notice and conditions. Should you violate conditions of this parole, you are subject to arrest, suspension of your parole.

  You waive extradition to the State of California from any state or territory of the United States or from the District of Columbia. You will not contest any effort to return you to the State of California.

  When the Board of Prison Terms determines, based upon psychiatric reasons, that you pose a danger to yourself or others, the Board may, if necessary for psychiatric treatment, order your placement in a community treatment facility or state prison or may revoke your parole and order your return to prison. You and your residence and any property under your control may be searched without a warrant by an agent of the Department of Corrections or any law enforcement officer.

  If another jurisdiction has lodged a detainer against you, you may be released to the custody of that jurisdiction. Should you be released from their custody prior to the expiration of your California parole, or should the detainer not be exercised, you are to immediately contact the nearest Department of Corrections' Parole and Community Service Division Office for instructions concerning reporting to a parole agent.

  You have been informed and have received in writing the procedure for obtaining a Certificate of Rehabilitation (4852.21 PC).

(continued)

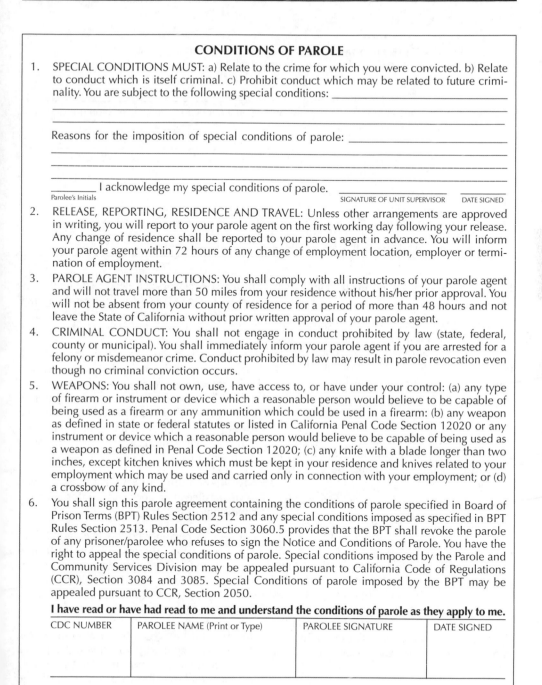

CONDITIONS OF PAROLE

1. SPECIAL CONDITIONS MUST: a) Relate to the crime for which you were convicted. b) Relate to conduct which is itself criminal. c) Prohibit conduct which may be related to future criminality. You are subject to the following special conditions: _____

_____

Reasons for the imposition of special conditions of parole: _____

_____

_____ I acknowledge my special conditions of parole. _____ _____
Parolee's Initials   SIGNATURE OF UNIT SUPERVISOR   DATE SIGNED

2. RELEASE, REPORTING, RESIDENCE AND TRAVEL: Unless other arrangements are approved in writing, you will report to your parole agent on the first working day following your release. Any change of residence shall be reported to your parole agent in advance. You will inform your parole agent within 72 hours of any change of employment location, employer or termination of employment.

3. PAROLE AGENT INSTRUCTIONS: You shall comply with all instructions of your parole agent and will not travel more than 50 miles from your residence without his/her prior approval. You will not be absent from your county of residence for a period of more than 48 hours and not leave the State of California without prior written approval of your parole agent.

4. CRIMINAL CONDUCT: You shall not engage in conduct prohibited by law (state, federal, county or municipal). You shall immediately inform your parole agent if you are arrested for a felony or misdemeanor crime. Conduct prohibited by law may result in parole revocation even though no criminal conviction occurs.

5. WEAPONS: You shall not own, use, have access to, or have under your control: (a) any type of firearm or instrument or device which a reasonable person would believe to be capable of being used as a firearm or any ammunition which could be used in a firearm: (b) any weapon as defined in state or federal statutes or listed in California Penal Code Section 12020 or any instrument or device which a reasonable person would believe to be capable of being used as a weapon as defined in Penal Code Section 12020; (c) any knife with a blade longer than two inches, except kitchen knives which must be kept in your residence and knives related to your employment which may be used and carried only in connection with your employment; or (d) a crossbow of any kind.

6. You shall sign this parole agreement containing the conditions of parole specified in Board of Prison Terms (BPT) Rules Section 2512 and any special conditions imposed as specified in BPT Rules Section 2513. Penal Code Section 3060.5 provides that the BPT shall revoke the parole of any prisoner/parolee who refuses to sign the Notice and Conditions of Parole. You have the right to appeal the special conditions of parole. Special conditions imposed by the Parole and Community Services Division may be appealed pursuant to California Code of Regulations (CCR), Section 3084 and 3085. Special Conditions of parole imposed by the BPT may be appealed pursuant to CCR, Section 2050.

I have read or have had read to me and understand the conditions of parole as they apply to me.

CDC NUMBER	PAROLEE NAME (Print or Type)	PAROLEE SIGNATURE	DATE SIGNED

(continued)

TO BE COMPLETED BY STAFF:
Does the inmate/parolee have a qualifying disability requiring effective communication?
☐ Yes   ☐ No
If yes, cite the source document and/or observations: _____
What type of accommodation/assistance was provided to achieve effective communication to the best of the inmate's/parolee's ability?

STAFF NAME (Print or Type)	STAFF SIGNATURE	DATE SIGNED

DISTRIBUTION ORIGINAL—CENTRAL FILE. CANARY—PAROLE AGENT, PINK—PAROLEE/ INMATE

Source: California Department of Corrections.

Parole Commission. *See* United States Parole Commission

parole contract. A statement of the conditions that a parolee is to observe while on parole. Violation of these conditions is grounds for revocation of parole and for the return of the parolee to the institution.

parole museum. *See* T. H. Pendergast parole museum

parole officer. An employee of a parole agency whose primary duties are the supervision of parolees and preparole investigation or planning.

parole revocation. The administrative action of a paroling authority removing a person from parole status in response to a violation of lawfully required conditions of parole. Such conditions include the prohibition against commission of a new offense and various technical provisions, such as complying with drug testing and reporting to the parole agent as directed, and prohibitions against associating with other felons or parolees. Parole revocation usually results in a return to prison.

parole supervision. Guidance, treatment, or regulation of a convicted adult who is obliged to fulfill conditions of parole or other conditional release, authorized and required by statute, performed by a parole agency, and occurring after a period of prison confinement.

parole supervisory caseload. The total number of clients registered with a parole agency or officer on a given date or during a specified period.

parole suspended. The withdrawal by a paroling authority or parole agent of a person's effective parole status, usually accompanied by a return to confinement, pending a determination of whether parole should be revoked or pending resolution of some problem that may require a temporary return to confinement.

parole violation. An act, or a failure to act, by a parolee that does not conform to the conditions of parole.

parolee. A person who has been conditionally released by a paroling authority from a prison prior to the expiration of his or her sentence, placed under the supervision of a parole agency, and required to observe conditions of parole.

paroling authority. A board or commission that has the authority to release on parole adults committed to prison, to revoke parole or other conditional release, and to discharge from parole or other conditional release status.

parricide. The murder of one's father, mother, or legal guardian. *See also* Borden, Lizzie; Menendez, Eric; Menendez, Kyle; matricide; patricide

participant observation. A type of research strategy in which a researcher gains access and develops intimate familiarity with a group of individuals for study. Generally, the groups attitudes, beliefs, practices, are documented through an intensive involvement of the subject in their natural setting over an extended period of time. See also ethnography, going native

parsimony (law of). The law of parsimony, also called the law of economy or Ockham's razor, proposes that a problem should be stated in its basic and simplest terms. Credit for outlining the law is usually given to William of Ockham (1284–1347?).

parties to offense. All persons culpably concerned in the commission of a crime, whether they directly commit the act constituting the offense or facilitate, solicit, encourage, aid, or abet its commission; also, in some penal codes, persons who assist one who has committed a crime to avoid arrest, trial conviction or punishment.

Part I offenses. In Uniform Crime Reports, the group of offenses, also called major offenses, for which UCR publishes counts of reported instances as "Index Crimes. Part I offenses are: 1. criminal homicide (murder and nonnegligent or voluntary manslaughter); 2. forcible rape (actual or attempted); 3. robbery (firearm, knife or cutting instrument, other dangerous weapon, or strong-arm); 4. aggravated assault (firearm, knife or cutting instrument, other dangerous weapon, hands, fist, feet, etc.—aggravated injury); 5. burglary (forcible entry, unlawful entry—no force, attempted forcible entry); 6. larceny theft (pocket-picking, purse-snatching, shoplifting, thefts from motor vehicles, theft of motor vehicle parts and accessories, theft of bicycles, theft from buildings, theft from coin-operated device or machine, all other); 7. motor vehicle theft; and 8. arson (added to the Part I offenses in 1979 by congressional action).

Part II offenses. In Uniform Crime Reports, crimes that are less serious than Part I offenses, with numbers continuing after the eight Part I categories: 9. other assault (in contrast with aggravated); 10. forgery and counterfeiting; 11. fraud; 12. embezzlement; 13. stolen property (buying, receiving, possessing); 14. vandalism; 15. weapons (carrying, possessing, etc.); 16. prostitution and commercialized vice; 17. sex offenses (except forcible rape, prostitution, and commercialized vice); 18. drug abuse violations; 19. gambling; 20. offenses against the family and children; 21. driving under the influence; 22. liquor law violations; 23. drunkenness; 24. disorderly conduct; 25. vagrancy; 26. all other offenses (except traffic law violations); 27. suspicion (no specific offense; suspect released); 28. curfew and loitering violations (juveniles); and 29. runaways (persons under 18 only). Uniform Crime Reports publishes both reported-crime and arrest data for Part I offenses, but only arrest data for Part II offenses.

party. (1) A person or group of persons constituting one side of an issue, undertaking, or dispute. (2) A person or persons constituting one or more sides of a contractual agreement.

party-dominated process. The aspect of the adversary system that gives to the judge the passive role of umpire and allows the adversaries (prosecution and defense) to be the major forces in the trial. In a party-dominated process, the judge cannot initiate or continue proceedings. The parties control the factual, and, to a large extent, the legal boundaries of a case.

paruresis A phobia in which the sufferer is unable to urinate in the (real or imaginary) presence of others, such as in a public restroom.

passer. A person who unlawfully uses the personal identifying information of another to obtain credit or commit a criminal act under false character; in effect, one who passes him or herself off as another person.

passive alcohol sensor. Small sensors that are built into or attached to portable police equipment (flashlights, clipboards, etc.) to detect the presence of alcohol in the ambient air of a vehicle. The concept of passive alcohol sensing dates from the early 1970s, becoming technically feasible since the 1990s. Early passive alcohol sensor prototypes had limitations for police applications, as the unit was not specific to alcohol, was sensitive to other contaminants, and would not hold a constant calibration. Later research developed a handheld tester for on-the-spot alcohol detection to determine probable cause for further mandatory testing (blood, breath, or urine) under the implied consent law. Research suggests the modern PAS is fairly accurate (about 70 percent) in identifying persons with BAL at or above 0.10. PAS are "passive" in that they do not require the "active" cooperation or consent by the suspect; they simply take a reading of alcohol in the air around a suspect. Since the PAS does not yield a specific blood alcohol level in a specific suspect, it is not submitted as *prima facie* evidence during prosecution. Rather, PAS readings are used by police as a field screening test, much like bloodshot eyes and slurred speech indicate possible intoxication and warrant further investigation. *See also* breathalyzer

passive intrusion sensor. A passive sensor in an intrusion-alarm system that detects an intruder within the range of the sensor. Examples are a sound-sensing detection system, a vibration detection system, an infrared motion detector, and an E-field sensor.

passive ultrasonic alarm system. An alarm system that detects the sounds in the ultrasonic frequency range caused by an attempted forcible entry into a protected structure. The system consists of microphones, a control unit containing an amplifier, filters, an accumulator, and a power supply. The unit's sensitivity is adjustable.

pastoral counseling. A special field that combines insights and procedures from religion, psychiatry, and the social sciences. Major seminaries offer courses in principles of psychology and methods of counseling. Clergy trained by such courses work with students, patients in hospitals, inmates of prisons, and members of the armed forces.

The nation's first "clergy malpractice" lawsuit was dismissed in midtrial, on May 16, 1985, by a Glendale, CA, superior court judge who ruled that any judicial effort to set standards for pastoral counseling would violate the First Amendment's separation of church and state.

patent. A form of property right giving an inventor of a new product, design, or process (or the owner of the patent, if sold) the sole legal right to use, not use, or dispose of the invention. Patents in the United States are issued for a period of 17 years by the U.S. Patent Office, with renewal possible after significant modification of the original design. One very large settlement in a patent-infringement suit was $55.8 million in *Pfizer Inc. v. International Rectifier Corp. and Rochelle Laboratories* over the antibiotic dioxycycline on July 5, 1983. In *Microsoft v. AT&T,* (2007), Microsoft admitted to violating an AT&T patent, incorporating into the Windows operating system, but argued that the U.S. patent jurisdiction did not extend outside the United States; the U.S.S.C. agreed, establishing that jurisdiction of U.S. patents extend only to U.S. borders, saving Microsoft from millions in damages to AT&T.

patent and copyright policy. Advice is supplied to the Department of Justice and other agencies on government patent policy by the Antitrust Division. Address: 950 Pennsylvania Avenue, NW, Washington, DC 20530. Web: http://www.justice.gov/atr/.

path analysis. A technique for estimating the effects that a set of independent variables has on a dependent variable from a set of observed correlations, given a set of hypothesized causal, asymmetric relations among the variables. Path diagrams indicate causality among variables with arrows. With causal ordering among the variables assumed, intercorrelations among them can be analyzed to obtain estimates of the path coefficients, one for each arrow. The path coefficients indicate the effect that each independent variable has on the dependent variable. The major limitation of this technique is the quality of the researcher's assumption regarding the causal ordering among the variables.

pathogenic. Causing disease.

pathologist. A person who is educated, trained, and certified/licensed in pathology, the area of medicine dealing with the nature and causes of illness or injury.

pathology. (1) The science dealing with causes, development, and effects of disease. (2) The disease or abnormal condition itself.

patricide. The murder of one's father.

Patriot Act. *See* USA PATRIOT ACT

patrol beat. An area to which a patrol is assigned and to which it has primary responsibility for responding to calls for police assistance.

patrol car. An automobile, usually modified with special equipment, used by law enforcement agencies in performing the patrol function. The first patrol car was a Model "T" Ford used in Detroit in 1909.

patrol district. A geographical area that consists of more than one patrol beat and that may have its own police station and vehicle maintenance facilities.

patrolman. (1) The law enforcement officer who walks a beat or patrols areas by motor vehicle. (2) An official rank of a police officer, generally the beginning rank.

patronage, political. The promise or provision of public sector jobs by politicians, usually to individuals who have made significant campaign contributions or otherwise aided the politician to be elected.

patron saints. Since the early days of Christianity, certain saints and angels have been regarded as patrons of specific occupations, groups, localities, and nations. Patron saints and their constituents include: falsely accused, St. Raymund Nonnatus; firemen, St. Florian; jurists, St. Catherine of Alexandria and St. John Capistrano; lawyers, St. Ivo and St. Thomas More; mentally ill, St. Dympna; motorcyclists, Our Lady of Grace; motorists, St. Christopher and St. Frances of Rome; policemen, St. Michael; prisoners, St. Dismas, St. Barbara, and St. Joseph Cafasso; and social workers, St. Louise de Marillac.

pauper. One without means; one supported at the public expense.

PCBs (polychlorinated hiphenyls). PCBs are a group of chemicals that were widely used before 1970 in the electrical industry as a coolant. They caused environmental problems as they do not break down and can spread through the water, soil, and air. They have been linked to cancer and reproductive disorders and can cause liver function abnormalities. Government action has resulted in the control of the use, disposal, and production of PCBs in nearly all areas of the world, including the United States.

PCP. *See* phencyclidine

PCR-based Short Tandem Repeat (STR). This method of nuclear DNA analysis is generally used by the FBI. It uses short repeated sequences of DNA, in particular segments which are polymorphic (having several possible types within a species). These regions of DNA are used to discriminate between unrelated individuals. The DNA regions (loci) used for this type of analysis are independent, meaning each one of the 13 loci can occur independently, and having specific pattern on one locus doesn't change the likelihood of patterns at any other locus. Thus, match probabilities for STR analysis are 1 in a quintillion (1 with 18 zeros after it) or more. According to the FBI, "the polymerase chain reaction (PCR) technique allows for the analysis of extremely small body fluid stains, as well as the analysis of samples with no visible staining (e.g., envelopes in an extortion case or a ski mask from a bank robbery). The results of the DNA analyses on evidentiary items are then compared to the results obtained from known blood or saliva samples submitted from the victims and/or suspects potentially involved in the alleged incident."

See also deoxyribo nucleic acid; DNA analysis; Restriction Fragment Length Polymorphism (RFLP) test; Polymerase Chain Reaction (PCR); Amplified Fragment Length Polymorphism (AmbFLP) method; Short Tandem Repeat on the Y-chromosome (Y-STR); and mitochondrial DNA (mtDNA)

peace bond. A bond or bail fixed by a magistrate to ensure that the person bonded will keep the peace and not injure someone against whom he or she has made threats or tried to harm. The peace bond is not available in all jurisdictions (it was declared unconstitutional by the state of Hawaii in 1970; it is used in Texas along with restraining orders and protective orders).

peaceful picketing. A right protected by Congress on June 24, 1936, with an act making it a felony to transport in interstate or foreign commerce persons to be employed to obstruct or interfere with the right of peaceful picketing during labor controversies. Amended in 1939. The provisions of the act do not apply to common carriers.

peace officers. This term is variously defined by state statutes, but generally includes sheriffs and their deputies, constables, marshals, members of municipal police forces, and other officers whose duty is to enforce and preserve the public peace.

Peace Officers' Memorial Day. A national observance day; May 15th of each year (during Police Week, established in 1962).

peculation. The wrongful conversion of property in one's custody or control to one's own use; embezzlement.

pecuniary value. Monetary value, such as that of a negotiable instrument, a commercial interest, or anything else whose primary significance is economic advantage.

pederastic. Pertaining to a man's erotic attraction to a boy.

pederasty. Erotic or sexual relationship between an older man and an adolescent boy; term often refers to anal sexual intercourse, usually defined in law as occurring between a man and a boy; sodomy.

pedestrian. Any person who is on foot or who is using a means of conveyance propelled by human power other than a bicycle. The term includes anyone who is operating a self-propelled wheelchair, tricycle, or motorized quadricycle because the individual is otherwise unable to move around because of disability.

pedomania. Additional term for pedophilia.

pedophile. An adult who experiences persistent feelings of sexual attraction to a prepubescent child, regardless of whether those urges are acted upon. This is in contract to a child molester, which typically denotes completion of a sexual act by an adult against a child. *See also* child molester

pedophilia. According to the *Diagnostic and Statistical Manual of the American Psychological Association,* pedophilia is a form of paraphilia in which an adult has intense sexual urges towards children, either acted upon or not, and those urges cause distress or disruption in the adult's life. In common usage, it refers to the use of a minor for sexual gratification by an adult, a criminal offense. The severity of the charge (misdemeanor vs. felony) is often determined by the relationship between perpetrator and victim, victim's age, type of sexual contact, and duration of criminal activity. Persons convicted of the crime of pedophilia, overwhelmingly males, although sexual conduct between adult females and non-adult males is known to occur (*See* Letourneau, Mary Kay). Pedophiles constitute a third of all institutionalized sex criminals, one of the largest classifications. Approximately two-thirds of the victims of pedophilic acts are prepubescent and adolescent girls, in about equal numbers. The act itself generally includes fondling, although it can progress to oral, genital, or anal. Contrary to general belief, the majority of pedophilic acts, especially those involving female victims, are perpetrated by relatives, neighbors, and acquaintances of the victim.

peeling. A system used by safe burglars, whereby the outer surface of the safe door is peeled off, thus making access to the locking device available.

Peel, Sir Robert. (1788–1850). Born in Bury, Lancashire, England, and educated at Oxford. In 1812, Peel accepted the post of chief secretary for Ireland and, during his term of office, made his reputation as an able and incorruptible administrator. He sought passage of the Peace Preservation Act of 1814, which made possible the formation of a body of national police, later to become known as the Royal Irish Constabulary, popularly called The Peelers. In 1822, he accepted a seat in the cabinet of Parliament. As the British Home Secretary in 1829, Peel introduced into Parliament an act for improving the police in and near London. He believed that a community needed a protective body of well-selected and trained men in order to prevent crime and institute social control. He reformed criminal laws by limiting their scope and reducing unfair penalties. Peel removed the death penalty from more than 100 offenses. Most important, he established 12 fundamental principles of quality policing that are still applicable today.

Peeping Tom. A popular name for a person who trespasses for the purpose of observing persons inside a dwelling. *See also* voyeurism

peer. (1) An equal. (2) A member of the British House of Lords. (3) Common wisdom asserts that a trial jury must be composed of persons who are peers (members of the general class) of the accused. This "right" is often asserted as a constitutional one. However, the constitution does *not* guarantee a jury of one's peers; it guarantees an *impartial* jury, often depicted as a jury of one's peers in the media.

Peltier, Leonard. On June 26, 1975, two FBI agents, Ronald Williams and Jack R. Coler, drove onto Indian land near Oglala, SD, a small village on the Pine Ridge Reservation. A shoot-out resulted in the deaths of both agents and a male Indian. Of the four

AIM members indicted for this civil disorder, one was released due to "weak evidence," and two others were acquitted in July 1976 for firing in self-defense. The fourth man, Leonard Peltier, was extradited from Canada, tried in 1977, convicted on two counts of first-degree murder, and sentenced to consecutive life terms in federal prison.

penal. Of or pertaining to punishment or penalties.

penal administration. The maintenance and management of institutions and programs (as probation and parole) for the punishment and correction of criminals. Personnel include prison and parole board staffs; wardens; guards; medical, pedagogical, and psychiatric staffs; and probation and parole officers.

penal codes. Many states have adopted penal or criminal codes, the purpose of which is to define what acts shall be punished as crimes. In some, the code is intended to cover the whole law, and no act is a crime unless it is expressly declared so. In others, the code does not entirely abrogate the common law, insofar as it makes acts crimes, but merely sets it aside for expressly prohibited acts, leaving common law in force for other acts.

penal laws. The set of statutes imposing penalties of confinement for the commission of prohibited acts, the terms of that confinement, and the operations of the places of confinement. In the United States, the dominant penal law is the prison system.

penal servitude. Punishment that consists of confinement and hard labor.

penalty. A punishment by fine, imprisonment, or both, inflicted for violation of a law.

penalty, death. *See* execution; punishment, capital

pendens (Lat.). Pending; hanging.

Pendleton Act. *See* merit system

penetration. The insertion of the penis or other object into a woman's vagina; in criminal law, the action is important in rape cases.

penile plethysmograph (PPG). Instrument which measures blood flow to the penis, either with a circumferential transducer, which measures the circumference of the penis, a volumetric air chamber, which measures the volume of the penis. It is a direct measure of sexual response and interest. The use of penile plethysmograph evidence was excluded in *United States v. Powers* (1995), as it did not meet the Daubert standard for scientific evidence. While it is not widely used as evidence in criminal prosecution today, it is often used in research and treatment on sex offenders. Multiple studies have suggested that penile phethysmographic responses to pictures of children was the single most accurate predictor of future sex offenses in convicted pedophiles.

penitentiary. An institution for the imprisonment of convicted offenders.

penitentiary science. Jean Jacques Vilain, who founded the Maison de Force built in Ghent in 1773, is called the father of penitentiary science.

Pennsylvania (separate) system. Based on Quaker beliefs, a penal system espousing the individual isolation of prisoners to avoid their harmful influences on others. This approach to corrections was symbolized by the Eastern State Penitentiary, erected in 1829 at Cherry Hill in Philadelphia. Resembling a medieval fortress and containing an individual, walled-in exercise yard at the rear of each cell, the prison was designed for "separate and solitary confinement at labor, with instruction in labor, morals, and religion." To further ensure isolation and anonymity, prisoners were enshrouded in hoods.

penology. The study of various programs, social structures, and administrative organizations for the treatment of criminal offenders, along with the evaluation of the effectiveness of such programs.

pen register. An electronic device which records all numbers dialed from a specified phone line. The name *pen register* is derived from an older, manual system of recording numbers dialed from a particular phone. *See also* dialed number recorders

Pentagon Papers. On June 13, 1971, a series of articles was launched by the *New York Times* and the *Washington Post,* based on documents called the Pentagon Papers, which detailed how the United States made key decisions regarding its involvement in the Vietnam War. The administration of President Richard Nixon obtained an injunction on June 15 against further articles in the series, but the Supreme Court disallowed the injunction on June 30. The Pentagon Papers' espionage trial of Dr. Daniel Ellsberg was dismissed by a federal judge on May 11, 1973, after disclosure that White House agents had committed burglary in seeking evidence.

penumbral right. A constitutional right that is not specifically articulated or guaranteed but is implied from other guarantees.

peonage. Derived from the Spanish word peón, a condition of enforced servitude in which individuals are deprived of liberty and compelled to labor to repay some debt or other obligation, real or imagined, against their will; laborers with no control over their working conditions.

People's Temple. Religious organization founded by Reverend Jim Jones in San Francisco in 1955. The group moved to Guyana, in a communist commune named Jonestown in honor of their leader. With nearly 1000 members, the organization sparked concerns for human rights abuses by relatives of the members, sparking congressional inquiry. In 1978, a delegation of U.S. Congress staff and reporters traveled to the commune, resulting in a shoot-out that killed five delegation members and resulted in the mass suicide of 909 People's Temple members. *See also* Jones, Reverend James "Jim" Warren

pepper spray. A nonlethal product containing capsicum oleoresin, the essence of hot chili peppers, as its active ingredient. Originally developed by the U.S. Forestry Service to incapacitate bears, pepper spray acts as an inflammatory agent rather than an irritant. Popular brand names are CAP-STUN and Mace.

per annum (Lat.). By the year.

per capita (Lat., lit.). By heads; per person; by or for each person.

per curiam (Lat., lit.). By the court; an opinion of the full court, rather than one of an individual judge.

per diem (Lat.). By the day.

peremptory challenge. In the selection of jurors, challenges made by either side to certain jurors without assigning any reason, and which the court must allow.

Pérez, Rafael (1967–). Pérez was a former member of the LAPD Community Resources Against Street Hoodlums (CRASH) team who was the catalyst for the Rampart Scandal in 1998. Pérez was charged with stealing nine pounds of cocaine from police evidence, and subsequently agreed to testify about serious corruption throughout CRASH in exchange for leniency. Pérez admitted to conspiracy in a bank robbery, theft, and resale of nearly $1,000,000 in cocaine, numerous assaults against suspects, and fabrication of evidence. His admissions implicated 70 officers, resulted in more than 100 vacated convictions, cost the LAPD $125 million in civil lawsuits, and resulted in the closure of CRASH amidst the scandal. Subsequently, Pérez was accused of being a gang member (Bloods) and the murder of rap artist Notorious B.I.G. in 1997. In accordance with his plea agreement, Perez was sentenced to five years in 2000; he was released in 2001. He was subsequently charged with possession of a firearm in 2001, for which he served five years in prison. In 2006, he pled no contest to perjury in a case related to his driver's license application, on which he used his new legal name (Ray Lopez) but not his previous. He was sentenced to probation. *See also* Community Resources Against Street Hoodlums (CRASH); Rampart Scandal

perfidious. False; untrustworthy; disloyal.

perfidity. Treachery or faithlessness.

perimeter security. Perimeter security systems are based on any or all of these components: (1) a fence or wall, (2) towers, (3) electronic detection, and (4) patrols. Due to high construction costs and advances in technology, new prison construction relies on security systems rather than masonry walls.

perjury. The intentional making of a false statement as part of testimony by a sworn witness in a judicial proceeding on a matter material to the inquiry.

permanent circuit. An alarm circuit that is capable of transmitting an alarm signal whether the alarm control is in access mode or secure mode; used, for example, on foiled fixed windows, tamper switches, and supervisory lines. *See also* permanent protection; supervisory alarm system

permanent protection. A system of alarm devices such as foil, burglar alarm pads, or lacing connected in a permanent circuit to provide protection whether the control unit is in the access mode or secure mode.

permit. An official paper identifying a person as one who is entitled to exercise some privilege under the law; also a license.

perpetrator. The chief actor in the commission of a crime, that is, the person who directly commits the criminal act. In law enforcement usage, culprit is a synonym. Where a crime involves two or more chief actors, they may be called coperpetrators, cohorts, or accomplices.

perquisites. Anything of value—such as a car and driver, generous expense account, or free parking—that is derived from a position of employment or office in addition to the regular salary; often shortened to perks.

per se (Lat.). By itself alone, or in and of itself.

Persico, Carmine "Junior" (1937–). Boss of the Colombo Crime Family convicted of murder and racketeering in the Mafia Commission Trial of 1985. Persico is currently serving a life sentence. *See also* Mafia; Mafia Commission Trial

persistent surveillance. A military term used to describe the ability to observe landscape changes over time and apply this knowledge in future circumstances.

persistent vegetative state. A condition of patients with severe brain damage who were in a coma and recover to a state of wakefulness without detectable awareness. Not to be confused with brain death. *See also* Schiavo, Terri

person. A human being, or a group of human beings considered a legal unit, having the lawful capacity to defend rights, incur obligations, prosecute claims, or be prosecuted or adjudicated. Examples of a legal unit constituting a legal person are a state, a territory, a government, a country, a partnership, a public or private corporation, or an unincorporated association.

personal property. Goods, money, and all movable property, as distinguished from real property—land and/or buildings.

personate. In law, a synonym for impersonate: with fraudulent intent, to assume the character and/or identity of another, without the latter's consent, and to gain some advantage or obtain something of value as a result. To pretend to be or assume the identity of another.

personnel security. A program or procedure whereby an organization seeks to protect its technology, materials, or equipment from loss or embezzlement by its own employees and nonemployees who have contact with personnel of the organization. Employees who are considered "not good risks" are precluded from access to certain types of information and materials.

PERT. *See* Program Evaluation and Review Technique

Peter Principle. A business theory formulated by Laurence Peter and suggesting that corporate employees tend to be promoted to their level of incompetence. The concept is that employees who perform their jobs well are rewarded with promotions, so that they ultimately reach positions just beyond their capabilities and skills. Since they no longer perform well in those jobs, promotions cease. The end result is that those who do their jobs poorly continue to do them, while those who do their jobs well are soon promoted out of them.

Peterson, Scott (1972–). Peterson was convicted of murdering his pregnant wife, Lacy Peterson on December 24, 2003. Peterson reported his wife missing on Christmas Eve when he returned home from a solo fishing trip in the Berkeley Marina. Peterson was not considered a suspect until police discovered a trail of inconsistencies and suspicious activities, including multiple affairs. Two weeks before Lacy went missing, he told a woman he was dating that his wife died, suggesting his intent to kill her. During one candlelight vigil for the missing Lacy, Scott was on the cell phone with his lover, stating he was traveling in Europe and making romantic plans. On April 14, 2004, the bodies of Lacy and the fetus, named Connor, were found north of the Berkeley Marina where Peterson was fishing the day of Lacy's disappearance. Peterson was apprehended in San Diego on April 18, in an apparent attempt to flee prosecution. He was convicted and sentenced to death. He is awaiting execution in California.

petit jury. A body at common law of 12 disinterested and impartial persons, chosen from the community in which the trial is held, who render a verdict on questions of fact submitted in the trial of a case. Later modified in many states by reduction in number of jurors, especially in civil cases, and by provisions for less-than-unanimous verdicts, except in the trial of persons accused of capital crimes. Called *petit* (Fr., small) because fewer in number than a grand jury; called also trial jury.

petite policy. *See* dual and successive prosecution policy

petition. (1) A written request made to a court asking for the exercise of its judicial powers, or asking for permission to perform some act for which the authorization of a court is required. (2) The First Amendment grants the privilege to petition the government for redress of grievances. The petition is the principal means by which an American citizen can inform an elected official of his or her opinions. Petition, in the form of letters to members of Congress, provides representatives with the opinions of their constituents.

petition not sustained. The finding by a juvenile court in an adjudicatory hearing that there is not sufficient evidence to sustain an allegation that a juvenile is a delinquent, status offender, or dependent.

pctit larceny. Also called petty larceny; any larceny that is less than grand larceny. *See also* larceny

petty jury. Petit jury.

peyote. A spineless cactus with a small crown or button that is dried and then swallowed. Peyote is a DEA Schedule I substance, and the active ingredient in peyote is mescaline. When eaten, mescaline affects the brain within 30 to 90 minutes, and effects may persist for up to 12 hours. The average dose brings about a state of introspection and insight described as metaphysical or spiritual in nature. It may produce clear and vivid hallucinations, including brightly colored lights, animals, and geometric designs. There is no delirium or amnesia, although there may be nausea. Three compounds are derived from mescaline: DOM (often referred to as DTP), TMA, and MMDA. These induce similar effects at higher dose, but may be toxic. Just as other churches use bread and wine as a sacrament, members of the Native American Church of North America, a 10,000-year-old faith with 250,000 members, use peyote in their religious sacraments, where it is seldom abused. Since 1996, federal law (42 USC §1996a) protects the cultivation and consumption of peyote for Native American religious purposes in all fifty states. Additionally, five states (Arizona, New Mexico, Colorado, Nevada, and Oregon) allow non-native Peyote use for religious purposes. Peyote has also been researched for its possible medicinal value, as it is a microbial inhibitor, protecting against fatal strains of bacteria in mice and in penicillin-resistant *Staphylococcus*.

pharmacognogy. The American Society of Pharmacognogy describes this field as the "study of the physical, chemical, biochemical and biological properties of drugs, drug substances, or potential drugs or drug substances of natural origin as well as the search for new drugs from natural sources."

pharmacology. The branch of science that deals with the study of the composition and uses of drugs and their effects on living systems.

phencyclidine (PCP). A psychedelic surgical anesthetic also called angel dust. It is manufactured as a tablet, capsule, liquid, flake, spray, or crystal-like white powder. PCP can be ingested, smoked, sniffed, or injected. It is often sprinkled on crack, marijuana, tobacco, or parsley and smoked. The greatest danger of this drug is what it causes users to do to themselves and others: It can trigger psychotic attacks, rendering victims temporarily violent. Half of all PCP deaths are from drowning, as the substance raises the body temperature and lends a hot, dry feeling to the skin, prompting users to swim. PCP chemicals associated with illegal laboratories include: cyclohexanone, sodium metabisulfite, potassium cyanide, piperidine, anhydrous ether, bromobenzene, magnesium turnings, iodine crystals, petroleum ether, hydrochloric acid, and sodium carbonate.

phenobarbital. A barbiturate, in white powder form, which has hypnotic and sedative properties. It was first marketed as Luminal, and is currently the most widely used anticonvulsant in the world, typically prescribed to treat seizures.

phenol. A poison or antiseptic-carbolic acid.

phenolphthalein test. A preliminary test to determine if a stain is blood. If a positive reaction is obtained, further confirmation tests are conducted. The use of phenolphthalein, hydrogen peroxide, and luminal replaced benzidine in forensic field work, as benzidine is highly carcinogenic.

phishing (also called phishing scam). Attempt to acquire sensitive information, including social security number, bank account number, credit card number, passwords, etc., by fraudulent misrepresentation as a legitimate and trustworthy entity via electronic communication.

phobia. A persistent, irrational fear of a specific object, activity, or situation that leads to a compelling desire to avoid it. *See* Table 37. Phobias, this page

phonoscopy. The study of voice prints, voiceprint analysis, and identification.

photoelectric alarm system. An alarm system that employs a light beam and photoelectric sensor to provide a line of protection. Any interruption of the beam by an intruder is detected by the sensor. Mirrors may be used to change the direction of the beam. The maximum beam length is limited by many factors, some of which are the light source intensity, number of mirror reflections, detector sensitivity, beam divergence, fog, and haze.

photoengraving. A method of producing etched printing plates by photographic means.

photogrammetry. The process of determining physical, geometric measurements from photographs. It requires the use of two cameras to produce photographs from slightly different but known points of reference. Precise measurements are determined from an analysis of the photographs.

photomacrograph. A photograph of an object large enough to be seen by the naked eye but in which the lens of a microscope enlarges the size and detail of the object. This process is used in the examination of the cut surfaces of metal wire, in tool mark examinations, or firearm examinations.

TABLE 37 PHOBIAS	
Phobia subject	**Phobia term**
Animals	Zoophobia
Beards	Pogonophobia
Books	Bibliophobia
Churches	Ecclesiaphobia
Clowns	Coulrophobia
Dreams	Oneirophobia
Flowers	Anthophobia
Flying	Aviophobia
Food	Sitophobia
Graves	Taphophobia
Infection	Nosemaphobia
Lakes	Limnophobia
Leaves	Phyllophobia
Lightning	Astraphobia
Men	Androphobia
Money	Chrometophobia
Music	Musicophobia
Public places	Agoraphobia
Sex	Genophobia
Shadows	Sciophobia
Spiders	Arachnophobia
Sun	Heliophobia
Touch	Haptephobia
Trees	Dendrophobia
Walking	Ambulophobia
Water	Hydrophobia
Women	Gynophobia
Work	Ergophobia
Writing	Graphophobia

photomicrograph. A photograph taken through a microscope of an object so small as to be invisible to the naked eye.

photo radar. *See* traffic enforcement cameras

photostat. The trademarked name of a camera that makes copies of documents, letters, or drawings, on sensitized paper; also the copies made by means of this camera.

Rights for this method of copying were sold in 1940, and the practice waned through the latter half of the twentieth century. In modern times, this is a reference to an antique copy machine.

physical security. The portion of security concerned with physical measures designed to safeguard personnel; to prevent unauthorized access to equipment, facilities, material, and documents; and to safeguard equipment, facilities, material, and documents against espionage, sabotage, damage, and theft.

pickpocket. Generally, a professional thief who specializes in stealing valuables from the garments of victims without their knowledge. This type of larceny requires some degree of criminal skill, including dexterity and speed. *See also* Moran, Thomas

PIE (Prison Industry Enhancement). Created by the United States Congress in 1868, PIE is a private-sector certification program that permits some states to sell prison-made goods in the open market.

Pills Anonymous. Support and self-help group for people addicted to prescription and nonprescription pills. Address: 1849 E. Guadalupe Road, Suite C-101-133, Tempe, Arizona 85283. Web site: www.pillsanonymous.org/.

pimp. A procurer; one who profits from finding customers for prostitutes. One who operates a prostitution business. *See also* pandering

Pinkerton, Allan. (1819–1884). Son of a Glasgow police sergeant, Pinkerton emigrated to the United States in 1842 and is considered the first professional detective in the United States. During a series of railway and express robberies in 1850, he opened his own firm (with E.G. Rucker as a partner), the Pinkerton National Detective Agency. He also organized the secret service division of the U.S. Army in 1861 and was made its first chief. Later, while employed by the Wilmington and Baltimore Railroad, he saved Abraham Lincoln's life by uncovering an assassination plot directed against the president.

PINS/CHINS/JINS/MINS. Acronyms used to name a class of juveniles often consisting of status offenders but variously defined in different jurisdictions. The INS portion of the acronym means in need of supervision, and P = Person, CH = Child, J = Juvenile, and M = Minor.

piquers. Criminals who use sharp instruments to stab their victims.

piracy. An act of robbery or violence committed at sea by individuals or groups from armed vessels, who are not acting under the authority of a state. According to the United Nations International Maritime Organization, 4,821 piracy events occurred worldwide between 1984–2008. In 2008, a total of 51 ships were hijacked by piracy, leading to six (6) crew deaths, forty-two (42) crew members injured/assaulted and 774 crew members taken hostage/kidnapped. As of 2009, thirty-eight (38) crew members and one (1) vessel remain missing. *See also* International Maritime Organization

pirate. One who commits robbery on the high seas.

pistol. (1) In popular usage, any firearm, usually short-barreled, designed to be held and fired in one hand. Pistols came into use early in the sixteenth century, when the wheel lock first made them practical; (2) more precisely, such a firearm in which the chamber is an integral part of the barrel, especially a self-loading pistol, as distinguished from a revolver.

Pizza Connection. This case, investigated by the FBI in the early 1980s, involved the smuggling and distribution of heroin from Southeast Asia's Golden Triangle by various elements of the Sicilian Mafia. The proceeds from East Coast heroin sales were collected from pizza parlors in Queens, NY. The money was then deposited in commodities accounts held by New York City brokerage firms and frequently transported to banks in gym bags and suitcases. In addition, some of the cash, usually in small-denomination bills, was taken to Bermuda on private jets. Money was then wire-transferred from New

York and Bermuda to Switzerland and from there to Italy, where it was used to buy more heroin. It was believed that at least $25.4 million was laundered in this case between 1980 and 1982. In 1984, 38 individuals were indicted. *See also* laundering money; Mafia

placement. The commitment or assignment of a person to a facility, or to any supervisory care or treatment program, as the result of either official or unofficial actions.

plagiarism. Theft of another's written work and/or ideas—whether intentional or accidental—and subsequent presentation of those words or ideas as the thief's own. Common ground rules: (1) You cannot use another writer's exact words without using quotation marks and offering a complete citation, indicating the source of the words so that a reader could find it in its original context. (2) It is unacceptable to edit or paraphrase another's words and present the revised version as your own work. (3) It is unacceptable to present another's ideas as your own, even if you use completely different words to express those ideas.

plain arch. A fingerprint pattern in which the ridges come in from one side and go out the other without recurving or turning back, and in which there is a smooth upward thrust of the lines at or near the center of the pattern. *See also* fingerprint patterns

plaintiff. A person who initiates a court action.

plain view rule. A procedure that permits police who are conducting a search to seize contraband if it is in plain view of the officers. Evidence seized in such a way may be admitted in a trial even if the search as a whole is found to be illegal.

plain whorl. A fingerprint pattern consisting of two deltas and one or more ridges.

planning. The process of articulating expectations or goals using current and past data, and structuring or operating in order to achieve those goals. The most common types of planning are *Reactive planning:* a response

to an immediate event, which may serve as a guide to future action in similar situations; *Contingency planning:* a method of responding to anticipated accidents, disasters, or other extraordinary events; *Operational efficiency planning:* a review of existing procedures in order to improve them; *Short-range planning:* solutions for immediate problems; *Long-range* or *Strategic planning:* the setting of goals for at least five years and creating methods to achieve them. *See also* Program Evaluation and Review Technique

plant security. The protection of a business or industrial plant from fire, burglary, sabotage, theft, or liability.

plaster of paris. A powdery substance used in police work for making casts of impressions in the earth and other soft surfaces. Such impressions are usually caused by shoe or tire imprints. Plaster of paris is composed of gypsum and can be obtained in pharmacies.

plasticized white phosphorus (PWP). A common ingredient in incendiary devices, PWP is produced by melting white phosphorus (WP) and stirring it into cold water. This produces small granules that are then mixed with a viscous solution of synthetic rubber. All the granules become coated with a film of rubber and thus are separated from one another. This rubbery mass is dispersed by an exploding munition, but does not break up to the extent that WP does.

platoon system. The division of police officers or fire personnel into shifts, or platoons, each of which is on duty during certain hours of a 24-hour day.

plea. A defendant's formal answer in court to the charge contained in a complaint, information, or indictment, that he or she is guilty or not guilty of the offense charged, or does not contest the charge. Among the possible pleas are *Initial* or *first plea:* the first plea to a given charge entered into the court record by or for the defendant; *Final plea:* the last plea to a given charge entered into the court record by or for the defendant; *Not-guilty* *plea:* a defendant's formal answer in court to the charge(s) contained in a complaint, information, or indictment, claiming that he or she did not commit the offense(s); *Not guilty by reason of insanity:* a defendant's formal answer in court to the charge(s) contained in a complaint, information, or indictment, claiming that he or she is not legally accountable for the offenses listed in the charging document due to insanity at the time they were committed; *Guilty plea:* a defendant's formal answer in court to the charge(s) contained in a complaint, information, or indictment, admitting that he or she did in fact commit the offense(s) listed; *Nolo contendere:* a defendant's formal answer in court to the charge(s) contained in a complaint, information, or indictment, stating that he or she will not contest the charge(s), but neither admits guilt nor claims innocence.

plea bargaining. The practice involving negotiation between prosecutor and defendant and/or his or her attorney, which often results in the defendant's entering of a guilty plea in exchange for the state's reduction of charges, or in the prosecutor's promise to recommend a more lenient sentence than the offender would ordinarily receive. Plea bargaining was allowed by the Supreme Court in *Brady v. United States.*, 197 U.S. 742 and by the California Supreme Court in *People v. West* (1970). Alaska abolished plea bargaining in 1975.

pleadings. Pleadings in criminal cases are comparatively simple, and, contrary to popular opinion, reversals of criminal cases on appeal are very infrequent. The pleadings used by the state in felony and some misdemeanor cases are the indictment and the information; in other misdemeanor cases, affidavits and complaints; by the defendant, usually an oral plea of guilty or not guilty. Other pleas, such as "former jeopardy' "autrefois acquit," "insanity," or "alibi" are available or required in particular states. Pleas in abatement, demurrers, motions to quash the indictment, and in arrest of judgment are also available under some circumstances.

pleasure-pain principle. The utilitarian concept that people endeavor to maximize pleasure (profit) and minimize pain (loss); making the anticipated penalty greater than the expected gain is believed to deter people from committing crimes.

pledge, legal. The process in which a debtor puts up or turns over to the creditor certain property to be held until the debt is satisfied, with property title remaining with the debtor. The creditor must have a lien on the property.

plenary. Full; entire; complete.

poach. To trespass, or to take game or fish illegally.

podophilia (also called foot fetish). A type of paraphilia in which sexual gratification is derived from feet. Podophilia, the most common form of fetish, can include touching, smelling, tickling, licking or any other sensory interaction with feet, including "foot jobs" (stimulation of the genitals with feet). *See also* paraphilia

podular units. Separate jail or prison areas within the facility and containing cells and at least one common recreational area. Pods can house varying numbers of prisoners and are observed by a centrally located guardian.

poena (Lat.). Punishment; penalty.

pogrom. A massacre or wholesale slaughter spontaneously generated or incited and organized by a government or ruling class against a group of unarmed persons because of popular hatred or some sort of prejudice. It refers especially to the large-scale killing of Jews in czarist Russia, which from time to time was carried out by the governing class.

points of identification. In fingerprints, identical or matching ridge formations on more than one set of or copies of prints, used, for example, when comparing a latent print with known prints of a person. Eight to 12 matching points of identification are enough to establish that two or more prints were made by the same person; some courts require a minimum of 12 points.

poison. A substance that on being applied to the human body, internally or externally, is capable of causing illness or death by destroying or damaging vital functions.

Polanski, Roman (1933–). Highly acclaimed film director and recipient of multiple Academy Awards for his work, dating back to 1962. Polanski's initial noteworthy connection to criminal justice was the 1969 murder of his actress and pregnant wife, Sharon Tate, who was murdered in the couple's home by followers of Charles Manson. He withdrew from directing for two years following the murder, then resumed his career in 1971. In 1977, he was arrested for sexually assaulting a 13-year-old girl in Los Angeles. Polanski pled guilty, then fled the United States to avoid prosecution. Polanski remained a fugitive from 1977 until he was arrested in 2009 in Switzerland, where he traveled to receive a lifetime achievement award at the Zurich Film Festival. In July 2010, Swiss authorities rejected the extradition request and declared him a "free man. *See also* extradition; Manson, Charles

police. As a means of social control, agents of the law charged with the responsibility of maintaining law and order among citizens. The policing function began to emerge in connection with military operations, and particularly for military occupation of conquered territories. Civil policing made its appearance in the form of the first guard system established by Pisistratus, ruler of Athens from 605 to 527 B.C. The Vigiles of Rome, in existence from 63 B.C. to A.D. 14, was the title of the first police-fire integrated service under Caesar. With the decline of central authority, organized police forces disappeared in Europe until the late Middle Ages. Until well into the seventeenth century, civil authorities relied for the most part on the military to curb civil disorders. By the nineteenth century, most European nations were well on the road to developing modern professional police forces. These were usually centralized and under the control of an interior minister. England, an exception to this pattern, developed decentralized British police forces under the jurisdiction of local authorities. The reforms of Sir Robert Peel instituted in 1829 are seen as the beginning of England's modern police system. The United States, which traces its law enforcement system to colonial times, also has a decentralized police system featuring independent local, county, state, and federal agencies, each with a high degree of autonomy. Police in western Europe, as well as in many parts of Asia, Africa, and Latin America, are usually under complete central control. There are also several kinds of private, industrial, and railroad police. *See also* Peel, Sir Robert

police advisory boards. A citizens' group overseeing general policies of the police; sometimes organized on a neighborhood basis. *See also* civilian review boards

Police Athletic League. A program of police officers working with young people of the community. One of the first such programs was established by New York City's police department.

police bureau of criminal alien investigation, first. Started by the New York City Police Department on December 23, 1930. Its purpose was to bring to the attention of the U.S. immigration authorities any undesirable aliens subject to deportation under immigration laws, either because of their criminal records or their illegal entry into the United States.

police bureau of identification, first. Established by Captain Michael Patrick Evans on January 1, 1884, for the Chicago Police Department. At its inception, only photographs were used. On June 1, 1887, the Bertillon system of identification was adopted; on November 1, 1904, the Sir E. R. Henry system of fingerprinting was added. Evans was in charge of the Bureau of Identification from its inception until his death on October 6, 1931. *See also* Bertillon method; Henry system

police civilian review boards. *See* civilian review boards; police advisory boards

police commission. Generally a body of appointed community members, approved by council, functioning to establish police policy and to review operational practices.

police corruption. Behavior by a police official that is unethical, dishonest, or criminal. Corruption is generally manifested in nine specific areas: (a) meals and services, (b) kickbacks, (c) opportunistic theft, (d) planned theft, (e) shakedowns, (f) protection, (g) case fixing, (h) private security, and (i) patronage. *See also* Community Resources Against Street Hoodlums (CRASH); Rampart Scandal; Serpico, Frank

police court. A municipal tribunal that tries those accused of violating local ordinances, acts as a tribunal for the preliminary examination and commitment of those accused of graver offenses, and is essentially equivalent to the criminal court of a justice of the peace in rural communities.

police decoys. In decoy operations, nonuniformed officers pose as potential high-risk victims—drunks, tourists, young women, the elderly, and the disabled—in high crime areas in order to attract and apprehend street criminals. *Blending* involves the use of police officers, posing as ordinary citizens, who are strategically placed in high-risk locations to observe and intervene should a crime occur. Among the more effective decoy and blending operations was New York City's Taxi-Truck Surveillance Unit, launched in 1970 to combat the growing number of nighttime assaults on truck and cab drivers. From 1970 to 1975, this approach reduced those assaults and robberies by almost 50 percent. *See also* SWAT

police department. A municipal—city, town, or village—law enforcement agency.

Police Executive Research Forum (PERF). A national organization of police chiefs from larger jurisdictions, the forum seeks to improve the professional quality of police services through discussion and debate among members, as well as research and development. Since larger jurisdictions encounter special problems in law enforcement, PERF provides a unique insight into cities with populations between 100,000 and 500,000. Address: 1120 Connecticut Ave., NW, Suite 930, Washington, DC 20036. Web site: http://www.policeforum.org/.

police jury. The administrative board of a parish in Louisiana, equivalent to a county's police commission elsewhere.

police power. The authority to legislate for the protection of the health, morals, safety, and welfare of the people. In the United States, police power is a reserved power of the states, provided for in state constitutions. The federal government can legislate for the welfare of its citizens only through specific congressional powers, such as taxation and the regulation of interstate commerce. Police power is the most important power exercised by individual state governments. Although resting in the executive branch of government, police power has been largely dependent on the judgment of the judiciary. During the twentieth century, the increasing power of both legal corporations and criminal enterprises whose business crosses state boundaries has created a greater need for federal authority. The Eighteenth, or Prohibition, Amendment (1920) was the most extensive attempt to grant police power to the federal government. In recent years further attempts have been made to exercise police powers on both national and state levels.

police review boards. A citizens' group composed of representatives of particular ethnic, racial, or other groups whose task is to investigate allegations of police misconduct.

police state. A state (as a totalitarian state or one operating under a dictatorship) that confers special powers over the rights of individuals upon its ordinary or secret police or military, vesting them with discretion to arrest, detain, incarcerate, and sentence individuals without formal trial or forms of law, and that refuses to be bound by established canons of due process or by the principle that the rights of individuals shall be adjudicated in established courts of justice.

police traffic squad, first. The famous old Broadway Squad of New York City was organized in 1860. This was the first unit of the police department to have special functions in traffic regulation. The members of the squad were stationed on the sidewalks along Broadway, from Bowling Green to 59th Street, at the intersections of the cross streets. It was their purpose to escort pedestrians across the streets and to stop traffic while so doing. The pavement of Broadway was of cobblestones, and most of the traffic consisted of slow-moving, horse-drawn vehicles.

police training school, first. Begun on July 29, 1935, by the Federal Bureau of Investigation, U.S. Department of Justice. The courses, similar to those given in the training bureau for newly appointed special agents of the FBI, provided a program of training for local and state law enforcement officials and included subjects under the following headings: scientific and technical; statistics, records, and report writing; firearms training and first aid; investigations, enforcement, and regulatory procedure; and police administration and organization. The course of training lasted for a period of 12 weeks and was given without cost to those enrolled. The first class consisted of 23 students.

police unions. At the local level these are collective bargaining units representing certain classes of employees. Rank and file (labor) employees in a police agency generally include officer through sergeant. Higher levels are represented by management-oriented associations. In some states, police unions have the right to "meet and confer, in good faith, with city management on all matters relating to wages and conditions of employment" a radical departure from the traditional practice of chiefs of police serving as sole bargaining representatives. At the county level, municipal associations may affiliate and network for common purposes. Umbrella labor organizations exist at the state level, providing services smaller

departments cannot afford, such as legal representation, false arrest and other insurance coverage, medical/dental plans, arbitration, and lobbying. At the national level, such as the National Association of Police Organizations, they monitor and lobby for favorable federal legislation. *See also* Fraternal Order of Police; International Brotherhood of Police Officers; International Brotherhood of Teamsters; International Union of Police Associations; National Association of Police Organizations

Police Week. Second or third week of May, proclaimed since 1962; includes Peace Officers' Memorial Day, May 15.

political question. Issues in a case that the court believes should be decided by a nonjudicial unit of government.

poll the jury. A procedure in court whereby each juror is asked to state his or her verdict and is required to make it known.

Pollutant Standard Index. The U.S. Environmental Protection Agency and the South Coast Air Quality Management District of El Monte, CA, devised the Pollutant Standard Index to monitor concentration of pollutants in the air and inform the public concerning related health effects. The scale measures the amount of pollution in parts per million and has been in use since 1978. Also called Air Quality Index, Air Pollution Index.

pollution control. At the federal level, the responsibility of a DOJ office that supervises the prosecution and defense of civil and criminal cases involving pollution abatement and environmental protection. Much of the caseload includes civil and criminal enforcement actions under the various environmental statutes. The rest is composed of litigation in which regulations or permits have been challenged by industry or environmental organizations. Address: Environmental Defense Section, Land and Natural Resources Division, P.O. Box 4390, Ben Franklin Station, Washington, DC 20044-4390. Web site: http://www.justice.gov/enrd/index.html.

polyandry. The practice of a woman's having more than one husband. *See also* polygamy

polygamy. A form of marriage in which one person has more than one spouse at the same time. The practices is generally illegal. There are three forms of polygamy: polygyny (one man with more than one wife); polyandry (one woman with more than one husband); and group marriage (multiple husbands and wives).

On July 1, 1862, polygamy, which was practiced by the Mormons in Utah, was made a federal crime by an act of Congress. The attempted federal enforcement caused decades of strife. Finally, on October 6, 1890, the Mormon Church renounced the practice, and on September 7, 1894, President Grover Cleveland proclaimed pardon and restoration of civil rights for persons disfranchised by antipolygamy laws. *See also bigamy,* Edmunds Act , *monogamy, polygyny, and polyandry*

polygraph. (Also called psychophysiological detection of deception (PDD) or lie detector in common usage). An analog or computerized instrument that measures physiological indices for the purpose of determining if a person is telling the truth or is being deceptive. Most modern polygraphs have three capacities for recording anatomical responses: the pneumograph, for recording respiration; the galvanograph, for recording skin electrical-resistance changes; and the cardiograph, for recording changes in blood pressure and pulse rate. Polygraphs are generally used for four purposes related to criminal justice: (1) police interrogations of criminal suspects; (2) as a screening tool for law enforcement and national security jobs; (3) post conviction treatment and supervision; and (4) employment screening in the private sector. The accuracy of polygraphs is highly contested within the scientific community. *See also* FBI Laboratory; polygraph, police interrogation; polygraph, security screening; polygraph, postconviction treatment and supervision; and polygraph, employment screening

polygraph, police interrogation. The first police department to use the polygraph was that of Berkeley, CA, in 1934; more than 75 years have passed, and its use is still widely contested today. In the United States, no defendant or witness can be compelled to take a polygraph test. However, police departments often gain consent to conduct such examinations, which may be admissible under *United States v. Scheffer (1998)*. While the *Scheffer* ruling indicated "there is simply no consensus that polygraph evidence is reliable" (referring to the 1993 standard for scientific evidence set in *Daubert v. Merrell Dow Pharmaceuticals*), individual states can decide about the use of polygraph evidence (if it obtained legally). As of 2007, 19 states allow polygraph evidence at trial, and it is admissible by judicial discretion within the federal court system.

polygraph, security screening. The Employee Polygraph Protection Act of 1988 (EPPA) permits the use of polygraphs for prescreening high security job applicants, such as those seeking employment in law enforcement agencies, national security, private security service firms (armored car, alarm, and guard) and pharmaceutical companies. However, a 2003 National Academy of Sciences report examined the use of polygraphs for such high-security screening— which are arguably more accurate than polygraphs administered in the field for other purposes—and found most research on point to be highly flawed and biased. The NAS discouraged the use of polygraphs as a screening tool for national security and police employment, as there is little evidence to support their accuracy. These findings mirrored the findings of a 1983 study conducted by the U.S. Congress. Nevertheless, it remains an almost universal tool in preemployment screening for state and law enforcement agents, and those requiring national security clearances.

polygraph, postconviction treatment, and supervision. The use of polygraphs in postconviction treatment and supervision of criminal offenders is common, especially for sex offenders. For example, the use of a polygraph is a standard part of sex offender treatment practiced at Coalinga State Hospital in California. Research suggests the combination of polygraph and penile plethysmograph (PPG) is the most accurate recidivism predictor for this population. *See also* penile plethysmograph, polygraph

polygraph, preemployment. The Employee Polygraph Protection Act of 1988 (EPPA) prevents employers from using polygraphs in most cases (exceptions are for security and pharmaceutical positions). Polygraphs cannot be used for routine hiring or job applicant screening, nor may polygraph results be used to discipline or fire employees. However, the act permits "polygraph testing of certain employees of private firms who are reasonably suspected of involvement in a workplace incident (theft, embezzlement, etc.) that resulted in specific economic loss or injury to the employer."

Polygraph Association, American. The mission of the American Polygraph Association is to provide "valid and reliable means to verify the truth and establish the highest standards of moral, ethical, and professional conduct in the polygraph field." Founded in 1966, the organization now boasts 3,200 members. Address: P.O. Box 8037, Chattanooga, TN 37414; telephone (800) APA-8037. Web site: http://www.polygraph.org/.

Polymerase Chain Reaction (PCR). A four-step "Quick Test" method of nuclear DNA analysis. Polymerase Chain Reaction (PCR) typing can be used on much smaller samples of DNA than the RFLP test. The steps include: (1) DNA is extracted from tissue or fluids and purified. (2) The intact DNA is combined with short fragments of known DNA, called primers, and other chemicals that cause the DNA to be replicated. The primers cause only certain segments of DNA to replicate. With 30 cycles of replication, the amount of DNA increases 1 million times. (3) Small quantities of the replicated DNA are applied to 8–10 spots on a reagent strip, each spot containing a different segment of

known DNA. If the replicated DNA contains a segment matching the known segment, a blue color appears on the spot. (4) The pattern of spots from a sample obtained at a crime scene is compared to that from a suspect. The PCR typing takes a week or less; chances of identical results from two different people are between 1 in 500 and 1 in 2,000 with the PCR test. *See also* Restriction Fragment Length Polymorphism (RFLP) test. *See also* Deoxyribo nucleic acid; DNA analysis; Restriction Fragment Length Polymorphism (RFLP) test; PCR-based Short Tandem Repeat (STR) method; Amplified Fragment Length Polymorphism (AmbFLP) method; Short Tandem Repeat on the Y-chromosome (Y-STR); and mitochondrial DNA (mtDNA)

Polymorphic. To have several shapes or forms. Term used in DNA analysis to describe multiple possible variations on a specific DNA marker or loci. *See also* Deoxyribo nucleic acid; DNA analysis; Restriction Fragment Length Polymorphism (RFLP) test; Polymerase Chain Reaction (PCR); PCR-based Short Tandem Repeat (STR) method; Amplified Fragment Length Polymorphism (AmbFLP) method; Short Tandem Repeat on the Y-chromosome (Y-STR); and mitochondrial DNA (mtDNA)

Polymorphism. Existence of two or more phenotypes within a species. Term used in DNA analysis to describe multiple possible variations on a specific DNA marker. *See also* Deoxyribo nucleic acid; DNA analysis; Restriction Fragment Length Polymorphism (RFLP) test; Polymerase Chain Reaction (PCR); PCR-based Short Tandem Repeat (STR) method; Amplified Fragment Length Polymorphism (AmbFLP) method; Short Tandem Repeat on the Y-chromosome (Y-STR); and mitochondrial DNA (mtDNA)

Ponzi, Charles (1882–1949). During the 1920s Ponzi, a $15-a-week stock clerk in Boston, told acquaintances he had found a way to make money by buying postal coupons in Spain for 1 cent and redeeming them in the United States for 5 cents. He promised investors a 50 percent return on their money in 45 days and 100 percent in 90 days. In fact, he simply paid off early investors with money obtained from later victims. Within a year, Ponzi had taken $15 million from gullible people and moved into a palatial home. Since then, any operation that pays off old investors from new investors' money is known as a "Ponzi scheme." *See also* Ponzi scheme

Ponzi Scheme. A common type of investment fraud in which early investors are paid with money from later investors. The parties who set the "Ponzi" in motion gain, while later investors suffer loss. *See also:* fraud, investment; Ponzi, Charles

poor laws. *See* Law, Elizabethan Poor; law, poor

popular justice. Attempts by local communities to devise informal and nonbureaucratic alternatives to the official justice system. These alternatives may include unofficial neighborhood or community courts and community patrols.

population. *See* sampling

pornography. Often equated in general usage with the ambiguous term obscenity, pornography has not been defined precisely enough to withstand legal challenges and court tests. Most attempts to define it refer to the portrayal of particular sexual acts or to excessive violence in sex. The ambiguity was perhaps best illustrated in *Jacobellis v. Ohio* (1964), in which U.S Supreme Court Justice Potter Stewart conceded that hard-core pornography was difficult to define, but that "I know it when I see it, and the motion picture involved in this case is not that." A landmark case was *Roth v. Alberts* in 1957, in which it was ruled that, in general, laws forbidding obscenity are constitutional. A three-part test evolved to define what is obscene: (1) the dominant theme of the material must appeal to a prurient interest in sex; (2) the material must be patently offensive in that it affronts contemporary community standards; (3) the material must be utterly without redeeming social value. In 1972 the second and third

criteria were changed by the Supreme Court in a decision holding that community standards were to be defined locally rather than nationally, and that material need not be "utterly without redeeming social value" to be pornographic, but need only be lacking, when "taken as a whole in serious literary, artistic, political or scientific value." *See also* pandering

pornography received through the mail. Receipt of unsolicited sexually oriented ads can be halted by filling out Form 2201 at your local post office. A mailer who sends sexually oriented ads to any person whose name has been on this postal list for 30 days is subject to legal action by the U.S. government. Notice for Prohibitory Order Against Sender of Pandering Advertisement in the Mails can also be filled out to stop any further mailings considered "erotically arousing or sexually provocative." Contact the nearest post office.

poroscopy. The study of the arrangement and individual characteristics of sweat pores as seen in fingerprint impressions as a means of fingerprint identification. These sweat-pore characteristics are especially important when there is only a fragment of the fingerprint impression available.

portrait parle (Fr., lit.). A speaking likeness; a means of recording the descriptions of persons, used in France.

port warden. Also called port police. Individual or group responsible for protecting a port against all hazards and keeping it safe and secure. For example, the Port Police Section of the Los Angeles, CA, Harbor Department is responsible for protecting the largest port in the Western Hemisphere; the LA Port Warden has safety and security responsibility for land and water patrol of approximately 11 square miles (28 miles of waterfront).

POSDCORB. Acronym for the primary management functions of planning, organizing, staffing, directing, coordinating, reporting, and budgeting.

positive evidence. Evidence that directly proves the fact or point at issue.

positive law. Law consisting of definite rules of human conduct with appropriate sanctions for their enforcement, both prescribed by a human superior or sovereign; defined by English jurist John Austin (1790–1859) and others of the positive school of jurisprudence, which owed much of its inspiration to the French social theorist, Auguste Comte.

posse. A company; a force; a body with legal authority.

posse *comitatus*. (1) The power of the county. (2) The whole body (under common law, all male persons over 15 years of age) that the sheriff may summon to assist him in law enforcement; also, any group that is actually summoned.

Posse Comitatus Act of 1878. Prohibits the use of military personnel for the purpose of assisting civil authorities in the execution of civil law enforcement. However, this federal law does not prohibit the use of a state's National Guard or Air National Guard troops if their use is authorized by the governor.

possession. Having certain articles prohibited by law constitutes the criminal offense of possession, such as possession of narcotics by persons not legally entitled to have them.

possession, writ of. A term generally used to designate any writ by which the sheriff is commanded to place a person in possession of real or personal property.

post. (1) A position. (2) A place of assignment for an officer. (3) To record or make a record of. (4) Afterward in time; following. (5) Postmortem. (6) Abbreviation for commission of Peace Officers Standards and Training, such as the one established in California in 1959.

postal robbery. *See* Jesse James Act

postconviction remedy. The procedure or set of procedures by which a person who has been convicted of a crime can challenge in court the lawfulness of the conviction judgment or penalty or of a correctional agency action, and thus obtain relief in situations where this cannot be done by a direct appeal.

posterity. Future generations or descendants.

post facto (Lat.). After the fact.

posthumous. Occurring to an individual after his or her death. A posthumous child is one born after the death of the father. A posthumous pardon occurs after the recipient is deceased.

postmortem. (1) Subsequent to death. (2) An autopsy.

postmortem lividity. *See* lividity, postmortem

post obit (Lat.). After death.

post-traumatic stress disorder (PTSD). Historically called shell shock or battle fatigue syndrome. According to the DSM IV, PTSD occurs after exposure to a traumatic event, wherein the victim has: persistent re-experiencing of the trauma (via flashbacks, dreams, or intense response when reminded of the trauma), persistent avoidance and emotional numbing, increased arousal levels, duration for at least one month, leading to significant impairment in life domains. PTSD can be triggered by a crisis or trauma that is beyond the usual or typical range of human experience, such as war or other kinds of violence.

potency. A measure of drug activity expressed in terms of the amount required to produce an effect of given intensity. Potency varies inversely with the amount of the drug required to produce its effect—thus the more potent the drug, the lower the amount required to produce the effect.

powder, black. A propellant for firearms ammunition, composed of charcoal, sulfur, and nitrate of potassium. It was used in firearms of the past but has been largely replaced by smokeless powder.

powder pattern. The pattern of powder deposited on an object when fired onto by a firearm. At contact range there is little or no powder deposited and what is there is in a small circle. As the distance between the gun muzzle and the object increases, the size of the powder pattern increases until a distance is reached where the discharge of powder particles does not reach the object. *See also* powder pattern test

powder pattern test. A crime laboratory test of garments to determine the pattern of powder residue and thus determine the distance between the muzzle of the weapon and the person shot. It is a useful test in homicide cases, especially where suicide is suggested or alleged.

powders. Three types of powders are used in weapon loading: black, semi-smokeless, and smokeless. Smokeless powders are divided into two types; the first is known as bulk, meaning that its charge corresponds in bulk, or nearly so, to the charge of black powder; the second is the dense type, which means that it is denser and of much less bulk.

powder, smokeless. A modern gunpowder consisting primarily of nitrocellulose or a combination of nitroglycerin and nitrocellulose.

power. The ability to do or act; political or national strength; great or marked ability to do or act; legal ability, capacity, or authority.

power of attorney. An instrument authorizing a person to act as the agent or attorney of the person granting it.

power of Congress. Unlike a state legislature, the U.S. Congress has no inherent powers; instead it derives them, including the power to define and punish crimes, from the Constitution. Under the Constitution, Congress may define and punish crimes in the District of Columbia, U.S. territories, and elsewhere within the jurisdiction of the federal government.

power of municipalities. By the weight of authority, municipal corporations may, by ordinance, prohibit and punish acts that are not prohibited and punishable as misdemeanors under the general statutes of a state or that may involve a common law offense. In some jurisdictions, however, this power cannot be exercised in the absence of express legislative authority.

prearraignment lockup. A confinement facility for arrested adults awaiting arraignment or consideration for pretrial release, in which the duration of stay is usually limited by statute to two days or until the next session of the appropriate court.

precedent. Decision by a court that may serve as an example or authority for similar cases in the future.

precept. (1) A process or warrant. (2) A writ directed to the sheriff or other officer directing him or her to do something.

precinct. (1) A minor division for police administration in a city or ward. (2) A county or municipal subdivision for casting votes in elections.

precipe (Lat.). A document containing the particulars of a writ.

precipitate reaction test. A chemical test involving the reaction of two substances in solution that produces an insoluble (the precipitate). In criminal justice, this term often refers to crime laboratory analysis, such as to determine if blood is of human origin.

predatory crime. Illegal activity, usually but not exclusively sex offenses, robbery or burglary, in which the offender preys upon, exploits, attacks, or in another way takes advantage of the victim. Juveniles and the elderly are often targets.

predisposition investigation. An investigation undertaken by a probation agency or other designated authority at the request of a juvenile court into the past behavior, family background, relationships, needs, and character/personality of a juvenile who has been adjudicated a delinquent, a status offender, or a dependent, in order to assist the court in determining the most appropriate disposition.

preempt. To move into a field or area and take possession or jurisdiction with priority ahead of others.

prefrontal cortex. Region of the brain that includes the anterior frontal lobes (in plain terms, the area right behind one's forehead). This region of the brain is responsible for planning and decision making

preliminary hearing. The proceeding before a judicial officer in which three matters must be decided: whether a crime was committed, whether the crime occurred within the territorial jurisdiction of the court, and whether there are reasonable grounds to believe that the defendant committed the crime. *See also* jurisdiction

preliminary jurisdiction. A criminal court has preliminary jurisdiction of an offense and may conduct criminal proceedings with respect to the offense when the proceedings lead or may lead to prosecution and final disposition of the case in a court having trial jurisdiction.

premeditation. A design to commit a crime or commit some other act before it is done; deliberation.

preponderance of evidence. Evidence that is the most impressive or convincing of any offered; the burden of proof required in a civil proceeding, which is less stringent than the requirement of "beyond a reasonable doubt," which is the requirement for criminal proceedings. For example, former pro football player O.J. Simpson was acquitted of murdering his ex-wife and her friend in his criminal trial, when a jury could not find him guilty beyond a reasonable doubt. A civil jury, however, found him liable for the two murders when evaluating the case using preponderance of evidence, the lesser burden of proof. Preponderance of evidence is also the standard required at probation or parole violation proceedings.

prescription. (1) Acquiring some advantage or title to property by possession for specified periods of time. (2) In law, something proscribed by negative prescription, such as the time limitations within which prosecutions must be commenced after the commission of a crime, and after which such prosecutions are said to be prescribed, or invalidated. (3) a physician's order to have certain medical tests, procedures, or to take certain controlled medication that is only available with the physician's authorization. *See also* statute of limitations

presentence investigation. An investigation undertaken by a probation agency or other designated authority at the request of a court into the past behavior, family circumstances, needs, educational/employment history and character/personality of an adult who has

been convicted of a crime, in order to assist the court in determining the most appropriate sentence. Presentencing information may reach the court in various ways. For example, a confidential report may be prepared in addition to the usually public presentence report, or the defendant may submit information.

presentence report (Sometimes called presentence investigation report, or PSI). A report prepared from the presentence investigation to aid the sentencing authority in determining an appropriate sentence following criminal conviction.

presentment. Historically, written notice of an offense taken by a grand jury from its own knowledge or observation; in current usage, any of several presentations of alleged facts and charges to a court or a grand jury by a prosecutor.

President's Crime Commission. Officially known as the President's Commission on Law Enforcement and Administration of Justice, the commission was established on July 25, 1965, by President Lyndon Johnson, who "declared war on crime." The commission, consisting of 19 commissioners, 63 staff members, 175 consultants, and hundreds of advisers, studied most aspects of the crime problem and the machinery of criminal justice. The commission released a series of task force reports on the police, courts, corrections, juvenile delinquency, organized crime, science and technology, drunkenness, narcotics and drugs, and the assessment of crime, all of which were summarized in its general report, *The Challenge of Crime in a Free Society*. The commission introduced the *Crime Commission Model,* which applied the systems approach to the process of criminal justice. It provided a conceptual framework and focused on the flow of cases between agencies. The main shortcoming is that it portrays a single justice system, handling all cases the same. *See* wedding cake model

press, freedom of the. Guaranteed in the First Amendment of the Constitution. Until 1925, this guarantee was generally considered to apply against infringement by Congress. As a result of the Supreme Court's decision in 1925 in the case of *Gitlow v. New York* (268 U.S. 652), the free press clause of the First Amendment has since been applied to the states as well. The principle of the freedom of the press was originally set down in North America in 1734 in the famous trial of Peter Zenger.

pressure. The application of force by one body on another. In criminal justice this can mean (1) coercion or pressure from others to engage in criminal acts one is not predisposed to commit, (2) pressure during police interrogation, which may be grounds for exclusion depending on circumstance. (3) In ballistics, the force exerted in the cartridge chamber and bore of a barrel by powder gases is known as the pressure and measured in pounds per square inch. The amount of pressure permissible in pistol and revolver charges is governed by safety factors. *See also* hydrostatic shock

pressure alarm system. An alarm system that protects a vault or other enclosed space by maintaining and monitoring a predetermined air pressure differential between the inside and outside of the space. Equalization of pressure resulting from opening the vault or cutting through will be sensed and will initiate an alarm signal.

presumed dead. *See* artificial presumption

presumption. Inference drawn from some fact or group of facts.

presumption, legal. The law providing that the judiciary shall assume certain facts exist from a set of circumstances. These assumptions or inferred facts persist until disproven. *See also* presumption, rebuttable

presumption of innocence. The defendant is presumed to be innocent and the burden is on the state to prove his guilt beyond a reasonable doubt. *See also* burden of proof

presumption, rebuttable. A legal presumption that relieves the person in whose favor it exists from the necessity of offering proof; however, it can be disproven or rebutted. Such is the presumption of innocence of an accused.

presumptive evidence. (1) The presumption of incapacity in a minor to act, which is conclusive and irrebuttable. (2) Evidence that may be disproved or rebutted by other evidence. Presumptions of fact can be determined by the judge from the existing evidence.

pretermit. To intentionally pass by, disregard, or take no action concerning. In relation to a grand jury, it means the jury passes a matter before it without finding a true bill or no true bill. This is brought about by lack of agreement among the grand jurors or by the intentional act of the grand jury. The next grand jury may consider the case.

pretexting. The unlawful acquisition of personal data, such as credit card verification and personal identification numbers, via the telephone directly from the intended victim of identity theft. As the name implies, pretexting is often perpetrated under the pretext of a legitimate purpose, such as a bank calling to verify personal information for security purposes.

pretrial conference. A meeting of the opposing parties in a case with the judicial officer prior to trial for the purposes of stipulating those things that are agreed upon and thus narrowing the trial to the things that are in dispute, disclosing the required information about witnesses and evidence, making motions, and generally organizing the presentation of motions, witnesses, and evidence. The matters dealt with in a pretrial conference may instead be taken up in a procedure called an omnibus hearing. In criminal proceedings, this type of pretrial activity takes place before the trial judge following an arraignment in which the defendant has pled not guilty. It may include consideration of reduction of the charges.

pretrial detention. Any period of confinement occurring between arrest or other holding to answer a charge, and the conclusion of prosecution.

pretrial discovery. Disclosure by the prosecution or the defense prior to trial of evidence or other information that is intended to be used in the trial.

pretrial publicity. Media information about a crime, a defendant, or a forthcoming trial that is sometimes claimed by the defense to be inordinate, prejudicial, and precluding a fair trial. It is often used by the defense in its request that the place of trial be moved (motion for a change of venue).

pretrial release. The release of an accused person from custody for all or part of the time before or during prosecution, upon his or her promise to appear in court when required. *See also* bail, own recognizance. *See* Table 3. Types of Pretrial Release, page 36.

pretrial screens. Steps in the criminal justice process to apply quality control to police arrests and prosecutors' charges to reduce the number of unwarranted trials.

Pretty Boy Floyd. *See* Floyd, Charles Arthur

prevalence of crime. Criminality measured in a given population during a specified period of time. For example, the prevalence of juvenile delinquency in a city or state in 2010 is the number of juveniles in that jurisdiction in 2010 who have ever been judged delinquent, relative to the total number of juveniles in that jurisdiction at that time.

preventive pretrial detention. A procedure that allows an individual to be held in police custody without benefit of bail. The practice of granting bail originated in thirteenth-century English common law and is guaranteed by the Eighth Amendment. Historically, the only condition for denying bail in other than capital cases has been that the accused might flee in order to avoid trial. Preventive detention allows the courts to detain individuals without possibility of bail on another condition: that an accused might, if set free, commit serious crimes while awaiting trial. *See also* bail

prima facie (Lat.). At first glance; without investigation or evaluation. That which, if not rebutted, is sufficient to establish a fact or case.

prima facie case. One in which the evidence in favor of a proposition is sufficient to support a finding in its favor, if all the evidence to the contrary is disregarded.

prima facie **evidence**. Evidence that is sufficient to support a fact or group of facts.

primary classification. Historically, a term used in classifying fingerprints. A numerical value is given to each of the 10 fingers, and that value is entered in the classification formula after the major division, such as 1/1.

primary deviance. Term coined by Lemert in reference to instances of minor deviance that do not necessarily evoke the label of "deviant." This is in contrast to secondary deviance, which refers to deviance committed after internalization of the deviant label. *See also* secondary deviance

primary evidence. Primary evidence is that kind of evidence which, under every possible circumstance, affords the greatest certainty of the fact in question. Thus, a written instrument is itself the best possible evidence of its existence and contents. It means original or firsthand evidence, the best evidence in the case; the evidence that is required in the first instance, and which must fail before secondary evidence can be admitted.

primogeniture. A social system centering on the firstborn child among all children born of the same parents. In law, primogeniture is the rule of inheritance and succession by the firstborn, particularly the firstborn son.

principal. A person held accountable for a crime. The person who actually commits the crime is a principal. In some states, persons who aid or assist the principal in committing a crime are also considered principals, even though they did not actively participate in the crime itself.

principal and accessories. Parties concerned in the commission of felonies are principals or accessories according to whether they are present or absent when the act is committed. Principals are either (a) principals in the first degree or (b) principals in the second degree. Accessories are either (a) before the fact or (b) after the fact.

principal in the first degree. A principal in the first degree is the person who actually perpetrates a deed, either by his or her own hand or through an innocent agent.

principal in the second degree. One who is actually or constructively present, aiding and abetting another in the commission of a deed: (a) he or she must be present, actually or constructively; (b) he or she must aid or abet the commission of the act; (c) there must be community of unlawful purpose at the time the act was committed; and (d) such purpose must be real on the part of the principal in the first degree.

principal registration. An historical system of classifying and identifying fingerprints based on all 10 fingers of the hands. *See also* Integrated Automated Fingerprint Identification System; single-fingerprint registration

principal's liability for acts of agent. As a rule, no person is criminally liable for the act of another unless he or she has previously authorized or assented to it; consequently a principal is not liable for acts of his or her agents or servants that were not authorized or assented to, although they are done in the course of employment.

prison. A state or federal confinement facility having custodial authority over adults sentenced to confinement.

prison, history of. Prisons are a relatively recent development. Until the reforms growing out of the eighteenth-century Enlightenment, those convicted of crime were more often fined, banished, publicly whipped, or executed than imprisoned. Although colonial jails were established in the seventeenth century, they hardly resembled the institutions that the term *prison* implies today. Such places were solely for detention and made no pretense of rehabilitation. Prisons as they are now known in America and Europe had their beginning in the eastern United States in the early nineteenth century. They were intended to stress reform instead of punishments and to correct the poor conditions and inmate idleness that characterized the jails. It was no accident that the first prison in Pennsylvania

was called a penitentiary, for the prisoner was kept in complete isolation so that, alone with his Bible and work, he could do penance. Auburn Prison in New York opened in 1819. Here, prisoners lived in separate cells but worked in groups. First introduced at Lewisburg, PA, in 1932, the Lewisburg plan, also termed the telephone-pole design, resembles a telephone pole with its crossarms; cellblocks and workshops are at right angles to a central corridor. This design provides flexibility in layout and coordination of elements for control and supervision of the inmates. The long connecting corridor (the pole) extends from the administrative building past dining rooms and shops, and is bisected by cell blocks.

European prisons developed largely after the Pennsylvania model, but, for economic reasons, most American prisons in the nineteenth century were patterned on the Auburn model. They evoked criticism by reformers in the 1870s, the "golden age of penal reform." In this decade, the National Prison Association was founded, one of its principles being that "reformation not vindictive suffering" should be the purpose of prisons. These theoretical advances were not followed in practice, although one lasting reform was parole. Reform received renewed impetus in the 1930s, when the federal prison system demonstrated that effective programs of rehabilitation could be established if qualified personnel were recruited. The era after World War II brought more reforms. Changes in California were so notable that American prisons once again served as models for those of Europe. However, beginning in the 1970s, the United States moved back towards a crime control model, with more offenders sentenced to prison under mandatory minimum laws, with few rehabilitation programs. Beginning around 2000, many state and federal prisons began to reintroduce prison rehabilitation programs, many aimed at drug and alcohol offenders. The United States has 53 prison systems, made up of those of the Federal Bureau of Prisons, the 50 states, the District of Columbia, and Puerto Rico. *See also* prison reform

Prison-Ashram Project. Founded in 1973, this organization sponsors workshops in prisons and universities, and a pen pal project to match people on the basis of spiritual interests. (An ashram is an institution similar to a monastery, except that most residents stay for only a brief period of time.) *Publishes Human Kindness Foundation* (quarterly newsletter). Address: P.O. Box 61619, Durham, NC 27715. Web site: http://www.humankindness.org/prisonashramproject.html.

prison commitment. A sentence of confinement to the jurisdiction of a state or federal confinement system for adults, of which the custodial authority extends to persons sentenced to more than a year of confinement, for a term expressed in years or for life, or to await execution of a death sentence.

prison community. Social structure, relationships, and processes in a prison: the quality of staff-staff, inmate-inmate, and inmate-staff relationships; class stratification, informal group life, leadership, folkways in prisoner society, and the role of gossip and public opinion as means of social control; the processes whereby the guards become institutionalized and the inmates "prisonized."

prison, discipline in. All those measures used by the prison administration—the grade system, degradation and advancement in grade, privileges and denial thereof, isolation in cell or in solitary cells, "good time," and so forth—designed to promote good behavior in the institution.

prisoner. A person in physical custody in a confinement facility, or in the personal physical custody of a criminal justice official while being transported to or between confinement facilities.

prison escape, largest. In February 1979 U.S. Army Colonel Arthur "Bull" Simons (ret.) led a band of 14 to break into Gasre prison, Teheran, Iran, to rescue two Americans. Some 11,000 other prisoners took advantage of this event and the national chaos, in what became history's largest jail break.

prison farms. Farms for convicts, of four general varieties: (a) those owned by counties or municipalities where misdemeanants are committed who would otherwise serve short terms in a county or city jail; (b) those run as auxiliaries to state prisons, partially as a means of segregating a special group of offenders, as for example, first offenders or habitual offenders, and partially to provide meat and vegetables for the prison kitchens; (c) those privately owned in the South, to which the states leased convicts at considerable profit and which assumed the responsibility for guarding and disciplining the men and providing their food and shelter in return for their labor (most of such farms having been abolished because of abuses); (d) those owned and operated by a number of southern states, including AR, LA, TX, and MS, as a basic part of their prison system, to which prisoners are sent from a receiving center that assigns them to different farms, according to their types.

prison, federal. The collection of prisons organized under the Federal Bureau of Prisons, responsible for managing offender convicted of federal crimes. *See also* Federal Bureau of Prisons

prison statistics, federal. From 1950 to 1980, the federal prison population increased less than 40 percent. From October 1980 to May 1989, the population almost doubled, growing from 24,162 to 48,017 inmates in 67 facilities. In September 1992 the inmate population was 70,998, or 144 percent of capacity. By 2000, federal prisons housed 145,125 inmates, or approximately 120 percent of capacity. By 2009, the federal inmate population grew to 206,784 inmates. Drug offenders account for more than half of all federal inmates, representing 54.2 percent, 57.4 percent and 52.0 percent of the federal inmate population in 1990, 2000 and 2009 respectively. Immigration offenses, which represented only 0.8 percent of the federal prison population in 1990, soared to 11.1 percent in 2009. Similarly, weapons offenders comprised 5.8 percent of the federal inmate population in 1990, 9.1 percent in 2000, and 15.1

TABLE 38 FEDERAL PRISONERS BY TYPE OF OFFENSE, 1990–2009			
Type of offense	1990	2000	2009
Drugs	54.2%	57.4%	52.0%
Robbery	13.3	7.1	4.6
Property	7.4	5.7	3.5
Extortion, bribery, fraud	7.4	5.1	4.9
Weapons, explosives, arson	5.8	9.1	15.1
Violent	5.8	2.6	2.9
Immigration	0.8	8.8	11.1
Courts or corrections	1.0	0.6	0.3
Sex offenses	0.8	0.8	3.7
National security	0.1	0.1	0.1
Continuing criminal enterprise	1.1	0.5	0.1
All others	2.2	2.0	1.5
TOTAL NUMBER OF INMATES	58,659	145,125	206,784

Source: U.S. Department of Justice, Federal Bureau of Prisons, *State of the Bureau 1990, 2000, and 2009*

in 2009. During this same period, imprisonment for robbery and extortion represented a decreasing percentage of the federal prison population. *See also* Federal Bureau of Prisons. *See* Table 38. Federal Prisoners by Type of Offense, 1990–2009, this page

Prison Fellowship International. Founded in 1976 and devoted to Christian ministry, both in prisons and in communities, for the welfare of inmates, ex-prisoners, and their families. Publishes *World Report* (bimonthly). Address: P.O. Box 17434, Washington, DC 20041. Web site: http://www.pfi.org.

Prison Fellowship Ministries. Founded in 1976. Affiliated with the American Correctional Association; Economic and Social Council of the United Nations; Evangelical Council for Financial Accountability; and Prison Fellowship International. Sponsors in-prison seminars and Bible studies, and sponsors Angel Tree, a program to deliver Christmas presents to children of incarcerated parents. Publishes *Inside Out Magazine, BreakPoint,* and *Justice eReport* (quarterly). Address: P.O. Box 1550, Merrifield, VA

22116-1550. Web site: http://www.prisonfellowship.org.

prison, industrial. A term, more common in Europe than in the United States, to designate a prison in which the inmates carry on production of useful articles, with a minimum emphasis upon vocational or other training intended to prepare the discharged prisoner for life in society. The inmates are those who are looked upon as relatively hopeless for reformatory methods. Originally it meant a prison for those sentenced to hard labor, as distinguished from those sentenced to simple imprisonment.

prison industrial complex. A pejorative term used to describes the business that has become prisons, including the multiple organizations and people involved in the construction, operation, and promotion of prisons nationwide. Eric Schlosser, one of the first to write critically about this issue in the current generation, wrote, "The 'prison-industrial complex' is not only a set of interest groups and institutions; it is also a state of mind. The lure of big money is corrupting

TABLE 39   ADULT CORRECTIONAL POPULATIONS, 1980–2008

Adult correctional populations, 1980–2008

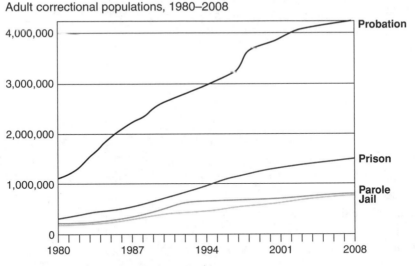

Source: Bureau of Justice Statistics Correctional Surveys.

the nation's criminal-justice system, replacing notions of safety and public service with a drive for higher profits. The eagerness of elected officials to pass tough-on-crime legislation—combined with their unwillingness to disclose the external and social costs of these laws—has encouraged all sorts of financial improprieties." This term is aligned with some critical criminological views on imprisonment, which often hold that high incarceration rates are not a function of high crime rates, but are due to the power differential between those who make laws (and benefit from high incarceration rates) and those who are affected by them.

prison information. General information is available on prisons, including statistics, such as percentage of population confined to institutions by offense, year, characteristics, and jurisdiction are available at the Bureau of Justice Statistics Web site: http://bjs.ojp.usdoj.gov/.

prisonization. The more indirect, negative effects of imprisonment—adopting, in greater or lesser degree, the values, orientation, and lifestyle of the prison subculture. *See also* prison psychosis

prison labor. As a tool within the correctional institution, labor by inmates has roots in both the retributive and rehabilitative philosophies. Some avow that prison labor should be as hard and unpleasant as possible, while others maintain that it should be useful and should train the inmate in marketable skills. Nearly all agree that it should be financially beneficial to the state. Methods of utilizing prison labor have ranged from a system of leasing prisoners and their labor to private users to a state-use system, in which the state retains control of the prisoners and their labor and alone uses their products.

Prison Ministry, International. Several organizations operate as "International Prison Ministries," which are generally non-profit, faith-based organizations that provide support and services to incarcerated persons. Examples include: International Network of Prison Ministries (http://prisonministry.net/); United Prison Ministries International (http://www.upmi.org/) and Prison Ministry International (http://www.prisonministryinternational.com/)

prison/parole population movement. Entries and exits of persons committed to prison, into or from prison facility systems into conditional release or supervisory programs.

prison psychosis. Historical term used to describe effects of incarceration on prisoners, manifesting in apathy, withdrawal, depression, rebellion, and violence. Personality changes of these sorts have been observed in prisons throughout the world. The longer the period of confinement, the more marked are the reactions. There is little opportunity for initiative; the prison atmosphere is repressive and the daily program, monotonous. Inmates are robbed of will. They compensate by day-dreaming and fantasizing or by marked aggressive behavior that sometimes takes the form of destroying everything in the cell. This kind of stupor or aggression has been labeled prison psychosis, a term not used to criticize its victims.

prison reform. Prison conditions in colonial America retained medieval characteristics. Punishments included whipping, the stocks, pillories, and dunking. Prisoners were confined to unsanitary quarters and not segregated by gender or age. The first prison reform society to bring about changes in prison administration was the Philadelphia Society for Alleviating the Miseries of Public Prisons, formed May 8, 1787, in the German School House on Cherry Street, Philadelphia, PA, by Quakers. The first president was William White. In 1791, the first penitentiary was established in Philadelphia. Overcrowded conditions, nevertheless, prevented any serious reform. It was not until the humanitarian revolt of the Jacksonian period that fundamental prison reform was undertaken. In 1824, the Auburn System of silent confinement was established. Correction houses and reform schools were founded to meet the special needs of juvenile offenders. By the opening of the Civil War, Auburn-type prisons had been established in all states except NJ and PA. The American Prison Association was founded in 1870 to carry out the ideas of such reformers as Enoch C. Wines and Zebulon R. Brockway. These leaders had been strongly influenced by the Irish penal system, which maintained rehabilitation rather

than punishment as the aim of imprisonment. In 1877, the New York State Reformatory at Elmira was opened under Brockway's administration to further this experiment. Youthful offenders were separated from hardened criminals and encouraged to reduce their terms through good conduct. Parole and probation were introduced to provide continuing supervision after release. The Elmira plan was quickly adopted in many northern and western states. In the twentieth century, psychology, psychiatry, sociology, and medicine have contributed to reform concepts in penology. These have emphasized occupational therapy, psychiatric care, social work, classification of inmates, the suspended sentence, and compensated labor. Post-release supervision has stressed adjustment to society through employment services, hospitalization, and family care.

prison riot. A temporary incident outside the normal operation of a prison, in which inmates rebel against guards or administration through collective defiance, often in response to a grievance or conditions of confinement.

prison riots, notable. In a four-day revolt in 1971 by 1,200 inmates of the Attica Correctional Facility in New York, prisoners held 38 guards hostage. During an assault by more than 1,000 NY state troopers and police to retake the prison, nine hostages and 28 inmates were killed. The New Mexico State Penitentiary Riot of February 2 and 3, 1980, is noted as one of the worst prison riots in U.S. history. The 36-hour rebellion claimed 33 lives and caused more than $50 million in damage. The penitentiary was restored to order by New Mexico National Guard troops, state police, Santa Fe County Sheriff personnel, and city police. From April 11 to 21, 1993, 409 maximum-security prisoners at the Southern Ohio Correctional Facility held five guards hostage. They surrendered after killing one guard and nine inmates. In April of 2007, the privately run Newcastle Correctional Facility in Indiana experienced a riot following the arrival of inmates from Arizona, under a contract between Arizona state prisons and the Newcastle private prison. The prison called in help from local police and fire departments to manage the riot. Once order was restored, nearly 100 inmates were transported to another facility and placed in segregation. A report on the incident focused blame on the Arizona prisoners and also the Newcastle institution, which was understaffed with "poorly trained personnel" and "very vague rules."

Prisons, Federal Bureau of, directors. First: Sanford Bates, 1930–1937; Second: James V. Bennett, 1937–1964; Third: Myrl E. Alexander, 1964–1970; Fourth: Norman A. Carlson, 1970–1987; Fifth: J. Michael Quinlan, 1987–1992; Sixth: Kathleen Hawk Sawyer, 1992–2003; seventh: Harley G. Lappin, 2003–present.

Prisons, Federal Bureau of, Library. A free publication, *Correctional Bookshelf,* is a bibliography of some of the books and periodicals in the library, covering such areas as administration and organization, programs for offenders, community corrections, jails, the prison social system, institutions for female offenders, and law and history. Reference and research services are also available. Contact: Federal Bureau of Prisons Archives, 320 First St., NW, Building 400, 3rd Floor, Washington, DC 20534. Web site: http://bop.library.net/.

prisons, receiving. Induction centers to which prisoners are sent for assignment to the particular prison or prison facilities that best suit them. Some prison systems have reception prisons; others have facilities at larger prisons. A reception center is designed to enable classification committees to assign each admitted offender to the proper custody, work, and education. During the period of reception, often called the period of quarantine or blackout dates, the offender is given any preventive and corrective medical attention necessary, interviewed for social and criminal background, examined psychologically, and processed for identification.

privacy, records. The Privacy Act of 1974 required the *Federal Register* to describe every system of records kept on individuals. There are five volumes devoted to explanations of these systems, including how a person can obtain copies of records. Further information can be found at this Department of Justice Web site: http://www.justice.gov/opcl/privacyact1974.htm.

privacy, right of. The right to be left alone; not to be interfered with as to conversations, activities within one's own home, or the possession and use of property. In 1983, a federal jury awarded $40 million to author-actress Jackie Collins for invasion of privacy by the magazine Alelina, which published nude photos in 1980 and incorrectly identified them as being of Collins.

private law. The law that regulates the relations of individuals to one another.

private probation. Post-incarceration monitoring owned and operated by private companies that contract with government agencies. Generally, private probation is a privilege, and as such, the fees are paid by the probationer.

private rehabilitation agency. An independent organization providing care and treatment services, such as housing or drug treatment, to convicted persons, juvenile offenders, or persons subject to judicial proceedings.

private right. A right enjoyed by the individual under law. Many such rights are enumerated in bills of rights of the federal and state constitutions.

private sector. In general, citizens' residential and business activities that are not part of the government or public sector. The first response to crime may come from any part of the private sector: individuals, families, neighborhood associations, business, industry, agriculture, educational institutions, the news media, or any other private service to the public. Public-sector involvement includes crime prevention and participation in the justice process once a crime has been committed and reported. Private crime prevention is more than providing private security, or burglar alarms, or participating in a neighborhood watch. It includes a moral commitment to stop criminal behavior by refusing to engage in it or condone it when it is committed by others. Citizens take part directly in the criminal justice process by reporting crime to the police, or by being reliable participants (such as witnesses or jurors) in criminal proceedings. As voters and taxpayers, citizens also participate in criminal justice through policymaking that affects how the process operates, the resources available to the process, and the process's goals and objectives. At every stage, from the original formulation of objectives, to political decisions about where to locate jails and prisons, the private sector has a role to play. Without such involvement, many feel that the criminal justice process cannot effectively serve the citizens it is designed to protect.

private security. A private patrol operator or operator of such a service within a premise's boundaries; a person other than an armored contract carrier, who, for any consideration whatsoever agrees to furnish, or furnishes a watchman, guard, patrolman, or other person to protect persons or property or to prevent the theft, unlawful taking, loss, embezzlement, misappropriation, or concealment of any goods, wares, merchandise, money, bonds, stocks, notes, documents, papers, or property of any kind or perform the service of such watchman, guard, or other person, for any said purposes.

private security agency. An independent or proprietary commercial organization whose activities include employee screening investigations, maintaining the security of persons or property, and/or performing the functions of detection and investigation of crime and criminals and apprehension of offenders.

privilege. A right or protection granted to persons in special statuses and not extended to others. Privileges may be held by the defendant, defense counsel, judge, spouse of the accused, and others.

privilege, absolute. A legal prohibition against prosecution for criminal libel, regardless of malice, generally limited to official participants in the governmental process.

This prohibition is based on the belief that the public benefits by having officials who are free to exercise their function with independence and without fear of litigation. *See also* libel and slander

privileged communications. Communication between parties with a confidential relationship, such that the communication's recipient is exempt from disclosure. No husband is compelled to disclose any communication made to him by his wife during the marriage, and no wife is compelled to disclose any communication made to her by her husband during the marriage. No one can be compelled to give evidence relating to any affairs of state, as to official communications between public officers upon public affairs, except with the permission of the officer at the head of the department concerned. In cases in which the government is immediately concerned, no witness can be compelled to answer any question, the answer to which would tend to discover the names of persons by or to whom information was given as to the commission of offenses. No *legal adviser* is permitted, whether during or after the termination of employment as such, unless with the client's express consent, to disclose any communication, oral or documentary, made to such legal adviser. The term legal adviser includes lawyers, their clerks, and interpreters between them and their clients. *See also* confidential communication

prize-promotion schemes. In such fraudulent schemes, the victim is typically told s/he has won a highly valuable prize, such as a car, or is a finalist for the prized item. The victim pays the fees or taxes associated with the prize but never actually receives it. *See also* telemarketing fraud

proactive. A broad criminal justice concept embracing the activities of planning, community involvement, and crime prevention with a view toward the future; as opposed to reactive.

probable cause. A set of facts and circumstances that would induce a reasonably intelligent and prudent person to believe that a particular person had committed a specific crime; reasonable grounds to make or believe an accusation.

probable evidence. Presumptive evidence.

probate. Proving and establishing a will.

probate court or surrogate's court. A state court having jurisdiction over probate (proving) of wills and administration of the estates of those who die intestate (without leaving a will), and supervision of financial matters relating to estates. In some states, probate courts have jurisdiction over the estates of minors and are thus called orphans' courts.

probation. The conditional freedom granted by a judicial officer to an alleged or adjudged adult or juvenile offender, as long as the person meets certain conditions of behavior. This form of judicial disposition was in use in all states by 1957. *See* Table 40. Sample Conditions of Probation, page 375

probation agency. A correctional agency of which the principal functions are juvenile intake; the supervision of adults and juveniles placed on probation status; the investigation of adults or juveniles; and the preparation of presentence or predisposition reports to assist the court in determining the proper sentence or juvenile court disposition.

Probation and Parole Association, American (APPA). Membership consists of practitioners in probation, parole, and community-based corrections from the United States and Canada. Publishes *Perspectives*. Address: APPA, P.O. Box 11910, Lexington, KY 40578. Web site: http://www.appa-net.org.

probationer. A person who is placed on probation and required by a court or probation agency to meet certain conditions of behavior, and who may or may not be placed under the supervision of a probation agency.

probation officer. An employee of a probation agency whose primary duties include one or more of the agency's functions.

probation revocation. A court order in response to a violation of conditions of probation, taking away a person's probationary

status and usually withdrawing the conditional freedom associated with the status.

probation supervisory caseload. The total number of clients registered with a probation agency on a given date or over a given period of time that have received grants of probation and are under active or inactive supervision.

probation supervisory population movement. Entries to and exits from the population for whom a probation agency has supervisory responsibility.

probation termination. The ending of the probation status of a given person by routine expiration of the probationary period, by special early termination by court, or by revocation.

probation violation. An act or failure to act by a probationer that does not conform to the conditions of his or her probation.

probation workload. The total set of activities required in order to carry out the probation agency functions of intake-screening of juvenile cases, referral of cases to other service agencies, investigation of juveniles and adults for the purpose of preparing predisposition or presentence reports, supervision or treatment of juveniles and adults granted probation, assistance in the enforcement of court orders concerning family problems such as abandonment and nonsupport cases, and such other functions as may be assigned by statute or court order.

probative value. Having value as proof; tending to prove or actually proving.

problem-oriented policing. A strategy to develop long-range plans to reduce recurrent crime and disorder problems and to assist in mobilizing public and private resources to that end. Requires the ability to analyze social problems, coordinate design solutions, appraise alternatives, advocate the adoption of programs, and monitor the results of cooperative efforts.

pro bono publico (commonly called *pro bono*). Translated from the Latin, "for the public good." The practice of voluntarily performing professional services without

text continues on page 376

TABLE 40. SAMPLE CONDITIONS OF PROBATION

INSTRUCTIONS:
1. Original to file
2. Copy to probationer

ORANGE COUNTY PROBATION DEPARTMENT
P.O. Box 10260, Santa Ana, CA 92711-0260

CASE NO. A- _____
COURT NO. _____

INSTRUCTIONS TO ADULT PROBATIONER

The Court Order made in this case is for your direction, guidance, and compliance. Only the Court has the authority to change this order. You are instructed to comply with the instructions of the Probation Officer.

You may be returned to the court or your probation may be revoked if the court "has reason to believe from the report of the probation officer or otherwise that the person has violated any of the conditions of his probation, has become abandoned to improper associates or a vicious life, or has subsequently committed other offenses, regardless whether he has been prosecuted for such offenses . . ." (1203.2 Penal Code)

In addition, you are instructed by the Probation Officer as follows: Probation officer to check appropriate boxes)

☐ 1. Report as required by the Probation Officer as follows:
     ☐ Once a month in person   ☐ Once a month in writing   ☐ or _____ in person.
     ☐ You are to report to the Probation Department the first Friday after release from custody.

☐ 2. Residence and employment to be approved by your probation officer. You are to notify your probation officer at least 72 hours prior to any change; giving new address where you are to be residing and employed. Also, give mailing address if different from above.

☐ 3. Do not associate with:
     ☐ Persons known by you to be illegal narcotic or drug users or sellers and stay away from places where users or sellers congregate.
     ☐ Minor children under the age of 18 unless in presence of responsible adults over 21 years of age unless approved by the probation officer.
     ☐ Anyone disapproved by Probation Officer.

☐ 4. You may not leave the state without the permission of your probation officer.

☐ 5. Registration: You are required by law to register pursuant to:
     ☐ 11590 Health & Safety Code   ☐ 290 Penal Code–Initial registration within 5 working days;
        within 30 days   re-registration, if residence changes, within 5 working days;
                                                                        annually, within 5 working days of birthday.

☐ 6. You are ordered to violate no law. Should you be arrested, you are directed to report such arrest to the Probation Officer immediately.

☐ 7. You are not to have firearms of any description in your possession during the period of probation.

☐ 8. Notify Probation Officer of all prescribed medication in your possession.

☐ 9. Other directions _____
     _____

☐ 10. Other directions _____
     _____

☐ 11. Other directions _____
     _____

Unless otherwise changed by Court Order, your probation will expire on _____.

I have received a copy of the Court's order and understand I must comply with the Probation Orders set forth therein. I have personally initialed the above boxes and understand each and every one outlined above. I hereby acknowledge receipt of and agree to comply with the above instructions.

Probationer: _____   _____

Date: _____   Deputy Probation Officer

F057-1117.12 (R6/98)   INSTRUCTIONS TO ADULT PROBATIONER

Source: Orange County Probation Department.

payment, generally to indigent persons who are in need of services but cannot pay for them. The American Bar Association recommends attorneys provide 50 hours of pro bono legal work annually, although the bar associations of several states recommend considerably less pro bono work.

procedural law. A branch of law that prescribes in detail the methods or procedures to be used in determining and enforcing the rights and duties of persons toward each other under substantive law. *See also* substantive law

procedural rights. Guarantees granted to every citizen by the Bill of Rights. Procedural rights are concerned with the methods by which citizens are protected against arbitrary actions by public officials. No one may be deprived of his or her life, liberty, property, or other rights except according to carefully stated procedures. No person may be tried or condemned without due process of law, and convictions may be rendered void if procedural errors occur. *See also* due process of law

procedure. Court procedure is a development from custom, while customs have their origin in the habits, mode of life, and special circumstances of the people among whom they prevail. The chief merit of any system of procedure lies in (a) the generality of its application; (b) the uniformity of its rules; and (c) the certainty of its course. Courts must adhere to established modes of procedure.

proceeding. Action in conducting judicial business in a court or before a judicial officer.

process. In law, generally defined as a means of compelling a defendant in an action to appear in court; a means whereby a court compels compliance with its demands, and, when actions were commenced by original writ instead of, as at present, by writ of summons, a means of compelling the defendant to appear by what was termed *original process,* so called to distinguish it from *mesne* or intermediate *process,* which was a writ or process issued during the progress of the suit.

The word process now commonly refers to all writs. The writ of summons is now used for commencing personal actions. Writs used to carry the judgments of the courts into effect and called *writs of execution* are also called *final process,* because they are usually issued at the end of a suit.

process in practice. A writ, summons, or order issued in a judicial proceeding to acquire jurisdiction of a person or his or her property, expedite the cause, or enforce the judgment.

procurement policy. An expressed or written statement that defines the terms, conditions, and other relevant criteria under which the user, such as a law enforcement agency, procures goods or services. In corporations, also called purchasing policy.

procuring. *See* pandering

productivity. A term used to describe the relationship between work accomplished and the resources used to accomplish it. The work to be done is often called input, while the results of efforts are called output. Productivity is measurable by a variety of means, and high productivity is often associated with job satisfaction or good morale. Frequent employee absence, overtime, turnover, disciplinary actions, and equipment abuse can all reduce productivity and/or indicate poor morale.

profession. Term often used to distinguish such careers as law, medicine, and theology from all other careers, which may be called trades, skills, labor, or by a variety of other names. In broader usage, the designation of any line of work as a profession depends on such criteria as: high admission standards, a specialized body of knowledge, advanced education, social acceptance, licensing, autonomy of performance, portability of skills, scholarly research and publication, lengthy training or apprenticeship, and trade groups or professional associations.

professional. In criminal justice usage: the humane constitutional application of legitimate authority in the best interests of the community; acknowledgment and adherence to the concepts and application of fiduciary trust and altruism; performance on the highest ethical plane.

professional crime. Regular participation in criminal activity that involves complex skills and relies on a specialized system of knowledge and organization. The *modus operandi* of professional crime usually emphasizes manipulating victims with cleverness rather than using force.

professionalization. Upgrading the standards of any occupation. In law enforcement, for example, professionalization includes rigorous admission standards, higher education, public acceptance, specialized training, ethical behavior, and a commitment to excellent community service and quality of life.

profiles, criminal. *See* National Center for the Analysis of Violent Crime

profiteer. One who demands and secures exorbitant profits in the sale of goods or services.

pro forma **(Lat.)**. For form's sake or as a matter of form.

Program Evaluation and Review Technique (PERT). A management technique of diagramming the logical, sequential steps in a program, operation, or function. This method, usually referred to as creating PERT charts, was applied to police investigations by Gilbert Burgoyne (LAPD ret.) in his application of VIA (Visual Investigative Analysis). *See also* link network diagrams

prohibition. Generally denotes the ban of alcoholic beverages containing 0.5 percent or more of alcohol. In a broader sense, the term applies to the ban by law of the manufacture and use of certain foods, clothes, and other articles considered injurious to the population. An example of a complete prohibition of the manufacture, transportation, and sale of liquor containing more than 0.5 percent alcohol was the Eighteenth Amendment ("The Great Social Experiment"), which was in effect from January 16, 1919, to December 5, 1933, when it was repealed by the Twenty-First Amendment. While it was in effect, Prohibition gave rise to organized crime and government corruption at all levels.

prohibition, writ of. In practice, the name of a writ issued by a superior court, directed to the judge and parties to a suit in an inferior court, commanding them to cease prosecution of the suit, because the original cause of the suit or collateral issue does not belong to that jurisdiction.

Project for Older Prisoners (POPS). Program operated out of George Washington law school that assists low-risk prisoners over the age of 55 in obtaining paroles, pardons, or alternative forms of incarceration. For more information, visit: http://www.law.gwu.edu/ACADEMICS/EL/CLINICS/Pages/POPS.aspx.

promulgate. To announce formally and officially or make known something such as a law.

proof. The method of establishing the truth of an allegation; establishment of a fact; evidence when used to establish a fact.

property. Property falls into two general categories: (a) real property, including things growing on, affixed to, and found in land; and (b) tangible and intangible personal property, including rights, privileges, interests, claims, and securities. The origin of the word property shows something about Western society's attitude toward possession. The Latin *proprius* means "one's own," and the French *propre* means "close" or "near."

property clerk. Law enforcement employee responsible for all property, lost or unclaimed, coming into police custody, and all evidence of crimes that is delivered to the police for safekeeping. Property unclaimed after a minimum of 90 days, or unclaimed evidence from crimes, upon disposition of the case and with the approval of the district attorney, is sold at public auction. Proceeds are generally turned over to the department pension or relief fund.

property rights. As developed in English common law and in the political philosophy of Thomas Hobbes and John Locke, this term refers to the right of ownership of private property against public restraint. Property rights, in the evolution of Anglo-American law, are now subject to public control when necessary to protect the public welfare. This has become particularly important in public utilities such as transportation, power, communication, and waterworks. Public restraints are based on reconciling police power with due process doctrines. *See also* Locke, John

proponent. One who makes a proposal; one who puts forward a document as a will for probate.

proprietary alarm system. An alarm system that is similar to a central station alarm system except that the equipment is located in a constantly manned guard room maintained by owners for their own internal security operations. The guards monitor the system and respond to all alarm signals, alert law enforcement agencies, or do both.

prosecute. To bring a matter or person into a court of law with a view to obtaining justice.

prosecution. (1) The conduct of a criminal proceeding before a judicial tribunal including all steps from the indictment or information to the final decision. (2) The party, usually the state, that conducts a criminal proceeding against an accused person.

prosecution agency. A federal, state, or local criminal justice agency or subunit whose principal function is the prosecution of alleged offenders.

prosecutor. An attorney who is the elected or appointed chief of a prosecution agency and whose official duty is to conduct criminal proceedings on behalf of the people against persons accused of committing criminal offenses. Also called district attorney, DA, state's attorney, county attorney, U.S. Attorney; any attorney deputized to assist the chief prosecutor.

prosecutorial screening decision. The decision of a prosecutor to submit a charging document to a court, seek a grand jury indictment, or decline to prosecute.

prosecutor's information. A written statement by a district attorney, filed with a local criminal court, accusing one or more defendants with the commission of one or more nonfelonious offenses. This accusation serves as a basis for prosecution.

prostitution. Offering or agreeing to engage in, or engaging in, a sex act with another in return for a fee. The California Penal Code defines it as anyone "who solicits or who engages in any act of prostitution (including) lewd acts between persons for money or other consideration." Prostitution is not illegal unless prohibited by state statute. Arizona is the only state in which prostitution is not banned, leaving the choice to each county in Arizona rather than prohibiting prostitution. Rhode Island then decriminalized prostitution in 1980, banned prostitution in December of 2009. The status of being a prostitute does not per se cause a person to forfeit any constitutional or legal rights. For example, a prostitute who has been raped can bring charges against the attacker. Prostitutes have created several special interest groups, such as COYOTE, Cast Off Your Old Tired Ethics (San Francisco), and DOLPHIN, Dump Obsolete Laws—Prove Hypocrisy Isn't Necessary (Honolulu). *See also* brothel; Fleiss, Heidi; madam; pandering

protest. Unconventional and often collective public action taken to show disapproval of, and the need for change in, some policy or condition. Protest may be aimed at the government, but it usually goes beyond voting to a variety of legal or illegal, peaceful or violent, forms of dissent.

provincial courts, criminal division. Criminal courts of limited jurisdiction located in urban areas in Canada.

provisional exit. An authorized temporary exit from prison for appearance in court, work furlough, hospital treatment, appeal proceedings, or other purposes that require absence with the expectation of return.

provocation. Incitement to commit an act.

provost marshal. A military officer whose duties correspond to those of a chief of police.

proxy. A person appointed to represent another; the document used by a shareholder or other individual authorizing someone to act on his or her behalf, such as in voting shares.

prurient. Having lustful interests or desires. This term is used in the legal definition of obscene or pornographic material.

psilocybin. Obtained from the so-called magic mushroom of Mexico, *Psilocybe Mexicana,* psilocybin is not as potent as LSD, but it can produce hallucinations and distortions of time and space at higher doses (5 to 15 mg). The drug was popular among Indians in Central America for religious use. Psilocybin sold on the streets is likely to be supermarket mushrooms sprayed with LSD or PCP.

psychedelic drug. Any drug with the ability to alter sensory perception. *See,* for example, LSD; psilocybin

psychiatric social worker. A professional who works with psychiatrists or psychologists to help patients with mental health disorders. Typical duties include interviewing patients and members of their families (interview reports are part of the background material used by doctors in diagnosis and planning treatment), counseling patients' families, and helping in rehabilitation programs. Required training for a psychiatric social worker consists of four years of college (B.S. degree) plus two years in an accredited school of social work (M.S.W.) and a period of supervised experience.

psychiatry. The specialized branch of medical practice that deals with the diagnosis, treatment, and prevention of mental and emotional disorders. A psychiatrist is a physician who is qualified through training and clinical experience in the specialty of psychiatry. Psychologists who work in criminal justice settings are called forensic psychiatrists.

psychoactive drug. Any chemical substance that alters mood or behavior as a result of alterations in the functioning of the brain. Classes of such drugs include:

Antidepressants, introduced in the early 1960s, are used to treat long-term clinical depression. Some common ones are tricyclic antidepressants (TCAs). They generally increase brain levels of norepinephrine, serotonin or both. First-generation TCAs Elavil (amitriptyline) and Tofranil (imi pramine) are used to treat depression and sleep disorders. Antidepressants that act to inhibit the enzyme monoamine oxidase are called MAO inhibitors. They increase the neurotransmitters that lead to emotional stability. MAO inhibitors can interact with hot dogs, cheese, alcoholic beverages, and other foods to produce dangerously adverse side effects. The newest antidepressants are serotonin reuptake blockers or serotonin uptake inhibitors. The best-known of these drugs is Prozac (fluoxetine). Lithium carbonate is still another type of antidepressant, often used to stabilize moods in bipolar disorder. *Antipsychotics* block the dopamine receptors in the brain. Also called major tranquilizers, they include: Thorazine (chlorpromazine), Trilafon (perphenazine), and Haldol (halperidol).

Antianxiety drugs, also called minor tranquilizers, act by depressing the limbic system and the gababenzodiazepine complex of the brain. Common examples are Librium (chlordiazepoxide), Valium (diazepam), and Xanax (alprazolam). This class of drugs is often misused, accounting for the majority of addicts among prescription-drug users. Stimulants, which were formerly prescribed as antidepressants and appetite suppressants, are now used primarily to treat both hyperactivity and narcolepsy. They can also supplement other treatments for depression. Common stimulants include Dexedrine, Ritalin, Cylert, and Pondimin.

psychological autopsy. A method of analysis used to determine state of mind of a person when a suicide is questionable.

psychological dependence. An emotional obsession or dependence of the mind; term generally used in reference to the compulsion to use illicit drugs that are not physically addicting.

psychological disorders. While mental health disorders are defined in the DSM, some psychological disorders are commonly associated with criminal justice. These include (see also): post-traumatic stress disorder, battered person syndrome, antisocial personality disorder, psychopathy, schizophrenia, and sociopathy.

psychological fact. In evidence, a fact perceived mentally rather than through documents or other physical evidence.

psychopathy. A life-long personality disorder characterized by absence of empathy, no conscience, and amoral behavior in a person who is able to appear normal. Although this term is not included in the current DSM-IV, it is clinically associated with (but separate from) antisocial personality disorder. Researcher Robert Hare developed the Psychopathy Checklist to screen for psychopathy, which is believed to be more prevalent in violent offenders than in the general population.

psychophysiological detection of deception (PDD). Term used by the U.S. federal government in reference to a polygraph. *See* polygraph

psychophysiology. Discipline that studies the physiological foundation of psychological process. Persons employed in this field often conduct research on the impact of emotional states on physical responses.

public defender. An attorney appointed by a court to represent individuals in criminal proceedings who do not have the resources to hire their own defense counsel. The appointment of public defenders is now required in most criminal cases as a result of the Supreme Court's *Gideon v. Wainwright* decision and later cases. Public defenders are not provided to defendants in civil suits.

public defender's organization. A federal, state, or local criminal justice agency or subunit whose principal function is to represent in court persons accused or convicted of a crime or crimes, and who are unable to hire private counsel. Since its beginnings in Los Angeles County in 1914, it has become the most typical method of representing indigent defendants in U.S. court systems. *See also* assigned counsel system

public interest disputes. Strikes that may jeopardize the national health and safety, or the public interest, such as strikes of police officers and firefighters, sometimes called emergency strikes. In order to protect the public in these situations, the emergency strike provisions of federal and state laws may be invoked. The Taft-Hartley Act provides for government intervention in such disputes.

public interest law. A term describing legal and quasi-legal (such as administrative) activities, rather than a branch of law. Such activities are undertaken to protect a sizable group of people or a community at large rather than a single individual; in this sense public interest law includes class action suits structured to spread legal costs among all affected people who are parties to the suit. Another definition of public interest law is the practice of law to accomplish social change. Major areas of such law have been environmental and consumer protection, but the term includes such traditional fields as legal aid. Consumer advocate Ralph Nader has been a leading figure in this type of legislation. *See also* class action

public law. (1) A general classification of law—the principal branches are constitutional, administrative, criminal, and international—that is concerned with the organization of the state; the relations between the state and the people who compose it; the responsibilities of public officers to the state, to each other, and to private persons; and the relations of states to one another. (2) A statute that applies to all people and in all locations in a state.

TABLE 41   GALLUP PUBLIC OPINION POLL ON THE DEATH PENALTY, 2009

Are you in favor of the death penalty for a person convicted of murder?

■ % in Favor   ▨ % Not in Favor

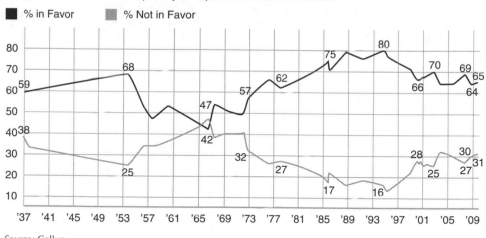

Source: Gallup.

public nuisance. An activity or set of conditions that negatively affects the rights, health, safety, or peace of others.

public opinion survey. A type of quantitative research instrument, usually conducted by telephone with random samples drawn from the population, to assess attitudes. Knowledge of the opinions of Americans on criminal justice issues is useful, for example, in revealing the public's mood and priorities, and such information may also assist in forecasting public pressure for legislative changes. *See also* Gallup poll; Harris poll. See Table 41. Gallup Public Opinion Poll on the Death Penalty, 2009, this page

public order offenses. Violations of the peace or order of the community or threats to the public health through unacceptable public conduct, interference with governmental authority, or violation of civil rights or liberties. Examples of such violations include prostitution, public drunkenness, minor weapons offenses, public sex, disturbing the peace, etc.

public relations. A specialty within the field of communications and/or marketing whose goal is to improve the public image of or promote public acceptance or support of an

organization or service or product. Primary public relations tactics include developing good relationships with media reporters and editors, targeting particular audiences within the public at large, staging news events, and generating publicity. Crisis public relations can be focused on helping an organization weather a problem situation such as bankruptcy or product tampering. Public relations conducted by large organizations is normally part of a larger communications program that includes marketing, advertising, lobbying, and customer, investor, and employee relations.

public safety department. An agency organized at the state or local level of government and incorporating, at a minimum, various law enforcement and emergency service functions. An example of this type of agency is the Canton, Michigan, Public Safety Department, which coordinates police, fire, and emergency management services within a single department.

public sector unions. Labor unions that represent employees in public service occupations, whose employers are generally local or state government. In 1962, President John F. Kennedy issued an executive order granting

TABLE 42   AMERICANS WHO BELIEVE INNOCENT PERSONS HAVE BEEN WRONGFULLY EXECUTED, 2009

How often do you think that a person has been executed under the death penalty who was, in fact, innocent of the crime he or she was charged with -- do you think this has happend in the past five years, or not?

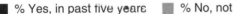

■ % Yes, in past five years   ▓ % No, not

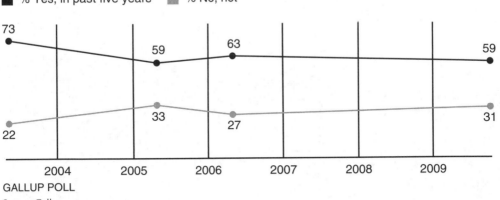

GALLUP POLL

Source: Gallup.

federal civil service employees the right to organize. Since the mid-1970s, public-sector unions have grown faster than those in the private sector. Public employees' unions differ from those in the private sector only in their types of employer and the tactics they use; many private-sector unions have members in public employment. Unions of educators, police, and firefighters are now common. Public-sector workers and their unions lack the protections granted by the National Labor Relations Act, and they cannot use the services of the National Labor Relations Board. Public employees are instead covered by various state labor laws, and at the federal level by the Civil Service Reform Act of 1978 and other legislation. Over 50 percent of federal employees are covered by collective bargaining agreements, and almost 40 percent at the state and local levels are so covered. *See also* collective bargaining

Puerto Rican Armed Forces of National Liberation (*Fuerzas Armadas de Liberación Nacional Puertorriqueña,* or FALN). An organization that advocated for the independence of Puerto Rico. Classified as a terrorist organization by the FBI, this organization is believed to be responsible for more than 100 bomb attacks in the United States between 1975–1983. In 1999, President Clinton offered clemency to eleven members, each of whom had served nearly twenty years imprisonment for federal conspiracy, firearms, and explosives convictions, on the condition that they renounce such violent activism.

pulling method. A safe-cracking technique involving a screw-type device with a long handle used by burglars to pull the combination wheel and its attached spindle from the safe. *See also* punching tool

Pullman strike. One of the most significant strikes in labor history, it began in May 1894 when the Pullman Palace Car Co. cut wages without reducing workers' rents in the company town of Pullman, IL. When the company refused to discuss grievances or arbitrate, Eugene Debs's American Railway Union joined the strike, and rail transportation in 27 states was paralyzed. The government used the Sherman Antitrust Act to obtain a blanket injunction against the union. Violence followed, and President Grover Cleveland sent federal troops to crush the strike. Debs emerged from jail a dedicated foe of American capitalism.

pump and dump scheme. A type of financial fraud in which the price of a specific stock is artificially inflated and misrepresented as more robust that it actually is. The intent in this kind of scheme is to sell cheap stock at an inflated price, leaving the buyer with nearly worthless investments.

punching tool. A tool used by safe burglars to batter away the safe lock and spindle so that the locking bars can be released and the safe opened. *See also* pulling method

punishment. In criminal law, any pain, penalty, suffering, or confinement inflicted upon a person by the authority of the law and the judgment and sentence of a court, for some crime or offense committed by him, or for his omission of a duty enjoined by law.

punishment, capital. Death penalty for crime; executions by the state for purposes of social control or defense. *See also* execution, methods of; lethal injection; electrocution; lethal gas; hanging; and firing squad. *See also* Table 24. Execution Methods in the United States, by State, 2010, page 173.

punishment, history of capital. A wide variety of crimes have come under the purview of the death penalty from ancient times to the present, and methods of execution have included hanging, crucifixion, quartering, beheading, gas, electric chair, lethal injection, and the firing squad. In England during the eighteenth century it was estimated that 240 crimes were punishable by death. Capital punishment was an early part of American colonial life. William Penn's Great Law of 1682, although essentially humanitarian, retained the death penalty for first degree murder. In the early 1840s reform movements such as the Anti-Gallows Societies and the National Society for the Abolition of Capital Punishment were formed. The first execution by electrocution occurred on August 6, 1890, at Auburn Prison, NY, when William Kemmler was put to death for murder. Caryl Chessman spent 12 years on death row in California before his execution in 1960. In 1972, the Supreme Court argued and decided three cases involving the use of capital punishment in a prejudicial manner. Each of the three petitioners was black and had been sentenced to death, with juries having

determined the sentence in each case. Lucius Jackson had been convicted of murder, and William Furman and Elmer Branch had been convicted of rape. All three eventually appealed their convictions to the Supreme Court. Prior to the ruling in *Furman v. Georgia* (408 U.S. 238), a total of 3,859 persons had been executed since 1930, when national statistics were first used. Of that total, 53.5 percent were black, lending credence to the charge that capital punishment had been used discriminately; only 32 were women. The largest single year for capital punishment in modern history was 1935, when 199 offenders were executed. The South used capital punishment more often than all the other regions of the nation combined—between 1930 and 1965, of 3,856 executed, 2,305 were in the South, 608 in the Northwest, 507 in the West, and 403 in the North Central states. The remaining 33 were federal prisoners. The last execution before the 1972 ruling took place in June 1967 in Colorado. *Furman v. Georgia* did not end the death penalty. In 1976 the Supreme Court in a 7–2 majority ruling (*Gregg v. Georgia* 428 U.S. 153)) upheld the constitutionality of new state capital punishment laws, which had been rewritten to avoid racial discrimination and to require separate consideration of the guilty-or-innocent decision and the penalty decision in potential capital cases. Convicted murderer Gary Gilmore was executed by a Utah firing squad on January 16, 1977, in the first exercise of capital punishment in the United States since 1967. Gilmore had opposed all attempts to delay his execution. At the time of Gilmore's death, there were approximately 450 persons under the death sentence, one in federal prison and the others in prisons in 23 states. Of that number, 233 had been sentenced to death in 1976, most under revised death penalty laws. In 2002 there were 3,557 death row inmates, and between 1977 and 2001, there were 743 executions. During those years, 270 died by causes other than execution, and 2,161 received other dispensation. In 2007, the U.S.S.C. considered the legality of lethal injection in *Baze v. Rees* (553 U. S. 35 (2008)), which effectively placed a moratorium on all executions in the United States while the case was pending. In April of 2008, the Court ruled that the 3-drug method of execution does not constitute cruel and unusual punishment, which effectively restored executions in the United States. In the remaining eight months of 2008, there were 32 executions in the United States, 18 of which were carried out in Texas. *See also* execution, methods of; death penalty rulings by the United States Supreme Court. See Table 24. Execution Methods in the United States, by State, 2010, page 173. *See* Table 21. Executions in the United States, page 132

punishment, corporal. (1) Bodily pain or suffering inflicted as punishment for crime, such as flogging. (2) The larger category of punishment that includes deportation or imprisonment, as distinguished from capital punishment or punishment by monetary penalty.

punishment, cruel and unusual. The Eighth Amendment to the Constitution says: "Excessive bail shall not be required nor excessive fines imposed, nor cruel and unusual punishment inflicted." Such punishment has been defined by the courts as those things that are cruel and inhuman, especially if such forms of punishment have not been specifically provided for by law; however, this definition is no guarantee that a particular punishment will not be determined cruel and unusual. The Court held that the use of convict guards in a penitentiary fell within this classification. Likewise, prison overcrowding which interferes with basic services (medical, mental health), is deemed a violation of eight amendment rights.

punishment, individualization of. Corrective treatment of offenders based on an analysis of the interrelated factors in the background and personality that led to the particular conflict with the law of each offender. Such treatment can be termed making the punishment fit the criminal rather than making the punishment fit the crime.

punishment, infamous. Punishment for what is held by society at a given time to be an infamous crime. The Supreme Court has decided that death, or imprisonment in a state prison for a term of years at hard labor, especially for treason or felony, are infamous punishments, and that disqualification for public office as a punishment for crime is infamous.

punishment, mitigation of. The reduction in severity of the sentence normally imposed for an offense because of some special aspect of, or surrounding circumstances in, the case.

punishment, purposes of. Criminologists generally reference four (or five) purposes of punishment. These are (see also) deterrence, incapacitation, rehabilitation, and retribution. Depending on the source and theoretical orientation, some also include restitution or reentry as a fifth purpose.

punitive damages. The awarding of damages in a tort action to punish the one at fault, usually but not always as a monetary award. Not all states allow such damages.

Pure Food and Drug Act. Federal law of 1906 supported by President Theodore Roosevelt in response to mounting criticism of the food preparation industries. It was passed in conjunction with the Meat Inspection Act. The food and drug act barred the sale or manufacture of adulterated or falsely labeled drugs and food involved in interstate commerce, while the meat act required federal inspection of meat plants engaged in interstate commerce. The campaign for the Pure Food and Drug Act had attacked the use of dyes and artificial preservatives in foods sold to the public. As early as 1898, public health officials banded together in the National Association of State Dairy and Food Departments to agitate for federal food controls, and in the Spanish-American War a huge public scandal over the "embalmed" beef supplied for U.S. troops aroused public outrage. However, the most effective propaganda came in 1906 with Upton Sinclair's shocking novel about the Chicago stockyards, *The Jungle*. Later amendments strengthened these reforms, and in 1938 the Wheeler-Lea Act required clearer labeling of food, drugs, and cosmetics and provided for prosecution of false advertisers.

push-out. Term that refers to a shoplifting practice wherein shoplifters fill up a shopping cart with items and goods to be stolen, and run past the registers and out of the store. Often, store clerks, who do not expect such a bold theft, are momentarily stunned, giving the pusher time to dump the contents of the cart into a waiting vehicle and leave.

pyromania. Usually referred to as pathological firesetting, the DSM categorizes pyromania as a type of impulse-control disorder characterized by the compulsion to start fires. This is distinct from arson or vandalism, which are generally characterized by malice and preplanning. Research from the 1940s introduced the "ego triad" of firesetting, animal cruelty, and enuresis (bedwetting), thought to be precursors to psychopathy and violent offending in adulthood (enuresis is no longer thought to be a predictor). *See also* MacDonald Triad

Q

quasi-judicial powers. Law-making powers granted by Congress to administrative and regulatory agencies. Although the doctrine of separation of powers calls for judicial powers to be exercised only by courts and judges, Congress can empower a commission or agency to hold hearings and make decisions that have the force of law.

quasi-military organization. Generally referring to law enforcement agencies modeled after the military: with strong emphasis on hierarchy, uniformity, chain-of-command, division of labor, accountability, and control. The structure is attributed to Sir Robert Peel, who in his Peelian Reform stated that police should be organized "along military lines."

Queer Nation. The organization formed during May 1990 in New York City after M-80 bombs were exploded in trash cans adjacent to a gay nightclub. Protesters formed a loose-knit organization dubbed Queer Nation that describes itself as "militant and uncompromising in the fight against homophobia in all its manifestations." *See also* ACT-UP

Questioned Document Examiners, American Society of. Founded in 1942, this organization aims "to foster education, sponsor scientific research, establish standards, exchange experience, and provide instruction in the field of questioned document examination, and to promote justice in matters that involve questions about documents." Address: P.O. Box 18298, Long Beach, CA 90807. Web site: http://www.asqde.org/.

questioned specimens. Physical evidence specimens, the origin or ownership of which is unknown; as contrasted with known specimens. For example, a bullet found in the body of a deceased is a questioned specimen, whereas one fired from a gun by an officer or a laboratory technician is a known specimen. The FBI Laboratory and some others number specimens and assign to each either a Q number, for questioned, or a K number, for known.

questionnaire. The most commonly used research tool to elicit information, in writing or by telephone, from respondents in surveys. Normally survey questions are carefully worded and ordered to avoid biasing respondents. Answers may be based on agree-disagree scales, rank-ordering of items, choosing preworded statements that most closely match the respondent's opinions, or open-ended questions requiring brief or one-word responses. All research questionnaires should be pretested for reliability and validity. *See also* Likert Scale; reliability

questions, lawful in cross-examination. When witnesses are cross-examined, they may be asked any questions that tend to (a) test their accuracy, veracity, or credibility or (b) damage their credibility. Witnesses have been compelled to answer such questions; the court has a right to exercise discretion in such cases and to refuse to compel such questions to be answered when the truth of the matter suggested would not, in the opinion of the court, affect the credibility of witnesses as to the matter to which they are required to testify.

quid pro quo (Lat., lit.). This for that; a phrase meaning a direct exchange of services or things of similar value.

quorum. A number or percentage of the officers or members of any body that has been determined as legally competent to transact business or make decisions on behalf of the entire organization.

quo warranto (Lat.). A proceeding requiring a person to show by what right he or she exercised any office or liberty.

R

racial profiling. Law enforcement practice of including racial and ethnic elements in determining whether or not a person is likely to have committed a crime. Although the practice has been used for centuries, it is criticized as being the basis of systemic discrimination in criminal justice. *See also* symbolic assailant

Racketeer Influenced and Corrupt Organizations (RICO). The federal RICO statute was enacted in 1970 and amended in 1986. Unlike other laws that address individual criminal acts such as murder or robbery, the RICO statutes were specifically designed to target overall and continuing operations of organized crime. RICO prohibits the use of racketeering activities or profits to acquire, conduct, or maintain the business of an existing organization or enterprise. Such activities are defined as any act or threat involving murder, kidnapping, gambling, arson, robbery, bribery, extortion, dealing in narcotics or dangerous drugs, fraud, and other crimes. The act provides for forfeiture of illegally obtained gains and interests in enterprises.

racketeering. The type of crime involving obtaining money illegally, especially through extortion, but also by bootlegging, fraud, or other criminal activities. In the twentieth century, racketeering became more common in large cities in prosecuting prostitution, gambling, liquor, and narcotics. Racketeering was vigorously enforced during the Prohibition era, when national gangster syndicates ruled over large empires of crime, extending their control into government, labor unions, and industry. Important rackets arose in poultry, laundries, milk, and other industries. Accompaniments to racketeering were bribes, bombings, assassinations, and corruption. *See also* Kefauver Investigation, mafia

radar. (1) Any of certain methods or systems of using beamed and reflected radio-frequency energy (radio waves) to detect and locate objects or to measure distance or altitude. (2) The electronic equipment, sets, or devices used in any such system. The term derives from the words *radio detection* and *ranging*. Most commonly police radar systems are used to detect speeding in traffic enforcement. The National Bureau of Standards has conducted tests in order to measure the reliability and performance of police radar systems. For further information on these tests, including details on devices that affect the reliability of radar systems, contact: National Bureau of Standards, Public Information Division, Department of Commerce, Washington, DC 20234.

Rader, Dennis Lynn (BTK Killer) (1946–). Serial killer who bound, tortured, and killed 10 people (hence the acronym BTK) between 1978–1991. Born in Kansas in 1946, Rader was the oldest of four brothers. Rader admits torturing animals as a child. After graduating high school, Rader attended one year of college and served in the Air Force from 1966–1970. Upon his discharge, he returned to the United States, earned his BS in Administration of Justice, gained employment at a security firm, and began killing. One noteworthy aspect of Rader's activities is that he maintained employment in the security field, including 14 years as Supervisor of his city's compliance department, zoning board, and animal advisory board. He was an engaged community member who was both a Cub Scout leader and president of his church congregation. Rader was identified as the BTK killer when, in 2004, he sent police a letter linking the BTK killer to a victim not yet attributed to him. DNA evidence from that lead, and additional clues from Rader's anonymous communication with police, led to his arrest in 2005. Rader pled guilty and was sentenced to 10 consecutive life sentences.

radial design. An architectural plan for penal institutions in which prisons are constructed in the form of wheels, with "spokes" or branches radiating from the center.

radical. One who advocates immediate and fundamental changes in governments and laws, especially laws relating to economic and social welfare.

radical criminology. A contemporary school of criminology that focuses on the political nature of crime and criminal law and that emphasizes the repressive function of the criminal justice system.

radicalism. A term derived from the Latin word *radix,* or root, radicalism literally means an attitude that goes to the heart or root of a problem or situation. Political radicalism represents an extreme difference from the point of view of those in power; that is, it questions the fundamentals of an economic or governmental system and implies advocacy of profound change in the institutions in question.

radio call letters. Generally those stations east of the Mississippi River begin with the letter "W" and the stations west of the Mississippi having the first letter as "K."

radio frequency motion detector. A sensor that detects the motion of an intruder through the use of a radiated, radio frequency,

electromagnetic field. The device operates by sensing a disturbance in the generated RF field caused by intruder motion, typically a modulation of the field referred to as a Doppler effect, which is used to initiate an alarm signal.

radio watch. Volunteer, mobile, citizen band (CB) radio operators and drivers who augment police surveillance and detection capacities. Screened CB volunteer operators are generally under the direct supervision of an official watch commander or supervisor and take no action other than notifying that official of suspicious activity or the location of a suspect.

railroad police. Largest private police group in the United States, numbering at least 10 separate organizations with an estimated 15,000 personnel in the United States and Canada, whose function is to protect the passengers, property, cargo, and reputation of the railroads.

railroad safety. The Office of Safety Programs inspects tracks, equipment, signals, and general railroad operations. It investigates accidents and complaints. Publishes a variety of safety reports, which includes a list of completed or pending judicial actions for the enforcement of any safety rules, regulations, orders, or standards issued. Address: U.S. Department of Transportation, Federal Railroad Administration, 1200 New Jersey Avenue, SE, Washington, DC 20590; web: http://www.fra.dot.gov/.

Railroad Strike. During the two-week Railroad Strike of 1877, service on two-thirds of the nation's rail lines in 11 states was disrupted, some 100 people died, and millions of dollars worth of property was destroyed.

Ramirez, Richard (1960–) (the Night Stalker). American serial killer responsible for more than a dozen murders and rapes with Satanic overtones in Southern California between 1984–1985. Unaware that he had been identified as the Night Stalker on August 30, Ramirez was recognized by an angry mob when he exited a Los Angeles bus on August 31, 1985. The mob pursued him, beating him into submission until police arrived. Ramirez was convicted of 13 counts of murder, five attempted murders, 11 sexual assaults, and 14 burglaries. He is awaiting execution in California. *See also* serial killer

Rampart Scandal. In 1998, two officers from the Rampart Community Resources Against Street Hoodlums (CRASH) unit came under scrutiny for beating and choking a suspect and covering up the abuse. Within months, another CRASH officer, Rafael Pérez, was accused of stealing nine pounds of cocaine from the LAPD evidence room. Perez testified for the prosecution in exchange for leniency, implicating widespread abuse in the CRASH division, including routine beatings, theft, abuse, falsifying reports, and cover-ups. The scandal included implications that several officers received money from Marion "Suge" Knight, CEO of Death Row Records with ties to the Bloods gang in LA; CRASH was also implicated in the 1997 murder of rapper "Notorious B.I.G.," Christopher Wallace. In all, nearly 70 officers were implicated, some of whom were indicted. The LAPD was named in more than 100 civil suits, which have cost the city an estimated $125 million to date. The scandal also called into question the validity of hundreds of convictions based on CRASH evidence, and to date, more than 100 convictions have been overturned as a result. The CRASH unit closed in 2000, amidst ongoing scandal. *See also* Bloods, Community Resources Against Street Hoodlums; Wallace, Christopher; Serpico, Frank

Ramsey, JonBenét Patricia (1990–1996). Six-year old girl found murdered in the basement of her home. Although the crime remains unsolved as of 2010, suspicion in the homicide centered around Ramey's parents, who were criticized for their promotion of their daughter in childhood beauty pageants, and her stepbrother, who was 9 years old at the time of her death. Two separate grand juries failed to indict the Ramseys. The case remains one of heated controversy, with some experts maintaining that the Ramseys got away with murder, and other equally qualified experts insisting that an intruder was responsible for the death, and the Ramseys have been wrongfully and relentlessly persecuted in the media.

Randolph, Edmund. Born in Williamsburg, VA, in 1793, Randolph served as the first U.S. attorney general under President George Washington from 1789 to 1794; he was secretary of state from 1794 to 1795, resigning after being falsely charged with accepting a bribe from France. Aaron Burr was his counsel and won an acquittal in Randolph's treason trial in 1807. He lived until 1813.

randomization. A technique for controlling variables that might confuse the relationship between the independent variable(s) and the dependent variable in an experimental situation. Randomization is accomplished by assigning the subjects to experimental and control groups in a random method, meaning each individual has an equal probability of being assigned to either type of group. This procedure guarantees with measurable probability that the characteristics associated with the individuals being observed, such as age, gender, or race, that might confuse or interfere with the relationship between the variables being tested, will be uniformly distributed among experimental and control groups.

ransom. The demanding of money for the redemption of captured persons or property.

rape. Unlawful sexual intercourse, by force or without legal or factual consent. Date rape is forcible rape in which the victim has consented to the company of the offender but has not agreed to have sexual intercourse. *See also* statutory rape

rap sheet. Popularized in many early crime movies and novels, rap is an acronym for record of arrest and prosecution.

Rastelli, Philip "Rusty" (1918–1991). Boss of the Bonano crime family prosecuted in the

1985 Mafia Commission Trial. Sentenced to 12 years in 1986, he was discharged from prison in July of 1991 for humanitarian reasons. He died of liver cancer in a New York hospital three days after his release. *See also* Mafia; Mafia Commission Trial

rate, crime. A measure of reported crime in given geographical areas or population groups, expressed in numbers proportionate to a population unit. Such rates may be crude (per 100,000 population), refined (per 100,000 persons capable of committing a crime), or specific (such as per 100,000 native-born males, 21–30 years of age). No generally accepted terminology to distinguish different types of rates exists. The unit of crime or criminality employed in computing these rates varies.

ratio level of measurement. *See* scale, ratio

rationalization. The process of explaining behavior or attitudes prompted by unrecognized motives; excuses or reasons that place the person in a more favorable light. In using this mechanism, an individual defends himself against truths that are uncomfortable or painful.

ratio scales. Measurement systems for intervals that have true, rather than arbitrary, zero points, allowing each outcome to be stated as *n* times greater or lesser than other outcomes. Fahrenheit and Centigrade scales both have arbitrary zero points, as do many other common systems.

Ray, James Earl (1928–1998). Convicted of assassinating Rev. Martin Luther King, Jr., in Memphis, TN, on April 4, 1968, Ray was the object of one of the most intensive manhunts in history when he was captured in London. Returned to Memphis, he initially pleaded guilty and then recanted his confession, claiming that he was victimized in a conspiracy. Sentenced to prison, he continued to deny his guilt until his death in a Nashville prison. By that time, he had convinced a group of Dr. King's heirs that the case should be reopened.

reaction time (RT). The interval between the beginning of a stimulus and the initiating of a response. For example, the length of time it takes to put one's foot on the brake is a measure of one's RT to a red light. The RT experiment was invented by the physiologist Hermann von Helmholtz more than 100 years ago.

real evidence. Evidence produced by actual inspection of material objects or physical characteristics.

reasonable man. Judicial review is sometimes guided by the precept that a "reasonable man" considering the evidence would make the same determination as the court. Reasonable-man standards are applied in administrative law matters and in determining patterned evasion of vice codes, racial equality laws, and other cases in which public sentiment may disagree with legal rules.

rebellion. The open, organized, and often armed resistance to government or authority. Like insurrection or revolt, rebellion does not imply the radical political and social changes of a revolution.

rebutting evidence. When the defense has produced new evidence that the prosecution has not dealt with, the court, at its discretion, may allow the prosecution to give evidence in reply to rebut or contradict it. When such rebutting evidence is given, the defense is entitled to comment on it. For example, evidence may be called to rebut or contradict an alibi.

recall. A procedure for dismissing elected officials before their term of office has officially terminated. *See also* impeachment

receiver. One who is legally appointed with custody of property belonging to others, pending judicial action; also sometimes an illegal activity, such as receiver of stolen goods, or fence.

reception. In criminal justice, the indoctrination and classification process used in the prison system for newly received inmates.

reception center. Correctional facility that performs intake functions for a system of prisons or jails. *See also* diagnosis or classification center

recidivism. The repetition of criminal behavior.

recidivism statutes. Laws that provide for increased penalties for persons who commit additional specific crimes after conviction for previous criminal acts. Included are career criminal and habitual criminal statutes.

recidivist. A person who has been convicted of one or more crimes and who is alleged or found to have subsequently committed another crime or series of crimes.

recognizance. Pledge by an individual charged with or found guilty of an offense to refrain from certain acts or to appear at a set time, usually in court.

record. (1) The records of a court: the formal history of the proceedings before it, entered by the clerk, which are the only evidence of what has been done by the court. They cannot be amended or contradicted. (2) A collection of information about an individual, including arrests and dispositions. (3) Any collection of data that pertains to a particular person, place, or thing.

record expungement. The process whereby a person who has a criminal record can request that the conviction be vacated.

"recovery-room" scheme. This type of fraud victimization is often perpetrated on victim who have been victimized by other telemarketing schemes. The recovery room scheme is generally based on the premise that the recovery company is associated with an official investigative or law enforcement agency tracking down the telemarketing fraud company that defrauded the victim in the first place. They convince victims that a court has secured their losses, which cannot be released until the victim files the proper fees. The victim pays the fee, but never recovers their earlier losses, thereby compounding the initial fraud. *See also* telemarketing fraud

recuse. (1) To challenge or object to a judge or other person officially involved in the trial of a case on the grounds that he or she is prejudiced, or has an interest in the case. (2) The nonparticipation of a judge or other official or person officially involved in the trial of a case because of personal interest, prejudice, or close relationship to an involved party.

redirect examination. The questioning of a witness, by the party who called him or her, after the witness has been cross-examined. In a criminal trial, the party offering a witness questions him or her first on direct examination. The opposing party questions on cross-examination, and the first party then questions on redirect examination.

Red Light Abatement Law. A California law enacted in 1913 and amended, stating that "any building or place used for the purpose of illegal gambling, lewdness, or prostitution is a nuisance that shall be enjoined, abated and prevented whether it is a public or private nuisance." Such abatement is a civil process, although contained in the penal code. This law has been a device to combat prostitution operating under the guise of massage parlors. If the police can show cause, the place of business can be closed for up to two years.

redress of grievances. The correction of abuses in the government of a state. The right of the individual to petition for redress of grievances, one of the oldest of British constitutional rights, is guaranteed in the First Amendment of the U.S. Constitution. Historically, such petitions were considered by the British parliament before it voted appropriations for governmental services.

Red Ribbon Week. A national, week-long campaign observed annually in October focused on the prevention of drug, alcohol, and tobacco use. *See also* Camarena, Enrique

reentry. Term that denotes the transition of offenders from prison to the community. The term encompasses efforts at treatment, education, housing, and vocational assistance aimed to ease the transition and provide former inmates with the services and support needed to refrain from criminal activity and resume a law-abiding life.

reeve. Historically, the top law enforcement officer of a district or shire in England. It was from "shire reeve" that the title sheriff evolved.

reflectoporn. Sexual practice that involves taking a naked photograph of oneself via a reflective surface such as a mirror or polished metal, then distributing the image in a public forum, often via the Internet. Reflectoporn reportedly began with the reflection of a naked man on a tea kettle auctioned on eBay. *See also* exhibitionism

reformatory. A correctional institution for youthful offenders; the term is based on the concept that juveniles who engage in criminal behavior can be reformed.

refreshing memory. A witness, while on the stand and testifying, may look at memoranda or other documents on any subject for the purpose of aiding his or her memory and recalling facts.

refugee. Traditionally a person fleeing his or her country to avoid persecution or hardship. Individual governments establish their own policies on the admission of refugees, despite the obligations imposed by United Nations conventions. Increasingly, states have begun to distinguish between political refugees, who are admitted, and those fleeing economic hardship, who are often refused entry.

regulation. (1) A rule or instruction to be followed by members of an organization. (2) Approved, accepted, or specified by the employing agency.

rehabilitate. To restore a person or thing to its original state or capacity, such as a slum area to a desirable neighborhood.

rehabilitation. A widely accepted but seldom achieved goal of penal systems, generally relying on three basic elements: (a) individualization—emphasis on the offender, not the violation; (b) indeterminacy—the release of the individual when cured rather than after a sentence has been served; (c) discretion—flexibility in managing the treatment of offenders.

Rehabilitation Act of 1973. Legislation covering recipients of federal contracts or financial assistance programs that prohibits discrimination on the basis of disability and requires affirmative action to include and accommodate disabled participants.

Rehabilitation of Errants, Citizens United for (CURE). Founded in 1972 for prisoners and former prisoners, their families, and others concerned with prison reform, CURE aims to reduce crime through reform of the criminal justice system. Address: CURE National, P.O. Box 2310, National Capitol Station, Washington, DC 20013. Web site: http://www.curenational.org/new/.

Reid, Richard Colvin (shoe bomber). (1973–). Born in South London, Reid's father was incarcerated for auto theft when Reid was born. Reid dropped out of school at the age of 16 and was arrested multiple times for minor offenses in the U.K. He converted to Islam in 1995 and began participating in extreme Islamic activities. In 1999 and 2000, Reid traveled to Pakistan and Afghanistan, where he reportedly received terrorist training by Al Qaeda. On December 11, 2001, Reid attempted to board an international flight from Paris to Miami, but he was delayed due to security concerns. He was permitted to board the flight the following day. During flight, Reid attempted to ignite his shoe, which was later found to contain sufficient explosives to cause the plane to crash. He pled guilty to eight counts of terrorism and is serving three life sentences in a federal super maximum security prison in Colorado. *See also* domestic terrorism; shoe bomber

release on own recognizance. The pretrial release of an arrested person on his or her pledge to reappear for trial at a later date, granted to those who are presumed likely to reappear. *See also* bail; Table 3. Types of Pretrial Release, page 36

release to parole. A release from prison by discretionary action of a paroling authority, conditional upon the parolee's fulfillment of specified conditions of behavior.

reliability. In statistical research, the consistency with which items are ordered on a measuring instrument to ensure that experiments can be replicated. That is, an instrument is reliable if, when no true change in a variable has occurred, items measured by the instrument will have the same relative placement in all experiments. *See also* replication

remand. *See* bind over

remedial. Curative, ameliorative; describes a level of social casework, group work, or custodial care that is above the merely palliative, in that the situation of the client becomes better than it was when the treatment was initiated and may even be brought into the range of average.

remission. In criminal justice, a release; pardon of an offense.

removal proceedings. A procedure used by the federal judicial system to transfer an accused from one judicial district to another, prior to his or her conviction for an offense. After a hearing on the matter, a federal judge signs a removal order, which authorizes a U.S. marshal to transfer the accused to another district.

reparation. The provision that a convicted offender make restitution to the victim in accordance with the damage the latter suffered. Thus, one of the conditions of probation in some jurisdictions is that the offender make weekly or periodic payments to the victim for the injury done.

reparole. A release to parole occurring after a return to prison from an earlier release to parole, on the same sentence of confinement.

repeal. The abrogation of a law by the enacting body, either by express declaration or implication by the passage of a later act whose provisions contradict those of the earlier law.

replevin. An action in court brought by an individual to recover possessions unlawfully taken or detained.

replication. The repetition or duplication of procedures followed in a particular study, in order to determine whether or not the findings obtained correspond to those of earlier studies. *See also* reliability

report. (1) The accurate recording of facts, usually transcribed in written form. (2) Data processing output that has high information content; more broadly, any planned and organized output from a system.

reprieve. The temporary postponement of the execution of a sentence, usually in order for an appeal to be brought.

requisition. In law, the demand made by one governor of another for a fugitive from justice.

research. An objective, painstaking, and careful investigation of a matter; a studious examination of a problem with a view toward finding facts.

research, applied. Scientific inquiry directed toward practical use or application.

research design. The strategy used by researchers to collect and analyze the data necessary to test hypotheses. Designing a study or experiment entails choosing the unit of analysis, determining the basic research method, selection and recruitment of subject, data collection procedures, and techniques for data analysis. The research methods most often used by criminologists are sample surveys, experiments, and field research.

research, pure. Inquiry directed toward the solution of a scientific problem of theory. The results may have no current practical application.

res gestae (Lat.). Events that speak for themselves; the words spoken by participants during an occurrence, rather than later in retelling; spontaneous words spoken during or immediately after an act, so that the speaker has no opportunity to rationalize or explain what was said. Any part of the *res gestae* is admissible as an exception to the hearsay rule.

resident. A person required by official action or his or her own acceptance of placement to reside in a public or private facility established for purposes of confinement, supervision, or care.

residential commitment. A sentence of commitment to a correctional facility for adults, in which the offender is required to reside at night but from which he or she is regularly permitted to depart during the day, unaccompanied by any official, usually for work, education, etc.

residential facility. A correctional facility from which residents are regularly permitted to depart, unaccompanied by any official, for the purposes of using community resources, such as schools or treatment programs, and seeking or holding employment.

resisting an officer. Active failure to comply, or obstructing a law enforcement officer in the performance of an official duty.

respondent. The person who formally answers the allegations stated in a petition that has been filed in a court; in criminal proceedings, the one who contends against an appeal. In research, anyone who answers a questionnaire or other survey instrument.

response time. The interval period between the receipt of information and the arrival of authorities.

restitution. A court requirement that an alleged or convicted offender pay money or provide services to the victim of the crime or provide services to the community.

restorative justice. A framework for justice reform that seeks to engage victims, offenders and their families, other citizens, and community groups both as clients of criminal justice services and as resources in an effective response to crime.

restraining order. An order, issued by a court of competent jurisdiction, forbidding a named person, or a class of persons, from doing specified acts.

Restriction Fragment Length Polymorphism (RFLP). Developed in 1985, the "Long Test" method of nuclear DNA analysis was termed the Restriction Fragment Length Polymorphism (RFLP) test. The RFLP test consists of seven steps: (1) DNA is extracted from body tissue or fluids, such as blood, collected from suspects and evidence. RFLP requires 50 nanograms of DNA. (2) The DNA is chemically cut into fragments using restriction enzymes. (3) The resulting fragments are placed in a gel and separated into bands by running an electric current through them, a process called electrophoresis. (4) The pattern, still invisible at this point, is transferred to a nylon membrane. (5) Radioactive DNA probes are applied to the membrane, which bind to matching DNA sequences. Excess, unattached DNA probes are washed away. (6) X-ray film is placed beside the membrane. The film is then developed, revealing a pattern of bands where the radioactive probe has bonded to the DNA fragments. This profile is the genetic fingerprint. (7) The final DNA fingerprint is a pattern of light and dark bands that looks like a supermarket bar code and is compared to DNA from other samples, such as blood found at a crime scene. This test requires much larger samples of DNA but is more definitive than the PCR test. The RFLP typing method takes four to six weeks. Chances of identical results from two different people are 1 in a million. This method has generally been replaced in favor of PCR-STR method. *See also* Deoxyribo nucleic acid; DNA analysis; Polymerase Chain Reaction (PCR); PCR-based Short Tandem Repeat (STR) method; Amplified Fragment Length Polymorphism (AmbFLP) method; Short Tandem

Repeat on the Y-chromosome (Y-STR); and mitochondrial DNA (mtDNA)

retaliation. The term applied to private vengeance for wrongs. The avenger attempts to make the offender suffer as much as the victim had suffered. The term carries the idea that punishment for an injury should be like the injury. *See also* revenge

retentionist. One who favors the retention or reinstitution of the death penalty, in contrast to the abolitionist, who favors its abolition.

retreatism. A mode of adaptation in Robert Merton's anomie theory in which the individual rejects both the goal of economic success and the legitimate means of attaining it. *See also* anomie

retreat to the wall. A phrase used in criminal justice to mean that an individual must avail him- or herself of any reasonable avenue of escape to eliminate the necessity of killing an assailant.

retribution. A concept that implies the payment of a debt to society and thus the expiation of one's offense is achieved through the vengeance of the criminal justice system. It was codified in the biblical injunction, "an eye for an eye, a tooth for a tooth."

reus. The individual formally accused of a crime.

revenge. The infliction of suffering upon an offender by a private individual who has been injured. It is a broader term than retaliation in that revenge has no limits as to kind or degree of suffering returned upon the offender. *See also* retaliation

reversal. The action of an appellate court in rendering judgment in a case under review that has the effect of invalidating a judgment of a lower court or tribunal or of requiring a new trial. Such action is usually based on an error by the lower court in interpreting the law applicable to the case.

Revia. Brand name for the generic drug naltrexone, used for the treatment of drug and alcohol addiction.

review. (1) A reexamination of some matter (as the findings of a board or the valuation of property by an assessor) by a higher officer or tribunal. (2) Reconsideration of applicable law in a judicial decision by a higher court.

review, writ of. A general designation of any form of process issuing from an appellate court and intended to bring up for review the record or decision of the lower court. In code practice, a substitute for, or equivalent of, the writ of *certiorari*.

revocation. In application to either probation or parole, the withdrawal of the privileges of either status because the behavior of the individual was in violation of the conditions agreed upon. In both instances, a body of case law has developed that defines the constitutional rights the probationer or parolee retains in revocation proceedings.

revolution. A far-ranging, pervasive, radical change in part, or in many parts, of society; the violent or nonviolent replacement of one power elite by another in the climactic phase of such a change.

ridge. A mark or line constituting part of a fingerprint.

ridge count. The number of ridges intervening between the delta and the core of a fingerprint. Ridges counted must cross or touch an imaginary line from the delta to the core. *See also* fingerprint patterns

Ridgway, Gary (1949–, Green River Killer). American serial killer responsible for the deaths of nearly 50 women in Washington in the years 1982–1998. Although he was a suspect as early as 1983, he passed a polygraph examination and was not charged. However, police retained DNA samples, which led to his arrest in 2001. Ridgway pled guilty to 48 murders in 2003 in a plea bargain in which Ridgway promised to help police locate victim remains provided he was not sentenced to death. Ridgway was sentenced to 48 consecutive life sentences plus 480 years and is currently incarcerated in Washington State Penitentiary in Wala Wala, Washington. *See also* serial killer

right of allocution. The right of the defendant to speak in his own defense before judgment is pronounced. *See also* allocution

right, political. Those individuals in the spectrum of political views who oppose drastic or radical change in society. Right-wing groups supporting the maintenance of the status quo are often termed conservatives, while those who advocate a return to an earlier set of conditions are termed reactionaries. *See also* conservative; leftists, political; liberals, political

Rights, Bill of. The first 10 amendments to the Constitution, prohibiting the federal government or, in certain amendments, the states, from interfering with political liberties and guaranteeing to persons charged with crime the protections of fair procedure. The Civil War amendments (Thirteenth, Fourteenth, and Fifteenth) are also commonly classed as part of the Bill of Rights. Most state constitutions also include the equivalent of the federal guarantees, and, when codified together, these are referred to as bills of rights. The phrase was used earlier in England in the course of the struggle between king and commoners and covers similar guarantees won by the people.

rights of accused. *See* rights of accused persons

rights of defendant. Those powers and privileges that are constitutionally guaranteed to every defendant.

right to bear arms. The right of citizens under the Second Amendment to the Constitution to possess arms in order to provide a militia. The courts have held that this right is not infringed by the Federal Firearms Act, or by statutes in most of the states that make unauthorized possession of lethal weapons a criminal offense.

right to counsel. A fundamental right of an accused person to be represented by an attorney at any stage of a criminal proceeding, including the rights (a) to have an attorney assigned as counsel by the court if the accused is financially unable to pay counsel fees, (b) to consult privately with counsel, and (c) of counsel to have sufficient time to prepare the case.

right-to-know laws. State laws that entitle genuine representatives of radio, television, newspapers, and magazines and certain other citizens access to official meetings, records, and other information. Although the First Amendment states that "Congress cannot make laws which threaten freedom of speech or freedom of the press," there is no enforceable constitutional right to know, nor is there any hard and fast regulation of what each branch of government and its agencies must disclose. *See also* Freedom of Information Act

right to release on bail. In common law it was within the discretion of the magistrate, judge, or court having jurisdiction and power to allow or deny bail in all cases. It could be allowed whenever it was deemed sufficient to ensure the appearance of the accused, but not otherwise, and was therefore always allowed in cases of misdemeanor, less frequently in cases of felony, and almost never in cases of felony punishable by death. It is now generally declared by the state constitutions, or provided by statute, that the accused shall have an absolute right to give bail in all cases except where the punishment may be death and in those cases, too, except where the proof of guilt is evident or the presumption great.

Rikers Island. Located in New York City, it is the largest penal colony in the nation. It consists of six facilities, each holding a separate population of offenders. The daily population of Rikers Island is about 14,000 inmates, plus an additional 5,000–7,000 guards on duty on a given day. Built in 1933 to house sentenced offenders, some of its cell blocks are the length of a football field.

riot. The coming together of a group of persons who engage in violent and tumultuous conduct, thereby causing or creating either a serious, imminent risk of injury to persons or property or public alarm. *See also* Draft Riots

Riot Act. A statute that originated in England for the purpose of dispersing unlawfully assembled persons. The statute states that if 12 persons or more are unlawfully assembled and disturbing the peace, they are guilty of a felony if they do not disperse within one hour when ordered to do so by a duly authorized officer.

riot-control agent. A chemical that produces temporary irritating or disabling effects when in contact with the eyes or when inhaled.

riot grenade. A grenade of plastic or other nonfragmenting material containing a charge of tear gas and a detonating fuse with short delay. The grenade functions and the gas is released by a bursting action.

riot gun. Any shotgun with a short barrel, especially one used in guard duty or to scatter rioters. A riot gun usually has a 20-inch cylindrical barrel.

riots, urban. Various uprising in metropolitan areas in the United State. Notable U.S. urban riots include the following. The anti-conscription (draft) riot of New York City from July 13 to 16, 1863, resulted in an estimated 1,200 deaths. The first ghetto riots in modern history occurred in the early 1960s in New York City's Brownsville, Bedford-Stuyvesant, and Harlem areas and were followed by the Watts riot in Los Angeles, CA, in August 1965. The Watts riot began with an alleged incident of police brutality and ended with 34 fatalities, 1,032 injuries, $40 million in property destroyed, 600 buildings damaged or demolished, and 4,000 arrests. By 1967 there had been 164 disorders (and 83 deaths); outbreaks of violence in Newark, NJ, and Detroit, MI, were especially serious. On April 29, 1992, following the reading of the Rodney King verdict, the nation's worst riot of the twentieth century broke out in an area of Los Angeles known as Mid-city. The three-day disorder spread from Hollywood to Long Beach, taking at least 53 lives, injuring 2,300 people, and damaging more than 1,100 stores, which were looted and/or burned. *See also* civil disturbances

"rip-and-tear" schemes. In an effort to avoid detection and prosecution, perpetrators of rip-and-tear schemes conduct their fraudulent calls from various locations, including pay phones and hotel rooms. Any number of schemes can be perpetrated this way, such as "prize promotion" scheme. The key here is that the perpetrator moves locations to avoid arrest. *See also* telemarketing fraud; prize promotion schemes.

ripping method. A method of opening safes by burglars. A can opener-type tool is used to remove the metal from the top, bottom, back, or side of a safe. *See also* pulling method

risk management. A business function that in large organizations is limited to the management of corporate property, liability, and casualty insurance and processing of claims. In smaller firms, risk management also includes loss prevention and loss control programs to contain employee or customer theft of merchandise and other company property.

Roberts, John Glover, Jr. (1955–). Born in Indiana, Glover graduated from Harvard University and Harvard Law School. Following law school, Roberts was a law clerk for William Rehnquist, then Chief Justice of the U.S. Supreme Court, subsequently working in the United States office of the Attorney General, Department of Justice, and Office of the White House Counsel before going into private practice. Glover was appointed as a DC Circuit Judge by President George W. Bush in 2003. On July 19, 2005, President George W. Bush nominated him as a U.S. Supreme Court Associate Justice to fill the planned vacancy of retiring Associate Justice Sandra Day O'Connor. Before Glover's confirmation, however, Chief Justice Rehnquist died unexpectedly on September 3, 2005; Bush withdrew his nomination for Roberts as Associate Justice and nominated Roberts as Chief Justice of the United States Supreme Court on September 6, 2005. Roberts was confirmed by the senate and sworn into office on September 29, 2005, the seventeenth Chief Justice of the United States Supreme Court.

robbery. The unlawful taking or attempted taking of property that is in the immediate possession of another, by force or threat of force. One of the largest amounts lost in a robbery was on November 25, 1983, when $35 million worth of gold in the form of 6,800 bars in 76 boxes were removed by six masked men from a vault of Brinks Mat Ltd. at Heathrow Airport, England. The greatest recorded train robbery occurred between 3:03 A.M. and 3:27 A.M. on August 8, 1963, when a General Post Office mail train from Glasgow, Scotland, was ambushed at Sears Crossing and robbed at Bridego Bridge near Mentmore, Buckinghamshire, England. The gang escaped with about 120 mailbags containing $6,053,103 worth of bank notes being taken to London for pulping. Only $961,654 was recovered. On April 29, 1985, $7.94 million in untraceable bills was taken from a Wells Fargo vault in New York City. The largest armored car robbery in the United States occurred in Jacksonville, FL, on April 4, 1997, when a Loomis armored-car driver fled with up to $20 million in used banknotes. The largest armed robbery was committed by five individuals in Los Angeles, CA, in September 1997. They escaped with $18.9 million in cash, in a takeover at Dunbar's armored truck depot. On June 18, 2001, Allen Pace III, a fired Dunbar Armored Co., security worker and mastermind of the heist, was sentenced to 24 years and two months in federal prison.

role playing. This procedure, which has a multitude of uses in clinical psychology, is widely used in sensitivity and therapeutic groups. The individual is required to adopt the role of another person and experience the world in a way that is not usual for him or her. This experience is designed to produce new insights into an individual's perception of his or her own behavior and that of others. Role playing has been effectively used, for example, in programs to establish better police-community relations. In such cases police play the roles of protesters, while protestors play those of police officers. This use of role playing is thought to increase empathy by providing individuals with some ability to relate to others' experiences. *See also* empathy

Roman legal system. A system that favored the interests of citizens with higher social status, similar to the Babylonian system. The law of the Twelve Tables (circa 450 B.C.) represented Rome's first attempts to codify the law and to satisfy the grievances of the lower classes; the tables set forth the citizen's basic rights. Roman procedure was highly formalized, with precise steps for filing courses of action and the drafting of pleas and remedies. After the fall of Rome, the Byzantine Empire, with its new capital at Constantinople, continued to develop sophisticated legal systems by codifying the Roman law. The Justinian Code (circa A.D. 530) consisted of four sections: the Code, the Digests, the Institutes, and the Novels. Adapting or absorbing previous laws, the Justinian Code represented a high point in reflective jurisprudence, revealing analytical thinking and authoritative commentary. The code later influenced the study of law in the first law school in Bologna, Italy, and at Oxford and Cambridge universities in England. Roman lawyers and magistrates also developed a system of equity, known as *jus gentium,* the law of nations. This system was to be used in cases involving foreigners. Although not equivalent to what we now refer to as international law, the system represents early attempts to solve conflict-of-laws questions. *See also* canon law; common law; Germanic law; Greek law; Mesopotamian laws and codes

Roscher system. A fingerprint classification system used through the 1990s, it was most commonly used Germany, where it was developed, and in Japan. *See also* fingerprint patterns, Henry classification, Juan Vucetich system

Rosewood Massacre. On January 1, 1923, a white mill worker's wife stated that her husband was assaulted by a black male. A posse was formed and marched to a small Florida town of Rosewood, the black section of town. When no suspect was found, the posse turned into a vigilante mob, pulling blacks from their homes and burning structures. The siege continued for six days with the mob growing to approximately 300 people. The official death toll was six blacks and two whites although it was alleged that many blacks were buried in mass graves. *See also* symbolic assailant

Routine Activities. Theory of crime proposed by Cohen and Felson (1979) which proposes three required elements necessary for a crime to occur: motivated offender, suitable target, and lack of a capable guardian. The omission of any one element will prevent crime.

Royal Canadian Mounted Police. The federal police force of Canada.

Ruby, Jack (1911–1967). Texas bar owner with reported mafia ties who killed Lee Harvey Oswald, President Kenney's alleged assassin, on November 24, 1963. Ruby's untimely murder of Oswald, who was in police custody when Ruby shot and killed him, has spawned debate about a possible conspiracy in the Kennedy assassination. Ruby died of lung cancer in 1967, awaiting trial. *See also* Oswald, Lee Harvey

Rudolph, Eric Robert. (the Olympic Park bomber) (1966–). Born in Florida in 1966, Rudolph moved to North Carolina with his mother and siblings after his father died in 1981. He dropped out of high school but subsequently earned his GED, and he attended college briefly before joining the U.S. Army in 1987. He was discharged for marijuana use in 1989. Rudolph committed four known bombings, including: the Olympic Park bombing in Atlanta, Georgia in 1996, which killed one and wounded 111; an abortion clinic in Atlanta in 1997, no casualties; a lesbian nightclub in 1997, wounding five; and an abortion clinic in Birmingham, Alabama in 1998, killing one and injuring one. Rudolph was a fugitive on the FBI's "Ten Most Wanted List" from 1998 until his capture in 2003. In a plea agreement to avoid the death penalty, Rudolph pled guilty and was sentenced to four consecutive life terms. He is incarcerated at the federal supermax prison in Colorado. *See also* Centennial Olympic Park bombing

rule of four. Prior to granting of *certiorari*, a potential case must pass the rule of four; that is, a case is accepted for Supreme Court review only if four or more members of the bench feel that it merits full consideration by the court. *See also certiorari*

rules. Social standards that are agreed upon by the members of a social organization and that concern acceptable and unacceptable actions but contain no moral implications.

runaway. A juvenile who has been judged by a judicial officer of a juvenile court to have committed the status offense of leaving the custody and home of his or her parents, guardians, or custodians without permission and failing to return within a reasonable length of time.

Rush, Benjamin. American psychiatrist, surgeon, and politician born in Philadelphia in 1746. After studying medicine at the University of Edinburgh, he became professor of chemistry at Dickinson College from 1769 to 1789. He was a signer of the Declaration of Independence. Regarded as the father of American psychiatry, Rush devoted much of his life to the reform of treatment for the mentally ill, particularly at Pennsylvania Hospital. Following his military career, he was the organizer and leader of the Philadelphia Society for Alleviating the Miseries of the Public Prisons, which was founded in 1787. In *An Enquiry Into the Effects of Public Punishment Upon Criminals,* 1787, he maintained that excessive cruelty served only to harden criminals. Opposed to capital punishment, he wrote *On Punishing Murder By Death* in 1792, condemning the practice as an offspring of monarchical divine right, a principle contrary to a republican form of government. Rush and his organization were influential in gaining penal reforms, including the establishment of the Walnut Street Jail, the first penitentiary. He is probably best known for advocating the penitentiary as a replacement for capital and corporal punishment. He lived until 1813.

S

sabotage. Willful acts designed to obstruct and interfere with the normal course of industrial operations by destroying their productive mechanisms. The purpose of sabotage in wartime is to interfere with the physical production of war goods. In labor, it is an intentional form of slowing or discontinuing production by using illegal and often violent means, sometimes including machine wrecking. The first recorded act of sabotage is said to have been the slipping of a workman's shoe into a loom to slow down production in the early days of the Industrial Revolution. In international law, sabotage may be punished by jail terms or death if the perpetrators are not lawful combatants.

Sacco-Vanzetti case. Celebrated trial and execution that has been considered a microcosm of the social, political, and economic issues of the 1920s. On April 15, 1920, two men were murdered in South Braintree, MA, in the course of a payroll robbery. On May 5, Nicola Sacco, a fish peddler, and Bartolomeo Vanzetti, a factory worker, were arrested for the crime. Both were Italian immigrants who were well known for their anarchist views. They were tried on July 14, 1921. From that time until their execution on August 23, 1927, the question of the justice of the trial, conviction, and execution of Sacco and Vanzetti agitated the country; the issue was whether or not members of unpopular minority groups are treated fairly by the American criminal justice system. To this day the case can arouse the most heated passions because the issue is still very much alive.

SADD. Founded as Students Against Driving Drunk, name changed to Students Against Destructive Decisions; see Students Against Destructive Decisions. *See also* MADD

Safer Society Foundation. National network/clearinghouse on sexual abuse prevention, assessment, and treatment programs. Address: P.O. Box 340, Orwell, VT 05733. Web site: http://www.safersociety.org/.

safe surrender law. Umbrella term for a variety of laws available in most jurisdictions which permit an overwhelmed parent to surrender their infants to designated facilities (such as hospitals and police stations). Such laws are designed to reduce infanticide. *See also* infanticide

Saint Valentine's Day Massacre. The murder of members of a gang of bootleggers in Chicago in 1929. This act against the "Bugs" Moran gang enabled Al Capone to consolidate his control in the city.

Salerno, Anthony "Fat Tony" (1911–1992). Boss of the Genovese crime family, Salerno was convicted of murder and racketeering in the 1985 Mafia Commission Trial. Sentenced to 100 years in 1986, Salerno died in custody in 1992. *See also* mafia; Mafia Commission Trial

saliva drug testing. The use of saliva samples to determine consumption of illicit substances in the preceding days/hours. *See also* drug monitoring, sweat patch, urine drug testing, hair testing

sally port. A double-gated security entrance into a jail or prison facility in which one gate is always closed. This permits identification, searches, and so forth, to be conducted before the remaining gate is opened.

salvia divinorum. A legal herb derived from a type of sage plant, salvia acts on kappa opioid receptors in the brain, causing periods of intense hallucinations which are relatively short in duration.

Sam Browne belt. A broad waistband of leather designed to carry police pistol, handcuffs, ammunition, and baton. The belt was designed by General Samuel J. Browne (1824–1901).

same act may be both a crime and a tort. In such a case the offender is subject both to a civil action by the state and to a civil action by the injured party. These two actions are separate and distinct; the object of the former is to punish as an example, of the latter, to compensate the injured party.

If the offense committed is a misdemeanor, either action may precede the other or both may be carried on at the same time. In case of a felony, the same rule applies generally in this country; but, in England and a few U.S. states, the civil action may not precede the criminal action. *See also* tort; Simpson, Orenthal James

same sex marriage. The legally sanctioned marriage of two persons of the same sex. Same sex marriage is not federally recognized in the United States, same-sex marriage is permitted in five states: Connecticut, Iowa, Massachusetts, New Hampshire, and Vermont. As of 2010, only a handful of nations have laws that afford equivalent status for same-sex and opposite-sex marriage.

sample. A part of a thing presented as evidence of the quality of the whole; a specimen.

sampling. The technique by which a researcher chooses some subset of a prespecified population to observe and measure, as a statistically valid representative group of the whole. A population is the aggregate of all individuals having some designated set of characteristics, such as all parents of pre-schoolers in Chicago or all inmates of Rikers Island Penitentiary.

sanction. A legal penalty assessed for the violation of law. Sanctions can include censure, community service, fines, forfeiture, suspension of privileges, probation, or incarceration. The term also includes social methods of obtaining compliance, such as peer pressure and public opinion.

sanctioned. (1) Socially permitted or approved. (2) Subject to social, particularly legal or conventional, restraints, prohibitions, or penalties.

sanity hearing. A procedure, ordered by the court or other official, for the purpose of determining whether a person is sane and legally capable of being held responsible for offenses.

sans (Fr.). Without.

satanic cult. A group of individuals usually allied with a charismatic leader who leads them to believe in him or her as a visible deity. The term also describes practitioners of satanic beliefs and black-mass worship. Practitioners believe that Satan was an archangel who protected the throne of God, and that because of his rebellious attitude, he and many other "fallen angels" were cast out of heaven. *See also* Church of Satan; Crowley, Aleister

satisfactory evidence. Evidence that is sufficient to produce a belief that a thing is true; credible evidence; evidence that is, in respect to its amount or weight, adequate or sufficient to justify the court or jury in adopting the conclusion in support of which it is adduced.

saving clause. An exception of a special thing out of general things mentioned in a statute.

Savings and Loan Crisis. Term that refers to the failure of hundreds of "savings and loan" institutions in the United States between approximately 1985–1992. The crisis was caused by a combination of factors, including federal deregulation and unsafe banking practices. In all, nearly 750 S & Ls failed and nearly 1,000 more received federal bail-out money, resulting in an estimated $160 billion loss, covered largely by state and federal insurance. The debacle is believed to be a key cause of the recession in the 1990s. *See also* Keating, Charles; Keating Five, Lincoln Savings and Loan

scaffold. A platform on which convicted criminals are executed by being hanged. Also termed the gallows.

scale, nominal. Nominal scales exist when one can say only whether or not the outcomes of a group of variables can be placed in the same measurement class; if response options are given on a nominal variable, they must be both exhaustive (cover all possible options) and mutually exclusive (the values cannot overlap). *See also* measurement, levels of; scale, interval; scale, ordinal; scale, ratio

scale, ordinal. An ordinal scale exists when, in addition to being able to establish equality among observations, one can say whether or not a particular outcome is greater than, less than, or equal to another outcome. Options on ordinal scales must be exhaustive, exclusive, and rank ordered. *See also* measurement, levels of; scale, interval; scale, nominal; scale, ratio

scale, interval. Interval scales, in addition to being able to order variable outcomes from low to high, can indicate by exactly how many units an outcome is greater or lesser than others, although the zero point for such comparisons is an arbitrary one. Thus, options on interval scales must be exhaustive, exclusive, distinguishable in rank, and values must be separated by equal units. *See also* measurement, levels of; scale, ordinal; scale, nominal; scale, ratio

scale, ratio. Ratio scales not only have equal intervals between values, as do interval scales, but they also have true rather than arbitrary zero points. Ratio variables must be exhaustive, exclusive, rank ordered, separated by equal units and have a "true zero" point. *See also* measurement, levels of; scale, ordinal; scale, nominal; scale, interval

scapegoat. A person or community that is made the undeserving object of aggressive energies of others, which are generated by the need to place blame for misfortunes they have experienced. The term derives from the goat allowed to escape after a Jewish chief priest had symbolically laid the sins of the people on it. (Lev. 16)

Scared Straight. On November 2, 1978, the film "Scared Straight!" was shown for the first time on public television (KTLA, Los Angeles). It showed the inside of the maximum-security state prison in Rahway, NJ, and followed 17 juvenile offenders "as they learn, at first hand, about the realities of prison life." The program won the Academy Award for best documentary in April 1979.

scatophilia (also called Scat). Paraphilia involving sexual pleasure from feces. *See also* coprophilia

schizophrenia. A mental illness characterized by delusions, hallucinations, disordered (confused) thinking and speech, bizarre or disorganized behavior, and inappropriate matching of emotion to context.

scientific management. The branch of classical management theory associated with U.S. industrial engineer Frederick Winslow Taylor (1856–1915). Taylor studied the physiological principles of work and was primarily concerned with discovering methods to improve efficiency and productivity. Techniques included detailed task performance instructions, extensive supervisory control, and economic incentives. In this model, workers were viewed as analogous to complex machines that must be well-programmed if they are to produce efficiently.

scintilla of evidence. A spark or shred of evidence. Any material evidence that, if true, would tend to establish an issue in the mind of a reasonable jury.

Scopes, John Thomas. John T. Scopes, a 24-year-old teacher in Dayton, TN, was charged with "undermining the peace and dignity of the state" by teaching his students the Darwinian theory of evolution, that man had descended from the apes. His famous trial is known as The Monkey Trial. Scopes was defended by Clarence Darrow but on July 21, 1925, was found guilty and fined $100. The decision was reversed on technical grounds by the Tennessee Supreme Court.

scopolamine. An alkaloid, produced from nightshade plants like belladonna, which creates a hypnotic state. It has been used in lie detection work to create a quasi-sleep in suspects who are then questioned, and will allegedly tell the truth as their inhibitions are removed. The value of this procedure is highly questionable. In recent years, it has also been used as a rape drug, as it is colorless and odorless. In addition, a recent study has found that scopolamine also works in certain doses to treat and quell sea sickness.

Scotland Yard. The popular name for the headquarters (established in 1829) of the London Metropolitan Police (MPO). The office was located in a building at Whitehall Place and took its name from the rear premises, Scotland Yard, through which the public had access to the building. The MPO is now located on Victoria Street.

Scottsboro cases (also called Scottsboro trials). On March 25, 1931, a group of nine young black men, ranging in age from 13 to 21 years, were riding in an open gondola car aboard a freight train crossing Alabama. Also aboard the train were seven other boys and two young women, all of whom were white. At some point a fight broke out between the two groups and six of the white boys were thrown from the train. A message was relayed, and as the train pulled into the station at Paint Rock, AL, a sheriff's posse was waiting. The two women, Victoria Price and Ruby Bates, claimed they had been raped by a number of the black youths. All nine were taken into custody and placed under military guard in the local jail at Scottsboro. The Scottsboro boys, as they became known in history, were indicted on March 31, arraigned on the same day, and entered pleas of not guilty. On the morning of the trial, a local attorney offered reluctantly to represent the defendants. Of the nine youths arrested, one had not been indicted because he was only 13. The remaining eight were joined into three groups for separate trials, each lasting a single day. Medical and other evidence was presented establishing that the two women had not been raped. The jury nevertheless sentenced all eight defendants to death. After conviction and sentence of death, the case remained pending for six years as a result of nationwide protest. The evidence was clear that the defendants were innocent of the charges, and many groups and individuals sought retrials on the basis of new evidence. A second trial was ordered by the U.S. Supreme Court in November 1932 and again in 1934 on the grounds that the defendants had been denied adequate counsel and that black citizens had been excluded from the juries at the three original trials. Continued appeals led to a decision in 1938 by the Court to deny new trials for four of the defendants (three eventually won parole, and one escaped). The other four had been released.

search and seizure. As the interpretation of the Fourth Amendment varies, it is necessary to study the statutes and case law governing each state. In California, for example, searches and seizures are considered reasonable if made under any of the following circumstances: (a) "With a valid search warrant"; or (b) "Incidental to a valid arrest made pursuant to a warrant of arrest or on probable cause (exception: a search warrant is required for materials having possible protection as free speech by the First Amendment)"; or (c) "By an officer lawfully on the premises (e.g., with probable cause to make an arrest; with consent; to render aid, in hot pursuit of escaping felon; pressing emergency; search of parolee's premises; or on public premises), though no arrest is in fact made, and who sees the evidence or contraband in plain sight"; or (d) "With consent voluntarily obtained"; or (e) "By an officer who searches a vehicle with reasonable cause to believe the vehicle contains contraband or evidence of crime even though not incidental to valid arrest (justified because of mobility)." On July 6, 1984, in a 6–3 decision, the Supreme Court ruled that police can conduct a "protective search" of the passenger area of a car without a warrant if they believe that concealed weapons are in the auto. Probable cause to believe a search will reveal contraband does not justify a search of a home or personal effects without a warrant, unless the search is incidental to a valid arrest based on probable cause.

search and seizure, unreasonable. Searches of persons and places and seizure of papers and effects without search warrants properly sworn to, issued by judicial officers, and, particularly, describing the place to be searched and the persons or things seized. Wiretapping and the use of a stomach pump are considered unreasonable searches; but blood tests for alcohol and seizures made immediately after a proper arrest, when objects wanted as evidence are in plain sight or the danger exists that offenders might escape because of the delay necessary to obtain a warrant, are not considered unreasonable. Since 1967 the courts have broadened the range of items that can be seized in a lawful search and used as evidence. The Fourth Amendment prohibits unreasonable searches and seizures, and the provision against self-incrimination in the Fifth Amendment prohibits the use of illegally seized articles as evidence against an accused person.

searching places outside of curtilage. Curtilage means the enclosed ground and buildings surrounding a dwelling. As a rule, no search warrant is needed for a lawful search of an open place not within the curtilage of, or in close proximity to, a dwelling, or unenclosed grounds not essential to the dwelling, where a search in no way invades or disturbs the privacy of a home or legitimate business.

search of curtilage or appurtenant premises. Usually considered to be a part of a dwelling, its curtilage or nearby premises, like the dwelling itself, cannot be searched without a valid search warrant.

search of place of business. While officers are vested with the same rights as the general public in entering a business establishment, a search warrant may be necessary to search an office or store or a room in a plant, and this rule extends to the premises of the business.

search warrant. A document issued by a judicial officer that directs a law enforcement officer to conduct a search at a specific location for specified property or persons relating to a crime(s), to seize the property or persons if found, and to account for the results of the search to the issuing judicial officer. On June 8, 1984, the Supreme Court voted 6–3 to expand police powers to obtain search warrants on the basis of anonymous tips; the court avoided ruling on whether illegally seized evidence could be admissible in court

if police acted in good faith. *See also* search and seizure

search warrant, second search (same warrant). A warrant once served cannot, of course, be used for the purpose of additional searches; but, where a search is continuous—not having been abandoned or completed—it will not be held void because the officers go over the premises a second time.

secondary classification. A term used in classifying fingerprints. In the classification formula, it follows the primary classification and is a code of two upper-case letters, such as T/W. It describes the type of pattern in each of the index fingers.

secondary deviance. A term describing the situation that arises when a person publicly labeled as a deviant for some initial behavior (primary deviance) begins to use deviant behavior, or a role based on it, as a means of defense or adjustment to the problems created by society's reactions to the primary behavior. *See also* primary deviance

secondary evidence. Evidence that is inferior to primary evidence, such as a copy of an instrument, or oral evidence of its contents. Either would be secondary to the original document.

secondhand evidence. Hearsay evidence.

Second Chance Act. Federal law passed in 2008 that provides federal aid to initiatives aimed at easing the transition from incarceration to the community.

secret. (1) Well-kept information or knowledge concerning a particular thing. (2) In government service, material or information that is disclosed without authority and that could result in serious damage to the nation by endangering its international relations; jeopardizing the effectiveness of a program or policy of great importance to the national defense; exposing important military or defense plans, technological developments of importance to the national defense, or information relative to important intelligence operations.

Secret Service. The Secret Service was founded in 1865 in order to prevent counterfeiting U.S. currency. Today however, under the direction of the secretary of the treasury, the service is responsible for the protection of the president and members of his immediate family, the president-elect, the vice president or other officer next in order of succession to the presidency, the vice president-elect, major candidates for the offices of president and vice president during their campaigns, the minor children of a former president until they reach age 16, and visiting heads of a foreign state or government. The Secret Service is also authorized to detect and arrest persons committing offenses against the laws of the United States relating to coins, obligations, and securities of the United States and foreign governments, and persons who forge government requests for transportation to be furnished by a common carrier. The director of the service is also responsible for the Protective Service and the Treasury Security Force. The FBI was created in 1908 under the Department of Justice to supplement the work of the Secret Service. It is currently under the Department of Homeland Security.

sector search. *See* zone search

Securities and Exchange Commission (SEC). Created by the Securities Exchange Act of 1934, independent federal agency that supervises all aspects of the securities industry—including brokers, investment companies, the stock exchanges, and the actions of corporate officials. The SEC, which consists of five members appointed by the president for five- year terms, was established by the Securities Exchange Act of 1934. The main purpose of the commission is to preserve the integrity of the securities industry. Generally emphasizing prevention of abuses over punishment, the SEC relies heavily on the industry for self-regulation. The mission of the SEC "is to protect investors, maintain fair, orderly, and efficient markets, and facilitate capital formation." Address: SEC Headquarters, 100 F Street, NE, Washington, DC 20549; Web: http://www.sec.gov/.

securities violations. In December 1988, the New York brokerage and investment banking firm of Drexel Burnham Lambert pleaded guilty to six felony counts of securities violations and was fined $650 million. Others involved in securities fraud cases and who have admitted to felonies are Ivan F. Boesky, Boyd L. Jefferies, Dennis B. Levine, and Martin Siegel.

security. (1) The restriction of inmate movement within a correctional facility, usually divided into maximum, medium, and minimum levels. (2) Measures taken for protection against espionage, observation, sabotage, annoyance, or surprise. (3) With respect to classified matter, the condition that prevents unauthorized persons from having access to official information that is safeguarded in the interests of national defense. (4) Item(s) deposited as a guarantee for payment of money. (5) Any of a wide variety of documents of monetary value, including but not limited to bills, stock certificates, bonds, certificates of deposit, checks, money orders, letters of credit, or certificates of interest in tangible or intangible property. Industrial security is a business function with the responsibility of safeguarding the physical plant, properties, and products of the business.

security and privacy. As an exception to the general right of U.S. citizens to security and privacy, the Supreme Court found in its 1976 *Paul v. Davis* decision that arrest records do not qualify for protection under the Constitution, because they do not relate to private conduct. This decision meant that confidentiality standards concerning criminal histories are largely a matter of legislative discretion.

security classifications. The following are used in the Department of Defense Industrial Security Program: *Confidential:* information or material for which unauthorized disclosure could reasonably be expected to cause damage to national security; *Restricted:* information concerning the design, manufacture, or utilization of atomic weapons; the production of special nuclear material;

and the use of special nuclear material in the production of energy; *Secret:* information or material whose unauthorized disclosure could [reasonably] be expected to cause serious damage to national security. *Top Secret:* information or material whose unauthorized disclosure could reasonably be expected to cause exceptionally grave damage to national security.

security for costs. The security that a defendant in an action may require of a plaintiff who does not reside within the jurisdiction of the court.

security index files. A card file maintained by the U.S. Civil Service Commission listing persons investigated by the commission and other agencies since 1939. Information from the index is available to investigators with a bona fide employment or investigative interest.

sedition. Issuing any false, scandalous, and malicious statement against the government, the President, or Congress with the intent to defame, disrupt, encourage contempt, or excite hatred of citizens for the United States. Laws against sedition, however, may not violate First Amendment guarantees. The United States faced its first conflict over sedition between 1798 and 1801, when there was a conflict between the Federalists and Republicans over defining the role of public criticism in a representative government. Historically, sedition laws were based on the philosophy that the government is superior to the people. With the election of President Thomas Jefferson in 1800, this idea was superseded by the Populist theory that the people are superior to the government and that First Amendment rights are stronger than sedition laws. Since that time Congress has revived the sedition laws only twice—during World War I and World War II.

seditious conspiracy. The agreement of two or more persons to act together in promoting unlawful means of changing the government or of encouraging the violation of law for the purpose of promoting disloyalty or disaffection to the government.

seduction. The offense of inducing someone to consent to sexual intercourse under promise of marriage or other promises or pretences.

segregation. In penology, the part of a prison where inmates are held in solitary confinement as punishment.

seizin. Possession of real estate or personal property.

seizure. The taking into custody, by a law enforcement officer or other person authorized to do so, of objects relating to, or believed to relate to, criminal activity. *See also* forfeiture

selective enforcement. The deploying of police personnel in ways to cope most effectively with existing or anticipated problems. If data show that residential burglaries occur most frequently in certain areas at certain times, officers are assigned to such areas at the critical times under a program of selective enforcement.

self-actualization. A concept attributed to Abraham Maslow, it has been described as the process of becoming all that one is capable of being, of developing into an individual who is motivated primarily by an unselfish need for growth rather than by the appraisals of others; a process of becoming conscious of one's unique self. *See also* Maslow's hierarchy of needs

self-defense. The protection of oneself or one's property from unlawful injury or the immediate risk of unlawful injury; the justification for an act that would otherwise constitute an offense and that the doer reasonably believed was necessary to protect self or property from immediate danger.

self-fulfilling prophecy. An event that was predicted, and then occurred because the prediction became the cause. For example, an individual who is convinced that something bad will happen may unconsciously cause the anticipated mishap. Some criminologists believe a person doesn't become deviant until so labeled by authorities. In this view, someone who has initially been labeled deviant, through arrest and conviction, may find the pattern of behavior difficult to alter.

self-incrimination. In constitutional terms, the process of becoming involved in or charged with a crime by one's own testimony. The Constitution prohibits forced self-incrimination under the Fifth Amendment. This amendment has been widely used by witnesses in congressional investigations of subversive or criminal activities, who refuse to answer questions on the grounds that such answers would be self-incriminating. In 1972 the Court upheld the constitutionality of the Organized Crime Control Law of 1970, which protects witnesses from prosecution only to the extent that what they say will not be used against them; they are still liable to prosecution on other evidence.

self-report studies. A modern survey technique designed to measure the number of criminals by asking respondents if they have committed crimes within a specific period. Although their truthfulness may be somewhat suspect even with firm pledges of confidentiality, as many as 91 percent of the respondents surveyed by some studies have admitted one or more criminal acts.

semiautomatic. A firearm or gun that uses part of the force of an exploding cartridge to extract the empty case and chamber the next round, but requires a separate pull of the trigger to fire each round; hence, the phrase semiautomatic fire.

Senate crime investigations. The first committee set up specifically to investigate crime was the Kefauver Committee of 1950–1951. The committee was aided by an executive order from President Harry Truman that gave it access to income tax returns, which were the starting point for many investigations. The committee discovered considerable evidence of a nationwide crime syndicate and its operations. Numerous Senate crime committees have been formed since 1950.

senior investment fraud. A type of investment fraud in which con artists target senior citizens, often with sale of unsecured promissory notes, or other investments that are either fraudulent or unsuitable. *See also* fraud, investment

sensitivity training (T-groups). Generic term for a variety of (primarily verbal) group-interaction experiences for individuals and organization staffs. The group sessions are intended to help people function more effectively in their jobs through understanding group dynamics, increasing awareness of their own and other people's feelings, becoming more direct in talking about those feelings, and exchanging feedback with others about styles of interaction.

sentence. (1) The penalty imposed by a court on a person convicted of a crime. (2) The court judgment specifying the penalty. imposed on a person convicted of a crime. (3) Any disposition of a defendant resulting from a conviction, including the court decision to suspend execution of a sentence.

sentence credit time. Time already spent in confinement in relation to a given offense(s), which is deducted at the point of admission on a sentence to jail or prison from the maximum jail or prison liability of the sentence for the offense(s).

sentence effective date. With respect to a term of confinement, the date from which time served is calculated, not necessarily coincident with the date sentence was pronounced or the date of entry to confinement after sentencing.

sentence, flat. Also called a straight sentence; a fixed sentence with no maximum or minimum range indicated.

sentence, indeterminate. A sentence to incarceration indicating a range of time between minimum date of parole eligibility and a maximum discharge date. A completely indeterminate sentence has a minimum of one day and a maximum of natural life.

sentence, maximum. The longest period of time the prisoner can be held in custody. The longest prison sentence was a 10,000-year sentence imposed on Dudley Wayne Kyzer,

40, on December 4, 1981, in Tuscaloosa, AL, for triple murder in 1976 that included his mother-in-law. A close second is the sentence imposed on Darron Bennalford Anderson of Oklahoma for rape, larceny, robbery, and kidnapping. Anderson was initially sentenced to 2,000 years; he appealed his sentence and was ordered to served 10,450 years. Upon further review, the court reduced his sentence to a total of 9,950 years. The longest time served was by Paul Geidel (born April 21, 1894), a 17-year-old porter employed by a New York City hotel. He was convicted of second-degree murder on September 5, 1911, and released from the Fishkill Correctional Facility in Beacon, NY, aged 85, on May 7, 1980, having served 68 years, eight months, and two days—the longest recorded term in U.S. history. He had first refused parole in 1974.

sentence, minimum. The shortest period of time an offender must spend in prison before becoming eligible for parole.

sentence review. The reconsideration of a sentence imposed on a person convicted of a crime, either by the same court that imposed the sentence or a higher court.

sentence, short. A sentence that runs from a few days to a few months, imposed on petty offenders who often cannot afford to pay a fine, if one is offered as an alternative to imprisonment. Short sentences are usually served in municipal or county jails, except in those few places where special institutions for misdemeanants are maintained.

sentence, suspended. Technically a sentence, but based on unconditional, unsupervised release of the convicted defendant.

sentencing councils. A panel of three or more judges sometimes used instead of a trial judge to determine a criminal sentence, in an attempt to make sentencing more uniform. Sentencing councils were first used in 1960 in the Eastern District of Michigan.

sentencing dispositions. Court dispositions of defendants after a judgment of conviction,

expressed as penalties, such as incarceration or payment of fines; or any of a number of alternatives to actually executed penalties, such as suspended sentences, grants of probation, or orders to perform restitution; or various combinations of the above.

sentencing hearing. A hearing during which the court or jury considers relevant information, such as evidence concerning aggravating or mitigating circumstances, for the purpose of determining a sentencing disposition for a person convicted of an offense(s).

sentencing jury. The trial jury attached to a court that imposes sentence.

sentencing postponed. The delay for an unspecified period of time, or to a remote date, of the court's pronouncement of any other sentencing disposition for a person convicted of an offense, in order to place the defendant in some status contingent on good behavior in the expectation that a penalty need never be pronounced or executed.

Sentencing Project, The. The project was founded in 1986 to provide defense attorneys with training in an effort to reduce reliance on incarceration; the Sentencing Project is a leading national organization working for a fair and effective criminal justice system by promoting reforms in sentencing law and practice, and alternatives to incarceration. The organization has provided technical assistance and helped to establish alternative sentencing schemes in more than 20 states. Address: 514 Tenth St., NW, Suite 1000, Washington, DC 20004. Web site: http://www.sentencingproject.org/template/index.cfm.

sentinel. A person charged with standing guard and giving notice of danger if it is threatened.

sentry. A guard, especially one who stands at a point where only properly authorized and identified persons are permitted to pass.

September 11 attacks. (also called 9/11). On the morning of September 11, 2001, terrorists hijacked four commercial airplanes, taking over the cockpit and flying the planes into the World Trade Center north tower (American Airlines Flight 11), the World Trade Center south tower (United Airlines Flight 175) and the Pentagon (American Air lines Flight 77). Passengers regained control of the fourth plane (United Airlines flight 93), which had an estimated target of the Capitol Building or the White House. This airplane crashed into a field in Pennsylvania. The estimated death toll of September 11 is 2,976 persons (excluding the 19 hijackers) from 77 countries. The attacks had a severe economic impact on the national and world economy, due to the six-day close of the stock markets and subsequent drop in stocks. The attacks cost the City of New York an estimated $22.75 billion dollars, including costs to clean up the WTC, repairing infrastructure, rebuilding the World Trade Center as smaller buildings, repairing other damaged buildings, and lost rent of the destroyed buildings. The attacks prompted the temporary closing of U.S. airspace for several days. It also spawned a series of hate crimes against persons who appeared to be of Middle Eastern descent in the United States. In response to the attack, the United States launched the U.S. "War on Terrorism" and subsequent military action, including deployment of military forces to Afghanistan beginning around October 7, 2001. The attacks also prompted the passage of the Homeland Security Act of 2002, which created the Department of Homeland Security, and the USA PATRIOT Act, to detect and prosecute terrorism and other crimes by allowing law enforcement to invade the privacy of citizens without judicial oversight in domestic intelligence gathering. The long term health effects of 9/11 are still not fully known. However, the World Trade center collapse alone produced thousands of tons of toxic debris, including known carcinogens. Multiple memorials have been erected in honor of the victims of the September 11 attacks, including the Tribute in Light, the Pentagon memorial, Flight 93 National Memorial, and the National September 11 Memorial & Museum (under construction). *See also* domestic terrorism

sepulture. Burial; interment.

sequester. To keep a jury together and in isolation from the public under charge of the bailiff during a trial; sometimes called separation of the jury. Also, to keep witnesses apart from other witnesses and therefore unable to hear their testimony.

sergeant. A police officer whose rank is higher than patrolman and lower than lieutenant. The sergeant is the first supervisory officer in the ascending chain of command. He is the line officer who is in closest contact with the field operations of a department.

serial killer. One who commits serial murder. *See also* serial murders

serial murders. The phenomenon of serial killings has been recognized since a man dubbed "Jack the Ripper" murdered seven London prostitutes in 1888. The FBI terms serial murders as the killing of several victims in three or more separate events. These may occur over several days, weeks, or years, and reveal similarities of pattern, such as where the murders occurred, the type of victim, or the method of killing. The elapsed time between murders separates serial killers from other multiple killers. John Wayne Gacy, a serial murderer, planned the separate killings of 33 boys and young men in Chicago over a span of two to three years in the late 1970s. Other serial murders have been attributed to Albert De Salvo, the Boston Strangler, although he was never charged with murder; Theodore Robert Bundy; Juan Carona; David Berkowitz, Son of Sam; Wayne Williams of Atlanta; and Randy Kraft. Aileen Wournos, a hitchhiking prostitute who killed six men, was executed in Florida by lethal injection on October 10, 2002. The FBI has compiled profiles of several types of repeat criminals, and analysts study data on more than 200 suspects each year. Professor Ronald Holmes of the University of Louisville is coauthor of a book on this subject titled *Serial Murder* from Sage Publications. *See also* Green River Task Force; mass murder; murder spree; National Center for the Analysis of Violent Crime; Table 43. Serial Killers in the United States, page 409–415

text continues on page 416

TABLE 43   SERIAL KILLERS IN THE UNITED STATES

Name	AKA	# of Victims	Year Convicted	Outcome
Charles Albright	"The Eyeball Killer," "Dallas Ripper," "Dallas Slasher"	3	1991	Life in prison.
Dale Anderson		2	1990	Life in prison.
John Eric Armstrong	"Baby doll" "Opie"	5	2001	Life in prison.
Margie Velma Barfield	"Death Row Granny," "Mamma Margie"	4	1978	Sentenced to death. Executed on November 2, 1984.
Herb Baumeister	"The I-70 Strangler"	16		Committed suicide before arrest. Died July 3, 1996.
Betty Lee Beets	"Texas Black Widow"	2	1985	Sentenced to death. Executed on February, 24 2000, at Huntsville State Prison in Huntsville, Texas.
Robert Berdella	"The Butcher of Kansas City"	6	1988	Life in prison. Died of a heart attack in 1992.
David Berkowitz	"Son of Sam"	6	1978	Serving 6 life sentences at Sullivan Correctional Facility in Fallsburg, New York.
Paul Bernardo		2	1995	Life in prison, chance at parole in 25 years.
Kenneth Alessio Bianchi	One of the "Hillside Stranglers"	12	1979	Life in prison.
Lawrence Bittaker	"Pliers"	5	1981	Sentenced to death. Awaiting execution in San Quentin Prison, California.
Warren James Bland		1	1993	Sentenced to death. Died of natural causes on August 30, 2001 before he could be executed.
Daniel Blank		6	1997	Sentenced to death.
William George Bonin	"The Freeway Killer"		1983	Sentenced to death. Executed on February, 23 1996.
Robert Charles Browne		8	1995	Sentenced to life in prison.
Jerome Brudos		3	1969	Three consecutive life sentences.
Judias Buenoano	"Black Widow"	4	1980, 1984, 1985	Sentenced to death. Executed March, 30 1998.

(continued)

Name	AKA	# of Victims	Year Convicted	Outcome
Ted Bundy			1979	Sentenced to death. Executed on January 24, 1989.
Angelo Buono, Jr.	One of the "Hillside Stranglers"	10	1983	Sentenced to life. Died of natural causes on September 21, 2002, while serving sentence.
Charles Rodney Campbell		3	1982	Sentenced to death. Executed on May 27, 1994.
John Cannan	"The Lady Killer"	1	1989	Sentenced to life in prison.
Harvey Louis Carignan	"The Want-Ad Killer"	13	1950, 1960, 1975, 1976	Sentenced to life in prison.
David Carpenter	"The Trailside Killer"	10	1984	Sentenced to death. Awaiting execution at San Quentin State Prison, California.
Richard Trenton Chase	"Dracula Killer," "The Vampire of Sacramento"	6	1979	Sentenced to death. Committed suicide while on death row. Died December 26, 1980.
Andrei Chikatilo	"Andrei the Great," "Butcher of Rostov," "The Red Ripper"		1992	Sentenced to death. Executed February 14, 1994.
Clark Hadden		2	1993	Sentenced to 60 years in prison.
Jill Coit	"The Louisiana Black Widow"	2	1995	Sentenced to life in prison and fined one million dollars.
Carroll Edward Cole	"Eddie"	13	1984	Sentenced to death. Executed December 6, 1985.
Alton Coleman		8	1985	Sentenced to death. Executed April 26, 2002.
John Norman Collins	"The Co-Ed Killer"	1	1970	Sentenced to life in prison.
Robert Otis Coulson	"Bob"	5	1994	Sentenced to death. Executed on June 25, 2002.
Rory Conde	"Tamiami Strangler"	6	1999	Sentenced to death. Awaiting execution at Union Correctional Institution.
Adolfo de Jesus Constanzo	"The Witch Doctor"			Killed before arrested on May 6, 1989.
Ray Copeland		5	1991	Sentenced to death. Died of natural causes in 1993.

(continued)

Name	AKA	# of Victims	Year Convicted	Outcome
Tammy Corbett		3	1990	Sentenced to life in prison.
Dean Corll	"Candy Man"	27		Killed before he was arrested on August 8, 1973.
Juan Corona	"The Machete Murderer"	25	1973	Serving 25 life sentences with chance of parole.
Antone Costa	"Lord Antone"	4	1970	Sentenced to life in prison. Committed suicide in cell in May 12, 1974.
Richard Francis Cottingham	"The Torso Killer"	5	1981, 1982, 1984	Sentenced to life in prison.
John Martin Crawford		4		Sentenced to 3 concurrent life sentences.
Theresa Cross Knorr		3	1995	Sentenced to two consecutive life terms.
Charles Cullen	"Killer Nurse," "Satan's Son"	29	2006	Sentenced to 11 consecutive life sentences.
Jesse James Cummings		2	1996	Sentenced to death.
Jeffrey Dahmer		16	1992	Sentenced to life in prison. He was killed on November 28, 1994 while serving his term.
James Daveggio	"Froggie"	4	2002	Sentenced to death. Awaiting execution at San Quesntin State Prison.
James Michael DeBardeleben	"Mall Passer"	8	1988	Sentenced to 375 years in prison.
Westley Allan Dodd	"The Van-couver Child Killer"	3	1990	Sentenced to death. Executed on January 5, 1993.
Brian James Dugan		2	1985	Sentenced to two life sentences, as well as 215 years.
Jon Scott Dunkle		4	1989	Sentenced to life without parole, and subsequently death. Awaiting execution at San Mateo Prison.
Paul Durousseau	"The Jackson-ville Serial Killer"	6	Pending	
Dr. Glennon Engleman	"The Killing Dentist"	7	1980	5 life terms.
Robery John Erler	"The Catch Me Killer"	1	1968	99.5 years.

(continued)

Name	AKA	# of Victims	Year Convicted	Outcome
Gary Charles Evans	"Red" "Gar" "Evans the air pirate"	5	Never convicted	Committed suicide before trial.
Richard March Evonitz		3	Never convicted	Committed suicide before arrest.
Larry Eyler	"The Highway Killer"	23	1986	Death sentence. Died of AIDS in 1994 while serving sentence.
Kendall Francois		8	1998	Eight consecutive 25 to life sentences.
Leonard Fraser	"The Bad Seed"	4	2003	4 life sentences.
Robert Fry		4	2001	Death.
John Wayne Gacy	"The Killer Clown"	33	1980	12 death sentences and 21 life sentences. Has been executed.
Charlene Williams		10	1982	16 years, 8 months.
Gerald Armond Gallego		10	1983	Death.
Edward Theordore Gein	"The American Psycho"	2	1968	Life in a mental Institution.
Kristen H. Gilbert		4	2001	4 consecutive life sentences, plus 20 years.
Lorenzo Gilyard		13	2007	Awaiting sentence.
David Allan Gore	"The Killing Cousins"	6	1985	Death penalty.
Vaugh Orrin Greenwood	"The Skid Row Slasher"	11	1976	Life.
Robert Hansen		17	1984	461 years plus life without parole.
Donald Harvey	"Angel of Death"	36	1987	Life in prison
Charles Ray Hatcher	"Crazy Charlie" "One Man Crime Wave" "Mr. Prince"	16	1984	50 years to life, without parole.
Gary Heidnik		2	1988	Death penalty, executed.
Raymont Hopewell	"Money"	5	2006	4 consecutive life sentences.
Waneta Ethel Hoyt		5	1996	75 years.

(continued)

Name	AKA	# of Victims	Year Convicted	Outcome
Keith Hunter Jesperson	"The Happy Face Killer"	8	1995	Life without parole.
Vincent Johnson	"Brooklyn Strangler"	6	2001	Life.
Genene Jones	"Killer Nurse"	11–46	1985	Life.
John Joubert	"Woodford Slasher"	3	1984	Death, executed by electric chair.
Joseph Kallinger	"The Shoemaker"	3	1976	Life.
Edmund Emil Kemper III	"Co-ed Murderer"	10	1973	Life.
Theresa Cross Knoor		3	1995	2 consecutive life terms.
Randy Craft	"Scorecard Killer"	16	1989	Death.
Rex Allen Krebs		2	1999	Death.
Derrick Todd Lee	"The Baton Rouge Serial Killer"	7–10	2004	Death.
William Darrell Lindsey	"Red Bird" "Crazy Bill"	7	1999	30 years.
Bobby Joe Long	"The Classified Ad Rapist"	10	1985	Death.
Henry Lee Lucas		3–600	1983	Death. In 1998 sentence was commuted to life in prison. Died of natural causes in 2001 while serving sentence.
Thomas Edward Luther		1	1996	65 years.
Lee Boyd Malvo	"Beltway Sniper"	13	2004	Life without parole.
Michael Dee Goyler	Michael Dee Mattson	5	1979	Death.
Kenneth Allen McDuff	"The Broomstick Killer"	5	1966, 1992	Death, executed by lethal injection.
John Allan Muhammad	"Beltway Sniper"	10	2003	Death.
Herbert Mullin		13	1973	Life.
Roy Norris		5	1980	Life with possibility of parole after 30 years.

(continued)

Name	AKA	# of Victims	Year Convicted	Outcome
Clifford Robert Olson Jr.		11	1982	11 Concurrent life sentences.
Colin Pitchfork	"Black Pad Killer"	2	1988	Double life in prison.
Robery Pickton	"Willie"	6	2007	Life in prison.
Cleophus Prince Jr.	"Clairemont Killer"	6	1993	Death.
Dorothea Helen Gray		19	1993	Life without parole.
Dennis Rader	"BTK"	10	2005	Life.
Richard Ramirez	"The Night Stalker"	14	1989	Death.
David Parker Ray		14	1999	224 years; died of heart attack in 2002 while serving his sentence.
Robert Ben Rhoades	"Whips and Chains"	4	1992	Life without parole.
Gary Leon Ridgway	"Green River Killer"	48	2003	Life without parole.
Joel Rifkin		17	1994	203 years to life.
John Edward Robinson Sr.	"Slavemaster"	8	2003	Death.
Adolph James Rode	"Cesar Barone"	5	1995	3 death sentences.
Glen Edward Rogers	"Casanova Killer" "The Cross Country Killer"	5	1997	Death.
Danny Rolling	"Gainesville Ripper"	8	1994	Death.
Randy Roth		2	1992	55 years.
George Waterfield Russell Jr.	"The Charmer" "East Side Killer" "Bellevue Killer"	3	1991	Life.
Charles Howard Schmid Jr.	"The Pied Piper of Tucson"	3	1966	Death.
Tommy Lynn Sells	"Coast to Coast Killer"	13	2000	Death.

(continued)

Name	AKA	# of Victims	Year Convicted	Outcome
Dr. Harold Frederick Shipman		200–357	2000	15 life sentences.
Anthony Allen Shore	"The Strangler"	5	2004	Death.
Robert Joseph Silveria Jr.	"The Boxcar Serial Killer" "Boxcar"	14	1998	Life in prison without parole.
Lemuel Smith		6	1979	2 life sentences.
Samuel L. Smithers		2	1999	Death penalty.
Eugene Paul Stano		41	1981	Death.
Richard Starrett	"Danny"	1	1989	5 consecutive life sentences.
Cary Stayner		4	2002	Death by lethal injection.
William Lester Suff	"Riverside Prostitute Killer" "Lake Elsinore Killer"	19	1995	Death.
Johann "Jack" Unterweger	"Poet of Death"	11	1994	Life in prison.
Faryion Wardrip	"Gonzo"	5	1999	Death.
Lesley Eugene Warren	"Babyface Killer"	4	1993	Death.
Fred Waterfield	"The Killing Cousins"	6	1985	2 consecutive life terms.
Carl Eugene Watts	"Coral" "The Sunday Morning Slasher"	More then 80	2004	Life; died of cancer in 2007 while serving his sentence.
James Edward Wood		1	1994	Death; died of natural causes in 2004 while serving sentence.
Stephan Gerald James Wright	"Ipswich Killer"	5	2008	Life in prison without parole.
Aileen Wuornos	"Damsel of Death"	7	1992	Death; executed in 2002.
Robert Lee Yates		15	2002	408 years in prison.
Robert Joseph Zani		2	1981	Life.

Compiled by Richard Porter, CSULB.

Serious and Violent Offender Reentry Initiative (SVORI). Sponsored by the Office of Justice Programs (OJP), U.S. Department of Justice, SVORI is a comprehensive federal effort to improve reentry outcomes in the areas of criminal justice, employment, education, health, and housing.

serious misdemeanor. A class of misdemeanors having more severe penalties than other misdemeanors, or being procedurally distinct; sometimes a statutory name for a type of misdemeanor having a maximum penalty much greater than the customary provisions for misdemeanors.

serology analysis. Forensic technique that involves the scientific examination of blood samples for evidence.

Serpico, Frank. A New York police officer who broke the code of silence regarding corruption in his department and was transferred to the Midtown Manhattan prostitution detail in retaliation. He released his story to the *New York Times,* in response to which the mayor convened the Knapp Commission to investigate the department during the summer of 1970. Serpico was shot in the face by a drug dealer but survived and continued his work with the commission. The group's findings were staggering: 15,000 officers were involved in some sort of corruption. In May 1972, after the commission had disbanded, a new scandal hit the New York Police Department: 20 plain-clothes police officers and three sergeants were indicted for accepting $250,000 a year in bribes from gamblers linked to organized crime.

service of process. The act of delivering a written summons or notice of a judicial proceeding to the person who will be affected by it.

session. A meeting; a sitting of a court, legislative body, or other assembly.

severance. In criminal proceedings the separation, for purposes of pleading and/or trial, of multiple defendants named in a single charging document, or of multiple charges against a particular defendant listed in a single charging document.

sexism. The domination and/or exploitation of one sex by the other, or generalized bias against a group of people based solely on their common gender. The term is usually used to mean the subordination of women by men through ideology, stereotyping, family structures, and unfair legislation.

sex offender. One who commits crime of a sexual nature, including, for example, forcible or statutory rape, fondling, sexual acts against a minor, indecent exposure, etc. While the term is often used loosely, it generally implies a serious sex offense and connotes required sex offender registration.

sex offender notification systems. Computerized systems that will automatically contact victims of sexual crimes that the perpetrators have escaped or are about to be released. Once victims have registered their telephone numbers, the systems are programmed to call, be activated by a code number, and play a taped message.

sex offender registration. Often grouped in a category called "Megan's Law," sex offender registration is the official reporting to local law enforcement agencies by persons convicted of sex offenses defined in state statutes. In many cases, sex offender registration is accompanied by community notification, which is often achieved via public-access Web site listing the names and descriptions of local sex offenders, often with an accompanying mug shot and street address. There have been several challenges to sex offender registration laws, but courts generally uphold the provisions. In *Smith v. Doe* (538 U.S. 84 (2003)), the Supreme Court denied petitioner's claim that an Alaska statue was unconstitutional *ex post facto* law, thereby affirming such statutes nationwide. In the same year, the Court ruled in *Connecticut Dept. of Public Safety v. Doe* (538 U.S. 1 (2003)), the Court held that sex-offender registration statutes were not a due process violation. While such laws were designed to protect children from sexual predation, some argue that they provide false security against stranger rape, as most sex crimes occur between a victim and a known or related offender. With the advent of sex registration laws, many sex offender registries are packed with listings of non-predatory, low-risk offenders, such as those convicted of consensual sex offenses such as statutory rape, sexting, solicitation for prostitution, or dogging (sex in public). This creates an unmanageable list of nonserious offenders that dilutes the tracking of more serious offenders. Further, assaults against and banishment of sex offenders, including those convicted of less-serious consensual sex crimes, may create more crime than registries prevent. *See also* Megan's Law

sex offenses. Defined by law as "offenses against chastity, common decency, morals, and the like," except prostitution, and commercialized vice.

sexting (combined from the words "sex" and "texting"). The act of sending, receiving, or viewing sexually explicit photographs, videos, and images electronically, usually via cell phone text. Sexting first emerged around 2005, and some research suggests sexting is a very common practice among teenagers, despite the fact that acts of sexting are tantamount to distribution of child pornography, a felony. Several teenagers have been indicted on such charges. In 2008, Ting-Yi Oei, a 60-year-old high school vice principal in Virginia, was charged with felony child pornography for investigating a sexting incident that occurred on campus in which he showed his principal an electronically confiscated "sexting" picture, which he then saved on his office computer per the principal's instruction. The judge dismissed the charge in 2009. The same year, the American Civil Liberties Union sued a Pennsylvania district attorney (*Miller, et al v. Skumanick* 605 F. Supp. 2d 634 (2009)) for threatening a group of teenage girls with criminal prosecution for sexting; in 2009, Vermont, Ohio, and Utah introduced legislation to legalize or reduce consensual sexting from a felony to a misdemeanor. *See also* sex offender

sexual deviations. Deviations such as exhibitionism and rape are penalized by law, but many other forms of sexual behavior are arbitrarily called deviant because they depart from what is considered normal by a society. Deviation is a label applied at a given time and does not imply a condemnation of everything so termed. Some authorities have suggested that sexual anomaly would be a preferable term.

sexual fetishism. A sexual arousal derived from the use of a nonliving object that is not part of normative stimulation. Generally, a fetish centers around a particular object (such as a shoe) that is not typically used for sexual gratification (thus excluding vibrators); sexual gratification is difficult to achieve without including the particular object in the sexual act. The most common fetish is podophilia, or foot fetish.

sexual harassment. The Supreme Court granted *certiorari* to review *Metitor Savings Bank v. Vinson* 477 U.S. 57 (1986)), heard the case the following March, and handed down its first sexual harassment decision on June 19, 1986. *Vinson* did not resolve all legal inconsistencies, but it did establish some important sexual harassment laws and deserves to be termed a landmark decision. Illinois defines sexual harassment as "any unwelcome sexual advances or requests for sexual favors or any conduct of a sexual nature when (1) submission to such conduct is made either explicitly or implicitly a term or condition of a person's employment; (2) submission to or rejection of such conduct by an individual is used as the basis for employment decisions affecting such individual; or (3) such conduct has the purpose or effect of substantially interfering with an individual's work performance or creating an intimidating, hostile, or offensive working environment" (Ill. Ann. State, ch. 68, Sec.2-102(E) [Smith-Hurd]). For another example of a state statute dealing expressly with sexual harassment, see Michigan's

Elliott-Larsen Act. Mich. Comp. Laws Ann., Sec. 37.211103 (h) (iii).

shakedowns. Forms of extortion in which officials accept money from citizens in lieu of enforcing the law. The term comes from the nineteenth-century British underworld, where shakedown was a common temporary substitute for a bed in many prostitutes' rooms; hence, their rooms also became known as shakedowns.

shall. In law this verb means must: mandatory actions or requirements. If the law states something shall be done, it is a positive and definite requirement. If the word may is used, discretion is allowed.

shanghai. To drug, intoxicate, or knock out someone in order to put him aboard ship as a seaman.

Sheldon, William (1898–1977) created a typology of somatotypes consisting of three body categories, each of which he related to a characteristic temperament. The endomorph was flabby and easygoing, the skinny ectomorph was inclined to be introspective, and the mesomorph was restless and tended to translate impulse into action.

shell game. A swindling game in which the operator manipulates a pea-sized object under three walnut shells. Victims wager they can tell which shell it is under. The object is generally concealed in the crook of the finger of the swindler, so that bettors always lose their money. The term is often used to connote any manipulative scheme that defrauds or misleads people.

sheriff. The elected chief officer of a county law enforcement agency, usually responsible for law enforcement in unincorporated areas and for the operation of the county jail; in some states, collects taxes. Sheriffs are popularly elected in all states except Rhode Island and are often not re-eligible. *See also* reeve

Sheriff's Association, National. Founded in 1940, it is a nonprofit organization dedicated to raising the level of professionalism among those in the criminal justice field. Publishes

Sheriff magazine (bimonthly). Address: 1450 Duke St., Alexandria, VA 22314. Web site: http://www.sheriffs.org/.

sheriff's department. A local law enforcement agency, organized at the county level, and directed by a sheriff, which exercises its law enforcement functions at the county level, usually within unincorporated areas, and operates the county jail in most jurisdictions. Sometimes referred to as the "SO" or Sheriff's Office.

Sherman Antitrust Act. An 1890 federal law providing that "every contract combination in the form of a trust or otherwise, or conspiracy in restraint of trade or commerce, is hereby declared to be illegal." Combinations of labor are included within the terms of this act, as are similar combinations of capital.

Sherman Report. A report by the National Advisory Commission on Higher Education for Police Officers, which criticized programs that concentrate heavily on training and that make a practice of employing law enforcement practitioners as part-time instructors.

shield law. (1) Protects professionals, such as doctors, lawyers, and ministers, from making public those facts that have been related to them in confidence by people who have sought their professional counsel. Journalists now cannot legally protect their news sources from public or court exposure and may contend that a shield law is necessary to ensure the flow of vital information. (2) The Supreme Court during May 1985 held that judges can be sued for violating constitutional rights and, if they lose, be forced to pay attorneys' fees. It affirmed an award against a Virginia magistrate who ordered two men jailed because they were unable to raise money for bail that she had illegally imposed on them for nonjailable misdemeanors. While permitting attorneys' fees against court officers, the justices left mostly intact the doctrine of judicial immunity, which shields judges, magistrates, and even prosecutors from damage suits related to their official acts. *See also* privileged communications

shock incarceration. Short-term, intensive incarceration followed by a specified term of community service. Historically, these were military-style boot camps designed for short-time and generally first-time offenders. The concept was first introduced in GA and OK during the early 1980s and grew to widespread use through the late 1990s. The boot-camp component has waned in recent years, although some elements of shock incarceration are still used nationwide.

shock probation. A type of split sentence used in some states, by which imprisoned offenders sentenced to long terms may be released to the community to serve the remainder of the sentence under supervision. It is hoped that the impact of the initial incarceration will have caused offenders to reevaluate their behavior. Failure to complete the probation satisfactorily generally results in reconfinement for the full duration of the sentence. *See also* split sentence

shoe bomber. On December 22, 2001, a passenger aboard American Airlines Flight 63 member attempted to ignite his shoe during flight. The passenger, Richard Colvin Reid was subdued on the airplane, arrested upon landing, and charged with interfering with flight crew. Upon subsequent examination, the sole of his shoe was found to contain a sufficient quantity of C-4 plastic explosives to cause the plane to crash. Reid was subsequently charged and pled guilty to eight counts of terrorism; he was sentenced to three consecutive life sentences. Reid, a self-admitted member of Al Qaeda, is currently incarcerated in a federal supermaximum security prison in Colorado. This crime led to requirement that U.S. airline passengers must remove their shoes for inspection before boarding airplanes. *See also* domestic terrorism; Reid, Richard Colvin

shoplifting. The theft of goods, wares, or merchandise from a store or shop (in retailing, such losses are included in the euphemism "inventory shrinkage"). Shoplifting has been the most common form of occasional property crime in the United States during the twentieth century, accounting for approximately 10 percent of all larceny theft. Shoplifting includes commercial shoplifters and so-called boosters, who steal merchandise to resell it, as well as pilferers, who steal for their own personal use. The pressures of inflation and recession in the late 1970s and early 1980s initiated higher levels of amateur shoplifting. During the 1979 Christmas season alone, it was estimated that shoplifting losses in the United States amounted to some $2 billion.

short ridge. In fingerprint patterns, a short, broken ridge or line. *See also* fingerprint patterns

Short Tandem Repeat on the Y-chromosome (Y-STR). Analysis of polymorphic regions on the Y-chromosome, which enables analysis of mixed samples of male-female DNA. This method is often used in genealogical testing. *See also* Deoxyribo nucleic acid; DNA analysis; Restriction Fragment Length Polymorphism (RFLP) test; Polymerase Chain Reaction (PCR); PCR-based Short Tandem Repeat (STR) method; Amplified Fragment Length Polymorphism (AmbFLP) method; and mitochondrial DNA (mtDNA)

shotgun. A smoothbore shoulder weapon that fires pellets or slugs. The usual classes are riot gun, skeet gun, and sporting gun.

shot pattern. The dispersion pattern of shot fired from a shotgun; pellets that separate from one another in flight. The shot pattern is determined by shooting at a target or other surface that will register the impact of the shots when they strike.

show cause. An order to appear in court and deliver reasons why certain circumstances continue either to be allowed or prohibited.

shrapnel. (1) Strictly speaking, small lead or steel balls contained in certain shells, which are discharged in every direction upon explosion of the shell. The system was invented by Lieutenant (later Gen.) Henry Shrapnel in 1784. (2) A term for munitions fragments.

sidewalk. That portion of a highway set apart by curbs, barriers, markings, or other delineations for pedestrian travel.

siege. The act or process of surrounding and attacking a fortified place so as to compel the surrender of its defenders and involving a prolonged effort to overcome resistance. One of the longest law enforcement sieges in American history was the 81-day standoff between the FBI and "freemen" in Jordan, Montana, extending from March 25 to June 13, 1996. Three other notable sieges were the 69-day American Indian Movement action at Wounded Knee in 1973; the 11-day standoff involving white separatist Randy Weaver and his family at Ruby Ridge, Idaho, in 1992; and the 51-day siege of the Branch Davidian compound near Waco, Texas, in 1993.

Siegel, Benjamin ("Bugsy," 1906–1947). American gangster involved in gambling and mafia bootlegging rackets during prohibition, Siegel was also a reported member of "Murder, Inc.," the Mafia's groups of organized assassins. He was known for his unpredictable, violent temper. From 1945–1947, he was responsible for the construction and opening of The Flamingo hotel in Las Vegas. Despite multiple delays and costs astronomically over budget, his life was spared due to the reported intervention of long time associate, Meyer Lansky. On June 20, 1947, Siegel was brutally murdered in his Beverly Hills home, reportedly in retaliation for his mismanagement of the Flamingo. *See also* Lansky, Meyer; Mafia; Murder Inc.

signal. (1) As applied to electronics, any transmitted electrical impulse. (2) Operationally, a type of message, the text of which consists of one or more letters, words, characters, signal flags, visual displays, or special sounds with prearranged meanings and which is conveyed or transmitted by visual, acoustical, or electrical means.

signal security. A generic term that includes both communications security and electronic security.

signals, 10-dash. A system of signals used in law enforcement that consists of the numeral 10 followed by other numbers. Such codes have prearranged meanings and are used frequently in radio communications.

silencer. A device designed to silence the explosive report caused by the discharge of cartridges by a small-arms weapon. It incorporates integral chambers or baffles that allow the gases to expand gradually.

"silver platter" doctrine. The name given to the controversial practice of circumventing rules prohibiting the introduction at federal trials of evidence illegally seized by federal officers. Federal officers exploited a loophole in the wording of a 1914 Supreme Court decision, *Weeks v. United States,* which said, "Evidence illegally seized by federal officers is inadmissible." Until curbed by the *Elkins v. United States* decision of 1960, federal police officers simply requested state or local officers to make seizures on their behalf. *See also* Court Cases: *Elkins v. United States; Weeks v. United States*

simple assault. Unlawful threatening, attempted inflicting, or inflicting of less than serious bodily injury, in the absence of a deadly weapon. *See also* aggravated assault

simple contract. A contract not under seal or record.

Simpson, Orenthal James "OJ" (1947–). A football hero and Heisman trophy winner, Simpson was charged with the 1994 murder of his ex-wife, Nicole Brown and her friend, Ron Goldman. While he was acquitted at criminal trial despite substantial evidence of ongoing domestic violence against his former wife and incriminating physical evidence at the scene, he was found responsible for the deaths in a 1999 civil suit. In August of 2007, rights to a book he was about to publish (*If I Did It*) was awarded to the Goldman family in partial payment of the civil suit. The following month, Simpson was arrested for armed robbery and kidnapping in Las Vegas. He was sentenced to 33 years in prison and is currently incarcerated in Nevada. *See also* domestic violence

simulated forgery. Forgery of writing accomplished by someone who practices the genuine writing until the forged writing is similar to the genuine.

simulation. Any model a researcher builds to convey his or her hypothesis of how variables interrelate. The simulation model is then used to make predictions, in contrast with the research technique of empirically examining relationships among variables and estimating relations among them based on data.

sine (Lat.). Without.

sine qua non. An indispensable thing; a necessity.

single action. A method of fire in some revolvers and shoulder arms in which the hammer must be cocked by hand, in contrast to double action, in which a single pull of the trigger both cocks and fires the weapon.

single-fingerprint registration. A system of classifying single fingerprints to permit identification of prints left at the scene of a crime. *See also* primary classification

Sing Sing. The New York State Penitentiary at Ossining, NY; the Ossining Correctional Facility.

Sirhan Sirhan. Convicted of assassinating Senator Robert F. Kennedy on June 5, 1968, in the pantry of the Ambassador Hotel in Los Angeles, CA. His release date was set for 1984, but revoked. In March of 2006, Sirhan was denied parole for the thirteenth time.

Situational Leadership Theory. Called "Life Cycle Theory" until the 1970s, situational leadership is a concept of leadership holding that the appropriate management style for a particular situation should be primarily dependent upon the maturity level of person or group supervised. Maturity is defined as a function of employees' general level of education, experience, motivation, desire to work, and willingness to accept responsibility.

sketching. The drawing or charting of objects, places, or scenes to show the details and/or relative positions of objects and other evidence.

skewness. In quantitative research, the amount by which a distribution departs from the symmetry of a bell-shaped curve. If the pattern of results has a longer tail on the right, it is said to be positively skewed; a long tail on the left indicates negative skewing.

skid. A controlled or uncontrolled slide by a vehicle, resulting from the loss of friction between the road surface and the tires.

skid marks. The marking or imprints left on a traveled surface by vehicle tires as a result of sliding or skidding. Calculations can be made of the direction and speed of a vehicle prior to a collision by examining the skid marks.

skin conductance. The measurement of autonomic activity in the skin, such as electrical impulses or perspiration. *See also* electroencephalograph, galvanometer

skyjacking. The hijacking of an airplane first occurred in the United States in 1961. The skyjacker typically: (a) wants to be flown to a destination other than that scheduled; (b) attempts to extort large sums of money from the airline; or (c) holds the passengers hostage for political purposes. Most U.S. skyjackings in the early 1960s involved people who wanted to fly to Cuba. From 1961 to 1968, there was an average of one skyjacking each month. The most recent notable skyjackings in the United States include the September 11 attacks on the World Trade Center and Pentagon, which resulted in suicide-crashes.

sky marshals. A group of officers who travel aboard passenger airplanes to protect against hijackers. Sky marshals are currently organized under the Federal Air Marshal Service (FAMS), Transportation Security Administration (TSA), a division of the U.S. Department of Homeland Security (DHS).

slander. The oral utterance or publication of a falsehood that is intended to defame a person or injure his or her reputation. *See also* libel and slander

Slaughterhouse Cases. 83 U.S. 36 (1873) was the first United States Supreme Court interpretation of the relatively new Fourteenth Amendment to the Constitution. It is viewed as a pivotal case in early civil rights law, reading the Fourteenth Amendment as protecting the "privileges or immunities" conferred by virtue of the federal United States citizenship to all individuals of all states within it, but not those privileges or immunities incident to citizenship of a state. Holding: Privileges and immunities of citizenship of the United States were to be protected by the Fourteenth Amendment not privileges and immunities of citizenship of a state.

slum. An area of urban blight marked by decaying buildings, abandoned businesses, widespread poverty, and accompanying social disorganization. Crime and violence and family disintegration are characteristic of slums. Renovation and rehabilitation are only partial solutions, for slums are symptoms of broad and deep problems of society.

small arms. All arms, including automatic weapons, up to and including those of .60 caliber and shotguns.

small claims court. A special court that provides expeditious, informal, and inexpensive adjudication of small contractual claims. In most jurisdictions, attorneys are not permitted for cases, and claims are limited to $1,500 ($2,000 in CA). Sometimes referred to as peoples' court.

Smith, Susan (1971–). South Carolina woman who gained national infamy when she reported a carjacking and kidnapping of her two sons, ages 1 and 3, by unknown male, black assailant on October 25, 1994. One week later, she confessed to killing both children by dumping her car into a local lake while the boys were restrained in their car seats. Smith was convicted and sentenced to thirty years, and she remains incarcerated in South Carolina. *See also* symbolic assailant

smoke bombs. Smoke bombs have a threefold purpose: they are used for screening movement, for creating an antipersonnel

effect in the open or in dug-in positions, and for making targets. They also have an incendiary effect, in that they will set fire to materials that are easily ignited, such as clothing, dry brush, and canvas. The bodies of the bombs are filled with plasticized white or white phosphorus. The functioning of a fuse and burster shatters the bomb on impact, dispersing the filler over a wide area. Atmospheric oxygen ignites the particles, which produce a dense white smoke.

smoke detector. A device that detects visible or invisible products of combustion. Types of smoke detectors include: ionization, photoelectric beam-type, photoelectric spot-type, and resistance bridge.

smoke grenade. A hand grenade or rifle grenade containing a smoke-producing mixture and used for screening or signaling. It is sometimes charged with colored smoke, such as red, green, yellow, or violet.

smuggle. To import or export without paying duty.

smuggling. Unlawful movement of goods across a national frontier or state boundary or into or out of a correctional facility.

sneeze gas. A gas that causes sneezing; specifically, diphenylchloroarsine.

sniperscope. An electronic device for use on a carbine or rifle that permits a shooter to aim at a target at night without being seen. Infrared rays illuminate the target, which is then viewed through a combination telescopic sight and fluorescent screen (in which all objects appear as various shades of green). The system was developed by the U.S. Army during World War II. It has an angle of view of 14 degrees and a range of 125 yards.

sobriety checkpoints. Temporary police locations in areas or on occasions noted for a high frequency of alcohol- or drug-impaired driving. *See also* driving under the influence cost recovery

social case work. A method of providing social services and personal counseling in order to improve the personal and family adjustments of clients. Each individual or family constitutes a case for the social worker.

social graph. The graph, diagram, or visual representation of the relationships between a given individual within a larger social network.

social indicators. Every three years, the book *Social Indicators* is published, providing statistical information about the population of the United States as a whole, including information on public safety. Contact: U.S. Census Bureau, 4600 Silver Hill Road, Washington, DC 20233.

Social Networking. (1) A type of analysis that includes diagramming relationships between an individual and other people based on the quality or frequency of their interactions upon some formal social graph; (2) also, the use of the Internet or similar electronic media to develop and maintain social relationships.

Social Networking sites. Internet-based locations such as Facebook, MySpace, Twitter, etc,. used primarily for social interactions. Law Enforcement agencies often use social networking sites to investigate criminal activity, background screening, and conduct internal (employee) investigations.

Social Security numbers. Numbers were first issued in 1936 by the Social Security Administration. The first three digits of numbers issued since 1972 have indicated the state of residence of the person to whom the number was issued. Address: Social Security Administration, Windsor Park Building, 6401 Security Building, Baltimore, MD 21235. Web site: http://www.ssa.gov/.

Society for the Reformation of Juvenile Delinquents. This organization opened the House of Refuge for young offenders in 1824, in New York City. It was the first institution in the United States whose function was to remove children from the primarily adult jails and prisons.

sociological law. A statement of scientifically established causal relations and of causal sequences and continuity; a social theory that has been proven. *See also* law

sociology. A term first used by Auguste Comte (1798–1857), who attempted to outline a new discipline modeled on the natural sciences. The scientific study of the phenomena arising out of the group relations of human beings; the study of humans and their human environment in relation to each other. Different schools of sociology lay varying emphasis on the related factors, some stressing the relationships themselves, such as interaction and association; while others emphasize human beings in their social relationships, focusing on the individual in varying roles and functions. It is uniformly recognized that the methods of sociology may be strictly scientific, and that the verified generalizations that are the earmark of true science are being progressively built up out of extensive and painstaking observation and analysis of the repetitious uniformities in group behavior.

sociopath. Antiquated term used colloquially to describe a person with an antisocial personality disorder or psychopathy.

sociopathy. Antiquated term for a set of characteristics similar to those described as psychopathy. The term derives from the first edition of the DSM (1952), with an implied etiology in bad parenting, compared psychopathy, which is a more empirically tested concept and is generally thought to be biologically based.

sodium amytal. So-called truth serum, this substance is also called amobarbital. Sodium amytal is a barbiturate derivative and is also considered a hypnotic. It was used in World War I and II, often to force confessions.

sodomy. (1) Scientifically, this term applies only to insertion of the penis into the rectum of another person. (2) In the laws of a number of states, however, sodomy includes oral-genital acts and bestiality: unlawful physical contact between the genitals of one person and the mouth or anus of another person or with the mouth, anus, or genitals of an animal. These laws were struck down by the U.S. Supreme Court in *Lawrence v. Texas* (decided June 2003), in which the Court held that laws proscribing behavior between consenting adults in the privacy of their own home were a denial of due process.

solicit. To ask earnestly; to petition.

solicitation. (1) *See* inchoate offense; (2) term sometimes used to reference the crime of solicitation for prostitution.

solicitor. A practitioner of the law who practices law in a court of chancery.

solicitor general (federal). Conducts and supervises government litigation in the Supreme Court. The Solicitor General determines the cases in which Supreme Court review will be sought by the government and the positions the government will take before the Court. He or she also reviews every case litigated by the federal government in which a lower court has decided against the United States to determine whether to appeal, and also decides whether the United States should file a brief as *amicus curiae* in any appellate court. For more information, contact: Office of the Solicitor General, DOJ, 950 Pennsylvania Ave., NW, Washington, DC 20530. Web site: http://www.justice.gov/osg/.

solicitor general (state). In states having no attorney general, the highest ranking law officer. Where there is an attorney general, the solicitor general is the next ranking law officer.

Son of Sam. *See* Berkowitz, David

Son of Sam Law. Type of law designed to keep criminals from profiting from their crimes, often by selling their stories. States can seize money earned from such arrangements and use it to compensate the criminal's victims.

Sotomayor, Sonia (1954–). Born in the Bronx, NY, Sotomayor graduated *summa cum laude,* from Princeton University and graduated from Yale Law School. Sotomayor was appointed as Judge of Southern New York U.S. District Court by President George H. W. Bush in 1992. President Bill Clinton nominated her as Judge of the U.S. Court of Appeals, Second Circuit, in 1998, and in May of 2009, President Barack Obama nominated her as Associate Justice to the U.S. Supreme Court. She was confirmed and sworn into office on August 6, 2009, and is the first Latina on the Court.

sound-sensing detection system. An alarm system that detects the audible sound caused by an attempted forcible entry into a protected structure. The system consists of microphones and a control unit containing an amplifier, accumulator, and a power supply. The unit's sensitivity is adjustable so that ambient noise or normal sounds will not initiate an alarm.

sovereign immunity. A doctrine under which a government and its subdivisions, in the conduct of governmental functions, is immune from civil liability resulting from wrongful acts of its agents. In 1946 the Federal Tort Claims Act abolished this immunity for the federal government; some states have also abolished the immunity, and courts in other states are striking it down.

SP. Abbreviation for: State Police, Shore Patrol (U.S. Navy), or Security Police.

spam. Unsolicited bulk e-mail for commercial gain. Spam is unlawful in some cases and many software programs automatically screen emails to remove spam.

span of control. Management principle suggesting that supervisors should supervise no more than three to six subordinates to remain effective. As the number of subordinates increases arithmetically, the number of possible interpersonal interactions increases geometrically. More generally, the term is used to describe any manager's level of responsibility in order to rank the job by comparison with others and/or determine the appropriate salary level.

special judge. A judge who is appointed to hear, and exercise all judicial functions for, a specific case. Special judges are appointed in addition to, not in lieu of, regularly appointed or elected judges. They conduct all criminal proceedings pertaining only to a specific case.

special verdict. A verdict by which the jury finds the facts only, leaving the judgment to the court.

specific deterrence. Sometimes called special deterrence, a strategy in which the punishment against one specific deviant serves as a specific example to prevent that offender from recidivating in the future. *See also* deterrence; general deterrence

specific intent. When a crime consists not merely in doing an act, but in doing it with a specific intent, the existence of that intent is an essential element of the case that must be proven; the existence of criminal intent is not presumed from the commission of the act.

special master. A master in chancery appointed to act as the representative of the court in some assigned action or transaction, such as collecting information, to aid the court in deciding if a constitutional violation has occurred, and to assist in developing or monitoring a remedial decree that involves constitutional violations. Prison inmates have been appointed as special masters to monitor consent decrees and report their findings to the court. *See also* consent decree, decree

specimen. An item of physical evidence, or that which might be evidence, in a criminal case, especially any item submitted to a crime laboratory. The laboratory may list or record the item as a questioned (Q) specimen or a known (K) specimen, according to its nature and whether it came from a known source.

spectrograph. A device used to photograph elements of the light spectrum. It is used in a crime laboratory to make a spectrogram, produced when various inorganic substances are examined to determine their composition,

and can detect the presence of minute quantities of materials.

speedy trial. The right of the defendant to have a prompt trial is guaranteed by the Sixth Amendment of the Constitution, which states, "In all criminal prosecution, the accused shall enjoy the right to a speedy and public trial." In 1970, the Supreme Court held that Florida did not give a defendant a speedy trial when he was not tried for six years while serving a term in federal prison, during which time the state maintained a detainer against him and the defendant repeatedly asked for a trial (*Dickey v. Florida*). Most states and the federal government (Speedy Trial Act of 1974, sponsored by Senator Sam J. Ervin of NC) have enacted statutes setting forth the time within which a defendant must be tried following the date of his or her arrest, detention, first appearance, or the filing of charges in court. Currently, if the accused is not brought to trial within 100 days, the case is dismissed. Jurisdictions differ, however, on whether dismissal on these grounds constitutes a bar to subsequent prosecution for the same offense(s).

spindle. A part of the combination-lock mechanism on a safe. The combination dial fits onto the outer end of the spindle, and its function is to turn the lock mechanism when the dial is rotated. On some types of safes, burglars gain entry by punching in or pulling out the spindle. *See also* pulling method; punching method

spiral rifling. The cutting of spiral grooves in the surface of the bore of a gun barrel. Invented about 1520 by G. Koller (or Kollner) of Vienna, this rifling imparts a rotary motion to the longitudinal axis of the bullet as it passes through the barrel, which is maintained during its flight. This rotation equalizes any defects or irregularities in the form of the bullet and in its density, thus tending to keep it in a straight course in its flight.

split sentence. A sentence explicitly requiring the convicted person to serve a period of confinement in a local, state, or federal facility followed by a period of probation. Shock probation is frequently used as another name for the split sentence, although neither term is recommended for reporting purposes.

spoils system. Practice by which political party loyalists are rewarded for their support with government offices. The Jacksonian senator William Marcy of New York proclaimed in 1831, "To the victor belong the spoils."

spontaneous declaration. An utterance made as a result of some sudden and/or shocking event, such as an accident or crime. *See also res gestae*

spoofing. The defeat or compromise of an alarm system by "tricking" or "fooling" its detection devices, such as by short-circuiting part or all of a series circuit, cutting wires in a parallel circuit, reducing the sensitivity of a sensor, or entering false signals into the system. Spoofing contrasts with circumvention.

spot protection. Protection of objects such as safes, art objects, or anything of value that could be damaged or removed from the premises.

spur. A ridge detail in a fingerprint, also called a hook; a hook-like ridge or small branch emanating from a single ridge line. *See also* fingerprint patterns

spy. Generally, anyone employed by a government to obtain secret information about another government; anyone who engages in espionage. *See also* Hanssen, Robert

staff. Personnel in the administrative functions of an organization and who are responsible for investigative, advisory, planning, accounting, and other functions.

staff functions. Doing things of an advisory, specialized, or technical nature that are not concerned directly with carrying out the main objectives of the organization or department. Such tasks include fiscal matters, personnel hiring and training, or planning and research.

stalking. A crime involving repeated following, spying on, or otherwise harassing someone such that the victim experiences a "credible threat" of bodily harm. California passed the first anti-stalking law in the United States in 1990. California Stalking law currently states, "any person who willfully, maliciously, and repeatedly follows or willfully and maliciously harasses another person and who makes a credible threat with the intent to place that person in reasonable fear for his or her safety, or the safety of his or her immediate family is guilty of the crime of stalking." As of 2010, all 50 states and the District of Columbia have some form of anti-stalking laws (sometimes called *criminal harassment* or *criminal menace*).

standard deviation. In a distribution of scores or observations gathered in a survey or experiment, two descriptive measures are particularly significant—indices of central tendency (mean, median, mode) and variability. The standard deviation is a measure of variability which reveals the degree to which scores in a distribution are clustered around the mean.

Standard Metropolitan Statistical Areas (SMSAs). *See* Metropolitan Statistical Areas

standard muzzle velocity. The velocity at which a given projectile is designed to leave the muzzle of a gun. The velocity is calculated on the basis of the particular gun, the propelling charge used, and the type of projectile fired from the gun. Firing tables are based on standard muzzle velocity.

standing. The qualifications needed to bring legal action. These qualifications relate to the existence of a controversy in which the plaintiff has suffered or is about to suffer an injury to or infringement upon a legal protected right that a court is competent to redress. Hence, a specific issue is said to have, or lack, legal standing.

standing order. An order that remains in force indefinitely, until it is amended or canceled.

star chamber proceeding. A secret proceeding in which a person is given little or no opportunity to present his or her case or defense, and in which the proceedings are conducted and conclusions reached without observing usual judicial formalities. The term comes from the Star Chamber, an English court established by King Charles I and abolished by Parliament in 1641. The Star Chamber had no jury and was permitted to apply torture.

Starkweather, Charles Raymond. On January 21, 1958, Starkweather set out on a murderous rampage across the American plains states. His mass slaughter lasted eight days and claimed the lives of 10 people. Three of the victims were the parents and baby sister of Charles's 14-year-old girlfriend, Carol Ann Fugate, who accompanied him on his trail of violence. Starkweather was electrocuted in the Nebraska State Penitentiary on June 14, 1959. The film *Nebraska* is based on this crime spree. *See also* serial murder

state and federal jurisdiction. The constitutional power of Congress to enact legislation, define crimes, and provide for their punishment implies that such legislation supersedes state statutes, and that the states cannot punish violations of federal law as offenses against the state. Where these provisions are not made explicit in federal laws, either expressly or by necessary implication, a state statute is not superseded by a federal law, and the same act may be punished as an offense against the United States and also as an offense against the state.

state constitutions. These differ materially from the U.S. Constitution. The state constitutions comprise, for the most part, restrictions or limitations of powers, whereas the federal document constitutes, for the most part, grants of powers.

state courts. The courts in the various states are created, and their jurisdiction is conferred and defined, by state statutes rather than federal or constitutional law.

state highway patrol. A state law enforcement agency whose principal functions consist of prevention, detection, and investigation

of motor vehicle offenses, and apprehension of traffic offenders.

state legislatures. These elected bodies have the inherent power to prohibit and punish any act as a crime, provided they do not violate the restrictions of the state and federal constitutions; and the courts cannot look further into the propriety of a penal statute than to ascertain whether the legislature had the power to enact it.

state police. A state law enforcement agency whose principal functions usually include maintaining statewide police communications, aiding local police in criminal investigation, police training, and guarding state property, and may include highway patrol. The earliest state police organization was the Texas Rangers, formed in 1835. In 1865 state constables were appointed in Massachusetts, with Connecticut adopting a similar force in 1903. The Arizona Rangers were established in 1901, followed by the New Mexico Mounted Police and the Pennsylvania State Police in 1905. The years after World War I saw a great expansion of state police forces: NY and MI in 1917; WV, 1919; NJ, 1921; and RI, 1925. Today all 50 states have some form of state police force.

state prisons. State prisons held 319,598 inmates at year end 1980. That figure rose to 743,382 in 1990 and 1,316,333 inmates in 2000. As of year-end 2006, there were 1,492,972 inmates in state prisons. These numbers do not include persons held in state jails (estimated at 766,010 in 2006), on probation (4,237,023 in 2006) or on parole (798,202 in 2006). *See also* Table 39. Adult Correctional Populations, 1980–2008, page 370; Table 44. United States Correctional Population, page 428

state's attorney. An officer, usually locally elected within a county, who represents the state in securing indictments and in prosecuting criminal cases; called a prosecuting attorney.

state's evidence. Testimony by a participant in the commission of a crime that incriminates

text continues on page 428

TABLE 44   UNITED STATES CORRECTIONAL POPULATION

Year	Probation Population	Jail Population	Prison Population	Parole Population	Total Correctional Population in the U.S.
1980	1,118,097	182,288	319,598	220,438	1,840,400
1985	1,968,712	254,986	487,593	300,203	3,011,500
1990	2,670,234	405,320	743,382	531,407	4,350,300
1995	3,077,861	507,044	1,078,542	679,421	5,342,900
2000	3,826,209	621,149	1,316,333	723,898	6,445,100
2005	4,166,757	747,529	1,448,344	780,616	7,051,900
2006	4,237,023	766,010	1,492,973	798,202	7,211,400

Source: Bureau of Justice Statistics.

others involved, given under the promise of immunity.

states' rights. As stated in the Tenth Amendment, "powers not delegated to the United States by the Constitution, nor prohibited by it to the States, are reserved to the States respectively, or to the people." In Article I, Section 8, however, the framers recognized the need for flexibility. This so-called elastic clause granted the federal government the power to enact legislation "necessary and proper for carrying into Execution the foregoing Powers." The battle about what is appropriately a concern of the states alone and what is a proper topic of federal legislation is a key and ongoing issue in American history and politics. Most key decisions limiting states' rights have been justified by the "due process" clause of the Fourteenth Amendment.

statistical analysis, multivariate. A set of techniques for analyzing the relationships among three or more variables. Multivariate analysis can have any of three major purposes: (1) to explain the variance in one dependent variable by two or more different independent variables; (2) to explain the variance in a set of dependent variables by some unmeasured construct; or (3) to explain a set of dependent variables by a set of independent variables.

statistical hypothesis. In research, a speculation as to the value of an unknown parameter in a population. The null hypothesis is the opposite of the hypothesis, which is ordinarily the conclusion that there is no relationship among or between the variables being tested. Because absolute proof of a scientific hypothesis is impossible, researchers rely on indirect proof by demonstrating that an observed sample statistic is so different from the results that would be predicted from the null hypothesis that it must be rejected in favor of the statistical hypothesis. However, there is always the possibility that the null hypothesis is true, and falsely rejecting it is called a Type I error; the opposite, or failing to reject a false null hypothesis, is called a Type II error. *See also* statistics

statistical inference. Generalized statements about the characteristics of a population made on the basis of information obtained from the study of one or more samples of the population. Such inference is necessary whenever a researcher wishes to test a hypothesis but cannot study an entire population. *See also* sampling

statistical model. One or more equations expressing the relationship between two or more variables. These equations must be capable of fitting in with observed data, and the precision of the fit is evaluated. Statistical models are expressions of hypothetical statements derived from theories; as such, they assume that the observable world works in the way predicted by the theory. If the model can be shown to fit observed data well, it lends support to the theory. A poor fit casts doubt on the theory.

statistical significance. A demonstration that the probability that a null hypothesis is true is very small. When a researcher states that a result is statistically significant at the 0.05 level, he or she means that the probability of obtaining a sample statistic as large as or larger than that achieved if the null hypothesis is true is less than 0.05, which is grounds for rejecting the null hypothesis. Statistical significance depends not only on the discrepancy between an observed sample statistic and hypothesized population parameter, but also on the size of the sample taken. Specifically, the larger the sample size, the easier it is to attain statistical significance. Care must be taken not to confuse statistical significance with substantive significance. Some substantively trivial relationships may well be statistically significant if one's sample size is large enough. For example, in a large enough sample of state prison inmates, a statistically significant number might have moles somewhere on their bodies—a substantively trivial relationship. *See also* statistics

statistical theory. Like a hypothesis, a theory states relationships in statistical as well as verbal terms in order to lend precision to research.

statistics. A method of analyzing data gathered from observations of samples in order to (1) describe the amount of variation in each of two or more variables; (2) describe relationships hypothesized to exist between or among the variables; and (3) make inferences from the results to the larger population from which the sample was drawn. A numerical value summarizing a characteristic of a sample (such as the sample mean) is called a sample statistic, whereas the comparable value computed in the population, such as the population mean, is called a population parameter.

status offense. Acts that are unlawful due to the status of the actor, not the act itself. Any act that is not a crime when committed by an adult is generally a status offense. Generally, status offenses are declared by statute to be an offense, but only when committed or engaged in by a juvenile, and that can be adjudicated only by a juvenile court. Typical status offenses are violation of curfew, running away from home, truancy, possession of or consuming alcohol, engaging in consensual sex below the legal age, "incorrigibility," "having delinquent tendencies," "leading an immoral life," and being "in need of supervision." Status offense ordinarily refers to juvenile conduct, but the term has also been used to refer to adults who were charged with the status offense of being vagrant or an addict.

status quo (Lat.). The situation in which a case was at any given date; sometimes referred to as *in status quo*. In general, the term connotes any existing condition or set of circumstances.

statute. A law enacted by, or with the authority of, a legislature.

statute law. An act of a legislature; a particular law enacted and established by the will of the legislative department of government; the written will of a legislature, solemnly expressed according to the forms necessary to constitute it a law of a state.

statute of limitations. A term applied to numerous statutes that set a limit on the length of time that may elapse between an event giving rise to a cause of action and the commencement of a suit to enforce that cause. The purpose is to settle people's affairs so that they are not forever subject to doubt. These statutory requirements simply mean that, within the prescribed period of the statute, an indictment, a complaint, or information must be filed. The time requirement does not run when the defendant is out of the state. Crimes specified as felonies have a three-year statute of limitations from time information is filed, not from filing of complaint. A one-year statute of limitations is specified for misdemeanors from the time a complaint is filed. When these time limits have expired, the defendant cannot be tried for the offense. This is jurisdictional, and a conviction after time has run out is void, even if the defendant does not plead this as a defense. The time starts to run from the date a crime was committed. The statute of limitations for the offense of "acceptance of bribe by a public official or employee" is six years. There is no statute of limitations for murder, embezzlement of public money, or falsification of public records. The federal statute of limitations regarding the liability to pay a fine expires (a) 20 years after the entry of the judgment or (b) on the death of the person fined.

statutes, repeal of. Except in jurisdictions where neither English nor American common law is in force, the general rule is that, if a statute is repealed without a saving clause, there can be no prosecution or punishment for a violation of it that occurred before the repeal. The repeal of an existing statute or law under which a proceeding is pending puts an end to the proceeding, unless it is saved by a proper saving clause in the repealing statute. Even when the statute is repealed after the accused has been convicted, judgment may be arrested, and, if an appeal from a conviction is pending when the statute is repealed, the judgment of conviction must be set aside and the indictment quashed. But a repeal after final judgment of an appellate court will neither vacate the judgment nor prevent the carrying out of the sentence.

statutory. Pertaining to a law or statute, that is, to a law enacted by a legislative body.

statutory rape. Consensual sexual intercourse with any female who is under the age of consent specified by statute. In some jurisdictions, the definition includes males as potential victims.

stay. A halting of judicial proceedings by court order.

stay ad interim (Lat.). A temporary stoppage of proceedings, pending the completion of another action or proceeding.

stay of execution. The stopping by a court of the carrying out or implementation of a judgment, that is, of a court order previously issued.

steal. To appropriate or take something of value that is the property of another, without the consent of the owner; to commit theft.

Stealth Retaliation. A nonviolent act of vengeance where the retaliator confiscates the wealth of a wrongdoer when no one is around to observe or prevent it.

Stephanie's Law (New York). Passed in 2003 "to amend the penal law, in relation to surreptitious surveillance without consent and disseminating an unlawful recording thereof and to amend the correction law, in relation to registration under the sex offender registration act." Laws of New York, 2003, Chapter 69. See also sex offender

stet (Lat.). Let it stand.

stereotype. An exaggerated or oversimplified set of beliefs about a particular category, especially a national, ethnic, or racial group of people. Stereotypes are a characteristic feature of prejudiced thinking. Biased people have a fixed mental image of the group or class against whom they are prejudiced, and that they apply to all members of the group or class without attempting to test their preconceptions against reality. The term is derived from the molded cast used in the printing process.

stigmata. In criminology, physical defects or characteristics that were once believed to be influential in producing or indicating criminal conduct. See also Lombroso, Cesare

stimulant. A drug or other substance that speeds up the physiological processes of the body. Sometimes referred to as "uppers," these drugs have a wide variety of types and effects. Prolonged and repeated usage has been known to cause physical and psychological dependence. Many stimulants are served over the counter like nicotine and caffeine. Others are illegal and on the DEA's scheduling of illicit drugs. Cocaine, crack, and amphetamines are examples of illicit stimulants.

sting operation. The typical sting involves using various undercover methods to control large-scale theft. Police officers pose as purchasers (fences) of stolen goods, setting up contact points and storefronts wired for sound and videotape. Perhaps the best known was the Washington, DC, sting operation in 1975, in which local police joined with the FBI and the Treasury Department in posing as members of the "New York Mafia." During a five-month period, they purchased some $2.4 million in stolen property (for $67,000) and arrested a total of 180 "customers."

stipend. A salary; fixed payment for work done.

stipulation. An agreement between attorneys representing opposing parties to perform or refrain from something in connection with a case in progress in court or pending court action.

Stockholm Syndrome. A term for misplaced empathy or compassion experienced by victims of terrorists, who may tend to identify with their captors or abductors, as was the case with a group held captive in a bank vault in Stockholm in August 1973. One of the female hostages later married her captor.

stolen property; buying, receiving, possessing. The terminology used in the annual Uniform Crime Reports to designate and measure the frequency of this type of offense.

stolen property offenses. The unlawful receiving, buying, distributing, selling, transporting, concealing, or possessing of the property of another by a person who knows that the property has been unlawfully obtained from the owner or other lawful possessor.

Stone, Harlan Fiske. American jurist (1872–1945) who was the eleventh Chief Justice of the Supreme Court. He began his law practice in New York City in 1899. In 1924 President Calvin Coolidge appointed Stone attorney general, and in 1925 he became an associate justice of the Supreme Court. In 1941 President Franklin Roosevelt,

ignoring partisan politics and Stone's basically Republican philosophy, selected him to succeed Charles Evans Hughes as chief justice. During World War II, he presided over cases of martial law, military courts, and treason. One of his more famous dissents (1935) involved the constitutionality of the first Agricultural Adjustment Act of the New Deal. Stone wrote that "while unconstitutional exercise of power by the government is subject to judicial restraint, the only check upon our exercise of power is our own sense of restraint."

Stonewall Riot. On June 28, 1969, New York City police conducted a routine raid at the Stonewall Inn, a gay bar in Greenwich Village. The officers had a search warrant to investigate reports that liquor was sold illegally, but patrons maintained the police harassed them because they were homosexual. A melee ensued, leading to the injury of 13 patrons and four policemen. Two more riots erupted that week; one the next day, involving hundreds of protesters. The Stonewall riots are considered the birth of the gay rights movement. The anniversary of the Stonewall riots is celebrated each year by gay rights activists and civil libertarians. *See also* gay; White Night

stop and frisk. The detaining of someone by a law enforcement officer for the purpose of investigation, accompanied by the officer's superficial examination of the person's body surface or clothing to discover weapons, contraband, or other objects relating to criminal activity. It is intended to stop short of any activity that could be considered a violation of a citizen's constitutional rights.

stoppage in transit. The right of a seller who has not yet been paid for his or her goods to stop the merchandise in transit after it has been removed from his or her possession.

strain-sensitive cable. An electrical cable that is designed to produce a signal whenever the cable is strained by a change in applied force. Typical uses including mounting it in a wall to detect any attempted forced entry through the wall, or fastening it to a fence to detect climbing on the fence, or burying it around a perimeter to detect walking or driving across the perimeter.

stratification. Often called social stratification, this is the divisions of persons into groups based on social class. It is more often a phenomenon that reflects systemic, unequal access to education and resources than a deliberate act by some group.

streaker. A person who engages in streaking.

streaking. The act of disrobing and running naked through a public place, often a college campus, for example. The practice, which can include the naked running of one person or a group of people, was more common in the 1960s and 1970s than today. The record for the largest number of streakers was set in 1974 at the University of Georgia, with 1,543 streakers. While it is generally a form of sophomoric humor, persons who engage in such activity are subject to prosecution. *See also* exhibitionism, sex offender

street. A way publicly maintained and open to the use of the public for purposes of vehicular travel. The term includes highway.

street crime. A class of offenses, sometimes formally defined as those that occur in public locations, are visible and assaultive, and thus constitute a special risk to the public and a special target for law enforcement preventive efforts and prosecutorial attention. Typically included are robbery, purse snatching, and any kind of assault outside a residence. *See also* treatment alternatives to street crime

stress. Stress is the emotional or physical strain an organism experiences due to change. Selye (1975) divided stress into two categories: eustress, created by positive or favorable change; and distress, caused by negative or unfavorable change. Stress occurs whenever individuals must adapt to demands placed on them. When they are placed under a great deal of adverse stress, they may no longer be able to function normally. Most frequently the result of prolonged distress is a breakdown in the hemostatic mechanisms that normally keep the body working as a whole.

An individual who is plagued by excessive tension and anxiety may develop headaches, ulcers, high blood pressure, or muscular ailments. These symptoms, generally referred to as psycho-physiological disorders, reflect true organic malfunctions that are caused by the body's efforts to cope with unusually high stress levels. Successfully dealing with stress involves such coping mechanisms as exercise, relaxation techniques, recreation, meditation, diet changes, and psychological counseling. *See also* general adaptation syndrome; Post Traumatic Stress Disorder (PTSD); Type-A personality

strict construction. Doctrine that the Constitution should have only its traditional literal meaning and that constitutional changes should be made through the amendment process.

strict liability. Category of laws under which a person is criminally and/or civilly liable for their actions in violation of said laws, regardless of their intent. Examples of strict liability laws in criminal justice include providing alcohol to persons under the legal drinking age and engaging in sexual relations with a person under the legal age of consent. In both examples, whether the offender was aware their victim was under the legal age for alcohol or sex is irrelevant; merely committing the act is sufficient for prosecution.

strike. A collective refusal by employees to work; a work stoppage. A " stoppage" is any interruption of employee activity lasting a full shift or day or longer and involving six or more workers. In 1981, 14,000 Minnesota state employees walked off their jobs. The strike lasted 22 days and resulted in wage increases. Although the first major police strike was in Boston in 1919, the police in Cincinnati, OH, had struck in September 1918. According to the Bureau of Labor Statistics, between 1970 and 1980, 215 police strikes occurred in U.S. cities, and job actions were threatened in many others. The Police Association of New Orleans led a 15-day strike that ended on March 4, 1979. The strike caused the city to reorganize the association, but the furor over cancellation of Mardi Gras turned public opinion against the union and resulted in no contract, 200 disciplinary actions, fines of $600,000, and disbanding of the Teamsters local. The first police strike in California was in 1969 in the city of Vallejo. On January 14, 1971, approximately 2,100 New York City police officers walked off the job. *See also* Boston police strike; job action; Railroad Strike

stripes. Chevrons used on uniforms to indicate an officer's rank.

strip search. (1) A search of a crime scene, usually outdoors, where the terrain to be searched is divided into strips and searched carefully strip by strip; generally followed by a grid search, which consists of dividing the area into strips at right angles to the lines used in the strip search. (2) A search of a person whose wearing apparel is removed so that both the clothing and the individual's body (including cavities) can be thoroughly examined. In *Safford Unified School Dist. #1 v. Redding* (2009), the USSC ruled that it was unconstitutional for school officials to strip search a 13-year-old student for ibuprofen; however, the court indicated strip searches could be warranted if the school officials strongly believed the student carried a dangerous drug or weapon. As of 2009, seven states forbid strip searches of children at school: California, Iowa, New Jersey, Oklahoma, South Carolina, Washington and Wisconsin.

Stroud, Robert Franklin ("Birdman of Alcatraz," 1887–1963). Convicted of manslaughter and sentenced to 12 years in 1909, Stroud committed multiple crimes in prison, including attacks on guards, assaults, extortion, and murder. He was sentenced to death for the murder of a guard, a sentence that was commuted to life in solitary confinement. After six years of segregation, he was transferred to the medical wing, where he died in 1963. He is nicknamed "Birdman" for his practice of raising sparrows and canaries in the 1930s while incarcerated at Leavenworth (he raised no birds subsequent to his transfer to Alcatraz in 1942).

struck jury. A trial jury of 12 secured by having opposing counsel each strike out 12 names from a list of 48 veniremen and thereafter eliminate 12 more from the list by exercising the right of challenge.

strychnine. A poison, bitter in taste, composed of white crystals, derived from *nux vomica* and certain other plants.

Students Against Destructive Decisions (SADD). Originally founded as Students Against Drunk Driving in 1981, SADD's mission is to "provide students with the best prevention tools possible to deal with the issues of underage drinking, other drug use, impaired driving and other destructive decisions." Address: SADD National, 255 Main Street, Marlborough, MA 01752. Web: http://www.sadd.org/.

Students Against Driving Drunk. *See* Students Against Destructive Decisions

Students for a Democratic Society (SDS). Student organization that was influential during the 1960s. It evolved from a small radical study group of socialists who attracted liberal and idealistic students disenchanted with the American establishment. SDS grew into the largest, most powerful national white leftist organization, which had, at its peak, an estimated 70,000 to 100,000 members. SDS became a major national force when it led white students to take action (mostly sit-ins and a few violent incidents) against racism, poverty, and war on major college campuses across the nation in the spring and summer of 1968. Due in large part to factionalism, SDS declined in power and influence by summer 1969, at which time a small, tightly organized, revolutionary fighting force of white youth, called Weathermen, emerged. They engaged in bombings, street fighting, and other offensive action. They were the first organization in recent years to stress publicly the importance of armed social protest in the United States. In 1970 the Weathermen moved underground. *See also* Weathermen

stun bomb. A device designed not to inflict permanent injury but to disable, for several seconds, those exposed to its concussive effect.

stun gun. A correctional riot control device that fires a flat shot bag with the ability to knock someone down without penetrating his or her body. The original model, manufactured by Nova Technologies of Austin, TX, was the handheld Nova XR 5000 Stun Gun, producing 45,000 volts of electricity and a bit larger than an electric razor, is said to be capable of immobilizing a person for up to 90 seconds. The Union City Police department was the first in California to employ stun guns.

St. Valentine's Day Massacre. *See* Saint Valentine's Day Massacre. *See also* Egan's rats

subject. (1) The person under investigation or about whom information is being sought by a peace officer. (2) In moulage or casting, the object or impression to be reproduced or cast.

sub justice. Under or before a judge or court undetermined.

suborn. To cause, persuade, or bribe a person to give false testimony while under oath in judicial matter.

subornation of perjury. Procuring another to commit legal perjury.

subpoena. A written order, issued by a judicial officer, prosecutor, defense attorney, or grand jury, requiring a specified person to appear in a designated court at a specified time in order to testify in a case under the jurisdiction of that court or to bring material to be used as evidence to that court. Subpoenas may be served in person by a law enforcement office or by another person authorized to do so, but generally not by a person involved in the action. In some jurisdictions some types of subpoenas may be served by mail or by telephone. Failure to obey a subpoena is contempt of court. A subpoena issued for the appearance of a hostile witness or person who has failed to appear in answer to a previous subpoena and authorizing a law enforcement officer to bring that person to the court is often called an instanter. A subpoena to serve as a witness is called a subpoena *testificatum*. A subpoena to bring material is called a subpoena *duces tecum.*

subrogation. The substitution of one person for another insofar as legal claims or rights are concerned.

sub rosa (Lat.). Privately, or in a manner not open to public scrutiny.

substantive evidence. Evidence offered for the purpose of proving a fact at issue, as opposed to evidence given for the purpose of discrediting a witness.

substantive felony. An independent felony; one not dependent on the conviction of another person for another crime.

substantive law. The part of law that creates, defines, and regulates rights.

substantive rights. Guarantees granted to all U.S. citizens under the Constitution. These rights, essential to personal liberty, are listed in the First, Thirteenth, and Fourteenth Amendments and include freedom of speech, press, religion, assembly, and petition. They also include freedom from involuntary servitude and equal protection under the law. These rights may be limited, but only in accordance with due process.

substitutionary evidence. Evidence allowed as a substitute for original or primary evidence.

subterfuge. Any plan, strategy, or action used to evade something unpleasant or difficult or to gain an unfair advantage.

suburb. From the Latin *sub urbe,* for below the city, a term meaning any community that is part of a metropolitan area but outside the city limits. Suburb has always implied proximity to the city, leading to the term exurb for dependent communities farther away from the urban center.

subversion. Demolition; overthrow; destruction; a cause of destruction or overthrow, especially of a government.

sue. To bring a lawsuit against another; to commence a legal action.

sufficiency of bail. The amount of bail is required to be enough, but not more than enough, to ensure the appearance of the accused.

sufficient evidence. Adequate evidence; such evidence in character, weight, or amount as will legally justify the judicial or official action demanded; according to circumstances, it may be *prima facie* or satisfactory evidence, according to the definition of these terms.

suicide. The human act of intentional, self-inflicted death. Self-killing is one of the 10 leading causes of death in most Western countries. The Centers for Disease Control (CDC) reported 34,000 in 2007. Approximately 33,000 suicides are recorded in the United States each year, but experts estimate the true number is closer to 40,000 annually. More men than women take their own lives by a ratio of three to one, but more women attempt suicide. Suicidologists are criminologists, sociologists, psychologists, and others who specialize in the study of suicide. A major preventive focus was provided in 1966 when the federal government established the Center for Studies of Suicide Prevention as part of the National Institutes of Mental Health. The first full-scale, professionally staffed suicide prevention center was established in Los Angeles in 1958.

Substance Abuse and Mental Health Services Administration (SAMHSA). Established in 1992, SAMHSA's mission is to "reduce the impact of substance abuse and mental illness on America's communities." To achieve this mission SAMHSA coordinates research through four agencies: Center for Mental Health Services (CMHS); Center for Substance Abuse Prevention (CSAP); Center for Substance Abuse Treatment (OSAT); and Office of Applied Studies (OAS). Address: SAMHSA's Health Information Network, P.O. Box 2345, Rockville, MD 20847-2345; Web: http://www.samhsa.gov/.

substance use disorder. The World Health Organization (WHO) defines a psychoactive substance use disorder as "mental and behavioural disorders due to psychoactive substance use. The term encompasses acute intoxication, harmful use, dependence syndrome, withdrawal state, withdrawal state with delirium, psychotic disorder and amnesic syndrome."

substance dependence. Defined by the DSM-IV as a maladaptive pattern of substance abuse, leading to clinically significant impairment or distress, as manifested by three (or more) specified criteria, occurring at any time in the same 12-month period.

Substantial Capacity Test. Type of insanity defense defined by the American Law Institute (ALI) around 1962 in the Model Penal Code. This standard defines insanity as a lack of substantial capacity to understand the wrongfulness of an act or conform one's behavior to law. *See also* insanity

summary proceeding. A judicial action, usually a judgment or decision, that is taken without benefit of a formal hearing. Summary decisions of the Supreme Court are those made without the Court's having heard oral arguments on the issue.

summons. A written order issued by a judicial officer requiring a person accused of a criminal offense to appear in a designated court at a specified time to answer the charge(s). A document issued by a law enforcement officer requiring court appearance of an accused person, is, in this terminology, classified as a citation.

sunset laws. Legislation enacted and designed to disband agencies that do not serve the public. The nation's first sunset law was enacted in 1976. Sunset legislation typically specifies that a government program will automatically expire, along with its administrative bureaucracy, after a certain number of years, often seven, in the expectation that it will have served its purpose within that time. The burden is then on the government and the program's advocates to justify the agency's existence beyond the expiration.

sunshine legislation. In recent years both state and federal governments have adopted significant legislation requiring that key meetings and hearings take place "in the sunshine"—or publicly—so that democratic participation and influence on government can be more effectively exercised at critical points in the policy-making process. Such laws are a reaction against government secrecy. In the Sunshine Act of 1977, the federal government required that some 50 executive agencies, regulatory commissions, advisory committees, and independent offices hold public meetings or publish minutes of their meetings. The act also banned all unofficial contracts between agencies and persons affected by them. Cabinet departments are exempted, but Congress has since passed rules requiring more sunshine on many of its internal deliberations.

suit. Prosecution of some claim or demand in a court of justice.

Sullivan Act. A law of New York State making it a felony to possess firearms without legal authority.

summary. (1) Done without delay or ceremony; done instantly or quickly; without formality. (2) In law, a hasty or arbitrary procedure, such as a trial without a jury.

summary jurisdiction. The jurisdiction of a court to give a judgment or make an order itself, forthwith; for example, to commit to prison for contempt; to punish malpractice in a solicitor; or, in the case of justices of the peace, a jurisdiction to convict offenders themselves instead of committing them for trial by jury.

Sundance Kid. *See* Longabaugh, Harry. *See also* Cassidy, Butch; Wild Bunch

supermax, supermaximum. Term used to reference prisons with the highest levels of security, generally reserved for the most hardened of offenders, including inmates who commit serious violence in lower-level institutions, and those who threaten the security of officers, prisons or the nation (e.g., terrorists). Conditions of confinement in such facilities often includes near-constant lock-down and solitary confinement. Human rights organizations have criticized supermax facilities as routinely violating Eighth amendment protections against cruel and unusual punishment, although supermax facilities remain in operation in nearly every state and the federal system.

superior court. (1) A court of record or general trial court in some states, superior to a justice of the peace or magistrate's court. (2) In other states, an intermediate court between the general trial court and the highest appellate court.

superior court warrant of arrest. In New York, a subpoena that a police officer delivers to the defendant.

supersede. To set aside; annul.

supersedeas, **writ of**. An order to stay the proceedings. It is either expressed by the issuance of a writ of *supersedeas,* or implied by the issuance of a writ, as of *certiorari.*

supervised probation. Guidance, treatment, or regulation by a probation agency of the behavior of a person who is subject to adjudication or who has been convicted of an offense, resulting from a formal court order or a probation agency decision. Supervision of adults may be in lieu of prosecution or judgment or after a judgment of conviction. Supervised probation may be a substitute for confinement or may occur after a period of confinement in jail or prison. Probation supervision differs according to the degree of intensity of supervision and amount of services provided to subjects. A common, broad distinction is between active supervision (contact between the agency and the client occurs on a regular basis) and inactive supervision (contact occurs only when initiated by the client or other interested party outside the probation agency and is not on a regular basis). Inactive cases are sometimes called "banked" cases.

supervision. Authorized and required guidance, treatment, and/or regulation of the behavior of a person who is subject to adjudication or who has been adjudicated to be an offender, performed by a correctional agency.

supervisory alarm system. An alarm system that monitors conditions or persons or both and signals any deviation from an established norm or schedule. Examples are the monitoring of signals from guard patrol stations for irregularities in the progression along a prescribed patrol route and the monitoring of production or safety conditions, such as sprinkler water pressure, temperature, or liquid level.

supporting evidence. Evidence that will bolster and strengthen such evidence as eyewitness testimony, transfer evidence, and statements of the accused. Supportive evidence includes such things as proof of motivation, similarity of *modus operandi* to other crimes known to have been committed by the accused, the accused having possession of the stolen property, and so forth.

suppression hearing. A hearing to determine whether or not the court will prohibit specified statements, documents, or objects from being introduced into evidence in a trial.

supra (Lat). Above; previously referred to.

supreme court, state. Usually the highest court in the state judicial system.

Supreme Court, U.S. Heads the judicial branch of the American government and is the nation's highest law court. It also performs a political function as the official interpreter and expounder of the Constitution. Because many of the most important provisions of the Constitution are extremely broad and offer much room for difference of interpretation (such as due process of law or equal protection of the laws), the Court's role in the political development of the American republic has been great, often exceeding that of the president or Congress. The Supreme Court was created by Article III of the Constitution and is headed by the Chief Justice of the United States. The size of the Court is determined by Congress; since 1869 it has been composed of nine justices appointed by the president with the advice and consent of the Senate. They serve during good behavior and are removable only by death, resignation, or impeachment. The Supreme Court is primarily an appellate court. It reviews decisions of the lower federal courts by writ of *certiorari,* a discretionary writ granted on the affirmative vote of four of the nine justices (Rule of Four). The Court also hears appeals against decisions of state supreme courts that involve interpretation of the Constitution, federal laws, or treaties. In addition, a few types of cases, principally suits between states, can be filed directly in the original jurisdiction of the Supreme Court without having gone through any other court. When President George Washington made his nominations for the Supreme Court in 1790, his six selections were all white, male, and Protestant. The first Roman Catholic justice appointed (in 1836) was Roger Brooke Taney, the son of a Maryland plantation owner. Another 80 years passed before the barrier against Jews was finally breached. In 1916 President Woodrow Wilson filled a vacant seat with Louis Dembitz Brandeis. The barrier against blacks fell in 1967 with President Lyndon B. Johnson's appointment of Thurgood Marshall, a former U.S. Court of Appeals judge. And after almost two centuries, the barrier against women also fell with the appointment of Sandra Day O'Connor, an Arizona Court of Appeals judge nominated by President Ronald W. Reagan in 1981 and confirmed by the Senate on September 28, 1981, by a unanimous vote. The 2009 appointment of Sonia Sotomayor is the first person of Latino descent on the court. *See* Table 45. United States Supreme Court, 2010 next page

surety. One who undertakes to become responsible for the debt of another; one who binds him- or herself for the performance of some act of another.

<table>
<tr><td colspan="4">**TABLE 45   UNITED STATES SUPREME COURT, 2010**</td></tr>
</table>

Justice	Year of Birth	Year of Appointment	Appointment Made by
John G. Roberts Jr., Chief Justice of the United States	1955	2003	President George W. Bush
Elena Kagan, Associate Justice	1960	2010	President Barack Obama
Antonin Scalia, Associate Justice	1936	1986	President Ronald Reagan
Clarence Thomas, Associate Justice	1948	1991	President George H. W. Bush
Ruth Bader Ginsberg, Associate Justice	1933	1993	President William Clinton
Stephen G. Breyer, Associate Justice	1938	1994	President William Clinton
Samuel Anthony Alito Jr., Associate Justice	1950	2006	President George W. Bush
Sonia Sotomayor, Associate Justice	1954	2009	President Barack Obama

Source: Supreme Court of the United States, *Biographies of the Current Justices of the Supreme Court.*

suretyship. An undertaking to answer for the debt, default, or miscarriage of another.

surprise. A procedural pleading available to parties to a trial when something unexpected, which could not be prevented by due diligence, develops. The side that is disadvantaged by such a development may plead surprise.

surreptitious. Covert, hidden, concealed, or disguised.

surrogate. A judicial officer who has jurisdiction over the probate of wills, the settlement of estates, and so forth.

surveillance. (1) Control of premises for security purposes through alarm systems, closed circuit television, or other monitoring methods. (2) Supervision or inspection of industrial processes by monitoring those conditions that could cause damage if not corrected. (3) Police investigative technique involving visual or electronic observation or listening directed at a person or place (such as stakeout, tailing suspects, or wiretapping). *See also* supervisory alarm system

surveillance cameras. Closed-circuit television (CCTV) which sends a specified signal to a specified place, often a looped recording device. Surveillance cameras are often used at banks and financial institutions, retail establishments with high value daily receipts (such as jewelry stores), and establishments with high volume foot traffic (such as gas stations and liquor stores). The National Institute of Standards and Technology created the Detection, Inspection, and Enforcement Technologies program to provide advice on how to select surveillance cameras for specific needs, including tips on storing processed film, improving photo quality, and selecting film and lens size. For information, contact: Office of Law Enforcement Standards Institute, National Institute of Standards and Technology, 100 Bureau Drive, M/S 8102, Gaithersburg, MD 20899-8102. Web site: http://www.eeel.nist.gov/oles/detection.html.

survey. A study that selects a sample from some larger population in order to ascertain the prevalence, incidence, and interrelations of selected variables. The survey is used primarily to determine the distribution of persons on some variable, such as the percentage of them opposed to capital punishment, and to determine other variables accompanying that opinion or position. A researcher begins by deciding what populations to study—from an entire country or state to a particular subgroup such as prisoners, women police officers, or juvenile arrestees. Next, the surveyor designates a sample of persons representing this population who will be studied. Depending on the research design, this may be a simple random sample, a stratified sample, a cluster sample, or a quota sample. Additionally, depending on research aims, a cross-sectional or panel study may be used. *See also* sampling

suspect. An adult or juvenile considered by a criminal justice agency to be one who may have committed a specific criminal offense but who has not yet been arrested or charged.

suspended sentence. A court disposition of a convicted person, pronouncing a penalty of a fine or commitment to confinement but unconditionally discharging the defendant or holding execution of the penalty in abeyance upon good behavior. *See also* deferred sentencing

suspension of judgment. A court action pronouncing a fine or a prison sentence followed by an order that, upon certain conditions, the payment of the fine, the prison term, or either of them need not be met.

suspicion. Category in the Uniform Crime Reports used to record and report arrests made on grounds of suspicion, in jurisdictions where the law permits, in which the arrestee is later released without being charged. Suspicion is not an offense.

Sutton, Willie. Willie "the actor" Sutton was America's most famous bank robber, who, during his half-century career, plundered almost 100 banks using a variety of ruses, disguises, pioneering safe-cracking techniques, and precision timing. He was arrested, for the fourth time, in New York for possession of a gun in 1952.

SWAT. An acronym for Special Weapons and Tactics. The forerunner was apparently New York City's Tactical Patrol Force (TPF). During the 1960s and 1970s, the TPFs

viewed their 1,000-member force as the elite of incorruptible law enforcement. In addition to mob and riot control, the TPFs swept into high crime areas to apprehend muggers and robbers, often using a variety of decoy units that readily blended into the street life. More visible and controversial are the newer, commando-style police units known as SWAT teams, carefully chosen and trained in the use of weapons and strategic invasion tactics and typically used in situations involving hostages, airplane hijackings, and prison riots. The first of these police units was the Philadelphia Police Department's 100-man SWAT squad, organized in 1964 in response to a growing number of bank robberies. That team, on May 19, 1985, in an effort to arrest members of a black radical group called MOVE, dropped a bomb on the group's "fortress," which resulted in the deaths of 11 people and left 270 homeless when 61 rowhouses burned. It was alleged that in the United States this was the first time that a home was bombed in pursuit of criminals. On May 3, 1988, a grand jury cleared Mayor W. Wilson Goode and all other city officials of criminal liability. But the jury referred to their actions as "morally reprehensible behavior," as well as "incompeten[t]" and "coward[ly]."

sweat patch. Drug testing method that collects nonvolatile components of perspiration, including controlled substances. Resembling a 2"x 3" bandage, the patch consists of a transparent cover, an absorption pad, and a release liner. A unique number is printed on the underside of the transparent cover to identify the patch. This cover allows small molecules such as water vapor, oxygen, and carbon dioxide to pass through it, while larger molecules, including controlled substances, are caught on the skin side of the patch in the absorbent pad. The patch can be worn on the outside of the upper arm or on the midriff, and after use is sent to a laboratory, where any drugs present are washed into an extraction solvent. The resulting liquid is tested by assays similar to those used for testing urine samples, with immunoassay technology used for screening. Positive results are confirmed with gas chromatography/mass spectometry. *See also* drug monitoring, saliva drug testing, urine drug testing, hair testing

swindler. One who defrauds others by cheating and deception or through fraudulent schemes.

symbolic assailant. Term that refers to depictions of unknown criminals as young men of minority descent, generally black or Latino; arguably, the media emphasizes such misconceptions by drawing attention to crimes meeting this stereotype and not providing similar coverage of crimes committed by other types of assailants. *See also* Smith, Susan

syndicate. A name applied to the Mafia and other organizations whose purpose is to accomplish unlawful or questionable objectives. It also applies to legal and legitimate organizations whose activities are joined together for business purposes.

T

table. A dual series of similar items—for example, the names of cities, their current crime rate, and one or more prior rates; a two-dimensional array.

tagging. (1) traditionally, this term refers to graffiti designed to indicate gang presence or territory, often committed by junior gang associates called "taggers." (2) The process of adding categorical information (usually one word or simple two-word phrases) that identifies some aspect of a Web resource

tales. Persons summoned as jurors.

talesman. A bystander who is chosen to serve on a jury when the jury is not filled by those who had been summoned for jury duty. The person chosen need not be present in court.

Taney, Roger Brooke (1777–1864). Taney was the fourth chief justice of the United States, whose decision in the Dred Scott case in 1857 became a controversial issue. Descended from a prominent Maryland Tidewater family, Taney studied law for three years in Annapolis. In 1836, as reward for his political loyalty, President Andrew Jackson appointed him chief justice, succeeding John Marshall. Taney held this position for nearly three decades. The Dred Scott case, which maintained that blacks did not possess rights of citizenship entitling them to sue in federal courts, caused the prestige of the Court to fall to its lowest point and, with it, the reputation of Taney, a position from which he never recovered. Although unpopular at his death in 1864, today Taney is considered one of the great justices by conservatives and liberals alike.

TASER. An acronym for Tom Swift's Electric Rifle (the "a" was added for phonetic purposes). The TASER was originally developed in 1970 by Jack Cover. As it initially used gunpowder for discharge, it was deemed a firearm. Further refinements led to the version introduced to law enforcement in early 1975, a neuro-muscular incapacitating device, designed as a nonlethal weapon resembling a handgun. In 1993, Cover merged with Rick and Tom Smith to form Air Taser, Inc.; the company became TASER International in 1993. TASER weapons are deployed as follows: once the trigger is depressed, two small barbed contacts, trailing fine conducting wires, are shot from one of the cassettes along the line of aim into the target. The dart-like contacts need not actually touch the skin. If the darts are imbedded in clothing, the electrical charge is capable of reaching the body, since the TASER provides a 1½-inch spark from its power supply. As of 2009, more than 14,200 law enforcement agencies in 40 countries use TASER devices. According to the TASER Web site, over 406,000 TASER devices have been sold to law enforcement agencies since February of 1998. For more information, contact: TASER International, Inc., 17800 N. 85th St., Scottsdale, AZ 85255-6311 USA. Web: http://www2.taser.com.

Task Force on Juvenile Justice and Delinquency Prevention. A group of persons, representing a wide variety of professional services and disciplines serving youth, appointed in 1975 to develop national standards for juvenile justice and delinquency prevention.

Tate, Lionel (1987–). In 2001, 14-year old Lionel Tate was sentenced to life imprisonment without parole for the 1999 death of his 6-year-old playmate and friend. Tate was only 12 at the time of the offense. Prosecutors claimed the battering death was a brutal, intentional crime, while the defense maintained Tate, who was demonstrating WWF wrestling maneuvers, accidentally killed his playmate. With this sentenced, Tate was the youngest person sentence to life imprisonment. In 2004, an appeals court vacated his conviction due to questions about his mental competency. Tate accepted a plea bargain of one year's house arrest and 10 years' probation, and was released from custody after five years' incarceration. A few months later, he violated his probation by carrying a 4-inch knife in his home. In 2005, Tate was charged with battery and armed robbery of a pizza delivery driver. Tate was sentenced to 30 years on the gun charge in 2006, and 10 years (concurrent) for the robbery. He remains incarcerated in Florida, with an anticipated release date in 2031. This case sparks heated debate. Some argue Tate is a hardened criminal whose robbery is further evidence that the initial life sentence was appropriate given his violent nature. They further argue that the justice system betrayed crime victims by letting Tate free to prey yet again. Others argue that the justice system betrayed young Tate by incarcerating the 12-year old youth with violent adult criminals following an accident, and that criminogenic experience has irrevocably shaped his life and will haunt him (in terms of further miscarriages of justice) forever.

Tate, Sharon (1943–1969). Tate was an American actress and pregnant wife of filmmaker Roman Polanski when she was murdered in her Los Angeles home by followers of Charles Manson in 1969. *See also* Manson, Charles; Polansky, Roman

tattooing. In law enforcement, gunpowder patterns; the marks left on the surface of a skin of the person who has been shot at fairly close range. They are caused by the residue of unburned powder in the propellant. From little or no pattern at contact range, the design or pattern increases in size with the increase in the distance of the muzzle of the weapon from the body, up to a distance from which none of the particles reach the body. The markings caused by these particles are black or red.

tax evasion. The crime of intentionally avoiding the payment of taxes using illegal means.

team policing (TP). A decentralized form of policing, popularized in the 1970s, that uses a self-contained group of officers who are permanently assigned to a neighborhood and are responsible for all its crime problems. These officers follow through to case or incident completion. The process relies on functional authority (individual expertise) rather than traditional rank structure. TP encourages community participation in solving crime, with less emphasis on response time and greater emphasis on follow-through for each case, and involves many nontraditional police methods. TP is no longer popular because (a) by increasing community participation and trust in law enforcement, it led to higher levels of crime-reporting, which appeared statistically as increases in crime; and (b) the law enforcement hierarchy perceived the method as reducing the control of middle- and senior-management officers.

Teapot Dome Scandal. An affair that disclosed corruption in high levels of government, shocking the American public. The findings of a Senate committee in October 1923, inquiring into how the rich naval oil reserves at Teapot Dome, WY, and Elk Hills and Buena Vista, CA, were leased to Harry F. Sinclair's Mammoth Oil Co. and Edward

L. Doheny's PanAmerican Petroleum and Transport Co. led to the prosecution for conspiracy and bribery of Senator Albert B. Fall of New York. As secretary of the interior under President Warren Harding, he had authorized the award of the leases to the two oil companies; he was confined in the New Mexico State Penitentiary at Santa Fe, but a $1 million fine was never paid. After his release, he lived in relative poverty until he died in 1944.

tear gas. A substance, usually liquid, that, when atomized and of a certain concentration, causes temporary but intense eye irritation and a blinding flow of tears in anyone exposed to it. Also called a lachrymator.

technical services. The specialized bureau in a traditionally organized police department responsible for communications, records, identification, laboratory activities, and temporary detention.

telegraph channel. A low-capacity communication channel with a maximum data transmission rate of 10 characters per second.

telephone. The first commercial telephone exchange in the United States, possibly in the world, opened in New Haven, CT, in 1876. The first police department to install a telephone exchange to replace the telegraph was that of Cincinnati, OH.

telephone channel. A medium-capacity communication channel with a maximum capacity of 300 characters per second.

telephone scatalogia. A type of virtual exhibitionism, in which sexual gratification is derived from fantasizing about or making obscene phone calls. While fantasies of this nature are not criminal, completing such calls is a criminal offense in many jurisdictions. *See also* exhibitionism, sex offender

teletypewriter. An electric typewriter that can be operated manually or by reading and reperforating paper tape; it is connected to a leased or dial-switched telegraph grade circuit for transmitting text and data messages in readable form. Teletypes were widely used by law enforcement officers until the 1990s.

temporary insanity. A type of insanity defense that asserts that the accused was insane at the time of the crime (and therefore not responsible for his actions) but is now sane.

Ten-Codes. Established around 1937, 10-codes are numeric codes used by law enforcement agencies to communicate common phrases. Although ten-codes remain in use in many U.S. jurisdictions, the practice is waning in favor of plain English communication. The officially suggested ten-codes by the Associated Public Safety Communications Officers is presented in Table 46. 10-Codes in the United States, page 443.

tender. To offer money in payment of a debt or in fulfillment of a contract.

Tent City. In 1993, the prisoner population in Maricopa County Jail, AZ, was reportedly the fourth largest jail system in the world. As actual capacity exceeded the maximum number of inmates allowed, inmates were routinely given early release due to the overcrowding. Sheriff Arpaio, elected in 1992, ordered that a Tent Jail be constructed utilizing inmate labor, some cement, and surplus military tents. The facility was assembled adjacent to an existing jail in Phoenix Arizona and can hold up to 2400 inmates. Placement in Tent City is a privilege. Inmates housed there must agree to work an assigned job and comply with the sheriff's grooming standards. Inmates who decline to work or refuse to groom themselves are relocated inside a hardened facility. Inmates live in tents year round, including summer months in which temperatures are well into the hundreds; they wear pink underwear and striped uniforms, and are fed two meals a day. Despite numerous allegations of humans rights violations, Tent City still exists today, and group tours are offered. Web: http://www.mcso.org/.

territorial court. Any one of a number of different courts established from time to time by Congress for territories subject to U.S. jurisdiction. These courts are legislative because their creation is an exercise of the power of Congress to make rules for U.S.

text continues on page 444

TABLE 46   10-CODES IN THE UNITED STATES

10-0 Caution
10-1 Unable to copy—
 change location
10-2 Signal good
10-3 Stop transmitting
10-4 Acknowledgment (OK)
10-5 Relay
10-6 Busy—stand by unless
 urgent
10-7 Out of service
10-8 In service
10-9 Repeat
10-10 Fight in progress
10-11 Dog case
10-12 Stand by (stop)
10-13 Weather—road report
10-14 Prowler report
10-15 Civil disturbance
10-16 Domestic disturbance
10-17 Meet complainant
10-18 Quickly
10-19 Return to . . .
10-20 Location
10-21 Call . . . by telephone
10-22 Disregard
10-23 Arrived at scene
10-24 Assignment
 completed
10-25 Report in person
 (meet) . . .
10-26 Detaining subject,
 expedite
10-27 Driver's license
 information
10-28 Vehicle registration
 information
10-29 Check for wanted
10-30 Unnecessary use of
 radio
10-31 Crime in progress
10-32 Man with gun
10-33 Emergency
10-34 Riot
10-35 Major crime alert
10-36 Correct time

10-37 (Investigate) suspicious vehicle
10-38 Stopping suspicious
 vehicle
10-39 Urgent—use light,
 siren
10-40 Silent run—no light,
 siren
10-41 Beginning tour of duty
10-42 Ending tour of duty
10-43 Information
10-44 Permission to
 leave . . . for . . .
10-45 Animal carcass at . . .
10-46 Assist motorist
10-47 Emergency road
 repairs at . . .
10-48 Traffic standard repair
 at . . .
10-49 Traffic light out at . . .
10-50 Accident (fatal, personal injury, property
 damage)
10-51 Wrecker needed
10-52 Ambulance needed
10-53 Road blocked at . . .
10-54 Livestock on highway
10-55 Suspected DUI
10-56 Intoxicated pedestrian
10-57 Hit and run (fatal, personal injury, property
 damage)
10-58 Direct traffic
10-59 Convoy or escort
10-60 Squad in vicinity
10-61 Isolate self for
 message
10-62 Reply to message
10-63 Prepare to make
 written copy
10-64 Message for local
 delivery
10-65 Net message
 assignment
10-66 Message cancellation

10-67 Clear for net message
10-68 Dispatch information
10-69 Message received
10-70 Fire
10-71 Advise nature of fire
10-72 Report progress on
 fire
10-73 Smoke report
10-74 Negative
10-75 In contact with . . .
10-76 En route . . .
10-77 ETA (estimated time
 of arrival)
10-78 Need assistance
10-79 Notify coroner
10-80 Chase in progress
10-81 Breathalyzer
10-82 Reserve lodging
10-83 Work school xing
 at . . .
10-84 If meeting . . . advise
 ETA
10-85 Delayed due to . . .
10-86 Officer/operator on
 duty
10-87 Pick up/distribute
 checks
10-88 Present telephone
 number of . . .
10-89 Bomb threat
10-90 Bank alarm at . . .
10-91 Pick up prisoner/
 subject
10-92 Improperly parked
 vehicle
10-93 Blockade
10-94 Drag racing
10-95 Prisoner/subject in
 custody
10-96 Mental subject
10-97 Check (test) signal
10-98 Prison/jail break
10-99 Wanted/stolen
 indicated

Source: Associated Public Safety Communications Officers.

property, under Article IV, Section 3 of the Constitution.

territorial jealousy. A concern with protecting the turf of one's own agency, which sometimes makes cooperation among criminal justice agencies difficult or impossible. Sometimes termed the *not-invented-here* or *NIH syndrome*.

territorial jurisdiction. The right of a state to exercise exclusive control over (a) all lands within its boundaries; (b) its territorial waters; (c) an extensive portion of the air space over its territory; and (d) all persons or things not covered by diplomatic immunity within any of the foregoing areas. Among the territories administered by the United States are: American Samoa; Baker, Howland, and Jarvis Islands; Canton and Enderburg Islands; Guam; Johnston Island; Kingman Reef; Midway Island; Navarra Island; Northern Mariana Islands; Palmyra Island; Puerto Rico; the U.S. Virgin Islands (St. Croix, St. John, and St. Thomas); and Wake Island.

territorial waters. The waters under the jurisdiction of a nation or state, including the offshore waters lying between its shores and the high seas, an area called the territorial belt or marginal sea; inland lakes and rivers entirely within the state; and boundary rivers, straits, lakes, and bays up to the middle point, measured from shore to shore. The jurisdiction of a state extends over territorial waters in matters of fishing rights, navigation, coastal trade, sanitation, and custom duties. Historically, the territorial belt was generally three to six miles, although some nations tried to enforce much wider limits. In December 1988 the United States became the 105th nation to proclaim a 12-mile limit, an action taken by President Ronald Reagan in accordance with the 1982 UN Law of the Sea Convention, created to curb Soviet spy ships. Ships of other nations have the right of innocent passage through the territorial waters of any nation as long as the vessels observe the navigation, customs, and sanitation regulations of the countries having jurisdiction. During war the marginal seas of neutral territories are off-limits to battling warships of the nations at war.

terrorism. The USA PATRIOT Act defines terrorism as "activities that (a) involve acts dangerous to human life that are a violation of the criminal laws of the U.S. or of any state, that (b) appear to be intended (i) to intimidate or coerce a civilian population, (ii) to influence the policy of a government by intimidation or coercion, or (iii) to affect the conduct of a government by mass destruction, assassination, or kidnapping, and (c) occur primarily within the territorial jurisdiction of the U.S." Major acts of terrorism with the United States as a main target are detailed in Table 47. U.S. Related Terrorist Attacks, 1980–Present, page 445–447.; *See also* bioterrorism; domestic terrorism; terrorism abroad

terrorism, domestic. The term "terrorism" means any activity that—(A) involves an act that—(i) is dangerous to human life or potentially destructive of critical infrastructure or key resources; and (ii) is a violation of the criminal laws of the United States or of any State or other subdivision of the United States; and (B) appears to be intended—(i) to intimidate or coerce a civilian population; (ii) to influence the policy of a government by intimidation or coercion; or (iii) to affect the conduct of a government by mass destruction, assassination, or kidnapping. (6 U.S.C. 101 (16))"

terrorism abroad. Acts of international terrorism rose from 322 incidents in 1994 to 440 in 1995, making that the worst year since 1991. However, the number of deaths involved was only 165 in 1995, down from 314 the prior year. The number of injuries was 6,291 in 1995, including approximately 5,500 people injured in a single incident, a gas attack in the Tokyo subway system that was attributed to the Aum Supreme Truth cult, a group based in Japan with branches in other nations. Attacks on U.S. government and military facilities peaked in 1986 at 200, declining to 39 in 1995. The greatest civilian death toll from a terrorist bomb was 329 killed when an Air India 747 was destroyed by a bomb over the North Atlantic while approaching Shannon, Ireland, on text continues on page 447

TABLE 47   U.S.-RELATED TERRORIST ATTACKS, 1980–PRESENT

Date:	Location:	Number of Victims Killed:	Details:
April 1983	Beirut	63	A suicide car bombing against the U.S. embassy; killed 17 Americans.
October 1983	Beirut	241	A suicide car bombing against the U.S. Marine barracks.
October 1983	France	58	An attack on a French Base killed 58 paratroopers.
November 1984	Bogota, Columbia	1	A bomb attack on the U.S. embassy killed a passerby after drug traffickers threatened U.S. officials.
April 1985	Madrid, Spain	18	A bomb exploded near a restaurant near a U.S. air base killing 18 Spaniards, wounding 82, including 15 Americans.
June 1985	San Salvador, El Salvador	13	13 people were killed in a machine gun attack at an outdoor café, including 4 U.S. Marines and 2 American businessmen.
June 1985	Mediterranean	0	A TWA airliner was hijacked over the Mediterranean; it led to a two-week hostage ordeal.
August 1985	Frankfurt, Germany	2	A car bomb at a U.S. military base killed two and injured 20 people. A U.S. soldier was murdered for his identity papers.
October 1985	Cruise liner: Achille Lauro	1	Palestinian terrorists hijacked the cruise liner Achille Lauro. An elderly wheelchair-bound American was killed and thrown overboard.
November 1985	Isle of Malta	61	Terrorists hijacked an Egyptian flight and killed one American. Egyptian commandos stormed the aircraft on the Isle of Malta and 60 people were killed.
December 1985	Rome & Vienna	20	Simultaneous suicide bomber attacks on the U.S. and Israeli check-in desks at Rome and Vienna international airports. 20 people, including the two terrorists are killed in the two attacks.
April 5, 1986	West Berlin	2	Bombing at the LaBelle discotheque in West Berlin. Killed one American and one German woman. Wounded 150, including 44 Americans.
April 1986	Athens, Greece	4	An explosion occurred on a TWA flight landing in Athens, Greece; four people are killed.

(continued)

Date:	Location:	Number of Victims Killed:	Details:
December 21, 1988	Lockerbie, Scotland	270	A bomb destroyed Pan Am Flight 103 over Lockerbie, Scotland. All 259 passengers are killed, including 189 Americans. 11 people on the ground are also killed.
February 1993	New York	6	A bomb in a van exploded in an underground parking garage in New York's World Trade Center; killed 6 people and wounded 1,042.
April 19, 1995	Oklahoma City	168	A car bomb destroyed the Murrah Federal Building in Oklahoma City; killed 168 people and wounded over 600.
November 13, 1995	Riyadh, Saudi Arabia	7	A car bomb in Riyadh, Saudi Arabia killed 7 people; five of them were American military and civilian advisors for the National Guard.
June 25, 1996	Dhahran, Saudi Arabia	19	A bomb on a fuel truck exploded outside a U.S. Air Force installation. 19 U.S. military personnel were killed in the Khubar Towers housing facility, and 515 were wounded, including 240 Americans.
July 27, 1996	Atlanta	1	A pipe bomb exploded during the Olympic games; it killed one person and wounded 111 more.
June 21, 1998	Beirut	0	Rocket-propelled grenades exploded near the U.S. embassy.
August 7, 1998	Nairobi, Kenya/ Dares Salaam, Tanzania	291 / 10	Terrorist bombs destroyed the U.S. embassies. In Nairobi, 291 people are killed, including 12 Americans. 5,000 were wounded including 6 Americans. In Dares Salaam, one U.S. citizen was wounded among the 10 killed and 77 injured.
October 12, 2000	Port of Aden, Yemen	17	A terrorist bomb exploded into the destroyer USS Cole in the port of Aden, Yemen. 17 sailors were killed and 39 were injured.
September 11, 2001	New York/ Washington D.C./ Shanksville, Pennsylvania	Approx. 5,245	Terrorists hijacked U.S. commercial airliners in a coordinated suicide attack. In New York, two of the airliners crashed into the World Trade Center's Twin Towers, which eventually collapsed. Approximately 5,000 people were killed.

(continued)

Date:	Location:	Number of Victims Killed:	Details:
September 2001	New York / Florida / Washington D.C.	5	In Washington, D.C. the third airliner crashed into the Pentagon, causing extensive damage. Approximately 200 people were killed. In Shanksville, PA, the fourth airliner crashed on its way towards Washington D.C. All 45 people on board were killed. Bruce Edwards Ivins sent letters containing the chemical agent Anthrax to various media offices and two U.S. senators. 5 people were killed and 17 infected.

Source: Center for Defense Information and Federal Bureau of Investigation. Compiled by Jennifer Doyle, CSULB.

June 23, 1985. In 1997, the U.S. government listed seven countries as perpetrators of state-sponsored terrorism: Iran, Iraq, Libya, North Korea, Sudan, Cuba, and Syria. In 1995, 440 acts of terrorism killed 163 people, while in 1996 there were 256 acts that killed 311 and wounded 2,652, making it one of the highest casualty years on record. In 2005, there were 11,153 terrorist incidents worldwide, 8,028 of which resulted in death or injury. In 2007, there were 14,499 terrorist attacks worldwide, resulting in more than 22,000 deaths. In 1996, President Clinton signed a bill that expanded the authority of U.S. courts to prosecute terrorists for crimes against Americans committed outside U.S. borders. Assistance is available to help design corporate security programs for businesses in foreign countries. Information is available on the security climate within a given country. *Countering Terrorism* is a free pamphlet providing security suggestions for U.S. business representatives abroad; it describes precautionary measures, as well as suggested procedures in case of kidnapping. Additional information is also available from: Bureau of Diplomatic Security, U.S. Department of State, 2201 C Street NW, Washington, DC 20520. Web: http://www.state.gov/m/ds/.

terrorist organizations, foreign. According to the USA PATRIOT Act (Section 219 of the INA), a foreign terrorist organization is: (1) a foreign organization; (2) one that engages in terrorist activity, as defined in section 212 (a)(3)(B) of the INA (8 U.S.C. § 1182(a) (3)(B)), or terrorism, as defined in section 140(d)(2) of the Foreign Relations Authorization Act, Fiscal Years 1988 and 1989 (22 U.S.C. § 2656f(d)(2)), or retain the capability and intent to engage in terrorist activity or terrorism; and (3) one whose terrorist activity or terrorism must threaten the security of U.S. nationals or the national security (national defense, foreign relations, or the economic interests) of the United States. The 2008 list of terrorist organizations identified by the U.S. Department of State is listed in Table 48. Foreign Terrorist Organizations, 2008, page 448.

terrorist targets worldwide. *See* Table 47. U.S.-Related Terrorist Attacks, 1980–Present, page 445–447; Table 48. Foreign Terrorist Organizations, 2008, page 448

Terror Warning Color Codes. The Homeland Security Advisory System, administered by the Department of Homeland Security, is a five-item color-coded scale that reflects the

---

TABLE 48   FOREIGN TERRORIST ORGANIZATIONS, 2008

1. Abu Nidal Organization (ANO)
2. Abu Sayyaf Group
3. Al-Aqsa Martyrs Brigade
4. Al-Shabaab
5. Ansar al-Islam
6. Armed Islamic Group (GIA)
7. Asbat al-Ansar
8. Aum Shinrikyo
9. Basque Fatherland and Liberty (ETA)
10. Communist Party of the Philippines/New People's Army (CPP/NPA)
11. Continuity Irish Republican Army
12. Gama'a al-Islamiyya (Islamic Group)
13. HAMAS (Islamic Resistance Movement)
14. Harakat ul-Jihad-i-Islami/Bangladesh (HUJI-B)
15. Harakat ul-Mujahidin (HUM)
16. Hizballah (Party of God)
17. Islamic Jihad Group
18. Islamic Movement of Uzbekistan (IMU)

19. Jaish-e-Mohammed (JEM) (Army of Mohammed)
20. Jemaah Islamiya organization (JI)
21. al-Jihad (Egyptian Islamic Jihad)
22. Kahane Chai (Kach)
23. Kongra-Gel (KGK, formerly Kurdistan Workers' Party, PKK, KADEK)
24. Lashkar-e Tayyiba (LT) (Army of the Righteous)
25. Lashkar i Jhangvi
26. Liberation Tigers of Tamil Eelam (LTTE)
27. Libyan Islamic Fighting Group (LIFG)
28. Moroccan Islamic Combatant Group (GICM)
29. Mujahedin-e Khalq Organization (MEK)
30. National Liberation Army (ELN)
31. Palestine Liberation Front (PLF)
32. Palestinian Islamic Jihad (PIJ)
33. Popular Front for the Liberation of Palestine (PFLP)

34. PFLP-General Command (PFLP-GC)
35. Tanzim Qa'idat al-Jihad fi Bilad al-Rafidayn (QJBR) (al-Qaida in Iraq) (formerly Jama'at al-Tawhid wa'al-Jihad, JTJ, al-Zarqawi Network)
36. al-Qa'ida
37. al-Qaida in the Islamic Maghreb (formerly GSPC)
38. Real IRA
39. Revolutionary Armed Forces of Colombia (FARC)
40. Revolutionary Nuclei (formerly ELA)
41. Revolutionary Organization 17 November
42. Revolutionary People's Liberation Party/Front (DHKP/C)
43. Shining Path (Sendero Luminoso, SL)
44. United Self-Defense Forces of Colombia (AUC)

Source: Office of the Coordinator for Counterterrorism, U.S. Department of State.

---

terrorism threat level in the United States. The levels include:

Red: Severe risk of terrorist attacks. Action includes increasing or redirecting personnel to address critical emergency needs; assigning emergency response personnel and prepositioning and mobilizing specially trained teams or resources; monitoring, redirecting, or constraining transportation systems; and closing public and government facilities.

Orange: High risk of terrorist attacks. Response for orange risk level includes coordinating necessary security efforts with federal, state, and local law enforcement agencies or any National Guard or other appropriate armed forces organizations; taking additional precautions at public events and possibly considering alternative venues or even cancellation; preparing to execute contingency procedures, such as moving to an alternate site or dispersing their workforce; and restricting threatened facility access to essential personnel only.

Yellow: Elevated condition, with significant risk of terrorist attacks. Yellow level results in increasing surveillance of critical locations; coordinating emergency plans as appropriate with nearby jurisdictions; assessing whether the precise characteristics of the threat require the further refinement of preplanned protective measures; and implementing, as appropriate, contingency and emergency response plans.

Blue: Guarded condition. General risk of terrorist attack. Actions for this level include checking communications with designated emergency response or command locations; reviewing and updating emergency response procedures; and providing the public with any information that would strengthen its ability to act appropriately.

Green: Low risk of terrorist attacks. Measures taken with green threat level include refining and exercising as appropriate preplanned protective measures; ensuring personnel receive proper training on the Homeland Security Advisory System and specific preplanned department or agency protective measures; and institutionalizing a process to assure that all facilities and regulated sectors are regularly assessed for vulnerabilities to terrorist attacks, and all reasonable measures are taken to mitigate these vulnerabilities. *See* Table 49. Homeland Security Advisory System, this page.

testamentary. Having to do with a will or testament; obtained by or through a will.

testimony. Evidence given by a witness, under oath or affirmation. All persons are competent to testify in cases except: if, in the opinion of the judge, they are prevented by extreme youth, disease affecting the mind, or any other cause of the same kind from recollecting the matter on which to testify, from understanding the questions put to them, from giving rational answers to those questions, or from knowing that they ought to speak the truth. Witnesses unable to speak or hear may give evidence by writing, signs, or any other manner in which they can make it intelligible, but the writing or signs must be made in open court. Evidence so given is deemed to be oral evidence. Generally, neither a husband nor wife can be compelled as a witness against the spouse, but the laws on this subject vary in different states. In most states, the accused is allowed to testify in his or her own behalf, but cannot be compelled to testify.

TABLE 49 HOMELAND SECURITY ADVISORY SYSTEM

Source: Department of Homeland Security.

Texas Rangers. A semimilitary, mounted police force first organized in 1836 as a local body of settlers with the purpose of defense against Indian attacks. When, in 1845, Texas was admitted to the union, the Rangers became the first official state police agency in America. During the Mexican War, they were reorganized by General Sam Houston, who built up their strength to a force of 1,600 men. They served in the Civil War as an element of the Confederate Army and were reorganized in the 1870s. As a police force at that time, the Rangers protected hundreds of miles of the Texas frontier against Indians, hold-up men, rustlers, and bandits. They operated without uniforms or standard procedures, being authorized as roving commissioners for specific duties. The Rangers were famous for their skill and ability and exercised great moral influence in the state. *See also* state police

Texas Syndicate. A group formed of Texas-born Mexican American inmates at San Quentin Prison in 1975. Membership spread to other California prisons and then to those in Texas.

thanatology. The study of death and dying.

theft. Generally, the taking of the property of another with intent to permanently deprive the rightful owner of possession; in the broadest legal usage, the name of the group of offenses featuring larceny, fraud, embezzlement, false pretenses, robbery, and extortion. Theft offenses can include larceny; shop-lifting; pick-pocketing; embezzlement; fraud; forgery; counterfeiting; confidence games; blackmail; usury; ransom; buying, receiving, or possessing stolen goods; plagiarism; removal of landmarks; and criminal bankruptcy. In March 1960 Miami's Trend-line Jewelry, a large wholesaler of precious metals, was the victim of a still-unknown and highly sophisticated group of thieves, who thwarted complex alarm systems that used sonar equipment and electric eyes and carried off thousands of 14-karat gold bracelets and ring mountings, plus over 800 pounds of gold and 3,000 pounds of silver. The $7 million loss was the largest theft of precious metals in the nation's history, exceeding even the Lufthansa robbery in 1978 at New York City's Kennedy Airport, in which thieves stole $5.8 million worth of currency and jewelry; and the famed 1950 Brinks robbery in Boston, which netted thieves some $2.8 million. The Philippine government announced on April 23, 1986, that it had identified $860.8 million that had been salted away by former president Ferdinand Marcos and his wife Imelda. The total allegedly stolen since November 1965 was believed to be between $5 and $10 billion.

Theory X and Theory Y. A nonempirical assumption by management theorist Douglas McGregor (1906–1964) regarding how managers perceive the people they direct. *Theory X,* the conventional concept, says that the

average human being has an inherent dislike of work and will avoid it if possible. Because people inherently dislike work, they must be coerced, controlled, and threatened with punishment to elicit adequate effort toward the achievement of company objectives. The average human being prefers to be directed, wishes to avoid responsibility, has relatively little ambition, and wants security above all. In *Theory Y* by contrast, the expenditure of physical and mental effort in work is as natural as play and rest. External control and the threat of punishment are not the only means for eliciting effort toward company objectives. Commitment to objectives is a function of the rewards associated with their achievement. The most significant types of rewards are ego satisfaction and self-actualization. The average human being will learn, under proper conditions, not only to accept but to seek responsibility. The human capacity to exercise a relatively high degree of imagination, ingenuity, and creativity in the solution of company problems is widely, not narrowly, distributed in the population. Under the conditions of modern industrial life, the intellectual potentialities of the average human being are only partially utilized. In an influential 1960 book, McGregor urged American industry to adopt Theory Y as quickly as possible in management, especially manufacturing operations.

Therapeutic Communities of America (TCA). Founded in 1975, the TCA is a chain of facilities that treats, among others, so-called "hard-core" substance abusers, clients who lack education, vocational skills, and family support systems, and who have criminal backgrounds and long histories of illicit-drug use. TCA offers residential and out-patient programs, crisis intervention, case management, education, and relapse prevention. Address: 1601 Connecticut Ave., NW, Suite 803, Washington, DC 20009. Web site: http://www.therapeuticcommunitiesofamerica.org/main/.

therapeutic community. A concept for treatment of people with emotional problems, especially in the rehabilitation of drug addicts. Centers for drug addicts include Synanon, Kinsman Hall, Odyssey House, and Phoenix House. They operate on the principle, similar to that of Alcoholics Anonymous, that recovered addicts can understand, relate to, and communicate effectively with addicts.

thief-takers. Private detectives who were paid by the Crown on a piecework basis. In England during the seventeenth century, highway robbery was prevalent and associated with persons such as Claude Duval, Jack Sheppard, Dick Turpin, and Captain Lightfoot. As a result, in 1693 an act of Parliament established a reward of 40 pounds sterling for the capture of any highwayman or road agent. The reward was payable upon conviction, and to the thief-taker also went the highwayman's horse, arms, money, and property, unless these were proven not to have been stolen. Thief-makers often became thief-takers. They would seduce youngsters into committing crimes, then have another thief-taker arrest the youth in the midst of the offense. Thief-takers were private individuals much like bounty hunters. However, thief-takers were usually hired by the Crown or by crime victims, while bounty hunters were paid by bail bondsmen to catch fugitives who skipped their court appearances and hence forfeited their bail.

THOR. An acronym for the Target Hardening and Opportunity Reduction project. This was one of the most comprehensive and well-funded of all Law Enforcement Assistance Administration-funded, community crime-prevention programs. Atlanta, GA, was one of eight cities selected for the anti-crime impact program.

T.H. Pendergast California Parole Museum. Located in Diamond Bar, California, the museum collects and organizes artifacts documenting the history of parole in California. Web: http://www.cdcr.ca.gov/Parole/Museum/index.html.

threat. The declaration by words or actions of an unlawful intent to do some injury to another, together with an apparent ability to do so.

Three Prisons Act. Passed by Congress in 1891, it authorized the establishment of three federal penitentiaries: first, Leavenworth, opened in 1895 and fully operational in 1906; second, Atlanta, opened in 1902; the territorial jail at McNeil Island, which had begun operations in 1875, was designated the third penitentiary in 1907 and has since been deactivated.

three-strikes laws. Although specific provisions vary by state, three-strikes laws are a type of mandatory minimum-sentencing structure in which judges have little or no discretion and must impose lengthy incarceration on defendants who have two serious or violent felonies on record prior to being convicted of a third. In California, for example, a defendant prosecuted under the three-strikes law must be sentenced to a term of 25 years-to-life for a third serious or violent felony conviction (a 2000 amendment allows drug treatment instead of life in prison for those convicted of a drug possession felony). Such laws are designed to incapacitate violent or career criminals, but they are controversial. Critics say they represent excessive and unnecessary punishment in many cases, as well as contributing to prison overcrowding. By 2010, 24 states had adopted such laws.

ticket-of-leave. Method of conditional release from prison, used in the 1840s by Alexander Maconochie of England and Sir Walter Crofton of Ireland. The ticket-of-leave allowed conditional release from prison.

time served. Generally, time spent in confinement in relation to conviction and sentencing for a given offense(s), calculated in accord with the rules and conventions specific to a given jurisdiction; also, total time served under correctional agency jurisdiction. "Dead time" or "nonrun time" is time that does not count as prison time served toward a required term in confinement or as time served on parole toward total time under correctional jurisdiction. Time elapsed after escape and before apprehension is dead time in counting time in confinement. Time spent out of confinement pending an appeal decision may also be declared dead time in counting prison time, depending on the rules of a jurisdiction or decisions made in individual cases. "Street time" is time spent on conditional release. If parole or other conditional release is revoked and the person reconfined, all or part of this time may become dead time in calculations of time served under correctional jurisdiction, according to administrative or court decision.

tokenism. The practice of permitting a very limited number of minority group members into schools, neighborhoods, businesses, and other organizations, often with the purpose of meeting only the minimum requirements of civil rights legislation or public opinion.

tong. *See* war, tong

top secret. In government service, information that is ranked of extreme importance and which if divulged without authority, might cause irreparable harm, which would bring about a break in diplomatic relations with another country, cause an armed attack upon the nation or its allies, or compromise military or defense plans or other developments vital to the national defense.

Top Ten Most Wanted Criminals. An FBI program in which 10 persons charged with major crimes are targeted through publication of their photos and descriptions. They are each the subject of an Identification Order. This program has proven effective, and many wanted persons have been identified by members of the public, which has resulted in their apprehension. John Dillinger was America's first "public enemy #1." In 1985, the Los Angeles Police Department established a similar program and took into custody its #1 suspect within two months. The syndicated TV show "America's Most Wanted," begun in the late 1980s, has further increased the effectiveness of the program. The list of FBI Top Ten Most Wanted Criminals can be accessed at: http://www.fbi.gov/ wanted/topten/fugitives/fugitives.htm.

tort. The breach of a duty to an individual that results in damage to him or her. Crime,

in minor misdemeanors and excluded from most databases of criminal and correctional proceedings.

traffic enforcement cameras. A system that uses a vehicle monitoring sensor and a camera to detect traffic law violation in the absence of traffic enforcement officers. Such systems include cameras to detect vehicles that exceed the speed limit, run red lights, travel in bus lanes, evade toll booths, violate "carpool" lane occupancy requirements, violate no-turn-on-red notices, and that are parked illegally. Various legal arguments have been raised, but the courts generally support the use of such devices. However, in some jurisdictions, laws require that the camera also record a photograph of the driver. Recent research has addressed the safety implications of traffic enforcement cameras, often suggesting that a reduction in one type of accident (e.g., right angle crashes) is replaced with an increase in a different type of accident (e.g., rear end collisions) following implementation of such devices, yielding an equivalent number of accidents. Nevertheless, they remain in usage in many jurisdictions.

traffic regulation, first. The first one-way traffic regulation appears to have been issued in New York City on December 17, 1791, when a regulation incidental to a performance at the John Street Theatre requested that "Ladies and Gentlemen will order their Coachmen to take up and set down with their Horse Heads to the East River, to avoid Confusion."

traffic signals. The use of mechanical devices to control traffic flow predates the invention of the automobile. One was installed outside the British Parliament in 1868 to regulate pedestrian traffic. This signal, and early American variations, had two semaphore arms, like a railroad signal, that acted as physical impediments to oncoming traffic. For night visibility, red and green gas lamps would signify when one could proceed or must stop. It is not clear where the first modern traffic signal to control automobile traffic was installed. Salt Lake City and St. Paul both lay claim to the event, but the green-red signal installed on Euclid Ave. in Cleveland in 1914 is generally credited with being the first of its kind. The mechanisms of signals are uniformly vertical, with the red light always on top to assist color-blind drivers.

transcript. The official description of a court proceeding recorded by the court reporter.

transfer. In criminal justice, the movement of a person from one correctional facility or caseload to another.

transfer hearing. A preadjudicatory hearing in juvenile court for the purpose of determining whether juvenile court jurisdiction should be retained over a juvenile alleged to have committed a delinquent act or whether it should be waived and the juvenile transferred to criminal court for prosecution as an adult.

transient. One who comes to a place for a temporary period of time and then moves on.

transit police. As most rapid transit systems cross jurisdictional boundaries, it was necessary to create special forces of transportation officers with law enforcement powers. The New York City Transit Police Department, policing over 700 miles of track and 460 stations, is the second largest police force in New York State, and one of the largest in the nation. It began in 1936 when Mayor LaGuardia signed a resolution creating the post of "special patrolman" on the subway system. These patrolmen were granted peace officer status in 1947 and the department made a separate entity in 1955.

transnational crime. Illegal activity involving more than one sovereign nation, or in which national borders are crossed, as in organized crime, money laundering, international terrorism, drug operations, and illegal traffic in armaments.

transponder warrant. A search warrant allowing the covert placement of a transponder (beeper) on property to track its movement.

Transportation Security Administration (TSA). Established in 2003, the TSA is an agency within the Department of Homeland Security that protects the nation's transportation systems by screening for dangerous devices in airports, rail cars, and subways. Address: Transportation Security Administration, 601 South 12th Street, Arlington, VA 20598; Web: http://www.tsa.gov/.

trap. (1) A device, usually a switch, installed within a protected area, which serves as secondary protection in the event a perimeter-alarm system is successfully penetrated. Examples are a trip-wire switch placed across a likely path for an intruder, a mat switch hidden under a rug, or a magnetic switch mounted on an inner door. (2) A volumetric sensor installed so as to detect an intruder in a corridor or pathway that is likely to be traveled. (3) A tracing device placed on a telephone line to identify the numbers from which calls are placed to that line; often used by law enforcement agencies and telephone companies in harassing call cases.

traverse method. A method of sketching a scene, especially an outdoor scene, where distances, contours, and locations of objects need to be shown. It requires the use of a sketchboard, a compass, and a telescopic surveying instrument.

treason. As cited in the Constitution: "Treason against the United States shall consist only in levying war against them, or in adhering to their enemies, giving them aid and comfort. No person shall be convicted of treason unless on the testimony of two witnesses in the same overt act or on confession in open court." A person convicted of treason is given the death penalty or sentenced to at least five years in prison and fined at least $10,000. The most recent U.S. treason case involved the October 2006 treason indictment against Adam Yahiye Gadahn, a U.S. citizen born in Oregon, for making videos as an al-Qaeda spokesman, threatening attacks on American soil.

Treatment Accountability for Safer Communities (TASC). A response to the problems of crime related to alcohol or drug abuse, TASC was developed over several years of testing, demonstration, and modification. It identifies substance-abusing offenders, refers them to community treatment resources, and monitors their treatment. TASC was initially conceived in the Special Action Office for Drug Abuse Prevention in the early 1970s; tested in Wilmington, DE, in 1972; and became operational that year in Philadelphia and Cleveland. For further information, contact: 1025 Connecticut Ave. NW, Suite 605, Washington, DC 20036. Web site: http://www.nationaltasc.org/.

treaty transfer. *See* deportation

trespass. Unlawful entry into someone's property.

trial. The examination in a court of the issues of fact and law in a case for the purpose of reaching a judgment. *Jury trial:* in criminal proceedings, a trial in which a jury is empanelled to determine the issues of fact in a case and to render a verdict of guilty or not guilty. *Nonjury trial:* in criminal proceedings, a trial in which there is no jury and in which a judicial officer determines all issues of fact and law in a case. (This type of trial is also called a judge trial, bench trial, or court trial.) *Trial on transcript:* also called trial by the record; a nonjury trial in which the judicial officer makes a decision on the basis of the record of pretrial proceedings in a lower court. *Consolidated trial:* one in which either two or more defendants named in separate charging documents are tried together or a given defendant is tried on charges contained in two or more charging documents.

trial court case. A case that has been filed in a court of general jurisdiction or a court of limited jurisdiction.

trial *de novo*. A new trial before a provincial court—criminal division—granted to a defendant in Canada following a successful appeal from a conviction on a summary offense by a justice of the peace. A trial *de novo* is a new trial, the rehearing of a case that has been appealed from a decision made in a court of limited jurisdiction.

trial judge. A judicial officer who is authorized to conduct jury and nonjury trials and who may or may not be authorized to hear appellate cases; the judicial officer who conducts a particular trial.

trial jury. A statutorily defined number of persons selected according to the law and sworn to determine, in accordance with the law as instructed by the court, certain matters of fact based on evidence presented in a trial, and to render a verdict. The size of a trial jury is set by statute and, depending upon jurisdiction, is 12 or a specific smaller number. Some jurisdictions specify a minimum of six jurors and allow for fewer if a juror falls ill.

tribunal. A court or other body in which decisions binding on litigants are made.

trifurcation. In fingerprinting, a single ridge line that divides into three lines. *See also* fingerprint patterns

triple (or treble) damages. A remedy in antitrust law (federal Sherman and Clayton Acts) whereby a competitor, damaged as a result of the proven illegal, anticompetitive behavior of a defendant, may recover from the defendant three times the amount of actual monetary damages sustained. In California Small Claims Court, a judgment for three times the face value of an insufficient funds check can be awarded to the defendant, with a limit of $2,000.

truancy law, first. The first state legislation was "an act to provide for the care and instruction of idle and truant children," enacted by New York on April 12, 1853. A fine of $50 was levied against parents whose children between the ages of 5 and 14 were absent from school.

truant. A juvenile who has been adjudicated by a judicial officer of a juvenile court as having committed the status offense of violating a compulsory school attendance law.

truant officer. An employee of a board of education who enforces compulsory school attendance laws; also called attendance officer.

true bill. An endorsement made by a grand jury on a bill of indictment submitted by a prosecuting officer when the grand jury finds that sufficient reason exists to bring an accused person to trial.

true negative. Finding in which an offender is predicted not to reoffend, and this ends up being true—he does not reoffend. *See also* false negative, false positive, and true positive

true positive. Situation in which an offender is predicted to reoffend and does indeed reoffend. *See also* false positive, false negative, true negative

trusty. An inmate of a jail or prison who has been entrusted with some custodial responsibilities or who performs other assistance services in the operation of the facility.

Truth-In-Lending Act. A detailed federal law of 1968 to protect consumers by enabling them to compare various credit terms realistically. The main provisions regarding installment buying and open-end credit plans (such as credit cards) call for clear and full disclosure of all credit charges and of conditions under which the creditor acquires security from the borrower. The act prevents the creditor from hiding lending violations and fraud behind a collection agency. The act's straightforward wording prohibits issuing unrequested credit cards and limits a cardholder's liability in the case of unauthorized card use to $50. Credit reports are open to review by their subjects, but issuing agencies cannot be prosecuted for including false information unless malice is proven.

Truth-In-Packaging Law. Federal legislation of 1966, also called the Fair Packaging and Labeling Act, is designed to help consumers compare products and be accurately informed. The law provides that all commodity labels must identify the product, give the name and place of business of the manufacturer, packer, or distributor, and list the net quantity of smaller packages. The law prohibits nonfunctional slack fill and regulates cents-off promotional labeling as well as size and type of labels.

Truth-in-Sentencing laws. Statutes passed in many states and in the federal code that require offenders to serve all or most of sentence time imposed by the court. Such laws are gaining popularity because, in many states, offenders have been serving 50 percent or less of the time to which they were sentenced, because of generous good-time policies and/or in efforts to avoid overcrowding in prisons. The federal system, for example, now requires that offenders serve 85 percent of the time imposed by judges. Most truth-in-sentencing laws do, however, provide for some time off for good behavior. *See also* Violent Offender Incarceration Truth in Sentencing.

TSA. *See* Transportation Security Administration

Tweed, William Marcy (Boss, 1823–1878). A New York political leader who came to symbolize the corruption of political bosses. He was one of the New York City aldermen known as the Forty Thieves, a congressman, and finally Grand Sachem of Tammany Hall (1863). The Tweed Ring monopolized all parts of the government. Contracts submitted to the city were approved only after payments of 10 to 85 percent went to the ring. In 1867 Tweed, as a state senator, broadened his system to include the legislature. When John Hoffman, Tweed's protégé, was elected governor in 1869, the ring's power encompassed all New York State. Their downfall was initiated by a series of cartoons by Thomas Nast, printed in *Harper's Weekly* from 1869 through 1871. Only when disgruntled ring members made documentary evidence available was a Committee of Seventy, led by Samuel Tilden, able to break the ring. Tweed served a short jail term then fled to Spain to avoid a trial to recover the stolen money. After extradition, he died in jail.

tweeker. Pejorative term used to reference those who smoke methamphetamines.

twist. In firearms, the inclination of the spiral grooves (rifling) to the axis of the bore of a weapon. It is expressed as the number of calibers of length in which the rifling makes one complete turn.

two-strikes law. A type of sentencing law that imposes lengthy prison terms (including life without parole) for persons convicted of their second serious or violent offense. *See* three-strikes laws

Type-A personality. A personality profile that was believed to lead to higher levels of stress and resulting heart disease than the contrasting Type B personality. According to this theory, Type A individuals tend to be competitive, hostile, impatient people who are constantly under stress, while Type B people demonstrate more patience and an ability to react to environmental demands and deal with stress more effectively. Later research has tended to show that only the underlying hostility of Type A personalities, rather than their competitiveness or impatience, is important in increasing the risk of heart disease. *See also* stress

Type-B personality. A personality profile that was believed to lead to lower levels of stress and stress-related disease than the contrasting Type A personality. Type B personalities are characterized as more patient, relaxed, and appear better able to react to environmental demands and stressors without the intensity characterizes the Type A personality.

typographic printing. A type of printing used in the making of paper currency, stock certificates, and similar items susceptible to counterfeiting. The typographic process allows for overprinting the permanent (intaglio) features with changeable characteristics such as serial numbers, seals, and authorizing signatures.

typology. A classification scheme containing two or more categories (types), based on characteristics of the things being classified that the classifier considers important. Typologies are useful in organizing data; any set of concepts can be used to classify. People can be grouped, for example, according to age, sex, race, weight, height, hair color, or shoe size.

U

ulnar loop. A fingerprint pattern.

ultrasonic motion detector. A sensor that detects the motion of an intruder through the use of ultrasonic generating and receiving equipment. The device operates by filling a space with a pattern of ultrasonic waves; the modulation of these waves by a moving object is detected and initiates an alarm signal.

ultraviolet light. Light located beyond the violet end of the visible spectrum. Sometimes referred to as black light. Used in law enforcement to detect certain fluorescent substances such as semen, invisible laundry marks, and other invisible writings. It is at the end of the spectrum opposite infrared light. An ultraviolet filter transmits ultraviolet light by the reflected ultraviolet light method.

ultra vires. An action beyond the legal power or authority of a corporation, governmental agency, or official.

Underwear Bomber. On December 25, 2009, a passenger on board Northwest Airlines Flight 263 from Amsterdam to Detroit ignited an incendiary device concealed in his underwear. Other passengers were alerted to the event when smoke and flames erupted in and around the seat occupied by the suspect, Umar Farouk Abdulmutallab. Other passengers quickly subdued Abdulmutallab and put out the fire. Adbulmutallab was arrested upon landing and is currently awaiting trial. No passengers were injured, although Abdulmutallab reported sustained serious burns to his groin area. *See also* domestic terrorism

Unibomber. University and Airline Bomber. Self-given title of an individual, now presumed to be Theodore Kaczynski, who perpetrated an 18-year rampage of letter bombs that killed three and injured 29 other people. The first bombing occurred on May 26, 1978, when a package found at the University of Illinois in Chicago was returned to the addressee at Northwestern University, where it exploded and injured one victim.

Between 1978 and 1985, several more people were injured by bombs planted at or mailed to addresses in Illinois, Utah, Tennessee, California, Washington, Michigan, and aboard an airplane. The first fatality occurred on December 11, 1985, when Hugh Scrutton was killed when he moved a bomb disguised as discarded lumber. On February 20, 1987, the Unabomber was seen in Salt Lake City wearing a hooded sweatshirt and aviator sunglasses while placing a bomb. There were no further attacks for six years. On June 22, 1993, University of California at San Francisco geneticist Charles Epstein was severely injured by a bomb mailed to his home. Two days later, Yale University computer scientist David Gelernter suffered extensive injuries when a bomb exploded in his office. On December 10, 1994, advertising executive Thomas Mosser was killed by a bomb sent to his home in New Jersey. On April 24, 1995, timber industry executive Gilbert P. Murray was killed when he opened a package in his Sacramento office. On June 27, 1995, the Unabomber threatened to blow up an airliner out of Los Angeles, which led to lasting changes in airport and postal security. On September 19, 1995, the Unabomber's 35,000-word, so-called manifesto against technology was published. Through information given by his brother, Theodore Kaczynski was taken into custody by federal officers on April 3, 1996. In April 1998, the 55-year-old former math professor, long a recluse, was sentenced to life in prison without parole. *See also* Kaczynski, Theodore John

Unibomber Attacks. Series of 16 U.S. bombings that occurred between 1978 and 1995. The bombings occurred via packages mailed to universities and airlines, resulting in three deaths and injuries to 23 people. In 1996, suspect Theodore Kaczynski was arrested following a tip from his brother, who recognized Kaczynski's writing and ravings from a manifesto the suspect sent to media. Kaczynski pled guilty and was sentenced to life in prison without the possibility of parole. *See also* Kaczynski, Theodore John; domestic terrorism

underground. An organized group of people who carry on some regular operation without effective discovery by those in authority; the network to which these people belong.

underground economy. Unreported, untaxed, unregulated, and often illegal economic transactions in goods and services that take place outside the official and legal economy. This includes the practice of tradeouts, where goods or services are traded by businesses without cash transactions or record. The underground economy consists of persons who report less income than earned and those who file no income tax returns. Drug trafficking and organized crime are major segments of this economy.

underground press. Much of the political and cultural dissent in the United States during the 1960s was expressed in some 500 weekly, monthly, and irregularly published non-establishment newspapers. Originating with New York's *The Village Voice* in 1955, the underground press flourished until the 1970s when many of its media disappeared.

underworld. A semipopular designation for the *sub rosa* existence of criminal activity, commercialized vice, gambling houses, places trafficking in contraband narcotics, and other interconnected illicit enterprises, such as bootlegging and numbers rackets. The criminal and pseudocriminal elements constitute an underworld to the extent that association and activity take place outside the bounds of respectable society; hence, they form a sort of pariah caste. *See also* organized crime

unfair and deceptive practices. Those activities of business firms that damage consumers and/or have an adverse effect on competition. Examples are bait-and-switch advertising, deceptive pricing, and misbranding and mislabeling. Under Section 5 of the original Federal Trade Commission Act, the FTC was authorized to proceed against business practices doing potential or actual damage to competition (a less rigorous test of damage than the restraint of trade provisions found in the Sherman Antitrust Act). With the Wheeler-Lea Act of 1938, the prohibition was extended to include unfair practices outside the normal antitrust category as well as practices unfair to the general consuming public.

unfair labor practices. Antiunion actions by employers. The 1930s marked a great turning point for organized labor, and no law aided its cause more than the Wagner Act (1935), which allowed unions to organize and bargain collectively. It also specified unfair labor practices in which employers were forbidden to engage. No comparable restrictions, however, were imposed on unions.

unfounding. The process in statistics of declaring that certain unsolved crimes were never crimes in the first place. *See also* defounding

Uniform Code of Military Justice. A comprehensive statement of the laws governing all the armed forces, containing 140 articles, signed by President Harry Truman and enacted by Congress. It replaced the Articles of War and the Articles for the Government of the Navy. (Articles 77 through 134 are considered the punitive articles.) The code also provides for a review of decisions of courts martial and for appeals to the United States Court of Military Appeals, which was created by the code.

Uniform Crime Reporting Program (UCR). In 1927, the International Association of Chiefs of Police (IACP) formed a committee to create a uniform system for gathering statistics on crimes known to the police. Led by August Vollmer and Bruce Smith, it was called the Committee on Uniform Crime Records; it developed the UCR, which was adopted by the IACP. In 1930 the FBI was authorized to serve as the national clearinghouse for the UCR. This was the first standardized crime-related record keeping on a national level. The national UCR program produces a major annual report called *Crime in the United States*. The bulk of the information in these reports relates to reported instances (offenses known to police) of the

FBI's Crime Index offenses, reported arrests for all crimes, and law enforcement agency employee data. The detail includes information concerning crimes cleared by arrest, arrests and dispositions of arrested persons, and dispositions of juveniles taken into custody. The reported crime and reported arrest data are categorized by geographical area and related to various factors. UCR also produces three other annual publications, *Law Enforcement Officers Killed, Assaults on Federal Officers, and Bomb Summary*. The FBI's Uniform Reporting Program offers its annual *Crime in the United States—Uniform Crime Reports*. These can be obtained online at www.fbi.gov/ucr/ucr.htm, or by writing the Uniform Crime Reporting Section, , FBI, 935 Pennsylvania Avenue, NW, Washington, DC 20535.

Uniform Juvenile Court Act. A 1968 act of Congress, which recommended standards for the processing of delinquent and status offenders in the juvenile justice system.

Uniform Parole Reports (UPR). UPR is a statistical program sponsored by the Bureau of Justice Statistics and administered by the National Council on Crime and Delinquency. It was established in 1964 by the National Institutes of Health. It has published statistical information on parolees, parole authority decisions, and parole agency workloads.

uniform state laws. Model statutes drafted by the Conference of Commissioners on Uniform Laws and enacted without amendment by all or several state legislatures, which are designed to substitute a series of uniform enactments for conflicting state laws on subjects like bills of lading, negotiable instruments, motor vehicle registration, and liability for accidents.

Unitarian Universalist Service Committee. This committee established the National Moratorium on Prison Construction in 1975. "NMPC works toward a halt to all prison and jail construction until alternatives to imprisonment are fully evaluated and implemented." The UUSC advances human rights and social justice around the world. Address: 698 Massachusetts Avenue, Cambridge, MA 02139. Web site: http://www.uusc.org/.

United Nations Criminal Justice Information Network. Established in 1989, UNCJIN provides the latest reports of research and activities of worldwide UN institutes, calendars of events and meetings, legislative and court updates, and UN World Crime Survey data. It publishes several directories, a bibliography of other criminal justice statistics, and a computerized selection of U.S. Bureau of Justice Statistics reports, available before they are printed. UNCJIN is funded in part by the U.S. Bureau of Justice Statistics and operates under the auspices of the UN Crime Prevention and Criminal Justice Branch, Vienna International Center, Austria. Address: Centre for International Crime Prevention, Office for Drug Control and Crime Prevention, P.O. Box 500, A-1400 Vienna Austria. Web site: http://www.uncjin.org/index.html.

United Nations Information Centre. Founded in 1946, under the Office of Public Information of the UN, the centre aims "to bring about an informed understanding of the United Nations, including its work in the field of criminal justice." This Center serves as the focal point for the UN news and information to increase understanding of the U.N. and its operations. Lists of UN publications in the field of criminal justice are printed in the United Nations Documents Indexes issued monthly. Address: 1775 K Street Northwest, Washington, DC 20006. Web site: http://www.unicwash.org/.

United Nations Standard Minimum Rules for the Treatment of Prisoners. Adopted on August 30, 1955, by the First United Nations Congress on the Prevention of Crime and the Treatment of Offenders, this document provides recommendations for the operation of penal facilities, as well as for the treatment of offenders.

United States Associate Attorney General. This office, under the Department of Justice,

"works to advise the Attorney General and the Deputy Attorney General in regards to policies and programs from a broad range of civil justice matters." Address: Office of the Associate Attorney General, Department of Justice, 950 Pennsylvania Avenue, NW, Washington, DC 20530-0001. Web site: http://www.justice.gov/asg/.

United States Attorneys. U.S. attorneys are the chief law enforcement representatives of the attorney general, in the federal judicial district. There is one in each federal judicial district, enforcing federal criminal law and handling most of the civil litigation in which the United States is involved. The attorneys are involved with white-collar crime, official corruption, narcotics, organized crime, and criminal and civil litigation. The position is appointive, and usually has one or more assistants carrying the title Assistant U.S. Attorney.

United States Attorneys, Executive Office for. This office provides general executive assistance and supervision to all officers of the U.S. Attorneys. Address: Executive Office for U.S. Attorneys, DOJ, 950 Pennsylvania Ave., NW, Room 2242, Washington, DC 20530. Web site: http://www.justice.gov/usao/eousa/index.html.

United States Bureau of Alcohol, Tobacco, Firearms and Explosives. The Bureau of Alcohol, Tobacco and Firearms was created under the Department of the Treasury in 1789 as a tax-collecting and enforcement branch. In 2003 the Bureau of Alcohol, Tobacco, Firearms and Explosives became part of the Department of Justice under the Homeland Security bill. The law enforcement functions of the ATF are now the responsibility of the Department of Justice, and the tax and trade functions remain under the Treasury Department with the new Alcohol and Tobacco Tax and Trade Bureau. The ATF enforces and administers laws regarding firearms and explosives, as well as those laws covering the production, use, and distribution of alcohol and tobacco products. The law enforcement office works with state and local agencies in curtailing the flow of firearms to criminal elements. For information concerning any activity in the Bureau of ATF, contact: Office of Public and Governmental Affairs, 99 New York Avenue, NE, Room 5N 540, Washington, DC 20226. Web site: http://www.atf.gov/.

United States Bureau of Prisons. *See* Federal Bureau of Prisons

United States Citizenship and Immigration Services. First established as the Bureau of Immigration under the Treasury Department in 1891, the service expanded to include naturalization functions in 1933, finally moving under the Justice Department in 1940. Currently, with approximately 11,000 employees, the service has a mission to "administer the immigration and naturalization laws relating to the admission, exclusion, deportation, and naturalization of aliens; inspect aliens to determine their admissibility into the United States; adjudicate requests of aliens for benefits under the law; guard against illegal entry into the United States; investigate, apprehend, and remove aliens in this country in violation of the law; and examine alien applicants wishing to become citizens." Address: U.S. Citizenship and Immigration Services, National Records Center, FOIA/PA office, P.O. Box 648010, Lee's Summit, MO 64064. Web site: http://www.uscis.gov/portal/site/uscis.

United States Claims Court. In 1855, the *Court of Claims* was established to oversee claims brought against the federal government. It was renamed the United States Court of Claims in 1948, and abolished in 1982.

United States Coast Guard (USCG). The Revenue Cutter Service was established in 1789 to deal with the problem of smuggling. According to its Web site the USCG was an autonomous unit of the public forces of the United States between 1967–2003, subject to the jurisdiction of the Department of Transportation in time of peace and of the Navy in time of war or national emergency. After 2003 however, the Coast Guard was placed under the jurisdiction of the U.S. Department of Homeland Security. Although it is especially charged with the enforcement of the customs, navigation, and neutrality laws, it serves as a general law enforcement agency on navigable waters and high seas and protects life and property at sea. It develops regulations on commercial vessel safety, recreational boating safety, port safety and security, and marine pollution. The U.S. Coast Guard, as authorized by a 1972 act of Congress, maintains three regional strike forces to assist in handling oil spills or hazardous substance leaks that are too large for other agencies to handle. These three strike forces make up the National Strike Force: the Pacific Strike Team, the Gulf Coast Strike Team; and the Atlantic Coast Strike Team When on land, the force works with the Environmental Protection Agency. For further information, contact: Commandant, U.S. Coast Guard, 2100 Second St., SW, Washington, DC 20593. Web site: http://www.uscg.mil/. *See also* high seas law enforcement

United States Code (USC). A consolidation and codification of all the general and permanent federal laws in effect, classified by subject matter under 50 titles, prepared under the direction of the Judiciary Committee of the House of Representatives. A revision has appeared every six years since 1926, and a supplementary volume is issued after each session of Congress. Many of the titles have been enacted as law and, when all have been enacted, the code will constitute the entire body of federal law.

United States Code Annotated (USCA). A commercially published edition of the U.S. Code.

United States Commissioner. A federal magistrate whose functions in the federal field are comparable to those in state matters of the justice of the peace. The officeholder is not a judge and does not hold court but may issue certain warrants, act as a committing official, set bail, and bind over for trial. All functions of the position are prescribed by statute.

United States Conference of Mayors. Organization that facilitates cooperation between cities and the federal government on urban social and health issues such as substance abuse, by providing mayors and municipal agencies with resources, technical assistance, and legislative services. Address: 1620 Eye St. NW, Washington, DC 20006. Web site: http://www.usmayors.org/default.asp.

United States Court of Claims. In 1855, the *Court of Claims* was established to oversee claims brought against the federal government. It was renamed the United States Court of Claims in 1948, and abolished in 1982.

United States Court of Customs and Patent Appeals. A specialized court established in 1909 as the U.S. Court of Customs Appeals, given its present title and duties in 1929, and consisting of five justices, which reviews (1) decisions of the U.S. Customs Court on classifications and duties on imported merchandise; (2) decisions of the Patent Office on applications for, and interference with, patents and trademarks; and (3) legal questions in findings of the U.S. Tariff Commission concerning unfair practices in import trade.

United States Customs and Border Protection. Determines and collects duties and taxes on merchandise imported into the United States, controls exporters and importers and their goods, and works to control smuggling and revenue fraud. Created as a division of the Department of the Treasury in 1927, the Customs Service is authorized to collect customs and revenue by the second, third, and fifth acts of the First Congress (1789). The service helps enforce environmental protection programs involving the discharge of oil or refuse into coastal waters, the safety standards of imported motor vehicles, and the regulation by quarantine of animals and plants entering the country. In 2003 the U.S. Customs Service changed its name to the U.S. Customs and Border Protection,

under the jurisdiction of the Department of Homeland Security. Today, the CBP works closely with the Drug Enforcement Administration and the Immigration and Naturalization Service. U.S. Customs maintains a force of special agents at 66 domestic and eight foreign offices. They investigate violations of customs and related laws and regulations—fraud, currency reporting violations, cargo theft, neutrality violations, narcotics, and bird smuggling. Address: 1300 Pennsylvania Ave., NW, Washington, DC 20299. Web site: http://www.cbp.gov/.

United States Customs Court. A court created in 1890 as the Board of the United States General Appraisers and given its present title in 1926, which consists of nine judges sitting in New York City, and which has sole jurisdiction over the interpretation of tariff laws, the classification of merchandise, and the determination of the dutiable valuation of imported goods. In 1956 it was made a court of record under Article III of the Constitution.

United States District Courts. Trial courts with original jurisdiction over diversity-of-citizenship cases and cases arising under U.S. criminal, bankruptcy, admiralty, patent, copyright, and postal laws. There are 94 district courts in the United States and Puerto Rico. Normally, one district judge presides over each trial, but three-judge district courts are necessary for the issuance of injunctions concerning certain subjects. From district courts, the normal course of appeals is to a court of appeals, but some decisions—holding statutes unconstitutional, certain criminal cases, and the injunction orders of three-judge district courts—may be appealed directly to the Supreme Court.

United States Fish and Wildlife Service. A division of the Department of the Interior, dating from the consolidation in 1940 of the Bureau of Biological Survey and the Bureau of Sport Fisheries and Wildlife, that carries on research and wildlife conservation programs and is charged especially with the preservation of the fishing industry; the enforcement of international agreements relating to fur seals and commercial fish; and the conservation, for economic and recreational purposes, of various kinds of wildlife. For further information, contact: U.S. Fish and Wildlife Service, 1849 C Street, NW, Washington, DC 20240. Web site: http://www.fws.gov/.

United States Internal Revenue Service. *See* Internal Revenue Service

United States Marshals Service. With approximately 4,942 employees, the service serves to apprehend federal fugitives, protect the federal judiciary, operate the Witness Security Program, transport federal prisoners, and seize property acquired by criminals through illegal activities. Address: United States Marshals Service, Department of Justice, 950 Pennsylvania Avenue, NW, Washington, DC 20530. Web site: http://www.usmarshals.gov/.

United States-Mexico border. This border extends 1,952 miles or 3,141 kilometers from Brownsville, TX (opposite Matamoros, Tamaulipas), to San Diego, CA (opposite Tijuana, Baja California Norte).

United States Parole Commission. An independent agency in the Department of Justice whose mission is to promote public safety and strive for justice and fairness in the exercise of its authority to release and supervise offenders under its jurisdiction. Its primary function is to administer a parole system for federal prisoners and develop federal parole policy. The commission is authorized to: grant or deny parole to any eligible federal prisoner; impose reasonable conditions on the release of any prisoner from custody or discretionary parole or mandatory release by operation of "good-time" laws; revoke parole or mandatory release; and discharge offenders from supervision and terminate their sentences prior to expiration. Address: Department of Justice, 5550 Friendship Blvd., Suite 420, Chevy Chase, MD 20815. Web site: http://www.justice.gov/uspc/.

United States Reports. The official printed record of cases heard and decided by the U.S. Supreme Court, which usually includes a statement of the essential facts of each case; the opinion of the Court, concurring and dissenting opinions, if any; the disposition of each case and occasionally an abstract of counsels' briefs. Originally, a series of reports, with volumes numbered consecutively, was issued during the incumbency of each successive court reporter. These are cited as Dallas (1790–1800), Cranch (1801–1815), Wheaton (1816–1827), Peters (1823–1843), Howard (1843–1860), Black (1861–1862), and Wallace (1863–1874). By 1874, when the number of volumes so identified totaled 90, the practice began of eliminating the reporter's name and citing them as United States Reports.

United States Secret Service. *See* Secret Service

United States Sentencing Commission. Established by the Comprehensive Crime Control Act of 1984, this independent commission in the judicial branch of the United States consists of seven voting members and one nonvoting member. The President, after consultation with representatives of judges, prosecuting attorneys, defense attorneys, law enforcement officials, senior citizens, victims of crime, and others interested in the criminal justice process, appoints the voting members of the commission, including its chairman, by and with the advice and consent of the Senate. At least three of the members are federal judges in regular active service selected after considering a list of six judges recommended to the president by the Judicial Conference of the United States. No more than four commission members may be members of the same political party. The purposes of the commission are to (a) establish sentencing policies and practices for the federal criminal justice system and (b) develop means of measuring the degree to which sentencing, penal, and correctional practices are effective in meeting the purposes of sentencing.

United States Statutes at Large. An official compilation of the acts and resolutions of each session of Congress published by the Office of the Federal Register in the National Archives and Records Service. It consists of two parts: the first comprises public acts and joint resolutions, the second, private acts and joint resolutions, concurrent resolutions, treaties, and presidential proclamations.

United States Supreme Court. *See* Supreme Court, U.S.

United States Trustee Program. Established in 1978 under the Bankruptcy Reform Act. Under this programs, officials are charged with administering bankruptcy cases in their respective regions. For further information, contact: Executive Office for U.S. Trustees, DOJ, 20 Massachusetts Ave., NW, Washington, DC 20530. Web site: http://www.justice.gov/ust/.

Uniting and Strengthening America by Providing Appropriate Tools Required to Intercept and Obstruct Terrorism Act of 2001. *See* USA PATRIOT Act.

unity of command. A traditional management principle recommending that employees should report directly only to one supervisor.

University of Chicago Center for Studies in Criminal Justice. Established in 1965 with goals to "conduct criminal justice research on the criminal justice system and to give specialized education at the graduate level." Address: Law School, 1111 East 60th St., Chicago, IL 60637. Web site: http://www.law.uchicago.edu/criminaljustice.

unlawful entry. A less serious crime than burglary, it involves entering an open or unlocked building without authority or legal right.

unlawful flight to avoid giving testimony. In federal law it is a felony to travel to another state or nation to avoid giving testimony as a material witness in a criminal proceeding in which a felony is charged under the state laws. The law is called the Fugitive Witness Act.

unlawful flight to avoid prosecution. A federal law making it a felony for any person, charged by a state with a felony, to travel to another state for the purpose of avoiding prosecution. Also called the Fugitive Felon Act.

unlicensed individuals selling securities. One of the most common types of investment fraud. The sale of securities is only legally permitted by those with a valid securities license; attempted sale of securities by an unlicensed person should (but usually does not) alert investors of likely fraud. *See also* fraud, investment

unregistered investment products. A type of investment fraud in which certain investment products that are closely regulated (e.g., pay telephone and ATM leasing contracts, and other investment contracts) are sold with the promise of low risk and high returns. *See also* fraud, investment

unsecured promissory notes. The sale of worthless promissory notes is a common type of investment fraud. *See also* fraud, investment

UOC. An abbreviation for the Uniform Offense Classifications, used by the FBI's National Crime Information Center to represent offense types in automated record systems of individual criminal histories.

UPR. *See* Uniform Parole Reports

urban riots. A form of civil disorder in which generally disorganized groups of citizens express their discontent through violence against property, law enforcement officers, or other persons. *See also* civil disorders; Civil Disorders, National Advisory Commission on; civil disturbances; King, Rodney; McDuffie, Arthur; Overtown see also Table 10. Urban Riots in the United States, page 80

usury. The charging of interest greater than that permitted by law in return for the loan of money. *See also* loan shark; loan sharking

text continues on page 471

TABLE 50 UNITED STATES SUPREME COURT JUSTICES

Name	Birth/death	President	Term	Chief Justice	Notable Decisions	Reason for Leaving
James Wilson	1742–1798	Washington	1789–1798	No	*Chisholm v. Georgia*	Death
John Jay	1745–1829	Washington	1789–1795	1789–1795	*Chisholm v. Georgia*	Resigned
William Cushing	1732–1810	Washington	1790–1810	No	*Madison v. Marbury, Chisholm v. Georgia*	Death
John Blair Jr.	1732–1800	Washington	1790–1795	No	*Chisholm v. Georgia*	Death
John Rutledge	1739–1800	Washington	1790–1791, 1795	1795		Resignation, term 2 rejection
James Iredell	1751–1799	Washington	1790–1799	No	*Chisholm v. Georgia*	Death
Thomas Johnson	1732–1819	Washington	1792–1793	No	*Chisholm v. Georgia*	Resignation
William Paterson	1745–1806	Washington	1793–1806	No	*Madison v. Marbury*	Death
Samuel Chase	1741–1811	Washington	1796–1811	No	*Madison v. Marbury*	Death
Oliver Ellsworth	1745–1807	Washington	1796–1800	1796–1800		Resignation
Bushrod Washington	1762–1829	J. Adams	1799–1829	No	*Madison v. Marbury, McCullouch v. Maryland*	Death
Alfred Moore	1755–1810	J. Adams	1800–1804	No	*Madison v. Marbury*	Resignation
John Marshall	1755–1835	J. Adams	1801–1835	1801–1835	*Madison v. Marbury, McCullouch v. Maryland*	Death
William Johnson	1771–1834	Jefferson	1804–1834	No	*McCullouch v. Maryland*	Death
Henry Brockholst Livingston	1757–1823	Jefferson	1807–1823	No	*McCullouch v. Maryland*	Death
Thomas Todd	1765–1826	Jefferson	1807–1826	No	*McCullouch v. Maryland, Gibbons v. Ogden*	Death
Gabriel Duvall	1752–1844	Madison	1811–1835	No	*McCullouch v. Maryland, Gibbons v. Ogden*	Resignation
Joseph Story	1779–1845	Madison	1812–1845	No	*McCullouch v. Maryland, Gibbons v. Ogden*	Death

Name	Birth/death	President	Term	Chief Justice	Notable Decisions	Reason for Leaving
Smith Thompson	1768–1843	Monroe	1823–1843	No	*Gibbons v. Ogden, Prigg v. Pennsylvania*	Death
Robert Trimble	1776–1828	J. Q. Adams	1826–1828	No		Death
John McClean	1785–1861	Jackson	1830–1861	No	*Dred Scott v. Sanford, Prigg v. Pennsylvania*	Death
Henry Baldwin	1780–1844	Jackson	1830–1844	No	*Prigg v. Pennsylvania*	Death
James Moore Wayne	1790–1867	Jackson	1835–1867	No	*Dred Scott v. Sanford, Prigg v. Pennsylvania*	Death
Roger B. Taney	1777–1864	Jackson	1836–1864	1836–1864	*Dred Scott v. Sanford, Prigg v. Pennsylvania*	Death
Phillip Pendleton Barbour	1783–1841	Jackson	1836–1841	No		Death
John McKinley	1780–1852	Van Buren	1838–1852	No	*Prigg v. Pennsylvania*	Death
Peter Vivian Daniel	1784–1860	Van Buren	1842–1860	No	*Dred Scott v. Sanford*	Death
Samuel Nelson	1792–1873	Tyler	1846–1872	No	*Dred Scott v. Sanford*	Retirement
Levi Woodbury	1789–1851	Polk	1845–1851	No		Death
Robert Cooper Grier	1794–1870	Polk	1846–1870	No	*Dred Scott v. Sanford*	Retirement
Benjamin Robbins Curtis	1809–1874	Filmore	1851–1877	No	*Dred Scott v. Sanford*	Resignation
John Archibald Campbell	1811–1889	Pierce	1853–1861	No	*Dred Scott v. Sanford*	Resignation
Nathan Clifford	1803–1881	Buchanan	1858–1881	No		Death
Noah Haynes Swayne	1804–1884	Lincoln	1862–1881	No		Retirement
Samuel Freeman Miller	1816–1890	Lincoln	1862–1890	No		Death

(continued)

Name	Birth/death	President	Term	Chief Justice	Notable Decisions	Reason for Leaving
David Davis	1815–1886	Lincoln	1862–1877	No		Resignation
Stephen Johnson Field	1816–1899	Lincoln	1863–1897	No	*Plessy v. Ferguson*	Retirement
Salmon P. Chase	1808–1873	Lincoln	1864–1873	1864–1873		Death
William Strong	1808–1895	Grant	1870–1880	No		Retirement
Joseph P. Bradley	1813–1892	Grant	1870–1892	No		Death
Ward Hunt	1810–1886	Grant	1873–1882	No		Retirement
Morrison Waite	1816–1888	Grant	1874–1888	1874–1888		Death
John Marshall Harlan	1833–1911	Hayes	1877–1911	No	*Plessy v. Ferguson*	Death
William Burnham Woods	1824–1887	Hayes	1881–1887	No		Death
Stanley Matthews	1824–1889	Garfield	1881–1889	No		Death
Horace Gray	1828–1902	Arthur	1882–1902	No	*Plessy v. Ferguson*	Death
Samuel Blatchford	1820–1893	Arthur	1882–1893	No		Death
Lucius Quintus Cincinnatus Lamar	1825–1893	Cleveland	1888–1893	No		Death
Melville Fuller	1833–1910	Cleveland	1888–1910	1888–1910	*Plessy v. Ferguson*	Death
David Josiah Brewer	1837–1910	B. Harrison	1890–1910	No	*Plessy v. Ferguson*	Death
Henry Billings Brown	1836–1913	B. Harrison	1891–1906	No	*Plessy v. Ferguson*	Retirement
George Shiras Jr.	1832–1924	B. Harrison	1892–1903	No	*Plessy v. Ferguson*	Retirement
Howell Edmunds Jackson	1832–1895	B. Harrison	1893–1895	No		Death

Name	Birth/death	President	Term	Chief Justice	Notable Decisions	Reason for Leaving
Edward Douglass White	1845–1921	Taft	1894–1921	1910–1921	*Plessy v. Ferguson*	Death
Rufus Wheeler Peckham	1838–1909	Cleveland	1896–1909	No	*Plessy v. Ferguson*	Death
Joseph McKenna	1843–1926	McKinley	1898–1925	1921	*Weeks v. United States*	Retirement
Oliver Wendell Holmes Jr.	1841–1935	T. Roosevelt	1902–1932	1930	*Powell v. Alabama, Weeks v. United States*	Retirement
William R. Day	1849–1923	T. Roosevelt	1903–1922	No	*Weeks v. United States*	Retirement
William Henry Moody	1853–1917	T. Roosevelt	1906–1910	No		Retirement
Horace Harmon Murton	1844–1913	Taft	1910–1914	No	*Weeks v. United States*	Death
Charles Evans Hughes	1862–1848	Taft	1910–1916	No	*Weeks v. United States*	Resignation
Wills Van Devanter	1859–1941	Taft	1911–1937	No	*Powell v. Alabama, Weeks v. United States*	Retirement
Joseph Rucker Lamar	1857–1916	Taft	1911–1916	No	*Weeks v. United States*	Death
Mahlon Pitney	1858–1924	Taft	1912–1922	No	*Weeks v. United States*	Resignation
James Clark McReynolds	1862–1946	Wilson	1914–1941	No	*Powell v. Alabama*	Retirement
Louis Brandeis	1856–1941	Wilson	1916–1939	No	*Powell v. Alabama*	Retirement
John Hessin Clarke	1857–1945	Wilson	1916–1922	No		Resignation
William Howard Taft	1857–1930	Harding	1921–1930	1921–1930		Resignation
George Sutherland	1862–1942	Harding	1922–1938	No	*Powell v. Alabama*	Retirement

(continued)

467

Name	Birth/death	President	Term	Chief Justice	Notable Decisions	Reason for Leaving
Pierce Butler	1866–1939	Harding	1923–1939	No	*Powell v. Alabama*	Death
Edward Terry Sanford	1865–1930	Harding	1923–1930	No		Death
Charles Evans Hughes	1862–1948	Hoover	1930–1941	1930–1941	*Powell v. Alabama*	Retirement
Harlan F. Stone	1872–1946	F. Roosevelt	1925–1946	1941–1946	*Korematsu v. United States*	Death
Owen Roberts	1875–1955	Hoover	1930–1945	No	*Korematsu v. United States*	Resignation
Benjamin N. Cardozo	1870–1938	Hoover	1932–1938	No		Death
Hugo Black	1886–1971	F. Roosevelt	1937–1971	1946	*Korematsu v. United States, Mapp v. Ohio*	Retirement
Stanley Forman Reed	1884–1980	F. Roosevelt	1938–1957	No	*Korematsu v. United States, Brown v. Board of Education*	Retirement
Felix Frankfurter	1882–1965	F. Roosevelt	1939–1962	No	*Korematsu v. United States, Brown v. Board of Education*	Retirement
William O. Douglas	1898–1980	F. Roosevelt	1939–1975	No	*Korematsu v. United States, Brown v. Board of Education*	Retirement
Frank Murphy	1890–1949	F. Roosevelt	1940–1949	No	*Korematsu v. United States, Betts v. Brady*	Death
James F. Byrnes	1879–1972	F. Roosevelt	1941–1942	No	*Betts v. Brady*	Resignation
Robert H. Jackson	1892–1954	F. Roosevelt	1941–1954	No	*Korematsu v. United States, Betts v. Brady*	Death
Wiley Blount Rutledge	1894–1949	F. Roosevelt	1943–1949	No	*Korematsu v. United States*	Death

Name	Birth/death	President	Term	Chief Justice	Notable Decisions	Reason for Leaving
Harold Hitz Burton	1888–1964	Truman	1945–1958	No	*Brown v. Board of Education*	Retirement
Fred M. Vinson	1890–1953	Truman	1946–1963	1946–1953	*Brown v. Board of Education, Mapp v. Ohio*	Death
Tom C. Clark	1899–1977	Truman	1949–1967	No	*Brown v. Board of Education, Mapp v. Ohio*	Retirement
Sherman Minton	1890–1965	Truman	1949–1956	No	*Brown v. Board of Education*	Retirement
Earl Warren	1891–1974	Eisenhower	1953–1969	1953–1969	*Brown v. Board of Education, Mapp v. Ohio*	Retirement
John Marshall Harlan II	1899–1971	Eisenhower	1955–1971	No	*Mapp v. Ohio, Gideon v. Wainright*	Retirement
William Brennan Jr.	1906–1997	Eisenhower	1956–1990	No	*Mapp v. Ohio, Miranda v. Arizona*	Retirement
Charles Evans Whitaker	1901–1973	Eisenhower	1957–1962	No	*Mapp v. Ohio*	Resignation
Potter Stewart	1915–1985	Eisenhower	1958–1981	No	*Mapp v. Ohio, Gideon v. Wainright*	Retirement
Byron White	1917–2002	Kennedy	1962–1993	No	*Gideon v. Wainright, Miranda v. Arizona*	Retirement
Arthur Goldberg	1908–1990	Kennedy	1962–1965	No	*Gideon v. Wainright*	Resignation
Abe Fortas	1910–1982	L. Johnson	1965–1969	No	*Miranda v. Arizona, Tinker v. Des Moines*	Resignation
Thurgood Marshall	1908–1993	L. Johnson	1967–1991	No	*Tinker v. Des Moines, Roe v. Wade*	Retirement
Warren E. Burger	1907–1995	Nixon	1969–1986	1969–1986	*Tinker v. Des Moines, Roe v. Wade*	Retirement

(continued)

Name	Birth/death	President	Term	Chief Justice	Notable Decisions	Reason for Leaving
Harry Blackmun	1908–1999	Nixon	1970–1994	No	*Roe v. Wade, U.S. v. Nixon*	Retirement
Lewis F. Powell Jr.	1907–1998	Nixon	1972–1987	No	*Roe v. Wade, U.S. v. Nixon*	Retirement
William Rehnquist	1924–2005	Reagan	1972–2005	1986–2005	*Roe v. Wade, U.S. v. Nixon*	Death
John Paul Stevens	1920–present	Ford	1975–present	2005	*U.S. v. Nixon, Regent of Univ. of Ca. vs. Bakke*	Retirement
Sandra Day O'Connor	1930–present	Reagan	1981–2006	No	*New Jersey v. T.L.O, Hazelwood v. Kuhlmeier*	Retirement
Antonin Scalia	1936–present	Reagan	1986–present	No	*Hazelwood v. Kuhlmeier, Texas v. Johnson*	Serving
Anthony Kennedy	1936–present	Reagan	1988–present	No	*Hazelwood v. Kuhlmeier, Texas v. Johnson*	Serving
David Hackett Souter	1939–present	G. H. W. Bush	1990–2009	No	*Ricci v. DeStephano, Grutter v. Bollinger*	Retirement
Clarence Thomas	1948–present	G. H. W. Bush	1991–present	No	*Ricci v. DeStephano, Grutter v. Bollinger*	Serving
Ruth Bader Ginsburg	1933–present	Clinton	1993–present	No	*Ricci v. DeStephano, Grutter v. Bollinger*	Serving
Stephen Breyer	1938–present	Clinton	1994–present	No	*Ricci v. DeStephano, Grutter v. Bollinger*	Serving
John G. Roberts	1955–present	G. W. Bush	2005–present	2005–present	*Ricci v. DeStephano*	Serving
Samuel Alito	1950–present	G. W. Bush	2006–present	No	*Ricci v. DeStephano*	Serving
Sonia Sotomayor	1954–present	Obama	2009–present	No	*Ricci v. DeStephano*	Serving
Elena Kagan	1960–present	Obama	2010–present	No	*Ricci v. DeStephano*	Serving

Compiled by Richard Porter, CSULB.

urine drug testing. The use of urine samples to determine the consumption of illicit substances in preceding hours/days. *See also* drug monitoring, saliva drug testing, sweat patch, hair testing

urolagnia (also called urophilia). Paraphilia involving sexual pleasure through urine or urination. *See also* golden shower

urophilia (also called urolagnia). Paraphilia involving sexual pleasure through urine or urination. *See also* golden shower

uroxicide. The killing of one's wife.

USA PATRIOT Act. Officially called the "Uniting and Strengthening America by Providing Appropriate Tools Required to Intercept and Obstruct Terrorism Act of 2001," this act is more commonly called the "PATRIOT Act." It was authorized by President George W. Bush in 2001 following the September 11 attacks in an effort to detect and prevent terrorism. Among other things, the PATRIOT Act: expands the definition of terrorism to include domestic terrorism; eases police access to search telephone, e-mail, medical, financial, and other records; expands the surveillance of financial transactions in the United States; facilitates foreign intelligence gathering in the United States; and provides law enforcement and immigration authorities wide discretion in detaining and deporting persons suspected of terrorist activities. Although various provisions of the Act were set to expire in 2005 due to sunset clause, it was re-authorized by President George W. Bush in 2006 and continues today.

USA on Watch. Established in 2002 by the National Sheriff's Association with support from the National Security Administration, Freedom Corps, Citizen Corps, and Department of Justice. According to its Web site, "USA on Watch empowers citizens to become active in homeland security efforts through participation in Neighborhood Watch groups." Address: USA on Watch, National Sheriffs' Association, 1450 Duke Street Alexandria, Virginia. 22314-3490 http://www.usaonwatch.org/. *See also* National Sheriffs' Association, neighborhood watch

United States Citizenship and Immigration Service. Formerly called United States Immigration and Naturalization Service, USCIS is the government agency that oversees lawful immigration to the United States. USCIS covers citizenship, immigration of family members, and working in the United States (green cards). Address: U.S. Citizenship and Immigration Services, National Records Center, FOIA/PA Office, P. O. Box 648010, Lee's Summit, MO 64064-8010; Web: http://www.uscis.gov/portal/site/uscis/.

United States Court of Appeals for the Federal Circuit. Established in 1982 with the merging of the United States Court of Customs and Patent Appeals and the appellate division of the United States Court of Claims, this court has jurisdiction over "international trade, government contracts, patents, trademarks, certain money claims against the United States government, federal personnel, veterans' benefits, and public safety officers' benefits claims." Address: 717 Madison Place, N.W., Washington, DC 20439; Web: http://www.cafc.uscourts.gov/.

United States Court of International Trade. Established in 1980 with the abolishment of the U.S. Customs Court Customs Court, this court provides judicial review of civil actions arising out of import transactions and federal statutes affecting international trade. Address: Clerk of the Court, United States Court of International Trade, One Federal Plaza, New York, New York 10278-0001; Web: http://www.cit.uscourts.gov/.

United States Department of Health and Human Services, Office of the Inspector General. Investigates and prosecutes health care fraud. To report suspected health care fraud: Office of Inspector General, Department of Health and Human Services, Attn: HOTLINE, PO Box23489, Washington, DC 20026; 1-800-447-8477; Web: http://oig.hhs.gov/fraud/hotline/.

United States Department of Transportation. Established in 1967, the mission of the U.S. DOT is to "serve the United States by ensuring a fast, safe, efficient, accessible and convenient transportation system that meets our vital national interests and enhances the quality of life of the American people." With more than 60,000 employees, the U.S. DOT operates 13 agencies that help ensure safety to persons traveling in the United States. The agencies include: Federal Aviation Administration (FAA); Federal Highway Administration (FHWA); Federal Motor Carrier Safety Administration (FMCSA); Federal Railroad Administration (FRA); Federal Transit Administration (FTA); Maritime Administration (MARAD); National Highway Traffic Safety Administration (NHTSA); Office of Inspector General (OIG); Office of the Secretary of Transportation (OST); Pipeline and Hazardous Materials Safety Administration (PHMSA); Research and Innovative Technology Administration (RITA); and Saint Lawrence Seaway Development Corporation (SLSDC); Surface transportation Board (STB). Address: U.S. Department of Transportation, 1200 New Jersey Ave, SE, Washington, DC 20590. Web: http://www.dot.gov/.

United States Equal Employment Opportunity Commission. The U.S. Equal Employment Opportunity Commission (EEOC) is responsible for enforcing federal laws that make it illegal to discriminate against a job applicant or an employee because of the person's race, color, religion, sex (including pregnancy), national origin, age (40 or older), disability, or genetic information. It is also illegal to discriminate against a person because the person complained about discrimination, filed a charge of discrimination, or participated in an employment discrimination investigation or lawsuit. Web: http://www.eeoc.gov/.

United States Fire Administration (USFA). USFA is an agency of the Department of Homeland Security created with the disbanding of the National Fire Prevention and Control Administration, the mission of the agency is to "provide national leadership to foster a solid foundation for our fire and emergency services stakeholders in prevention, preparedness, and response." Web site:http://www.usfa.dhs.gov/.

United States Immigration and Customs Enforcement (ICE). Formed in 2003, ICE is the largest investigative agency in the U.S. Department of Homeland Security (DHS). The mission of ICE is "to protect the security of the American people and homeland by vigilantly enforcing the nation's immigration and customs laws." There are four divisions under ICE: Office of Detention and Removal Operations (DRO), Office of Investigations (OI), Office of Intelligence (Intel), and Office of International Affairs (OIA). Address: Immigration and Customs Enforcement, department of Homeland Security, 500 12th St, SW, Washington, DC 20536 Web: http://www.ice.gov/.

United States Immigration and Naturalization Service. Existed 1870–2003. Became U.S. Citizenship and Immigration Service in 2003. *See* U.S. Citizenship and Immigration Service

United States Sentencing Commission. The United States Sentencing Commission is an independent agency in the judicial branch of government. Its principal purposes are: (1) to establish sentencing policies and practices for the federal courts, including guidelines to be consulted regarding the appropriate form and severity of punishment for offenders convicted of federal crimes; (2) to advise and assist Congress and the executive branch in the development of effective and efficient crime policy; and (3) to collect, analyze, research, and distribute a broad array of information on federal crime and sentencing issues, serving as an information resource for Congress, the executive branch, the courts, criminal justice practitioners, the academic community, and the public. The U.S. Sentencing Commission was created by the Sentencing Reform Act provisions of the Comprehensive Crime Control Act of 1984. Web: http://www.ussc.gov/.

V

Vacutainer. Trade name for a blood collection system used for laboratory testing of blood for its alcohol content.

vagrancy. Except where defined by statute, the behavior of a person without permanent social attachments; aimless wandering of an individual without visible means of legitimate self-support. In common law, vagrancy means wandering about from place to place by an idle person who has no visible means of support, subsists on charity, and does not work, though able to do so. But the connotations of vagrancy have been extended by statutory regulations to include other forms of behavior. Vagrancy is the broadest of offense categories, which could include: prostitution, gambling, fortune-telling, drunkenness, begging, and many other forms of behavior deemed socially undesirable, if not dangerous. Though the charge of vagrancy may not be sustained if the alleged offender has regular employment or is wandering in search of it, in times of economic recession, convictions for vagrancy increase sharply. The vagueness of vagrancy laws was demonstrated on May 2, 1984, when the California Supreme Court struck down the vagrancy law in a 7–2 decision, holding that the state cannot give police power to arrest persons who fail to produce proper identification on demand.

vagrant. An unattached, itinerant, and indigent person. Several types are variously described on the basis of behavior or appearance, as in this old text: "The hobo works and wanders; the tramp dreams and wanders; and the bum drinks and wanders." The hobo, an itinerant worker who may occasionally panhandle, is now virtually nonexistent. Homeless indigent types change from one period to another and are different in different localities. Vagrants are perceived to be a problem to the security of a community because they are homeless, voteless, and without local interests, and there is strong presumption that they are or may become offenders.

Valentine's Day. Named after St. Valentine, patron saint of lovers, who was a third-century Roman bishop who defied imperial law by performing marriage rites for military-eligible young men and their brides and advising them to pursue domestic, rather than army, life. Roman law decreed that young men were better soldiers if they remained single. St. Valentine's activities led to his execution by Roman authorities on February 14, 269.

Valium and Librium. Prescription drugs that act as sedatives and minor tranquilizers. They are central nervous system depressants and directly affect the brain, relaxing large skeletal muscles and causing tranquility or sleepiness. Both are commonly prescribed and often abused.

values. A term distinguished from attitudes, needs, or wants that refers to the degree to which an event is perceived to be positive or negative. As guides to behavior, values link actions to attitudes, needs, or interests. Some investigators link values to what ought to be, in contrast to what is. As a result, much values research has addressed morals and ethics. The three major theories of how people acquire values are psychoanalytic, social learning, and perceptual. Many law enforcement agencies have adopted organizational values statements to clarify their mission, vision, and purposes.

vandalism. Willfully destroying or defacing the property of another. The word is derived from Vandals, the Germanic tribe responsible for destroying Rome in the fifth century. Vandalism in the United States is predominantly, though not exclusively, perpetrated by juveniles and is responsible for losses of millions of dollars each year. The City of New York spent $10 million in 1973 to paint and clean surfaces defaced by graffiti.

VanHouten, Leslie (1949–). Manson follower convicted of the La Bianca murders in Los Angeles in 1969. Initially sentenced to death, her sentence was commuted to life in

1972. She remains incarcerated in California. *See also* Manson, Charles

variable. A dynamic trait or characteristic that can change in value or magnitude from case to case. The term is contrasted with constant, a static and unchanging characteristic. Variables can be qualitative, such as male or female; quantitative and stated numerically, such as age or height; continuous, involving such uninterrupted progressions as aging or traveling certain distances; or discrete. A discrete variable can be quantitative or qualitative; if it is quantitative, its values increase or decrease by definite steps. A continuous variable must be quantitative, but not all quantitative variables are discrete.

variable annuity sales practices. A type of investment fraud, often perpetrated against senior citizens, in which the sale of securities accompanies high surrender fees and steep sales commissions agents. *See also* fraud, investment

VASCAR. Abbreviation for Visual Average Speed Computer and Recorder. An electronic device, manually activated, that measures quantities of distance and time and computes the resultant speed. Used in several states by the highway patrol.

vehicle. A device by means of which any person or property can be propelled, moved, or drawn on a highway, except a device moved exclusively by human power or used exclusively on stationary rails or tracks.

vehicle identification number (VIN). A permanent and unique number assigned to, and placed on, each vehicle by an automotive manufacturer for identification purposes. It may indicate the vehicle's model, engine displacement, place and year of manufacture, and sequence in the manufacturer's production.

vehicle theft. Unauthorized taking of a motor vehicle belonging to another person. *See also* Cargo CATS; Community Effort to Combat Auto Theft; Operation Guatemalan Auto Theft Enforcement

venireman. A member of a jury; a juror summoned by a writ of *venire facias.*

venue. The locality in which a suit may be tried.

Vera Institute of Justice. Formerly the Vera Foundation, a research organization with objectives "to achieve a more equal and fair criminal justice system." It was founded in October 1961 in New York by Louis Schweitzer. The Manhattan Bail Project, the Bronx Sentencing Project, the Manhattan Bowery Project, the Victim/Witness Assistance Project, and the Court Employment Project are well-known endeavors of the Institute. Address: 233 Broadway, 12th Floor, New York, NY 10279. Web site: http://www.vera.org.

verbal judo. In law enforcement, managing a person's behavior only through verbal commands and responses, rather than physical restraint. It is a noncombative method of easing tension and encouraging compliance. In some law enforcement agencies, verbal judo training is mandatory.

verdict. The decision of the jury in trials of either civil or criminal cases.

verdict, directed. A jury decision rendered by an order of a trial judge; in modern criminal procedure the directed verdict is always to acquit, although it may be limited to specific counts or specific defendants.

vibration detection system. An alarm system that employs one or more contact microphones or vibration sensors fastened to the surfaces of the area or object being protected to detect excessive levels of vibration. The contact microphone system consists of microphones, a control unit containing an amplifier and an accumulator, and a power supply. The unit's sensitivity is adjustable so that ambient noises or normal vibrations will not initiate an alarm signal. In a vibration sensor system, the sensor responds to excessive vibration by opening a switch in a closed-circuit system.

ViCAP. *See* Violent Criminal Apprehension Program

vicarious strain. Stress or strain experienced by those around an individual who is experiencing primary strain.

vicarious liability. Liability for the actions of another in the absence of fault, as where the persons neither knew of, encouraged, nor assisted in the act(s) of the other; usually imposed because of a person's general duty of supervision over another. There are several situations in which the theory of vicarious liability has been applied: negligent appointment or hiring, negligent retention (of an employee), negligent assignment, negligent supervision, negligent entrustment, and failure to train. *See also* negligent

vice, commercialized. As customarily used in sociological studies and crime statistics, the business of prostitution. Prostitution shows varying degrees of commercialization, ranging from independent conduct of prostitution by individuals to exploitation of prostitutes in brothels or syndicated houses of prostitution. In some Asian countries the business of prostitution has been accepted as an institution, with practitioners called business girls. In Western countries, it is either tolerated through police policy or has illegal status; in the latter case it is the object of suppressive measures of law enforcement.

vice squad. A special detail of police agents, charged with raiding and closing houses of prostitution and gambling resorts. Vice squads are likely to become unusually active in selective enforcement or law and order campaigns. *See also* Red Light Abatement law

vicinage. The county, district, or subdivision in which a court has the power or authority to hear cases.

victim. A person who has been killed or suffered physical or mental anguish or loss of property as a result of an actual or attempted criminal offense committed by another person.

Victim and Witness Protection Act of 1984. The federal VWP Act and state laws protect crime victims and witnesses against physical and verbal intimidation where such intimidation is designed to discourage reporting of crimes and participation in criminal trials. Laws generally protect all subpoenaed witnesses but may also protect persons the offender believes will be called to testify or who may have knowledge of the crime. Some laws also permit courts to forbid defendants from communicating with or approaching victims and witnesses.

Victim Assistance Program. A synthesis of several years of experience with prosecutor- or police-based victim-witness programs, rape crisis centers, domestic violence programs, and other independent victim assistance projects. The program incorporates recommendations, developed by the 1982 President's Task Force on Victims of Crime, that have an immediate impact on victims. The goals are to improve the treatment of victims of crime by providing assistance and services necessary to speed their recovery from a criminal act and to support and aid them as they move through the criminal justice process. Address: Office for Victims of Crime Resource Center, National Criminal Justice Reference Service, P.O. Box 6000, Rockville, MD 20849-6000. Web site: http://www.ojp.usdoj.gov/ovc/ovcres/welcome.html.

victim compensation. State compensation programs are funded with state-administered funds. The 1984 federal Victims of Crime Act provides for federal grants to assist states that have established qualifying victim compensation programs. Forty-four states, the District of Columbia, and the U.S. Virgin Islands provide compensation for medical bills and lost wages for victims. In general, awards may be made to persons injured as a direct result of the crime. If the victim dies, payments to cover burial and related expenses are generally available to dependent survivors. In many cases, good Samaritans—persons injured while trying to prevent a crime or apprehend an offender—are also eligible for payment. Most states establish upper limits on payments and do not provide compensation for property losses In general, payment can be made whether or not the offender has been apprehended or convicted, but most states require that the crime be reported to proper authorities. *See also* Victims of Crime Act; *see* Table 51. State Compensation Programs to Help Victims of Violent Crime, pages 477–483

Victim-Offender Reconciliation Program (VORP). Name for a type of program that mediates for victims and offenders, to allow offenders to take responsibility and victim to receive restitution.

victimization. The harming of any single victim in a criminal incident. The first national victimization survey was conducted in 1965 by the University of Chicago. More detailed surveys were undertaken in medium- and high-crime areas in Washington, DC; Boston; and Chicago by the Bureau of Social Science Research in Washington and the Survey Research Center of the University of Michigan.

victimless crimes. Illegal acts that harm no one, or where harm occurs, it is negated by the informed and legal consent of the participants in the crime. In this context, harm can take several forms: (1) harm to the person, (2) harm to property, (3) psychological harm, (4) social harm, and (5) harm to an individual's freedom. The category commonly includes gambling, individual drug use, prostitution, and consensual sexual acts.

victimology. The study of the psychological and dynamic interrelationships between victims and offenders, with a view towards crime prevention. Interest in the study of the victim arose in the 1849s, and the works of such scholars as Mendelsohn (1947) and Von Hentig (1948) underlined the importance of studying criminal-victim relationships in understanding crime.

victim precipitation. A criminal act in which the victim was responsible, at least in part, for initiating, encouraging, or escalating the altercation that resulted in his/her own loss, injury, or death.

Victims of Crime Act. On October 12, 1984, President Ronald W. Reagan signed into law the Victims of Crime Act, which established a Crime Victims Fund in the Treasury Department that can receive up to $100 million annually from four sources: criminal fines collected from convicted federal defendants; new penalty assessments imposed on convicted federal defendants; forfeited appearance bonds, bail bonds, and collateral security posted by federal criminal defendants; and literary profits due certain convicted federal defendants. The money collected is used to help the victims of crimes to cope with their trauma and possible financial troubles caused by the crimes committed against them. Address: Office for Victims of Crime, Office of Justice Programs, 810 7th Street, NW, Washington, DC 20531. Web site: http://www.ojp.usdoj.gov/ovc/. *See also* Office for Victims of Crime

victim-witness programs. County- and/or state-funded agencies to provide assistance to victims or witnesses of crime available within the office of the district attorney in most urban areas.

victim/witness relocation program. *See* Witness Protection Plan

video surveillance. Electronic cameras capable of viewing targeted areas, which fall into two categories, clearly visible systems and those hidden from view.

vigilante. An individual or member of a group who undertakes to enforce the law and/or maintain morals without legal authority. From the 1760s through the beginning of the twentieth century, vigilante activity was an almost constant factor in American life. The better-known vigilante groups, such as the South Carolina Moderators (1767) and the East Texas Regulators (1840–1856), were highly structured and served in all phases of their own criminal justice proceedings. *See also* lynching

text continues on page 484

TABLE 51 STATE COMPENSATION PROGRAMS TO HELP VICTIMS OF VIOLENT CRIME

State	Victim compensation board location	Maximum financial award	To qualify, victim must					Contact information
			Show financial need	Report to police within . . .	Cooperate with law enforcement	File claim within . . .		
Alabama	State Crime Victim Compensation Commission	$15,000	No	72 hours	Yes	1 year		http://www.acvcc.state.al.us/
Alaska	State Department of Administration	Not specified	No	5 days	Yes	2 years		http://doa.alaska.gov/vccb/
Arizona	State Criminal Justice Commission	$20,000	No	72 hours	Yes	2 years		http://www.acjc.state.az.us/
Arkansas	State Attorney General's Office	$25,000	No	72 hours	Yes	1 year		http://www.ag.arkansas.gov/crime_safety_crime_victims_reparations.html
California	State Victim Compensation and Government Claims Board	Not specified	No	Yes, time unspecified	Yes	1 year		http://www.vcgcb.ca.gov/
Colorado	State Department of Public Safety	$20,000	No	72 hours	Yes	1 year		http://dcj.state.co.us/ovp/
Connecticut	State Judicial Branch	$25,000	No	5 days	Not specified	2 years		http://www.jud.ct.gov/crimevictim/
Delaware	State Attorney General's Office	$50,000	No	72 hours	Yes	1 year		http://attorneygeneral.delaware.gov/VCAP/
District of Columbia	Superior Court of D.C. Crime Victim Compensation Program	$25,000	No	7 days	Yes	1 year		http://dccourts.gov/dccourts/superior/cvcp.jsp

(continued)

477

State	Victim compensation board location	Maximum financial award	Show financial need	Report to police within . . .	Cooperate with law enforcement	File claim within . . .	Contact information
Florida	State Attorney General's Office	Not specified	Yes	72 hours	Yes	1 year	http://myfloridalegal.com/victims
Georgia	State Criminal Justice Coordinating Council	$25,000	No	72 hours	Not specified	1 year	http://cjcc.ga.gov/victimDetails.aspx?id=62
Hawaii	State Department of Public Safety	Not specified	No	Without undue delay	Not specified	18 months	http://hawaii.gov/cvcc
Idaho	State Crime Victim Compensation Agency	$25,000	No	72 hours	Yes	1 year	http://www.crimevictimcomp.idano.gov/
Illinois	State Attorney General's Office	$27,000	No	72 hrs.– 7 days, depending on crime	Yes	2 years	http://www.ag.state.il.us/victims/cvc.html
Indiana	State Criminal Justice Institute	$15,000	No	72 hours	Yes	180 days	http://www.in.gov/cji/2348.htm
Iowa	State Attorney General's Office	Approx $60,000	No	72 hours	Yes	2 years	http://www.state.ia.us/government/ag/helping_victims/index.html
Kansas	State Attorney General's Office	$25,000	No	72 hours	Yes	2 years	http://www.ksag.org/page/crime-victims-compensation-board
Kentucky	State Crime Victim Compensation Board	$25,000	No	48 hours	Yes	5 years	http://cvcb.ky.gov/

State	Victim compensation board location	Maximum financial award	Show financial need	Report to police within . . .	Cooperate with law enforcement	File claim within . . .	Contact information
Louisiana	State Commission on Law Enforcement and Administration of Criminal Justice	$25,000	No	72 hours	Yes	1 year	http://www.lcle.state.la.us/programs/cvr.asp
Maine	State Attorney General's Office	$15,000	No	5 days	Yes	3 years	http://www.maine.gov/ag/crime/victims_compensation/index.shtml
Maryland	State Department of Public Safety and Correctional Services	$45,000	No	48 hours	Not specified	3 years	http://www.dpscs.state.md.us/victimservs/vs_cicb.shtml
Massachu-setts	State Attorney General's Office	$25,000	No	5 days	Yes	3 years	http://www.mass.gov/?pageID=cagoterminal&L=3&L0=Home&L1=Victim+and+Witness+Assistance&L2=Victims+of+Violent+Crime&sid=Cago&b=terminalcontent&f=victim_Victim_Compensation&csid=Cago
Minnesota	State Office of Justice Programs	$50,000	No	30 days	Yes	3 years	http://www.dps.state.mn.us/OJP/
Michigan	State Department of Community Health	$15,000	No	48 hours	Yes	1 year	http://www.michigan.gov/mdch/0,1607,7-132-54783_54853--,00.html

(continued)

State	Victim compensation board location	Maximum financial award	Show financial need	Report to police within . . .	Cooperate with law enforcement	File claim within . . .	Contact information
Mississippi	State Attorney General's Office	$20,000	No	72 hours	Yes	36 months	http://www.ago.state.ms.us/index.php/sections/victims/victim_compensation
Missouri	Department of Public Safety	$25,000	No	48 hours	Yes	2 years	http://www.dps.mo.gov/cvc/
Montana	Department of Justice	$25,000	No	72 hours	Yes	1 year	http://www.doj.mt.gov/victims/victimcompensation.asp
Nebraska	State Crime Commission	$10,000	No	3 days	Yes	2 years	http://www.ncc.state.ne.us/services_programs/crime_victim_reparations.htm
Nevada	State Department of Administration	$35,000	No	5 days	Yes	1 year	http://www.voc.nv.gov/
New Hampshire	Department of Justice	$10,000	No	5 days	Yes	1 year	http://doj.nh.gov/victim/compensation.html
New Jersey	State Attorney General	$25,000	No	3 months	Yes	2 years	http://www.njvictims.org/
New Mexico	State Crime Victims Reparation Commission	Not specified	No	Yes, no date specified	Yes	2 years	http://www.cvrc.state.nm.us/
New York	State Crime Victim's Board	$45,000	No	1 week	Yes	1 year	http://www.cvb.state.ny.us/home.aspx

State	Victim compensation board location	Maximum financial award	Show financial need	Report to police within . . .	Cooperate with law enforcement	File claim within . . .	Contact information
North Carolina	State Department of Crime Control and Public Safety	$35,000	No	72 hours	Not specified	2 years	http://www.nccrime control.org/Index2. cfm?a=000003,000016
North Dakota	State Department of Corrections and Rehabilitation	$25,000	No	72 hours	Yes	1 year	http://www.nd.gov/docr/ programs/victims/vic-comp.html
Ohio	State Attorney General's Office	$50,000	No	72 hours	Yes	2 years	http://www.ohioattor-neygeneral.gov/Services/ Victims/Victims-Compensation-Application
Oklahoma	State District Attorney Council	Not specified	No	72 hours	Yes	1 year	http://www.ok.gov/dac/ Victims_Services/Vic-tims_Compensation_ Program/index.html
Oregon	State Attorney General	$20,000	No	72 hours	Yes	6 months	http://www.doj.state. or.us/crimev/comp.shtml
Pennsylvania	State Commission on Crime and Delinquency	Not specified	No	3 days	Not specified	2 years	http://www.portal.state. pa.us/portal/server.pt/ community/available_ser-vices/14558/financial_ assistance/600143
Rhode Island	State Treasure Department	$25,000	No	10 days	Yes	1 year	http://www.treasury.state. ri.us/crimevictim/

(continued)

State	Victim compensation board location	Maximum financial award	Show financial need	Report to police within . . .	Cooperate with law enforcement	File claim within . . .	Contact information
South Carolina	State Governor's Office	$15,000	No	Yes, no time specified	Not specified	Not specified	http://www.sova.sc.gov/
South Dakota	State Department of Social Services	$15,000	No	Not specified	Yes	1 year	http://www.sdvictims.com/
Tennessee	State Criminal Injuries Compensation Fund	$30,000	No	48 hours	Yes	1 year	http://treasury.tn.gov/injury/
Texas	State Attorney General's office	$125,000	No	Within reasonable time	Yes	3 years	http://www.oag.state.tx.us/victims/about_comp.shtml
Utah	State Commission on Criminal and Juvenile Justice	$50,000	No	Must be reported, but no time specified	Yes	Not specified	http://www.crimevictim.state.ut.us/
Vermont	State Attorney General's office	$10,000	No	Must be reported, but no time specified	Not specified	Not specified	http://www.ccvs.state.vt.us/joomla/index.php?option=com_content&task=category&sectionid=5&id=16&Itemid=33
Virginia	State Worker's Compensation System	$15,000	No	120 hours	Yes	1 year	http://www.cicf.state.va.us/
Washington	State Department of Labor and Industry	$50,000	No	1 year	Yes	2 years	http://www.lni.wa.gov/claimsins/crimevictims/default.asp

State	Victim compensation board location	Maximum financial award	Show financial need	Report to police within . . .	Cooperate with law enforcement	File claim within . . .	Contact information
West Virginia	State legislature	$50,000	No	72 hours	Yes	2 years	http://www.legis.state.wv.us/joint/victims/main.cfm
Wisconsin	State Attorney General	$40,000	No	5 days	Yes	1 year	http://www.doj.state.wi.us/cvs/CVCompensation/Compensation_Brochure.asp
Wyoming	State Attorney General	$15,000	No	As soon as possible	Yes	1 year	http://victimservices.wyoming.gov/vcomp.htm

Vinson, Frederick Moore (1890–1953). Born in 1890, Vinson was the twelfth Chief Justice of the United States, noted for his support of the broad interpretation of the powers of the federal government. He began his law practice in 1911 in his hometown of Louisa, KY. He became an influential congressman, supporting Franklin Roosevelt's New Deal. In 1938, President Roosevelt appointed Vinson to the U.S. Circuit Court of Appeals for the District of Columbia. In 1943, he moved to the executive branch, serving in several posts, including secretary of the treasury (1945–1946). He was appointed to the Supreme Court by President Harry S. Truman in 1946. Vinson's failure to unite a faction-ridden court led critics to consider him one of the less successful justices.

violence. Expression of verbal, physical, social, or political force. In criminal justice, violence generally refers to the use of physical force in violation of criminal law; violent offenses generally include: murder, attempted murder, assault, battery, and robbery. Forcible rape, while requiring physical force, is generally categorized as a sexual crime.

violent confiscation. A form of retaliation that generally involves both violence and resource confiscation.

Violent Crime Control and Law Enforcement Act of 1994. A 1994 act of Congress dealing with crime and law enforcement, this is the largest crime bill in the history of the United States. Among the major provisions, the act provided for 200,000 additional police officers, nearly $10 billion in prison funding, and more than $6 billion for prevention programs. *See also* Brady Handgun Violence Prevention Act; Bureau of Alcohol, Tobacco, Firearms and Explosives (ATF); Federal Assault Weapons Ban of 1994; Federal Firearms Act of 1938; Firearm Owners' Protection Act of 1986; Gun Control Act of 1968; National Firearms Act of 1934; Omnibus Crime Control and Safe Streets Act of 1968

Violent Criminal Apprehension Program (ViCAP). ViCAP is the FBI's nationwide data information center that is responsible for collecting, sorting, and analyzing information about crimes throughout the United States.

Violent Offender Incarceration Truth-in-Sentencing (VOI/TIS). From 1996–2001, federal funds were provided to states to build or expand prison bed capacity to accommodate persons convicted of violent crime. These funds prompted many jurisdictions to establish "truth-in-sentencing" statutes, which in effect lengthened prison terms for violent offenders.

Virginia Tech massacre. Name given to the April 16, 2007, shootings at Virginia Polytechnic Institute and State University in Blacksberg, Virginia. During the siege, a lone gunman, later identified as Seung-Hui Cho, opened fire in two separate incidents, killing 32 people and wounding at least 23 more. Cho, who reportedly suffered from mental health issues, shot and killed himself, ending the siege.

virus. Defined by Microsoft as "computer programs or scripts that attempt to spread from one file to another on a single computer and/or from one computer to another, using a variety of methods, without the knowledge and consent of the computer user."

vitiate. To impair the quality of.

voice identification. The ability to distinguish individual voice patterns using telecommunications technology. Banks use this technique to protect currency and securities transfers made by telephone. It is also used in adult and juvenile community supervision programs.

voiceprint. A spectrographic record of the energy output produced by the sound of words or sounds made by a person when speaking. Allegedly, it is distinctive for each person.

voir dire (Fr.). The preliminary examination of a prospective juror in order to determine his or her qualifications to serve as a juror.

VOI/TIS. *See* Violent Offender Incarceration Truth in Sentencing

Vollmer, August. Born in 1876, Vollmer began his distinguished law enforcement career in 1905 when he was elected town marshal for the city of Berkeley, CA. He assisted in the creation of the State Bureau of Criminal Identification. He promoted a police school in conjunction with the University of California, San Jose, in 1916. He was appointed Professor of Police Administration at the University of Chicago in 1929, accepting a full professorship at the University of California in 1931. Vollmer introduced the bicycle for patrol (soon to be followed by motorcycles), radio-equipped police cars, and the police telephone-callbox system. During his career, he served as a consultant to survey and reorganize police departments in 75 American and foreign cities. He inaugurated the use of automatic tabulating machinery to marshal the facts of crime and established the first scientific crime-detection laboratory. He is considered the "father of modern American police" and the "dean of American police chiefs." He lived until 1955. The August Vollmer University is located in Santa Ana, CA.

Volstead Act. Also known as the National Prohibition Act; passed by Congress in 1919. Its enactment was a result of the authorization conferred upon Congress by the Eighteenth Amendment. The law prohibited the manufacture, transportation, and sale of beverages containing more than 0.5 percent alcohol. It fixed penalties for sales of liquor and provided for injunctions against public places that dispensed liquor in violation of the law. Private stocks bought before the act went into effect could be retained. The act was roundly condemned by a large segment of the American people as an invasion of their constitutional rights. The most unfortunate consequences of its passage were the development of widespread political corruption and the emergence of organized crime. The act was repealed by the passage of the Twenty-First Amendment in 1933.

voluntariness. The state of having autonomy over one's actions; it is allegedly diminished or negated by such conditions as physical or psychological duress, illness, hypnosis, or mental defect.

volunteer. One who serves or acts, usually without compensation, of his or her own free will or accord.

Volunteers of America. Established in 1896, a nonprofit organization comprised of 16,000 staff and more than 70,000 volunteers who provide service to vulnerable groups in the United States, "including at-risk youth, the frail elderly, men and women returning from prison, homeless individuals and families, people with disabilities, and those recovering from addictions." Address: 1660 Duke Street, Alexandria, Virginia 22314, Web: http://www.voa.org/default.aspx. *See also* AmeriCorps; Corporation for National and Community Service (CNCS)

vomiting agents. War gases and mob- and riot-control gases, such as DA, DM, and DC. These three vomiting agents are normally solids that, when heated, vaporize and then condense to form toxic aerosols. Under field conditions, vomiting agents cause great discomfort to their victims; when released indoors, they may cause serious illness or death.

von Brunn, James Wenneker. (1920–2010). Born in St. Louis Missouri, James Brunn was an artistic child who earned a degree in journalism from Washington University in 1943. Brunn's arrest record dates back to the 1960s, when he was incarcerated for resisting arrest, fighting, and drunk driving. He was arrested in 1981 for taking employees of the Federal Reserve Board hostage, for which he served six years in prison. He was reportedly a white supremacist who denied the Holocaust occurred. On June 10, 2009, Brunn reportedly shot and killed a security guard at the Holocaust Memorial Museum in Washington, DC. Brunn was arrested at the scene. A judge ordered a psychological evaluation of Brunn in September of 2009. He died on January 10, 2010, while incarcerated. *See also* Holocaust Memorial Museum shooting

vote of no confidence. An extralegal and nonbinding procedure used by police labor associations and unions to voice their dissatisfaction with agency personnel such as the chief of police and appointed officials such as city managers regarding leadership or policy. In some instances such votes may influence community and political decisions.

voting laws. The Voting Section of the Civil Rights Division, Department of Justice, enforces voting laws designed to ensure that all qualified citizens have the opportunity to register and vote without discrimination on account of race, color, membership in an ethnic minority group, or age. It also enforces the overseas Citizens Voting Rights Act. Address: Chief, Voting Section, Civil Rights Division, Room 7254—NWB, DOJ, 950 Pennsylvania Avenue, NW, Washington, DC 20530. Web site: http://www.justice.gov/crt/voting/.

voyeurism. Commonly called a "peeping tom." At one time voyeurism was defined only as looking at individual people, while observing sexual acts was called *scoptophilia* or *scotophilia*. This distinction is no longer made. Voyeurism is the compulsive interest in, or practice of, spying on other people engaged in sexual activity for one's own sexual gratification. This can involve a variety of behaviors, including viewing strangers engaged in sexual acts from a distance, through peep-holes or mirrors, and with the use of hidden camera. Typically, voyeurism (sexual spying without videotaping) is treated as a nuisance case in criminal justice and is often prosecuted as trespassing. However, research in the 1980s suggested that voyeuristic behavior suggests the potential for escalating sexual offenses, particularly when such activity demonstrates advance planning, as in the use video equipment. Thus, several jurisdictions now treat instances of voyeurism more seriously than in the past. Videotaping sexual acts without the consent of both parties is a crime (*see,* for example Stephanie's Law). *See also* exhibitionism, Peeping Tom, sex offender

W

WACO. Area located between Dallas and Austin, Texas, and the site of a 50-day standoff between February 28 -April 19, 1993. The siege began when federal agents attempted to serve a search warrant, prompted by concerns over possible weapons and child abuse offenses, at the Branch Davidian Compound, led by leader David Koresh. After the initial raid, which resulted in an intense battle leaving 10 dead and dozens of persons injured, the Branch Davidian Compound was locked down, leading to the 50-day standoff. At one point, 19 children were released. The incident ignited on April 19, 1993, when federal forces used tear gas in an attempt to flush out the remaining persons inside the compound, an act precipitated by law enforcement concerns of ongoing child abuse and the threat of mass suicide. The compound ignited in flame, either due to deliberate arson by Davidian members or due to the federal tank assault, leaving 50 adults and 25 children dead. Only nine persons survived.

wage and hour enforcement. The Wage and Hour Division of the Department of Labor administers and enforces federal labor laws on minimum wage, overtime pay, recordkeeping, youth employment and special employment, and enforces regulations established by Congress through the Fair Labor and Standards Act. It has the authority to conduct investigations and gather data on wages, hours, and other employment conditions, as well as supervise the payment of back wages. Address: Wage and Hour Division, Department of Labor, 200 Constitution Ave., NW, Washington, DC 20210. Web site: http://www.dol.gov/whd/index.htm.

Waite, Morrison "Mott" Remick (1816–1888). Sixth chief justice of the United States, who is generally regarded as having had only fair capabilities. Born in Connecticut in 1816, Waite was educated at Yale. He moved to Ohio to practice law and soon became successful as a bank and railroad lawyer. Waite was loyal to President Abraham Lincoln and in 1874 was appointed chief justice by President Ulysses S. Grant. Waite died in office in 1888.

wait, lie in. To conceal oneself, or stay hidden, ready to attack. A Louisiana statute provides that lying in wait with a dangerous weapon with intent to commit a crime constitutes an attempt to commit the offense intended.

walking line. An imaginary line that, in normal and ideal walking, fuses with the direction line and runs along the inner sides of both heelprints. It is one of the elements of an individual's walking profile.

walking picture. The study of the characteristics of footprints left by a person walking. Included in this study are the direction line, the walking line, and the foot line.

Wallace, Christopher George Tatore (aka **Notorious B.I.G., Biggie Smalls, Biggie, Frank White**). (1972–1997). Wallace was born in Brooklyn and raised during the crack cocaine epidemic of the 1980s. He released his debut album in 1994, at the age of 22, and was tremendously popular hip hop artist. At this time, there was fierce rivalry between East coast/West coast hip hop artists, and Wallace reportedly maintained an intense rivalry with rapper Tupac Shakur. In September of 1996, Shakur was murdered in a drive-by shooting in Las Vegas, and Wallace was implicated in the murder, but never charged. On March 8, 1997, Wallace appears at the Soul Train Music Awards in Los Angeles. Following the event, he attended a party, which he left around 12:30 A.M. on March 9. En route to his hotel room around 12:45 A.M., Wallace was killed in a drive-by shooting. He was seated in the passenger seat of his vehicle, stopped at a red light, when an unknown black male pulled up next to him and fired four bullets into Wallace's torso. He died within the hour. Various theories exist about Wallace's death, including the East coast/West coast rapper rivalry; another plausible theory was detailed in the book

LAbyrinth (2002) based on information from an LAPD insider. According to this theory, Marion "Suge" Knight conspired with LAPD CRASH officers to kill Wallace and fabricate an East Coast/West coast rap rivalry to cover it up. The theory further suggests that LAPD did not fully investigate links with Knight's Death Row Records. While the murder has never been solved, relatives of Wallace filed wrongful death lawsuit against the city of Los Angeles, naming LAPD CRASH officers Rafael Perez and Nino Durden as conspirators in Wallace's murder and accusing the LAPD of a cover-up. *See also* Perez, Rafael; Community Resources Against Street Hoodlums; Rampart Scandal

Wall Street bombing. On September 16, 1920, Wall Street in New York was bombed by dynamite, killing 38 and injuring 143 persons. No arrests or convections resulted, but the incident is believed to be an act committed by Galleanist anarchists. *See also* domestic terrorism

Walnut Street Jail. Erected in Philadelphia in 1773, it was later called a penitentiary. Unlike previous prisons, it received convicted felons from a statewide area and kept its prisoners at hard labor in solitary confinement. It was expected that prisoners in solitary confinement could meditate on their evil ways and become penitent, leading to the term *penitentiary*. This institution served as a model of humane penal reform that was widely adopted by European penologists. Among the characteristics that were most impressive were the facts that prisoners were paid for their work, men and women prisoners were separated, corporal punishment was forbidden, and religious instruction was required.

Walsh, Adam John (1974–1981). Walsh was a Florida boy abducted from a department store while shopping with his mother; he was later found murdered. Walsh's abduction and death garnered national attention and prompted his father, John Walsh, to became one of the nation's most fierce victim's advocates.

wanton. Reckless; malicious; without regard to the rights of others.

war crimes. During World War II, the first statement by the United Nations that war crimes would be punished after the war was made in the Moscow Declaration on October 30, 1943. Subsequently the UN Commission for the Investigation of War Crimes was established to compile lists of suspected war criminals. It classified two groups of crimes: those against the nationals of a state, the trials of whom were to be held by national courts or military tribunals, and those international in scope, to be tried by special international courts under military law. In August 1945 the United States, the United Kingdom, France, and the Soviet Union adopted a statute for trying the principal Nazi civil and military leaders. These nations established the Nuremberg Tribunal, which opened its hearing on November 20, 1945. War crimes had been defined as plotting aggressive war, atrocities against civilians, genocide, slave labor, looting of occupied countries, and the maltreatment and murder of war prisoners. During June of 1946, concurrent trials were held in German and Japanese courts, which by 1950 had tried more than 8,000 war criminals and executed 2,000 of them. Altogether about 150,000 war criminals—members of the Gestapo, SS, and their collaborators—were suspected of crimes against humanity. Only about 40,000 were ever formally charged, and only about 10,000 were convicted. There may be as many as 50,000 Nazi criminals still alive around the world—about 10,000 in the United States and over 3,000 in Canada. The best known is Josef Mengele, dubbed by his victims as the Angel of Death. Rewards for his capture total more than $2.3 million, including $1 million each from the Friends of the Wiesenthal Center and the *Washington Times*. According to June 1985 reports, Mengele lived in Brazil for at least 15 years and allegedly drowned on February 7, 1979, at Bertioga, about 47 miles from São Paulo. The body was said to have been buried the next day under the name of Wolfgang Gerhard, an Austrian who served in the German army.

warden. The official in charge of operating a prison; the chief administrator of a prison; the prison superintendent.

Wardens and Superintendents, North American Association of. Founded in 1870; this organization promotes improved prison management and prison conditions through training and networking. Publishes *The Grapevine* (bimonthly). Address: P.O. Box11037, Albany, NY 12211. Web site: http://naaws.corrections.com/.

War on Terror, War on Terrorism. Phrase coined by President George W. Bush in response to U.S. actions following the September 11 attacks. The term references U.S. military conflict in the middle east, including the invasion of Afghanistan in 2001, deployment to the Philippines in 2002, deployment of UN forces to the Horn of Africa beginning in 2002, and the 2003 invasion of Iraq. Although military presence is ongoing as of 2010, the term "War on Terror" has been replaced with the term "Overseas Contingency Operation" in the Obama administration.

warrant. In criminal proceedings, any of number of writs, issued by a judicial officer that direct law enforcement officers to perform specified acts and afford them protection from damage in carrying them out. *See also* execution and return of warrant; execution of the warrant; search and seizure

Warren Commission. The commission assigned to report on the assassination of President John F. Kennedy, headed by Chief Justice Earl Warren. It was established by executive order in November 1963 to study and report on the Kennedy shooting and subsequent shooting of Lee Harvey Oswald, the man arrested in connection with the assassination. The September 1964 commission report, submitted to President Lyndon B. Johnson, rejected the possibility of an assassination conspiracy, finding that Oswald acted alone. The commission further determined that Jack Ruby, the man convicted of killing Oswald, also acted alone. Several other theories had been postulated, several of which still have substantial following.

Warren, Earl. (1891–1974). Fourteenth chief justice of the United States from 1953 to 1969. Not since John Marshall has a chief justice been credited with engendering as many social and political changes as Earl Warren, who was appointed by President Dwight D. Eisenhower. Born in Los Angeles in 1891, Warren graduated from the University of California Law School at Berkeley. From 1920 on he spent his entire career in appointive and elective political offices: deputy district attorney, attorney general, and governor of California. He was also the Republican candidate for vice president in 1948. The so-called Warren Revolution began in 1954, when Warren argued that state-imposed segregation of public schools was unconstitutional because it fostered feelings of inferiority (*Brown v. Board of Education of Topeka*). The Warren Court expanded First Amendment freedoms and the requirements for counsel for defendants (*Gideon v. Wainwright,* 1963), ruled on the necessity of informing defendants of particular rights (*Miranda v. Arizona,* 1966), invalidated illegally seized evidence at trial (*Mapp v. Ohio,* 1961), and outlawed prayers in public schools (*Engel v. Vitale,* 1962). Warren died in 1974.

war, tong. Violent conflict between rival Chinese groups or tongs. Such groups or societies in the United States are a transfer from China, where they are based upon kinship, district, or other forms of affiliation. They often serve useful purposes in business or social welfare. But through business rivalry, or efforts to control illicit forms of gain in relation to vice, gambling, or opium traffic, some of the tongs become involved in criminal violence. Membership in the tongs may consist, in part, of merchants who are forced to join in order to get protection from rival tongs who seek control over their businesses.

Washington, DC sniper. *See* Beltway sniper attacks

watch and ward. During the reign of Edward I (1272–1307), the first police forces —the watch and ward—were created in England. They appeared in the larger walled towns of England, usually under the control of the constable and with responsibility to protect the town against fire, to guard the gates, and to arrest those who committed offenses at night. Thus, they were equivalent to today's night watchmen or private security guards. The first night watch in the United States was established in Boston, MA, in 1636.

watchdog committee. Congressional special committee, or a subcommittee of a standing committee, charged with investigation, in contrast with the standing committee's routine consideration of bills. Watchdog committees are usually authorized by each house independently, although on occasion both houses have acted concurrently to set up a joint watchdog committee. The committees have inquired into lobbying activities, corrupt practices and campaign expenditures, and government stockpiling of strategic materials.

waterboarding. A controversial interrogation technique in which the subject is restrained to a board, with legs slightly elevated, with water poured over the head and breathing passages. This method, deemed torture by the United Nations, that causes a sensation similar to drowning and has the potential for brain damage and death, was used by the United States against extra judicial prisoners in the War on Terror.

Watergate Affair. One of the most sensational political scandals of the twentieth century, involving numerous prominent Republicans. During the 1972 Presidential campaign, the Democrats had their party headquarters in the Watergate Complex in Washington, DC. In June 1972 burglars, originally thought to be anti-Castro Cuban refugees who opposed George McGovern, were caught in Democratic headquarters. The Nixon administration and the Republican campaign organization at first denied complicity, but, following President Richard M. Nixon's landslide reelection and the conviction of the burglars, more revealing details began to emerge. In addition to wide-ranging financial irregularities, the affair involved the use of independent government agencies for partisan, political purposes and widened the gulf between the executive branch and Congress, which held its own investigation into Watergate. Maurice Stans, ex-secretary of commerce, and John N. Mitchell, ex-attorney general, as well as John Ehrlichman and H. R. Haldeman, the president's top White House advisers, and the president's personal lawyer and his White House counsel were all implicated. The Nixon administration's effort to cover up its involvement provoked the Justice Department and Senate to investigate even further, and, in 1973, impeachment proceedings were begun against Nixon. When the Supreme Court ordered him to hand over tape recordings that implicated him in the coverup, Nixon resigned in 1974. Several of his top officials were convicted for their parts in the Watergate affair and were sentenced to prison. Nixon was eventually granted a general pardon by his successor, Gerald R. Ford.

watermark. A design worked into certain kinds of paper. It can be seen by holding the paper against a bright light and is usually put there by the paper manufacturer, whose logo it may be.

Watson, Charles Denton "Tex" (1945–). Manson follower convicted of the Tate/La Bianca murders in California in 1969. His death sentence was commuted to life in 1972. He remains incarcerated in California. *See also* Manson, Charles

weapon. An instrument used in fighting; an instrument of offensive or defensive combat. The term is chiefly used in law in the statutes prohibiting the carrying of concealed or deadly weapons. *See also* nonlethal weapons

weapon identification. *See* Criminalistics Laboratory Information System

weapons: carrying, possessing, and so forth. The name of the Uniform Crime Reports category used to record and report arrests for offenses relating to the regulation of the manufacture, sale, distribution, possession, use, or transportation of deadly weapons and accessories.

weapons of mass destruction (WMD). According to the United States Code, a WMD is "any weapon or device that is intended, or has the capability, to cause death or serious bodily injury to a significant number of people through the release, dissemination, or impact of: (A) toxic or poisonous chemicals or their precursors; (B) a disease organism; or (C) radiation or radioactivity 50 U.S.C. 2302(1)".

Weathermen. A militant faction of the Students for a Democratic Society (SDS). It splintered from SDS in June 1969 at Ann Arbor, MI. *See also* Students for a Democratic Society

wedding cake model. This criminal justice model was formulated by Lawrence Friedman and Robert V. Percival. The "cake" model consists of four layers: (1) celebrated cases, (2 & 3) serious felonies, and (4) misdemeanors. The fourth layer far outnumbers the felonies. The celebrity cases receive massive media coverage and give the public a distorted view of the actual criminal justice system. *See* crime commission model

Weed and Seed Operation. On July 20, 1992, the U.S. attorney general created the Executive Office for Weed and Seed as an arm of the Office of the Deputy Attorney General. Operation Weed and Seed is a neighborhood revitalization program that coordinates law enforcement with social services, housing, and community redevelopment programs. The purpose is to "weed out" undesirable elements through aggressive law enforcement and to "seed" neighborhoods through economic revitalization and restoration.

Welch, Joseph Nye. Born in Primghar, Iowa, on October 22, 1890, Welch graduated from Grinnell College and Harvard Law School and was admitted to the Massachusetts bar in 1918. He gained national fame in 1954 as special counsel for the U.S. Army in the congressional McCarthy hearings on the spread of Communism and Communist plots in the United States then being alleged by Senator Joseph McCarthy. When McCarthy made a particularly nasty accusation, Welch responded with the most memorable statement to come out of the sessions: "Until this moment, Senator, I think I never really gauged your cruelty or recklessness... Have you no sense of decency?" The hearings were McCarthy's undoing. Welch returned to his law practice in Boston, a national figure. He died in Hyannis, MA, on October 6, 1960.

Wells Fargo and Co. Founded in 1852 by Henry Wells and William G. Fargo as a joint stock association, Wells Fargo was actually a banking institution, an express and mail-carrying service, and a stage line that operated out of more than 100 offices in the western mining districts. The company carried millions of dollars in gold dust in an area beset with bandits and, since it had advertised that there would never be a loss to any customer, it was forced to structure its own elaborate security system. Treasure boxes and express coaches were protected by armed guards, and outlaws who held up Wells Fargo banks and carriers were relentlessly hunted down by specially trained and equipped couriers and agents.

Werther effect. Additional term for the copycat syndrome in which people are spurred to commit suicide by media reports of others who have done so. Werther was a character in a novel by Goethe who committed suicide, and the story was said to have triggered imitative deaths throughout Europe in the nineteenth century.

Western States Information Network. Established by Congress in 1981 as one of six regional intelligence systems in the United States. WSIN serves the narcotics intelligence needs of law enforcement agencies in Alaska, California, Hawaii, Oregon, and Washington.

WETIP. Acronym for We Turn In Pushers, founded in 1972. Conducts a program for witnesses who wish to remain anonymous. Address: P.O. Box1296, Rancho Cucamonga, CA 91729: (800) 78-CRIME, (800) 47-ARSON, and (800) US-FRAUD. Web site: https://www.wetip.com/.

Wharton Rule. Legal restriction that two people who agree to commit a crime cannot be prosecuted as conspirators when the crime naturally requires the participation of two people, such as dueling or adultery.

whistleblowers. *See* False Claims Act

white-collar crime. Nonviolent crime for financial gain committed by means of deception by persons whose occupational status is entrepreneurial, professional, or semiprofessional and who use their special occupational skills and opportunities; also, nonviolent crime for financial gain using deception and committed by anyone having special technical and professional knowledge of business and government, irrespective of the person's occupation. The term was first used by criminologist Edwin H. Sutherland to cover business crimes such as embezzlement, price fixing, and antitrust violations. Actual instances of white-collar crime are prosecuted as the offenses defined in statutes under such headings as theft, fraud, and embezzlement. On May 2, 1985, the brokerage firm of E. F. Hutton wrote at least $4 billion in overdrafts—cheating 400 banks of tens of millions in interest. The case resulted in a $2 million fine. According to the U.S. Department of Justice, white-collar criminals rake in a minimum of $200 billion annually, far overshadowing the $11 billion cost of violent crimes. Criminal acts played a part in half of the more than 100 bank and savings and loan failures in 1989. Specific white-collar crimes include embezzlement, bribery, fraud (including procurement fraud, stock fraud, fraud in government programs, and investment and other schemes), theft of services, theft of trade secrets, tax evasion, and obstruction of justice. *See also* securities violations

White, Edward Douglass (1845–1921). Eighth chief justice of the United States, appointed by President Grover S. Cleveland. He is noted for opinions reflecting a conservative and nationalistic viewpoint. Born in Louisiana in 1845, White was admitted to the bar in 1868. In 1874 he was elected to the state senate and served on the Louisiana

Supreme Court from 1879 to 1880 before his election to the U.S. Senate in 1890. White served as an associate justice from 1894 to 1910, when he was elevated to chief justice by President William H. Taft. His chief distinction lies in his dissenting opinion in the Income Tax Cases and his concurring and dissenting opinions in the Insular Cases.

White Night. On May 21, 1979, after former San Francisco county supervisor Dan White was convicted of voluntary manslaughter rather than murder for killing Mayor George Moscone and gay supervisor Harvey Milk, thousands of gay men and women attacked San Francisco City Hall, smashing windows and torching patrol cars. Police, in a retaliatory action, stormed the Castro, the city's gay ghetto. *See also* Queer Nation

white slave traffic. A term meaning selling or procuring others for the purpose of prostitution. The federal law known as the Mann Act punishes, by the fine of $5,000 or imprisonment for five years or both, any person who knowingly transports, or causes to be transported or assists in obtaining transportation for, any woman or girl for the purpose of prostitution or debauchery or for any other immoral purpose or with the intent to do so, in interstate or foreign commerce. The act includes inducing, enticing, or coercing a woman or girl to go from one place to another in interstate or foreign commerce for immoral purposes. The act received the cooperation of many foreign nations at the Paris conference on May 18, 1904. It has been used as an instrument for blackmail by prostitutes working bordering states and has proven difficult to enforce, although it is a very effective weapon for the suppression of the vice it was designed to suppress. The importation of women from foreign countries for the purpose of prostitution or for any other immoral purpose is prohibited by the federal law governing aliens and immigration; the law prohibits such traffic and includes within its scope the keeping, controlling, or harboring of any woman imported for such purposes.

Whitewater Scandal. Political controversy ignited in 1992 over the involvement of President William Clinton and his wife Hillary in the 1998 failure of the Whitewater Development Corporation and Madison Guaranty Savings and Loan. The Whitewater Development Corporation and Madison S&L were operated by Clinton associates Jim & Susan McDougal, who allegedly borrowed more than one million dollars from their own S&L to fund business development, in violation of federal law. In all, 15 people were convicted of various fraud and conspiracy charges, including the Arkansas Governor who succeeded Clinton, although the Clintons were never indicted. When he left office in January 2001, President Clinton pardoned four persons involved in the debacle.

Whitman, Charles (1941–1966). Texas college student responsible for murdering his mother and his wife, then shooting 46 people from a tower at the University of Texas, Austin. In all, 16 persons died and 32 sustained injuries. Whitman was killed by police during his sniper attack, although a suicide note was found on his body. Autopsy revealed a brain tumor, which may have played a role in his sudden violence. *See also* Columbine

Wild Bunch, also called the Doolin–Dalton Gang, name refers to a group of Wild West outlaws, including: Bill Doolin, George Newcomb, Charley Pierce, Oliver Yantis, Bob Dalton, Emmett Dalton, Jack Dalton, Gratton Dalton, William "Bill" Dalton, "Tulsa" Jack Blake, "Dynamite" Dan Clifton, Roy Daugherty, George "Red Buck" Waightman, Richard "Little Dick" West, and William "Little Bill" Raidler. *See also* Cassidy, Butch; Sundance Kid

Wickersham Commission. Informal name for the National Commission on Law Observance and Enforcement, which was created by President Herbert Hoover in 1931 as the first national commission to deal with crime and the police. It ultimately produced a series of 13 reports, on the following subjects: Observance and Enforcement of Prohibition, Enforcement of the Prohibition Laws of the U.S., Criminal Statistics, Prosecution, Enforcement of the Deportation Laws of the United States, The Child Offender in the Federal System of Justice, Progress on the Study of the Federal Courts, Criminal Procedure, Crime and the Foreign Born, Lawlessness in Law Enforcement, Cost of Crime, Causes of Crime, and Police. The report on police noted that the average police chief's term was too short and that his responsibility to political officials made his position insecure. The commission also felt there was a lack of competent, efficient, and honest patrolmen. It said that no intensive effort was being made to educate, train, and discipline prospective officers, or to eliminate those shown to be incompetent. The commission found that with perhaps two exceptions, police forces in cities with populations over 300,000 had neither an adequate communications system nor the equipment necessary to enforce the law effectively. It said that the police task was made much more difficult by the excessively rapid growth of U.S. cities in the prior 50 years, and by the tendency of different ethnic groups to retain their languages and customs in large cities. The report added that there were too many duties cast upon each officer and patrolman. The commission report also excoriated the police for the practice of giving suspects the "third degree," and expressed concern about whether or not criminal investigations were conducted lawfully.

Williams, Stanley Tookie III (1953–2005). Born in Louisiana in 1953, Williams was the father of the Crips gang. Williams was a nefarious gang leader believed to be responsible for dozens of murders, robberies, and drug crimes during the operation of his criminal organization. He was convicted of four murders and sentenced to death in 1979. By 1993, Williams renounced his gang and began writing books aimed at deterring youth involvement in gangs. William's request for commutation was rejected, and he was executed by lethal injection in California on December 13, 2005.

Wilson, Orlando W. A police reformer who has often been credited with the promotion of police professionalism. Wilson learned police reform while a patrolman under August Vollmer at Berkeley, CA, in 1921. He was police chief in Wichita, KS, in 1928 and convinced the Kansas League of Municipalities to create a statewide police training school in 1931, and to appoint him the director. He drafted the Square Deal Code of Wichita, which has since been adopted as a code of ethics by the International Association of Chiefs of Police. By 1939 Wilson had achieved national prominence, but he had also irritated too many Wichita politicians. He resigned as Chief of Police and accepted a professorship in police administration at the University of California, Berkeley, and founded the first professional school of criminology there after World War II ended. As dean, Wilson became an extremely influential reformer. Wilson was appointed Chief of Police for Chicago in 1960 and retired in 1967.

witness. Anyone called to testify by either side in a trial. The witness is sworn in and offers evidence deemed relevant to the case. More broadly, a witness is anyone who has observed an event.

witness, alibi. *See* alibi

witness, character. *See* character

witness, expert. *See* expert testimony

witness list. A list of all individuals intended to be called as witnesses by either side in trial. It is usually demanded of the prosecution by the defense during discovery, so that counsel for the accused can adequately prepare a case and not be taken by surprise. In many jurisdictions, the defense must furnish a list of alibi and expert witnesses it intends to call.

Witness Protection Plan (WPP). This program was established in 1970 under Title V of the Organized Crime Control Act. It provides for the health, safety, and welfare of witnesses who have offered valuable testimony in investigations or prosecutions of organized crime. Services are provided to witnesses and their families by the U.S.

Marshals Service. (Between 1974 and 1978, an estimated 10 percent of all murders linked to organized crime were of prosecution witnesses.) The Witness Security Reform Act was passed in 1984, extending protection under the WPP to witnesses who provided information in other serious crimes not involving organized crime. Since 1971, WPP has protected, relocated, and given new identities to more than 8,200 witnesses and 9,800 of their family members.

WMD. *See* weapons of mass destruction

Workaholics Anonymous. Support and self-help group for people who feel they are addicted to their jobs or to spending time in the offices. Address: World Service Organization, P.O. Box289, Menlo Park, CA 94026-0289. Web site: http://www.workaholics-anonymous.org/.

work release (furlough) programs. Change in prisoners' status to minimum custody with permission to work outside prison. Many such prisoners are housed in local communities. The concept was first applied in Wisconsin in 1913 but did not receive much support until the 1950s. Work release, work furlough, house arrest, and electronic monitoring are all economical alternatives to incarceration and prison overcrowding. They also provide a supervised transition period from prison to life on the outside.

World Court. Formally known as the International Court of Justice, the court was formed in 1945 by the United Nations to deal with disputes involving international law. Its 15 judges are elected for nine-year terms from UN countries under rules ensuring a political balance. It sits in the Peace Palace built in The Hague, the Netherlands, in 1903 with money donated by industrialist Andrew Carnegie. Although the court has had no power to enforce its rulings over the past four decades, it has decided barely 50 cases and given a dozen advisory opinions. The United States has been involved directly in only five cases, winning the most important in 1980 when the court condemned Iran's seizure of the U.S. embassy in Teheran and demanded the release of 50 American hostages. Iran ignored the findings. The United States won another victory in the 1960s when the court told the Soviet Union to pay its share of costs for Mideast peacekeeping forces approved by the General Assembly. Moscow refused. The most recent case was Nicaragua's charge that the CIA was trying to "overthrow or destabilize" the Sandinista government by supplying aid, money, and training to contra forces. In April 1985 the United States stated that it would not accept, for the next two years, the court's jurisdiction on matters concerning Central America.

World Trade Center Attack (2001). Destruction of the north and south towers of the World Trade Center on the morning of September 11, 2001. The World Trade Center attack occurred as part of a broader act of terrorism, which included the hijacking of four planes on that date, which crashed into the two towers of the World Trade Center, the Pentagon, and a field in Pennsylvania (final destination believed to be the U.S. Capital building or White House). *See also* September 11 attacks, domestic terrorism

World Trade Center bombing (1993). On February 26, 1993, the World Trade Center in New York was attacked by bombing, resulting in six deaths and more than 1,000 injuries. The attack was perpetrated by Ramzi Yousef and six associates, Mohammad Salameh, Abdul Yasin, Mahmoud Abouhalima, Ahmen Ajaj, Nidal Ayyad, and Eyad Ismoil, who planted the bomb in an underground parking garage beneath the World Trade Center. The culprits were apprehended when FBI found a vehicle identification number (VIN) in the wreckage, which was matched to a rental van reportedly stolen the day before the attack. The van was rented by suspect Mohammad Salameh (eventually sentenced to 240 years), who was arrested March 4, 1993, while attempting to obtain the return of his $400 deposit from the rental company. Additional clues led to the arrest of three more suspects, Nidal Ayyad (240 years), Mahmoud Abouhalima (240 years), and

Ahmed Ajaj (115 years), and the discovery of a storage locker containing explosives and cyanide gas. Further investigation uncovered the goal of the bombing—to topple one tower by bomb, and have the second tower collapse due to the explosion and debris. The FBI also uncovered plans to orchestrate simultaneous bombings of U.S. international flights. Yousef, believed to be the leader, was arrested in Pakistan in 1995 and extradited to the United States. Yousef and the sixth conspirator, Ismoil, it were subsequently convicted and sentenced to life without parole and 240 years, respectively. Abdul Yasin remains at large, although he was reportedly in prison in Iraq in 2002, under Sadam Hussein. This was the first Middle Eastern terrorist attack on American soil, and a prelude to the September 11, 2001 attacks. *See also* terrorist, September 11

Wournos, Aileen (1956–2002). Female serial killer believed responsible for the deaths of at least seven men in Florida between 1989–1990. Wournos claimed each of her victims attempted to rape or kill her when she was working as a prostitute, arguing self-defense for each murder. She was convicted in 1992 and sentenced to death. Wournos was executed by lethal injection on October 9, 2002. *See also* serial killer

wrongful conviction. The erroneous conviction of person who is factually innocent of the crime for which he is charged. According to the Innocence Project, the most common sources of wrongful conviction include: Eyewitness Misidentification; Unvalidated or Improper Forensic Science; False Confessions/Admissions; Government Misconduct; Informants or Snitches; and Bad Lawyering. *See also* false imprisonment

X

xenophobe. A person who fears, mistrusts, and dislikes foreigners or things he or she perceives as strange and foreign. *See also* hate crimes

text continues on page 497

TABLE 52 WORLDWIDE PRISON POPULATION AND INCARCERATION RATES, 2010

Country	Estimated Prison Population	Incarcerated rate (inmates per 100,000)
United States	2,186,230	738
Russia	869,814	611
St. Kitts and Nevis	214	547
Turkmenistan	22,000	489
Cuba	55,000	487
Belize	1,359	487
Bahamas	1,500	462
Belarus	41,583	426
Dominica	289	419
Barbados	997	367
Panama	11,649	364
Ukraine	165,716	356
Suriname	1,600	356
Botswana	—	348
Maldives	1,125	343
Kazakhstan	46,292	340
South Africa	157,402	335
Estonia	4,463	333
St. Vincent/ Grenadines	367	312
Saint Lucia	503	303
Trinidad and Tobago	3,851	296
Latvia	6,676	292
Kyrgyzstan	15,744	292
United Arab Emirates	8,927	288
Georgia	11,731	276
Mongolia	6,698	269
Namibia	4,814	267
Grenada	237	265
Tunisia	26,000	263

(continued)

Country	Estimated Prison Population	Incarcerated rate (inmates per 100,000)	Country	Estimated Prison Population	Incarcerated rate (inmates per 100,000)
Thailand	164,443	256	Lesotho	2,924	156
Swaziland	2,734	249	Bulgaria	11,436	148
Moldova	8,876	247	Spain	64,215	145
Chile	39,916	240	Dominican Republic	12,725	143
Lithuania	8,124	240	Malaysia	35,644	141
Seychelles	193	239	Brunei	529	140
Poland	87,901	230	Argentina	54,472	140
Antigua and Barbuda	176	225	Zimbabwe	18,033	139
Azerbaijan	18,259	219	Colombia	62,216	134
Iran	147,296	214	Saudi Arabia	28,612	132
Gabon	2,750	212	Fiji	1,113	131
Israel	13,909	209	Kuwait	3,500	130
Libya	11,790	207	Kenya	47,036	130
Mauritius	2,464	205	Netherlands	22,013	128
Guyana	1,524	199	Algeria	42,000	127
Mexico	214,450	196	Australia	25,353	126
Uruguay	6,947	193	Peru	35,642	126
Brazil	361,402	191	Cameroon	20,000	125
New Zealand	7,620	186	United Kingdom	88,458	124
Czech Republic	18,950	185	Samoa	223	123
Uzbekistan	48,000	184	Portugal	12,870	121
Jamaica	4,913	182	Myanmar	60,000	120
Costa Rica	7,782	181	China	1,548,498	118
Cape Verde	755	178	Tonga	128	114
Morocco	54,542	175	Sri Lanka	23,413	114
El Salvador	12,176	174	Tanzania	43,911	113
Hong Kong	11,580	168	Albania	3,491	111
Lebanon	5,971	168	Philippines	89,639	108
Luxembourg	768	167	Canada	34,096	107
Romania	35,429	164	Madagascar	20,294	107
Tajikistan	10,804	164	Austria	8,766	105
Honduras	11,589	161	Vietnam	88,414	105
Slovakia	8,493	158	Italy	61,721	104
Hungary	15,720	156	Jordan	5,589	104
			Macedonia	2,026	99

Country	Estimated Prison Population	Incarcerated rate (inmates per 100,000)
Nicaragua	5,610	98
South Korea	45,882	97
Germany	78,581	95
Bahrain	701	95
Uganda	26,126	95
Ecuador	12,251	93
Belgium	9,597	91
Turkey	65,458	91
Greece	9,984	90
Armenia	2,879	89
Egypt	61,845	87
Malta	352	86
Paraguay	5,063	86
France	52,009	85
Switzerland	6,111	83
Bolivia	7,710	83
Yemen	14,000	82
Sweden	7,450	82
Sao Tome & Prinicipe	155	82
Croatia	3,594	81
Oman	2,020	81
Denmark	4,198	77
Cyprus	580	76
Finland	3,954	75
Venezuela	19,853	74
Ireland	3,080	72
Laos	4,020	69
Papua New Guinea	4,056	69
Norway	3,048	66

Country	Estimated Prison Population	Incarcerated rate (inmates per 100,000)
Slovenia	1,301	65
Vanuatu	138	65
Togo	3,200	65
Japan	79,055	62
Solomon Islands	297	62
Dijbouti	384	61
Bosnia & Herzegovina	1,526	59
Syria	10,599	58
Cambodia	8,160	58
Guatemala	7,227	57
Pakistan	89,370	57
Qatar	465	55
Ghana	12,736	55
Senegal	5,360	55
Bangladesh	71,200	50
Indonesia	99,946	45
Haiti	3,670	43
Timor-Leste	320	41
Iceland	119	40
Congo	918	38
Sudan	12,000	36
Gambia	450	32
India	332,112	30
Comoros	200	30
Nigeria	40,444	30
Mauritania	815	25
Nepal	7,135	26

Compiled by Richard Porter, CSULB.

x-ray. This technique is used in some examinations conducted by a crime laboratory. The process was invented by German professor Wilhelm Roentgen in 1895 by accident. He received the Nobel Prize in 1901 for his work.

XXY syndrome (Klinefelter's syndrome). The most common sex chromosome disorder, this is a syndrome in which males have an extra Y chromosome. The disorder goes undetected for many affected, although it is associated with microorchidism (small testicles), low testosterone, and reduced fertility. There is no documented link between XXY syndrome and criminality.

XYY syndrome. An aneuploidy (abnormal number) of the sex chromosomes in which a human male receives an extra Y chromosome, giving a total of 47 chromosomes instead of the more usual 46. There are no unusual physical features or medical problems associated with XYY syndrome, although XYY men tend towards increased growth in early childhood and are at greater risk of delayed speed and learning difficulties than other males. Men with XYY are slightly taller in adulthood and have normal sexual development and fertility. A 1965 study reported linkage between XYY and criminal propensity, which was subsequently debunked. In 1966, Richard Speck cited XYY syndrome as a defense in his case. Speck claimed the extra "Y" chromosome cause "maleness," making him overly aggressive and prone to violence for which he should not be blamed. Speck lost his case and his appeals and was sentenced for the murders of eight nurses. Today, no linkage between XYY and criminality has been demonstrated.

Y

youth. A person from the age of adolescence to full maturity. As a collective term, youth refers especially to young persons of high school and early college age. Persons aged 15 through 24 are usually considered the youth group by researchers dealing with census data. The National Youth Administration considered persons aged 16 through 25 as eligible for assistance.

youth correction authority. An administrative agency for the treatment of convicted youthful offenders. Designed by a committee of the American Law Institute and described in a model act approved by the institute in 1940, the agency meets many of the demands for reform in penal treatment urged by social scientists and lawyers in recent times. The model act was, with modifications, adopted by California in 1914.

Youth Correction Authority Act. A model act, published by the American Law Institute in 1940, which served as an impetus to several state youth authority laws. Among other proposals, the act gave ultimate sentencing authority to an administrative board, and provided for an indefinite commitment until the maximum age of 25.

Youth Crime Watch of America. Organization that trains students, teachers, school administrators, and other community members to develop youth-led crime prevention groups. Offers a video and accompanying manual, "Guns and Teens." Address: 9200 Dadeland Blvd., Suite 417, Miami, FL 33156. Web site: http://www.ycwa.org/.

Z

Zenger, Peter (1697–1746). A German-born immigrant to the United States, Zenger was a printer who published critical views of the colonial government in the Americas, prompting his arrest and prosecution for libel in 1734. He was acquitted because his allegations were factually true. Zenger's case is heralded as an early victory for free speech in America. *See also* press, freedom of

zero-based budgeting (ZBB). A procedure requiring departments and agencies to justify all annual expenditures by starting each cost category at 0 rather than using the prior year's expenditures as a framework. More traditional budgeting requires justification of changes from the prior year's expenditures. Under ZBB, money allocated each year is based on predetermined department or agency goals as they relate to proposed expenditures.

Zodiak Killer. Name given to the killer of seven young men and women in the California Bay area in 1968–1969. The killer was named for a series of letters and ciphers mailed to police subsequent to his crimes.

The killer was never apprehended, and the case remains unsolved as of 2010.

zone search. A method of searching a crime scene where the area to be searched is divided into sectors and each one is carefully examined. This is also called a sector search.

zoning. The division of municipalities into distinct districts, the use of each of which is regulated by statute. Zoning laws specify what types of buildings may be constructed and to what use existing buildings and land may be devoted—residential, commercial, light industrial, mixed, and other categories. In addition, zoning laws may regulate the height and densities of buildings, as well as their size in relation to amount of property and the placement of buildings on lots. Zoning is the main procedure local government uses to control the socioeconomic character and the development of a community. The first comprehensive zoning ordinance was adopted in New York City in 1916 and patterned on earlier, smaller-scope ordinances in Boston and Los Angeles. The Supreme Court approved zoning as a proper use of governmental powers when it was challenged in 1926. The enactment of zoning laws falls under the police power of communities to protect the health, safety, and welfare of the citizens.

zoophilia. Unnaturally strong attachment to specific animals for generating sexual pleasure through stroking, petting, or smelling. The practice of sexual relations between humans and animals.

zoosadism. The practice of deriving sexual pleasure through killing or torturing animals. Zoosadism in childhood is considered a warning sign for more serious conduct in adulthood, and is one of the "McDonald triad" associated with sociopathy.

TABLE 53   CRIMINOLOGY AND CRIMINAL JUSTICE GRADUATE PROGRAMS

Institution (United States unless otherwise noted)	Program Name	Web site	Masters Degree	Doctorate Degree
American University, Washington, D.C.	School of Public Affairs	http://www.american.edu/spa/	Yes	Ph.D
Arizona State University	Justice and Social Inquiry	http://justice.clas.asu.edu/	Yes	Ph.D
University of Cincinnati, Ohio	College of Education, Criminal Justice, and Human Services	http://www.cech.uc.edu/criminal_justice	Yes	Ph.D
Florida State University	College of Criminology and Criminal Justice	http://criminology.fsu.edu/index.php	Yes	Ph.D
George Mason University, Virginia	Administration of Justice	http://adj.gmu.edu/	Yes	Ph.D
University of Illinois at Chicago	Criminology, Law, and Justice	http://www2.las.uic.edu/depts/cjus/	Yes	Ph.D
Indiana University	Criminal Justice	http://www.indiana.edu/~crimjust/	Yes	Ph.D
Indiana University of Pennsylvania	Criminology	http://www.iup.edu/criminology	Yes	Ph.D

(continued)

Institution (United States unless otherwise noted)	Program Name	Web site	Masters Degree	Doctorate Degree
University of California, Irvine	Criminology, Law, and Society	http://cls.soceco.uci.edu/	Yes	Ph.D
City University of New York	John Jay College of Criminal Justice	http://www.jjay.cuny.edu/	Yes	Ph.D
University of Delaware	Sociology and Criminal Justice	http://www.udel.edu/soc/grad.html	Yes	Ph.D
University of Maryland	Criminology and Criminal Justice	http://www.ccjs.umd.edu/	Yes	Ph.D
Michigan State University	Criminal Justice	http://www.cj.msu.edu/	Yes	Ph.D
University of Missouri, St. Louis	Criminology and Criminal Justice	http://www.umsl.edu/~ccj/	Yes	Ph.D
University of Nebraska Omaha	Criminology and Criminal Justice	http://www.unomaha.edu/criminaljustice/index.php	Yes	Ph.D
North Dakota State University	Criminal Justice and Political Science	http://www.ndsu.edu/cjps/	Yes	Ph.D
Northeastern University, Massachusetts	Criminal Justice	http://www.cj.neu.edu/	Yes	Ph.D
Penn State University	Sociology and Crime, Law and Justice	http://www.sociology.psu.edu/	Yes	Ph.D
Oregon State University	Criminology and Criminal Justice	http://www.pdx.edu/hatfieldschool/criminology-and-criminal-justice-master-science	Yes	Ph.D
Rutgers University, New Jersey	School of Criminal Justice	http://rutgers-newark.rutgers.edu/rscj/	Yes	Ph.D
Sam Houston State University, Texas	College of Criminal Justice	http://www.cjcenter.org/	Yes	Ph.D
University of South Carolina	Criminology and Criminal Justice Department	http://www.cas.sc.edu/crju/	Yes	Ph.D
University of South Florida	Department of Criminology	http://criminology.usf.edu/	Yes	Ph.D
University of Southern Mississippi	School of Criminal Justice	http://www.cj.usm.edu/	Yes	Ph.D
State University of New York, Albany	School of Criminal Justice	http://www.albany.edu/scj/	Yes	Ph.D
Temple University, Pennsylvania	Criminal Justice Department	http://www.temple.edu/cj/	Yes	Ph.D

(continued)

Institution (United States unless otherwise noted)	Program Name	Web site	Masters Degree	Doctorate Degree
Washington State University	Criminal Justice Department	http://libarts.wsu.edu/crimj/graduate-studies/	Yes	Ph.D
Andrew Jackson University, Alabama	Criminal Justice Department	http://www.aju.edu/jrc/jrc_index.asp	Yes	No
Faulkner University, Alabama	MCJ Online Department	http://www.faulkner.edu/admissions/graduate/mcj/academicinformation.asp	Yes	No
Jacksonville State University, Alabama	College of Criminal Justice	http://www.jsu.edu/	Yes	No
Troy University, Alabama	Criminal Justice and Social Sciences	http://troy.troy.edu/artsandsciences/criminaljustice/index.html	Yes	No
University of Alabama	Criminal Justice Department	http://www.cj.ua.edu/	Yes	No
University of North Alabama	Department of Criminal Justice	http://www.una.edu/criminaljustice/	Yes	No
University of Alaska	Criminal Justice Department	http://www.uaf.edu/catalog/current/programs/justice_admin.html	Yes	No
University of Arkansas	Department of Criminal Justice	http://ualr.edu/criminaljustice/	Yes	No
University of Northern Arizona	Department of Criminology and Criminal Justice	http://www4.nau.edu/academiccatalog/2009/Educational_Programs/SBS/Criminal_Justice/MSCrimJustTP.htm	Yes	No
California State University, Fresno	Department of Criminology	http://www.csufresno.edu/criminology/	Yes	No
California State University, Long Beach	Department of Criminal Justice	http://www.csulb.edu/colleges/chhs/departments/criminal-justice/	Yes	No
California State University, Sacramento	Division of Criminal Justice	http://www.hhs.csus.edu/cj/	Yes	No
California State University, San Bernardino	Criminal Justice Department	http://criminaljustice.csusb.edu/	Yes	No

(continued)

Institution (United States unless otherwise noted)	Program Name	Web site	Masters Degree	Doctorate Degree
California State University, Stanislaus	Criminal Justice	http://cjwww.csustan.edu/cj/cjhome.html	Yes	No
Claremont Graduate School, California	Center for Policy and Politics	http://www.cgu.edu/pages/1.asp	Yes	No
California State University, San Diego	Justice Studies Department	http://arweb.sdsu.edu/es/admissions/ab/criminaljusticeadmin.htm	Yes	No
California State University, San Jose	Justice Studies Department	http://www.sjsu.edu/justicestudies/	Yes	No
University of California, Berkeley	Sociology Department	http://sociology.berkeley.edu/	Yes	No
University of Colorado, Boulder	Department of Sociology	http://socsci.colorado.edu/SOC/	Yes	No
University of Denver	Program of legal Administration	http://www.law.du.edu/index.php/msla	Yes	No
Central Connecticut State University	Criminal Justice	http://finalsite.ccsu.edu/page.cfm?p=4084	Yes	No
University of New Haven, Connecticut	Public Management and Forensic Science	http://www.newhaven.edu/5921/	Yes	No
George Washington University, Washington, D.C.	Criminal Justice Department	http://www.gwu.edu/learn/undergraduate programs/explore undergraduate programs/fulllistof academicofferings/criminaljustice	Yes	No
Florida Atlantic University	School of Criminology	http://www.fau.edu/dcj/	Yes	No
Florida International University	Criminal Justice Department	http://cj.fiu.edu/	Yes	No
University of Central Florida	Department of Criminal Justice and Legal Studies	http://www.cohpa.ucf.edu/crim.jus/	Yes	No
University of North Florida	Sociology	http://www.unf.edu/coas/ccj/	Yes	No
University of South Florida	Criminology Department	http://criminology.usf.edu/certificate/	Yes	No

(continued)

Institution (United States unless otherwise noted)	Program Name	Web site	Masters Degree	Doctorate Degree
Albany State University, Georgia	Criminal Justice Department	http://www.potentialrealized.org/admin/academic-affairs/divisions/science-health/criminal-justice/index.dot	Yes	No
Armstrong Atlantic State University, Georgia	Department of Government	http://www.armstrong.edu/Majors/degree/criminal_justice1	Yes	No
Georgia State University	Criminal Justice Department	http://chhsweb.gsu.edu/cj/	Yes	No
Valdosta State University, Georgia	Criminal Justice	http://www.valdosta.edu/crju/	Yes	No
University of Hawaii at Manoa	Sociology Department	http://www2.soc.hawaii.edu/css/dept/soc/	Yes	No
Chaminade University, Hawaii	Program in Criminal Justice Administration	http://www.chaminade.edu/criminal-justice/mscja.php	Yes	No
Boise State University	Department of Criminal Justice	http://cja.boisestate.edu/	Yes	No
Chicago State University	Department of Criminal Justice	http://www.csu.edu/CriminalJustice/	Yes	No
Illinois State University	Criminal Justice Department	http://criminaljustice.illinoisstate.edu/	Yes	No
Western Illinois University	School of Law Enforcement and Justice Administration	http://www.wiu.edu/users/mileja/	Yes	No
Indiana State University	Department of Criminology and Criminal Justice	http://web.indstate.edu/ccj/	Yes	No
Indiana University, Purdue	School of Public and Environmental Affairs	http://www.spea.iupui.edu/	Yes	No
Washburn University, Kansas	Criminal Justice and Legal Studies	http://www.washburn.edu/sas/cj/	Yes	No
Wichita State University	School of Community Affairs	http://webs.wichita.edu/?u=criminal justice&p=/index	Yes	No
Eastern Kentucky University	College of Justice and Safety	http://www.justice.eku.edu/cj/	Yes	No
University of Louisville, Kentucky	Justice Administration	https://louisville.edu/justiceadministration/	Yes	No

(continued)

Institution (United States unless otherwise noted)	Program Name	Web site	Masters Degree	Doctorate Degree
Grambling State University, Louisiana	Criminal Justice	http://www.gram.edu/ liberalarts/crimjustice/	Yes	No
Loyola University, New Orleans	Criminal Justice	http://css.loyno.edu/ criminaljustice/	Yes	No
University of Louisiana at Monroe	Criminal Justice	http://www.ulm.edu/ criminaljustice/	Yes	No
Southern University New Orleans	Criminal Justice	http://www.suno.edu/ Colleges/Arts_and_Sciences/Social_Sciences/ Criminal_Justice/grad/	Yes	No
University of Baltimore	Division of Criminal Justice	http://www.ubalt. edu/cla_template. cfm?page=56	Yes	No
University of Maryland	Department of Criminology and Criminal Justice	http://www.ccjs.umd. edu/	Yes	No
American International University, Massachusetts	Criminal Justice	http://www.aic. edu/academics/aes/ criminal_justice	Yes	No
Boston University	Criminal Justice	http://www.bu.edu/ online/online_programs/graduate_ degree/master_criminal_justice/index.html	Yes	No
Harvard University	Criminal Justice Policy and Management	http://www.hks.harvard.edu/criminal justice/index.htm	Yes	No
Suffolk University	Crime and Justice Studies	http://www.law.suffolk. edu/academic/joint/ criminal.cfm	Yes	No
University of Massachusetts, Lowell	Criminal Justice and Criminology	http://www.uml.edu/ college/arts_sciences/ criminaljustice/default. html	Yes	No
Northern Michigan University	Criminal Justice	http://webb.nmu. edu/Departments/ CriminalJustice/	Yes	No
Wayne State University	Criminal Justice	http://www.clas. wayne.edu/CRJ/	Yes	No
St. Cloud State University	Criminal Justice	http://www. stcloudstate.edu/ criminaljustice/	Yes	No

(continued)

Institution (United States unless otherwise noted)	Program Name	Web site	Masters Degree	Doctorate Degree
University of Central Missouri	Criminal Justice	http://www.ucmo.edu/cj/	Yes	No
Columbia College, Missouri	Criminal Justice	http://www.ccis.edu/onlineMSCJ/	Yes	No
University of Missouri, Kansas City	Criminal Justice and Criminology	http://cas.umkc.edu/cjc/#	Yes	No
Southeastern Missouri State University	Criminal Justice and Sociology	http://www5.semo.edu/criminal/	Yes	No
University of Nebraska, Lincoln	Criminal Justice	http://bulletin.unl.edu/graduate/Criminal_Justice	Yes	No
University of Nevada, Las Vegas	Criminal Justice	http://criminaljustice.unlv.edu/	Yes	No
College of New Jersey	Criminology	http://www.tcnj.edu/~lawj/	Yes	No
Monmouth University, New Jersey	Criminal Justice	http://www.monmouth.edu/academics/criminal_justice/default.asp	Yes	No
New Mexico State University	Criminal Justice	http://www.nmsu.edu/~crimjust/	Yes	No
Buffalo State University, New York	Criminal Justice	http://www.buffalo-state.edu/gradprog.xml?bpid=15	Yes	No
Niagara University, New York	Criminology and Criminal Justice	http://www.niagara.edu/crj/	Yes	No
Appalachian State University, North Carolina	Criminal Justice and Criminology	http://www.pscj.appstate.edu/mscjc/	Yes	No
East Carolina University	Criminal Justice	http://www.ecu.edu/che/just/index.html	Yes	No
Fayetteville State University, North Carolina	Criminal Justice	http://www.uncfsu.edu/crimjust/	Yes	No
Methodist University, North Carolina	Justice Administration	http://www.methodist.edu/MJA/	Yes	No
North Carolina Central University	Criminal Justice	http://www.nccu.edu/Academics/sc/socialsciences/criminaljustice/	Yes	No

(continued)

Institution (United States unless otherwise noted)	Program Name	Web site	Masters Degree	Doctorate Degree
University of North Carolina	Criminal Justice	http://www.uncc.edu/gradmiss/catalog/CriminalJustice.htm	Yes	No
Western Carolina University	Criminology and Criminal Justice	http://www.wcu.edu/4975.asp	Yes	No
Minot State University, North Dakota	Criminal Justice	http://www.minotstateu.edu/cjgrad/	Yes	No
Bowling Green State University, Ohio	Criminal Justice	http://www.bgsu.edu/departments/dhs/crju/index.html	Yes	No
Kent State University, Ohio	Justice studies	http://www.kent.edu/cas/justice/	Yes	No
University of Toledo, Ohio	Criminal Justice	http://www.utoledo.edu/hshs/criminaljustice/gradmaja.html	Yes	No
Xavier University, Ohio	Criminal Justice	http://www.xavier.edu/criminal-justice-grad/	Yes	No
University of Central Oklahoma	Criminal Justice	http://www.libarts.uco.edu/sociology/	Yes	No
Oklahoma City University	Criminal Justice	http://www.okcu.edu/petree/soc/	Yes	No
Marywood University, Pennsylvania	Criminal Justice	http://cwis.marywood.edu/departments/socsci/criminaljustice/mscj.html	Yes	No
Mercyhurst College, Pennsylvania	Criminal Justice	http://crjs.mercyhurst.edu/	Yes	No
Shippensburg University, Pennsylvania	Criminal Justice	http://www.ship.edu/Criminal_Justice/	Yes	No
St. Joseph's University, Pennsylvania	Criminal Justice	http://www.sju.edu/academics/cas/grad/criminaljustice/	Yes	No
Villanova University, Pennsylvania	Criminology, Law, and Society	http://www.villanova.edu/artsci/sociology/graduate/	Yes	No
West Chester University, Pennsylvania	Criminal Justice	http://www.wcupa.edu/_academics/sch_sba/u-cj.html	Yes	No

(continued)

Institution (United States unless otherwise noted)	Program Name	Web site	Masters Degree	Doctorate Degree
Widener University, Pennsylvania	Criminal Justice	http://www.widener.edu/academics/collegesandschools/artsandsciences/graddegrees/criminaljustice	Yes	No
The Citadel, South Carolina	Criminal Justice	http://www.citadel.edu/pscj/	Yes	No
University of South Carolina	Criminology and Criminal Justice	http://www.cas.sc.edu/crju/	Yes	No
East Tennessee State University	Criminal Justice and Criminology	http://www.etsu.edu/crimjust/	Yes	No
University of Memphis	Criminology and Criminal Justice	http://www.memphis.edu/cjustice/	Yes	No
Middle Tennessee State University	Criminal Justice	http://www.mtsu.edu/criminaljustice/	Yes	No
Tennessee State University	Criminal Justice	http://www.tnstate.edu/interior.asp?mid=2330&ptid=1	Yes	No
University of Tennessee Chattanooga	Criminal Justice	http://www.utc.edu/Academic/CriminalJustice/	Yes	No
University of Tennessee Knoxville	Criminal Justice	http://web.utk.edu/~utsocdep/criminal_justice.html	Yes	No
Texas State University	Criminal Justice	http://www.cj.txstate.edu/	Yes	Ph.D
Sul Ross State University, Texas	Criminal Justice	http://www.sulross.edu/pages/3166.asp	Yes	No
University of Texas Arlington	Criminology and Criminal Justice	http://www.uta.edu/criminology/	Yes	No
Weber State University, Utah	Criminal Justice	http://www.weber.edu/cj/	Yes	No
Norfolk State University, Virginia	Criminal Justice	http://sola.nsu.edu/macj/	Yes	No
Old Dominion University, Virginia	Criminal Justice	http://al.odu.edu/sociology/	Yes	Ph.D
Radford University, Virginia	Criminal Justice	http://crju-web.asp.radford.edu/	Yes	No
Seattle University, Washington	Criminal Justice	http://www.seattleu.edu/artsci/macj/default.aspx	Yes	No

(continued)

Institution (United States unless otherwise noted)	Program Name	Web site	Masters Degree	Doctorate Degree
Washington State University	Criminal Justice	http://libarts.wsu.edu/ crimj/graduate-studies/ index.asp	Yes	Ph.D
Marshall University, West Virginia	Criminal Justice and Criminology	http://www.marshall. edu/criminal-justice/	Yes	No
University of Wisconsin, Milwaukee	Criminal Justice	http://www4.uwm.edu/ hbssw/criminal_justice/	Yes	No
University of Cape Town (South Africa)	Criminology	http://www.criminol-ogy.uct.ac.za/	Yes	Ph.D
Australian Institute of Technology	Criminology	http://www.aic.gov.au/	Yes	Ph.D
Griffith University (Australia)	Criminology and Criminal Justice	http://www.griffith. edu.au/arts-lan-guages-criminology/ school-criminology-criminal-justice	Yes	No
University of Melbourne (Australia)	Criminal Justice	http://www.ssps. unimelb.edu.au/ research/criminology	Yes	Ph.D
University of Western Australia	Criminal Justice	http://courses.hand-books.uwa.edu.au/ courses/c2/2051	Yes	No
University of Toronto (Canada)	Centre for Criminology	http://link.library. utoronto.ca/uoftdi-rectory/dept_details. cfm?id=CRIM	Yes	No
Simon Fraser University (Canada)	Criminal Justice	http://www.sfu.ca/ criminology/	Yes	Ph.D
University of Alberta (Canada)	Sociology (Criminal Justice)	http://www.sociology. ualberta.ca/graduate. cfm	Yes	Ph.D
Oxford University (England)	Criminology and Criminal Justice	http://www.law.ox.ac. uk/postgraduate/msc. php	Yes	No
University of Leicester (England)	Criminology	http://www2.le.ac. uk/departments/ criminology	Yes	No

Compiled by Richard Porter, CSULB.

REFERENCES

_____. (1988). *The police dictionary and encyclopedia.* Springfield, IL: Charles C. Thomas.

_____. (1989). *When do fish sleep?* New York: Harper Perennial.

_____. (1991). *Do penguins have knees?* New York: Harper Perennial.

9/11 Commission Report. (2004). *The attack looms. National Commission on Terrorist attacks upon the United States.* Retrieved February 22, 2010, from http://govinfo.library.unt.edu/911/report/911Report_Ch7.htm

Abadinsky, H. (1993). *Drug abuse. In Annual editions: Criminal justice 85/86; 86/87; 87/88; 88/89; 89/90; 90/91; 91/92; 92/93; 93/94.* Guilford, CT: Dushkin Publishing Group.

Abel, E. L., & Sokol, R. J. (1987). Incidence of fetal alcohol syndrome and economic impact of FAS-related anomalies: Drug alcohol syndrome and economic impact of FAS-related anomalies. *Drug and Alcohol Dependency, 19*(1), 51–70.

About.com. (n.d.). *Glossary of terrorism terms.* Retrieved January 29, 2010, from http://terrorism.about.com/od/glossaryof terrorismterms/Glossary_of_Terrorism_Terms.htm

ACA Code of Ethics. (n.d.). Retrieved March 6, 2010, from http://www.wca2.org/ethics.html

Adam Walsh Child Protection and Safety Act, Pub.L. 109-248 (2006).

Adamic, L. (1934). *Dynamite: The story of class violence in America.* Edinburgh: AK Press.

Adams, R., Rohe, W., & Arcury, R. (2002). Implementing community-oriented policing: Organizational change and street officer attitudes. *Crime & Delinquency, 48*(3), 399–430.

Aggrawal, A. (2009). *Forensic and medico-legal aspects of sexual crimes and unusual sexual practices.* Boca Raton: CRC Press.

Ahuja, G. (2006, April 18). Sex offender registries: Putting lives at risk? *ABC News.* Retrieved April 6, 2010, from http://abc news.go.com/US/story?id=1855771&page=1

Alvarez-Machain v. United States, 331 F.3d 604, 610 (9th Cir. 2003).

America's Most Wanted. (2010). *The grim sleeper.* Retrieved March 6, 2010, from http://www.amw.com/fugitives/brief.cfm?id=60381

American Academy of Pain Medicine (2001). *Definitions related to the use of opioids for the treatment of pain.* Retrieved March 19, 2010, from http://www.painmed.org/pdf/definition.pdf

American Bar Association. (2006). ABA model rule 6.1 voluntary *pro bono publico* service Accessed March 29, 2010 at: http://www.abanet.org/legalservices/probono/rule61.html

American Foundation for Suicide Prevention. (2010). Retrieved March 16, 2010, from http://www.afsp.org/index.cfm?fuseaction=home.viewpage&page_id=050FEA9F-B064-4092-B1135C3A70DE1FDA

American Gaming Association. (1999). *Is legalized gambling a $600 billion industry or a $50 billion industry.* Retrieved February 22, 2010, from at http://www.americangaming.org/Industry/factsheets/general_info_detail.cfv?id=11

American Gaming Association. (2009). *Gaming revenue: Current year data.* Retrieved April 6, 2010, from http://www.american-gaming.org/Industry/factsheets/statistics_detail.cfv?id=7

American Heart Association Guidelines for Cardiopulmonary Resuscitation and Emergency Cardiovascular Care [Electronic Version]. (2005). *Circulation, 112*(24), Retrieved March 6, 2010, from http://circ.ahajournals.org/content/vol112/24_suppl/

American Psychiatric Association. (1994). *Diagnostic and statistical manual of mental disorders: (DSM-IV).* Washington, DC: American Psychiatric Association.

American Psychiatric Association. (2000). *Diagnostic and statistical manual of mental disorders (DSM-IV-TR).* (4th ed.) Washington DC: American Psychiatric Association.

American Psychiatric Society. (2000). *Diagnostic and statistical manual of mental disorders.* (4th ed.), Text revision. Washington, DC: American Psychiatric Association.

American Society of Pharmacognosy. (2010). *About the ASP.* Retrieved March 12, 2010, from http://www.pharmacognosy.us/?page_id=73

Amunts, K., Kedo, O., Kindler, M., Pieperhoff, P., Mohlberg, H., Shah, N., Habel, U., Schneider, F., Zilles, K. (2005). "Cytoarchitectonic mapping of the human amygdala, hippocampal region and entorhinal cortex: intersubject variability and probability maps." *Anat Embryol (Berl) 210* (5-6): 343–52.

Anderson, J. (2009, September 3). Two bicycle riders charged with DUI on same day. *St. Petersburg Times.* Retrieved March 6, 2010, from http://www.tampabay.com/news/publicsafety/accidents/two-bicycle-riders-charged-with-dui-on-same-day/1033308

Anti-Defamation League. (n.d.). *About the Ku Klux Klan.* Retrieved February 28, 2010, from http://www.adl.org/learn/ext_us/kkk/default.asp?LEARN_Cat=Extremism&LEARN_SubCat=Extremism_in_America&xpicked=4&item=kkk

Anti-Drug Abuse Act, Pub. L. No. 100-690, 102 Stat. 4181 (1988).

Appel, J. M. (2009). What I want for Christmas: Mass clemency. *Huffington Post.* Retrieved March 10, 2010, from http://www.huffingtonpost.com/jacob-m-appel/what-i-want-for-christmas_b_402639.html

Appointment of Officials, 28 U.S.C. § 534 (n.d.).

Arbery, V. (1999). Washington's farewell address and the form of the American regime. In G. L. Gregg II and Matthew Spalding (Eds.) *Patriot safe: George Washington and the American political tradition.* Intercollegiate Studies Institute.

Arbisi, P. A., Sellbom, M., & Ben-Porath, Y. S. (2008). Empirical correlates of the MMPI-2 restructured clinical (RC) scales in psychiatric inpatients. *Journal of Personality Assessment, 90,* 122-128.

Arizona Gun List. (n.d.). *Ammunition types.* Retrieved March 4, 2010, from http://arizonagunlist.com/ammunition_types.html

Armed Career Criminal Act, 18 U.S.C. 924 § (1984).

Asante, M. K. (2002). *100 Greatest African Americans: A Biographical Encyclopedia.* Amhert, NY: Prometheus Books.

Ashcroft v. Free Speech Coalition, 535 U.S. 234 (2002).

Associated Press. (1985). Producer of sex films convicted of pandering. *New York Times.* Retrieved February 22, 2010, from http://www.nytimes.com/1985/05/25/movies/producer-of-sex-films-convicted-of-pandering.html

Associated Press. (1996). Conviction quashed in Heidi Fleiss case. *New York Times.* Retrieved March 19, 2010, from http://www.nytimes.com/1996/05/30/us/conviction-quashed-in-heidi-fleiss-case.html?pagewanted=1

Associated Press. (2009). *Kevorkian criticizes attack on right-to-die group.* Retrieved March 6, 2010, from http://www.mlive.com/news/index.ssf/2009/02/kevorkian_criticizes_attack_on.html

Associated Press. (2010). Medical marijuana lawyer files complaint on raid. *KRDO.* Retrieved April 9, 2010, from http://www.krdo.com/Global/story.asp?S=11984413

Atkins v. Virginia, 536 U.S. 304 (2002).

Automobile Association of America. (2010). *AAA's DUI JusticeLink.* Retrieved February 24, 2010, from http://www.aaaduijusticelink.com/Main/Default.asp?CategoryID=16&SubCategoryID=1&ContentID=7

Avrich, P. (1991). *Sacco and Vanzetti: The anarchist background.* Princeton: Princeton University Press.

Avrich, P. (1996). *Anarchist voices: An oral history of anarchism in America.* Princeton: Princeton University Press.

Ayala, J. (2009). *Examining preparedness and coordination efforts of first responders along the southwest border: Statement before the U.S. House of Representatives committee on Homeland Security.* Retrieved March 2, 2010, from http://homeland.house.gov/SiteDocuments/20090331101052-40943.pdf

Badley, T. (2006). *Annual editions: Violence and terrorism.* (3rd ed.). Guilford, CT: McGraw-Hill/Dushkin.

Bardsley, M. (1997). Life & death in prison. *Crime Library—Courtroom Television Network, LLC.* Retrieved March 15, 2010, from http://www.trutv.com/library/crime/notorious_murders/famous/loeb/7b.html

Bardsley, M. (n.d.). True crime library: The Hillside Stranglers. *True TV.* Retrieved January 29, 2010, from http://www.trutv.com/library/crime/serial_killers/predators/stranglers/rampage_1.html

Bardwell, B., & Arrigo, B. A. (2002). *Criminal competency on trial: The case of Colin Ferguson.* Durham, NC: Carolina Academic Press.

Bartlett, J. M., & Stirling, D. (2003). A short history of the polymerase chain reaction. *Methods Mol Biol. 226,* 3–6.

Bartol, C. R. & Bartol, A. M. (2006). *Current perspectives in forensic psychology and criminal justice.* Los Angeles: Sage Publications.

Baze v. Rees, 553 U.S. 35 (2008).

Bell, R. (2008). *Strategy 360: 10 steps to creating a complete game plan for business and life.* Owners Manual Press.

Belluck, P. (2003, January 31). Threats and responses: The bomb plot: Unrepentant shoe bomber is given a life sentence. *New York Times.* Retrieved March 14, 2010, from http://www.nytimes.com/2003/01/31/us/threats-responses-bomb-plot-unrepentant-shoe-bomber-given-life-sentence-for.html?pagewanted=1

Benjamin, D. & Simon, S. (2003). *The Age of Sacred Terror.* New York: Random House.

Bennett, J. W., & Klich, M. (2003). *Mycotoxins. Clinical Microbiology Reviews, 16*(3), 497–516.

Ben-Porath, Y. S., & Tellegen, A. (2008). MMPI-2-RF (Minnesota multiphasic personality inventory-2-restructured form). *Pearson PsychCorp.* Retrieved March 6, 2010, from http://psychcorp.pearsonassessments.com/HAIWEB/Cultures/en-us/Productdetail.htm?Pid=PAg523&Mode=summary

Benson, J., Joy, J. E., & Watson, S. J. (Eds.). (1999). *Marijuana and medicine: Assessing the science base.* Washington, DC: National Academy Press.

Bentley, E. & Rich, F. (2002). *Thirty years of treason: Excerpts from hearings before the house committee on un-American activities, 1938-1968.* New York: Nation Books.

Bevel, T, Gardner, R., & Bloodstain, M. (2008). *Pattern analysis with an introduction to crime-scene reconstruction.* (3rd ed.). CRC Press.

Bhat, V. J., Vikram, P., & Kumar, G. P. (2005). Reliability of postmortem lividity as an indicator of time since death in cold stored bodies. *Medico Legal Update, 5*(4).

Bidinotto, R. (1988, July). Getting away with murder. *Reader's Digest.*

Biography Channel. (n.d.). *Notorious crime profiles: Leopold and Loeb, partners in crime.* Retrieved March 23, 2010, from http://www.biography.com/notorious/crimefiles.do?action=view&profileId=262929&catId=259455

Black, C. (1999). First lady opposes presidential clemency for Puerto Rican nationalists. *Time.* Retrieved March 3, 2010, from http://cgi.cnn.com/ALLPOLITICS/stories/1999/09/05/senate.2000/hillary.puerto.rico/

Black, W. K. (2005). *The best way to rob a bank is to own one.* Austin: University of Texas Press.

Blackledge, C. (2003). *The story of V: A natural history of female sexuality.* New Brunswick, New Jersey: Rutgers University Press.

Blatchford, C. (2009). *The black hand: The bloody rise and redemption of "Boxer" Enriquez, a Mexican Mob Killer.* New York: Harper Collins.

Bohm, R. M., & Haley, K. N. (2010). *Introduction to Criminal Justice* (6th ed.). New York: McGraw-Hill.

Bonanno, J. (1983). *A man of honor: The autobiography of Joseph Bonanno.* New York: St Martin's Paperbacks.

Boone, K. B., Swerdloff, R. S., Miller, B. L., et al. (2001). Neuropsychological profiles of adults with Klinefelter syndrome. *Journal of International Neuropsychological Society, 7*(4), 446–56.

Bopp, W. J., & Schultz, D. O. (1972). *Short history of American law enforcement.* Thomas, Springfield, IL.

Boumediene v. Bush, 553 U.S. 723 (2008).

Boyes, R. B. (2010). Absent Roman Polanski wins best director at Berlin Film Festival. *Times Online.* Retrieved March 29, 2010, from http://entertainment.timesonline.co.uk/tol/arts_and_entertainment/film/article7035310.ece

Bradford, J. M. W. (1999). The paraphilias, obsessive compulsive spectrum disorder, and the treatment of sexually deviant behaviors. *Psychiatric Quarterly, 70*(3), 209–219.

Brady Center to Prevent Gun Violence. (n.d.). Retrieved March 6, 2010, from http://www.bradycenter.org/

Brady Handgun Violence Prevention Act, Pub.L. 103-159, 107 Stat. 1536 (1993).

Brantingham, P. J. & Brantingham, P. L. (1991). *Environmental criminology.* Prospect Heights, IL: Waveland Press.

Brayton, E. (2006). Religious right targeting gay-straight clubs. *Science Blogs.* Retrieved April 21, 2010, from http://scienceblogs.com/dispatches/2006/05/religious_right_targeting_gays.php

Brewer v. Williams, 430 U.S. 387 (1977).

Brown, W. M. (1980). Polymorphism in mitochondrial DNA of humans as revealed by restriction endonuclease analysis. *Proc Natl Acad Sci USA, 77,* 3605–3609.

Brown, W. M., George, M. Jr., & Wilson, A. C. (1979). Rapid evolution of mitochondrial DNA. *Proc Natl Acad Sci USA, 76,* 1967–1971.

Brush, P. (2002, May 28). Court will review cross burning ban. *CBS News.* Retrieved March 23, 2010, from http://www.cbsnews.com/stories/2002/05/28/supremecourt/main510317.shtml

Bryant, T. (2005). *The life & times of Hammurabi.* Bear: Mitchell Lane Publishers, Hockessin, DE.

Buck, M. L. (2004). Therapeutic uses of codeine in pediatric patients. *Pediatric Pharmacotherapy, 10*(4).

Bugliosi, V. & Gentry, C. (1974). *Helter skelter: The true story of the Manson murders.* New York: Bantam Books.

Bugliosi, V. (2007). *Reclaiming history: The assassination of President John F. Kennedy.* New York: W. W. Norton & Company.

Bureau of Alcohol, Tobacco, Firearms and Explosives. (n.d.). *ATF's history.* Retrieved March 14, 2010, from http://www.atf.gov/about/history/

Bureau of Justice Statistics. (2008). Methods of execution in states authorizing the death penalty. *Sourcebook of Criminal Justice Statistics Online.* Retrieved March 26, 2010, from http://www.albany.edu/sourcebook/pdf/t6872008pdf

Bureau of Prisons Inmate Locator (2010). Retrieved March 23, 2010, from http://www.bop.gov/iloc2/InmateFinderServlet?Transaction=NameSearch&needingMoreList=false&FirstName=Abdul&Middle=&LastName=Murad&Race=U&Sex=M&Age=&x=85&y=20

Bureau of Prisons. (n.d.). *Quick facts about the Bureau of Prisons.* Retrieved March 22, 2010, from http://www.bop.gov/news/quick.jsp

Burek, D., Koek, K. E., & Novallo, A. (Eds.). (1989). *Encyclopedia of associations.* Detroit, MI: Gale Research.

Burns, J. F. (2009, December 30). Terror inquiry looks at suspect's time in Britain. *The New York Times.* Retrieved February 22, 2010, from http://www.nytimes.com/2009/12/30/world/europe/30nigerian.html?_r=1&hp.

Butler, J. M. (2005). *Forensic DNA typing: Biology, technology, and genetics of STR markers.* (2nd ed.). Burlington, MA: Academic Press.

Butler, J. D. (1896). British convicts shipped to American colonies [electronic version]. *American Historical Review.* Retrieved February 23, 2010, from http://www.dinsdoc.com/butler-1.htm

Cahill, T. (1986). *Buried dreams: Inside the mind of a serial killer.* New York: Bantam Books.

Calavita, K., & Pontell, H. N. (1997). *Big money crime: Fraud and politics in the savings and loan crisis.* Los Angeles: University of California Press.

California Department of Corrections and Rehabilitation. (2005). *Stanley Williams.* Retrieved March 15, 2010, from http://www.cdcr.ca.gov/News/docs/StanleyWilliams.pdf

California Department of Corrections and Rehabilitation. (2010). *Inmate visiting guidelines.* Retrieved March 23, 2010, fromhttp://www.cdcr.ca.gov/visitors/docs/inmatevisitingguidelines.pdf

California Department of Mental Health. (2010). *Coalinga State Hospital: Model sex offender treatment.* Retrieved March 30, 2010, from http://www.dmh.ca.gov/Services_and_Programs/State_Hospitals/Coalinga/Treatment.asp

California fires rage, visible in space. (2007, October 23). *National Geographic.* Retrieved March 23, 2010, from http://news.nationalgeographic.com/news/2007/10/photogalleries/wildfire-pictures/

California Good Samaritan Act, Ann.Cal. Bus. & Prof.Code §2395 (n.d.).

California Proposition 83. (2006). Retrieved January 13, 2010, from http://vote2006.sos.ca.gov/voterguide/pdf/prop83_text.pdf

Canadian Criminal Justice Association. (n.d.). Retrieved March 3, 2010, from http://www.ccja-acjp.ca/en/

Cannons of police ethics: Institute for Criminal Justice Ethics. (n.d.). Cannons of police ethics. http://www.lib.jjay.cuny.edu/cje/html/codes/codes-usa-organizational/canon.html

Capeci, J.& Mustain, G. (1996). *Gotti: Rise and Fall.* New York: Onyx.

Carlo, P. (1996). *The night stalker: The life and crimes of Richard Ramirez.* New York: Pinnacle Books.

Carlo, P. (2006). *The Ice Man: Confessions of a mafia contract killer.* New York: St. Martin's Press.

Catalano, S. M. (2005). Bureau of Justice Statistics, National Crime Victimization Survey, criminal victimization, 2004. *U.S. Department of Justice, Office of Justice Programs.*

Cave, D. (2009, May 29). In Puerto Rico, Supreme Court pick with island roots becomes a superstar. *The New York Times.* Retrieved February 16, 2010, from http://www.nytimes.com/2009/05/30/us/politics/30puerto.html

CCCEH study of the effects of 9/11 on pregnant women and newborns. (2006). *World Trade Center Pregnancy Study.* Columbia University. Retrieved February 12, 2010, from http://www.familiesofseptember11.org/docs/CCCEH%20Study%20Intro.pdf

Center for Defense Information (2010). *Terrorism Project.* Retrieved April 22, 2010, from http://www.cdi.org/terrorism/chronology.html

Center for Disease Control and Prevention. (2007) *Methamphetamine Use and Risk for HIV/AIDS.* Retrieved March 20, 2010, from http://www.cdc.gov/hiv/resources/factsheets/meth.htm

Center for Disease Control and Prevention. (2010). *Suicide information.* Retrieved March 20, 2010, from http://www.cdc.gov/ViolencePrevention/suicide/index.html

Center for Disease Control and Prevention. (2010). *Tobacco information.* Retrieved March 16, 2010, from http://www.cdc.gov/tobacco/data_statistics/fact_sheets/fast_facts/index.htm

Centers for Disease Control. (2010). *Suicide in 2006.* Retrieved April 2, 2010, from http://webappa.cdc.gov/cgi-bin/broker.exe

Central Intelligence Agency. (2007). *Biological warfare.* Retrieved April 2, 2010, from https://www.cia.gov/library/reports/general-reports-1/iraq_wmd_2004/chap6.html

Cernak, I. (2005). Blast (Explosion)-induced neurotrauma: A myth becomes reality.

Restorative Neurology and Neuroscience, 23, 139–140.

Cernak, I., Wang, Z., Jiang, J., Bian, X., & Savic, J. (2001). Cognitive deficits following blast injury induced neurotrauma. *Brain Injury, 15*(7), 593–612.

Cernak, I., Wang, Z., Jiang, J., Bian, X., & Savic, J. (2001). Ultrastructural and functional characteristics of blast injury-induced neurotrauma. *The Journal of Trauma, 50,* 695–706.

Certification of Failure to Testify or Produce; Grand Jury, 2 U.S.C. §194 (n.d.).

Champion, D. J., & Rush, G. E. (1997). *Policing in the community.* Englewood Cliffs, NJ: Prentice Hall.

Chase, A. (2003). *Harvard and the unabomber: The education of an American terrorist.* New York: Norton.

Chermak, S. M., & Bailey, F. Y. (2007). *Crimes and trials of the century.* Westport, Connecticut: Greenwood Publishing Group.

Chibbaro, L. (2010). Couples plan courthouse visits to celebrate D.C. marriage law. *D.C. Agenda.* Retrieved March 15, 2010, from http://www.dcagenda.com/2010/02/24/couples-plan-courthouse-visits-to-celebrate-d-c-marriage-law/

Chidester, D. (2004). *Salvation and suicide: Jim Jones, the people's temple and Jonestown (religion in North America)* (2nd rev. ed.). Bloomington, Indiana: Indiana University Press.

Chin, G. J. (2004). Reconstruction, felon disenfranchisement and the right to vote: Did the fifteenth amendment repeal section 2 of the fourteenth? *Georgetown Law Journal, 92,* 259.

Christiansen, J. (2006). Anti-gay abuse seen to pervade U.S. schools. *Planet OutNet work.* Retrieved March 17, 2010, from http://web.archive.org/web/20070301145035/ http://www.gay.com/news/article.html?2006/04/26/1

Cieslak, T. J., & Christopher, G. W. (2007). Medical management of potential biological casualties: A stepwise approach. In Dembek, Zygmunt F., *Medical Aspects of Biological Warfare.* Washington, DC: The Borden Institute.

Civil Asset Fofeiture Reform Act, Pub. L. 106-185,114 Stat.202 (2000).

Clark County Prosecuting Attorney. (n.d.). *Methods of execution.* Retrieved April 2, 2010, from http://www.clarkprosecutor.org/html/death/methods.htm

Clark County Prosecutor. (1996). *William Bonin.* Retrieved April 2, 2010, from http://www.clarkprosecutor.org/html/death/US/bonin322.htm

Closing arguments today in Texas dragging-death trial. (1999). *CNN.* Retrieved March 5, 2010, from http://www.cnn.com/US/9902/22/dragging.death.03/

CNN reporter Eric Phillips interviews Sheriff Arpario and a juvenile offender. (2004, March 11). *CNN.* Retrieved February 17, 2010, from http://transcripts.cnn.com/TRANSCRIPTS/0403/11/lt.01.html

CNN Wire. (2008). *Lennon's killer denied parole.* Retrieved April 2, 2010, from http://cnnwire.blogs.cnn.com/2008/08/12/lennons-killer-denies-parole/

CNN. (1998). *Last World Trade Center bombing conspirator sentenced.* Retrieved March 15, 2010, from http://www.cnn.com/US/9804/03/wtc.bombing/

CNN. (2007, October 26). *Fire deaths, damage come into focus as evacuees cope.* Retrieved March 14, 2010, from http://www.cnn.com/2007/us/10/26/fire.wildfire.ca/index.html?eref=onion

CNN. (2009). *Polanski arrested in connection with sex charge.* Retrieved April 2, 2010, from http://www.cnn.com/2009/SHOWBIZ/Movies/09/27/zurich.roman.polanski.arrested/index.html

CNN. (2009). *U.S. formally asks for Polanski extradition.* Retrieved April 2, 2010, from http://www.cnn.com/2009/SHOWBIZ/Movies/10/23/polanski.extradition/index.html

CNN. (2010). *Fort Hood shootings.* Retrieved April 2, 2010, from http://www.cnn.com/SPECIALS/2009/fort.hood.shootings/

Cohen, L. E., & Felson, M. (1979). Social change and crime rate trends: A routine activity approach. *American Sociological Review 44*(4), 588.

Cole, D. (1991). *Encyclopedic dictionary of economics* (4th ed.). Guilford, CT: Dushkin Publishing Group.

Cole, G. F. (1983). *The American system of criminal justice* (3rd ed.). Pacific Grove, CA: Brooks/Cole.

Cole, L. A. (2009). *The anthrax letters: A bioterrorism expert investigates the attacks that shocked America—Case closed?* Sky horse Publishing.

Coleman v. Schwarzenegger, 2:90-cv-00520-LKK-JFM (E.D. Cal.) (2009).

Commission for Review of FBI Security Programs. (2002). *A review of FBI security programs.* U.S. Department of Justice. Retrieved March 16, 2010, from http://www.fas.org/irp/agency/doj/fbi/webster-report.html

Comprehensive Drug Abuse Prevention and Control Act, Pub. L. No. 91-513, 84 Stat. 1236 (1970).

Connecticut Dept. of Public Safety v. Doe, 538 U.S. 1 (2003).

Cornwell, P. (2002). *Portrait of a killer—Jack the Ripper: Case closed.* New York: G.P. Putnam's Son's.

Courtney, M., & Courtney, A. (2007). Experimental observations of incapacitation via ballistic pressure wave without a wound channel. Retrieved March 16, 2010, from http://www.ballisticstestinggroup.org/lotor.pdf

Cox, S. M., & Wade, J. E. (1985). *The criminal justice network: An introduction.* Dubuque, Iowa : W.C. Brown Publishers

Cross, I. B. (1974). *History of the labor movement in California.* University of California Printing.

Crossland, J. (2006, January 1). Churchill: execute Hitler without trial. *The Sunday Times.* Retrieved April 4, 2010, from http://www.timesonline.co.uk/article/0,,2087-1965607,00.html

Dahmer, L. (1994). *A father's story.* New York: William Morrow and Co.

Dalby, J. T. (1988). Is telephone scatologia a variant of exhibitionism? *International Journal of Offender Therapy and Comparative Criminology, 32,* 45–49.

Daniels, M. W. (2003). *Revised definitions of metropolitan statistical areas, new definitions of micropolitan statistical areas and combined statistical areas, and guidance on uses of the statistical definitions of these areas.* Office of Management and Budget. Retrieved April 2, 2010, from http://www.whitehouse.gov/omb/bulletins_b03-04/

Daubert v. Merrell Dow Pharmaceuticals, 509 U.S. 579 (1993).

Daubert v. Merrell Dow Pharmaceuticals, Inc., 43 F.3d 1311 (1995).

Davis, A. (2003). *Are prisons obsolete?* Cambridge: Open Media.

De Sola, R. (1982). *Crime dictionary* (revised and expanded ed.). New York: Facts on File Publications.

DEA Web site. (n.d.). Retrieved March 10, 2010, from http://www.justice.gov/dea/pubs/abuse/5-stim.htm

DeAngelis, F. J. (1980). *Criminalistics for the investigator.* Mission Hills, CA: Glencoe.

Department of Defense industrial security program manual. (1984). Washington, DC: Defense Investigative Service.

Debs, E. V. (1926, November 1). As it must to all men, death came last week to Eugene Victor Debs, socialist [electronic version]. *Time.* Retrieved April 6, 2010, from http://www.time.com/time/magazine/article/0,9171,722648,00.html

Defensible space. (n.d.). Retrieved February 7, 2010, from http://www.defensiblespace.com/

Denschlag, D., Clemens, T., Kunze, M., Wolff, G., & Keck, C. (2004). Assisted reproductive techniques in patients with Klinefelter syndrome: A critical review. *Fertility and Sterility, 82*(4)X, 775–779.

Denschlag, D., MD, Clemens, T., MD, Kunze, M., MD, Wolff, G., MD & Keck, C., MD (2004). Assisted reproductive techniques in patients with Klinefelter syndrome: A critical review. *Fertility and Sterility, 82*(4), 775–779.

DePalma, A. (2006, May 13). Tracing lung ailments that rose with 9/11 dust. *The New York Times*. Retrieved March 15, 2010, from http://www.nytimes.com/2006/05/13/nyregion/13symptoms.html

Department of Homeland Security. (2007). *Plain language guide: Making the transition from 10-codes to plain language*. Retrieved March 15, 2010, from http://www.safecomprogram.gov/NR/rdonlyres/5945AFE3-ADA9-4189-83B0-4D8218D0CA2F/0/PlainLanguageGuide.pdf

Department of Justice. (2004). Intimate partner violence. *Bureau of Justice Statistics*.

Department of Justice. (2008). *Federal Advisory Committee on Juvenile Justice annual report*. Retrieved February 9, 2010, from http://www.facjj.org/annualreports/FACJJ%20Annual%20Report%2008.pdf

Department of Justice. (2009). *Former shipping executive sentenced to 48 months in jail for his role in antitrust conspiracy*. Retrieved March 16, 2010, from http://www.justice.gov/atr/public/press_releases/2009/242030.htm

Department of Justice. (n.d.). *About the office*. Retrieved February 20, 2010, from http://www.justice.gov/asg/about-oaag.html

Department of Justice. (n.d.). *DOJ's community relations service*. Retrieved April 5, 2010, from http://www.justice.gov/crs/

Department of Justice. (n.d.). *Enrique Camerena bio*. Retrieved April 16, 2010, from http://www.justice.gov/dea/agency/10bios.htm

Designation and Custody Classification. (n.d.). Retrieved February 4, 2010, from http://www.bop.gov/policy/progstat/5100_008.pdf

Di Maio, V. J., & Di Maio, D. (2001). *Time of Death. In: Forensic Pathology*. (2nd ed.). New York: CRC Press.

DiMaio , V. J., & DiMaio, D. (2001). *Forensic pathology*. (2nd ed.). New York: CRC Press.

District in Which to Sue Corporation, 15 U.S.C. § 22 (n.d.).

Dizard III, W. P. (2006). FBI plans major database upgrade. *Government Computer News*.

DNA test results. (2006, March 15). Retrieved March 15, 2010, from http://www.thejeffreymacdonaldcase.com/html/gov_dna_2006-03-15.html#top

Documents on the Grand Alliance. (1943). Tehran conference: Tripartite dinner meeting November 29, 1943 Soviet Embassy, 8:30 PM. Retrieved March 7, 2010 from http://teachingamericanhistory.org/library/index.asp?document=906

Dodge, C. D. (1997). *Due process advocacy*. Office of Juvenile Justice of Delinquency Prevention. Retrieved April 9, 2010, from http://www.ncjrs.gov/pdffiles/fs9749.pdf

Dogging hotspot to be policed. (2009, February 9). BBC. Retrieved February 12, 2010, from http://news.bbc.co.uk/2/hi/uk_news/england/wear/7878889.stm

Douglas, J., & Olshaker, M. (2002). The cases that haunt us. New York: Simon and Schuster.

Driver, G. R., & J. C. Miles (2007). *The Babylonian laws*. Eugene, WA: Wipf and Stock.

Drug-Toting Semi-Sub Nabbed In Tampa-Based Probe. (2008, September 13). *The Tampa Tribune*. Retrieved March 15, 2010, from http://www2.tbo.com/content/2008/sep/15/coast-guard-nabs-drug-toting-semi-sub-tampa-based-/

Duhaime.org. (n.d.). McNaughten rules. Retrieved March 10, 2010, from http://duhaime.org/LegalDictionary/M/MNaghtenRules.aspx

Dupont, J. *The common law abroad: Constitutional and legal legacy of the British empire*. Wm. S. Hein Publishing.

Duties of the United States Sentencing Commission, 28 U.S.C. § 994 (n.d.).

Eastern State Penitentiary. (n.d.). Retrieved April 18, 2010, from http://www.easternstate.org/

Easton, N. (2005, March 23). Rights groups for disabled join in fight. *Boston Globe*. Retrieved March 15, 2010, from http://www.boston.com/news/nation/washington/articles/2005/03/23/rights_groups_for_disabled_join_in_fight/

Eldefonso, E., Coffey, A. R., & Grace, R. C. (1982). *Principles of law enforcement* (3rd ed.). New York: John Wiley & Sons.

Electronic Communications Privacy Act, ECPA Pub. L. 99-508, Oct. 21, 1986, 100 Stat. 1848, 18 U.S.C. § 2510 (1986).

Elie, M. P., Baron, M. G., & Birkett, J. W. (2008). Enhancement of microcrystalline identification of γ-Hydroxybutyrate. *Journal of Forensic Sciences, 53*(1), 147–160.

Employee Polygraph Protection Act, 29 USC §2001 et seq. 29 CFR Part 801 (1998).

Encyclopedic dictionary of American history (4th ed.). (1991). Guilford, CT: Dushkin Publishing Group.

Encyclopedic dictionary of psychology (4th ed.). (1991). Guilford, CT: Dushkin Publishing Group.

Encyclopedic dictionary of sociology (4th ed.). (1991). Guilford, CT: Dushkin Publishing Group.

Engert, G. J. (1964). International Corner. *Identification News, 14*(1).

English, T. J. (2005). *Paddy whacked: The untold story of the Irish American gangster.* New York: HarperCollins.

Enrique S. Camarena Education Foundation Inc. (n.d.) Retrieved March 17, 2010, from http://www.camarenafoundation.org/index.htm

Epilepsy Foundation. (n.d.). *Phenobarbital.* Retrieved March 20, 2010, from http://www.epilepsyfoundation.org/answerplace/Medical/treatment/medications/typesmedicine/phenobarbital.cfm

Erlet, S. (2009). Pro-life news: Obama, abortion, conscience, assisted suicide, final exit, Catholic, Casey. *LifeNews.com.* Retrieved February 21, 2010, from http://www.lifenews.com/nb188.html

Esposito, R., & Ross, B. (2009, December 28). Accused bomber Abdulmutallab's underwear, explosive packet and detonator. *ABC News.* Retrieved March 24, 2010, from http://abcnews.go.com/Blotter/northwest-airlines-flight-253-bomb-photos-exclusive/story?id=9436297

Establishment of Office of Justice Programs, 42 U.S.C. § 3711 (n.d.).

Evans, S. P., & Skinner, K. (2002). *The ultimate Jack the Ripper sourcebook: An illustrated encyclopedia.* London: Constable and Robinson.

Executive Office of the President, Office of Management and Budget. (2008). *Update of statistical area definitions and guidance on their uses.* Retrieved February, 19, 2010, from http://www.whitehouse.gov/omb/assets/omb/bulletins/fy2009/09-01.pdf

Exemplary Rehabilitation Certificates, 29 U.S.C. §§ 601–605 Repealed.

F. C. (1995). *The unabomber manifesto: Industrial society & its future.* Jolly Roger Pr.

Facilities 1992. Washington, DC: U.S. Department of Justice, Federal Bureau of Prisons.

Fairchild, H. P. (1977). *Dictionary of sociology and related sciences.* New York: Philosophical Library.

False Claims Act Legal Center. (2010). *Statistics.* Retrieved March 15, 2010, from http://www.taf.org/statistics.htm

False Claims Act, 31 U.S.C. § 3729–3733 (1863).

Family legal guide. (1981). Pleasantville, NY: Reader's Digest Association.

Fay, J. J. (1987). *Security dictionary.* Stoneham, MA: Butterworth Publishers.

Federal Assault Weapons Ban (AWB), HR 3355 (1994).

Federal Bureau of Investigation. (2010). *Amerithrax investigation.* Retrieved April 22, 2010, from http://www.fbi.gov/anthrax/amerithraxlinks.htm

Federal Bureau of Investigation (2010). *Questioned documents.* Retrieved March 13, 2010, from http://www.fbi.gov/hq/lab/html/qdu1.htm

Federal Bureau of Investigation. (1973). *Mexican mafia.* Retrieved March 16, 2010, from http://foia.fbi.gov/mafia_mexican/mafia_mexican_part01.pdf

Federal Bureau of Investigation. (1992). *National incident based reporting system.* Retrieved February 22, 2010, from http://www.fbi.gov/ucr/faqs.htm

Federal Bureau of Investigation. (2000). *National incident-based reporting system, Volume 1:Data collection guidelines.* Retrieved February 26, 2010, from http://www.fbi.gov/ucr/nibrs/manuals/v1all.pdf

Federal Bureau of Investigation. (2000). *Safe street violence crime initiative report.* Retrieved March 6, 2010, from http://www.fbi.gov/publications/safestreets/ssgu00.pdf

Federal Bureau of Investigation. (2001). *Congressional testimony of Louis J. Freeh.* Retrieved March 8, 2010, from http://www.fbi.gov/congress/congress01/freeh051001.htm.

Federal Bureau of Investigation. (2001). *Congressional testimony: Threat of terrorism to the United States.* Retrieved March 22, 2010, from http://www.fbi.gov/congress/congress01/freeh051001.htm

Federal Bureau of Investigation. (2002). *Congressional testimony on "the threat of eco-terrorism."* Retrieved March 22, 2010, from http://www.fbi.gov/congress/congress02/jarboe021202.htm

Federal Bureau of Investigation. (2003). *FBI facts and figures.* Retrieved March 16, 2010, from http://www.fbi.gov/libref/facts figure/orgcrime.htm

Federal Bureau of Investigation. (2004). *2004 Uniform Crime Report.* Retrieved March 19, 2010, from http://www.fbi.gov/ucr/cius_04/documents/CIUS_2004_Section4.pdf

Federal Bureau of Investigation. (2004). *Operation greylord.* Retrieved March 29, 2010, from http://www.fbi.gov/page2/march04/greylord031504.htm

Federal Bureau of Investigation. (2004). *Protecting America from terrorist attack: Meet the National Joint Terrorism Task Force.* Retrieved March 22, 2010, from http://www.fbi.gov/page2/july04/njttf070204.htm

Federal Bureau of Investigation. (2004). *Uniform crime reporting handbook.* Retrieved March 13, 2010, from http://www.fbi.gov/ucr/handbook/ucrhandbook04.pdf

Federal Bureau of Investigation. (2008). *FBI 100: The legend of 'Machine Gun Kelly'.* Retrieved March 22, 2010, from http://www.fbi.gov/page2/sept08/kelly_092608.html

Federal Bureau of Investigation. (2008). *Headline archives: First strike, global terror in America.* Retrieved April 6, 2010, from http://www.fbi.gov/page2/feb08/tradebom_022608.html

Federal Bureau of Investigation. (2008). *Integrated automated fingerprint identification system (IAFIS).* Retrieved March 29, 2010, from http://www.fbi.gov/hq/sjisd/iafis.htm

Federal Bureau of Investigation. (2009). *FBI top ten stories of the week ending October 23, 2009.* Retrieved March 16, 2010, from http://www.fbi.gov/pressrel/pressrel09/topten_102309.htm

Federal Bureau of Investigation. (2009). *Norte Valle cartel kingpin and former FBI top ten fugitive Diego Montoya Sanchez sentenced to 45 years for cocaine trafficking, murder, and racketeering charges.* Retrieved February 27, 2010 from http://miami.fbi.gov/dojpressrel/pressrel09/mm102109.htm

Federal Bureau of Investigation. (2009). Press release: *Mortgage fraud surge investigation nets more than 100 individuals throughout middle district of Florida.* Retrieved March 29, 2010, from http://tampa.fbi.gov/dojpressrel/2009/ta110409.htm

Federal Bureau of Investigation. (2010). *Top ten most wanted criminals.* Retrieved March 16, 2010, from http://www.fbi.gov/wanted/topten/fugitives/fugitives.htm

Federal Bureau of Investigation. (n.d.). *Dr. Snow.* Retrieved February 22, 2010, from http://philadelphia.fbi.gov/dr_snow.htm

Federal Bureau of Investigation. (n.d.). *Disaster squad.* Retrieved March 26, 2010, from http://www.fbi.gov/hq/lab/disaster/disaster.htm

Federal Bureau of Investigation. (n.d.). *Famous cases: George "Machine Gun" Kelly.* Retrieved March 16, 2010, from http://www.fbi.gov/libref/historic/famcases/kelly/kelly.htm

Federal Bureau of Investigation. (n.d.). *Taking legible fingerprints.* Retrieved March 16,

2010, from http://www.fbi.gov/hq/cjisd/takingfps.html

Federal Bureau of Prisons. (2010). *Conjugal visits: General information*. Retrieved March 7, 2010, from http//www.bop.gov/inmate_locator/conjugal.jsp

Federal Communications Commission. (2005). *FCC amended report to Congress on the deployment of e911 phase II services by tier III service providers*. Retrieved March 15, 2010, from http://hraunfoss.fcc.gov/edocs_public/attachmatch/DOC-257964A1.pdf

Federal Communications Commission. (n.d.). *Wireless 911 services*. Retrieved February 27, 2010, from http://www.fcc.gov/cgb/consumerfacts/wireless911srvc.html

Federal Firearms Act, ch. 850, 52 Stat. 1252 (1938).

Federal Trade Commission. (2010). *Consumer sentinel network databook*. Retrieved March 17, 2010, from http://www.ftc.gov/sentinel/reports/sentinel-annual-reports/sentinel-cy2009.pdf

Federally Protected Activities, 18 U.S.C. § 245 (n.d.).

Feeney, M. (1996, November 16). Alger Hiss dead at 92. *Boston Globe*. Retrieved March 16, 2010, from http://nl.newsbank.com/nl-search/we/Archives?p_product=BG&p_theme=bg&p_action=search&p_max docs=200&p_topdoc=1&p_text_direct-0=0EADDC78A3348618&p_field_direct-0=document_id&p_perpage=10&p_sort=YMD_date:D&s_trackval=GooglePM

Feldman, D. (1987). *Why do clocks run clockwise?* New York: Harper & Row.

FEMA. (2010). *National fire academy completes management curriculum overhaul*. Retrieved March 15, 2010, from http://www.usfa.dhs.gov/media/press/2010releases/012010.shtm

Fido, M. (1987). *The crimes, detection and death of Jack the Ripper*. London: Weidenfeld & Nicolson.

Fiercewireless. (2007). *Sprint, Alltell, USC fined for missed e911 deadline*. Retrieved

March 13, 2010, from http://www.fierce-wireless.com/story/sprint-alltel-usc-fined-missed-e911-deadline/2007-08-31

FindLaw. (n.d.). *The "irresistible impulse" test*. Retrieved January 27, 2010, from http://criminal.findlaw.com/crimes/more-criminal-topics/insanity-defense/irresistible-impulse-test.html

Fins, J., Schiff, N. (2005, September 1). In brief: The afterlife of Terri Schiavo [Electronic Version]. *The Hastings Center Report*. Retrieved March 14, 2010, from http://www.medscape.com/viewarticle/511647

Firearm Owners' Protection Act (FOPA), Pub. L. No. 99-308, 100 Stat. 449, 18 U.S.C. § 921 (1986).

Firearms, 18 U.S.C. Chp. 44.

FirearmsID.com. (n.d.). *Bullet basics 1- materials*. Retrieved January 16, 2010, from http://www.firearmsid.com/Bullets/bullet1.htm

Firestorm claims 9th victim. (2007, November 8). NBCSandiego.com (KNSD). Retrieved April 7, 2010, from http://www.nbcsandiego.com/news/1456772/detail.html?dl=headlineclick

Fischer, R. G., Fradella, H. F., & Ireland, C. (2009). Sex, violence, and the boundaries of the defense of consent. *Criminal Law Bulletin, 45*(6), 1137–1155.

Flaccus, G. (2007, October 24). 1,500 Homes lost; $1B loss in San Diego area. *Seattle Times*. Retrieved March 23, 2010, from http://www.seattletimes.newsource.com/html/nationworld/2003971082_wildfires24.html

Fleiss, H. and Labi, N. (2003). In defense of prostitution. *Legal Affairs*. Retrieved March 6, 2010, from http://www.legalaffairs.org/issues/September-October-2003/feature_fleiss_sepoct03.msp

Fleming, D. O., & Hunt, D. L. (2000). *Biological safety: Principles and practices*. Herndon, VA: ASM Press.

Flight to avoid prosecution of giving testimony, 18 U.S.C. § 1-49-1073 (n.d.).

Florida Department of Corrections. (2010). *Corrections offender network-inmate population information detail: Lionel Tate.* Retrieved March 26, 2010, from http://www.dc.state.fl.us/ActiveInmates/Detail.asp?Bookmark=1&From=list&SessionID=528400228

Florida House Bill 1877 (2005). "Jessica's law." Retrieved March 25, 2010, from http://www.myfloridahouse.gov/Sections/Documents/loaddoc.aspx?FileName=_h1877er.doc&DocumentType=Bill&BillNumber=1877&Session=2005

Florida International University. (2000). *National counternarcotics center training program south Florida needs assessment.* Retrieved April 8, 2010, from http://www.fiu.edu/~ tcs/itct/itct.pdf

Florida v. Powell, 559 U. S. _____ (2010).

Folley, V. L. (1976). *American law enforcement* (2nd ed.). Rockleigh, NJ: Holbrook.

Fox, V. (1977). *Introduction to corrections.* Englewood Cliffs, NJ: Prentice Hall.

Forbidden Explosives, 49 CFR § 173.54 (n.d.).

Ford v. Wainwright, 477 U.S. 399 (1986).

Fox, F. (1999, September 17). Justice in Jasper. *Texas Observer.* Retrieved March 18, 2010, from http://web.archive.org/web/20050123091932/http:/www.texasobserver.org/showArticle.asp?ArticleID=275

Fox, M. (2009). Susan Atkins, Manson Follower, Dies at 61. *New York Times.* Retrieved March 9, 2010, from http://www.nytimes.com/2009/09/26/us/26atkins.html?_r=1

Frank T. (1985, May 27). It looks just like a war zone. *TIME magazine.* Retrieved March 24, 2010, from http://www.time.com/time/magazine/article/0,9171,956982,00.html

Fraud and Misuse of Visas, Permits, and Other Documents, 18 U.S.C. § 1546 (n.d.).

Freund, K., Watson, R., & Rienzo, D. (1988). The value of self-reports in the study of voyeurism and exhibitionism. *Annals of Sex Research, 2,* 243–262.

Frey, A. (2005). *Witness: For the prosecution of Scott Peterson.* New York: Harper Collins.

Fricke, C. W. (1968). *5000 criminal definitions, terms, and phrases.* Los Angeles: Legal Books.

Frye v. United States, 293 F. 1013 (D.C. Cir. 1923).

Fuchs, C. (2002). Biggie and Tupac review. *PopMatters.* Retrieved March 28, 2010, from http://www.popmatters.com/film/reviews/b/biggie-and-tupac.shtml

Fugitive Felon Act, 18 U.S.C. § 1073 (1961).

Full Faith and Credit, 28 U.S.C. § 1738 A (n.d.).

Furedy, J. J., & Heslegrave, R. J. (1988). Validity of the lie detector. *Criminal Justice and Behavior, 15*(2), 219–246.

Furman v. Georgia, 408 U.S. 238 (1972).

Gale Group. (1998). *West's encyclopedia of American law.* (2nd ed.). St. Paul, MN: West Group Publishing.

Gallup. (2010). *Corporate history.* Retrieved March 6, 2010, from http://www.gallup.com/corporate/1357/corporate-history.aspx

Garber, N. J., Miller, J. S., Abel, E., Eslambolchi, S., & Korukonda, S. K. (2005). The Impact of red light cameras (photored enforcement) on crashes in Virginia. *Virginia Transportation Research Council.* Retrieved April 4, 2010, from http://www.virginiadot.org/vtrc/main/online_reports/pdf/07-r2.pdf

Gardner, R. J. M., & Sutherland, G. R. (2004). *Chromosome abnormalities and genetic counseling.* (3rd ed.). Oxford: Oxford University Press.

Garner, B. A. (Ed.). (2004). *Black's law dictionary.* (8th ed.). St. Paul, Minnesota: West Group.

Garza, A. O. (2008). US-Mexican officials launch Armas Ceuzadas program. *US Embassy in Mexico.* Retrieved April 6, 2010, from http://www.usembassy-mexico.gov/eng/releases/ep080609armas.html

Gates, A. (2006, September 11). Buildings rise from rubble while health crumbles. *The New York Times.* Retrieved January 16, 2010, from http://www.nytimes.

com/2006/09/11/arts/television/11dust. html?ref=nyregionspecial3

Geis, G., & Bienen, L. B. (1998). *Crimes of the century.* Boston: Northeastern University Press.

Geller, W. A. (Ed.). (1991). *Local government police management* (3rd ed.). International City Management Association.

Geodakyan V. A. (2000). Evolutionary chromosomes and evolutionary sex dimorphism. *Biology Bulletin, 27,* 99–113.

Germann, A. C., Day, F. D., & Gallati, R. J. (1981). *Introduction to law enforcement and criminal justice.* Springfield, IL: Charles C. Thomas.

Gettleman, J., & Halbfinger, D. M. (2003, June 1). Suspect in '96 Olympic bombing and 3 other attacks is caught. *The New York Times.* Retrieved April 4, 2010, from http://www.nytimes.com/2003/06/01/us/ suspect-in-96-olympic-bombing-and-3-other-attacks-is-caught.html?sec= &spon=&pagewanted=all

Giannini, A. J., Colapietro, G., Slaby, A. E., Melemis, S. M., & Bowman, R. K. (1998). Sexualization of the female foot as a response to sexually transmitted epidemics: *Psychological Report, 83*(2), 491–498.

Gibson, D. C. (2004) *Clues from killers: Serial murder and crime scene messages.* Westport, Connecticut: Praeger.

Gideon, L., & Sung, H. (2010). *Rethinking corrections: Rehabilitation, reentry and reintegration.* Thousand Oaks, CA: Sage.

Glossarist. (n.d.). *Terrorism.* Retrieved January 20, 2010, from http://www.glossarist. com/glossaries/government-politics-mili tary/terrorism.asp

Glover, M. (2010, January 21). US Supreme Court ruling reverses Iowa campaign law. *ABC News.* Retrieved April 5, 2010, from http://abcnews.go.com/Business/wire Story?id=9627211

Glover, S., & Lait, M. (2003). Ex-chief refuses to discuss Rampart. *Times.* Retrieved March 29, 2010, from http://www.streetgangs. com/topics/rampart/082303ramparks. html

Goldfarb, R. L., & Singer, L. R. (1973). *After conviction.* New York: Simon & Schuster.

Gregory, R. H., & Van Horn, R.L. (1981). *Automatic data-processing systems* (2nd ed.). Belmont, CA: Wadsworth.

Goldman Family. (2007). *If I did it: Confessions of the killer.* New York: Beaufort books.

Gollmar, R. H. (1981). *Edward Gein.* New York: Pinnacle Books.

Gonzalez, A. (2010). Whale trainer died of drowning, blunt force trauma. *Ravalli Republic.* Retrieved March 29, 2010, from http://www.ravallirepublic.com/news/ national/article_d81c5760-3d49-11df-8a09-001cc4c03286.html

Gonzalez, R. (2007). Acute and non-aute effects of cannabis on brain functioning and neuropsychological performance. *Neuropsychology Review, 17*(3), 47–61.

Good Samaritan Act, A.R.S. § 9-500.02 (n.d.).

Good Samaritan Act, D.C. 1981 §2-1344 (n.d.).

Good Samaritan Act, K.S.A. §65-2891 (n.d.).

Good Samaritan Immunity, A.C.A. § 17-95-101 (n.d.).

Good Samaritan Law, C.G.S.A. §52-557b (n.d.).

Good Samaritan Law, CRS title 13-21-108 (n.d.).

Good Samaritan Statute, LSA-R.S. 37:1731 (n.d.).

Goodhart, A. L. (1946). The legality of the Nuremberg trials. *Juridical Review.*

Goodnough, B. (2003, December 11). Youngster given life term for killing gets new trial. *The New York Times.*

Governors Committee on the Medical Aspects of the Charles Whitman Catastrophe. (1966). *Press conference.* Retrieved January 15, 2010, from http://alt.cimedia.com/ statesman/specialreports/whitman/find ings.pdf

Graham, J. M., Jr., Bashir, A. S., Stark, R. E., Silbert, A., & Walzer, S. (1988). Oral and written language abilities of XXY boys: Implications for anticipatory guidance. *Pediatrics, 81*(6), 795–806.

Grand Larceny, Vir. Stat.§ 18.2-95, Code of Virginia (1950).

Granville, J. (2003). Dot.con: The dangers of cyber crime and a call for proactive solutions. *Australian Journal of Politics and History, 49*(1), 102–109.

Greenberg, B., & Kunich, J. C. (2002). *Entomology and the law: Flies as forensic indicators.* Cambridge: Cambridge University Press.

Greer, G. W., (2000, February 11). In re: the guardianship of Theresa Marie Schiavo, Incapacitated, File No. 90-2908GD-003. *Florida Sixth Judicial Circuit.* Retrieved March 23, 2010, from http://abstractappeal.com/schiavo/trialctorder02-00.pdf

Griffin, D. N. (2006). *The battle for Las Vegas: The law vs. the mob.* Las Vegas, NV: Huntington Press.

Guard killed during shooting at Holocaust Museum. (2009, June 10). *CNN.* Retrieved January 30, 2010, from http://edition.cnn.com/2009/CRIME/06/10/museum.shooting/index.html

Guard slain in museum shoot-out ID'd; Gunman hospitalized. (2009. June 10). *WJLA-TV.* Retrieved March 21, 2010, from http://www.wjla.com/news/stories/0609/630674.html

Guffey, C. J. (2007). Laser technology: revolutionizing CSI work. *Forensic Magazine.* Retrieved January 14, 2010, from http://www.forensicmag.com/articles.asp?pid=171

Guinness book of world records. (1988). New York: Sterling.

Gulam, H., & Devereaux, J. (2007). A brief primer on good Samaritan law for health care professionals. *Austin Health Review,* (31), 478–482.

Gun Control Act, Pub. L. No. 90-618, 82 Stat. 1213 (1968).

Hague Convention Declaration III—On the Use of Bullets Which Expand or Flatten Easily in the Human Body July 29, 1899.

Hale, C. D. (1977). *Fundamentals of police administration.* Rockleigh, NJ: Holbrook.

Holmes, R.M. (1991). *Sex crimes.* Newbury Park: Sage.

Halpern, S. (2008). Can't remember what I forgot: Rape, robbery, memory. *Psychology today.* Retrieved January 14, 2010, from http://www.psychologytoday.com/blog/cant-remember-what-i-forgot/200808/rape-robbery-memory

Halpern, S. (2008). *Rape, robbery, memory. Can't Remember What I Forgot: The Good News From The Front Lines of Memory Research.* Retrieved March 16, 2010, from http://www.psychologytoday.com/blog/cant-remember-what-i-forgot/200808/rape-robbery-memory.

Hamid, H., El-Mallakh, R. S., & Vandeveir, K. (2005). Substance abuse: Medical and slang terminology. *South Medical Journal, 98*(3), 350–362.

Hamilton, A. (2006, January 18). New life, identity await Fortier as he leaves prison. *The Dallas Morning News.* Retrieved March 27, 2010, from http://www.dallasnews.com/sharedcontent/dws/dn/latestnews/stories/011906dntexfortier.1742cf8f.html

Hammond, S. D. (2008). *Recent developments trends, and milestones in the antitrust division's criminal enforcement program.* U.S. Department of Justice. Retrieved March 8, 2010, from http://www.justice.gov/atr/public/speeches/232716.htm

Handel, R. W., & Archer, R. P. (In Press). An investigation of the psychometric properties of the MMPI-2 restructured clinical (RC) scales with mental health inpatients. *Journal of Personality Assessment.*

Hanser, R. D. (2010). *Community corrections.* Thousand Oaks, CA: Sage.

Hanson, R. K., & Bussière, M. T. (1998). Predicting relapse: A meta-analysis of sexual offender recidivism studies. *Journal of Consulting and Clinical Psychology, 66,* 348–362.

Hanson, R. K., & Morton-Bourgon, K. E. (2005). The characteristics of persistent sexual offenders: A meta-analysis of recidivism studies. *Journal of Consulting and Clinical Psychology, 73,* 1154–1163.

Hanson, S. (2010). Combating maritime piracy. *Council on Foreign Relations.* Retrieved March 14, 2010, from http://www.cfr.org/publication/18376/combating_maritime_piracy.html

Harris, F. R., & Curtis, L. A. (eds.). (1998). *Locked in the poorhouse: Crisis, race, and poverty in the United States.* Lanham, MD: Rowman & Littlefield Publishers Inc.

Harvey, M. (2009). California dreaming of full marijuana legalisation. *The Times Online.* Retrieved March 17, 2010, from http://business.timesonline.co.uk/tol/business/industry_sectors/health/article 6851523.ece

Hazelwood, R. R., & Hazelwood, J. (1989). The serial rapist: His characteristics and victims. *FBI Law Enforcement Bulletin,* 18–25.

Health Care Fraud, 18 U.S.C. § 1347 (n.d.).

Henry, E. R., Sr. (1900). *Classification and uses of fingerprints* [Electronic version]. London: George Rutledge & Sons, Ltd. Retrieved March 22, 2010, from http://www.clpex.com/Information/Pioneers/henry-*classification.pdf*

Herridge, C., McCaleb, I., & Associated Press. (2006). American Al Qaeda member to be indicted for treason. *Fox news.* Retrieved March 7, 2010, from http://www.foxnews.com/story/0,2933,219861,00.html

Hersey, P., & Blanchard, K. H. (1969). *Management of organizational behavior—utilizing human resources.* New Jersey: Prentice Hall.

Hersey, P., & Blanchard, K. H. (1969). Life cycle theory of leadership. *Training and Development Journal, 23*(5), 26–34.

Hersey, P., & Blanchard, K. H. (1977). *Management of organizational behavior—utilizing human resources.* (3rd ed.). New Jersey: Prentice Hall.

Hershey, M. (1989). The campaign and the media. In G.M. Pomper (Ed.), *The election of 1988* (pp. 95–96). Chatham, N.J.: Chatham House.

Hess, P. (2008, August 24). Pentagon's intelligence arm steps up lie-detector efforts. *Arizona Daily Star.*

Hill, G. N., & Hill, K. T. (2005). *Insanity defense. Farflex.* Retrieved January 30, 2010, from http://legal-dictionary.thefreedictionary.com/Plea+of+temporary+insanity

Hills, C. (2008). *Gambling in the United States.* Retrieved February 25, 2010, from http://www.citizenlink.org/FOSI/gambling/cog/A000007294.cfm

Hinduja, S., & Patchin, J. W. (2007). Offline consequences of online victimization: School violence and delinquency. *Journal of School Violence, 6*(3), 89–112.

Hinduja, S., & Patchin, J. W. (2008). Cyberbullying: An exploratory analysis of factors related to offending and victimization. *Deviant Behavior, 29*(2), 129–156.

Hinduja, S, Patchin, J. W. (2009). *Bullying beyond the schoolyard: Preventing and responding to cyberbullying.* Thousand Oaks, CA: Corwin Press.

Hiss, A. (1988). *Recollections of a life.* New York: Little Brown & Co.

Holmes, R. M., & De Burger, J. (1988). *Serial murder.* Newbury Park, CA: Sage Publications.

Holstege, C. P and Boyle, J. S. (2008). *CBRNE—vomiting agents—Dm, Da, Dc.* Retrieved February 25, 2010, from http://emedicine.medscape.com/article/833391-overview

Homeland Security Act, Pub. L. No. 107–296, 116 Stat. 2135 (2002).

Homeland Security. (2010). *Homeland Security,* U. S. Department of (2010). Homeland security *advisory system.* Retrieved March 13, 2010, from http://www.dhs.gov/files/programs/Copy_of_press_release_0046.shtm

Horn, D. (2003). Pandering conviction voided. *Cincinnati Enquirer.* Retrieved February 28, 2010, from http://www.enquirer.com/editions/2003/05/31/loc_dute31.html

Horwitz, R. (2003). *Sniper: Inside the hunt for the killers who terrorized the nation.* New York: Ballantine Books.

Hosking, G. (2004). *Russian and the Russian: A history.* Cambridge: Harvard University Press.

How Bush Won. (1998, November 21). *Newsweek.*

How He Won. (1992, November/December). *Newsweek.*

Iacono, W. G. (2001). Forensic "lie detection": Procedures without scientific basis (PDF). *Journal of Forensic Psychology Practice.*

Retrieved January 30, 2010, from http://www.psych.umn.edu/faculty/iacono/2001%20forensic%20lie%20detection%20-%20procedures%20without%20scientific.pdf

Iborra, F. J., Kimura, H., & Cook, P. R. (2004). The functional organization of mitochondrial genomes in human cells. *BMC Biol.,*2, 9.

Immunity Act, 18 U.S.C. § 2486 (1954).

Immunity from Civil Liability, 210 ILCS 50/3.150 (n.d.).

Inciardi, J.A. (1993). *Criminal justice* (4th ed.). Fort Worth, TX: Harcourt Brace Jovanovich College Publishers.

Indictment in U.S. v. Abdulmutallab. (2010, January 6). *CBS News.* Retrieved March 18, 2010, from http://www.cbsnews.com/htdocs/pdf/Abdulmutallab_Indictment.pdf

Influencing, Impeding, or Retaliating Against a Federal Official by Threatening or Injuring a Family Member, 18 U.S.C. § 115 (n.d.).

Inquiry Begun on Klan Ties Of 2 Icons at Virginia Tech. (1997, November 16). *NY Times.* Retrieved March 17, 2010, from http://www.nytimes.com/1997/11/16/us/inquiry-begun-on-klan-ties-of-2-icons-at-virginia-tech.html

Inside Indiana Business. (2007). *Investigation continues into New Castle Correctional Facility uprising.* Retrieved March 17, 2010, from http://www.insideindianabusiness.com/newsitem.asp?ID=22970&ts=true

International Child Abduction Remedies, 42 U.S.C. § 11601 et seq. (n.d.).

International Maritime Organization. (2009). *Report on acts of piracy and armed robbery against ships, annual report 2008. United Nations.* Retrieved February 18, 2010, from http://www.imo.org/includes/blastDataOnly.asp/data_id%3D25550/133.pdf

International Narcotics Control Board. (2008). *List of narcotic drugs under international control.* Retrieved April 18, 2010, from http://www.incb.org/incb/yellow_list.html.

International Task Force on Euthanasia and Attempted Suicide (2009). *Failed attempts to legalize euthanasia/assisted suicide in the United States.* Retrieved March 16, 2010, from http://www.internationaltaskforce.org/usa.htm

Interpol a list of the 77 countries whose citizens died as a result of the attacks on September 11, 2001 (2002). Retrieved March 27, 2010, from http://www.interpol.int/public/ICPO/speeches/20020911List77Countries.asp

Jacob Wetterling Crimes Against Children and Sexually Violent Offender Registration Program, 42 U.S.C. 14071 (n.d.).

Jacobson, M. (2007). ThemMan who didn't shoot Malcolm X. *New York Magazine.* Retrieved March 2, 2010, from http://nymag.com/news/features/38358/

James v. Commonwealth, 12 Serg. & Rawle 220 (Penn., 1824).

James, W., Berger, T., & Elston, D. (2005). *Andrews' diseases of the skin: Clinical dermatology.* (10th ed.). New York: Saunders.

Jauch, E., Cadena, R. S., & Kuo, J. D. (2010). Inhalants. *Web MD.* Retrieved March 29, 2010, from http://emedicine.medscape.com/article/1174630-overview

Jensen, T. (2008). Judge who rigged murder cases dies. *Chicago Tribune.* Retrieved April 3, 2010, from http://www.chicagobreakingnews.com/2008/10/judge-who-rigged-murder-cases-dies.html

Jerry Lee Center of Criminology. (2010). *History of Criminology at University of Pennsylvania.* Retrieved March 16, 2010, from http://www.sas.upenn.edu/jerrylee/history.htm

Johnson, C., Sheridan, M. B., & Branigin, W. (2008, August 6). Officials say scientist was solely responsible for anthrax attacks. *The Washington Post.* Retrieved February 6, 2010, from http://www.washingtonpost.com/wp-dyn/content/article/2008/08/06/AR2008080601400.html

Johnson, T. (2006). *Taming Mal De Mer: A review of current knowledge on the prevention and the treatment of sea sickness.* Center for Disease Control. Retrieved February 22, 2010, from www.cdc.gov

niosh/docs/2006-114/pdfs/2006-114m. pdf

Join Together. (1996). *Fixing a failing system.*

Joint Service Committee on Military Justice. (2008). *Manual for courts-martial United States.* Retrieved January 18, 2010, from http://www.jag.navy.mil/documents/ mcm2008.pdf

Jones, K. L., & Smith, D. W. (1975). The fetal alcohol syndrome. *Teratology, 12*(1), 1–10.

Jones, K. L., & Smith, D. W. (1973). Recognition of the fetal alcohol syndrome in early infancy. *Lancet, 2,* 999–1001.

Joy, C. B., Adams, C. E., & Lawrie, S. M. (2006). Haloperidol versus placebo for schizophrenia. *Cochrane Database System Review* (4), CD003082.

Judge of the United States Courts—Sotomayor, Sonia. (n.d.). *Federal Judicial Center.* Retrieved February 8, 2010, from http://www.fjc.gov/servlet/tGetInfo? jid=2243

Judge recommends life in solitary for World Trade Center plotter. (1998). *The Minnesota Daily Online.* Retrieved March 17, 2010, from http://web.archive.org/ web/20070930181524/http://www.mn daily.com/daily/1998/01/09/world_nation/ wn2.ap/

Judicial and Statutory Definitions of Words and Phrases [electronic version]. (1914). Retrieved February 21, 2010, from Http:// books.google.com/books?id=NGU8 AAAAIAAJ&pg=PA763&dq=%22 Under+color+of+authority%22+- wikipedia&as_brr=1&client=firefox-a# v=onepage&q=%22Under%20color %20of%20authority%22%20-wiki pedia&f=false

Julien, R. M. (1981). *A primer of drug action* (3rd ed.). New York: W.H. Freeman and Company.

Juvenile Justice and Delinquency Prevention Act, Pub. L. 93–415 42 U.S.C. § 5601 et seq. (1974).

Kadish, S. H. (Ed.). (1983). *Encyclopedia of crime and justice* (Vol. 4). New York: The Free Press.

Kamphuis, J. H., Arbisi, P. A., Ben-Porath, Y. S., & McNulty, J. L. (2010). Detecting comorbid axis-II status among inpatients using the MMPI-2 restructured clinical scales. *European Journal of Psychological Assessment.*

Kane, J. N. (1975). *Famous first facts of records.* Bronx, NY: H.W. Wilson.

Kenucky Good Samaritan Statute, K.R.S. §411.148 (n.d.).

Keppel, R. (2004). *The Riverman: Ted Bundy and I hunt for the Green River Killer.* New York: Pocket Books.

Kershaw, I. (2008). *Hitler: A biography.* New York: W. W. Norton & Co.

Kessler, R. (1988, April 17). Moscow's role in the CIA: How a swinging Czech superspy stole America's most sensitive secrets. *Washington Post,* C1.

Kevorkian released from prison after 8 years. (2007, June 1). *MSNBC.* Retrieved February 22, 2010, from http://www.msnbc. msn.com/id/18974940/

Khan, A. (1994). Lessons, from Malcolm X: Freedom by Any Means Necessary. *Howard Law Journal, 38,* 80.

Kibble, H. (2009). *Law enforcement responses to Mexican drug cartels: Testimony before the Judiciary Subcommittee on Crime and Drugs and the Senate Caucus on International Narcotics Control.* Retrieved March 7, 2010, from http://www. dhs.gov/ynews/testimony/testimony_ 1237397860176.shtm

Kidnapping, International Parental Kidnapping, 18 U.S.C. § 1204 (n.d.).

King, J. (1999). *The life and death of pretty boy Floyd.* Kent, Ohio: Kent State University Press.

Kirk, J. (2007) Supreme Court sides with Microsoft in AT&T case. *Computer World.* Retrieved March 16, 2010, from http://www.computerworld.com/s/article/ 9018258/Supreme_Court_sides_with_ Microsoft_in_AT_T_case?nlid=8& source=NLT_PM

Klaus, P. (2004). *Carjacking, 1993–2002. Bureau of Justice Statistics.* Retrieved August 15, 2010 from http://bjs.ojp.usdoj. gov/index.cfm?ty=pbdetail&iid=476

Klein, P. (1987). Sex-Film maker loses appeal of conviction in pandering case. *Los Angeles Times.* Retrieved March 26, 2010, from http://articles.latimes.com/1987-01-07/local/me-2323_1

Knapp, A., & Wright, V. (2006). *The government and politics of France.* New York: Routledge.

Knickerbocker, B. (2007, February 9). Anti-immigrant sentiments fuel Ku Klux Klan resurgence. *Christian Science Monitor.* Retrieved April 3, 2010, from http://www.csmonitor.com/2007/0209/p02s02-ussc.html

Knight, S. (1976). *Jack the Ripper: The final solution.* London: Bounty Books.

Knox, G. (2004). *Gang threat analysis: The black disciples.* Peotone, IL: National Gang Crime Research Center.

Kosserev, I., Crawshaw, R. (1994). Medicine and the gulag. *BMJ, 309*(6970), 1726–1730.

Krash, A. (1961). *The Durham rule and judicial administration of the insanity defense in the District of Columbia* [Electronic version]. Retrieved March 17, 2010, from http://www.jstor.org/pss/794426

Kratowski, P., & Walker, D. (1984). *Criminal justice in America: Process and issues* (2nd ed.). New York: Random House.

Kuznia, R. (2009, May 26). Hispanics praise selection of Sotomayor for Supreme Court; Republicans wary. *Hispanic Business.* Retrieved January 31, 2010, from http://www.hispanicbusiness.com/news/2009/5/26/hispanics_praise_selection_of_sotomayor_for.htm

Laundering of Monetary Instruments, 18 U.S.C. § 1956 (n.d.).

Law Enforcement Training Network. (2010). Retrieved March 18, 2010, from http://www.letn.com.

LawGlossary.net. (n.d.). *Substantial capacity test.* Retrieved January 20, 2010, from http://www.lawglossary.net/definition/2818-Substantial_Capacity_Test

Lawrence v. Texas, 539 U.S. 558 (2003).

Laws, D. R., & O'Donohue, W. T. (2008). *Sexual deviance: Theory, assessment, and treatment.* New York: Guilford Press.

Lee, J. (2006, November 6). Samuel Bowers, 82, Klan leader convicted in fatal bombing, dies. *NY Times.* Retrieved February 2, 2010, from http://www.nytimes.com/2006/11/06/us/06bowers.html

Leeb, R. T., Paulozzi, L., Melanson, C., Simon, T., & Arias, I. (2008). Child maltreatment surveillance: Uniform definitions for public health and recommended data elements, version 1.0. Atlanta (GA). *Centers for Disease Control and Prevention, National Center for Injury Prevention and Control.*

Leet, D. A., Smith, A. M., & Rush, G. E. (1997). *Gangs, graffiti and violence: A realistic guide to the scope and nature of gangs in America.* Incline Village, NV: Copperhouse.

Legal Aid Ontario. (2010). *Getting legal help: Am I eligible for aid?* Retrieved January 26, 2010, from http://www.legalaid.on.ca/en/getting/eligibility.asp

Leopold, N. F. (1958). *Life plus 99 years.* Garden City, NY: Doubleday.

Lesko, M. (1983). *Information USA.* New York: Viking.

Letters. (1973, December 31). *Time Magazine.*

Lettice, J. (2005, September 15). Gatso 2: Rollout of UK's 24x7 vehicle movement database begins. *The Register.* Retrieved February 4, 2010, from http://www.theregister.co.uk/2005/11/15/vehicle_movement_database/

Levenson, J. S., & Cotter, L. P. (2005). The effect of Megan's Law on sex offender reintegration. *Journal of Contemporary Criminal Justice, 21*(1), 49–66.

Levenson, J. S., D'Amora, D. A., & Hern, A. L. (2007). Megan's law and its impact on community re-entry for sex offenders. *Behavioral Sciences & the Law, 25*(4), 587–602.

Levesque, W. R. (2003, November 8). Schiavo's wishes recalled in records. *St. Petersburg Times Online.* Retrieved March 27, 2010, from http://www.sptimes.com/2003/11/08/Tampabay/Schiavo_s_wishes_reca.shtml

Lindberg, L., Brauer, S., Wollmer, P., Goldberg. L., Jones, A. W., & Olsson S.G. (2007). Breath alcohol concentration determined with a new analyzer using free exhalation predicts almost precisel—

the arterial blood alcohol concentration. *Forensic Science International, 168*(2-3), 200–207.

Linden, M. G., & Bender, B. G. (2002). Fifty-one prenatally diagnosed children and adolescents with sex chromosome abnormalities. *Am J Med Genet, 110*(1), 11–18.

Linden, M. G., Bender, B. G., & Robinson, A. (2002). Genetic counseling for sex chromosome abnormalities. *Am J Med Genet, 110* (1), 3–10.

Linder, D. O. (1997). *The Leopold and Loeb trial: A brief account.* Retrieved January 31, 2010, from http://www.law.umkc.edu/faculty/projects/ftrials/leoploeb/Accountoftrial.html

Linedecker, C. L. (1980). *The man who killed boys: A true story of mass murder in a Chicago suburb.* New York: St. Martin's Press.

Listverse. (n.d.). *The 10 most famous successful assassinations.* Retrieved March 22, 2010, from http://listverse.com/2007/10/28/the-10-most-famous-successful-assassinations/

Littlejohn, R. F. (1983). *Crisis management: A team approach.* New York: American Management Association.

Live Science. (n.d.). *Top 10 crazy cults.* Retrieved March 29, 2010, from http://www.livescience.com/strangenews/top-10-crazy-cults-1.html

Los Angeles Judge Reinstates Biggie Smalls Wrongful Death Lawsuit. (2008, May 9). *XXL.* Retrieved March 24, 2010, from http://www.xxlmag.com/online/?p=21396

Los Angeles Times ruins yield five more bodies. (1910, October 3). *New York Times.*

Loving v. Virginia, 388 U.S. 1 (1967).

Luft, G., & Korin, A. (2004). Terrorism goes to sea. *Foreign Affairs Council on Foreign Relations.* Retrieved March 15, 2010, from http://www.foreignaffairs.com/articles/60266/gal-luft-and-anne-korin/terrorism-goes-to-sea

Luft, J. (1969). *Of human interaction.* Palo Alto, CA: National Press.

Maas, P. (1996). *Underboss: Sammy the bull Gravano's story of life in the mafia.* New York City: HarperCollins

MacDonald, J. M. (1963). The threat to kill. *American Journal of Psychiatry, 120*(2), 125–130.

Machado, C. (2007). *Brain death: A reappraisal.* New York: Springer.

Madariaga, I. (2005). *Ivan the terrible: First Tsar of Russia.* London: Yale University Press.

Mahony, E. (1999). *Puerto Rican independence: The Cuban connection.* Hartford, Connecticut: The Hartford Courant.

Malcolm X Killer Heads Mosque. (1998, March 31). *BBC News.* Retrieved January 26, 2010, from http://news.bbc.co.uk/2/hi/americas/71838.stm

Malvo: Muhammad 'made me a monster'; Younger man cross-examined by former mentor in sniper trial. (2006, May 23). *CNN.* Retrieved March 16, 2010, from http://www.cnn.com/2006/LAW/05/23/sniper.trial/index.html

Mannheim, H. (Ed.). (1972). *Pioneers in criminology.* Montclair, NJ: Patterson Smith.

Maricopa County Sheriff's Office. (n.d.). Retrieved January 28, 2010, from http://www.mcso.org/

Marriott, T. (2005). *Jack the ripper: The 21st century investigation.* London: John Blake.

Martin, J. A. (1980). *Law enforcement vocabulary.* Springfield, IL: Charles C. Thomas.

Martin, M., & Gelber, L. (1981). *Dictionary of American history.* New York: Philosophical Library.

Martinez v. California Court of Appeals, 528 U.S. 152 (2000).

Martinson, R. 1974. What works? Questions and answers about prison reform. *The Public Interest, 35,* 22–54.

Matera, D. (2005). *John Dillinger: The life and death of America's first celebrity criminal.* New York: Carroll & Graf Publishers.

Mathias, W., Rescoria, R. C., & Stephens, E. (1980). *Foundations of criminal justice.* Englewood Cliffs, NJ: Prentice Hall.

Mauer, M. (1995). *"Young Black Americans and the criminal justice system: Five years later."* The Sentencing Project.

Mayer, R. G. (2005). *Embalming: history, theory, and practice.* New York: McGraw-Hill.

McCain, J., & Salter, M. (2002). *Worth the fighting for.* New York: Random House.

McCleary, J. A., Sypherd, P. S., & Walkington, D. L. (1960). Antibiotic activity of an extract of Peyote [Lophophora Williams ii (Lemaire) Coulter]. *Economic Botany, 14,* 247–249.

McCormick, C. H. (2005). *Hopeless cases: The hunt for the red scare terrorist bombers.* University Press of America.

McDonnell, P. (1997). Fleiss sentenced to prison for attempted pandering. *Los Angeles Times.* Retrieved January 18, 2010, from http://articles.latimes.com/1997-02-11/local/me-27513_1_federal-prison-sentence

McEwen, J. T. (1989). *"Dedicated computer crime units."* Washington, DC: National Institute of Justice.

McFadden, R. D. (1996, May 26). Prisoner of rage—a special report.; From a child of promise to the unabomber suspect. *The New York Times.* Retrieved January 30, 2010, from http://query.nytimes.com/gst/fullpage.html?res=9B05E7D91139F935A15756C0A960958260&pagewanted=all

McLaughlin, E. C. (2010, March 4). Sniper's apology brings closure, no justice. *CNN.* Retrieved February 2, 2010, from http://www.cnn.com/2010/CRIME/03/04/malvo.sniper.confession/

McNerthney, C. (2009, May 24). Inside the Mary Kay Letourneau "hot for teacher" night. *The Big Blog Seattle Post-Intelligencer.* Retrieved March 6, 2010, from http://blog.seattlepi.com/thebigblog/archives/169396.asp?source=mypi

Medicine: Drug Detector. (1956, December 24). *Time Magazine.* Retrieved January 26, 2010, from http://www.time.com/time/magazine/article/0,9171,808859,00.html

Mercy Medical Cannabis Resource Center. (2010). *DEA: "It's still a violation of federal law, we're still going to continue to investigate and arrest people."* Retrieved January 30, 2010, from http://mercycenters.org/links/Colorado.html

Meudt, H. M., & Clarke, A. C. (2007). Almost forgotten or latest practice? AFLP applications, analyses and advances. *Trends Plant Sci, 12*(3), 106–117.

Mexican Mafia: Prison Gang Profile. (2006). *Insideprison.com.* Retrieved March 22, 2010, from http://www.insideprison.com/mexican-mafia-prison-gang.asp

Microsoft v. AT&T, 550 U.S. 437 (2007).

Miller v. California, 413 U.S. 15 (1973).

Miller, et al v. Skumanick, 605 F. Supp. 2d 634 (M.D. Pa. 2009).

Miller, G. (2010). Muslim cleric Aulaqui is 1st U.S. citizen on list of those CIA is allowed to kill. *Washington Post.* Retrieved April 10, 2010, from http://www.washingtonpost.com/wp-dyn/content/article/2010/04/06/AR2010040604121.html

Missing Children Findings, 42 U.S.C. § 5771 (n.d.).

Missing Children Reporting Requirement, 42 U.S.C. § 5779 (n.d.).

Mitchell, D. (2008, May 31). Legitimizing marijuana. *The New York Times.* Retrieved January 26, 2010, from http://www.nytimes.com/2008/05/31/technology/31online.html

Model Penal Code and Commentaries. (1985). *Philadelphia, Pa. : The Institute alphabetize under American Law Institute.*

Moeller, F. G., & Dougherty, D. M. (2001). Antisocial personality disorder, alcohol, and aggression. *Alcohol Research & Health.* National Institute on Alcohol Abuse and Alcoholism. Retrieved January 14, 2010, from http://pubs.niaaa.nih.gov/publications/arh25-1/5-11.pdf

Moir, R. (2003). Defining malware: FAQ. *Microsoft TechNet.* Retrieved February 29, 2010 from http://technet.microsoft.com/en-us/library/dd632948.aspx

Moldea, D. (1978). *The Hoffa wars: Teamsters, rebels, politicians and the mob.* New York: Paddington Press.

Monke, J. (2004). Agroterrorism: Threats and preparedness. *U.S. Congress.* Retrieved February 8, 2010, from http://www.fas.org/irp/crs/RL32521.pdf

Montaldo, C. (2006, May 25). Malvo outlines snipers' plan of terror. *About.com.*

Retrieved March 9, 2010, from http://crime.about.com/b/a/256952.htm

Morris, A. (2008). ALS—Alternative light source use in forensic nursing. *On The Edge.* International Association of Forensic Nursing. Retrieved January 4, 2010, from http://www.iafn.org/displaycommon.cfm?an=1&subarticlenbr=158

Morris, J. E. (2001). Malcolm X's critique of the education of black people. *The Western Journal of Black Studies, 25*(2).

Morris, M. (2005). Casting a wide net: Lifting fingerprints from difficult surfaces. *Forensic Magazine,* August/September.

Moser, C., & Kleinplatz, P. J. (2005). DSM-IV-TR and the paraphilias: An argument for removal. *Journal of Psychology and Human Sexuality, 17*(3/4), 91–109.

Mueller, U. G., & Wolfenbarger, L. L. (1999). AFLP genotyping and fingerprinting. *Trends Ecol. Evol. (Amst.), 14*(10), 389–394.

Munro, N. B., Ambrose, K. R., & Watson, A. P. (1994). Toxicity of the organophosphate chemical warfare agents GA, GB, and VX: Implications for public protection. *Environmental Health Perspectives, 102*(1).

Murray, J. G. (1965). *The madhouse on Madison Street.* Chicago: Follett Publishing Company.

Murton, T., & Hayams, J. (1969). *Accomplices to the crime.* New York: Grove.

Narcotic agonist analgesics. *Drug Facts and Comparisons.* EFacts [electronic version]. (2004). Available from Wolters Kluwer Health, Inc.

Nash, J. R. (1995). *Bloodletters and badmen.* New York: M Evans and Company.

Nash, N. (1989). Collapse of Lincoln savings leaves scars for rich, poor and the faithful. *New York Times.* Retrieved January 7, 2010, from http://www.nytimes.com/1989/11/30/us/collapse-of-lincoln-savings-leaves-scars-for-rich-poor-and-the-faithful.html

Nash, N. (1989). Greenspan's Lincoln savings regret. *New York Times.* Retrieved January 9, 2010, from http://www.nytimes.com/1989/11/20/business/greenspan-s-lincoln-savings-regret.html

Nash, N. C. (1989, November 30). Collapse of Lincoln savings leaves scars for rich, poor and the faithful. *The New York Times.* Retrieved March 15, 2010, from http://query.nytimes.com/gst/fullpage.html?res=950DE1D81131F933A05752C1A96F948260

National Advisory Committee for Juvenile Justice and Delinquency Prevention. (1980). 3.132 Representation by counsel—for the juvenile. *Standards for the Administration of Juvenile Justice.* Washington, DC: Office of Juvenile Justice and Delinquency Prevention, U.S. Department of Justice.

National Alliance for Model State Drug Laws. (2010). Retrieved April 8, 2010, from http://www.namsdl.org/home.htm

National Association of Police Organizations. (2010). Retrieved March 18, 2010, from http://www.napo.org

National Association of State Alcohol/Drug Abuse Directors. (2010). Retrieved March 18, 2010, from http://www.nasadad.org/index.php?doc_id=2

National Center for Missing and Exploited Children. (2010). *Federal Statutes.* Retrieved March 3, 2010, from http://www.missingkids.com/missingkids/servlet/PageServlet?LanguageCountry=en_US&PageId=1615

National Commission on Terrorist Attacks Upon the United States. (n.d.). Retrieved March 1, 2010, from http://govinfo.library.unt.edu/911/

National Counterterrorism Center. (2007). *Country reports on terrorism 2006, United States.* Retrieved March 25, 2010, from http://terrorisminfo.mipt.org/pdf/Country-Reports-Terrorism-2006.pdf

National Counterterrorism Center. (2008). *2007 report on terrorism.* Retrieved January 22, 2010, from http://terrorisminfo.mipt.org/pdf/NCTC-2007-Report-on-Terrorism.pdf

National Crime Prevention Council. (2010). Retrieved April 18, 2010, from http://www.ncpc.org/about

National Criminal Justice Reference Service. (2010). Retrieved April 12, 2010, from http://www.ncjrs.gov

National Defense Authorization Act, H.R. 2647 (2010).

National Firearms Act, 26 U.S.C. ch.53 (1934).

National Highway Traffic Safety Administration. (2008). *Traffic safety facts 2007 data: Alcohol impaired driving DOT 810 985.* Retrieved January 15, 2010, from http://www-nrd.nhtsa.dot.gov/Pubs/810985.PDF

National Highway Transportation Safety Administration. (1996). *Passive alcohol sensors tested in 3 states for youth alcohol enforcement.* Retrieved January 15, 2010, from http://www.nhtsa.dot.gov/people/outreach/traftech/pub/tt121.pdf

National Institute of Drug Abuse. (2009) *Marijuana.* Retrieved March 18, 2010, from http://www.drugabuse.gov/Infofacts/marijuana.html

National Institute of Drug Abuse. (2009) *Ritalin.* Retrieved April 16, 2010, from http://www.drugabuse.gov/InfoFacts/ADHD.html

National Institute of Justice. (1984). *A network of knowledge.* (Directory of Criminal Justice Information Sources). Queenstown, MD: Aspen Systems.

National Institute of Justice. (1984). *National criminal justice thesaurus.* Washington, DC: Author.

National Institute of Standards and Technology. (2010). *Detection, inspection, and enforcement technologies.* Retrieved April 9, 2010, from http://www.eeel.nist.gov/oles/detection.html

National Institute on Aging. (n.d.). *What is dementia.* Retrieved March 19, 2010, from http://www.nia.nih.gov/HealthInformation/

National Institute on Drug Abuse. (2010). *NIDA InfoFacts: Hallucinogens—LSD, reyote, psilocybin, and PCP.* Retrieved March 4, 2010, from http://www.nida.nih.gov/infofacts/hallucinogens.html

National Institutes on Drug Abuse (2008). *Drugs of Abuse.* Retrieved February 22, 2010, from http://www.nida.nih.gov/drugpages/

National Institutes on Drug Abuse. (2010). *Inhalants.* Retrieved March 16, 2010, from http://www.drugabuse.gov/drugpages/inhalants.html

National Narcotics Act, Pub. L. No. 98-473, 98 Stat. 2168 (1984).

National Police Bloodhound Association. (n.d.). Retrieved February 23, 2010, from http://www.npba.com/

National Research Council of the National Academies. (2003). *The Polygraph and Lie Detection* [Electronic version]. National Academies Press: Washington DC. Retrieved March 27, 2010, from http://www.nap.edu/openbook.php?record_id=10420&page=R1

National Research Council. (2003). *The polygraph and lie detection.* Committee to review the scientific evidence on the polygraph. Division of behavioral and social sciences and education. Washington, DC: The National Academies Press.

National Sheriffs' Association. (n.d.). *About NSA.* Retrieved January 27, 2010, from http://www.sheriffs.org/about/AboutNSA.asp

Naturalization, Citizenship or Alien Registry, 18 U.S.C. § 1015 (n.d.).

Nelson, M., & Bayliss, S. H. (2006). *Exquisite corpse: Surrealism and the Black Dahlia murder.* New York: Bulfinch Press.

Neville, J. F. (2004). *Twentieth-century cause cèlébre: Sacco, Vanzetti, and the press, 1920–1927.* Westport, CN: Praeger.

New York Times. (1910, October 2). *Fire kills 19, unions accused.*

New York v. Ferber, 458 U.S. 747 (1982).

Newman, A., Eligon, J. (2010). Killer of Malcolm X granted parole. *The New York Times.* Retrieved March 14, 2010, from http://cityroom.blogs.nytimes.com/2010/03/19/killer-of-malcolm-x-granted-parole/

Newman, O. (1996). Creating defensible spaces. *U.S. Department of Housing and Urban Development Office of Policy Development and Research.* Retrieved March 5, 2010, from http://www.huduser.org/publications/pdf/def.pdf

Newport, F. (2009). *In U.S. Two-Thirds Continue to Support Death Penalty. Gallup.* Retrieved April 29, 2010, from http://www.gallup.com/poll/123638/In-U.S.-Two-Thirds-Continue-Support-Death-Penalty.aspx

Nice, R. (1965). *Dictionary of criminology.* New York: Philosophical Library.

Nix v. Williams, 467 U. S. 431 (1984).

Nobel Foundation. (n.d.). *The nomination database for the Nobel Prize in Peace, 1901–1955.* Retrieved March 3, 2010, from http://nobelprize.org/nomination/peace/nomination.php?action=show&showid=1347

Noble v. Union River Logging R Co, 147 U.S. 165 (1893).

Nonmedical Good Samaritan Civil Immunity, 42 Pa.C.S.A. § 8 332 (n.d.).

North American Association of Wardens and Superintendents. (2010). Retrieved April 9, 2010, from http://naaws.corrections.com/index.html

North American Police Work Dog Association. (n.d.). Retrieved January 26, 2010, from http://www.napwda.com/

North Carolina Volunteer Health Care Professional, G.S. 90-21.16 (n.d.).

Nude eBayer flashes 19inch monitor. (2005, July 1). *The Register.* Retrieved March 14, 2010, from http://www.theregister.co.uk/2005/07/01/ebay_monitor_flash/

O'Connor, P. G. (2007). Alcohol abuse and dependence. In: Goldman, L., & Ausiello, D. Eds.) *Cecil Medicine.* (23rd ed.) Philadelphia, Pa: Saunders Elsevier.

O'Connor, J. D. (2005, May 31). I'm the guy they called Deep Throat. *Vanity Fair.* Retrieved April 19, 2010, from http://www.vanityfair.com/politics/features/2005/07/deepthroat200507?printable=true&currentPage=all

O'Neil, A. (2008, November 14). Jury awards $2.5 million to teen beaten by Klan members. *CNN.* Retrieved March 16, 2010, from http://www.cnn.com/2008/CRIME/11/14/klan.sued.verdict/index.html

Obituary for Oscar Newman. (2004, April). Retrieved March 5, 2010, from http://www.rootsweb.ancestry.com/~nygreen2/daily_mail_obituaries_april_2004.htm

Obituary: Dr. Bruce Edwards Ivins. (2008, July 31). *Frederick News-Post.* Retrieved March 13, 2010, from http://www.fredericknewspost.com/sections/local/obit_detail.htm?obitID=24497

Office of Applied Studies. (2009). *Trends in adolescent inhalant use: 2002 to 2007.* Rockville, MD: Substance Abuse and Mental Health Services.

Office of National Drug Control Policy. (1998). *Title III—High intensity drug trafficking areas.* Retrieved March 4, 2010, from http://www.whitehousedrugpolicy.gov/hidta/cf~va.html

Office of National Drug Control Policy. (2000) *Methadone.* Retrieved April 8, 2010, from http://www.whitehousedrugpolicy.gov/publications/factsht/methadone/index.html.

Office of Technology Assessment. (1983). *Scientific validity of polygraph testing: A research review and evaluation* [Electronic version]. Washington, DC: U.S. Congress. Retrieved April 17, 2010, from http://www.fas.org/sgp/othergov/polygraph/ota/

Office of the Associate Attorney General. (2010). Retrieved April 6, 2010, from http://www.justice.gov/asg/about-oaag.html

Office of the Attorney General, State of California. (2010). *Missing Persons Resources.* Retrieved March 27, 2010, from http://ag.ca.gov/missing/resource.php

Office of the Attorney General, State of California. (n.d.). *Campaign against marijuana planting.* Retrieved January 23, 2010, from http://ag.ca.gov/bne/camp.php

Office of the Coordinator for Counterterrorism. (2008). Foreign terrorist organizations. *U.S. Department of State.* Retrieved March 27, 2010, from http://merln.ndu.edu/archivepdf/terrorism/state/103392.pdf

Office of the Deputy Attorney General, U.S. Dept. of Justice, Washington DC 20530. (2009, October 19). *Investigations and prosecutions in states authorizing the medical use of marijuana.* Retrieved January 27, 2010 from http://www.justice.gov/opa/documents/medical-marijuana.pdf

Office of the Press Secretary. (2006). President signs H.R. 4472, the Adam Walsh Child Protection and Safety Act of 2006. *White House.* Retrieved April 6, 2010, from http://georgewbush-whitehouse.archives.gov/news/releases/2006/07/20060727-6.html

Office of the Solicitor General. (2010). *About the office of the solicitor general.* Retrieved March 22, 2010, from http://www.justice.gov/osg/about_us.htm

Official Web site of Fort Hood, Texas. (2010). *Fort Hood news releases.* Retrieved March 25, 2010, from http://www.hood.army.mil/news.releases.aspx

Ohio v. Sharma. CR 06-09-3248 (2007).

Olsen, K. R. (2007). Carbon monoxide section of poisoning. In S. J. McPhee et al., eds., *Current Medical Diagnosis and Treatment,* (46th ed.). New York: McGraw-Hill.

Omnibus Crime Control and Safe Streets Act, Pub.L. 90-351, June 19, 1968, 82 Stat. 197, 42 U.S.C. § 3711 (1968).

Palmer, J. W. (1984). *Constitutional rights of prisoners.* Cincinnati, OH: Anderson.

Paris Adult Theatre I v. Slaton, 413 U.S. 49 (1973).

Parker, D. R. (1992). The Oakland-Berkeley hills fire: An overview. *Oakland Office of Fire Services.* Retrieved February 22, 2010, from http://www.sfmuseum.org/oakfire/overview.html

Parker, K. D., and Hine, C. H. (1965). Urine screening techniques employed in the detection of users of narcotics and their correlation with the nalline test. *Journal of Forensic Science.*

Parker, K. D., and Hine, C. H. (1967). Manual for the determination of narcotics and

dangerous drugs in the urine. *Psychopharmacology Bulletin.* Retrieved March 6, 2010, from https://www.unodc.org/unodc/en/data-and-analysis/bulletin/bulletin_1967-01-01_2_page006.html

Patchin, J. W., & Hinduja, S. (2006). Bullies move beyond the schoolyard: A preliminary look at cyberbullying. *Youth Violence and Juvenile Justice, 4*(2), 148–169.

Paulson, M. (2009, May 26). Sotomayor would be sixth Catholic justice. *The Boston Globe.* Retrieved March 4, 2010, from http://www.boston.com/news/local/articles_of_faith/2009/05/sotomayor_would.html

PBS Frontline. (2001). *Rampart scandal timeline.* Retrieved March 3, 2010, from http://www.pbs.org/wgbh/pages/frontline/shows/lapd/scandal/cron.html

PBS. (1977). Remembering Vietnam: Carter's pardon. *Online NewsHour.* Retrieved March 22, 2010 from http://www.pbs.org/newshour/bb/asia/vietnam/vietnam_1-21-77.html

PBS. (n.d.). *From Daniel M'Naughten to John Hinckley: A brief history of the insanity defense.* Retrieved March 4, 2010, from http://www.pbs.org/wgbh/pages/frontline/shows/crime/trial/history.html

Pearson, A. (2004, March 5). 1974: Univ. 'cracks' streaking record. *The Red and Black.* Retrieved March 3, 2010, from http://media.www.redandblack.com/media/storage/paper871/news/2004/03/05/News/1974-Univ.cracks.Streaking.Record-2576112.shtml

Pelisek, C. (2008). Grim sleeper returns: He's murdering Angelenos as COPS hunt his DNA. *LA Weekly.* Retrieved January 30, 2010, from http://www.laweekly.com/2008-08-28/news/grim-sleeper/

Pelicciotti, J. M. (1988). *Title VII liability for sexual harassment in the workplace.* Alexandria, VA: International Personnel Management Association.

People v. Freeman, 46 Cal.3d 419, 758 P.2d 1128; 250 Cal.Rptr. 598 (1988).

Persons Rendering Emergency Care Exempt From Liability, 16 Del.C. §6801 (a) (n.d.).

Petersilia, J., & Turner, S. (1990). Comparing intensive and regular supervision fo high-risk probationers: Early results from an experiment in California. *Crime & Delinquency, 36*(1), 87–110.

Pfeifer, W., Jr. (2009, September 4). Too many registered sex offenders make dangerous sex offenders difficult to track. *The Examiner.* Retrieved January 29, 2010, from http://www.examiner.com/x-16813-Legal-News-Examiner~y2009m9d4-Too-many-registered-sex-offenders-makes-dangerous-sex-offenders-difficult-to-track

Philadelphia Held Liable For Firebomb Fatal to 11. (1996, June 25). *The New York Times.* Retrieved March 28, 2010, from http://query.nytimes.com/gst/fullpage.html?res=9E0DEFDE1239F936A15755C0A960958260&sec=&spon=&pagewanted=all

Philadelphia, city officials ordered to pay $1.5 million in MOVE case. (1996, June 24). *CNN.* Retrieved January 27, 2010, from http://www.cnn.com/US/9606/24/move.vertict/

Philips, C. (2006). LAPD Renews search for rapper's killer. *Los Angeles Times.* Retrieved January 31, 2010, from http://www.lapd.com/article.aspx?&a=4084

Philips, C. (2007). Slain rapper's family keeps pushing suit. *Los Angeles Times.* Retrieved January 31, 2010, from http://www.latimes.com/entertainment/news/business/la-me-biggie4feb04,1,5807757.story?coll=la-headlines-business-enter

Plata v. Schwarzenegger, 556 F.Supp. 2d 1087 (N.D. Cal. 2008).

Pokin, S. (2007, November 11). "My Space" hoax ends with suicide of Dardenne Prairie teen. *Suburban Journals.* Retrieved March 1, 2010, from http://suburbanjournals.stltoday.com/articles/2007/11/11/news/sj2tn20071110-1111stc_pokin_1.ii1.txt

Potter, D. (2009, November 10). DC sniper Muhammad executed for 2002 attacks. *Yahoo news.* Retrieved March 17, 2010, from http://news.yahoo.com/s/ap/us_sniper_execution

Powell, J. G. F. (1984). A note on the use of the praenomen. *The Classical Quarterly, New Series, 34*(1), 238–239.

Powell, M. and Kovaleski, S. F. (2009, June 4). Sotomayor rose on merit alone, her allies say. *The New York Times.* Retrieved March 15, 2010, from http://www.nytimes.com/2009/06/05/us/politics/05judge.html

Procurement of Citizenship or Naturalization Unlawfully, 18 U.S.C. § 1425 (n.d.).

Protection and Preservation of Traditional Religions of Native Americans, 42 USC §1996a (n.d.).

Protection of Offices and Employees of the United States, 18 U.S.C. §1114 (n.d.).

Providing or Possessing Contraband in Prison, 18 U.S.C. § 1791 (n.d.).

Psychwest. (n.d.). *What is a mental state at time of offense (MSO) evaluation.* Retrieved January 30, 2010, from http://www.psychwest.com/ForensicSanity.html

Pursley, R. D. (1987). *Introduction to criminal justice* (4th ed.). New York: Macmillan.

Pynes, J. (2004). *Human resourcesmManagement for public and nonprofit organizations.* (2nd ed.). Hoboken, NJ: John Wiley and Sons.

Quick, J. (1973). *Dictionary of weapons and military terms.* New York: McGraw-Hill.

Quinones, S. (2007, April 7). Jimmy Lee Smith, infamous 'Onion Field' cop killer, dead at 76. *Los Angeles Times.*

Raab, S. (1994, September 26). Signing for your sentence: How will it pay off? Ex-crime underboss may find out today what he gets for turning U.S. Witness. *The New York Times.* Retrieved April 1, 2010, from http://www.nytimes.com/1994/09/26/nyregion/singing-for-your-sentence-will-it-pay-off-ex-crime-underboss-may-find-today-what.html?scp=1&sq=gravano%20scibetta&st=cse

Rand, M. (2009) National crime victimization survey, criminal victimization, 2008. *Bureau of Justice Statistics Bulletin.* U.S. Department of Justice, Office of Justice Programs.

Rechtsmed, Z. (1990). Cartoid and vertebral artery circulation in forcarin choke holds in Doppler sonography [Electronic Version]. *Journal of Legal Medicine, 103*(5), 369–377. Retrieved March 14, 2010, from http://www.medscape.com/medline/abstract/2192520

Reelect Sheriff Joe Arpaio, Background Information. (n.d.). Retrieved March 1, 2010, from http://www.sheriffjoe.org/index.php?option−com_content&task=view&id=14&Itemid=29

Reflectoporn hits auction site. (2003, September 9). *The Mirror.* Retrieved March 16, 2010, from http://www.mirror.co.uk/news/latest/content_objectid=13386628_method=full_siteid=50143_headline=-Get-your-bids-out-name_page.html

Refusal of Witness to Testify or Produce Papers, 2 U.S.C. § 192 (n.d.).

Regalado Cuellar v. United States, 552 U.S. 973 (2007).

Reid, S.T. (1996). *Criminal justice* (4th ed.). Guilford, CT: Brown & Benchmark

Reisine, T., & Pasternak, G. (1996). Opioid analgesics and antagonists. In J. G. Hardman & L. E. Limbird (Eds.), Goodman and Gilman's The Pharmacological Basis of Therapeutics. (9th ed.). New York: McGraw-Hill.

Religion-cults.com. (n.d.). Retrieved January 31, 2010, from http://www.religion-cults.com/

Report of the President's Commission on the Assassination of President John F. Kennedy. (1964). United States Government Printing Office. Retrieved February 26, 2010, from http://www.archives.gov/research/jfk/warren-commission-report/index.html

Ressler, R. K., Revocation of Naturalization, 8 U.S.C. § 1451 (n.d.).

Richey, W. (2010). Supreme Court rules that police can ad lib Miranda warnings. *Christian Science Monitor.* Retrieved March 23, 2010, from http://www.csmonitor.com/USA/Justice/2010/0223/Supreme-Court-rules-that-police-can-ad-lib-Miranda-warnings

Roberts, J. C., O'Conner, J. V., & Ward, E. E. (2005). Modeling the effect of nonpenetrating ballistic impact. *The Journal of Trauma, 58,* 1241–1251.

Roberts, J. C., Ward, E. E., Merkle, A. C., & O'Conner, J. V. (2007). Assessing behind armor blunt trauma. *The Journal of Trauma, 62,* 1127–1133.

Roberts, M. (2010). Medical marijuana lab raided by DEA during introduction of Senator Chris Romer's doctor-patient bill. *Denver Westwood Blog.* Retrieved March 26, 2010, from http://blogs.westword.com/latestword/2010/01/medical_marijuana_bill_about_d.php

Rosoff, S., Pontell, H., & Tillman, R. (2010). *Profit without honor: White collar crime and the looting of America* (5th ed.). Saddle River, N.J.: Prentice Hall.

Ross, B., & Esposito, R. (2005, October 6). Investigation continues: Security breach at the White House. *ABC News.* Retrieved February 18, 2010, from http://abcnews.go.com/WNT/Investigation/story?id=1190375

Ross, R. S. (1996). *American national government* (4th ed.). Guilford, CT: Dushkin Publishing Group.

Ruane, M. E., Duggan, P., & Williams, C. (2010, June 6). At a monument of sorrow, a burst of deadly violence. *The Washington Post.* Retrieved March 29, 2010, from http://www.washingtonpost.com/wp-dyn/content/article/2009/06/10/AR2009061001768.html?hpid=topnews

Ruberg, B. (2008). Social networking terms you should know. *Forbes.com.* Retrieved February 26, 201, http://www.forbes.com/2008/10/22/tech-starter-kit-ent-tech-cx_br_1022socialnetworkingglossary.html

Rubin, S. (1973). *Law of criminal correction* (2nd ed.). St. Paul, MN: West.

Ruckman, P. S., Jr. (1997). Executive clemency in the United States: Origins, development, and analysis (1900–1993). *Presidential Studies Quarterly, 27,* 251–271.

Rumbelow, D. (2004). *The complete Jack the Ripper: Fully revised and updated.* New York: Penguin Books.

Russ, D. (2009, April 13). Ohio to address 'sexting' laws. *WKYC-TV.*

Safford Unified School Dist. #1 v. Redding, 129 S. Ct. 2633 (2009).

Saiki, R. K., Scharf, S., Faloona, F., Mullis, K. B., Horn, G. T., Erlich H. A., & Arnheim, N. (1985). Enzymatic amplification of beta-globin genomic sequences and restriction site analysis for diagnosis of sickle cell anemia. *Science, 230*(4732), 1350–1354.

Saiki, R. K., Gelfand, D. H., Stoffel, S., Scharf, S. J., Higuchi, R., Horn, G. T., Mullis, K. B., & Erlich, H. A. (1988). Primer-directed enzymatic amplification of DNA with a thermostable DNA polymerase. *Science, 239:* 487–491.

Salottolo, L. A. (1976). *Modern police service encyclopedia* (2nd ed.). New York: ARCO.

Sansone, S. J. (1977). *Modern photography for police and firemen.* Cincinnati, OH: Anderson.

Savage, D. G. (2009). *Strip search case in Arizona: Supreme Court declares strip-search of student unconstitutional.* Retrieved February 27, 2010, from http://www.sheldensays.com/stripsearchcase.htm

Scaduto, A. (1976). *Scapegoat: The lonesome death of Bruno Richard Hauptmann.* New York: Putnam.

Schachtman, T. (1992). *Whoever fights monsters: My twenty years tracking serial killers for the FBI.* New York: St. Martin's Press.

Schechter, H. (1998). D*eviant: The shocking true story of Ed Gein, the original psycho.* New York: Simon and Schuster.

Schlosser, E. (1998, December). The prison-industrial complex. *The Atlantic Monthly.* Retrieved January 31, 2010, from http://www.theatlantic.com/issues/98dec/prisons.htm.

Schram, M. (1990, May 28). The making of Willie Horton. *The New Republic.*

Schultes, R. E. (2008). The appeal of peyote (*Lophophora Williamsii*) as a medicine [electronic version]. *American Ethnography Quasimonthly.* Retrieved January 30, 2010, from http://www.americanethnography.com/article_sql.php?id=20

Scientific Working Group on Bloodstain Pattern Analysis (2009). Scientific working group on bloodstain pattern analysis: *Guidelines for developing standard operating procedures for bloodstain pattern analysis.* Retrieved April 22, 2010, from http://www.swgstain.org/

Scott, G. G. (2005). *Homicide by the rich and famous: A century of prominent killers.* Westport, CT: Greenwood Publishing Group.

Scott, Sir H. (Ed.). (1961). *Crime and criminals.* New York: Hawthorne Books.

Sears, L. R. (2001). Punishing the saints for their "peculiar institution": Congress on the constitutional dilemmas. *Utah Law Review 2001,* 581-658.

Secret Service. (2010). *Who we are.* Retrieved from http://www.secretservice.gov/whoweare.shtml

Seiter, R. P. (2010). *Corrections: An introduction.* Upper Saddle River, NJ: Pearson.

Sellbom, M., Ben-Porath, Y. S., & Bagby, R. M. (In Press). Personality and psychopathology: Mapping the MMPI-2 restructured clinical (RC) scales onto the five factor model of personality. *Journal of Personality Disorders.*

Sellbom, M., Ben-Porath, Y. S., Baum, L. J., Erez, E., & Gregory, C. (2008). Predictive validity of the MMPI-2 restructured clinical (RC) scales in a batterers' intervention program. *Journal of Personality Assessment, 90,* 129–135.

Selye, H. (1975). Confusion and controversy in the stress field. *U.S. National Library of Medicine.* Retrieved January 15, 2010, from http://www.ncbi.nlm.nih.gov/pubmed/1235113

Senna, J. J., & Siegel, L. J. (1990). *Introduction to criminal justice* (5th ed.). St. Paul, MN: West Publishing.

Sentence of Fine, 18 U.S.C. § 3571 (n.d.).

Sentencing Classification of Offenses, 18 U.S.C. § 3559 (n.d.).

Sentencing project. (2010). *About us.* Retrieved April 9, 2010, from http://www.sentencingproject.org/template/page.cfm?id=2

Serpick, E. (2002). Review: Rappers' deaths probed in 'LAbyrinth'. *Entertainment Weekly.* Retrieved February 28, 2010, from http://archives.cnn.com/2002/SHOWBIZ/

books/04/15/ew.rec.book.labyrinth/index.html

Shariat, S., Mallonee, S., & Stephens-Stidham, S. (1998). Summary of reportable injuries in Oklahoma. *Oklahoma State Department of Health.* Retrieved January 17, 2010, from http://web.archive.org/web/20080110063748/http://www.health.state.ok.us/PROGRAM/injury/Summary/bomb/OKCbomb.htm

Shepard, C. (1999). *The injured at Columbine High School.* Retrieved March 15, 2010, from http://acolumbinesite.com/victim/injured.html

Sherman, C., & Lehr, D. (2003). *A rose for Mary: The hunt for the Boston strangler.* Boston, MA: Northeastern University Press.

Sherwin, A. (2006). Gay means rubbish, says BBC. *Times newspaper.* Retrieved February 26, 2010, from http://entertainment.timesonline.co.uk/tol/arts_and_entertainment/article671972.ece

Sills, D. (Ed.). (1977). *International encyclopedia of social sciences.* New York: Macmillan.

Silva, J. (2008). Carriers push E-911 lawsuit in court despite winning deadline extension. *RCR wireless.* Retrieved March 2, 2010, from http://www.fiercewireless.com/story/sprint-alltel-usc-fined-missed-e911-deadline/2007-08-31

Sleven, C. (2010). Colorado medical marijuana lab raided by DEA while owners attended Senate hearing on MMJ. *The Huffington Post.* Retrieved March 17, 2010, from http://www.huffingtonpost.com/2010/01/28/colorado-medical-marijuan_10_n_440545.html

Smith v. Doe, 538 U.S. 84 (2003).

Smith, E., & Zurcher, A. (1968). *Dictionary of American politics* (2nd ed.). New York: Harper & Row.

Smith, G. (1999). WTC bombers are resentenced. *Daily News.* Retrieved February 13, 2010, from http://www.nydailynews.com/archives/news/1999/10/14/1999-10-14_wtc_bombers_are_resentenced.html

Smith, J. D. (2004). *100 Most infamous criminals.* New York: Metro Books.

Smith, S. (2008, April 28). 9/11 "Wall Of Heroes" to include sick cops. *CBS News.* Retrieved February 15, 2010, from http://www.cbsnews.com/stories/2008/04/28/national/main4049362.shtml

Sodhi, J. S., & Kaur, J. (2005). The forgotten Indian pioneers of fingerprint science. *Current Science, 88*(1), 185–191.

Solis, D. (2009). U.S. cuts back on sedating deportees with Haldol. *Seattle Times.* Retrieved March 5, 2010, from http://seattletimes.nwsource.com/html/nationworld/2008590327_deport05.html

Sosa v. Alvarez-Machain, 542 U.S. 692 (2004).

Soto, O. R. (2006, June 17). 36 indicted in Mexican Mafia crackdown. *San Diego Union-Tribune.* Retrieved January 29, 2010, from http://legacy.signonsandiego.com/news/metro/20060617-9999-1n17mafia.html

Sourcebook of Criminal Justice Statistics (1992). Washington, DC: U.S. Department of Justice, Office of Justice Programs, Bureau of Justice Statistics.

Sourcebook of Criminal Justice Statistics. (2008). Methods of execution in states authorizing the death penalty. Retrieved March 22, 2010, from http://www.albany.edu/sourcebook/pdf/t6872008.pdf

Southern Poverty Law Center vs. Imperial Klans of America. (2007, July 25). *Southern Poverty Law Center.* Retrieved February 27, 2010, from http://www.splcenter.org/legal/docket/files.jsp?cdrID=69&sortID=2

Spalding, L. H. (1998). Florida's 1997 chemical castration law: A return to the dark ages. *Florida State University Law Review, 25,* 117–139.

Spalding, M. (2001). The Command of its own fortunes: Reconsidering Washington's farewell address. In William D. Pederson, Mark J. Rozell, Ethan M. Fishman, eds. *George Washington: Foundation of presidential leadership and character.* Westport, Connecticut: Praeger.

Stalking, California PC 646.9 (n.d.).

State Finance and Procurement, M.L. 5-309 (n.d.).

State of California. (2003). *Cedar fire: Final update.* Retrieved February 18, 2010, from http://www.fire.ca.gov/cdf/incidents/cedar%20fire_120/incident_info.html

Stephanie's Law. (2003). State of New York. Retrieved February 28, 2010, from http://criminaljustice.state.ny.us/legalservices/ch69_2003_stephanie_vidvoy.htm

Stevens, J. P. (2009, November 9). Muhammad v. Kelly, application for stay and on petition for a Writ of Certiorari to the United States Court of Appeals for the Fourth Circuit. *Supreme Court of the United States.* Retrieved January 19, 2010, from http://www.supremecourt.gov/opinions/09pdf/09-7328.pdf

Stevenson, R. J. (2000). *The boiler room and other telephone sales scams.* Chicago: University of Illinois Press.

Stimulants. (n.d) *In the Controlled Substances Act.* Retrieved April 7, 2010, from http://www.justice.gov/dea/pubs/abuse/5-stim.htm

Stoff, D. M., Breiling, J., and Maser, J. D. (1997). *Handbook of Antisocial Behavior.* New York: Wiley.

Stone, A. C., Starrs, J. E., & Stoneking, M. (2001). Mitochondrial DNA analysis of the presumptive remains of Jesse James. *J. Forensic Sci, 46*(1), 173–176.

Street Law, Inc. (2010). *Landmark cases of the U.S. Supreme Court.* Retrieved April 19, 2010, from http://www.landmarkcases.org/

Substance Abuse and Crime Prevention Act, Prop. 36 (2000).

Suicide and Mental Health Association International. (n.d.). *Glossary of forensics terminology.* Retrieved April 4, 2010, from http://suicideandmentalhealthassociationinternational.org/forensicsgloss.html

Sullivan, R. (2003). *LAbyrinth: A detective investigates the murders of Tupac Shakar and Notorious BIG, the implications of Death Row Records' Suge Knight, and the origins of the Los Angeles Police Scandal.* New York: Grove Press.

Sullivan, R. (2005, December 5). The unsolved mystery of the Notorious B.I.G. *Rolling Stone.* Retrieved February 27, 2010, http://www.rollingstone.com/news/story/8898338/the_unsolved_mystery_of_the_notorious_big.

Sullivan, T., & Maiken, P. T. (2000). *Killer clown: The John Wayne Gacy murders.* New York: Pinnacle Books.

Suneson, A. Hansson, H. A., & Seeman, T. (1987). Peripheral high-energy missile hits cause pressure changes and damage to the nervous system: Experimental studies on pigs. *The Journal of Trauma, 27*(7), 782–789.

Suneson, A., & Hansson, H. A. (1990). Pressure wave injuries to the nervous system caused by high energy missile extremity impact: Part II. Distant effects on the central nervous system. A light and electron microscopic study on pigs. *The Journal of Trauma, 30*(3), 295–306.

Suneson, A., Hansson, H. A., & Seeman, T. (1988). Central and peripheral nervous damage following high-energy missile wounds in the thigh. *The Journal of Trauma, 28*(1), 197–203.

Supreme Court of the United States. (n.d.). Retrieved April 1, 2010, from http://www.supremecourt.gov/

Supreme Court. (2010). *Biographies of the Supreme Court of the United States.* Retrieved April 17, 2010, from http://www.supremecourt.gov/about/biographies.aspx

Surveillance. (n.d). In *Detection, Inspection, and Enforcement Technologies.* Retrieved April 7, 2010, from http://www.eeel.nist.gov/oles/detection.html

Suspect is seized in Capital in threat at Federal Reserve. (1981, December 8). *The New York Times.* Retrieved March, 6, 2010, from http://www.nytimes.com/1981/12/08/us/suspect-is-seized-in-capital-in-threat-at-federal-reserve.html?n=Top%2FReference%2FTimes%20Topics%2FSubjects%2FH%2FHostages

Sutherland, E. H., & Cressey, D. R. (1966). *Principles of criminology* (7th ed.). Philadelphia: J.B. Lippincott.

Sykes B. (1999). *The human inheritance: genes, language and evolution.* Oxford: Oxford University Press.

Takeoff. (1973, December 10). *Time Magazine.*

TASER International. (2009). *Press kit.* Retrieved March 27, 2010, from http://www2.taser.com/company/pressroom/Pages/PressKit.aspx

Tatum, G. H. (1977). Combatting crime: full utilization of the police officer and CSO (community service officer) concept. *Police Chief, 44*(4), 46–87.

Taylor, A. (2001). *American colonies.* London: Penguin.

Telecommunications Industry Association. (n.d.). *TIA-942: Data center standards overview.* Retrieved March 17, 2010, from http://www.adc.com/us/en/Library/Literature/102264AE.pdf

Terri Schiavo biography and timeline. (2007, March 27). *Bay News 9.* Retrieved March 6, 2010, from http://www.baynews9.com/content/36/2005/3/31/76457.html

Testimony of Alger Hiss. (1948). *Hearings regarding communist espionage in the United States government. United States House of Representatives.* Retrieved February 26, 2010, from http://74.125.95.132/search?q=cache:BGQinnn2ruAJ:www.law.umkc.edu/faculty/projects/ftrials/hiss/8-17testimony.html+%22I+was+a+Communist+and+you+were+a+Communist%22&cd=5&hl=en&ct=clnk&gl=us

Testimony of Michael Braun, Drug Enforcement Administration. (2006). *Counternarcotics Strategies in Latin America.* Retrieved March 16, 2010, from http://www.justice.gov/dea/pubs/cngrtest/ct033006.html

Texas Code of Criminal Procedure. (n.d.). Proceedings before magistrates to prevent offenses. Retrieved March 18, 2010, from http://www.statutes.legis.state.tx.us/Docs/CR/htm/CR.7.htm

The Black Supremacists. (1959, August 10). *Time.* Retrieved March 3, 2010, from http://www.time.com/time/magazine/article/0,9171,811191-1,00.html

The United States Department of Labor. The Employee Polygraph Protection Act, 29 U.S.C. § 2001 (1988). Accessed 3-29-10 at: http://www.dol.gov/compliance/laws/comp-eppa.htm

The Lincoln Savings and Loan Investigation: Who Is Involved. (1989, November 22). *The New York Times.* Retrieved February 23, 2010, from http://query.nytimes.com/gst/fullpage.html?res=950DE4D91230F931A15752C1A96F948260

The Man Who Got Away. (2002, May 31). *60 Minutes.* Retrieved January 27, 2010, from http://www.cbsnews.com/stories/2002/05/31/60minutes/main510795.shtml

The National Archives. (n.d.). Retrieved January 31, 2010, from http://www.archives.gov/

The Privacy Act, 5 U.S.C. § 552a (1974).

The Sentencing Project. (2010). Retrieved April 18, 2010, from http://www.sentencingproject.org/template/page.cfm?id=2

The Sentencing Project. (n.d.). *Felony Disenfranchisement.* Retrieved March 9, 2010, from http://www.sentencingproject.org/template/page.cfm?id=133

The World Factbook. (2007). *Prison population and incarceration rate—2007 rankings.* Retrieved February 23, 2010, from http://www.allcountries.org/ranks/prison_incarceration_rates_of_countries_2007.html

Theft of Livestock, 18 U.S.C. § 667 (n.d.).

Therapeutic Communities of America. (2010). *About TCA.* Retrieved February 27, 2010, from http://www.therapeuticcommunitiesofamerica.org/main/AboutTCA/tabid/56/Default.aspx

Therapeutic Communities of America. (2010). Retrieved April 19, 2010, from http://www.therapeuticcommunitiesofamerica.org/main/AboutTCA/tabid/56/Default.aspx.

Thomas, J. (1997, December 28). December 21–27; Nichols found guilty in Oklahoma City case. *The New York Times.* Retrieved March 17, 2010, from http://www.nytimes.com/1997/12/28/weekinreview/december-21-27-nichols-found-guilty-in-oklahoma-city-case.html

Thomas-Lester, A. (2005, June 14). A Senate apology for history on lynching: Vote condemns past failure to act. *Washington Post.* Retrieved March 18, 2010, from http://www.washingtonpost.

com/wp-dyn/content/article/2005/06/13/AR2005061301720.html

Timeline: Investigation and court case. (2006, May 24). *CBC News.* Retrieved March 20, 2010, from http://www.cbc.ca/news/background/sniper/timeline_investigation.html

Timeline: The shoe bomber case. (2002, January 7). *CNN.* Retrieved March 16, 2010, from http://www.cnn.com/2002/US/01/07/reid.timeline/index.html.

Transportation of Stolen Goods, Securities, Moneys, Fradulent State Tax Stamps, or Articles Used in Counterfeiting, 18 U.S.C. § 2314 et seq.

Travis, J. (2005). *But they all come back: Facing the challenges of prisoner reentry.* Washington, DC: The Urban Institute Press.

Trefousse, H. L. (1989). *Andrew Johnson: A biography.* New York: W.W. Norton & Co.

Trentacoste, M. F. (2005). Safety evaluation of red-light cameras. *U.S. Department of Transportation, Federal Highway Administration.* Retrieved March 23, 2010, from http://www.tfhrc.gov/safety/pubs/05048/index.htm

Trex, E. (2008). 6 presidential siblings and the headaches they caused. *Mental Floss.* Retrieved March 19, 2010, from http://blogs.static.mentalfloss.com/blogs/archives/21323.html?cnn=yes

Trex, E. (2009). 11 notable presidential pardons. *CNN.* Retrieved March 19, 2010, from http://www.cnn.com/2009/LIVING/wayoflife/01/05/mf.presidential.pardons/

Tully, J. C. H. (1998). *Prisoner 1167: The madman who was Jack the Ripper.* New York: Carroll & Graf Pub.

Twenty-one killed and more injured in the dynamited 'Times' building. (1910, October 2). *Los Angeles Times.*

Tyler C. C., & Kerkvliet, G. J. (2004). What is the true number of victims of the postal anthrax attack of 2001? *Journal of the American Osteopathic Association,* 104(11).

U.S v. James Wenneker von Brunn. (2009). *FindLaw.* Retrieved January 31, 2010, from http://news.findlaw.com/hdocs/docs/crim/us-von-brunn61109cmp.html

U.S. Census Bureau. (2010). *Participant statistical areas program (PSAP) criteria for the 2010 census and beyond.* Retrieved March 29, 2010, from http://www.census.gov/geo/www/psap2010/psapcriteria.html

U.S. Coast Guard. (n.d.). *Pacific strike team.* Retrieved January 31, 2010, from http://www.uscg.mil/hq/nsfweb/PST/pstdefault.asp

U.S. Customs and Border Patrol. (n.d.). *Canine information.* Retrieved January 31, 2010, from http://www.cbp.gov/xp/cgov/border_security/port_activities/canines/

U.S. Customs and Border Protection. (n.d.). *About CBP.* Retrieved January 31, 2010, from http://www.cbp.gov/xp/cgov/about/

U.S. Department of Commerce. (2009). *Minority business development agency.* Retrieved March 28, 2010, from http://www.mbda.gov/

U.S. Department of Justice (2010). Amber alert. *Office of Justice Programs.* Retrieved April 3, 2010, from http://www.amberalert.gov/

U.S. Department of Justice and Federal Trade Commission. (2007). *Antitrust enforcement and intellectual property rights: promoting innovation and competition.*

U.S. Department of Justice, Bureau of Justice Statistics (2008). *Criminal Victimization in the United States, 2006 Statistical Tables.* Retrieved April 15, 2010, from http://bjs.ojp.usdoj.gov/index.cfm?ty=pbdetail&iid=1094

U.S. Department of Justice, Bureau of Justice Statistics (2010). *Capital Punishment, 2008—Statistical Tables, NCJ 228662, Table 2* [Online]. Retrieved April 15, 2010, from: http://bjs.ojp.usdoj.gov/content/pub/pdf/cp08st.pdf

U.S. Department of Justice, Federal Bureau of Prisons (2000). *State of the Bureau 1990.* Washington, DC: U.S. Department of Justice.

U.S. Department of Justice. (1976). *Law enforcement and private security sources*

U.S. Department of Justice. (2000). *Clemency Regulations.* Retrieved March 15, 2010, from http://www.justice.gov/pardon/clemency.htm

U.S. Department of Justice. (2004). Violent offender incarceration and truth-in-sentencing (VOI/TIS) Program. *Bureau of Justice Assistance.* Retrieved March 30, 2010, from http://www.ojp.usdoj.gov/BJA/grant/voitis.html

U.S. Department of Justice. (2009). *2008 Hate Crime Statistics.* Retrieved March 23, 2010, from http://www.fbi.gov/ucr/hc2008/index.html

U.S. Department of Justice. (2010). *Fraud statistics: 1986–2008.* Retrieved March 28, 2010, from http://www.taf.org/FCA-stats-DoJ-2008.pdf

U.S. Department of Justice. (2010). *What is telemarketing fraud.* Retrieved March 6, 2010, from http://www.justice.gov/criminal/fraud/telemarket/ask/whatis.html

U.S. Department of Justice. (n.d.). *Executive office for the organized crime drug enforcement task force.* Retrieved March 23, 2010, from http://www.usdoj.gov/criminal/ocdetf.html

U.S. Department of Justice. (n.d.). *Sex offender sentencing, monitoring, apprehending, registering, and tracking (SMART).* Retrieved March 24, 2010, from http://www.ojp.usdoj.gov/smart/

U.S. Department of Justice. *Insanity defense reform act of 1984.* Retrieved March 22, 2010, from http://www.justice.gov/usao/eousa/foia_reading_room/usam/title9/crm00634.htm

U.S. Department of Justice: Bureau of Justice Statistics. (1981). *Dictionary of criminal justice data terminology: Terms and definitions proposed for interstate and national data collection and exchange: Report of work performed by Search Group, Inc.*

U.S. Department of Justice: Bureau of Justice Statistics. (1990). *Drugs and crime facts.* Washington, DC: Author.

U.S. Department of Justice: Bureau of Justice Statistics. (2006). *Adults on probation, in jail or prison, and on parole.* Retrieved April 22, 2010, from http://www.albany.edu/sourcebook/pdf/t612006.pdf

U.S. Department of Justice: Bureau of Justice Statistics. (2009). *Prisoners executed under civil authority.* Accessed April 20, 2010, from: http://www.albany.edu/sourcebook/pdf/t6852009.pdf

U.S. Department of the Treasury. (2002). Remarks of under-secretary Jimmy Gurulé 2002 national money laundering strategy roll out. *Office of Public Affairs.* Retrieved January 27, 2010, from http://www.treas.gov/press/releases/po3287.htm

U.S. Department of Veterans Affairs. (2010). Agent Orange: Information about Agent Orange, possible health problems, and related VA benefits. *Office of public health and environmental hazards.* Retrieved February 26, 2010, from http://www.publichealth.va.gov/exposures/agentorange/

U.S. Drug Enforcement Agency. (n.d.). *D.E.A programs: Organized crime drug enforcement task force.* Retrieved March 16, 2010, from http://www.dea.gov/programs/ocdetf.htm

U.S. Equal Employment Opportunity Commission. (n.d.). Retrieved January 18, 2010, from http://www.eeoc.gov/policy/vii.html

U.S. General Accounting Office. (1985). *Coordination of federal drug interdiction efforts. Report to the Chairman, Subcommittee on Government Information, Justice and Agriculture committee on government operations.* Retrieved March 17, 2010, from http://archive.gao.gov/d8t2/127418.pdf

U.S. Government Accountability Office. (2002). *Welfare reform: Implementation of fugitive felon provisions should be strengthened.* Retrieved March 3, 2010, from http://www.gao.gov/products/gao-02-716

U.S. Immigrations and Customs Enforcement. (2009). *Armas Cruzadas fact sheet.* Retrieved March 17, 2010, from http://www.ice.gov/pi/news/factsheets/armas_cruzadas.htm

U.S. v. McVeigh. (n.d.). Oklahoma State Courts Network. Retrieved March 3, 2010, from http://www.oscn.net/applications/oscn/DeliverDocument.asp?CiteID=151372

USA PATRIOT Act, P.L. 107-56 (2001).

Uniform Child Custody Jurisdiction Act, 9 U.L.A. at 123 (1988).

Uniform Child Custody Jurisdiction and Enforcement Act, 9 U.L.A. at 115 (1997).

Unitarian Universalist Service Committee. (2010). Retrieved April 9, 2010, from http://www.uusc.org/

United Nations Treaty Collection. (1989). Convention on the rights of the child. Retrieved March 29, 2010, from http://treaties.un.org/Pages/ViewDetails.aspx?src=TREATY&mtdsg_no=IV-11&chapter=4&lang=en

United States Bureau of Alcohol, Tobacco, and Firearms and Explosives. (2010). Retrieved March 29, 2010, from http://www.atf.gov/about/history/

United States Citizenship and Immigration Services. (n.d.). Retrieved March 17, 2010, from http://www.uscis.gov/portal/site/uscis

United States Coast Guard. (2010). Retrieved April 17, 2010, from http://www.uscg.mil/top/about/

United States Coast Guard. (n.d.). *About us.* Retrieved February 27, 2010, from http://www.uscg.mil/top/about/

United States Congress (1985). *Continued review of the administration's drug interdiction efforts: Hearings before a House subcommittee of the committee on government operations: March 21, 22, 23; June 14; August 1; and September 6, 1984.* NCJ 111631.

United States Court of Appeals for the Federal Circuit. (2010). Retrieved March 15, 2010, from http://www.cafc.uscourts.gov/

United States Court of International Trade. (2010). Retrieved March 27, 2010, from http://www.cit.uscourts.gov/

United States Customs and Border Protection. (2010). Retrieved April 19, 2010, from http://www.cbp.gov/xp/cgov/about/

United States Department of Justice. (2002). *Joint terrorism task force.* Retrieved March 3, 2010, from http://www.justice.gov/jttf/

United States Department of Justice. (2010). *Privacy act of 1974.* Retrieved January 13, 2010, from http://www.justice.gov/opcl/privacyact1974.htm

United States Department of Justice. (2010). Retrieved March 29, 2010, from http://www.justice.gov/osg/about_us.htm

United States Department of Justice. (n.d.). *Telemarketing fraud.* Retrieved March 1, 2010, from http://www.justice.gov/criminal/fraud/telemarket/ask/schemes.html#charity

United States Department of Transportation. (2010). Retrieved January 17, 2010, from http://www.dot.gov/

United States House of Representatives. (2010). *The permanent standing House Committee on UnAmerican Activities.* Retrieved March 16, 2010, from http://clerk.house.gov/art_history/highlights.html?action=view&intID=198

United States Immigration Support. (n.d.). *Information about deportation from the United States.* Retrieved March 1, 2010, from http://www.usaimmigrationsupport.com/u-s-visas/information-about-deportation-from-the-united-states.html

United States Marshals. (2010). *Witness security program United States Marshals Service.* Retrieved April 13, 2010, from http://www.usmarshals.gov/witsec/index.html

United States Parole Commission. (2010). Retrieved March 17, 2010, from http://www.justice.gov/uspc/

United States Parole Commission. (n.d.). *The mission of the parole commission.* Retrieved March 30, 2010, from http://www.justice.gov/uspc/

United States Police Canine Association. (n.d.). Retrieved January 30, 2010, from http://www.uspcak9.com/

United States Reports Project. (n.d.). *United States reports: Landmark cases.* Retrieved February 26, 2010, from http://www.unitedstatesreports.org/landmarkcases/index.htm

United States Secret Service. (2010). Retrieved April 9, 2010, from http://www.secretservice.gov/whoweare.shtml

United States Securities and Exchange Commission. (2007). *Portrait of a "boiler room."* Retrieved March 13, 2010, from http://www.sec.gov/investor/links/toptips.htm#boiler

United States v. Alvarez-Machain, 504 U.S. 655 (1992).

United States v. Henderson, D. C. Docket No. 03-00065-CR-FTM-29-SPC (2005). Retrieved March 15, 2010, from http://www.ca11.uscourts.gov/opinions/ops/200411545.pdf

United States v. Morelund, 258 U.S. 433 (1922).

United States v. Persico, Langella, Persico, DeRoss, Scarpati, Russo, Cataldo, McIntosh, 646 F. Supp. 752 (1986). Retrieved March 26, 2010, from http://www.ipsn.org/court_cases/us_v_persico_1986-09-25.htm

United States v. Powers, 59 F.3d 1460 (4th Cir. 1995).

United States v. Richard Colvin Reid Indictment (PDF). (2002). *U.S. District Court, District of Massachusetts.* Retrieved January 23, 2010, from http://www.fas.org/irp/news/2002/01/reidindictment.pdf

United States v. Santos, 553 U.S. 507 (2008).

United States v. Scheffer, 523 U.S. 303 (1998).

United States v. Williams, 553 U. S. 285 (2008).

United States Witness Protection Program, 18 U.S.C.A 3521 et. seq. (n.d.).

Uptime Institute. (n.d.). *Data center site infrastructure tier standard: Topology.* Retrieved January 31, 2010, from http://uptimein stitute.org/index.php?option=com_ docman&task=doc_download&gid=82

Uptime Institute. (n.d.). *Data center site infrastructure tier standard: Topology* [PDF]. Retrieved January 31, 2010, from http://professionalservices.uptimeinsti tute.com/UIPS_PDF/TierStandard.pdf

Utah lawmakers OK bill on 'sexting.' (2009, March 11). *Associated Press.*

Van Slambrouck, P. (2000, November 28). On death row, an author and Nobel nominee. *Christian Science Monitor,* p. 1.

Vergano, D. (2002, September 9). Telling the truth about lie detectors. *USA Today.* Retrieved March 15, 2010, from http://www.usatoday.com/news/nation/2002-09-09-lie_x.htm

Vermont considers legalizing teen 'sexting.' (2009, April 13). *Associated Press.*

Violent Crime Control and Law Enforcement Act, H.R. 3355, Pub.L. 103–322 (1994).

Virginia Tech. (2010). *Blood alcohol concentration effects.* Retrieved March 2, 2010, from http://www.alcohol.vt.edu/students/alcoholeffects/index.htm

Vold, G. B., & Bernard, T. J. (1986). *Theoretical criminology* (3rd ed.). New York: Oxford University Press.

Vos, P., Hogers, R., Bleeker, M., et al (1995). AFLP: A new technique for DNA fingerprinting. *Nucleic Acids Res, 23*(21), 4407–4414.

Wage and Hour Division. (2010). *About WHD.* Retrieved March 30, 2010, from http://www.dol.gov/whd/index.htm

Walker, M. (1993). An American tale. *Entertainment Weekly.* Retrieved March 15, 2010, from http://www.ew.com/ew/article/0,307346,00.html

Walker, S. (1989). *Sense and nonsense about crime: A policy guide* (2nd ed.). Pacific Grove, CA: Brooks/Cole.

Walls, H. J. (1974). *Forensic science: An introduction to scientific crime detection.*

Wang, Q., Wang, Z., Zhu, P., & Jiang, J. (2004). Alterations of the myelin basic protein and ultrastructure in the limbic system and the early stage of trauma-related stress disorder in dogs. *The Journal of Trauma, 56*(3), 604–610.

War casualties pass 9/11 death toll. (2006, September 22). *CBS News.* Retrieved March 16, 2010, from http://www.cbs news.com/stories/2006/09/22/terror/ main2035427.shtml

Warner, J. (2010). Medical marijuana lab in Colorado Springs latest to be raided by DEA. *Denver Westwood Blogs.* Retrieved March 4, 2010, from http://blogs. westword.com/latestword/2010/02/ another_dea_lab_application_an.php

Washington and Lee University School of Law. (2007). *Ranking of US. law journals by impact factor.* Retrieved January 21, 2010, from http://lawlib.wlu.edu/LJ/index.aspx

Watson, B. (2007). *Sacco and Vanzetti: The men, the murders, and the judgment of mankind.* New York: Viking Press.

Waugh, D. (2007). Egan's rats: The untold story of the gang that ruled prohibition-era *St. Louis.* Nashville: Cumberland House.

Weber, H. R. (2007, August 30). Former Olympic park guard Jewell dies. *The Washington Post.* Retrieved February 26, 2010, from http://www.washingtonpost.com/wp-dyn/content/article/2007/08/30/AR2007083000324.accessed

Wedge, T. W. (1988). *The Satan hunter.* Canton, OH: Daring Books.

Weisskopf, M. (2001). A pardon, a Presidential library, a big donation. *Time.* Retrieved March 14, 2010, from http://www.time.com/time/nation/article/0,8599,101652,00.html

Welchans, S. (2005). Megan's Law: Evaluations of sexual offender registries. *Criminal Justice Policy Review, 16*(2), 123–140.

Wellek, A. (Ed.). (1991). *Encyclopedic dictionary of American government* (4th ed.). Guilford, CT: Dushkin Publishing Group.

West, D. M. (1993). *Air wars: Television advertising in election campaigns, 1952–1992.* Washington, DC: Congressional Quarterly Press.

Weston, P. B., & Wells, K. M. (1981). *The administration of justice* (4th ed.). Englewood Cliffs: NJ: Prentice Hall.

What was found in the dust. (2006, September 5). *New York Times.* Retrieved March 15, 2010, from http://www.nytimes.com/imagepages/2006/09/05/nyregion/20060905_HEALTH_GRAPHIC.html

Whisenand, P. M. (1981). *The effective police manager.* Englewood Cliffs, NJ: Prentice Hall.

Whisenand, P. M., & Ferguson, R. F. (1973). *The managing of police organizations.* Englewood Cliffs, NJ: Prentice Hall.

Whisenand, P. M., & Rush, G. E. (1988). *Supervising police personnel: Back to the basics.* Englewood Cliffs, NJ: Prentice Hall.

Whisenand, P. M., & Rush, G. E. (1993). *Supervising police personnel: The fifteen responsibilities.* Englewood Cliffs, NJ: Prentice Hall.

White, G. E. (2005). *Alger Hiss's looking-glass wars: The covert life of a Soviet spy.* New York: Oxford University Press.

White, R. (2003). Environmental issues and the criminological imagination. *Theoretical Criminology, 7*(4), 483–506.

Whitehead, M., & Rivett, M. (2006). *Jack the ripper.* Harpenden, Hertfordshire: Pocket Essentials.

Wiesner, R. J., Ruegg, J. C., & Morano, I. (1992). Counting target molecules by exponential polymerase chain reaction, copy number of mitochondrial DNA in rat tissues. *Biochim Biophys Acta,183,* 553–559.

Williams, C. (2008, September 15). Vehicle spy-cam data to be held for five years. *The Register.* Retrieved March 27, 2010, from http://www.theregister.co.uk/2008/09/15/anpr_five_years/

Williams, T., & Price, H. (2005). *Uncle Jack.* London: Orion.

Willman, D. (2008, August 1). Apparent suicide in anthrax case. *Los Angeles Times.* Retrieved March 4, 2010, from http://www.latimes.com/news/nationworld/nation/la-na-anthrax1-2008aug01,0,2864223.story?page=1

Willman, D. (2008, September 18). Senators question FBI's handling of anthrax inquiry. *Los Angeles Times.* Retrieved March 4, 2010, from http://www.latimes.com/news/nationworld/nation/la-na-anthrax18-2008sep18,0,2539984.story

Wilson, J. R., & Wilson, J. A. (1992). *Addictionary.* New York: Simon & Schuster.

Wire and Electronic Communications Interception and Interception of Oral Communications, Definitions, 18 U.S.C. § 2510 (n.d.).

Wolfe, D. H. (2005). *The Black Dahlia files: The mob, the mogul, and the murder that transfixed Los Angeles.* New York: Regan Books.

Woods, G. (1993). *Drug abuse in society: A reference handbook.* Santa Barbara, CA: ABC-CLIO.

Woodward, B. (2005, June 2). How Mark Felt became "Deep Throat." *Washington Post.* Retrieved March 15, 2010, from http://www.washingtonpost.com/wp-dyn/content/article/2005/06/01/AR2005060102124_pf.html

World almanac and book of facts. (1988). New York: Newspaper Enterprise Association.

World health organization. (n.d.). *Disability.* Retrieved January 17, 2010, from http://www.who.int/topics/disabilities/en/

Wournos, A. (2004). *Monster: My true story.* London: John Blake Publishing.

Wuornos, A., & Berry-Dee, C. (2006). *Monster: My true story.* London: John Blake Publishing.

Wygant, D. B., Boutacoff, L. A., Arbisi, P. A., Ben-Porath, Y. S., Kelly, P. H., & Rupp, W. M. (2007). Examination of the MMPI-2 restructured clinical (RC) scales in a sample of bariatric surgery candidates. *Journal of Clinical Psychology in Medical Settings, 14,* 197–205.

You and the law: A practical guide to everyday law and how it affects you and your family. (1971). Pleasantville, NY: Reader's Digest Association.

Zetter, K. (2009). 'Sexting' hysteria falsely brands educator as child pornographer. *Wired.com.* Retrieved March 19, 2010, from http://www.wired.com/threatlevel/2009/04/sexting-hysteri/

Zimring, F. E., Hawkins, G., & Kamin, S. (2001). *Punishment and democracy: Three strikes and you're out in California.* New York: Oxford University Press.

Part II

SUMMARIES OF SUPREME COURT CASES AFFECTING CRIMINAL JUSTICE

Summaries of
United States Supreme Court
Cases Affecting Criminal Justice

Judy Hails, J.D., LL.M.

Department of Criminal Justice
California State University, Long Beach

PREFACE

The United States Supreme Court has decided hundreds of cases that relate to criminal justice. This summary includes cases decided through April 1, 2010. Although it focuses on cases decided in the last 50 years, other landmark cases have been included for the sake of completeness. Due to their historical impact, some cases have been included even though they have been subsequently overruled. The need to keep this volume to a manageable size has necessitated deletion of some of the less important cases included in prior editions.

The materials in this summary are organized by topic. Cases within each topic are chronological, with the most recent cases appearing first. When looking up a case, it will be necessary to glance through the more recent cases to determine if the holding has been modified or overruled. It must be emphasized that these brief summaries are presented as a reference point, not as a substitute for studying the text of the cases. A complete alphabetical index to all cases is at the end of the section.

Each Supreme Court case has three citations:

U.S. United States Reports (official published source of United States Supreme Court decisions)

L.Ed. United States Supreme Court Reports, Lawyers Edition (published by Lawyers Co-operative Publishing Company)

S.Ct. Supreme Court Reporter (published by West Publishing Company)

Current L.Ed. citations contain the reference "2d," which refers to the Second Series (volumes were numbered sequentially until 1957; then the Second Series was initiated starting with volume 1 L.Ed. 2d). The Supreme Court Reporter has one number for each term of the Supreme Court; the entire term is paginated consecutively, but for ease in binding, two or three volumes appear on the shelf (130 S.Ct. will be bound as 130, 130A, and 130B). United States Reports usually are printed later than the other two sources; an example of a citation for a case that has not appeared yet in the official reports is *Arizona v. Gant* ___ U.S. ___, 129 S.Ct. 1710, 173 L.Ed. 2d 485 (2009).

A student looking for the text of a Supreme Court decision should check to see which of these reference works the local library has. Due to the fact that Supreme Court opinions are printed verbatim in each of them, it is not necessary to look up a case in more than one source. Once this is determined, the number preceding the abbreviated title of the book is the volume number, the number following it is the page number, and the number in parentheses is the year the case was decided. For example, the citation for *Miranda v. Arizona* is 384 U.S. 436, 16 L.Ed. 2d 694, 86 S.Ct. 1602 (1966). *Miranda* can be found starting on page 436 of volume 384 of the United States Reports; page 694 of volume 16 of the United States Supreme Court Reports, Lawyers Edition, Second Series; or page 1602 of volume 86 of the Supreme Court Reporter.

U.S. SUPREME COURT SUMMARIES–TABLE OF CONTENTS

I FIRST AMENDMENT ISSUES

A. *Freedom of Speech*

Citizens United v. Federal Election Commission ___ U.S. ___, 175 L.Ed. 2d 753, 130 S.Ct. 876 (2010): The Court, in an opinion by Kennedy, portions of which were signed by 8 justices, held that a federal law that prohibited corporations and unions from using their general treasury funds to make independent expenditures for "electioneering communication" or for speech that expressly advocates the election or defeat of a candidate violated the First Amendment.

United States v. Williams 553 U.S. 285, 170 L.Ed. 2d 650, 128 S.Ct. 1830 (2008): The Court, 7–2 in an opinion by Scalia, held that 18 U.S.C. §2252A(a)(3)(B), which generally prohibits offers to provide and requests to obtain child pornography, does not violate the First Amendment. Its definitions track *New York v. Ferber,* 458 U.S. 747, and *Miller v. California,* 413 U.S. 15.

Morse et al. v. Frederick 551 U.S. 393, 168 L.Ed. 2d 290, 127 S.Ct. 2618 (2007): The Court, in an opinion by Roberts for 5 justices, held that schools may take steps to safeguard students from speech that can reasonably be regarded as encouraging illegal drug use. School officials did not violate the First Amendment by confiscating the banner reading "BONG HiTS 4 JESUS" and suspending the student.

Garcetti et al. v. Ceballos 547 U.S. 410, 164 L.Ed. 2d 689, 126 S.Ct. 195 (2006): The Court, in a 5–4 opinion by Kennedy, held that for First Amendment purposes, when public employees make statements pursuant to their official duties, they are not speaking as citizens and the Constitution does not insulate their communications from employer discipline.

Rumsfeld v. Forum for Academic and Institutional Rights, Inc. 547 U.S. 47, 164 L.Ed. 2d 156, 126 S.Ct. 1297 (2006): The Court, in an 8–0 opinion by Roberts, held that Congress could require law schools receiving federal funds to provide equal access to military recruiters without violating the schools' freedoms of speech and association. The law schools had sought to exclude recruiters because of discrimination against gays and lesbians in the military.

Federal Election Commission v. Beaumont 539 U.S. 146, 156 L.Ed. 2d 179, 123 S.Ct. 2200 (2003): The Court, 7–2 in an opinion by Souter, held the First Amendment was not violated by federal law that prohibited corporations from making "a contribution or expenditure in connection with" certain federal elections but did not prohibit corporations from establishing, administering, and soliciting contributions to a separate fund (such as PACs) to be used for political purposes.

Virginia v. Hicks 539 U.S. 113, 156 L.Ed. 2d 148, 123 S.Ct. 2191 (2003): The Court, in a unanimous opinion by Scalia, held that Richmond Redevelopment and Housing Authority's policy which authorized the Richmond police to serve notice on any person lacking "a legitimate business or social purpose" for being on the premises and to arrest any person for trespassing who remains or returns after having been so notified does not violate the First Amendment's overbreadth doctrine.

Illinois ex rel. Madigan, Attorney General of Illinois v. Telemarketing Associates, Inc. 538 U.S. 600, 155 L.Ed. 2d 793, 123 S.Ct. 1829 (2003): The Court, in a unanimous opinion by Ginsburg, held that the First Amendment does not prohibit states from maintaining fraud actions when fundraisers make false or misleading representations designed to deceive donors about how their donations will be used.

Virginia v. Black 538 U.S. 343, 155 L.Ed. 2d 535, 123 S.Ct. 1536 (2003): The Court, in an opinion by O'Connor for 5 justices, held that state laws that make it a crime to burn a cross with the intent to intimidate someone do not violate the First Amendment.

Republican Party of Minnesota v. White 536 U.S. 765, 153 L.Ed. 2d 694, 122 S.Ct. 2528 (2002): The Court, 5–4 in an opinion by Scalia, held that prohibiting candidates for judicial office from announcing their views on disputed legal or political issues violates the First Amendment.

Watchtower Bible & Tract Soc'y of New York, Inc. v. Village of Stratton 536 U.S. 150, 153 L.Ed. 2d 205, 122 S.Ct. 2080 (2002): The Court, in an opinion by Stevens for 6 justices, held that a village ordinance that made it a misdemeanor to engage in door to door advocacy without first obtaining a permit violated the First Amendment as it applies to religious proselytizing, anonymous political speech, and the distribution of handbills.

Ashcroft v. Free Speech Coalition 535 U.S. 234, 152 L.Ed. 2d 403, 122 S.Ct. 1389 (2002): The Court, in an opinion by Kennedy for 5 justices, held that provisions of the Child Pornography Prevention Act of 1996 (CPA), which extends the federal prohibition on child pornography to include "any visual depiction, including any photograph, film, video, picture, or computer or computer-generated image or picture" that "is, or appears to be, of a minor engaging in sexually explicit conduct" is overbroad and unconstitutional because it prohibits distribution of material that is not obscene under the *Miller* standard.

Thomas v. Chicago Park District 534 U.S. 316, 151 L.Ed. 2d 783, 122 S.Ct. 775 (2002): The Court, in a unanimous opinion by Scalia, held that a content-neutral permit scheme regulating uses of a public forum need not contain procedures for prompt judicial review. The ordinance involved content-neutral time, place, and manner regulations.

Lorillard Tobacco Co. v. Reilly 533 U.S. 525, 150 L.Ed. 2d 532, 121 S.Ct. 2404 (2001): The Court, in an opinion by O'Connor, parts of which represented the views of all of the justices, held that Massachusetts' regulations which prohibit advertising of smokeless tobacco and cigars within 1,000 feet of a school or playground violate the First Amendment because they were not carefully calculated to balance the costs and benefits associated with the burden on speech imposed.

Federal Election Commission v. Colorado 533 U.S. 431, 150 L.Ed. 2d 461, 121 S.Ct. 2351 (2001): The Court, 5–4 in an opinion by Souter, held the limitations on political campaign contributions both directly to candidates and to political parties in the Federal Election Campaign Act of 1971 were valid.

Good News Club v. Milford Central School 533 U.S. 98, 150 L.Ed. 2d 151, 121 S.Ct. 2093 (2001): The Court, 6–3 in an opinion by Thomas, held that the school violated the Club's free speech rights when it excluded the Club from meeting after hours at the school because its proposed activities were the equivalent of religious worship.

Bartnicki v. Vopper 532 U.S. 514, 149 L.Ed. 2d 787, 121 S.Ct. 1753 (2001): The Court, 6–3 in an opinion by Stevens, held that the First Amendment protects a radio commentator's disclosure of information, obtained by an illegal wiretap conducted by a private person who was not involved in the suit, about labor negotiations involving a local high school.

Shaw v. Murphy 532 U.S. 223, 149 L.Ed. 2d 420, 121 S.Ct. 1475 (2001): The Court, in a unanimous opinion by Thomas, held that inmates do not possess a First Amendment right to provide legal assistance to other inmates if doing so violates a prison rule that is based on a legitimate penological interest in maintaining order in the prison.

Legal Services Corporation v. Velazquez 531 U.S. 533, 149 L.Ed. 2d 63, 121 S.Ct. 1043 (2001): The Court, 5–4 in an opinion by Kennedy, held that federal legislation which prohibited Legal Services Corporation from funding any organization that represented clients in an effort to amend or otherwise challenge existing welfare law violated the First Amendment.

Hill v. Colorado 530 U.S. 703, 147 L.Ed. 2d 597, 120 S.Ct. 2480 (2000): The Court, 6–3 in an opinion by Stevens, held that a state law which made it unlawful for any person within 100 feet of a health care facility's entrance to "knowingly approach" within 8 feet of another person, without that person's consent, in order to pass "a leaflet or handbill to, display a sign to, or engage in oral protest, education, or counseling with [that] person" did not impose a undue burden on speech-related conduct. The code section was applied in a content-neutral manner.

Boy Scouts of America v. Dale 530 U.S. 640, 147 L.Ed. 2d 554, 120 S.Ct. 2446 (2000): The Court, 5–4 in an opinion by Rehnquist, held that New Jersey's attempt to apply a public accommodations law to require the Boy Scouts to admit an avowed homosexual and gay rights activist violated the organization's First Amendment right of expressive association.

California Democratic Party v. Jones 530 U.S. 567, 147 L.Ed. 2d 502, 120 S.Ct. 2402 (2000): The Court, 7–2 in an opinion by Scalia, held that California's blanket primary, which forced parties to open their candidate selection process to persons wholly unaffiliated with the party, violated a political party's First Amendment right of association.

Board of Regents, University of Wisconsin System v. Southworth 529 U.S. 217, 146 L.Ed. 2d 193, 120 S.Ct. 1346 (2000): The Court, in an opinion by Kennedy for 6 justices, held that the First Amendment permits a public university to charge students an activity fee used to fund a program to facilitate extracurricular student speech, provided that the program is viewpoint neutral.

Nixon v. Shrink Missouri Government PAC 528 U.S. 377, 145 L.Ed. 2d 886, 120 S.Ct. 897 (2000): The Court, 6–3 in an opinion by Souter, held that a Missouri statute imposing limits on contributions to candidates for state office infringed upon speech and association guarantees of the First Amendment and equal protection clause.

Greater New Orleans Broadcasting Assn., Inc. v. United States 527 U.S. 173, 144 L.Ed. 2d 161, 119 S.Ct. 1923 (1999): The Court, in an opinion by Stevens for 8 justices, held that a FCC regulation which prohibited the broadcast of advertisements for private casino gambling that was legal in the states where it was located violated the First Amendment.

Buckley v. American Constitutional Law Foundation 525 U.S. 182, 142 L.Ed. 2d 599, 119 S.Ct. 636 (1999): The Court, in an opinion by Stevens for 5 justices, held that a Colorado law violated the First Amendment by requiring ballot initiative-petition circulators to be registered voters in the state and wear identification badges bearing their names; initiative proponents were also required to report the names and addresses of all paid circulators and the amount paid to circulators.

Arkansas Educational Television Commission v. Forbes 523 U.S. 666, 140 L.Ed. 2d 875, 118 S.Ct. 1633 (1998): The Court, 6–3 in an opinion by Kennedy, held that a state-owned public television broadcast of a candidate debate that excluded independent candidates with little popular support did not violate the candidate's First Amendment rights. The decision was a reasonable, viewpoint-neutral exercise of journalistic discretion.

Schenck v. Pro-Choice Network of Western New York 519 U.S. 357, 137 L.Ed. 2d 1, 117 S.Ct. 855 (1997): The Court, in an opinion by Rehnquist for 5 justices, held that a 15-foot "fixed buffer zone" around doorways, driveways, and parking lots in an injunction against pickets at an abortion clinic did not violate the First Amendment, but a 15-foot "floating buffer zone" around any person or vehicle entering or leaving the building violated the First Amendment. The size of the buffer zones depends on the layout of the location in question.

O'Hare Truck Service, Inc. v. City of Northlake 518 U.S. 712, 135 L.Ed. 2d 874, 116 S.Ct. 2353 (1996): The Court, 7–2 in an opinion by Kennedy, held that the government cannot retaliate against a contractor or a regular provider of services for exercising the rights of political association or expression of political allegiance.

Board of County Commissioners, Wabaunsee County v. Umbehr 518 U.S. 668, 135 L.Ed. 2d 843, 116 S.Ct. 2342 (1996): The Court, 7–2 in an opinion by O'Connor, held that the

First Amendment protects independent contractors from termination of at-will government contracts in retaliation for their exercise of freedom of speech.

44 Liquormart, Inc. and Peoples Super Liquor Stores, Inc. v. Rhode Island and Rhode Island Liquor Stores Association 517 U.S. 484, 134 L.Ed. 2d 711, 116 S.Ct. 1495 (1996): The Court, in an opinion by Stevens for 6 justices, held that statutory prohibition against advertisements that provide the public with accurate information about retail prices of alcoholic beverages violates the First Amendment.

Rosenberger v. Rector and Visitors of the University of Virginia 515 U.S. 819, 132 L.Ed. 2d 700, 115 S.Ct. 2510 (1995): The Court, 5–4 in an opinion by Kennedy, held that the University of Virginia violated the First Amendment right to free speech when it paid the printing costs for publications by some student organizations but denied funding for petitioner's paper because of its religious orientation.

Florida Bar v. Went for It, Inc. 515 U.S. 618, 132 L.Ed. 2d 541, 115 S.Ct. 2371 (1995): The Court, 5–4 in an opinion by O'Connor, held that the Florida Bar's prohibition on personal injury lawyers sending targeted direct-mail solicitations to victims and their relatives for 30 days following an accident or disaster did not violate the First Amendment. The Court noted that this case involved pure commercial advertising and that the actions of lawyers have always been subject to extensive regulation by the states.

Hurley v. Irish-American Gay, Lesbian, and Bisexual Group of Boston 515 U.S. 557, 132 L.Ed. 2d 487, 115 S.Ct. 2338 (1995): The Court, in a unanimous opinion by Souter, held Massachusetts violated the First Amendment rights of private citizens who organized a St. Patrick's Day parade when it required that the organization include a group of marchers imparting a message that the organizers did not wish to convey.

McIntyre v. Ohio Elections Commission 514 U.S. 334, 131 L.Ed. 2d 426, 115 S.Ct. 1511 (1995): The Court, in an opinion by Stevens for 6 justices, held that an Ohio statute that prohibits the distribution of anonymous campaign literature violates the First Amendment.

Madsen v. Women's Health Center, Inc. 512 U.S. 753, 129 L.Ed. 2d 593, 114 S.Ct. 2516 (1994): The Court, in an opinion by Rehnquist for 6 justices, upheld an injunction on demonstrations at abortion clinics that established a 36-foot buffer zone around the clinic entrances and driveway and noise restrictions. A provision that applied to all persons acting "in concert" with protesters was upheld. The following were found unconstitutional: 36-foot buffer zone as applied to private property on the back and side of the clinic; restriction on using "images observable" to patients during clinic hours; prohibition against uninvited approaches of persons seeking the services of the clinic; and prohibition against picketing within 300 feet of the residences of clinic staff.

City of LaDue v. Gilleo 512 U.S. 43, 129 L.Ed. 2d 36, 114 S.Ct. 2038 (1994): The Court, in a unanimous opinion by Stevens, held that a content-neutral city ordinance that prohibited nearly all signs in residential areas violated the First Amendment rights of residents.

United States v. Edge Broadcasting Co. 509 U.S. 418, 125 L.Ed. 2d 345, 113 S.Ct. 2696 (1993): The Court, in an opinion by White for 7 justices, held that a statute in a state in which lotteries were illegal, which prohibited the broadcast of information about lotteries operated in states where they are legal, did not violate the First Amendment protection of commercial speech.

Wisconsin v. Mitchell 508 U.S. 47, 124 L.Ed. 2d 436, 113 S.Ct. 2194 (1993): The Court, in a unanimous decision by Rehnquist, held that a "hate crime" law that permitted enhancement of a sentence if the defendant selected the victim due to race, religion, color, disability, sexual orientation, national origin, or ancestry was not an impermissible infringement of free speech because battery, the conduct forbidden by the statute, is not protected by the First Amendment.

El Vocero de Puerto Rico v. Puerto Rico 508 U.S. 147, 124 L.Ed. 2d 60, 113 S.Ct. 2004 (1993): The Court, in a unanimous *per curiam* opinion, held that a rule requiring preliminary hearings to be held in private unless the defendant requests otherwise violates the First Amendment.

City of Cincinnati v. Discovery Network, Inc. 507 U.S. 410, 123 L.Ed. 2d 99, 113 S.Ct. 1505 (1993): The Court, 6–3 in an opinion by Stevens, held that a city ordinance prohibiting distribution of commercial publications in freestanding news racks on public property, enacted in the interest of safety and maintaining the attractive appearance of streets and sidewalks, violated First Amendment protection of commercial speech.

International Society for Krishna Consciousness v. Lee 505 U.S. 672, 120 L.Ed. 2d 541, 112 S.Ct. 2701 (1992): The Court, 5–4 in an opinion by Rehnquist, held that solicitation inside a public airport terminal could be restricted.

Lee v. International Society of Krishna Consciousness 505 U.S. 830, 120 L.Ed. 2d 669, 112 S.Ct. 2709 (1992): The Court, 5–4 in a *per curiam* opinion, held that distribution of literature within a public airport terminal could not be restricted.

R. A. V v. City of St. Paul, Minnesota 505 U.S. 377, 120 L.Ed. 2d 305, 112 S.Ct. 2538 (1992): The Court, 5–4 in an opinion by Scalia, held a "hate crime" ordinance unconstitutional because statutes attempting to regulate "fighting words" must be content-neutral.

Forsyth County, Georgia v. The Nationalist Movement 505 U.S. 123, 120 L.Ed. 2d 101, 112 S.Ct. 2395 (1992): The Court, 5–4 in an opinion by Blackmun, held that basing parade permit fees on the anticipated amount of hostility generated by the demonstration was unconstitutional because it tied the amount of the fee to the content of the speech and lacked adequate procedural safeguards.

Simon & Schuster Inc. v. Members of the New York State Crime Victims Board 502 U.S. 116, 116 L.Ed. 2d 476, 112 S.Ct. 501 (1991): The Court, 6–2 in an opinion by O'Connor, held that a Son of Sam law, which prohibited convicted criminals from profiting from publishing their stories, violates the First Amendment because it was not content-neutral.

Barnes v. Glen Theatre, Inc. 501 U.S. 560, 115 L.Ed. 2d 504, 111 S.Ct. 2456 (1991): The Court, without a majority opinion, held that a city ordinance prohibiting nude dancing as entertainment did not violate the First Amendment.

United States v. Eichman 496 U.S. 310, 110 L.Ed. 2d 287, 110 S.Ct. 2404 (1990): The Court, in an opinion by Brennan for 5 justices, held that the Flag Protection Act was unconstitutional because it criminally proscribed expressive conduct because of its likely impact.

Florida Star v. B. J. F. 491 U.S. 524, 105 L.Ed. 2d 443, 109 S.Ct. 2603 (1989): The Court, in an opinion by Marshall for 5 justices, held that imposing civil penalties for publication of the name of a sex crime victim in violation of Florida law violated the First Amendment. The Court set out a three-point test: whether the newspaper lawfully obtained truthful information about a matter of public significance; whether the sanctions protected a need to further a state interest of the highest order; and whether the statute was overbroad or underinclusive.

Johnson v. Texas 491 U.S. 397, 105 L.Ed. 2d 342, 109 S.Ct. 2533 (1989): The Court, 5–4 in an opinion by Brennan, held that a state statute prohibiting burning the United States flag in protest violated the First Amendment by restricting expressive conduct.

City of Dallas v. Stanglin 490 U.S. 19, 104 L.Ed. 2d 18, 109 S.Ct. 1591 (1989): The Court, 7–2 in an opinion by Rehnquist, held that the First Amendment does not prohibit regulation of purely social conduct. The case involved local ordinance regulating dance halls attended by juveniles.

Frisby v. Schultz 487 U.S. 474, 101 L.Ed. 2d 420, 108 S.Ct. 2495 (1988): The Court, 5–4 in an opinion by O'Connor, held that the First Amendment was not violated by a local ordinance that prohibited picketing focused on a single residence.

City of Houston v. Hill 482 U.S. 451, 96 L.Ed. 2d 398, 107 S.Ct. 2502 (1987): The Court, in an opinion by Brennan for 5 justices, held that an ordinance that made it unlawful to ". . . willfully or intentionally interrupt a city policeman . . . by verbal challenge during an investigation" facially violated the First Amendment because it did not deal with "core criminal conduct." The First Amendment protects a significant amount of verbal criticism and challenge directed at police officers.

Arcara v. Cloud Books, Inc. 478 U.S. 697, 92 L.Ed. 2d 568, 106 S.Ct. 3172 (1986): The Court, in an opinion by Burger for 6 justices, held that an adult bookstore is not immune from health laws authorizing closure of a premises found to be used as a place for prostitution and lewdness.

Los Angeles City Council v. Taxpayers for Vincent 466 U.S. 789, 80 L.Ed. 2d 772, 104 S.Ct. 2118 (1984): The Court, 6–3 in an opinion by Stevens, held that a local ordinance prohibiting posting of signs on public property during political campaigns did not violate the First Amendment.

Connick v. Myers 461 U.S. 138, 75 L.Ed. 2d 708, 103 S.Ct. 1684 (1983): The Court, 5–4, in an opinion by White, held that the First Amendment did not require a public employer to tolerate action by an employee that the employer reasonably believed would disrupt the office, undermine the authority of the employer, and destroy close working relationships within the office.

Village of Hoffman Estates v. Flipside, Hoffman Estates, Inc. 455 U.S. 489, 71 L.Ed. 2d 362, 102 S.Ct. 2023 (1982): The Court, in an opinion by Marshall for 7 justices, upheld an ordinance requiring businesses to obtain licenses if they sell any items that are "designed or marketed for use with illegal cannabis or drugs."

Village of Schaumberg v. Citizens for Better Environment 444 U.S. 620, 63 L.Ed. 2d 73, 100 S.Ct. 826 (1980): The Court, 8–1 in an opinion by White, held that an ordinance that barred solicitation of charitable contributions unless at least 75% of the money collected went to charitable purposes violated the First Amendment.

Hynes v. The Mayor and Council of the Borough of Oradell 425 U.S. 610, 48 L.Ed. 2d 243, 96 S.Ct. 1755 (1976): The Court, in an opinion by Burger for 5 justices, held that cities may regulate soliciting and canvassing by the use of narrowly drawn ordinances.

Greer v. Spock 424 U.S. 828, 47 L.Ed. 2d 505, 96 S.Ct. 1211 (1976): The Court, 6–2 in an opinion by Stewart, held that civilians do not have a generalized constitutional right to make political speeches or distribute political leaflets at a military post.

Gooding v. Wilson 405 U.S. 518, 31 L.Ed. 2d 408, 92 S.Ct. 1103 (1972): The Court, 6–2 in an opinion by Brennan, held the Court held a statute unconstitutional that made it an offense to use "opprobrious words or abusive language tending to cause a breach of the peace" but did not limited it to "fighting words."

Brandenburg v. Ohio Overruled *Whitney v. California* (1927). 395 U.S. 444, 23 L.Ed. 2d 430, 89 S.Ct. 1827 (1969): The Court, in a *per curiam* opinion, held the Ohio Criminal Syndicalism Act unconstitutional because it punished "advocacy" of force or lawlessness that is neither directed at inciting or producing imminent lawless action nor likely to incite or produce such action.

Shuttleworth v. City of Birmingham 394 U.S. 147, 22 L.Ed. 2d 162, 89 S.Ct. 935 (1969): The Court, in an opinion by Stewart, found an ordinance that conferred "virtually unbridled and absolute power to prohibit any 'parade, procession,' or 'demonstration' on the city's streets or public ways" unconstitutional on its face

Cameron v. Johnson 390 U.S. 611, 20 L.Ed. 2d 182, 88 S.Ct. 1335 (1966): The Court held, 7–2, that picketing cannot be made a crime, but blocking the entrance to a public building can.

Cox v. Louisiana 379 U.S. 536, 13 L.Ed. 2d 471, 85 S.Ct. 453 (1965): The Court, 6–3 in an opinion by Goldberg, rejected the notion that the First and Fourteenth Amendments afford the same kind of freedom to those who would communicate ideas by conduct such as patroling, marching, and picketing and those who communicate ideas by pure speech.

Poulos v. New Hampshire 345 U.S. 195, 97 L.Ed. 1105, 73 S.Ct. 760 (1953): The Court held that a state or municipality may require a permit to conduct a meeting in a public park.

Dennis v. United States 341 U.S. 494, 95 L.Ed. 1137, 71 S.Ct. 857 (1951): The Court held that teaching and advocating the overthrow of the government is protected by the First Amendment except when it advocates "a rule of principle to incite persons to such action, all with the intent to cause the overthrow or destruction of the Government of the United States by force and violence as speedily as circumstances will permit."

Kovacs v. Cooper 336 U.S. 77, 93 L.Ed. 513, 69 S.Ct. 448 (1949): The Court held that the state or municipality may prohibit the operation of sound trucks and loud speakers on public streets.

Chaplinsky v. New Hampshire 315 U.S. 568, 86 L.Ed. 1031, 62 S.Ct. 766 (1942): The Court held unanimously that states may punish "fighting words."

Cox v. New Hampshire 312 U.S. 569, 85 L.Ed. 1049, 61 S.Ct. 762 (1941): The Court held unanimously that states may regulate parades incident to regulating streets for traffic purposes.

Gitlow v. New York 268 U.S. 652, 69 L.Ed. 1138, 45 S.Ct. 625 (1925): The Court upheld the validity of New York's Criminal Anarchy Act of 1902.

Schenck v. United States 249 U.S. 47, 63 L.Ed. 470, 39 S.Ct. 247 (1919): Holmes enunciated his famous clear-and-present danger test. The well-known words about shouting "Fire!" in a crowded theater are used to illustrate a situation in which free speech may be limited.

B. Freedom of the Press

Gentile v. State Bar of Nevada 501 U.S. 1030, 115 L.Ed. 2d 888, 111 S.Ct. 2720 (1991): The Court, 5–4 in an opinion by Rehnquist, held that a rule that prohibited attorneys from making statements to the press that posed a substantial likelihood of material prejudice to the case did not violate the First Amendment.

Florida Star v. B. J. F. 491 U.S. 524, 105 L.Ed. 2d 443, 109 S.Ct. 2603 (1989): The Court, in an opinion by Marshall for 5 justices, held that imposing civil penalties for publication of the name of the victim of a sex crime in violation of Florida law violated the First Amendment.

Press-Enterprise Company v. Superior Court of California for the County of Riverside 478 U.S. 1, 92 L.Ed. 2d 1, 106 S.Ct. 2735 (1986): The Court, in an opinion by Burger for 7 justices, held that any limitation on access to the preliminary hearing must be narrowly tailored to serve First Amendment interests.

Press-Enterprise Company v. Superior Court of California, Riverside County 464 U.S. 501, 78 L.Ed. 2d 629, 104 S.Ct. 819 (1984): The Court, in an opinion by Burger for 8 justices, held that closure of *voir dire* of the jury may be allowed rarely and only on a showing of cause that outweighs the value of openness.

Richmond Newspapers, Inc. v. Virginia 448 U.S. 555, 65 L.Ed. 2d 973, 100 S.Ct. 2814 (1980): 7 justices, although unable to agree upon an opinion, held that the trial judge's order, at request of defendant and without objection by the prosecution, that a murder trial be closed to the public and press violated the First Amendment.

Gannett Co., Inc. v. DePasquale 443 U.S. 368, 61 L.Ed. 2d 608, 99 S.Ct. 2898 (1979): The Court, in an opinion by Stewart for

5 justices, held that where the trial judge had adequately considered the balance of the defendant's right to a fair trial against the right of the press and public to attend a suppression hearing, the order closing the hearing to the press and public was constitutional.

Zurcher v. The Stanford Daily 436 U.S. 547, 56 L.Ed. 2d 525, 98 S.Ct. 1970 (1978): The Court, 5–3 in an opinion by White, held First Amendment protections of the press did not require that evidence in the hands of third-party press be obtained by the use of subpoena *duces tecum* rather than a search warrant.

Landmark Communications, Inc. v. Virginia 435 U.S. 829, 56 L.Ed. 2d 1, 98 S.Ct. 1535 (1978): The Court, in an opinion by Burger for 6 justices, held that the First Amendment did not prohibit punishing members of the press for divulging or publishing truthful information regarding an official commission's confidential proceedings.

Oklahoma Publishing Company v. District Court in and for Oklahoma County, Oklahoma 430 U.S. 308, 51 L.Ed. 2d 355, 97 S.Ct. 1045 (1977): The Court, in a unanimous *per curiam* opinion, held that a pretrial order that enjoined members of the news media from publishing, broadcasting, or disseminating in any manner the name or picture of a 11-year-old defendant in a juvenile court case violated the free press guarantee of the First and Fourteenth Amendments.

Nebraska Press Association v. Stuart 427 U.S. 539, 49 L.Ed. 2d 683, 96 S.Ct. 2791 (1976): The Court, in an opinion by Burger for 5 justices, held that a court order prohibiting the publication or broadcasting of accounts of confessions or admissions made by the accused or facts strongly implicating him, was unconstitutional. The trial judge had not adequately considered alternatives to prior restraint that might have mitigated the adverse effect of pretrial publicity. Prohibition on reporting and commenting on court proceedings held in public is clearly invalid.

Pell v. Procunier 417 U.S. 817, 41 L.Ed. 2d 495, 94 S.Ct. 2800 (1974): The Court, 6–3 in an opinion by Stewart, held that denying the press the right to conduct face-to-face interviews with inmates did not violate the First Amendment because other avenues were available to the media.

Branzburg v. Hayes 408 U.S. 665, 33 L.Ed. 2d 626, 92 S.Ct. 2646 (1972): The Court, 5–4 in an opinion by White, held that news reporters have no constitutional privilege to refuse to appear before a grand jury and identify their sources or information received in confidence.

C. Obscenity and Related Issues

Ashcroft v. American Civil Liberties Union et al. 542 U.S. 656, 159 L.Ed. 2d 690, 124 S.Ct. 2783 (2004): The Court, 5–4 in an opinion by Kennedy, enjoined enforcement of the Child Online Protection Act (COPA), 47 U.S. C. §231, which, among other things, imposes a $50,000 fine and 6 months in prison for the knowing posting for "commercial purposes" Internet content that is "harmful to minors," but provides an affirmative defense to commercial Web speakers who restrict access to prohibited materials by "requiring use of a credit card" or "any other reasonable measures that are feasible under available technology." Respondents asserted that blocking and filtering software is a less restrictive alternative, and the government had not shown it would be likely to disprove that contention at trial.

City of Littleton, Colorado v. Z. J. Gifts D-4, L.L.C., dba Christal's 541 U.S. 774, 159 L.Ed. 2d 84, 124 S.Ct. 2219 (2004): The Court, in an opinion by Breyer for 5 justices, held that ordinary "judicial review" rules suffice to assure a prompt judicial decision on the denial of a an "adult business" license as long as the courts remain sensitive to the need to prevent First Amendment harms and administer those procedures accordingly. No separate administrative review is required under these circumstances.

United States v. American Library Association, Inc. 539 U.S. 194, 156 L.Ed. 2d 221, 123 S.Ct. 2297 (2003): The Court, without a majority opinion, held that the federal Children's Internet Protection Act, which requires all libraries that receive federal assistance in order to provide Internet service to their clients to install software to block obscene or pornographic images and to prevent minors from accessing material harmful to them, does not violate the First Amendment. Adults could ask the librarian to disable the filters.

United States v. Playboy Entertainment Group, Inc. 529 U.S. 803, 146 L.Ed. 2d 865, 120 S.Ct. 1878 (2000): The Court, 5–4 in an opinion by Kennedy, held that Section 505 of the Telecommunications Act of 1996, which required cable television operators providing channels "primarily dedicated to sexually oriented programming" either to "fully scramble or otherwise fully block" those channels or to limit their transmission to between 10:00 P.M. and 6:00 A.M. when children are unlikely to be viewing, violated the First Amendment because it was not the least restrictive means for addressing the problem.

Reno v. American Civil Liberties Union 521 U.S. 844, 138 L.Ed. 2d 874, 117 S.Ct. 2329 (1997): The Court, in an opinion by Stevens for 7 justices, held that portions of the Communications Decency Act of 1996 that attempted to protect minors from dissemination of "indecent" and "patently offensive" communications on the Internet violated the First Amendment because the act infringed upon the free speech rights of adults.

Osborne v. Ohio 495 U.S. 103, 109 L.Ed. 2d 98, 110 S.Ct. 1691 (1990): The Court, 6–3 in an opinion by White, held that states have sufficient interest in the prevention of sexual exploitation of children to regulate possession and viewing of child pornography. A statute must require *scienter* and not be overbroad; mere nudity cannot be banned.

New York v. P. J. Video 475 U.S. 868, 89 L.Ed. 2d 871, 106 S.Ct. 1610 (1986): The Court, in an opinion by Rehnquist for 6 justices, held that search warrants for allegedly obscene materials do not require a higher standard of probable cause than for items not protected by the First Amendment.

City of Renton v. Playtime Theaters 475 U.S. 41, 89 L.Ed. 2d 29, 106 S.Ct. 925 (1986): The Court, 6–3 in an opinion by Rehnquist, held that the First Amendment was not violated by a zoning ordinance that required adult movie theaters to be at least 1,000 feet from any residence, church, park, or school.

New York v. Ferber 458 U.S. 747, 73 L.Ed. 2d 1113, 102 S.Ct. 3348 (1982): The Court, in an opinion by White for 5 justices, held that child pornography is unprotected by the First Amendment if it involves *scienter* and a visual depiction of sexual conduct by children without serious literary, artistic, political, or scientific value.

Cooper v. Mitchell Brothers' Santa Ana Theater 454 U.S. 90, 70 L.Ed. 2d 262, 102 S.Ct. 172 (1981): The Court, 6–3 in a *per curiam* opinion, held that states were free to decide whether or not to use the beyond-a-reasonable-doubt standard of proof in civil obscenity cases such as public nuisance abatement of theaters showing obscene movies.

Young v. American Mini Theaters, Inc. 427 U.S. 50, 49 L.Ed. 2d 310, 96 S.Ct. 2440 (1976): The Court, 5–4, in an opinion by Stevens, held the city's interest in regulating the use of property for commercial purposes was adequate to support licensing and zoning restrictions that would not permit an adult theater to be located within 1,000 feet of any two other "regulated uses" (10 different kinds of establishments in addition to adult theaters were considered to be "regulated uses").

Miller v. California 413 U.S. 15, 37 L.Ed. 2d 419, 93 S.Ct. 2607 (1973): The Court, in an opinion by Burger for 5 justices, held that the First Amendment does not protect obscene matter. This case established the test for obscenity: the average person, applying contemporary community standards, would find that the work, taken as a whole, appealed to prurient interest; the work depicted or described, in a patently offensive way, sexual conduct specifically defined by the applicable state law, as written or authoritatively construed; and, the work, taken as a whole, lacked serious literary, artistic, political, or scientific value.

D. Freedom of Religion

Pleasant Grove City, Utah v. Summum ___ U.S. ___, 172 L.Ed. 2d 853, 129 S.Ct. 1125 (2009): The Court, in an opinion by Alito for 8 justices, held that the placement of a display of the Ten Commandments along with other permanent monument in a public park is a form of government speech and is therefore not subject to scrutiny under the Free Speech Clause. The display does not need to represent all points of view. This case does not address application of the Establishment Clause.

Gonzales v. O Centro Espirita Beneficente Uniao Do Vegetal et al. 546 U.S. 418, 163 L.Ed. 2d 1017, 126 S.Ct. 1211 (2006): The Court, 8–0 in an opinion by Roberts, held that the Religious Freedom Restoration Act of 1993 (RFRA) requires the Government to demonstrate that the compelling interest test is satisfied through application of the challenged law to the particular claimant whose sincere exercise of religion is being substantially burdened; this test cannot be met by a categorical showing that the Controlled Substance Act applies.

McCreary County, Kentucky, et al. v. American Civil Liberties Union of Kentucky et al. 545 U.S. 844, 162 L.Ed. 2d 729, 125 S.Ct. 2722 (2005): The Court, 5–4 in an opinion by Souter, held that when determining if a government entity has violated the Establishment Clause by posting the Ten Commandments in the courthouse, scrutinizing purpose makes practical sense where an understanding of official objective emerges from readily discoverable fact set forth in a statute's text, legislative history, and implementation or comparable official act. Courts may look to the legislative body's prior attempts to enact similar ordinances when determining intent for enacting the current law.

Van Orden v. Perry 545 U.S. 677, 162 L.Ed. 2d 607, 125 S.Ct. 2854 (2005): The Court, 'n a plurality opinion by Rehnquist, held that isplay of the Ten Commandments on the state capitol grounds in an area containing numerous other historical monuments did not violate the Establishment Clause.

Cutter et al. v. Wilkinson 544 U.S. 709, 161 L.Ed. 2d 1020, 125 S.Ct. 2113 (2005): The Court, in a unanimous opinion by Ginsberg, held that Section 3 of the Religious Land Use and Institutionalized Persons Act of 2000 (42 U.S. C. §2000cc -1(a)(1)-(2)) does not violate the Establishment Clause of the First Amendment. The act does not elevate accommodation of religious observances over a penal institution's need to maintain order and safety.

Locke v. Davey 540 U.S. 712, 158 L.Ed. 2d 1, 124 S.Ct. 1307 (2004): The Court, 7–2 in an opinion by Rehnquist, held that a state's exclusion of the pursuit of a devotional theology degree from its otherwise inclusive scholarship aid program does not violate the Free Exercise Clause.

Zelman v. Simon-Harris 536 U.S. 639, 153 L.Ed. 2d 604, 122 S.Ct. 2460 (2002): The Court, 5–4 in an opinion by Rehnquist, held that an Ohio school voucher program which allowed parents to select private schools for their children did not violate the Establishment Clause even though 96% of the students participating in the program were enrolled in religiously affiliated schools. The opinion emphasized that the parents, not the government, selected the schools.

Mitchell v. Helms 530 U.S. 793, 147 L.Ed. 2d 660, 120 S.Ct. 2530 (2000): The Court, without a majority opinion, held that the fact that school vouchers were used to attend a high school with a religious affiliation did not mean the program involved violated the Establishment Clause.

Santa Fe Independent School District v. Doe 520 U.S. 290, 147 L.Ed. 2d 295, 120 S.Ct. 2266 (2000): The Court, 6–3 in an opinion by Stevens, held that the school district's policy of permitting student-led, student-initiated prayer at football games violated the Establishment Clause.

City of Boerne v. Flores 521 U.S. 507, 138 L.Ed. 2d 624, 117 S.Ct. 2157 (1997): The

Court, 6–3 in an opinion by Kennedy, invalidated the Religious Freedom Restoration Act of 1993. It was seen as disrupting the separation of powers created by the Constitution because it prohibited "government" from "substantially burdening" a person's exercise of religion even if the burden results from a rule of general applicability unless the government can demonstrate the burden (1) is in furtherance of a compelling governmental interest; and (2) is the least restrictive means of furthering that compelling governmental interest.

Agostini v. Felton overruled *Aguilar v. Felton* (1985) and portions of *School District of Grand Rapids v. Ball* (1985) 521 U.S. 203, 138 L.Ed. 2d 391, 117 S.Ct. 1997 (1997): The Court, 5–4 in an opinion by O'Connor, held that the use of public school employees for remedial education in private schools as part of the Elementary and Secondary Education Act of 1965 did not violate the establishment clause of the First Amendment.

Church of the Lukumi Babalu Aye, Inc. v. City of Hialeah 508 U.S. 520, 124 L.Ed. 2d 472, 113 S.Ct. (1993): The Court, in an opinion by Kennedy relevant parts of which represented the views of 7 justices, held that an ordinance that subjects a person to criminal punishment if he/she "unnecessarily or cruelly . . . kills any animal" violated the Free Exercise Clause because it was both overbroad and underinclusive; analogous nonreligious conduct was not covered. The Court found that the object of the ordinance was suppression of the central element of the Santeria worship service.

Employment Division, Department of Human Resources of Oregon v. Smith 494 U.S. 872, 108 L.Ed. 2d 876, 110 S.Ct. 1595 (1990): The Court, in an opinion by Scalia for 5 justices, held defendant could be denied unemployment compensation when he was fired based on use of peyote in violation of Oregon's law. The Court rejected defendant's argument that the ingestion of peyote for sacramental purposes at a ceremony of the Native American Church was protected by the Free Exercise Clause.

II SECOND AMENDMENT ISSUES

District of Columbia v. Heller ___ U.S. ___, 171 L.Ed. 2d 637, 128 S.Ct. 2783 (2008): The Court, 5–4 in an opinion by Scalia, held that the Second Amendment protects an individual's right to possess a firearm unconnected with service in a militia. A statute that totally prohibits use of a firearm for self-defense in one's own home is unconstitutional. Requirements that a gun be disassembled or have a trigger lock in place at all times makes the use of a firearm in self defense impossible and therefore is unconstitutional.

III FOURTH AMENDMENT ISSUES

A. Aerial Surveillance

Florida v. Riley 488 U.S. 445, 102 L. Ed. 2d 835, 109 S. Ct. 693 (1989): The Court, in a plurality opinion by White, held that the defendant could not claim a reasonable expectation of privacy when a police officer observed marijuana growing through a missing panel in the roof of a greenhouse behind a mobile home from a helicopter flying at 400 feet in navigable airways.

Dow Chemical Company v. United States 476 U.S. 227, 90 L.Ed. 2d 226, 106 S.Ct. 1819 (1986): The Court, in an opinion by Burger for 5 justices, held that the Environmental Protection Agency's aerial photography of Dow's 2,000-acre plant complex from navigable airspace without a warrant was not a search under the Fourth Amendment.

California v. Ciraolo 476 U.S. 207, 90 L.Ed. 2d 210, 106 S.Ct. 1809 (1986): The Court, in an opinion by Burger for 5 justices, held that the Fourth Amendment was not violated by aerial observation without a warrant from an altitude of 1,000 feet of a fenced-in backyard within the curtilage of a home.

B. Arrest and Booking

Arizona v. Gant ___ U.S. ___, 173 L.Ed. 2d 485; 129 S.Ct. 1710 (2009): The Court, 5–4 in an opinion by Stevens, restricted police searches of the passenger compartment a vehicle incident to a recent occupant's arrest to situations where there is a reasonable belief that the arrestee might access the vehicle at the time of the search or that the vehicle contains evidence of the offense for which the person was arrested.

Devenpeck v. Alford 543 U.S. 146, 160 L.Ed. 2d 537, 125 S.Ct. 588 (2004): The Court, in a unanimous opinion by Scalia, held that an arrest is valid if there is probable cause to believe the suspect committed a crime even though it is not related to the reason the suspect was originally detained.

Thornton v. United States 541 U.S. 615, 124 S.Ct. 2127, 158 L.Ed. 2d 905 (2004): The Court, 7–2 in an opinion by Rehnquist, held that an officer has the right to search the passenger compartment of a vehicle incident to the arrest of a person who exited the vehicle moments before the encounter with the police and was next to the vehicle when arrested.

Maryland v. Pringle 540 U.S. 366, 157 L.Ed. 2d 769, 124 S.Ct. 795 (2003): The Court, in a unanimous opinion by Rehnquist, held that where there is a reasonable inference from the facts that any or all of the car's occupants had knowledge of cocaine found in the vehicle compartment and they all exercised dominion and control over it, there is probable cause to believe each committed the crime of possession of cocaine.

Atwater v. City of Lago Vista 532 U.S. 318, 149 L.Ed. 2d 549, 121 S.Ct. 1536 (2001): The Court, 5–4 in an opinion by Souter, held the Fourth Amendment does not forbid a warrantless custodial arrest authorized by state law for a minor criminal offense, such as a misdemeanor seatbelt violation punishable only by a fine.

Wilson v. Layne 526 U.S. 603, 143 L.Ed. 2d 818, 119 S.Ct. 1692 (1999): The Court, in an opinion by Rehnquist that was unanimous in part, held that plaintiffs' Fourth Amendment privacy rights were violated when the media were allowed to accompany officers executing an arrest warrant in his home.

Knowles v. Iowa 525 U.S. 113, 142 L.Ed. 2d 92, 119 S.Ct. 484 (1998): The Court, in a unanimous opinion by Rehnquist, held that when there is no custodial arrest, reasonable suspicion of danger to the officer is required to justify any type of search when issuing a traffic citation.

Minnesota v. Olson 495 U.S. 91, 109 L.Ed. 2d 85, 110 S.Ct. 1684 (1990): The Court, in an opinion by White for 7 justices, held that the suspect's rights under the Fourth Amendment were violated by police entry, without a warrant or consent, into a home where the suspect was an overnight guest.

Maryland v. Buie 494 U.S. 325, 108 L.Ed. 2d 276, 110 S.Ct. 1093 (1990): The Court, in an opinion by White for 7 justices, held that incident to an arrest the officers could, as a precautionary matter and without probable cause or reasonable suspicion, look for people hiding in closets and other places immediately adjoining the place of arrest. To go beyond that area, there must be reasonable suspicion that the area to be swept harbors an individual posing a danger to those on the scene.

Welsh v. Wisconsin 466 U.S. 740, 80 L.Ed. 2d 732, 104 S.Ct. 2091 (1984): The Court, in an opinion by Brennan joined by 5 other justices, held that absent exigent circumstances, a warrantless nighttime entry into the home of an individual to arrest him for a civil, nonjailable traffic offense is prohibited by the Fourth Amendment.

Illinois v. Lafayette 462 U.S. 640, 77 L.Ed. 65, 103 S.Ct. 2605 (1983): The Court, in an opinion by Burger for 7 justices, held that routine inventory and search of any container or article in the possession of a person during booking at a police station was reasonable.

Washington v. Chrisman 455 U.S. 1, 70 L.Ed. 2d 778, 102 S.Ct. 812 (1982): The Court, 6–3 in an opinion by Burger, held that a police officer has the right to monitor the movements of a person following his/her arrest.

Stegald v. United States 451 U.S. 204, 68 L.Ed. 2d 38, 101 S.Ct. 1642 (1981): The Court, in an opinion by Marshall joined by 5 justices, held that defendant's right of privacy had been invaded when, absent consent or exigent circumstances, officers entered his house to search for another person whom they had a warrant to arrest.

Payton v. New York 445 U.S. 573, 63 L.Ed. 2d 639, 100 S.Ct. 1371 (1980): The Court, 6–3 in an opinion by Stevens, held that, except in exigent circumstances, police are prohibited from making warrantless, nonconsensual entry into a suspect's home in order to make a felony arrest.

Michigan v. DeFillipo 443 U.S. 31, 61 L.Ed. 2d 343, 99 S.Ct. 2627 (1979): The Court, 6–3 in an opinion by Burger, held that warrantless arrest in good-faith reliance on an ordinance was valid regardless of fact that ordinance was later held to be unconstitutional.

Pennsylvania v. Mimms 434 U.S. 106, 54 L.Ed. 2d 331, 98 S.Ct. 330 (1977): The Court, 6–3 in a *per curiam* opinion, held that when a police officer lawfully stops a motorist for a traffic violation, the officer may order the motorist out of the car. "Pat down" search for weapons requires reasonable suspicion that the person is armed.

United States v. Santana 427 U.S. 38, 49 L.Ed. 2d 300, 96 S.Ct. 2406 (1976): The Court, 7–2 in an opinion by Rehnquist, held that a person in the threshold of his/her house was in a public place and could be arrested without a warrant. Police may pursue suspect into house if suspect attempts to avoid arrest.

United States v. Watson 423 U.S. 411, 46 L.Ed. 2d 598, 96 S.Ct. 820 (1976): The Court, in an opinion by White joined by 4 justices, held that a felony arrest could be made without a warrant in a public place even though there were no exigent circumstances.

United States v. Edwards 415 U.S. 800, 39 L.Ed. 2d 771, 94 S.Ct. 1234 (1974): The Court, 5–4 in an opinion by White, held that sending clothing worn at the time of booking to a crime laboratory for examination did not violate the suspect's rights.

Gustafson v. Florida 414 U.S. 260, 38 L.Ed. 2d 456, 94 S.Ct. 488 (1973): The Court,

6–3 in an opinion by Rehnquist, held that a full search incident to a custodial arrest is allowed even though the officer did not fear for his/her own safety and no physical evidence of the offense could be revealed by the search.

United States v. Robinson 414 U.S. 218, 38 L.Ed. 2d 427, 94 S.Ct. 467 (1973): The Court upheld, 6–3, searches incident to custodial arrests for traffic code violations. Court rejected argument that a search incident to an arrest must be based on belief that search will produce weapon, evidence of crime, or contraband.

Whiteley v. Warden 401 U.S. 560, 28 L.Ed. 2d 306, 91 S.Ct. 1031 (1971): The Court, 6–3 in an opinion by Harlan, held that a police radio broadcast based on an affidavit insufficient for issuance of an arrest warrant cannot furnish probable cause to arrest the suspect described in the broadcast.

Vale v. Louisiana 399 U.S. 30, 26 L.Ed. 2d 409, 90 S.Ct. 1969 (1970): The Court, 7–2 in an opinion by Stewart, held that an arrest outside the house, even if made on the front steps as the suspect was about to enter the house, did not justify the search of the house as part of the search incident to the arrest.

Chimel v. California overruled *Harris v. United States* (1947) and *United States v. Rabinowitz* (1950) 395 U.S. 752, 23 L.Ed. 2d 685, 89 S.Ct. 2034 (1969): The Court, 6–2 in an opinion by Stewart, held that a search incident to a lawful arrest in a home must be limited to "the area into which an arrestee might reach in order to grab a weapon or other evidentiary items."

Davis v. Mississippi 394 U.S. 721, 22 L.Ed. 2d 676, 89 S.Ct. 1394 (1969) held that fingerprints taken as a result of an illegal arrest were inadmissible in evidence.

Schmerber v. California 384 U.S. 757, 16 L.Ed. 2d 908, 86 S.Ct. 1826 (1966): The Court, 5–4 in an opinion by Brennan, held that in a driving under the influence case the prosecution can introduce the analysis of a blood sample taken without the consent of the accused or a warrant without violating his Fourth, Fifth, Sixth, and Fourteenth Amendment rights.

C. Border Searches

United States v. Flores-Montano 541 U.S. 149, 158 L.Ed. 2d 311, 124 S.Ct. 1582 (2004): The Court, in a unanimous opinion by Rehnquist, held that federal customs agents had authority to remove, disassemble, and reassemble the fuel tank of a vehicle entering the United States.

United States v. Arvizu 534 U.S. 266, 151 L.Ed. 2d 740, 122 S.Ct. 744 (2002): The Court, in a unanimous opinion by Rehnquist, held that a border patrol agent was allowed to stop a vehicle on a rural road based on reasonable suspicion that the occupants of the vehicle were engaging in illegal activities related to smuggling.

United States v. Montoya de Hernandez 473 U.S. 531, 87 L.Ed. 2d 381, 105 S.Ct. 3304 (1985): The Court, in an opinion by Rehnquist for 6 justices, held that detention of a traveler at the international border, beyond the scope of the routine Customs search and inspection, is justified at its inception if Customs' agents, reasonably suspect that the traveler is smuggling contraband in his/her alimentary canal. Incommunicado detention for almost 16 hours prior to seeking a search warrant to allow suspect, who refused to be X-rayed, to have a bowel movement was justified under the circumstances.

Immigration and Naturalization Service v. Delgado 466 U.S. 210, 80 L.Ed. 2d 247, 104 S.Ct. 1758 (1984): The Court, in an opinion by Rehnquist for 6 justices, held that INS "factory surveys" did not constitute detention or seizure under the Fourth Amendment. "Factory surveys" consisted of entering factories, pursuant to a warrant, and questioning employees regarding immigration or citizenship status.

United States v. Villamonte-Marquez 462 U.S. 579, 77 L.Ed. 2d 22, 103 S.Ct. 2573 (1983): The Court, 6–3 in an opinion by Rehnquist, held that the Fourth Amendment is not violated when Customs' agents board vessels to conduct document checks without suspicion that a statute is being violated.

United States v. Cortez 449 U.S. 411, 66 L.Ed. 2d 621, 101 S.Ct. 690 (1981): The Court, in an opinion by Burger for 7 justices, held that border patrol officers investigating a specific person for smuggling aliens into the United States could stop a vehicle based on reasonable suspicion for the purpose of questioning the occupants about their citizenship, immigration status, and the reasons for their presence in the area.

United States v. Ramsey 431 U.S. 606, 52 L.Ed. 2d 617, 97 S.Ct. 1972 (1977): The Court, in an opinion by Rehnquist for 6 justices, held that customs officers could open and search mail entering the United States without probable cause or a warrant.

United States v. Martinez-Fuerte 428 U.S. 543, 49 L.Ed. 2d 1116, 96 S.Ct. 3074 (1976): The Court, in an opinion by Powell for 7 justices, held that the Fourth Amendment was not violated by stops of vehicles at permanent border patrol checkpoints for brief questioning of their occupants regarding immigration status, even though there was no reason to believe that the particular vehicle contained illegal aliens.

United States v. Brignoni-Ponce 422 U.S. 873, 45 L.Ed. 2d 607, 95 S.Ct. 2574 (1975): The Court, in an opinion by Powell, held that a car may be briefly stopped at roving border patrol checkpoints for questioning and investigation based on reasonable suspicion that it may contain aliens who are illegally in the country. The officer may question the driver and passengers about their citizenship and immigration status and may ask them to explain suspicious circumstances. Any further detention or search must be based on consent or probable cause.

United States v. Ortiz 422 U.S. 891, 45 L.Ed. 2d 623, 95 S.Ct. 2585 (1975): The Court, in an opinion by Powell for 6 justices, held that the search of a car at a fixed checkpoint requires consent, probable cause, or a warrant.

Almeida-Sanchez v. United States 413 U.S. 266, 37 L.Ed. 2d 596, 93 S.Ct. 2535 (1973): The Court, in an opinion by Steward for 5 justices, held that a search of an automobile at a roving border patrol checkpoint without a search warrant, consent, or probable cause to believe there was evidence in the automobile violated the Fourth Amendment.

D. Car and Other Vehicle Searches

Arizona v. Gant ___ U.S. ___, 173 L.Ed. 2d 485, 129 S.Ct. 1710 (2009): The Court, 5–4 in an opinion by Stevens, restricted police searches of the passenger compartment of a vehicle incident to a recent occupant's arrest to situations where there is a reasonable belief that the arrestee might access the vehicle at the time of the search or that the vehicle contains evidence of the offense for which the person was arrested.

Brendlin v. California 551 U.S. 249, 168 L.Ed. 2d 132, 127 S.Ct. 2400 (2007): The Court, in a unanimous opinion by Souter, held that when police make a traffic stop both passengers and the driver are seized for Fourth Amendment purposes and may challenge the stop's constitutionality.

Thornton v. United States 541 U.S. 615, 158 L.Ed. 2d 905, 124 S.Ct. 2127 (2004): The Court, 7–2 in an opinion by Rehnquist, held that an officer has the right to search the passenger compartment of a vehicle incident to the arrest of a person who exited the vehicle moments before the encounter with the police and was next to the vehicle when arrested.

Florida v. White 526 U.S. 559, 143 L.Ed. 2d 748, 119 S.Ct. 1555 (1999): The Court, 7–2 in an opinion by Thomas, held that the Fourth Amendment does not require the police to obtain a search warrant before seizing an automobile from a public place when there is probable cause to believe that the automobile is subject to forfeiture.

Wyoming v. Houghton 526 U.S. 295, 143 L.Ed. 2d 408, 119 S.Ct. 1297 (1999): The Court, 7–2 in an opinion by Scalia, held that when police officers conduct a probable cause search of a car, the officers may inspect property found in the car that belong to passengers if, based on its size and shape, it is capable of concealing the items that are the object of the search.

Pennsylvania v. Labron 518 U.S. 938, 135 L.Ed. 2d 1031, 116 S.Ct. 2485 (1996): The Court, 7–2 in a *per curiam* opinion, held that an officer's right to search a car without a warrant was not contingent upon there being exigent circumstances necessitating rapid action.

California v. Acevedo overruled *Arkansas v. Sanders* (1979) 500 U.S. 565, 114 L.Ed. 2d 619, 111 S.Ct. 1982 (1991): The Court, 5–4 in an opinion by Blackmun, held that police may conduct a warrantless search of a closed container in a vehicle if there is probable cause that it contains evidence.

Florida v. Wells 495 U.S. 1, 109 L.Ed. 2d 1, 110 S.Ct. 1632 (1990): The Court, in an opinion by Rehnquist for 5 justices, held that the search of closed containers during the inventory of an automobile is only valid if the law enforcement agency has a policy regulating the actions of its officers in this type of situation.

Colorado v. Bertine 479 U.S. 367, 93 L.Ed. 2d 739, 107 S.Ct. 738 (1987): The Court, in an opinion by Rehnquist for 7 justices, held that the search of a closed backpack found in an impounded vehicle during a warrantless inventory search of the vehicle did not violate the Fourth Amendment.

New York v. Class 475 U.S. 106, 89 L.Ed. 2d 81, 106 S.Ct. 960 (1986): The Court, in an opinion by O'Connor for 5 justices, held that the Fourth Amendment was not violated by a police officer's finding a gun while reaching into a car to move papers obscuring the vehicle's identification number (VIN).

California v. Carney 471 U.S. 386, 85 L.Ed. 2d 406, 105 S.Ct. 2066 (1985): The Court, in an opinion by Burger for 6 justices, held that readily mobile motor homes fall under the vehicle exception to the Fourth Amendment.

Michigan v. Long 463 U.S. 1032, 77 L.Ed. 2d 1201, 103 S.Ct. 3469 (1983): The Court, in an opinion by O'Connor for 5 justices, held that during a stop of a vehicle on reasonable suspicion an officer may search of the passenger compartment, limited to those areas in which a weapon may be, if the officer reasonably believes that the suspect is dangerous and may gain immediate control of weapons.

New York v. Belton 453 U.S. 454, 69 L.Ed. 2d 768, 101 S.Ct. 2860 (1981): The Court, in an opinion by Stewart for 5 justices, held that incident to a lawful custodial arrest of the occupant of a vehicle, an officer may search the entire passenger compartment including glove compartment, console, luggage, and clothing. Decision was limited by *Arizona v. Gant* (2009).

South Dakota v. Opperman 428 U.S. 364, 49 L.Ed. 2d 1000, 96 S.Ct. 3092 (1976): The Court, 5–4 in an opinion by Burger, held routine inventories of cars taken into police custody do not violate the Fourth Amendment.

Chambers v. Maroney 399 U.S. 42, 26 L.Ed. 2d 419, 90 S.Ct. 1975 (1970): The Court held that if the officer has probable cause to believe that a car contains evidence of a crime and the car is mobile, the officer may search the car without a warrant at the scene or move it to the police station or impound lot and search it there.

Cooper v. California 386 U.S. 58, 17 L.Ed. 2d 730, 87 S.Ct. 788 (1967): The Court, 5–4, held that a search of an automobile is reasonable when it is impounded based on forfeiture statues.

Preston v. United States 376 U.S. 364, 11 L.Ed. 2d 777, 84 S.Ct. 881 (1963): A unanimous Court held that to qualify as a search incident to an arrest, an automobile must be searched at the time and place of arrest.

Carroll v. United States 267 U.S. 132, 69 L. Ed. 543, 45 S. Ct. 280 (1925): The Court, 5–2

in an opinion by Taft, held that the warrantless seizure of contraband in a vehicle did not violate the Fourth Amendment if search was done based on probable cause that the vehicle contains contraband.

E. Closed Containers

United States v. Chadwick 433 U.S. 1, 53 L.Ed. 2d 538, 97 5. Ct. 2476 (1977): The Court, 7–2, in an opinion by Burger, held that a warrant was necessary to search a closed container even though it had been legally seized. Exceptions that allow officers to open closed containers without obtaining a search warrant: probable cause search of vehicle (*California v. Acevedo*), inventory of a vehicle (*Florida v. Wells* and *Colorado v. Bertine*), search of car incident to lawful arrest (*New York v. Belton*), and search conducted during booking (*Illinois v. Lafayette*).

F. Consent Searches

Georgia v. Randolph 547 U.S. 103, 164 L.Ed. 2d 208, 126 S.Ct. 1515 (2006): The Court, 5–4 in an opinion by Souter, held that a physically present co-occupant's stated refusal to permit entry renders warrantless entry invalid as to him even though the another co-occupant consented to the search.

Ohio v. Robinette 519 U.S. 33, 136 L.Ed. 2d 347, 117 S.Ct. 417 (1996): The Court, 8–1 in an opinion by Rehnquist, held that voluntary consent obtained from a lawfully detained person before he is advised that he is "free to go" is valid.

Florida v. Bostick 501 U.S. 429, 115 L.Ed. 2d 389, 111 S.Ct. 2382 (1991): The Court, in a 6–3 opinion by O'Connor, held that a police officer may approach a person on a bus without cause and request consent to search luggage.

Florida v. Jimeno 500 U.S. 248, 114 L.Ed. 2d 297, 111 S.Ct. 1801 (1991): The Court, 7–2 in an opinion by Rehnquist, held that consent to search a vehicle includes consent to search closed containers found in the vehicle unless restrictions were placed on the consent when it was given.

Illinois v. Rodriguez 497 U.S. 177, 111 L.Ed. 2d 148, 110 S.Ct. 2793 (1990): The Court, in an opinion by Scalia for 6 justices, held that a consent search was valid when consent was obtained from a third party whom the police, at the time of the entry, reasonably believed possessed common authority over the premises.

United States v. Matlock 415 U.S. 164, 39 L.Ed. 2d 242, 94 S.Ct. 988 (1974) a majority of the Court in an opinion by White upheld the introduction into evidence of materials seized during the warrantless search of a bedroom because the common law wife of the defendant had consented to the search.

Schneckloth v. Bustamonte 412 U.S. 218, 36 L.Ed. 2d 854, 93 S.Ct. 2041 (1973): The Court, 7–2 in an opinion by White, held that advisement of Fourth Amendment rights is not necessary as a prerequisite to a consent search in a noncustodial situation. The standard for the evaluation of consent is voluntariness based on the totality of the circumstances.

Bumper v. North Carolina 391 U.S. 543, 20 L.Ed. 2d 797, 88 S.Ct. 1788 (1968): The Court, 7–2 in an opinion by Stewart, held that valid consent was not obtained when permission to enter was given immediately after officers informed the occupant that they had a search warrant for the premises.

Stoner v. California 376 U.S. 483, 11 L.Ed. 2d 856, 84 S.Ct. 889 (1964): The Court held that the search of defendant's hotel room without his consent and without a warrant violated his constitutional rights even though the hotel clerk gave consent to search.

G. Plain View and Open Fields Doctrines

Kyllo v. United States 533 U.S. 27, 150 L.Ed. 2d 94, 121 S.Ct. 2038 (2001): The Court, 5–4 in an opinion by Scalia, held that use of a device that is not in general public use, such as thermal imaging, to explore details of a private home that would otherwise be unknown without physical intrusion, is a

search under the Fourth Amendment and presumptively unreasonable if done without a warrant.

California v. Hodari D. 499 U.S. 621, 113 L.Ed. 2d 690, 111 S.Ct. 1547 (1991): The Court, 7–2 in an opinion by Scalia, held that the seizure of an item discarded by a person who was being pursued by the police did not violate the Fourth Amendment where the police had not touched the person in order to make an arrest at the time the item was discarded.

Horton v. California 496 U.S. 128, 110 L.Ed. 2d 112, 110 S.Ct. 2301 (1990): The Court, in an opinion by Stevens for 7 justices, held that evidence does not need to be inadvertently discovered in order to be covered by the Plain View Doctrine.

California v. Greenwood 486 U.S. 35, 100 L.Ed. 2d 30, 108 S.Ct. 1625 (1988): The Court, in an opinion by White for 6 justices, held that the Fourth Amendment does not prohibit warrantless search and seizure of garbage left for collection outside the curtilage of a home.

Arizona v. Hicks 480 U.s. 321, 94 L.Ed. 2d 347, 107 S.Ct. 1149 (1987): The Court, in an opinion by Scalia for 6 justices, held that moving a stereo found in plain view in order to obtain its serial number was a "search" covered by the Fourth Amendment.

United States v. Dunn 480 U.S. 294, 94 L.Ed. 2d 326, 107 S.Ct. 1134 (1987): The Court, in an opinion by White for 6 justices, held that peering into a barn that was not within the curtilage of a dwelling without a search warrant did not violate the Fourth Amendment because observations made from open fields do not violate any other privacy expectations.

Oliver v. United States 466 U.S. 170, 80 L.Ed. 2d 214, 104 SQ. 1735 (1984): The Court, in an opinion by Powell for 5 justices, held that Fourth Amendment protections do not extend to open fields (areas not immediately surrounding a home).

Texas v. Brown 460 U.S. 730, 75 L.Ed. 2d 502, 103 SQ. 1319 (1983): The Court although unable to agree upon an opinion, held that seizure of evidence in plain view did not violate the warrant requirement of the Fourth Amendment.

H. Stop-and-Frisk

Safford School District #1 v. Redding ___ U.S. ___, 174 L.Ed. 2d 354, 129 S.Ct. 2633 (2009): The Court, in an opinion by Souter for 6 justices, held that even though a teacher had sufficient suspicion to legally search a student's backpack and outer clothing for contraband pills, searching the student's underwear violated the Fourth Amendment because the teacher did not have cause to believe the student was currently concealing, in her underwear, pills that were dangerous to students.

Arizona v. Johnson ___ U.S. ___, 172 L.Ed. 2d 694,129 S.Ct. 781 (2009): The Court, in a unanimous opinion by Ginsburg, held that the frisk of a passenger in a car that was stopped pursuant to *Terry v. Ohio* was reasonable if the officer had reasonable suspicion that the person had a weapon.

Illinois v. Caballes 543 U.S. 405, 160 L.Ed. 2d 842, 125 S.Ct. 834 (2005): The Court, 6–3 in an opinion by Stevens, held that a dog sniff that reveals no information other than the location of a contraband substance, conducted during a lawful traffic stop, does not violate the Fourth Amendment.

Hiibel v. Sixth Judicial District Court, Nevada 542 U.S. 177, 159 L.Ed. 2d 292, 124 S.Ct. 2451 (2004): The Court, 5–4 in an opinion by Kennedy, held that a state may require a suspect to disclose his/her name during a *Terry* stop.

United States v. Knights 534 U.S. 112, 151 L.Ed. 2d 497, 122 S.Ct. 587 (2001): The Court, in a unanimous opinion by Rehnquist, held that the warrantless search of a person on probation, based on reasonable suspicion and authorized by a condition of probation, satisfied the Fourth Amendment.

Florida v. J. L. 529 U.S. 266, 146 L.Ed. 2d 54, 120 S.Ct. 1375 (2000): The Court, in a unanimous opinion by Ginsburg, held that an anonymous tip that a person is carrying a gun is not, without more, sufficient to justify a police officer's stop and frisk of that person.

Illinois v. Wardlow 528 U.S. 119, 145 L.Ed. 2d 570, 120 S.Ct. 673 (2000): The Court, 5–4 in an opinion by Rehnquist, held that the fact that a suspect fled when police vehicles converged on the area where he was established reasonable suspicion that he was involved in criminal activity.

Maryland v. Wilson 519 U.S. 408, 137 L.Ed. 2d 41, 117 S.Ct. 882 (1997): The Court, 7–2 in an opinion by Rehnquist, held that police officers may routinely order passengers out of vehicles that are legally stopped. No showing of suspicion or probable cause regarding the passengers' activities need be present.

Whren v. United States 517 U.S. 806, 135 L.Ed. 2d 89, 116 S.Ct. 1769 (1996): The Court, in a unanimous opinion by Scalia, held that the constitutionality of detention of a motorist at a traffic stop depends on objective reasonableness, not the subjective motivation of the individual officers.

Minnesota v. Dickerson 508 U.S. 366, 124 L.Ed. 2d 334, 113 S.Ct. 2130 (1993): The Court, in an opinion by White, held that an officer may seize nonthreatening contraband detected during a protective patdown search under *Terry v. Ohio* only if, by the object's contour or mass, its identity is immediately apparent. This has been called the plain feel rule.

Alabama v. White 496 U.S. 325, 110 L.Ed. 2d 301, 110 S.Ct. 2412 (1990): The Court, in an opinion by White for 6 justices, held that the *Gates* "totality of the circumstances" test could be used to evaluate reasonable suspicion.

Pennsylvania v. Bruder 488 U.S. 9, 102 L.Ed. 2d 172, 109 S.Ct. 205 (1988): The Court, in a *per curiam* opinion for 7 justices, held that no *Miranda* warnings are required during a routine traffic stop.

Michigan v. Chesternut 486 U.S. 567, 100 L.Ed. 2d 565, 108 S.Ct. 1975 (1988): The Court, in a unanimous opinion by Blackmun, held that an "investigatory pursuit" of a suspect during which officers drove alongside the suspect, but did not stop him, did not amount to a seizure within the meaning of the Fourth Amendment.

Hayes v. Florida 470 U.S. 811, 84 L.Ed. 2d 705, 105 S.Ct. 1643 (1985): The Court, in an opinion by White for 5 justices, held that absent probable cause, a warrant, or consent, police cannot transport a suspect to the police station for fingerprinting.

United States v. Sharpe 470 U.S. 675, 84 L.Ed. 2d 605, 105 S.Ct. 1568 (1985): The Court, in an opinion by Burger for 6 justices, held that the Fourth Amendment imposes no rigid time limitations on investigative detentions. Given the circumstances of the case, a 20-minute stop was not unreasonable.

New Jersey v. T.L.O. 469 U.S. 325, 83 L.Ed. 2d 720, 105 S.Ct. 733 (1985): The Court, in an opinion by White relevant parts of which were signed by 8 justices, held that the Fourth Amendment applies to searches by public school officials. Probable cause is not required but school officials must reasonably believe that a student is currently violating, or has violated, a school regulation or the law.

United States v. Hensley 469 U.S. 221, 83 L.Ed. 2d 604, 105 S.Ct. 675 (1985): The Court, in a unanimous decision by O'Connor, held that police officers may make an investigative stop in objective reliance on a "wanted flyer" issued by another police department so long as the flyer is supported by reasonable suspicion that the wanted person had committed an offense.

Michigan v. Long 463 U.S. 1032, 77 L.Ed. 2d 1201, 103 S.Ct. 3469 (1983): The Court, in an opinion by O'Connor for 5 justices, held that a search of the passenger compartment of a vehicle for weapons is permissible during a *Terry* stop when the officer reasonably believes the occupant(s) are dangerous and may gain immediate access to weapons inside the vehicle. The fact officers intended to release the suspect is immaterial.

United States v. Place 462 U.S. 696, 77 L.Ed. 2d 110, 103 S.Ct. 2637 (1983): The Court, in an opinion by O'Connor for 6 justices, held that the Fourth Amendment was not violated by temporary detention of personal luggage based on reasonable suspicion for the purpose of allowing a dog trained in narcotics detection to sniff it.

Brown v. Texas 443 U.S. 47, 61 L.Ed. 2d 357, 99 S.Ct. 2637 (1979): The Court, in a unanimous opinion by Burger, held a Texas law was invalid insofar as it allowed officers to require a person to identify him/herself when there was no reasonable suspicion that the person was, or had been, engaged in criminal activity.

Dunaway v. New York 442 U.S. 200, 60 L.Ed. 2d 824, 99 S.Ct. 2248 (1979): The Court, in an opinion by Brennan for 6 justices, held that a suspect cannot be transported to a police station for interrogation without consent or probable cause to arrest.

Delaware v. Prouse 440 U.S. 648, 59 L.Ed. 2d 660, 99 S.Ct. 1391 (1979): The Court, 8–1 in an opinion by White, held that police may not stop the driver of a vehicle in order to check his driver's license and car registration absent at least reasonable suspicion that the driver is unlicensed, the vehicle is unregistered, or it is otherwise subject to seizure for violation of the law.

Terry v. Ohio 392 U.S. 1, 20 L.Ed. 2d 889, 88 S.Ct. 1868 (1968): The Court, 8–1 in an opinion by Warren, held that a person may be detained without probable cause to make an arrest if there is reasonable suspicion that criminal activity is afoot. Reasonable suspicion must be based on specific, articulable facts from which reasonable inferences may be drawn. Based on reasonable suspicion that the officer or others in the area are in danger, a "frisk" may be justified to discover guns, knives, clubs, or other hidden instruments for assault of the police officer. The "frisk" must be limited in scope to a patdown of the outer clothing of the suspect for weapons.

I. Warrants

United States v. Grubbs 547 U.S. 90, 164 L.Ed. 2d 195, 126 S.Ct. 1494 (2006): The Court, in an opinion by Scalia for 5 justices, held that anticipatory warrants are not categorically unconstitutional. They require the magistrate to determine (1) that it is *now probable* that (2) contraband, evidence of a crime, or a fugitive *will be* on the described premises (3) when the warrant is executed.

Muehler v. Mena 544 U.S. 93, 161 L.Ed. 2d 299, 125 S.Ct. 1465 (2005): The Court, in an opinion by Rehnquist for 5 justices, held that handcuffing a person while a search warrant was executed was reasonable under the facts of the case. The governmental interest in minimizing risk of harm to both officers and occupants outweighs the marginal intrusion when executing a warrant for weapons.

Groh v. Ramirez 540 U.S. 551, 157 L.Ed. 2d 1068, 124 S.Ct. 1284 (2004): The Court, 5–4 in an opinion by Stevens, held that a search warrant that failed to describe any items to be seized was not valid. The application for the warrant and the supporting affidavit identified specific items but these documents were not incorporated by reference nor were they attached to the warrant at the time it was executed.

Illinois v. McArthur 531 U.S. 326, 148 L.Ed. 2d 838, 121 S.Ct. 946 (2001): The Court, 8–1 in a decision by Breyer, held that the brief seizure of the premises to prevent destruction of evidence while officers obtained a search warrant was permissible under the Fourth Amendment.

Griffin v. Wisconsin 483 U.S. 868, 97 L.Ed. 2d 709, 107 S.Ct. 3164 (1987): The Court, in an opinion by Scalia for 5 justices, held that the warrantless search of a probationer's home by probation officers, conducted pursuant to a valid regulation governing probationers, was "reasonable" within the meaning of the Fourth Amendment.

New York v. Burger 482 U.S. 691, 96 L.Ed. 2d 601, 107 S.Ct. 2636 (1987): The Court, in an opinion by Blackmun for 6 justices, held that the warrantless search of an automobile junkyard conducted pursuant to state statutes falls within the exception for warrantless administrative inspections of pervasively regulated industries.

New York v. P J. Video 475 U.S. 868, 89 L.Ed. 2d 871, 106 S.Ct. 1610 (1986): The Court, in an opinion by Rehnquist for 6 justices, held that the same standard of probable cause should be used for obtaining a search warrant authorizing the seizure of allegedly obscene material as is required for items not protected by the First Amendment.

Winston v. Lee 470 U.S. 753, 84 L.Ed. 2d 662, 105 S.Ct. 1611 (1985): The Court, in an opinion by Brennan for 6 justices, held that to obtain a court order for surgical removal of a bullet for evidentiary purposes there must be a compelling showing of need for the evidence and the medical risk to the suspect was low.

Illinois v. Andreas 463 U.S. 765, 77 L.Ed. 2d 1003, 103 S.Ct. 3319 (1983): The Court, 6–3 in an opinion by Burger, held that no warrant was required to reopen a package containing drugs that had been discovered at an airport by customs inspectors. The package had been resealed, delivered to the addressee, and kept under surveillance except for about 30–45 minutes between delivery to the defendant and his arrest.

Illinois v. Gates replaced the "two-pronged test" of *Aguilar* (1964) and *Spinelli* (1969) 462 U.S. 213, 76 L.Ed. 2d 527, 103 S.Ct. 2317 (1983): The Court, in an opinion by Rehnquist for 5 justices, held that evaluation of the reliability of an informant in search warrant cases should be based on the "totality of the circumstances." Prior reliability does not have to be established if the information provided is sufficiently detailed and has indicia of credibility.

Michigan v. Summers 452 U.S. 692, 69 L.Ed. 2d 340, 101 S.Ct. 2587 (1981): The Court, 6–3 in an opinion by Stevens, held that a valid warrant for the search of a dwelling implicitly contains the authority to detain the occupants of the premises while the warrant is being lawfully executed.

Ybarra v. Illinois 444 U.S. 85, 62 L.Ed. 2d 238, 100 S.Ct. 338 (1979): The Court, 6–3 in an opinion by Stewart, held that the search of patrons of a bar during the execution of a search warrant authorizing the seizure of narcotics found in the bar or on the person of the bartender violated the Fourth Amendment.

Franks v. Delaware 438 U.S. 154, 57 L.Ed. 2d 667, 98 S.Ct. 2674 (1978): The Court, 7–2 in an opinion by Blackmun, held that a defendant could attack the validity of a search warrant based on the fact that officers had knowingly and intentionally, or with reckless disregard of the truth, used false statements in the affidavit supporting said warrant. If the defendant establishes by a preponderance of the evidence that such false statements were in the affidavit, the remaining untainted information in the affidavit must be reevaluated to determine if there is probable cause to support the issuance of the warrant.

Mincey v. Arizona 437 U.S. 385, 57 L.Ed. 2d 290, 98 S.Ct. 2408 (1978): The Court, in an opinion by Stewart for 7 justices, held that there is no "murder scene" exception to the warrant requirement authorizing police to remain at the location without consent.

Michigan v. Tyler 436 U.S. 499, 56 L.Ed. 2d 486, 98 S.Ct. 1942 (1978): The Court, although unable to agree upon an opinion, held that no search warrant was required when firefighters entered a building to extinguish a fire, or to conduct an investigation of the cause of the fire immediately after the fire was out and for a reasonable amount of time thereafter.

Marshall v. Barlow's Inc. 436 U.S. 307, 56 L.Ed. 2d 305, 98 S.Ct. 1816 (1978): The Court, 5–3 in an opinion by White, held nonconsensual inspections by Occupational Safety and Health Administration inspectors violated the Fourth Amendment unless conducted pursuant to a search warrant or

an administrative warrant as described in *Camara*.

Connally v. Georgia 429 U.S. 245, 50 L.Ed. 2d 444, 97 S.Ct. 546 (1977): The Court, in a unanimous *per curiam* opinion, held a state law unconstitutional that permitted the issuance of search warrants by an unsalaried justice of the peace who received a fee when a search warrant was issued, but none if the application for a warrant was denied.

United States v. Miller 425 U.S. 435, 48 L.Ed. 2d 71, 96 S.Ct. 1619 (1976): The Court, 7–2, in an opinion by Powell, held that bank records could be subpoenaed for use in a criminal case; a search warrant was not required.

Coolidge v. New Hampshire 403 U.S. 443, 29 L.Ed. 2d 564, 91 S.Ct. 2022 (1971): The Court, in an opinion by Stewart, held that search warrants must be issued by a "neutral and detached magistrate." State law designating a deputy attorney general or a police captain as justices of the peace and authorizing them to issue search warrants was unconstitutional.

Spinelli v. United States replaced by the "totality of the circumstances test" in *Illinois v. Gates* (1983) 393 U.S. 110, 21 L.Ed. 2d 637, 89 S.Ct. 584 (1969): The Court, 5–3 in an opinion by Harlan, applied the two-pronged *Aguilar* test to cases where the informant had not been previously proven to be reliable.

Camara v. Municipal Court Overruled *Frank v. Maryland* (1959) 387 U.S. 523, 18 L.Ed. 2d 930, 87 S.Ct. 1727, and *See v. Seattle* 387 U.S. 541, 18 L.Ed. 2d 943, 87 S.Ct. 1737 (1967): The Court, in an opinion by White for 6 justices, held that health and fire inspectors are not entitled to search a home or business without warrant or consent. Probable cause for a administrative warrant can be established by showing a reasonable legislative purpose or administrative standards for conducting an inspection of the area.

McCray v. Illinois 386 U.S. 300, 18 L.Ed. 2d 62, 87 S.Ct. 1056 (1967): The Court, 5–4 in an opinion by Stewart, held that a reliable informant's identity generally need not be disclosed pretrial on a motion to suppress.

Aguilar v. Texas replaced by the "totality of the circumstances test" in *Illinois v. Gates* (1983) 378 U.S. 108, 12 L.Ed. 2d 723, 84 S.Ct. 1509 (1964): The Court held that the magistrate issuing the warrant must be advised: (1) of the underlying circumstances from which the affiant concluded that probable cause existed; and (2) of the underlying circumstances from which the affiant concluded that the informant, whose identity need not be revealed in the affidavit, was "credible" or his/her information "reliable." This case established the so-called "*Aguilar* two-prong test*."*

J. Wiretapping and Electronic Surveillance

United States v. Karo 468 U.S. 705, 82 L.Ed. 2d 530, 104 S.Ct. 3296 (1984): The Court, in a plurality opinion by White, held that the installation of an electronic beeper in a container with the consent of the person who owned it does not violate the Fourth Amendment rights of the purchaser who had no knowledge that it contained a monitoring device. Monitoring the beeper after it entered the residence of the purchaser, and was out of view from common areas, violated the right of privacy of the suspect.

United States v. Knotts 460 U.S. 276, 75 L.Ed. 2d 55, 103 S.Ct. 1081 (1983): The Court, in an opinion by Rehnquist for 5 justices, held that the monitoring of a beeper, installed inside a container of chloroform, did not invade the suspect's reasonable expectation of privacy.

Smith v. Maryland 442 U.S. 735, 61 L.Ed. 2d 220, 99 S.Ct. 2577 (1979): The Court, 5–3 in an opinion by Blackmun, held that installation and use of a pen register at telephone company offices did not violate the suspect's ·easonable expectation of privacy and did not

require the authorization of a warrant. NOTE: Congress later enacted 18 U.S.C. §3121 et al. requiring a court order to install a pen register.

Dalia v. United States 441 U.S. 238, 60 L.Ed. 2d 177, 99 S.Ct. 1682 (1979): The Court, in an opinion by Powell for 5 justices, held that the right to covertly enter a private premises in order to install an electronic listening device was implicit in an electronic surveillance warrant issued under Title III of the Omnibus Crime Control and Safe Streets Act.

United States v. Caceres 440 U.S. 741, 59 L.Ed. 2d 733, 99 S.Ct. 1465 (1979): The Court, 7–2 in an opinion by Stevens, held that tape recorded nontelephonic conversations between the defendant and an IRS agent were admissible despite the fact that the conversations were recorded in violation of agency regulations and without the defendant's consent.

United States v. New York Telephone Company 434 U.S. 159, 54 L.Ed. 2d 376, 98 S.Ct. 364 (1977): The Court, in an opinion by White for 5 justices, held that a telephone company must comply with a federal court order requiring it to assist law enforcement officers by installing a pen register.

United States v. United States District Court, Eastern Michigan 407 U.S. 297, 32 L.Ed. 2d 752, 92 S.Ct. 2125 (1972): The Court, 6–2 in an opinion by Powell, refused to approve warrantless electronic monitoring of domestic "subversives."

Katz v. United States overruled *Olmstead v. United States* (1928) 389 U.S. 347, 19 L.Ed. 2d 576, 88 S.Ct. 507 (1967): The Court, 8–1 in an opinion by Stewart, held that the Fourth Amendment "protects people, not places," and as a result, electronic eavesdropping constitutes a "search" and "seizure" and is subject to the warrant requirements of the Fourth Amendment.

Osborn v. United States 385 U.S. 323, 17 L.Ed. 2d 394, 87 S.Ct. 429 (1966): The Court, 7–2 in an opinion by Stewart, held that a tape recording of incriminating conversation, obtained by a "friend" of the defendant, was admissible even though no warrant was obtained. Tapes of privileged conversations between defendant and attorney would not be admissible.

Hoffa v. United States 385 U.S. 293, 87 S.Ct. 408, 17 L.Ed. 2d 374 (1966): The Court, in an opinion by Stewart, held that the Fourth Amendment does not protect a wrongdoer's misplaced belief that a person to whom he voluntarily speaks will not reveal what was said in confidence.

K. Other Fourth Amendment Issues

1. Use of Force

Graham v. Connor 490 U.S. 386, 104 L.Ed. 2d 443, 109 S.Ct. 1865 (1989): The Court, in an opinion by Rehnquist for 6 justices, held that in Civil Rights Act suits under 42 U.S.C. §1983 allegations of excessive force in a nonprison setting should be analyzed under the Fourth Amendment's "objective reasonableness" standard.

Tennessee v. Garner 471 U.S. 1, 85 L.Ed. 2d 1, 105 S.Ct. 1694 (1985): The Court, in an opinion by White for 6 justices, held that the Fourth Amendment prohibits the use of deadly force by police officers to prevent the escape of a suspected felon unless the officer has probable cause to believe that the suspect poses a significant threat of death or serious physical injury to the officer or another person.

2. Drug Testing

Board of Education of Independent School District No. 92 of Pottawatomie County v. Earls 536 U.S. 822, 153 L.Ed. 2d 735, 122 S.Ct. 2559 (2002): The Court, 5–4 in an opinion by Thomas, upheld a school district's policy requiring students participating in all forms of extracurricular activities to submit to random drug testing.

Ferguson v. City of Charleston 532 U.S. 67, 149 L.Ed. 2d 205, 121 S.Ct. 1281 (2001): The Court, 6–3 in an opinion by Stevens, held that a state hospital's performance of a diagnostic test without the patient's consent to obtain evidence of drug use for law enforcement purposes is an unreasonable search.

Chandler v. Miller 520 U.S. 305, 137 L.Ed. 2d 513, 117 S.Ct. 1295 (1997): The Court, 8–1 in an opinion by Ginsburg, held that Georgia's requirement that candidates for state office pass a drug test violated the candidate's Fourth Amendment rights.

Vernonia School District 47J v. Acton 515 U.S. 646, 132 L.Ed. 2d 564, 115 S.Ct. 2386 (1995): The Court, 6–3 in an opinion by Scalia, held that random drug testing of students who participate in the school's athletics programs did not violate the Fourth Amendment.

Skinner v. Railway Labor Executives' Association 489 U.S. 602, 103 L.Ed. 2d 639, 109 S.Ct. 1402 (1989): The Court, in an opinion by Kennedy for 6 justices, held that regulations of the Federal Railroad Administration that mandate blood and urine tests of employees involved in specified train accidents did not violate the Fourth Amendment because the employees subject to testing discharge duties fraught with such risks of injury to others that even a momentary lapse of attention could have disastrous consequences.

National Treasury Employees Union v. Raab 489 U.S. 656, 103 L.Ed. 2d 685, 109 S.Ct. 1384 (1989): The Court, in an opinion by Kennedy for 5 justices, held that the Fourth Amendment was not violated by a practice of the United States Customs Service that required an urinalysis test of employees who sought transfer or promotion to positions involving drug interdiction or the mandatory carrying of firearms.

3. Trash Searches

California v. Greenwood 486 U.S. 35, 100 L.Ed. 2d 30, 108 S.Ct. 1625 (1988): The

Court, in an opinion by White for 6 justices, held that the Fourth Amendment does not prohibit warrantless search and seizure of garbage left for collection outside the curtilage of a home.

4. Police Checkpoints

Illinois v. Lidster 540 U.S. 419, 157 L.Ed. 2d 843, 124 S.Ct. 885 (2004): The Court, 6–3 in an opinion by Breyer, held that checkpoints established to seek information from the public do not require a warrant or probable cause.

City of Indianapolis v. Edmond 531 U.S. 32, 148 L.Ed. 2d 333, 121 S.Ct. 447 (2000): The Court, 6–3 in an opinion by O'Connor, held that checkpoints designed to interdict unlawful drugs on city streets were established with the primary purpose of crime control, and therefore stops made without reasonable suspicion violated the Fourth Amendment.

Michigan Department of State Police v. Sitz 496 U.S. 444, 110 L.Ed. 2d 412, 110 S.Ct. 2481 (1990): The Court, in an opinion by Rehnquist for 5 justices, held that sobriety checkpoints set up on public streets do not violate the Fourth Amendment.

5. Knock and Announce

Hudson v. Michigan 547 U.S. 586, 165 L.Ed. 2d 56, 126 S.Ct. 2159 (2006): The Court, 5–4 in an opinion by Scalia, held violation of the "knock-and-announce" rule while executing a search warrant does not require suppression of evidence found during an otherwise valid search.

United States v. Banks 540 U.S. 31, 157 L.Ed. 2d 343, 124 S.Ct. 521 (2003): The Court, in a unanimous decision by Souter, held that a 15–20 second delay to allow the suspect to answer the door after the officers announced their presence was sufficient.

United States v. Ramirez 523 U.S. 65, 140 L.Ed. 2d 191, 118 S.Ct. 992 (1998): The

Court, in a unanimous opinion by Rehnquist, reaffirmed that "no-knock" entries are justified when police officers have a "reasonable suspicion" that knocking and announcing their presence before entering would "be dangerous or futile, or . . . inhibit the effective investigation of the crime."

Richards v. Wisconsin 520 U.S. 385, 137 L.Ed. 2d 615, 117 S.Ct. 1416 (1997): The Court, in a unanimous opinion by Stevens, held that it was an error to make a blanket exclusion from the "knock-notice" requirement for the execution of search warrants in felony drug investigations.

Wilson v. Arkansas 514 U.S. 927, 131 L.Ed. 2d 976, 115 S.Ct. 1914 (1995): The Court, in a unanimous opinion by Thomas, held that the common-law "knock and announce" principle forms a part of the reasonableness inquiry under the Fourth Amendment.

6. Emergency Assistance

Michigan v. Fisher ___ U.S. ___, 175 L.Ed. 2d 410, 130 S.Ct. 546 (2009): The Court, 7–2 in a *per curiam* opinion, held that warrantless entry into a home to render aid, prevent violence, or restore order does not violate the Fourth Amendment as long as the officer has objectively reasonable cause at the time of entry to believe that the assistance is necessary.

Brigham City, Utah v. Stuart 547 U.S. 398, 164 L.Ed. 2d 650, 126 S.Ct. 1943 (2006): The Court, in a unanimous opinion by Roberts, held that officers may make warrantless entry to render emergency assistance to occupants of private property who are seriously injured or threatened with such injury.

7. Other Issues

Samson v. California 547 U.S. 843, 165 L.Ed. 2d 250, 126 S.Ct. 2193 (2006): The Court, 6–3 in an opinion by Thomas, held that the Fourth Amendment does not prohibit a police officer from conducting a suspicion-less search of a parolee.

O'Connor v. Ortega 480 U.S. 709, 94 L.Ed. 2d 714, 107 S.Ct. 1492 (1987): The Court, in an opinion by O'Connor for 5 justices, held a public employee has a reasonable expectation of privacy in a desk and file cabinets which were not shared with any other employees and where personal materials were kept.

IV IDENTIFICATION PROCEDURES

Manson v. Brathwaite 432 U.S. 98, 53 L.Ed. 2d 140, 97 S.Ct. 2243 (1977): The Court, 7–2 in an opinion by Blackmun, permitted the introduction into evidence of pretrial identification of the defendant, based on the totality of the circumstances when only one photograph was displayed, even though the method of making the identification was suggestive and unnecessary.

United States v. Ash 413 U.S. 300, 37 L.Ed. 2d 619, 93 S.Ct. 1568 (1973): The Court, 6–3 in an opinion by Blackmun, held that a defendant has no right to the presence of counsel at a pretrial photographic lineup.

Neil v. Biggers 409 U.S. 188, 34 L.Ed. 2d 401, 93 S.Ct. 375 (1972): The Court, in an opinion by Powell for 7 justices, held that a stationhouse identification based on the viewing of a single suspect was admissible into evidence based on the totality of the circumstances. The factors to be considered include: the opportunity of the witness to view the criminal at the time of the crime; the witness's degree of attention to the suspect during the crime; the accuracy of the witness's prior description of the criminal; the level of certainty demonstrated by the witness at the confrontation; and the length of time between the crime and the confrontation.

Kirby v. Illinois 406 U.S. 682, 32 L.Ed. 2d 411, 92 S.Ct. 1877 (1972) in a plurality opinion by Stewart, the Court held that after the formal charge is made (whether by preliminary hearing, indictment, information, or arraignment) a person is entitled to have counsel present at a lineup.

Gilbert v. California 388 U.S. 263, 18 L.Ed. 2d 1178, 87 S.Ct. 1951 (1967): The Court clearly indicates that testimony that is the direct result of an illegal lineup is inadmissible.

United States v. Wade 388 U.S. 218, 18 L.Ed. 2d 1149, 87 S.Ct. 1926 (1967) held that the Sixth Amendment right to counsel applies to indicted defendants who are required to participate in lineups.

V FIFTH AMENDMENT ISSUES

A. Self-Incrimination

1. Confessions

Berghuis v. Thompkins ___ U.S. ___, 176 L. Ed. 2d 1098, 130 S. Ct. 2250 (2010) the Court, 5–4 in an opinion by Kennedy, held that if the State establishes that *Miranda* warnings were given and understood, a suspect's uncoerced statement establishes an implied waiver.

Florida v. Powell ___ U.S. ___, 175 L.Ed. 2d 1009, 130 S.Ct. 1195 (2010): The Court, 7–2 in an opinion by Ginsburg, held that a judge determining whether the *Miranda* warnings were given correctly should consider whether the officer's statements reasonably conveyed the warnings required by *Miranda*.

Maryland v. Shatzer ___ U.S. ___, 175 L.Ed. 2d 1045, 130 S.Ct. 1213 (2010): The Court, in an opinion by Scalia for 7 justices, held that after a suspect invoked *Miranda* and requested an attorney, the suspect could make a valid *Miranda* waiver without an attorney present if there had been at least a 14-day break in custody before police again sought a *Miranda* waiver. If the suspect is incarcerated for other reasons, returning the suspect to the general population is considered a break in custody.

Corley v. United States ___ U.S. ___, 173 L.Ed. 2d 443, 129 S.Ct. 1558 (2009): The

Court, 5–4 in an opinion by Souter, held that 18 U.S. C. §3501, enacted in response to *Miranda v. Arizona,* did not change the *McNabb-Mallory* rule which makes voluntary confessions inadmissible in federal court if the suspect was not taken before a magistrate in a timely manner.

United States v. Patane 542 U.S. 630, 159 L.Ed. 2d 667, 124 S.Ct. 2620 (2004): The Court, in a plurality opinion by Thomas, concluded that failure to give a suspect *Miranda* warnings does not require suppression of the physical fruits of the suspect's unwarned but voluntary statements.

Missouri v. Seibert 542 U.S. 600, 159 L.Ed. 2d 643, 124 S.Ct. 2601 (2004): The Court, in a plurality opinion by Souter, concluded that when *Miranda* warnings were intentionally delayed until midway through the interrogation session, both the statements made before and after the warnings were inadmissible. Interrogating officer used pre-*Miranda* admissions during the post-*Miranda* session.

Yarborough v. Alvarado 541 U.S. 652, 158 L.Ed. 2d 938, 124 S.Ct. 2140 (2004): The Court, 5–4 in an opinion by Kennedy, held that courts do not have to specifically consider the suspect's age and inexperience when deciding whether a person is "in custody" for *Miranda* purposes.

Dickerson v. United States 530 U.S. 428, 147 L.Ed. 2d 405, 120 S.Ct. 2326 (2000): The Court, 7–2 in an opinion by Rehnquist, held a law passed by the U.S. Congress designed to negate *Miranda* was unconstitutional.

Stansbury v. California 511 U.S. 318, 128 L.Ed. 2d 293, 114 S.Ct. 1526 (1994): The Court, in a unanimous *per curiam* opinion, held that for the purposes of *Miranda,* the initial determination of custody depends on the objective circumstances of the interrogation, not on the subjective views of either the officer or the person being questioned.

Davis v. United States 512 U.S. 452, 129 L.Ed. 2d 362, 114 S.Ct. 2350 (1994): The Court, in an opinion by O'Connor for 5

justices, held that the suspect's Fifth Amendment rights were not violated when officers asked a suspect who made a valid *Miranda* waiver to clarify his ambiguous remark about talking to a lawyer.

McNeil v. Wisconsin 501 U.S. 171, 115 L.Ed. 2d 158, 111 S.Ct. 2204 (1991): The Court, in a 6–3 opinion by Scalia, held that a defendant's invocation of his Sixth Amendment right to counsel during a judicial proceeding to set bail and schedule a preliminary examination did not constitute an invocation of the *Miranda* right to counsel.

Arizona v. Fulminante 499 U.S. 279, 113 L.Ed. 2d 302, 111 S.Ct. 1246 (1991): The Court, 5–4 in an opinion by White, held that a confession obtained by a prison informant, under circumstances where there was a credible threat of physical harm by other inmates unless the informant intervened, was coerced and violated due process. The Harmless Error Rule applies if a coerced confession was introduced at trial.

Minnick v. Mississippi 498 U.S. 146, 112 L.Ed. 2d 489, 111 S.Ct. 486 (1990): The Court, 6–2 in an opinion by Kennedy, held that questioning may not resume without an attorney present if a person invoked the *Miranda* right to counsel.

Illinois v. Perkins 496 U.S. 292, 110 L.Ed. 2d 243, 110 S.Ct. 2394 (1990): The Court, in an opinion by Kennedy for 7 justices, held that *Miranda* warnings were not required when a suspect is unaware that he/she is speaking to a law enforcement officer and voluntarily gives a statement.

Pennsylvania v. Bruder 488 U.S. 9, 102 L.Ed. 2d 172, 109 S.Ct. 205 (1988): The Court, in a *per curiam* opinion for 7 justices, held that no *Miranda* warnings are required during a routine traffic stop.

Patterson v. Illinois 487 U.S. 285, 101 L.Ed. 2d 261, 108 S.Ct. 2389 (1988): The Court, in an opinion by White for 5 justices, held that giving *Miranda* admonitions and obtaining a valid waiver prior to post-arraignment interrogation is sufficient to apprise the defendant of the nature of his/her Sixth Amendment right to counsel and of the consequences of abandoning that right.

Arizona v. Roberson 486 U.S. 675, 100 L.Ed. 2d 704, 108 S.Ct. 2093 (1988): The Court, in an opinion by Stevens for 6 justices, held that *Edwards v. Arizona* applies regardless of the crime being investigated or agency involved in subsequent interrogation sessions.

Colorado v. Spring 479 U.S. 364, 93 L.Ed. 2d 954, 107 S.Ct. 851 (1987): The Court, in an opinion by Powell for 7 justices, held that the suspect's awareness of all possible subjects of questioning in advance of interrogation is not relevant in determining whether *Miranda* waiver was valid.

Connecticut v. Barrett 479 U.S. 523, 93 L.Ed. 2d 920, 107 S.Ct. 828 (1987): The Court, in an opinion by Rehnquist for 6 justices, held that the Fifth Amendment does not require suppression of an oral confession where suspect was given *Miranda* warnings and agreed to make oral, but not written, statements without an attorney present.

Colorado v. Connelly 479 U.S. 157, 93 L.Ed. 2d 473, 107 S.Ct. 515 (1986): The Court, in an opinion by Rehnquist for 5 justices, held that coercive police activity is a necessary predicate to finding a confession was not voluntary.

Kuhlman v. Wilson 477 U.S. 436, 91 L.Ed. 2d 364, 106 S.Ct. 2616 (1986): The Court, in an opinion by Powell, pertinent parts of which were signed by 6 justices, held that in order to reverse a conviction defendant must demonstrate that the police and their jailhouse informant took some action beyond mere passive listening to defendant's incriminating remarks.

Crane v. Kentucky 476 U.S. 683, 90 L.Ed. 2d 636, 106 S.Ct. 2142 (1986): The Court, in a unanimous opinion by O'Connor, held that a defendant may introduce evidence about the physical and psychological circumstances under which the confession was obtained in order to show the confession

was untrustworthy; this is independent of a *Miranda* issues.

Moran v. Burbine 475 U.S. 412, 89 L.Ed. 2d 410, 106 S.Ct. 1135 (1986): The Court, in an opinion by O'Connor for 6 justices, held that the failure of police to inform suspect of his attorney's telephone call did not affect validity of uncoerced waiver of *Miranda* rights.

Oregon v. Elstad 470 U.S. 298, 84 L.Ed. 2d 222, 105 S.Ct. 1285 (1985): The Court, in an opinion by O'Connor for 6 justices, held an uncoerced confession admissible where police officers had properly administered *Miranda* and obtained a waiver even though the officers had previously obtained damaging statements from the defendant in violation of *Miranda.*

Berkemer v. McCarty 468 U.S. 420, 82 L.Ed. 2d 317, 104 S.Ct. 3138 (1984): The Court, in an opinion by Marshall for 8 justices, held that *Miranda* warnings are required prior to custodial interrogation regardless of the severity of the offense being investigated.

New York v. Quarles 467 U.S. 649, 81 L.Ed. 2d 550, 104 S.Ct. 2626 (1984): The Court, in an opinion by Rehnquist for 5 justices, held that an overriding consideration of public safety justified the officer's failure to provide *Miranda* warnings before asking questions regarding the location of a weapon the defendant had apparently abandoned immediately prior to arrest.

Minnesota v. Murphy 465 U.S. 420, 79 L.Ed. 2d 409, 104 S.Ct. 1136 (1984): The Court, in an opinion by White for 6 justices, held that a probation officer does not have to give *Miranda* warnings prior to meetings required as a condition of probation.

Taylor v. Alabama 457 U.S. 687, 73 L.Ed. 2d 314, 102 S.Ct. 2664 (1982): The Court, in an opinion by Marshall for 5 justices, held a confession obtained during custodial interrogation after an illegal arrest should be inadmissible unless the confession is sufficiently an act of free will to purge the taint of the illegal arrest.

California v. Prysock 453 U.S. 355, 69 L.Ed. 2d 696, 101 S.Ct. 2806 (1981): The Court, 6–3, in a *per curiam* opinion, held police do not need to give a verbatim rendition of *Miranda* warnings so long as the suspect is fully advised of his rights and no suggestion of any limitation of those rights is made.

Edwards v. Arizona limited by *Minnick v. Mississippi* (1990) 451 U.S. 477, 68 L.Ed. 2d 378, 101 S.Ct. 1880 (1981): The Court, in an opinion by White for 6 justices, held custodial interrogation can only be resumed after a suspect has requested a lawyer if the suspect has had an opportunity to consult with a lawyer or if the suspect initiates the conversation.

Rhode Island v. Innis 446 U.S. 291, 64 L.Ed. 2d 297, 100 S.Ct. 1682 (1980): The Court, in an opinion by Stewart for 5 justices, held *Miranda* warnings are required whenever a suspect in custody is subjected to either express questioning or its functional equivalent. Any words or actions on the part of the police that they should know are reasonably likely to elicit an incriminating response are covered.

Fare v. Michael C. 442 U.S. 707, 61 L.Ed. 2d 197, 99 S.Ct. 2560 (1979): The Court, in an opinion by Blackmun for 5 justices, held that a juvenile's request to speak with his probation officer did not per se constitute an invocation of his Fifth Amendment right against self-incrimination.

North Carolina v. Butler 441 U.S. 369, 60 L.Ed. 2d 286, 99 S.Ct. 1755 (1979): The Court, 5–3 in an opinion by Stewart, held validity of a waiver of *Miranda* rights should be determined by looking at the facts to see if the defendant knowingly and voluntarily waived his rights. An explicit waiver is not required.

Brewer v. Williams 430 U.S. 387, 51 L.Ed. 2d 424, 97 S.Ct. 1232 (1977): The Court, in an opinion by Stewart for 5 justices, held that indirect questioning of a suspect, after arraignment and without counsel present, violated his right to counsel.

Oregon v. Mathiason 429 U.S. 492, 50 L.Ed. 2d 714, 97 S.Ct. 711 (1977): The Court, in a *per curiam* opinion for 6 justices, held that *Miranda* warnings were not required prior to interrogation of a parolee who voluntarily came to the police station and was allowed to leave the station without being arrested.

Michigan v. Mosley 423 U.S. 96, 46 L.Ed. 2d 313, 96 S.Ct. 321 (1975): The Court, in an opinion by Stewart for 5 justices, held statements made by a suspect who was in custody during an interrogation session two hours after invoking *Miranda* may be used in court if the right of the suspect to cut off questioning was scrupulously honored.

Brown v. Illinois 422 U.S. 590, 45 L.Ed. 2d 416, 95 S.Ct. 2254 (1975): The Court held, in an opinion by Blackmun, that the mere giving of the warnings required by *Miranda* does not dissipate the taint of a defendant's illegal arrest and render statements given after the arrest admissible.

Harris v. New York 401 U.S. 222, 28 L.Ed. 2d 1, 91 S.Ct. 643 (1971): The Court, 5–4 in an opinion by Burger, held that a confession obtained in violation of *Miranda* may be used to impeach a defendant who testifies in court.

Orozco v. Texas 394 U.S. 324, 22 L.Ed. 2d 311, 89 S.Ct. 1095 (1969): The Court, 6–2 in an opinion by Black, held that once an accused is in custody, regardless of where he/she is being held, *Miranda* warnings must be given if a statement, or evidence derived therefrom, is to be admissible.

Gardner v. Broderick 392 U.S. 273, 20 L.Ed. 2d 1082, 88 S.Ct. 1913 (1968): The Court held that a policeman who refused to waive his Fifth Amendment privilege against self-incrimination cannot be dismissed from office solely because of his refusal. Compare *Lachance v. Erikson* (1998).

Miranda v. Arizona 384 U.S. 436, 16 L.Ed. 2d 694, 86 S.Ct. 1602 (1966): The Court, 5–4 in an opinion by Warren, held that prior to custodial interrogation the following warnings must be given: (1) you have the right to remain silent; (2) anything you say can be used in a court of law against you; (3) you have the right to have an attorney with you during the interrogation; (4) if you are unable to hire an attorney one will be provided for you without cost during questioning.

Escobedo v. Illinois 378 U.S. 478, 12 L.Ed. 2d 977, 84 S.Ct. 1758 (1964): The Court held "that when the process shifts from investigatory to accusatory and its purpose is to elicit a confession . . . the accused must be permitted to consult with his lawyer."

Malloy v. Hogan overruled *Adamson v. California* (1947) 378 U.S. 1, 12 L.Ed. 2d 653, 84 S.Ct. 1489 (1964): The Court, 7–2, made the self-incrimination privilege of the Fifth Amendment applicable to the states through the due process clause of the Fourteenth Amendment.

Massiah v. United States 377 U.S. 201, 12 L.Ed. 2d 246, 84 S.Ct. 1199 (1964): The Court held, 6–3, that interrogation of an indicted defendant without counsel present, or a waiver of counsel, violates the Sixth Amendment right to counsel. *McLeod v. Ohio* (1965) made the Massiah doctrine binding on the states under the Fourteenth Amendment.

2. Other Self-Incrimination Issues

United States v. Hubbell 530 U.S. 27, 147 L.Ed. 2d 24, 120 S.Ct. 2037 (2000): The Court, 8–1 in an opinion by Stevens, held that while previously produced documents are not covered by the Fifth Amendment, the act of complying with a subpoena that requires a person to produce his/her own documents falls within the privilege against self-incrimination.

United States v. Balsys 524 U.S. 666, 141 L.Ed. 2d 575, 118 S.Ct. 2218 (1998): The Court, 7–2 in an opinion by Souter for 5 justices, held that a person could not claim the Fifth Amendment privilege against

self-incrimination based on fear of prosecution by a foreign nation.

United States v. Dunnigan 507 U.S. 87, 122 L.Ed. 2d 445, 113 S.Ct. 1111 (1993): The Court, in a unanimous opinion by Kennedy, held United States Sentencing Commission Guidelines, which permit imposition of an enhanced sentence if the Court finds the defendant committed perjury at trial, do not violate the Fifth Amendment right to give testimony in one's own behalf.

Doe v. United States 487 U.S. 201, 101 L.Ed. 2d 184, 108 S.Ct. 2341 (1988): The Court, in an opinion by Blackmun for 8 justices, held that the Fifth Amendment was not violated by a court order compelling a target of a grand jury investigation to authorize foreign banks to disclose records of his accounts.

Allen v. Illinois 478 U.S. 364, 92 L.Ed. 2d 296, 106 S.Ct. 2988 (1986): The Court, in an opinion by Rehnquist for 5 justices, held that the Fifth Amendment guarantee against compulsory self-incrimination does not apply to proceedings under the Illinois Sexually Dangerous Person Act because they are civil proceedings.

South Dakota v. Neville 459 U.S. 553, 74 L.Ed. 2d 748, 103 S.Ct. 916 (1983): The Court, 7–2 in an opinion by O'Connor, held that the admission into evidence of the fact that defendant refused to submit to a blood-alcohol test did not offend the privilege against self-incrimination.

Andresen v. Maryland 427 U.S. 463, 49 L.Ed. 2d 627, 96 S.Ct. 2737 (1976): The Court, 7–2 in an opinion by Blackmun, held that the privilege against self-incrimination was not violated by the admission into evidence of personal files seized during a search of defendant's law office pursuant to a search warrant.

Fisher v. United States 425 U.S. 391, 48 L.Ed. 2d 39, 96 S.Ct. 1569 (1976): The Court, in an opinion by White for 6 justices, held the privilege against self-incrimination did not bar the enforcement of a summons for the production of records prepared by the defendant's accountant and held by the defendant's attorney.

Griffin v. California 380 U.S. 609, 14 L.Ed. 2d 106, 85 S.Ct. 1229 (1965): The Court held, 6–2, that the Fifth Amendment forbids a state prosecutor's comments on failure of a defendant to take the stand and explain evidence. It also bars a jury instruction that such silence may be evidence of guilt.

B. Double Jeopardy

Yeager v. United States ___ U.S. ___, 174 L.Ed. 2d 78, 129 S.Ct. 2360 (2009): The Court, 6–3 in an opinion by Stevens, held that an apparent inconsistency between a jury's verdict of acquittal on some counts and its failure to return a verdict on other counts does not affect the acquittals' preclusive force under the double jeopardy clause.

Smith v. Massachusetts 543 U.S. 462, 160 L.Ed. 2d 914, 125 S.Ct. 1129 (2005): The Court, 5–4 in an opinion by Scalia, held that once a judge entered a mid-trial acquittal, reconsideration of the issue and sending the case to the jury violated double jeopardy.

United States v. Lara 541 U.S. 193, 158 L.Ed. 2d 420, 124 S.Ct. 1628 (2004): The Court, 7–2 in an opinion by Breyer, held that prosecution by an Indian tribe of a nonmember for a crime of violence against a police officer and by the federal government for assault on a federal officer who made the arrest does not violate double jeopardy.

Seling v. Young 531 U.S. 250, 148 L.Ed. 2d 734, 121 S.Ct. 727 (2001): The Court, 8–1 in an opinion by O'Connor, upheld Washington's law authorized civil commitment of "sexually violent predators." A civil law cannot be deemed punitive "as applied" to a single individual in violation of double jeopardy and *ex post facto* clause.

Monge v. California 524 U.S. 721, 141 L.Ed. 2d 615, 118 S.Ct. 2246 (1998): The Court, 5–4 in an opinion by O'Connor, held that the double jeopardy clause does not prohibit

retrial of the recidivism issue where a bifurcated trial was held and the defendant was convicted of the substantive offense but an appellate court ruled that insufficient evidence of the prior offense was introduced at the sentencing hearing.

Hudson v. United States 522 U.S. 93, 139 L.Ed. 2d 450, 118 S.Ct. 488 (1997): The Court, in an opinion by Rehnquist, held that the double jeopardy clause does not bar criminal prosecution of a defendant who has been previously subjected to civil administrative proceedings that resulted in monetary penalties and occupational debarment for violation of federal banking statutes.

United States v. Watts 519 U.S. 148, 136 L.Ed. 2d 554, 117 S.Ct. 633 (1996): The Court, in a *per curiam* opinion for 7 justices, held that a federal judge sentencing a convicted defendant could consider facts from cases that resulted in acquittals because the federal sentencing guidelines permit consideration of evidence established by a preponderance of the evidence.

United States v. Ursery 518 U.S. 267, 135 L.Ed. 2d 549, 116 S.Ct. 2135 (1996): The Court, in an opinion by Rehnquist for 5 justices, held that civil forfeiture proceedings that are separate from the criminal charges relating to the same transaction do not constitute "punishment," and therefore do not violate the double jeopardy clause.

Witte v. United States 515 U.S. 389, 132 L.Ed. 2d 351, 115 S.Ct. 2199 (1995): The Court, in an opinion by O'Connor for 6 justices, held that double jeopardy was not violated by a federal cocaine conviction, even though the facts that gave rise to the prosecution had previously been considered when sentencing the defendant on a federal marijuana offense.

United States v. Felix 503 U.S. 378, 118 L.Ed. 2d 25, 112 S.Ct. 1377 (1992): The Court, 7–2 in an opinion by Rehnquist, held introduction of "prior acts evidence" at one trial does not bar the same acts from being the subject of criminal charges at a later trial. For double jeopardy purposes, charges of conspiracy are distinct from the underlying offense, and prosecution for the underlying offense does not bar later prosecution for the conspiracy.

United States v. Halper 490 U.S. 435, 104 L.Ed. 2d 487, 109 S.Ct. 1892 (1989): The Court, in a unanimous opinion by Blackmun, held that under the double jeopardy clause a defendant who already has been punished in a criminal prosecution may be subjected to additional civil sanctions to the extent that they may fairly be characterized as remedial, but not if they are for deterrence or retribution.

Ricketts v. Adamson 483 U.S. 1, 97 L.Ed. 2d 1, 107 S.Ct. 2860 (1987): The Court, in an opinion by White for 5 justices, held that double jeopardy was not violated by prosecution of the defendant for first-degree murder following his breach of a plea agreement under which he had pled guilty to a lesser offense.

Smalis v. Pennsylvania 476 U.S. 140, 90 L.Ed. 2d 116, 106 S.Ct. 1745 (1986): The Court, in a unanimous opinion by White, held that the trial judge's granting of a defense demurrer at the end of the prosecution's case was an acquittal under the double jeopardy clause.

Morris v. Mathews 475 U.S. 237, 89 L.Ed. 2d 187, 106 S.Ct. 1032 (1986): The Court, in an opinion by White for 5 justices, held that the double jeopardy clause was not violated when a judge modified a jeopardy-barred conviction and imposed a sentence for a lesser-included offense that was not jeopardy-barred.

Heath v. Alabama 474 U.S. 82, 88 L.Ed. 2d 387, 106 S.Ct. 433 (1985): The Court, in an opinion by O'Connor for 7 justices, held that under the "dual sovereignty" doctrine successive prosecutions by two states for the same conduct are not barred by the double jeopardy clause.

Arizona v. Rumsey 467 U.S. 203, 81 L.Ed. 2d 164, 104 S.Ct. 2305 (1984): The Court, 7–2 in an opinion by O'Connor, held that double

jeopardy barred the state from seeking the death penalty when the case was remanded by the appellate court for resentencing after the original trial judge imposed a life sentence without possibility of parole instead of the death sentence due to misconception of the state's law on aggravating circumstances.

Oregon v. Kennedy 456 U.S. 667, 72 L.Ed. 2d 416, 102 S.Ct. 2083 (1982): The Court, in an opinion by Rehnquist for 5 justices, held that double jeopardy does not bar a retrial after a trial ends due to prosecutorial or judicial misconduct unless the conduct in question was intended to provoke the defendant into moving for a mistrial.

Bullington v. Missouri 451 U.S. 430, 68 L.Ed. 2d 270, 101 S.Ct. 1852 (1981): The Court in an opinion by Blackmun, held that where the penalty phase of a capital case was tried before a jury, and the jury sentenced the defendant to life imprisonment, the prosecution is barred from seeking the death penalty at retrial.

Hudson v. Louisiana 450 U.S. 40, 67 L.Ed. 2d 30, 101 S.Ct. 970 (1981): The Court, in a unanimous opinion by Powell, held that retrial was barred by double jeopardy when the trial court had granted a new trial because the state had failed to prove its case as a matter of law.

United States v. Scott 437 U.S. 82, 57 L.Ed. 2d 65, 98 S.Ct. 2187 (1978): The Court, 5–4 in an opinion by Rehnquist, held that double jeopardy does not apply in a case where the first trial was terminated at the request of the defendant.

Crist v. Bretz 437 U.S. 28, 57 L.Ed. 2d 24, 98 S.Ct. 2156 (1978): The Court, 6–3 in an opinion by Stewart, held that jeopardy attaches when the jury is impaneled and sworn.

Burks v. United States 437 U.S. 1, 57 L.Ed. 2d 1, 98 S.Ct. 2141 (1978): The Court, 8–0 in an opinion by Burger, held that double jeopardy prohibits the retrial of a defendant who has had a conviction reversed solely for lack of sufficient evidence to sustain the jury's verdict. Defendant's motion for a new trial does not waive the double jeopardy defense.

United States v. Wheeler 435 U.S. 313, 55 L.Ed. 2d 303, 98 S.Ct. 1079 (1978): The Court, 8–0 in an opinion by Stewart, held that under the "independent sovereign" doctrine double jeopardy did not bar prosecutions by the United States and the Navajo Tribe for the same offense even though the tribal court was enforcing federal law.

Arizona v. Washington 434 U.S. 497, 54 L.Ed. 2d 717, 98 S.Ct. 824 (1978): The Court, in an opinion by Stevens for 5 justices, held that double jeopardy did not bar a retrial where the judge granted a motion for a mistrial based on misconduct by defense attorney during his opening statement.

Harris v. Oklahoma 433 U.S. 682, 53 L.Ed. 2d 1054, 97 S.Ct. 2912 (1977): The Court, in a unanimous *per curiam* opinion, held that when a conviction for a greater crime could not be had without a conviction for a lesser crime, double jeopardy barred prosecution for the lesser crime after conviction for the greater.

Breed v. Jones 421 U.S. 519, 44 L.Ed. 2d 346, 95 S.Ct. 1779 (1975): The Court, unanimously in an opinion by Burger, held that prosecution of a juvenile as an adult after the adjudicatory hearing in Juvenile Court was barred by double jeopardy.

Benton v. Maryland overruled *Palko v. Connecticut* (1937) 395 U.S. 784, 23 L.Ed. 2d 707, 89 S.Ct. 2056 (1969): The Court, 6–2 in an opinion by Marshall, held that the double jeopardy clause of the Fifth Amendment is applicable to the states.

C. Indictment

Hurtado v. California 110 U.S. 516, 28 L.Ed. 232, 4 S.Ct. 292 (1884): The Court held that the due process clause of the Fourteenth Amendment does not require a state to use an indictment or presentment of a grand jury in prosecution for murder or other offenses.

VI SIXTH AMENDMENT ISSUES

A. Right to Counsel

Padilla v. Kentucky ___ U.S. ___, 176 L.Ed. 2d 284, 130 S.Ct. 1473 (2010): The Court, 7–2 in an opinion by Stevens, held that prior to the entry of a guilty plea counsel is required to inform the defendant about the collateral risk of deportation.

Kansas v. Ventris ___ U.S. ___, 173 L.Ed. 2d 801, 129 S.Ct. 1841 (2009): The Court, 7–2 in an opinion by Scalia, held that voluntary statements obtained in violation of the defendant's right to counsel can be used to impeach the defendant at trial.

Knowles v. Mirzayance ___ U.S. ___, 173 L.Ed. 2d 251, 129 S.Ct. 1411 (2009): The Court, in an opinion by Thomas parts of which represented a unanimous Court, held that when a state inmate raises the issue of ineffective assistance of counsel in a federal *habeas corpus* proceeding, a federal court may reverse the state court only if the lower court's decision was unreasonable.

Rothgery v. Gillespie County, Texas 554 U.S. 191, 171 L.Ed. 2d 366, 128 S.Ct. 2578 (2008): The Court, 8–1 in an opinion by Souter, held that a criminal defendant's initial appearance before a magistrate judge, where he learns the charge against him and his liberty is subject to restriction, marks the initiation of adversary judicial proceedings and triggers the Sixth Amendment right to counsel whether or not a prosecutor was aware of the proceeding or involved in it.

Indiana v. Edwards 554 U.S. 164, 171 L.Ed. 2d 345, 128 S.Ct. 2379 (2008): The Court, 7–2 in an opinion by Breyer, held that states may insist upon representation by counsel for a defendant who is competent to stand trial but whose severe mental illness renders him/her not competent to proceed *pro per.*

United States v. Gonzalez-Lopez 548 U.S. 140, 165 L.Ed. 2d 409, 126 S.Ct. 2557 (2006): The Court, 5–4 in an opinion by Scalia, held that a trial court's erroneous deprivation of a criminal defendant's choice of counsel without providing alternatives warrants a reversal of the conviction.

Halbert v. Michigan 545 U.S. 605, 162 L.Ed. 2d 552, 125 S.Ct. 2582 (2005): The Court, 6–3 in an opinion by Ginsburg, held that due process and equal protection clauses require the appointment of counsel for indigent defendants who seek first-tier appellate review of their guilty pleas.

Bradshaw v. Stumpf 545 U.S. 175, 162 L.Ed. 2d 143, 125 S.Ct. 2398 (2005): The Court, in a unanimous opinion by O'Connor, held that a statement on the record that the elements of the crime had been explained to the defendant by the defense attorney was sufficient to establish that the defendant knowingly entered a guilty plea; the judge does not need to inform the defendant of the elements of the crime.

Iowa v. Tovar 541 U.S. 77, 158 L.Ed. 2d 209, 124 S.Ct. 1379 (2004): The Court, in a unanimous opinion by Ginsburg, held that a trial judge is not required to specifically advise the defendant who is seeking to be a *pro per* that waiving counsel's assistance entails the risk that a viable defense will be overlooked and deprives the defendant of the opportunity to obtain an independent opinion on whether it is wise to plead guilty.

Fellers v. United States 540 U.S. 519, 157 L.Ed. 2d 1016, 124 S.Ct. 1019 (2004): The Court, in a unanimous opinion by O'Connor, held that statements officers deliberately elicited from petitioner at his home were not admissible at trial because they were obtained after petitioner had been indicted, outside the presence of counsel, and in the absence of any waiver of his Sixth Amendment rights.

Alabama v. Shelton 535 U.S. 654, 152 L.Ed. 2d 888, 122 S.Ct. 1764 (2002): The Court, 5–4 in an opinion by Ginsburg, held that a judge may not impose a suspended sentence that may "end up in the actual deprivation of a person's liberty" unless the defendant was accorded the right to counsel in the prosecution for the crime charged.

Mickens v. Taylor 535 U.S. 162, 152 L.Ed. 2d 291, 122 S.Ct. 1237 (2002): The Court, 5–4 in an opinion by Rehnquist, held that to justify reversal because the trial court failed to inquire into a potential Sixth Amendment conflict of interest, the defendant must establish that he/she was adversely affected by counsel's performance.

Texas v. Cobb 532 U.S. 162, 149 L.Ed. 2d 321, 121 S.Ct. 1335 (2001): The Court, 5–4 in an opinion by Rehnquist, held that the Sixth Amendment right to counsel is "offense-specific": errors that are "factually related" to one offense do not necessarily extend to related offenses.

Glover v. United States 531 U.S. 198, 148 L.Ed. 2d 604, 121 S.Ct. 696 (2001): The Court, in a unanimous opinion by Kennedy, held that the defendant is entitled to a new sentencing hearing when ineffective assistance of counsel at the sentencing hearing resulted in an increase in the length of the defendant's sentence.

Roe v. Flores-Ortega 528 U.S. 470, 145 L.Ed. 2d 985, 120 S.Ct. 1029 (2000): The Court, 6–3 in an opinion by O'Connor, held that when evaluating a claim that counsel was constitutionally ineffective for failing to file a notice of appeal, the defendant must establish that there is a reasonable probability that, but for counsel's deficient behavior, he would have timely appealed.

Smith v. Robbins 528 U.S. 259, 145 L.Ed. 2d 756, 120 S.Ct. 746 (2000): The Court, 5–4 in an opinion by Thomas, held that procedures described in *Anders v. California* (1967) for the withdrawal of appointed appellate counsel are not the exclusive permissible method for handling such cases.

Martinez v. Court of Appeal of California 528 U.S. 152, 145 L.Ed. 2d 597, 120 S.Ct. 684 (2000): The Court, 8–1 in an opinion by Stevens, held that there is no constitutional right to self-representation on direct appeal from a criminal conviction.

Nichols v. United States overruled *Baldasar v. Illinois* (1980) 511 U.S. 738, 128 L.Ed. 2d 745, 114 S.Ct. 1921 (1994): The Court, 6–3 in an opinion by Rehnquist, held that the use of a prior misdemeanor conviction in order to impose a longer sentence for a new conviction was valid even though the defendant was not represented by counsel in the case involving the misdemeanor conviction.

Godinez v. Moran 509 U.S. 389, 125 L.Ed. 2d 321, 113 S.Ct. 2680 (1993): The Court, in an opinion by Thomas for 5 justices, held that the competency standard for a defendant to plead guilty and for waiver of the right to counsel are the same as the competency standard for standing trial. The defendant also needs to make the decision knowingly and voluntarily.

Powell v. Texas 492 U.S. 680, 106 L.Ed. 2d 551, 109 S.Ct. 3146 (1989): The Court, in a unanimous *per curiam* opinion, held that while a defendant's raising an insanity defense may give the prosecution the right to have the defendant examined by prosecution experts, conducting such evaluation without prior notice to defense counsel violates the Sixth Amendment.

Wheat v. United States 486 U.S. 153, 100 L.Ed. 2d 140, 108 S.Ct. 1692 (1988): The Court, in an opinion by Rehnquist for 5 justices, held refusal to permit an attorney to represent two defendants despite defendant's waiver of the right to conflict-free counsel was within the discretion of the trial judge both in cases where the judge sees an actual conflict of interest and where a potential for such a conflict exists.

Pennsylvania v. Finley 481 U.S. 551, 95 L.Ed. 2d 539, 107 S.Ct. 1990 (1987): The Court, in an opinion by Rehnquist for 5 justices, held that there is no constitutional right to appointed counsel when mounting a collateral attack on a conviction, such as *habeas corpus* proceedings.

Smith v. Murray 477 U.S. 527, 91 L.Ed. 2d 434, 106 S.Ct. 2661 (1986): The Court, in an opinion by O'Connor for 5 justices, held that a deliberate tactical decision not to raise an issue on direct appeal bars its introduction in a writ of *habeas corpus* absent a showing that there is a probability that counsel's

procedural default resulted in the conviction of an innocent person.

Nix v. Whiteside 475 U.S. 157, 89 L.Ed. 2d 123, 106 S.Ct. 988 (1986): The Court, in an opinion by Burger for 5 justices, held Sixth Amendment right to counsel was not violated by attorney who refused to cooperate with defendant's wishes to present perjured testimony.

Maine v. Moulton 474 U.S. 159, 88 L.Ed. 2d 481, 106 S.Ct. 477 (1985): The Court, in an opinion by Brennan for 5 justices, held that statements obtained by codefendant who had decided to cooperate with police after indictment and wear a concealed microphone during a conference with defense attorneys were inadmissible as a violation of the Sixth Amendment right to counsel.

Evitts v. Lucey 469 U.S. 387, 83 L.Ed. 2d 821, 105 S.Ct. 830 (1985): The Court, in an opinion by Brennan for 7 justices, held that defendant has due process right to effective assistance of counsel on first appeal.

Strickland v. Washington 466 U.S. 668, 80 L.Ed. 2d 674, 104 S.Ct. 2052 (1984): The Court, in an opinion by O'Connor for 7 justices, established the standard for reversing a conviction based on ineffective assistance of trial counsel: (1) counsel was not functioning as the counsel guaranteed by the Sixth Amendment; and (2) there is a reasonable probability that, except for counsel's errors, the outcome of the trial would have been different.

Jones v. Barnes 463 U.S. 745, 77 L.Ed. 2d 987, 103 S.Ct. 3308 (1983): The Court, in an opinion by Burger for 6 justices, held that counsel who is appointed to handle an appeal for a criminal defendant does not have a constitutional duty to raise every nonfrivolous issue requested by the defendant.

Lassiter v. Department of Social Services of Durham County, North Carolina 452 U.S. 18, 68 L.Ed. 2d 640, 101 S.Ct. 2153 (1981): The Court, in an opinion by Stewart for 5 justices, held that under Fourteenth Amendment due process clause the decision to appoint counsel at a hearing to terminate parental status should be determined by the trial court on a case-by-case basis.

Cuyler v. Sullivan 446 U.S. 335, 64 L.Ed. 2d 333, 100 S.Ct. 1708 (1980): The Court, in an opinion by Powell for 7 justices, held that joint representation of codefendants by one attorney does not require automatic reversal. The trial judge is not required to appoint separate attorneys unless there is reason to believe that a conflict exists.

Scott v. Illinois 440 U.S. 367, 59 L.Ed. 2d 383, 99 S.Ct. 1158 (1979): The Court, 5–4 in an opinion by Rehnquist, held that the Sixth Amendment right to counsel requires that any defendant who is sentenced to imprisonment have been represented by counsel at trial.

Holloway v. Arkansas 435 U.S. 475, 55 L.Ed. 2d 426, 98 S.Ct. 1173 (1978): The Court, 6–3 in an opinion by Burger, held that automatic reversal was required where the trial judge, over timely objection, improperly required codefendants to be represented by the same counsel.

Moore v. Illinois 434 U.S. 220, 54 L.Ed. 2d 424, 98 S.Ct. 458 (1977): The Court, in an opinion by Powell for 7 justices, held that the fact the rape victim identified the defendant at his preliminary hearing where he was not represented by counsel was inadmissible at trial.

Weatherford v. Bursey 429 U.S. 545, 51 L.Ed. 2d 30, 97 S.Ct. 837 (1977): The Court, 7–2, in an opinion by White, held that presence of an undercover agent at a pretrial conference between the accused and his attorney did not violate the accused's Sixth Amendment rights where he attended the meetings in order to maintain his cover and did not reveal anything learned at the meetings.

Geders v. United States 425 U.S. 80, 47 L.Ed. 2d 592, 96 S.Ct. 1330 (1976): The Court, in a unanimous opinion by Burger, held that denying the defendant the right to consult with counsel during a 17-hour, overnight recess in the case violated the right to counsel.

Middendorf v. Henry 425 U.S. 25, 47 L.Ed. 2d 556, 96 S.Ct. 1281 (1975): The Court, 5–3 in an opinion by Rehnquist, held that a summary court-martial was not a "criminal proceeding" for purposes of the right to counsel.

Faretta v. California 422 U.S. 806, 45 L.Ed. 2d 562, 95 S.Ct. 2525 (1975). The Court, 6–3 in an opinion by Stewart, held that the Sixth Amendment guarantees self-representation to a criminal defendant who voluntarily and intelligently waives the right to the assistance of counsel and insists on conducting his own defense.

Gerstein v. Pugh 420 U.S. 103, 43 L.Ed. 2d 541, 95 S.Ct. 854 (1975): The Court, in an opinion by Powell, held that the defendant does not have the right to be present or the right to be represented by counsel at a probable cause hearing.

Ross v. Moffitt (1974) 417 U.S. 600, 41 L.Ed. 2d 341, 94 S.Ct. 2437 (1974): The Court, 6–3 in an opinion by Rehnquist, held that states do not have to provide counsel for indigents wishing to make discretionary appeals to the state's highest court or to the United States Supreme Court.

Gagnon v. Scarpelli 411 U.S. 778, 36 L.Ed. 2d 656, 93 S.Ct. 1756 (1973): The Court, 8–1 in an opinion by Powell, held that under some circumstances the state may be required to assign counsel at probation revocation hearings.

Argersinger v. Hamlin 407 U.S. 25, 32 L.Ed. 2d 530, 92 S.Ct. 2006 (1972): The Court, 6–3 in an opinion by Douglas, held that all indigent defendants facing a possible jail sentence are entitled to be represented by appointed counsel in their trial. See also, *Scott v. Illinois* (1979) and *Nichols v. United States* (1994)

Coleman v. Alabama 399 U.S. 1, 26 L.Ed. 2d 387, 90 S.Ct. 1999 (1970): The Court, in an opinion by Brennan, held that a preliminary hearing is a "critical stage" where an indigent defendant has a constitutional right to the appointment of counsel.

Brady v. United States 397 U.S. 742, 25 L.Ed.2d 747, 90 S.Ct. 1463 (1970) (together with *McMann v. Richardson,* 397 U.S. 759, 25 L.Ed. 2d 763, 90 S.Ct. 1441, and *Parker v. North Carolina* 397 U.S. 790, 25 L.Ed. 2d 785, 90 S.Ct. 1458): The Court held that a defendant has the right to the presence of counsel during the plea bargaining process.

Johnson v. Avery 393 U.S. 483, 21 L.Ed. 2d 718, 89 S.Ct. 747 (1969): The Court invalidated a prison regulation that prohibited an inmate acting as a "jailhouse lawyer" for other inmates if no other legal assistance were available.

Mempha v. Rhay 389 U.S. 128, 19 L.Ed. 2d 336, 88 S.Ct. 254 (1967): The Court held that an indigent defendant who is to be sentenced as a part of probation revocation proceedings must have counsel provided for him/her.

Anders v. California 386 U.S. 738, 18 L.Ed. 2d 493, 87 S.Ct. 1396(1967): The Court, 6–3 in an opinion by Clark, held that if appointed appellate counsel, after a conscientious examination of the record, finds the case to be wholly frivolous, he may so advise the court and request permission to withdraw. The request should be accompanied by a brief referring to anything in the record that might arguably support the appeal.

Douglas v. California 372 U.S. 353, 9 L.Ed. 2d 811, 83 S.Ct. 814 (1963): The Court, 6–3, held that there is an absolute right to the assistance of counsel during the first appeal.

Gideon v. Wainwright 372 U.S. 335, 9 L.Ed. 2d 799, 83 S.Ct. 792 (1963): The Supreme Court included the Sixth Amendment right to be represented by counsel when a person is being tried for a crime in a state court among the fundamental rights guaranteed by the Fourteenth Amendment. Indigent defendants have the right to have counsel assigned by the court.

Griffin v. Illinois 351 U.S. 12, 100 L.Ed. 891, 76 S.Ct. 585 (1956): The Court, 5–4, held that the due process and equal protection clauses of the Fourteenth Amendment require that all indigent defendants be furnished a transcript, or a record of sufficient completeness, needed for an appeal.

B. Grand and Petit Juries

1. Trial Juries

Presley v. Georgia ___ U.S. ___, 175 L.Ed. 2d 675, 130 S.Ct. 721 (2010): The Court, in a 7–2 *per curiam* opinion, held that the public has the right to be present during *voir dire* of the jury. If the trial court has an overriding interest in closing *voir dire,* it is incumbent upon it to consider all reasonable alternatives.

Rivera v. Illinois ___ U.S. ___, 173 L.Ed. 2d 320, 129 S.Ct. 1446 (2009): The Court, in a unanimous opinion by Ginsburg, held that where all jurors seated in a criminal case are qualified and unbiased, the due process clause does not require automatic reversal of a conviction because the trial court made a good-faith error in denying the defendant's peremptory challenge to a juror.

Snyder v. Louisiana 552 U.S. 472, 128 S.Ct. 1203, 170 L.Ed. 2d 175 (2008): The Court, 7–2 in an opinion by Alito, found clear error in rejecting a *Batson* objection to the striking of a juror, where the judge did so without asking the prosecutor for an explanation for the alleged racial discriminatory use of a peremptory challenge.

Miller-El v. Dretke 545 U.S. 231, 162 L.Ed. 2d 196, 125 S.Ct. 2317 (2005): The Court, 6–3 in an opinion by Souter, held that a case of discrimination under *Batson* was shown where the prosecution excluded 91% of the eligible African Americans from the jury panel, more extensively questioned potential African American jurors, allowed white jurors to remain on the panel who had the same personal experiences, and repeatedly shuffled the jury cards in an attempt to prevent African Americans from being seated in the jury box.

Johnson v. California 545 U.S. 162, 162 L.Ed. 2d 129, 125 S.Ct. 2410 (2005): The Court, in an opinion by Stevens for 7 justices, held that a defendant satisfies *Batson*'s first step by producing evidence sufficient to permit the trial judge to draw an inference that discrimination has occurred. At this stage, it is not necessary to show discrimination "more likely than not" occurred.

Lewis v. United States 518 U.S. 322, 135 L.Ed. 2d 590, 116 S.Ct. 2163 (1996): The Court, 7–3 in an opinion by O'Connor, held that a defendant in a federal criminal prosecution has the right to a jury trial only if the sentence for a charge exceeds six months; sentences for lesser offenses cannot be aggregated in order to trigger the right to a jury trial.

J. E. B. ex rel. T. B. 511 U.S. 127, 128 L.Ed. 2d 89, 114 S.Ct. 1419 (1994): The Court, 6–3 in an opinion by Blackmun, held that the Fourteenth Amendment equal protection clause prohibits the use of peremptory challenges by state actors on the basis of gender.

Sullivan v. Louisiana 508 U.S. 275, 124 L.Ed. 2d 182, 113 S.Ct. 2078 (1993): The Court, in a unanimous opinion by Scalia, held that failure to give the jury an adequate instruction on "proof beyond a reasonable doubt" violates the defendant's right to a jury trial and is a fundamental error requiring reversal.

Georgia v. McCollum 505 U.S. 42, 120 L.Ed. 2d 33, 112 S.Ct. 2348 (1992): The Court, 6–3 in an opinion by Blackmun, held that the Constitution prohibits a criminal defendant from engaging in purposeful discrimination on the grounds of race in the exercise of peremptory challenges.

Hernandez v. New York 500 U.S. 352, 114 L.Ed. 2d 395, 111 S.Ct. 1859 (1991): The Court, 6–3 although unable to agree on a majority opinion, held the equal protection clause was not violated by the exclusion of Hispanic jurors based on fear that they would rely on their own knowledge of Spanish rather than the translation of the court's interpreter.

Powers v. Ohio 499 U.S. 400, 113 L.Ed. 2d 411, 111 S.Ct. 1364 (1991): The Court, 7–2 in an opinion by Kennedy, held that a white

defendant had standing to have a conviction reversed due to violation of the equal protection clause if the prosecutor used peremptory challenges to exclude prospective black jurors.

Blanton v. City of North Las Vegas, Nevada 489 U.S. 538, 103 L.Ed. 2d 550, 109 S.Ct. 1289 (1989): The Court, in a unanimous opinion by Marshall, held that for offenses with a maximum sentence of six months or less, the defendant is entitled to a jury trial only if he/she can demonstrate that any additional statutory penalties, viewed in conjunction with the maximum authorized period of incarceration, are so severe that they clearly reflect a legislative determination that the offense in question is a "serious" one. The fact that increased penalties are imposed for repeat offenses is not to be considered.

Batson v. Kentucky 476 U.S. 79, 90 L.Ed. 2d 69, 106 S.Ct. 1712 (1986): The Court, in an opinion by Powell for 7 justices, held the equal protection clause forbids prosecutorial use of peremptory challenges to exclude potential jurors solely on account of their race or on the assumption that black jurors as a group will be unable to impartially consider the state's case against a black defendant. To establish a prima facie case the defendant must show: he/she is a member of a cognizable racial group; and the prosecutor has exercised peremptory challenges to remove members of defendant's race from the jury. Once the defense makes a prima facie showing, the burden shifts and the state must give a neutral explanation for challenging jurors.

Burch v. Louisiana 441 U.S. 130, 60 L.Ed. 2d 96, 99 S.Ct. 1623 (1979): The Court, in an opinion by Rehnquist for 6 justices, held that conviction by a nonunanimous six-person jury in a state criminal trial for a nonpetty offense violated the Sixth and Fourteenth Amendments.

Duren v. Missouri 439 U.S. 357, 58 L.Ed. 2d 579, 99 S.Ct. 664 (1979): The Court, 8–1 in an opinion by White, held that a state statute that exempted women but not men from jury service upon request violated the male defendant's Sixth and Fourteenth Amendment rights to a jury drawn from a fair cross-section of the community.

Ballew v. Georgia 435 U.S. 223, 55 L.Ed. 2d 234, 98 S.Ct. 1029 (1978): The Court, although unable to agree upon an opinion, unanimously agreed that a jury of less than six persons in a criminal trial violated the Sixth and Fourteenth Amendments.

Ristaino v. Ross 424 U.S. 589, 47 L.Ed. 2d 258, 96 S.Ct. 1017 (1976): The Court, in an opinion by Powell for 5 justices, held that the defendant had the right to have prospective jurors questioned regarding their racial prejudices only if the facts of the case suggested a significant likelihood that racial prejudice might infect the defendant's trial.

Taylor v. Louisiana 419 U.S. 522, 42 L.Ed. 2d 690, 95 S.Ct. 692 (1975): The Court, in an opinion by White for 7 justices, held that the exclusion of women from jury service unless they volunteered violated the Sixth and Fourteenth Amendments. Both male and female defendants have standing to object to this type of unconstitutional procedure.

Johnson v. Louisiana 406 U.S. 356, 32 L.Ed. 2d 152, 92 S.Ct. 1620 (1972): The Court, 6–3, in an opinion by White, held that a state law allowing nonunanimous jury verdicts in criminal trials utilizing a 12-person jury panel did not violate the Sixth Amendment. A minimum of 9 out of 12 votes were needed to convict.

McKiever v. Pennsylvania (*In re Barbara Burns* et al.), 403 U.S. 528, 29 L.Ed. 2d 647, 91 S.Ct. 1976 (1971): The Court, 6–3 in an opinion by Blackmun, held that the Sixth Amendment does not require trial by jury in state juvenile delinquency proceedings.

Williams v. Florida 399 U.S. 78, 26 L.Ed. 2d 446, 90 S.Ct. 1893 (1970): The Court, in an opinion by White, held that the traditional 12-person jury was the result of historical accident and that smaller juries are permissible under the Sixth Amendment.

Singer v. United States 380 U.S. 24, 13 L.Ed. 2d 630, 85 S.Ct. 783 (1965): The Court, in a unanimous opinion by Warren, held that a criminal defendant does not have the right to be tried without a jury if the prosecution requests a jury.

2. Grand Juries

Campbell v. Louisiana 523 U.S. 392, 140 L.Ed. 2d 551, 118 S.Ct. 1419 (1998): The Court, in an opinion by Kennedy pertinent portions of which represented the unanimous opinion of the Court, held that a white criminal defendant had standing to raise equal protection and due process objections to discrimination against black persons in the selection of grand jurors.

United States v. Williams 504 U.S. 36, 118 L.Ed. 2d 352, 112 S.Ct. 1735 (1992): The Court, 5–4 in an opinion by Scalia, held that the government has no duty to disclose "substantially exculpatory evidence" in its possession to the grand jury when seeking an indictment.

Butterworth v. Smith 494 U.S. 624, 108 L.Ed.2d 572, 110 S.Ct. 1376 (1990): The Court, in a unanimous opinion by Rehnquist, held that a Florida law that prohibited a grand jury witness from disclosing his/her own testimony after the term of the grand jury had ended violated the First Amendment.

Rose v. Mitchell 443 U.S. 545, 61 L.Ed. 2d 739, 99 S.Ct. 2993 (1979): The Court, in an opinion by Blackmun joined in pertinent parts by 5 justices, held that discrimination in the selection of members of a grand jury is valid ground for setting aside a criminal conviction even though a guilty verdict had been rendered by a properly selected trial jury.

C. Trial See Section I B. Freedom of the Press for cases involving the First Amendment right to access to trials.

1. Public Access to Trial

Waller v. Georgia 467 U.S. 39, 81 L.Ed. 2d 31, 104 S.Ct. 2210 (1984): The Court, in a unanimous opinion by Powell, held that the right to a public trial under the Sixth and Fourteenth Amendments applies to pretrial hearings held to determine whether evidence should be suppressed.

Globe Newspaper Company v. Superior Court for the County of Norfolk 457 U.S. 596, 73 L.Ed. 2d 248, 102 S.Ct. 2613 (1982): The Court, in an opinion by Brennan for 5 justices, held that a statute providing for exclusion of the general public from the trials of specified sexual offenses involving victims under the age of 18 was unconstitutional.

Gannett Co., Inc. v. DePasquale 443 U.S. 368, 61 L.Ed. 2d 608, 99 S.Ct. 2898 (1979): The Court, in an opinion by Stewart for 5 justices, held that where the trial judge had adequately considered the balance of the defendant's right to a fair trial against the right of the press and public to attend a suppression hearing, the order closing the hearing to the press and public was constitutional.

2. Publicity

Chandler v. Florida 449 U.S. 560, 66 L.Ed. 2d 740, 101 S.Ct. 802 (1981): The Court, in an opinion by Burger for 6 justices, held that states could experiment with the use of electronic media and still photographic coverage of public judicial proceedings without violating the constitutional rights of the defendant.

Nebraska Press Association v. Stuart 427 U.S. 539, 49 L.Ed. 2d 683, 96 S.Ct. 2791 (1976): The Court, in an opinion by Burger for 5 justices, held that a court order prohibiting the publication or broadcasting of confessions, admissions made by the accused, or facts strongly implicating him was unconstitutional. Prohibition of reporting and commenting on court proceedings that were held in public is invalid.

Murphy v. Florida 421 U.S. 794, 44 L.Ed. 2d 589, 95 S.Ct. 2031 (1975): The Court, in an opinion by Marshall for 7 justices, held that

denial of a motion for change of venue on grounds of pretrial publicity did not violate the defendant's constitutional rights where the defendant had failed to show that the setting of the trial was inherently prejudicial or that the jury selection process permitted an inference of actual prejudice.

3. Plea Bargaining

Godinez v. Moran 509 U.S. 389, 125 L.Ed. 2d 321, 113 S.Ct. 2680 (1993): The Court, in an opinion by Thomas for 5 justices, held that the mental competency standard for pleading guilty and for waiver of the right to counsel is the same as the competency standard for standing trial.

United States v. Broce 488 U.S. 563, 102 L.Ed. 2d 927, 109 S.Ct. 757 (1989): The Court, in an opinion by Kennedy for 6 justices, held that the entry of guilty pleas foreclosed the defendant's right to challenge those pleas by collateral attack on double jeopardy grounds.

Ricketts v. Adamson 483 U.S. 1, 97 L.Ed. 2d 1, 107 S.Ct. 2860 (1987): The Court, in an opinion by White for 5 justices, held that double jeopardy was not violated by prosecution of the defendant for first-degree murder following his breach of a plea agreement under which he had pled guilty to a lesser offense.

Mabry v. Johnson 467 U.S. 504, 81 L.Ed. 2d 437, 104 S.Ct. 2543 (1984): The Court, in a unanimous opinion by Stevens, held that the defendant's acceptance of a proposed plea bargain the prosecutor erroneously made does not create a constitutional right to have the bargain enforced by the trial court.

Corbitt v. New Jersey 439 U.S. 212, 58 L.Ed. 2d 466, 99 S.Ct. 492 (1978): The Court, in an opinion by White for 5 justices, upheld a New Jersey law that made a sentence of life imprisonment mandatory upon jury conviction for first-degree murder but allowed lesser sentences if the defendant entered a plea.

4. Speedy Trial

Vermont v. Brillon ___ U.S. ___, 173 L.Ed. 2d 231, 129 S.Ct. 1283 (2009): The Court, 7–2 in an opinion by Ginsburg, held that when evaluating a Sixth Amendment denial of speedy trial motion, delays sought by both retained and assigned counsel are ordinarily attributable to the defendant they represent.

Doggett v. United States 505 U.S. 647, 120 L.Ed. 2d 520, 112 S.Ct. 2686 (1992): The Court, 5–4 in an opinion by Souter, held that in cases with extraordinary delays, the longer the delay the less other evidence of prejudice is needed.

United States v. Lovasco 431 U.S. 783, 52 L.Ed. 2d 752, 97 S.Ct. 2044 (1977): The Court, 8–1 in an opinion by Marshall, held that the right to a speedy trial based on due process was not denied where the delay between the commission of the crime and the initiation of prosecution was for the purpose of investigating the offense.

Dillingham v. United States 423 U.S. 64, 46 L.Ed. 2d 205, 96 S.Ct. 303 (1975): The Court, 7–1 in a *per curiam* opinion, held that a showing of actual prejudice was not necessary in order for preindictment delay to violate the Sixth Amendment right to a speedy trial.

Barker v. Wingo 407 U.S. 514, 33 L.Ed. 2d 101, 92 S.Ct. 2182 (1972): The Court, in an opinion by Powell, held that violation of the Sixth Amendment right to a speedy trial is judged by weighing four factors, no one of which is conclusive: length of delay, reason for delay, defendant's assertion of his right, and prejudice to the defendant.

5. Confrontation and Cross-Examination

Melendez-Diaz v. Massachusetts ___ U.S. ___, 174 L.Ed. 2d 314, 129 S.Ct. 2527 (2009): The Court, 5–4 in an opinion by Scalia, held that introduction of certified reports from the state's forensics laboratory at trial, without the person who conducted the tests to testify, violated the defendant's right to confront witnesses against him.

Davis v. Washington 547 U.S. 813, 165 L.Ed. 2d 224, 126 S.Ct. 2266 (2006): The Court, in an opinion by Scalia for 8 justices, held that statements are testimonial, and admissible only if the declarant is available for cross-examination, when the circumstances objectively indicate that they were obtained when there was no ongoing emergency, and that the primary purpose of the questioning was to establish past events potentially relevant to criminal prosecution.

Holmes v. South Carolina 547 U.S. 319, 164 L.Ed. 2d 503, 126 S.Ct. 1727 (2006): The Court, in a unanimous opinion by Alito, held that a criminal defendant's federal constitutional rights were violated by a rule precluding the defendant's introduction of evidence of third-party guilt if the prosecution introduced forensic evidence that, if believed, strongly supports a guilty verdict.

Crawford v. Washington 541 U.S. 36, 158 L.Ed. 2d 177, 124 S.Ct. 1354 (2004): The Court, in an opinion by Scalia for 7 justices, held that the defendant's Sixth Amendment right to confront witnesses is violated when testimonial hearsay is admitted at trial without the hearsay declarant testifying.

Lilly v. Virginia 527 U.S. 116, 144 L.Ed. 2d 117, 119 S.Ct. 1887 (1999): The Court, 6–3 in an opinion by Stevens, held that the defendant's confrontation clause rights were violated when the state was allowed to introduce the statements of a principal to the crime who invoked the Fifth Amendment during trial. The statements were admitted under the hearsay exception for declarations against penal interest of an unavailable witness.

United States v. Scheffer 523 U.S. 303, 140 L.Ed. 2d 413, 118 S.Ct. 1261 (1998): The Court, in an opinion by Thomas pertinent parts of which represented the views of 8 justices, held that a rule which prohibits the introduction of testimony regarding polygraph examinations does not violate the defendant's right to present a defense.

White v. Illinois 502 U.S. 346, 116 L.Ed. 2d 848, 112 S.Ct. 736 (1992): The Court, 7–2 in an opinion by Rehnquist, held that the confrontation clause is not violated by admitting hearsay without showing that the declarant is unavailable under the "spontaneous declaration" or "statements made in the course of securing medical treatment" exceptions to the hearsay rule.

Michigan v. Lucas 500 U.S. 145, 114 L.Ed. 2d 205, 111 S.Ct. 1743 (1991): The Court, 6–3 in an opinion by O'Connor, held the Sixth Amendment was not violated when the trial court refused to allow evidence of prior sexual conduct between a defendant in a rape case and the victim. The Court rejected a *per se* rule that preclusion is unconstitutional.

Maryland v. Craig 497 U.S. 836, 111 L.Ed. 2d 666, 110 S.Ct. 3157 (1990): The Court, in an opinion by O'Connor for 5 justices, held that the confrontation clause of the Sixth Amendment did not categorically prohibit the victim in a child abuse case from testifying against a defendant at trial by one-way closed circuit television. The Court found it significant that all other elements of confrontation were preserved. The requisite finding of necessity to deny face-to-face confrontation must be made on a case-specific basis.

Idaho v. Wright 497 U.S. 805, 111 L.Ed. 2d 638, 110 S.Ct. 3139 (1990): The Court, in an opinion by O'Connor for 5 justices, rejected Idaho's "residual hearsay exception." To be admissible against the defendant under the confrontation clause, hearsay evidence must possess indicia of reliability by virtue of its inherent trustworthiness, not by reference to other evidence at trial.

James v. Illinois 493 U.S. 307, 107 L.Ed. 2d 676, 110 S.Ct. 648 (1990): The Court, in an opinion by Brennan for 5 justices, held that statements that were the product of an illegal arrest could not be used to impeach a defense witness who is not the defendant in the case.

Olden v. Kentucky 488 U.S. 227, 102 L.Ed. 2d 513, 109 S.Ct. 480 (1988): The Court, in a *per curiam* opinion for 8 justices, held that in a case involving rape, the trial court's refusal to allow cross-examination of the victim regarding possible motive to lie deprived the defendant of his Sixth Amendment rights.

Coy v. Iowa 487 U.S. 1012, 101 L.Ed. 2d 857, 108 S.Ct. 2798 (1988): The Court, in an opinion by Scalia for 6 justices, held that placing a screen to block the defendant from the sight of the witnesses violated the defendant's Sixth Amendment right to face-to-face confrontation of the witnesses against him/her.

Rock v. Arkansas 483 U.S. 44, 97 L.Ed. 2d 37, 107 S.Ct. 2704 (1987): The Court, in an opinion by Blackmun for 5 justices, held that a state's *per se* evidentiary rule prohibiting the admission of hypnotically refreshed testimony violated the defendant's constitutional right to testify on his/her own behalf.

Kentucky v. Stincer 482 U.S. 730, 96 L.Ed. 2d 631, 107 S.Ct. 2658 (1987): The Court, in an opinion by Blackmun for 6 justices, held that exclusion of the defendant, but not defense counsel, from proceedings held to determine the competency of child witnesses to testify did not violate either the confrontation clause of the Sixth Amendment or the due process clause of the Fourteenth Amendment.

Richardson v. Marsh 481 U.S. 200, 95 L.Ed. 2d 176, 107 S.Ct. 1702 (1987): The Court, in an opinion by Scalia for 6 justices, held that the confrontation clause is not violated by the admission of a nontestifying codefendant's confession with a proper limiting instruction when the confession was redacted to eliminate the defendant's name and any reference to his/her existence.

Cruz v. New York 481 U.S. 186, 95 L.Ed. 2d 162, 107 S.Ct. 1714 (1987): The Court, in an opinion by Scalia for 5 justices, held that, where a nontestifying codefendant's confession incriminating the defendant is not directly admissible against the defendant, the confrontation clause bars its admission at their joint trial even if the jury is instructed not to consider it against the defendant, and even if the defendant's own confession is admitted against him/her.

Pennsylvania v. Ritchie 480 U.S. 39, 94 L.Ed. 2d 40, 107 S.Ct. 989 (1987): The Court, in an opinion by Powell pertinent parts of which were signed by 5 justices, held that in a child molestation case the due process clause gives the defendant the right to have the court conduct an *in camera* review of records of the agency handling child abuse. Due process does not require that the defense be given full access to confidential materials.

Crane v. Kentucky 476 U.S. 683, 90 L.Ed. 2d 636, 106 S.Ct. 2142 (1986): The Court, in a unanimous opinion by O'Connor, held that a defendant may introduce evidence about the physical and psychological circumstances under which a confession was obtained in order to show lack of trustworthiness of the confession; this is independent of ruling on *Miranda* issues.

Lee v. Illinois 476 U.S. 530, 90 L.Ed. 2d 514, 106 S.Ct. 2056 (1986): The Court, in an opinion by Brennan for 5 justices, held that a confession of a codefendant and alleged accomplice inculpating the accused is viewed with suspicion and presumptively unreliable; use of such confession against an accused at trial without benefit of cross-examination violates Sixth Amendment right of confrontation if the presumption of unreliability is not overcome by a showing of sufficient independent indicia of reliability. The harmless error rule is used in these types of cases.

Delaware v. Van Arsdall 475 U.S. 673, 89 L.Ed. 2d 674, 106 S.Ct. 1431 (1986): The Court, in an opinion by Rehnquist for 6 justices, held that the Sixth Amendment was violated by cutting off all questioning about an event which the prosecution conceded occurred, that the jury might reasonably have found furnished the witness with a motive for favoring the prosecution in his testimony.

United States v. Inadi 475 U.S. 387, 89 L.Ed. 2d 390, 106 S.Ct. 1121 (1986): The Court, in an opinion by Powell for 7 justices, held that the confrontation clause of the Sixth Amendment does not require the prosecution to show that a nontestifying coconspirator is unavailable to testify as a condition for admission of that coconspirator's out-of-court statements that were made in furtherance of the conspiracy.

Delaware v. Fensterer 474 U.S. 15, 88 L.Ed. 2d 15, 106 S.Ct. 292 (1985): The Court, in an opinion by Burger for 7 justices, held that the confrontation clause contains no guarantee that prosecution witnesses will refrain from giving testimony marred by forgetfulness, confusion, or evasion.

Ohio v. Roberts 448 U.S. 56, 65 L.Ed. 2d 597, 100 S.Ct. 2531 (1980): The Court, 6–3 in an opinion by Blackmun, held that use of the transcript of the testimony of a witness at the preliminary hearing did not violate the defendant's Sixth Amendment right to confrontation.

Davis v. Alaska 415 U.S. 308, 39 L.Ed. 2d 347, 94 S.Ct. 1105 (1974): The Court, 6–3 in an opinion by Burger, held that a defendant in a criminal case had the right to cross-examine a witness for impeachment purposes regarding a conviction that occurred while the witness was a juvenile.

Bruton v. United States overruled *Delli Paoli v. United States* (1957) 391 U.S. 123, 20 L.Ed. 2d 476, 88 S.Ct. 1620 (1968): The Court, in an opinion by Brennan, held that a confession of one defendant cannot be used at a joint trial in which it might prejudice a codefendant because of the substantial risk that the jury, despite instructions to the contrary, looked to the incriminating extrajudicial statements in determining the non-confessing codefendant's guilt.

6. Prosecutor's Misconduct

Darden v. Wainwright 477 U.S. 168, 91 L.Ed. 2d 144, 106 S.Ct. 2464 (1986): The Court, in an opinion by Powell for 5 justices, held that the relevant question when evaluating the prosecutor's comments in closing arguments is whether they "so infected the trial with unfairness as to make the resulting conviction a denial of due process."

Fletcher v. Weir 455 U.S. 603, 71 L.Ed. 2d 490, 102 S.Ct. 1309 (1982): The Court, in a *per curiam* opinion for 7 justices, held that cross-examination of a defendant regarding his/her post-arrest silence did not violate due process when the silence was not attributable to invocation of *Miranda* rights.

Carter v. Kentucky 450 U.S. 288, 67 L.Ed. 2d 241, 101 S.Ct. 1112 (1981): The Court, 8–1 in an opinion by Stewart, held that a defendant has the right to have a cautionary instruction given to the jury explaining that an inference of guilt cannot be drawn from the defendant's failure to testify at trial.

Jenkins v. Anderson 447 U.S. 23, 65 L.Ed. 2d 86, 100 S.Ct. 2124 (1980): The Court, in an opinion by Powell for 5 justices, held that use of pre-arrest silence to impeach a defendant who testified at his/her own trial did not violate either the Fifth Amendment right to remain silent or the Fourteenth Amendment right to fundamental fairness.

Doyle v. Ohio 426 U.S. 610, 49 L.Ed. 2d 91, 96 S.Ct. 2240 (1976): The Court, 6–3 in an opinion by Powell, held that impeachment based on the failure of the defendants to make a timely allegation during custodial interrogation, after having been apprised of their *Miranda* rights, that they had been framed violated due process.

Malloy v. Hogan overruled *Adamson v. California* (1947) 378 U.S. 1, 12 L.Ed. 2d 653, 84 S.Ct. 1489 (1964): The Court held, 7–2, that the states, like the federal government, cannot compel incriminating testimony.

7. Role of Judge and Jury

Taylor v. Illinois 484 U.S. 400, 98 L.Ed. 2d 798, 108 S.Ct. 646 (1988): The Court, in an opinion by Stevens for 5 justices, held that the trial judge must consider alternative sanctions for discovery violations and not arbitrarily exclude key testimony.

California v. Brown 479 U.S. 538, 93 L.Ed. 2d 934, 107 S.Ct. 837 (1987): The Court, in an opinion by Rehnquist for 5 justices, held that an instruction given during the penalty phase of a capital murder trial informing jurors that they "must not be swayed by mere sentiment, conjecture, sympathy, passion, prejudice, public opinion or public feeling" did not violate the Eighth and Fourteenth Amendments.

8. Security in the Courtroom

Illinois v. Allen 397 U.S. 337, 25 L.Ed. 2d 353, 90 S.Ct. 1057 (1970): The Court, in an opinion by Black, held that an extremely disruptive defendant has no Sixth Amendment right to remain in the courtroom during his/her trial.

VII SENTENCING (non-death penalty)

A. Role of Jury

Oregon v. Ice ___ U.S.___, 172 L.Ed. 2d 517, 129 S.Ct. 711 (2009): The Court, 5–4 in an opinion by Ginsburg, held that the Sixth Amendment is not violated when states allow judges, rather than juries, to determine whether sentences should be consecutive or concurrent.

Cunningham v. California 549 U.S. 270, 166 L.Ed. 2d 856, 127 S.Ct. 856 (2007): The Court, 6–3 in an opinion by Ginsburg, held that California's sentencing law violated a defendant's Sixth and Fourteenth Amendment right to a jury trial because it places sentence-elevating factfinding within the judge's province. The law established 3 sentences for each crime and allowed the judge to consider aggravating and mitigating circumstances before selecting the sentence.

Blakely v. Washington 542 U.S. 296, 159 L.Ed. 2d 403, 124 S.Ct. 2531 (2004): The Court, 5–4 in an opinion by Scalia, held that the Sixth Amendment right to trial by jury was violated because the facts supporting an exceptional sentence were neither admitted by petitioner in his plea agreement nor found by a jury.

Apprendi v. New Jersey 530 U.S. 466, 147 L.Ed. 2d 435, 120 S.Ct. 2348 (2000): The Court, 5–4 in an opinion by Stevens, held that any fact that increases the penalty for a crime beyond the prescribed statutory term, other than a prior conviction, must be submitted to a jury and proved beyond a reasonable doubt.

B. Sentencing Guidelines and Judicial Discretion

Spears v. United States ___ U.S. ___, 172 L.Ed. 2d 596, 129 S.Ct. 840 (2009): The Court, in a *per curiam* opinion for 7 justices, held that U.S. district courts are entitled to reject the federal sentencing guidelines and impose sentences that vary categorically from the Guidelines for crack cocaine.

Greenlaw v. United States 554 U.S. 237, 171 L.Ed. 2d 399, 128 S.Ct. 2559 (2008): The Court, 6–3 in an opinion by Ginsburg, held that the U.S. Court of Appeals could not order an increase in a sentence on its own initiative.

Kimbrough v. United States 552 U.S. 85, 169 L.Ed. 2d 481, 128 S.Ct. 558 (2007): The Court, 7–2 in an opinion by Ginsburg, held that a U.S. district court judge must consider the range of sentences in the Federal sentencing guidelines, but the judge may determine that, in the particular case, a within-Guidelines sentence is "greater than necessary" to serve the objectives of sentencing.

Gall v. United States 552 U.S. 38, 169 L.Ed. 2d 445, 128 S.Ct. 586 (2007): The Court, 7–2 in an opinion by Stevens, held that a U.S. district court judge must consider the extent of any departure from the federal sentencing guidelines and must explain the appropriateness of an unusually lenient or harsh sentence and give sufficient justifications. The Court of Appeals may not require "extraordinary" circumstances or employ a rigid mathematical formula to determine whether the justification required for a specific sentence is adequate.

Rita v. United States 551 U.S. 338, 168 L.Ed. 2d 203, 127 S.Ct. 2456 (2007): The Court, in an opinion by Breyer, parts of which were joined by 7 other justices, held that when a U.S. district court judge gives a sentence within the range specified by the federal sentencing guidelines, an appellate court should apply a nonbinding presumption that the sentence is reasonable.

United States v. Booker 543 U.S. 220, 160 L.Ed. 2d 621, 125 S.Ct. 738 (2005): The Court, in opinions by Stevens and Breyer, portions of each representing the views of 5 justices, held that legislation making the federal sentencing guidelines mandatory is incompatible with the Sixth Amendment right to have the jury determine sentencing factors.

C. Recidivist Statutes

Ewing v. California 538 U.S. 11, 155 L.Ed. 2d 108, 123 .Ct. 1179 (2003): The Court, without a majority opinion, held that California's "three strikes" law did not violate the cruel and unusual punishment clause of the Eighth Amendment even though it allowed a life sentence based on a third strike that was a non-violent property crime which the judge had the discretion to reduce to a misdemeanor.

Solem v. Helm 463 U.S. 277, 77 L.Ed. 2d 637, 103 S.Ct. 3001 (1983): The Court, 5–4 in an opinion by Powell, held that a sentence of life imprisonment without possibility of parole, given under a habitual criminal statute, for the crime of passing a "no account" check for $100 by a person with 7 prior nonviolent felony convictions, violated the Eighth Amendment.

Rummel v. Estelle 445 U.S. 263, 63 L.Ed. 2d 382, 100 S.Ct. 1133 (1980): The Court, 5–4 in an opinion by Rehnquist, held that a life sentence with possibility of parole imposed pursuant to a recidivist statute did not violate the cruel and unusual punishment clause.

D. Other Sentencing Issues

United States v. Bajakajian 524 U.S. 321, 141 L.Ed. 2d 314, 118 S.Ct. 2028 (1998): The Court, 5–4 in an opinion by Thomas, held that forfeiture of $357,144, which defendant attempted to transport out of the United States as a penalty for violation of the federal law for which the maximum fine was $5,000, violated the Eighth Amendment excessive fines clause.

Harmelin v. Michigan 501 U.S. 957, 115 L.Ed. 2d 836, 111 S.Ct. 2680 (1991): The Court, 5–4 in an opinion by Scalia, held that the Eighth Amendment is not violated in non-capital cases by severe mandatory sentences.

Hunter v. Underwood 471 U.S. 222, 85 L.Ed. 2d 222, 105 S.Ct. 1916 (1985): The Court, in a unanimous opinion by Rehnquist, declared an Alabama statute unconstitutional that disenfranchised a person convicted of a misdemeanor involving moral turpitude.

Hutto v. Davis 454 U.S. 370, 70 L.Ed. 2d 556, 102 S.Ct. 703 (1982): The Court, in a *per curiam* opinion for 5 justices, held a sentence of two consecutive 20-year prison terms and two fines of $10,000 for conviction of possession and distribution of 9 ounces of marijuana did not violate the cruel and unusual punishment clause. The Court refused to note disparity in sentencing schemes between this and other crimes in the state, or disparity between sentences for similar crimes in other states.

Robinson v. California 370 U.S. 660, 8 L.Ed. 758, 82 S.Ct. 1417 (1962): The Court held that addiction to drugs is a disease and cannot be criminally punished where there is no evidence of possession of drugs or violation of any other law.

VIII DEATH PENALTY

A. General Principles

Kennedy v. Louisiana ___ U.S. ___, 171 L.Ed. 2d 525, 128 S.Ct. 2641 (2008): The Court, 5–4 in an opinion by Kennedy, held that execution for the crime of raping a child violates the Eighth Amendment.

Roper v. Simmons 543 U.S. 551, 161 L.Ed. 2d 1, 125 S.Ct. 1183 (2005): The Court, 5–4 in an opinion by Kennedy, held the Eighth Amendment prohibits execution if the offense was committed before the defendant's 18th birthday. *Stanford v. Kentucky* (1989) overruled.

Tennard v. Dretke 542 U.S. 274, 159 L.Ed. 2d 384, 124 S.Ct. 2562 (2004): The Court, 6–3 in an opinion by O'Connor, held evidence of defendant's low IQ was relevant mitigating evidence similar to evidence of mental retardation in *Penry v. Lynaugh.*

Atkins v. Virginia 536 U.S. 304, 153 L.Ed. 2d 335, 122 S.Ct. 2242 (2002): The Court, 6–3 in an opinion by Stevens, held that execution of mentally retarded criminals violates the Eighth Amendment.

Kelly v. South Carolina 534 U.S. 246, 151 L.Ed. 2d 670, 122 S.Ct. 726 (2002): The Court, 5–4 in an opinion by Souter, held that in a state where the jury can only recommend execution or life in prison without parole, a defendant in a capital murder case was entitled to have the jury informed that if he were not sentenced to death, he would be ineligible for parole.

Shafer v. South Carolina 532 U.S. 36, 149 L.Ed. 2d 178, 121 S.Ct. 1263 (2001): The Court, 7–2 in an opinion by Ginsburg, held that whenever future dangerousness is at issue in a capital sentencing proceeding, due process requires that the jury be informed that a life sentence carries no possibility of parole.

Calderon v. Coleman 525 U.S. 141, 142 L.Ed. 2d 521, 119 S.Ct. 500 (1998): The Court, 5–4 in a *per curiam* opinion, held that in a death penalty case the Court will intervene only if it finds that an error, in the whole context of the particular case, had a substantial and injurious effect or influence on the jury's verdict.

Ohio Adult Parole Authority v. Woodard 523 U.S. 272, 140 L.Ed. 2d 387, 118 S.Ct. 1244 (1998): The Court, in an opinion by Rehnquist pertinent parts of which were unanimous, held that there were no violations of the Fifth Amendment when death-row inmates seeking clemency were given the choice of testifying at a voluntary clemency hearing or allowing adverse inferences to be drawn from failure to testify.

Gray v. Netherland 518 U.S. 152, 135 L.Ed. 2d 457, 116 S.Ct. 2074 (1996): The Court, 5–4 in an opinion by Rehnquist, held that a defendant in a capital case does not have a special right to notice of the evidence that will be used against him at the penalty phase of the hearing.

Harris v. Alabama 513 U.S. 504, 130 L.Ed. 2d 1004, 115 S.Ct. 1031 (1995): The Court, 8–1 in an opinion by O'Connor, upheld an Alabama law that vests capital sentencing authority in the trial judge but required the judge to consider an advisory jury verdict without specifying the weight that the judge must give the advisory verdict.

McCleskey v. Kemp 481 U.S. 279, 95 L.Ed. 2d 262, 107 S.Ct. 1756 (1987): The Court, in an opinion by Powell for 5 justices, held that a complex statistical study that indicated that black defendants received the death penalty more often than whites, especially when the victim was white, was not sufficient to demonstrate that racial considerations enter into capital sentencing determinations. The defendant must show purposeful discrimination in his own case.

Tison v. Arizona 481 U.S. 137, 95 L.Ed. 2d 127, 107 S.Ct. 1676 (1987): The Court, in an opinion by O'Connor for 5 justices, held that the death penalty can be constitutionally imposed in felony-murder cases, if there was major participation in the felony combined with reckless indifference to human life.

Ford v. Wainwright 477 U.S. 399, 91 L.Ed. 2d 335, 106 S.Ct. 2595 (1986): The Court, in an opinion by Marshall for 5 justices, held

the Eighth Amendment prohibits execution of a prisoner who is insane.

Caldwell v. Mississippi 472 U.S. 320, 86 L.Ed. 2d 231, 105 S.Ct. 2633 (1985): The Court, in an opinion by Marshall for 5 members, held that it is unconstitutional to rest a death sentence on a determination by a jury who has been led to believe that the responsibility for determining the appropriateness of the defendant's execution rests with the state's Supreme Court.

Spaziano v. Florida 468 U.S. 447, 82 L.Ed. 2d 340, 104 S.Ct. 3154 (1984): The Court, in an opinion by Blackmun held that a system that allows the judge to impose the death penalty after the jury recommended life imprisonment was not unconstitutional.

Pulley v. Harris 465 U.S. 37, 79 L.Ed. 2d 29, 104 S.Ct. 871 (1984): The Court, in an opinion by White for 6 justices, held that in death penalty cases appellate courts are not required to compare the sentence in the case before them with sentences imposed in similar cases.

California v. Ramos 463 U.S. 992, 77 L.Ed. 2d 1171, 103 S.Ct. 3446 (1983): The Court, in an opinion by O'Connor for 5 justices, held that in death penalty cases instructing the jury that a sentence of life imprisonment without parole could be commuted by the governor to a sentence allowing parole did not violate the Constitution.

Enmund v. Florida 458 U.S. 782, 73 L.Ed. 2d 1140, 102 S.Ct. 3368 (1982): The Court, 5–4, in an opinion by White, held that the death penalty was unconstitutionally imposed in a felony murder case where the defendant had aided and abetted the felony but had not killed, attempted to kill, intended to kill, or contemplated that life would be taken during the commission of the felony.

Hammett v. Texas 448 U.S. 725, 65 L.Ed. 2d 1086, 100 S.Ct. 2905 (1980): The Court, 6–3, in a *per curiam* opinion, allowed a prisoner sentenced to death to withdraw petition for hearing by the Supreme Court which the prisoner's counsel had filed without his consent.

Beck v. Alabama 447 U.S. 625, 65 L.Ed. 2d 392, 100 S.Ct. 2382 (1980): The Court, in an opinion by Stevens for 6 justices, held that in a capital case it was reversible error to fail to give a jury instruction on a lesser included noncapital offense when the evidence would support a conviction for such offense.

Coker v. Georgia 433 U.S. 584, 53 L.Ed. 2d 982, 97 S.Ct. 2861 (1977): The Court, 7–2, in an opinion by White for 4 justices, held that the imposition of the death penalty for the rape of an adult female was unconstitutional.

Gregg v. Georgia 428 U.S. 153, 49 L.Ed. 2d 859, 96 S.Ct. 2909 (1976): The Court, 7–2, affirmed a death penalty but was unable to agree on an opinion.

Furman v. Georgia 408 U.S. 238, 33 L.Ed. 2d 346, 92 S.Ct. 2726 (1972): The Court, in 9 separate opinions, held that the manner in which the death penalty was imposed and carried out under the laws of Georgia and Texas was cruel and unusual punishment in violation of the Eighth and Fourteenth Amendments.

Louisiana ex rel. Francis v. Resweber 329 U.S. 459, 91 L.Ed. 422, 67 S.Ct. 374 (1947): The Court, 5–4, held that a second attempt to execute a defendant after an unsuccessful attempt due to mechanical failure of the electric chair did not violate the Eighth Amendment.

B. Assistance of Counsel and Other Services

Bobby v. Van Hook ___ U.S. ___, 175 L.Ed. 2d 255, 130 S.Ct. 13 (2009): The Court, in a unanimous *per curiam* opinion, held that the test for ineffective assistance of counsel at the sentencing phase of a capital murder case reflects standards in effect in the community at the time of the trial. ABA guidelines are not binding on the reviewing court.

Florida v. Nixon 543 U.S. 175, 160 L.Ed. 2d 565, 125 S.Ct. 551 (2004): The Court, in a unanimous opinion by Ginsburg, held that counsel's failure to obtain the defendant's express consent to a strategy of conceding guilt in a capital trial should be judged by an objective reasonableness standard and does not require automatic reversal.

Wiggins v. Smith 539 U.S. 510, 156 L.Ed. 2d 471, 123 S.Ct. 2527 (2003): The Court, 7–2 in an opinion by O'Connor, held that in a death penalty case tried before a jury, counsel's failure to conduct a reasonable investigation into mitigating factors involving the defendant's troubled childhood, diminished mental capacity, and difficult adult life violated the defendant's right to effective assistance of counsel.

Williams v. Taylor 529 U.S. 362, 146 L.Ed. 2d 389, 120 S.Ct. 1495 (2000): The Court, 6–3 in an opinion by Stevens, held that the defendant was denied the constitutionally guaranteed right to effective assistance of counsel when his trial lawyers failed to investigate and present substantial mitigating evidence to the sentencing jury in a death penalty case.

Ake v. Oklahoma 470 U.S. 68, 84 L.Ed. 2d 53, 105 S.Ct. 1087 (1985): The Court, in an opinion by Marshall for 8 justices, held that in capital case an indigent defendant is entitled to an appointed psychiatrist if prosecution intends to use psychiatric evidence to establish defendant's future dangerousness.

C. Jury Selection

Morgan v. Illinois 504 U.S. 719, 119 L.Ed. 2d 492, 112 S.Ct. 2222 (1992): The Court, 6–3 in an opinion by White, held that due process was violated when a trial judge in a capital case refused to ask potential jurors during *voir dire* if they would automatically impose the death penalty upon conviction.

Lockhart v. McCree 476 U.S. 162, 90 L.Ed. 2d 137, 106 S.Ct. 1758 (1986): The Court, in an opinion by Rehnquist for 5 justices, held the Constitution does not prohibit the removal for cause, prior to the guilt phase of a bifurcated capital trial, of prospective jurors whose opposition to the death penalty is so strong that it would prevent or substantially impair the performance of their duties as jurors at the sentencing phase of the trial.

Turner v. Murray 476 U.S. 28, 90 L.Ed. 2d 27, 106 S.Ct. 1683 (1986): The Court, in an opinion by White for 5 justices, held that a defendant in a capital case who is accused of an interracial crime is entitled to have prospective jurors informed of the race of the victim and questioned about racial bias.

Wainwright v. Witt 469 U.S. 412, 83 L.Ed. 2d 841, 105 S.Ct. 844 (1985): The Court, in a opinion by Rehnquist for 6 justices, held a juror may be excluded in a death penalty case if personal views on capital punishment would prevent or substantially impair the performance of duties as a juror in accordance with the jury instructions and oath.

Witherspoon v. Illinois 391 U.S. 510, 20 L.Ed. 2d 776, 88 S.Ct. 1770 (1968): The Court, in an opinion by Stewart for 5 justices, held that an sentence of death cannot be carried out if the jury that imposed or recommended it was chosen by excluding prospective jurors for cause simply because they voiced general objections to the death penalty, or expressed conscientious or religious scruples against its infliction.

D. Guilt Phase—Special Circumstances

Brown v. Sanders 546 U.S. 212, 163 L.Ed. 2d 723, 126 S.Ct. 884 (2006): The Court, 5–4 in an opinion by Scalia, held that in a case where the state alleged four separate "special circumstances" in a death penalty prosecution, the jury's consideration of two that were invalid did not violate the defendant's Eighth Amendment rights because the remaining two were sufficient to satisfy *Furman*'s narrowing requirement and alone rendered Sanders death eligible.

Sumner v. Shuman 483 U.S. 66, 97 L.Ed. 2d 56, 107 S.Ct. 2716 (1987): The Court, in an opinion by Blackmun for 6 justices, held that a state statute that made the death penalty mandatory for prison inmates who are convicted of murder while serving a life sentence without possibility of parole violates the Eighth and Fourteenth Amendments.

Roberts (Harry) v. Louisiana 431 U.S. 633, 52 L.Ed. 2d 637, 97 S.Ct. 1993 (1977): The Court, 5–4, in a *per curiam* opinion, held that a statute violated the Eighth Amendment by mandating a death sentence for killing a peace officer.

E. Penalty Phase—Mitigating Circumstances

Brewer v. Quarterman 550 U.S. 286, 167 L.Ed. 2d 622, 127 S.Ct. 1706 (2007): The Court, 5–4 in an opinion by Stevens, held that the defendant's right to have mitigating circumstances considered was violated when the judge rejected the defense's request for a jury instruction on his history of mental illness.

Ayers v. Belmontes 549 U.S. 7, 166 L.Ed. 2d 334, 127 S.Ct. 469 (2006): The Court, 5–4, in an opinion by Kennedy, held that a trial judge's instructions to the jury to consider "any other circumstance which extenuates the gravity of the crime even though it is not a legal excuse for the crime" adequately allowed the jury to consider all mitigating circumstances.

Kansas v. Marsh 548 U.S. 163, 165 L.Ed. 2d 429, 126 S.Ct. 2516 (2006): The Court, 5–4 in an opinion by Thomas, held that a state may direct imposition of the death penalty when it has proved beyond a reasonable doubt that either mitigating factors outweigh aggravators or that the two are in equipoise.

Ring v. Arizona 536 U.S. 584, 153 L.Ed. 2d 556, 122 S.Ct. 2428 (2002): The Court, 7–2 in an opinion by Ginsburg, held that when finding of "aggravating factors" in a death penalty case is the equivalent of elevating the crime to a greater offense, the jury, not the judge, must decide if the "aggravating factors" have been proven.

Tuilaepa v. California 512 U.S. 967, 129 L.Ed. 2d 750, 114 S.Ct. 2630 (1994): The Court, in an opinion by Kennedy for 6 justices, held that juries can be required to consider a relevant, open-ended factor, such as the circumstances of the crime, without being required to answer a factual question; and it was not a flaw to fail to instruct jurors how to weigh any of the facts.

Johnson v. Texas 509 U.S. 350, 125 L.Ed. 2d 290, 113 S.Ct. 2658 (1993): The Court, 5–4 in an opinion by Kennedy, held that in the penalty phase of a capital murder case the defendant must be allowed to introduce evidence that his/her youth contributed to the crime, but the judge is not required to give a specific instruction telling the jury to consider this as a mitigating circumstance.

Arave v. Creech 507 U.S. 463, 123 L.Ed. 2d 188, 113 S.Ct. 1534 (1993): The Court, 7–2 in an opinion by O'Connor, held that an aggravating circumstance of "utter disregard for human life" was valid in light of the consistent narrowing definition given to the term by the state's Supreme Court.

Sochor v. Florida 504 U.S. 527, 119 L.Ed. 2d 326, 112 S.Ct. 2114 (1992): The Court, 7–2 in an opinion by Souter, held that failure to make a timely objection to a jury instruction on an invalid aggravating circumstance in a capital sentencing hearing waives the right to appeal that jury instruction.

Dawson v. Delaware 503 U.S. 159, 117 L.Ed. 2d 309, 112 S.Ct. 1093 (1992): The Court, 8–1 in an opinion by Rehnquist, held that admission of evidence at a penalty phase of a capital trial of defendant's membership in the Aryan Brotherhood did not violate his First Amendment rights.

Payne v. Tennessee 501 U.S. 808, 115 L.Ed. 2d 720, 111 S.Ct. 2597 (1991): The Court, 6–3 in an opinion by Rehnquist, held that the Eighth Amendment does not bar the introduction of victim-impact evidence during the penalty phase of a capital case.

Lewis v. Jeffers 497 U.S. 764, 111 L.Ed. 2d 606, 110 S.Ct. 3092 (1990): The Court, in an opinion by O'Connor for 5 justices, held that the "fundamental constitutional requirement" of "channeling and limiting . . . the sentencer's discretion in imposing the death penalty" has been met if a state adopted a constitutionally narrow construction of a facially vague aggravating circumstance and applied that construction to the facts of the particular case.

Walton v. Arizona 497 U.S. 639, 111 L.Ed. 2d 511, 110 S.Ct. 3047 (1990): The Court, in an opinion by White relevant parts of which represented the opinion of 5 justices, held: (1) Arizona's capital sentencing law, which allowed the judge rather than the jury to decide what aggravating and mitigating circumstances are present, was constitutional; and (2) an aggravating circumstance of "especially heinous, cruel or depraved" was not unconstitutional because the state's Supreme Court had defined these terms sufficiently by stating "a crime is committed in an especially cruel manner when the perpetrator inflicts mental anguish or physical abuse before the victim's death" . . . and "mental anguish includes a victim's uncertainty as to his ultimate fate."

Clemons v. Mississippi 494 U.S. 738, 108 L.Ed. 2d 725, 110 S.Ct. 1441 (1990): The Court, in an opinion by White for 5 justices, held that a state appellate court may uphold a death sentence that was based in part on an invalid or improperly defined aggravating circumstance if it does one of the following: (1) reweighs the aggravating and mitigating evidence utilizing the appropriate standards; or (2) finds that the harmless error rule applies.

McKoy v. North Carolina 494 U.S. 433, 108 L.Ed. 2d 369, 110 S.Ct. 1227 (1990): The Court, in an opinion by Marshall for 5 justices, held that a requirement that jurors only consider mitigating circumstances on which the jury unanimously agreed violated the defendant's right to have mitigating evidence considered.

Boyde v. California 494 U.S. 370, 108 L.Ed. 2d 316, 110 S.Ct. 1190 (1990): The Court, in an opinion by Rehnquist for 5 justices, held that a jury instruction that required jurors to vote for the death penalty if the aggravating circumstances outweighed the mitigating circumstances was constitutional.

Blystone v. Pennsylvania 494 U.S. 299, 108 L.Ed. 2d 255, 110 S.Ct. 1078 (1990): The Court, in an opinion by Rehnquist for 5 justices, held that requiring the jury to impose the sentence of death if it finds at least one aggravating circumstance and no mitigating circumstances is constitutional.

Mills v. Maryland 486 U.S. 367, 100 L.Ed. 2d 384, 108 S.Ct. 1860 (1988): The Court, in an opinion by Blackmun for 5 justices, held a capital punishment statute was unconstitutional because it required jurors to unanimously agree on mitigating circumstances before the balance of aggravating and mitigating circumstances could be considered.

Maynard v. Cartwright 486 U.S. 356, 100 L.Ed. 2d 372, 108 S.Ct. 1853 (1988): The Court, in a unanimous opinion by White, held that a statute that listed "especially heinous, atrocious or cruel" as an aggravating circumstance in capital murder cases failed to adequately instruct juries on what justified imposition of the death penalty.

Lawenfield v. Phelps 484 U.S. 231, 98 L.Ed. 2d 568, 108 S.Ct. 546 (1988): The Court, in an opinion by Rehnquist for 5 justices, held that the fact that an aggravating circumstance used to determine eligibility for the death penalty duplicated one of the elements of the crime does not violate any constitutional rights.

Booth v. Maryland 482 U.S. 496, 96 L.Ed. 2d 440, 107 S.Ct. 2529 (1987): The Court, in an opinion by Powell for 5 justices, held that introducing a "Victim Impact Statement," which described the personal characteristics of the victim and emotional impact of the crimes on the victim's family as well as the family's opinions of the defendant and characterization of the crimes, during the penalty phase of a capital case introduced irrelevant information and created a constitutionally unacceptable risk that the jury might impose the death penalty in an arbitrary and capricious manner.

Hitchcock v. Dugger 481 U.S. 393, 95 L.Ed. 2d 347, 107 S.Ct. 1821 (1987): The Court, in a unanimous opinion by Scalia, held that

instructing the sentencing jury that they could only consider statutory mitigating circumstances clearly violated the defendant's Eighth Amendment rights.

California v. Brown 479 U.S. 538, 93 L.Ed. 2d 934, 107 S.Ct. 837 (1987): The Court, in an opinion by Rehnquist for 5 justices, held that an instruction given during the penalty phase of a capital murder trial informing jurors that they "must not be swayed by mere sentiment, conjecture, sympathy, passion, prejudice, public opinion or public feeling" did not violate the Eighth and Fourteenth Amendments.

Skipper v. South Carolina 476 U.S. 1, 90 L.Ed. 2d 1, 106 S.Ct. 1669 (1986): The Court, in an opinion by White for 6 justices, held the defendant's right to introduce mitigating evidence at the penalty phase of a capital case was violated by the judge's refusal to allow testimony regarding defendant's good behavior in jail during the seven months that he awaited trial.

Wainwright v. Goode 464 U.S. 78, 78 L.Ed. 2d 187, 104 S.Ct. 378 (1983): The Court, 7–2 in a *per curiam* opinion, held that the act of the trial court in considering aggravating circumstances not authorized by state statute did not require reversal because the state procedures did not produce an arbitrary or freakish sentence. Similar results: *Barclay v. Florida* 463 U.S. 939, 77 L.Ed. 2d 1134, 103 S.Ct. 3418 (1983), and *Zant v. Stephens* 462 U.S. 862, 77 L.Ed. 2d 235, 103 S.Ct. 2733 (1983).

Marshall v. Lonberger 459 U.S. 422, 74 L.Ed. 2d 646, 103 S.Ct. 843 (1983): The Court, 5–4 in an opinion by Rehnquist, held that the use of a guilty plea, knowingly and voluntarily made in a prior case, to establish an aggravating circumstance in the current murder case, was constitutional.

Eddings v. Oklahoma 455 U.S. 104, 71 L.Ed. 2d 1, 102 S.Ct. 869 (1982): The Court, 5–4 in an opinion by Powell, held that a death sentence was unconstitutional because the state court found, as a matter of law, that it could not consider the defendant's unhappy child-hood and emotional disturbance as mitigat-ing circumstances.

F. *Federal* Habeas Corpus

Lonchar v. Thomas 517 U.S. 314, 134 L.Ed. 2d 440, 116 S.Ct. 1293 (1996): The Court, in an opinion by Breyer for 5 justices, held that a death-row defendant's first federal *habeas corpus* petition cannot be dismissed due to the fact that a stay of execution must be granted; it must be reviewed within the framework of the *habeas corpus* rules and settled precedents.

Schlup v. Delo 513 U.S. 298, 130 L.Ed. 2d 808, 115 S.Ct. 851 (1995): The Court, in an opinion by Stevens for 5 justices, held that when a death-row inmate files a *habeas corpus* petition based on actual innocence in order to avoid the procedural bar to consider-ation of the merits of his constitutional claim, the inmate must show a constitutional viola-tion probably resulted in the conviction of a petitioner who is actually innocent.

McFarland v. Scott 512 U.S. 849, 129 L.Ed. 2d 666, 114 S.Ct. 2568 (1994): The Court, in an opinion by Blackmun signed by 5 justices, held that an indigent inmate who has been sentenced to death may apply to federal court and have an attorney appointed to handle federal *habeas corpus* proceedings under 28 U.S.C. §2254 or 2255. If granted, a district court can order a stay of execution to allow appointed counsel to prepare the case.

Herrera v. Collins 506 U.S. 390, 122 L.Ed. 2d 203, 113 S.Ct. 853 (1993): The Court, in an opinion by Rehnquist for 5 justices, held that in a death-penalty case seeking *habeas corpus,* a claim of innocence must be evalu-ated in light of all the previous proceedings in the case, particularly evidence produced at the trial and the fact that the issue was raised for the first time several years after the trial.

Dobbs v. Zant 506 U.S. 357, 122 L.Ed. 2d 103, 113 S.Ct. 835 (1993): The Court, in a *per curiam* opinion for 5 justices, held that in a state *habeas corpus* proceeding involv-ing a defendant who had been sentenced to death, it was error to refuse to consider the transcript of the sentencing hearing when evaluating a claim of ineffectiveness of trial counsel.

Delo v. Stokes 495 U.S. 320, 109 L.Ed. 2d 325, 110 S.Ct. 1880 (1990): The Court, in a *per curiam* opinion expressing the views of 5 members, held that a stay of execution pend-ing disposition of second or successive fed-eral *habeas* petitions should be granted only when there are "substantial grounds upon which relief might be granted."

G. Retrials and Double Jeopardy

Sattazahn v. Pennsylvania 537 U.S. 101, 154 L.Ed. 2d 588, 123 S.Ct. 732 (2003): The Court, 5–4 in an opinion by Scalia, held that there was no double jeopardy bar to seeking the death penalty on retrial when the defen-dant received a life sentence at his first trial due to a state law which required that the defendant be given a life sentence if the jury was unable to reach a unanimous verdict at the penalty phase of a capital murder trial.

Schiro v. Farley 510 U.S. 222, 127 L.Ed. 2d 47, 114 S.Ct. 783 (1994): The Court, 7–2 in an opinion by O'Connor, held that the jury's failure to return a verdict at the sentencing phase of a bifurcated death penalty trial is tantamount to an acquittal for double jeop-ardy purposes only if the record establishes that the issue was actually and necessar-ily decided in the defendant's favor. This is determined by an examination of the entire record.

Poland v. Arizona 476 U.S. 147, 90 L.Ed. 2d 123, 106 S.Ct. 1749 (1986): The Court, in an opinion by White for 6 justices, held the double jeopardy clause does not bar a sec-ond capital sentencing proceeding when, on appeal from a sentence of death, the review-ing court finds the evidence insufficient to support the only aggravating factor on which the sentencing judge relied but does not find the evidence insufficient to support the death penalty.

Bullington v. Missouri 451 U.S. 430, 68 L.Ed. 2d 270, 101 S.Ct. 70 (1981): The Court, 5–4.

in an opinion by Blackmun, held that the imposition of the death penalty at the retrial of a defendant who had successfully sought a new trial after a conviction for murder with a sentence of life imprisonment was barred by double jeopardy.

IX DUE PROCESS ISSUES

A. General Standards

Deck v. Missouri 544 U.S. 622, 161 L.Ed. 2d 953, 125 S.Ct. 2007 (2005): The Court, 7–2 in an opinion by Breyer, held that having the defendant in shackles during the penalty phase of a capital murder case violated his due process rights.

Connecticut Department of Public Safety v. Doe 538 U.S. 1, 155 L.Ed. 2d 98, 123 S.Ct. 1160 (2003): The Court, in an opinion by Rehnquist for 8 justices, held that "Megan's Law" which requires sex offenders to register and makes their names, addresses, and photographs available to the public, does not violate due process. Mere injury to reputation, even if defamatory, does not constitute the deprivation of a liberty interest.

Victor v. Nebraska 511 U.S. 1, 127 L.Ed. 2d 583, 114 S.Ct. 1239 (1994): The Court, in an opinion by O'Connor, part of which was unanimous, held that precise wording of jury instructions on proof beyond a reasonable doubt does not matter as long as there is no reasonable likelihood that the jury understands the instruction to allow conviction based on proof insufficient to meet the due process standard.

Sullivan v. Louisiana 508 U.S. 275, 124 L.Ed. 2d 182, 113 S.Ct. 2078 (1993): The Court, in a unanimous decision by Scalia, held that failure to give the jury an adequate instruction on "proof beyond a reasonable doubt" violates the defendant's right to a jury trial and is a fundamental error requiring reversal.

Parke v. Raley 506 U.S. 20, 121 L.Ed. 2d 391, 113 S.Ct. 517 (1992): The Court, in an opinion by O'Connor for 8 justices, held that requiring defendants charged under recidivist statutes to bear the burden of proof when challenging the use of prior guilty pleas did not violate due process.

De Shaney v. Winnabego County Department of Social Services 489 U.S. 189, 103 L.Ed. 2d 249, 109 S.Ct. 998 (1989): The Court, in an opinion by Rehnquist for 6 justices, held that while the state has a duty to protect a person from harm when it restrains that individual's freedom to act on his own behalf, it has no due process duty to protect a person's liberty interest against harm inflicted under other circumstances. The county was found to have no liability under 42 U.S.C. §1983 for Children's Protective Services failure to heed signs of abuse and remove a child from the home.

Martin v. Ohio 480 U.S. 228, 94 L.Ed. 2d 267, 107 S.Ct. 1098 (1987): The Court, in an opinion by White for 5 justices, held that a state law that declares that self-defense is an affirmative defense and places the burden of proof on the defendant does not violate the due process clause.

Patterson v. New York 432 U.S. 197, 53 L.Ed. 2d 281, 97 S.Ct. 2319 (1977): The Court, 5–3 in an opinion by White, held that a state law did not violate due process when it required the defendant to bear the burden of persuasion on an affirmative defense that was a separate issue and did not serve to negate any facts of the crime that the state had the burden of proving.

Mullaney v. Wilbur 421 U.S. 684, 44 L.Ed. 2d 508, 95 S.Ct. 1881 (1975): The Court, in a unanimous opinion by Powell, held that due process requires that the prosecution prove every fact necessary to constitute the crime charged beyond a reasonable doubt. Requiring the defendant to establish heat of passion on sudden provocation by a preponderance of the evidence violated due process.

Rochin v. California 342 U.S. 165, 96 L.Ed. 183, 72 S.Ct. 205 (1952): The Court held that evidence obtained by tactics that shock the conscience or offend the sense of justice must be excluded on due process grounds.

B. Detention

County of Riverside v. McLaughlin 500 U.S. 44, 114 L.Ed. 2d 49, 111 S.Ct. 1661 (1991): The Court, 5–4 in an opinion by O'Connor, held that arraignments, which are also used as probable cause hearings to satisfy *Gerstein v. Pugh,* satisfied the Fourth Amendment if they are held within 48 hours of arrest. Interpreting 48 hours to mean 48 hours plus weekends and court holidays was not constitutionally permissible.

Schall v. Martin 467 U.S. 253, 81 L.Ed. 2d 207, 104 S.Ct. 2403 (1984): The Court, in an opinion by Rehnquist for 5 justices, held pretrial detention of accused juveniles delinquents did not violate due process. The law in question required that probable cause be established that the juvenile committed the offense and provided other procedural safeguards during a 17-day maximum confinement.

Gerstein v. Pugh 420 U.S. 103, 43 L.Ed. 2d 54, 95 S.Ct. 854 (1975): The Court, in a unanimous opinion by Powell, held persons arrested without a warrant are entitled to a timely hearing before a neutral judge to determine probable cause for detention. The hearing does not have to include the full panoply of adversary safeguards and is not a "critical stage" at which the defendant had a right to have counsel present. Confrontation and cross examination are not required.

C. Discovery

Banks v. Dretke 540 U.S. 668, 157 L.Ed. 2d 1166, 124 S.Ct. 1256 (2004): The Court, in an opinion by Ginsburg for 7 justices, held that it is ordinarily incumbent on the state to set the record straight when police or prosecutors conceal significant exculpatory or impeaching material in the state's possession.

United States v. Ruiz 536 U.S. 622, 153 L.Ed. 2d 586, 122 S.Ct. 2450 (2002): The Court, in an opinion by Breyer for 8 justices, held that the Constitution does not require the government to disclose material impeachment evidence prior to entering into a plea agreement with a criminal defendant.

Strickler v. Greene 527 U.S. 263, 144 L.Ed. 2d 286, 119 S.Ct. 1936 (1999): The Court, 7–2 in an opinion by Stevens, held that a defendant did not have a right to have a conviction reversed due to violation of *Brady v. Maryland* if the defendant received a trial resulting in a verdict worthy of confidence.

Bracy v. Gramley 520 U.S. 899, 138 L.Ed. 2d 97, 117 S.Ct. 1793 (1997): The Court, in a unanimous opinion by Rehnquist, held that district court judges should fashion appropriate discovery orders in federal *habeas corpus* suits when "good cause" is shown.

Arizona v. Youngblood 488 U.S. 51, 102 L.Ed. 2d 281, 109 S.Ct. 333 (1988): The Court, in an opinion by Rehnquist for 5 justices, held that unless a criminal defendant can show bad faith on the part of the police, failure to preserve potentially useful evidence does not constitute a denial of due process of law.

Taylor v. Illinois 484 U.S. 400, 98 L.Ed. 2d 798, 108 S.Ct. 646 (1988): The Court, in an opinion by Stevens for 5 justices, held that the trial judge can apply appropriate sanctions but must not arbitrarily exclude key evidence due to discovery violations.

Pennsylvania v. Ritchie 480 U.S. 39, 94 L.Ed. 2d 40, 107 S.Ct. 989 (1987): The Court, in an opinion by Powell pertinent parts of which were signed by 5 justices, held that in a child molestation case, the due process clause gives the court the right to conduct an *in camera* review of pertinent records of the agency handling child abuse prior to releasing them to the defense attorney. Due process does not require full access to confidential materials.

United States v. Bagley 473 U.S. 667, 87 L.Ed. 2d 481, 105 S.Ct. 3375 (1985): The Court, in an opinion by Blackmun pertinent parts of which represented the views of 5 justices, held that a conviction would be reversed for failure to provide items during discovery in compliance with *Brady v. Maryland* only if the withheld evidence was material in the sense that its suppression undermined confidence in the outcome of the trial.

California v. Trombetta 467 U.S. 479, 81 L.Ed. 2d 413, 104 S.Ct. 2528 (1984): The Court, in a unanimous opinion by Marshall, held that due process does not require law enforcement agencies to preserve breath samples of suspected drunk drivers.

United States v. Agurs 427 U.S. 97, 49 L.Ed. 2d 342, 96 S.Ct. 2392 (1976): The Court, 7–2 in an opinion by Stevens, held that the due process right to a fair trial required a prosecutor to volunteer exculpatory matter to the defense.

Brady v. Maryland 373 U.S. 83, 10 L.Ed. 2d 215, 83 S.Ct. 1194 (1962): The Court, in an opinion by Douglas for 6 justices, held the prosecutor's failure to comply with the defense's timely request for a copy of an accomplice's confession violated the defendant's due process rights.

D. Filing Additional Charges and Imposing Greater Sentences

Alabama v. Smith 490 U.S. 794, 104 L.Ed. 2d 865, 109 S.Ct. 2201 (1989): The Court, in an opinion by Rehnquist for 8 justices, held that the difference in sentences cannot be presumed to be the result of vindictiveness even though the original trial judge presides over the retrial.

Texas v. McCullough repudiated language in *North Carolina v. Pearce* (1969) 475 U.S. 134, 89 L.Ed. 2d 104, 106 S.Ct. 976 (1986): The Court, in an opinion by Burger for 5 justices, held that due process was not violated when the defendant received a longer sentence after a retrial than at the original trial. The Court repudiated language in *North Carolina v. Pearce* (1969) permitting a harsher sentence only if there had been relevant conduct of the defendant subsequent to the original sentencing.

Thigpen v. Roberts 468 U.S. 27, 82 L.Ed. 2d 23, 104 S.Ct. 2916 (1984): The Court, 6–3 in an opinion by White, held that the prosecution of the driver for felony manslaughter, after he had exercised his right to appeal a misdemeanor conviction based upon the same criminal acts, violated due process.

United States v. Goodwin 457 U.S. 368, 73 L.Ed. 2d 74, 102 S.Ct. 2485 (1982): The Court, in an opinion by Stevens for 6 justices, held that filing additional felony charges based on conduct already the subject of a misdemeanor complaint, immediately after the defendant refused to plea bargain, did not trigger a presumption that the prosecutor's conduct was vindictive.

Bordenkircher v. Hayes 434 U.S. 357, 54 L.Ed. 2d 604, 98 S.Ct. 663 (1978): The Court, 5–4 in an opinion by Stewart, held that due process was not violated when a prosecutor carried out a threat, made during plea bargaining, to reindict the defendant on more serious charges if the defendant refused to plead guilty to the original offense.

E. Forfeiture Proceedings

United States v. Bajakajian 524 U 5 321, 141 L.Ed. 2d 314, 118 S.Ct. 2028 (1998): The Court, 5–4 in an opinion by Thomas, held that forfeiture of $357,144, which defendant attempted to transport out of the United states, as a penalty for violation of the federal law for which the maximum fine was $5,000, violated the Eighth Amendment excessive fines clause.

Bennis v. Michigan 516 U.S. 442, 134 L.Ed. 2d 68, 116 S.Ct. 1560 (1996): The Court, 5–4 in an opinion by Rehnquist, held that a Michigan court did not offend due process clause or the taking clause of the Fifth Amendment when it ordered the forfeiture of an automobile in which the husband engaged in sexual activity with a prostitute. Forfeiture was based on a public nuisance law with no offset for the wife's interest in the car notwithstanding her lack of knowledge of her husband's activity.

United States v. James Daniel Good Real Property 510 U.S. 43, 126 L.Ed. 2d 490, 114 S.Ct. 492 (1993): The Court held, 5–4 in an opinion by Kennedy, that in civil forfeiture proceedings against real property, a party has the right to notice and a hearing before the property is seized except in exigent circumstances. The Court approved *Calero-Toledo v. Pearson Yacht Leasing Co.* (1974), which permitted seizure of personal property prior to giving notice if the property was of a type that could be removed to another jurisdiction, destroyed, or concealed, if advance warning of confiscation were given.

United States v. One Assortment of 89 Firearms 465 U.S. 354, 79 L.Ed. 2d 361, 104 S.Ct. 1099 (1984): The Court, in a unanimous opinion by Burger, held that the acquittal of a gun owner on charges involving firearms does not preclude a later forfeiture proceeding against the same firearms.

F. Insanity and Competence to Stand Trial

Clark v. Arizona 548 U.S. 735, 165 L.Ed. 2d 842, 126 S.Ct. 2709 (2006): The Court, 6–3 in an opinion by Souter, held that due process does not prohibit Arizona's use of an insanity test stated solely in terms of the capacity to tell whether an act charged as a crime was right or wrong.

Sell v. United States 539 U.S. 166, 156 L.Ed. 2d 197, 123 S.Ct. 2174 (2003): The Court, 6–3 in an opinion by Breyer, held that the Constitution allows the government to administer antipsychotic drugs to render a mentally ill defendant competent to stand trial on serious criminal charges. The treatment must be medically appropriate; substantially unlikely to have side effects that may undermine the trial's fairness; and, taking account of less intrusive alternatives, is necessary to significantly further important governmental trial-related interests.

Cooper v. Oklahoma 517 U.S. 348, 134 L.Ed. 2d 498, 116 S.Ct. 1373 (1996): The Court, in a unanimous opinion by Stevens, held that an Oklahoma law establishing a presumption that a defendant in a criminal case is competent unless incompetence is established by clear and convincing evidence violates due process because the defendant could be put on trial even though it is more likely than not that he/she is incompetent.

Shannon v. United States 512 U.S. 573, 129 L.Ed. 2d 459, 114 S.Ct. 2419 (1994): The Court, 7–2 in an opinion by Thomas, held that the federal Insanity Defense Reform Act of 1984 does not require the judge to give an instruction as to the consequences of a verdict of not guilty by reason of insanity unless there is a specific need for it, such as a witness or prosecutor stating that the defendant will go free if found not guilty by reason of insanity.

Medina v. California 505 U.S. 437, 120 L.Ed. 2d 353, 112 S.Ct. 2572 (1992): The Court, 5–4 in an opinion by Kennedy, held that a statute that required the party raising the issue of competency to stand trial to prove the issue by a preponderance of the evidence was constitutional.

Foucha v. Louisiana 504 U.S. 71, 118 L.Ed. 2d 437, 112 S.Ct. 1780 (1992): The Court, 5–4 in an opinion by White part of which was the opinion of the Court, held that defendants acquitted on a plea of not guilty by reason of insanity could be held in a mental hospital only so long as they were dangerous to themselves or others.

Riggins v. Nevada 504 U.S. 127, 118 L.Ed. 2d 479, 112 S.Ct. 1810 (1992): The Court, 6–3 in an opinion by O'Connor, held that a criminal defendant could be forced to take antipsychotic drugs only so long as medically necessary. Administration of such drugs violates the right to counsel where the drugs interfere with the defendant's ability to communicate with counsel and assist with the defense.

Washington v. Harper 494 U.S. 210, 108 L.Ed. 2d 178, 110 S.Ct. 1028 (1990): The Court, in an opinion by Kennedy for 6 justices, held that the due process clause permits the state to administer antipsychotic drugs against an inmate's will if the inmate has a serious mental illness and is dangerous to him/herself or others and the treatment is in the inmate's medical interest. Procedural due process was satisfied by a policy that provided for: hearing by a committee composed of one psychiatrist, one psychologist, and the prison superintendent; inmate had the right to be present and cross-examine witnesses; inmate had right to lay advisor but was not represented by counsel. Hearing does not need to be conducted in accordance with rules of evidence; "clear, cogent, and convincing" standard of proof is not required.

Jones v. United States 463 U.S. 354, 77 L.Ed. 2d 694, 103 S.Ct. 3043 (1983): The Court, 5–4 in an opinion by Powell, held that a finding of insanity by a preponderance of the evidence at a criminal trial was sufficient to commit a defendant to a mental institution until the person regains sanity or is no longer a danger. The length of the detention is not tied to the sentence that the person could have received if convicted for the offense charged.

Drope v. Missouri 420 U.S. 162, 43 L.Ed. 2d 103, 95 S.Ct. 896 (1975): The Court, in a unanimous opinion by Burger, held there was sufficient evidence of incompetence on the trial record to require that the judge order such an examination and failure to do so violated the defendant's due process right to a fair trial.

G. Intoxication Defense

Montana v. Egelhoff 518 U.S. 37, 135 L.Ed. 2d 361, 116 S.Ct. 2013 (1996): The Court, 5–4 in an opinion by Scalia, held that a Montana law that provided that voluntary intoxication "may not be taken into consideration in determining the existence of mental state which is an element of a criminal offense" did not violate due process.

H. Liberty Interest in Private Conduct

Lawrence v. Texas overruled *Bowers v. Hardwick* (1986) 539 U.S. 558, 156 L.Ed. 2d 508, 123 S.Ct. 2472 (2003): The Court, 6–3 in an opinion by Kennedy, held that a Texas statute making it a crime for two persons of the same sex to engage in certain intimate sexual conduct violates the due process clause. The Constitution gives homosexual persons the liberty to choose to enter upon relationships in the confines of their homes and their own private lives.

I. Parole and Probation

Board of Pardons v. Allen 482 U.S. 369, 96 L.Ed. 2d 303, 107 S.Ct. 2415 (1987): The Court, in an opinion by Brennan for 6 justices, held that Montana statutes which state that, subject to specified restrictions, the Board of Pardons "shall release on parole . . . any person . . . when in its opinion there is reasonable probability that the prisoner can be released without detriment to the prisoner or the community" created a liberty interest in parole release that is protected under the due process clause of the Fourteenth Amendment.

Kelly v. Robinson 479 U.S. 36, 93 L.Ed. 2d 216, 107 S.Ct. 353 (1986): The Court, in an opinion by Powell for 7 justices, held that any condition a state criminal court imposed as part of a criminal sentence, including restitution, cannot be discharged in bankruptcy.

Gagnon v. Scarpelli 411 U.S. 778, 36 L.Ed. 2d 656, 93 S.Ct. 1756 (1973): The Court, 8–1 in an opinion by Powell, held that "a probationer, like a parolee, is entitled to a preliminary and a final revocation hearing, under the conditions specified in *Morrissey.*" Where "special circumstances" exist the state authority may be required to assign counsel at the hearing.

Morrissey v. Brewer 408 U.S. 471, 33 L.Ed. 2d 484, 92 S.Ct. 2593 (1972): The Court, in an opinion by Burger, held that due process establishes the right of a parolee to a preliminary and final hearing before parole can be revoked.

J. Presumptions

Carella v. California 491 U.S. 623, 105 L.Ed. 2d 218, 109 S.Ct. 2419 (1989): The Court, in a *per curiam* opinion for 5 justices, held that a jury instruction which said a person "shall be presumed to have embezzled" a rental car if it was not returned within five days of the expiration of the rental agreement, and that "intent to commit theft by fraud is presumed" from failure to return rented property within 20 days of demand, created mandatory presumptions that violate due process.

Francis v. Franklin 471 U.S. 307, 85 L.Ed. 2d 344, 105 S.Ct. 1965 (1985): The Court, in an opinion by Brennan for 5 justices, held that a jury instruction was unconstitutional if a reasonable juror, in the context of the jury charge as a whole, could have concluded that there was a mandatory presumption that shifted the burden of persuasion to the defendant on the crucial element of intent.

Sandstrom v. Montana 442 U.S. 510, 61 L.Ed. 2d 39, 99 S.Ct. 2450 (1979): The Court, in a unanimous opinion by Brennan, held that in a trial for deliberate homicide, a jury instruction that "the law presumes that a person intends the ordinary consequences of his voluntary acts" violated due process. The instruction could be assumed to state a conclusive presumption and thus modify the prosecution's burden of proof and shift the burden of persuasion to the defendant to prove that he lacked the requisite mental state.

County Court of Ulster County, New York v. Allen 442 U.S. 142, 60 L.Ed. 2d 777, 99 S.Ct. 2213 (1979): The Court, in an opinion by Stevens for 5 justices, held that a permissive presumption that a firearm in an automobile is in the illegal possession of all persons then occupying the vehicle does not violate due process. Permissive presumptions are allowed if there is a rational connection between the basic fact that the prosecution proved and the ultimate fact presumed and that the latter is more likely than not to flow from the former.

Kentucky v. Whorton 441 U.S. 786, 60 L.Ed. 2d 640, 99 S.Ct. 2088 (1979): The Court, 6–3 in a *per curiam* opinion, held failure to give a jury instruction on the presumption of innocence did not *per se* require reversal. Due process requires a review of the totality of the circumstances including the jury instructions given, arguments of counsel, and the weight of the evidence of guilt.

K. Sexually Violent Predators

Kansas v. Crane 534 U.S. 407, 151 L.Ed. 2d 856, 122 S.Ct. 867 (2002): The Court, 7–2 in an opinion by Breyer, held that in order to commit a person as a dangerous sexual offender there must be proof that the offender

has serious difficulty in controlling behavior; proof of total or complete lack of control is not required.

Kansas v. Hendricks 521 U.S. 346, 138 L.Ed. 2d 501, 117 S.Ct. 2072 (1997): The Court, 5–4 in an opinion by Thomas, held that Kansas's Sexually Violent Predator law did not violate due process. The law permitted confinement of sexually violent predators in a mental health facility based on proof beyond a reasonable doubt that the person had past sexually violent behavior and a present mental condition that creates a likelihood of such conduct in the future if the person is not incapacitated. The Sexually Violent Predator Act provided for a hearing prior to the end of the prison term. Confinement in a mental health facility was permitted until the person's "abnormality or personality disorder has so changed that the person is safe to be at large" but yearly reviews were mandated.

L. Vagueness

Chicago v. Morales 527 U.S. 41, 144 L.Ed. 2d 67, 119 S.Ct. 1849 (1999): The Court, 6–3 in an opinion by Stevens, held that Chicago's Gang Congregation Ordinance, which encompassed a great deal of harmless behavior and gave officers absolute discretion to determine what activities constitute loitering, violates the requirement that legislation establish minimal guidelines to govern law enforcement.

Kolender v. Lawson 461 U.S. 352, 75 L.Ed. 2d 903, 103 S.Ct. 1855 (1983): The Court, 7–2, in an opinion by O'Connor, held that a loitering statute requiring "credible and reliable" identification upon request by the police was unconstitutionally vague. Failure to specify the type of identification required was found to encourage arbitrary enforcement of the law.

City of Mesquite v. Aladdin's Castle, Inc. 455 U.S. 283, 71 L.Ed. 2d 152, 102 S.Ct. 1070 (1982): The Court, in an opinion by Stevens for 7 justices, held a city licensing ordinance permitting the denial of a license for the operation of coin-operated amusement establishments if the applicant had any "connection with criminal elements" was not unconstitutionally vague.

M. Other Issues

Town of Castle Rock, Colorado v. Gonzales 545 U.S. 748, 162 L.Ed. 2d 658, 125 S.Ct. 2796 (2005): The Court, 7–2 in an opinion by Scalia, held that there is no due process property interest in having police enforce a restraining order in a domestic violence case.

Rogers v. Tennessee 532 U.S. 451, 149 L.Ed. 2d 697, 121 S.Ct. 1693 (2001): The Court, 5–4 in an opinion by O'Connor, held that retroactive application of a decision abolishing the year and a day rule for criminal homicide did not deny petitioner the due process of law. The due process clause does not incorporate the specific prohibitions of the *ex post facto* clause.

Neder v. United States 527 U.S. 1, 144 L.Ed. 2d 35, 119 S.Ct. 1827 (1999): The Court, in a unanimous opinion by Rehnquist, held that the harmless error rule should be applied in a case where the jury instructions omitted an element of an offense.

County of Sacramento v. Lewis 523 U.S. 833, 140 L.Ed. 2d 1043, 118 S.Ct. 1708 (1998): The Court, in an opinion by Souter for 6 justices, held that only an intent to cause harm unrelated to the legitimate object of arrest will establish a violation of due process based on arbitrary conduct that shocks the conscience.

Lachance v. Erikson 522 U.S. 262, 139 L.Ed. 2d 695, 118 S.Ct. 753 (1998): The Court, in a unanimous opinion by Rehnquist, held that the due process clause does not prohibit sanctioning a federal employee for making false statements to a federal agency regarding his/her alleged employment-related misconduct.

Washington v. Glucksberg 521 U.S. 702, 138 L.Ed. 2d 772, 117 S.Ct. 2258 (1997): The Court, in an opinion by Rehnquist for 5 justices, held that Washington's law prohibiting "causing" or "aiding" a suicide did not

offend the Fourteenth Amendment due process clause. See also, *Vacco v. Quill* (1997)

Goeke v. Branch 514 U.S. 115, 131 L.Ed. 2d 152, 115 S.Ct. 1275 (1995): The Court, in a unanimous *per curiam* opinion, held that Missouri did not violate the defendant's constitutional rights when it dismissed a direct appeal because the defendant was a fugitive at the time the appeal was scheduled to be heard.

X EQUAL PROTECTION ISSUES
See Section VI B Trial Juries for equal protection issues related to juries.

Parents Involved in Community Schools v. Seattle School District No. 1 551 U.S. 701, 168 L.Ed. 2d 508,127 S.Ct. 2738 (2007): The Court, in a plurality opinion by Roberts, held that the school district's policy of assigning students based on race did not pass the strict scrutiny test. The school districts have not carried its heavy burden of showing that the interest it sought to achieve justifies the extreme means chosen. The school district could not rely on the need to remedy past discrimination because the Seattle schools had never been racially segregated by law or under court order to desegregate.

Johnson v. California 543 U.S. 499, 160 L.Ed. 2d 949, 125 S.Ct. 1141 (2005): The Court, 5–3 in an opinion by O'Connor, held that the strict scrutiny standard applies to issues involving racial segregation of prisons. California's policy of racially segregating prisons because gang affiliation was frequently along racial lines was deemed a violation of equal protection.

Vacco v. Quill 521 U.S. 793, 138 L.Ed. 2d 834, 117 S.Ct. 2293 (1997): The Court, in an opinion by Rehnquist for 5 justices, held that laws enacted by the state making assisted suicide a crime do not violate equal protection. See also, *Washington v. Glucksberg* (1997)

Romer v. Evans 517 U.S. 620, 134 L.Ed. 2d 855, 116 S.Ct. 1620 (1996): The Court, 6–3 in an opinion by Kennedy, held that

"Amendment 2" of the Colorado constitution, which repealed all local ordinances prohibiting discrimination on the basis of sexual orientation, violated the equal protection clause of the Fourteenth Amendment. It concluded that the classification of homosexuals in "Amendment 2" did not further a proper legislative end but made them unequal to everyone else.

United States v. Armstrong 517 U.S. 456, 134 L.Ed. 2d 687, 116 S.Ct. 1480 (1996): The Court, 8–1 in an opinion by Rehnquist, held that an African American defendant who sought discovery on his claim that the U.S. attorney singled him out for prosecution on the basis of race failed to satisfy the threshold showing that the government declined to prosecute similarly situated suspects of other races.

Bearden v. Georgia 461 U.S. 660, 76 L.Ed. 2d 221, 103 S.Ct. 2064 (1983): The Court, in an opinion by O'Connor for 5 justices, held that automatic revocation of probation for failure to pay a fine, without first determining that the probationer had not made sufficient bona fide efforts to pay the amount due or that adequate alternative forms of punishment existed, was a violation of equal protection.

Michael M. v. Superior Court of Sonoma County 450 U.S. 464, 67 L.Ed. 2d 437, 101 S.Ct. 1200 (1981): The Court, in an opinion by Rehnquist for 4 justices with 2 concurring opinions, held that statutory rape laws that punish only males do not violate equal protection. The state's interest in preventing teenage pregnancies was found to be sufficient to justify the laws.

Estelle v. Dorrough 420 U.S. 534, 43 L.Ed. 2d 377, 95 S.Ct. 1173 (1975): The Court, in a *per curiam* opinion expressing the views of 5 justices, held that a Texas statute that provided for automatic dismissal of pending appeals if the defendant felon escaped from prison for more than ten days while the appeal was pending did not violate equal protection.

Douglas v. California 372 U.S. 353, 9 L.Ed. 2d 811, 83 S.Ct. 814 (1963): The Court held, 6–3, that there is an absolute right to the assistance of counsel during the first appeal under the equal protection clause of the Fourteenth Amendment.

Grifin v. Illinois 351 U.S. 12, 100 L.Ed. 891, 76 S.Ct. 585 (1956): The Court held, 5–4, that the due process and equal protection clauses of the Fourteenth Amendment require that all indigent defendants be furnished a transcript, or record of sufficient completeness, for an appeal.

XI JUVENILE COURT PROCEEDINGS

Graham v. Florida ___ U.S. ___, 176 L.Ed. 2d 825,130 S. Ct. 2011 (2010): The Court, 6-3 in an opinion by Kennedy, held that sentencing a juvenile to life in prison without the possibility of parole in a non-homicide crime violates the Eighth Amendment.

Roper v. Simmons 543 U.S. 551, 161 L.Ed. 2d 1, 125 S.Ct. 1183 (2005): The Court, 5–4 in an opinion by Kennedy, held that the Eighth Amendment prohibits execution for offenses committed before the defendant's 18th birthday. Overruled *Stanford v. Kentucky*.

Schall v. Martin 467 U.S. 253, 81 L.Ed. 2d 207, 104 S.Ct. 2403 (1984): The Court, in an opinion by Rehnquist for 5 justices, held that a law authorizing pretrial detention of accused juvenile delinquents did not violate due process. This statute authorized detention only if a court found that there was a serious risk that the juvenile might commit a crime before the return date.

Smith v. Daily Mail Publishing Co. 443 U.S. 97, 61 L.Ed. 2d 399, 99 S.Ct. 2667 (1979): The Court, in an opinion by Burger for 7 justices, held that a law that made it a crime to truthfully publish legally obtained names of alleged juvenile delinquents violated the First Amendment.

Breed v. Jones 421 U.S. 519, 44 L.Ed. 2d 346, 95 S.Ct. 1779 (1975): The Court, in a unanimous opinion by Burger, held that the transfer hearing (waiver of Juvenile Court jurisdiction) must be held prior to the adjudicatory hearing to avoid double jeopardy.

McKiever v. Pennsylvania (In *re Barbara Burrus et al.*), 403 U.S. 528, 29 L.Ed. 2d 647, 91 S.Ct. 1976 (1971): The Court, 6–3 in an opinion by Blackmun, held that the Sixth Amendment does not require trial by jury in state juvenile delinquency proceedings.

In re Winship 397 U.S. 358, 25 L.Ed. 2d 368, 90 S.Ct. 1068 (1970): The Court, 5–3 in an opinion by Brennan, held that the due process clause requires proof of guilt beyond a reasonable doubt at the adjudicatory stage of a juvenile delinquency proceeding in which a youth is charged with an act that would constitute a crime if committed by an adult.

In re Gault 387 U.S. 1, 18 L.Ed. 2d 527, 87 S.Ct. 1428 (1967): The Court held that the due process clause of the Fourteenth Amendment applies at the adjudicatory stage of a juvenile court proceeding; juveniles are entitled to substantially the same rights that are accorded to an adult in a criminal court.

Kent v. United States 383 U.S. 541, 16 L.Ed. 2d 84, 86 S.Ct. 1045 (1966): The Court, 5–4 in an opinion by Fortas, held that a juvenile court must conduct a hearing prior to the entry of a waiver order transferring jurisdiction to a criminal court. (The opinion is decided on statutory grounds as an interpretation of the District of Columbia Juvenile Court Act).

XII RIGHTS OF THE INCARCERATED

Wilkins v. Gaddy ___ U.S. ___, 175 L.Ed. 2d 995, 130 S.Ct. 1175 (2010): The Court, in a *per curiam* opinion, held that in a §1983 case based on use of excessive force in prison in violation of the Fourth Amendment the inmate must prove not only that the assault actually occurred but also that it was carried out "maliciously and sadistically" rather than as part of "a good-faith effort to maintain or restore discipline." Serious injuries are not required.

Haywood v. Drown ___ U.S. ___, 173 L.Ed. 2d 920, 129 S.Ct. 2108 (2009): The Court, 5-4 in an opinion by Stevens, held that a New York law that replaced both state and federal suits, including §1983 cases by prisoners against correctional officers, with a procedure requiring cases be filed in a state Court of Claims violated the Supremacy Clause of the Constitution.

Jones v. Bock 549 U.S. 199, 166 L.Ed. 2d 798, 127 S.Ct. 910 (2007): The Court, in a unanimous opinion by Roberts, held that the exhaustion of state remedies required in Prison Litigation Reform Act of 1995 (PLRA) is an affirmative defense; a case should not be dismissed solely because the prisoner failed to allege in the complaint that all administrative remedies had been pursued.

Beard v. Banks 548 U.S. 521, 165 L.Ed. 2d 697, 126 S.Ct. 2572 (2006): The Court, in a plurality opinion by Breyer, held that a policy forbidding level 2 federal inmates from accessing newspapers, magazines, and photographs did not violate the First Amendment.

Woodford v. Ngo 548 U.S. 81, 165 L.Ed. 2d 368, 126 S.Ct. 2378 (2006): The Court, 6-3 in an opinion by Alito, held that the exhaustion of state remedies requirement of Prison Litigation Reform Act of 1995 (PLRA) is not satisfied by the filing of a grievance in an untimely manner.

Wilkinson v. Austin 545 U.S. 209, 162 L.Ed. 2d 174, 125 S.Ct. 2384 (2005): The Court, in a unanimous opinion by Kennedy, held that inmates have a constitutionally protected liberty interest in avoiding assignment to "supermax" facilities.

Wilkinson v. Dotson 544 U.S. 74, 161 L.Ed. 2d 253, 125 S.Ct. 1242 (2005): The Court, 8-1 in an opinion by Breyer, held that state prisoners may bring §1983 actions for declaratory and injunctive relief challenging the constitutionality of state parole procedures.

Overton v. Bazzetta 539 U.S. 126, 156 L.Ed. 2d 162, 123 S.Ct. 2162 (2003): The Court, in an opinion by Kennedy for 7 justices, held limitations on visitation that are rationally related to legitimate penological interests are constitutional even if respondents have a constitutional right of association that survived incarceration.

Hope v. Pelzer 536 U.S. 730153 L.Ed. 2d 666, 122 S.Ct. 2508 (2002): The Court, 6–3 in an opinion by Stevens, held that prison guards could not assert the defense of qualified immunity at the summary judgment phase of a §1983 case when the Eighth Amendment violation involved was obvious on the facts alleged.

Porter v. Nussle 534 U.S. 516, 152 L.Ed. 2d 12, 122 S.Ct. 983 (2002): The Court, in a unanimous opinion by Ginsburg, held that the exhaustion of state remedies requirement in the Prison Litigation Reform Act of 1995 applies to all inmate suits about prison life.

Booth v. Churner 532 U.S. 731, 149 L.Ed. 2d 958, 121 S.Ct. 1819 (2001): The Court, in a unanimous opinion by Souter, held that under the Prison Litigation Reform Act of 1995 an inmate filing an action under 42 U.S.C. §1983 seeking only monetary damages must, prior to filing the §1983 action, complete any prison administrative process capable of addressing the inmate's complaint and providing some form of relief, even if this process does not make specific provision for monetary relief.

Edwards v. Balisok 520 U.S. 641, 137 L.Ed. 2d 906, 117 S.Ct. 1584 (1997): The Court, in a unanimous opinion by Scalia, held that the inmate's claim for declaratory relief and money damages based on allegations of deceit and bias on the part of the decision maker at a prison disciplinary hearing that necessarily imply the invalidity of the punishment imposed, but not insufficiency of the facts establishing the violation of prison rules, is not cognizable under §1983.

Young v. Harper 520 U.S. 143, 137 L.Ed. 2d 270, 117 S.Ct. 1148 (1997): The Court, in a unanimous opinion by Thomas, held that a state program to release prison inmates early on "preparole" in order to alleviate overcrowding was functionally similar to parole; therefore the procedural protections set forth

in *Morrissey v. Brewer* (1972) apply to revocation proceedings.

Sandin v. Conner 515 U.S. 472, 132 L.Ed. 2d 418, 115 S.Ct. 2293 (1995): The Court, 5–4 in an opinion by Rehnquist, held that the defendant's confinement in disciplinary segregation did not present the type of atypical, significant deprivation that affords inmates the right to a disciplinary hearing under the due process clause.

Farmer v. Brennan 511 U.S. 825, 128 L.Ed. 2d 811, 114 S.Ct. 1970 (1994), the Court, 8–1 in an opinion by Souter, held that a prison official may be liable under the Eighth Amendment based on "deliberate indifference" for denying humane conditions of confinement only if he knows that inmates face a substantial risk of serious harm and disregards that risk by failing to take reasonable measures to abate it.

Helling v. McKinney 509 U.S. 25, 125 L.Ed. 2d 22, 113 S.Ct. 2475 (1993): The Court, 7–2 in an opinion by White, held that an inmate stated a cause of action under the Eighth Amendment by alleging that prison officials had, with deliberate indifference, exposed him to levels of environmental tobacco smoke that pose an unreasonable risk of serious damage to his future health.

McCarthy v. Madigan 503 U.S. 140, 117 L.Ed. 2d 291, 112 S.Ct. 1081 (1992): The Court, 6–3 in an opinion by Blackmun, held that a federal prisoner does not have to exhaust administrative remedies before filing a *Bivens* suit for monetary damages because neither Congress nor the federal Bureau of Prisons has made an adequate administrative remedy available.

Hudson v. McMillian 503 U.S. 1, 117 L.Ed. 2d 156, 112 S.Ct. 995 (1992): The Court, 6–3 in an opinion by O'Connor, held that use of excessive physical force against a prisoner may constitute cruel and unusual punishment even though the inmate does not suffer serious injury. The core judicial inquiry is whether force was applied in a good-faith effort to maintain or restore discipline, or maliciously and sadistically to cause harm.

Rufo v. Inmates of the Suffolk County Jail 502 U.S. 367, 116 L.Ed. 2d 867, 112 S.Ct. 748 (1992): The Court, 5–3 in an opinion by White, held that in a jail-overcrowding case, a party seeking modification of a consent decree must establish that a significant change in facts or law warrants revision of the decree and that the proposed modification is suitably tailored to the changed circumstances.

Wilson v. Seiter 501 U.S. 294, 115 L.Ed. 2d 271, 111 S.Ct. 2321 (1991): The Court, in 5–4 opinion by Scalia, held that claims that the conditions of confinement constitute cruel and unusual punishment in violation of the Eighth Amendment should be judged by the "deliberate indifference" standard.

Thornburgh v. Abbot 490 U.S. 401, 104 L.Ed. 2d 459, 109 S.Ct. 1874 (1989): The Court, in an opinion by Blackmun for 6 justices, held that regulations that permit the Federal Bureau of Prisons to reject incoming publications found to be detrimental to institutional security are valid if they are "reasonably related to a legitimate penological interest."

West v. Atkins 487 U.S. 42, 101 L.Ed. 2d 40, 108 S.Ct. 2250 (1988): The Court, in an opinion by Blackmun for 8 justices, held that a physician who is under contract with the state to provide medical services to inmates at a state prison hospital on a part-time basis acts "under color of state law."

O'Lone v. Shabazz 482 U.S. 342, 96 L.Ed. 2d 282, 107 S.Ct. 2400 (1987): The Court, in an opinion by Rehnquist for 5 justices, held that a prison regulation that prohibited inmates on outside work details from returning to the main prison building during the day, and thereby prevented them from attending Muslim religious services that the Koran dictated be held during the early afternoon on Fridays, did not violate their First Amendment rights. Prison officials need only show that the regulation was reasonably related to the security interest of the prison and do not have to show that there is no other reasonable alternative that would not infringe on First Amendment rights.

Turner v. Safley 482 U.S. 78, 96 L.Ed. 2d 64, 107 S.Ct. 2254 (1987): The Court, in an opinion by O'Connor for 5 justices, held that the test of reasonable relationship to legitimate penological objectives, not strict scrutiny, is used to determine if prison rules that affect only inmates are constitutional. A content-neutral rule prohibiting inmate-to-inmate correspondence was upheld but a regulation that amounted to an almost complete ban on the decision to marry was held not reasonably related to legitimate penological objectives.

Whitley v. Albers 475 U.S. 312, 89 L.Ed. 2d 251, 106 S.Ct. 1078 (1986): The Court, in an opinion by O'Connor for 5 justices, held that where a prison security measure that poses significant risks to the safety of inmates and prison staff was used during a disturbance, the inquiry must focus on whether the actions were taken in a good faith effort to maintain or restore discipline or maliciously and sadistically for the purpose of causing harm.

Davidson v. Cannon 474 U.S. 344, 88 L.Ed. 2d 677, 106 S.Ct. 668 (1986): The Court, in an opinion by Rehnquist for 5 justices, held that neither procedural nor substantive due process is violated by a lack of due care (simple negligence) by prison officials.

Daniels v. Williams 474 U.S. 327, 88 L.Ed. 2d 662, 106 S.Ct. 662 (1986): The Court, in an opinion by Rehnquist for 6 justices, held that negligent acts of correctional officers that lead to unintended loss of property or injury do not violate inmates' due process rights.

Superintendent v. Hill 472 U.S. 445, 86 L.Ed. 2d 356, 105 S.Ct. 2768 (1985): The Court, in an opinion by O'Connor, relevant parts of which were signed by all 9 justices, held that due process is satisfied if the record relied on by a prison disciplinary board to revoke goodtime credits contains any evidence that could support the conclusion reached by the disciplinary board.

Ponte v. Real 471 U.S. 491, 85 L.Ed. 2d 553, 105 S.Ct. 2192 (1985): The Court, in an opinion by Rehnquist for 6 justices, held that when prison officials deny an inmate the right to call witnesses at a disciplinary hearing, their reason for denying the request need not be made a part of the administrative record of that disciplinary hearing. If an inmate brings suit to challenge the denial of a request to call witnesses, the prison officials may be required to state in court their reasons for denying the request.

Block v. Rutherford 468 U.S. 576, 82 L.Ed. 2d 438, 104 S.Ct. 3227 (1984): The Court, in an opinion by Burger for 5 justices, held that a total prohibition on contact visits by pretrial detainees at a jail is a reasonable response to legitimate security interests and does not violate the Fourteenth Amendment.

Hudson v. Palmer 468 U.S. 517, 82 L.Ed. 2d 393, 104 S.Ct. 3194 (1984): The Court, in an opinion by Burger for 5 justices, held that an inmate did not have a reasonable expectation of privacy in his/her cell entitling him/her to Fourth Amendment protections against unreasonable searches and seizures. The Court also found no due process violation where the inmate had been deprived of property by a state employee but state law provided for a meaningful postdeprivation remedy for the loss.

United States v. Gouveia 467 U.S. 180, 81 L.Ed. 2d 146, 104 S.Ct. 2292 (1984): The Court, in an opinion by Rehnquist for 6 justices, held that inmates were not constitutionally entitled to appointed counsel while in administrative segregation prior to initiation of adversary judicial proceedings.

Ohm v. Wakinekona 461 U.S. 238, 75 L.Ed. 2d 813, 103 S.Ct. 1741 (1983): The Court, in an opinion by Blackmun for 6 justices, held that an inmate was denied due process by a transfer to an out-of-state prison without a hearing only if the state statutes involved sufficiently limit official discretion in the placement of prisoners to create a liberty interest subject to protection under the due process clause.

Jago v. Van Curen 454 U.S. 14, 70 L.Ed. 2d 13, 102 S.Ct. 31 (1981): The Court, in a *per curiam* opinion for 5 justices, held that the revocation of a parole date, prior to release of the inmate on parole, did not require a hearing.

Rhodes v. Chapman 452 U.S. 337, 69 L.Ed. 2d 59, 101 S.Ct. 2392 (1981): The Court, in an opinion by Powell for 5 justices, held that double celling at a prison does not constitute cruel and unusual punishment unless there is evidence that the conditions in question inflict unnecessary or wanton pain, or are disproportionate to the severity of crimes warranting imprisonment.

Hughes v. Rowe 449 U.S. 5, 66 L.Ed. 2d 163, 101 S.Ct. 173 (1980): The Court, in a *per curiam* opinion for 5 justices, held that an inmate's allegation that he had been unnecessarily confined to segregation was adequate to require a response by the defendant rather than a dismissal outright. The Court also held that attorney fees should not have been awarded to the defendant-state without a finding that the prisoner's action was groundless or without foundation.

Carlson v. Green 446 U.S. 14, 64 L.Ed. 2d 15, 100 S.Ct. 1468 (1980): The Court, in an opinion by Brennan for 5 justices, held that the mother of a deceased inmate could maintain a *Bivens* suit against federal prison officials even though an action under the Federal Tort Claims Act was also available.

Viteck v. Jones 445 U.S. 480, 63 L.Ed. 2d 552, 100 S.Ct. 1254 (1980): The Court, in an opinion by White joined in pertinent parts by 4 other justices, held that an involuntary transfer of a prisoner to a mental hospital required a hearing that included written notice of the transfer, an adversary hearing before an independent decision maker, written findings, and effective and timely notice of these rights.

Greenholtz v. Inmates of the Nebraska Penal and Correctional Complex 442 U.S. 1, 60 L.Ed. 2d 668, 99 S.Ct. 2100 (1979): The Court, in an opinion by Burger for 5 justices, upheld Nebraska's procedures for granting parole which included: a preliminary hearing where the inmate is permitted to appear before the board and present letters and statements on his/her own behalf, and a final hearing where the inmate is allowed to call witnesses, present evidence, and be represented by private counsel of his choice. Inmates were notified in advance of the month of the hearing but not the exact day. The Court also found that due process does not mandate that the parole board specify the particular evidence on which it relied in ruling against parole.

Bell v. Wolfish 441 U.S. 520, 60 L.Ed. 2d 447, 99 S.Ct. 1861 (1979): The Court, in an opinion by Rehnquist for 5 justices, held: double bunking of pretrial inmates did not violate their constitutional rights under the circumstances (length of confinement, length of time in cell per day, physical conditions in jail); a rule that books could be received by inmates only if they were mailed directly from the publisher was a rational response by prison administrators to security risks; restrictions on receipt of packages to one package per year were not unreasonable based on security and sanitation requirements; cell searches did not violate the rights of inmates; visual body cavity searches conducted after visits and without probable cause were legal. The case stressed reliance on the prison administration for determining a rational reason for a prison rule.

Houchins v. KQED, Inc. 438 U.S. 1, 57 L.Ed. 2d 553, 98 S.Ct. 2588 (1978): The Court, although unable to agree upon a decision, agreed that the press did not have a right to access jails superior to that of the general public.

Procunier v. Navarette 434 U.S. 555, 55 L.Ed. 2d 24, 98 S.Ct. 855 (1978): The Court, in an opinion by White for 7 justices, held that in suits under 42 U.S.C. §1983, prison officials were entitled to qualified immunity.

Bounds v. Smith 430 U.S. 817, 52 L.Ed. 2d 72, 97 S.Ct. 1491 (1977): The Court, in an opinion by Marshall for 6 justices, held that

prisoners must have access to an adequate law library if no adequate form of legal assistance was provided for them.

Estelle v. Gamble 429 U.S. 97, 50 L.Ed. 2d 251, 97 S.Ct. 285 (1976): The Court, in an opinion by Marshall for 7 justices, held that deliberate indifference to a prisoner's serious medical needs constituted cruel and unusual punishment in violation of the Eighth Amendment.

Montanye v. Haymes 427 U.S. 236, 49 L.Ed. 2d 466, 96 S.Ct. 2543 (1976): The Court, in an opinion by White for 6 justices, held that there was no due process right to a hearing prior to the transfer of an inmate from one prison facility to another, absent some right or justifiable expectation rooted in state law that the inmate would not be transferred except for misbehavior or some other specific event.

Meachum v. Fano 427 U.S. 215, 49 L.Ed. 2d 451, 96 S.Ct. 2532 (1976): The Court, in an opinion by White for 6 justices, held that due process did not require a hearing prior to transferring an inmate from a medium security institution to a maximum security facility.

Baxter v. Palmigiano 425 U.S. 308, 47 L.Ed. 2d 810, 96 S.Ct. 1551 (1976): The Court, in an opinion by White for 6 justices, held that during a prison disciplinary hearing: an inmate has no due process right to retained or appointed counsel regardless of the charges; the Fifth Amendment does not prohibit the drawing of adverse inferences from the inmate's failure to testify at the hearing; inmates do not have a right to confront and cross-examine the witnesses against them.

Wolff v. McDonnell 418 U.S. 539, 41 L.Ed. 2d 935, 94 S.Ct. 2963 (1974): The Court, in an opinion by White for 6 justices, held that in major prison disciplinary proceedings, due process requires that written notice of the charges be given to the inmate; the fact-finder make written statements of the evidence relied upon and reasons for the disciplinary action taken; the inmate be allowed to call witnesses and present documentary evidence except when doing so would be unduly hazardous to institutional security or correctional goals. Due process does not require confrontation and cross-examination of adverse witnesses or the right to counsel. The Court upheld a regulation allowing guards to open incoming mail from an attorney if done in the presence of the inmate.

Pell v. Procunier 417 U.S. 817, 41 L.Ed. 2d 495, 94 S.Ct. 2800 (1974): The Court, 6–3 in an opinion by Stewart, held that a prison regulation prohibiting face-to-face press interviews did not violate the First Amendment because other avenues were available to the media.

Johnson v. Avery 393 U.S. 483, 21 L.Ed. 2d 718, 89 S.Ct. 747 (1969): The Court held that if no other legal assistance is available, prison regulation cannot prohibit an inmate from acting as a "jailhouse lawyer" for other inmates.

XIII USE OF ILLEGALLY OBTAINED EVIDENCE

A. Exclusionary Rule

Herring v. United States _____ U.S. _____, 172 L.Ed. 2d 496, 129 S.Ct. 695 (2009): The Court, 5–4 in an opinion by Roberts, held that evidence seized during the search incident to an arrest on a recalled warrant that remained in the police data base fell under the "good faith" exception to the exclusionary rule.

Sanchez-Llamas v. Oregon 548 U.S. 331, 165 L.Ed. 2d 557, 126 S.Ct. 2669 (2006): The Court, in an opinion by Roberts signed by 5 justices, held that the exclusionary rule did not require suppression of a confession where prior to the obtaining the confession officers failed to inform a foreign national that he had the right to have his Consulate informed of his detention (Article 36(1)(b) of the Vienna Convention on Consular Relations).

Hudson v. Michigan 547 U.S. 586, 165 L.Ed. 2d 56, 126 S.Ct. 2159 (2006): The Court, in

an opinion by Scalia, various parts of which were signed by 5 justices, held that violation of "knock-and-announce" during the execution of a search warrant did not make otherwise legally seized evidence inadmissible under the exclusionary rule.

Pennsylvania Board of Probation and Parole v. Scott 524 US 357, 141 L.Ed. 2d 344, 118 S.Ct. 2014 (1998): The Court, 5–4 in an opinion by Thomas, held that the exclusionary rule does not apply to parole revocation hearings.

Arizona v. Evans 514 U.S. 1, 131 L.Ed. 2d 34, 115 S.Ct. 1185 (1995): The Court, 7–2 in an opinion by Rehnquist, held that the "good faith" exception to the exclusionary rule applies to evidence seized incident to an arrest resulting from an inaccurate computer record indicating that there was an outstanding arrest warrant for the suspect, regardless of whether police or court personnel were responsible for the record's continued presence in the police computer.

New York v. Harris 495 U.S. 14, 109 L.Ed. 2d 13, 110 S.Ct. 1640 (1990): The Court, in an opinion by White for 5 justices, held that the exclusionary rule does not bar admission of statements obtained outside the suspect's home after a probable cause arrest was made inside the residence in violation of *Payton v. New York*. Statements would not be admissible if coerced, *Miranda* had been violated, or counsel had been denied under *Edwards v. Arizona*.

James v. Illinois 493 U.S. 307, 107 L.Ed. 2d 676, 110 S.Ct. 648 (1990): The Court, in an opinion by Brennan for 5 justices, held that statements that were the product of an illegal arrest could not be used to impeach a defense witness other than the defendant.

Murray v. United States 487 U.S. 533, 101 L.Ed. 2d 472, 108 S.Ct. 2529 (1988): The Court, in an opinion by Scalia for 4 justices (7 justices participated in the decision), held that evidence seen during an illegal entry but seized during the execution of a search warrant at a later time was admissible if the search pursuant to the warrant was genuinely independent source of the evidence seized.

Illinois v. Krull 480 U.S. 340, 94 L.Ed. 2d 364, 107 S.Ct. 1160 (1987): The Court, in an opinion by Blackmun for 5 justices, held that the "good faith" exception to the exclusionary rule applies to searches conducted by police officers acting in objectively reasonable reliance upon a statute authorizing warrantless administrative searches even though the statute was later found to violate the Fourth Amendment.

Immigration and Naturalization Service v. Lopez-Mendoza 468 U.S. 1032, 82 L.Ed. 2d 778, 104 S.Ct. 3479 (1984): The Court, 5–4, in an opinion by O'Connor for 4 justices and joined in pertinent part by Burger, held that the exclusionary rule does not apply in civil deportation proceedings.

Massachusetts v. Sheppard 468 U.S. 981, 82 L.Ed. 2d 737, 104 S.Ct. 3424 (1984): The Court, in an opinion by White for 6 justices, held that when deciding if the exclusionary rule should be applied to evidence obtained during the execution of a defective search warrant that appeared valid on its face, the sole issue before the court is whether the officers reasonably believed that the search they conducted was authorized by a valid warrant.

United States v. Leon 468 U.S. 897, 82 L.Ed. 2d 677, 104 S.Ct. 3405 (1984): The Court, 6–3 in an opinion by White, held that evidence seized under a facially valid warrant executed in good faith should be admissible except in the unusual cases in which exclusion will further the purposes of the exclusionary rule. This has been called the "good faith" exception to the exclusionary rule.

Segura v. United States 468 U.S. 796, 82 L.Ed. 2d 599, 104 S.Ct. 3380 (1984): The Court, in an opinion by Burger relevant parts of which were joined by 5 justices, held that notwithstanding an earlier illegal entry, the Fourth Amendment did not require suppression of evidence later taken from a private residence pursuant to valid search warrant because the warrant was issued on information obtained by police before the illegal entry was made. This decision is the basis for the "independent source" exception to the exclusionary rule.

New York v. Quarles 467 U.S. 649, 81 L.Ed. 2d 550, 104 S.Ct. 2626 (1984): The Court, in an opinion by Rehnquist for 5 justices, held that an overriding consideration of public safety justified the officer's failure to provide *Miranda* warnings before asking questions regarding the location of a weapon the defendant had apparently abandoned immediately prior to arrest. This decision is the basis for the "public safety" exception to the exclusionary rule.

Nix v. Williams 467 U.S. 431, 81 L.Ed. 2d 377, 104 S.Ct. 2501 (1984): The Court, in an opinion by Burger for 6 justices, held that the body of a murder victim, which was found after the defendant was illegally interrogated, was admissible on the grounds it would inevitably have been discovered even if no violation of any constitutional or statutory provisions had taken place. Prosecutor must show inevitability of discovery by preponderance of evidence. This decision is the basis for the "inevitable discovery" exception to the exclusionary rule.

Wainwright v. Sykes 433 U.S. 72, 53 L.Ed. 2d 594, 97 S.Ct. 2497 (1977): The Court, in an opinion by Rehnquist for 6 justices, held that the defendant waives the right to challenge the voluntariness of a confession unless a timely objection is made. This waiver will preclude review on federal *habeas corpus* unless the defendant can establish "cause" or "prejudice" and show a miscarriage of justice.

United States v. Janis 428 U.S. 433, 49 L.Ed. 2d 1046, 96 S.Ct. 3021 (1976): The Court, 5–3 in an opinion by Blackmun, held that the exclusionary rule did not make evidence illegally seized by the Los Angeles Police Department inadmissible in a civil tax case brought against the defendant by the Internal Revenue Service.

Oregon v. Haas 419 U.S. 823, 43 L.Ed. 2d 570, 95 S.Ct. 1215 (1975): The Court, in an opinion by Blackmun, allowed voluntary statements obtained in violation of *Miranda* to be used for impeachment.

Mapp v. Ohio overruled *Wolf v. Colorado* (1949). 367 U.S. 643, 6 L.Ed. 2d 1081, 81 S.Ct. 1684 (1961): The Court, in a 5–4 opinion, held that the Fourth Amendment exclusionary rule is applicable to the states through the due process clause of the Fourteenth Amendment.

Elkins v. United States 364 U.S. 206, 4 L.Ed. 2d 1169, 80 S.Ct. 1437 (1960): The Court in a 5–4 decision overturned the so-called "silver platter" doctrine which had permitted evidence seized by police during an illegal search while investigating a state crime to be turned over to federal authorities and introduced in federal court so long as federal agents did not participate in the illegal search.

Wolf v. Colorado overruled by *Mapp v. Ohio* (1961) 338 U.S. 25, 93 L.Ed. 1782, 69 S.Ct. 1359 (1949): The Court, 5–4 in an opinion by Frankfurter, stated that the Fourth Amendment applied to the states, but declined to ban use of the illegally seized evidence in state courts.

Weeks v. United States 232 U.S. 383, 58 L.Ed. 652, 34 S.Ct. 341 (1914): The Court, in a unanimous opinion by Day, held that in a federal prosecution the Fourth Amendment barred the use of evidence secured through an illegal search and seizure by federal officers.

Boyd v. United States 116 U.S. 616, 39 L.Ed. 746, 6 S.Ct. 524 (1886) is the first case where the Court excluded evidence seized by federal officers in violation of the Fourth Amendment.

B. Fruit of the Poisonous Tree and Related Doctrines

Taylor v. Alabama 457 U.S. 687, 73 L.Ed. 2d 314, 102 S.Ct. 2664 (1982): The Court, in an opinion by Marshall for 5 justices, held a confession obtained through custodial interrogation, after an illegal arrest, should be inadmissible unless the confession is sufficiently an act of free will to purge the taint of the illegal arrest.

United States v. Havens 446 U.S. 620, 64 L.Ed. 2d 559, 100 S.Ct. 1912 (1980): The Court, in an opinion by White for 5 justices, held that illegally seized evidence could be used to impeach the defendant's statements made on direct examination during a criminal trial.

United States v. Crews 445 U.S. 463, 63 L.Ed. 2d 537, 100 S.Ct. 1244 (1980): The Court held in an opinion by Brennan, pertinent parts of which represented a majority, that an in-court identification is not made inadmissible solely because the defendant's original arrest was illegal.

United States v. Ceccolini 435 U.S. 268, 55 L.Ed. 2d 268, 98 S.Ct. 1054 (1978): The Court, in an opinion by Rehnquist for 5 justices, emphasizing the role of the witness's free will, held that statements made by an eyewitness were sufficiently removed from the illegal search to dissipate the taint.

Brown v. Illinois 422 U.S. 590, 45 L.Ed. 2d 416, 95 S.Ct. 2254 (1975): The Court, in an opinion by Blackmun, held that the mere giving of the *Miranda* warnings does not dissipate the taint of a defendant's illegal arrest and render admissible statements given after the arrest.

Wong Sun v. United States 371 U.S. 471, 9 L.Ed. 2d 441, 83 S.Ct. 407 (1963): The Court, in an opinion by Brennan for 5 justices, held that the defendant's statements were admissible because the connection between an illegal arrest and the statements had "become so attenuated as to dissipate the taint."

C. Standing

Minnesota v. Carter 525 U.S. 83, 142 L.Ed. 2d 373, 119 S.Ct. 469 (1998): The Court, in an opinion by Rehnquist for 5 justices, held that a person who visits a residence for a brief period for business-related purposes lacks the expectation of privacy needed to challenge an illegal entry and search by the police. The Court reaffirmed the holding in *Minnesota v. Olson.*

United States v. Padilla 508 U.S. 77, 123 L.Ed. 2d 635, 113 S.Ct. 1936 (1993): The Court, in a unanimous *per curiam* opinion, held that co-conspirators have standing if their personal expectation of privacy is invaded but refused to give a co-conspirator standing based on his/her supervisory role in the conspiracy or joint control over the place or property involved in the search or seizure.

Minnesota v. Olson 495 U.S. 91, 109 L.Ed. 2d 85, 110 S.Ct. 1684 (1990): The Court, 7–2 in an opinion by White, held that overnight guests in a house have an expectation of privacy protected by the Fourth Amendment.

Rawlings v. Kentucky 448 U.S. 98, 65 L.Ed. 2d 633, 100 S.Ct. 2556 (1980): The Court, in an opinion by Rehnquist for 5 justices, held that Fourth Amendment standing issues should be analyzed in terms of the defendant's reasonable expectation of privacy. Where the defendant had given items to a friend to hold in her purse, the defendant could no longer claim a reasonable expectation of privacy in them.

United States v. Salvucci 448 U.S. 83, 65 L.Ed. 2d 619, 100 S.Ct. 2547 (1980): The Court, 7–2, in an opinion by Rehnquist, held that defendants charged with crimes of possession do not have "automatic standing" to challenge the legality of the search. Standing must rest on reasonable expectation of privacy. Overruled *Jones v. United States* (1960).

Rakas v. Illinois 439 U.S. 128, 58 L.Ed. 2d 387, 99 S.Ct. 421 (1978): The Court, 5–4, in an opinion by Rehnquist, held the defendants lacked standing to challenge the illegal search of the car they had been occupying immediately before the search. The fact that they were in the car with the permission of the owner did not establish a reasonable expectation of privacy in particular areas of the car, namely under the front seat and in the glove compartment.

XIV CIVIL RIGHTS ACT AND CONSTITUTIONAL TORTS See XII Right of the Incarcerated for Civil Rights Act cases involving inmates and prison conditions.

District Attorney's Office for the Third Judicial District et al. v. Osborne ___ U.S. ___, 174 L.Ed. 2d 38, 129 S.Ct. 2308 (2009): The Court, 5–4 in an opinion by Roberts, held that *Brady* rights to pretrial disclosure do not extend to post-conviction proceedings and §1983 suits.

Van de Kamp v. Goldstein ___ U.S. ___, 172 L.Ed. 2d 706, 129 S.Ct. 855 (2009): The Court, in a unanimous opinion by Breyer, held that supervisory prosecutors were entitled to absolute immunity in respect to a claim that they failed to properly train or supervise prosecutors or to establish an information system containing potential impeachment material about informants because these actions are "intimately associated with the judicial phase of the criminal process."

Fitzgerald v. Barnstable School Committee ___ U.S. ___, 172 L.Ed. 2d 582, 129 S.Ct. 788 (2009): The Court, in a unanimous opinion by Alito, held that Title IX does not preclude a §1983 action alleging unconstitutional gender discrimination in schools.

Scott v. Harris 550 U.S. 372, 167 L.Ed. 2d 686, 127 S.Ct. 1769 (2007): The Court, 8–1 in an opinion by Scalia, held that the attempt to terminate the chase initiated by the respondent by forcing the respondent off the road was reasonable because the chase posed a substantial and immediate risk of serious physical injury to others. The officer was entitled to summary judgment.

Wallace v. Kato 549 U.S. 1362, 167 L.Ed. 2d 807, 127 S.Ct. 2090 (2007): The Court, 7–2 in an opinion by Scalia, held that the statute of limitations applicable to a §1983 case based on a false arrest, where the arrest was followed by criminal proceedings, begins to run at the time the claimant is detained pursuant to legal process.

Chavez v. Martinez 538 U.S. 760, 155 L.Ed. 2d 984, 123 S.Ct. 1994 (2003): The Court, without a majority opinion, held that a person could not bring a §1983 case based on the fact that he was repeatedly questioned in violation of *Miranda* when no charges were filed against him and the statements were not used in court. A majority of the justices agreed that the repeated questioning, after being asked to stop by the person and medical staff, of a person who was severely injured could be a substantive due process violation and remanded the case for further development of the facts as they relate to this issue.

Inyo County, California v. Paiute-Shoshone Indians of Bishop Community of the Bishop Colony 538 U.S. 701, 155 L.Ed. 2d 933, 123 S.Ct. 1887 (2003): The Court, in an opinion by Ginsburg for 8 justices, held that the tribe could not sue under §1983 to vindicate a claim that search warrants could not be used because the tribe, as a sovereign, had immunity from the County's process. It was also noted that tribes, like states, were immune from being sued under §1983.

Lapides v. Board of Regents of University System of Georgia 535 U.S. 613, 152 L.Ed. 2d 806, 122 S.Ct. 1640 (2002): The Court, in a unanimous opinion by Breyer, held that a state waives its Eleventh Amendment immunity when the state removes a §1983 case from state court to federal court.

Correctional Services Corp. v. Malesko 534 U.S. 61, 151 L.Ed. 2d 456, 122 S.Ct. 515 (2001): The Court, 5–4 in an opinion by Rehnquist, held that *Bivens* cannot be extended to confer a right of action for damages against a private entity acting under color of federal law.

Saucier v. Katz 533 U.S. 194, 150 L.Ed. 2d 272, 121 S.Ct. 2151 (2001): The Court, 8–1 in an opinion by Kennedy, held that a qualified immunity ruling should be made early in the proceedings; immunity is an entitlement not to stand trial, not a defense from liability.

Kalina v. Fletcher 522 U.S. 118, 139 L.Ed. 2d 471, 118 S.Ct. 502 (1997): The Court, in a unanimous opinion by Stevens, held that a prosecutor does not have absolute immunity in §1983 suits for false statements in affidavits when he/she assumes the role of complaining witness and signs an affidavit supporting the application for an arrest warrant.

Richardson v. McKnight 521 U.S. 399, 138 L.Ed. 2d 540, 117 S.Ct. 2100 (1997): The Court, 5–4 in an opinion by Breyer, held that guards employed by a private firm operating the state's prisons were not entitled to qualified immunity in Civil Rights Act cases.

Board of the County Commissioners of Bryan County, Oklahoma v. Brown 520 U.S. 397, 137 L.Ed. 2d 626, 117 S.Ct. 1382 (1997): The Court, 5–4 in an opinion by O'Connor, held that a person seeking to recover from a municipality under §1983 for actions of employees must demonstrate that a municipality's decision reflects deliberate indifference to the risk that a violation of a particular constitutional or statutory right will follow the decision. The official's failure to adequately scrutinize the applicant's background constitutes "deliberate indifference" only where adequate scrutiny would lead a reasonable policy maker to conclude that the plainly obvious consequence of the decision to hire the applicant would be the deprivation of a third party's federally protected rights.

Heck v. Humphrey 512 U.S. 477, 129 L.Ed. 2d 383, 114 S.Ct. 2364 (1994): The Court, in an opinion by Scalia for 5 justices, held that in a Civil Rights Act case under §1983 that alleged malicious prosecution, the plaintiff must show that his/her case ended in his/her favor (acquittal, reversed on direct appeal, conviction expunged by executive order, declared invalid by a state or federal court on *habeas corpus*).

Buckley v. Fitzsimmons 509 U.S. 259, 125 L.Ed. 2d 209, 113 S.Ct. 2606 (1993): The Court, in an opinion by White for 5 justices, held that prosecutors have qualified immunity for acts performed during the investigative phase of a case and for statements made to the press.

Farrar v. Hobby 506 U.S. 103, 121 L.Ed. 2d 494, 113 S.Ct. 566 (1992): The Court, in an opinion by Thomas for 5 justices, held that in a §1983 case, a plaintiff who receives nominal damages is a prevailing party and eligible to receive attorney's fees under 42 U.S.C. § 1988, but awarding attorney fees is not appropriate when there is only a "technical" victory.

Denton v. Hernandez 504 U.S. 25, 118 L.Ed. 2d 340, 112 S.Ct. 1728 (1992): The Court, 7–2 in an opinion by O'Connor, held that *in forma pauperis* suits under §1983 can be dismissed as frivolous, without requiring the defendant to answer, if the facts alleged rise to the level of the irrational or the wholly incredible, whether or not there are judicially noticeable facts available to contradict them. They may not be dismissed simply because the court finds the plaintiff's allegations unlikely.

Hunter v. Bryant 502 U.S. 224, 116 L.Ed. 2d 589, 112 S.Ct. 534 (1991): The Court, 5–3 in a *per curiam* opinion, held Secret Service agents were entitled to immunity from *Bivens* suits when making an arrest if a reasonable officer would have believed that probable cause existed for the arrest.

Hafer v. Melo 502 U.S. 21, 116 L.Ed. 2d 301, 112 S.Ct. 358 (1991): The Court, in a unanimous opinion by O'Connor, held that a state official could be held personally liable under §1983 if constitutional rights were violated when firing employees.

Mireles v. Waco 502 U.S. 9, 116 L.Ed. 2d 9, 112 S.Ct. 286 (1991): The Court, 5–4 in a *per curiam* opinion, held that a judge has absolute immunity under §1983 for actions performed in his/her judicial capacity even if he/she authorized or condoned excessive force by police officers to carry out the judge's orders.

Burns v. Reed 500 U.S. 478, 114 L.Ed. 2d 547, 111 S.Ct. 1934 (1991): The Court, 6–3 in an opinion by White, held that a prosecutor has absolute immunity for actions at a probable cause hearing to determine if a

warrant should be issued but only qualified immunity for advice given to police regarding the investigation.

West Virginia University Hospitals, Inc. v. Casey 499 U.S. 83, 113 L.Ed. 2d 68, 111 S.Ct. 1138 (1991): The Court, 6–3 in an opinion by Scalia, held that 42 U.S.C. §1988, which permits the prevailing party to collect attorney fees from the opposing side, does not allow recovery of fees for services rendered by expert witnesses and consultants on handling the case. Experts appearing at trial are entitled to fees set in 28 U.S.C. §1920 and 1921.

Venegas v. Mitchell 495 U.S. 82, 109 L.Ed. 2d 74, 110 S.Ct. 1679 (1990): The Court, in a unanimous opinion by White, held that contingent fee contracts for the representation of a plaintiff filing a civil rights action under §1983 are valid. Section 1988 limits what a defendant can be ordered to pay but does not control what the plaintiff may contract to pay.

Will v. Michigan Department of State Police 491 U.S. 58, 105 L.Ed. 2d 45, 109 S.Ct. 2304 (1989): The Court, in an opinion by White for 5 justices, held that a state is not a "person" within the meaning of §1983. Suits against state officials in their official capacity are in fact suits against the state and are barred by the Eleventh Amendment unless the state waived its immunity or Congress has exercised its power under Section 5 of the Fourteenth Amendment to override that immunity (which the Court found Congress had not done).

Graham v. Connor 490 U.S. 386, 104 L.Ed. 2d 443, 109 S.Ct. 1865 (1989): The Court, in an opinion by Rehnquist for 6 justices, held that in suits under §1983, allegations of excessive force in a nonprison setting should be analyzed under the Fourth Amendment's "objective reasonableness" standard, not a substantive due process standard.

Brower v. County of Inyo 489 U.S. 593, 103 L.Ed. 2d 628, 109 S.Ct. 1378 (1989): The Court, in an opinion by Scalia for 5 justices, held that the act of placing a roadblock across all lanes of traffic in order to stop a fleeing suspect was sufficient to establish a seizure under the Fourth Amendment. If such a seizure was unreasonable, it would establish liability under §1983.

City of Canton, Ohio v. Harris 489 U.S. 378, 103 L.Ed. 2d 412, 109 S.Ct. 1197 (1989): The Court, in an opinion by White for 6 justices, held that a municipality has liability under §1983 for constitutional violations resulting from its failure to train municipal employees only if its failure to train evidences deliberate indifference to the constitutional rights of its inhabitants.

De Shaney v. Winnebago County Department of Social Services 489 U.S. 189, 103 L.Ed. 2d 249, 109 S.Ct. 998 (1989): The Court, in an opinion by Rehnquist for 6 justices, held that while the state has a duty to protect individuals from harm when it restrains their freedom to act on their own behalf, it has no due process duty to protect a person's liberty interest against harm inflicted by other means. The county had no liability under §1983 for injuries after Children's Protective Services failed to heed signs of abuse and remove the child from the home.

Felder v. Casey 487 U.S. 131, 101 L.Ed. 2d 123, 108 S.Ct. 2302 (1988): The Court, in an opinion by Brennan for 7 justices, held that §1983 preempts a Wisconsin statute requiring that that before any suit may be brought in state court against a state or local governmental entity or officer, the plaintiff must notify the governmental defendant of the circumstances giving rise to the claim, the amount of the claim, and his/her intent to hold the named defendant liable.

West v. Atkins 487 U.S. 42, 101 L.Ed. 2d 40, 108 S.Ct. 2250 (1988): The Court, in an opinion by Blackmun for 8 justices, held that a physician who is under contract with the state to provide medical services to inmates at a state prison hospital on a part-time basis acts "under color of state law."

Anderson v. Creighton 483 U.S. 635, 97 L.Ed. 2d 523, 107 S.Ct. 3034 (1987): The

Court, in an opinion by Scalia for 6 justices, held that a federal law enforcement officer who participates in a search that violates the Fourth Amendment may not be held personally liable for money damages if a reasonable officer could have believed that the search comported with the Fourth Amendment.

Hewitt v. Helms 482 U.S. 755, 96 L.Ed. 2d 654, 107 S.Ct. 2672 (1987): The Court, in an opinion by Scalia for 5 justices, held that in order to be entitled to attorney fees in an action under §1983, a litigant must be a "prevailing party." A court's conclusion that the inmate's constitutional rights were violated by prison officials who are immune from suit does not justify the awarding of attorney's fees. Neither does the fact that prison officials decided to change their regulations as a result of the lawsuit even though the court did not order them to do so.

Newton v. Rummery 480 U.S. 386, 94 L.Ed. 2d 405, 107 S.Ct. 1187 (1987): The Court, in an opinion by Powell, relevant portions of which were signed by 5 justices, held that in most cases a court properly may enforce an agreement in which a criminal defendant voluntarily released his/her right to file an action under §1983 in return for a prosecutor's dismissal of pending criminal charges.

City of Riverside v. Rivera 477 U.S. 561, 91 L.Ed. 2d 466, 106 S.Ct. 2686 (1986): The Court, without a majority opinion, held that attorneys' fees under 42 U.S.C. §1988 do not have to be proportionate to the size of the monetary recovery in the case.

City of Los Angeles v. Heller 475 U.S. 796, 89 L.Ed. 806, 106 S.Ct. 1571 (1986): The Court, in a *per curiam* opinion for 6 justices, held that there is no authorization for an award of damages against a municipality based on the actions of one of its officers when the jury concluded that the officer inflicted no constitutional harm.

Pembaur v. City of Cincinnati 475 U.S. 469, 89 L.Ed. 2d 452, 106 S.Ct. 1292 (1986): The Court, in an opinion by Brennan for 6 justices, held that a municipality could be liable under §1983 based on a policy decision if, and only if, officials responsible for establishing final policy with respect to the subject matter in questions made a deliberate choice to follow a course of action after considering various alternatives.

Malley v. Briggs 475 U.S. 335, 89 L.Ed. 2d 271, 106 S.Ct. 1092 (1986): The Court, in an opinion by White for 7 justices, held that an officer who obtained an arrest warrant has immunity from suits under §1983 for an arrest made pursuant to that warrant except where the warrant application is so lacking in indicia of probable cause as to render the officer's belief in its existence unreasonable.

Cleavinger v. Saxner 474 U.S. 193, 88 L.Ed. 2d 507, 106 S.Ct. 496 (1985): The Court, in an opinion by Blackmun for 6 justices, held that members of a federal prison's Institutional Discipline Committee who hear cases in which inmates are charged with rules infractions are entitled to qualified immunity from liability for actions that violate the U.S. Constitution as long as they follow the clear constitutional requirements of *Wolff v. McDonnell*.

City of Oklahoma City v. Tuttle 471 U.S. 808, 85 L.Ed. 2d 791, 105 S.Ct. 2427 (1985): The Court, without a majority opinion, held that a single isolated incident of excessive force by a police officer cannot establish an official policy of inadequate training that is sufficient to render a municipality liable for damages under §1983.

Tower v. Glover 467 U.S. 914, 81 L.Ed. 2d 758, 104 S.Ct. 2820 (1984): The Court, in an opinion by O'Connor, held that public defenders do not have absolute immunity from liability in §1983 suits.

Pulliam v. Allen 466 U.S. 522, 80 L.Ed. 2d 565, 104 S.Ct. 1970 (1984): The Court, 5–4 in an opinion by Blackmun, held that judicial immunity under 42 U.S.C. §1988 does not bar an award of attorney's fees.

Smith v. Wade 461 U.S. 30, 75 L.Ed. 2d 632, 103 S.Ct. 1625 (1983): The Court, 5–4 in an opinion by Brennan, held that punitive

damages could be awarded in a Civil Rights Act suit when the defendant was shown to have an evil motive or intent, or when it was demonstrated that the defendant was reckless or had callous indifference to federally protected rights.

Briscoe v. Lahue 460 U.S. 325, 75 L.Ed. 2d 96, 103 S.Ct. 1108 (1983): The Court, in a 6–3 opinion by Stevens, held that a person convicted in state court based on perjured testimony by a police officer may not bring suit under §1983 against the police officer.

Polk County v. Dodson 454 U.S. 312, 70 L.Ed. 2d 509, 102 S.Ct. 445 (1981): The Court, 8–1 in an opinion by Powell, held that for purposes of suits under §1983, the public defender does not act "under color of state law."

City of Newport v. Fact Concerts 453 U.S. 247, 69 L.Ed. 2d 616, 101 S.Ct. 2748 (1981): The Court, 6–3 in an opinion by Blackmun, held that cities are immune from punitive damage awards under §1983.

Carlson v. Green 446 U.S. 14, 64 L.Ed. 2d 15, 100 S.Ct. 1468 (1980): The Court, in an opinion by Brennan for 5 justices, held that the mother of a deceased inmate could maintain a *Bivens* suit against federal prison officials even though an action under the Federal Tort Claims Act was also available.

Moore v. Sims 442 U.S. 415, 60 L.Ed. 2d 994, 99 S.Ct. (1979): The Court, 5–4 in an opinion by Rehnquist, held that it was improper for a federal court to issue an injunction in a Civil Rights Act suit when proceedings were pending in state court.

Procunier v. Navarette 434 U.S. 555, 55 L.Ed. 2d 24, 98 S.Ct. 855 (1978): The Court, in an opinion by White for 7 justices, held that in suits under §1983, prison officials were entitled to qualified immunity.

Imbler v. Pachtman 424 U.S. 409, 47 L.Ed. 2d 128, 96 S.Ct. 984 (1976): The Court, in an opinion by Powell for 5 justices, held that a state prosecutor has absolute immunity from civil rights actions under §1983 for actions taken while initiating and pursuing criminal prosecutions.

Rizzo v. Goode 423 U.S. 362, 46 L.Ed. 2d 561, 96 S.Ct. 598 (1976): The Court, 5–3 in an opinion by Rehnquist, held that an injunction requiring the development of an improved system for handling citizen complaints against police officers was improvidently entered. Factors considered in determining that no order should be made include: no pattern of violations of citizens' constitutional rights was shown; only a few officers appeared to be involved in these violations; no link between the misconduct and official department policy was shown; the total number of incidents involved (20 in 12 months) was small in comparison with the size of the city and the police department (city of 3,000,000 with 7,500 officers).

Hicks v. Miranda 422 U.S. 332, 45 L.Ed. 2d 223, 95 S.Ct. 2281 (1975): The Court, 5–4 in an opinion by White, held that a federal court must not interfere with pending state criminal prosecutions unless there are exceptional circumstances creating a threat of irreparable great and immediate injury.

Wood v. Strickland 420 U.S. 308, 43 L.Ed. 2d 214, 95 S.Ct. 992 (1975): The Court, 5–4, in an opinion by White, held that in civil rights actions under §1983, a public official is liable for violations of civil rights if he/she knew, or should have known, that the actions taken violated constitutional rights, or if the violation was done with malicious intent to cause deprivation of constitutional rights or injury. Qualified immunity applies if the defendant can show both objective and subjective good faith in the performance of his/her duties.

Allee v. Medrano 416 U.S. 802, 40 L.Ed. 2d 566, 94 S.Ct. 2191 (1974): The Court held that a federal court had the authority to issue an injunction in a Civil Rights Act case when there was no interference with a pending state prosecution, if the plaintiff had demonstrated a pattern of police misconduct and irreparable injury would result if an injunction was not issued.

Bivens v. Six Unknown Named Agents of Federal Bureau of Narcotics 403 U.S. 388, 29 L.Ed. 2d 619, 91 S.Ct. 1999 (1971): The Court, 6–3, in an opinion by Brennan, held that a civil remedy could be based directly on the Fourth Amendment. Civil suits to recover damages for violation of constitutional rights by federal officers who are not covered by the Civil Rights Act have become known as *"Bivens"* cases or constitutional torts.

Younger v. Harris 401 U.S. 37, 27 L.Ed. 2d 699, 91 S.Ct. 746 (1971): The Court, 5–4 in an opinion by Black, held that issuing an injunction was improper in a case of good faith enforcement of a possibly unconstitutional statute.

Pierson v. Ray 386 U.S. 547, 18 L.Ed. 2d 288, 87 S.Ct. 1213 (1967): The Court, 8–1 in an opinion by Warren, held that judges have absolute immunity for their judicial acts; police have conditional immunity for acts done in good faith based on probable cause.

XV *HABEAS CORPUS* IN FEDERAL COURTS TO REMEDY CONSTITUTIONAL WRONGS

Boumediene et al. v. Bush 553 U.S. 723, 171 L.Ed. 2d 41, 128 S.Ct. 2229 (2008): The Court, 5–4 in an opinion by Kennedy, held that inmates held in the wake of 9/11 are not barred from seeking the writ of *habeas corpus* or invoking the suspension clause's protections because they have been designated as enemy combatants or because of their detention at Guantanamo.

Munaf v. Geren 553 U.S. 674, 171 L.Ed. 2d 1, 128 S.Ct. 2207 (2008): The Court, in a unanimous opinion by Roberts, held that the *habeas* statute extends to American citizens held overseas by American forces operating subject to an American chain of command. Federal district courts, however, may not exercise their *habeas* jurisdiction to enjoin the United States from transferring individuals alleged to have committed crimes, who are detained within the territory of a foreign sovereign, to that sovereign for criminal prosecution.

Panetti v. Quarterman 551 U.S. 930, 168 L.Ed. 2d 662, 127 S.Ct. 2842 (2007): The Court, 5–4 in an opinion by Kennedy, held that a federal *habeas corpus* petition should be granted where petitioner, who had a well-documented history of mental illness, filed a motion under Texas law after an execution date was set, claiming for the first time that he was incompetent to be executed because of mental illness.

Hamdan v. Rumsfeld 548 U.S. 557, 165 L.Ed. 2d 723, 126 S.Ct. 2749 (2006): The Court, in an opinion by Stevens, portions of which were signed by 5 justices, held that "enemy combatants" housed at Guantanamo have the right to *habeas corpus* review.

House v. Bell 547 U.S. 518, 165 L.Ed. 2d 1, 126 S.Ct. 2064 (2006): The Court, 5–4 in an opinion by Kennedy, held that when deciding to grant a *habeas corpus* petition based on actual innocence after the default period has expired, the federal court must assess how reasonable jurors would react to the overall, newly supplemented record.

Hamdi v Rumsfeld 542 U.S. 507, 159 L.Ed. 2d 578, 124 S.Ct. 2633 (2004): The Court, in a plurality opinion by O'Connor, held that due process demands that a citizen held in the United States as an enemy combatant be given a meaningful opportunity to contest the factual basis for that detention before a neutral decision maker.

Rasul v. Bush 542 U.S. 466, 159 L.Ed. 2d 548, 124 S.Ct. 2686 (2004): The Court, 6–3 in an opinion by Stevens, held that the jurisdiction of U.S. district courts to hear *habeas* challenges under 28 U.S.C. §2241, extends to aliens held in a territory over which the United States exercises plenary and exclusive jurisdiction but not "ultimate sovereignty."

Massaro v. United States 538 U.S. 500, 155 L.Ed. 2d 714, 123 S.Ct. 1690 (2003): The Court, in a unanimous opinion by Kennedy, held that an ineffective assistance of counsel claim may be brought in a collateral proceeding under §2255 whether or not the petitioner could have raised the claim on direct appeal.

Bell v. Cone 535 U.S. 685, 152 L.Ed. 2d 914, 122 S.Ct. 1843 (2002): The Court, 8–1 in an opinion by Rehnquist, held that a state inmate filing federal *habeas corpus* and alleging violation of the right to counsel due to trial attorney's incompetence must overcome the presumption that the challenged action might be considered sound trial strategy; the claimant must also show that the state court that reviewed the case applied the standard in an objectively unreasonable manner.

Zadvydas v. Davis 533 U.S. 678, 150 L.Ed. 2d 653, 121 S.Ct. 2491 (2001): The Court, 5–4 in an opinion by Breyer, held that in cases where an alien has been ordered removed from the country, Section 2241 *habeas* proceedings are available as a forum for statutory and constitutional challenges to the length of post-removal-period detention.

Bracy v. Gramley 520 U.S. 899, 138 L.Ed. 2d 97, 117 S.Ct. 1793 (1997): The Court, in a unanimous opinion by Rehnquist, held that district court judges should fashion appropriate discovery orders in federal *habeas corpus* suits when "good cause" was shown.

Felker v. Turpin 518 U.S. 651, 135 L.Ed. 2d 827, 116 S.Ct. 2333 (1996): The Court, in a unanimous opinion by Rehnquist, held that restrictions on filing *habeas corpus* contained in the Antiterrorism and Effective Death Penalty Act of 1996 did not preclude the Supreme Court from entertaining an application for *habeas corpus* relief, although it does affect the standards governing the granting of such relief.

Thompson v. Keohane 516 U.S. 99, 133 L.Ed. 2d 383, 116 S.Ct. 457 (1995): The Court, 7–2 in an opinion by Ginsburg, held that when a defendant files federal *habeas corpus* to challenge the failure to give *Miranda* rights, federal judges should conduct an independent review of the question of whether the defendant was "in custody" when interrogated.

Garlotte v. Fordice 515 U.S. 65, 132 L.Ed. 2d 36, 115 S.Ct. 1948 (1995): The Court, 7–2 in an opinion by Ginsburg, held a prisoner is "in custody," and thus eligible to file a petition for federal *habeas corpus,* when serving consecutive sentences even though the sentence for the case being considered has already been completed.

Duncan v. Henry 513 U.S. 364, 130 L.Ed. 2d 865, 115 S.Ct. 887 (1995): The Court, in a *per curiam* opinion for 5 justices, held that a state inmate may not file for federal *habeas corpus* relief unless the federal issue involved was raised on direct appeal in state courts.

O'Neal v. McAninch 513 U.S. 432, 130 L.Ed. 2d 947, 115 S.Ct. 992 (1995): The Court, 6–3 in an opinion by Breyer, held that when a federal judge considers a *habeas corpus* petition applying the harmless error rule to constitutional issues, the case should be decided in the inmate's favor if there is grave doubt about whether the error had a "substantial and injurious effect or influence in determining the jury's verdict." "Grave doubt" means that, in the judge's mind, the matter is so evenly balanced that he/she feels him/herself in virtual equipoise as to the harmlessness of the error.

Withrow v. Williams 507 U.S. 680, 123 L.Ed. 2d 407, 113 S.Ct. 1745 (1993): The Court, in an opinion for 5 justices, held that the logic behind *Stone v. Powell,* which denied federal *habeas corpus* relief to prisoners making Fourth Amendment claims if the state courts provided a full and fair chance to litigate the issues, cannot be used to deny federal *habeas corpus* review of a state prisoner's claims that a conviction rests on statements obtained in violation of *Miranda.*

Brecht v. Abrahmson 507 U.S. 619, 123 L.Ed. 2d 353, 113 S.Ct. 1710 (1993): The Court, in an opinion by Rehnquist for 5 justices, held that the standard for determining whether *habeas corpus* should be granted when post-*Miranda* silence was used for impeachment is whether the violation of the right to remain silent had substantial and injurious effect or influence in determining the jury's verdict.

Keeney v. Tamayo-Reyes 504 U.S. 1, 118 L.Ed. 2d 318, 112 S.Ct. 1715 (1992): The Court, 5–4 in an opinion by White, held a defendant filing federal *habeas corpus* to challenge a state court conviction was entitled to an evidentiary hearing if he/she could show cause for his/her failure to develop the facts in state court proceedings and that actual prejudice resulted from that failure. A hearing is mandated if it is shown that a fundamental miscarriage of justice would result from failure to hold a federal evidentiary hearing.

McCleskey v. Zant 499 U.S. 467, 113 L.Ed. 2d 517, 111 S.Ct. 1454 (1991): The Court, 6–3 in an opinion by Kennedy, held that raising issue(s) in a second or subsequent petition for federal *habeas corpus,* when the issue(s) were not raised in the first petition, is an abuse of the writ and merits dismissal of the case.

Lozada v. Deeds 498 U.S. 430, 112 L.Ed. 2d 956, 111 S.Ct. 860 (1991): The Court, 7–2 in a *per curiam* opinion, held that a defendant who made a substantial showing that no appeal was filed in state court due to ineffective assistance of counsel was entitled to a certificate of probable cause so that federal *habeas corpus* could be pursued.

Smith v. Murray 477 U.S. 527, 91 L.Ed. 2d 434, 106 S.Ct. 2661 (1986): The Court, in an opinion by O'Connor for 5 justices, held that a deliberate tactical decision not to raise an issue on direct appeal bars its introduction in a writ of *habeas corpus* absent a showing that there is a probability that counsel's procedural default resulted in the conviction of an innocent person.

Murray v. Carrier 477 U.S. 478, 91 L.Ed. 2d 397, 106 S.Ct. 2639 (1986): The Court, in an opinion by O'Connor for 5 justices, held that an inmate petitioning for a writ of *habeas corpus* on the grounds of ineffective assistance of appellate counsel needs to establish that there was some external impediment that might have prevented counsel from raising the appropriate claims in the appellate briefs. The federal courts retain the authority to consider cases in which there is a probability that the defendant was factually innocent.

Cardwell v. Taylor 461 U.S. 571, 76 L.Ed. 2d 333, 103 S.Ct. 2015 (1983): The Court, in a *per curiam* opinion for 7 justices, held that a claim that a confession was inadmissible as the product of an illegal arrest could not be raised in federal court if the petitioner had had an opportunity for a full and fair hearing on that claim in state court.

Engle v. Isaac 456 U.S. 107, 71 L.Ed. 2d 783, 102 S.Ct. 1558 (1982): The Court, in an opinion by O'Connor for 5 justices, held that the petitioners had forfeited their constitutional claims by not complying with the state's contemporaneous objection rule.

Rose v. Lundy 455 U.S. 509, 71 L.Ed. 2d 379, 102 S.Ct. 1198 (1982): The Court, in an opinion by O'Connor joined in pertinent parts by 5 other justices, held federal district courts must dismiss *habeas corpus* petitions that contain any claims for relief that have not been exhausted in state courts. Petitioner has the option of returning to state court to seek relief for previously unexhausted claims or amending federal petition to eliminated unexhausted state claims.

Duckworth v. Serrano 454 U.S. 1, 70 L.Ed. 2d 1, 102 S.Ct. 18 (1981): The Court, 8–1 in a *per curiam* opinion, held that a claim of ineffective assistance of counsel was not an exception to the requirement that a petitioner must exhaust state court relief prior to filing in federal court.

Jackson v. Virginia 443 U.S. 307, 61 L.Ed. 2d 560, 99 S.Ct. 2781 (1979): The Court, in an opinion by Stewart for 5 justices, held that when the petitioner who has met the exhaustion requirement alleges that a state court conviction rests upon insufficient evidence, the federal court must consider whether there is sufficient evidence to justify a rational trier of the facts finding guilt beyond a reasonable doubt.

Wainwright v. Sykes 433 U.S. 72, 53 L.Ed. 2d 594, 97 S.Ct. 2497 (1977): The Court, in an opinion by Rehnquist for 6 members

of the Court, held that a state may utilize a contemporaneous objection rule whereby the defendant waives the right to challenge the voluntariness of a confession unless a timely objection to its voluntariness is made. This waiver will preclude review on federal *habeas corpus* unless the defendant can establish "cause" or "prejudice" and show a miscarriage of justice.

Stone v. Powell 428 U.S. 465, 49 L.Ed. 2d 1067, 96 S.Ct. 3037 (1976): The Court, 6–3 in an opinion by Powell, held that when a state has provided an opportunity for full and fair litigation of a Fourth Amendment claim, a state prisoner may not be granted federal *habeas corpus* relief on the ground that the evidence was obtained in violation of the Fourth Amendment.

Leflcowitz v. Newsome 420 U.S. 283, 43 L.Ed. 2d 196, 95 S.Ct. 886 (1975): The Court, 5–4, in an opinion by Stewart, held that where state law allows a defendant to plead guilty without forfeiting a right to appeal specified constitutional issues, the defendant is also not foreclosed from pursuing those constitutional claims in federal *habeas corpus* proceedings.

Peyton v. Rowe 391 U.S. 54, 88 S. Ct. 1549, 20 L. Ed. 2d 426 (1968): The Court, in a unanimous opinion by Warren, held that a prisoner serving consecutive sentences was in custody under any one of the sentences for purposes of *habeas corpus* relief under 28 U.S.C.S. §2241(c)(3).

XVI OTHER CONSTITUTIONAL ISSUES

A. Ex Post Facto Laws

Stogner v. California 539 U.S. 607, 156 L.Ed. 2d 544, 123 S.Ct. 2446 (2003): The Court, 5–4 in an opinion by Breyer, held that a law which retroactively extended the statute of limitations on crimes involving sexual molestation of children violated the *ex post facto* clause when it revived previously time-barred prosecutions.

Smith v. Doe 538 U.S. 84, 155 L.Ed. 2d 164, 123 S.Ct. 1140 (2003): The Court, 6–3 in an opinion by Kennedy, held that Alaska's Sex Offender Registration Act is nonpunitive, and therefore its retroactive application does not violate the *ex post facto* clause.

Carmell v. Texas 529 U.S. 513, 146 L.Ed. 2d 577, 120 S.Ct. 1620 (2000): The Court, 5–4 in an opinion by Stevens, found a violation of the prohibition against *ex post facto* laws because testimony was admitted at trial based on a law passed after the crime occurred, which allowed a rape conviction to be sustained based solely on the testimony of the victim if the victim was under 18.

Garner v. Jones 529 U.S. 244, 146 L.Ed. 2d 236, 120 S.Ct. 1362 (2000): The Court, 6–3 in an opinion by Kennedy, held that when applying changes in sentencing guidelines and possibility of release on parole, the controlling inquiry in *ex post facto* analysis is whether application of the new rules creates a sufficient risk of increasing the measure of punishment, such as prolonging incarceration, attached to the crime.

Lynce v. Mathis 519 U.S. 433, 137 L.Ed. 2d 63, 117 S.Ct. 891 (1997): The Court, in an opinion by Stevens for 7 justices, held that a Florida law that retroactively canceled release credits for prison inmates violated the *ex post facto* clause.

California Department of Corrections v. Morales 514 U.S. 499, 131 L.Ed. 2d 588, 115 S.Ct. 1597 (1995): The Court, 7–2 in an opinion by Thomas, held that amended rules that permitted the Board of Prison terms to decrease the frequency of parole suitability hearings were not *ex post facto* laws when applied to inmates who were sentenced prior to the date the amendments went into effect.

Collins v. Youngblood 497 U.S. 37, 111 L.Ed. 2d 30, 110 S.Ct. 2715 (1990): The Court, in an opinion by Rehnquist for 6 justices, held that a Texas statute, passed after defendant's crime, that allowed the reformation of an improper jury verdict did not violate the *ex post facto* clause.

Miller v. Florida 482 U.S. 423, 96 L.Ed. 2d 351, 107 S.Ct. 2446 (1987): The Court, in a unanimous opinion by O'Connor, held that revisions of Florida's sentencing guidelines between the time the crime was committed and the date of sentencing in a manner that increased the defendant's presumptive sentence violated the *ex post facto* clause.

B. Jurisdiction over the Military

Solorio v. United States 483 U.S. 435, 97 L.Ed. 2d 364, 107 S.Ct. 2924 (1987): The Court, in an opinion by Rehnquist for 5 justices, held that the jurisdiction of a court-martial convened pursuant to the Uniform Code of Military Justice to try a member of the armed forces is not limited to cases where there is a "service connection" with the offense. The offenses must be committed while the service person was on active duty but the acts do not need to occur on post. Overruled *O'Callahan v. Parker* (1969).

C. Other Issues

Cuomo v. Clearing House Association, L.L.C. ___ U.S. ___, 174 L.Ed. 2d 464, 129 S.Ct. 2710 (2009): The Court, in an opinion by Scalia for 5 justices, held that the Comptroller of the Currency's regulation preempt state law enforcement investigation of banks is not a reasonable interpretation of the National Banking Act.

Gonzales v. Oregon 546 U.S. 243, 163 L.Ed. 2d 748, 126 S.Ct. 904 (2006): The Court, 6–3 in an opinion by Kennedy, held that the Controlled Substance Act does not allow the U.S. Attorney General to prohibit doctors from prescribing regulated drugs for use in physician-assisted suicide under state law permitting the procedure.

Gonzales v. Raich 545 U.S. 1, 162 L.Ed. 2d 1, 125 S.Ct. 2195 (2005): The Court, 6–3 in an opinion by Stevens, held that Congress had the power under the commerce clause to prohibit the local cultivation and use of marijuana for medicinal purposes even though it was authorized in California's Compassionate Use Act.

New Mexico ex rel. Ortiz v. Reed 524 U.S. 151, 141 L.Ed. 2d 131, 118 S.Ct. 1860 (1998): The Court, in a unanimous *per curiam* opinion, held that under the extradition clause, the asylum state is not permitted to litigate issues regarding the legality of the penal system (including parole revocation) of the demanding state.

Printz v. United States 521 U.S. 898, 138 L.Ed. 2d 914, 117 S.Ct. 2365 (1997): The Court, 5–4 in an opinion by Scalia, held that Congress does not have the authority to order states to enforce federal regulations; neither may it conscript local officials to do so. Congress could not mandate that local law enforcement officials conduct background checks before a person could purchase firearms under the Brady Bill.

United States v. Lopez 514 U.S. 549, 131 L.Ed. 2d 626, 115 S.Ct. 1624 (1995): The Court, 5–4 in an opinion by Rehnquist, held that provisions of the Gun-Free School Zones Act of 1990 that made it a federal offense "for any individual knowingly to possess a firearm at a place that the individual knows, or has reasonable cause to believe, is a school zone" were invalid because Congress exceeded its authority under the commerce clause. The act neither regulates a commercial activity nor contains a requirement that the possession be connected in any way to interstate commerce.

INDEX OF CASES

Q

R

S

APPENDIX A

DOCTORAL PROGRAMS IN CRIMINAL JUSTICE

The American University
School of Public Affairs
4400 Massachusetts Avenue, NW
Washington, DC
(Ph.D. programs with concentration in justice,
law, and society available in departments of
Political Science, Public Administration, and
Sociology

Arizona State University
School of Justice Studies
Tempe, AZ 85287

Bowling Green State University
Sociology Department
Bowling Green, OH 43403

Claremont Graduate School
Center for Politics and Policy
Claremont, CA 91711

Florida State University
School of Criminology
Tallahassee, FL 32306

Indiana University of Pennsylvania
Criminology Department
Indiana, PA 15705

John Jay College of Criminal Justice
Criminal Justice Program
New York, NY 10019

Michigan State University
School of Criminal Justice
East Lansing, MI 48824

Pennsylvania State University
Administration of Justice
University Park, PA 16802

Portland State University
Administration of Justice Department
P.O. Box 751
Portland, OR 97207

Rutgers University
School of Criminal Justice
Newark, NJ 07102

Sam Houston State University
College of Criminal Justice
Huntsville, TX 77341

State University of New York at Albany
School of Criminal Justice
Albany, NY 12222

Temple University
Department of Criminal Justice
Philadelphia, PA 19122

University of California at Berkeley
Jurisprudence and Social Policy
Berkeley, CA 94720

University of California at Irvine
Program in Social Ecology
Irvine, CA 92717

University of Delaware
Sociology and Criminal Justice
Newark, DE 19716

University of Illinois at Chicago
Criminal Justice Department
1007 West Harrison Street
Chicago, IL 60607

University of Maryland
Institute of Criminal Justice and Criminology
College Park, MD 20742-8235

University of Missouri–St. Louis
Department of Criminology and Criminal Justice
8001 Natural Bridge Road
St. Louis, MO 63121

University of Nebraska at Omaha
Director of Graduate Studies
Department of Criminal Justice
Omaha, NE 68182

University of New Haven
Public Safety & Professional Studies
300 Orange Avenue
West Haven, CT 06516

Western Michigan University
Sociology and Criminology
Kalamazoo, MI 49008

School of Criminology
University of Montreal
C.P. 6128, Montreal, Quebec H3C 3J7 Canada

APPENDIX B

FORENSIC AGENCIES AND ORGANIZATIONS

American Academy of Forensic Sciences
225 South Academy Boulevard
Colorado Springs, CO 80910

American Board of Forensic Entomology
University of Missouri–Columbia
Columbia, MO 65211

American Board of Forensic Psychiatry
c/o Medical and Chirurgical Faculty of Maryland
1211 Cathedral Street, Baltimore, MD 21201

American Board of Odontology
c/o Homer R. Campbell, D.D.S.
6800 C Montgomery, NE
Albuquerque, NM 87109

American Board of Pathology
c/o 112 Lincoln Center
5401 West Kennedy Boulevard
Box 24695, Tampa, FL 33623

American Society of Crime Laboratory Directors
c/o Jerry Chisum
California Department of Justice
2213 Blue Gum Avenue
Modesto, CA 95351

American Society of Forensic Odontology
c/o Dr. James D. Woodward
School of Dentistry, University of Louisville
Louisville, KY 40292

American Society of Questioned Document
Examiners
1415 Esperson Building
Houston, TX 77002

Armed Forces Institute of Pathology
Washington, DC 20306

Center for Human Toxicology
University of Utah
Salt Lake City, UT 84112

Drug Enforcement Administration
Forensic Science Section

1405 I Street, NW
Washington, DC 20537

FBI Laboratory Division
10th Street and Pennsylvania Avenue, NW
Washington, DC 20535

Federal Bureau of Investigation
Training Academy
Forensic Science Research Training Center
Quantico, VA 22135

Forensic Sciences Foundation
Suite 201, 225 South Academy Boulevard
Colorado Springs, CO 80910

Independent Association of Questioned
Document Examiners
518 Guaranty Bank Building
Cedar Rapids, IA 52401

International Association for Identification
Box 139
Utica, NY 13503

International Association of Coroners and
Medical Examiners
2121 Adelbert Road
Cleveland, OH 44106

International Reference Organization in
Forensic Medicine and Sciences
c/o Dr. William G. Eckert Laboratory
St. Francis Hospital
Wichita, KS 67214

Milton Helpern Institute of Forensic Medicine
520 First Avenue
New York, NY 10016

National Association of Medical Examiners
1402 S. Grand Boulevard
St. Louis, MO 63104

U.S. Department of the Treasury
Bureau of Alcohol, Tobacco, and Firearms
Forensic Science Laboratory
1401 Research Boulevard
Rockville, MD 20850

World Association of Document Examiners
111 North Canal Street
Chicago, IL 60606

APPENDIX C

CRIMINAL JUSTICE WEB SITES

This compilation is a sampling rather than a comprehensive guide to Web sites that may be of interest to students, instructors, and professionals in law enforcement and related fields. They can be sources for news, trends, statistics, research, and people with specialized knowledge and experience. Note that some URLs may have changed since the listing was compiled and that new sites are created frequently.

U.S. GOVERNMENT
Department of Justice:

http://www.icpsr.umich.edu/NACJD/.html (National Archive of Criminal Justice Data)

http://www.ojp.usdoj.gov/bjs (Office of Justice Programs, Bureau of Justice Statistics)

http://www.ojp.usdoj.gov/nij (Office of Justice Programs, National Institute of Justice)

http://www.ojp.usdoj.gov/ovc (Office for Victims of Crime)

http://www.justnet.org/Pages/home.aspx (Justice Technology Information Network)

http://www.usdoj.gov/marshals (United States Marshals)

http://www.usdoj.gov/dea/index.htm (Drug Enforcement Administration)

http://www.cops.usdoj.gov. (Community Oriented Policing Services)

Other federal organizations:

http://www.fbi.gov/ucr (FBI's Uniform Crime Reports)

http://www.fbi.gov/vicap (FBI's Violent Criminal Apprehension Program)

http://www.nida.nih.gov (National Institute on Drug Abuse)

www.atf.treas.gov (Treasury Department's Bureau of Alcohol, Tobacco and Firearms)

http://www.bop.gov (Bureau of Prisons)

http://www.ncjrs.org (National Criminal Justice Reference Service)

http://www.lab.fws.gov (Fish and Wildlife Service's forensic science site)

http://www.albany.edu/sourcebook (Criminal Justice Statistics)

LAW AND JUSTICE ORGANIZATIONS

http://www.law.cornell.edu (Legal Information Institute)

http://www.uic.edu/depts/lib/specialcoll/services/lhsc/ead/011-34-01f.html (Office of International Criminal Justice)

http://www.splcenter.org/?ref=logo (Southern Poverty Law Center)

http://193.123.144.14/interpol.com (Interpol)

http://www.nafi.org/ (National Association of Fire Investigators) http:www.asc41.com/ (American Society of Criminology)

http://aclu.org/issues/criminal/hmcj.html (ACLU's criminal justice home page)

http://www.terrorism.com

http://crimetimes.org/ (sponsored by the Wacker Foundation)

PRIVATE ORGANIZATIONS

http://www.coplink.com/HOME.htm (news of and for the law enforcement community)

http://www.noblenatl.org (National Organization of Black Law Enforcement Executives)

http://www.corrections.com/aja (American Jail Association)

http://www.criminaljusticepress.com (publisher)

LINKS TO OTHER CRIMINAL JUSTICE AND RELATED SITES

http://www.tencore.com/rw/row_ho10. htm#links (compiled by Roy A. Walker, Ph.D, University of Illinois Police Training Institute)

http://www.apbnews.com/ (police and crime news)

http://www.policeforum.org/ (sponsored by the Police Executive Research Forum)

APPENDIX D

JURIED/REFEREED JOURNALS

(Journals that have outside experts judge submitted manuscripts on merit alone, without knowledge of the author's identity.)

ADVANCES IN CRIMINOLOGICAL THEORY (annually). Affiliation: School of Criminal Justice, Rutgers University, 15 Washington St., Newark, NJ 07102. (201) 648-5073.

AMERICAN JOURNAL OF CRIMINAL JUSTICE (Spring/Fall). Affiliation: The Southern Criminal Justice Association. Published by the School of Justice Administration, College of Urban and Public Affairs, University of Louisville, Louisville, KY 40292. (502) 588-6567.

AMERICAN JOURNAL OF CRIMINAL LAW (3 times a year). Managing Editor, 727 E. 26th St., Austin, TX 78705. (512) 471-9200.

AMERICAN JOURNAL OF POLICE (quarterly). Affiliation: Police Executive Research Forum (PERF) and Police Section of the Academy of Criminal Justice Sciences. Published by AMP, the University of Nebraska–Omaha, Department of Criminal Justice, Omaha, NE 68182-0149.

CRIME AND DELINQUENCY Published by Sage (quarterly). Submit manuscripts to Don Gibbons, Ph.D., 1100 S.W. Hillcroft, Portland, OR 97225.

CRIMINAL JUSTICE AND BEHAVIOR Published by Sage (quarterly). Submit manuscripts to CJB, Curt R. Bartol, Ph.D., Dept. of Psychology, Castleton State College, Castleton, VT 05735.

CRIMINAL JUSTICE ETHICS (semiannually). Affiliation: John Jay College of Criminal Justice, 899 Tenth Ave., New York, NY 10019 (212) 237-8415.

CRIMINAL JUSTICE JOURNAL (semiannually). Affiliation: Western State University College of Law, 2121 San Diego Ave., San Diego, CA (619) 298-3111.

CRIMINAL JUSTICE POLICY REVIEW (quarterly). Affiliation: Department of Criminology, Indiana University of Pennsylvania, Indiana, PA 15701. (412) 357-2471.

CRIMINAL JUSTICE REVIEW (Spring/Fall). Affiliation: American Society for Public Administration. Published by the College of Public and Urban Affairs, Georgia State University, Atlanta, GA 30303-3091. (404) 651-3515.

CRIMINOLOGY (quarterly). Affiliation: American Society of Criminology. Published by ASC, 1314 Kinnear Road, Columbus, OH 43212. (614) 292-9207.

GANG JOURNAL: AN INTERDISCIPLINARY RESEARCH QUARTERLY Affiliation: Department of Criminal Justice, Chicago State University, 95th St. at King Drive, HWH 329, Chicago, IL 60628. (312) 995-2108.

HOMICIDE STUDIES Published by Sage (quarterly). Submit manuscripts to HSIIJ, M. Dwayne Smith, Ph.D., Dept. of Sociology, University of North Carolina at Charlotte, Charlotte, NC 28223.

INTERNATIONAL JOURNAL OF LAW AND PSYCHIATRY (quarterly). Affiliation: International Academy of Law and Mental Health. Published by Pergamon Press, c/o Osgoode Hall Law School, York University, 4700 Keele St., Downsview, Ontario M3J 2R5, Canada.

INTERNATIONAL JOURNAL OF OFFENDER THERAPY AND COMPARATIVE CRIMINOLOGY Published by Sage (quarterly). Submit manuscripts to IJOTCC, George B. Palermo, M.D., 925 East Wells St., Milwaukee, WI 53202.

JOURNAL FOR JUVENILE JUSTICE AND DETENTION SERVICES (biannually). Affiliation: National Juvenile Detention Association. Contact JJJDS, Dept. of Correctional and Juvenile Justice Studies, Eastern Kentucky University, 105 Stratton Bldg., Richmond, KY 40475-3102. (606) 622-1155.

JOURNAL OF CONTEMPORARY CRIMINAL JUSTICE Published by Sage (quarterly). Affiliation: Department of Criminal Justice,

California State University, Long Beach. For themes and guest editors, contact George E. Rush, Ph.D., Dept. of Criminal Justice, 1250 Bellflower Boulevard, Long Beach, CA 90840.

JOURNAL OF CORRECTIONAL EDUCATION (quarterly). Published by Karez, McGing, and Associates. 26 E. Exchange St., St. Paul, MN 55101 (612) 224-3340.

JOURNAL OF CRIME AND JUSTICE (biannually). Affiliation: Midwestern Criminal Justice Association. Published by JCJ, Bowling Green State University, Criminal Justice Program, Bowling Green, OH 43403.

JOURNAL OF CRIMINAL JUSTICE EDUCATION (Spring/Fall). Affiliation: Academy of Criminal Justice Sciences. Published by theSchool of Criminal Justice, State University of New York at Albany, Albany, NY 12222. (518) 455-6322.

JOURNAL OF INTERPERSONAL VIOLENCE Published by Sage (monthly). Submitmanuscripts to JIV, Jon R. Conte, Ph.D., School of Social Work, University of Washington, 410115th Ave., NE, Mailstop 354900, Seattle, WA 98195.

JOURNAL OF OFFENDER REHABILITATION (quarterly). Affiliation: Newhouse Center for Law and Justice, Rutgers State University, 15 Washington St., Newark, NJ 07102 (908) 753-4030.

JOURNAL OF POLICE AND CRIMINAL PSYCHOLOGY (semiannually). Affiliation: Department of Criminal Justice, Southwest Texas State University, San Marcos, TX 78666 (512) 245-2174.

JOURNAL OF PRISON AND JAIL HEALTH (semiannually). Affiliation: Department of Social Medicine, Montefiore Hospital and Medical Center, 111 E. 210th St., Bronx, NY 10467 (212) 920-6226.

JOURNAL OF QUANTITATIVE CRIMINOLOGY (quarterly). Printed by Plenum Publishing Corporation. Published by JQC, College of Criminal Justice, Northeastern University, 360 Huntington Ave., Boston, MA 02115.

JOURNAL OF RESEARCH ON CRIME AND DELINQUENCY (quarterly). Published by Sage. Send manuscripts to JRCD, Mercer Sullivan, Ph.D., School of Criminal Justice, 15 Washington Street, Rutgers Campus at Newark, Newark, NJ 07102.

JUDICATURE: THE JOURNAL OF THE AMERICAN JUDICATURE SOCIETY (bimonthly). Published by AJS, 25 East Washington Street, Chicago, IL 60602. (312) 558-6900.

JUSTICE QUARTERLY (quarterly). Affiliation: Academy of Criminal Justice Sciences (ACJS). Published by ACJS, 402 Nunn Hall, Northern Kentucky University, Highland Heights, KY 41076-1448. (606) 572-5634.

POLICE PRACTICE AND RESEARCH (quarterly). Affiliation: International Police Executive Symposium. Submit manuscripts to PPR, Arvind Verma, Dept. of Criminal Justice, Indiana University, Bloomington, IN 47405.

POLICE STUDIES: THE INTERNATIONAL REVIEW OF POLICE DEVELOPMENT (quarterly). Affiliation: Police Section of the Academy of Criminal Justice Sciences. Published by Police Studies, John Jay College of Criminal Justice, Office of Publications, 899 10th Ave., New York, NY 10019.

POLICING (quarterly). Published by Police Review Publishing Company, 14 St. Cross Street, London E1N 8FE, England.

PRISON JOURNAL: AN INTERNATIONAL FORUM ON INCARCERATION ANDALTERNATIVE SANCTIONS (quarterly). Published by Sage. Send manuscripts to TPPJI-FIAS, Alan Harlan, Ph.D., Dept. of Criminal Justice, Gladfelter Hall, 5th Floor, Temple University, Philadelphia, PA 19122.

SOCIOLOGY AND SOCIAL RESEARCH JOURNAL (quarterly). No affiliation. Published by the Department of Sociology, University of Southern California, University Park, Los Angeles, CA 90089-2539. (213) 743-2658.

THE JUSTICE PROFESSIONAL (Spring/Fall). No affiliation. Printed by Wyndham Hall

Press. Published by Department of Sociology and Social Work, Pembroke State University, Pembroke, NC 28372. (919) 521-4214.

THEORETICAL CRIMINOLOGY (quarterly). Affiliation: Department of Criminology, University of Southern Maine, 1 Chamberlain Ave., Portland, ME 04103.

TRAUMA, VIOLENCE, & ABUSE: A REVIEW JOURNAL (TVAR) (quarterly). Published by Sage. Submit manuscripts to TVAR, Jon R. Conte, Ph.D., School of Social Work, University of Washington, 4101 15th Ave., NE, Mailstop 354900, Seattle, WA 98195.

VIOLENCE AGAINST WOMEN: AN INTERNATIONAL AND INTERDISCIPLINARY JOURNAL (monthly). Published by Sage. Submit manuscripts to VAWIIJ, Claire M. Renzetti, Ph.D., Dept. of Sociology, St. Joseph's University, Philadelphia, PA 19131.

WOMEN IN CRIMINAL JUSTICE (biannual). Published by The Haworth Press, Inc., 10 Alice Street, Binghamton, NY 13904-1580. (800) 342-9678.